LEGAL FOUNDATIONS

of a

FREE SOCIETY

LEGAL
FOUNDATIONS
of a
FREE SOCIETY

STEPHAN KINSELLA

**PAPINIAN
PRESS**
HOUSTON

Papinian Press • Houston, Texas

Cover Design & Interior Formatting by Susi Clark of Creative Blueprint Design

Main text font is Adobe Caslon; headers are LeMonde

ISBN Paperback   979-8-9890306-1-3
ISBN Hardcover   979-8-9890306-0-6
ISBN Ebook   979-8-9890306-2-0

To Ethan, and his generation, in hopes that they and their descendants live in a freer world.

Sir, I have found you an argument; but I am not obliged to find you an understanding.

—Samuel Johnson

even if the libertarian ethic and argumentative reasoning must be regarded as ultimately justified, this still does not preclude that people will act on the basis of unjustified beliefs either because they don't know, they don't care, or they prefer not to know. I fail to see why this should be surprising or make the proof somehow defective. More than this cannot be done by propositional argument.

—Hans-Hermann Hoppe

Contents

Foreword

The question as to what is justice and what constitutes a just society is as old as philosophy itself. Indeed, it arises in everyday life even long before any systematic philosophizing is to begin.

All throughout intellectual history, one prominent answer to this question has been to say that it is "might" that makes "right." Or more specifically: that what is right or wrong, just or unjust, is unilaterally decreed by a State qua territorial monopolist of violence. The self-contradictory nature of this "decisionist" position, i.e. of "legal positivism," comes to light once we ask its proponents for a reason or evidence as to why we should believe the proposition that "might makes right" to be true and correct. By virtue of providing any such reason or evidence, however, and thus seeking—ultimately—unanimous agreement regarding the validity of the proposition in question, any such proponent implicitly acknowledges the presence of other reasonable and sensible persons and, importantly, that the question of right or wrong, true or not-true, then, is not a matter of "might" or "fiat," but a question to be decided on the basis of common reason and experience instead. Yet reason and experience demonstrate, contrary to the proponent's initial claim, that "might does *not* make right." That "might is might" and "right is right," but "no might can ever *make* a right."

Aside from the decisionism championed by legal positivists, the most prominent answer in modern times to the question under consideration, then, has come from so-called social-contracts theorists.

According to them, what is just or not is determined by the terms of a contract concluded and agreed upon by all members of a society. — Yet this solution opens more questions than it answers and ends in a tangle of confusion. For one, no such contract has ever been concluded anywhere. Yet in the absence of any such contract, would people still be able to distinguish between right and wrong? Obviously, one would think so, because otherwise they would not even be able to rightfully conclude a—indeed any—valid contract. Put differently: there first must be a contractor—a person—and then there must be something rightfully owned and to be contracted by this person—private or personal property—before there can ever be a valid contractual agreement. Thus, personhood and private property logically—or more precisely: praxeologically—precede contracts and contractual agreements; and hence, trying to construct a theory of justice on the foundation of contracts is a fundamental praxeological error.

Moreover, with personhood and private property as the praxeological foundation of contracts, then, any universal, all-encompassing and -including social contract as imagined by social-contract theorists is impossible. Rather: on this basis, all contracts are contracts between identifiable and enumerable persons and concerning identifiable and enumerable things or matters. No contract can bind anyone other than the actual contractors, and no contract can concern things or matters other than those specified in the contract. Accordingly: Real persons with their various real, separate and exclusive properties simply *cannot—praxeologically* cannot—conclude a contract as fancied by social contract theorists.

For such a contract to be conceivable, a "new person" must be invented. A fictitious person, that can do what no real person can! This "new person," invented for the purpose by social contract theorists, then, is invariably some wildly unrealistic, severely "dis-embodied" entity, i.e., a person without any bodily needs or appetites; "pure" reason, if you will, freed from all constraints of time and place. — The theorists then ask what arrangement of the world such persons would agree on as just. And they then spin out an answer as to what they believe this agreement between such entities to be, and why. — Any such answer, however, whatever it may be, is always arbitrary, because the only thing that can possibly be known about fictitious people and an agreement among them is whatever has already been invested in such beings from the very outset, per assumption. Indeed, as John Rawls, the most celebrated modern social contract theorist, has admitted with captivating frankness, he had simply "define(d) the original position [of fictitious people placed behind a 'veil of ignorance,' *HHH*] so that we get the desired solution."[1] While the results that Rawls gets from his assumptions concerning the original position agree largely with the political views of the social democratic left, other social contract theorists, with different assumptions about the original meeting-of-the-minds, such as James M. Buchanan and his fictitious constructs of "conceptual contracts" and "quasi-unanimity," for instance, have proposed answers more closely associated with the political right. Still other theorists have presented yet other results. Demonstrating, then, that the intellectual endeavors of social contract theorists, however ambitious and sophisticated they may appear, are ultimately no more than idle mental exercises: deriving wildly unrealistic conclusions from wildly unrealistic assumptions, i.e., examples of "garbage-in-and-garbage-out."

But there is another, more sinister aspect to the idea of a social contract that comes to light once anyone of the various contractual agreements as fancied by social contract theorists is actually put to the test, implemented and enforced. Because implementing and enforcing the terms of a contract that no real person had or could have agreed on means, in effect, that all *real* contracts between *real* people are superseded and replaced by the terms of some alleged agreement among fictitious people as the ultimate judge in matters of right and wrong. The word "contract," then, with its positive connotations, is used by social contract theorists to advance a program that is actually destructive of all contracts. They declare non-contracts and non-agreements to be contracts and agreements and contracts and agreements to be non-contracts and non-agreements. — Thus, ultimately, social contract theory turns out barely less arbitrary than the decisionism of legal positivists. For its proponents, the question of right or wrong may not be considered a matter of mere decree as for some strict positivists. Instead, for them, it is the intuitions and fancies of some philosophers

---

[1] John Rawls, *A Theory of Justice*, revised ed. (Cambridge, Mass.: Harvard University Press, 1999), p. 122.

that are supposed to do the job. But this is hardly less arbitrary, one would think! And, of course, since no real person had or could have agreed to any so-called social contract, its enforcement then always requires an agency not itself founded on agreement and contract but on disagreement, violence and coercion instead: a State. And just like legal positivists, then, social contract theorists invariably turn out to be statists, too, assigning and entrusting the role of the ultimate arbiter of right and wrong to the State qua territorial monopolist of violence.

Another popular answer to the question under consideration is that of utilitarianism. Utilitarians essentially contend that the very rules that maximize or promise to maximize total social utility or bring about the greatest happiness to the greatest number of people are and should be considered just. Apart from other difficulties connected with its consequentialism, however, this answer can be quickly dismissed as fatally flawed for the simple reason that there exist no units of utility or happiness, and hence, that any interpersonal comparison of utility or happiness and any aggregation of individual utility or happiness to "social utility" or "social happiness" must be considered impossible (or, if still invoked, as entirely arbitrary).

With the answers of legal positivists, social contract theorists and utilitarians all rejected as fundamentally flawed, however popular they may be, the only remaining answer, then, comes from the old, pre-modern intellectual tradition of natural law and natural rights. It is also in this nowadays rather unfashionable intellectual tradition, broadly conceived, that Stephan Kinsella's here presented work must be placed.

Natural law and rights theorists contend that the principles of just human conduct can be discovered from the study of human nature. On the one hand, such study reveals that humans are endowed with *reason*, as manifested by the indisputable fact that they can speak and communicate with one another, from person to person, in a common language. On the other hand, this study shows that humans are also *actors* (and in combination then: *reasonable actors*). Speaking and communicating itself are purposeful activities directed at a goal. Yet even if and when we are not speaking or communicating but do things silently, we are still acting and cannot but act as long as we are not asleep, comatose or dead.

Further, this study also reveals the "deep structure" of human action, i.e. what all actions of all humans have in common. Every individual actor (and only individuals act!), whatever he does, pursues a goal or end the attainment of which he considers more satisfying than the satisfaction to be expected from acting differently. Every actor is thereby placed in a given environment, at a specific point in time and space, with specific external surroundings of men and materials, and equipped with his own nature-given bodily makeup and mental endowment; and every action, then, whatever it may be, invariably aims to alter an actor's specific present situation to his personal advantage and greater satisfaction. In any case, to reach his goals, whatever they may be, an actor invariably must employ *means*. At a minimum, he must employ his own physical body and brain (plus the body's standing room) as means for the attainment of some expected bodily or psychic gain, and he must thereby use up some time that he also could have used differently.

Generally, however, a person's actions involve more than the purposeful use of one's physical body and mind. It involves also various elements of the external world that, unlike a person's own body, can only be indirectly controlled by means of one's directly controlled body. Such elements of the external world that can be indirectly controlled and manipulated by a person and that are recognized or believed by an actor to be suitable for the attainment of his ends are called *means*. Those elements of the external world beyond or believed to be beyond human control on the other hand are referred to as *external conditions* under which a person's actions are to take place. The choice of means employed by a person for the attainment of his ends is always a matter of *ideas*, i.e. of reason and reasoning. An actor always chooses such an allocation and arrangement of means that he believes to bring about some desired result. The choice of means is validated by their result. A person's actions then are always guided by some ideas about cause and effect: performing A, B and C will lead to X, Y and Z. But man is not infallible and a person's ideas concerning cause and effect or the interconnectedness and regularity of events may be false, and a person's action based on these ideas then will lead to failure rather than the anticipated success, inducing the person to learn, i.e. to revisit and possibly revise his original ideas.

Given this insight into the general human condition, it becomes immediately clear what a human ethic or a theory of justice worth its salt must accomplish. It must give an answer to the question of what am I and what is every other person permitted (or not permitted) to do, right now and right here, wherever a person may find himself and whatever his external surroundings of men and materials may be. More specifically, what is a person permitted (or not permitted) to do in an interaction with another person? And: what external entities is a person permitted (or not permitted) to bring under his control to be used as means toward his personal ends?

Because no person can ever *stop* acting, from his beginnings as a person until his very end (except when asleep, comatose or dead), these questions arise again and again, without end, for everyone, wherever and whenever he may find himself and must act. Obviously, then, an answer to pressing questions such as these cannot wait for the establishment of the institution of a State, the conclusion of a contract (which would actually have to *presuppose* a valid answer to these very questions in order to make it a *valid* contract) or the arrival of some future consequences. Instead, the answer must be discoverable and recognizable from the very outset, from the first, immediate insight into the nature of man as a *reasonable actor*. And indeed, this is so once the purpose, the ultimate end, of all reason and reasoning is recognized and acknowledged. As already noted, human reason is manifested in the indisputable fact that one person can *communicate* with another person in a *common* language (and different languages are inter-translatable). The purpose of speaking and communicating with one another, then, even if and when expressing one's disagreement with another person's say-so in meaningful words, is to guide or coordinate the actions of different persons by words or meaningful symbols alone. This endeavor may succeed and words help guide or coordinate the actions of different persons to mutual satisfaction. Or the endeavor may fail. But in any case, the goal of speaking and communicating is always and invariably the same: to maintain peace and seek peaceful cooperation or coexistence—and in reverse: to *avoid conflict*, i.e., physical clashes or conflagrations of people that are destined to result whenever and wherever two or more people pursue their own different goals with the help of one and the same person's body or one and the same indirectly controlled or controllable external means of action at the same time.

The objective for a human ethic or a theory of justice, then, is the discovery of such rules of human conduct that make it possible for a—indeed, any—bodily person to act—indeed, to live his entire active life—in a world made up of different people, a "given" external, material environment, and various scarce—rivalrous, contestable or conflict-able—material objects useable as means toward a person's ends, without ever running into physical clashes with anybody else.

Essentially, these rules have been known and recognized since eternity. They consist of three principal components. First, *personhood* and *self-ownership*: Each person owns—exclusively controls—his physical body that only he and no one else can control *directly* (any control over another person's body, by contrast, is invariably an *in-direct* control, presupposing the prior direct control of one's own body). Otherwise, if body-ownership were assigned to some indirect body-controller, conflict would become unavoidable as the direct body-controller *cannot* give up the direct control over his body as long as he is alive. Accordingly, any physical interference with another person's body must be consensual, invited and agreed to by such a person, and any non-consensual interference with his body constitutes an unjust and prohibited invasion.

Second, *private property* and *original appropriation*: Logically, what is required to avoid all conflict regarding external material objects used or usable as means of action, i.e. as goods, is clear: every good must always and at all times be owned privately, i.e. controlled exclusively by some specified person. The purposes of different actors then may be as different as can be, and yet no conflict will arise so long as their respective actions involve exclusively the use of their own private property. And how can external objects become private property in the first place without leading to conflict? To avoid conflict from the very start, it is necessary that private property be founded through *acts of original appropriation*, because only through *actions*, taking place in time and space, can an objective—intersubjectively ascertainable—link be established between a particular person and a particular object. And only the *first* appropriator of a previously unappropriated thing can acquire this thing as his property *without conflict*. For, by definition, as the *first* appropriator he *cannot* have run into conflict with anyone else in appropriating the good in question, as everyone else appeared on the scene only *later*. Otherwise, if exclusive control is assigned instead to some *late-comers*, conflict is not avoided but contrary to the very purpose of reason made unavoidable and permanent.

Third, *exchange* and *contract*: Other than per original appropriation, property can only be acquired by means of a voluntary—mutually agreed upon—exchange of property from some previous owner to some later owner. This transfer of property from a prior to a later owner can either take the form of a direct or "spot" exchange, which may be bi- or multi-lateral as when someone's apples are exchanged for another's oranges, or it may be unilateral as when a person makes a gift to someone else or when someone pays another person with his property now, on the spot, in the expectation of some future services on the part of the recipient. Or else the transfer of property can take the form of contracts concerning not just present but in particular also prospective, future-dated transfers of property titles. These contractual transfers of property titles can be unconditional or conditional transfers, and they too can involve bi- or multi-lateral as well as unilateral property transfers. Any acquisition of property other than through original appropriation or voluntary or contractual exchange and transfer from a previous to a later owner is unjust and prohibited by reason. (Of course, in addition to these normal property acquisition rules, property can also be transferred from an aggressor to his victim as rectification for a previous trespass committed.)

Drawing on the long, but in today's world largely forgotten or neglected, intellectual tradition of natural law and natural rights theory with its three just briefly sketched principal components, then, the most elaborate, systematic, rigorous and lucid presentation of a theory of justice up until then had been developed in the course of the second half of the 20th century by economist-philosopher Murray N. Rothbard, culminating in his *Ethics of Liberty*, originally published in 1982. Unfortunately, but not entirely surprisingly, however, his work was typically either completely ignored or else dismissed out of hand by the gatekeepers and high priests of academia. The anarchist conclusions ultimately arrived at by Rothbard in his works appeared simply outlandish in an ideological environment molded overwhelmingly by tax-funded intellectuals and steeped to the hip in statism or *étatisme*. Among academic big shots, only Harvard philosopher Robert Nozick in his *Anarchy, State and Utopia* acknowledged his intellectual debt to Rothbard and seriously tried to refute his anarchist conclusions—but miserably failed.

While Rothbard's work largely fell on deaf ears within academia, then, it exerted considerable influence outside of it, in the public at large. Indeed, through his work Rothbard became the founder of the modern libertarian movement, attracting a sizable popular following far exceeding that of any mainstream academic in numbers. As for the further development of a natural-law and -rights based theory of justice, however, this very success turned out to be a rather mixed blessing. On the one hand, the movement inspired by Rothbard likely helped dampen and slow down the popularity and growth of statism, but it manifestly failed in halting or even reversing the long-run historical trend toward ever increasing state power. On the other hand (and that may well be one of the reasons for this failure), the larger the movement grew in numbers, the greater also the confusion and the number of intellectual errors spread and committed by its followers. The pure theory of justice as presented by Rothbard was increasingly watered down, misunderstood, misinterpreted or downright falsified, whether for short-run tactical gains, out of ignorance or plain cowardice. As well, all too often sight was lost of the fundamentally important distinction between the core, the foundational principles of a theory on the one hand and its application to various peripheral—often far-fetched or merely fictional—practical problems on the other; and far too much effort and time, then, has been spent on debating peripheral issues the solution of which may well be arguable, but which is of minor importance in the larger scheme of things and helps distract public attention and concentration away from those questions and issues that truly matter and count.

In this situation, then, more than 40 years after the first publication of Rothbard's *Ethics of Liberty* and characterized by much practical disappointment and increasing theoretical confusion, the publication of Stephan Kinsella's present work must be considered a most welcome sign of renewed hope and new, refreshing intellectual inspiration.

Indeed, with this work, that has been in the making for more than two decades, Kinsella has produced no less than an intellectual landmark, establishing himself as the leading legal theorist and the foremost libertarian thinker of his generation. While following in Rothbard's footsteps, Kinsella's work does not merely rehash what has been said or written before. Rather, having absorbed as well all of the relevant literature that has appeared during the last few decades since Rothbard's passing, Kinsella in the following offers some fresh perspectives and an innovative approach to the age-old quest for justice, and he adds several highly significant refinements and improvements and some centrally important new insights to the theories of personhood, property and contract, most famously some radical criticism and rejection of the idea of "intellectual property" and "intellectual property rights."

Henceforth, then, all essential studies in the philosophy of law and the field of legal theory will have to take full account of the theories and criticisms expounded by Kinsella.

Hans-Hermann Hoppe
Istanbul, May 2023

Preface

The issue of what property rights we have, or should have, what laws are just and proper, has long confronted mankind, and continues to be the subject of debate today. This book seeks to address these issues, with an approach that keeps in mind the nature and reality of human life—that we are purposeful human actors living in a world of scarcity and facing the possibility of interpersonal conflict—and the purpose of law and property norms: to enable us to live together, in society, peacefully and cooperatively. The goal is to vindicate the private law as developed in the decentralized systems of the Roman and common law, with an emphasis on consistency, principle, and the inviolable rights of the individual. In short, to argue for a private law system informed by libertarian principles.

Thus, in these pages, I try to explain what libertarianism *is*, why individual self-ownership and property rights are justified, how the law ought to deal with criminals and tortfeasors, how property rights should be understood so that errors such as intellectual property (IP), taxes, and the drug war can be exposed, and, finally why a consistent libertarianism implies that a stateless society, sometimes called anarchy, offers the best hope for a free and just social order. I explore the nature of law and legislation, and subject various aspects of positive law, as well as other theories of law, including that of other libertarians, to criticism and appraisal.

These arguments are premised on the thesis that just law is anchored in core principles of self-ownership plus ownership of external scarce resources as governed by principles of original appropriation, contractual title transfer, and rectification. The developed legal system of an advanced, free society is the detailed working out of the implications and applications of these basic principles to various practical and recurring situations in human interactions. This book looks from numerous angles at why these principles are important and how adhering to them consistently can help us achieve a freer society and adjudge the legitimacy of concrete laws and legal systems.

As to how this book came about: I've been intensely interested in—some might say obsessed with—libertarian ideas for over forty years, since high school. It has become a life passion and an avocation of sorts. A calling, though not a career.[1] After starting, as so many libertarians of my generation have, with the ideas of Ayn Rand,[2] I soon discovered the work of Austrian economists and anarcho-libertarians, such as Ludwig von Mises, Murray Rothbard, and Hans-Hermann Hoppe, whose ideas are my greatest influence.

I started publishing on matters of libertarian theory in 1992, fresh out of law school.[3] I tried to use my knowledge of the law—both the English common law and the Roman law, as embodied in the civil law of most European countries and my own home state, Louisiana—and Austrian economics and libertarian principles, to advance libertarian theory where I thought I could contribute. I first wrote on rights and punishment theory in the early 1990s (see chapters 5 and 22), and then on related areas like legislation (chapter 13), contract and inalienability theory (chapters 9 and 10), and so on. In 2001, I published "Against Intellectual Property,"[4] which was controversial and influential, so I've become known by many libertarians primarily for my IP arguments. As the essays in the current volume illustrate, however, IP is not my

---

[1] See comments from Gary North about calling vs. career, mentioned in chapter 24.

[2] Jerome Tuccille, *It Usually Begins with Ayn Rand* (Stein and Day, 1971). See also chapters 1 and 25.

[3] Stephan Kinsella, "Estoppel: A New Justification for Individual Rights," *Reason Papers* No. 17 (Fall 1992): 61–74. See chapter 5.

[4] Kinsella, "Against Intellectual Property," first published in the *Journal of Libertarian Studies* 15, no. 2 (Spring 2001): 1–53; later republished as a monograph by the Mises Institute in 2008 and in an edition by Laissez-Faire books in 2012 (*AIP*).

sole area of interest. My interest in and passion for libertarian ideas has always been driven by my love of philosophy, truth, justice, logic, consistency, and economics. This book includes several chapters on IP but also covers other aspects of libertarian legal theory, such as rights theory and others noted above.

By 2010 or so, most of the theory-laden articles that became the chapters in this book had been published, so around that time I thought of collecting some of these articles in a single book, since they covered a large and complementary number of interrelated topics, such as rights and punishment theory, contract theory, causation and responsibility, intellectual property, anarchy, legislation, and so on. But I kept putting the project off. I felt I was missing some material that should be in such a book, such as a general overview of libertarianism itself, and an update of the intellectual property material I had initially published in 2001. I eventually wrote these articles (now chapters 2, 14, and 15), so I felt it was time to finally assemble and complete this book.

The twenty-five chapters are based on articles published over an almost thirty-year period, from 1994 to 2022, with one chapter (15) being formally published for the first time here (2023). I decided to omit some articles I had published before, as they are a bit too focused on American-specific issues like the US Constitution, federalism, and so on, and also for space reasons.[5] I also did not include any purely legal publications—those related to my vocation, not my avocation—such as those found at my legal website www.KinsellaLaw.com. I included only writing having to do with libertarian issues.

Most of these articles were published in scholarly journals or in online publications. A few chapters are more conversational in tone, as they were based on interviews or transcripts of speeches (e.g. chapters

---

[5] For example I considered including, but ultimately decided against, articles such as: Patrick Tinsley, Stephan Kinsella & Walter Block, "In Defense of Evidence and Against the Exclusionary Rule: A Libertarian Approach," *Southern U. L. Rev.* 32 no. 1 (2004): 63–80; Kinsella, "A Libertarian Defense of Kelo and Limited Federal Power," *LewRockwell.com* (June 27, 2005); *idem*, "Supreme Confusion, Or, A Libertarian Defense of Affirmative Action," *LewRockwell.com* (July 4, 2003); Walter Block, Stephan Kinsella & Hans-Hermann Hoppe, "The Second Paradox of Blackmail," *Bus. Ethics Q.* 10, no. 3 (July 2000): 593–622; Walter Block, Roy Whitehead & N. Stephan Kinsella, "The Duty to Defend Advertising Injuries Caused by Junk Faxes: An Analysis of Privacy, Spam, Detection and Blackmail," *Whittier L. Rev.* 27, no. 4 (2006): 925–49.

17 and 23–25). Even with these, I have added extensive references and cross-references where appropriate.

I divided the book into six sections. Part I—Libertarianism covers my own introduction to libertarianism, an overview of libertarianism, and my take on anarchism. Part II—Rights concerns arguments for self-ownership, property rights, and punishment theory. Part III—Libertarian Legal Theory has chapters building on the theory in previous chapters to apply to various laws and libertarian issues, like causation and responsibility (chapter 8), contract and inalienability theory (chapters 9–11), and a long chapter on the pitfalls of legislation as a way of making law (chapter 13) (I probably should have turned this one into a PhD dissertation…).

Part IV—Intellectual Property contains a chapter presenting the basic case against IP (chapter 14), basically a streamlined and somewhat updated version of *AIP*, followed by chapter 15, which summarizes other IP arguments and issues that I wrote and spoke on after *AIP*. I also include some of my discussion with, and commentary on the views of, my pro-IP libertarian friend, the late J. Neil Schulman, and a piece on the nature of scarce and nonscarce goods, which is relevant to the IP issue.

Part V—Reviews contains four book reviews or review essays providing libertarian commentary on various books on law or political philosophy. Finally, Part VI—Interviews & Speeches is less formal and contains two interviews and a speech assessing the last five or six decades of the libertarian movement.

For those who want to skip the more extraneous material and focus on the core libertarian theory chapters, I recommend chapters **2–12**, **14–15**, and **18**.

I have revised all the material in the book, which was required since many of the original articles used different citation formats and also because some of my thinking and terminology has changed over the years. Several chapters are significantly revised or expanded, which in a few cases led to very long footnotes, since it would have been too disruptive to rewrite the article to integrate the extra commentary into the text; in some cases I moved very long footnotes to an appendix.

Although the chapters were all written separately and at different times over three decades, many of them build on (or anticipated) others.

For example, in chapter 10, originally published 1998–99, I outlined a sketch of a view of contracts, inalienability, and so on (note 48), and wrote "Elaboration of these ideas will have to await a subsequent article." I did so in 2003, in the article which became chapter 9. Thus, I was able to piece together several articles in a fairly systematic form since they either built on or anticipated each other and were written to be consistent with each other and all flowing from the same core principles and reasoning.

I have added extensive cross-references pointing to related discussion in other chapters. There is a bit of redundancy in some of the chapters since they were published independently. However, it is my view that the repetition that does exist in some articles can help reinforce a given argument or idea or show it from a different angle.

In one case I now disagree with something I originally wrote; I retained the original text and added an explanatory note (chapter 13, Part III.C). And in chapter 9 (Part III.C), I note that, regarding my earlier criticism of Rothbard's argument for inalienability: "I now think it is possible that his approach is more compatible with my own than I originally realized." But otherwise, I today still stand by most of the original content of those articles, in terms of substance. However, as noted several places in the text, I often now use terminology somewhat differently, e.g., the term *state* instead of *government*; *rivalrous* or *"conflictable"* instead of *scarce*; using the word *property* to refer to the relation between humans with respect to owned resources, instead of referring to the owned resource itself, and so on. I have in some cases updated the text to my current, preferred usage, but not always since it would have been too drastic and tedious.

I have also included a table of contents for some of the chapters where I thought it would be useful. And as noted above, in several chapters I moved very long footnotes to an appendix.

I have tried to conform references to a more or less uniform citation style of my own preference (a modified version of Chicago style), although my main goal was to simply provide sufficient information for the reader to locate the cited work, not to conform to some arbitrary format (and also not to obsess over consistency). In this, I am influenced by the citation policy of the second incarnation of the legal journal *The Greenbag*: "Citations should be accurate, complete, and unobtrusive.

Familiar sources need no citation. Authors may use whatever citation form they prefer; we will make changes only to keep footnotes from looking like goulash."[6]

I have also included hyperlinks for online versions of cited material where possible. If we lived in a copyright-free world, everything would be online and readers could easily find any cited work with a search. Alas. For my own work that I reference, since it is mostly available on my own website, I provide an initial hyperlink in the title but do not type out the URL in the text. Almost all of my work referenced in the text can be found at www.StephanKinsella.com/publications, www.StephanKinsella.com/lffs, or www.c4sif.org. I have liberally used permalinks via www.perma.cc in cases where I suspected future possible linkrot or where the original URL is overlong.

I debated various titles for this work. Titles like *Freedom and the Law* and *Liberty and Law* were already taken.[7] I considered at one time calling this work *The Ethics of Action*, as an amalgamation and nod to similar titles by other authors[8] and to evoke a recurring theme in my writing: an exploration of the ethics that guide action and of ethics implied by certain classes of action (see the argumentation ethics and estoppel theory of rights I advance in chapters 5 and 6). But in the end, this seemed too inscrutable and only applicable to a small part of this book's content, so for years I planned on using the title *Law in a Libertarian World: Legal Foundations of a Free Society*. In the end, some trusted colleagues urged me to drop the main title and use the subtitle instead. I have.

---

6 See Kinsella, "Cool Footnote Policy," *StephanKinsella.com* (June 14, 2002).

7 Bruno Leoni, *Freedom and the Law* (Indianapolis: Liberty Fund, expanded 3d. ed. 1991 [1961]; https://oll.libertyfund.org/title/kemp-freedom-and-the-law-lf-ed); Giovanni Sartori, *Liberty and Law* (Menlo Park, Ca.: Institute for Humane Studies, 1976).

8 Such as: Murray N. Rothbard, *The Ethics of Liberty* (New York: New York University Press, 1998); *idem, The Logic of Action* (Edward Elgar, 1997), later republished as *Economic Controversies* (Auburn, Ala.: Mises Institute, 2011; https://mises.org/library/economic-controversies); Michael Polanyi, *The Logic of Liberty* (Chicago: University of Chicago Press, 1980); G.B. Madison, *The Logic of Liberty* (New York: Greenwood Press, 1986); and others such as James M. Buchanan, *The Limits of Liberty: Between Anarchy and Leviathan*, vol. 7 in *The Collected Works of James M. Buchanan* (Indianapolis: Liberty Fund, 2000 [1975]). Interestingly, Jan Narveson's excellent *The Libertarian Idea* (Philadelphia: Temple University Press, 1988) is part of the "Ethics and Action" series edited by Tom Regan. I mention this in chapter 8, at n.11.

The length of the book turned out to be larger than expected, but I have chosen to publish this book as one volume instead of breaking it into two. I think this will be easier for the reader, given the extensive cross-references between chapters, and should make for a lower cost. My goal was never sales. It was only to help advance libertarian theory by making these thoughts accessible to whoever might be interested now or in the future. Thus, in addition to print (both hard and softcover) and ebook versions for sale on major platforms, I am of course posting a free digital version online at www.StephanKinsella.com/lffs, and with a Creative Commons Zero license. Anyone is free to republish this work, or translate it, or make audio versions, without asking my permission.

I have published in the past with various publishing houses, such as the Mises Institute, Oceana Publications, Oxford University Press, and so on, but for this book I have decided to self publish, under my own imprint, Papinian Press (www.PapinianPress.com), for a variety of reasons. First, my own procrastination has delayed this project for over a decade, so I was reluctant to add yet another year to this project by engaging a normal publisher. Second, I saw no benefit to using a mainstream publisher. I do not need their delays or "helpful suggestions," which would no doubt urge me to water down my arguments or make them more mainstream. No, thank you. And I have no career or academic ambitions to burnish by using a prestigious press. Also, I wanted freedom to release this book totally open source, free of any copyright restrictions, and to post free online versions, which most publishers would balk at. I'm frankly tired of the dinosaur legacy publishing industry. Finally, I may use the Papinian Press imprint for future book projects, so am glad to use this book to kick it off.

The imprint, by the way, is named after the third-century Roman jurist Papinian (Aemilius Papinianus), who also adorned the advertisement for my 2011 Mises Academy course on libertarian legal theory.[9]

---

[9] See www.PapinianPress.com and Kinsella, "KOL018 | "Libertarian Legal Theory: Property, Conflict, and Society: Lecture 1: Libertarian Basics: Rights and Law" (Mises Academy, 2011)," *Kinsella on Liberty Podcast* (Feb. 20, 2013).

The reason I admire Papinian, in addition to his being a great jurist:

> Papinian is said to have been put to death for refusing to compose a justification of Caracalla's murder of his brother and co-Emperor, Geta, declaring, so the story goes, that "it is easier to commit murder than to justify it."[10]

Papinian bravely chose death in the name of justice; and his formulation *"it is easier to commit murder than to justify it"* brilliantly encapsulates the distinction between *committing* an action and normatively *justifying* the action. It emphasizes the importance of justifying interpersonal violence, and the difference between description and prescription, between fact and value, between is and ought—insights which play a crucial role in my own defenses of rights (see chapters 5–7).

Although this book is written in English, many of the articles from which it derives have been translated into other languages, and some have audio versions available. They are online at www.StephanKinsella.com/translations and www.StephanKinsella.com/media.

I refer readers to www.StephanKinsella.com/lffs for errata, links to my own publications referenced in the book, and for supplementary material.

It is my hope that readers and future scholars will benefit from the arguments offered in these pages.

Stephan Kinsella
Houston, June 2023

---

[10] Barry Nicholas, *An Introduction to Roman Law*, rev. ed. (Oxford University Press, 1962), p. 30 n.2; see also chapter 5, n.1.

Acknowledgments

As noted in the Preface, I've been intensely involved in libertarianism for over forty years and, for almost thirty years, with the Mises Institute. I've been fortunate to have learned from thinkers from the past such as Rothbard, Mises, Ayn Rand, Milton Friedman, Frederic Bastiat, and many others,[1] but also from countless friends, mentors, colleagues, co-authors, acquaintances, interlocutors, discussants, and so on over the last forty years. It would be impossible to try to thank them all by name. Nonetheless I would like to try to express my appreciation for some special people and groups that have meant so much to me. I apologize in advance for those I have inadvertently omitted.

First and foremost, to my wife of thirty years, Cindy, and to all my close friends and family, for tolerating my libertarian obsessions and libertarian macho flashes for decades, and for listening to me argue, explain, and explore ideas.[2] To my son Ethan, to whom this book is dedicated, for inspiring me and enriching my life, and for also loving liberty and goodness. And to my trainer and friend, Stephanie Rakoczy, for letting me vent about all matters libertarian for many years now in between squats and pushups. I am grateful to my birth mother, Gail Doiron McGehee, for blessing me with my adoptive parents; to my

---

[1] Many of them included in the works listed in Stephan Kinsella, "The Greatest Libertarian Books," *StephanKinsella.com* (Aug. 7, 2006).

[2] See Michael Cloud, "The Late, Great Libertarian Macho Flash," *benbachrach.com* (1978; preserved at https://perma.cc/KY9P-V7K7). See also Jeff Wood, "The Triumphant Return of Libertarian Macho Flash," *medium.com* (March 8, 2017; https://perma.cc/KE6W-WQK4).

mom for taking me to the library as much as I wanted; to my dad for driving me to school so far away in another parish for so many years; and to Mrs. Reinhardt, a librarian at Catholic High School in Baton Rouge, for recommending that I read *The Fountainhead*.

This book would not be possible without the understanding of property rights I've arrived at, and this in turn would not be possible without the work of Hans-Hermann Hoppe, whom I have also been fortunate to call a close friend. His support, friendship, guidance, and example of personal and intellectual integrity over the years mean more to me than I can properly express. My life would not be the same, nor this book possible, without him.

I've had a host of libertarian friends and friend groups that I've learned and benefitted from, or had support from, over the years, including my longtime friend Jack Criss, Jr.; the "Las Vegas crew"—former students of Rothbard and Hoppe, and now my good friends: Doug French (and Deanna Forbush), Jeff Barr, Lee Iglody, Jim Yohe, Joe Becker; others such as Juan Fernando Carpio; Greg and Joy Morin; Konrad Graf, Michael Conaghan, Jacob Huebert, Gene Healy, Gary Chartier, Gerard Casey, Richard Storey, Tom Woods, Michael Malice, Bob Murphy, Roderick Long, Jan Narveson, Frank van Dun, Robert Bradley, Jr.; Gil Guillory, Paul Edwards, Jacob Lovell, Rob Wicks, Greg Rome, Brian Martinez, Dick Clark, Isaac Bergman, Daniel Coleman, Timo Virkkala, and many others in my "Libertarian Forum" crowd (you know who you are); James Cox and Daniel Rothschild; many friends and scholars from the Property and Freedom Society and from countless Mises Institute events and conferences since 1995, including Lew Rockwell, David Gordon, Tom DiLorenzo, Peter Klein, Jeff Herbener, Joe Salerno, Sean Gabb, and others; correspondents from years ago such as Johan Ridenfeldt and Chris Whitten; co-authors and friends such as Patrick Tinsley, Jeff Tucker, and Walter Block, the first two of whom co-authored chapters with me in this volume. Thanks also to Nelson Loftin, for nudging me over several years to complete this book.

My dear friend Guido Hülsmann, whom I met on a bus from the Atlanta airport to the Mises Institute in Auburn in 1995 when we were both going there to meet Hans-Hermann Hoppe, has been an important friend and influence, both personally and intellectually.

My friend Wendy McElroy has also been an inspiration and sounding board and helped me see the light on IP.

The notes for various chapters in this book also thank various commentators.

I would also like to thank Randy Barnett, and several LSU law professors, such as Saúl Litvinoff, Glenn Morris, William Hawkland, Alain Levasseur, Robert Pascal, and John Devlin, for inspiration, support, and guidance in my earlier years in law school and in the beginning years of my legal practice and scholarly and educational endeavors (Litvinoff and Pascal were not my professors but they became friends and correspondents after law school). I learned a great deal at the LSE about international law and legal scholarship from professor and now Baroness Rosalyn Higgins, later President of the International Court of Justice; she inspired and informed much of my subsequent legal publications on international law.

I am also grateful to my intellectual adversaries, who have forced me to hone, refine, and clarify my arguments to counter and explain the errors in theirs.

P.J. Doland, a fellow libertarian and web-designer with www.DancingMammoth.com, has graciously hosted and helped me run my own websites and others I manage over the years, all in the service of liberty, which were invaluable in collecting, publishing, and assembling material used in the preparation of this book. Since I haltingly started this book project about fifteen years ago, I've had the assistance of several people, including Lisa Eldridge and Rosemary Denshaw (transcriptions); Justina Clark, Harry David, Lauren Barlow, and Carly Catt (copyediting); Susi Clark, of www.creativeblueprintdesign.com, for cover design, typesetting and publishing assistance; and Susan Bruck (proofreading, indexing, and bibliography).

The image on the back cover of the book is based on a painting by my childhood friend John Wax, of www.JohnWaxArt.com, which itself was based on photographs of a statue by H.C. Andersen.[3] To get permission and arrange a private photographer at the Andersen Musuem in Rome, I was fortunate to have the help of my Italian libertarian

---

3 See Kinsella, "The Story of a Libertarian Book Cover," *StephanKinsella.com* (March 4, 2011).

friend and scholar, Roberta Modugno, and my Italian-speaking Canadian libertarian attorney friend Daniel Roncari.

To all these, and many others not mentioned, I am grateful.

PART I

LIBERTARIANISM

1

How I Became a Libertarian

First published as part of the *LewRockwell.com* autobiography series initiated by Walter Block, as "How I Became A Libertarian," *LewRockwell.com* (December 18, 2002). Later included as "Being a Libertarian" in *I Chose Liberty: Autobiographies of Contemporary Libertarians* (compiled by Walter Block; Mises Institute 2010). Additional biographical pieces may be found at www.stephankinsella.com/publications/#biographical.

Unlike many libertarians who dally with socialism before seeing the light, I have never been attracted to leftism. Indeed, although I of course welcome former pinkos to our ranks, I'm always a bit suspicious of anyone who could ever be swayed by that bunk.

Born in 1965, I was reared in a small town near Baton Rouge, Louisiana. My natural aversion to leftism stems from this upbringing. The milieu—if South Louisiana can be said to have one—was nominally Democratic, but relatively apolitical, culturally conservative, and Catholic. I can't recall ever meeting any open or hardcore leftists until college.

There were other contributing factors that made me ripe for libertarianism. For one, I have always been strongly individualistic and merit-oriented. This is probably because I was adopted and thus have always tended to cavalierly dismiss the importance of "blood ties" and any inherited or "unearned" group characteristics. This made me an ideal candidate to be enthralled by Ayn Rand's master-of-universe "I don't need anything from you or owe you anything" themes.

Another factor is my strong sense of outrage at injustice, which probably developed as a result of my hatred of bullies and bullying. I was frequently attacked by them as a kid, because I was small for my age, bookish, and a smartass. Not a good combination.

I attended Catholic elementary and high school in Baton Rouge. I had a love-hate relationship with Mrs. Reinhardt, Catholic High School's librarian. When she was not expelling me and my cronies from the library for pulling pranks, she would recommend books to me, as she knew I was an avid reader of both fiction and nonfiction. One day she recommended Ayn Rand's *The Fountainhead* to me.[1] (I believe this was in 1982, when I was a junior in high school—the same year Rand died.)

"Read this. You'll like it," she told me. *Ex nihilo*—something. Rand's ruthless logic of justice appealed to me. I was thrilled to see a more-or-less rigorous application of reason to fields outside the natural sciences. I think this helped me to avoid succumbing, in college, to the simplistic and naïve empiricism-scientism that most of my fellow engineering classmates naturally absorbed. Mises's dualistic epistemology and criticism of monism-positivism-empiricism, which I studied much later, also helped shield me from scientism.

By my first year of college (1983), where I studied electrical engineering, I was a fairly avid "Objectivist" style libertarian. I had read Henry Hazlitt's *Economics in One Lesson*[2] and some of Milton Friedman's works, but I initially steered clear of "libertarian" writing. Since Rand was so right on so many things, I at first assumed she—and her disciples Peter Schwartz and Leonard Peikoff—must be right in denouncing libertarianism as the enemy of liberty.

And yet in my reading I kept coming across libertarians, whose views seemed virtually identical to Rand's "capitalist" politics. Finally, out of exasperation at trying to reconcile Rand's denunciation of libertarians with their seemingly similar views, I read Rothbard's *For a New*

---

[1] Ayn Rand, *The Fountainhead* (New York: Signet, 1996). See also Jerome Tuccille, *It Usually Begins with Ayn Rand* (Stein and Day, 1971); and "Libertarianism After Fifty Years: What Have We Learned?" (ch. 25).

[2] Henry Hazlitt, *Economics in One Lesson* (New York: Three Rivers Press, 1988; https://fee.org/resources/economics-in-one-lesson).

Liberty,[3] and then several other works, such as Nozick, the Tannehills, David Friedman, etc.[4] Before long I realized Rand's minarchism was flawed. Individual rights entail anarcho-capitalism; a state, even a minarchist one, necessarily violates the individual rights that Rand so passionately championed. Rand made a lot of sense on a lot of issues, but her arguments in favor of government were strained.

I remember attending my only Objectivist conference, in Dallas, with my good friend Jack Criss (a libertarian radio talk show host from Jackson, Mississippi). Entitled "Meeting of the Minds," the conference showcased Objectivist stars David Kelley, John Ridpath, and Alan Gotthelf. This was in March 1989, I believe, before David Kelley had been purged from official Objectivist circles for daring to praise Barbara Branden's biography *The Passion of Ayn Rand.*[5] I had corresponded with Kelley who was gracious enough to take time to reply (this was before email) to my questions. I have always admired and respected Kelley.

I had several stimulating conversations with him at the conference, mostly on epistemology and philosophy. But I remember at a reception one of the students telling how he had taken his copy of *The Passion of Ayn Rand* and burned it in a private ceremony in his mom's back yard when he realized how "evil" it was. I think he sought to gain points among his audience by relating this tale. I recall Jack and I looking at each other with cocked eyebrows. "Book burning." Yes. Well. That was the last and only Objectivist conference I ever attended.

In the late-80s I started publishing columns in the LSU student newspaper, *The Daily Reveille*, from an explicitly libertarian perspective. As my interests became more sharply political and philosophical, my girlfriend (later wife) and friends urged me to consider law school. I was by this time in engineering grad school. Unlike many attorneys, I was not one of those who had always wanted to be a lawyer. In fact it never occurred to me until my girlfriend suggested it over dinner, when I was wondering what degree I could pursue next, so as to avoid

---

[3] Murray N. Rothbard, *For a New Liberty,* 2d ed. (Auburn, Ala.: Mises Institute, 2006; https://mises.org/library/new-liberty-libertarian-manifesto).

[4] And many of the works listed in Stephan Kinsella, "The Greatest Libertarian Books," *StephanKinsella.com* (Aug. 7, 2006).

[5] Barbara Branden, *The Passion of Ayn Rand* (New York: Anchor, 1987).

having to enter the workforce. At the time I thought one had to have a pre-law degree and many prerequisite courses that engineers would lack; and I feared law school would be difficult. I remember my girl-friend's chemical engineer father laughing out loud at my concern that law school might be more difficult than engineering. In retrospect, I can say that law school is not easy, it is a lot of work—but it is not that conceptually difficult. Lots of morons graduate from law school.

By 1988 I was in law school and becoming a more well-round-ed libertarian, having read by this time Rothbard, Mises, Bastiat, the Tannehills, and a non-trivial portion of the books offered in the *Laissez-Faire Books* catalog. In that year there were two significant events in my life, from a libertarian perspective. One was Hans-Hermann Hoppe's controversial and provocative article in *Liberty*, "The Ultimate Justification of the Private Property Ethic."[6] In this article Hoppe sets forth his "argumentation ethics," which holds that the libertarian private property ethic is implied in the very activity of argumentation—because those engaged in argumentation already presuppose the value of conflict-avoidance and the ability to control property and thus, those arguing in favor of socialism contradict themselves.

The second thing was that I encountered the legal principle of "estoppel" in my contracts class. This is the ubiquitous legal principle that precludes someone from asserting a legal claim or position that is inconsistent with earlier statements or behavior. I remember sitting in contracts class, as Professor Morris lectured on this topic, thinking "Eureka!" to myself, as I began to see that the concept of estoppel meshed perfectly with libertarian logic (and also with Hoppe's argu-mentation ethics). The libertarian non-aggression principle holds that force may only be used *in response* to (initiated) force. There is a nice

---

[6] Hans-Hermann Hoppe, "The Ultimate Justification of the Private Property Ethic," *Liberty* 2, no. 1, September 1988), p. 20, republished as "On the Ultimate Justification of the Ethics of Private Property," chap. 13 in *The Economics and Ethics of Private Property: Studies in Political Economy and Philosophy* (Auburn, Ala.: Mises Institute, 2006 [1993]; www.hanshoppe.com/eepp). See also Stephan Kinsella, "Argumentation Ethics and Liberty: A Concise Guide," *StephanKinsella.com* (May 27, 2011), and other material available at www.StephanKinsella.com/lffs.

symmetry here. One may use force, if and only if it is in response to initiated force (aggression).[7]

I saw in class that day that the principle of estoppel could help explain and justify the non-aggression rule. Force was justified against an aggressor, because having used force himself he would be estopped from objecting to retaliation. For him to assert that force is wrong—which he must do in order to object to retaliation—would contradict the "force is permissible" maxim underlying his own act of aggression. He is "estopped" from asserting a claim inconsistent with that underlying his earlier behavior.

My estoppel theory complements and draws on Hoppe's argumentation ethics. For years I believed that I first came up with my estoppel theory and then read Hoppe's work and linked the two together. Now I am not so sure and think that I first read and absorbed Hoppe's argumentation ethic, which made me fixate on the similar logic of estoppel when I coincidentally studied it in law school shortly thereafter.

I was at King's College London in 1991, pursuing a master's degree in law, when I produced the first draft of a paper arguing estoppel

---

[7] For more on this, see "A Libertarian Theory of Punishment and Rights" (ch. 5) and "Dialogical Arguments for Libertarian Rights (ch. 6); also Stephan Kinsella, "The Genesis of Estoppel: My Libertarian Rights Theory," *StephanKinsella.com* (March 22, 2016). For more on argumentation ethics, *see* chaps. 5 and 6, as well as "Defending Argumentation Ethics" (ch. 7); "The Undeniable Morality of Capitalism" (ch. 22); Hans-Hermann Hoppe, "The Ethical Justification of Capitalism and Why Socialism Is Morally Indefensible," chap. 7 in Hans-Hermann Hoppe, *A Theory of Socialism and Capitalism: Economics, Politics, and Ethics* (Auburn, Ala.: Mises Institute, 2010 [1989]; www.hanshoppe.com/tsc); *idem*, "From the Economics of Laissez Faire to the Ethics of Libertarianism," "The Justice of Economic Efficiency," and "On the Ultimate Justification of the Ethics of Private Property," chaps. 11–13 in *The Economics and Ethics of Private Property*; *idem*, "Of Common, Public, and Private Property and the Rationale for Total Privatization," in *The Great Fiction: Property, Economy, Society, and the Politics of Decline* (Second Expanded Edition, Mises Institute, 2021; www.hanshoppe.com/tgf); *idem*, "PFP163 | Hans Hermann Hoppe, 'On The Ethics of Argumentation' (PFS 2016)," *The Property and Freedom Podcast*, ep. 163 (June 30, 2022); Stephan Kinsella, "Argumentation Ethics and Liberty: A Concise Guide," *StephanKinsella.com* (May 27, 2011); *idem*, "Hoppe's Argumentation Ethics and Its Critics," *StephanKinsella.com* (Aug. 11, 2015); Frank van Dun, "Argumentation Ethics and the Philosophy of Freedom," *Libertarian Papers* 1, art. no. 19 (2009; www.libertarianpapers.org); Marian Eabrasu, "A Reply to the Current Critiques Formulated Against Hoppe's Argumentation Ethics," *Libertarian Papers* 1, 20 (2009; www.libertarianpapers.org); Norbert Slenzok, "The Libertarian Argumentation Ethics, the Transcendental Pragmatics of Language, and the Conflict-Freedom Principle," *Analiza i Egzystencja* 58 (2022), 35–64.

can help justify libertarian rights. Somewhat naïvely, I submitted it to King's College Law School's law review, whereupon it was summarily rejected. Not daunted, I submitted an improved draft to Tibor Machan for his journal *Reason Papers*. I had read many of Machan's works, including his *Human Rights and Human Liberties*[8] and *Individuals and Their Rights*,[9] and he had been kind enough to respond to several of my letters. I remember speaking with him one night, about the submission, from a students' pay telephone at King's College in London, and then getting drinks at a pub with friends, none of them knowing or able to appreciate that I had just spoken with a "famous" libertarian writer whose books I had read. "Estoppel: A New Justification for Individual Rights" was published in the Fall 1992 issue of *Reason Papers*.[10]

Another shift in my libertarian life occurred in 1994, when I first met Lew Rockwell, Hans Hoppe, and Murray Rothbard. But let me back up. After finally completing my nine years of higher education, I had to earn a living. So in 1992 I started practicing law in Houston. When Hoppe's second English-language book, *The Economics and Ethics of Private Property*, came out in 1993,[11] I decided to do a review essay for a law review; the review was published in 1994 in the *St. Mary's Law Journal*.[12] I promptly sent it to Hoppe, who sent back a warm thank you note.

By mid-1994 I had moved to Philadelphia (I was there for three years, until I returned to Houston in 1997, where I reside today), and resolved to attend the John Randolph Club meeting in October 1994, near Washington, D.C., which was a gathering of paleoconservatives from the *Chronicles* crowd and several libertarians associated with the Mises Institute, part of a short-lived attempt at yet another libertarian-

---

[8] Tibor R. Machan, *Human Rights and Human Liberties: A Radical Reconsideration of the American Political Tradition* (Chicago: Burnham Inc Pub, 1975).

[9] Tibor R. Machan, *Individuals and Their Rights* (Chicago: Open Court Publishing, 1989).

[10] See also Kinsella, "The Genesis of Estoppel: My Libertarian Rights Theory" and chapters 5–7 in this volume. Tibor became a good friend. He passed away in 2016. See Kinsella, "Remembering Tibor Machan, Libertarian Mentor and Friend: Reflections on a Giant," *StephanKinsella.com* (April 19, 2016).

[11] Hoppe, *The Economics and Ethics of Private Property*.

[12] Stephan Kinsella, "The Undeniable Morality of Capitalism," *St. Mary's L. J.* 25, no. 4 (1994): 1419–47, included as chapter 22 in this volume.

conservative "fusionism."[13] My primary goal was to meet Hoppe, Rothbard, and Rockwell. I was thrilled to meet them and other scholars associated with the Mises Institute, and was able to get Murray to autograph my copy of *Man, Economy, and State*,[14] which he inscribed *"To Stephan: For Man & Economy, and against the state —Best regards, Murray Rothbard."* Well, I know the nicer one-volume edition is out now, but just try to get me to part with my musty, tattered two-volume copy. Rothbard unfortunately passed away in January 1995, just two months later, but I was happy that I was able to meet him.

Since then I have attended many Mises Institute conferences, including every one of the annual Austrian Scholars Conferences, initiated, if I am not mistaken, in 1995. Over the years I gained more appreciation for Mises and Austrian economics, and for the unparalleled scope of Rothbard's scholarly contributions to economics and political philosophy, and related fields. I am now not only an anarcho-libertarian, but a Misesian-Austrian. I have gained an increasingly deeper respect for Lew Rockwell and the singular achievement that is the Mises Institute. It has become my intellectual home.

---

[13] See references in Kinsella, "The Three Fusionisms: Old, New, and Cautious," *StephanKinsella.com* (Jan. 16, 2022).

[14] Murray N. Rothbard, *Man, Economy, and State, with Power and Market*, Scholars ed., 2d ed. (Auburn, Ala.: Mises Institute, 2009; https://mises.org/library/man-economy-and-state-power-and-market).

2

What Libertarianism Is

Originally published in *Property, Freedom, and Society: Essays in Honor of Hans-Hermann Hoppe* (Guido Hülsmann & Stephan Kinsella, eds., Mises Institute, 2009). The original author's note thanked "fellow Hoppe aficionados Juan Fernando Carpio, Paul Edwards, Gil Guillory, Manuel Lora, and Patrick Tinsley for helpful comments."

PROPERTY, RIGHTS, AND LIBERTY

Libertarians tend to agree on a wide array of policies and principles. Nonetheless it is not easy to find consensus on what libertarianism's defining characteristic is, or on what distinguishes it from other political theories and systems.

Various formulations abound. It is said that libertarianism is about: individual rights; property rights;[1] the free market; capitalism; justice;

---

[1] Although the term "private property rights" is widely used, property rights are in a sense necessarily *public*, since the borders or boundaries of property must be *publicly visible* so that non-owners can avoid trespass. For more on this aspect of property borders, see Hans-Hermann Hoppe, *A Theory of Socialism and Capitalism: Economics, Politics, and Ethics* (Auburn, Ala.: Mises Institute, 2010; www.hanshoppe.com/tsc), pp. 167–68; "A Libertarian Theory of Contract: Title Transfer, Binding Promises, and Inalienability" (ch. 9), at n.38; "Law and Intellectual Property in a Stateless Society" (ch. 14), Part II.C, note 7 and accompanying text, text at notes 24–25, and Part III.B; Stephan Kinsella, *Against Intellectual Property* (Auburn, Ala.: Mises Institute, 2008), pp. 30–31, 49; "Selling Does Not Imply Ownership, and Vice-Versa: A Dissection" (ch. 11), text at n.24. *See also idem*, "How To

the nonaggression principle. Not all these will do, however. Capitalism and the free market describe the catallactic conditions that arise or are permitted in a libertarian society, but do not encompass other aspects of libertarianism. And individual rights, justice, and aggression collapse into property rights. As Murray Rothbard explained, individual rights *are* property rights.[2] And justice is just giving someone his due—which, again, depends on what his rights are.[3]

The nonaggression principle is also dependent on property rights, since what aggression is depends on what our (property) rights are. If you hit me, it is aggression *because* I have a property right in my body. If I take from you the apple you possess, this is trespass, aggression, only *because* you own the apple. One cannot identify an act of aggression without implicitly assigning a corresponding property right to the victim.[4]

Think About Property (2019)," *StephanKinsella.com* (April 25, 2021); and Randy E. Barnett, "A Consent Theory of Contract," *Colum. L. Rev.* 86 (1986; www.randybarnett.com/pre-2000): 269–321, at 291, 303.

[2] Murray N. Rothbard, "'Human Rights' as Property Rights," in *The Ethics of Liberty* (New York: New York University Press, 1998; https://mises.org/library/human-rights-property-rights); *idem, For a New Liberty*, 2d ed. (Auburn, Ala.: Mises Institute, 2006; https://mises.org/library/new-liberty-libertarian-manifesto), p. 42 *et pass.* See also "*Against Intellectual Property* After Twenty Years: Looking Back and Looking Forward" (ch. 15), Part IV.B.

[3] "Justice is the constant and perpetual wish to render every one his due.… The maxims of law are these: to live honestly, to hurt no one, to give every one his due." J.A.C. Thomas, ed., *The Institutes of Justinian: Text, Translation, and Commentary*, J.A.C. Thomas, trans. (Amsterdam: North-Holland Publishing Company, 1975).

[4] The standard libertarian litany is that the nonaggression principle (the NAP; sometimes also called the nonaggression axiom by libertarians, in an idiosyncratic usage of the term "axiom," no doubt inspired by Ayn Rand's idiosyncratic use of the term axiom) prohibits the initiation of force against the person *or property* of someone else—*or threats* thereof, *or fraud*. Some libertarians or libertarian critics argue that trespass to owned resources, fraud, and threats do not quite fit into the NAP because these things are not actually "aggression," as the term is properly understood. (See, e.g., the criticisms of libertarianism for being unable to explain why fraud may be prohibited, by James Child and Benjamin Ferguson, as discussed in "A Libertarian Theory of Contract" (ch. 9), Part III.E. The NAP in a literal sense prohibits hitting or using someone's body ("aggression") without their permission, which implies self- or body-ownership. Thus, the NAP implies self-ownership, and vice-versa. They are merely different ways of expressing the same view: owning one's body implies that aggression against it is impermissible; the prohibition against aggression implies self/body-ownership. (See also "On Libertarian Legal Theory, Self-Ownership and Drug Laws" (ch. 23).)

The rationale for body-ownership, however, is extended by libertarians to develop similar property rights in external resources; and also to prohibit threats and fraud. (See ibid.) Thus, in my view, the term "nonaggression principle" is an acceptable shorthand for basic

So, as descriptive terms for our political philosophy, capitalism and the free market are too narrow, and justice, individual rights, and aggression all boil down to, or are defined in terms of, property rights.

What of property rights, then? Is this what differentiates libertarianism from other political philosophies—that we favor property rights, and all others do not? Surely such a claim is untenable. After all, a property right is simply the *exclusive right to control a scarce resource*—what I often refer to now as *conflictable* resources.[5] Property rights specify which persons own—have the right to control—various scarce resources in a given region or jurisdiction. Yet everyone and every political theory advances *some* theory of property. None of the various forms of socialism deny property rights; each socialism will specify an owner for every scarce resource.[6] If the state nationalizes an industry, it is asserting ownership of these means of production. If the state taxes you, it is implicitly asserting ownership of the funds taken. If my land is transferred to a private developer by eminent domain statutes, the developer is now the owner. If the law allows a recipient of racial discrimination to sue his employer for a sum of money—he is the (new)

---

libertarian property rights principles—self-ownership plus ownership of external resources based on original appropriation, and fraud and threats—as long as it is kept in mind that in literal terms it refers to body-ownership and that the other property rights are extensions of and based on this primary property right. See also Kinsella, "Aggression and Property Rights Plank in the Libertarian Party Platform," *StephanKinsella.com* (May 30, 2022); *idem*, "KOL259 | "How To Think About Property", New Hampshire Liberty Forum 2019," *Kinsella on Liberty Podcast* (Feb. 9, 2019); "On Libertarian Legal Theory, Self-Ownership and Drug Laws" (ch. 23); "Libertarianism After Fifty Years: What Have We Learned?" (ch. 25); Kinsella, "KOL229 | Ernie Hancock Show: IP Debate with Alan Korwin," *Kinsella on Liberty Podcast* (Nov. 16, 2017); *idem*, "KOL161 | Argumentation Ethics, Estoppel, and Libertarian Rights: Adam Smith Forum, Moscow (2014)," *Kinsella on Liberty Podcast* (Nov. 7, 2014).

[5] In revising this chapter, this footnote grew to unmanageable length. I have placed the relevant commentary in Appendix I, below.

[6] For a systematic analysis of various forms of socialism, from Socialism Russian-Style, Socialism Social-Democratic Style, the Socialism of Conservatism, the Socialism of Social Engineering, see Hoppe, *A Theory of Socialism and Capitalism*, chaps. 3–6. Recognizing the common elements of various forms of socialism and their distinction from libertarianism (capitalism), Hoppe incisively defines socialism as "an institutionalized interference with or aggression against private property and private property claims." Ibid., p. 2. See also the quote from Hoppe in note 14, below.

owner of the money.[7] If the state conscripts someone, or imprisons them as the penalty for refusing to serve in the military, or for failure to pay taxes, or for using illegal narcotics, then the state is claiming legal ownership of the person's body.

Protection of and respect for property rights is thus not unique to libertarianism. Every legal system defines and enforces some property rights system. What is distinctive about libertarianism is its *particular property assignment rules*—its view as to *who is the owner* of each contestable, conflictable resource, and how to determine this.

LIBERTARIAN PROPERTY RIGHTS

A system of property rights assigns a particular owner to every scarce (conflictable) resource.[8] These resources obviously include natural resources such as land, fruits of trees, and so on. Objects found in nature are not the only scarce resources, however. Each human actor has, controls, and is identified and associated with a unique human body, which is also a scarce resource.[9] Both human bodies and non-human

---

[7] Even the private thief, by taking your watch, is implicitly acting on the maxim that *he* has the right to control it—that he is its owner. He does not deny property rights—he simply differs from the libertarian as to *who the owner is*. In fact, as Adam Smith observed: "If there is any society among robbers and murderers, they must at least, according to the trite observation, abstain from robbing and murdering one another." Adam Smith, *The Theory of Moral Sentiments* (Indianapolis: Liberty Fund, [1759] 1982), II.II.3.

[8] As Hoppe points out in the Foreword, regarding the principle of "*private property and original appropriation*: Logically, what is required to avoid all conflict regarding external material objects used or usable as means of action, i.e. as goods, is clear: every good must always and at all times be owned privately, i.e. controlled exclusively by some specified person."

Note also that it is *only* scarce (conflictable) things that can be owned, that is, be the subject of property rights. For example, as noted in the section *"IP Rights as Negative Easements"* in "*Against Intellectual Property* After Twenty Years" (ch. 15), information or knowledge (recipes, in general), as a non-scarce, non-conflictable thing, *cannot* be owned; any law *purporting* to assign property rights in such things is just a *disguised* reassignment of property rights in existing conflictable resources (money, factories, printing presses, etc).

[9] As Hoppe observes, even in a paradise with a superabundance of goods:
every person's physical body would still be a scarce resource and thus the need for the establishment of property rules, i.e., rules regarding people's bodies, would exist. One is not used to thinking of one's own body in terms of a scarce good, but in imagining the most ideal situation one could ever hope for, the Garden of Eden, it

scarce resources are desired for use as means by actors in the pursuit of various goals.[10]

Accordingly, any political or legal system must assign ownership rights in human bodies as well as in external things.

The libertarian view is that individual rights—property rights—are assigned according to a few simple principles: *self-ownership*, in the case of human bodies; and, in the case of previously-unowned external things (conflictable resources), in accordance with principles of *original appropriation*, *contractual title transfer*, and *rectification*.[11] Let us discuss

---

becomes possible to realize that one's body is indeed the prototype of a scarce good for the use of which property rights, i.e., rights of exclusive ownership, somehow have to be established, in order to avoid clashes.

Hoppe, *A Theory of Socialism and Capitalism*, pp. 8–9. *See also* Hans-Hermann Hoppe, "Of Common, Public, and Private Property and the Rationale for Total Privatization," in *The Great Fiction: Property, Economy, Society, and the Politics of Decline* (Second Expanded Edition, Mises Institute, 2021; www.hanshoppe.com/tgf); Hans-Hermann Hoppe, "On The Ethics of Argumentation," *Property and Freedom Podcast* (episode 163; 2016; www.PropertyAndFreedom.org); and "Causation and Aggression" (ch. 8) (discussing the use of other humans' bodies as means).

N.b.: *correlating* (not: equating) an actor's "self" or person with his corporeal body is not mystical or incoherent, as some (even *soi-disant* libertarian!) critics confusingly maintain, any more than it is mystical to conceptually distinguish the mind from the brain. See "How We Come to Own Ourselves" (ch. 4), at n.1 *et pass.*

10 See "Causation and Aggression" (ch. 8).

11 As Narveson writes:

Robert Nozick has most usefully divided the space for principles on the subject of property into three classes: (1) *initial acquisition*, that is, the acquisition of property rights in external things from a previous condition in which they were unowned by anyone in particular; (2) *transfer*, that is, the passing of property (that is to say, property rights) from one rightholder to another; and (3) *rectification*, which is the business of restoring just distributions of property when they have been upset by admittedly unjust practices such as theft and fraud.

Jan Narveson, *The Libertarian Idea*, reissue ed. (Broadview Press, 2001), p. 69. See also Robert Nozick, *Anarchy, State, and Utopia* (New York: Basic Books, 1974), ch. 7, section I; Roderick T. Long, "Why Libertarians Believe There is Only One Right," *C4SS.org* (April 7, 2014; https://c4ss.org/content/25648) ("Libertarian property rights are, famously, governed by principles of justice in initial appropriation (mixing one's labour with previously unowned resources), justice in transfer (mutual consent), and justice in rectification (say, restitution plus damages)"); and Gary Chartier, *Anarchy and Legal Order: Law and Politics for a Stateless Society* (Cambridge University Press, 2013), at 64–65, *et seq.*, elaborating on the "baseline possessory rules" corresponding to original appropriation and contractual title transfer. Regarding transfers made for purposes of rectification, see ibid., chap. 5, "Rectifying Injury," esp. §II.C.2, and "A Libertarian Theory of Punishment and Rights" (ch. 5), at Parts IV.B and IV.G.

these in turn in the following sections. Note that in this chapter I aim mostly to *describe* libertarian principles, not necessarily to justify them; subsequent chapters provide further arguments in support of these principles.

PROPERTY IN BODIES

Let us consider first the libertarian property assignment rules with respect to human bodies, and the corresponding notion of aggression as it pertains to bodies.[12]

Libertarians often refer to the non-aggression principle, or NAP, as their prime value. As Ayn Rand said, "So long as men desire to live together, no man may *initiate*—do you hear me? No man may *start*—the use of physical force against others."[13] Or, as Rothbard put it:

See also Kinsella, "The Limits of Libertarianism?: A Dissenting View," *StephanKinsella.com* (April 20, 2014); *idem*, "KOL345 | Kinsella's Libertarian "Constitution" or: State Constitutions vs. the Libertarian Private Law Code (PorcFest 2021)," *Kinsella on Liberty Podcast* (June 26, 2021).

[12] This issue is discussed in further detail in "How We Come to Own Ourselves" (ch. 4); see also "A Libertarian Theory of Punishment and Rights" (ch. 5).

[13] Ayn Rand, "Galt's Speech," in *For the New Intellectual*, quoted in "Physical Force" entry, *The Ayn Rand Lexicon: Objectivism from A to Z*, Harry Binswanger, ed. (New York: New American Library, 1986; https://perma.cc/L4YA-96CC). Ironically, Objectivists often excoriate libertarians for having a "contextless" concept of aggression—that is, that "aggression" or "rights" is meaningless unless these concepts are embedded in the larger philosophical framework of Objectivism—despite Galt's straightforward, physicalist definition of aggression as the initiation of physical force against others. In "Q&A on Libertarianism," *The Ayn Rand Lexicon* (http://aynrandlexicon.com/ayn-rand-ideas/ari-q-and-a-on-libertarianism.html), for example, (someone at) the Ayn Rand Institute writes:

> The "libertarians," in this usage of the term, plagiarize Ayn Rand's non-initiation of force principle and convert it into an axiom, denying the need for and relevance of philosophical fundamentals—not only the underlying ethics, but also the underlying metaphysics and epistemology…. libertarianism declares that the value of liberty and the evil of initiating force are self-evident primaries, needing no justification or even explanation—leaving undefined such key concepts as "liberty," "force," "justice," "good," and "evil." It claims compatibility with all views in metaphysics, epistemology, and ethics—even subjectivism, mysticism, skepticism, altruism, and nihilism—substituting "hate the state" for intellectual content.

See also Peter Schwartz, "Libertarianism: The Perversion of Liberty," in Ayn Rand, *The Voice of Reason: Essays in Objectivist Thought* (Meridian, 1990) and the "Libertarians" entry in The Ayn Rand Lexicon (http://aynrandlexicon.com/).

The libertarian creed rests upon one central axiom: that no man or group of men may aggress against the person or property of anyone else. This may be called the "nonaggression axiom." "Aggression" is defined as the initiation of the use or threat of physical violence against the person or property of anyone else. Aggression is therefore synonymous with invasion.[14]

But as noted above, Rand own's formulation in support of the NAP—"no man may *initiate*—do you hear me? No man may *start*—the use of physical force against others"—relies on rudimentary concepts like physical force and the initiation thereof, which do not really require much explanation; rather, her theory builds on these fairly uncontroversial concepts. Just as her theory can use these basic concepts as building blocks, libertarians can coherently use these principles in articulating what we oppose, without lapsing into subjectivism, nihilism, etc. People can communicate with language without adopting the whole of Objectivism, after all. See also Walter Block's response to Schwartz: "Libertarianism vs. Objectivism: A Response to Peter Schwartz," *Reason Papers* No. 26 (Summer 2003; https://reasonpapers.com/archives/): 39–62.

[14] Rothbard, *For a New Liberty*, p. 23. See also *idem*, "Property and Criminality," in *idem*, *The Ethics of Liberty*: "The fundamental axiom of libertarian theory is that each person must be a self-owner, and that no one has the right to interfere with such self-ownership" (p. 60), and "What … aggressive violence means is that one man invades the property of another without the victim's consent. The invasion may be against a man's property in his person (as in the case of bodily assault), or against his property in tangible goods (as in robbery or trespass)" (p. 45). Hoppe writes:

> If … an action is performed that uninvitedly invades or changes the physical integrity of another person's body and puts this body to a use that is not to this very person's own liking, this action … is called *aggression*.… Next to the concept of action, *property* is the most basic category in the social sciences. As a matter of fact, all other concepts to be introduced in this chapter—aggression, contract, capitalism and socialism—are definable in terms of property: *aggression* being aggression against property, *contract* being a nonaggressive relationship between property owners, *socialism* being an institutionalized policy of aggression against property, and *capitalism* being an institutionalized policy of the recognition of property and contractualism.

Hoppe, *A Theory of Socialism and Capitalism*, pp. 22, 18.

In earlier years of the modern libertarian movement (see "Libertarianism After Fifty Years: What Have We Learned?" (ch. 25); Kinsella, "Foreword," in Chase Rachels, *A Spontaneous Order: The Capitalist Case For A Stateless Society* (2015; https://archive.org/details/ASpontaneousOrder0)), what most libertarians now refer to as the non-aggression principle was sometimes called the non-aggression axiom, probably because of Rand's somewhat idiosyncratic use of the term axiom in her philosophy. See "Axioms" entry *The Ayn Rand Lexicon* (http://aynrandlexicon.com/lexicon/axioms.html). Rothbard himself, who was initially heavily influenced by Rand, sometimes uses this phraseology, as can be seen in the passages quoted above. Not all libertarians believe the NAP is "axiomatic" in Rand's sense—a proposition that is self-evidently true because its denial results in contradiction—but all consistent and coherent libertarians oppose the legitimacy of aggression, for whatever reasons, and thus favor the non-aggression *principle* (i.e., self-ownership), at least to a large extent.

In other words, libertarians maintain that the only way to violate rights is by *initiating* force—that is, by committing aggression. (Libertarianism also holds that, while the initiation of force against another person's body is impermissible, force used *in response* to aggression—such as defensive, restitutive, or retaliatory/punitive force—is justified.[15]) Now in the case of the body, it is clear what aggression is: invading the borders of someone's body, commonly called battery, or, more generally, *using the body of another without his or her consent.*[16] The very notion of interpersonal aggression presupposes property rights in bodies—more particularly, that each person is, at least *prima facie*, the owner of his own body.[17]

Non-libertarian political philosophies have a different view. In these systems, each person has some limited rights in his own body, but not complete or exclusive rights. Society or the state, purporting to be society's agent, has certain rights in each citizen's body, too. This partial slavery is implicit in state actions and laws such as taxation, conscription, and drug prohibitions.[18] The libertarian says that each person is the full owner of his body: he has the right to control his body, to decide whether or not he ingests narcotics, joins an army, pays taxes, and so on. Those various non-libertarians who endorse any such state prohibitions, however, necessarily maintain that the state, or society, is at least a partial owner of the body of those subject to such laws—or even a complete owner in the case of conscriptees or

---

[15] See "A Libertarian Theory of Punishment and Rights" (ch. 5).

[16] The following terms and formulations may be considered as roughly synonymous, depending on context: aggression; initiation of force; trespass; invasion; unconsented to (or uninvited) change in the physical integrity (or use, control or possession) of another person's body or property. See also Kinsella, "Aggression and Property Rights Plank in the Libertarian Party Platform"; *idem*, "Hoppe on Property Rights in Physical Integrity vs Value," *StephanKinsella.com* (June 12, 2011). For further discussion of how to define the concept of "rights," see "Dialogical Arguments for Libertarian Rights" (ch. 6), n.22 and accompanying text, *et pass.*

[17] "*Prima facie*," because some rights in one's body are arguably forfeited or lost in certain circumstances, e.g. when one commits a crime, thus authorizing the victim to at least use defensive force against the body of the aggressor (implying the aggressor is to that extent not the owner of his body). For more on this see "A Libertarian Theory of Contract" (ch. 9), Part III.B; "Inalienability and Punishment: A Reply to George Smith" (ch. 10); and "Knowledge, Calculation, Conflict, and Law" (ch. 19), at n.81 and accompanying text.

[18] See Robert W. McGee, "The Body as Property Doctrine," in Christoph Lütge, ed., *Handbook of the Philosophical Foundations of Business Ethics* (Springer, 2013).

non-aggressor "criminals" incarcerated for life or executed. Libertarians believe in *self*-ownership. Non-libertarians—statists—of all stripes advocate some form of slavery.[19]

SELF-OWNERSHIP AND CONFLICT AVOIDANCE

Without property rights, there is always the possibility of conflict over contestable resources. By assigning an owner to each resource, legal systems make possible conflict-free use of resources by establishing public, visible boundaries that non-owners can avoid. Libertarianism does not endorse just any property assignment rule, however.[20] It favors *self*-ownership over *other*-ownership (slavery).[21]

The libertarian seeks property assignment rules *because* he values or accepts various *grundnorms* such as justice, peace, prosperity, cooperation, conflict-avoidance, civilization.[22] The libertarian view is that

---

[19] Similarly, Hoppe argues:

There can be no socialism without a state, and as long as there is a state there is socialism. The state, then, is the very institution that puts socialism into action; and as socialism rests on aggressive violence directed against innocent victims, aggressive violence is the nature of any state.

Hoppe, *A Theory of Socialism and Capitalism*, p. 177.

[20] On the importance of the concept of scarcity and the possibility of conflict for the emergence of property rules, see Hoppe, *A Theory of Socialism and Capitalism*, pp. 20–21, 160, *et pass.*; and the discussion thereof in Kinsella, "Thoughts on the Latecomer and Homesteading Ideas; or, Why the Very Idea of 'Ownership' Implies that only Libertarian Principles are Justifiable," *Mises Economics Blog* (Aug. 15, 2007).

[21] See also "How We Come to Own Ourselves" (ch. 4).

[22] "Grundnorm" was legal philosopher Hans Kelsen's term for the hypothetical basic norm or rule that serves as the basis or ultimate source for the legitimacy of a legal system. See Hans Kelsen, *General Theory of Law and State*, Anders Wedberg, trans. (Cambridge, Mass.: Harvard University Press, 1949). I employ this term to refer to the fundamental norms presupposed by civilized people, e.g., in argumentative discourse, which in turn imply libertarian norms.

That the libertarian *grundnorms* are, in fact, necessarily presupposed by all civilized people to the extent they are civilized—during argumentative justification, that is—is shown by Hoppe in his "argumentation ethics" defense of libertarian rights. See Hoppe, *A Theory of Socialism and Capitalism*, chap. 7; "Dialogical Arguments for Libertarian Rights" (ch. 6); and "Defending Argumentation Ethics" (ch. 7).

For discussion of *why* people (to one extent or the other) *do* value these underlying norms, see Kinsella, "The Division of Labor as the Source of Grundnorms and Rights," *Mises Economics Blog* (April 24, 2009), and *idem*, "Empathy and the Source of Rights," *Mises*

self-ownership is the only property assignment rule compatible with these *grundnorms*; it is implied by them. As Professor Hoppe has shown, the assignment of ownership to a given resource must not be random, arbitrary, particularistic, or biased if it is to actually be a property norm that can serve the function of conflict-avoidance.[23] Property title has to be assigned to one of competing claimants based on "the existence of an objective, intersubjectively ascertainable link between owner and the" resource claimed.[24] In the case of one's own body, it is the unique relationship between a person and his body—*his direct and immediate control* over his body, and the fact that, at least in some sense, a body *is* a given person and vice versa—that constitutes the objective link sufficient to give that person a claim to his body superior to typical third party claimants.

Moreover, any outsider who claims another's body cannot deny this objective link and its special status, since the outsider also necessarily presupposes this in his own case. This is so because in seeking dominion over the other, in asserting ownership over the other's body, he has to presuppose his own ownership of his body, which demonstrates he

---

Economics Blog (Sept. 6, 2006). See also "A Libertarian Theory of Punishment and Rights" (ch. 5), text at notes 3 and 77:

> Civilized people are also concerned about *justifying* punishment. They want to punish, but they also want to know that such punishment is justified. They want to be able to punish legitimately—hence the interest in punishment theories.... Theories of punishment are concerned with justifying punishment, with offering decent people who are reluctant to act immorally a reason why they may punish others. This is useful, of course, for offering moral people guidance and assurance that they may properly deal with those who seek to harm them.

[23] See Hoppe, *A Theory of Socialism and Capitalism*, pp. 157–65. See also "A Libertarian Theory of Punishment and Rights" (ch. 5), Parts III.C "Punishing Aggressive Behavior" and III.D "Potential Defenses by the Aggressor"; "Defending Argumentation Ethics" (ch. 7); Kinsella, "The problem of particularistic ethics or, why everyone really has to admit the validity of the universalizability principle," *StephanKinsella.com* (Nov. 10, 2011); "How We Come to Own Ourselves" (ch. 4), n.15; and "Dialogical Arguments for Libertarian Rights" (ch. 6), n.43 and accompanying text.

[24] Hoppe, *A Theory of Socialism and Capitalism*, p. 23. *See also* "Selling Does Not Imply Ownership, and Vice-Versa: A Dissection" (ch. 11). For further discussion of the necessity of objective property rules that can determine what resources may be used *now*, without having to wait for the approval of late-comers, see "How We Come To Own Ourselves" (ch. 4), n.14 and accompanying text.

does place a certain significance on this link, at the same time that he disregards the significance of the other's link to his own body.[25]

Libertarianism realizes that only the self-ownership rule is universalizable and compatible with the goals of peace, cooperation, and conflict avoidance. We recognize that each person is *prima facie* the owner of his own body because, by virtue of his unique link to and connection with his own body—his direct and immediate control over it—he has a better claim to it than anyone else.

PROPERTY IN EXTERNAL THINGS

Libertarians apply similar reasoning in the case of other scarce resources—namely, external objects in the world that, unlike bodies, were at one point *unowned*. In the case of bodies, the idea of aggression being impermissible immediately implies self-ownership. In the case of external objects, however, we must identify who the owner *is* before we can determine what constitutes aggression.

As in the case with bodies, humans need to be able to use external objects as means to achieve various ends. Because these things are scarce, there is also the potential for conflict. And as in the case with bodies, libertarians favor assigning property rights so as to permit the peaceful, conflict-free, productive use of such resources. As in the case with bodies, then, property is assigned to the person with the best claim or link to a given scarce resource—with the "best claim" standard based on the goals of permitting peaceful, conflict-free human interaction and use of resources.

Unlike human bodies, however, external objects are not parts of one's identity, are not directly controlled by one's will—and, significantly, they are *initially unowned*.[26] Here, the libertarian realizes that the relevant

---

[25] For elaboration on this point, see "How We Come To Own Ourselves" (ch. 4), the sections "Direct Control" and "Summary"; "Defending Argumentation Ethics" (ch. 7); "Law and Intellectual Property in a Stateless Society" (ch. 14), Part II.C; Hoppe, *A Theory of Socialism and Capitalism*, chaps. 1, 2, and 7. See also the quote by Auberon Herbert and the related citation to Rothbard in "How We Come to Own Ourselves" (ch. 4), n.7.

[26] For further discussion of the difference between bodies and things homesteaded for purposes of rights, see "A Libertarian Theory of Contract" (ch. 9), Part III.B; and

objective link is *original appropriation*—the transformation or embordering of a previously unowned resource, Lockean homesteading,
the first use or possession of the thing.[27] Under this approach, the first

---

"How We Come to Own Ourselves" (ch. 4). See also Kasper Lippert-Rasmussen, "Against
Self-Ownership: There are No Fact-Insensitive Ownership Rights Over One's Body,"
Philosophy & Public Affairs 36, no. 1 (2008): 86–118, at 88–89 (footnotes omitted):

> [R]ight- and left-libertarians ... agree that:
>
> *The Asymmetry Thesis*: Ownership of external resources is intrinsically
> different, morally, from ownership of one's mind and body.
>
> For example, each person enters the world owning himself or herself, but own-
> ership of external resources is acquired through personal exercise of the moral
> power to acquire such ownership.
>
> Nozick's subscription to the asymmetry thesis is evident in his admittedly rather
> sketchy, but broadly Lockean, account of how one can become the owner of an un-
> owned external object, for he offers no comparable account of how one can become
> the owner—morally speaking—of one's own—nonmorally speaking—mind and
> body. Absent special circumstances, such as organ theft, one simply starts owning
> oneself. Similarly, Otsuka thinks that ownership of external things is conditional
> upon the satisfaction of an egalitarian proviso enjoining equal opportunities for
> welfare; he assumes that ownership of oneself is not conditional in this sense.

Citing Robert Nozick, *Anarchy, State, and Utopia* (Oxford: Basil Blackwell, 1974), pp.
174–82 and Michael Otsuka, *Libertarianism Without Inequality* (Oxford: Oxford University Press, 2003), pp. 22–29.

See also Olle Torpman, "Mid-Libertarianism and the Utilitarian Proviso," *J. Value Inquiry*
(Sept. 2, 2021; https://philpapers.org/rec/TORMAT-4), at §1.1 (last emphasis added):

> Libertarianism's most salient thesis concerns full moral self-ownership, accord-
> ing to which every person has fundamental moral rights to anything that counts
> as herself—including her body parts, organs, blood, eggs, sperms, stem cells,
> thoughts, etc. We may call these *personal resources*. Most versions of libertarianism
> also allow people to gain moral ownership over natural resources (i.e., non-per-
> sonal resources)—such as land, minerals, water, air, etc. We may call these *external
> resources*. While the rights to our personal resources are natural and thus *in need of
> no acquisition, the rights to external resources must somehow be acquired...*

Citing Eric Mack, "The Natural Right of Property," *Social Philosophy and Policy* 27, no. 1
(2010): 53–78, at 54, and Bas van der Vossen, "What counts as original appropriation?,"
Politics, Philosophy & Economics 8, no. 4 (2009): 355–373, at 368.

[27] "Original appropriation" is the broader concept for the acquisition of previously-
unowned scarce (conflictable) resources, including land or realty (immovables), while
"homesteading" is sometimes used as a subset of original appropriation that involves
immovables (land), such as a "homestead." However, homesteading is often used more
generally and in this book I often use "homesteading" synonymously with original appropriation to refer to appropriation of any type of unowned, conflictable resource, whether
movable or immovable.

On the nature of appropriation of unowned scarce resources, see Hoppe's and de Jasay's
ideas quoted and discussed in Kinsella, "Thoughts on the Latecomer and Homesteading
Ideas," and note 32, below. In particular, see Hoppe, *A Theory of Socialism and Capitalism*, pp.
24, 160–62, 169–71; and Anthony de Jasay, *Against Politics: On Government, Anarchy, and*

(prior) user of a previously unowned thing has a prima facie better claim than a second (later) claimant solely by virtue of his being earlier.

Why is appropriation the relevant link for determination of ownership? First, keep in mind that the question with respect to such scarce resources is: who is the resource's *owner*? Recall that ownership is the *right* to control, use, or possess,[28] while possession is *actual* control—"the *factual authority* that a person exercises over a corporeal thing."[29] The question is not who has physical possession; it is who has ownership. Thus, asking who is the owner of a resource presupposes *a distinction* between ownership and possession—between the *right* to control (or exclude) (ownership, or property rights), and *actual* control (possession; economic dominion). And the answer has to take into account the nature of previously-unowned things: to wit, that they must at some point become owned by a first owner.

Order (London & New York: Routledge, 1997), pp. 158 *et seq.*, 171 *et seq.*, *et pass*. De Jasay is also discussed extensively in "Review of Anthony de Jasay, *Against Politics: On Government, Anarchy, and Order*" (ch. 20). De Jasay's argument presupposes the value of justice, efficiency, and order. Given these goals, he argues for three principles of politics: (1) *if in doubt, abstain from political action* (pp. 147 *et seq.*); (2) *the feasible is presumed free* (pp. 158 *et seq.*); and (3) *let exclusion stand* (pp. 171 *et seq.*). In connection with principle (3), "let exclusion stand," de Jasay offers insightful comments about the nature of homesteading or appropriation of unowned goods. De Jasay equates property with its owner's "excluding" others from using it, for example by enclosing or fencing in immovable property (land) or finding or creating (and keeping) movable property (corporeal, tangible objects). He concludes that since an appropriated thing has no other owner, *prima facie* no one is entitled to object to the first possessor claiming ownership. Thus, the principle means "let ownership stand," i.e., that claims to ownership of property appropriated from the state of nature or acquired ultimately through a chain of title tracing back to such an appropriation should be respected. This is consistent with Hoppe's defense of the "natural" theory of property. Hoppe, *A Theory of Socialism and Capitalism*, pp. 20–24 & chap. 7. For further discussion of the nature of appropriation, see Jörg Guido Hülsmann, "The A Priori Foundations of Property Economics," *Q.J. Austrian Econ.* 7, no. 4 (Winter 2004; https://mises.org/library/priori-foundations-property-economics-0): 51–57.

[28] See note 5 and accompanying text, above, and Appendix I.

[29] A.N. Yiannopoulos, *Louisiana Civil Law Treatise, Property* (West Group, 4th ed. 2001), § 301 (emphasis added); see also Louisiana Civil Code (https://www.legis.la.gov/legis/Laws_Toc.aspx?folder=67&level=Parent), art. 3421 ("Possession is the *detention or enjoyment of a corporeal thing*, movable or immovable, that one holds or exercises by himself or by another who keeps or exercises it in his name" (emphasis added)). See also discussion of this point in "Selling Does Not Imply Ownership, and Vice-Versa: A Dissection" (ch. 11), at n.35 *et pass*.

The answer must also take into account the presupposed goals of those seeking this answer: rules that permit conflict-free use of resources. For this reason, the answer cannot be whoever has the *resource or whoever is able to take it* is its owner. To hold such a view is to adopt a might makes right system where ownership collapses into possession for want of a distinction.[30] Such a "system," far from avoiding conflict, makes conflict inevitable.[31]

Instead of a might-makes-right approach, from the insights noted above it is obvious that *ownership presupposes the prior-later distinction*: whoever any given system specifies as the owner of a resource *has a better claim than latecomers*.[32] If he does not, then he is not an owner, but merely the current user or possessor, in a might-makes-right world in which there is no such thing as ownership—which contradicts the presuppositions of the inquiry itself. If the first owner does not have a better claim than latecomers, then he is not an owner, but merely a possessor, and there is no such thing as ownership. More generally, latecomers' claims are inferior to those of prior possessors or claimants, who either homesteaded the resource or who can trace their title back to the homesteader or earlier owner.[33] The crucial importance of the prior-later distinction to libertarian theory is why Professor Hoppe repeatedly emphasizes it in his writing.[34]

---

[30] See, in this connection, the quote from Adam Smith in note 7, above.

[31] This is also, incidentally, the reason the mutualist "occupancy" position on land ownership is unlibertarian and unjust. In revising this chapter, this footnote grew to unmanageable length. I have placed the relevant commentary in Appendix II, below.

[32] See Kinsella, "Thoughts on the Latecomer and Homesteading Ideas."

[33] See Louisiana Code of Civil Procedure, art. 3653, providing:

To obtain a judgment recognizing his ownership of immovable property…, the plaintiff … shall:

(1) Prove that he has acquired ownership from a previous owner or by acquisitive prescription, if the court finds that the defendant is in possession thereof; or

(2) Prove a better title thereto than the defendant, if the court finds that the latter is not in possession thereof.

When the titles of the parties are traced to a common author, he is presumed to be the previous owner.

See also Louisiana Civil Code, arts. 526, 531–32; Yiannopoulos, *Louisiana Civil Law Treatise, Property*, §§ 255–79 & 347 *et pass.*

[34] See, e.g., Hoppe, *A Theory of Socialism and Capitalism*, pp. 168–71; idem, *The Economics and Ethics of Private Property: Studies in Political Economy and Philosophy* (Auburn, Ala.: Mises Institute, 2006 [1993]; www.hanshoppe.com/eepp), pp. 327–30; see also discussion of these and related matters in Kinsella, "Thoughts on the Latecomer and Homesteading

Thus, the libertarian position on property rights is that, in order to permit conflict-free, productive use of scarce resources, property titles to particular resources are assigned to particular owners. As noted above, however, the title assignment must not be random, arbitrary, or particularistic; instead, it has to be assigned based on "the existence of an objective, intersubjectively ascertainable link between owner and the" resource claimed.[35] As can be seen from the considerations presented above, the link is the physical transformation or embordering

---

Ideas"; "Defending Argumentation Ethics" (ch. 7), the section "Objective Links: First Use, Verbal Claims, and the Prior-Later Distinction." In particular, for further discussion of the necessity of objective property rules that can determine what resources may be used *now*, without having to wait for the approval of latecomers, see "How We Come To Own Ourselves" (ch. 4), n.14 and accompanying text.

See also, in this connection, de Jasay, *Against Politics*, further discussed and quoted in Kinsella, "Thoughts on the Latecomer and Homesteading Ideas," as well as in "Review of Anthony de Jasay, *Against Politics*" (ch. 20). See also de Jasay's argument (note 27, above) that since an appropriated thing has no other owner, *prima facie* no one is entitled to object to the first possessor claiming ownership. De Jasay's "let exclusion stand" idea, along with the Hoppean emphasis on the prior-later distinction, sheds light on the nature of homesteading itself. Often the question is asked as to what types of acts constitute or are sufficient for homesteading (or "embordering" as Hoppe sometimes refers to it); what type of "labor" must be "mixed with" a thing; and to what property does the homesteading extend? What "counts" as "sufficient" homesteading? We can see that the answer to these questions is related to the issue of what is the thing in dispute. In other words, if *B* claims ownership of a thing possessed (or formerly possessed) by *A*, then the very framing of the dispute helps to identify what the thing is in dispute, and what counts as possession of it. If *B* claims ownership of a given resource, he wants the right to control it, to a certain extent, and according to its nature. Then the question becomes, did someone else previously control "it" (whatever is in dispute), according to its nature; i.e., did someone else already homestead it, so that *B* is only a latecomer? This ties in with de Jasay's "let exclusion stand" principle, which rests on the idea that if someone is actually able to control a resource such that others are excluded, then this exclusion should "stand." Of course, the physical nature of a given scarce resource and the way in which humans use such resources will determine the nature of actions needed to "control" it and exclude others. See also on this Rothbard's discussion of the "relevant technological unit" in Murray N. Rothbard, "Law, Property Rights, and Air Pollution," in *Economic Controversies* (Auburn, Ala.: Mises Institute, 2011; https://mises.org/library/economic-controversies); also B.K. Marcus, "The Spectrum Should Be Private Property: The Economics, History, and Future of Wireless Technology," *Mises Daily* (Oct. 29, 2004, https://mises.org/library/spectrum-should-be-private-property-economics-history-and-future-wireless-technology) and *idem*, "Radio Free Rothbard," *J. Libertarian Stud.* 20, no. 2 (Spring 2006; https://mises.org/library/radio-free-rothbard): 17–51.

[35] Hoppe, *A Theory of Socialism and Capitalism*, p. 23.

of the original homesteader, or a chain of title traceable by contract back to him.[36]

As Hoppe summarizes self-ownership rights and property rights in external resources based in original appropriation and contractual title transfer:

> But who owns what scarce resource as his private property and who does not? First: Each person owns his physical body that only he and no one else controls *directly* (I can control your body only in-directly, by first directly controlling my body, and vice versa) and that only he direct-ly controls also in particular when *discussing and arguing* the question at hand. Otherwise, if body-ownership were assigned to some indirect body-controller, conflict would become unavoidable as the direct body-con-troller *cannot* give up his direct control over his body as long as he is alive; and in particular, otherwise it would be impossible that any two persons, as the contenders in any property dispute, could ever *argue and debate* the question whose will is to prevail, since arguing and debating *presupposes* that both, the proponent and the opponent, have exclusive control over their respective bodies and so come to the correct judgment *on their own*, without a fight (in a conflict-free form of interaction).

> And second, as for scarce resources that can be controlled *only* indirectly (that must be appropriated with our own nature-given, i.e., un-appro-priated, body): Exclusive control (property) is acquired by and assigned to that person, who appropriated the resource in question *first* or who acquired it through voluntary (conflict-free) exchange from its *previous* owner. For only the first appropriator of a resource (and all later owners connected to him through a chain of voluntary exchanges) can possibly acquire and gain control over it without conflict, i.e., peacefully. Other-wise, if exclusive control is assigned instead to *latecomers*, conflict is not

---

36 To be clear, this does *not* mean that ownership or title can be established only if one can trace one's title back to "Adam" or the first homesteader. See the "common author" rules noted in note 33, above; Kinsella, "Rothbard on the 'Original Sin' in Land Titles: 1969 vs. 1974," *StephanKinsella.com* (Nov. 5, 2014); *idem*, "Mises, Rothbard, and Hoppe on the 'Orig-inal Sin' in the Distribution of Property Rights," *StephanKinsella.com* (Oct. 7, 2014); and "Libertarianism After Fifty Years: What Have We Learned?" (ch. 25). Many libertarians are tripped up by this issue. See, e.g. R.W. Bradford, "A Contrast of Visions," *Liberty* 10, no.4 (March 1997; https://perma.cc/7FDT-G7FD): 57–63, at 58.

On the title transfer theory of contract, see "A Libertarian Theory of Contract" (ch. 9); Williamson M. Evers, "Toward a Reformulation of the Law of Contracts," *J. Libertarian Stud.* 1, no. 1 (Winter 1977; https://mises.org/library/toward-reformulation-law-contracts): 3–13; Rothbard, "Property Rights and the Theory of Contracts," in *The Ethics of Liberty* (https://mises.org/library/property-rights-and-theory-contracts).

avoided but contrary to the very purpose of norms made unavoidable and permanent.[37]

CONSISTENCY AND PRINCIPLE

Not only libertarians are civilized. Most people give some weight to some of the above considerations. In their eyes, a person is the owner of his own body—usually. A homesteader owns the resource he appropriates—unless the state takes it from him "by operation of law."[38] This is the principal distinction between libertarians and non-libertarians: libertarians are consistently opposed to aggression, defined in terms of invasion of property borders, where property rights are understood to be assigned on the basis of self-ownership, in the case of bodies, and on the basis of prior possession or homesteading and contractual transfer of title, in the case of other things (plus transfers for purposes of rectification).

This framework for rights is motivated by the libertarian's consistent and principled valuing of peaceful interaction and cooperation—in short, of civilized behavior. A parallel to the Misesian view of human action may be illuminating here. According to Mises, human action is

---

[37] Hans-Hermann Hoppe "A Realistic Libertarianism," *LewRockwell.com* (Sept. 30, 2013; https://www.hanshoppe.com/2014/10/a-realistic-libertarianism/); see also similar argument in *idem*, "Of Common, Public, and Private Property and the Rationale for Total Privatization," at pp. 85–87.

[38] State laws and constitutional provisions often pay lip service to the existence of various personal and property rights, but then take them back by recognizing the right of the state to regulate or infringe the right so long as it is "by law" or "not arbitrary." See, e.g., *Constitution of Russia*, art. 25 ("The home shall be inviolable. No one shall have the right to get into a house against the will of those living there, except for the cases established by a federal law or by court decision") and art. 34 ("Everyone shall have the right to freely use his or her abilities and property for entrepreneurial or any other economic activity not prohibited by the law"); *Constitution of Estonia*, art. 31 ("Estonian citizens shall have the right to engage in commercial activities and to form profit-making associations and leagues. The law may determine conditions and procedures for the exercise of this right"); *Universal Declaration of Human Rights*, art. 17 ("Everyone has the right to own property alone as well as in association with others.... No one shall be arbitrarily deprived of his property"); art. 29(2) ("In the exercise of his rights and freedoms, everyone shall be subject only to such limitations as are determined by law solely for the purpose of securing due recognition and respect for the rights and freedoms of others and of meeting the just requirements of morality, public order and the general welfare in a democratic society").

aimed at alleviating some felt uneasiness.[39] Thus, means are employed, according to the actor's understanding of causal laws, to achieve various ends—ultimately, the removal of some *felt uneasiness.*

Civilized man feels uneasy at the prospect of violent struggles with others. On the one hand, he wants, for some practical reason, to control a given scarce resource and to use violence against another person, if necessary, to achieve this control. On the other hand, he also wants to avoid a wrongful use of force. Civilized man, for some reason, feels reluctance, uneasiness, at the prospect of violent interaction with his fellow man. Perhaps he has reluctance to violently clash with others over certain objects because he has empathy with them.[40] Perhaps the instinct to cooperate is a result of social evolution. As Mises noted,

> There are people whose only aim is to improve the condition of their own ego. There are other people with whom awareness of the troubles of their fellow men causes as much uneasiness as or even more uneasiness than their own wants.[41]

Whatever the reason, because of this uneasiness, when there is the potential for violent conflict, the civilized man seeks justification for the forceful control of a scarce resource which he desires but which some other person opposes. Empathy—or whatever spurs man to adopt the libertarian *grundnorms*—gives rise to a certain form of uneasiness, which gives rise to *ethical action.* Civilized man may be defined as he who seeks justification for the use of interpersonal violence. When the inevitable need to engage in violence arises—for defense of life or property—civilized man seeks justification. Naturally, since this justification-seeking is done by people who are inclined to reason and peace (justification is after all a peaceful activity that necessarily takes place during discourse),[42] what they seek are rules that are fair, potentially acceptable to all, grounded in the nature of things, and universalizable, and that per-

---

[39] Ludwig von Mises, *Human Action: A Treatise on Economics*, Scholar's ed. (Auburn, Ala: Mises Institute, 1998; https://mises.org/library/human-action-0), pp. 13–14, *et pass.*

[40] For further discussion of the role of empathy in the adoption of libertarian *grundnorms*, see note 22, above.

[41] Mises, *Human Action*, p. 14.

[42] As Hoppe explains, "Justification—proof, conjecture, refutation—is *argumentative* justification." Hoppe, *The Economics and Ethics of Private Property*, p. 384; also ibid., p. 413; and Hoppe, *A Theory of Socialism and Capitalism*, p. 155 *et pass.*

mit conflict-free use of resources. Libertarian property rights principles emerge as the only candidate that satisfies these criteria. Thus, if civilized man is he who seeks justification for the use of violence, the libertarian is he who is *serious* about this endeavor. He has a deep, principled, innate opposition to violence, and an equally deep commitment to peace and cooperation.

For the foregoing reasons, libertarianism may be said to be the political philosophy that *consistently* favors social rules aimed at promoting peace, prosperity, and cooperation.[43] It recognizes that the only rules that satisfy the civilized *grundnorms* are the self-ownership principle and the Lockean homesteading principle, applied as consistently as possible.

And as I have argued elsewhere, because the state necessarily commits aggression, the consistent libertarian, in opposing aggression, is also an anarchist.[44]

APPENDIX I
"PROPERTY"—CONCEPT AND TERMINOLOGY

As noted above, the material here was originally intended to appear in footnote 5, above. Due to its length, I include this material in this appendix.

Concept and Definition of "Property"

As Professor Yiannopoulos explains:

> *Property* is a word with high emotional overtones and so many meanings that it has defied attempts at accurate all-inclusive definition. The English word *property* derives from the Latin *proprietas*, a noun form of *proprius*, which means one's own. In the United States, the word *property* is fre-

---

[43] For this reason Henry Hazlitt's proposed name "cooperatism" for the freedom philosophy, has some appeal, to me at least. *See* Kinsella, "The new libertarianism: anti-capitalist and socialist; or: I prefer Hazlitt's 'Cooperatism,'" *StephanKinsella.com* (June 19, 2009).

[44] See "What It Means to Be an Anarcho-Capitalist" (ch. 3); also Jan Narveson, "The Anarchist's Case," in *Respecting Persons in Theory and Practice* (Lanham, Md.: Rowman & Littlefield, 2002; https://perma.cc/2P24-H4JL).

quently used to denote indiscriminately either the *objects* of rights … or the *rights* that persons have *with respect to things*. Thus, lands, automobiles, and jewels are said to be property; and rights, such as ownership, servitudes, and leases, are likewise said to be property. This latent confusion between rights and their objects has its roots in texts of Roman law and is also encountered in other legal systems of the western world. *Accurate analysis should reserve the use of the word property for the designation of rights that persons have with respect to things.*

Property may be defined as an *exclusive right to control an economic good…*; it is the name of a concept that refers to the rights and obligations, privileges and restrictions that govern the relations of man with respect to *things of value*. People everywhere and at all times desire the possession of things that are necessary for survival or valuable by cultural definition and which, as a result of the demand placed upon them, *become scarce*. Laws enforced by organized society control the competition for, and guarantee the enjoyment of, these desired things. What is guaranteed to be one's own is property.…

[Property rights] *confer a direct and immediate authority over a thing.*[45]

In this book, I endeavor to use the term "property" to refer to rights a person has with respect to a given thing or resource, instead of to the thing itself, but on occasion (partly due to the fact that many of these chapters are over 20 years old and I did not want to rewrite everything completely), I will employ the more colloquial usage where "property" refers to the object or resource or thing owned. It is sometimes necessary to avoid the inconvenience of nonstandard language in order to communicate (just as I use the term "intellectual property" in discussing

---

[45] Yiannopoulos, *Louisiana Civil Law Treatise, Property*, §§ 1, 2 (citations omitted; last two emphases in first paragraph added; first emphasis of second paragraph in original and remaining emphasis added; emphasis added in third paragraph). See also Louisiana Civil Code, art. 477 ("Ownership is the right that confers on a person direct, immediate, and exclusive authority over a thing. The owner of a thing may use, enjoy, and dispose of it within the limits and under the conditions established by law"). See also *"Against Intellectual Property After Twenty Years"* (ch. 15), n.31 and accompanying text; J.W. Harris, *Property and Justice* (Oxford University Press, 1996), pp. 9, 11–13, *et pass.* (discussing different uses of the term "property"); and "A Libertarian Theory of Contract" (ch. 9), n.1. See also Kinsella, "Libertarian Answer Man: Self-ownership for slaves and Crusoe; and Yiannopoulos on Accurate Analysis and the term 'Property'; Mises distinguishing between juristic and economic categories of 'ownership,'" *StephanKinsella.com* (April 3, 2021).

modern patent and copyright law, even though I dislike the term,[46] so that people understand what I'm referring to).

"Things"

As Yiannopoulos notes:

> Accurate definition of the word *things* is indispensable in view of the fact that only things in the legal sense may be objects of property rights.... In most legal systems, including common law jurisdictions, Louisiana, and legal systems of the French family, the word things applies both to physical objects and incorporeals [intangibles]. In legal systems following the model of the German Civil Code, however, the word things applies only to corporeal objects that are susceptible of appropriation.[47]

Thus, the concept of "thing" in the civil law (*res* under Roman law; *bien* (good) and *chose* (corporeal thing) under French law; *Sache* under German law) denotes certain objects of rights in the law.

Things are also divided into different types, such as common, public, and private; corporeals and incorporeals; and movables and immovables.[48] Things are divided into other types, as well, such as things in commerce and out of commerce, consumable and non-consumable, and so on.[49]

The civil law concept of things, especially private things, more or less corresponds to the notion of economic goods, or appropriable objects having a pecuniary value, which itself is close to the concept of *conflictable* (contestable, rivalrous, scarce) resources I use in this book to refer to the types of things that can be the subject of property rights—that can be owned (see the section "Conflictable vs. Scarce," below). They are

---

[46] See Kinsella, "Intellectual Properganda," *Mises Economics Blog* (Dec. 6, 2010); "*Against Intellectual Property* After Twenty Years" (ch. 15), Part IV.I. See also the discussion of Böhm-Bawerk on the use of inaccurate terms, in "On the Logic of Libertarianism and Why Intellectual Property Doesn't Exist" (ch. 24), n.32.

[47] Yiannopoulos, *Louisiana Civil Law Treatise, Property*, § 2 (emphasis added).

[48] Louisiana Civil Code, arts. 448, 453. See also J.W. Harris, "The Elusiveness of Property," in Peter Wahlgren, *Perspectives on Jurisprudence: Essays in Honor of Jes Bjarup* (Stockholm Institute for Scandinavian Law, 2005; https://perma.cc/SW6Z-FYTV), p. 128 (discussing different views on whether property rights only include tangible or corporeal things or whether it is broader).

[49] See Yiannopoulos, *Louisiana Civil Law Treatise, Property*, §§ 1–2, 12–16, 18–44.

things that can be used by acting man as means of action—possessed—and in society, that can be owned (property rights).[50]

Property as a Right to Exclude

Technically speaking, a property right is not a right to *control* a resource but a *right to exclude others from using the resource*. Ironically, this is how patent rights work, although most non-specialists have trouble understanding this; having a patent on an invention does *not* allow the inventor to make or use it, but only to *prevent others* from doing so.[51] I have explained elsewhere why property rights do not give the owner a right to control or use the resource.[52] However, for our purposes in this chapter, this distinction is not particularly germane.

---

[50] Emanuele Martinelli, "On Whether We Own What We Think" (draft, 2019; https://www.academia.edu/93535130/On_Whether_We_Own_What_We_Think), p. 6 ("Thing is taken to be 'anything one could use'"). On the distinction between possession and ownership, see the section "Property in External Things," above.

[51] See 35 U.S.C. §271, https://www.law.cornell.edu/uscode/text/35/271; *Connell v. Sears, Roebuck Co.*, 722 F.2d 1542, 1547 (Fed. Cir. 1983; https://casetext.com/case/connell-v-sears-roebuck-co) ("the right to exclude recognized in a patent is but the essence of the concept of property"), citing *Schenck v. Nortron Corp.*, 713 F.2d 782 (Fed. Cir. 1983; https://casetext.com/case/carl-schenck-ag-v-nortron-corp); Bitlaw, "Rights Granted Under U.S. Patent Law," https://www.bitlaw.com/patent/rights.html; see also Thomas W. Merrill, "Property and the Right to Exclude," *Neb. L. Rev.* 77 (1998; https://scholarship.law.columbia.edu/faculty_scholarship/3553): 730–55, p. 749 and n.10 and related text, in particular; Harris, *Property and Justice*; James Y. Stern, "The Essential Structure of Property Law," *Mich. L. Rev.* 115, no. 7 (May 2017; https://repository.law.umich.edu/mlr/vol115/iss7/2/): 1167–1212, p. 1171 n.15, referencing and comparing *Bloomer v. McQuewan*, 55 U.S. 539, 549 (1852) ("The franchise which the patent grants, consists altogether in the right to exclude every one from making, using, or vending the thing patented, without the permission of the patentee. This is all that he obtains by the patent."), Robert Patrick Merges & John Fitzgerald Duffy, *Patent Law and Policy: Cases and Materials* (6th ed. 2013), p. 49 ("Unlike other forms of property, however, a patent includes only the right to exclude and nothing else." (emphasis omitted), and Frank H. Easterbrook, "Intellectual Property Is Still Property," *Harv. J.L. & Pub. Pol'y* 13, no. 1 (Winter 1990; https://chicagounbound.uchicago.edu/journal_articles/309/): 108–118, p. 112 ("[A] right to exclude in intellectual property is no different in principle from the right to exclude in physical property.").

[52] See "*Against Intellectual Property* After Twenty Years" (ch. 15), n.62 and Part IV.H *et pass.* See also Kinsella, "The Non-Aggression Principle as a Limit on Action, Not on Property Rights," *StephanKinsella.com* (Jan. 22, 2010) and *idem*, "IP and Aggression as Limits on Property Rights: How They Differ," *StephanKinsella.com* (Jan. 22, 2010).

Property as a Right between People

Moreover, as noted in "A Libertarian Theory of Contract" (ch. 9), n.1, property rights can be conceived of not as a right between a human actor and an owned object, but rather as a right *as between human actors*, but *with respect to particular (owned) resources*.

As Judge Alex Kozinski writes:

> But what is property? That is not an easy question to answer. I remember sitting in my first-year property course on the first day of class when the professor … asked the fundamental question: What are property rights? … I threw up my hand and without even waiting to be called on I shouted out, "Property rights define the relationship between people and their property."
>
> Professor Krier stopped dead in his tracks, spun around, and gave me a long look. Finally he said: "That's very peculiar, Mr. Kozinski. Have you always had relations with inanimate objects? Most people I know have relations with other people."
>
> That was certainly not the last time I said something really dumb in class, but the lesson was not lost on me. Property rights are, of course, a species of relationships between people. At the minimum, they define the degree to which individuals may exclude other individuals from the use and enjoyment of their goods and services….[53]

Conflictable vs. Scarce

As noted elsewhere, in recent years I tend to emphasize the rivalrous or "conflictable" nature of ownable resources to avoid the inevitable equivocation when the term "scarce" is used. When I refer to scarce resources in this book it is to be understood as meaning conflictable resources.[54]

---

[53] Alex Kozinski, "Of Profligacy, Piracy, and Private Property," *Harv. J.L. & Pub. Pol'y.* 13, no. 1 (Winter 1990; https://perma.cc/Z8AD-634V): 17–21, p. 19. See further references in "A Libertarian Theory of Contract" (ch. 9), n.1.

[54] See *"Against Intellectual Property* After Twenty Years" (ch. 15), text at n.29. On the term "conflictable," see Kinsella, "On Conflictability and Conflictable Resources," *StephanKinsella.com* (Jan. 31, 2022); see also "How We Come to Own Ourselves" (ch. 4), text at n.10; "A Libertarian Theory of Punishment and Rights" (ch. 5), at n.62; "Dialogical Arguments for Libertarian Rights" (ch. 6), at n.6; "Causation and Aggression" (ch. 8), at n.19.

APPENDIX II
MUTUALIST OCCUPANCY

As noted above, the material here was originally intended to appear in footnote 31, above. Due to its length, I include this material in this appendix.

As pointed out in the text above, any workable and just legal system must distinguish ownership from possession, and must recognize the prior-later distinction. Instead of a might-makes-right approach, the owner of a resource has a better claim than latecomers. If he does not, then he is not an owner, but merely the current user or possessor, in a might-makes-right world in which there is no such thing as ownership.

I have observed that this is also the reason the mutualist "occupancy" position on land ownership is unlibertarian and unjust. Mutualist Kevin Carson writes:

> For mutualists, *occupancy and use* is the only legitimate standard for establishing ownership of land, regardless of how many times it has changed hands. An existing owner may transfer ownership by sale or gift; but the new owner may establish legitimate title to the land *only by his own occupancy and use*. A change in occupancy will amount to a change in ownership…. The *actual occupant is considered the owner of a tract of land*, and any attempt to collect rent by a self-styled ["absentee"] landlord is regarded as a *violent invasion of the possessor's absolute right of property*.[55]

Thus, for mutualism, the "actual occupant" is the "owner"; the "possessor" has the right of property. If a homesteader of land stops personally using or occupying it, he loses his ownership. Carson contends this is compatible with libertarianism:

> [A]ll property rights theories, including Lockean, make provision for *adverse possession and constructive abandonment of property*. They differ only in degree, rather than kind: in the "stickiness" of property…. There is a large element of convention in any property rights system—Georgist, mutualist, and both proviso and nonproviso Lockeanism—in determining what constitutes transfer and abandonment.[56]

---

55 Kevin A. Carson, *Studies in Mutualist Political Economy* (Self-published: Fayetteville, Ark., 2004; http://mutualist.org/id47.html), chap. 5, sec. A (emphasis added).
56 Kevin A. Carson, "Carson's Rejoinders," *J. Libertarian Stud.* 20, no. 1 (Winter 2006; https://mises.org/library/carsons-rejoinders): 97–136, p. 133 (emphasis added).

In other words, Lockeanism, Georgism, and mutualism are all types of libertarianism, differing *only in degree*. In Carson's view, the gray areas in issues like adverse possession and abandonment leave room for mutualism's "occupancy" requirement for maintaining land ownership.[57]

But the concepts of adverse possession and abandonment cannot be stretched to cover the mutualist occupancy requirement. The mutualist occupancy view is essentially a *use* or *working* requirement, which is distinct from doctrines of adverse possession and abandonment. The doctrine of abandonment in positive law and in libertarian theory is based on the idea that ownership *acquired* by *intentionally* appropriating a previously unowned thing may be lost when the owner's intent to own terminates. Ownership is acquired by a merger of possession and intent to own. Likewise, when the intent to own ceases, ownership does too—this is the case with both abandonment of ownership *and* transfer of title to another person, which is basically an abandonment of property "in favor" of a particular new owner.[58]

The legal system must therefore develop rules to determine when property has been abandoned, including default rules that apply *in the absence of clear evidence*. Acquisitive prescription is based on an implicit presumption that the owner has abandoned his property claims if he does not defend it within a reasonable time period against an adverse possessor. But such rules apply to *adverse* possessors—those who possess the property *with the intent to own* and in a sufficiently public fashion that the owner knows or should know of this.[59] The "public" requirement means that the possessor possesses the property openly as *owner*, adverse or hostile to the owner's ownership—which is *not* the case when, for example, a lessee or employee uses an apartment or manufacturing facility

---

[57] For a critique of Georgism, see Rothbard, "The Single Tax: Economic and Moral Implications," in *Economic Controversies*.

[58] See "A Libertarian Theory of Contract" (ch. 9), Part III.A; also Louisiana Civil Code, art. 3418 ("A thing is abandoned when its owner relinquishes possession with the intent to give up ownership") and art. 3424 ("To acquire possession, one must *intend to possess as owner* and must take *corporeal possession* of the thing"; emphasis added).

[59] See Yiannopoulos, *Louisiana Civil Law Treatise, Property*, § 316; see also Louisiana Civil Code, art. 3424 ("To acquire possession, one must *intend to possess as owner* and must take corporeal possession of the thing"; emphasis added) and art. 3476 (to acquire title by acquisitive prescription, "The possession must be continuous, uninterrupted, peaceable, *public*, and unequivocal"; emphasis added); see also art. 3473.

under color of title and *permission* from the owner. Rules of abandonment and adverse possession are default rules that apply when the owner has *not* made his intention sufficiently clear—by neglect, apathy, death, absence, or other reason.

In fact, the very idea of abandonment rests on the distinction between ownership and possession. Property is more than possession; it is a right to possess, originating and sustained by the owner's *intention* to possess as owner. And abandonment occurs when the intent to own terminates. This happens even when the (immediately preceding) owner temporarily maintains possession but has lost ownership, as when he gives or sells the thing to another party.[60]

Clearly, default abandonment and adverse possession rules are categorically different from a working requirement, whereby ownership is lost in the *absence of use*.[61] Ownership is not lost by nonuse, however, and a working requirement is *not* implied by default rules regarding abandonment and adverse possession. See, e.g., Louisiana Civil Code, art. 481 (emphasis added): "The ownership and the possession of a thing are distinct.… Ownership exists independently of any exercise of it and *may not be lost by nonuse*. Ownership is lost when acquisitive prescription accrues in favor of an adverse possessor." Carson is wrong to imply that abandonment and adverse possession rules can yield a working (or *use* or *occupancy*) requirement for maintaining ownership. In fact, these are distinct legal doctrines. Thus, when a factory owner contractually allows workers to use it, or a landlord permits tenants to live in an apartment, there is no question that the owner *does not intend to abandon* the property, and there is no *adverse* possession (and if there were, the owner could institute the appropriate action to eject them and

---

[60] As I argue in "A Libertarian Theory of Contract" (ch. 9), Part III.A at n.31 and accompanying text *et seq.*

[61] See, e.g., Louisiana Mineral Code, § 27 (http://law.justia.com/louisiana/codes/21/87935.html) ("A mineral servitude is extinguished by: … prescription resulting from nonuse for ten years").

regain possession).[62] There is no need for "default" rules here to resolve an ambiguous situation.[63]

A final note here: I cite positive law here not as an argument from authority, but as an illustration that even the positive law carefully distinguishes between possession and ownership—and also between a *use* or *working* requirement to maintain ownership, and the potential to lose title by abandonment or adverse possession—to illustrate the flaws in Carson's view that an occupancy requirement is just one variant of adverse possession or default abandonment rules. Furthermore, the civilian legal rules cited derive from legal principles developed over the ages in largely decentralized fashion, and can thus be useful in our own libertarian efforts to develop concrete applications of abstract libertarian principles.[64]

---

[62] See Yiannopoulos, *Louisiana Civil Law Treatise, Property*, §§ 255, 261, 263–66, 332–33, 335 *et pass.*; Louisiana Code of Civil Procedure (https://www.legis.la.gov/legis/Laws_Toc.aspx?folder=68&level=Parent), arts. 3651, 3653 & 3655; Louisiana Civil Code, Arts. 526 & 531).

[63] For another critique of Carson, see Roderick T. Long, "Land-Locked: A Critique of Carson on Property Rights," *J. Libertarian Stud.* 20, no. 1 (Winter 2006; https://mises.org/library/land-locked-critique-carson-property-rights): 87–95.

[64] See "Legislation and the Discovery of Law in a Free Society" (ch. 13); also "Knowledge, Calculation, Conflict, and Law" (ch. 19), the section "The Third-Order Problem of Knowledge and the Common Law," text at n. 24 *et seq.* (discussing Randy Barnett's views on the distinction between abstract legal rights and more concrete rules that serve as guides to action). I discuss some of this also in "A Critique of Mutualist Occupancy," *StephanKinsella.com* (Aug. 2, 2009).

3

What It Means To Be an Anarcho-Capitalist

Originally published at *LewRockwell.com* (Jan. 20, 2004; https://perma.cc/
QAJ6-KHKN); reprinted in Keith Knight, ed., *The Voluntaryist Handbook:
A Collection of Essays, Excerpts, and Quotes* (2022; https://perma.cc/N8UX-4PX4).
See also Kinsella, "The Irrelevance of the Impossibility of Anarcho-
Libertarianism," *Mises Economics Blog* (Aug. 20, 2009).

Butler Shaffer's recent LRC article, "What is Anarchy?,"[1] prompted discussion on the *Reason* blog and inspired me to set down a few ideas I've also had along these lines.

Libertarian opponents of anarchy are attacking a straw man. Their arguments are usually utilitarian in nature and amount to "but anarchy won't work" or "we need the (things provided by the) state." But these attacks are confused at best, if not disingenuous. To be an anarchist does not mean you think anarchy will "work" (whatever that means), nor that you predict it will or "can" be achieved. It is possible to be a pessimistic anarchist, after all. To be an anarchist only means that you believe that aggression is not justified, and that states necessarily employ aggression. And, therefore, that states, and the aggression they necessarily employ, are unjustified. It's quite simple, really. It's an ethical view, so no surprise it confuses utilitarians.

---

[1] Butler Shaffer, "What Is Anarchy?," *LewRockwell.com* (Jan. 13, 2004; www.lewrockwell.com/shaffer/shaffer60.html).

Accordingly, anyone who is not an anarchist must maintain either: (a) aggression is justified; or (b) states (in particular, minimal states) do not necessarily employ aggression.

Proposition (b) is plainly false. States always tax their citizens, which is a form of aggression. They always outlaw competing defense agencies, which also amounts to aggression. (Not to mention the countless victimless crime laws that they inevitably, and without a single exception in history, enforce on the populace. Why minarchists think minarchy is even possible boggles the mind.)

As for (a), well, socialists and criminals also feel aggression is justified. This does not make it so. Criminals, socialists, and anti-anarchists have yet to show how aggression—the initiation of force against innocent victims—is justified. No surprise; it is not possible[2] to show this.[3] But criminals don't feel compelled to justify aggression; why should advocates of the state feel compelled to do so?

Conservative and minarchist-libertarian criticism of anarchy on the grounds that it won't "work" or is not "practical" is just confused. Anarchists don't (necessarily) predict anarchy will be achieved—I for one don't think it will. But that does not mean states are justified.

Consider an analogy. Conservatives and libertarians all agree that private crime (murder, robbery, rape) is unjustified, and "should" not occur. Yet no matter how good most men become, there will always be at least some small element who will resort to crime. Crime will always be with us. Yet we still condemn crime and work to reduce it.

Is it logically possible that there could be no crime? Sure. Everyone could voluntarily choose to respect others' rights. Then there would be no crime. It's easy to imagine. But given our experience with human nature and interaction, it is safe to say that there will always be crime. Nevertheless, we still proclaim crime to be evil and unjustified, in the face of the inevitability of its recurrence. So to my claim that crime is immoral, it would just be stupid and/or insincere to reply, "but that's an impractical view" or "but that won't work," "since there will always be crime." The fact that there will always be crime—that not everyone will voluntarily respect others' rights—does not mean that it's "impractical"

---

2 "Defending Argumentation Ethics" (ch. 7).
3 "Dialogical Arguments for Libertarian Rights" (ch. 6).

to oppose it; nor does it mean that crime is justified. It does not mean there is some "flaw" in the proposition that crime is wrong.

Likewise, to my claim that the state and its aggression is unjustified, it is disingenuous and/or confused to reply, "anarchy won't work" or is "impractical" or "unlikely to ever occur."[4] The view that the state is unjustified is a normative or ethical position. The fact that not enough people are willing to respect their neighbors' rights to allow anarchy to emerge, i.e., the fact that enough people (erroneously) support the legitimacy of the state to permit it to exist, does not mean that the state, and its aggression, are justified.[5]

Other utilitarian replies like "but we need a state" do not contradict the claim that states employ aggression and that aggression is unjustified. It simply means that the state-advocate does not mind the initiation of force against innocent victims—i.e., he shares the criminal/socialist mentality. The private criminal thinks his own need is all that matters; he is willing to commit violence to satisfy his needs; to hell with what is right and wrong. The advocate of the state thinks that his opinion that "we" "need" things justifies committing or condoning violence against innocent individuals. It is as plain as that. Whatever this argument

---

[4] Another point: In my view, we are about as likely to achieve minarchy as we are to achieve anarchy. I.e., both are remote possibilities. What is striking is that almost every criticism of "impracticality" that minarchists hurl at anarchy is also true of minarchy itself. Both are exceedingly unlikely. Both require massive changes in views among millions of people. Both rest on presumptions that most people simply don't care much about.

[5] Though the case for anarchy does not depend on its likelihood or "feasibility," any more than the case against private crime depends on there never being any acts of crime, anarchy is clearly possible. There is anarchy among nations, for example. There is also anarchy within government, as pointed out in a seminal and neglected JLS article by Alfred G. Cuzán, which argues that even the government itself is in anarchy, internally—the President does not literally force others in government to obey his commands, after all; they obey them voluntarily, due to a recognized, hierarchical structure. Government's (political) anarchy is not a good anarchy, but it demonstrates anarchy is possible—indeed, that we never really get out of it. See Alfred G. Cuzán, "Do We Ever Really Get Out of Anarchy?," *J. Libertarian Stud.* 3, no. 2 (Summer 1979; https://mises.org/library/do-we-ever-really-get-out-anarchy): 151–58. And Shaffer makes the insightful point that we are in "anarchy" with our neighbors. If most people did not already have the character to voluntarily respect most of their neighbors' rights, society and civilization would be impossible. Most people are good enough to permit civilization to occur, despite the existence of some degree of public and private crime. It is conceivable that the degree of goodness could rise—due to education or more universal economic prosperity, say—sufficient to make support for the legitimacy of states evaporate. It's just very unlikely.

is, it is not libertarian. It is not opposed to aggression. It is in favor of something else—making sure certain public "needs" are met, despite the cost—but not peace and cooperation. The criminal, gangster, socialist, welfare-statist, and even minarchist all share this: they are willing to condone naked aggression, for some reason. The details vary, but the result is the same—innocent lives are trampled by physical assault. Some have the stomach for this; others are more civilized—libertarian, one might say—and prefer peace over violent struggle.

As there are criminals and socialists among us, it is no surprise that there is a degree of criminal-mindedness in most people. After all, the state rests upon the tacit consent of the masses, who have erroneously accepted the notion that states are legitimate. But none of that means the criminal enterprises condoned by the masses are justified.

It's time for libertarians to take a stand. Are you for aggression, or against it?[6]

---

[6] For discussion of other aspects of anarchist libertarian theory, see references in "Legislation and the Discovery of Law in a Free Society" (ch. 13), n.25, and others listed in Kinsella, "The Greatest Libertarian Books," *StephanKinsella.com* (Aug. 7, 2006) and Hans-Hermann Hoppe, "Anarcho-Capitalism: An Annotated Bibliography," *LewRockwell.com* (Dec. 31, 2001; https://archive.lewrockwell.com/hoppe/hoppe5.html).

PART II

RIGHTS

4

How We Come to Own Ourselves

Originally published in *Mises Daily* (Sep. 7, 2006). The illustrating photo chosen by an editor at Mises.org for the original article inspired the image used on the back cover of this book. See my post "The Story of a Libertarian Book Cover," *StephanKinsella.com* (March 4, 2011).

The primary social evil of our time is lack of respect for self-ownership rights. It is what underlies both private crime and institutionalized crime perpetrated by the state. State laws, regulations, and actions are objectionable *just because* the state is claiming the legal right to control how someone's body is to be used.[1]

---

[1] As will become clear, by "self-ownership," I am referring to a person's ownership *of his body*, where the person (or actor or agent) is conceptually distinct from his body, just as one's mind is conceptually distinct from one's brain, even if a mind is not possible without a brain and a person cannot exist without a body. Other terms such as "self-body-ownership" might be used instead, but they are unwieldy. Some libertarians object to the concept of self-ownership or body-ownership, maintaining that it implies some mystical belief where the "person," or perhaps his soul, is some spirit that owns and "inhabits" or "occupies" the body. For an example of a silly objection along these lines, Leland Yeager claims my advocacy of self-ownership involves some kind of mind-body dichotomy mistake. *See* Stephan Kinsella "Yeager and Other Letters Re Liberty article 'Intellectual Property and Libertarianism,'" *StephanKinsella.com* (Jan. 23, 2010); *idem*, "Intellectual Property and Libertarianism," *Mises Daily* (Nov. 17, 2009). This is nonsense. Self-ownership simply specifies that each person has the right to control his body; it is the opposite of other-ownership, or domination and slavery. Nothing could be more libertarian. *See* "What Libertarianism Is" (ch. 2), text at notes 12 and 13; *see also* Stephan Kinsella, "'Libertarians'

When the state drafts a man or threatens him with imprisonment if he violates its narcotics laws, for example, it is assuming partial control of his body, contrary to his self-ownership rights. Moreover, laws such as tax laws or fines for failure to comply with arbitrary state decrees (e.g., economic regulations, anti-discrimination rules) also violate self-ownership rights, to the extent they threaten to imprison or harm the body of the person, and in any case violate the person's derivative property rights in the expropriated resources.

After all, although self-ownership is more fundamental than rights in external resources—one must own oneself, one's body, in order to own other things—self-ownership is rendered meaningless if the right to own private property in external resources is not also respected.[2] This

---

Who Object to 'Self-Ownership,'" *StephanKinsella.com* (July 19, 2022); Roderick T. Long, "Getting Self-Ownership in View" (Paper presented to the PPE conference, March 2019, New Orleans; https://perma.cc/U4AU-F996); *idem*, "This Self Is Mine," *Austro-Athenian Empire Blog* (July 8, 2014; https://perma.cc/VKP7-9F4D). See also Hans-Hermann Hoppe, "The Idea of a Private Law Society," *Mises Daily* (July 28, 2006; https://mises.org/library/idea-private-law-society) ("Outside of the Garden of Eden, in the realm of all-around scarcity, the solution [to the problem of social order] is provided by four inter-related rules.... First, every person is the proper owner of his own physical body. Who else, if not Crusoe, should be the owner of Crusoe's body? Otherwise, would it not constitute a case of slavery, and is slavery not unjust as well as uneconomical?"); and *idem*, *The Great Fiction: Property, Economy, Society, and the Politics of Decline* (Second Expanded Edition, Mises Institute, 2021; www.hanshoppe.com/tgf), chap. 11, Part II.

2 As Professor Hoppe explains, a person's body is "the very prototype of a scarce good." Hans-Hermann Hoppe, *The Economics and Ethics of Private Property: Studies in Political Economy and Philosophy* (Auburn, Ala.: Mises Institute, 2006 [1993]; www.hanshoppe.com/eepp), p. 335; see also *idem*, *A Theory of Socialism and Capitalism: Economics, Politics, and Ethics* (Auburn, Ala.: Mises Institute, 2010 [1989]; www.hanshoppe.com/tsc), pp. 19 & 21 *et pass.*, pp. 158–60. Once property rights are established in one's body (self-ownership), the argument can then be extended to other, external, previously-unowned scarce resources. See generally Hoppe, *The Economics and Ethics of Private Property*, pp. 335–36, *et pass.* and *idem*, *A Theory of Socialism and Capitalism*, pp. 19 & 21 *et pass.*, pp. 158–60 (re body rights) and p. 160 *et seq.* for property rights in external resources. The self-ownership or body-ownership rule can be formulated as "Nobody has the right to uninvitedly aggress against the body of any other person and thus delimit or restrict anyone's control over his own body." Hoppe, *A Theory of Socialism and Capitalism*, p. 159. But "conflicts over bodies, for whose possible avoidance the nonaggression principle formulates a universally justifiable solution, make up only a small portion of all possible conflicts." *Ibid.*, at 159–60. For conflicts related to the use of other resources:

> norms are needed, too, as it could come to conflicting evaluations regarding their use. But in fact, any other norm must be logically compatible with the nonaggression principle in order to be justified itself, and, mutatis mutandis, every norm that could be shown to be incompatible with this principle would have to be considered

is why Murray Rothbard insisted that all "human rights" are property rights: that is, ownership rights in scarce resources, whether self-ownership rights in one's body, or property rights in external objects.[3]

Now as the examples above show, all political theories advocate some form of property rights, since they specify certain owners of various types of resources.[4] State policies that tax, conscript, or imprison or fine individuals for failure to comply with various regulations in effect assign partial ownership in the subjects' bodies or other owned resources to the state. The state claims a partial ownership right in these resources.[5]

All political systems assign owners to resources according to some assignment rule. What sets libertarianism apart is its own unique property-assignment rule: the rule that specifies that individuals, not the state, are owners of their own bodies and other external scarce resources.

FIRST USE AND HOMESTEADING OF UNOWNED RESOURCES

It is, therefore, crucial that libertarian theory have a sound basis for property rights and for its unique property assignment rules.

---

invalid. In addition, as the things with respect to which norms have to be formulated are scarce goods—just as a person's body is a scarce good—and as it is only necessary to formulate norms at all because goods are *scarce* and not because they are *particular kinds* of scarce goods, the specifications of the nonaggression principle, conceived of as a special property norm referring to a specific kind of good, must in fact already contain those of a *general* theory of property.

Ibid., at 160. See also "A Libertarian Theory of Punishment and Rights" (ch. 5), Part III.F, "Property Rights" (extending the body- or self-ownership rights established by the preceding estoppel analysis to external scarce resources).

For my attempt at a concise formulation of the libertarian view on self-ownership and external property rights, see Stephan Kinsella, "Aggression and Property Rights Plank in the Libertarian Party Platform," *StephanKinsella.com* (May 30, 2022).

[3] Murray N. Rothbard, "'Human Rights' as Property Rights," in *The Ethics of Liberty* (New York: New York University Press, 1998; http://mises.org/rothbard/ethics/fifteen.asp). See also Kinsella, "Aggression and Property Rights Plank in the Libertarian Party Platform."

[4] See "What Libertarianism Is" (ch. 2) for more on this.

[5] This is ultimately also the core injustice of intellectual property laws: they are non-consensual negative easements granted by the state. See "*Against Intellectual Property After Twenty Years: Looking Back and Looking Forward*" (ch. 15), Part IV.B.

Relying on some version of the Lockean notion of *homesteading* or *original appropriation*—an individual *appropriating* something *unowned* from the state of nature, thereby becoming the owner—libertarianism rightly focuses on the concept of *first use* of a *previously unowned scarce resource* as the key test for determining ownership of it.[6]

One's initial impression might be that first use is the bedrock principle of libertarian property assignment, that is, that it decides questions of ownership of *all* scarce resources, both human bodies and external things. The owner of a plot of land is its first user (or his descendent in title), just as the first user of a body is its owner. This would mean that self-ownership rests on the first use principle, or homesteading.

PARENTS AS FIRST OWNERS

And what is wrong with relying on first use as the basis for self-ownership? To be sure, with respect to most claimants to one's body—a robber or state trying to conscript, say—one is indeed the "first user," or a prior user, and thus has a better claim to the body than the outsider.[7] But what about one's parents? Is one really the *first user* of one's body? Was one's

---

[6] For more on the importance of and reasons for first use being the touchstone of property ownership, see "Defending Argumentation Ethics" (ch. 7), especially the section "Objective Links: First Use, Verbal Claims, and the Prior-Later Distinction," and the references in "A Libertarian Theory of Contract: Title Transfer, Binding Promises, Inalienability" (ch. 9) to various writings by Hans-Hermann Hoppe on this issue; also Stephan Kinsella, "The Essence of Libertarianism? 'Finders Keepers,' 'Better Title,' and Other Possibilities," *StephanKinsella.com* (Aug. 31, 2005); idem, "Thoughts on Intellectual Property, Scarcity, Labor-Ownership, Metaphors, and Lockean Homesteading," *Mises Economic Blog* (May 26, 2006); "Selling Does Not Imply Ownership, and Vice-Versa: A Dissection" (ch. 11); idem, "KOL259 | 'How To Think About Property,' New Hampshire Liberty Forum 2019," *Kinsella on Liberty Podcast* (Feb. 9, 2019). Two subsidiary rules are contractual title transfer and transfer as a result of rectification for a tort. For more on this, see "What Libertarianism Is" (ch. 2), n.11 and accompanying text *et pass.*

[7] Writes Hoppe: "While I can cite in favor of my property claim regarding my body the objective fact that I was the body's first occupant—its first user—anyone else who claims to have the right to control this body can cite nothing of the sort." *A Theory of Socialism and Capitalism*, p. 23. See also Kinsella, "Intellectual Property and Libertarianism":

the libertarian property-assignment rule for bodies is that each person owns his own body. Implicit in the idea of self-ownership is the belief that each person has a *better claim* to the body that he or she directly controls and inhabits than do others. I have a better claim to the right to control my body than you do, because it is *my*

body simply lying around unowned, in state of nature, waiting for some occupant to swoop down and appropriate it?

No, obviously not. One's body was in the care of—and in a sense produced by—one's parents, in particular one's mother. So if we maintain that "first use" always determines the answer to the question "who owns this resource?," for any resource at all, then it would seem that parents *do* own their children. The mother owns the physical matter and bits of food and nourishment that assemble into the zygote, embryo, fetus, and then baby, just as the owner of an apple tree owns the apples that fall and the owner of a cow owns the calves it produces.

So, when does the child become a self-owner? Or does he? The libertarian seems to be faced with a dilemma.

POSSIBLE SOLUTIONS TO THE DILEMMA

Several possible arguments might be put forward to avoid the uncomfortable specter of children in bondage, slaves owned by their parents. First, it could be noted that the main political issue in society concerns third parties who want to dominate and control others. Slaveowning parents do not seem to pose the most pressing danger. For the typical case of conflict, the first-use principle suffices to prove self-ownership

---

body; I have a unique link and connection to my body that others do not, and that is prior to the claim of any other person.

Anyone other than the original occupant of a body is a *latecomer* with respect to the original occupant. Your claim to my body is inferior in part because *I had it first*. The person claiming your body can hardly object to the significance of what Hoppe calls the "prior-later" distinction, since he adopts this very rule with respect to his own body—he has to presuppose ownership of his own body in order to claim ownership of yours.

As for this latter point, Auberon Herbert writes: "If the entities do not belong to themselves, then we are reduced to the most absurd conclusion. A or B cannot own himself; but he can own, or part own, C or D." Auberon Herbert, "Part XI," in Auberon Herbert & J. H. Levy, *Taxation and Anarchism: A Discussion between the Hon. Auberon Herbert and J.H. Levy* (London: The Personal Rights Association, 1912; https://perma.cc/LX8H-MZFH), p. 37, quoted in Murray N. Rothbard, *Man, Economy, and State, with Power and Market*, Scholar's ed., second ed. (Auburn, Ala.: Mises Institute, 2009; https://mises.org/library/man-economy-and-state-power-and-market), chap. 2, § 13, p. 185.

See also "Law and Intellectual Property in a Stateless Society" (ch. 14), Part II.C. For more on the prior-later distinction, see references in note 6, above.

of one's body vis-à-vis the third party claimant. Still, this leaves open the possibility of parents owning their children.

Second, it could be argued that even if the parent does own the child, in *most* cases a decent parent would voluntarily manumit the child at a suitable age. This is probably true, but the possibility of a brutal parent selling his son or daughter into slavery is still unsettling.

Third, it is not difficult to envision a scenario in which most lines of descent, at some point, become permanently "liberated" or "manumitted" by the benevolent actions of a key ancestor. Great-great-great-Grand-dad manumits his child on the condition that he free his issue, and so on. In this way, eventually all or most lines of descent become freed by some distant act in the past of a benevolent ancestor. But still, this leaves open the possibility that some might not; and, in any event, it admits that at some points in time, child-slavery exists and is permissible.

Finally, and to me most decisive: it could be argued that the parent has various *positive obligations* to his or her children, such as the obligation to feed, shelter, educate, etc. The idea here is that libertarianism does not oppose "positive rights"; it simply insists that they be *voluntarily incurred*. One way to do this is by contract, or so some would argue;[8] another is by trespassing against someone's property. Now, if you pass by a drowning man in a lake you have no enforceable (legal) obligation to try to rescue him; but if you push someone in a lake you have a positive obligation to try to rescue him, to mitigate the harm resulting from your tort. If you don't attempt the rescue, you could be liable for homicide.

Likewise, if your voluntary actions bring into being an infant with natural needs for shelter, food, care, and with human rights, it is akin to throwing someone into a lake. In both cases you create a situation where another human is in dire need of help and without which he will perish. By creating this situation of need you incur an obligation to provide for those needs. And surely this set of positive obligations to one's child would encompass the obligation to manumit the child at a certain point. This last argument is, to my mind, the most attractive,

---

8 But see "A Libertarian Theory of Contract" (ch. 9), arguing that contracts do not give rise to binding obligations but only result in transfers of title to owned (alienable) resources. In which case a mere promise or "contract" could not, in and of itself, give rise to any positive obligations or corresponding positive rights.

but it is also probably the least likely to be accepted by most libertarians, who generally seem opposed to positive obligations, even if they are incurred as the result of one's actions. Rothbard, for example, puts forward several objections to such an approach.[9]

OBJECTIVE LINK: THE REAL TOUCHSTONE

All this said, it turns out that these Herculean efforts are unnecessary. The dilemma arises only if it is assumed that "first use" determines ownership not only for homesteaded resources, but also for bodies.

However, the "first use" rule is merely the result of the application of the more general principle of *objective link* to the case of objects that may be homesteaded from an unowned state. Recall that the purpose of property rights is to permit conflicts over scarce (rivalrous, conflictable) resources to be avoided.[10] To fulfill this purpose, property titles to particular resources are assigned to particular owners. The assignment must not, however, be random, arbitrary, or biased, if it is to actually be a property norm and possibly help conflict to be avoided. What this means is that title has to be assigned to one of the competing claimants based on "the existence of an objective, intersubjectively ascertainable link between owner and the" resource claimed.[11]

Thus, it is the concept of *objective link* between claimants and a claimed resource that determines property ownership. First use is merely what constitutes the objective link in the case of previously unowned resources. In this case, the only objective link to the thing is that between the first user—the appropriator—and the thing. Any other supposed link is not objective, and is merely based on verbal decree, or on some type of formulation that violates the prior-later

---

[9] See Murray N. Rothbard, "Children and Rights," in *The Ethics of Liberty* (New York: New York University Press, 1998; http://mises.org/rothbard/ethics/fourteen.asp). See also Kinsella, "Objectivists on Positive Parental Obligations and Abortion," *The Libertarian Standard* (Jan. 14, 2011).

[10] On the term "conflictable," see Kinsella, "On Conflictability and Conflictable Resources," *StephanKinsella.com* (Jan. 31, 2022); also "*Against Intellectual Property* After Twenty Years: Looking Back and Looking Forward" (ch. 15), at n.29; "What Libertarianism Is" (ch. 2), Appendix I.

[11] Hoppe, *A Theory of Socialism and Capitalism*, p. 23.

distinction. But the prior-later distinction is crucial if property rights are to actually establish rights and make conflict avoidable. Moreover, ownership claims cannot be based on mere verbal decree, as this also would not help to reduce conflict, since any number of people could simply decree their ownership of the thing.[12]

So for homesteaded things—previously unowned resources—the objective link *is* first use. It has to be, by the nature of the situation.

Human Bodies

But for human bodies, matters are somewhat different. As noted above, one is not really the "first user" of one's body in the same sense as one is the first user of a previously unowned thing that one appropriates. It's not as if the body was just lying, unoccupied and unused, in the wild, waiting for an occupant to homestead it. And moreover, as noted above, the occupant is not exactly the first user of his body, with respect to his parents.

Additionally, to homestead an *unowned* resource *presupposes one already has a body*, which one uses to *act* in the world and to homestead such unowned things. But this is not the case for "homesteading" one's body. One has no body before one gains rights to it.[13]

Direct Control

If "first use" is not the ultimate test for the "objective link" in the case of body ownership, what is? It is the unique relationship between a person and "his" body—his *direct and immediate control* over the body, and the fact that, at least in some sense, a body *is* a given person and vice-versa (as it is impossible to imagine a person that does not have a body, without accepting groundless religious conceptions). This is

---

12 Hoppe elaborates on these themes in chaps. 1, 2, and 7 of *A Theory of Socialism and Capitalism*.

13 For further discussion of the difference between bodies and previously unowned things, see "A Libertarian Theory of Contract" (ch. 9), Part III.B *et pass*. As Hoppe points out, "any indirect control of a good by a person presupposes the direct control of this person regarding his own body; thus, in order for a scarce good to become justifiably appropriated, the appropriation of one's directly controlled 'own' body *must already be presupposed as justified*." Quoted in text at note 17, below.

what constitutes the objective link sufficient to give that person better title to his body than any third party claimant, even his parents.[14] (This link is only a presumption, it is defeasible, as noted below, since it may be severed or forfeited by a person committing an act of aggression that gives the victim rights over the aggressor's body, for purposes of self-defense, restitution, or retribution.)

Moreover, any outsider who claims another's body cannot deny this objective link and its special status, since the outsider also necessarily presupposes this in his own case. This is so because in seeking dominion over the other, in asserting ownership over the other's body, he has to presuppose his own ownership of his body, which demonstrates he does place a certain significance on this link, at the same time that he disregards the significance of the other's link to his own body. (Notice that if a victim seeks dominion over the body of his aggressor for purposes of self-defense or proportional punishment, his claim of ownership over the aggressor's body is not incompatible with a claim of self-ownership, since the cases are different. It is not inconsistent to claim that the special link between an innocent person and his body gives him the best claim over that body, and to also claim that this no longer holds for an aggressor because he has committed aggression. This distinction is neither arbitrary nor particularizable; it is grounded in the nature of things.)[15]

---

[14] In revising this chapter, this footnote grew to unmanageable length. I have placed the relevant commentary in the Appendix, below.

[15] For more on this, see especially the text following n.37 in chapter 7; also "A Libertarian Theory of Punishment and Rights" (ch. 5), Parts III.C "Punishing Aggressive Behavior" and III.D "Potential Defenses by the Aggressor"; Hoppe, *A Theory of Socialism and Capitalism*, pp. 157–65; "What Libertarianism Is" (ch. 2), the section "Self-ownership and Conflict Avoidance"; "Dialogical Arguments for Libertarian Rights" (ch. 6), n.43 and accompanying text; and Stephan Kinsella, "The problem of particularistic ethics or, why everyone really has to admit the validity of the universalizability principle," *StephanKinsella.com* (Nov. 10, 2011). Although Hoppe has not directly addressed this issue, I believe this is compatible with his argumentation ethics. Note that in the quote in note 17 below, he states: "every attempt of an indirect control of my body by another person must, unless I have *explicitly agreed to it*, be regarded as unjust(ified)" (emphasis added). I believe the forfeiture of rights that results from voluntarily committing aggression can be subsumed under the "explicitly agreed to" provision; indeed, I have been reluctant to separate out rectification as a third principle of property rights allocation, in addition to original appropriation and contractual transfer, since rectification can be thought of as a special case of contractual transfer since aggression is a voluntary

The basic point about the primacy of the "direct" link over an "indirect" link (*ceteris paribus*—see the point above about punishment of criminals) was first suggested to me by Hoppe. As might be apparent to those familiar with Hoppe's argumentation ethics,[16] the Hoppean theory implies the logical priority of direct versus indirect control over one's body. In fact, the argument made above (that any outsider who claims another's body cannot deny the objective link between person and body) is merely an application of Hoppe's argumentation ethics approach. It turns out Hoppe made a similar argument in a German publication in 1987:

> The answer to the question what makes my body "mine" lies in the obvious fact that this is not merely an assertion but that, for everyone to see, this *is* indeed the case. Why do we say "This is my body"? For this, a twofold requirement exists. On the one hand it must be the case that the body called "mine" must indeed (in an intersubjectively ascertainable way) express or "objectify" my will. Proof of this, as far as my body is concerned, is easy enough to demonstrate: When I announce that I will now lift my arm, turn my head, relax in my chair (or whatever else) and these announcements then become true (are fulfilled), then this shows that the body which does this has been indeed appropriated by my will.

---

action that results in changes of ownership, just as normal contracts do. However, due to its special characteristics, it is worth calling it out as a third principle, if its relationship to the first two principles (homesteading and contract) is kept in mind. See, e.g., my formulation in Kinsella, "Aggression and Property Rights Plank in the Libertarian Party Platform."

[16] For more on argumentation ethics, see "Dialogical Arguments for Libertarian Rights" (ch. 6); "Defending Argumentation Ethics" (ch. 7); "The Undeniable Morality of Capitalism" (ch. 22); Hoppe, "The Ethical Justification of Capitalism and Why Socialism Is Morally Indefensible," chap. 7 in *A Theory of Socialism and Capitalism; idem*, "From the Economics of Laissez Faire to the Ethics of Libertarianism," "The Justice of Economic Efficiency," and "On the Ultimate Justification of the Ethics of Private Property," chaps. 11–13 in *The Economics and Ethics of Private Property; idem*, "Of Common, Public, and Private Property and the Rationale for Total Privatization," in *The Great Fiction; idem*, "PFP163 | Hans Hermann Hoppe, 'On The Ethics of Argumentation' (PFS 2016)," *The Property and Freedom Podcast*, ep. 163 (June 30, 2022); Stephan Kinsella, "Argumentation Ethics and Liberty: A Concise Guide," *StephanKinsella.com* (May 27, 2011); *idem*, "Hoppe's Argumentation Ethics and Its Critics," *StephanKinsella.com* (Aug. 11, 2015); Frank van Dun, "Argumentation Ethics and the Philosophy of Freedom," *Libertarian Papers* 1, art. no. 19 (2009; www.libertarianpapers. org); Marian Eabrasu, "A Reply to the Current Critiques Formulated Against Hoppe's Argumentation Ethics," *Libertarian Papers* 1, art. no. 20 (2009; www.libertarianpapers.org); Norbert Slenzok, "The Libertarian Argumentation Ethics, the Transcendental Pragmatics of Language, and the Conflict-Freedom Principle," *Analiza i Egzystencja* 58 (2022), 35–64.

If, to the contrary, my announcements showed no systematic relation to my body's actual behavior, then the proposition "this is my body" would have to be considered as an empty, objectively unfounded assertion; and likewise this proposition would be rejected as incorrect if following my announcement not my arm would rise but always that of Müller, Meier, or Schulze (in which case one would more likely be inclined to consider Müller's, Meier's, or Schulze's body "mine"). On the other hand, apart from demonstrating that my will has been "objectified" in the body called "mine," it must be demonstrated that my appropriation has *priority* as compared to the possible appropriation of the same body by another person.

As far as bodies are concerned, it is also easy to prove this. We demonstrate it by showing that it is under my *direct* control, while every other person can objectify (express) itself in my body only *indirectly*, i.e., by means of their own bodies, and direct control must obviously have logical-temporal priority (precedence) as compared to any indirect control. The latter simply follows from the fact that any indirect control of a good by a person presupposes the direct control of this person regarding his own body; thus, in order for a scarce good to become justifiably appropriated, the appropriation of one's directly controlled "own" body must already be *presupposed* as justified. It thus follows: If the justice of an appropriation by means of direct control must be presupposed by any further-reaching indirect appropriation, and if only I have direct control of my body, then no one except me can ever justifiably own my body (or, put differently, then property in/of my body cannot be transferred onto another person), and every attempt of an indirect control of my body by another person must, unless I have explicitly agreed to it, be regarded as unjust(ified).[17]

---

[17] Informal translation (by Hans-Hermann Hoppe) from, *Eigentum, Anarchie und Staat* (Manuscriptum Verlag, 2005; originally published in 1987; www.hanshoppe.com/eigentum), pp. 98–100. See also the similar, but later, quote in "Defending Argumentation Ethics" (ch. 7), at n.35; and *idem, Economy, Society, and History* (Auburn, Ala.: Mises Institute, 2021; https://www.hanshoppe.com/esh/), pp. 7–8 (discussing each human's unique connection to his own body). See also Emanuele Martinelli, "On Whether We Own What We Think" (draft, 2019; https://www.academia.edu/93535130/On_Whether_We_Own_What_We_Think), p. 3: regarding Locke's notion of self-ownership, "the basic intuition is that no one could metaphysically control another one's body and mind." See also Locke, *Second Treatise on Civil Government*, chap. 5, "Of Property"; and Richard A. Epstein, "Possession as the Root of Title," *Georgia L. Rev.* 13 (1979; https://chicagounbound.uchicago.edu/journal_articles/1236/) 1221–43, p. 1227 (citation omitted; emphasis added):

Why does labor itself create any rights in a thing? The labor theory rests at least upon the belief that each person owns himself. Yet that claim, unless it be accepted as bedrock and unquestioningly, must be justified in some way.... The obvious line

And as Hoppe adds in the Foreword, "if body-ownership were assigned to some indirect body-controller, *conflict would become unavoidable* as the direct body-controller cannot give up the direct control over his body as long as he is alive" (emphasis added). In other words, direct control has logical-temporal priority as compared to any indirect control, since otherwise conflict is unavoidable, contrary to the very purpose of property norms.

Summary

Perhaps it is time to summarize the (interrelated) reasons why direct control is the relevant link for determining ownership of human bodies, and why self-ownership is thus justified:

1. First, it is intuitively obvious; it's the "natural" position. Who better to own my body than me? (See Hoppe's discussion of this in *A Theory of Socialism and Capitalism*, at p. 21 *et seq.*) As Locke wrote, "every man has a property in his own person: this no body has any right to but himself."[18]

2. The arguments made by both Rothard and Hoppe, in the Appendix, below, rejecting the only two possible alternatives to self-ownership: the "communist" alternative of Universal and Equal Other-ownership, which is unworkable and would lead to the death of the human race; and other-ownership (slavery, domination), which is not universalizable.

3. The prior-later distinction, noted above (see notes 6, 7): It is difficult to deny that a person has a claim to self-ownership based on his direct control of his body. This is the objective link *par excellence*. As Hoppe writes, "While I can cite in favor of my property claim regarding my body the objective fact that I was the body's first occupant—its first user—anyone else who claims to have the right to control this body can cite nothing of the sort." (note 7, above) Anyone claiming a right to enslave this person via indirect control always comes along later. Indirect control of a person is impossible unless he is a person. When he becomes a person, his direct control makes him the first owner of his body. The would-be

---

for justification is that *each person is in possession of himself,* if not by choice or conscious act, then *by a kind of natural necessity.*

[18] Locke, *Second Treatise on Civil Government,* §25.

enslaver is thus a latecomer, in violation of the prior-later distinction. Thus, a property norm assigning property rights in a latecoming-indirect controller cannot be justifiable since it would, like any property norm violating the prior-later distinction, generate rather than reduce conflict.

4.   Related to the universalizability points made in point 2 above: human actors who seek to own external resources presuppose they already own their own bodies. This right did not come from homesteading, but is based on some other reason (e.g., direct control). Thus, when the slaver attempts to dominate and own another person, he must claim self-ownership rights in himself—on *some* basis. Whatever the basis for the would-be enslaver's claim to self-ownership, he cannot deny that similarly situated other persons do not have this same right.

5.   Perhaps most decisively, as Hoppe argues in previous work (quote at note 17, above), and as he emphasizes in a related comment in the Foreword: "if body-ownership were assigned to some indirect body-controller, *conflict would become unavoidable* as the direct body-controller cannot give up the direct control over his body as long as he is alive." As I discuss also in chapter 7 (note 35, text following note 36), what Hoppe is pointing out here is that assigning ownership over a person (the direct body-controller) to an enslaver (the indirect body-controller), *necessarily generates conflict* because the enslaved person maintains his direct control over his body—as Rothbard points out, his will remains "inalienable" (see chapter 9, Part III.C). In other words, direct control has priority as compared to any indirect control, since otherwise conflict is unavoidable, contrary to the *very purpose* of property norms. A norm that generates conflict cannot be considered a property norm aimed at reducing conflict, and thus cannot be justified. For this reason, direct control has logical-temporal precedence over indirect control, and the only justified property norm is self-ownership.[19]

---

[19] I discuss this also in Kinsella, "On the Obligation to Negotiate, Compromise, and Arbitrate," *StephanKinsella.com* (April 6, 2023). See also related discussion in "Defending Argumentation Ethics" (ch. 7), text following n.36; "Law and Intellectual Property in a Stateless Society" (ch. 14), Part II.C.

Returning to the Child

So, who owns a child's body? We may say that initially, before the child has rights (say, as a very early stage fetus), the mother owns the growing fetus that is part of her body and that was produced by her body.[20] Once the child is recognized as having rights, the child owns his own body because of his direct control over it, but the parents serve as presumptive guardians who can make decisions on the child's behalf. (The presumption can be overcome if the parents are abusive, meaning some other adults would be selected as the guardians/parents.) When the child reaches a sufficient level of maturity, he or she becomes an adult, so to speak, and the parents' guardianship ends. [21]

Hoppe recognized this basic conclusion in his 1989 treatise, where he wrote:

> It is worth mentioning that *the ownership right stemming from production finds its natural limitation only when, as in the case of children, the thing produced is itself another actor-producer. According to the natural theory of property, a child, once born, is just as much the owner of his own body as anyone else.* Hence, not only can a child expect not to be physically aggressed against but as the owner of his body a child has the right, in particular, to abandon his parents once he is physically able to run away from them and say "no" to their possible attempts to recapture him. Parents only have special rights regarding their child—stemming from their unique status as the child's producers—insofar as they (and no one else) can rightfully claim to be the child's trustee as long as the child is physically unable to run away and say "no."[22]

---

[20] For those who believe human rights start from conception, the mother would never be seen as the owner of the fetus. But I do not believe this can be argued from purely rational principles.

[21] To be clear, humans do not literally homestead or appropriate their bodies as they homestead or appropriate unowned external resources. In the original article upon which this chapter is based, I referred to the child at some point appropriating or "homesteading" his body, but this was meant only as an analogy. Before the child has rights, the body is owned by the mother as it is part of her. After the child is recognized as having rights, but before he or she has full capacity, the parents are the presumptive agents for and guardians of the child. For more on the distinction between self- or body-ownership and ownership of external resources, see "A Libertarian Theory of Contract" (ch. 9); "Selling Does Not Imply Ownership, and Vice-Versa: A Dissection" (ch. 11); *idem*, "Aggression and Property Rights Plank in the Libertarian Party Platform"; *idem*, "KOL259 | 'How To Think About Property.'"

[22] Hoppe, *A Theory of Socialism and Capitalism*, pp. 24–25, n.12 (emphasis added).

Here Hoppe adopts the Rothbardian approach, which uses the child's capacity to run away and say "no" as a sort of rule of thumb for indicating when a child fully appropriates his body.[23] But a more general conception of body-appropriation may be developed by considering the following. First, as Hoppe emphasizes, to appropriate means to *bring under control*.[24]

Hoppe also argues that rights are held by *rational agents*—those who are "capable of communicating, discussing, arguing, and in particular, [who are] *able to engage in an argumentation of normative problems*."[25] This implies that a person reaches adulthood, or "appropriates" his body and gains full ownership rights to it, when he reaches the point where he is a rational agent in this sense. (The act of gaining full self-ownership rights may be regarded as a type of homesteading or appropriation of one's body—reaching adulthood, so to speak—so long as it is kept in mind that it is a special type of homesteading: not homesteading *by* a body-owner *of* an *unowned* (non-agent) resource, but the establishment of an objective link constituted by direct and immediate control of the body by a rational agent. The child becomes a full self-owner or body-owner, when he reaches sufficient rational agency to be rights-bearing and independent, *because* he has direct control over his body. It is the union of these two characteristics that gives him a proprietary right over his body: rational agency + direct control. Animals also have direct control over their bodies but can be owned because they have no rational agency, that is, no rights. Both characteristics are needed for the young human to become a self-owning adult, so to speak.)

Obviously, there are other issues that could be explored here: when and exactly how does a child homestead himself, or reach adulthood; and exceptions to the *prima facie* case, such as where a person commits a crime which in some sense severs his objective link or transfers it to his victim (creating a "superior" link on behalf of the victim), so that the victim has the right to retaliate. But it should be clear that what

---

[23] Rothbard, "Children and Rights." Again, this "appropriation" is not the same as a body-owning actor homesteading or appropriating an unowned, external resource. See note 21, above.

[24] Hans-Hermann Hoppe, "Four Critical Replies," in *The Economics and Ethics of Private Property*, p. 405.

[25] Hoppe, *A Theory of Socialism and Capitalism*, pp. 18–19, n.5.

distinguishes libertarianism from all competing political theories is its scrupulous adherence—informed by sound, i.e., Austrian, economics—to the idea that property rights in scarce resources must be assigned to the person with the best objective link to the resource in question; and that, in the case of bodies, the link is the natural connection to and relationship between the occupant and the body, while for all other resources, the objective link is first use and contractual transfer.

APPENDIX
DIRECT CONTROL AND OBJECTIVE LINKS

As noted above, the material here was originally intended to appear in footnote 14, above. Due to its length, I include this material in this appendix.

In the text above, I noted that "first use" is not the ultimate test for the "objective link" in the case of body ownership, but that rather it is a person's *direct and immediate control* over his body. See also, on this, Rothbard, who argues in favor of self-ownership because the only logical alternatives are "(1) the 'communist' one of Universal and Equal Other-ownership, or (2) Partial Ownership of One Group by Another—a system of rule by one class over another."[26] However, Alternative (2) cannot be universal, as it is partial and arbitrary; and Alternative (1) either breaks down in practice and reduces to Alternative (2), or, if actually implemented, would result in the death of the human race. As Rothbard writes:

> Can we picture a world in which *no* man is free to take *any* action whatsoever without prior approval by *everyone else* in society? Clearly no man would be able to do anything, and the human race would quickly perish. But if a world of zero or near-zero self-ownership spells death for the human race, then any steps in that direction also contravene the law of what is best for man and his life on earth.[27]

---

[26] Murray N. Rothbard, "Interpersonal Relations: Ownership and Aggression," in *The Ethics of Liberty* (https://mises.org/library/crusoe-social-philosophy), p. 45.
[27] Ibid., p. 46.

Hoppe also writes on this:

> If a person A were *not* the owner of his own body and the places and goods originally appropriated and/or produced with this body as well as of the goods voluntarily (contractually) acquired from another previous owner, then only two alternatives exist. Either *another* person B must be recognized as the owner of A's body as well as the places and goods appropriated, produced or acquired by A, or else *all* persons, A and B, must be considered equal co-owners of all bodies, places and goods.
>
> In the first case, A would be reduced to the rank of B's slave and object of exploitation.... such a ruling must be discarded as a human ethic equally applicable to everyone qua human being (rational animal). From the very outset, any such ruling can be recognized as not universally acceptable and thus cannot claim to represent law. For a rule to aspire to the rank of a law—a *just* rule—it is necessary that such a rule apply equally and universally to everyone.
>
> Alternatively, in the second case of universal and equal co-ownership, the requirement of equal law for everyone is fulfilled. However, this alternative suffers from another even more severe deficiency, for if it were applied, all of mankind would instantly perish. (And since every human ethic must permit the survival of mankind, this alternative must be rejected.)
>
> … This insight into the praxeological impossibility of "universal communism," as Rothbard referred to this proposal, brings us immediately to an alternative way of demonstrating the idea of original appropriation and private property as the only correct solution to the problem of social order.[28]

And in another work, Hoppe adds:

> What is wrong with this idea of dropping the prior-later distinction as morally irrelevant? First, if the late-comers, i.e., those who did not in fact do something with some scarce goods, had indeed as much of a right to them as the first-comers, i.e., those who did do something with the

---

[28] Hans-Hermann Hoppe, "Rothbardian Ethics," in *The Economics and Ethics of Private Property*, pp. 383–84. See also similar comments in David Boaz, *The Libertarian Mind: A Manifesto for Freedom* (New York: Simon & Schuster, 2015), p. 140. See also related discussion in "Law and Intellectual Property in a Stateless Society" (ch. 14), n.27 and "Defending Argumentation Ethics" (ch. 7), at n.31. See also R.W. Bradford's inane criticism of this reasoning in R.W. Bradford, "A Contrast of Visions," *Liberty* 10, no.4 (March 1997; https://perma.cc/7FDT-G7FD): 57–63, at 57–58.

scarce goods, then literally no one would be allowed to do anything with anything, as one would have to have all of the late-comers' consent prior to doing whatever one wanted to do. Indeed, as posterity would include one's children's children—people, that is, who come so late that one could never possibly ask them—advocating a legal system that does not make use of the prior-later distinction as part of its underlying property theory is simply absurd in that it implies *advocating death* but must presuppose life to advocate anything. Neither we, our forefathers, nor our progeny could, do, or will survive and say or argue anything if one were to follow this rule. In order for any person—past, present, or future—to argue anything it *must be possible to survive now*. Nobody can wait and suspend acting until everyone of an indeterminate class of late-comers happens to appear and agree to what one wants to do. Rather, insofar as a person finds himself alone, he must be able to act, to use, produce, consume goods straightaway, prior to any agreement with people who are simply not around yet (and perhaps never will be).[29]

Marxist philosopher G.A. Cohen acknowledges:

> people can do (virtually) nothing without using parts of the external world. If, then, they require the leave of the community to use it, then, effectively…, they do not own themselves, since they can do nothing without communal authorization.[30]

Regarding this remark by Cohen, libertarian philosopher Jan Narveson comments: "It is testimony to the strength of our position that even someone so ideologically opposed gives it clear recognition as an argument that must be confronted."[31]

John Locke also rejected the idea that people can only use unowned resources by getting the consent of everyone else as absurd:

> By making an explicit consent of every commoner, necessary to any one's appropriating to himself any part of what is given in common, children or servants could not cut the meat, which their father or master

---

[29] Hoppe, *A Theory of Socialism and Capitalism*, pp. 169–70 (emphasis added). See also idem, "The Ethics and Economics of Private Property," in *The Great Fiction*, p. 17.

[30] G.A. Cohen, "Self-Ownership, World-Ownership, and Equality," in Frank Lucash, ed., *Justice and Equality, Here and Now* (Ithaca, N.Y.: Cornell University Press, 1986), pp. 113–14; also in G.A. Cohen, *Self-ownership, Freedom, and Equality* (Cambridge University Press, 1995), pp. 93–94.

[31] Jan Narveson, *The Libertarian Idea*, reissue ed. (Broadview Press, 2001), p. 74.

had provided for them in common, without assigning to every one his peculiar part.[32]

For a point related to those mentioned above, see Hoppe, in the Foreword:

> [It is] clear what a human ethic or a theory of justice worth its salt must accomplish. It must give an answer to the question of what am I and what is every other person permitted (or not permitted) to do, right now and right here, wherever a person may find himself and whatever his external surroundings of men and materials may be.

---

[32] John Locke, *Second Treatise on Civil Government* (1690; https://www.johnlocke.net/2022/07/two-treatises-of-government.html), §29.

5

A Libertarian Theory of
Punishment and Rights

I published my first article on libertarian theory, "Estoppel: A New Justification for Individual Rights," in *Reason Papers* in 1992.[*] An expanded treatment was published in the *Journal of Libertarian Studies* in 1996 and a similar version in the *Loyola of Los Angeles Law Review*.[†] This chapter is based on the latter article, also incorporating some material from the *JLS* article. There I thanked "Professor Hans-Hermann Hoppe and Jack Criss for helpful comments on an earlier draft."

[*] Stephan Kinsella, "Estoppel: A New Justification for Individual Rights," *Reason Papers* No. 17 (Fall 1992): 61–74.

[†] Stephan Kinsella, "Punishment and Proportionality: The Estoppel Approach," *J. Libertarian Stud.* 12, no.1 (Spring 1996; https://mises.org/library/punishment-and-proportionality-estoppel-approach-0): 51–73 and *idem*, "A Libertarian Theory of Punishment and Rights," *Loy. L.A. L. Rev.* 30, no. 2 (1997; https://digitalcommons.lmu.edu/llr/vol30/iss2/): 607–45.

[I]t is easier to commit murder than to justify it.[1]

I. INTRODUCTION

Punishment serves many purposes. It can deter crime and prevent the offender from committing further crimes. It can even rehabilitate some criminals—except, of course, if it is capital punishment. It can satisfy a victim's longing for revenge or a relative's desire to avenge. Punishment can also be used as a lever to obtain restitution or rectification for some of the damage caused by the crime. For these reasons, the issue of punishment is and always has been a vital concern to civilized people. They want to know the effects of punishment and effective ways of carrying it out.[2]

Civilized people are also concerned about *justifying* punishment. They want to punish, but they also want to know that such punishment is justified. They want to be able to punish legitimately—hence the interest in punishment theories.[3] As pointed out by Murray Rothbard in his short but insightful discussion of punishment and proportionality, however, the theory of punishment has not been adequately developed, even by libertarians.[4]

---

[1] Barry Nicholas, *An Introduction to Roman Law*, rev. ed (Oxford: Oxford University Press, 1962), p. 30 n.2 (quoting Papinian (Aemilius Papinianus)). Papinian, a third-century Roman jurist, is considered by many to be the greatest of Roman jurists. "Papinian is said to have been put to death for refusing to compose a justification of Caracalla's murder of his brother and co-Emperor, Geta, declaring, so the story goes, that 'it is easier to commit murder than to justify it.'" Ibid. For further references and discussion of this story, see Edward D. Re, "The Roman Contribution to the Common Law," *Fordham L. Rev.* 29, no. 3 (1960; https://ir.lawnet.fordham.edu/flr/vol29/iss3/2/): 447–94, at 452 n.21.

[2] See H.L.A. Hart, *Punishment and Responsibility: Essays in the Philosophy of Law* (Oxford: Oxford University Press, 1968), p. 73, discussing various reasons why people engage in punishment.

[3] The distinction between the effects or utility of punishment and the reason we have a right to punish has long been recognized. See, e.g., William Blackstone, *Commentaries on the Laws of England* (Oxford Edition, Wilfrid Prest, General Editor, 2016), bk 4, chap. 1, at pp. *7-*13 (Oxford edition pp. 4-8); F.H. Bradley, *Ethical Studies*, 2d ed. (Oxford: Clarendon Press, 1927), pp. 26–27; Hart, *Punishment and Responsibility*, pp. 73–74.

[4] Murray N. Rothbard, "Punishment and Proportionality," in *The Ethics of Liberty* (New York: New York University Press, 1998; https://mises.org/library/punishment-and-proportionality-0), at p. 85 ("Few aspects of libertarian political theory are in a less satisfactory

In conventional theories of punishment, concepts of restitution, deterrence,[5] retribution, and rehabilitation are often forwarded as justifications for punishment, even though they are really the effects or purposes of punishment.[6] This reversal of logic is not surprising given the consequentialist, result-oriented type of thinking that is so prevalent nowadays. Nevertheless, the effects of punishment or the uses to which it might be put do not justify punishment.

Take the analogous case of free speech rights as an example. Modern-day liberals and other consequentialists typically seek to justify the First Amendment right to free speech on the grounds that free speech promotes political discourse.[7] But, as libertarians—the most systematic

---

state than the theory of punishment.... It must be noted, however, that *all* legal systems, whether libertarian or not, must work out some theory of punishment, and that existing systems are in *at least* as unsatisfactory a state as punishment in libertarian theory."). This chapter appeared in substantially the same form in "Punishment and Proportionality," in Randy E. Barnett & John Hagel III, eds., *Assessing the Criminal: Restitution, Retribution, And the Legal Process* (Cambridge, Mass.: Ballinger, 1977), chap. 11, pp. 259–70. *See also* Rothbard's article "King on Punishment: A Comment," *J. Libertarian Stud.* 4, no. 2 (Spring 1980; https://mises.org/library/king-punishment-comment-1): 167–72 (commenting on J. Charles King, "A Rationale for Punishment," *J. Libertarian Stud.* 4, no. 2 (Spring 1980; https://mises.org/library/rationale-punishment-0): 151–65). For additional discussion of various punishment-related theories, see Robert James Bidinotto, ed., *Criminal Justice? The Legal System Vs. Individual Responsibility* (Irvington-on-Hudson, New York: Foundation for Economic Education, Inc., 1994; https://perma.cc/KW2G-4JF5); Gertrude Ezorsky, ed., *Philosophical Perspectives on Punishment* (Albany: State University of New York Press, 1972); Stanley E. Grupp, ed., *Theories of Punishment* (Bloomington: Indiana University Press, 1971); and Hart, *Punishment and Responsibility.*

[5] This includes both prevention and incapacitation.

[6] Rehabilitation is also sometimes referred to as reform. For discussion of various punishment-related theories, see Barnett & Hagel III, eds., *Assessing the Criminal*; Robert James Bidinotto, "Crime and Moral Retribution," in *Criminal Justice?*, pp. 181–86, discussing various utilitarian strategies of crime control and punishment; Hart, *Punishment and Responsibility*; Ezorsky, ed., *Philosophical Perspectives on Punishment*; Grupp, ed., *Theories of Punishment*; Matthew A. Pauley, "The Jurisprudence of Crime and Punishment from Plato to Hegel," *Am. J. Jurisprudence* 39, no. 1 (1994; https://scholarship.law.nd.edu/ajj/vol39/iss1/6/): 97–152; and Ronald J. Rychlak, "Society's Moral Right to Punish: A Further Exploration of the Denunciation Theory of Punishment," *Tul. L. Rev.* 65, no. 2 (1990): 299–338, at pp. 308–31.

[7] See, e.g., *Mills v. Alabama*, 384 U.S. 214 (1966), p. 218: "[T]here is practically universal agreement that a major purpose of [the First] Amendment was to protect the free discussion of governmental affairs"; *Roth v. United States*, 354 U.S. 47 (1957), p. 484, stating that a purpose of the right to free speech is "to assure unfettered interchange of ideas for the bringing about of political and social changes desired by the people"; John Hart Ely, *Democracy and Distrust: A Theory of Judicial Review* (Cambridge, Mass.: Harvard University Press, 1980),

and coherent school of modern political philosophy and the contemporary heirs of the classical liberal Founding Fathers—have explained, there is a right to free speech simply because it does not involve aggression against others, not because it "promotes political discussion."[8]

---

p. 112, stating that the "central function" of the First Amendment is to "assur[e] an open political dialogue and process"; see also Ronald D. Rotunda & John E. Nowak, *Treatise on Constitutional Law: Substance and Procedure*, vol. 4, 2d ed. (St. Paul, Minn.: West Publishing, 1992), §§ 20.6 & 20.30, discussing various defenses of freedom of speech and reasons for providing a lower standard of constitutional protection to "commercial speech" than to normal speech. *See also* the entry "Case Categories: Commercial Speech," *The First Amendment Encyclopedia* (https://perma.cc/QY39-K9NP).

[8] We do not even have a direct or independent right to free speech. The right to free speech is merely shorthand for one positive result of the right to own private property: If I am situated on property (resources) I have a right to be on, for example in my home, I am entitled to do *anything* on or with that resource (property) that does not invade others' rights, whether it be skeet shooting, barbecuing, or communicating with others. Thus, the right to free speech is only indirect and does not in turn justify property rights, which are logically at the base of the right to free speech. See Rothbard, "'Human Rights' as Property Rights," in *The Ethics of Liberty* (https://mises.org/library/human-rights-property-rights), pp. 113–17; Murray N. Rothbard, *For a New Liberty: The Libertarian Manifesto*, rev. ed. (New York: Libertarian Review Foundation, 1985; https://mises.org/library/new-liberty-libertarian-manifesto), pp. 42–44, discussing the relation between free speech rights and property rights. In like manner, if there is a right to punish, there is only indirectly a "right" to deter crime, and any indirect right to deter, rehabilitate, or retaliate, which is based on the right to punish, can hardly justify or limit the logically prior right to punish.

Technically speaking, a property right is not a right to control a resource but a right to exclude others from using the resource. But this distinction is not material here. See *"Against Intellectual Property* After Twenty Years: Looking Back and Looking Forward" (ch. 15), n.62 and Part IV.H, *et pass.* See also Stephan Kinsella, "The Non-Aggression Principle as a Limit on Action, Not on Property Rights," *StephanKinsella.com* (Jan. 22, 2010) and *idem*, "IP and Aggression as Limits on Property Rights: How They Differ," *StephanKinsella.com* (Jan. 22, 2010); and "What Libertarianism Is" (ch. 2), at n.2 and accompanying text.

Regarding the use of the term "property" to refer to a resource, see *"Against Intellectual Property* After Twenty Years" (ch. 15), at n. 31 and accompanying text, cautioning against use of "property" to refer to the object of a property rights rather than the rights agents have with respect to owned things. This and some other chapters (originally authored years ago) sometimes use "property" in this colloquial sense, but it should be kept in mind that in such cases, it should be understood that the word "property" refers to the thing (resource) owned. The civil law has a broad understanding of the concept of a "thing," which can be owned or the subject of legal rights; see Louisiana Civil Code (https://www.legis.la.gov/legis/Laws_Toc.aspx?folder=67&level=Parent), art. 448: "Division of things. Things are divided into common, public, and private; corporeals and incorporeals; and movables and immovables." Incidentally this exhaustive classification schema implies that intellectual property rights are (private) "incorporeal movables." See also Kinsella, "Are Ideas Movable or Immovable?", *C4SIF Blog* (April 8, 2013).

This analogy highlights the fact that the purpose to which a right holder might put the right is not necessarily what justifies the right in the first place. Turning back to punishment, if individuals have a right to punish, the purpose for which a person exercises this right—for example, for revenge, for restitution, or for deterrence—and the consequences that flow from it may well be irrelevant to the question of whether the right claimed can be justified.[9]

In this chapter I will attempt to explain how and why punishment can be justified. The right to punish discussed herein applies to property crimes such as theft and trespass as well as to bodily-invasive crimes such as assault, rape, and murder. I will develop a retribution-ist, or *lex talionis*, theory of punishment, including related principles of proportionality. This theory of punishment is largely consistent with the libertarian-based *lex talionis* approach of Murray Rothbard.[10] I will not follow the approach of some theorists who derive principles of punishment from a theory of rights or from some other ethical or utilitarian theory. Instead, I will follow the opposite approach in which justifying punishment itself defines and justifies our rights.[11]

---

[9] Others, of course, have recognized the distinction between the effects or utility of punishment and the justification of the *right* to punish. See, e.g., Blackstone, *Commentaries on the Laws of England*, bk 4, pp. *7–*19, discussing in separate subsections (1) the right or power to punish; (2) the object or end of punishment, for example, rehabilitation, deterrence, or incapacitation; and (3) the degree, measure, or quantity of punishment; Bradley, *Ethical Studies*, pp. 26–27 ("Having once the right to punish, we may modify the punishment according to the useful and the pleasant."); Hart, *Punishment and Responsibility*, p. 74 ("[W]e must distinguish two questions commonly confused. They are, first 'Why do men in fact punish?' This is a question of fact to which there may be many different answers.... The second question, to be carefully distinguished from the first, is 'What justifies men in punishing? Why is it morally good or morally permissible for them to punish?'").

[10] Professors Barnett and Hagel state that Rothbard's punishment theory, "with its emphasis on the victim's rights, ... is a significant and provocative departure from traditional retribution theory which, perhaps, merits a new label." Randy E. Barnett & John Hagel III, "Introduction to 'Part II: Criminal Responsibility: Philosophical Issues,'" in Barnett & Hagel III, eds., *Assessing the Criminal*, at p. 179.

[11] What this means is that we determine the content of our rights, by determining when the use of force is justified, since rights are considered to be claims that are legitimately enforceable, instead of the opposite approach of defining rights first which then implies which use of force is justified. The central question that I seek to address is: when is the use of force justified; the contours of rights *follows from* the answer to this question.

II. PUNISHMENT AND CONSENT

What does it mean to punish? Dictionary definitions are easy to come by, but in the sense that interests those of us who want to punish, punishment is the infliction of physical force on a person in response to something that the person has done or has failed to do.[12] Thus, punishment comprises physical violence committed against a person's body, against any property (resource) that a person legitimately owns, or against any rights that a person has.[13] It is a *use of* someone's body or owned resource without their currently-expressed consent, that is, over their expressed objection. Punishment is distinct from aggression, in that it is *for*, or *in response to*, some action, inaction, feature, or status of the person punished; otherwise, it is simply random violence or aggression, unconnected with some previous action or inaction of the one punished.[14] Naked aggression against an innocent victim is not punishment; it is simply aggression. When we punish a person, it is because we consider that person to be a wrongdoer of some sort. We typically want to teach that person or others a lesson or exact vengeance or restitution for what that person has done.

If wrongdoers always consented to the infliction of punishment in response to the perpetration of a crime or tort, we would not need to justify punishment. It would be justified by the very consent of the purported wrongdoer. As the Roman jurist Ulpian summarized this commonsense insight centuries ago, "there is no affront [or injustice] where the victim consents."[15] The need to justify punishment only arises

---

12 See, e.g., *American Heritage Dictionary*, 3d ed. (Boston: Houghton Mifflin, 1992), p. 1469, defining "punishment" as a "penalty imposed for wrongdoing: '*The severity of the punishment must ... be in keeping with the kind of obligation which has been violated*' (Simone Weil)."

13 See *Black's Law Dictionary*, 6th ed. (St. Paul, Minn.: West Publishing, 1990), p. 1234, defining "punishment" as "[a]ny fine, penalty, or confinement inflicted upon a person.... [Or a] deprivation of property or some right."

14 See ibid. "Punishment" is "inflicted upon a person by the authority of the law and the judgment and sentence of a court, for some crime or offense committed by him, or for his omission of a duty enjoined by law."

15 Ulpian, "Edict 56," in *The Digest of Justinian*, translation edited by Alan Watson (Philadelphia: University of Pennsylvania Press, 1985), Vol. 4, 47.10.1.5 (p. 258) (in Latin: "*nulla iniuria est, quae in uolentem fiat*"). As Richard Epstein explains:

The case for the recognition of consent as a defense in case of the deliberate infliction of harm can also be made in simple and direct terms. The self-infliction

when a person resists and refuses to consent to being punished. As philosopher John Hospers notes, the very thing that is troublesome about punishment "is that in punishing someone, we are forcibly *imposing* on him something against his will, and of which he may not approve."[16]

I will thus seek to justify punishment exactly where it needs to be justified: the point at which we attempt to inflict punishment upon people who oppose it. In short, I will argue that society may justly punish those who have initiated force, in a manner proportionate to their

---

of harm generates no cause of action, no matter why inflicted. There is no reason, then, why a person who may inflict harm upon himself should not, prima facie, be allowed to have someone else do it for him.
Richard A. Epstein, "Intentional Harms," *J. Legal Stud.* 4 (1975): 391–442, at 411.

[16] John Hospers, "Retribution: The Ethics of Punishment," in Barnett & Hagel III, eds., *Assessing the Criminal*, p. 190. That said, we must be clear that the core of the libertarian ethic and the notion of aggression and rights does not center around the vague concept of "imposing cost," contra the theory of J.C. Lester, in his *Escape from Leviathan: Liberty, Welfare and Anarchy Reconciled* (New York: St. Martin's Press, 2000), or "causing harm," as per T. Patrick Burke, *No Harm: Ethical Principles for a Free Market* (New York: Paragon House, 1994). On Lester, see Kinsella, "'Aggression' versus 'Harm' in Libertarianism," *Mises Economics Blog* (Dec. 16, 2009) (criticizing Lester's approach, his opposition to "justificationism," and his focus on "imposed cost" instead of aggression as the key libertarian principle); see also David Gordon & Roberta A. Modugno, "Review of J.C. Lester's *Escape from Leviathan: Liberty, Welfare, and Anarchy Reconciled*," *J. Libertarian Stud.* 17, no. 4 (2003, https://mises.org/library/review-jc-lesters-escape-leviathan-liberty-welfare-and-anarchy-reconciled-0): 101–109. On Burke, see Kinsella, "Book Review," *Reason Papers* No. 20 (Fall 1995; https://reasonpapers.com/archives/), p. 135–46; *idem*, "'Aggression' versus 'Harm' in Libertarianism." See also Kinsella, "Hoppe on Property Rights in Physical Integrity vs Value," *StephanKinsella.com* (June 12, 2011). As Rothbard points out:
Legal and political theory have committed much mischief by failing to pinpoint physical invasion as the only human action that should be illegal and that justifies the use of physical violence to combat it. The vague concept of "harm" is substituted for the precise one of physical violence. Consider the following two examples. Jim is courting Susan and is just about to win her hand in marriage, when suddenly Bob appears on the scene and wins her away. Surely Bob has done great "harm" to Jim. Once a nonphysical-invasion sense of harm is adopted, almost any outlaw act might be justified. Should Jim be able to "enjoin" Bob's very existence?
Murray N. Rothbard, "Law, Property Rights, and Air Pollution," in *Economic Controversies* (Auburn, Ala.: Mises Institute, 2011; https://mises.org/library/economic-controversies), p. 374 (footnotes omitted). Rothbard criticizes, in this regard, John Stuart Mill, F.A. Hayek, and Robert Nozick. See ibid., p. 374 notes 13 & 14. See also *idem, Man, Economy, and State, with Power and Market*, Scholar's ed., second ed. (Auburn, Ala.: Mises Institute, 2009; https://mises.org/library/man-economy-and-state-power-and-market), chap. 2, § 12, p. 183 (just law can only prohibit invasion of the *physical* person and property of others, not injury to "values" of property).
See also related discussion in "Dialogical Arguments for Libertarian Rights" (ch. 6), n.3.

initiation of force and to the consequences thereof, because they cannot coherently object to such punishment. In brief, it makes no sense for them to object to punishment because this requires that they maintain that the infliction of force is unjustified, which is contradictory because they intentionally initiated force themselves. Thus, they are dialogically *estopped*, to use related legal terminology, or precluded, from denying the legitimacy of their being punished and from withholding their consent.[17] As argued below, this reasoning may be used to develop a theory of punishment and rights.

III. PUNISHMENT AND ESTOPPEL

A. Legal Estoppel

Estoppel is a well-known common law principle that prevents or precludes someone from making a legal claim that is inconsistent with prior conduct if some other person has changed position detrimentally in reliance on the prior conduct (referred to as "detrimental reliance").[18] Estoppel thus denies a party the ability to assert a fact or right that the party otherwise could. Estoppel is a widely applicable legal principle that has countless manifestations.[19] Roman law and its modern heir, the civil law, contain the similar doctrine "*venire contra proprium factum,*" or "no one can contradict his own act."[20] Under this principle, "no one is allowed to ignore or deny his own acts, or the consequences

---

[17] For an earlier presentation of the argument presented in this chapter, see Kinsella, "Estoppel: A New Justification for Individual Rights." See also "How I Became a Libertarian" (ch. 1); Kinsella, "The Genesis of Estoppel: My Libertarian Rights Theory," *StephanKinsella. com* (March 22, 2016); and "Dialogical Arguments for Libertarian Rights" (ch. 6).

[18] See, e.g., *Allen v. Hance,* 161 Cal. 189 (1911), p. 196; *Highway Trailer Co. v. Donna Motor Lines, Inc.,* 217 A.2d 617 (N.J. 1966), p. 621; *Black's Law Dictionary,* p. 551.

[19] For example, there is estoppel by deed, equitable estoppel, promissory estoppel, and judicial estoppel. See "Estoppel and Waiver," *American Jurisprudence,* 2d ed., vol. 28 (St. Paul, Minn.: West Publishing, 1966), § 1.

[20] Vernon V. Palmer, "The Many Guises of Equity in a Mixed Jurisdiction: A Functional View of Equity in Louisiana," *Tul. L. Rev.* 69, no. 1 (1994): 7–70, at 55. See also Ulpian, "Edict 3," in *The Digest of Justinian,* Vol. I, 2.2.1, p. 42 (Section title: "The Same Rule which Anyone Maintains against Another is to be Applied to Him"):

thereof, and claim a right in opposition to such acts or consequences."[21] Estoppel may even be applied if a person's silent acquiescence in the face of a duty to speak amounts to a representation.[22] The principle behind estoppel can also be seen in common sayings such as "actions speak louder than words," "practice what you preach," and "put your money where your mouth is," all of which embody the idea that actions and assertions should be consistent.[23] As Lord Coke stated, the word "estoppel" is used "because a man's own act or acceptance stoppeth or closeth up his mouth to allege or plead the truth."[24]

This edict has the greatest equity without arousing the just indignation of anyone; for who will reject the application to himself of the same law which he has applied or caused to be applied to others? 1. "If one who holds a magistracy or authority establishes a new law against anyone, he himself ought to employ the same law whenever his adversary demands it. If anyone should obtain a new law from a person holding a magistracy or authority, whenever his adversary subsequently demands it, let judgment be given against him in accordance with the same law." The reason, of course, is that what anyone believed to be fair, when applied to another, he should suffer to prevail in his own case.

21 Saúl Litvinoff, "Still Another Look at Cause," *La. L. Rev.* 48, no. 1 (1987; https://digitalcommons.law.lsu.edu/lalrev/vol48/iss1/5/): 3–28, at 21.

22 See, e.g., *Duthu v. Allements' Roberson Mach. Works, Inc.*, 393 So. 2d 184, 186-87 (La. Ct. App. 1980); *Blofsen v. Cutaiar*, 333 A.2d 841, 843–44 (Pa. 1975).

23 Recall also the saying "'What you do speaks so loud I can't hear what you are saying.'" Clarence B. Carson, *Free Enterprise: The Road to Prosperity* (New Rochelle: America's Future, 1985; https://fee.org/articles/free-enterprise-the-key-to-prosperity/). For a recent example of a use of the basic logic behind this notion, see Cheyenne Ligon, Jack Schickler & Nikhilesh De, "Hodlonaut Wins Norwegian Lawsuit Against Self-Proclaimed 'Satoshi' Craig Wright," *Coindesk.com* (Oct. 20, 2022; https://perma.cc/QLV9-VSLM), discussing a recent Norwegian case concerning a dispute over whether Craig S. Wright is really Satoshi Nakamoto, the pseudonymous creator of Bitcoin, and the claims of Magnus Granath, known on Twitter as "Hodlonaut," that Wright is not Nakamoto and is instead a "fraud" and a "scammer." The court ruled for Granath, employing, in part, estoppel-like reasoning:
"Wright has come out with a controversial claim, and must withstand criticism from dissenters," [Judge Engebrigtsen] added, concluding that Granath's statements were lawful, not defamatory.
Engebrigtsen also appeared to take up the idea that Twitter is a naturally rough-and-tumble environment where users should have a thick skin, after Granath's lawyers noted that Wright had also tweeted strong words such as "cuck" and "soy boy."
"Wright himself uses coarse slang and derogatory references, and so, in the court's view, must accept that others use similar jargon against him," the judgment said.

24 "Estoppel and Waiver," *American Jurisprudence* 28 (1966), § 1, quoting Lord Coke. In the remainder of this chapter, the expression "estoppel" or "dialogical estoppel" refers to the more general, philosophical estoppel theory developed herein, as opposed to the traditional theory of legal estoppel, which will be denoted "legal estoppel."

For legal estoppel to operate, there usually must have been detrimental reliance by the person seeking to estop another.[25] Proof of detrimental reliance is required because until a person has relied on another's prior action or representation, the action or representation has not caused any harm, and thus, there is no reason to estop the actor from asserting the truth or from rejecting the prior conduct.[26]

As an example, in the recent case *Zimmerman v. Zimmerman*, a daughter sued her father for tuition fee debts she had incurred during her second and third years at college.[27] In this case, when the daughter was a senior in high school, the father promised to pay her tuition fees and related expenses if she attended a local college (Adelphi University). However, the promise was a "mere" promise, because it was not accompanied by the requisite legal formalities such as consideration, and therefore did not constitute a normally binding contract. Nevertheless, during her first year at college, her father paid her tuition for her, as he had promised. However, he failed to pay her tuition during the second and third years, although he repeatedly assured her during this time that he would pay the tuition fees when he had the money. This resulted in the daughter's legal obligation to pay approximately $6,700 to Adelphi. In this case, although the promise itself did not give rise to an enforceable contract (because of lack of legal formalities such as consideration), it was found that the father should have reasonably expected that his daughter would rely on his promise, and that she did in fact rely on the promise, taking substantial action to her detriment or disadvantage (namely, incurring a debt to Adelphi). Therefore, the daughter was awarded an amount sufficient to cover the unpaid tuition. The father was, in effect, estopped from denying that a contract was formed, even though one was not.[28]

---

[25] See *Bellsouth Adver. & Publ'g Corp. v. Gassenberger*, 565 So.2d 1093 (La. Ct. App. 1990), p. 1095.

[26] See *Dickerson v. Colegrove*, 100 U.S. 578 (1879), p. 580.

[27] *Zimmerman v. Zimmerman*, 447 N.Y.S.2d 675 (App. Div. 1982).

[28] The concept of "detrimental reliance" actually involves circular reasoning, however, for reliance on performance is not "reasonable" or justifiable unless one already knows that the promise is enforceable, which begs the question. See "A Libertarian Theory of Contract: Title Transfer, Binding Promises, and Inalienability" (ch. 9), Part. I.E. However, the legitimacy of the traditional legal concept of detrimental reliance is irrelevant here.

B. Dialogical Estoppel

As can be seen, the heart of the idea behind legal estoppel is consistency. A similar concept, "dialogical estoppel," can be used to justify the libertarian conception of rights because of the reciprocity inherent in the libertarian tenet that force is legitimate only in response to force and because of the consistency that must apply to aggressors trying to argue why they should not be punished.[29] The basic insight behind this theory of rights is that people who initiate force cannot consistently object to being punished. They are dialogically, so to speak, "estopped" from asserting the impropriety of the force used to punish them because of their own coercive behavior. This theory also establishes the validity of the libertarian conception of rights as being strictly negative rights against aggression.

The point at which punishment needs to be justified is when we attempt to inflict punishment upon a person who opposes it. Thus, using a philosophical, generalized version of dialogical estoppel, I want to justify punishment in just this situation by showing that an aggressor is estopped from objecting to punishment. Under the principle of dialogical estoppel, or simply "estoppel," a person is estopped from making certain claims during discourse if these claims are inconsistent and contradictory. To say that a person is estopped from making certain claims means that the claims cannot possibly be right because they are contradictory. It is to recognize that his assertion is simply wrong because it is contradictory.

Applying estoppel in this manner perfectly complements the purpose of dialogue. Dialogue, discourse, or argument—terms that are used interchangeably herein—is by its nature an activity aimed at finding truth. Anyone engaged in argument is necessarily endeavoring to discern the truth about some particular subject; otherwise, there is no dialogue occurring but mere babbling or even physical fighting. This cannot be denied. Any person arguing long enough to deny that truth

---

[29] As used herein, "'[a]ggression' is defined as the *initiation* of the use or threat of physical violence against the person or property of anyone else." Rothbard, *For a New Liberty*, p. 23, emphasis added. See also Kinsella, "What Libertarianism Is" (ch. 2), at n.9, *et pass.*; Kinsella, "Aggression and Property Rights Plank in the Libertarian Party Platform," *StephanKinsella.com* (May 30, 2022).

is the goal of discourse contradicts this denial because that person is asserting or challenging the truth of a given proposition. Thus, asserting that something is true that cannot be true is incompatible with the purpose of discourse. Anything that clearly cannot be true is contrary to the truth-finding purpose of discourse and, consequently, is impermissible within the bounds of the discourse.

Contradictions are certainly the archetype of propositions that cannot be true. A and not-A cannot both be true simultaneously and in the same respect.[30] This is why participants in discourse must be consistent. If an arguer does not need to be consistent, truth-finding cannot occur. And just as the traditional legal theory of estoppel mandates a sort of consistency in a legal context, the more general use of estoppel can be used to require consistency in discourse. The theory of estoppel that I propose is nothing more than a convenient way to apply the requirement of consistency to arguers—those engaged in discourse, dialogue, debate, discussion, or argumentation. Because discourse is a truth-finding activity, any such contradictory claims should be disregarded since they cannot possibly be true. Dialogical estoppel is thus a rule of discourse that rejects any inconsistent, mutually contradictory claims because they are contrary to the very goal of discourse. This rule is based solely on the recognition that discourse is a truth-seeking activity and that contradictions, which are necessarily untrue, are incompatible with discourse and thus should not be allowed.[31] The validity of this rule is undeniable because it is necessarily presupposed by any participant in discourse.

---

[30] On the impossibility of denying the law of contradiction, see Aristotle, *Metaphysics*, Richard Hope, trans. (New York: Columbia University Press, 1952), p. 68 ("It is impossible for the same thing at the same time to belong and not to belong to the same thing and in the same respect."); Hans-Hermann Hoppe, *A Theory of Socialism and Capitalism: Economics, Politics, and Ethics* (Mises, 2010 [1989]; www.hanshoppe.com/tsc), p. 142 n.108; Tibor R. Machan, *Individuals and Their Rights* (Chicago: Open Court Publishing, 1989), p. 77; Douglas B. Rasmussen & Douglas J. Den Uyl, *Liberty and Nature: An Aristotelian Defense of Liberal Order* (La Salle, Ill.: Open Court, 1991), p. 50; Ludwig von Mises, *Human Action: A Treatise on Economics*, Scholar's ed. (Auburn, Ala.: Mises Institute, 1998; https://mises.org/library/human-action-0), p. 36; see also Leonard Peikoff, *Objectivism: The Philosophy of Ayn Rand* (New York: Plume, 1991), pp. 6–12, 118–21, explaining the law of identity and its relevance to knowledge; Ayn Rand, *Atlas Shrugged* (New York: Signet 1992), pp. 942–43, discussing identity, or "A is A," and the law of contradiction.

[31] Because discourse is a peaceful, cooperative, conflict-free activity, as well as an inquiry into truth, *aggression* itself is also incompatible with norms presupposed by all participants in discourse. Indeed, it is this realization that Professor Hoppe builds on in his brilliant

There are various ways that contradictions can arise in discourse. First, an arguer's position might be explicitly inconsistent. For example, if a person states that A is true and that not-A is also true, there is no doubt that the person is incorrect. After all, as Ayn Rand repeatedly emphasized, A is A; the law of identity is indeed valid and unchallengeable.[32] It is impossible for him[33] to coherently and intelligibly assert that two contradictory statements are true; it is impossible for these claims to both be true. Thus, he is estopped from asserting them and is not heard to utter them because they cannot tend to establish the truth, which is the goal of all argumentation.[34]

"argumentation ethics" defense of individual rights. For more on argumentation ethics, *see* chaps. 5–7 and 19; Hans-Hermann Hoppe, "The Ethical Justification of Capitalism and Why Socialism Is Morally Indefensible," chap. 7 in Hoppe, *A Theory of Socialism and Capitalism*; *idem*, "From the Economics of Laissez Faire to the Ethics of Libertarianism," "The Justice of Economic Efficiency," and "On the Ultimate Justification of the Ethics of Private Property," chaps. 11–13 in *The Economics and Ethics of Private Property: Studies in Political Economy and Philosophy* (Mises, 2006 [1993]; www.hanshoppe.com/eepp); *idem*, "Of Common, Public, and Private Property and the Rationale for Total Privatization," in *The Great Fiction: Property, Economy, Society, and the Politics of Decline* (Second Expanded Edition, Mises Institute, 2021; www.hanshoppe.com/tgf); *idem*, "PFP163 | Hans Hermann Hoppe, 'On The Ethics of Argumentation' (PFS 2016)," *Property and Freedom Podcast*, ep. 163 (June 30, 2022); Stephan Kinsella, "Argumentation Ethics and Liberty: A Concise Guide," *StephanKinsella.com* (May 27, 2011); *idem*, "Hoppe's Argumentation Ethics and Its Critics," *StephanKinsella.com* (Aug. 11, 2015); Frank van Dun, "Argumentation Ethics and the Philosophy of Freedom," *Libertarian Papers* 1, 19 (2009; www.libertarianpapers.org); Marian Eabrasu, "A Reply to the Current Critiques Formulated Against Hoppe's Argumentation Ethics," *Libertarian Papers* 1, 20 (2009; www.libertarianpapers.org); Norbert Slenzok, "The Libertarian Argumentation Ethics, the Transcendental Pragmatics of Language, and the Conflict-Freedom Principle," *Analiza i Egzystencja* 58 (2022), 35–64.

[32] Ayn Rand, *Atlas Shrugged* (New York: Signet 1992), pp. 942–43.

[33] It is the general policy of the *Loyola of Los Angeles Law Review* to use gender-neutral language. The author, however, has chosen not to conform to this policy. [Note: this footnote was inserted by the journal after I refused to change my text. I left this footnote in as reminder of the political correctness and language battles that were already beginning to rear their heads back in 1997, when the original paper was published.]

[34] More than once, I have had the frustrating and bewildering experience of having someone actually assert that consistency is not necessary for truth, that mutually contradictory ideas can be held by a person and be true at the same time. When faced with such a clearly incorrect opponent, one can do little more than try to point out the absurdity of the opponent's position. Beyond this, though, a stubborn opponent must be viewed as having renounced reason and logic and is thus simply unable or unwilling to engage in meaningful discourse. See Peikoff, *Objectivism: The Philosophy of Ayn Rand*, pp. 11–12, discussing when to abandon attempts to communicate with stubbornly irrational individuals. The mere fact that individuals can choose to disregard reason and logic does not contradict the estoppel theory any more than a criminal who chooses to murder another thereby "proves" that the victim had no right to life. As R.M. Hare stated:

As Wittgenstein noted, "What we cannot speak about we must pass over in silence."[35]

An arguer's position can also be inconsistent without explicitly maintaining that A and not-A are true. Indeed, rarely will an arguer assert both A and not-A explicitly. However, whenever an arguer states that A is true, and also necessarily holds that not-A is true, the inconsistency is still there, and he is still estopped from explicitly claiming that A is true and implicitly claiming that not-A is true. The reason is the same as above: he cannot possibly be right that explicit A and implicit not-A are both true. Now he might, in some cases, be able to remove the inconsistency by dropping one of the claims. For example, suppose he asserts that the concept of gross national product is meaningful and a minute later states the exact opposite, apparently contradicting the earlier assertion. To avoid inconsistency, he can disclaim the earlier statement, thereby necessarily maintaining that the previous statement was incorrect. But it is not always possible to drop one of the assertions if it is unavoidably presupposed as true by the arguer. For example, the speaker might argue that he never argues. However, since he is currently arguing, he must necessarily, at least implicitly, hold or recognize that he sometimes argues. We would not recognize the contradictory claims as permissible in the argument because contradictions are untrue. The speaker would be estopped from maintaining these two contradictory claims, one explicit and one implicit, and he could not drop the second claim—that he sometimes argues—for he cannot help but hold this view while engaged in argumentation itself. To maintain an arguable—

Just as one cannot win a game of chess against an opponent who will not make any moves—and just as one cannot argue mathematically with a person who will not commit himself to any mathematical statements—so moral argument is impossible with a man who will make no moral judgements at all…. Such a person is not entering the arena of moral dispute, and therefore it is impossible to contest with him. *He is compelled also—and this is important—to abjure the protection of morality for his own interests.*

R.M. Hare, *Freedom and Reason* (New York: Oxford University Press, 1963), p. 101, emphasis added. For other, similar quotes, see Kinsella, "Quotes on the Logic of Liberty," *StephanKinsella.com* (June 22, 2009), the Appendix, below, and the quote by Arendt in "Dialogical Arguments for Libertarian Rights" (ch. 6), n.19.

[35] Ludwig Wittgenstein, *Tractatus Logico-Philosophicus*, D.F. Pears & B.F. McGuinness, trans. (London: Routledge & Paul Kegan, 1961), p. 151.

that is, possibly true—position, he would have to renounce the first claim that he never argues.

Alternatively, if this person was so incoherent as to argue that he somehow does not believe or recognize that arguing is possible, despite engaging in it, he would still be estopped from asserting that argumentation is impossible. For even if he does not actually *realize* that argumentation is possible—or, what is more likely, does not actually admit it—it still cannot be the case that argumentation is impossible if someone is indeed arguing.

We know this to be true whether or not others admit or recognize this. Thus, if someone asserts that argumentation is impossible, this assertion contradicts the undeniable presupposition of argumentation—that argumentation *is* possible. This person's proposition is facially untrue. Again, the person would be estopped from asserting such a claim since it is not even possibly true; the assertion flies in the face of undeniably true facts of reality.

Thus, because dialogue is a truth-finding activity, participants are estopped from making explicitly contradictory assertions since they subvert the goal of truth-seeking by being necessarily false. For the same reason, arguers are estopped from asserting one thing if (1) it contradicts something else that they necessarily maintain to be true; (2) it contradicts something that is necessarily true because it is a presupposition of discourse; or (3) it is necessarily true as an undeniable feature of reality or human existence. Further, no one can disagree with these general conclusions without self-contradiction, for anyone disagreeing with anything is a participant in discourse and, therefore, necessarily values truth-finding and consistency.

C. Punishing Aggressive Behavior

The conduct of individuals can be divided into two types: (1) coercive or aggressive—that is, the initiation of force—and (2) noncoercive or nonaggressive. This division is purely descriptive and does not presume that aggression is invalid, immoral, or unjustifiable. It only assumes that at least some human action can be objectively classified as either aggressive or nonaggressive.[36] Thus, there are two types of behavior for which we might attempt to punish a person: aggressive and nonaggressive.[37] I will examine each in turn to show that punishment of aggressive behavior is legitimate while punishment of nonaggressive behavior is illegitimate.

The clearest and most severe instance of aggression is murder, so let us take this as an example. In what follows I will assume that the victim B, or B's agent, C, attempts to punish a purported wrongdoer A.[38] Suppose that A murders B, and C convicts and imprisons A. In order for A to object to his punishment, A must claim that C should not and must not treat him this way; that he has a *right*[39] to not be punished or, at least, that the use of force is *wrong* so that C should, therefore, not

---

[36] Other divisions could of course be proposed as well, but they do not result in interesting or useful results. For example, one could divide human conduct into jogging and not jogging, but to what end? Although such a division would be valid, it would produce uninteresting results, unlike the aggressive/nonaggressive division, which produces relevant results for a theory of punishment, which necessarily concerns the use of force. See Ludwig von Mises, *Epistemological Problems of Economics*, 3d ed., George Reisman, trans. (Auburn, Ala.: Mises Institute, 2003; https://mises.org/library/epistemological-problems-economics); *idem, Human Action*, pp. 65–66; *idem, The Ultimate Foundation of Economic Science: An Essay on Method* (Princeton, N.J.: D. Van Nostrand Company, Inc., 1962; https://mises.org/library/ultimate-foundation-economic-science), explaining in all three works that experience can be referenced to develop interesting laws based on the fundamental axioms of praxeology, rather than irrelevant or uninteresting—though not invalid—laws). See also "Knowledge, Calculation, Conflict, and Law" (ch. 19), at n.65 and Kinsella, "Mises: Keep It Interesting," *StephanKinsella.com* (Oct. 16, 2010).

In any event, it is clear that some actions can objectively be characterized as aggressive. See above, Part III.D.1.

[37] To be more precise, if society attempts to punish a person, it is either for aggressive behavior or for not(aggressive behavior). Not(aggressive behavior) is a residual category that includes both nonaggressive behavior, such as speaking or writing, and also nonbehavioral categories such as status, race, age, nationality, skin color, and the like.

[38] In principle, any right of a victim to punish the victimizer may be delegated to an heir or to a private agent such as a defense agency—or to the state, if government is valid, a question that does not concern us here.

[39] On this subject, Alan Gewirth has noted:

Now these strict "oughts" involve normative necessity; they state what, as of right, other persons *must* do. Such necessity is also involved in the frequently noted use of "due" and "entitlement" as synonyms or at least as components of the substantive use of "right." A person's rights are what belong to him as his due, what he is entitled to, hence what he can rightly demand of others.

Alan Gewirth, "The Basis and Content of Human Rights," *Georgia L. Rev.* 13 (1979): 1150. For discussion of Alan Gewirth's justification of rights and its relation to estoppel, see "Dialogical Arguments for Libertarian Rights" (ch. 5), the section "Pilon and Gewirth on the Principle of Generic Consistency," esp. n.39 and accompanying text; also Kinsella,

punish him.[40] However, such a claim is blatantly inconsistent with what must be A's other position: because A murdered B, which is clearly an act of aggression, his actions have indicated that he also holds the view that "aggression is *not* wrong."

Thus, because of his earlier actions, A is estopped from claiming that aggression is wrong.[41] He cannot assert contradictory claims and is estopped from doing so. The only way for A to maintain consistency is to drop one of his claims. If A retains only the claim "aggression is proper," then he is failing to object to his imprisonment; thus, the question of justifying the punishment does not arise. By claiming that aggression is proper, A consents to his punishment. If, on the other hand, A drops his claim that "aggression is proper" and retains only his claim that "aggression is wrong," he indeed could object to his imprisonment. As we shall see below, it is impossible for him to drop the claim that "aggression is proper" just as it would be impossible for him to avoid maintaining that he exists or that he can argue.

To restate, A cannot consistently claim that murder is wrong, for it contradicts his view that murder is *not* wrong, evidenced by or made manifest in his previous act of murder. A is estopped from asserting such inconsistent claims. Therefore, if C attempts to kill A, A has no grounds for objecting since he cannot now say that such a killing by C is "wrong," "immoral," or "improper" or that it would violate his "rights." And if A cannot complain if C proposes to kill him, then, *a fortiori*, he

---

"Estoppel: A New Justification for Individual Rights," p. 71 n.9; see also Hare, *Freedom and Reason*, § 2.5 (discussing usage of concepts "ought" and "wrong").

[40] If a skeptic were to object to the use of moral concepts here—for example, wrong, should, etc.—it should be noted that it is the criminal, A, who introduces normative, rights-related terminology when A tries to object to A's punishment. Randy Barnett makes a similar point in a different context. Professor Barnett argues that those who claim that the U.S. Constitution justifies certain government regulation of individuals are themselves making a normative claim, which may thus be examined or criticized from a moral point of view by others. See Randy E. Barnett, "Getting Normative: The Role of Natural Rights in Constitutional Adjudication," *Constitutional Commentary* 12 (1995; www.randybarnett.com/pre-2000): 93–122, at 100–01; see also *idem*, "The Intersection of Natural Rights and Positive Constitutional Law," *Connecticut L. Rev.* 25 (1993; http://www.randybarnett.com/pre-2000): 853–68, discussing the unavoidable connection between natural law and positive law in constitutional adjudication.

[41] If A cannot even claim that aggression—the *initiation* of force—is wrong, then, *a fortiori*, A cannot make the subsidiary claim that retaliatory or responsive force is wrong.

surely cannot complain if *C* merely imprisons him.[42] Thus, we can legitimately apply force to—punish—a murderer in response to the crime. (And of course, if an aggressor may be punished after the fact, force used in self-defense is, *a fortiori*, obviously justified.)[43]

---

[42] Although *A* may not complain that his imminent execution by *C* would violate his rights, this does not necessarily mean that *C* may legitimately execute him. It only means that *A*'s complaint may not be heard and that *A*'s rights are not violated by being executed. A third party *T*, however, may have another legitimate complaint about A's execution, one which does not assert *A*'s rights but rather takes other factors, such as the special nature of the defense agency *C*, into account—especially if the defense agency is a government (a state). For example, *T* may argue that the state, as an inherently dangerous and powerful entity, should not be allowed to kill even murderers because giving such power to the state is so inherently dangerous and threatening to innocent, non-estopped people, like *T*, that it amounts to an aggression and a violation of *T*'s rights. Further, if the state deems itself to be *B*'s agent, *B*'s heir may conceivably object to the state's execution of *A*, claiming the sole right to execute or otherwise punish *A*. For lesser crimes, such as assault, where the victim *B* remains alive, *B* himself may object to the state's administering punishment to the aggressor.

Similarly, after applying estoppel solely to the relationship between the defense agency, *C*, and a defendant, *A*, the exclusionary rule—whereby a court may not use evidence if it is illegally obtained—would fall. If *A* actually committed the crime, it cannot violate his rights for the court to discover this fact, even if the evidence was illegally obtained; *A* would still be estopped from complaining about his punishment. However, a third party can conceivably argue that it is too dangerous for a defense agency, *C*, to have a system which gives it incentives to illegally search people and that the exclusionary rule is therefore a necessary procedural or prophylactic rule required in order to protect *innocent* people from *C*'s dangerousness—this is especially true if *C* is a *governmental* defense agency. In essence, the argument would be that prosecutions by the state or other defense agencies, without an exclusionary rule to temper the danger of such prosecutions, could amount to aggression or a standing threat against innocent third parties. For a related discussion, see Part III.D.3, and note 50, below. See also Patrick Tinsley, Stephan Kinsella & Walter Block, "In Defense of Evidence and Against the Exclusionary Rule: A Libertarian Approach," *Southern U. L. Rev.*, 32 no. 1 (2004; www.walterblock.com/publications), pp. 63–80.

Whether such arguments of third parties could be fully developed is a separate question beyond the scope of this chapter. I merely wish to point out that other complaints about certain government actions are not automatically barred just because the specific criminal cannot complain. Just because *C*'s imprisonment of *A* does not aggress against *A* does not necessarily show that such action does not aggress against others.

[43] See, e.g., Rothbard, "Self-Defense," in *The Ethics of Liberty* (https://mises.org/library/right-self-defense); Thomas Aquinas, *Summa Theologica* (New Advent, https://www.newadvent.org/summa), *Secunda Secundæ Partis*, Question 64, art. 7:

> Nothing hinders one act from having two effects, only one of which is intended, while the other is beside the intention. Now moral acts take their species according to what is intended, and not according to what is beside the intention, since this is accidental.... Accordingly the act of self-defense may have two effects, one is the saving of one's life, the other is the slaying of the aggressor. Therefore this act, since

Because the essence of rights is their legitimate enforceability, this establishes a right to life—that is, to not be murdered. It is easy to see how this example may be extended to less severe forms of aggression, such as assault and battery, kidnapping, and rape.[44]

D. Potential Defenses by the Aggressor

A might assert several possible objections to this whole procedure. None of them bear scrutiny, however.

1. The Concept of Aggression

First, *A* might claim that the classification of actions as either aggressive or not aggressive is invalid. We might be smuggling in a norm or value judgment just by describing murder as "aggressive" rather than merely describing the murder without evaluative overtones. This smuggled norm might be what apparently justifies the legitimacy of punishing *A*, thus making the justification circular and, therefore, faulty. However, in order to object to our punishment of him, *A* must admit the validity of describing some actions as forceful—namely, his imminent punishment. If he denies that any actions can be objectively described as being coercive, he has no grounds to object to imprisonment, for he cannot even be certain what constitutes punishment, and we may proceed to punish him. The moment he objects to this use of force, he cannot help admitting that at least some actions can be objectively

---

one's intention is to save one's own life, is not unlawful, seeing that it is natural to everything to keep itself in "being," as far as possible. And yet, though proceeding from a good intention, an act may be rendered unlawful, if it be out of proportion to the end. Wherefore if a man, in self-defense, uses more than necessary violence, it will be unlawful: whereas if he repel force with moderation his defense will be lawful, because ... "it is lawful to repel force by force, provided one does not exceed the limits of a blameless defense." Nor is it necessary for salvation that a man omit the act of moderate self-defense in order to avoid killing the other man, since one is bound to take more care of one's own life than of another's.

[44] For a recent book-length treatment of ideas related to Hoppe's argumentation ethics and my estoppel approach advanced in this chapter, see Pavel Slutskiy, *Communication and Libertarianism* (Springer, 2021). In revising this chapter, this footnote grew to unmanageable length. I have placed the relevant commentary in the Appendix, below.

classified as involving force. Thus, he is estopped from objecting on these grounds.

2. Universalizability

It could also be objected that the estoppel principle is being improperly applied and that *A* is not, in fact, asserting inconsistent claims. Instead of having the contradictory views that "aggression is proper" and "aggression is improper," *A* could claim to hold the consistent positions that "*aggression by me* is proper" and "aggression by others against me is improper." However, we must recall that *A*, in objecting to *C*'s imprisonment of him, is engaging in argument. He is arguing that *C should not*—for some good reason—imprison him, and so he is making normative assertions. But as Professor Hans-Hermann Hoppe points out:

> Quite commonly it has been observed that argumentation implies that a proposition claims *universal* acceptability, or, should it be a norm proposal, that it is "universalizable." Applied to norm proposals, this is the idea, as formulated in the Golden Rule of ethics or in the Kantian Categorical Imperative, that only those norms can be justified that can be formulated as general principles which are valid for everyone without exception.[45]

This is so because propositions made during argumentation claim universal acceptability. "[I]t is implied in argumentation that everyone who can understand an argument must in principle be able to be convinced by it simply because of its argumentative force…"[46] Thus, universalizability is a presupposition of normative discourse, and any arguer violating the principle of universalizability is maintaining inconsistent positions—that universalizability is required and that it is not—and is thus estopped from doing so. Only universalizable normative propositions are consistent with

---

[45] Hoppe, *A Theory of Socialism and Capitalism*, p. 157, footnote omitted; see also n. 119 *et pass.* For further discussion of universalizability, see Hare, *Freedom and Reason*, §§ 2.2, 2.7, 3.2, 6.2, 6.3, 6.8, 7.3, 11.6, *et pass.*; also Stephan Kinsella, "The problem of particularistic ethics or, why everyone really has to admit the validity of the universalizability principle," *StephanKinsella.com* (Nov. 10, 2011); "Dialogical Arguments for Libertarian Rights" (ch. 6), notes 42–43 and accompanying text; "What Libertarianism Is" (ch. 2), the section "Self-ownership and Conflict Avoidance"; and "How We Come to Own Ourselves" (ch. 4), n.15.

[46] Hoppe, *The Economics and Ethics of Private Property*, p. 316.

the principle of universalizability necessarily presupposed by the arguer in entering the discourse. As Hare points out:

> Offenses against the thesis of universalizability are logical, not moral. If a person says 'I ought to act in a certain way, but nobody else ought to act in that way in relevantly similar circumstances', then ... he is abusing the word 'ought' he is implicitly contradicting himself.... [A]ll [the thesis of universalizability] does is to force people to choose between judgements which cannot both be asserted without self-contradiction.[47]

The proper way, then, to select the norm that the arguer is asserting is to ensure that it is universalizable. The view that "aggression *by me* is proper" and "aggression by the state against me is improper" clearly does not pass this test. The view that "aggression is or is not proper" is, by contrast, perfectly universalizable and is thus the proper form for a norm. An arguer cannot escape the application of estoppel by arbitrarily specializing otherwise inconsistent views with liberally sprinkled "for me only's."[48]

Furthermore, even if *A* denies the validity of the principle of universalizability and maintains that he can particularize norms, he cannot object if *C* does the same. If *A* admits that norms may be particularized, *C* may simply act on the particular norm that "It is permissible to punish *A*."

3. Time

---

[47] Hare, *Freedom and Reason*, § 3.2, p. 32; see also ibid., § 11.6, p. 216 ("It is part of the meanings of the moral words that we are logically prohibited from making different moral judgements about two cases when we cannot adduce any difference between the cases which is the ground for the difference in moral judgements.").

[48] As Hoppe notes, particularistic rules,
> which specify different rights or obligations for different classes of people, have no chance of being accepted as fair by every potential participant in an argumentation for simply formal reasons. Unless the distinction made between different classes of people happens to be such that it is acceptable to both sides as grounded in the nature of things, such rules would not be acceptable because they would imply that one group is awarded legal privileges at the expense of complementary discriminations against another group. Some people, either those who are allowed to do something or those who are not, therefore could not agree that these were fair rules.

Hoppe, *A Theory of Socialism and Capitalism*, pp. 164–65, footnote omitted.

A could also attempt to rebut this application of estoppel by claiming that he, in fact, *does* currently maintain that aggression is improper and that he has changed his mind since the time when *B* was murdered. Thus, there is no inconsistency or contradiction because he does not simultaneously hold both contradictory ideas and is not estopped from objecting to imprisonment.[49]

But this is a simple matter to overcome. First, *A* is implicitly claiming that the passage of time should be taken into account when determining what actions to impute to him. But then, if this is true, all *C* needs to do is administer the punishment and afterwards assert that all is in the past and that *C*, like *A*, now condemns its prior action. Since the impermissible action is "in the past," it can no longer be imputed to *C*. Indeed, if such an absurd simultaneity requirement is operative, at every successive moment of the punishment, any objection or defensive action by *A* is directed at actions in the immediate past and thus become immediately irrelevant and past-directed. Therefore, the irrelevance of the mere passage of time cannot be denied by *A*,[50] for in order to effectively object to being punished, *A* must presume that the passage

---

[49] See Hare, *Freedom and Reason*, § 6.9, p. 108, discussing the simultaneity requirement with respect to contradictory statements.

[50] This is not to say that the passage of time cannot be relevant for other reasons. Just as capital punishment does not violate the rights of the executed murderer, it can conceivably be objected to on the grounds of the danger posed by such a practice to innocent people. See note 42, above. So punishment after a long period of time does not violate the rights of actually guilty criminals but may arguably constitute a threat to innocent people—because of the relative unreliability of stale evidence, faded memories, etc. But these are procedural or structural, not substantive, concerns, the discussion of which is beyond the scope of this chapter. My focus here is the basic principles of rights that must underlie any general justification of punishment, even if other procedural or systemic features also need to be taken into account after a prima facie right to punish is established. Thus, this chapter also does not consider such questions as the danger of being a judge in one's own case, as these are separate concerns. For discussion of the risks of individuals acting as judge, jury, and executioner, see Robert Nozick, *Anarchy, State, and Utopia* (New York: Basic Books, 1974), pp. 54–146. On the danger of being a judge in one's own case, see *"The Theodosian Code,"* in *The Theodosian Code and Novels and the Sirmondian Constitutions*, Clyde Pharr, trans. (Princeton, N.J.: Princeton University, 1952), § 2.2.1; John Locke, Second Treatise on Civil Government (1690; https://www.johnlocke.net/2022/07/two-treatises-of-government.html), §13 (When men are "judges in their own cases," it can be objected that "selflove will make men partial to themselves and their friends: and on the other side, ill nature, passion, and revenge will carry them too far in punishing others.").

of time does not make a difference to imputing responsibility-incurring actions to individuals.[51]

Second, in objecting to punishment in the present, *A* necessarily maintains that force must not and should not occur. Even if he really does no longer believe that murder is proper, by his own current view, the earlier murder was still improper. He necessarily denounces his earlier actions and is estopped from objecting to his punishment imposed on that murderer—namely, himself. To maintain that a murderer should not be punished is inconsistent with a claim that murder should not and must not occur.

Third, even if *A* argues that he never held the view that "murder is not wrong" and that he murdered despite holding it to be wrong,[52] he still admits that murder is wrong and that he, in fact, did murder *B* and still ends up denouncing his earlier action. Thus, *A* is again estopped from objecting to the punishment as in the situation where he claims to have changed his mind. Finally, if *A* maintains that it is possible to administer force while simultaneously holding it to be wrong, the same applies to *C*. So even if *C* is convinced by *A*'s argument that it would be wrong to punish *A*, *C* may go ahead and do so despite this realization, just as *A* himself claims to have done.[53] Thus, whether *A* currently holds

---

[51] For a similar argument by Hoppe regarding why any participant in argument contradicts himself if he denies the relevance of the passage of time in another context, specifically if he denies the validity of the "prior-later" distinction which distinguishes between prior homesteaders and later latecomers, see Hoppe, *A Theory of Socialism and Capitalism*, pp. 169–71. For a discussion of performative contradictions, see Roy A. Sorensen, *Blindspots* (New York: Oxford University Press, 1988).

[52] Whether someone can genuinely believe something is impermissible and yet do it anyway is questionable. As Hare has pointed out, "If a man does what he says he ought not to, ... then there is something wrong with what he says, as well as with what he does." Hare, *Freedom and Reason*, § 5.9.

[53] Any other similar argument of *A*'s would also fail. For example, *A* could defend himself by asserting that there is no such thing as free will, so that he was determined to murder *B*, and thus cannot be blamed for doing so. However, note that the estoppel theory nowhere assumed the existence of free will, so such an argument is irrelevant. Moreover, if *A* is correct that there is no free will, then *C* is similarly predestined to do whatever he will, and if this includes punishing *A*, how can *C* be blamed? The logic of reciprocity is inescapable. R.P. Phillips has called such a type of axiom a "boomerang principle ... for even though we cast it away from us, it returns to us again." R.P. Phillips, *Modern Thomistic Philosophy: An Explanation for Students*, vol. 2 (Westminster, Md.: The Newman Press, 1962 [1934–35]), p. 37, quoted in Murray N. Rothbard, "Beyond Is and Ought," *Liberty* 2,

both views, or only one of them, he is still estopped from objecting to the imprisonment.

Thus, we can see that applying the principle of estoppel would not hinder the prevention and punishment of violent crimes. The above murder analysis can be applied to any sort of coercive, violent crime. All the classical violent crimes would still be as preventable under the proposed scheme as they are today. All forms of aggression—rape, theft, murder, assault, trespass—would still be legitimately punishable crimes. A rapist, for example, could only complain about being imprisoned by saying that his rights are being violated by the aggressive imprisonment, but he would be estopped from saying that aggression is wrong. In general, any aggressive act—one involving the initiation of violence—would cause an inconsistency with the actor later claiming that he should not be imprisoned or punished in some manner.

E. Punishing Nonaggressive Behavior

As seen above, punishment of aggression can be justified because the use of force in response to force cannot sensibly be condemned as a violation of the rights of the original aggressor. Is it ever legitimate to punish someone for *non*aggressive behavior? If not, then this means that rights can only be negative rights against the initiation of force. As argued below, no such punishment is ever justified because punishment is the application of force to which a person is not estopped from objecting unless that person has initiated force. Otherwise, there is no inconsistency. Thus, nonaggressive force, consented-to force, and actions not involving force may not be punished.

First, a nonaggressive use of force, such as retaliation against aggression, cannot be justly punished. If someone were to attempt to punish B for retaliating against aggressor A, B is *not* estopped from objecting. There is nothing inconsistent or nonuniversalizable about maintaining both that (1) the use of retaliatory force in response to the initiation of force is proper—the implicit claim involved in retaliation against A—and (2) the use of force not in response to the initiation of force is improper—the basis for *B*'s objection to his own punishment. In short, the initiation of force is different from retaliatory force; retaliation is not aggression. *B* can easily show that the maxim of his action is "the use of force against an aggressor is legitimate," which does not contradict "the use of force against nonaggressors is illegitimate." Rather than being a particularizable claim that does not pass the universalizability test, *B*'s position is tailored to the actual nature of his prior action. The universalizability principle prevents only arbitrary, biased statements not grounded in the nature of things.[54] Thus, the mere use of force is not enough to estop someone from complaining about being punished for the use of force. It is only aggression, that is, *initiated* force, that estops a person from complaining about force used against that person.

Similarly, if *A* uses force against *B* with *B*'s permission, *A* is not an aggressor and thus may not be punished. *A* may consistently assert that "using force against someone is permissible if they have consented" and that "using force against someone is impermissible if they have not consented." For example, suppose that *A* slaps *B* after *B* has given consent. Is *A* estopped from objecting if *B* attempts to slap him back? Obviously, *A* is not estopped because he may consistently assert that "slapping someone is permissible if they have consented" and that "slapping someone is impermissible if they have not consented." These are not inconsistent statements, and neither is barred by the universalizability principle because it rests on the recognition that the nature of a consented-to act is different than one objected to. Thus, although uninvited physical force estops the initiator thereof from complaining of punishment, invited or consented-to physical force does not.

Other actions do not involve force or aggression at all, so there is no ground for punishing this behavior either. Suppose publisher *P* publishes a patently pornographic magazine, and some entity, such as the state, punishes him for this by conviction and imprisonment. Clearly, the state has committed naked aggression against him. Following the analysis of Part III.C, unless *P* is estopped from complaining about the

---

[54] See Part III.D.2, above.

punishment, the state itself may be punished, demonstrating that it has violated his rights. [55]

P has only published pornography, which is not aggression; he has not engaged in any activity nor necessarily made any claim that would be inconsistent with claiming that aggression is wrong. Thus, it is not inconsistent to simultaneously maintain that (1) it is legitimate to publish pornography and (2) it is illegitimate to aggress against a person. *P* is not estopped from complaining about his confinement.[56]

Unlike the case of retaliation against aggression, however, the state has not administered force in response to *P*'s initiation of force and is estopped from objecting to the proposed use of force against it. The state's punishment of *P* is, therefore, not legitimate. Thus, it can be seen that punishment of any nonaggressive behavior is illegitimate and unjustified, as are laws prohibiting such behavior, since laws are themselves backed by and manifestations of force.[57]

F. Property Rights

---

[55] *P* will usually not be able, in practice, to successfully retaliate or defend himself against the state, but might and right are independent concepts. Thus, this fact of the state's greater might is irrelevant in the same way that *B*'s murder does not "prove" that there is not a right to life. After all, there is a difference between *may* and *can*.

[56] *P* could, perhaps, be dialogically estopped from complaining about other pornographers engaging in pornography, but here he is complaining about his being kidnapped by the state.

[57] Lawrence Crocker discusses a similar use of "moral estoppel" in preventing a criminal from asserting the unfairness of being punished in certain situations. Crocker, "The Upper Limit of Just Punishment," p. 1067. Crocker's theory, while interesting, is not developed along the same lines as the estoppel theory developed herein, nor does Crocker seem to realize the implications of estoppel for justifying only the libertarian conception of rights. Rather than focusing on the reciprocity between the force used in punishment and the force of an aggressive act by a wrongdoer, Crocker claims that a person who has "treated another person or society at large in a fashion that the criminal law prohibits" is "morally estopped" from asserting that his punishment would be unfair. Ibid. However, Crocker's use of estoppel is too vague and imprecise, for just because one has violated a criminal law does not mean that one has committed the aggression which is necessary to estop him from complaining about punishment. The law must first be valid for Crocker's assumption to hold, but as the estoppel theory indicates, a law is valid only if it prohibits aggression. Thus, it is not the mere violating of a law that estops a lawbreaker from complaining about being punished—the law might be illegitimate—it is the initiation of force. Crocker is also discussed in "Dialogical Arguments for Libertarian Rights" (ch. 6).

So far, the right to punish actors who initiate invasions of victims' bodies has been established, which corresponds to a right in one's own body, or self-ownership. Although there is not space here to provide a detailed justification for rights in scarce resources outside one's body—property rights—I will briefly outline such a justification in this section. Because rights in one's own body have been established, property rights may be established by building on this base. This may be done by pointing out that rights in one's body are meaningless without property rights and vice versa.[58]

For example, imagine that a thief admits that there are rights to self-ownership but that there is no right to property. If this is true, we can easily punish him simply by depriving him of external property, namely food, air, or space in which to exist or move. Clearly, the denial of his property through the use of force can physically harm his body just as direct invasion of the borders of his body can. The physical, bodily damage can be done fairly directly, for example, by snatching every piece of food out of his hands until he dies—why not, if there are no property rights? Or it can be done somewhat more indirectly by infringing upon his ability to control and use the external world, which is essential to his survival. Such property deprivation could continue until his body is severely damaged—implying, since this is tantamount to physical retaliation in its effect on him, that physical retaliation in response to a property crime is permissible—or until he objected to such treatment, thereby granting the validity of property rights. Just as one can commit an act of aggression against another with one's body—for example, one's fist—or with external property—a club, gun, bomb, poison—so one's self-ownership rights can be aggressed against in a limitless variety of ways by affecting one's property and external environment.

---

[58] This has been recognized even by the U.S. Supreme Court. As the Court recognized:
[t]he right to enjoy property without unlawful deprivation ... is in truth a "personal" right.... In fact, a fundamental interdependence exists between the personal right to liberty and the personal right in property. Neither could have meaning without the other. That rights in property are basic civil rights has long been recognized.
Lynch v. Household Fin. Corp., 405 U.S. 538 (1972), p. 552. But see the famous (or infamous, to some of us) footnote 4 in *United States v. Carolene Products Co.*, which implies that economic and property rights are less fundamental than personal rights. 304 U.S. 144 (1938), p. 152 n.4.

Professor Hoppe's "argumentation ethics" defense of individual rights also shows that the right to homestead is implied in the right to self-ownership. First, Hoppe establishes self-ownership by focusing on propositions that cannot be denied in discourse in general.[59] Anyone engaging in argumentation implicitly accepts the presupposed right of self-ownership of all listeners and even potential listeners. Otherwise, the listener would not be able to consider freely and accept or reject the proposed argument.

Second, because participants in argumentation indisputably need to use and control the scarce resources in the world to survive, and because their scarcity makes conflict over their use possible, norms are needed to determine the proper owner of these goods so as to avoid conflict. This necessity for norms to avoid conflicts in the use of scarce resources is itself undeniable by those engaged in argumentation—which is to say, undeniable—because anyone who is alive in the world and participating in the practical activity of argumentation cannot deny the value of being able to control scarce resources or the value of avoiding conflicts over such scarce resources. But there are only two fundamental alternatives for acquiring rights in unowned property: (1) by doing something with the property which no one else had ever done before, such as the mixing of labor or homesteading; or (2) by mere verbal declaration or decree. The second alternative is arbitrary and cannot serve to avoid conflicts. Only the first alternative, that of Lockean homesteading, establishes an objective link between a particular person and a particular scarce resource; thus, no one can deny the Lockean right to homestead unowned resources.

As Hoppe points out, since one's body is itself a scarce resource, it is "the *prototype* of a scarce good for the use of which property rights, i.e. rights of exclusive ownership, somehow have to be established, in order to avoid clashes."[60] Thus, the right to homestead external scarce resources is implied in the fact of self-ownership since "the specifications of the nonaggression principle, conceived of as a special property norm referring to a specific kind of good, must in fact already contain

---

[59] For further details see note 31, above.
[60] Hoppe, *A Theory of Socialism and Capitalism*, p. 19.

those of a *general* theory of property."[61] For these reasons, whether self-ownership is established by Hoppe's argumentation ethics or by the estoppel theory—both theories that focus on the dynamics of discourse—such rights imply the Lockean right to homestead, which no aggressor could deny any more than he could deny that self-ownership rights are justified.

I will, for the remainder of this chapter, place property rights and rights in one's body on the same level, both warranting punishment for their invasion. Thus, under the estoppel theory one who aggresses against another's body or against another's external property is an aggressor, plain and simple, who may be treated as such.

IV. TYPES OF PUNISHMENTS AND THE BURDEN OF PROOF

A. Proportional Punishment

Just because aggressors can legitimately be punished does not necessarily mean that all concerns about proportionality may be dropped. At first blush, if we focus only on the initiation of force itself, it would seem that a victim could make a prima facie case that since the aggressor initiated force—no matter how trivial—the victim is entitled to use force against the aggressor, even including execution of the aggressor. Suppose A uninvitedly slaps B lightly on the cheek in response to a rude remark by B. Is B entitled to execute A in return? A, it is true, has initiated force, so how can he complain if force is to be used against him? But A is not estopped from objecting to being killed. A may, perfectly consistently, object to being killed since he may maintain that it is wrong to kill. This in itself is not inconsistent with A's implicit view that it is legitimate to lightly slap others. By sanctioning slapping, A does not necessarily claim that killing is proper because usually—as in this example—there is nothing about slapping that rises to the level of killing.

---

[61] Ibid., p. 160.

It is proper to focus on the consequences of aggression in determining to what extent an aggressor is estopped because the very reason people object to aggression, or wish to punish aggressors for it, is just because it has certain consequences.[62] Aggressive action, by physically interfering with the victim's person, is undesirable because, among other reasons, it can (1) cause pain or injury; (2) interfere with the pursuit of goals in life; or (3) simply create a risky, dangerous situation in which pain, injury, or violence are more likely to result. Aggression interferes with one's physical control over one's life, that is, over one's own body and external property.

Killing someone obviously brings about the most undesirable level of these consequences. Merely slapping someone, by contrast, does not in normal circumstances. A slap has relatively insignificant consequences in all these respects. Thus, *A* does not necessarily claim that aggressive killing is proper just because he slaps *B*. The universalization requirement does not prevent him from reasonably narrowing his implicit claim from the more severe "aggression is not wrong" to the less severe "minor aggression, such as slapping someone, is not wrong." Thus, *B* would be justified in slapping *A* back but not in killing *A*. I do not mean that *B* is justified *only* in slapping *A* and no more, but certainly *B* is justified at least in slapping *A*, and is not justified in killing him; this would be murder. These outside boundaries, at least, we know.

In general, while the universalization principle prevents arbitrary particularization of claims—for example, adding "for me only's"—it does not rule out an objective, reasonable statement of the implicit claims of the aggressor tailored to the actual nature of the aggression and its necessary consequences and implications. For example, while it is true that *A* has slapped *B*, he has not attempted to take *B*'s life; thus, he has never necessarily claimed that "murder is not wrong," so he is not

---

[62] Analogously, this is why scarcity (conflictability) is the defining characteristic of property. Taking another's good has the effect of depriving the owner of it because it is scarce; if goods were infinitely abundant then it would not be possible to "take" them because the taking would have no consequence at all, and thus, the concepts of property and scarcity would not arise. *See* Hoppe, "Of Common, Public, and Private Property and the Rationale for Total Privatization." On the term "conflictable," see Stephan Kinsella, "On Conflictability and Conflictable Resources," *StephanKinsella.com* (Jan. 31, 2022); also *"Against Intellectual Property* After Twenty Years" (ch. 15), Part III; "What Libertarianism Is" (ch. 2), n.5.

estopped from asserting that murder is wrong.[63] Since a mere slapper is not estopped from complaining about his imminent execution, he can consistently object to being executed, which implies that *B* would become a murderer if he were to kill *A*.

In this way, we can see a requirement of proportionality—or, more properly, of reciprocity along the lines of the *lex talionis* or the law of retaliation[64]—accompanies any legitimate punishment of an aggressor. "As the injury inflicted, so must be the injury suffered."[65] There are, thus, limitations to the amount of punishment the victim may administer to the aggressor, related to the extent of the aggression committed by the aggressor, because it is the nature of the particular act of aggression that determines the extent of the estoppel working against the aggressor. The more serious the aggression and the consequences that flow from it, the more the aggressor is estopped from objecting to punishment. Consequently, a greater level of punishment may legitimately be applied.

B. The Victim's Options

At this point, we have established the basic right to one's body and to property homesteaded or acquired from a homesteader, as well as the contours of the basic requirement of proportionality in punishment. This chapter now presents a further consideration of the various types of punishment that can be justly administered.

As has been shown, a victim of aggression may inflict on the aggressor at least the same level or type of aggression previously inflicted by the aggressor. In determining the maximum amount and type of punishment

---

[63] This said, I do not mean to deny that something like the "eggshell skull rule" is compatible with the analysis offered herein. According to this legal rule, a tortfeasor is liable for all consequences of their tort, even if the victim has an unusual vulnerability. For example, if *A* lightly slaps *B* on the head in a way that would cause only minor damage to most people, but *B*'s thin skull causes him to die, then *A* is liable for the homicide even though he did not intend to kill *B*, since the battery was intentional (or negligent). See https://en.wikipedia.org/wiki/Eggshell_skull.

[64] The classic formula of the *lex talionis* is "life for life, eye for eye, tooth for tooth, hand for hand, foot for foot, burn for burn, wound for wound, stripe for stripe." *Exodus* 21: 23–25; see also *Deuteronomy* 19: 21 (calling for "life for life, eye for eye, tooth for tooth, hand for hand, foot for foot"); *Leviticus* 24: 17–21 (calling for "broken limb for broken limb, eye for eye, tooth for tooth").

[65] *Leviticus* 24: 20. See also the Aquinus quote in note 43, above.

that may be applied, the distinction between victim and victimizer must be kept in mind, and we must recognize that, for most victims—those who are not masochists or sadists—punishing the wrongdoer does not genuinely make the victim whole and does not directly benefit the victim very much, if at all. A victim who has been shot in the arm by a robber and who consequently loses his arm is clearly entitled, if he wishes, to amputate the robber's own arm. But this, of course, does not restore the victim's arm; it does not make him whole. Perfect restitution is always an unreachable goal, for crimes cannot be undone.

This is not to say that the right to punish is therefore useless, but we must recognize that the victim remains a victim even after retaliating against the wrongdoer. No punishment can undo the harm done. For this reason, the victim's range of punishment options should not be artificially or easily restricted. This would further victimize him. The victim did not choose to be made a victim and did not choose to be placed in a situation where he has only one narrow punishment option—namely, eye-for-an-eye retaliation. On the contrary, the responsibility for this situation is entirely that of the aggressor who by his action has damaged the victim. Because the aggressor has placed the victim in a no-win situation where being restricted to one narrow type of remedy may recompense the victim even less than other remedies, the aggressor is estopped from complaining if the victim chooses among varying types of punishment, subject to the proportionality requirement.

In practice this means that, for example, the victim of assault and battery need not be restricted to only having the aggressor beaten—or even killed. The victim may abhor violence, and might choose to forego any punishment at all if his only option was to either beat or punish the aggressor. The victim may prefer, instead, to simply be compensated monetarily out of any—current or future—property of the wrongdoer. Or, if the victim believes he will gain more satisfaction from using force against the aggressor in a way different than the manner in which the aggressor violated the victim's rights—for example, taking property of an aggressor who has beaten the victim—the aggressor is estopped from complaining about this as long as proportionality is satisfied.

The nonequivalence of most violent crimes makes this conclusion clearer. Suppose that A, a man, rapes B, a woman. B would be entitled to rape A in retaliation or to have A raped by a professional, private punishing company. But the last thing in the world that a rape victim might want is to be involved in further sexual violence, and this alone would give her a right to insist on other forms of punishment. To limit her remedy to having *A* raped would be to inflict further damage on her. *B* can never be made whole, but at least her best remedy—in her opinion—of a variety of imperfect remedies need not be denied her. She has done nothing to justify denying her such options.

And in this case there simply is no equivalent. The only remotely similar equivalent is the forcible anal rape of *A*, but even this is vastly different from the rape of a woman. If nothing else, a woman might reasonably consider rape much more of a violation than would a man "similarly" treated, for these acts give rise to different consequences for the victim, a point that we need not belabor. Thus, if there is no possibility of exact "eye-for-an-eye" style retaliation for a given act of aggression, such as is the case with rape, then our conclusion must be either that (1) *B* may not punish *A*, or (2) *B* may punish *A* in another manner. Clearly, the latter alternative is the correct one, for a rapist is estopped from denying the right of his victim to punish him and is also estopped from claiming a benefit because there is no equivalent punishment. Furthermore, the absence of an equivalent punishment is a direct result of *A*'s aggression. If *B* acts to mitigate the damage done to her by *A*—which includes not only the rape, but placing *B* in a situation where her remedies will all be inadequate and where there is not even an equivalent punishment possible—*A* is estopped from objecting. Thus, for example, *B* may choose, instead, to have *A*'s penis amputated or even his arm or leg. Or *B* may choose instead to have *A* publicly flogged, displayed, and imprisoned for some length of time or even enslaved for a time and put to work earning money for *B*. Alternatively, *B* may threaten *A* with the most severe punishment she has the right to inflict and allow *A* to buy his way out of the punishment—or reduce its severity—with as much money as he is able or willing to offer.[66]

---

[66] For a discussion of Jefferson's attempts at devising proportional punishments, see Walter Kaufman, "Retribution and the Ethics of Punishment," in Barnett & Hagel III, eds., *Assessing the Criminal*, p. 223. For recent examples of judges' attempts at creative punishment to "fit the crime," see Judy Farah, "Crime and Creative Punishment," *Wall Street J.*, March 15, 1995, p. A15; Andrea Gerlin, "Quirky Sentences Make Bad Guys

Further, even if such rape of a man is somewhat equivalent to the rape of a woman, the rape of an *innocent* person, *B*, is typically much more of an offense than is a similar violation of a criminal, *A*, who evidently does not abhor aggression as much. *A*, the rapist, may even be a masochist and enjoy being beaten or sodomized, so a more or less equal amount of physical punishment of *A* would not really damage or truly punish *A* as badly as *A* has damaged *B*. Because *A* is a criminal, he is also likely accustomed to a lifestyle where force is used more routinely so that "equal" punishment of *A* would not damage *A* to the extent it would damage *B*, who is unused to such violence. For these reasons, *B* is entitled to inflict a greater amount of punishment on *A* than *A* inflicted on *B*, if only to more or less equalize the actual level of damage inflicted.[67] Thus, if *A* permanently damages *B*'s arm, *B* may be entitled to damage both of *A*'s arms or even all of *A*'s limbs.[68]

Squirm," *Wall Street J.* (August 4, 1994), p. B1, B12; see also Richard A. Posner, "An Economic Theory of the Criminal Law," *Colum. L. Rev.* 85 (1985): 1212, discussing different ways to vary the severity of punishment.

[67] Of course, values are subjective, so damage can never be exactly equated. On the subjective theory of value, see Rothbard, *Man, Economy, and State, with Power and Market*, chap. 1, § 5.A, pp. 17–21; Alexander H. Shand, *The Capitalist Alternative: An Introduction to Neo-Austrian Economics* (New York: New York University Press, 1984); Mises, *Epistemological Problems of Economics*, p. 89; Mises, *Human Action*, pp. 94–97, 200–206, 331–33. But again this is not the *victim's* fault, and if her only option is to attempt to measure or balance a difficult-to-balance equation—for example, by trying to equate somewhat quantifiable physical aspects of force, such as the magnitude and type of force and the physical consequences thereof—she cannot be blamed and the aggressor may not complain. For an illustrative theory proposing to attribute fault and liability according to objective factors such as force and momentum in a situation such as an automobile collision, see the sections on causation and causal defenses, respectively, in Richard A. Epstein, *A Theory of Strict Liability: Toward a Reformation of Tort Law* (San Francisco: Cato Institute, 1980; https://perma.cc/PVV6-U3Y7), pp. 15–49; Richard A. Epstein, "Defenses and Subsequent Pleas in a System of Strict Liability," *J. Legal Stud.* 3 (1974), pp. 174–85. Further, if the aggressor *A* were seriously to maintain that force against *A* and force against *B* were wholly incommensurable, he could never meaningfully object to being punished—for to object to punishment, *A* must maintain that such force is unjust and that some level and type of force could be justly used to prevent his punishment. But this implies at least some commensurability. If *A* really maintains incommensurability, *B* may take him at his word and posit that *B*'s punishment of *A* justifies *no* retaliatory force on *A*'s part—which means that *A* is not effectively claiming that he has a right to not be punished because rights are legitimately enforceable.

[68] Just how much greater the punishment may be than the original aggression, and how this is determined, is discussed in further detail in Part IV.G, below.

Alternatively, a victim is entitled to take by force a certain amount or portion of the aggressor's property if this type of response to aggression would better satisfy the victim or if the victim prefers this remedy for any reason at all, including greed, malice, or sadism—the victim's motivation is not the aggressor's rightful concern. Of course, a mixture would be permissible as well. A woman might, in response to being raped by a man, seize all of the ravisher's $10,000 estate and have him publicly beaten and enslaved for some number of years until his forced labor earns her $100,000 more—assuming that this overall level of punishment is roughly equivalent to the rape.

Along the same lines, a property aggressor, such as a thief, may be dealt with any number of ways. The victim may satisfy himself solely out of the aggressor's property, if this is possible, or through corporal punishment of the aggressor, if this better satisfies the victim—as discussed in further detail below. In short, any rights or combinations of rights of an aggressor may be ignored by a victim in punishing the aggressor—implying that the aggressor actually does not have these purported "rights"—as long as general bounds of proportionality are considered.

C. Enhancing Punishment Due to Other Factors

Other factors may be considered that increase the amount of punishment that may be inflicted on the aggressor over and above the type of damage initially inflicted by the aggressor. As explained above with regard to rape, aggression against an innocent, peaceful person may cause more psychic damage to the victim than would an equivalent action against the aggressor. Also, as Rothbard explains, a criminal, such as thief A, has not only stolen something from victim B, but he has "also put B into a state of fear and uncertainty, of uncertainty as to the extent that B's deprivation would go. But the penalty levied on A is fixed and certain in advance, thus putting A in far better shape than was his original victim."[69] The criminal has also imposed other damages, such as

---

[69] Rothbard, "Punishment and Proportionality," pp. 85, 88, n.6 (and at pp. 259–70 in Rothbard's chapter of the same name in Barnett & Hagel III, eds., *Assessing the Criminal*). See also Walter Block, "Toward a Libertarian Theory of Guilt and Punishment for the Crime of Statism," *J. Libertarian Stud.* 22, no. 1 (2011; https://mises.org/library/

interest, and even general costs of crime prevention—for who can such costs be blamed on and recouped from if not criminals when they are caught? As Kant observed, "whoever steals anything makes the property of all insecure."[70]

General bounds of proportionality are also satisfied when the consequences and potential consequences to the victim that are caused by the aggression are taken into account. Thus, some crimes may be punished capitally if their consequences are serious enough—for example, stealing a man's horse when his survival depends on it, which was capitally punished in the frontier West for the same reason.[71] (This is one point on which I disagree with Rothbard, however, who argues that "it should be quite clear that, under libertarian law, capital punishment would have to be confined strictly to the crime of murder. For a criminal would only lose his right to life if he had first deprived some victim of that same right. It would not be permissible, then, for a merchant whose bubble-gum had been stolen, to execute the convicted bubble-gum thief."[72] For one could imagine rare situations where theft of bubble-gum could legitimately be punished by execution, if the theft somehow endangered the life of its owner.[73])

---

toward-libertarian-theory-guilt-and-punishment-crime-statism): 665–75; *idem*, "Radical Libertarianism: Applying Libertarian Principles to Dealing With the Unjust Government, Part I," *Reason Papers* No. 27 (Fall 2004; https://reasonpapers.com): 113–30; and *idem*, "Radical Libertarianism: Applying Libertarian Principles to Dealing with the Unjust Government, Part II," *Reason Papers* 28 (Spring 2006; https://reasonpapers.com): 117–33; and Rothbard, "King on Punishment," p. 167.

[70] Immanuel Kant, *The Philosophy of Law*, W. Hastie, trans. (Edinburgh: T&T Clark, 1887), p. 197, quoted in Immanuel Kant, "Justice and Punishment," in Ezorsky, ed., *Philosophical Perspectives on Punishment*, p. 105.

[71] See *People v. Borja*, 22 Cal.Rptr.2d 307 (Ct. App. 1993), p. 309, superseded by 860 P.2d 1182, 24 Cal.Rptr.2d 236 (1993); *Guido v. Koopman*, 1 Cal.App.4th 837 (Ct. App. 1991), p. 842, discussing the critical importance of horses for transportation and survival in the old West. This brings to mind the reported exchange "many years ago between the Chief Justice of Texas and an Illinois lawyer visiting that state. 'Why is it,' the visiting lawyer asked, 'that you routinely hang horse thieves in Texas but oftentimes let murderers go free?' 'Because,' replied the Chief Justice, 'there never was a horse that needed stealing!'" *People v. Skiles*, 450 N.E.2d 1212 (Ill. App. Ct. 1983), p. 1220.

[72] Rothbard, "Punishment and Proportionality," p. 85.

[73] However, it is a separate question (and beyond the scope of this chapter) whether the merchant would have a right to kill the bubble-gum thief who, caught in the act, refused to abandon his attempt at theft.

D. Graduated Scale of Punishment

Some would object to the use of the severe penalty of capital punishment for crimes other than the most serious or heinous, such as murder, mass-murder, or genocide. Many thus favor a scale of punishment having more severe punishments for the most serious crimes with capital punishment reserved for murderers or serial-killers and the like.[74] Perhaps some feel that a mass murderer, serial killer, child killer, or cop killer should be punished more harshly than a more typical murderer of one adult and that if capital punishment is "wasted" on more mundane murderers or criminals, there will be nothing more severe left to impose on the really bad guys; there will be no deterrent effect left to deter extra acts of aggression committed by those who have already placed themselves in the category of deserving the death penalty. Of course, even if such a scale with gradations of punishment would provide a "better" deterrent effect, this does not mean that one does not have the right to punish a given criminal in a certain way. Such utilitarian reasoning is beside the point. If we had to save the more severe punishments for, say, mass murderers, this in effect incorrectly attributes a right to life to other murderers who simply do not have such a right.

Also, it should be realized that punishment of murderers is always an imperfect remedy since the victim remains murdered, so that whether the murderer remains underpunished even after being executed—like a regular murderer—or *very* underpunished—like a mass murderer—this is an unfortunate but simply irrelevant and inescapable fact. Furthermore, punishment actually *can* be made more and more severe, practically without limit, for greater and greater crimes. Death after torture is worse punishment than mere death, and a longer period or greater amount of physical pain being inflicted is more severe punishment than a shorter period or lesser amount. The severity of punishment can be varied, then, by varying the length of imprisonment, by inflicting more or less physical

---

[74] See, e.g., Letter from Ayn Rand to John Hospers, April 29, 1961, in Ayn Rand, *Letters of Ayn Rand*, Michael S. Berliner, ed. (New York: Plume, 1995), pp. 544, 559, arguing for "a proportionately scaled series of punishments," and that "the punishment deserved by armed robbery would depend on its place in the scale which begins with the lightest misdemeanor and ends with murder."

pain, and by many other methods. For example, for prison inmates, the severity of punishment can be adjusted by varying the size of the prison cell, temperature, and quality of food.[75]

E. Property Crimes

Aggression can also take the form of a property crime. For example, where A has stolen $10,000 from B, B is entitled to recoup $10,000 of A's property. However, the recapture of $10,000 is not punishment of A but merely the recapture by B of his own property. B then has the right to take another $10,000 of A's property, or even a higher amount if the $10,000 stolen from B was worth much more to B than to A—for example, if A has a higher time preference or less significant plans to use the money than B, which is likely, or if A has more money than B, which is unlikely.[76] This amount may also be enhanced to take into account other damages, such as interest, general costs of crime preven-

---

[75] See Posner, "An Economic Theory of the Criminal Law," p. 1212, discussing different ways to vary the severity of punishment.

[76] However, where the thief is poorer than the victim, as is usually the case, this does not mean that the victim is not entitled to recoup the entire $10,000. For example, if the $10,000 stolen is only 1% of the victim's estate and the thief's estate is only $10,000 total—after the victim has retaken his own $10,000 from the thief—it is not the case that the victim is limited to 1% of $10,000—$100. Because it is the thief who caused the harm, the victim should have the option of selecting the higher of (a) the amount that was stolen, or (b) a higher amount that is equivalent in terms of damage done. For further suggestions along these lines, such as Stephen Schafer's view that punishment "'should … be equally burdensome and just for all criminals, irrespective of their means, whether they be millionaires or labourers,'" see Randy E. Barnett, "Restitution: A New Paradigm of Criminal Justice," in Barnett & Hagel III, eds., *Assessing the Criminal*, pp. 349, 363–64, quoting Stephen Schafer, *Compensation and Restitution to Victims of Crime*, 2d ed. (Montclair, N.J.: Patterson Smith, 1970), p. 127. It should be noted that Rothbard's view of restitution and retribution is slightly different from the principles discussed above. *See* Rothbard, "Punishment and Proportionality," at 86.

Further, suppose that A, the victim, was about to use the $10,000 to save his own or another's life: for example, as a ransom for his daughter's kidnapper or to pay for a medical procedure to save his daughter's life. Theft of the $10,000 from a sufficiently poor person, or at a crucial time, could very well lead to death—the kidnapper murders the daughter because he was not paid. In this case it is very possible that execution of the thief could be justified since the consequences of this theft were even more severe than normal, especially in the case where the thief was aware of the potentially life-endangering consequences of the theft. For the principle that a criminal or tortfeasor "takes his victim as he finds him," see note 83, below, and accompanying text.

tion, and compensation for putting the victim into a state of fear and uncertainty.[77] It may also be enhanced to account for the uncertainty as to what the exact amount of retaliation or restitution ought to be, as this uncertainty is *A*'s fault, not *B*'s. Alternatively, at the victim's option, corporal punishment may be administered by *B* *instead* of taking back his own $10,000—indeed, this may be the only option where the thief is penniless or the stolen property is spent or destroyed.

F. Why Assault, Threats, and Attempts Are Aggression

This method of analyzing whether a proposed punishment is proper also makes it clear just why the threat of violence or assault is properly treated as an aggressive crime. Assault is defined (in some legal systems) as putting someone in fear of receiving a battery—a physical beating—or an attempted battery.[78] Suppose *A* assaults *B*, such as by pointing a gun at him or threatening to beat him. Clearly *B* is entitled to do to *A* what *A* has done to *B*—*A* is estopped from objecting to the propriety of being threatened or assaulted. But what does this mean? To assault is to manifest an intent to cause harm and to apprise *B* of this so that he *believes* *A* will inflict this harm—otherwise it is something like a joke or acting, and *B* is not actually in apprehension of being coerced. Now *A* was able to actually put *B* in a state of fear—of receiving a battery—by threatening *B*. But because of the nature of assault, the only way *B* can really make *A* fear a retaliatory act by *B* is if *B* *really means it*

---

[77] See note 69, above, and accompanying text.

[78] See *Mason v. Cohn*, 438 N.Y.S.2d 462 (N.Y. Sup. Ct. 1981), p. 464; *Black's Law Dictionary*, 6th ed. (St. Paul, Minn.: West Publishing, 1990), p. 114. The Louisiana Criminal Code defines assault as "an attempt to commit a battery, or the intentional placing of another in reasonable apprehension of receiving a battery." *Louisiana Revised Statutes Annotated*, § 14:36 (https://legis.la.gov/legis/Laws_Toc.aspx?folder=75&level=Parent). A battery is defined as "the intentional use of force or violence upon the person of another; or the intentional administration of a poison or other noxious liquid or substance to another." Ibid., § 14:33. Assault can thus also include an attempted battery, which need not put the victim in a state of apprehension of receiving a battery—for example, the victim may be asleep and be unaware that another has just swung a club at his head, but missed. This second definition of assault is ignored for our present purposes.

For some of my thoughts on how negligence law might develop in a private-law society, see Stephan Kinsella, "The Libertarian Approach to Negligence, Tort, and Strict Liability: Wergeld and Partial Wergeld," *Mises Economics Blog* (Sep. 1, 2009).

and is able to convince A of this fact. Thus, B must actually be—or be capable of being—willing to carry out the threatened coercion of A, not just mouth the words, otherwise A will know B is merely engaged in idle threats, merely bluffing. Indeed, B can legitimately go forward with the threatened action if only to make A believe it. Although A need not actually use force to assault B, because of the nature of retaliation, there is simply no way for B to assault A in return without actually having the right to use force against A. Because the very situation is caused by A's action, he is estopped from objecting to the necessity of B using force against him.[79] Likewise, if A attempts to harm B but fails, then B is entitled to "attempt" to harm A; for the attempt to be a real attempt, it must be possible for B to succeed. And so on.

G. The Burden of Proof

As seen in the preceding discussion, the victim of a violent crime has the right to select different mixtures and types of punishments. The actual extent or severity of punishment that may be permissibly inflicted, consistent with principles of proportionality and the burden of proof in this regard, is discussed in this section.

Theories of punishment are concerned with justifying punishment, with offering decent people who are reluctant to act immorally a reason why they may punish others. This is useful, of course, for offering moral people guidance and assurance that they may properly deal with those who seek to harm them. We have established so far a prima facie case for the right to proportionately punish an aggressor in response to acts of violence, actions which invade the borders of others' bodies or legitimately acquired property. Once this burden is carried, however,

---

[79] See also Pavel Slutskiy, "Threats of the Use of Force: 'Mere Speech' or Rights Violation?," in *idem, Communication and Libertarianism*. For a discussion of why fraud is a type of rights violation, see "A Libertarian Theory of Contract" (ch. 9), Part III.E.

See also Rothbard's argument for why threats (and fraud) count as types of aggression:
Defensive violence, therefore, must be confined to resisting invasive acts against person or property. But such invasion may include two corollaries to actual physical aggression: *intimidation*, or a direct threat of physical violence; and *fraud*, which involves the appropriation of someone else's property without his consent, and is therefore "implicit theft."

Rothbard, "Self-Defense," p. 77.

it is just to place the burden of proof on the aggressor to show why a proposed punishment of him is disproportionate or otherwise unjustified. The justice of this point is again implied by the logic of estoppel. The aggressor was not put in the position of justifying how much force he could use against the victim before he used such force; similarly, the victim should not be put in the position of justifying how much force is the appropriate level of retaliatory force to use against the aggressor before retaliating.

As pointed out above, because it is the aggressor who has put the victim into a situation where the victim has a limited variety and range of remedies, the aggressor is estopped from complaining if the victim uses a type of force against the aggressor that is different from the aggressor's use of force. The burden of proof and argument is therefore on the aggressor to show why any proposed, creative punishment is *not* justified by the aggressor's aggression. Otherwise, an additional burden is being placed on the victim in addition to the harm already done him. If the victim wants to avoid shouldering this additional burden, the aggressor is estopped from objecting because it was the aggressor who placed the victim in the position of having the burden in the first place. If there is a gray area, the aggressor ought not be allowed to throw his hands up in mock perplexity and escape liability; rather, the line ought to come down on the side of the gray that most favors the victim unless the aggressor can further narrow the gray area with convincing theories and arguments, for the aggressor is the one who brings the gray into existence.

This is similar to the issue of proportionality itself. Although proportionality or reciprocity is a requirement in general, if a prima facie case for punishment can be established—as it can be whenever force is initiated—the burden of proof lies with the aggressor to demonstrate that *any* proposed use of force, even including execution, mutilation, or enslavement, exceeds bounds of proportionality. As mentioned above, in practice there are several clear areas: murder justifies execution; minor, nonarmed, nonviolent theft does not.[80] Exceeding known appropriate levels of retaliation makes the retaliator an aggressor to the extent of the excess amount of force used. But there are indeed gray areas in which

---

[80] See Part IV.A, above.

it is difficult, if not impossible, to precisely delimit the exact amount of maximum permissible punishment. However, this uncertain situation, this grayness, is caused by the aggressor. The victim is placed in a quandary and might underpunish, or underutilize his right to punish, if he has to justify how much force he can use. Or he might have to expend extra resources in terms of time or money—for example, to hire a philosopher or lawyer to figure out exactly how much punishment is warranted—which would impermissibly increase the total harm done to the victim.

It is indeed difficult to determine the bounds of proportionality in many cases. But we do know one thing: force has been initiated against the victim, and thus force, in general, may be used against the victim- izer. Other than for easy or established cases, any ambiguity or doubt must be resolved in favor of the victim unless the aggressor bears his burden of argument to explain why the proposed punishment exceeds his own initial aggression.[81] Unless the maximum permissible level of retaliation is clearly established or persuasively argued by the aggressor, there should be no limitations on the victim's right to retaliate. Fur- ther, suppose the aggressor is not able to show why the victim may not execute him, even for a nonkilling act of aggression, and thus the aggressor is executed. If the aggressor's heirs should later successfully

---

[81] Many crimes would have established or generally accepted levels or at least ranges of permissible punishment—for example, as worked out by a private justice system of a free society or by specialists writing treatises on the subject. For further discussion of the role of judges or other decentralized law-finding fora, and of legislatures, in the development of law, see "Legislation and the Discovery of Law in a Free Society" (ch. 13). No doubt litigants in court or equivalent forums, especially the defendant, would hire lawyers to present the best arguments possible in favor of punishment and its permissible bounds. In a society that respects the general libertarian theory of rights and punishment developed herein, one could even expect lawyers to specialize in arguing whether a defendant is estopped from asserting a particular defense, whether a given defense is capable of being made universal or particular when the burden of proof for each side has been satisfied, and the like.

With regard to the concept of making a prima facie case and switching the burden of proof from the plaintiff to the defendant, Richard Epstein has set forth a promising theory of pleadings and presumptions whereby one party who wishes to upset the initial balance must establish a prima facie case that may be countered by a defense, which may be met with a second round of prima facie arguments, and so on. See Richard A. Epstein, "Pleading and Presumptions," *U. Chicago L. Rev.* 40 (1973), p. 556. For its application to the fields of torts and intentional harms, see *idem, A Theory of Strict Liability; idem,* "Defenses and Subsequent Pleas in a System of Strict Liability"; and *idem,* "Intentional Harms."

show that the type of aggression perpetrated by the aggressor did not, in fact, warrant capital punishment, still the victim has committed no aggression. To so hold would be to require victims to err on the side of underpunishing in cases of doubt in order to avoid potential liability in the future if it turns out that the aggressor could have made a better defensive argument. For the fact that there is a doubtful question is the aggressor's fault, and if he does not resolve it—either because of laziness, incompetence, bad luck, or tactics designed to make the victim unsure of how much he may punish—the victim should not be further harmed by this fact, which he would be if he were forced to take the risk that he might underpunish when punishing in the gray area.

Thus, several factors may be taken into account in coming up with an appropriate punishment. Suppose that an aggressor kidnaps and cuts off the hand of the victim. The victim is clearly entitled to do the same to the aggressor. But if the victim wishes to cut off the aggressor's foot instead—for some reason—he is, prima facie, entitled to do this. The victim would also be entitled to cut off both of the aggressor's hands unless the aggressor could explain why this is a higher amount of coercion than his own.[82] Merely cutting off one of the aggressor's hands might actually not be as extreme as was the aggressor's own action. For example, the victim may have been a painter. Thus, the consequence of the aggressive violence might be that, in addition to endangering the victim's very life and causing pain, the victim suffers a huge amount of mental and financial damage. It might take cutting off all four of the aggressor's limbs or even decapitating him to inflict that much damage on him. We know that it is permissible to employ violence against an aggressor. How much? Let the aggressor bear the burden of figuring this out.

As mentioned above with respect to rape, the victim may be squeamish about violence itself and thus recoil at the idea of eye-for-an-eye. If that is the victim's nature, the victim should not be penalized further by being forced to administer *lex talionis*. The aggressor must take his

---

[82] Admittedly, it is difficult to know how this argument would proceed or even what would qualify as a good argument. But such concerns are the aggressor's worry, not the victim's. And there is an easy way to avoid being placed in this position: do not initiate force against your fellow man.

victim as he finds him[83] and is estopped from complaining because he placed the victim in the situation where the victim's special preferences can only be satisfied by a nonreciprocal punishment. Thus, the victim may instead choose to seize a certain portion of the aggressor's property. The amount of the award that is "equal" to the damage done is of course difficult to determine, but, if nothing else, similar principles could be used as are used in today's tort and criminal justice system. If the amount of damages is uncertain or seems "too high," it must be recalled that the aggressor himself originated this state of uncertainty, and thus he cannot now be heard to complain about it.

Alternatively, a more objective damage award could be determined by the victim bargaining away his right to inflict corporal punishment against the aggressor in return for some or all of the aggressor's property.[84] This might be an especially attractive—or the least unattractive—alternative for a person victimized by a very rich aggressor. The established award for chopping someone's hand off might normally be, say, $1 million. However, this would mean that a billionaire could commit such crimes with impunity. Under the estoppel view of punishment, the victim, instead of taking $1 million of the aggressor's money, could kidnap the aggressor and threaten to exercise his right to, say, chop off both of the aggressor's arms, slowly, and with pain. A billionaire may be willing to trade half, or even all, his wealth to escape this punishment.

For poor aggressors, there is no property to take as restitution, and the mere infliction of pain on the aggressor may not satisfy some victims.

---

[83] This is an ancient principle of justice. For example:
It is well settled in our jurisprudence that a defendant *takes his victim as he finds him* and is responsible for all natural and probable consequences of his tortious conduct. Where defendant's negligent action aggravates a preexisting injury or condition, he must compensate the victim for the full extent of his aggravation.
American Motorist Ins. Co. v. American Rent-All, Inc., 579 So.2d 429 (La. 1991), p. 433, emphasis added, citation omitted.
[84] See also Kinsella, "Fraud, Restitution, and Retaliation: The Libertarian Approach," *StephanKinsella.com* (Feb. 3, 2009). Admittedly, this presupposes that the victim has the primary right of retribution against the aggressor so that she may *forgive* him. This topic is ripe for further development, and in fact has been explored in a recent paper. See Łukasz Dominiak, Igor Wysocki & Stanisław Wójtowicz, "Dialogical Estoppel, Erga Omnes Rights, and the Libertarian Theory of Punishment and Self-Defense," *J. Libertarian Stud.* 27, no. 1 (March, 2023; https://perma.cc/RP8Z-VE3C): 1–24.

They would be entitled to enslave the aggressor or sell him into slavery or for medical testing to yield the best profit possible.[85]

V. CONCLUSION

The ways in which punishment can be administered are rich and various, but all the typically-cited goals of punishment could be accommodated under the view of punishment set forth above. Criminals could be incapacitated and deterred, even rehabilitated, perhaps, according to the victim's choice. Restitution could be obtained in a variety of ways, or, if the victim so chooses, retribution or revenge. Though it is difficult to precisely determine the boundaries of proportionality, justice requires that the aggressor be held responsible for the dilemma he has created as well as for the aggression he has committed.

APPENDIX
THE JUSTICE OF RESPONSIVE FORCE

In Part III.C above, I discussed the legitimacy of punishing aggressors, that is, the justice of *responsive* force—force that is *in response to* aggression, or initiated force. As noted above, the material here was originally intended to appear in footnote 44, above. Due to its length, I include this material in this appendix.

As noted in "Dialogical Arguments for Libertarian Rights" (ch. 6), "Defending Argumentation Ethics" (ch. 7), and "The Undeniable Morality of Capitalism" (ch. 22), Hans-Hermann Hoppe has defended the right to self-defense and retaliatory force in his argumentation ethics. For a recent book-length treatment of ideas related to Hoppe's argumentation ethics and my estoppel approach advanced in this chapter, see Pavel Slutskiy, *Communication and Libertarianism* (Springer, 2021), and further references in these chapters.

---

[85] *But see* Kinsella, "Fraud, Restitution, and Retaliation: The Libertarian Approach," discussing practical problems with an actual institutionalized retributionist system and how the theoretical case for punitive rights could play a role in a restitution-based system. For a related commentary related to disputes in general, see Kinsella, "On the Obligation to Negotiate, Compromise, and Arbitrate," *StephanKinsella.com* (April 6, 2023).

Others have previously recognized the justice of using force against one who has used force. Law professor Lawrence Crocker writes:

> Suppose ... that A and B are shipwrecked on a deserted island. A makes use of the only firearm salvaged from the wreck to force B to build him a shelter. If B gains control of the gun, it will not be unfair for B to use it to force A to return the favor.[86]

Libertarian philosopher John Hospers opined that when an aggressor initiates force, "the victim is entitled to respond according to the rule (*'The use of force is permissible'*) that the *aggressor himself* has implicitly laid down."[87] According to Herbert Morris:

> If I say the magic words "take the watch for a couple of days" or "go ahead and slap me," have I waived my right not to have my property taken or a right not to be struck or have I, rather, in saying what I have, simply stepped into a relation in which the rights no longer apply with respect to a specified other person? These observations find support in the following considerations. The right is that which gives rise, when infringed, to a legitimate claim against another person. What this suggests is that the right is that sphere interference with which *entitles us to complain* or gives us a right to complain. From this it seems to follow that a right to bodily security should be more precisely described as "a right that others not interfere *without permission*." And there is the corresponding duty not to interfere unless provided permission. Thus when we talk of waiving our rights or "giving up our rights" in such cases we are not waiving or giving up our right to property nor our right to bodily security, for we still, of course, possess the right not to have our watch taken without permission. *We have rather placed ourselves in a position where we do not possess the capacity*, sometimes called a right, *to complain* if the person takes the watch or slaps us.[88]

Or as Hegel wrote:

---

[86] Lawrence Crocker, "The Upper Limit of Just Punishment," *Emory L. J.* 41 (1992): 1059–1110, at 1068.

[87] Hospers, "Retribution: The Ethics of Punishment," p. 191 (emphasis added).

[88] Herbert Morris, "Persons and Punishment," in *On Guilt and Innocence: Essays in Legal Philosophy and Moral Psychology* (Berkeley: University of California Press, 1976), p. 52 (emphasis added); see also pp. 31, 52, *et pass.*, discussing the right to bodily integrity and the waiver of this right.

The injury [the penalty] which falls on the criminal is not merely *implicitly* just—as just, it is *eo ipso* his implicit will, an embodiment of his freedom, his right; on the contrary, it is also a right *established* within the criminal himself, i.e., in his objectively embodied will, in his action. The reason for this is that *his action* is the action of a rational being and this implies that *it is something universal* and that *by doing it the criminal has laid down a law which he has explicitly recognized in his action* and under which in consequence he should be brought as under his right.[89]

Thus, under Hegel's philosophy, "when a criminal steals another person's property, he is not only denying that person's right to own that piece of property, he is denying the right to property in *itself*."[90]

Charles King, discussing the moral acceptability of using force against force, states that when another initiates force,

[w]ith him we are returned to the first-stage state of nature and may use force against him. In so doing we do not violate his rights or in any other way violate the principle of right, because he has broken the *reciprocity* required for us to view such a principle [of rights] as binding. In this we find the philosophic grounding for the moral legitimacy of the practice of punishment. Punishment is just that practice which raises the price of violation of the principle of right so as to give us all good reason to accept that principle.[91]

Or as Locke writes:

In transgressing the law of nature, the offender declares himself to live by another rule than that of reason and common equity ... and so he becomes dangerous to mankind, ... every man ... by the right he hath to preserve mankind in general, may restrain, or where it is necessary, destroy things noxious to them, and so may bring such evil on any one, who hath transgressed that law, as may make him repent the doing of it. ... [A] criminal, who having renounced reason, the common rule and measure God hath given to mankind, hath, by the unjust violence and slaugh-

---

[89] G.W.F. Hegel, "Punishment as a Right," in Ezorsky, ed., *Philosophical Perspectives on Punishment*, at 107 (emphasis in last sentence added, brackets in original) (excerpted from G.W.F. Hegel, *The Philosophy of Right*, T.M. Knox, trans. (New York: St. Martin's Press, 1969), § 100).

[90] Pauley, "The Jurisprudence of Crime and Punishment from Plato to Hegel," pp. 140–41, citing Peter J. Steinberger, "Hegel on Crime and Punishment," *Am. Pol. Science Rev.* 77, no. 4 (Dec. 1983): 858–70, p. 860.

[91] King, "A Rationale for Punishment," p. 154 (emphasis added).

ter he hath committed upon one, declared war against all mankind, and therefore may be destroyed as a lion or a tiger, one of those wild savage beasts, with whom men can have no society nor security.[92]

Other quotes can be listed briefly here:

Tibor Machan: "[I]f someone attacks another, that act carries with it, as a matter of the logic of aggression, the implication that from a rational moral standpoint the victim may, and often should retaliate." [93]

Jan Narveson: "[T]hose who do not want peace, or want it only for others in relation to themselves rather than vice versa, are on their own and may in principle be dealt with by any degree of violence we like."[94]

Rasmussen & Den Uyl, "[W]hen someone is punished for having violated others' rights, it is not the case that the criminal has alienated or otherwise lost his rights; rather, it is the case that the criminal's choice to live in a rights-violating way is being respected."[95]

Randy Barnett: "It has been noted that one who wishes to extinguish or convey an inalienable right may do so by committing the appropriate wrongful act and thereby forfeiting it."[96]

Others are collected at Kinsella, "Quotes on the Logic of Liberty."

---

[92] Locke, *Second Treatise on Civil Government*, §11.

[93] Machan, *Individuals and Their Rights*, p. 176.

[94] Jan Narveson, *The Libertarian Idea*, p. 230, reissue ed. (Broadview Press, 2001). See also p. 159, subsection entitled "Being Able to Complain."

[95] Rasmussen & Den Uyl, *Liberty and Nature*, p. 85.

[96] Randy E. Barnett, "Contract Remedies and Inalienable Rights," *Social Pol'y & Phil.* 4, no. 1 (Autumn 1986; https://perma.cc/2RTU-L7EQ): 179–202, p. 186 (citing Diana T. Meyers, *Inalienable Rights: A Defense* (New York: Columbia University Press, 1985), p. 14). For more on forfeiture, see references in "Knowledge, Calculation, Conflict, and Law" (ch. 19), n.81 and "A Libertarian Theory of Punishment and Rights" (ch. 5), n.88.

6

Dialogical Arguments for Libertarian Rights

After publishing articles on my estoppel-based theory of rights[*] and Hans-Hermann Hoppe's "argumentation ethics" defense of libertarian rights[†] between 1992 and 1996, I published an article surveying estoppel, argumentation ethics, and similar theories in the *Journal of Libertarian Studies* in 1996, entitled "New Rationalist Directions in Libertarian Rights Theory."[††] An updated version of this article was published as "Dialogical Arguments for Libertarian Rights" in *The Dialectics of Liberty* in 2019.[§] This chapter is based on the latter piece, and is updated still further.[**]

---

[*] Stephan Kinsella, "Estoppel: A New Justification for Individual Rights," *Reason Papers* No. 17 (Fall 1992): 61–74 and the pair of articles that form the basis of "A Libertarian Theory of Punishment and Rights" (ch. 5). See also "How I Became a Libertarian" (ch. 1) and Stephan Kinsella, "The Genesis of Estoppel: My Libertarian Rights Theory," *StephanKinsella.com* (March 22, 2016).

[†] See "The Undeniable Morality of Capitalism" (ch. 22) and Stephan Kinsella, "Book Review: *The Economics and Ethics of Private Property: Studies in Political Economy and Philosophy* by Hans-Hermann Hoppe," *The Freeman: Ideas on Liberty* (November 1994; https://perma.cc/5J2V-R5R6) (each reviewing Hans-Hermann Hoppe, *The Economics and Ethics of Private Property: Studies in Political Economy and Philosophy* (Auburn, Ala.: Mises Institute, 2006 [1993]; www.hanshoppe.com/eepp)), and "A Libertarian Theory of Punishment and Rights" (ch. 5). See also "Defending Argumentation Ethics" (ch. 7). For more on argumentation ethics, see the references in note 15 to "How We Come to Own Ourselves" (ch. 4).

[††] Stephan Kinsella, "New Rationalist Directions in Libertarian Rights Theory," *J. Libertarian Stud.* 12, no. 2 (Fall 1996): 313–26. For a recent book-length exploration of some of the arguments discussed in this chapter, see Pavel Slutskiy, *Communication and Libertarianism* (Springer, 2021).

[§] Stephan Kinsella, "Dialogical Arguments for Libertarian Rights," in Roger Bissell, Chris Sciabarra & Ed Younkins, eds., *The Dialectics of Liberty* (Lexington Books, 2019).

[**] The term "dialogical" in my title refers to discourse, or dialogue, which features in many of the theories discussed here, including Hoppe's discourse or argumentation ethics and

Classical liberals and libertarians believe that individuals have rights, even if there is debate about just why we have them or how this can be proved. Robert Nozick opened his book *Anarchy, State, and Utopia* with the assertion: "Individuals have rights, and there are things no person or group may do to them (without violating their rights)."[1] Yet, he did not offer a proof of this assertion, for which he has drawn criticism. It is commonly assumed that Nozick's argument is not *complete* until a proof of rights is offered.[2] Other theorists have offered, over the years, various reasons—utilitarian, natural law, pragmatic, and the like—why we should respect others' rights, why we should recognize that individuals have certain rights.[3]

many others mentioned in this chapter. As noted in "Defending Argumentation Ethics" (ch. 7) and "The Undeniable Morality of Capitalism" (ch. 22), Hoppe's discourse ethics was influenced by the discourse ethics of Jürgen Habermas, Hoppe's PhD advisor, and Karl-Otto Apel. Interestingly, although Rawls says, of his own "original position," "[l]ike Habermas's ideal discourse situation, it is a dialogue; indeed, an omnilogue, … Habermas sometimes says that the original position is monological and not dialogical; that is because all the parties have, in effect, the same reasons and so they elect the same principles." John Rawls, *Political Liberalism*, expanded ed. (New York: Columbia University Press, 2005), p. 383. For our purposes, I think the term dialogue or dialogical suffices.

[1] Robert Nozick, *Anarchy, State, and Utopia* (New York: Basic Books, 1974), p. ix.
[2] See e.g., Thomas Nagel, "Libertarianism Without Foundations," *Yale L. J.* 85 (1975; https://perma.cc/SZP3-XPBM): 136–49 (reviewing Nozick, *Anarchy, State, and Utopia*). See also Tibor R. Machan, *Individuals and Their Rights* (La Salle, Ill.: Open Court, 1989), p. xiii ("In a way this book is a response to Thomas Nagel's criticism of [Nozick], a criticism often endorsed by others, to wit, that libertarianism lacks moral foundations."); Loren E. Lomasky, *Persons, Rights, and the Moral Community* (New York: Oxford University Press, 1987), p. 9, who says that Nozick declines "to offer *any* systematic rationale for the vaguely specified collection of rights he takes to be basic" (footnote omitted).
[3] See, e.g., Ludwig von Mises, *Liberalism: In the Classical Tradition*, 3d ed., Ralph Raico, trans. (Irvington-on-Hudson, N.Y.: Foundation for Economic Education, 1985; https://mises.org/library/liberalism-classical-tradition); Murray N. Rothbard, *The Ethics of Liberty* (Atlantic Highlands, N.J.: Humanities Press, 1982); *idem, For A New Liberty: The Libertarian Manifesto*, rev'd ed. (New York: Libertarian Review Foundation, 1985; https://mises.org/library/new-liberty-libertarian-manifesto); Ayn Rand, *Capitalism: The Unknown Ideal* (New York: Signet, 1967); *idem, The Virtue of Selfishness: A New Concept of Egoism* (New York: Signet, 1964); Machan, *Individuals and Their Rights*; Jan Narveson, *The Libertarian Idea*, reissue ed. (Broadview Press, 2001); Lomasky, *Persons, Rights, and the Moral Community*; Douglas B. Rasmussen & Douglas J. Den Uyl, *Liberty and Nature: An Aristotelian Defense of Liberal Order* (La Salle, Ill.: Open Court, 1991).
   Randy Barnett contends that consequentialist arguments for rights need not be utilitarian. See Randy E. Barnett, "Of Chickens and Eggs—The Compatibility of Moral

For instance, an economic case can be made for respecting the liberty of others. Given that you are a decent person and generally value your fellow man and wish everyone to live a satisfying life, you will tend to be in favor of the free market and liberty, at least if you understand basic economic principles.[4] But the success of arguments such as these depends on other people accepting particular premises, such as valuing the general well-being of others, without which the argument is incomplete. Skeptics can always deny the validity of the premises even if they cannot refute free-market economics.

There can be no doubt that a rigorous argument for individual rights would be useful. In recent years, interest has been increasing in rationalist, dialectical, or dialogical rights theories or related theories, some of which promise to provide fruitful and unassailable defenses of individual rights. These arguments typically examine the implicit claims that are necessarily presupposed by action or discourse. They then proceed deductively or conventionally from these core premises,

---

Rights and Consequentialist Analyses," *Harv. J. L. & Pub. Pol'y* 12 (1989; www.randybarnett.com/pre-2000): 611–36, and *idem*, "Introduction: Liberty vs. License," in *The Structure of Liberty: Justice and the Rule of Law*, 2d ed. (Oxford, 2014). Some libertarian theorists provide arguments other than traditional deontological, principled, or natural rights, and utilitarian, empirical, or consequentialist, approaches. For example, Michael Huemer argues for a type of intuitionism in his *Ethical Intuitionism* (Palgrave Macmillan, 2007). In his *Escape from Leviathan: Liberty, Welfare and Anarchy Reconciled* (New York: St. Martin's Press, 2000), J.C. Lester opposes "justificationist" arguments for liberty and advances a critical-rationalist, "conjecturalist" approach influenced by Karl Popper's empiricist-positivist views. Patrick Burke proposes "causing harm" as the main linchpin of libertarian justice. See T. Patrick Burke, *No Harm: Ethical Principles for a Free Market* (New York: Paragon House, 1994). On Lester, see David Gordon & Roberta A. Modugno, "Review of J.C. Lester's *Escape from Leviathan: Liberty, Welfare, and Anarchy Reconciled*," *J. Libertarian Stud.* 17, no. 4 (2003, https://mises.org/library/review-jc-lesters-escape-leviathan-liberty-welfare-and-anarchy-reconciled-0): 101–109; and Kinsella, "'Aggression' versus 'Harm' in Libertarianism," *Mises Economics Blog* (Dec. 16, 2009) (criticizing Lester's approach, his opposition to "justificationism," and his focus on "imposing costs" instead of aggression as the key libertarian principle). On Burke, see Kinsella "Book Review," *Reason Papers* No. 20 (Fall 1995; https://reasonpapers.com/archives/), p. 135–46, and *idem*, "'Aggression' versus 'Harm' in Libertarianism." See also Kinsella, "Hoppe on Property Rights in Physical Integrity vs Value," *StephanKinsella.com* (June 12, 2011). See also "A Libertarian Theory of Punishment and Rights" (ch. 5), n.16, including the quote by Rothbard criticizing the "harm" approach and Mill, Hayek, and Nozick.

4 See Kinsella, "The Division of Labor as the Source of Grundnorms and Rights," *Mises Economics Blog* (April 24, 2009), and *idem*, "Empathy and the Source of Rights," *Mises Economics Blog* (Sept. 6, 2006).

or axioms, to establish certain apodictically true conclusions. Several such arguments are surveyed below.

ARGUMENTATION ETHICS

Let us first discuss Hans-Hermann Hoppe's pathbreaking "argumentation ethics" defense of libertarian rights.[5] Hoppe shows that basic rights are implied in the activity of argumentation itself, so that anyone asserting any claim about anything necessarily presupposes the validity of rights. Hoppe first notes that any truth at all (including norms such as individual rights to life, liberty, and property) that one would wish to discuss, deny, or affirm will be brought up in the course of an argumentation, that is to say, will be brought up in dialogue. If participants in argumentation necessarily accept particular truths, including norms, in order to engage in argumentation, they could never challenge these norms in an argument without thereby engaging in a performative contradiction. This would establish these norms as literally incontestable truths.

Hoppe establishes self-ownership by pointing out that argumentation, as a form of action, implies the use of the scarce resources of one's body. One must have control over, or own, this scarce resource in order to engage in meaningful discourse. This is because argumentation is, by its very nature, a *conflict-free* way of interacting, since it is an attempt to find what the truth *is*, to establish truth, to persuade or be persuaded by the force of words alone. If one is threatened into accepting the statements or truth-claims of another, this does not tend to get at the truth, which is undeniably a goal of argumentation or discourse. Thus, anyone engaging in argumentation implicitly presupposes the right of self-ownership of other participants in the argument, for otherwise the other would not be able to consider freely and accept or reject the

---

5 *See* Hans-Hermann Hoppe, *A Theory of Socialism and Capitalism: Economics, Politics, and Ethics* (Auburn, Ala.: Mises Institute, 2010 [1989]; www.hanshoppe.com/tsc), ch. 7; *idem*, "From the Economics of Laissez Faire to the Ethics of Libertarianism," "The Justice of Economic Efficiency," and "On the Ultimate Justification of the Ethics of Private Property," chaps. 11–13 in *The Economics and Ethics of Private Property*, esp. pp. 314–22. See also "Defending Argumentation Ethics" (ch. 7) and other references in note 15, below.

proposed argument. Only as long as there is at least an implicit recognition of each individual's property right in his or her own body can true argumentation take place. When this right is not recognized, the activity is no longer argumentation, but threat, mere naked aggression, or plain physical fighting. Thus, anyone who denies that rights exist contradicts himself since, by his very engaging in the cooperative and conflict-free activity of argumentation, he necessarily recognizes the right of his listener to be free to listen, think, and decide. That is, any participant in discourse presupposes the non-aggression principle, the libertarian view that one may not initiate force against others. Thus, according to Hoppe, anyone who would ever deny the ethics underlying the free market is already, by his very engaging in the civilized activity of discourse, presupposing the very ethic that he is challenging. This is a powerful argument because, instead of seeking to persuade someone to accept a new position, it points out to him a position that he already maintains, a position that he *necessarily* maintains. Opponents of liberty undercut their own position as soon as they begin to state it.

Hoppe then extends his case for self-ownership to external resources, to show that property rights in external scarce resources, in addition to self-ownership rights, are also presupposed by discourse. As he argues, "one's body is indeed the *prototype* of a scarce good for the use of which property rights, that is, rights of exclusive ownership, somehow have to be established, in order to avoid clashes."[6] As Hoppe explains,

> The compatibility of this principle with that of nonaggression can be demonstrated by means of an argumentum a contrario. First, it should be noted that if no one had the right to acquire and control anything except his own body … then we would all cease to exist and the problem of the justification of normative statements … simply would not exist. The existence of this problem is only possible because we are alive, and our existence is due to the fact that we do not, indeed cannot, accept

---

[6] Hoppe, *A Theory of Socialism and Capitalism*, at 19. In recent years I have tried to emphasize that "scarce" in this technical economic sense does not mean merely "rare" but rivalrous, or "not-superabundant," and have sometimes employed the term "conflictability" to avoid confusion and to forestall equivocation. See Stephan Kinsella, "On Conflictability and Conflictable Resources," *StephanKinsella.com* (Jan. 31, 2022); also "*Against Intellectual Property* After Twenty Years: Looking Back and Looking Forward" (ch. 15), text at n.29; "What Libertarianism Is" (ch. 2), n.5.

a norm outlawing property in other scarce goods next and in addition to that of one's physical body. Hence, the right to acquire such goods must be assumed to exist.[7]

Next, Hoppe argues that the only ownership rule that is compatible with self-ownership and the presuppositions of discourse is the Lockean original-appropriation rule.[8] Hoppe's basic point here is that self-ownership rights are established just because one's body is itself a scarce (conflictable) resource, so other scarce resources must be similarly ownable.[9]

Looked at from another angle, participants in argumentation indisputably need to use and control the scarce resources in the world to survive; otherwise, they would perish. But because their scarcity makes conflict over the uses of resources possible, only norms that determine the proper ownership can avoid conflict over these scarce goods. That such norms are valuable cannot be denied, because anyone who is alive in the world and participating in the practical activity of argumentation cannot deny the value of being able to control scarce resources and the value of avoiding conflicts over such scarce (i.e., conflictable) resources.

So no one could ever deny that norms for determining the ownership of scarce goods are useful for allowing conflict-free exploitation of such resources. But, as Hoppe points out, there are only two fundamental alternatives for acquiring rights in unowned property: (1) by doing something with things with which no one else had ever done anything before, that is, the Lockean concept of mixing of labor, or homesteading; or (2) simply by verbal declaration or decree. However, a rule that allows property to be owned by mere verbal declaration cannot serve to avoid conflicts, since any number of people could at any time assert conflicting claims of ownership over any particular scarce resource. Only the first alternative, that of Lockean homesteading, establishes an objective (or, as Hoppe sometimes calls it, intersubjectively ascertainable) link between a particular person and a particular scarce resource, and thus no one can deny the Lockean right to homestead unowned resources.

---

[7] Ibid., at 161.

[8] Ibid., at 160–69.

[9] See note 21, below, for one view of the U.S. Supreme Court regarding the connection between property and other rights.

Argumentation Ethics and Natural Rights

Before closing this section let me emphasize that Hoppe offered his theory as an improvement on traditional natural rights arguments. For one, by focusing on argumentation instead of action,[10] he seeks to avoid one weakness of previous arguments:

> It has been a common quarrel with the natural rights position, even on the part of sympathetic readers, that the concept of human nature is far "too diffuse and varied to provide a determinate set of contents of natural law."[11]

Hoppe is also critical of classical natural rights reasoning insofar as it violates the is-ought gap. As he writes: "[O]ne can readily subscribe to the almost generally accepted view that the gulf between 'ought' and 'is' is logically unbridgeable."[12] Argumentation ethics attempts to sidestep this issue by remaining in the realm of is-statements:

---

[10] See text at note 46, below.

[11] Hoppe, *A Theory of Socialism and Capitalism*, p. 156 n.118, quoting Alan Gewirth, "Law, Action, and Morality," in *Georgetown Symposium on Ethics: Essays in Honor of Henry B. Veatch*, R. Porreco, ed. (New York: University Press of America, 1984), p. 73); see also "The Undeniable Morality of Capitalism" (ch. 22), at n. 31. This point should not be confused with:

> H.L.A. Hart's notion of the minimum content of the natural law [which Hart] introduces to show that the constraints on the nature of law imposed by the human condition are very weak indeed, whereas Barnett invokes Hart's notion in support of what, at first blush, might seem to be the opposite conclusion, i.e., that fundamental problems of human nature impose very strong constraints on the content of the law. This seeming opposition is dissolved once we appreciate that Hart introduced his idea to show that nature imposes very weak constraints on the concept of law, that is, on what can count as a "law," from the point of view of philosophical analysis.... Barnett uses Hart's terminology for the very different purpose of showing that nature imposes very strong constraints on what laws can be justified.... Barnett would not claim that his argument establishes that compliance with his liberal conception of justice is required for a norm to count as a law.

Lawrence B. Solum, "The Foundations of Liberty" [review of the first edition of Barnett's *The Structure of Liberty*], *Mich. L. Rev.* 97, no. 6 (May 1999; https://repository.law.umich.edu/mlr/vol97/iss6/26/): 1780–1812, p. 1782 n.4 (citations omitted). See also H.L.A. Hart, *The Concept of Law* 3d ed. (Oxford: Oxford University Press, 2012 [1961]), chap. IX, §2, "The Minimum Content of Natural Law"; Barnett, *The Structure of Liberty: Justice and the Rule of Law*, pp. 11–12 (discussing this aspect of Hart's work) and 332–34 (discussing Solum's criticism of Barnett in this regard).

[12] Hoppe, *A Theory of Socialism and Capitalism*, p. 163 (citing W.D. Hudson, ed., *The Is-Ought Question* (London: Macmillan, 1969)).

Here the praxeological proof of libertarianism has the advantage of offering a completely value-free justification of private property. It remains entirely in the realm of is-statements, and nowhere tries to derive an ought from an is. The structure of the argument is this: (a) justification is propositional justification—a priori true is-statement; (b) argumentation presupposes property in one's body and the homesteading principle—a priori true is-statement; and (c) then, no deviation from this ethic can be argumentatively justified—a priori true is-statement.[13]

Thus, as Hoppe writes:

> The relationship between our approach and a "natural rights" approach can now be described in some detail, too. The natural law or natural rights tradition of philosophic thought holds that universally valid norms can be discerned by means of reason as grounded in the very nature of man. It has been a common quarrel with this position, even on the part of sympathetic readers, that the concept of human nature is far "too diffuse and varied to provide a determinate set of contents of natural law." ... Furthermore, its description of rationality is equally ambiguous in that it does not seem to distinguish between the role of reason in establishing empirical laws of nature on the one hand, and normative laws of human conduct on the other....
>
> In recognizing the narrower concept of argumentation (instead of the wider one of human nature) as the necessary starting point in deriving an ethic, and in assigning to moral reasoning the status of a priori reasoning, clearly to be distinguished from the role of reason performed in empirical research, our approach not only claims to avoid these difficulties from the outset, but claims thereby to be at once more straightforward and rigorous. Still, to thus dissociate myself from the natural rights tradition is not to say that I could not agree with its critical assessment of most of contemporary ethical theory; indeed I do agree with H. Veatch's complementary refutation of all desire (teleological, utilitarian) ethics as well as all duty (deontological) ethics.... Nor do I claim that it is impossible to interpret my approach as falling in a "rightly conceived" natural rights tradition after all. What I claim, though, is that the following approach is clearly out of line with what the natural rights approach has actually come to be, and that it owes nothing to this tradition as it stands.[14]

---

13 Hoppe, *The Economics and Ethics of Private Property*, p. 345. See also "The Undeniable Morality of Capitalism" (ch. 22), at n. 31.

14 Hoppe, *A Theory of Socialism and Capitalism*, pp. 156–57, n.118 (citations omitted). It should be noted that other thinkers have glimpsed the idea that the requirements of human reason and reasoning/discourse itself can help to inform which norms can be justified, but

And this, perhaps, part of the reason why Rothbard gave a wholehearted endorsement to Hoppe's argumentation ethics:

> In a dazzling breakthrough for political philosophy in general and for libertarianism in particular, he [Hoppe] has managed to transcend the famous is/ought, fact/value dichotomy that has plagued philosophy since the days of the scholastics, and that had brought modern libertarianism into a tiresome deadlock. Not only that: Hans Hoppe has managed to establish the case for anarcho-capitalist, Lockean rights in an unprecedentedly hard-core manner, one that makes my own natural law/natural rights position seem almost wimpy in comparison.[15]

---

none of them recognize the crucial importance of scarcity and praxeological action as Hoppe does, so their arguments only go so far or end in error (e.g. supporting welfare rights). See, e.g., Solum, "The Foundations of Liberty," p. 1809 ("The justification for a conception of justice can be limited to the resources of public reason, the common reason of all the rational and reasonable members of a community."); Rawls, *Political Liberalism*, Lectures IV and VI, and Part Four; Barnett, *The Structure of Liberty: Justice and the Rule of Law*, pp. 332–34.

See also Hoppe's criticism of Gewirth's argument for rights in the section "Pilon and Gewirth on the Principle of Generic Consistency," below.

[15] Murray N. Rothbard, "Beyond Is and Ought," *Liberty* 2, no. 2 (Nov. 1988; https://perma.cc/A5UU-P64A): 44–45, at 44. The late Leland Yeager claimed that Rothbard, who died in January 1995, had changed his mind before his death regarding the validity of Hoppe's argument, even after endorsing it in 1988. Leland B. Yeager, "Book Review," *Rev. Austrian Econ.* 9, no. 1 (1996; https://perma.cc/UDC3-UQ3Z): 181–88 (reviewing Murray N. Rothbard, *Economic Thought Before Adam Smith* and *Classical Economics*, vols. 1 and 2 of *An Austrian Perspective on the History of Economic Thought* (Aldershot, England and Brookfield, Vt.: Edward Elgar, 1995; https://perma.cc/3ABN-9FD2)). Yeager asserts that, based on language in this posthumously-published treatise:

> Rothbard no longer endorses Hans-Hermann Hoppe's claim to derive libertarian policy positions purely from the circumstances of discussion itself, without any appeal to value judgments…. On the contrary, and as he had done earlier, Rothbard now correctly observes that policy recommendations and decisions presuppose value judgments as well as positive analysis. (p. 185)

There is no doubt that Yeager himself sees no merit in Hoppe's argumentation ethics. See Leland B. Yeager, "Raw Assertions," *Liberty* 2, no. 2 (Nov. 1988; https://perma.cc/A5UU-P64A): 45–46. However, Yeager provides no evidence for his contention about Rothbard's change of mind. It is undoubtedly wrong.

Hoppe's argumentation ethics has drawn a number of critics and defenders since its debut in the mid-1980s, and continues to attract attention. See generally Stephan Kinsella, "Argumentation Ethics and Liberty: A Concise Guide," *StephanKinsella.com* (May 27, 2011); and *idem*, "Hoppe's Argumentation Ethics and Its Critics," *StephanKinsella.com* (Aug. 11, 2015). See also Chris Matthew Sciabarra, *Total Freedom: Toward a Dialectical Libertarianism* (Penn State University Press, 2000), pp. 367–69 (discussing Hoppe's argumentation ethics as well as my own estoppel views and other dialectical approaches); and Bissell, Sciabarra & Younkins, "Introduction," in Bissell, Sciabarra & Younkins, eds., *The Dialectics of Liberty* (discussing the estoppel theory). Several scholars have responded to Bob Murphy &

ESTOPPEL

Another rationalist-oriented justification of rights is an argument
I developed based on the common-law concept of estoppel.[16] As one
legal treatise explains:

> The word *estoppel* means "not permitted to deny." If A makes a statement
> of fact that B relies on in some substantial way, A will not be permitted
> to deny it (that is, A will be estopped), if the effect of A's denial would be
> to injure the party who relies on it.[17]

Thus, under the traditional *legal* principle of estoppel, a person may be
prevented, or estopped, from maintaining something (for example in
court) inconsistent with his previous conduct or statements. For instance,
if a father promises his daughter that he will pay her college tuition for
her, and the daughter relies on this promise to her detriment, for example by enrolling in college and becoming obligated to the college for her

---

Gene Callahan, "Hans-Hermann Hoppe's Argumentation Ethic: A Critique," *Anti-state.
com* (Sept. 19, 2002), republished in substantially similar form as "Hans-Hermann Hoppe's
Argumentation Ethic: A Critique," *J. Libertarian Stud.* 20, no. 2 (2006; https://mises.org/
library/hans-hermann-hoppes-argumentation-ethic-critique): 53–64, including: "Defending
Argumentation Ethics" (ch. 7); Frank van Dun, "Argumentation Ethics and the Philosophy
of Freedom," *Libertarian Papers* 1, art. no. 19 (2009; www.libertarianpapers.org); Marian
Eabrasu, "A Reply to the Current Critiques Formulated Against Hoppe's Argumentation
Ethics," *Libertarian Papers* 1, art. no. 20 (2009; www.libertarianpapers.org); Walter Block,
"Rejoinder to Murphy and Callahan on Hoppe's Argumentation Ethics," *J. Libertarian Stud.*
22, no. 1 (2011; www.walterblock.com); and Norbert Slenzok, "The Libertarian Argumen-
tation Ethics, the Transcendental Pragmatics of Language, and the Conflict-Freedom
Principle," *Analiza i Egzystencja* 58 (2022), 35–64.

Hoppe re-presented his argument and responded to a variety of critics in his 2016
speech, at "PFP163 | Hans Hermann Hoppe, 'On The Ethics of Argumentation' (PFS
2016)," *The Property and Freedom Podcast*, ep. 163 (June 30, 2022), stating:

> Some later critics, in particular Robert Murphy and Gene Callahan, who apparently
> accepted my libertarian conclusion but rejected my way of deriving it (without,
> however, proposing any alternative reason for their own libertarian "beliefs"), were
> argumentatively demolished by Stephan Kinsella, Frank van Dun and also Marian
> Eabrasu.

16 See references at note *, above.

17 Bernard F. Cataldo, et al., *Introduction to Law and the Legal Process*, 3d ed. (New York:
John Wiley and Sons, 1980), p. 479. See also American Law Institute, *Restatement (Second)
of Contracts* (St. Paul, Minn.: American Law Institute Publishers, 1981), §90; Louisiana
Civil Code (https://www.legis.la.gov/legis/Laws_Toc.aspx?folder=67&level=Parent), art.
1967. See also references in Part III.A of "A Libertarian Theory of Punishment and Rights"
(ch. 5).

tuition, then she may be able to recover some of her expenses from her father, even if his original promise is not enforceable as a normal contract (for example, because there was no consideration).[18] The father would be estopped from denying that a contract was formed, even though, technically, one was not.

Drawing on this legal terminology and concept, the approach I advance may be termed "dialogical" estoppel, or simply estoppel. The estoppel principle shows that an aggressor contradicts himself if he objects to others' enforcement of their rights. Thus, unlike Hoppe's argumentation ethics approach, which focuses on presuppositions of discourse in general, and which shows that any participant in discourse contradicts himself if he denies these presuppositions, the estoppel theory focuses on the discourse between an aggressor and his victim about punishment of the aggressor and seeks to show that the aggressor contradicts himself if he objects to his punishment.

What would it mean to have a right? Whatever else rights might be, certainly it is the case that rights are legitimately enforceable; that is, one who is physically able to enforce his right *may not* be prevented from doing so. In short, having a right allows one to legitimately punish the violator of the right or to legitimately use force to prevent another from violating the right. The only way one could be said *not* to have a right would be if the attempt to punish a violator of the right is for some reason unjustifiable. But clearly this problem itself can arise only when the alleged criminal *objects* to being punished, for if criminals consented to punishment, we would not face the problem of justifying punishing them.[19]

---

[18] See, for example, *Zimmerman v. Zimmerman*, 447 N.Y.S.2d 675 (App. Div. 1982), from which this example was derived. For another recent example concerning a Bitcoin-related defamation lawsuit, see "A Libertarian Theory of Punishment and Rights" (ch. 5), at n.23.

[19] Of course, an accused criminal need not engage in discourse with his accuser at all. But if the criminal is to put forward an objection to his punishment, he must engage in argumentation and thus be subject to the rules of argumentation. As Hare noted in a similar context:

Just as one cannot win a game of chess against an opponent who will not make any moves—and just as one cannot argue mathematically with a person who will not commit himself to any mathematical statements—so moral argument is impossible with a man who will make no moral judgments at all.... Such a person is not entering the arena of moral dispute, and therefore it is impossible to contest with him. *He is compelled also—and this is important—to abjure the protection of morality for his own interests.*

The estoppel argument contends that we have rights just because no aggressor could ever meaningfully object to being punished. Thus, if the only potential obstacle to having a legitimately enforceable right is the unconsenting criminal, and if he is estopped from objecting to his punishment, then the right may be said to exist, or be justified, since, in effect, the criminal cannot deny this.

So why is this the case? Why is a criminal estopped in this manner? Consider: if *B* is a violent aggressor, such as a murderer or rapist, how could he *not* consent to any punishment that *A*, the victim (or the victim's agent), attempts to inflict? To object to his punishment, *B* must engage in discourse with *A*; he must at least temporarily adopt the stance of a peaceful, civilized person trying to persuade *A*, through the use of reason and consistent, universalizable principles, to provide reasons as to why *A* should not punish him. But to do this, *B* must in essence claim that *A* should not use force against him (*B*), and to do this, *B* must claim that it is wrong, or unjustifiable, to use force. But since he *has* initiated force, he has admitted that (he believes that) it is proper to use force, and *B* would contradict himself if he were to claim the opposite. Since contradictions are always false[20] and since an undeniable goal of discourse is to establish truth, such contradictions are ruled out of bounds in discourse, since they cannot tend to establish truth. Thus, *B* is estopped from making this contradictory assertion, and is therefore unable to object to his punishment.

R.M. Hare, *Freedom and Reason* (Oxford: Clarendon Press, 1963), § 6.6 (emphasis added). See also Hannah Arendt's justification of the execution of Adolf Eichmann:

[J]ust as you [Eichmann] supported and carried out a policy of not wanting to share the earth with the Jewish people and the people of a number of other nations—as though you and your superiors had any right to determine who should and who should not inhabit the world—we find that no one, that is, no member of the human race, can be expected to want to share the earth with you. This is the reason, and the only reason, you must hang.

Hannah Arendt, *Eichmann in Jerusalem: A Report on the Banality of Evil* (Penguin, 2006), p. 279.

For other, similar quotes, see Kinsella, "Quotes on the Logic of Liberty," *StephanKinsella. com* (June 22, 2009).

20 *See* "A Libertarian Theory of Punishment and Rights" (ch. 5), n.29 and accompanying text.

Under the estoppel theory, then, we may enforce our rights against violent aggressors, since they cannot object to the enforcement of rights without self-contradiction.[21]

RIGHTS-SKEPTICISM

A third type of rights argument concerns the very nature of rights themselves and shows how any rights-skeptic contradicts himself whenever he denies that rights exist. It is similar to the estoppel approach outlined above, although the discourse under examination need not involve an aggressor. Instead, this argument focuses on rights-skeptics who deny the existence of rights, rather than on actual criminals who object to being punished in particular instances for a given crime.

If any right at all exists, it is a right of A to have or do X without B's preventing it; and, therefore, A can legitimately use force against B to en*force* the right.[22] A is concerned with the enforceability of his right

---

[21] As Hoppe's argumentation ethics approach grounds self-ownership rights and then is extended to cover property rights, so the estoppel argument may also be extended to cover property rights and the Lockean homesteading principle, essentially by showing that self-ownership rights presuppose the right to homestead, because one is meaningless without the other. See "A Libertarian Theory of Punishment and Rights" (ch. 5), Part III.F. As the U.S. Supreme Court has recognized, "The right to enjoy property without lawful deprivation ... is in truth a 'personal' right.... In fact, a fundamental *interdependence* exists between the personal right to liberty and the personal right in property. *Neither could have meaning without the other.* That rights in property are basic civil rights has long been recognized." *Lynch v. Household Fin. Corp.*, 405 U.S. 538, 552 (1972) (emphasis added). But see the famous (infamous, to some of us) footnote 4 in *United States v. Carolene Products Co.*, 304 U.S. 144, 152 n.4 (1938) (implying that economic and property rights are less fundamental than personal rights).

[22] Many definitions of the concept "rights" have been offered. See, e.g., Antony Flew, *A Dictionary of Philosophy*, rev'd 2d ed. (New York: St. Martin's Press, 1984), p. 306 (defining "rights"); idem, "What is a 'Right'?", *Georgia L. Rev.* 13 (1979): 1117–41; Alan Gewirth, "The Basis and Content of Human Rights," *Georgia L. Rev.* 13 (1979): 1143–70, at 1148; Wesley N. Hohfeld, *Fundamental Legal Conceptions as Applied in Judicial Reasoning*, W.W. Cook, ed. (New Haven, Conn.: Yale University Press, 1946), p. 30 *et passim* (discussing four senses of "rights" and explaining that a right is a three-term relation between a right-holder, a type of action, and one or more other persons); Albert Kocourek, *Jural Relations* (Indianapolis: Bobbs-Merrill, 1927), p. 7; Lomasky, *Persons, Rights, and the Moral Community*, p. 101; Machan, *Individuals and Their Rights*, pp. 1–2; Narveson, *The Libertarian Idea*, chap. 5; Nozick, Anarchy, State, and Utopia, pp. 29–30; Ayn Rand, "Man's Rights," in Rand, *The*

to *X*, and this enforceability is all that *A* requires in order to be secure in his right to *X*. For a rights-skeptic meaningfully to challenge *A*'s asserted right, the skeptic must challenge the *enforceability* of the right, instead of merely challenging the existence of the right. Nothing less will do. If the skeptic does not deny that *A*'s proposed enforcement of his purported right is legitimate, then the skeptic has not denied *A*'s right to *X*, because what it *means* to have a right is to be able to legitimately enforce it. If the skeptic maintains, then, that *A* has no right to *X*, indeed, no rights at all since there are no rights, the skeptic must also maintain that *A*'s enforcement of his purported right to *X* is not justified.

But the problem faced by the skeptic here is that he assumes that enforcement—that is, the use of force—*requires* justification. *A*, however, cares not that the rights-skeptic merely challenges *A*'s use of force against *B*. The rights-skeptic must do more than express his *preference* that *A* not enforce his right against *B*, for such an expression does not attack the legitimacy of *A*'s enforcing his right against *B*. The only way

---

Virtue of Selfishness, pp. 29–30; Rasmussen and Den Uyl, *Liberty and Nature*, p. 111. One of the clearest, non-tautological definitions of rights of which I am aware is Sadowsky's:

> When we say that one has the right to do certain things we mean this and only this, that it would be immoral for another, alone or in combination, to stop him from doing this by the use of physical force or the threat thereof. We do not mean that any use a man makes of his property within the limits set forth is necessarily a *moral* use.

James A. Sadowsky, "Private Property and Collective Ownership," in *The Libertarian Alternative*, Tibor R. Machan, ed. (Chicago: Nelson-Hall Co., 1974), pp. 120–21. Whatever the definition, however, it seems clear that the concept of rights and the concept of enforceability are mutually dependent in the sense discussed in the text.

Note: I now am of the view that rights are best viewed as metanorms that direct us as to which laws are just, not directly to personal behavior. Most libertarians would view rights as a subset of morality; not everything that is immoral should be illegal, but every rights violation is necessarily immoral. I believe the sets are intersecting sets only. Just as some immoral actions are not rights violations, some rights violations might be morally mandatory (breaking into a cabin to feed your baby in the middle of a storm). I do believe *most* rights violations are immoral, though libertarianism itself cannot make this determination. For more on rights as metanorms, see Douglas B. Rasmussen & Douglas J. Den Uyl, "Why Individual Rights? Rights as Metanormative Principles," in *Norms of Liberty: A Perfectionist Basis for Non-Perfectionist Politics* (Pennsylvania State University Press, 2005):

> An individual's right to liberty is thus not in essence a normative principle. Rather, it is a metanormative principle. In other words, it is concerned with the creation, interpretation, and justification of a political/legal context in which the possibility of the pursuit of flourishing is secured.

for the skeptic meaningfully to challenge *A*'s enforcement action is to acknowledge that *B* may use force to prevent *A*'s (illegitimate) enforcement action. And here the rights-skeptic (perversely) undercuts his own position, because by recognizing the legitimacy of *B*'s use of force against *A*, the rights-skeptic effectively attributes rights to *B* himself, the right not to have unjustifiable force used against him. In short, for anyone to meaningfully maintain that *A* has no rights against *B* on the grounds that no rights exist, he must effectively attribute rights to *B* so that *B* may defend himself against *A*'s purportedly unwarranted enforcement action.

More common-sensically, this demonstration points out the inconsistency on the part of a rights-skeptic who engages in discourse about the propriety of rights at all. If there are no rights, then there is no such thing as the justifiable or legitimate use of force, but neither is there such a thing as the unjust use of force. But if there is no unjust use of force, what is it, exactly, that a rights-skeptic is concerned about? If individuals delude themselves into thinking that they have natural rights, and, acting on this assumption, go about enforcing these rights as if they are true, the skeptic has no grounds to complain. To the extent the skeptic complains about people enforcing these illusory rights, he begins to attribute rights to those having force used against them. Any rights-skeptic can only shut up, because he contradicts himself the moment he objects to others' acting as if they have rights.[23]

---

[23] Indeed, another way to respond to a rights-skeptic would be to propose to physically harm him. If there are no rights, as he maintains, then he cannot object to being harmed. So, presumably, any rights-skeptic would change his position and admit there were rights (if only so as to be able to object to being harmed)—or there would soon be no more rights-skeptics left alive to give rights-advocates any guff. See also Murray Rothbard, "On the Duty of Natural Outlaws to Shut Up," *New Libertarian* (April 1985; https://mises.org/library/duty-natural-outlaws-shut):

> The nihilists remind me of the classic bore at college bull sessions: "Nyah, nyah, prove to me that this chair exists!" Trying desperately for "proof" accomplishes nothing, of course, to wipe the mocking smile off the face of the Outlaw. In a deep sense, and on many levels, the proper riposte is to hit the Outlaw over the head with the chair. For one thing, the purpose of philosophic discourse is, or should be, to arrive mutually at the truth, not to engage in parlor games or verbal fencing. To engage in such games, to be a bravura pest for pest's sake, is to put oneself outside the realm of rational discourse. (But this, of course, is a moral as well as factual statement!)

OTHER RATIONALIST-RELATED THEORIES

In addition to the three approaches discussed above, other arguments, which also point out the inherent presuppositions of discourse or action, are briefly discussed below.

G.B. Madison and Argumentation Ethics–Related Theorists

One approach that is similar to Hoppe's argumentation ethics is that of philosopher G.B. Madison. Madison argues that

> the various values defended by liberalism are not arbitrary, a matter of mere personal preference, nor do they derive from some natural law. … Rather, they are nothing less and nothing more than what could be called the *operative presuppositions* or intrinsic features and demands of communicative rationality itself. In other words, they are values that are implicitly recognized and affirmed by everyone by the very fact of their engaging in communicative reason. This amounts to saying that no one can rationally deny them without at the same time denying reason,

---

See also Hans-Hermann Hoppe, "In Defense of Extreme Rationalism," in *The Great Fiction: Property, Economy, Society, and the Politics of Decline* (Second Expanded Edition, Mises Institute, 2021; www.hanshoppe.com/tgf), p. 310:

> Why should we follow [McCloskey's] advice of paying attention to talk and not resorting to violence, particularly in view of the fact that what is advocated here is talk of the sort where anything goes and where everything said is just as good a candidate for one's attention as anything else? It certainly is not evident that one should pay much attention to talk if that is what talk is all about! Moreover, it would be downright fatal to follow this ethic. For any viable human ethic must evidently allow people to do things other than talk, if only to have a single human survivor who could possibly have any ethical questions; McCloskey's talk-ethic, however, gives us precisely such deadly advice of never to *stop* talking or stop listening to others talk. In addition, McCloskey himself and his fellow hermeneuticians must admit that they can have no objective ground for proposing their ethic anyway. For if there are no objective standards of truth, then it must also be the case that one's ethical proposals cannot claim to be objectively justifiable either. But what is wrong, then, with not being persuaded by all of this and, rather than listening further, hitting McCloskey on the head straightaway rather than waiting until he perishes from following his own prescription of endless talk? Clearly, if McCloskey were right, nothing could be said to be objectively wrong with this.

The arguments directed here against rights-skeptics also apply, *mutatis mutandis*, to radical pacifists—that is, to those who claim not just that pacifism is preferred morally or tactically, but that victims of aggression are not entitled to use force in self-defense or that victims somehow violate the rights of their aggressors.

without self-contradiction, without in fact abandoning all attempts to persuade the other and to reach agreement.[24]

These implicitly recognized values include a renunciation of the legitimacy of violence. Thus, "it is absolutely impossible for anyone who claims to be rational, which is to say human, outrightly to defend violence."[25]

Madison continues:

> [Paul] Ricoeur writes: "… *violence is the opposite of discourse.…* Violence is always the interruption of discourse: discourse is always the interruption of violence." That violence is the opposite of discourse means that it can never justify itself—and is therefore not justifiable—for only through discourse can anything be justified. As the theory of rational argumentation and discussion, liberalism amounts, therefore, to a rejection of power politics.[26]

---

[24] G.B. Madison, *The Logic of Liberty* (New York: Greenwood Press, 1986), p. 266.

[25] Ibid., p. 267. See also Kinsella, "Quotes on the Logic of Liberty," and n. 19, above. Madison and Hoppe both draw on the "discourse ethics" of Jürgen Habermas and Karl-Otto Apel. See, e.g., Jürgen Habermas, "Discourse Ethics: Notes on a Program of Philosophical Justification," and Karl-Otto Apel, "Is the Ethics of the Ideal Communication Community a Utopia? On the Relationship between Ethics, Utopia, and the Critique of Utopia," both in Seyla Benhabib & Fred Dallmayr, eds., *The Communicative Ethics Controversy* (Cambridge, Mass.: MIT Press, 1990). Douglas Rasmussen has criticized both Habermas's discourse ethics and Hoppe's argumentation ethics. *See* Douglas B. Rasmussen, "Political Legitimacy and Discourse Ethics," *International Philosophical Quarterly* 32 (1992; https://perma.cc/MK59-QEVV): 17–34 (on Habermas) and *idem*, "Arguing and Y-ing," *Liberty* 2, no. 2 (Nov. 1988; https://perma.cc/A5UU-P64A): 50 (on Hoppe). The latter article was part of a symposium, "Breakthrough or Buncombe" (pp. 44–53), containing discussion of Hoppe's argumentation ethics by several libertarian theorists, and Hoppe's reply, "Utilitarians and Randians *vs* Reason" (53–54). This reply and replies to other critics are included in "Appendix: Four Critical Replies" in Hoppe, *The Economics and Ethics of Private Property*; see also subsequent response to critics in *idem*, "PFP163 | Hans Hermann Hoppe, 'On The Ethics of Argumentation' (PFS 2016)."

[26] Madison, *The Logic of Liberty*, pp. 267 & 274, n. 37 (quoting Paul Ricoeur, *Main Trends in Philosophy* (New York: Holmes and Meier, 1979), pp. 226–76). Madison also notes that Frank Knight made a similar point. Madison quotes Knight's statement, in his book *Freedom and Reform* (Indianapolis: Liberty Press, 1982), pp. 473–74, that:
> The only "proof" that can be offered for the validity of the liberal position is that we are discussing it and its acceptance is a presupposition of discussion, since discussion is the essence of the position itself. From this point of view, the core of liberalism is a faith in the ultimate potential equality of men as the basis of democracy.
See also Frank H. Knight, *On the History and Method of Economics* (Chicago: University of Chicago Press, 1956), p. 268; Kinsella, "Quotes on the Logic of Liberty."

Madison, like Hoppe, argues that the fact-value gap can be bridged by an appeal to the nature of discourse:

> the notion of *universal human rights and liberties* is not an … arbitrary value, a matter of mere personal preference…. On the contrary, it is nothing less and nothing more than the operative presupposition or intrinsic feature and demand of communicative rationality itself.[27]

In a sense, notes Madison, Thomas Jefferson was not so far off in calling our rights "self-evident."

The general thrust of Madison's argument seems sound, although it is not as consistent or fully developed as Hoppe's argumentation ethics. While Hoppe shows that the nonaggression principle (i.e., self-ownership plus the right to homestead external resources) itself is directly implied by any discourse or argumentation, Madison's train of logic seems more muddled. For instance, he argues that, because discourse has "priority" over violence, this validates the Kantian claim that people ought to be treated as ends rather than means, which is the principle of human dignity. The principle of freedom from coercion then follows from the principle of human dignity. Madison does not specify in any more detail than this the libertarian principles that can be derived from such an approach,[28] although, to be fair, Madison stresses that his remarks are intended only "to indicate the way in which liberalism must seek to" defend the values it advocates.[29]

Frank van Dun similarly suggests that part of "the ethics of dialogue" is that we ought to respect the "dialogical rights of others—their right to speak or not to speak, to listen or not to listen, to use their own judgment."[30] Van Dun argues that "principles of private property and uncoerced exchange" are also presupposed by participants in discourse

---

[27] Madison, *The Logic of Liberty*, p. 269.
[28] Madison does maintain that the supreme "ought" or demand of liberalism is "that conflicts of interest and differences of opinion should be resolved through free, open, peaceful discussion aimed at consensus and not by recourse to force." Ibid., p. 266.
[29] Ibid., pp. 269–70.
[30] Frank van Dun, "Economics and the Limits of Value-Free Science," *Reason Papers* 11 (Spring 1986): 24; see also *idem*, "On the Philosophy of Argument and the Logic of Common Morality," in *Argumentation: Approaches to Theory Formation*, E.M. Barth & J.L. Martens, eds. (Amsterdam: John Benjamins, 1982), p. 281; *idem*, "Argumentation Ethics and The Philosophy of Freedom."

and later defended Hoppe's argumentation ethics.[31] Jeremy Shearmur also proposes[32] that a Habermasian argument may be developed to justify individual property rights and other classical liberal principles, although this argument is different in approach from that of Hoppe, Madison, and Van Dun, and is, in my view, much weaker than Hoppe's approach.[33]

Other theories that are briefly worth mentioning here include Paul Chevigny's theory that the nature of discourse may be used to defend the right to free speech[34] and Tibor Machan's view that discourse in general and political dialogue in particular rest on individualist prerequisites or presuppositions.[35]

---

[31] Van Dun, "Economics and the Limits of Value-Free Science," p. 28; *idem*, "Argumentation Ethics and The Philosophy of Freedom."

[32] Jeremy Shearmur, "Habermas: A Critical Approach," *Critical Review* 2 (1988): 39–50, at 47; see also *idem*, "From Dialogue Rights to Property Rights: Foundations for Hayek's Legal Theory," *Critical Review* 4 (1990): 106–32.

[33] See also Shearmur, "From Dialogue Rights to Property Rights," pp. 106–32.

[34] See Paul G. Chevigny, "Philosophy of Language and Free Expression," *N.Y. U. L. Rev.* 55 (1980): 157–94; Michael Martin, "On a New Argument for Freedom of Speech," *N.Y. U. L. Rev.* 57 (1982): 906–19; Paul G. Chevigny, "The Dialogic Right of Free Expression: A Reply to Michael Martin," *N.Y. U. L. Rev.* 57 (1982): 920–31. See also Rodney J. Blackman, "There is There There: Defending the Defenseless with Procedural Natural Law," *Ariz. L. Rev.* 37 (1995): 285–353, which defends a procedural natural-law position on the grounds that, as we normally use language and define "law," "law" has a procedural component that, if adhered to, limits a government's arbitrary and irrational use of power. Blackman contends that language users implicitly accept this normative, procedural aspect of what is described as law; they use a definition of law that also limits what state power can be classified as law. Of course, H.L.A. Hart argues that some types of rules or arbitrary commands enforced by a given regime are too unlawlike to be considered even positive law. See Hart, *The Concept of Law*, chap. II, §2; chap. IX, §3. A somewhat similar argument may be found in Randy E. Barnett, "Getting Normative, the Role of Natural Rights in Constitutional Adjudication," *Constitutional Commentary* 12 (1995; www.randybarnett.com/pre-2000): 93–122, where Barnett argues that those who claim that the U.S. Constitution justifies certain government regulation of individuals are themselves introducing normative claims into discourse, and thus cannot object, on positivist or *wertfrei* grounds, to a moral or normative criticism of their position. See also *idem*, "The Intersection of Natural Rights and Positive Constitutional Law," *Connecticut L. Rev.* 25 (1993; www.randybarnett.com/pre-2000): 853–68.

[35] Tibor R. Machan, "Individualism and Political Dialogue," *Poznan Studies in the Philosophy of Science and the Humanities* 46 (June 1996; https://www.stephankinsella.com/wp-content/uploads/texts/machan_dialogue.pdf): 45–55. Several other related theories are mentioned in "The Undeniable Morality of Capitalism" (ch. 22), n.29, e.g. Lawrence B. Solum, "Freedom of Communicative Action: A Theory of the First Amendment Freedom

Murray Rothbard, who was very enthusiastic about Hoppe's argumentation ethics, was also hopeful that Hoppe's argumentation ethics
or axiomatic approach could be further extended. As Rothbard stated:

> A future research program for Hoppe and other libertarian philosophers
> would be (a) to see how far axiomatics can be extended into other spheres
> of ethics, or (b) to see if and how this axiomatic could be integrated into
> the standard natural law approach.[36]

The various perspectives of Hoppe, Madison, Van Dun, and others
on a similar theme indicate that Rothbard may indeed be correct that
this type of rationalist thinking can be further extended in libertarian
or ethical theory.[37]

---

of Speech," *Northwestern U. L. Rev.* 83 (1989; https://scholarship.law.georgetown.edu/
facpub/1954/): 54–135.

[36] Rothbard, "Beyond Is and Ought," p. 45. For some efforts in this direction, see
Konrad Graf, "Action-Based Jurisprudence: Praxeological Legal Theory in Relation to
Economic Theory, Ethics, and Legal Practice," *Libertarian Papers* 3, art. no. 19 (2011;
http://libertarianpapers.org/19-action-based-jurisprudence-praxeological-legal-theory-
relation-economic-theory-ethics-legal-practice/). See also Kinsella, "Extreme Praxeology,"
StephanKinsella.com (Jan. 19, 2007). Van Dun also seems to have a somewhat broader
conception of the normative or moral implications of discourse ethics than Hoppe explores
in his argumentation ethics. See Van Dun, "Argumentation Ethics and the Philosophy
of Freedom."

[37] Madison notes that "it should be possible to derive in a strictly systematic fashion all
of the ... universal values" necessary to defend liberalism. Madison, *The Logic of Liberty*, p.
268. Concerning extending Hoppe's discourse ethics to natural law, it should be pointed
out that both Hoppe and Madison appear skeptical of the validity of classic natural law
theory. Madison states that rights are not "a requirement of some natural law existing independently of the reasoning process and discernible only by metaphysical insight into the
'nature of things'" (p. 269); Hoppe states, as noted in text at note 11, above: "It has been a
common quarrel with the natural rights position, even on the part of sympathetic readers,
that the concept of human nature is far 'too diffuse and varied to provide a determinate set
of contents of natural law'"; see also notes 10–14, above, and accompanying text; and "The
Undeniable Morality of Capitalism" (ch. 22). However, Machan, accepting the validity of
action-based ethical theories (similar to Pilon's and Gewirth's approach, discussed below),
but not purely-argumentation-based theories, also maintains that "human action needs
to be understood by reference to human nature." Machan, "Individualism and Political
Dialogue," p. 46. See also more of the quote by Machan in note 46 below.

Crocker's Moral Estoppel Theory

In a theory bearing some resemblance to the estoppel theory discussed above, law professor Lawrence Crocker proposes the use of "moral estoppel" in preventing a criminal from asserting the unfairness of being punished in certain situations. Crocker's theory, while interesting, is not rigorous, and Crocker does not seem to realize the implications of estoppel for justifying only the *libertarian* conception of rights. Rather than focusing on the reciprocity between the force used in punishment and the force of an aggressive act by a wrongdoer, Crocker claims that a person who has "treated another person or the society at large in a fashion that the criminal law prohibits" is "morally estopped" from asserting that his punishment would be unfair.[38] However, Crocker's use of estoppel is too vague and imprecise, and relies on a legal positivist conception of law, for just because one has violated a criminal law does not mean that one has committed the aggression that is necessary to estop him from complaining about punishment. A breached law must first be legitimate (just) for Crocker's assumption to hold, but as the estoppel theory indicates, a law is legitimate only if it prohibits aggression. Crocker's theory seems to assume that any law is valid, even those that do not prohibit the initiation of force.

Pilon and Gewirth on the Principle of Generic Consistency

Another rights theory that bears mention here is that of Roger Pilon. Pilon has developed a libertarian version of the theory propounded by his teacher Alan Gewirth.[39] Although he disagrees with the non-libertarian conclusions that Gewirth draws from his own rights theory, Pilon builds "upon much of the justificatory groundwork he [Gewirth] has

---

[38] Lawrence Crocker, "The Upper Limit of Just Punishment," *Emory L. J.* 41 (1992): 1059–1110, at 1067.

[39] See Roger A. Pilon, "Ordering Rights Consistently: Or What We Do and Do Not Have Rights To," *Georgia L. Rev.* 13 (1979; https://perma.cc/FYX4-CFNH): 1171–96; *idem, A Theory of Rights: Toward Limited Government* (Ph.D. dissertation, University of Chicago, 1979; https://perma.cc/DGS3-W4UA). See also Alan Gewirth, *Moral Rationality* (The Lindley Lecture, Univ. of Kansas, 1972; https://core.ac.uk/download/pdf/213402925. pdf); also *idem*, "The Basis and Content of Human Rights," and *idem*, *Reason and Morality* (Chicago: University of Chicago Press, 1978).

134 | PART 2: Rights

established, for I believe he has located, drawn together, and solved some of the most basic problems in the theory of rights."[40]

To determine what rights we have, Pilon (following Gewirth) focuses on "what it is we necessarily claim about ourselves, if only implicitly, when we act."[41] Pilon argues that all action is *conative*, that is, an agent acts voluntarily and for purposes which seem good to him. Pilon argues that the prerequisites of successful action are "voluntariness and purposiveness," the so-called generic features that characterize all action. Thus, an agent cannot help valuing these generic features and even making a rights-claim to them, according to Pilon/Gewirth. From this conclusion, it is argued that all agents also necessarily claim rights against coercion and harm. And since it would be inconsistent to maintain that one has rights for these reasons without also admitting that others have these rights too (since the reasoning concerning the nature of action applies equally to all purposive actors), such rights-claims must be universalizable.[42] As Gewirth writes, the

> voluntariness and purposiveness which every agent necessarily has in acting, and which he necessarily claims as rights for himself on the ground that he is a prospective agent who wants to fulfill his purposes, he must also, on pain of self-contradiction, admit to be rights of his recipient.[43]

Thus, an agent in any action makes a rights-claim to be free from coercion and harm, since such rights are necessary to provide for the generic features of action, which an agent also necessarily values, and the agent also necessarily grants these rights to others because of the universalizability requirement.

---

[40] Pilon, "Ordering Rights Consistently," p. 1173.

[41] Ibid., p. 1177.

[42] Ibid., p. 1179.

[43] Gewirth, *Moral Rationality*, p. 20. On universalizability, see also Kinsella, "The problem of particularistic ethics or, why everyone really has to admit the validity of the universalizability principle," *StephanKinsella.com* (Nov. 10, 2011); Hoppe, *A Theory of Socialism and Capitalism*, p. 157 and n. 119 *et pass.*; Hare, *Freedom and Reason*, § 11.6 ("It is part of the meanings of … moral words that we are logically prohibited from making different moral judgements about two cases, when we cannot adduce any difference between the cases which is the ground for the difference in moral judgements"). See also "What Libertarianism Is" (ch. 2), the section "Self-ownership and Conflict Avoidance"; "How We Come to Own Ourselves" (ch. 4), n.15; and "A Libertarian Theory of Punishment and Rights" (ch. 5), Part III.D.2.

From this point, Pilon/Gewirth develops a sort of modern categorical imperative, which is called the "Principle of Generic Consistency" (PGC). The PGC is: "Act in accord with the generic rights of your recipients as well as of yourself," and "Recipients are those who stand opposite agents, who are 'affected by' or 'recipients of' their actions."[44] Under Pilon's libertarian working of the PGC:

> [T]he PGC does not require anyone to *do* anything. It is addressed to agents, but it does not require anyone to be an agent who has recipients. An individual can "do nothing" if he chooses, spending his life in idle contemplation. Provided there are no recipients of this behavior, he is at perfect liberty to perform it. And if there are recipients, the PGC requires only that he act in accord with the generic rights of those recipients, *i.e.*, that he not coerce or harm them.[45]

Pilon extends his reasoning and works the PGC to flesh out more fully just what (primarily libertarian) rights we do have.

All this is well done, except for one crucial error. As Hoppe points out, it is *argumentation*, not action, that is the appropriate starting point for such an analysis, because:

> [F]rom the correctly stated fact that in action an agent must, by necessity, presuppose the existence of certain values or goods, it does not follow that such goods then are universalizable and hence should be respected by others as the agent's goods by right.... Rather, the idea of truth, or of universalizable rights or goods only emerges with argumentation as a special subclass of actions, but not with action as such, as is clearly revealed by the fact that Gewirth, too, is not engaged simply in action, but more specifically in argumentation when he wants to convince us of the necessary truth of his ethical system.[46]

---

44 Ibid., p. 1184.
45 Ibid.
46 Hoppe, *The Economics and Ethics of Private Property*, pp. 315–16, n. 18. For further criticism and discussion of the Gewirthian argument, see Machan, *Individuals and Their Rights*, pp. 197–99; Alisdair MacIntyre, *After Virtue* (Notre Dame, Ind.: University of Notre Dame Press, 1981), pp. 64–65; Henry Veatch, *Human Rights: Fact or Fancy?* (Baton Rouge: Louisiana State University Press, 1985), pp. 159–60; and Jan Narveson, "Gewirth's *Reason and Morality*: A Study in the Hazards of Universalizability in Ethics," *Dialogue* 19 (1980): 651–74. Perhaps somewhat ironically, given his criticisms of Gewirth, Machan seems to agree with Gewirth/Pilon on this issue rather than Hoppe, claiming that

> [D]iscourse is not primary. Instead, it is human action itself that is primary, with discourse being only one form of human action. It is the presuppositions of human

It is possible that, despite this error, much of Pilon's work is salvageable by, in effect, moving it to an argumentation context, such as is done in the estoppel approach where an aggressor must engage in argumentation to object to his punishment and is therefore subject to the unique constraints of argumentation. In other words, the weak link in Pilon's PGC chain may be able to be repaired by considering claims made *about* prior actions when the agent later objects to punishment, for an objection to being punished requires the agent to enter into the special subclass action of argumentation, to which criteria such as universalizability do apply.

CONCLUSION

Under the three theories outlined above—argumentation ethics, estoppel theory, and the self-contradictions of rights-skeptics—we can see that the relevant participant in discourse cannot deny the validity of individual rights. These rationalist-oriented theories offer very good defenses of individual rights, defenses that are more powerful than many other approaches, because they show that the opponent of individual rights, whether criminal, skeptic, or socialist, presupposes that they are true. Critics must enter the cathedral of libertarianism even to deny that it exists. This makes criticism of libertarian beliefs hollow: for if someone asks why we believe in individual rights, we can tell them to look in the mirror and find the answer there.

---

action that require certain political principles to be respected and protected. And human action needs to be understood by reference to human nature.

Machan, "Individualism and Political Dialogue," p. 45. In my view, Hoppe's criticisms of Pilon/Gewirth, as well as his criticism of classical natural rights arguments (see note 37, above), applies also to Machan.

7

Defending Argumentation Ethics

This chapter is based on an article originally published in 2002 on the now-defunct site *Anti-state.com*, as a response to an article by Robert P. Murphy and Gene Callahan (hereinafter, MC), on the same forum, which was critical of Hoppe's argumentation ethics.[*]

I intend here to provide a short guide to the relevant literature followed by a limited response to MC's critique of Hans-Hermann Hoppe's argumentation ethics.

---

[*] My article was "Defending Argumentation Ethics: Reply to Murphy & Callahan," *Anti-state.com* (Sept. 19, 2002), which is thesis of this chapter. It was a response to Robert P. Murphy & Gene Callahan, "Hans-Hermann Hoppe's Argumentation Ethic: A Critique," *Anti-state.com* (Sept. 19, 2002; archived at https://tinyurl.com/5n62x6zc and https://perma.cc/D395-3JSW). The original links for both our pieces are bad (as this was a *libertarian* publication, 'natch) but MC later published a substantially similar version of their article as "Hans-Hermann Hoppe's Argumentation Ethic: A Critique," *J. Libertarian Stud.* 20, no. 2 (Spring 2006; https://mises.org/library/hans-hermann-hoppes-argumentation-ethic-critique): 53–64. In the later version of their paper they did not respond to my critique. As their earlier paper is no longer online, in this chapter I will reference the later article for quotes and page citations, and sometimes with in-line citations.

I later debated my longtime friend Bob Murphy, whose work I greatly respect and admire, on this topic. See Kinsella, "KOL278 | Bob Murphy Show: Debating Hans Hoppe's 'Argumentation Ethics," *Kinsella on Liberty Podcast* (Nov. 24, 2019).

See also various responses to MC and other criticisms of Hoppe, cited in "Dialogical Arguments for Libertarian Rights" (ch. 6), n.15, including Frank van Dun, "Argumentation Ethics and the Philosophy of Freedom," *Libertarian Papers* 1, art. no. 19 (2009; www.libertarianpapers.org); Marian Eabrasu, "A Reply to the Current Critiques Formulated

BACKGROUND

Hoppe published several pieces expounding his "argumentation ethics" defense of libertarian rights, including "The Ultimate Justification of the Private Property Ethic" in *Liberty* magazine in 1988,[1] which resulted in a large number of commentaries from several libertarian thinkers.[2] Over the next few years, Hoppe's theory was intensely debated and commented on by several libertarians. Several replies and reviews, for example, were published in *Liberty* and elsewhere, by libertarians such as Murray Rothbard, David Gordon, Tibor Machan, David Friedman, Loren Lomasky, David Osterfeld, Sheldon Richman, Leland Yeager,

---

Against Hoppe's Argumentation Ethics," Libertarian Papers 1, art. no. 20 (2009; www. libertarianpapers.org); Walter Block, "Rejoinder to Murphy and Callahan on Hoppe's Argumentation Ethics," *J. Libertarian Stud.* 22, no. 1 (2011; https://mises.org/library/ rejoinder-murphy-and-callahan-hoppes-argumentation-ethics): 631–39; and Norbert Slenzok, "The Libertarian Argumentation Ethics, the Transcendental Pragmatics of Language, and the Conflict-Freedom Principle," *Analiza i Egzystencja* 58 (2022), 35–64. Hoppe re-presented his argument and responded to a variety of critics in his 2016 speech, at "PFP163 | Hans Hermann Hoppe, 'On The Ethics of Argumentation' (PFS 2016)," *The Property and Freedom Podcast*, ep. 163 (June 30, 2022) (which includes a transcript).

---

[1] See Hans-Hermann Hoppe, "The Ultimate Justification of the Private Property Ethic," *Liberty* 2, no. 1 (Sept. 1988; https://perma.cc/6TYM-BJRZ): 20–22, republished as "On the Ultimate Justification of the Ethics of Private Property," ch. 13 in Hoppe, *The Economics and Ethics of Private Property: Studies in Political Economy and Philosophy* (Auburn, Ala.: Mises Institute, 2006 [1993]; www.hanshoppe.com/eepp). See also Hoppe, "From the Economics of Laissez Faire to the Libertarianism" and "The Justice of Economic Efficiency," chaps. 11–12 in *The Economics and Ethics of Private Property*; *idem*, "The Ethical Justification of Capitalism and Why Socialism Is Morally Indefensible," in *A Theory of Socialism and Capitalism: Economics, Politics, and Ethics* (Auburn, Ala.: Mises Institute, 2010 [1989]; www.hanshoppe.com/tsc); and later pieces such as *idem*, "Of Common, Public, and Private Property and the Rationale for Total Privatization," in *The Great Fiction: Property, Economy, Society, and the Politics of Decline* (Second Expanded Edition, Mises Institute, 2021; www.hanshoppe.com/tgf). I discuss argumentation ethics in "Dialogical Arguments for Libertarian Rights" (ch. 6); "The Undeniable Morality of Capitalism" (ch. 22); Kinsella, "Argumentation Ethics and Liberty: A Concise Guide," *StephanKinsella.com* (May 27, 2011); and *idem*, "Hoppe's Argumentation Ethics and Its Critics," *StephanKinsella.com* (Aug. 11, 2015).

[2] See the symposium "Breakthrough or Buncombe," *Liberty* 2, no. 2 (Nov. 1988; https:// perma.cc/A5UU-P64A): 44–53.

David Ramsay Steele, Douglas Rasmussen, David Conway, and others. Hoppe responded to many of these pieces at length.[3]

Several of the replies to Hoppe were unusually nasty and unfair. Some were shocked anyone would argue for "untrammeled anarchism" and others were turned off by the idea that libertarian rights could be rigorously proved.[4] Others badly misconstrued Hoppe's argument. Still others, like Rothbard, recognized that Hoppe's theory was a revolutionary advance in libertarian theory, as have a growing number of adherents over the years. As Rothbard wrote:

> In a dazzling breakthrough for political philosophy in general and for libertarianism in particular, he [Hoppe] has managed to transcend the famous is/ought, fact/value dichotomy that has plagued philosophy since the days of the scholastics, and that had brought modern libertarianism into a tiresome deadlock. Not only that: Hans Hoppe has managed to establish the case for anarcho-capitalist, Lockean rights in an unprecedentedly hard-core manner, one that makes my own natural law/natural rights position seem almost wimpy in comparison.[5]

---

3 See Hoppe, "Appendix: Four Critical Replies," in *The Economics and Ethics of Private Property*; see also *idem*, "PFP163 | Hans Hermann Hoppe, 'On The Ethics of Argumentation' (PFS 2016)." See also references in note *, above.

4 See, e.g., Loren Lomasky, "The Argument from Mere Argument," *Liberty* 3, no. 1 (Sept. 1989; https://perma.cc/38XS-ZDEL): 55–57; Hoppe's reply, "Intimidation by Argument— Once Again," *Liberty* 3, no. 2 (Nov. 1989; https://perma.cc/4382-RKSQ): 37–39, republished as "Intimidation by Argument" section III in "Appendix: Four Critical Replies" (to Lomasky's complaint that Hoppe's treatise is "no less than a manifesto for untrammeled anarchism," Hoppe responds, "Only someone advocating the trammeling of private property rights would take offense"); and Rothbard's response to Lomasky, "Hoppephobia," originally published in *Liberty* 3, no. 4 (March 1990; https://perma.cc/JT7K-YTUJ): 11–12, reprinted at *LewRockwell.com* (Oct. 4, 2014; https://perma.cc/5HH6-2P78):
 [Lomasky] is shocked and stunned that Hoppe is not simply a defender of existing capitalism; his book is "no less than a manifesto for untrammeled anarchism." Well, heavens to Betsy! Anarchism! One wonders where Lomasky has been for the last 20 years! Perhaps the knowledge has not yet penetrated to the fastnesses of Minnesota, but anarchism has been a vibrant part of the libertarian dialogue for a long time, as most readers of *Liberty* well know.
5 Murray N. Rothbard, "Beyond Is and Ought," *Liberty* 2, no. 2 (Nov. 1988; https://perma.cc/8LZR-DN6Y; also https://mises.org/library/beyond-and-ought): 44–45, 44. The hapless Leland Yeager later dishonestly tried to claim that Rothbard disavowed his earlier support for Hoppe's argumentation ethics before his death. See "Dialogical Arguments for Libertarian Rights" (ch. 6), n.15. Yeager was also confused about self-ownership and knowledge and the calculation problem. On the former, see "How We Come to Own Ourselves" (ch. 4), n.1; regarding the latter issue, see "Legislation and the Discovery of Law

Since the original article upon which this chapter is based was published, there have been many more contributions expanding on and defending Hoppe's argumentation ethics. In the years since Hoppe's theory was first published, several scholars have worked to defend, clarify and extend it.[6] I have also commented and built on Hoppe's work in my own writing.[7]

To fully appreciate Hoppe's argument and to fairly evaluate MC's critique, I suggest reading Hoppe's own work[8] and various secondary sources.[9]

LIBERTARIAN RIGHTS

The central question here is: does Hoppe's theory establish that there are libertarian rights?

Scarce (conflictable) resources are those things over which there can be conflict; two or more individuals may want to use or control a given scarce resource at the same time, but only one of them can, because use by one excludes use by the other. Thus, as Hoppe explains, a theory of interpersonal ethics must be a theory of property rights, "a theory of the assignment of rights of exclusive control over scarce

---

in a Free Society" (ch. 13), at n.66. See also "The Undeniable Morality of Capitalism" (ch. 22), n.2, criticizing Yeager.

6 See Kinsella, "Argumentation Ethics and Liberty: A Concise Guide."

7 See, e.g., "Dialogical Arguments for Libertarian Rights" (ch. 6); "The Undeniable Morality of Capitalism" (ch. 22); "A Libertarian Theory of Punishment and Rights" (ch. 5); also Kinsella, "Argumentation Ethics and Liberty: A Concise Guide."

8 A good starting point would be: chapters 1 and 2 of *A Theory of Socialism and Capitalism* (discussing notions of scarcity, aggression, property, norms, and justification); chap. 7 of *A Theory of Socialism and Capitalism*, "The Ethical Justification of Capitalism and Why Socialism Is Morally Indefensible" (esp. pp. 154–71); "Appendix: Four Critical Replies"; and "PFP163 | Hans Hermann Hoppe, 'On The Ethics of Argumentation' (PFS 2016)." See also related material in Kinsella, "Argumentation Ethics and Liberty: A Concise Guide."

9 In particular, some of the works cited in "Dialogical Arguments for Libertarian Rights" (ch. 6), n.15, including Van Dun, "Argumentation Ethics and the Philosophy of Freedom"; Eabrasu, "A Reply to the Current Critiques Formulated Against Hoppe's Argumentation Ethics"; Block, "Rejoinder to Murphy and Callahan on Hoppe's Argumentation Ethics"; and Slenzok, "The Libertarian Argumentation Ethics, the Transcendental Pragmatics of Language, and the Conflict-Freedom Principle." See also Kinsella, "Hoppe's Argumentation Ethics and Its Critics."

means."[10] The purpose of rights is to specify which individual has the right to control a given scarce resource, so that conflicts may be avoided. The person who has the right to control a given scarce resource—its owner—is the person who is *justified* in using the resource, in excluding others, and in enforcing this exclusion against non-owners who would act in disregard of the owner's property rights.

Everyone has at least an implicit view of rights. An aggressor—or at least one who would try to justify his aggression—maintains that he is entitled to a given scarce resource "because" he is strong enough to take it. Others, such as socialists, believe that the state is entitled to the means of production "because"—well, because they are the state, "because" capitalists "exploit" workers, and so on. Mainstream liberal-democratic types believe that, for example, the poor are entitled to property formerly owned by the not-poor, "because" the property is transferred from the latter to the former by means of a democratic process, which is "legitimate." Everyone assigns each disputed scarce resource to *some* owner—whether to a thief, the state, or a relatively-poor "needy" person—for *some* reason.

The libertarian view is that each person presumptively owns his own body, and for other, previously-unowned resources, the owner is determined in accordance with the principles of original appropriation and contractual title transfer. Thus, under libertarianism, an individual has (a) a right to the exclusive control of the scarce resource of his body, sometimes called "self-ownership"; and (b) a right to the exclusive control of other, previously-unowned scarce resources that are originally appropriated by the individual or by his ancestor-in-title.[11]

---

[10] Hoppe, *A Theory of Socialism and Capitalism*, p. 158 n.120; also p. 18 *et pass*. See also Kinsella, "On Conflictability and Conflictable Resources," *StephanKinsella.com* (Jan. 31, 2022); Hoppe, "Of Common, Public, and Private Property and the Rationale for Total Privatization." See also Kinsella, "KOL259 | "How To Think About Property", New Hampshire Liberty Forum 2019," *Kinsella on Liberty Podcast* (Feb. 9, 2019), and "Selling Does Not Imply Ownership, and Vice-Versa: A Dissection" (ch. 11).

[11] For more on this, see "What Libertarianism Is" (ch. 2), at n.4 et pass. For my attempt at a concise formulation of the libertarian view on self-ownership and external property rights, see Stephan Kinsella, "Aggression and Property Rights Plank in the Libertarian Party Platform," *StephanKinsella.com* (May 30, 2022). See also references in "How We Come To Own Ourselves" (ch. 4), n.6.

So the question is, does Hoppe's theory establish that the libertarian view of rights, as opposed to competing views, is the correct one?

HOPPE'S THEORY: LET'S TRY AGAIN

I do not intend here to restate Hoppe's entire argument, as I believe it has been adequately explicated and defended already by Hoppe in the literature referenced above. And he has already replied to numerous criticisms, including arguments similar to those leveled by MC.[12] Instead, I will try to show, as simply as possible, why Hoppe succeeds. I'll then address, in view of this, a few of MC's concrete critiques, but it should be clear by this point why I think their criticism is off base.

Hoppe starts by noting that if any proposed theory of rights is going to be justified, it has to be justified in the course of an argument (discourse). As Hoppe writes:

> Whether or not persons have any rights and, if so, which ones, can only be decided in the course of argumentation (propositional exchange). Justification—proof, conjecture, refutation—is *argumentative* justification. Anyone who denied this proposition would become involved in a performative contradiction because his denial would itself constitute an argument. Even an ethical relativist must accept this first proposition, which has been referred to as the *a priori of argumentation.*[13]

---

[12] See Hoppe, "PFP163 | Hans Hermann Hoppe, 'On The Ethics of Argumentation' (PFS 2016)"; *idem,* "Appendix: Four Critical Replies." See also references in note *, above.

[13] Hoppe, *The Economics and Ethics of Private Property,* p. 384. *See also idem, A Theory of Socialism and Capitalism,* pp. 154–55:

> [I]t must be presupposed of *any* intellectual position, that it is meaningful and can be argued with regard to its cognitive value, simply because it is presented in a language and communicated. To argue otherwise would already implicitly admit its validity. One is forced, then, to accept a rationalist approach towards ethics for the very same reason that one was forced to adopt a rationalist instead of an empiricist epistemology....
> The above argument shows us that any truth claim—the claim connected with any proposition that it is true, objective, or valid (all terms used synonymously here)— is and must be raised and decided upon in the course of an argumentation. And since it cannot be disputed that this is so (one cannot communicate and argue that one cannot communicate and argue), and it must be assumed that everyone knows what it means to claim something to be true (one cannot deny this statement

I fail to see how MC can disagree with this without falling into contradiction. It follows that if any norms, ethics, facts, or rules of discourse are *necessarily presupposed* by participants in argumentation simply by virtue of arguing, then no theory that contradicts these presupposed facts or norms could ever be justified. By contrast, any proposed theory that is consistent with, indeed implied by, these presuppositions, would have to be seen as irrefutably justified. This type of reasoning is called the "apriori of communication and argumentation," and was pioneered by German philosophers Jürgen Habermas (Hoppe's PhD advisor) and Karl-Otto Apel, although, unlike Hoppe's approach, this method was applied by them to reach non-libertarian (social-democratic) results.

And there certainly are norms presupposed by argumentative justification as such. As Hoppe writes,

> [A]rguing never just consists of free-floating propositions claiming to be true. Rather, argumentation is always an activity, too. But given that truth claims are raised and decided upon in argumentation and that argumentation, aside from whatever is said in its course, is a practical affair, it follows that intersubjectively meaningful norms must exist—precisely those which make some action an argumentation—which have special cognitive status in that they are the practical preconditions of objectivity and truth.
>
> Hence, one reaches the conclusion that norms must indeed be assumed to be justifiable as valid. It is simply impossible to argue otherwise, because the ability to argue so would in fact presuppose the validity of those norms which underlie any argumentation whatsoever. [14]

Again, I fail to see how MC can disagree with any of this, in general. Rather, the disagreement is over what norms are actually implicit in the activity of argumention—that is, over what participants in discourse *must presuppose to be true* in order to participate in argumentation. Whatever these presuppositions are, they rule out of court any proposed norms inconsistent with them. And, any such normative presuppositions, or norms deduced from these presuppositions, would have to be considered to be ultimately and irrefutably justified, as their validity could never be coherently denied.

---

without claiming its negation to be true), this has been aptly called "the a priori of communication and argumentation."

[14] Hoppe, *A Theory of Socialism and Capitalism*, p. 155.

UNIVERSALIZABILITY

So let's see what Hoppe contends. First, any norm proposed in argumentation is presumed to be *universalizable*. Writes Hoppe:

> Quite commonly it has been observed that argumentation implies that a proposition claims *universal* acceptability, or, should it be a norm proposal, that it is "universalizable." Applied to norm proposals, this is the idea, as formulated in the Golden Rule of ethics or in the Kantian Categorical Imperative, that only those norms can be justified that can be formulated as general principles which are valid for everyone without exception.[15]

In other words, any proposed norm—that is, an attempted justification for a given action—is not justified if it is not universalizable. This rule is presupposed by the very attempt to argumentatively justify something, because "argumentation implies that everyone who can understand an argument must in principle be able to be convinced of it *simply because of its argumentative force.*" Because the universalizability principle is an inherent feature of argumentation in general, "the universalization principle of ethics can now be understood and explained as grounded in the wider 'apriori of communication and argumentation.'"[16] I.e., no one can deny that only universalizable norms can be justified.[17]

So, we have our first presupposition: that only universalizable ethics can be possible candidates for being justified.[18] By the same token, so-called "particularizable" norms are not justifiable. However:

---

[15] Ibid., p. 157.

[16] Ibid.

[17] See also Kinsella, "The problem of particularistic ethics or, why everyone really has to admit the validity of the universalizability principle," *StephanKinsella.com* (Nov. 10, 2011); "What Libertarianism Is" (ch. 2), the section "Self-ownership and Conflict Avoidance"; "How We Come to Own Ourselves" (ch. 4), n.15; "A Libertarian Theory of Punishment and Rights" (ch. 5), Part III.D.2; and "Dialogical Arguments for Libertarian Rights" (ch. 6), n.43 and accompanying text.

[18] Murphy *appears* to concede this point that universalizability is an undeniable requirement for normative justification; he simply thinks it isn't useful. In the informal discussion on *Anti-state.com* following my original response article, there was this exchange:

> Kinsella: "No one, that I can see, has been *denying* that fundamental moral principles should be universalizable."
> Murphy: "*Right*. All I (and I think Gene) have argued is that 'universalizability' doesn't really help much in deciding between concrete systems. At a formal level, socialism doesn't imply 'I have the right to hit you but you don't have the right to hit me' anymore than capitalism does. Socialism really says, 'I have the right to hit you

[T]he universalization principle only provides a purely formal criterion for morality. To be sure, checked against this criterion all proposals for valid norms which would specify different rules for different classes of people could be shown to have no legitimate claim of being universally acceptable as fair norms, unless the distinction between different classes of people were such that it implied no discrimination, but could instead be accepted as founded in the nature of things again by everyone. But while some norms might not pass the test of universalization, if enough attention were paid to their formulation, the most ridiculous norms, and what is of course even more relevant, even openly incompatible norms could easily and equally well pass it. For example, "everybody must get drunk on Sundays or be fined" or "anyone who drinks alcohol will be punished" are both rules that do not allow discrimination among groups

---

if the elected government [or whatever] says it's legitimate,' and capitalism really says, 'I have the right to hit you in defense of my property rights.' So the issue boils down to whether socialism and capitalism can be justified on other grounds. I.e., the universalization principle doesn't give us any help in picking between the two. Archived at https://tinyurl.com/54rzjcnp and https://perma.cc/UU8S-2APB (emphasis added).

Callahan, by contrast, does not appear to even grant the universalizability requirement. From our exchange at the same page:

lee_mccracken: "does this 'universalizability' principle imply that there can't be special moral duties (say, the duties of parents to children or vice versa)? Hoppe says that such principles could be found to be universally acceptable if they are 'grounded in the nature of things', but I'm not quite sure what this means. Can anyone explain that further?"

Callahan: "My cynical view: 'the nature of things' means whatever you want it to in order to get to the conclusion you want anyway."

Kinsella: "Right. As [] I suspected, you do not seem to accept the validity of the universalizability principle. Which, as I indicated, leads to skepticism, which of course goes hand in hand with cynicism.... Gene, I'd ask you to confirm or deny that you reject the universalizability principle—but I won't hold out hope that you will do this. But if you would confirm it, I'd say—you are subject to this criticism (about the nature of things) yourself. And if you deny it, I'd ask you—do you really realize the implications of such a denial?"

Callahan did not to respond to this direct question.

Murphy is correct that some socialist norms can be universalized, as Hoppe himself explicitly notes (see text at note 19). However, as Hoppe points out, this does not mean that all invalid norms can be reformulated to avoid violating universalizability, and can serve as a first-level "filter" for eliminating some particularizable norms; nor that the universalizability criterion is useless for, if one is forced to reformulate an apparently particularized (and thus facially invalid) norm to avoid this problem, it exposes the nature of the claimed norm more clearly so that it can be compared to other, more substantive, norms necessarily presupposed by any participants in argumentative justification. See text at note 20 below, *et pass*. See also Eabrasu, "A Reply to the Current Critiques Formulated Against Hoppe's Argumentation Ethics," p. 11 *et pass*.

of people and thus could both claim to satisfy the condition of universalization.

Clearly then, the universalization principle alone would not provide one with any positive set of norms that could be demonstrated to be justified.[19]

But even though universalizability is merely a formal requirement, it does eliminate many proposed norms, such as those underlying most versions of socialism which amount to "I can hit you but you cannot hit me" particularizable rules.

[T]he property theory implicit in socialism does not normally pass even the first decisive test (the necessary if not sufficient condition) required of rules of human conduct which claim to be morally justified or justifiable. This test, as formulated in the so-called golden rule or, similarly, in the Kantian categorical imperative, requires that in order to be just, a rule must be a *general* one applicable to every single person in the same way. The rule cannot specify different rights or obligations for different categories of people (one for the red-headed, and one for others, or one for women and a different one for men), as such a "particularistic" rule, naturally, could never, not even in principle, be accepted as a fair rule by everyone. Particularistic rules, however, of the type "I can hit you, but you are not allowed to hit me," are ... at the very base of all practiced forms of socialism.[20]

Thus universalizability acts as a first-level "filter" that weeds out all particularistic norms. This reduces the universe of possibly justified normative claims but does not finish the job since many incompatible and unethical norms could be reworded in universalizable ways.

It is for this reason that Hoppe next examines other, more substantive, presuppositions inherent in argument itself. These are then used in a second filtering process to reject additional proposed norms, those that are universalizable but incompatible with the other presuppositions of discourse. And, because some of these presuppositions turn out to be presupposed *norms*, Hoppe then shows that the libertarian conception of rights can be deduced from these presupposed norms and facts.

---

[19] Hoppe, *A Theory of Socialism and Capitalism*, pp. 157–58 (emphasis added).
[20] Ibid., p. 14.

SUBSTANTIVE FACTS AND NORMS
PRESUPPOSED IN ARGUMENTATION

The universalization principle filters out many possible norms, but many possible, mutually incompatible, and nonlibertarian candidates remain ("anyone who drinks alcohol will be punished").

> However, there are other positive norms implied in argumentation aside from the universalization principle. In order to recognize them, it is only necessary to call three interrelated facts to attention. First, that argumentation is not only a cognitive but also a *practical affair*. Second, that argumentation, as a form of action, implies the use of the *scarce resource* of one's body. And third, that argumentation is a *conflict-free* way of interacting.[21]

Participants in discourse cannot deny the existence of scarcity (discourse is a form of action, after all, and action implies scarce resources, in one's body and in external objects or means of action) nor the possibility of conflict over these scarce resources. They also value the ability to participate in argument (they are engaging in it, after all) and thus its *practical preconditions*, namely the ability to actually use scarce resources in order to survive (for argumentation is not possible without survival). And because argumentation/discourse is a cooperative, civilized, peaceful activity, and because "justifying *means* justifying without having to rely on coercion,"[22] participants in discourse necessarily value being able to use scarce resources in a conflict-free way. One adopting a civilized, peaceful stance and trying to justify a norm cannot coherently advocate non-peaceful norms. In fact, the very attempt to justify a resource allocation norm is an *attempt to settle conflicts* with regard to the use of that resource. Thus, a participant in discourse could never justify the proposition that there is no value to being able to use resources, or that conflict should not be avoided, or that cooperation and peacefulness are bad things. Valuing the avoidance of conflicts also presupposes the value of attempting to find rules that make conflict avoidance possible. I.e., property rules.

---

21 Ibid., p. 158 (emphasis added).
22 Ibid., p. 159.

Accordingly, participants in discourse, in particular those seeking to justify proposed norms, implicitly recognize the value and legitimacy of assigning specified property owners to specified scarce resources— for reasons that are universalizable and that make conflict-avoidance possible. However, property rights make conflict avoidance possible by establishing perceivable boundaries to resources indicating the resource's borders and who the owner is, and by basing the assignment on universalizable rules that could be accepted as fair by all potential participants in discourse, in argumentative justification. For this reason, the assignment of property rights has to be based on some *objective link* between the claimant and a particular resource.[23]

What all this means is that anyone ever attempting to (argumentatively) justify any norm is already presupposing a host of norms and argumentative rules. The substantive presupposed norms rule out many proposed norms, even if they are universalizable. For example, a rule such as "no one should ever be able to use any scarce resource" could never be justified. It is incompatible with the speaker's evident value for the ability to use scarce resources, because he has to (be able to) use the scarce resource of his body in order to engage in any activity, including argumentation. And he, or someone, had to be able to use other scarce resources such as food, shelter, etc., so that the arguers are alive and able to argue (remember, discourse is a practical affair, and requires the speakers to be alive, to have control of their bodies and their standing room, etc.).

In addition, a rule specifying that all resources, or even some resources, should have no owner at all, simply does not allocate ownership in the scarce resources at issue, i.e., it does not fulfill its function of conflict-avoidance. Unless property rights are allocated to someone, conflict over each scarce resource is possible; that is the nature of scarcity. (As a practical matter, most such rules also imply that if a given resource should not be "owned," then some person or agency is authorized to

---

[23] See, on this, "How We Come To Own Ourselves" (ch. 4), references in n.6; also Kinsella, "KOL259 | "How To Think About Property", New Hampshire Liberty Forum 2019"; "Selling Does Not Imply Ownership, and Vice-Versa: A Dissection" (ch. 11); *idem*, "Aggression and Property Rights Plank in the Libertarian Party Platform"; also Hoppe, "Of Common, Public, and Private Property and the Rationale for Total Privatization." See also "What Libertarianism Is" (ch. 2).

prevent others from using the thing. In which case the rule is, in reality, assigning ownership to the agency with control and would need to be justified. For example, the public forests are said (by some libertarians) to be "unowned," but the federal government prevents homesteaders from moving in. Clearly here the federal government is asserting ownership. The necessity of justifying this cannot be avoided by the fiction that the property is not owned.)

There is no way any norm can be justified that does not seek to assign ownership of every scarce resource to particular owners, based on an objective link between the owner and the owned resource. No rule could ever be justified if it refrains from deciding who owns a particular resource or if it specifies that no one owns a resource. And any justification offered has to be universalizable. The reasons for all these requirements should be clear by now, as discussed above. Particular owners must be assigned to each and every scarce resource—this is what any theory of property—any ethic—has to do. There must be an objective link between the owner and the resource, so that conflicts can be avoided, and also to comply with universalizability. "Every" scarce resource must be owned by someone, for conflict-avoidance and other reasons given above.

To this point the case is fairly general, and only establishes the framework for examining various competing norms. The libertarian insistence on objective links between resources and owners, and its particular view of what constitutes such objective links, is what completes the case.

OBJECTIVE LINKS: FIRST USE, VERBAL CLAIMS, AND THE PRIOR-LATER DISTINCTION

So now we come to libertarianism. It turns out that libertarianism is the only theory of rights that satisfies the presuppositions of discourse, because only it advocates assigning ownership by means of objective links between the owner and the resource in question.

Hoppe first establishes property rights in bodies. As noted above,[24] argumentation is a *conflict-free* way of interacting, and justifying

---

[24] See text at notes 21–22, above.

means justifying without having to rely on coercion. In other words, the nonaggression principle is presupposed in argumentation. Thus, in the case of one's own body, the rule of "self-ownership" is implied, since saying that a participant in discourse is not permitted to aggress against the body of other participants is tantamount to recognizing a property right in each participant's body. The nonaggression principle and self- (body-) ownership are just different ways of expressing the same idea. The objective link here is each person's control over and identification with his own body.[25]

As for previously-unowned, external scarce resources, the objective link that is relevant to property rights is first use, or original appropriation. Only the norm assigning ownership in a thing to its *first user*, or his transferee in title, could fulfill this requirement, or the other presuppositions of argumentation.

There is clearly an objective link between the person who first begins to use something, and emborders it, and all others in the world. Everyone can see this. No goods are ever subject to conflict unless they are first acquired by someone. The first user and possessor of a good is either its owner or he is not. If he is not, then who is? The person who takes it from him by force? If forcefully taking possession from a prior owner entitles the new possessor to the thing, then *there is no such thing as ownership*, but only mere possession.[26] But such a rule—that a later user may acquire something by taking it from the previous owner—does not avoid conflicts, it rather authorizes them. It is nothing more than mights-makes-right writ large. This is not what peaceful, cooperative, conflict-free argumentative justification is about.

What about the person who verbally *declares* that he owns the good that another has appropriated? Again, this rule is not justifiable because it does not avoid conflicts—because everyone in the world can simultaneously decree that they own any thing. With multiple claimants for a piece of property, each having an "equally good" verbal decree, there is no way to avoid conflict by allocating ownership to a particular person.

---

[25] See also "How We Come To Own Ourselves" and "What Libertarianism Is" (ch. 2).

[26] On the distinction between possession and ownership, see "What Libertarianism Is" (ch. 2), at notes 22–24 and accompanying text, *et pass.*

No way, other than an objective link, that is, which again shows why there must be an objective link between the claimant and the resource.

As Hoppe states:

> Hence, the right to acquire such goods must be assumed to exist. Now, if this is so, and if one does not have the right to acquire such rights of exclusive control over unused, nature-given things through one's own work, i.e., by doing something with things with which no one else had ever done anything before, and if other people had the right to disregard one's ownership claim with respect to such things which they had not worked on or put to some particular use before, then this would only be possible if one could acquire property titles not through labor, i.e., by establishing some objective, intersubjectively controllable link between a particular person and a particular scarce resource, but simply by verbal declaration; by decree.... The separation is based on the observation that some particular scarce resource had in fact—for everyone to see and verify, as objective indicators for this would exist—been made an expression or materialization of one's own will, or, as the case may be, of someone else's will.[27]

As Hoppe notes, assigning ownership based on verbal decree would be incompatible with the "nonaggression principle regarding bodies," which is presupposed due to the cooperative, peaceful, conflict-free nature of argumentative justification. Moreover, it would not address the problem of conflict avoidance, as explained above.

Thus, Hoppe is correct, when he writes:

> Hence, one is forced to conclude that the socialist ethic is a complete failure. In all of its practical versions, it is no better than a rule such as "I can hit you, but you cannot hit me," which even fails to pass the universalization test. And if it did adopt universalizable rules, which would basically amount to saying "everybody can hit everybody else," such rulings could not conceivably be said to be universally acceptable on account of their very material specification. Simply to say and argue so must presuppose a person's property right over his own body. Thus,

---

[27] Hoppe, *A Theory of Socialism and Capitalism*, pp. 161–62; see also pp. 169–71. See also Hoppe, "Appendix: Four Critical Replies," in *The Economics and Ethics of Private Property*, p. 412:

> if actors were not entitled to own physical resources other than their bodies, and if they as moral agents ... were to follow this prescription, they would be dead and no problem whatsoever would exist. For ethical problems to exist, then, ownership in other things must be justified.

only the first-come-first-own ethic of capitalism can be defended effectively as it is implied in argumentation. And no other ethic could be so justified, as justifying something in the course of argumentation implies presupposing the validity of precisely this ethic of the natural theory of property.[28]

In other words, cognition and truth-seeking as such have a normative foundation, and the normative foundation on which cognition and truth rest is the recognition of private property rights.[29]

MURPHY'S & CALLAHAN'S CRITIQUE

I am really at a loss as to where MC would part company with this theory. Do they deny, for example, that there is scarcity in the world or that conflicts are possible? I doubt it. Do they deny that universalizability is a requirement for justified norms? I doubt it, unless they are also ethical skeptics, in which case I wonder why they consider themselves libertarians.[30] Do they deny that rights have to be justified, and that justification has to occur during argument? Such a denial would be a neat trick, as it would itself be an argument. Do they maintain that participants in discourse do not presuppose *any* truths?—or do they just say that none of these are *normative*? Or do they think that argumentation is not a conflict-free way of interacting?—in which case they would seem to think bashing someone over the head or stealing their wallet is also a form of peaceful, cooperative discourse.

Or, do they think it is coherent for a participant in the peaceful, cooperative activity of discourse, while searching with the other for a universalizable, conflict-avoiding property allocation rule, to advocate socialism, or any other non-libertarian approach? If they are libertarians surely there must be *some* advantage to libertarian rights that would factor in to such a generalized argumentative justification context. Or, would MC seriously maintain that a norm could be argumentatively

---

[28] Ibid., p. 171.

[29] Hoppe, *The Economics and Ethics of Private Property*, p. 345.

[30] As noted above (note 18), Murphy seems to acknowledge the universalizability principle, and is a libertarian, while Callahan appears to reject it and apparently, as far as I am aware, no longer considers himself a libertarian (or Austrian).

justified, if the norm, if followed, would render human life, and thus argumentative justification itself, impossible?[31]

---

[31] See also Rothbard's criticism of the "communist" rule of universal equal and other-ownership:

> Can we picture a world in which no man is free to take any action whatsoever without prior approval by everyone else in society? Clearly no man would be able to do anything, and the human race would quickly perish. But if a world of zero or near-zero self-ownership spells death for the human race, then any steps in that direction also contravene the law of what is best for man and his life on earth.

Murray N. Rothbard, "Interpersonal Relations: Ownership and Aggression," in *The Ethics of Liberty* (New York: New York University Press, 1998), pp. 45–46, at 46, reproduced in substantially similar form in *idem*, "A Crusoe Social Philosophy," *Mises Daily* (December 7, 2021; https://mises.org/library/crusoe-social-philosophy). See also related discussion in "How We Come to Own Ourselves" (ch. 4), n.14 and "Law and Intellectual Property in a Stateless Society" (ch. 14), n.27.

For a related insight regarding the importance of the prior-later distinction and the necessity that property rights be able to answer the question of who can use what resource *now*, rather than waiting for some future information, otherwise people would not be able to survive because they could not use resources to produce and consume in the present, see Hoppe, "From the Economics of Laissez Faire to the Ethics of Libertarianism," in *The Economics and Ethics of Private Property*, pp. 328–30; Hoppe, "On the Ultimate Justification of the Ethics of Private Property," in *The Economics and Ethics of Private Property*, p. 345 ("Nobody advocating a wait-for-the-outcome ethic would be around to say anything if he took his own advice seriously. Also, to the extent that utilitarian proponents are still around, they demonstrate through their actions that their consequentialist doctrine is and must be regarded as false. Acting and proposition-making require private property rights now and cannot wait for them to be assigned only later."); Hoppe, "Appendix: Four Critical Replies," in *The Economics and Ethics of Private Property*, p. 407; *idem*, "The Ethics and Economics of Private Property," in *The Great Fiction*, at section III, "Misconceptions and Clarifications." See also Rothbard, "Beyond Is and Ought" (emphasis added):

> In the modern libertarian movement, only the natural-rights libertarians have come to satisfyingly absolute libertarian conclusions. The different wings of "consequentialists"—whether emotivists, utilitarians, Stirnerites, or whatever—have tended to buckle at the seams. If, after all, one has to *wait for consequences to make a firm decision*, one can hardly adopt a consistent, hard-nosed stance for liberty and private property in every conceivable case.

See also Hoppe, "The Justice of Economic Efficiency," in *The Economics and Ethics of Private Property*, at 337:

> While every person can have control over whether or not his actions cause the physical integrity of something to change, control over whether or not one's actions affect the value of someone's property to change rests with other people and their evaluations. One would have to interrogate and come to an agreement with the entire world population to make sure that one's planned actions would not change another person's evaluations regarding his property. Everyone would be long dead before this could ever be accomplished.

For more on the prior-later distinction, see "What Libertarianism Is" (ch. 2), at notes 32–36 and accompanying text, *et pass.*

MC do not attempt to debunk argumentation ethics in general, or, alternatively, to show just what ethics *are* implied in argumentation (and why these are not the ones that Hoppe proposes). Do they believe *any* norms are implied in argumentation? If not, they would seem to reject the entire edifice of work in this regard, including work by Jürgen Habermas, Karl-Otto Apel, Frank van Dun, G.B. Madison, Alan Gewirth, Roger Pilon, Tibor Machan, and others discussed in "Dialogical Arguments for Libertarian Rights" (ch. 6).

On the other hand, if they accept that argumentation implies *some* norms, which are they? Do these norms support libertarianism? Socialism? Or are they only non-rights-related interpersonal norms, like "be nice" or "don't lie"?[32] Are these argumentatively-presupposed norms at least consistent with libertarianism? MC write:

> Hoppe next invokes the "ethics of argumentation," which was developed by Habermas and Apel…. They contend that whenever people are engaged in debate, they have implicitly agreed to a certain set of norms, for example, that they will restrict themselves to peaceful means in their efforts to persuade other participants of their contentions. [54]

It is not clear whether MC are merely paraphrasing this basic insight or whether they agree with it. If they do, are there *no* implications to be drawn from this? Does it place no constraints whatsoever on the legitimacy of norms propositionally advanced in the course of (peaceful!) argument? After all, later they say "Hoppe has shown that bashing someone on the head is an illogical form of argumentation." (p. 58) Does this concede that argumentation does presuppose some norms? It's not clear.

It seems to me that if MC accept any form of argumentation ethics as valid—that is, if there are some norms implied in discourse—then, as libertarians who believe libertarian norms *are* (somehow) justified, they would have to believe that the argumentative norms are at least compatible with, if not the grounding for, libertarian rights. That is, if you accept that there are some norms presupposed by argumentative justification, *and* if you yourself accept libertarian norms, you must

---

32 Van Dun does seem to have a somewhat broader conception of the scope of discourse ethics type reasoning than Hoppe or myself. See Van Dun, "Argumentation Ethics and the Philosophy of Freedom," p. 32 n.73, regarding the "right to lie."

believe that the norms of argumentation ethics are at least compatible with, and possibly relevant to, the greater set of libertarian norms.

Universalizability

What about universalizability? I am not sure if MC really reject the universalizability requirement—but if they do, I fail to see how they can themselves adhere to any notion of rights; rejecting universalizability means that any norm whatsoever can be proposed by simply making up a particularistic reason for it. Without the universalizability principle, literally "anything goes," which of course leads to ethical relativism and/or skepticism. I will assume that MC are not ethical relativists or skeptics and thus do not reject universalizability. But I am not sure they fully appreciate this principle.

Consider this comment by MC:

> To simply declare that ownership rights must be "universalizable" is no help, either; after all, communists could cite the same principle to "prove" that everyone should have equal shares to all property. [59 n.3]

MC write here as if they are totally unaware that Hoppe has explicitly stated that "the universalization principle only provides a *purely formal criterion for morality*."[33] Of course, even if socialism's principles were reformulated in a completely universalizable way, it will still be inconsistent with other norms presupposed in argumentation, as noted above.

And regarding universalizability, MC also state:

> Our final point in this section is to note that, even setting aside all of the above difficulties, it's still the case that Hoppe has only proven self-ownership for the individuals in the debate. This is because, even on Hoppe's own grounds, someone denying the libertarian ethic would only be engaging in contradiction if he tried to justify his preferred doctrine to its "victims."

> For example, so long as Aristotle only argued with other Greeks about the inferiority of barbarians and their natural status as slaves, then he would not be engaging in a performative contradiction. He could quite consistently grant self-ownership to his Greek debating opponent, while

---

[33] Hoppe, *A Theory of Socialism and Capitalism*, p. 157 (emphasis added).

denying it to those whom he deems naturally inferior.... Aristotle need only contend [that] barbarians [] are not as rational as Greeks. [58, 59]

Do MC think that merely "deeming" or "contending" something to be so is automatically compatible with universalizability? I believe they are simply misapplying the universalizability principle here (or, rather, failing to apply it). For Aristotle to grant rights to himself and Greeks, but not to other individuals, would simply be particularistic. He would have to show that there is some reason, objectively grounded in the nature of things, that justifies rights in Greeks but not in other people identical to Greeks in all respects *except for* their Greekness. Again, either the universalizability requirement is taken seriously, or it is not. If not, the door to ethical skepticism is opened wide.[34]

Moreover, I would assume MC themselves do *not* agree that one can mount a viable argument that Greeks have rights (for some reason) but other humans do not. So why would they think it's "consistent" to make such an argument, when even they would (presumably) disagree with such an argument?

Entire Body vs. Parts of the Body

One criticism MC make is the argument that Hoppe has not succeeded in arguing for ownership of one's entire body, but, at best, only parts of it:

> At best, all Hoppe has proven is that it would be a performative contradiction for someone to deny in an argument that his debating opponent (and perhaps those in the same "class") own the body parts (such as eyes, brain, and lungs) necessary for debate, for the duration of the debate. This is a far cry from showing that it would be a contradiction for someone to deny the case for libertarianism. In particular, a collectivist could argue that people can rightfully be forced to give up a kidney, or go to war, if such actions would help the rest of society. [60]

---

34 See also, on this "Greek" issue, Van Dun, "Argumentation Ethics and the Philosophy of Freedom," pp. 24–25. See also Eabrasu, "A Reply to the Current Critiques Formulated Against Hoppe's Argumentation Ethics," pp. 17–23; Block, "Rejoinder to Murphy and Callahan on Hoppe's Argumentation Ethics," p. 635–36; Slenzok, "The Libertarian Argumentation Ethics, the Transcendental Pragmatics of Language, and the Conflict-Freedom Principle," p. 55 *et pass.*

Hoppe has subsequently responded to this type of argument:

> Some critics have argued that this does not demonstrate a person's own-
> ership of his entire body, but at best only of parts of it. Why? Because to
> argue it is not necessary to use all body parts. And true enough, you do
> not need two kidneys, two eyes or an appendix to argue. Indeed, you also
> do not need your body hair or even arms and legs to argue. And hence,
> according to such critics, you cannot claim to be the lawful owner of
> your two kidneys or eyes, your legs and arms. Yet this objection does not
> only appear silly on its face—after all, it implies the recognition of these
> "un-necessary" parts as *natural parts of one unitary body* rather than as sep-
> arate, stand-alone entities. More importantly, it involves, philosophically
> speaking, a category mistake. The critics simply confuse the *physiology* of
> argumentation and action with the *logic* of argumentation and action.
> And this confusion is particularly surprising coming from economists,
> and even more so from economists familiar also with praxeology. For the
> fundamental distinction made in economics between "labor" and "land"
> as the two originary means of production, which corresponds exactly to
> the distinction made here between "body" and "external world," is also
> not a physiological or physicalistic distinction, but a praxeological one.
>
> The question to be answered is not: which body parts are physiologi-
> cally necessary requirements for one person arguing with another person.
> Rather, the question is: which parts of my body and which parts of your
> body can I or you argumentatively justify as my or your lawful possessions.
> And to this a clear and unambiguous answer exists. I am the lawful owner
> of my nature-given body with everything naturally in it and attached to
> it, and you are the lawful owner of your entire nature-given body. Any
> argument to the contrary would land its proponent in a performative or
> dialectic contradiction. For me to say, for instance, in an argumentation
> with you, that you do not rightfully own all of your nature-given body is
> contradicted by the fact that in so arguing, not fighting, with you, I must
> recognize and treat you as another person with a separate body and recog-
> nizably separate physical boundaries and borders from me and my body.
> To argue that you do not lawfully own your entire natural body, which
> you actually possess and have peacefully taken into possession before
> I could have possibly done so indirectly by means of my natural body, is
> to advocate conflict and bodily clash and hence contrary to the purpose
> of argumentation: of peacefully resolving a present conflict and avoiding
> future conflict.[35]

---

[35] Hoppe, "PFP163 | Hans Hermann Hoppe, 'On The Ethics of Argumentation' (PFS 2016)." See also a similar quote in "How We Come to Own Ourselves" (ch. 4), at n.17.

Arguing With Your Slave

MC introduce supposed "counterexamples" of God and slavery. Take the slavery case. They recognize that

> Hoppe and Rothbardian libertarians in general do *not* believe in universal self-ownership. In particular, they believe that *criminals* may be rightfully enslaved to pay off their debts to victims (or their heirs). [62]

Well, of course! Hoppe is a libertarian. To advocate self-ownership means that a person has the right to control his body, as a default or *prima facie* matter. But if someone commits aggression, of course the victim now is a partial "owner" of the aggressor's body, because he has a right to use force against it. So consider a man who now "owns" an aggressor who, say, murdered the man's wife. Of course, the owner could engage in debate with the slave, but only by granting the slave the right to use his body for purposes of argument. But how does this change the fact that no one can argumentatively deny the normative presuppositions that imply libertarianism? Let's assume the owner is libertarian. He believes in the need for property rules and conflict-avoidance. He believes any norms have to be universalizable. If he advocated socialism, his argument would be incompatible with necessary argumentative presuppositions of peace, prosperity, and conflict-avoiding prosperity— because socialist rules are either not universalizable or are not based on objective links between owner and resource.

But his claim that he has a right to wield force against the slave is perfectly justified. It is universalizable, because the different treatment of the slave-aggressor and the master-victim is not arbitrary but is grounded in the objective fact of the act of aggression. It is compatible with objectively assigning property rights, because it is a way of *enforcing* objectively assigned property rights that are violated.[36]

See also Van Dun, "Argumentation Ethics and the Philosophy of Freedom," p.20 n.46, p.23 n.55, and accompanying text, *et pass.*; Eabrasu, "A Reply to the Current Critiques Formulated Against Hoppe's Argumentation Ethics," pp. 13–15; Block, "Rejoinder to Murphy and Callahan on Hoppe's Argumentation Ethics," p. 633; Slenzok, "The Libertarian Argumentation Ethics, the Transcendental Pragmatics of Language, and the Conflict-Freedom Principle," pp. 55–56 *et pass.*

[36] See "A Libertarian Theory of Punishment and Rights" (ch. 5) and "Dialogical Arguments for Libertarian Rights" (ch. 6). See also Hoppe's rejection of a similar "slavery"

And another way to look at this issue is this. As pointed out in chapter 4 (n.17), and as alluded to by Hoppe in the quote at note 35, above, and also his comments in the Foreword, the reasons for the self-ownership norm is that a person's direct control over his own body has logical-temporal priority over the control by another person which must be *indirect*. Since the person always maintains direct control,

---

argument in Hoppe, "Appendix: Four Critical Replies," in *The Economics and Ethics of Private Property*, section II, "Utilitarians and Randians vs. Reason," pp. 404 *et seq.* and also in Hoppe, "PFP163 | Hans Hermann Hoppe, 'On The Ethics of Argumentation' (PFS 2016)":

> [M]atters are quite different when it comes to an argumentation between slave master and slave about the subject of slavery, i.e., the conditions under which their argumentation takes place. In this case, if the slave master would say to the slave "let's not fight but *argue* about the justification of slavery," and he would thereby recognize the slave as another, separate and independent person with his own mind and body, he would have to let the slave go free and leave. And if he would say instead "so what, I have recognized you momentarily as another independent person with your own mind and body, but now, at the end of our dispute, I deny you ownership of the means necessary to argue with me and prevent you from leaving anyway," *then* he would be involved in a performative or dialectic contradiction.

See also Slenzok, "The Libertarian Argumentation Ethics, the Transcendental Pragmatics of Language, and the Conflict-Freedom Principle," p. 57 *et pass.*

Of course, as I noted in the text above, if the slave had committed aggression against the master-owner, then the owner would not be involved in contradiction by treating the slave differently than himself. See also, on this issue, Van Dun, "Argumentation Ethics and the Philosophy of Freedom," pp. 26–27; also p. 24 (emphasis added):

> [Hoppe's] argument is that when A and B enter into an argumentation both of them do so under the dialectically valid presumptions of rationality, innocence, and self-ownership—presumptions that will hold *until there is proof that they should be withdrawn.*

And ibid., p. 16 n.34 (emphasis added):

> [MC] assert "We cannot convince you of anything by clubbing you, but we may quite logically try to convince you that we should have the right to club you" (M&C, p.58). True, *they may try to convince me that they ought to have the right to punish me for my crimes, if I have committed any.* There is a good chance that they will succeed. But how on earth do they hope to convince me by means of logical arguments that they should have the right to club me, *regardless of what I may have done or will do?* If the (unqualified) statement "We have a right to club you" were justifiable then clubbing a person would be a justifiable action also in an argumentation.

See also ibid., p. 26 n.62:

> Obviously, as noted before, there may be cases where the use of force to deprive another of his freedom is justified, for example to make him pay for his crimes, or to stop him from completing the crime he is in the process of committing. One may be justified in using uninvited force against such persons. However, these are not paradigmatic cases of the sort of slavery to which Friedman or Murphy and Callahan refer.

another person attempting to control the person's body by indirect control (basically, coercion) will always, necessarily, generate conflict. But the purpose of property norms is to reduce conflict or allow conflict to be avoided. So one of the reasons the slavery-norm cannot be accepted as justified is that it generates conflict. (There are other, interrelated reasons as well, such as: someone claiming ownership of another by indirect control claims ownership of his own body due to direct control; so it is contradictory to deny the same right to the other person.)

Now when the victim of a crime seeks to enslave the criminal, it is true that this will be a conflict: the indirect control of the victim will clash with the direct control of the criminal over his own body. Yet it is too late to avoid conflict; the criminal's criminal act was already an act of conflict. So now we do not have two peaceful people seeking a conflict-reducing norm to allow them to live peacefully together. Now we have a victim of aggression and conflict who seeks to obtain some kind of rectification from the aggressor, *even if* that involves violently coercing or dominating the aggressor, overwhelming his direct control with indirect control via coercion. So there is no contradiction in Hoppe's theory in opposing the slavery-norm as being contradictory and granting the legitimacy of a type of slavery in limited situations. In the first case, Hoppe is observing that a property norm aimed at reducing conflict cannot be justified if it sets up conflict. In the second case, conflict has already happened and now the victim is not seeking to avoid conflict but is instead seeking restitution.[37]

God as Slaveowner

As for God—you can't just *posit* that God owns everyone and "therefore" we are not self-owners. Moreover, even if God *does* own us, then this would be because God has some objective link that gives him a better claim or title to a person's body than this person has—some kind of logical-temporal priority that takes precedence over the person's own claims to own his body because of his direct control of his body. If we

---

[37] See further discussion of this matter at "How We Come To Own Ourselves" (ch. 4), the sections "Direct Control" and "Summary"; "Law and Intellectual Property in a Stateless Society" (ch. 14), Part II.C.

are positing this kind of magic, then God himself might have a sort of "super" direct control over our bodies that gives him a better claim. For example, as Hoppe points out (note the text I have italicized):

> The answer to the question what makes my body "mine" lies in the obvious fact that this is not merely an assertion but that, for everyone to see, this *is* indeed the case. Why do we say "this is my body"? For this a twofold requirement exists. On the one hand it must be the case that the body called "mine" must indeed (in an intersubjectively ascertainable way) express or "objectify" my will. Proof of this, as far as my body is concerned, is easy enough to demonstrate: When I announce that I will now lift my arm, turn my head, relax in my chair (or whatever else) and these announcements then become true (are fulfilled), then this shows that the body which does this has been indeed appropriated by my will. If, to the contrary, my announcements showed no systematic relation to my body's actual behavior, then the proposition "this is my body" would have to be considered as an empty, objectively unfounded assertion; and likewise this proposition would be rejected as incorrect if following my announcement not my arm would rise but always that of Müller, Meier, or Schulze (*in which case one would more likely be inclined to consider Müller's, Meier's, or Schulze's body "mine"*).[38]

Now Hoppe's italicized example here is not intended to be realistic, anymore than the hypothetical construct of the "evenly rotating economy," or ERE, employed by Mises and Rothbard; or the magical world of the Garden of Eden or the Land of Cockaigne (or Schlaraffenland), in which there is no scarcity or conflict possible, but in which human action is also virtually inconceivable.[39] (This is unlike Robinsonades, which analyze the economic implications of the actions of Crusoe alone on his island, which is not unrealistic at all, just highly simplified.)[40]

---

38 Quoted in "How We Come to Own Ourselves" (ch. 4), at n.17.

39 See the criticism of the ERE in Jörg Guido Hülsmann, "A Realist Approach to Equilibrium Analysis," *Q.J. Austrian Econ.* 3, no. 4 (Winter 2000; https://mises.org/library/realist-approach-equilibrium-analysis): 3–51. On the Schlaraffenland construct, see Hoppe, "Of Common, Public, and Private Property and the Rationale for Total Privatization," in *The Great Fiction*, p. 86; Hoppe, *A Theory of Socialism and Capitalism*, p. 219. See also the Wikipedia entry for "Cockaigne," https://en.wikipedia.org/wiki/Cockaigne. These are both discussed in "On Libertarian Legal Theory, Self-Ownership and Drug Laws" (ch. 23), at notes 16–17.

40 See Ludwig von Mises, *The Ultimate Foundation of Economic Science: An Essay on Method* (Princeton, N.J.: D. Van Nostrand Company, Inc., 1962; https://mises.org/library/ultimate-foundation-economic-science), p. 41; *idem, Epistemological Problems of Economics,*

It was merely a way to emphasis the crucial centrality of direct control with a somewhat unrealistic and whimsical hypothetical. Likewise, until someone can prove there is a God, and that he owns us, I fail to see the relevance of this example. In any case, as Locke argues, God "gave" self-ownership to each person, "manumitting" them in a sense.[41] Notes Van Dun in this regard:

> Assume that Murphy and Callahan refer to a theist in the Judeo-Christian tradition: Would God claim justifiable possession or control of a creature that He put out of his Garden when He discovered that it was capable of reason and free will? What does all the biblical talk about Covenants mean if we are asked to consider a covenant between an owner and his property?[42]

Van Dun also observes that MC

> fail to note the difference between arguing about God and arguing with God. The question of God's ownership would have to be decided in an argumentation with God, not with any self-proclaimed representative of God, who would have a hard time proving his credentials anyway—so much so that it is doubtful that he would ever get to discuss the question of God's ownership itself. The same applies to discussions about Society or The People's having ultimate ownership of our bodies or other things.[43]

Moreover, the purpose of property rights and human law is to govern interpersonal behavior among human beings, here on earth. Even if there is a God out there that has some kind of super-ownership claim over us, as his subjects or creations, within the human realm and among other humans, we are still self-owners *vis-à-vis* each other. As

---

3d ed., George Reisman, trans. (Auburn, Ala.: Mises Institute, 2003), pp. 14–16, 30–31, 87–88; *idem, Human Action: A Treatise on Economics*, Scholar's ed. (Auburn, Ala.: Mises Institute, 1998; https://mises.org/library/human-action-0), p. 64 *et seq.* See also Hoppe, *A Theory of Socialism and Capitalism*, p. 142, as quoted in "Causation and Aggression" (ch. 8), n.4. See also related discussion in "Knowledge, Calculation, Conflict, and Law" (ch. 19), at n.65, and "A Libertarian Theory of Punishment and Rights" (ch. 5), n.36.

[41] See John Locke, *Second Treatise on Civil Government* (1690; https://www.johnlocke.net/2022/07/two-treatises-of-government.html), §25: "every man has a property in his own person: this no body has any right to but himself."

[42] Van Dun, "Argumentation Ethics and the Philosophy of Freedom," p. 21 n.50.

[43] Ibid., p. 21.

Walter Block observes, "libertarianism is a theory that concerns the relationship between man and man, not between man and God."[44]

Thus, the positing of a hypothetical God in no way refutes the conclusion that only the libertarian norms, including especially self-ownership, can be argumentatively justified amongst fellow humans.

Claims Made During Argumentation Only

MC try to make much of their notion that propositions advanced "during" argument are not subject to the presuppositions of argument if the rule is designed to be applied in a non-argumentative context. But propositions *can only* be justified during argumentation. A participant in discourse cannot deny that conflict-avoidance is good. *When he seeks to justify something*, it is always some action he seeks to justify. The justification takes place at one time; the action to be justified, at another. So what? Are MC saying that *no* action can ever be justified, other than argument itself? Consider an act of theft, or property acquisition, or rape: all non-argumentative actions. Obviously, these actions are not justifying-actions, because they are not arguments. The only time they could possibly be justified, or criticized, is at another time, during argument. In any event, this critique seems to miss the point. As Hoppe notes: "In the same way as the validity of a mathematical proof is not restricted to the moment of proving it, so is the validity of the libertarian property theory not limited to instances of argumentation. If correct, the argument demonstrates its universal justification."[45]

Thus, if two people seek to agree upon a fair, universalizable rule for assigning property rights in scarce resources to individuals in a way that would allow conflict to be avoided and the resources to be used—of course the rule they are considering will be applicable to future property disputes. I am baffled at how they could think otherwise.[46]

---

44 Block, "Rejoinder to Murphy and Callahan on Hoppe's Argumentation Ethics," p. 636.

45 Hoppe, *The Economics and Ethics of Private Property*, p. 406.

46 See also Hoppe, "PFP163 | Hans Hermann Hoppe, 'On The Ethics of Argumentation' (PFS 2016)":

Another "objection" to my argument from argumentation, advanced repeatedly and by several opponents in a seemingly most serious manner, actually better qualifies as a joke. It boils down to the claim that, even if true, my argument is irrelevant and inconsequential. Why? Because the ethics of argumentation is valid and binding only at the moment and for the duration of argumentation itself and even then only for those actually participating in it. Curiously, these critics do not notice that this thesis, if it were true, would have to apply to itself, too, and hence, render their own criticism irrelevant and inconsequential also. Their criticism itself then would be just talk for the sake of talking, without any consequence outside of talking. For, according to their own thesis, what they say about argumentation is true only when and while they are saying it and has no relevance outside the context of argumentation; and moreover, that what they say to be true is true only for the parties actually involved in argumentation or even only for *them alone*, if and insofar as there is no *actual* opponent and they say what they say in an internal dialog only to themselves. But why, then, should anyone waste his time and pay attention to such private "truths"?

For others' criticism of this "duration" part of MC's argument, see Van Dun, "Argumentation Ethics and the Philosophy of Freedom," p. 7 n.20, p. 19 n.43, and accompanying text, *et pass.*; Eabrasu, "A Reply to the Current Critiques Formulated Against Hoppe's Argumentation Ethics," pp. 15–17; Block, "Rejoinder to Murphy and Callahan on Hoppe's Argumentation Ethics," p. 633–34; Slenzok, "The Libertarian Argumentation Ethics, the Transcendental Pragmatics of Language, and the Conflict-Freedom Principle," p. 55.

PART III

LIBERTARIAN LEGAL THEORY

8

Causation and Aggression

In 2001, I presented a paper entitled "Reinach and the Property Libertarians on Causality in the Law" at a Mises Institute symposium on Adolf Reinach and Murray Rothbard.[*] I later collaborated with Patrick Tinsley on an article based on this paper, published in 2004 in a related symposium issue in *The Quarterly Journal of Austrian Economics*.[†] This chapter is a substantially revised version of that article.[††]

[*] "Reinach and Rothbard: An International Symposium," Ludwig von Mises Institute, Auburn, Ala. (March 29–30, 2001; https://perma.cc/396W-HJEL). The other presenters were Walter Block, Guido Hülsmann (also the director), Hans-Hermann Hoppe, Larry J. Sechrest, and Barry Smith.

[†] Stephan Kinsella & Patrick Tinsley, "Causation and Aggression," *Q. J. Austrian Econ.* 7, no. 4 (Winter 2004): 97–112. Then a law student, and a former student of Walter Block's at Holy Cross, Tinsley is now a practicing attorney at Fletcher Tilton, PC (https://perma.cc/8LS5-AGN4). This article was included in a symposium issue (vol. 7, no. 4, Winter 2004), on "Austrian Law and Economics: The Contributions of Reinach and Rothbard," which contained contributions based mainly on the papers presented at the 2001 symposium. For other articles in that issue, see note 66, below—I've moved them to the end to avoid awkward formatting issues. Also: when "we" is used in this chapter, it is retained from the original article.

[††] My co-author Tinsley has reviewed the changes made in this chapter and fully agrees with them.

For an application of the causation ideas in this chapter to related issues, see Kinsella, "Corporate Personhood, Limited Liability, and Double Taxation," *The Libertarian Standard* (Oct. 18, 2011); Kinsella, "KOL100 | The Role of the Corporation and Limited Liability In a Free Society" (PFS 2013); also Kinsella, "KOL382 | FreeTalkLive at PorcFest: Corporations, Limited Liability, and the Reno Reset," *Kinsella on Liberty Podcast* (June 23, 2022); *idem*, "KOL354 | CDA §230, Being "Part of the State," Co-ownership, Causation, Defamation, with Nick Sinard," *Kinsella on Liberty Podcast* (Aug. 3, 2021).

For other related material published after the original article, see *idem*, "Intellectual Property and the Structure of Human Action," *StephanKinsella.com* (Jan. 6, 2010); *idem*, "KOL021 | 'Libertarian Legal Theory: Property, Conflict, and Society, Lecture 4: Causation, Aggression, Responsibility' (Mises Academy, 2011)," *Kinsella On Liberty Podcast* (Feb. 21, 2013 [Feb. 21, 2011]).

PRAXEOLOGY AND LEGAL ANALYSIS:
ACTION VS. BEHAVIOR

For libertarians, the purpose of a legal system is to establish and enforce rules that facilitate and support peaceful, conflict-free interaction between individuals, i.e., property rights. In short, the law should prohibit aggression—the unconsented-to use of someone's owned resources, or "property"—by identifying and protecting private property rights.[1] Because aggression is a particular kind of human action—action that intentionally violates or threatens to violate the physical integrity of another person or another person's property without that person's consent[2]—it can be successfully prohibited only if the law is based on a sound understanding of the nature of human action more generally.[3]

Praxeology, the general theory of human action, studies the universal features of human action and draws out the logical implications of the undeniable fact that humans act.[4] Praxeology is central to Austrian

---

[1] See generally "What Libertarianism Is" (ch. 2) and Kinsella, "How To Think About Property (2019)," *StephanKinsella.com* (April 25, 2021); and Hans-Hermann Hoppe, *Economy, Society, and History* (Auburn, Ala.: Mises Institute, 2021; https://www.hanshoppe.com/esh/), pp. 2, 10–12, *et pass.* See also "What Libertarianism Is" (ch. 2), Appendix I (regarding the use of the term property to refer to the rights actors have with regard to resources, instead of the resources themselves, and also regarding the nature of a property right as a right to exclude, not a right to use).

[2] For discussion of the distinction between an action's intentionality or purposiveness (thus distinguishing it from mere behavior, such as a reflexive or involuntary response), which factors into responsibility and liability, and its motive or actual purpose, which factors into the appropriate punishment, see Kinsella, "Hate Crime—Intentional Action and Motivations," *StephanKinsella.com* (July 9, 2009). See also text at note 8, below.

[3] As described elsewhere in this book, aggression means nonconsensual use of another's owned resources, so is dependent upon the prior and more fundamental concept of property rights. In other words, to determine what actions constitution aggression, one must first know who owns what. See "What Libertarianism Is" (ch. 2), at notes 6, 9, 11, and accompanying text *et pass.*; also Kinsella, "How To Think About Property (2019)"; *idem*, "Aggression and Property Rights Plank in the Libertarian Party Platform," *StephanKinsella.com* (May 30, 2022). In any case, aggression is always an action, and thus in order to identify and analyze property rights violations, an analysis of *action* is necessary. See *idem*, "The Non-Aggression Principle as a Limit on Action, Not on Property Rights," *StephanKinsella.com* (Jan. 22, 2010) and *idem*, "IP and Aggression as Limits on Property Rights: How They Differ," *StephanKinsella.com* (Jan. 22, 2010).

[4] As Hoppe writes:
   Essentially, economic analysis consists of: (1) an understanding of the categories of action and an understanding of the meaning of a *change* in values, costs, technological knowledge, etc.; (2) a description of a situation in which these categories

economics, the "hitherto best elaborated part" of the science of praxeology.[5] However, other disciplines can benefit from the insights of praxeology. Hans-Hermann Hoppe has already extended praxeology to the field of political ethics.[6] The related discipline of legal theory, which also concerns ethical implications of human action, can also benefit from the insights of praxeology.[7]

In the context of legal analysis, one important praxeological doctrine is the distinction between action and mere behavior. The difference between action and behavior boils down to intent. Action is an individual's *intentional* intervention in the physical world, via certain selected *means*, with the *purpose* of attaining a state of affairs that is preferable to the conditions that would prevail in the absence of the action. Mere behavior, by contrast, is a person's physical movements that are not undertaken intentionally and that do not manifest any purpose, plan, or design. Mere

---

assume concrete meaning, where definite people are identified as actors with definite objects specified as their means of action, with definite goals identified as values and definite things specified as costs; and (3) a deduction of the consequences that result from the performance of some specified action in this situation, or of the consequences that result for an actor if this situation is changed in a specified way. And this deduction must yield a priori-valid conclusions, provided there is no flaw in the very process of deduction and the situation and the change introduced into it being given, and a priori-valid conclusions about reality if the situation and situation-change, as described, can themselves be identified as real, because then their validity would ultimately go back to the indisputable validity of the categories of action.

Hans-Hermann Hoppe, *A Theory of Socialism and Capitalism: Economics, Politics, and Ethics* (Auburn, Ala.: Mises Institute, 2010 [1989]; www.hanshoppe.com/tsc), p. 142. See also Ludwig von Mises, *Human Action: A Treatise on Economics*, Scholar's ed. (Auburn, Ala.: Mises Institute, 1998; https://mises.org/library/human-action-0), pp. 3, 15–16, 480; *idem*, *The Ultimate Foundation of Economic Science: An Essay on Method* (Princeton, N.J.: D. Van Nostrand Company, Inc., 1962; https://mises.org/library/ultimate-foundation-economic-science); and Hans-Hermann Hoppe, *Economic Science and the Austrian Method* (Auburn, Ala.: Mises Institute, 1995; www.hanshoppe.com/esam).

See also "A Libertarian Theory of Punishment and Rights" (ch. 5), n.36 and "Knowledge, Calculation, Conflict, and Law" (ch. 19), at n.65, regarding the need to select relevant facts and assumptions when applying such reasoning to result in interesting and useful results.

[5] Mises, *Human Action*, p. 3.

[6] See Hoppe, *A Theory of Socialism and Capitalism*, chap. 7 and, generally, "Dialogical Arguments for Libertarian Rights" (ch. 6) and "Defending Argumentation Ethics" (ch. 7).

[7] See also Kinsella, "The Other Fields of Praxeology: War, Games, Voting… and Ethics?," *StephanKinsella.com* (Aug. 5, 2006).

behavior cannot be aggression; aggression must be deliberate, it must be an action.[8]

In order to better understand this distinction between action and behavior, we may focus on the role of causality in explaining each. Human action involves two-fold causality. On the one hand, human action requires that time-invariant causal relations govern the physical world. Otherwise, a given means could not be said to *achieve* a desired result. "As no action could be devised and ventured upon without definite ideas about the relation of cause and effect, teleology presupposes causality."[9]

And on the other hand, human action requires that those time-invariant causal relations can be understood and exploited by an individual whose actions are not themselves subject to time-invariant causal relations. Otherwise, there would be nothing to distinguish human action from blind natural forces. In such a world, laws and norms would be pointless, because no one could be considered responsible for his actions—human beings would not be actors but passive conduits for mechanical processes.[10]

To some extent, of course, human beings are just that. Not everything we do is intentional; we also exhibit what is mere (i.e., non-purposeful) *behavior.* Our hearts beat, our eyes blink, and we fall asleep—all without any intention on our part. In these cases, we can understand the behavior in terms of time-invariant physical causes. There is no need to apply the concept of an actor deliberately choosing and employing means for the

---

[8] See, on this, note 2, above, and accompanying text.

[9] Mises, *The Ultimate Foundation of Economic Science*, p. 8. See also Kirzner on the employment by human actors of scarce means to achieve ends:

In a market system each member of the society is free to act, within very wide limits, as he sees fit. Moreover, the system operates within a framework of law which recognizes individual rights to private property. This means that each individual is free at each moment to employ the means available to him for the purpose of furthering his own ends, providing only that this should not invade the property rights of others.

Israel M. Kirzner, *Market Theory and the Price System* (Princeton, N.J.: D. Van Nostrand Co., Inc., 1963; https://mises.org/library/market-theory-and-the-price-system-0), p. 13.

[10] On the impossibility of explaining human action in terms of time-invariant causal relations, see Hoppe, "In Defense of Extreme Rationalism," in *The Great Fiction*, pp. 330–31; Hoppe, *A Theory of Socialism and Capitalism*, pp. 134–36; and Jörg Guido Hülsmann, "Facts and Counterfactuals in Economic Law," *J. Libertarian Stud.* 17, no. 1 (2003; https://mises.org/library/facts-and-counterfactuals-economic-law-1): 61–64.

purpose of attaining a desired end. We can understand human behavior exactly the same way we can understand any nonhuman natural (i.e., nonteleological) process. But unlike most natural processes, human beings are capable of more than mere behavior; they are capable also of action, of purposeful behavior.

As legal theorists, therefore, we cannot accept an entirely mechanistic picture of the world. Legal theorizing is concerned with the ethical or normative implications of action.[11] It asks whether an actor should be held responsible for the consequences of his actions and what rights to respond his actions give rise to on the part of the recipients of his action. And to hold someone responsible for the consequences of his actions is implicitly to invoke the two-fold concept of causality expressed above. For there even to be consequences in the first place, the physical world must be governed by time-invariant causal relations. And to hold an actor responsible for those consequences, we must determine that they can be traced back to his own deliberate use of means to achieve a desired result: his "action" cannot itself be a merely mechanical response to physical stimuli; he is the author, or "cause," of the results achieved.[12] In other words, like Austrian economics, legal theory must presuppose both time-invariant causation (an actor could not *employ means* to attain his goal otherwise) and agent-causation in which the actor himself is the *cause* of results that he intended to achieve by the use of certain means (the actor is not *acting* otherwise).

The law, therefore, in prohibiting aggression, is concerned with prohibiting aggressive *action*—nonconsensual violations of property

---

[11] In fact, as noted in the Preface, at one point I considered entitling this book *The Ethics of Action*—a title and meaning distinct from, but inspired by, similar titles such as Murray N. Rothbard, *The Ethics of Liberty* (New York: New York University Press, 1998) and *idem*, *The Logic of Action* (Edward Elgar, 1997, later republished as *Economic Controversies* (Auburn, Ala.: Mises Institute, 2011; https://mises.org/library/economic-controversies)); also Michael Polanyi, *The Logic of Liberty* (Routledge, 1951); G.B. Madison, *The Logic of Liberty* (New York: Greenwood Press, 1986); and James M. Buchanan, *The Limits of Liberty: Between Anarchy and Leviathan*, vol. 7 in *The Collected Works of James M. Buchanan* (Indianapolis: Liberty Fund, 2000 [1975]).

[12] As Mises wrote, "Action is purposive conduct. It is not simply behavior, but behavior begot by judgments of value, aiming at a definite end and *guided by ideas concerning the suitability or unsuitability of definite means.*" Mises, *The Ultimate Foundation of Economic Science*, p. 34 (emphasis added). See also the quote by Holmes in note 14, below.

boundaries that are the product of deliberate action. Analyzing action in view of its praxeological structure is essential.

AGGRESSION AND THE IMPLICIT CONCEPT OF CAUSALITY

Hitting someone without permission is an example of the kind of aggression libertarians oppose. If it is illegal to hit someone, however, this means that it is illegal to *cause* another person to be hit; that is to say, it is illegal to use physical objects, including one's fist, in a way that will cause unwanted physical contact with another person. Therefore, if *A* does *intentionally* (and uninvitedly) hit *B*, he can be held responsible for the action—the aggression can be imputed to him and he can be lawfully punished for it—because *A*'s decision to hit his victim was not itself conditioned by strictly physical laws. It was volitional. *A*—not some impersonal force of nature, and not some other person—was the cause of the aggression against *B*. *A*'s aggression is an action.[13]

The general question facing libertarians, then, is whether a particular actor, by his action, intentionally *caused* the prohibited result—an uninvited border-crossing. Implicitly, the libertarian prohibition on the initiation of force is a prohibition on willfully *causing* an unwanted intrusion.

---

[13] In my view, one need not take a stand on the interminable (and somewhat pointless and intractable) free will debate to hold these views. It does not matter if humans "really" have "genuine" free will in the causal realm in order to usefully characterize their actions teleologically. We conscious and self-aware humans are aware of the external world via our senses and reason, but also aware of an internal perspective by which we characterize our own actions as involving choice and goals. In order to understand, interact with, and predict the behavior or conduct of other humans, it is reasonable and useful for us to assume they have a similar internal perspective, since they are biologically similar to us, and thus, to interpret their motions as actions in pursuit of goals, as opposed to mere causal behavior. To the extent we adopt a teleological perspective to characterize other humans' actions, categories of choice, opportunity cost, time preference, and so on are unavoidable. Though I do not consider it relevant to the arguments made in this chapter (or this book), I view my perspective on free will and determinism/causality as a type of compatibilism, but a unique one informed by Misesian dualism. It is no more spooky to refer to an actor's "choice" than it is to conceptually distinguish the mind from the brain or the person from his body, as it is undeniably a conceptually useful, and probably unavoidable, way to characterize what other humans do.

Where *A*'s action—not mere behavior—is the cause of aggression against *B*, we might simply say that "*A* killed *B*." But if we unpack this statement, we will usually find that *A* did not directly kill *B*; some intermediate means was employed to achieve that end (hence the causal aspect of action). Action is not just intentional; it is the intentional use of *means* to attain a desired end. For example, *A* deliberately loaded his gun, deliberately pointed the gun at *B* and then deliberately squeezed the trigger, causing a bullet to discharge into *B*'s heart. Why say that *A* killed *B*? Why not say that the *bullet* killed *B*, whereas *A* merely squeezed a trigger? Why connect *A*'s action of squeezing a trigger with the resulting harm to *B*? In some contexts, of course, *A*'s action would be irrelevant. To a medical examiner conducting an autopsy, for instance, the bullet is the cause of *B*'s death, and who fired it and why is beside the point. But that does not change the fact that in a legal and normative context we trace the chain of causation back to *A*'s intentional action of squeezing the trigger. There is, after all, a causal connection between the immediate action and the means employed on the one hand, and the harmful consequence on the other hand.[14]

In praxeological terms, we can say that *A*'s goal or end was to kill *B*; he selected a means—the gun—calculated and designed, according to known laws of cause and effect in the physical world (the causal

---

[14] See also Frank van Dun, "Against Libertarian Legalism: A Comment on Kinsella and Block," *J. Libertarian Stud.* 17, no. 3 (2003; https://mises.org/library/against-libertarian-legalism-comment-kinsella-and-block-0): 63–90, p. 78 ("Few are likely to believe a progressive lawyer who argues that, while his client admittedly did aim his gun at the victim and pulled the trigger, it was the bullet that killed the victim.").

As Justice Oliver Wendell Holmes noted:

An act is always a voluntary muscular contraction, and nothing else. The chain of physical sequences which it sets in motion or directs to the plaintiff's harm is no part of it, and very generally a long train of such sequences intervenes.... When a man commits an assault and battery with a pistol, his only act is to contract the muscles of his arm and forefinger in a certain way, but it is the delight of elementary writers to point out what a vast series of physical changes must take place before the harm is done.

Oliver Wendell Holmes, Jr., *The Common Law* (Boston: Little, Brown, 1881), p. 91.

For further discussion of causation in the law, see Richard A. Epstein, "An Analysis of Causation," in *A Theory of Strict Liability: Toward a Reformation of Tort Law* (San Francisco: Cato Institute, 1980; https://perma.cc/PVV6-U3Y7); Tony Honoré, "Causation in the Law," *The Stanford Encyclopedia of Philosophy*, Edward N. Zalta, ed. (2001; https://perma.cc/3JJ6-VD29); H.L.A. Hart & Tony Honoré, *Causation in the Law,* 2d ed. (Oxford: Clarendon Press, 1985).

realm), to achieve that goal. *A*'s action was intended to cause *B*'s death, and the action employed means that did, in fact, result in *B*'s death. As shorthand we say that *A* killed *B*, but implicit in this account is that *A* undertook an intentional action employing means and exploiting causal laws (causal realm) to achieve his desired result (teleological realm).[15]

At this point, we might want to revisit the issue of intent. Why should we concern ourselves with *A*'s *intent*? If we objectively determine that *A*'s actions caused the death of *B*, what should it matter what *A* intended to do—or whether *A* intended to do anything at all?

Intent matters because without intent there is no action and without action there is no actor to whom we may impute legal responsibility. If *A* did not intend to do anything at all, then we cannot determine that *A*'s actions caused the death of *B*—because *A took* no action. Intent is a necessary ingredient in human action; if there is no intent, then there is no action, only behavior: involuntary physical movements guided by deterministic (or perhaps random) causal relations.

The role of law in a free society is to protect the rights of nonaggressors and, where those rights are violated, to compensate the victims and punish the aggressors. But aggression must be intentional—otherwise, there is no reason to attribute it to a particular human actor instead of an impersonal natural force. For person *A* to be the cause of *B*'s death, *B* must have died as the result of a series of events initiated by *A*'s willful action. If, on the other hand, *B* dies as the result of a thoroughly deterministic process unconnected with any willful action, then there is no

---

[15] The causal aspect of a prohibited act of aggression is sometimes made explicit and is sometimes simply implicit. As an example of the former, see New York Penal Law §105.05: "Conspiracy in the fifth degree," which provides:

A person is guilty of conspiracy in the fifth degree when, with intent that conduct constituting:

1. a felony be performed, he agrees with one or more persons to engage in *or cause* the performance of such conduct; or

2. a crime be performed, he, being over eighteen years of age, agrees with one or more persons under sixteen years of age to engage in *or cause* the performance of such conduct.

New York Penal Law §105.05 (https://perma.cc/FEV5-KBK3; emphasis added).

In the case of torts, the mandate is: do not unreasonably act so as to *cause harm* to another. In crimes such as rape, theft, and burglary, the causal aspect may only be implied. But theft occurs, for example, when the actor's voluntary act *causes* movement (asportation) of the goods stolen. Rape includes the crime of *causing* another's penis to be inserted into victim, and so on.

one to punish; no one caused B's death. To punish A's unintentional bodily movement would be like punishing lightning for destruction of property or punishing a flood for assault. A can murder B, whereas lightning (or a flood, or a cougar, or an involuntary human reflex) cannot.

PUNISHING AGGRESSION

There is another, closely related reason why intent matters for the assessment of criminal guilt. A guilty criminal—that is, an aggressor—may be lawfully punished. Or, to put it another way, an aggressor cannot meaningfully object when his aggression is met with physical force in response. After all, his aggressive actions conclusively demonstrate that he does not find nonconsensual physical force objectionable. In common law terms, we may say that by virtue of his own violence against others, an aggressor is "estopped" from objecting to (proportional) violence against himself.[16] But to punish someone is to engage in an *intentional* act. As an intentional act, punishment is only justified in response to an intentional act of violence; this is the elegant symmetry of libertarian ethics. Neither an unintentional movement, nor an intentional act of *nonaggression*, can justify the use of force. We may punish A if he intentionally strikes B, but not if B is struck by lightning; and we may punish A if he intentionally shoots B with a gun, but not if he shoots B with a camera. If we do punish A for nonaggression, we become aggressors ourselves—because nonaggressive action cannot estop A from mounting a coherent objection to the use of violence against him. Thus we can say that when an aggressor intentionally and uninvitedly attempts to (or does) impair the physical integrity of another's person or property, he gives his victim the right to punish him, because he can no longer withhold his consent to physical force in response to his initiatory force.[17]

---

[16] For a libertarian theory of punishment grounded in the insight that an aggressor may be punished because and insofar as his own use of violence deprives him of the ability to mount a coherent objection, see "A Libertarian Theory of Punishment and Rights" (ch. 5) and "Dialogical Arguments for Libertarian Rights" (ch. 6).

[17] In other words, initiatory force, or aggression, is unjust; but responsive force is justifiable. For further discussion of how to characterize the nature of aggression—as trespass, or invasion of borders, or unconsented use or altering the physical integrity, of owned resources,

COMPLICATING THE PICTURE:
CAUSATION, COOPERATION, AND HUMAN MEANS

Compared to many real-world cases of murder, the above example in which *A* deliberately shoots *B* is simple and straightforward. After all, *A*'s chosen means of carrying out his aggression against *B* was a gun—an inanimate object enmeshed in a web of causal relations but incapable of initiating a causal sequence on its own. As the well-known slogan goes, guns don't kill people, people kill people. There is little difficulty in laying the moral and legal responsibility for the murder on *A*, therefore, because only *A* engaged in an action. Only *A* made a choice to which moral and legal blame could attach. The means that *A* employed—the gun and its ammunition—were physical objects completely bound by causal laws.

What about actions that involve other humans? As Mises observed:

> A means is what serves to the attainment of any end, goal, or aim. Means are not in the given universe; in this universe there exist only things. A thing becomes a means when human reason plans to employ it for the attainment of some end and human action really employs it for this purpose. Thinking man sees the serviceableness of things, i.e., their ability to minister to his ends, and acting man makes them means.... It is human meaning and action which transform them into means.[18]

Now in these comments Mises is primarily concerned with the use of nonhuman scarce resources as the things employed as means. But there is no reason that other humans cannot also be one's means, in a sense. What else does it mean to "employ" a worker, or to cooperate with others to produce wealth? In fact, as Mises commented in *Socialism*:

> [I]n the means of production *men serve as means*, not as ends. For liberal social theory proves that each single man sees in all others, first of all,

see "What Libertarianism Is" (ch. 2), notes 9 & 11 and accompanying text; also Kinsella, "Aggression and Property Rights Plank in the Libertarian Party Platform." See also Hoppe, *A Theory of Socialism and Capitalism*, p. 23 n.11 & 165–68; also Hans-Hermann & Walter Block, "Property and Exploitation," *Int'l J. Value-Based Mgt* 15, no. 3 (2002; https://perma.cc/UQ8U-UM35): 225–36; Rothbard, "Law, Property Rights, and Air Pollution," in *Economic Controversies*, p. 375; *idem, Man, Economy, and State, with Power and Market*, Scholar's ed., second ed. (Auburn, Ala.: Mises Institute, 2009; https://mises.org/library/man-economy-and-state-power-and-market), chap. 2, § 12, p. 183; Kinsella, "Hoppe on Property Rights in Physical Integrity vs Value," *StephanKinsella.com* (June 12, 2011).
 18 Mises, *Human Action*, p. 92. See also Hoppe, *Economy, Society, and History*, p. 8 *et seq.*

only means to the realization of his purposes, while he himself is to all others a means to the realization of their purposes; that finally, by this reciprocal action, in which each is simultaneously means and end, the highest aim of social life is attained—the achievement of a better existence for everyone.[19]

There is no doubt that cooperative, productive action is possible, in which case multiple actors cooperate with each other and, in a sense, employ each other as means to achieve mutual and/or separate goals. But not all cooperative action is productive and peaceful. It is also possible for multiple actors to collaborate or conspire together to trespass against others' property rights.

In analyzing action through the lens of the praxeological means-ends structure to determine if it amounts to aggression, we ask if the actor employed *means* to achieve the end of invading the borders of another's property or body—in other words, we ask if he *caused* the border invasion or trespass. The means employed can be inanimate or nonhuman means governed solely by causal laws (a gun), *or* it can include other humans who are employed (used) as means to achieve the illicit end desired. The latter category includes both innocent humans that one employs to cause a border invasion as well as culpable humans that one conspires (cooperates) with to achieve the illicit end.

Consider the following case in which an aggressor employs an innocent human as one of his means. A terrorist builds a letter-bomb and mails it to his intended victim via courier. The courier has no idea that

---

19 Ludwig von Mises, *Socialism: An Economic and Sociological Analysis*, J. Kahane, trans. (Indianapolis, Ind: Liberty Fund, 1981; https://oll.libertyfund.org/title/kahane-socialism-an-economic-and-sociological-analysis), chap. 30, §1, p. 390 (emphasis added).

To be clear, there is a distinction between the nonhuman scarce means of action employed by actors, and other humans employed to help achieve one's ends. Only the former are ownable things. (See "A Libertarian Theory of Contract: Title Transfer, Binding Promises, and Inalienability" (ch. 9) and "Selling Does Not Imply Ownership, and Vice-Versa: A Dissection" (ch. 11).) Because of confusion and often equivocation surrounding the term *scarce*, e.g., in the intellectual property context ("good ideas are pretty scarce, so IP must be legitimate"), in recent years I have tried to emphasize the rivalrous or "conflictable" nature of the types of resources, things, or entities that may be subject to property rights. See Kinsella, "On Conflictability and Conflictable Resources," *StephanKinsella.com* (Jan. 31, 2022); also *"Against Intellectual Property* After Twenty Years: Looking Back and Looking Forward" (ch. 15), at n. 29; "What Libertarianism Is" (ch. 2), Appendix I.

the package he is delivering contains a lethal device. When the addressee dies in an explosion after he opens the package, whom should we hold responsible? The obvious answer is: the terrorist. Why not the courier? Or the victim himself? After all, the courier is causally connected to the killing, as is the victim. The courier delivered the package; the victim opened it. But because he did not know he was carrying a bomb, the courier did not have the intent to aggress against the victim. Instead, he was connected to the killing only as a means. When the bomb exploded, it was the terrorist's action, not the courier's, that was completed. The courier simply handed over a package. The terrorist, by contrast, intentionally used means—the bomb materials, but also the unwitting courier—to cause his victim's death. It is no different than if the terrorist used a nonhuman robot or drone to deliver the bomb. This case would be similar to the gun example, but not significantly different from the case in which a human courier was employed. From the point of view of both the victim, and the terrorist, whether the means employed was an innocent human or a nonhuman mechanistic delivery mechanism is irrelevant. The victim opposes being harmed in both cases; and the terrorist achieves his end, in both cases.[20]

In fact, the victim's own actions play a role in this scenario—after all, he opens the package, "causing" it to explode. We would not hesitate to say that the terrorist killed the victim, even though there is a significant time lag between the terrorist's initial actions and the ensuing result, *and even though the victim's own volitional actions were part of the chain of events.* So why not blame the victim? After all, he is the one who set off the bomb by opening the package. But this is obviously absurd. The victim did not intend to kill himself!

It is true that the positive law has long recognized that one accused of a crime or tort is not responsible if the damage was really caused by an "intervening act" that breaks the chain of causal connection" between the actions of the accused and the damage that occurred.[21] The idea is that the intervening act is the true cause of the harm caused. But this is the case only if the event is superseding cause—that is, an *unforeseeable*

---

[20] See also the "evil midget" example in the text at note 26, below.

[21] I trust my readers can google, but see e.g. https://en.wikipedia.org/wiki/Intervening_cause.

intervening cause. In other words, an intervening force only breaks the chain of causal connection when it is *unforeseeable*. As the *Restatement (Second) of Torts* provides, "The intervention of a force which is a normal consequence of a situation created by the actor's ... conduct is not a superseding cause of harm which such conduct has been a substantial factor in bringing about." [22]

But it is simply not the case that when an actor (whom we may in general refer to as a "boss" or "inciter") induces another human to aggress against a victim, that the act of aggression is "unforeseeable" merely because the intermediary has free will. [23] When a terrorist uses a courier to deliver a letter bomb, it is not unforeseeable that the victim will receive it; and it is not unforeseeable that the victim will open it. If I hire a hit-man to kill someone, I am doing so because I hope and expect the victim to be killed. If I send my underling to rob a bank, I am doing it to have the bank robbed. If a woman persuades her lover to murder her husband, and he does, she gets the result she wanted; can we really say the outcome was "unforeseeable"? [24] Thus, the fact that there are other humans with free will who are part of the chain of events does not excuse the instigator. This is, admittedly, how the positive law reasons, but I think this is reasonable and compatible with libertarian-based principles of rights, causation, and responsibility.

---

[22] *Restatement (Second) of Torts*, § 443 (1965).

[23] In this chapter I will use various terms, such as "instigator," inciter, boss, and the like, to refer to the person who attempts to persuade or induce another human, whom I will often refer to as an intermediary, underling, henchman and so on, to directly commit an act of aggression against some innocent victim.

[24] The example given on Wikipedia is as follows:

An intervening cause will generally absolve the tortfeasor of liability for the victim's injury *only if* the event is deemed a *superseding cause*. A *superseding cause* is an *unforeseeable* intervening cause. By contrast, a *foreseeable* intervening cause typically does *not* break the chain of causality, meaning that the tortfeasor is still responsible for the victim's injury—unless the event leads to an unforeseeable result.

For example…, if a defendant had carelessly spilled gasoline near a pile of cigarette butts in an alley behind a bar, the fact that a bar patron later carelessly threw a cigarette butt into the gasoline would be deemed a foreseeable intervening cause, and would not absolve the defendant of tort liability. However, if the bar patron *intentionally* threw the cigarette butt into the gasoline because he wanted to see it ignite, this intentional act would likely be deemed unforeseeable, and therefore superseding.

https://en.wikipedia.org/wiki/Intervening_cause.

We submit that the case of an intentional border-crossing being carried out in part through human actors as opposed to through exclusively inanimate or nonhuman means poses no special praxeological problems. Whether the terrorist handed the bomb to his victim directly or through an innocent third party, the legal analysis remains the same. We look to see who intentionally employed means to cause an unwanted invasion against another. The means can be nonhuman or inanimate means, or another human, whether innocent or acting in coordination with the actor. In this case, the (innocent) courier was the terrorist's *means* of killing the victim. It is simply confused to claim, as some do, that the terrorist in this case is not a cause of the killing because the chain of causation is "broken" by the "intervening" acts of another human (the courier) with free will. The acts of the courier do not *absolve* the terrorist; to the contrary, they *implicate* him, since he used the courier and his actions to cause damage to the victim.

In the cases mentioned above, only innocent parties—the courier, or the victim himself—are employed as the malfeasor's means of committing aggression. Although here we find the terrorist alone responsible for the killing, it will not always be the case that an act of aggression "belongs" to just one person. For example, consider a bank heist in which there are several participants. One of them drives the getaway car; another handles crowd control; a third directs the action by walkie-talkie; and a fourth actually steals the money. The one who takes by force money that does not belong to him is clearly guilty of robbery. But most libertarians would agree that his companions are no less guilty. Most libertarians would recognize this as a "simultaneous" criminal conspiracy that renders all of its participants independently and jointly responsible. And that is our conclusion as well. But how can we justify that conclusion, inasmuch as only one person actually took possession of the stolen money?

The key is causation. Each of these actors had the goal that the bank's and customers' property be seized and each intentionally used means—including one another—to attain this goal. In other words, *each* bank robber that was part of the conspiracy was a cause of the robbery. Each had intent to achieve, and employed means to attain, the illicit end.[25]

Consider the following example: A purchases a remote-controlled tank. With the remote control he can steer the tank and fire its cannon. He directs the tank to blow down the walls of a neighbor's house, destroying the house and killing the neighbor. No one would deny that A is the cause of the killing and is guilty of murder and trespass. However, after the rampage, a hatch opens in the tank, and an evil midget jumps out. It turns out, you see, that the midget could see on a screen which buttons were pressed on the remote control, and he would operate the tank accordingly. We submit that A is equally liable in both cases. From his point of view, the tank was a "black box" that he used to attain his end, regardless of whether there was a human will somewhere in the chain of causation. No one can plausibly argue that we cannot determine A's liability until we know whether there was a midget, or mere machinery, in the tank. (Of course, the evil midget, if there is one, is also liable.)[26] In general, one can be liable for acts commited by another, if one is employing them as means to commit aggression. As Frank van Dun argues,

> Hitler, Churchill, Roosevelt, Stalin, and their likes were not innocent practitioners of free speech at a time when a lot of their compatriots were blowing up towns and villages and people. The general who, in his search of scapegoats for a defeat, sends a handful of privates to the firing-squad is not exonerated by the fact that some other privates actually fired the shots that killed their convicted colleagues.[27]

In other words, the simple fact that a person's actions are mediated through other persons does not mean he should not be held liable for them. The driver of the getaway car is responsible for the robbery because he is intentionally engaged in a "simultaneous" criminal conspiracy to commit the heist. The mob boss who orders a crime is liable for his

---

[25] Frank van Dun's discussion of "social causation" is also relevant here. See Van Dun, "Against Libertarian Legalism," pp. 64, 79. It is discussed in further detail in the text below.

[26] For a critique of our reasoning here, see Matt Mortellaro, "Causation and Responsibility: A New Direction," *Libertarian Papers* 1, art. no. 24 (2009; https://mises.org/library/causation-and-responsibility-new-direction), p. 11 *et seq.* This paper also criticizes other aspects of the reasoning in our original article.

[27] Van Dun, "Against Libertarian Legalism," p. 78.

underling's actions. The political leader who orders military actions is responsible for them. People can conspire—collaborate, cooperate—to commit crimes.

Moreover, the conspiracy or joint action need not even be simultaneous. In the terrorist example, the bomb did not detonate until long after the terrorist had handed it over to the courier. Nevertheless, he used the courier as an unwitting "partner" in a temporal "conspiracy" to kill the intended victim. In situations such as these, other human actors (including the victim) can be means to an end. It should be emphasized, of course, that this is a general rule; the analysis in each situation must be case-specific and take relevant facts and context into account. Whether a given person is considered to be "in" or "out" of the conspiracy—an intentional actor or an unwitting dupe—will depend on the circumstances surrounding the particular case.

Generally, however, the libertarian position is that what is impermissible—and properly punishable—is *action that is aggression*. This means action characterized by the following structure: the actor intentionally employs some means (which can be mere objects but could also include other actors, whether innocent or not) calculated to cause an invasion of the physical borders of a nonaggressor's person or property.

LIBERTARIAN OBJECTIONS

Virtually no one has a quarrel with the notion that an actor is the "cause" of a result if he employs nonhuman means to attain this result. However, as indicated above, some, including some libertarians, assume that if another *person* is employed as the means, somehow the "chain" of causation is "broken." For example, A somehow persuades C to plant a bomb under B's car, which kills B. Some libertarians maintain that, while C is responsible for B's murder, A is not, because C's actions were undertaken with "free will," thereby "breaking the chain of causation." They argue that what C did was commit murder, while A committed a mere speech act, which does not in and of itself aggress against anyone's person or property. Similar arguments are made for someone inciting a mob to lynch someone—"mere incitement" is not, according to this view, and never can be, a crime. You are not responsible for what a mob does, even if they act on your instructions, since its members have free will.

Consider, for example, Walter Block's approach to these issues.[28] Block follows Rothbard in maintaining *categorically* that "inciting" others to commit a crime (such as a riot) is simply not a crime. Rather, as Rothbard maintains, "'Inciting to riot' … is a pure exercise of a man's right to speak without being thereby implicated in a crime."[29] Block points out that the rioters have "free will"[30]—unlike an inanimate object such as a bullet—and therefore the inciter is not responsible for the riot. This reasoning can be extended to absolve various mob bosses, political leaders, and the like, who merely instruct underlings or intermediaries to engage in aggressive acts. Hence the libertarian joke that Hitler's defense to war crimes would be, "I just gave orders."[31]

---

[28] See, e.g., Walter Block, "Reply to 'Against Libertarian Legalism' by Frank van Dun," *J. Libertarian Stud.* 18, no. 2 (2004; https://mises.org/library/reply-against-libertarian-legalism-frank-van-dun): 1–30, at pp. 3–16.

[29] Murray N. Rothbard, "Self-Defense," in *The Ethics of Liberty* (New York: New York University Press, 1998; https://mises.org/library/right-self-defense): p. 81; see also *idem*, "'Human Rights' As Property Rights," in ibid. (https://mises.org/library/human-rights-property-rights), pp. 113–15.

[30] Block, "Reply to 'Against Libertarian Legalism,'" p. 16.

[31] Libertarian, or "voluntaryist," Jack Lloyd:
[I]f we assume that Hitler did not murder anyone and, on top of that, we assume for the sake of argument that Hitler had no other partaking in initiations of force whether it was receipt of stolen goods or rape, could Hitler be held to account for the murders that took place under his watch?
In this Steel-Man-case scenario, Hitler would not be culpable for an initiation of force. Rather, the people who did the actual initiations and threats of force would be culpable, whether it was just pointing guns to threaten people into railcars or using physical violence to massacre people in concentration camps.
Jack Lloyd, "Justice and Voluntaryism," *Voluntaryist Association* (Dec. 7, 2022; https://perma.cc/2FZJ-U4EX).
The perversity of the joke noted in the text illustrates why this reasoning is flawed. Imagine a Jewish woman conscripted to be Hitler's cleaning lady at the height of World War II, with her family being imprisoned in a concentration camp. If one night she is cleaning Hitler's office while he is there alone and has the chance to kill him, some libertarians literally argue this action would be murder since Hitler is not himself an aggressor (!). I trust the absurdity and perverseness of this position is apparent to most readers. *Of course* the enslaved Jewish woman, in the hypothetical above, has a right to kill Hitler, in self-defense and defense of others, implying Hitler must be an aggressor, even though he "only gives orders." Thus, not all speech-acts are nonaggressive.
See also the related discussion in Kinsella, "KOL149 | IP And Beyond With Stephan Kinsella—Non-Aggression Podcast," *Kinsella on Liberty Podcast* (Aug. 30, 2014).

Rothbard and Block are assuming here that the rioter *cannot* be the means of the inciter, *because the rioter has free will*; they assume that having another human in the chain of causation breaks the chain. But as explained above, there is no reason other humans cannot serve as means for one's action.

Ad Hoc Exceptions

Understandably, libertarians who advance such views are uncomfortable with the implications—with the idea that presidents and political leaders, mob bosses, people who hire hit men, and so on, are not liable. To avoid these difficulties, they advance various *ad hoc* exceptions to their "incitement is never a crime, it's just free speech" or "the free will of the intermediary breaks the chain of causation" arguments.[32] Walter Block, for example, argues that the "instigator" of actions directly committed by an intermediary can be liable if (a) he threatens or coerces the intermediary to commit the crime,[33] (b) he contractually pays the intermediary money to commit the crime,[34] (c) he "orders"

---

[32] Somewhat similarly, Rothbard also tried to ameliorate the unacceptable consequences of some of his contract views in *The Ethics of Liberty*. He first argues (correctly, to my mind; see "A Libertarian Theory of Contract" (ch. 9)) that voluntary slavery contracts are invalid because the human body or will is inalienable. (See ibid., Part III.C.) Yet he also then argues that failure to repay a debt is "implicit theft" and that, therefore, in principle, debtor's prison is justified. (Rothbard is in error here, as I discuss in ibid.) If someone may be imprisoned for failing to pay a contractual debt (on the basis of the "implicit theft" characterization), this is just another way one can, in fact, alienate one's body by contract. In other words, the positions "the body is inalienable" and "debtor's prison is justified" are contradictory. Perhaps sensing this, Rothbard tries to minimize the latter view by simply asserting that imprisoning an "implicit thief"—the debtor—is somehow necessarily disproportionate and "excessive" punishment. See ibid., Part III.D.

Lloyd, quoted in note 31, above, also tries to minimize the implications of absolving a Hitler from liability. He writes:

> But that Hitler may escape a direct consequence over physical initiations of force does not mean, "no justice." ... Justice is brought by holding the order-followers accountable for their harms and by exposing Hitler's role.... The social and economic ramifications are themselves a toll on him and his ability [to] live and should not be discounted in the calculation.

For some of us, probably most of us, this is pretty thin gruel.

[33] Block, "Reply to 'Against Libertarian Legalism,'" p. 15.

[34] Ibid., p. 17.

the intermediary to commit the crime,[35] or (d) he is "in" a "criminal conspiracy with" the other person, whatever that means.[36] So if you coerce someone, or pay them, or "order" them, or "conspire with" them, you are liable for the intermediary's crimes. With so many exceptions to the rule that one is simply not responsible for the actions of others,

---

[35] Ibid., p. 15 (footnotes omitted):

According to Van Dun's interpretation of my viewpoint, they [Hitler, Stalin, et al] would therefore be "guilty" of no more than exercising their free speech rights, and should be considered innocent of all wrongdoing.

However, Van Dun reckons in the absence of threats. To reiterate, the libertarian legal code proscribes not only invasive acts, but also intimidation. Hitler, Stalin, et al. were not merely engaging in their free speech rights. Rather, they were issuing orders to their subordinates to maim and kill innocent people. Implicit in these commands was the threat that if they were not obeyed, those who failed to carry out these orders would be summarily dealt with.

Here Block seems to imply that "orders" necessarily include a threat. In this case, the "orders" exception noted above seems to collapse into the first exception, where the instigator threatens of coerces the intermediary. But see Walter Block, "Reply to Frank van Dun's 'Natural Law and the Jurisprudence of Freedom,'" *J. Libertarian Stud.* 18, no. 2 (Spring 2004; https://mises.org/library/reply-frank-van-duns-natural-law-and-jurisprudence-freedom): 65–72, p. 67, which seems to distinguish orders from threats, with the conjunction "or," although it is somewhat ambiguous: "A gang leader does not merely *incite* his followers to criminal behavior, he *orders* them to do it, or *threatens* that if they do not, they will be visited with physical sanctions."

[36] See Walter Block, "Were Manson, Hitler, Criminals? Yes.", *LewRockwell.com* (Feb. 1, 2017; https://www.lewrockwell.com/lrc-blog/manson-hitler-criminals-yes/) ("Were Manson, Hitler merely inciting? No, they were 'involved in a plan or conspiracy with others to commit various crimes.'"); Łukasz Dominiak & Walter E. Block, "Libertarian Theory of Bribery and Incitement: A Reformulation," *MEST Journal* 5 no. 2 (July 15, 2017; http://www.walterblock.com/wp-content/uploads/2017-bribery-and-incitement.pdf): 95-101, p. 98 (emphasis added):

From Rothbard's point of view, inciting to crime "is a pure exercise of a man's right to speak without being thereby implicated in the crime. On the other hand, it is obvious that if Green happened to be *involved in a plan or conspiracy with others to commit various crimes*, and that then Green *told them to proceed*, he would then be just as implicated in the crimes as are the others—more so, if he were the mastermind who headed the criminal gang."

Mortellaro also seems to advance a view which would absolve a mafia boss or a Hitler in some cases, but then tries to make an exception in cases of conspiracy or collaboration. See Mortellaro, "Causation and Responsibility," p. 16:

With regard to the necessity of the inciter, it would seem that the hitman has the ability and means to engage in the crime without the help of the inciter. Indeed, unless the inciter plays some other role—if he helps hide the hitman from the authorities, drives the getaway car, picks the lock on the target's door, or something actually involved in the crime itself, then and only then would he have been necessary for the hitman to carry out the crime.

the rule itself is questionable. Moreover, there is no clear reason given for any of these exceptions; they are all apparently supposed to be intuitively obvious cases, but there is no unifying theme between them. These exceptions are *ad hoc* and not based on any general theory.[37]

For example, if an instigator is usually off the hook for actions committed by an intermediary, because the intermediary has free will, why does coercion or monetary payment make a difference? If you coerce someone, or pay him, he still has free will. Whether the instigator threatens, or merely persuades, the intermediary, he still does not "determine" the intermediary's actions, since in both cases, he has free will.[38] In fact, legal systems do not absolve someone from liability for crime just because they are coerced, in recognition of the fact that even coerced agents have choice and culpability.

Furthermore, why is contractual, *monetary* payment some special exception? What about other types of contract, such as a contract for services, or other forms of inducement, such as the promise of sex or getting in the instigator's good graces? We cannot understand why paying someone to murder a victim makes the payer responsible, while there is categorically no responsibility for inducing or persuading someone to commit the murder. Focusing on monetary payment as a special exception seems contrary to the Rothbardian view of contracts

---

37 See also Mortellaro, "Causation and Responsibility," p. 14 (footnote omitted):
   Kinsella goes on in his paper to criticize the inconsistency of some of the defenders of the Rothbardian position for making ad hoc exceptions to the theories which they support. This will be discussed in greater detail below, but suffice to say for now that I am entirely in agreement with Kinsella on this point and can bring no substantive objection to his criticisms.

38 As Mortellaro notes:
   [W]hy should we assume that the hitman's actions are determined? Why should we assume that by the mere act of offering money the inciter is able to take control of the hitman's body and make him do the dirty work? The same argument which underpins the Blockian and Rothbardian support for the right to incite-by-words can be used to bolster the right to incite-by-monetary-payment.
   Mortellaro, "Causation and Responsibility," p. 16. See also Van Dun, "Against Libertarian Legalism," p. 64 n.3 ("there is such a thing as one person causing another to do something without actually using compulsion or force to make him do it and without having him agree to a contractual obligation to do it."). Moreover, as noted in the text, under the Rothbardian title-transfer theory of contracts advocated in these pages, contracts do not give rise to obligations anyway, but only cause title to owned resources to be transferred. See "A Libertarian Theory of Contract" (ch. 9).

as mere title transfers (in which money is just one type of thing that can contractually be transferred), and also contrary to the Austrian view of the subjective nature of value (because people can be motivated by things other than title transfers; the end of action need not be obtaining ownership of something).

As for the former point: a contract is simply alienation to property: it is simply a property title transfer. It is not a "binding obligation."[39] Yet Block does seem to rely on the conventional view of contracts as "binding obligations" or promises, instead of as mere transfers of title to alienable owned resources (Rothbard's view, which Block elsewhere seems to support), to support his *ad hoc* "incitement-by-monetary-payment" exception. As he writes:

> However, if Van Dun *paid* me for this information, e.g., the hikers *paid and therefore contractually obligated* the local yokel to tell the truth, then we would have entirely a different matter. Then he would be guilty of a contract violation that resulted in death, a very serious matter indeed.[40]

Block's use of the language "contractually obligated" indicates he is not here viewing a contract as a mere transfer of ownership of a resource, but rather as some kind of promise giving rise to a legally-enforceable or binding obligation—contrary to the Rothbard-Evers title-transfer theory of contract.

As for the latter point: paying someone is simply one means of inducing them to do something—to obtain money that they subjectively value. They could be induced or persuaded by giving them other things they value, such as gratitude, or a service. Whether a woman pays a hitman money to kill her husband or persuades him to do so for sexual favors should not make a difference. To focus on the payment of money, or coercion, as exceptions, is simply *ad hoc* and also ignores the Rothbardian view of contracts, as well as the Austrian view of the subjective nature of value.[41]

---

[39] See "A Libertarian Theory of Contract" (ch. 9).
[40] Block, "Reply to Frank van Dun's 'Natural Law and the Jurisprudence of Freedom,'" p. 66.
[41] See also Mortellaro, "Causation and Responsibility," p. 16, criticizing Rothbard and Block for the *ad hoc* exception of "incitement-by-monetary-payment" as being inconsistent with their objection to "incitement-by-words" and also as being "in tension with the Austrian theory of value, namely, that it is entirely subjective ... we have no reason to condemn money payments while turning a blind eye to psychic value."

As for Block's view that an instigator can be liable for the intermediaries actions if he "orders" him, it is not clear what the rationale is, although Block's comments suggest he means here an order coupled with a threat, in which case this exception collapses into the first.[42] Why can't the person who incites the mob be characterized as "ordering" them to lynch someone, if ordering does not require threats? If ordering does not require threats, then why would this reasoning not apply to an inciter?

As for the final exception—liability in the case of being part of a criminal conspiracy—there is no definition provided and no clear explanation of why this makes one culpable.[43] No reason is given as to why we can't characterize the person inciting a lynch mob as being part of a criminal conspiracy with the lynchers.

As noted above with the Hitler example, even with these exceptions, many "instigators" would not technically be culpable for actions taken by their subordinates.[44] Block attempts to find a way out of absolving a Hitler or other political leader, or mob boss, army general, and the like from liability for actions of their subordinates by simply assuming or positing that they are always, necessarily, threatening their subordinates, so that the first exception applies. As he writes:

> [T]he libertarian legal code proscribes not only invasive acts, but also intimidation. Hitler, Stalin, et al. were not merely engaging in their free speech rights. Rather, they were issuing orders to their subordinates to maim and kill innocent people. Implicit in these commands was the threat that if they were not obeyed, those who failed to carry out these orders would be summarily dealt with.[45]

---

[42] See note 35, above.

[43] Block attempts to clarify the principle in Walter Block, "Rejoinder to Kinsella and Tinsley on Incitement, Causation, Aggression and Praxeology," *J. Libertarian Stud.* 22, no. 1 (2011; https://mises.org/library/rejoinder-kinsella-and-tinsley-incitement-causation-aggression-and-praxeology): 641–64, p. 652, but he simply restates his rule in other terms, without any basis or justification. He writes:

> There are no exceptions here. The arm's length rule of cooperation, collusion, aiding and abetting, is exceptionless. Of course, it is sometimes a delicate matter to determine where on the arm's length continuum any particular case lies.

But what are the criteria for "colluding" or "cooperation"? Why are these even the criteria? Why isn't the inciter who whips a mob into a lynching frenzy "colluding" with them?

[44] See note 31 and accompanying text, above, *et pass.*

[45] See note 35, above.

But this is simply a convenient, yet false, assumption. First, not every underling is literally threatened with physical punishment if he does not obey orders. Second, even if the underling is threatened, the threat does not necessarily come *from the boss*, but rather from others in the hierarchy or organization. Did Hitler *literally*, personally threaten any of his generals or subordinates *himself*? Did President Truman threaten his generals or, indirectly, the airmen who dropped nuclear bombs on Japan? Simply assuming every leader or boss is necessarily "threatening" the underlings is unrealistic and just too convenient of an assumption to let one wriggle out of the uncomfortable consequences of this *ad hoc* theorizing. (And, again, even when the underling is threatened, this *still* does not mean his actions were "determined"; he still has the same free will that a non-coerced intermediary has.) We would argue that the leaders in these social or institutional hierarchies are responsible for the crimes committed by subordinates, even if they don't threaten them.

In sum, it is a mistake to conclude that someone can be responsible for the actions of others *only* in the cases of the exceptions of coercion, monetary payment, orders + threats, or criminal conspiracy. It makes more sense to scrutinize actions in terms of the more generalizable praxeological means-end framework set forth above. This framework easily justifies all the "exceptions" noted above, and more. In each case, the malfeasor (wrongdoer) had a prohibited end in mind (some type of property invasion), and employs means that attain this end. The fact that the means in these examples were other people simply does not prevent the action from being classified as aggression.

Fixed Pie of Responsibility and Joint and Several Liability

The reluctance to attribute responsibility to the instigator of a crime, unless one of the exceptions is met, may be due to confusion about the nature of responsibility for torts or crimes. First, as noted above, some believe that the intermediary or underling's free will breaks the chain of causation so that the instigator is not liable. But since cooperative action (for good or evil) is possible, and humans can employ other humans as means to accomplish ends, this is not a tenable objection.

In addition, some libertarians seem to believe that holding the instigator or inciter liable would relieve the underling or henchman of responsibility, which they understandably oppose. We may refer to this as the "fixed pie of responsibility" fallacy. For example, libertarian author Jack Lloyd seems to implicitly adopt such reasoning; note the use of the word "rather" here: "In this Steel-Man-case scenario, Hitler would not be culpable for an initiation of force. *Rather*, the people who did the actual initiations and threats of force would be culpable...."[46] The word "rather" implies it has to be *either* Hitler, *or* his underlings, that is responsible. But why can't it be both?

Block also seems to implicitly accept such an approach. He writes:

> Van Dun tries to make an analogy between the triggerman and the bullet, on the one hand, and the inciter and the rioter, on the other. He argues that the gunman is really responsible for the murder, not the bullet that actually kills, because the former came first in the causal chain, and so was responsible for the effect of the latter. This conclusion is true enough. But then he maintains that precisely the same relationship obtains between the inciter and the rioter who murders. To do so, however, he would have to say that, after all, the inciter, too, is responsible for the murder, not the rioter who actually kills, because the former came first in the causal chain, and was thus responsible for the effect of the latter.
>
> When put in this way, the problems with the analogy are apparent. First, no one in his right mind would hold the bullet guilty of anything. It is an inanimate object, for all of its destructive power. Yet, it would be the rare analyst, even one as intent upon incarcerating the *inciter* as is Van Dun, who would allow the *rioter* off scot-free, as he would the bullet. That is, no one would even think to "punish" the bullet for its evil deed.[47]

Note the language "he would have to say that, after all, the inciter, too, is responsible for the murder, *not the rioter who actually kills*" (emphasis added) and the criticism that by holding the inciter responsible, the rioter would have to be let off "scot-free." But there is no basis for this contention. Just because the inciter or instigator is culpable does *not* mean the rioter or underling is off the hook. It is perfectly possible to hold them *both* fully liable; this is what joint and several liability means.[48]

---

46 See Lloyd, "Justice and Voluntaryism," quoted in note 31, above (emphasis added).
47 Block, "Reply to 'Against Libertarian Legalism,'" p. 16.
48 Block adds:
Second, and not unrelated, the rioter is a human being, presumably with free will; no one could say the same of a piece of lead. Third, there are many cases in which

With this "fixed pie of liability" assumption, some might object that each malfeasor is responsible only for his pro-rata "part" of the crime. Maybe the instigator is 60% responsible and the underling 40% responsible. And so on. These critics mistakenly assume that there is some fixed 100 percent bucket of liability for a crime, which cannot be shared jointly by multiple parties. They thus are leery of attributing some responsibility to the boss because they think that this would reduce the liability of the underling. But there is no conceptual problem with having multiple parties *each fully liable* for the same act of aggression, under the notion of joint and several liability. It is not clear why my opponents here do not realize that this doctrine can play a useful role as part of the analysis of collective action. As an example, suppose *A* and *B* jointly borrow money from *C*. If *A* is unable to pay his share later, it is not as if *C* can only pursue *B* for half the amount owed; he can pursue each debtor for 100% of the amount owed (barring contractual terms to the contrary).[49]

---

an inciter incites until his lungs give out, and no subsequent riot takes place, further attesting to the distinction between free will and inanimate objects that mars Van Dun's analogy. But, apart from a misfire, bullets always discharge when fired. According to Van Dun, the inciter "fires off" the rioter in much the same way as the shooter does to the bullet. This is not at all the case. To be logically consistent, Van Dun would have to hold the inciter guilty of a crime even when no subsequent riot ensued.

Ibid., p. 16 (footnote omitted). I have already argued above that the "free will" of the rioter does not mean the inciter is innocent; after all, in other cases in which Block does believe the instigator is liable, such as coercion or monetary payment, the intermediary still has free will. But consider here Block's final sentence, criticizing Van Dun because someone who *attempts* to incite a riot that does not happen, under Van Dun's approach, would presumably still be guilty of a crime. Block points this out as if this conclusion is obviously wrong or unjust. But why is it wrong? If you try to shoot someone but miss, you can still be guilty of attempted murder, a lesser crime than actual murder, perhaps, but a punishable offense nonetheless. The libertarian view of rights and aggression prohibits not only trespass, battery, and so on, but also *assault* (which is *attempted* battery, or putting someone in fear of receiving a battery), *threats*, and the like. See "A Libertarian Theory of Punishment and Rights" (ch. 5), Part IV.F, "Why Assault, Threats, and Attempts Are Aggression"; and Kinsella, "Stalking and Threats as Aggression," *StephanKinsella.com* (Jan. 10, 2021). So, yes, someone who tries to whip a mob up into lynching someone, even if he fails, might be guilty of attempted aggression.

49 See, e.g., Saúl Litvinoff, *The Law of Obligations: Part I: Obligations in General*, 2d ed. (St. Paul, Minn.: West Publishing Company, 2001), § 7.13 (citing 2 Williston, *A Treatise on the Law of Contracts*, 3d ed. (1959), pp. 316, 320 and *Restatement (Second) of Contracts* (1981), § 289), and §7.26 *et seq*. See also the similar concept of "solidary obligation" in the civil law. See Litvinoff, *The Law of Obligations*, § 7.61; Louisiana Civil Code (https://

Likewise, just as one criminal can harm multiple victims and be unable to be punished by, or render full restitution to, each victim—so multiple criminals can each be fully—jointly and severally—liable for the damage done to the victim. There is simply no reason to maintain that there is a finite "pie" of "criminal harm" that has to be distributed piecemeal to multiple criminals who collaborate to harm someone. It is the victim's rights that matter most, not that of individual criminals.[50] Suppose two criminals cooperate to rob someone of $10,000 worth of property and then they spend the money. Suppose they are later apprehended; the first is penniless and the second has assets. The second should be forced to pay the victim the full $10,000 owed,[51] not only half on the grounds that his partner owes the other $5,000 to the victim. Why should the victim, as opposed to the bankrupt criminal's partner in crime, be left holding the bag? Thus it is just to hold both the mob boss, and his henchman, fully liable and responsible for a murder committed by the henchman but ordered by the boss.

"Mere" Speech and Causation

Related to the above-noted arguments is the notion that "mere" speech cannot be aggression since it does not actually invade others' property borders. It is true that a speech act *per se* is not an act of aggression: it does not intentionally cause the person or property of another to be physically and nonconsensually infringed upon.[52] (Shooting a gun, or

---

www.legis.la.gov/legis/Laws_Toc.aspx?folder=67&level=Parent), art. 1794 ("An obligation is solidary for the obligors when each obligor is liable for the whole performance. A performance rendered by one of the solidary obligors relieves the others of liability toward the obligee."); Alain A. Levasseur, *Louisiana Law of Obligations in General: A Précis*, 3d ed. (LexisNexis, 2009), chap. 3, in particular §§ 3.2.1, 3.2.2, 3.3.1; and *idem, Louisiana Law of Obligations in General: A Comparative Civil Law Perspective, A Treatise* (Durham, NC: Carolina Academic Press, 2020), chap. 3, ¶ 117 *et seq.*

50 For more on this approach, see "A Libertarian Theory of Punishment and Rights" (ch. 5), Part IV.B, "The Victim's Options," *et pass.*

51 Of course, more than $10,000 would arguably be owed, but this is not relevant here. (For more on this issue, see "A Libertarian Theory of Punishment and Rights" (ch. 5), Part IV.C, "Enhancing Punishment Due to Other Factors.")

52 For a discussion of how this doctrine works itself out in the context of voluntary slave contracts, see "A Libertarian Theory of Contract" (ch. 9) and "Inalienability and Punishment: A Reply to George Smith" (ch. 10), the section "Inalienability." It is ironic that Block generally opposes the notion that speech acts (such as incitement) can give rise to liability, except for

swinging your first, is also not *per se* an act of aggression!) But some speech acts can be classified as acts of aggression in the context in which they occur because they constitute the speaker's use of means calculated to inflict intentional harm, and because of the social and institutional hierarchies involved. One clear example of this is threats of force. The threat to stab someone does not actually pierce the victim's skin; it is a "mere" speech-act, but it is still regarded as aggression. Offering to pay money to someone to assassinate someone would be another example. But these are not mere *ad hoc* exceptions; they are the result of the application of the more general means-end analysis.[53]

In other cases, the act of speaking—communicating—and the other people with whom the speaker communicates serve as one's means to achieve a certain end. The firing squad commander who yells "Fire!" is as responsible for the ensuing execution as the riflemen themselves.[54] This is not because his spoken word was physically the cause of the victim's

---

the *ad hoc* exceptions of monetary payment and coercion, yet in his view of voluntary slavery, the uttering of the words "I hereby promise to be your slave" justify the "master's" use of force against the purported "slave"—as if his words had committed a type of aggression against the "master" that justifies the use of (responsive) force against the promisor.

[53] See "A Libertarian Theory of Punishment and Rights" (ch. 5), Part IV.F, "Why Assault, Threats, and Attempts Are Aggression"; Kinsella, "Stalking and Threats as Aggression."

[54] This argument should not be conflated with Justice Oliver Wendell Holmes's famous (and flawed) example of liability for shouting "Fire" in a crowded theater, which he used to argue that First Amendment free speech rights are not absolute. As Rothbard notes:

> [C]ouching the analysis in terms of a "right to free speech" instead of property rights leads to confusion and the weakening of the very concept of rights. The most famous example is Justice Holmes's contention that no one has the right to shout "Fire" falsely in a crowded theater, and *therefore* that the right to freedom of speech cannot be absolute, but must be weakened and tempered by considerations of "public policy." And yet, if we analyze the problem in terms of *property* rights we will see that no weakening of the absoluteness of rights is necessary.
> For, logically, the shouter is either a patron or the theater owner. If he is the theater owner, he is violating the property rights of the patrons in quiet enjoyment of the performance, for which he took their money in the first place. If he is another patron, then he is violating both the property right of the patrons to watching the performance *and* the property right of the owner, for he is violating the terms of his being there. For those terms surely include not violating the owner's property by disrupting the performance he is putting on. In either case, he may be prosecuted as a violator of property rights; therefore, when we concentrate on the *property* rights involved, we see that the Holmes case implies no need for the law to weaken the absolute nature of rights.

Rothbard, "'Human Rights' As Property Rights," p. 114 (references omitted).

death. His voice did not propel the bullets forward—and it did not have to. Instead, the firing squad commander is responsible for the execution because of what the command "Fire!" *signifies* in the context and social hierarchy in which it was uttered; it signifies that the commander intends for the victim to die and is choosing to employ efficacious means—his firing squad—calculated to achieve that goal. The firing squad commander isn't "merely" speaking; he is intentionally colluding with the shooters for the purpose of killing the victim. Likewise the American president who orders a bomb be dropped is causing the bombing; he is employing the pilot and other underlings as his means. By being part of a certain organization or hierarchy and having certain relationships with other people, as a practical matter he is in a position to use other people to achieve his ends.[55]

Consider the car-bomb scenario discussed above. When *A* persuades *C* to plant the bomb, his words do not physically cause *B*'s car to explode. And they do not even physically cause *C* to plant the bomb—*C* voluntarily chooses to do so. The fact that *C*'s action was voluntary, however, does not mean that *A*'s action—persuading someone to plant a car-bomb—cannot itself be considered aggression. To the contrary, *A* is an aggressor because his actions demonstrated the intent to kill *B* and the use of means calculated to do just that. So what if his chosen means included another person and his intervening will?

---

[55] In this regard, see also Frank van Dun's discussion of "social causation." Van Dun, "Against Libertarian Legalism," pp. 64, 79. Block, in responding to some of Van Dun's criticisms, writes:

> The essence of Van Dun's criticism of my article is that while all physically invasive acts must be characterized as unjustified aggression and prohibited by law, there is a second type of aggression, call it for want of a better term "mental aggression," which should also, in addition to physical aggression, be considered legally illicit. Examples of this, as we shall analyze below, include libel, lying, making false accusations to the police, blackmail, "hate" speech, and negative "social causation" such as incitement to riot, gang leaders or dictators ordering their henchmen to commit crimes (of physical invasion), etc....
>
> Further instances of "mental aggression" might include shunning, boycotting, cutting "dead," refusing to deal with, buy from, sell to, etc. It is difficult to see how any libertarian could favor the outlawry of such behavior, but this would seem to be the implication of Van Dun's theory.

Block, "Reply to 'Against Libertarian Legalism,'" p. 3 and n.7 (footnote omitted). I agree with Block's criticism of Van Dun here, except for the social causation part, where I agree with Van Dun.

Let us return to the incitement example. In order to determine whether the inciter is responsible, we ask whether the inciter *used the mob as his means* to attain the violent acts committed by the rioting mob. For the inciter's action to be considered aggression, he would have to *intend* the prohibited result; and he would have to have *chosen means* that resulted in the rioting. We do not maintain that the inciter is necessarily responsible in every case; the question turns on many specific facts and the context. What we maintain is that the inciter is not off the hook *merely because* the rioters had free will. The question to be answered is: was the mob the *means* of the inciter? Was the inciter a cause of the mob rioting, or of their ensuing havoc?

As Van Dun keenly observes:

> Who should take credit for the poem: the blind poet, or his girlfriend who lovingly typed the manuscript (which she could have refused to do)? And if the blind poet really is the author of the poem, why should the rabble-rousing demagogue not be the author of the riots he incites?

> Why should we require libertarian judges to turn a blind eye to real processes of "social causation" when we know that advertisers, educators, politicians, and agitators are very much aware of them—and willing to use them for their purposes? It is not just in a libertarian world that each person is responsible for his own acts; it is true in every world. However, we should not take that as an excuse for disregarding the complex causal processes that go on in the real world, whatever legal code is in force. A libertarian judge has to confront the facts. Reality does not yield to theory. It is all right for a judge to remind a man charged with participating in a violent mob that he is responsible for his own actions, but only after he has determined what the man's own *actions*—not merely his bodily movements—really were. If the man was forced (coerced, compelled) by another to participate, we have one sort of case. If he got paid to smash windows, we have another sort of case. If he was manipulated in any other way, surely we cannot just pretend that then everything was the same as if he was not manipulated in any way—and treat the manipulator as if he was just an innocent bystander.[56]

---

[56] Van Dun, "Against Libertarian Legalism," p. 79. For a recent real-world example, see Ellen Moynihan & Larry McShane, "Bronx mom charged with luring ex-boyfriend to his shooting death by current beau," *New York Daily News* (Mar 15, 2023; https://perma.cc/79Z8-UV8L).

The same question is asked in a variety of situations: did the general kill people, using his troops as means to this end? Did the manager use his employee as a means to attain some end? Did the wife kill her husband by using her lover (or a hired hit-man) as the means to attain this goal? If someone votes in favor of socialism (or speaks out in favor of it), are they a cause of the ensuing acts of aggression by state agents? If a witness lies on the witness stand, resulting in a criminal defendant wrongly being imprisoned, has he caused harm to the defendant, through means of jurors, jailers, and the judicial system?[57] In other words, was the first party a *cause* of the result that was actually committed by an intermediate person?

Although there will be easy cases, we do not suggest that merely formulating the issue in this manner makes the correct answer easy to find in every situation. Such questions must take into account relevant facts and the context, custom, social hierarchies and realities, and depend on the sense of justice of the judge or jury—of the community. Looking at actions from the praxeological point of view, however, helps us look in the right place and ask the right questions. No doubt, in cases where the intermediate actor is coerced, or paid, by the first party, it is easier to see that the first party is the cause of the threatened or remunerated action.[58] But it is simply arbitrary to restrict cause to cases where the intermediate actor is threatened, or paid cash.

---

[57] See Thomas Aquinas, *Summa Theologica* (New Advent; https://www.newadvent.org/summa), *Secunda Secundæ Partis*, Question 64, art. 6, Reply to Objection 3 (emphasis added):
> If the judge knows that man who has been convicted by false witnesses, is innocent he must, like Daniel, examine the witnesses with great care, so as to find a motive for acquitting the innocent: but if he cannot do this he should remit him for judgment by a higher tribunal. If even this is impossible, he does not sin if he pronounce sentence in accordance with the evidence, for *it is not he that puts the innocent man to death, but they who stated him to be guilty.*

[58] In cases where the victim's own actions, or those of an innocent intermediate party like the courier (as in the letter-bomb case) are part of the chain of causation, the instigator is solely liable. In cases where someone collaborates with other malefactors to commit an act of aggression, as in a bank robbery, the co-conspirators each have joint and several liability.

CAUSE-IN-FACT, PROXIMATE CAUSE, AND ACTION

Before turning to Reinach's views on causation, a brief discussion of the contrast between conventional legal theories and that laid out here is in order. In general, in the common law, to be responsible, an actor needs to be both the cause-in-fact (or "but-for" cause) of a prohibited result, and also the "proximate" (or "legal") cause (referred to as "culpability" in continental legal systems).[59] Both need to be satisfied. One is a cause-in-fact of a result if "but for" the person's actions, the result would not have occurred. There are various tests for proximate cause, but basically

---

[59] As Francis Bacon wrote in his treatise *Maxims of the Law*, regarding *causa proxima*, or proximate cause: "'In jure non remota causa, sed proxima spectatur' (In law not the remote, but the proximate cause is looked at)." Patrick J. Kelley, "Proximate Cause in Negligence Law: History, Theory and the Present Darkness," *Washington U. L. Q.* 69, no. 1 (Jan. 1991; https://openscholarship.wustl.edu/law_lawreview/vol69/iss1/6/): 49–105, at 54. See also International Risk Management Institute, "The History of Proximate Causation" (https://www.irmi.com/articles/expert-commentary/the-history-of-proximate-causation).

The Model Penal Code (1985), §2.03 (https://archive.org/details/ModelPenalCode_ALI), which codifies a dominant test for causation in the law, provides:

Section 2.03. *Causal Relationship Between Conduct and Result; Divergence Between Result Designed or Contemplated and Actual Result or Between Probable and Actual Result.*

(1) Conduct is the cause of a result when:
   (a) it is an antecedent but for which the result in question would not have occurred; and
   (b) the relationship between the conduct and result satisfies any additional causal requirements imposed by the Code or by the law defining the offense.

(2) When purposely or knowingly causing a particular result is an element of an offense, the element is not established if the actual result is not within the purpose or the contemplation of the actor unless:
   (a) the actual result differs from that designed or contemplated, as the case may be, only in the respect that a different person or different property is injured or affected or that the injury or harm designed or contemplated would have been more serious or more extensive than that caused; or
   (b) the actual result involves the same kind of injury or harm as that designed or contemplated and is not too remote or accidental in its occurrence to have a [just] bearing on the actor's liability or on the gravity of his offense.

(3) When recklessly or negligently causing a particular result is an element of an offense, the element is not established if the actual result is not within the risk of which the actor is aware or, in the case of negligence, of which he should be aware unless:
   (a) the actual result differs from the probable result only in the respect that a different person or different property is injured or affected or that the probable injury or harm would have been more serious or more extensive than that caused; or

the idea is that the results had to be intended, or somewhat foreseeable to the actor, and not too "remote" (hence "proximate," meaning near or close) from the person's action. It is sometimes said that the result had to follow as a natural, direct, and immediate consequence of the action, with no "intervening cause" breaking the connection between the action and the result. For example, a murderer's mother is a cause-in-fact of the murders he commits, for without her actions (giving birth to him) the murders would not have been committed. Yet she is not a proximate cause of the murders and therefore not responsible.

In our case, when we ask if someone was the cause of a certain aggression, we are asking whether the actor did choose and employ means to attain the prohibited result. For there to be "cause" in this sense, obviously there has to be cause-in-fact or "but-for" causation—this is implied by the notion of the means employed "attaining" or resulting in the actor's end. Intentionality is also a factor, because action has to be intentional to be an action (the means is chosen and employed intentionally; the actor intends to achieve a given end).[60]

(b) the actual result involves the same kind of injury or harm as the probable result and is not too remote or accidental in its occurrence to have a [just] bearing on the actor's liability or on the gravity of his offense.

(4) When causing a particular result is a material element of an offense for which absolute liability is imposed by law, the element is not established unless the actual result is a probable consequence of the actor's conduct.

[60] Notice that this analysis helps to explain why damages or punishment is greater for intentional crimes than for negligent torts that result in similar damage. Keep in mind that punishment is an action, and a fully intentional one; it is not negligent, or "partially intentional." Punishment is an intentional action that aims at punishing the body of the aggressor or tortfeasor. In punishing a criminal, the punishment is justified because the criminal himself intentionally violated the borders of the victim; the punishment is therefore symmetrical (see "A Libertarian Theory of Punishment and Rights" (ch. 5)). However, in punishing a mere tortfeasor, the punishment is fully intentional, but the negligent action being punished is only "partially" intentional, so to speak. In order to make the punishment or response to a torfeasor proportionate, since the tort was only partly intentional but the punishment will be fully intentional, therefore, the damages (intentionally) inflicted (or extracted) have to be reduced to some degree to make the punishment more proportionate overall. As an example, if a criminal intentionally murders someone, it would (in principle) be symmetrical for the victim's heirs to have him killed. But if a tortfeasor accidentally kills someone, the punishment inflicted on him would have to be an order of magnitude lower since his action was not fully intentional while that of the punisher would be. Walter Block argues that if it were technologically feasible to "suck the life out of" a criminal, or even a negligent tortfeasor, to bring the victim back to life, this would be justified. See Roy Whitehead & Walter Block, "Taking the Assets

REINACH AND CAUSATION

Reinach provides a framework for the analysis of legal causation which, although it employs different terminology, is largely compatible with the Austrian-praxeological view presented above.[61] Reinach states:

> Every action which is a condition for an outcome is, in relation to the intentional crime, a cause of this outcome in the sense of the criminal law. … Disregarding exceptional cases of the law, the characterized principle is fully valid. It is then also to be said: if the action is a sound [*zurechnungsfähigen*] condition of an unlawful outcome, and if an intention is also given in relation to this outcome, then the agent is customarily punished. … That an outcome is brought about means that it is brought about by an action which sets a condition for the outcome; to bring about intentionally means to bring about via an action that sets a condition. The latter condition brings about the outcome. Intention is a striving for an outcome via an action, or mediated by an action. This outcome itself can of course be a means to another outcome. The death of a human being can be striven for in order to obtain the things left behind which the murderer subsequently is entitled to. But the outcome is "striven" for, also when it is not a final goal, but in that case is "striven" for as a means towards a final goal. There are however several kinds of strivings: one can hope for, desire [*ersehnen*], or fear for [*befürchten*] a result. These are all "strivings" for a result, but not a striving in our sense. It is a striving "in relation to that to which it is applied"; for us it is a matter of striving for an outcome with the awareness that something can be contributed [such as to control] to its occurrence. Such a striving is called an act of will [*Wollen*]. To cause something intentionally means to set a condition for an outcome through a voluntary action such that

---

of Criminals to Compensate Victims of Violence: A Legal and Philosophical Approach," *J. Law in Society* 5 (2003; http://www.walterblock.com/publications/): 229–253, p. 249 *et seq.* Since this is so far-fetched and probably would never be possible, I state no opinion on this argument but do not find it relevant.

For some of my thoughts on how negligence law might develop in a private-law society, see Kinsella, "The Libertarian Approach to Negligence, Tort, and Strict Liability: Wergeld and Partial Wergeld," *Mises Economics Blog* (Sep. 1, 2009).

[61] See Hans-Hermann Hoppe, "Property, Causality, and Liability," *Q. J. Austrian Econ.* 7, no. 4 (Winter 2004; https://mises.org/library/property-causality-and-liability-1): 87–95, also included in Hoppe, *The Great Fiction: Property, Economy, Society, and the Politics of Decline*, Second Expanded Edition (Auburn, Ala.: Mises Institute, 2021; https://www.hanshoppe.com/tgf/), for an excellent discussion of Reinach's views on causation.

> this condition of course in combination with other conditions brings
> about the outcome.... Intention is to will an outcome.[62]

This analysis is strikingly compatible with the Austrian understanding of action. Reinach's use of "cause" and "condition" is similar to the proximate cause and "cause-in-fact" test discussed above. Reinach maintains that an action that intends the outcome to occur (i.e., desires a given end or goal), and "causes" this outcome to occur by an action (i.e., employs a means to attain this goal), then the actor should be punished for the action, which is a crime.

Using Reinach's causal analysis, one would, as in the analysis presented above, not necessarily absolve someone of responsibility simply because another human is used to help "cause" the unlawful end. Reinach's paper is full of interesting and illuminating examples and applications of causation framework. In one colorful example, A sends B into a forest in the hopes that he will be struck by lightning.[63] Reinach contrasts this case with one in which A is able to calculate precisely where and when a tree will be struck by lightning, and, with malicious intent, sends B to be at the fateful place where lightning strikes. In both cases, Reinach argues, A is the "cause" (our "cause-in-fact") of B's death, since B's death would not have occurred but for A's having sent him into the forest. Nevertheless, Reinach concludes that A may be punished only in the second case and not in the first. The difference hinges upon A's intent. In the first case, A hoped for B to die, but it was simply wishful thinking: he had no control over the lightning, and no knowledge of any objective likelihood that it would strike where it did.

---

[62] Adolf Reinach, "On the Concept of Causality in the Criminal Law," *Libertarian Papers* 1, art. no. 35 (2009 [1905]; http://libertarianpapers.org/35-concept-causality-criminal-law/), pp. 27–28. In our original article, Tinsley and I relied on the then-unpublished translation of Reinach's article. I subsequently published a revised version of the translation in *Libertarian Papers*. I have updated the references in this chapter as well as the quoted passages to conform to the published version of the translation.

Another important work by Reinach not discussed in this chapter is Adolf Reinach, "The A Priori Foundations of the Civil Law," in *Aletheia* 3 (1983; https://philarchive.org/rec/REITAP-9): 1–142, which volume also includes other important commentary on Reinach, e.g. by Husserl and others. See also Kevin Mulligan, ed., *Speech Act and Sachverhalt: Reinach and the Foundations of Realist Phenomenology* (Dordrecht/Boston/Lancaster: Martinus Nijhoff Publishers, 1987).

[63] Ibid., pp. 11, 27, 31–33.

In praxeological terms, A's action in the first case cannot be construed as "killing" B, because he did not really intend B to die and did not employ any means expected to attain such a goal, any more than a rain dance causes it to rain or sticking pins in a voodoo doll harms the "victim." A's action is not calculated to cause harm to B; in fact, A does not expect and has no reason to expect that B will die as a result of going into the forest. As Reinach puts it, "the intention fails if the outcome is only hoped for, but the intention is present if it is expected with certainty."[64] Thus the praxeological view and Reinach's framework are consistent in this case.

In the second case, A has more than an empty wish: he has certain knowledge that sending B into the forest will result in B's being struck by lightning. Here Reinach finds A to have the intent necessary to be held responsible for B's death. Likewise, praxeologically, A's action now becomes more than simply "dispatching B into the forest." With the knowledge that sending B into the forest will cause his death, A's action rises to the level of "intentionally killing B." This is because, if A knows for certain that sending B into the forest will result in B's death by lightning, then A has the requisite intent to attain the goal of B's death, and his action employs means (namely, sending B into the forest) that do attain this goal.

This example can be a useful tool for separating criminal aggressors from their noncriminal sympathizers. Earlier we pointed out that the rule that allows one person to be responsible for another person's aggressive actions is a general one that must be applied cautiously and on a case-by-case basis, taking context and circumstances into account. The lightning example can help clarify our intuitions about which actions are aggressive and which are not. It is aggression when one person intentionally uses another as a means to cause an unwanted property violation; it is not aggression when one person merely hopes for a property violation to occur but does not intentionally use means to accomplish it. The Israeli government, for example, recently assassinated Hamas founder Sheik Ahmed Yassin.[65]

---

[64] Ibid., p. 28.
[65] See https://en.wikipedia.org/wiki/Ahmed_Yassin.

Putting aside the question of whether Yassin was an innocent victim or a deserving target, we can surely acknowledge that there are many people—especially in the United States and Israel—who wanted to see Yassin killed. But only a very small number of these people intended to kill Yassin themselves or to assist his killers in any way. The lesson of Reinach's lightning example is that the people who simply hoped that Yassin would die, or who rejoiced when he was killed, are not responsible for his killing. They gave his killers silent support and sympathy, but they did not intentionally act with the purpose of killing him. The team of assassins themselves, and the Israeli government that sponsored them, are responsible for the killing, but not the citizens who opinion polls show approve of the assassination.

This result is compatible with the framework advocated herein. The subtle insights, analysis, and examples provided in Reinach's century-old paper are clearly still useful in constructing a praxeologically sound theory of legal causation today.[66]

---

[66] As pointed out in note †, above, our paper "Causation and Aggression" was published in a symposium issue on "Austrian Law and Economics: The Contributions of Reinach and Rothbard," in *Quarterly J. Austrian Econ.* 7, no. 4 (Winter 2004). In addition to our paper, the symposium issue included the following (plus two additional papers not presented at the original in-person symposium): Jörg Guido Hülsmann, "Editorial," https://mises.org/library/editorial-special-symposium-issue-austrian-law-and-economics-0, pp. 3–6; Laurent Carnis, "Pitfalls of the Classical School of Crime," https://mises.org/library/pitfalls-classical-school-crime-0, pp. 7–18 (this paper does not deal with Reinach); Larry J. Sechrest, "Praxeology, Economics, and Law: Issues and Implications," https://mises.org/library/praxeology-economics-and-law-issues-and-implications-0, pp. 19–40; Jörg Guido Hülsmann, "The A Priori Foundations of Property Economics," https://cdn.mises.org/qjae7_4_4.pdf, pp. 41–68; Walter Block, "Austrian Law and Economics: The Contributions of Adolf Reinach and Murray Rothbard," https://mises.org/library/austrian-law-and-economics-contributions-adolf-reinach-and-murray-rothbard-law-economics-and, pp. 69–85; Hoppe, "Property, Causality, and Liability"; and Leo Zailbert, "Toward Meta-Politics," https://mises.org/library/toward-meta-politics-0, pp. 113–28.

Barry Smith's original paper presented at the in-person symposium, "The *A Priori* Ontology of Social Reality," was never published. In private correspondence with Smith (Nov. 25, 2022), he stated that although he has lost track of the original symposium piece he presented, one of his subsequent papers contains many of the pertinent elements of the argument of that presentation: Barry Smith, "An Essay on Material Necessity," Philip Hanson & Bruce Hunter, eds., *Return of the A Priori* (*Canadian J. Philosophy*, Supplementary Volume 18, 1993; https://philpapers.org/archive/SMIAEO-2.pdf): 301–322; and that a much later paper concerning these issues is Barry Smith & Wojciech Żełaniec, "Laws of Essence or Constitutive Rules? Reinach vs. Searle on the Ontology of Social Entities," in Francesca De Vecchi, ed., *Eidetica del Diritto e Ontologia Sociale. Il Realismo di Adolf Reinach* (Milan: Mimesis, 2012; https://perma.cc/LR2P-NLXW): 83–108.

9

A Libertarian Theory of Contract:
Title Transfer, Binding Promises, and Inalienability

While in law school in Louisiana (the only civil law state in the US), I was
introduced to the Roman and civil law* and also to contract law and theory.
It was during my first-year contracts class, in 1988, that I conceived of my
"estoppel" based theory of rights.† I also became interested in the Rothbard-Evers
title-transfer theory of contract.†† I presented a paper on this topic in 1999,
integrating the views of Rothbard and Evers with various concepts from the
civil law and the common law.§ I later published an article on this in the
Journal of Libertarian Studies, upon which this chapter is based.**

* Discussed in "Legislation and the Discovery of Law in a Free Society" (ch. 13).
† See "How I Became a Libertarian" (ch. 1), n.6 and accompanying text; "A Libertarian
Theory of Punishment and Rights" (ch. 5).
†† See Murray N. Rothbard, "Property Rights and the Theory of Contracts," in *The Ethics
of Liberty* (New York: New York University Press, 1998; https://mises.org/library/property-
rights-and-theory-contracts); and Williamson M. Evers, "Toward a Reformulation of the
Law of Contracts," *J. Libertarian Stud.* 1, no. 1 (Winter 1977; https://mises.org/library/

I. INTRODUCTION

A. Property and Contract

A system of property rights specifies how to determine which individuals own—have the right to control—particular scarce resources. By having a just, objective rule for allocating control of scare resources to particular owners, resource use conflicts may be reduced. Nonowners can simply refrain from invading the borders of the owned resources—that is, avoid using the thing without the owner's consent.[1] Using a property rights

---

toward-reformulation-law-contracts): 3–13. See also Kinsella, "Justice and Property Rights: Rothbard on Scarcity, Property, Contracts...," *The Libertarian Standard* (Nov. 19, 2010), discussing the origins of the Rothbard-Evers contract theory.

§ Stephan Kinsella, "A Libertarian Theory of Contracts," Austrian Scholars Conference, Mises Institute, Auburn, Ala. (April 17, 1999); also *idem*, "The Theory of Contracts," Rothbard Graduate Seminar, Mises Institute, Auburn, Ala. (July 28–Aug. 2, 2002; https://perma.cc/RQ5Z-S2GE).

** Stephan Kinsella, "A Libertarian Theory of Contracts: Title Transfer, Binding Promises, and Inalienability," *J. Libertarian Stud.* 17, no. 2 (Spring 2003): 11–37. Related articles or discussions published after the original article include "Selling Does Not Imply Ownership, and Vice-Versa: A Dissection" (ch. 11); and various *Kinsella on Liberty Podcast* episodes, e.g.: "KOL225 | Reflections on the Theory of Contract (PFS 2017)" (Sep. 17, 2017); "KOL197 | Tom Woods Show: The Central Rothbard Contribution I Overlooked, and Why It Matters: The Rothbard-Evers Title-Transfer Theory of Contract" (Dec. 3, 2015); "KOL146 | Interview of Williamson Evers on the Title-Transfer Theory of Contract" (Aug. 5, 2014); "KOL020 | "Libertarian Legal Theory: Property, Conflict, and Society: Lecture 3: Applications I: Legal Systems, Contract, Fraud" (Mises Academy, 2011)" (Feb. 21, 2013).

---

[1] As noted previously, technically speaking, property rights are best viewed as rights to *exclude others* from using a resource rather than a right to use; and the term property, to be precise, should be used to refer to the (ownership) relationship between a human owner and an object (scarce, conflictable resource), not to the owned material object itself. Thus, your car is not your "property"; you have a property right *in* your car. On all this, and on the use of terms like conflictable or rivalrous to refer to ownable scarce resources, see Kinsella, "On Conflictability and Conflictable Resources," *StephanKinsella.com* (Jan. 31, 2022); *"Against Intellectual Property* After Twenty Years: Looking Back and Looking Forward" (ch. 15), at n.62; and "What Libertarianism Is" (ch. 2), at n.5.

Even more precisely still, property rights can be conceived of as rights *between human actors*, but *with respect to particular resources*, although this distinction makes little difference for our present purposes. On this point see, e.g., Emanuele Martinelli, "On Whether We Own What We Think" (draft, 2019; https://www.academia.edu/93535130/On_Whether_We_Own_What_We_Think), p. 6 ("Property is a relation between a person and a thing.");

scheme, it is at least possible for conflict to be avoided or reduced. This is the very purpose and function of property rights: to respond to the practical problem of conflict in a world of multiple actors.[2]

Under the libertarian approach, people are self-owners, that is, they own their bodies. As for external resources, that is, previously-unowned conflictable resources, the first to use an *unowned* scarce resource—the homesteader—becomes its owner.[3] This is called original appropriation or, sometimes, usually in the case of real (immovable) property,

---

Svetovar Pejovich, "Towards an Economic Theory of the Creation and Specification of Property Rights," in Henry G. Manne, ed., *Economics of Legal Relationships* (West Group, 1975), p. 40 (emphasis in original) ("[P]roperty rights are defined not as relations between men and things but, rather as *the behavioural relations among men that arise from the existence of things and pertain to their use.*"; quoted in Boudewijn Bouckaert, "What is Property?", *Harv. J.L. & Pub. Pol'y* 13, no. 3 (Summer 1990): 775–816, at 795); Andrew Koppelman, *Burning Down the House* (St. Martin's Press, 2022), p. 79 ("It's sometimes said that property is a relation between a person and a thing, but that's confused. Property rights are relations between people. If I legitimately own something (rather than merely possessing it, as might be true of stolen goods), everyone else on the planet has an obligation to keep their hands off it. If that's going to be true, then there has to be some reasonable basis for thinking that they have that obligation."); and Alex Kozinski, "Of Profligacy, Piracy, and Private Property," *Harv. J.L. & Pub. Pol'y.* 13, no. 1 (Winter 1990; https://perma.cc/Z8AD-634V): 17–21, p. 19:

> But what is property? That is not an easy question to answer. I remember sitting in my first-year property course on the first day of class when the professor ... asked the fundamental question: What are property rights? ... I threw up my hand and without even waiting to be called on I shouted out, "Property rights define the relationship between people and their property."
> Professor Krier stopped dead in his tracks, spun around, and gave me a long look. Finally he said: "That's very peculiar, Mr. Kozinski. Have you always had relations with inanimate objects? Most people I know have relations with other people."
> That was certainly not the last time I said something really dumb in class, but the lesson was not lost on me. Property rights are, of course, a species of relationships between people. At the minimum, they define the degree to which individuals may exclude other individuals from the use and enjoyment of their goods and services....

See also "*Against Intellectual Property* After Twenty Years: Looking Back and Looking Forward" (ch. 15), at n.62; and "What Libertarianism Is" (ch. 2), at n.5 and Appendix I.

2 See "What Libertarianism Is" (ch. 2); and other references in note 4, below.

3 See John Locke, *Second Treatise on Civil Government* (1690; https://www.johnlocke.net/2022/07/two-treatises-of-government.html), chap. 5, "Of Property"; "What Libertarianism Is" (ch. 2); "How We Come to Own Ourselves" (ch. 4); "A Libertarian Theory of Punishment and Rights" (ch. 5); Kinsella, "Aggression and Property Rights Plank in the Libertarian Party Platform," *StephanKinsella.com* (May 30, 2022).

homesteading. The first possessor has better title in the resource than any possible challenger, who is always, with respect to him, a latecomer.[4]

But property rights are not only acquired; they may be lost or transferred to others. For example, the owner may abandon the thing so that it once more becomes unowned and available for appropriation by a new homesteader. Likewise, the owner may give or sell the resource to another. The owner might also commit a crime or tort, thereby forfeiting his rights to the resource, in favor of the victim.[5]

Property theory concerns not only the initial acquisition of property rights in conflictable resources, but also their loss and transfer. Tort and punishment theory, as subsets of general property theory, describe how acts of aggression or negligence change ownership rights to scarce resources.[6] Contract theory specifies how rights are transferred as the

---

[4] The owner of a given resource is said to have a title to the resource, i.e., is entitled to use it. It is a property right since it becomes an extension of the owner's ability to interact with the world, i.e., one of his attributes or "properties"; he is the proprietor or has a proprietary interest in the thing. As Bouckaert writes:

> [T]he definition of property is simultaneously simple and complex. It is simple because we can distinguish a generally accepted common-sense notion of property; that is, something that belongs to somebody in a legitimate way, something that is "proper" to somebody.

Boudewijn Bouckaert, "What is Property?", *Harv. J.L. & Pub. Pol'y* 13, no. 3 (Summer 1990): 775–816, at 775.

On the function of property rights, see generally Hans-Hermann Hoppe, *A Theory of Socialism and Capitalism: Economics, Politics, and Ethics* (Auburn, Ala.: Mises Institute, 2010; www.hanshoppe.com/tsc), chaps. 1, 2, and 7, esp. pp. 13–15 & 18–30, discussing notions of scarcity, aggression, norms, property, and justification; *idem*, "Of Common, Public, and Private Property and the Rationale for Total Privatization," in *The Great Fiction: Property, Economy, Society, and the Politics of Decline* (Second Expanded Edition, Mises Institute, 2021; www.hanshoppe.com/tgf). See also the discussion of Hoppe's work on this topic in "Defending Argumentation Ethics" (ch. 7). On the prior-later distinction, see "What Libertarianism Is" (ch. 2), at notes 32–36 and accompanying text, *et pass.*; "Defending Argumentation Ethics" (ch. 7), the section "Objective Links: First Use, Verbal Claims, and the Prior-Later Distinction."

[5] For more on the issue of abandonment and a criticism of the Mutualist-libertarian position on it, see "What Libertarianism Is" (ch. 2), n.31 and accompanying text and Appendix II. For further discussion of the issue of "forfeiting" or waiving rights, see "Knowledge, Calculation, Conflict, and Law" (ch. 19), n.81 and "A Libertarian Theory of Punishment and Rights" (ch. 5), n.88 and Appendix: The Justice of Responsive Force.

[6] Invasions of the borders—uninvited use—of others' owned resources by a tortfeasor or aggressor results in a transfer of rights from the wrongdoer to the victim. By attacking someone, the aggressor transfers some rights in his body and/or property to the victim, for purposes of defense, punishment, and/or restitution. See "Inalienability and Punishment:

result of voluntary agreement between the owner and others. While some voluntary agreements are said to be "enforceable," others are not. The question for libertarians concerns when and why agreements are legally enforceable. In other words, how are (property) rights voluntarily (consensually) transferred?

B. Overview of Contract

Contracts are used in exchange—from simple barter to complex exchanges such as loans and employment contracts. In economics, exchange has to do with the motivations of the actor and his view of opportunity costs. In the positive law, in both the common law and civil law, a contract is seen as a relation between two or more parties which includes legally *enforceable obligations* between them.

Contracts result from *agreement* or *promises* between the parties, e.g., one party promises to another to do (or not do) something, or to give some (owned or ownable) thing to the other party. The promise may be made in exchange for things given or promised by the second party. The promises may be future-oriented and based on certain conditions. Agreements may be simple or complex; contemporaneous or future-oriented; unilateral donations or bilateral and reciprocal.

Not all agreements or promises result in a binding contract or legally enforceable obligations. Only those meeting certain criteria are, depending on the legal system.[7] For example, in the common law, there must

---

A Reply to George Smith" (ch. 10); "Defending Argumentation Ethics" (ch. 7); and "A Libertarian Theory of Punishment and Rights" (ch. 5). In causing damage to another's property through negligence (the commission of a tort), the tortfeasor becomes liable to the victim. In both cases, the wrongdoer loses rights, not because of any voluntary agreement, but by virtue of his action. Re negligence, see Kinsella, "The Libertarian Approach to Negligence, Tort, and Strict Liability: Wergeld and Partial Wergeld," *Mises Economics Blog* (Sep. 1, 2009).

[7] Agreement is a broader term than contract, because not all agreements are enforceable, and a given agreement might lack an essential element of a contract. See, e.g., also Louisiana Civil Code (https://www.legis.la.gov/legis/Laws_Toc.aspx?folder=67&level=Parent), art. 1906: "A contract is an agreement by two or more parties whereby obligations are created, modified, or extinguished." See also ibid., art. 1757: "Obligations arise from contracts and other declarations of will." Thus, "A contract is, therefore, a juridical act because by their 'agreement,' or exchange of wills, the parties to it *create, modify or extinguish obligations.*" Alain A. Levasseur, *Louisiana Law of Conventional Obligations: A Précis* (LexisNexis, 2010),

be *consideration*; in the civil law, there must be *cause*. The parties must have capacity. And so on. If the promises or agreement made results in a contract, the force of law can be brought to bear to enforce the contract—the agreement may be "enforced." In modern legal systems, when one party breaches the contract (fails to render the agreed-upon performance), the other party may sue to have appropriate "remedies" awarded. The remedies usually include an award of money, called damages.

Under the positive law, contractual obligations may be classified as obligations *to do*, *not to do*, or *to give*.[8] An obligation *to give* may be viewed as a transfer of title to property, as it is an obligation to give ownership of a thing to another. An obligation *to do* is an obligation to perform a specific action, such as an obligation to sing at a wedding or paint someone's house. It is significant for our purposes that courts usually will *not* order *specific performance* (forcing the breaching or unwilling party to perform the contract), on the grounds that the plaintiff can usually be adequately compensated with money damages.[9] Further, money damages do not impose a heavy burden on the court to supervise performance, while specific performance would. Specific performance would often be counterproductive. Consider a singer who refuses to perform a promised contract, for example. If ordered to perform, the singer might well give

---

"Introduction"; see also *idem*, *Louisiana Law of Obligations in General: A Comparative Civil Law Perspective, A Treatise* (Durham, NC: Carolina Academic Press, 2020), chap. 1, ¶ 17 *et pass.*

For useful definitions of various legal terms used in this chapter, see *Dictionary.law.com* and the latest edition of *Black's Law Dictionary*; also Gregory Rome & Stephan Kinsella, *Louisiana Civil Law Dictionary* (New Orleans, La.: Quid Pro Books, 2011).

8 See Louisiana Civil Code, arts. 1756 and 1986, describing obligations to do (an act) and obligations to give; also Levasseur, *Louisiana Law of Conventional Obligations: A Précis*, chap. 3, art. 3; chap. 6 (preamble); chap. 8 (preamble); Saúl Litvinoff, *The Law of Obligations: Part I: Obligations in General*, 2d ed. (St. Paul, Minn.: West Publishing Company, 2001), § 1.4; Randy E. Barnett, "Contract Remedies and Inalienable Rights," *Social Policy and Philosophy* 4, no. 1 (Autumn 1986; https://tinyurl.com/44adafte): 179–202, at p. 189; *idem*, "Rights and Remedies in a Consent Theory of Contract," in R.G. Frey & C. Morris, eds., *Liability and Responsibility: Essays in Law and Morals* (Cambridge University Press, 1991), p. 158; and, more generally, Alain A. Levasseur, *Louisiana Law of Obligations in General: A Précis*, 3rd ed. (LexisNexis, 2009); *idem*, *Louisiana Law of Obligations in General: A Comparative Civil Law Perspective, A Treatise*; and Saúl Litvinoff, *Obligations*, vol. 1 (St. Paul, Minn.: West Publishing Company, 1969).

9 Barnett, "Contract Remedies and Inalienable Rights," pp. 180–82; *idem*, "Rights and Remedies in a Consent Theory of Contract," pp. 154–55. On the availability of specific performance in civil-law systems, see Louisiana Civil Code, art. 1986; and Litvinoff, *Obligations*, vol. 2, pp. 301–302.

a shabby performance. For these and other reasons, in such cases, the singer would be ordered to pay monetary damages to the other party instead of ordered to sing.

Even an agreement to sell a piece of property, such as a barrel of apples or a car, will usually not be enforced with specific performance; instead, the court would order the promisor (obligor) to pay the promisee (obligee) a sum of money.

So-called "specific performance" is typically granted only in the case of unique property, such as a particular portrait, or in the case of real estate, because each parcel of land is unique. But note that, even in this case, specific performance results in the transfer of title to the unique property from the owner to the other party, which supports the Rothbard-Evers title-transfer theory of contract advocated below.

Thus, in modern positive law, "breach of contract"—failing to render the contractual obligations—results in a transfer of property—sometimes unique goods such as real property, but usually money—from the breaching party to the promisee. Contracts are enforced today *not* by forcing a party to perform the promised action but by threatening to transfer some of the promisor's owned resources to the promisee *if* the promisor does not perform. For an agreement to be enforceable under modern legal systems *means that* some of one party's owned resources (whether money or some other owned good, usually a unique good such as land or a painting) can be forcibly transferred to the other party.

What this means is that, in reality, in modern contract law, there are really no contractual obligations "to do" anything. It also means contract breach is really impossible, as contracts are not enforceable obligations to do things. There are only obligations to transfer title to resources, either directly (agreement to pay a sum of money) or as a consequence of failure to perform a promised action (a conditional obligation to pay a sum of money if the promised performance does not occur).

It should be noted that, despite the lack of a legal compulsion to perform a contract, the institution of contract is alive and well. The legal threat of transfer of some of the promisor's resources (commonly called "property") in the event of default, combined with reputation effects, is apparently sufficient to render contracting a useful institution.

At a minimum, contract theory purports to justify the transfer of title to the property of parties to a contract. And in the case of specific performance, debtors' prison, and voluntary slavery, contract theory must justify the use of force against the parties. Not surprisingly, then, a variety of arguments have been set forth attempting to explain why agreements may be enforced.[10]

C. Speech, Promises, and Libertarianism

The question especially interests libertarians. By endorsing a given theory of contract, we are, in effect, supporting the transfer of property rights from the owner to others, in certain circumstances.

Why does making a promise or agreeing or "committing" to do something result in a transfer of rights from the promisor to the promisee? To many—even to many libertarians—it seems to be elementary and obvious: if you promise to do something, you may be forced to do it. Some libertarians and laymen assume that an individual has some power or ability to legally "bind" or obligate himself by simply promising to do something. However, this assumption is groundless. Not all promises are enforceable, nor should they be.

As a general matter, libertarians hold that the use of force is permissible only in *response* to *initiated* force. Or, more generally, an owner of a resource is entitled to use force to defend his ownership rights in his body and in resources he or she owns. Ownership of an external resource means that the owner can withhold consent (exclude) others or invite them to use the resource.

In other words, viewed in property terms, a resource may be used only with the *consent* of its owner. Unprovoked aggression against another is a use of his resource (or his body) without his consent and is

---

10   Randy E. Barnett, "A Consent Theory of Contract," *Colum. L. Rev.* 86 (1986; www.randybarnett.com): 269–321 (as well as the version thereof incorporated into *idem*, "Rights and Remedies in a Consent Theory of Contract") provides a useful discussion of the multitude of contract theories which have been proposed. For a recent work discussing contract theory, see Harry N. Scheiber, ed., *The State and Freedom of Contract* (Stanford, Calif.: Stanford University Press, 1999). See also Richard Craswell, "Contract Law: General Theories," section 4000 in *Encyclopedia of Law & Economics* (Cambridge: Cambridge University Press, 2000); Morris R. Cohen, "The Basis of Contract," *Harv. L. Rev.* 46 (1933): 573; Charles Fried, *Contract as Promise* (Cambridge, Mass: Harvard University Press, 1982); and Charles J. Goetz & Robert E. Scott, "Enforcing Promises: An Examination of the Basis of Contract," *Yale L. J.* 89, no. 7 (June 1980; https://scholarship.law.columbia.edu/faculty_scholarship/249/): 1261–1322.

therefore prohibited. As a result of the act of aggression, the victim becomes entitled to use the aggressor's property (or body) for, e.g., purposes of punishment. That is, by committing aggression—using a victim's property without consent—some or all of the aggressor's property rights are transferred to the victim. Because the aggressor used the victim's property as if it were his own (although it is not), the victim may use the aggressor's property as if it is his own.[11] This is why initiated force (aggression) is impermissible, while responsive force—force in response to aggression—is not.

It is impermissible to use force in response to *non*-invasive actions, since this would be itself initiated force. Speech is (generally) non-aggressive, for example, because it does not invade others' property borders, so it does not justify the use of responsive force.[12] Libertarians oppose censorship and recognize a free-speech right because speech, *per se*, does not aggress (usually). The recipient of noxious or unwanted speech is free to ignore it and go about his business. The boundaries of his body and property are not invaded by speech, and his actions are not physically restrained by the mere words of others.

The same holds true of promises, at least at first glance. As even mainstream contract theorists have pointed out, a "mere promise" is not sufficient to create a binding contractual obligation.[13]

For example, consider a budding singer who asks his famous actor friend to attend the singer's concert. The famous actor says, "I'll be there." The singer is pleased, hoping that the actor's fame will add publicity to the event. To the singer's disappointment, though, the actor fails to show up. Did the actor violate any of the singer's rights? Of course not. What if the actor had said, "I promise to attend your concert"? The actor told,

---

[11] See "A Libertarian Theory of Punishment and Rights" (ch. 5), "Dialogical Arguments for Libertarian Rights" (ch. 6), "Inalienability and Punishment" (ch. 10), and "Defending Argumentation Ethics" (ch. 7).

[12] I say "generally" because speech acts can certainly be one means by which a person causes aggression. For example, a crime lord ordering an underling to murder someone is complicit in murder, as is the captain of a firing squad murdering an innocent man when he states, "Ready, aim, fire!" In general, however, speech does not cause invasion of others' property. These issues are discussed in further detail in "Causation and Aggression" (ch. 8).

[13] See, e.g., Shael Herman, "Detrimental Reliance in Louisiana Law—Past, Present, and Future (?): The Code Drafter's Perspective," *Tul. L. Rev.* 58 (1984): 707–57, p. 711 ("No legal system supposes that all promises should be enforced. Identifying which promises deserve judicial enforcement is crucial to any system of laws.").

or promised, the singer that he would go to the concert, but he did not by these speech-acts aggress against the singer or his property.

A promise, then, would seem to be unenforceable unless it somehow gives rise to or involves an act of aggression, that is, it somehow causes an uninvited use—invasion of the borders—of another's property. But a promise seems to be merely a speech-act; it does not appear to aggress against anyone.

If promises are not aggression, then the only other way that promises could be enforceable is if the promise resulted in a transfer of property rights from the promisor to the promisee. Then the promisee could "enforce" the contract by simply using the (former) property of the promisor, title to which has transferred to the promisee.

However, to state that promises transfer property title begs the question that contract theory asks: Why does a promise serve to transfer title?

D. Consideration

Many theories have been set forth in an attempt to explain or justify why the law enforces contracts, and why it makes some promises "binding" or enforceable. It is only a special type of promise, or a promise plus *something else*, that results in a legally binding contract under today's legal systems.

Under the common-law doctrine of bargained-for consideration, (an enforceable) contract requires a promise and *consideration*—something of value received in exchange for the promise.[14] This is why a dollar, or ten dollars, is often given (or stated to be given) by one party who is receiving something from another party. The consideration may be another promise or something else of value. For example, in a bilateral contract, the parties obligate themselves reciprocally so that each one's promised obligation serves as the consideration for the other's

---

[14] Saúl Litvinoff, "Still Another Look at Cause," *La. L. Rev.* 48, no. 1 (Sep. 1987; https://digitalcommons.law.lsu.edu/lalrev/vol48/iss1/5/): 3–28, pp. 18–19; *Restatement of the Law Second, Contracts 2d* (St. Paul, Minn.: American Law Institute Publishers, 1981), § 71; Barnett, "A Consent Theory of Contract," pp. 287–91; *idem*, "Rights and Remedies in a Consent Theory of Contract," pp. 148–49, *et pass.*

promise.[15] The value of the consideration given need not match the value of the thing received. In fact, even consideration as small as a "peppercorn" will suffice.[16]

Yet the antiquated doctrine of consideration has long been criticized.[17] It would prevent a contract from being formed in some situations that it seems they should be, such as gratuitous (gift) promises and even some commercial promises.[18] Further, if a mere promise (naked promise, or *nudum pactum*) is not enforceable, why does it become enforceable just because the promisee gives something small in return? Given that only a token amount of consideration—a "mere peppercorn"—is sufficient to make a promise enforceable, doesn't the doctrine of consideration elevate form over substance? Why can we not dispense with the formality and make mere promises, or at least promises with some kind of sufficient formality, enforceable? Further, under Austrian value theory, how can we say the thing given in return "has a value" to the recipient?[19] Maybe he accepts it only as a formality to satisfy the courts.

From the libertarian point of view, receiving consideration for a promise does not turn the promise into an act of aggression, nor is it

---

15 See Louisiana Civil Code, arts. 1908–1909, describing unilateral and bilateral obligations. In civil law systems, "consideration" is not required, but there must be a lawful "cause" which is "the reason why" a party obligates himself. See Louisiana Civil Code, arts. 1966 & 1967; Litvinoff, "Still Another Look at Cause"; Herman, "Detrimental Reliance in Louisiana Law," p. 718; Malcolm S. Mason, "The Utility of Consideration—A Comparative View," *Columbia L. Rev.* 41 (1941): 825–48; Jon C. Adcock, Note, "Detrimental Reliance," *La. L. Rev.* 45, no. 3 (Jan. 1985; https://digitalcommons.law.lsu.edu/lalrev/vol45/iss3/5/): 753–70. For a discussion of further differences between common law and civil law legal systems, see "Legislation and the Discovery of Law in a Free Society" (ch. 13); and Rome & Kinsella, *Louisiana Civil Law Dictionary*.

16 *King County v. Taxpayers of King County*, 133 Wash. 2d 584; 949 P.2d 1260 (Wa.S.Ct. 1997), at n.3. Yet as noted above, with inflation, people often nowadays use $10 instead of $1 in some attempt to satisfy the gods.

17 See Barnett, "A Consent Theory of Contract," pp. 287–91, and *idem*, "Rights and Remedies in a Consent Theory of Contract," pp. 148–49, *et pass.*, for discussion and criticism of the bargain theory of consideration. See also Mason, "The Utility of Consideration."

18 See Mason, "The Utility of Consideration," pp. 832–42.

19 See Ludwig von Mises, *Human Action: A Treatise on Economics*, Scholar's ed. (Auburn, Ala.: Mises Institute, 1998; https://mises.org/library/human-action-0), 94–96 and 102–103; Murray N. Rothbard, "Toward a Reconstruction of Utility and Welfare Economics," in *idem*, *Economic Controversies* (Auburn, Ala.: Mises Institute, 2011; https://mises.org/library/economic-controversies).

clear how it causes the promise to effectuate a transfer of title any better than a naked promise would.

E. Promissory Estoppel and Detrimental Reliance

The requirement of consideration can sometimes lead to seemingly harsh results, because some promises will be unenforceable if there is no consideration, but they will be relied upon by the promisee. A classic example is the grandfather who promises his granddaughter he will pay her tuition if she goes to college. However, in exchange, she gives nothing of legally recognized value, so there is no consideration and, thus, no binding contract. Halfway through her college career, the old man may change his mind and stop paying. What is the granddaughter to do? Can she sue to enforce the promise to pay for her tuition? Under the standard theory of contract, she cannot prevail, because consideration is missing.

The equitable doctrine of promissory estoppel is used in common law systems to form an alternative basis for enforcement of contracts.[20] This doctrine seeks to protect the "expectations" or "reliance interest" of the promisee.[21] The *Restatement (Second) of Contracts*, for example, provides:

> A promise which the promisor should reasonably expect to induce action or forbearance on the part of the promisee or a third person and which does induce such action or forbearance is binding if injustice can

---

[20] Barnett, "A Consent Theory of Contract," p. 276 n.25 discusses the role of detrimental reliance in enforcing promises that would otherwise be unenforceable for lack of consideration. Herman, "Detrimental Reliance in Louisiana Law," p. 713 n.19, discusses the use of promissory estoppel in common law jurisdictions as a substitute for consideration. See also Litvinoff, "Still Another Look at Cause," p. 19. Thomas P. Egan, "Equitable Doctrines Operating Against the Express Provisions of a Written Contract (or When Black and White Equals Gray)," *DePaul Bus. L. J.* 5 (1993): 261–312, at pp. 263–69 & 305–10, discusses the historical and philosophical basis of contract law and the development of the doctrine of promissory estoppel. For additional discussion of promissory estoppel and detrimental reliance, see Randy E. Barnett & Mary E. Becker, "Beyond Reliance: Promissory Estoppel, Contract Formalities, and Misrepresentations," *Hofstra L. Rev.* 15 (1987; www.randybarnett. com/pre-2000): 443–97; Adcock, "Detrimental Reliance"; and Christian Larroumet, "Detrimental Reliance and Promissory Estoppel as the Cause of Contracts in Louisiana and Comparative Law," *Tul. L. Rev.* 60, no. 6 (1986): 1209–30.

[21] See Evers, "Toward a Reformulation of the Law of Contracts"; and Rothbard, "Property Rights and the Theory of Contracts," p. 133.

be avoided only by enforcement of the promise. The remedy granted for breach may be limited as justice requires.[22]

Similarly, the Louisiana Civil Code provides:

> A party may be obligated by a promise when he knew or should have known that the promise would induce the other party to rely on it to his detriment and the other party was reasonable in so relying. Recovery may be limited to the expenses incurred or the damages suffered as a result of the promisee's reliance on the promise.[23]

If there is "detrimental reliance," promissory estoppel can be invoked to enforce the promise. Even though there is technically not a valid contract, because, for example, the promisee gave no consideration, the promisor is "estopped" to deny this because this would work a hardship on the promisee.[24] In the case of the granddaughter, she can prevail in court under this theory. In this way, detrimental reliance is used as an alternative ground for contract enforcement. The idea of protecting the expectations or reliance interests of promisees is also sometimes seen as the primary justification for enforcing contracts.

The theory of detrimental reliance rests on the notion that a promise sets up an "expectation" of performance in the mind of the promisee which induces him to act because he "reasonably relies" on this expectation. But this is confused. Every time someone acts, he is "relying" on some understanding of reality. This reliance might be quite ridiculous or unreasonable. Thus, all detrimental reliance theories and doctrines inevitably qualify the theory by saying that a promise is enforceable only if the promisee *reasonably* or *justifiably* relied on the promise.[25] If the reliance is not reasonable, it is not really the promisor's "fault" that

---

[22] American Law Institute, *Restatement (Second) of Contracts* § 90(1) (1979). Civil law systems provide similar grounds for enforcement of promises. The idea of detrimental reliance can be found in Roman law and in the Latin maxim *venire contra proprium factum* (no one can contradict his own act). Herman, "Detrimental Reliance in Louisiana Law," p. 714.

[23] Louisiana Civil Code, art. 1967. See also Litvinoff, "Still Another Look at Cause," pp. 18–28.

[24] See Litvinoff, "Still Another Look at Cause," pp. 23–24. For further discussion of promissory estoppel, see "A Libertarian Theory of Punishment and Rights" (ch. 5), Part. III.A, "Legal Estoppel."

[25] Barnett, "A Consent Theory of Contract," p. 275.

the promisee relied. The promisor could not have anticipated outlandish reliance.

One major problem with this doctrine, however, is its circularity. In deciding whether to rely on a given promise, a reasonable person would take into account whether promises, in a given legal system, are enforceable. If promises without consideration are known to be unenforceable, for example, it would be unreasonable to rely on them because it is known that the promisor is not obligated to keep his promise. Thus, reliance depends on enforceability. Yet, the detrimental reliance doctrine makes enforceability itself depend on reliance, hence the circularity.[26] As such, conventional theories of contract enforcement are defective.

For the libertarian, another problem with detrimental reliance is that it is not explained why a person's "reliance" on the statements or representations of another gives the relying person a *right* to rely on them. Why can a person be forced to perform or liable for failure to perform a promise just because it is "relied on" by another? The default assumption for the libertarian is that you rely on the statements of others at your own risk.

As we see, then, the mainstream theories proposed to date that are purported to justify and explain the institution of contract have been, by and large, inconsistent and unsatisfying.

II. THE TITLE-TRANSFER THEORY OF CONTRACT

A. Evers-Rothbard Title-Transfer Theory

A much better grounding for contract law is found in the writings of libertarian theorists Murray Rothbard and Williamson Evers, who advocate a *title-transfer* theory of contract.[27] As Rothbard and Evers point

---

[26] For discussions of the circularity of reliance theories of promising, see F.H. Buckley, "Paradox Lost," *Minn. L. Rev.* 72 (1988; https://scholarship.law.umn.edu/mlr/1293/): 775–827, at p. 804; Barnett, "A Consent Theory of Contract," pp. 274–75, 315–316; and Barnett & Becker, "Beyond Reliance," pp. 446–47, 452.

[27] The theory discussed in this section is largely based on that developed by Rothbard, "Property Rights and the Theory of Contracts," and Evers, "Toward a Reformulation of the

out, a binding contract should be considered as one or more *transfers of title to (alienable) property*, usually title transfers exchanged for each other. A contract should have nothing to do with promises, which at most serve as *evidence* of a transfer of title. A contract is nothing more than a way to give something you own to another.

Title may be conveyed without ever promising anything. I can, for example, manually give you a dollar in payment for a soda. No words need be exchanged. Or I can simply state my intention to give you something I own: "I hereby give you my car," or even "I hereby give you my car in three days." There need be no "promise" involved. In general, title is transferred by manifesting one's intent to transfer ownership or title to another.[28] A promise can be one way of doing this, but it is not necessary. Rothbard and Evers seem to have a fixation on the word "promise" and do not agree that a promise can convey title. They appear to think that because a promise is not enforceable, it therefore cannot serve to transfer title to property.[29] However, a promise can be intended

---

Law of Contracts," although I suggest some additions and changes. I also discuss the origin of the Rothbard-Evers contract theory in my post "Justice and Property Rights." Randy Barnett has also contributed important insights to the theory of contracts. See Barnett, "A Consent Theory of Contract"; *idem*, "Rational Bargaining Theory and Contract: Default Rules, Hypothetical Consent, the Duty to Disclose, and Fraud," *Harv. J. L. & Pub. Pol'y* 15 (1992; www.randybarnett.com/pre-2000): 783–803; and *idem*, "The Sound of Silence: Default Rules and Contractual Consent," *Va. L. Rev.* 78 (1992; www.randybarnett.com/pre-2000): 821–911.

[28] Evers, "Toward a Reformulation of the Law of Contracts," p. 12 n.20, endorses making "objectively observable conduct symbolizing consent the standard for determining whether consent has been given." See also Barnett, "A Consent Theory of Contract," p. 303: "Only a general reliance on objectively ascertainable assertive conduct will enable a system of entitlements to perform its alloted boundary-defining function." And, on p. 305, emphasis in the original: "The consent that is required [to transfer rights to alienable property] is a *manifestation of an intention to alienate rights.*"

[29] Rothbard, "Property Rights and the Theory of Contracts," p. 141; and Evers, "Toward a Reformulation of the Law of Contracts," p. 6. But see also Murray N. Rothbard, *Man, Economy, and State, with Power and Market*, Scholar's ed., 2d ed. (Auburn, Ala.: Mises Institute, 2009; https://mises.org/library/man-economy-and-state-power-and-market), p. 177:

Contract must be considered as an agreed-upon exchange between two persons of two goods, present or future.... Failure to fulfill contracts must be considered as theft of other's property. Thus, when a debtor purchases a good in exchange for a promise of future payment, the good cannot be considered his property until the agreed contract has been fulfilled and payment is made.... An important consideration here is that contract not be enforced because a promise has been made and understood to convey title, and thus can operate to do so. In certain contexts, the making of a promise can be one way to manifest one's intent to transfer title. Contracts always involve communication and some type of language, when the owner of a resource communicates his consent to allow someone else to use or have his resource. Language is always contextual. There is no reason that use of the word "promise" cannot be intended to signify an intent to give contractual permission or consent.

Ultimately, contracts are enforceable simply by recognizing that the transferee, instead of the previous owner, is the current owner of the property. If the previous owner refuses to turn over the property transferred, he is committing an act of aggression (trespass, use of the property of another without permission) against which force may legitimately be used.

B. Conditional Transfers of Title

The simplest title transfers are contemporaneous and manual. For example I hand a beanie baby to my niece as a gift. However, most transfers are not so simple, and are conditional. Any future-oriented title transfer in particular is necessarily conditional, since the future is uncertain. For example, before dinner, I tell my niece that she gets the beanie baby after dinner *if* she behaves during dinner. The transfer of title is future-oriented and conditional upon certain events taking place. *If* my niece behaves, *then* she acquires title to the beanie baby. Future transfers of title are usually expressly conditioned upon the occurrence of some future event or condition.

---

that is not kept. It is not the business of the enforcing agency or agencies in the free market to enforce promises merely because they are promises; its business is to enforce against theft of property, and contracts are enforced because of the implicit theft involved. Evidence of a promise to pay property is an enforceable claim, because the possessor of this claim is, in effect, the owner of the property involved, and failure to redeem the claim is equivalent to theft of the property. See also ibid., pp. 176–80; and Rothbard, "Property Rights and the Theory of Contracts," pp. 137–38.

In addition, because the future is not certain,[30] all future-oriented title transfers are necessarily conditioned upon the item to be transferred *existing* at the designated time of transfer. Title to something that does not exist cannot be transferred. Consider the situation where I own no hamster but tell my niece, "Here, I give this hamster to you." In this case, "this hamster" has no referent so no title is transferred. Likewise, the future beanie baby transfer is conditional not only on the expressly stated condition—the niece performing the specified action (behaving)—but also on the unstated condition that the beanie baby *exists* at the designated future transfer time. During dinner, the cat might destroy it, or it might be lost, or consumed by fire. In this case, even if the niece behaves, there is no beanie baby left for her to acquire. In effect, when agreeing to a future title transfer, the transfer is inescapably accompanied by a condition: "I transfer a thing to you at a certain time in the future—if, of course, the thing exists."

Like future title transfers, title exchanges are also necessarily conditional. This is true even of a simple, contemporaneous exchange. I hand you my dollar and you hand me your chocolate bar. Because it is an *exchange* rather than two unrelated transfers, the title transfers are each conditional. I give my dollar to you only on the condition that you give your chocolate bar to me, and vice-versa. Exchange contracts quite often involve at least one future title transfer which is given in exchange for either a contemporaneous or future title transfer by the other party. In this case, each title transfer is conditional upon the other title transfer being made. Also, any future title transfers are conditional upon the future existence of the thing to be transferred.

Many types of contracts can be formed by imposing various conditions on the title transfers involved. For example, suppose that we make the following wager: *If* the horse Starbucks finishes first, *then* I transfer to you $100; otherwise, the $10 you gave me remains mine to keep. In this case, you transferred title to $10 to me at the moment of the wager, conditioned on my agreeing, at the moment of the wager, to a future, conditional transfer of $100 to you. I transferred title to $100 to you in the future, on two conditions: the explicit condition that Starbucks

---

30 See Hans-Hermann Hoppe, "On Certainty and Uncertainty, Or: How Rational Can Our Expectations Be?", in *The Great Fiction*.

wins, and the implied condition that I have title to $100 at the designated future payment time (and that we both exist!).

In a loan contract, the creditor conveys title to money (the principal) to the debtor in exchange for a present agreement to a future transfer of money (principal plus interest) from the debtor to the creditor. For example, Jim borrows $1000 now from Bank to be repaid in a year with $100 interest. Analyzed in terms of title transfers, Bank transfers title to $1000 of its money to Jim in the present in exchange for (conditioned on) Jim contemporaneously agreeing to a title transfer to future property; and Jim's future title transfer is executed in exchange for the contemporaneous $1000 title transfer.[31]

A contract in which payment is to be made for the performance of a service, such as an employment arrangement, is not an exchange of titles, because the employee does not transfer any title. Although it may be referred to as an exchange of title for services, such a contract is better viewed as a conditional, future transfer of title to the monetary payment, conditioned upon the specified services being performed. That is, *if* you mow my lawn, *then* title to this gold coin transfers to you. Again, the transfer of title in this case is both expressly conditional and future-oriented. Title to the coin transfers only if the lawn is mowed, and if I still own the coin.[32]

---

[31] One problem with using US dollars as an example is that the USD system is a fiat currency, and it is not clear anymore what exactly is "owned" by people holding dollar bills of various denominations or federal-government insured bank-accounts with fiat dollars. The reader can substitute owned gold coins instead of fiat for conceptual clarity. As I have argued, even bitcoins are not properly ownable, and the status of ownership of state-created fiat money is even murkier. See Kinsella, "Nobody Owns Bitcoin," *StephanKinsella.com* (April 21, 2021). But we assume here $1000 represents title to a certain amount of something ownable, like gold.

As for so-called "conveyances," it is interesting to note one difference in the common law and the civil law is that, in the civil law, "Land is not 'conveyed' by deed but is sold." Patrick H. Martin & J. Lanier Yeates, "Louisiana and Texas Oil & Gas Law: An Overview of the Differences," *La. L. Rev.* 52, no. 4 (March 1992; https://digitalcommons.law.lsu.edu/lalrev/vol52/iss4/3/): 769–860, at 787. See also "Legislation and the Discovery of Law in a Free Society" (ch. 13), Part V.B, discussing the relative superiority of the civil law in its more streamlined conception of real property rights. See also ibid, Part III.C.4, re Hoppe's comments about the relative merits of the civil law system over the common law system.

[32] Part of the confusion here stems from conflating the economic-descriptive-*wertfrei* realm and the normative realm of law and rights. In human action—in praxeological terms—there is employment of means, which requires control of resources. Every action requires choice among possible ends and this requires losing the next-highest valued end, which is

Also, as evident in the beanie baby example above, the title-transfer theory of contract permits gift contracts (donations) as well as exchanges. The common law is reluctant to enforce gift contracts because of the lack of consideration. Under the rubric of "hard cases make bad law" (such as the grandfather promising to pay his granddaughter's tuition), such systems use the circular theory of promissory estoppel to enforce such contracts.

The title-transfer theory of contract, on the other hand (like the civil law), does not discriminate between gratuitous and onerous contracts[33]—between donations (gifts) and mutual exchanges. The owner of property may convey title to another, for any reason, whether pecuniary, charitable, or arbitrary, by manifesting and communicating his intent to do so. Gifts of property or title exchanges are all operative and, thus, enforceable.

C. Enforcement of Promises

Although a variety of contractual arrangements can be constructed using conditional transfers of title, there would seem to be no way to compel someone to perform an agreed-upon *action*, such as a service— the promise "to do" or "not to do" as opposed to the promise "to give." The only way to actually en*force* a promise to perform a given action is to have the right to inflict, well, physical *force*, as either punishment or inducement to perform, on the defaulting party's body. A promise to paint a house or sing at a party, for example, can be enforced only by threatening to use force against the promisor to force him to perform, or by punishing him afterwards for failing to perform.

---

reflected in the economic concept of opportunity cost. This could be viewed as a primordial type of exchange, that even Crusoe could engage in: he "exchanges" the chance to spend a night in leisure for the opportunity to catch more fish in the future (by spending his Friday night, no pun intended, to make a fishing net). In society, *A* might exchange something he controls with *B*; each benefits *ex ante*. When there are property rights and a developed legal system, then sales, exchange, and so on have a legal aspect and exchange refers to legal owners transferring their ownership over ownable, scarce resources to someone else, usually reciprocally and conditionally.

[33] See Louisiana Civil Code, arts. 1909 & 1910, describing gratuitous and onerous contracts.

However, under libertarian theory, there are only three ways that it is permissible to use force against the body of another: if he consents to the force, if he is committing or has committed aggression, or if his body is owned by someone else.

As noted above, the making of a promise is not the commission of aggression. At most, promises are evidence of an intent to transfer title. Therefore, there is no aggression to justify the enforcement option. Assuming the promisor does not consent to being punished, the second option is likewise unavailable. The third option assumes that the promisor has, in effect, transferred his rights in his body to the promisee, i.e., sold himself into slavery. However, although one may be considered to be a self-owner, one's body is inalienable.[34]

Therefore, contracts involve only conditional transfers of title to scarce resources external to the body. Promises cannot actually be enforced. The inability of the title-transfer theory to enforce promises might be seen, by some, as a defect of the theory. These critics predict chaos and the loss of the ability to have binding commitments. However, as noted above, even in modern legal systems, there is almost never enforcement of contractual obligations "to do" things. The primary enforcement mechanism utilized is to order the party in breach of contract to pay money damages to the other party, not to perform the promised service. The inability to "enforce" promises in today's legal system has not resulted in the death of contract.

The same result can be obtained under the title-transfer theory of contract by using conditional title-transfers to provide for "damages" to "enforce" promises to perform. When a contract to do something is to be formed and the parties want there to be an incentive for the specified action to be performed, the parties agree to a *conditional* transfer of title to a specified or determinable sum of monetary damages, where the transfer is conditional upon the promisor's *failure* to perform.[35]

---

[34] See Part III below.

[35] See Rothbard, "Property Rights and the Theory of Contracts," pp. 138–141; Evers, "Toward a Reformulation of the Law of Contracts," p. 9; Barnett, "A Consent Theory of Contract," p. 304 n. 143; *idem*, Barnett, "Contract Remedies and Inalienable Rights," pp. 190–91, 197; and *idem*, "Rights and Remedies in a Consent Theory of Contract," pp. 145, 170, discussing similar performance-enforcing schemes through title-transfers to "money damages," which Rothbard and Evers refer to as a performance bond.

This provides a result similar to today's system where the party who fails to perform owes monetary damages to the other party.

For example, if Karen wants to "hire" Ethan to paint her house, she agrees to pay Ethan $3,000 on a specified future day X if he has painted her house by that day. In other words, Karen makes the following conditional conveyance of title: "I hereby transfer title to $3,000 to Ethan on day X *if* he has painted my house (and *if* I own $3,000)." But such a unilateral arrangement only obligates Karen. She may want to give Ethan an extra incentive to perform (in addition to the prospect of payment and his promise-keeping reputation). For example, she may be planning an important business-related poolside party at her house, for which it is important that various promisors perform certain actions, such as mowing the lawn, cleaning the house and the pool, and showing up to serve as waiters and chefs. She would like to be able to obtain *damages* from Ethan in the event of nonperformance, and can, thus, contract with him so that he agrees to pay a specified or determinable sum of money *in the event that* he does not perform.

In sum, conditional title transfers can be used to provide for damages payable upon nonperformance of a promised service. This provides for almost the same type of enforcement mechanism used in modern legal systems today, in which contracts are widely used and relied upon. Indeed, although this approach to contracts seems odd to those used to the conventional "binding promises" view of contract, it is not really new. As Randy Barnett observes:

> Viewing contract law as part of a more general theory of individual entitlements that specifies how resources may be rightly acquired (property law), used (tort law), and transferred (contract law) is not new.[36]

---

36 Barnett, "A Consent Theory of Contract," p. 292, and *idem*, "Rights and Remedies in a Consent Theory of Contract," p. 137. See also Morton J. Horwitz, *The Transformation of American Law, 1780–1860* (Harvard University Press, 1977), p. 162:
> [A]s late as the eighteenth century contract law was still dominated by a *title theory of exchange*…
> To modern eyes, the most distinctive feature of eighteenth century contract law is the subordination of contract to the law of property. In Blackstone's *Commentaries* contract appears for the first time in Book II, which is devoted entirely to the law of property. Contract is classified among such subjects as descent, purchase, and occupancy as one of the many modes of transferring title to a specific thing.…

III. CLARIFICATIONS AND APPLICATIONS

A. Transfer of Title to Homesteaded Resources

The title-transfer theory of contract assumes that the property owner can transfer title in the property to others, by manifesting his intent to do so. The theory takes for granted that ownership of homesteaded property is *alienable* by the will of the owner. Writes Rothbard: "The right of property *implies* the right to make contracts about that property: to give it away or to exchange titles of ownership for the property of another person."[37]

Yet, we must ask, why does manifesting one's intent to transfer title actually do it? Why does the owner have the power or capacity to do this? This power is implied by several interrelated aspects of the ownership of homesteaded property. First, note that the owner, who has the sole right to control the resource, can permit others to use it. For example, he can lend his car or hammer to his neighbor. This highlights the distinction between *ownership* and *possession*. The owner has rights to a thing even if he does not possess it. Note also that "permitting" others to use one's property is done by manifesting (communicating) one's consent to the borrower. The manifested consent of the owner of a good to permit its use by others is what distinguishes a licit use (such as a loan) from an illicit act (such as theft); it is what distinguishes invited guests from trespassers. In short, because the owner of property has the

---

As a result of the subordination of contract to property, eighteenth century jurists endorsed a title theory of contractual exchange according to which a contract functioned to transfer title to the specific thing contracted for. Thus, Blackstone wrote that where a seller fails to deliver goods on an executory contract, "the vendee may seize the goods, or have an action against the vendor for detaining them." Similarly, in the first English treatise on contract, Powell wrote of the remedy for failure to deliver stock on an executory contract as being one for specific performance.

See also Evers, "Toward a Reformulation of the Law of Contracts," p. 7: "[Lysander] Spooner and other legal philosophers like Immanuel Kant have constructed theories of the law of contracts based on property titles rather than on promise." Referring to Lysander Spooner, *Poverty: Its Illegal Causes, and Legal Cure, Part 1* (1846; http://www.lysanderspooner.org/works), pp. 100–101; and Immanuel Kant, *The Philosophy of Law: An Exposition of the Fundamental Principles of Jurisprudence as the Science of Right* (Edinburgh: T.&T. Clark, 1887; https://oll.libertyfund.org/title/hastie-the-philosophy-of-law), p. 101.

[37] Rothbard, "Property Rights and the Theory of Contracts," p. 133, emphasis added.

right to control it, he can, through a sufficiently objective manifestation or communication of his consent, permit others to possess the thing while he maintains ownership. In this way, "contract" is just a consequence or application of ownership rights; the owner has the right to exclude or deny permission to others to use the owned resource, or he can consent to it. This must somehow be communicated by language.

Second, homesteaded property was at one time *acquired*. It can, therefore, also be abandoned. One is not stuck with something forever just because one once homesteaded it. But acquiring and abandoning both involve a manifestation of the owner's intent. Recall that the very purpose of property rights in scarce resources is to prevent conflicts over the use of resources. Thus, property rights have an unmistakably public aspect: the property claimed has boundaries visible (manifested) to others.[38] One essential aspect of property is that it publicly demarcates one's bounds of ownership so others can avoid using it. If the bounds are secret or unknowable, conflicts cannot be avoided. To know *that* a thing is owned by another and to avoid uninvited use of the other's property, the property's borders must be publicly known.

In fact, one reason that the first *possessor* of a scarce resource acquires title to it is the need for borders to be objective and public. The result of using a thing—either by transforming the thing in an apparent way up to certain borders or by setting up a publicly discernible border around the property—can be objectively apparent to others. This is why Hoppe refers to acts of original appropriation as "embordering" or "produc[ing] borderlines for things."[39]

Acquiring is an action by which one manifests intent to own the thing by setting up public borders.[40] Likewise, property is abandoned,

---

[38] In this sense all property is "public," not "private." See also "What Libertarianism Is" (ch. 2), n.1. On the objective function of property rules, see Hoppe, *A Theory of Socialism and Capitalism* and *idem*, *The Economics and Ethics of Private Property: Studies in Political Economy and Philosophy* (Auburn, Ala.: Mises Institute, 2006, www.hanshoppe.com/eepp); also Barnett, "A Consent Theory of Contract," p. 303: "Only a general reliance on objectively ascertainable assertive conduct will enable a system of entitlements to perform its alloted boundary-defining function"; for similar comments, see *idem*, "Rights and Remedies in a Consent Theory of Contract," p. 144.

[39] Hoppe, *A Theory of Socialism and Capitalism*, p. 24, also pp. 167–68.

[40] This insight calls to mind Rosalyn Higgins's observation that "Law, far from being authority battling against power, is the interlocking of authority with power." Rosalyn Higgins, *Problems and Process: International Law and How We Use It* (Clarendon Press;

and title thereto is lost, when the owner manifests an intent to abandon and, thereby, to relinquish ownership. This intention is not manifested merely by suspending possession or transferring it to another, since possession can be suspended without losing ownership. Thus, a farmer who leaves his homesteaded farm for a week to buy supplies in a far away city does not thereby lose ownership, nor has he manifested any intent to abandon his farm. For these reasons, an owner of acquired property does not abandon property merely by not-possessing it, but he *does* have the power and the right to abandon it by manifesting his intent to do so.

Ownership of acquired property includes the right to use the property, to permit (license) others to use it (maintain ownership while giving possession to another), and to abandon ownership by manifesting the intent to do so. Combining these aspects of ownership, it is clear that an owner of property can transfer title to another by "abandoning" the good in favor of a designated new owner. If one can abandon title to property to the world in general, then *a fortiori* one can do "less" and simply abandon it "in favor" of a given person.[41]

Reprint edition, 1995), p. 4 (quoted in Kinsella, "Book Review of Rosalyn Higgins, *Problems and Process: International Law and How We Use It* (1994)," *Reason Papers* No. 20 (Fall 1995): 147–53, at 149). Likewise, ownership of a resource involves both the intent to own ("authority") and the initial possession and/or embordering ("power").

[41] The theory for transferring property advocated herein bears a conceptual resemblance to the common-law practice of "quitclaiming" and also to the Roman law doctrine of "*traditio*." *Traditio* was a legal mechanism used to transfer ownership of certain types of *things* (*res nec mancipi*) by physically transferring possession or control of the thing, coupled with intent to transfer. See, e.g., W.W. Buckland, *A Text Book of Roman Law from Augustus to Justinian*, 3d ed. rev'd by Peter Stein, reprint with corrections (Cambridge University Press, 1975), at LXXXIII, pp. 226–27; also Gaius, *Institutes of Roman Law*, with a translation and commentary by Edward Poste, 4th ed., revised and enlarged by E.A. Whittuck (Oxford: 1904; https://oll.libertyfund.org/title/gaius-institutes-of-roman-law), Book II, §19 (p. 133), §§ 24–26 (pp. 136–39), §§ 40–41 (p. 153), §65 (p. 164), and §95 (p. 174); and Alan Watson, *Failures of the Legal Imagination* (University of Pennsylvania Press, 1988; https://archive.org/details/failuresoflegali0000wats), p. 90 *et pass*. (For a brief discussion of the concept of "thing" in the civil and Roman law, see "What Libertarianism Is" (ch. 2), Appendix I.)

As for quitclaim deeds: conventional conveyances of property operate by a deed, but a quitclaim deed operates by way of a *release*, similar to abandonment. It is intended to pass any title or right owned by the transferor to the transferee, without warranting that anything is, in fact, owned. See Gregory Michael Anding, Comment, "Does This Piece Fit?: A Look at the Importation of the Common-Law Quitclaim Deed and After-Acquired Title Doctrine into Louisiana's Civil Code," *La. L. Rev.* 55, no. 1 (Summer 1994; https://

Consider the case where the owner abandons the property outright. In this case, it once more becomes unowned and available for appropriation by a new homesteader, i.e., the next person to possess it. For example, suppose one lends his car or hammer to a neighbor and then abandons the item. In this case, the neighbor at first has possession, but not title, to the object. When the owner abandons it, the car, or hammer, becomes unowned again. As an unowned resource, it is now subject to re-appropriation by the next possessor, who happens to be the neighbor who is already in possession.[42] By combining the power to permit others to use property with the power to abandon—both rights or powers of *owners*—it is possible to transfer title to a particular transferee.

Another way to look at it is to consider the general rule that the first possessor has better title in the property than other challengers who are, compared to the first possessor, latecomers. If property is abandoned conditionally in favor of a particular transferee, then the transferee has "better title" because, as between these parties, the previous owner has abandoned it, and, thus, does not have better title. And as between the transferee and any third party, the transferee benefits from the prior title of the previous owner because, from the point of view of the third parties, the transferee is a licensee of the prior owner and/or an earlier possessor than the third parties.[43]

---

digitalcommons.law.lsu.edu/lalrev/vol55/iss1/8/): 159–77; and *Black's Law Dictionary*, defining "quitclaim." The quitclaim is a type of abandonment "in favor" of another, which effectively functions as a conveyance or transfer of the title. See also Louisiana Civil Code, art. 2502:

Art. 2502. Transfer of rights to a thing
A person may transfer to another whatever rights to a thing he may then have, without warranting the existence of any such rights. In such a case the transferor does not owe restitution of the price to the transferee in case of eviction, nor may that transfer be rescinded for lesion.
Such a transfer does not give rise to a presumption of bad faith on the part of the transferee and is a just title for the purposes of acquisitive prescription.
If the transferor acquires ownership of the thing after having transferred his rights to it, the after-acquired title of the transferor does not inure to the benefit of the transferee.

[42] The owner need not wait until the owner-to-be has possession to make the transfer. For example, the owner could make his abandonment conditional upon the desired recipient possessing the property.

[43] See also "What Libertarianism Is" (ch. 2), notes 33 and 36, for more on this issue.

As an analogy, consider a person sitting in a tree with his loaf of bread. Below him, others occasionally pass. He can eat the bread if he wishes, or hold onto it, or, if he wants, he can just drop it, abandoning it to whichever passerby seeks to pick it up. This would be analogous to outright abandonment. Or he can toss it to a particular friend in the crowd, thus abandoning it and "guiding it" to a desired recipient at the same time, who can then re-homestead it.

This is the reason why an owner can transfer title to others: scarce unowned resources are acquired and can be abandoned. Property that can be abandoned by manifesting's one's consent to undo or cease a previous acquisition can be given to particular others.

B. Property in the Body

Under libertarian principles, an individual has the sole right to control his body as well as scarce resources originally appropriated by the individual or by his ancestor in title. Since ownership means the right to control (to exclude), an individual may be said to own his body and homesteaded resources he has acquired. He is a "self-owner" as well as an owner of acquired resources.

Now, in the case of acquired resources, the rights of ownership include the right to transfer title to others because one can *abandon*, by manifested intent, a previously unowned resource that was *acquired* by manifested intent. In other words, rights in acquired resources may be alienated at will because of the way in which they come to be owned.

By contrast, although one may be said to own—rightfully control—one's body, the same reasoning regarding acquisition, abandonment, and alienability does not apply. The act of acquisition presupposes that there is an individual *doing the acquiring* and an *unowned thing* acquired by possessing it. But how can someone "acquire" his body? One's body is part of one's very identity. The body is not some unowned resource that is acquired *by* the intentional embordering action of some external, already existing acquirer. Or as Professor Hoppe points out, "any indirect control of a good by a person presupposes the direct control of this person regarding his own body; thus, in order for a scarce good to become justifiably appropriated, the appropriation of one's directly controlled 'own' body *must already be presupposed as justified.*"[44]

Because the body is not some unowned resource that an already existing individual chooses to acquire, it makes little sense to say that it can be abandoned by its owner. And since alienation of property derives from the power to abandon it, the body is inalienable. A manifestation of intent to "sell" the body is without effect because a person cannot, merely by an act of will, abandon his or her body. Title to one's body is inalienable, and it is not subject to transfer by contract.

C. Rothbard on Inalienability[45]

Rothbard, viewing contracts as transfers of title to alienable property, rejected the enforceable-promises view of contracts, with *mere promises* being unenforceable. He also maintained that rights to control—i.e., one's ownership of, or title to—one's body were inalienable.

These views are not unrelated. In fact, promises being unenforceable necessarily implies the inalienability of the body, and vice versa. If promises were enforceable, then one could be punished or coerced into performing the action that had been promised, implying some rights in the body had been alienated merely by making the promise. Likewise, if one could alienate title to one's body by an act of will, this would mean that promises could be enforceable. For example, one could make a conditional transfer of title to one's body *if* one does not perform a specified service. This would justify punishment or coercion against the promisor's body, which is now owned by the promisee. Thus, alienability of the body and the enforceable promises view of contract go hand in hand. One implies the other.

---

[44] See the Hoppe quote in "How We Come to Own Ourselves" (ch. 4), at n.17 (emphasis added). For further discussion of these issues, see "What Libertarianism Is" (ch. 2), the sections "Property in Bodies" and "Property in External Things," and, in particular, n.26; and "How We Come to Own Ourselves" (ch. 4).

[45] Note: In my original article, first presented in 1999 and published in 2003, in the above section, I criticized some aspects of Rothbard's argument for inalienability. I now think it is possible that his approach is more compatible with my own than I originally realized. I retain in this chapter most of the original critique in this section (revised and updated), and follow it with an addendum, below (Part III.C.1), explaining my current view.

So Rothbard, in rejecting the enforceable-promises theory of contract, has to also reject body alienability. As he does. However, this conclusion is apparently inconsistent with other strands of his rights theory. Rothbard wrote that "[t]he right of property *implies* the right to make contracts about that property."[46] Since he also views individuals as "self-owners," meaning that one owns one's body, then one has "the right to make contracts about that property," according to his earlier pronouncement. (This is, in fact, Walter Block's view.)[47] To avoid accepting body alienability, Rothbard must find a reason why the body, although owned, is *not* alienable—even though the owner of property "can make contracts about it."

What argument does he produce to show that our bodies are not alienable? Like other libertarians, Rothbard, in essence, argues that slavery or other personal service contracts are not enforceable because there is some sort of logical *impossibility* involved in voluntarily alienating one's rights to one's body.[48] He reasons that it is literally impossible to

---

[46] Rothbard, "Property Rights and the Theory of Contracts," p. 133, emphasis added. But other passages indicate he did not think this applied to bodies:

> The basic reason is that the only valid transfer of title of ownership in the free society is the case where the property is, in fact and in the nature of man, alienable by man. All physical property owned by a person is *alienable*, i.e., in natural fact it can be given or transferred to the ownership and control of another party. I can give away or sell to another person my shoes, my house, my car, my money, etc. But there are certain vital things which, in natural fact and in the nature of man, are inalienable, i.e., they *cannot* in fact be alienated, even voluntarily. Specifically, a person cannot alienate his *will*, more particularly his control over his own mind and body. Each man has control over his own mind and body. Each man has control over his own will and person, and he is, if you wish, "stuck" with that inherent and "inalienable ownership. Since his will and control over his own person are inalienable, then so also are his *rights to* control that person and will. That is the ground for the famous position of the Declaration of Independence that man's natural rights are inalienable; that is, they cannot be surrendered, even if the person wishes to do so.

Ibid., pp. 134–35.

[47] See various references in "Selling Does Not Imply Ownership, and Vice-Versa: A Dissection" (ch. 11); see also Kinsella, "Thoughts on Walter Block on Voluntary Slavery, Alienability vs. Inalienability, Property and Contract, Rothbard and Evers," *StephanKinsella. com* (Jan. 9, 2022).

[48] Murray N. Rothbard, "Interpersonal Relations: Ownership and Aggression," in *The Ethics of Liberty* (New York: New York University Press, 1998), pp. 40–41, reproduced in *idem*, "A Crusoe Social Philosophy," *Mises Daily* (December 7, 2021; https://mises.org/library/crusoe-social-philosophy); Rothbard, "Property Rights and the Theory of Contracts,"

transfer one's actual will to another, so a promise to do so is null and void; title thereto cannot be transferred. It is like contracting to sell the sun to someone. Such a contract, having an impossible object, would be null and void from the outset.

The problem with this view is that it assumes that a person's will has to be transferred in order for him to become a slave, or for others to have the right to control his body. But this is not necessary. Rather, the slave owner need only have the *right* to use force against the recalcitrant slave. It is true that one cannot alienate *direct* control of his body; one person can only have indirect control of another's body. Yet, we own animals, even though the animals retain direct control over their actions. The owner exerts indirect control over the animal's actions, e.g., by coercing or otherwise manipulating the animal to get the animal to do what the owner desires.

Likewise, aggressors may be jailed or punished—in short, "enslaved"—by the victim or his agent or heirs.[49] In effect, the aggressor's body is owned by his victim. This is despite the fact that the jailed aggressor still retains a will and direct control of his body; the jailer can only exert indirect control over him. The "impossibility" of an aggressor alienating his will does not prevent him from alienating *title* to his body—giving someone else the right to exert (admittedly indirect) control over his body—by committing an act of aggression.

It would seem, therefore, that the impossibility of alienating one's will does not prevent a person from being owned by others, or others from having *rights* to control the person's body. Thus, the impossibility of alienating the will should not be a barrier to making contracts regarding the right to control one's body.

---

pp. 134–36. See also Randy E. Barnett, *The Structure of Liberty: Justice and The Rule of Law*, 2d ed. (Oxford University Press, 2014), pp. 78–82; *idem*, "Contract Remedies and Inalienable Rights," pp. 186–95; *idem*, "Rights and Remedies in a Consent Theory of Contract," pp. 156 *et seq.*; Tibor R. Machan, *Human Rights and Human Liberties* (Chicago: Nelson Hall, 1975), pp. 116–17; George H. Smith, "A Killer's Right to Life," *Liberty* 10, no. 2 (Nov. 1996; https://perma.cc/8U8C-ZTAR): 49–54 & 68–69, at 68; *idem*, "Inalienable Rights?" *Liberty* 10, no. 6 (July 1997; https://perma.cc/4CUE-KG7G): 51–56.

[49] For further discussion of the theory of inalienability and the legitimacy of punishment, see "Inalienability and Punishment" (ch. 10) and "A Libertarian Theory of Punishment and Rights" (ch. 5).

Rothbard's error was to presume that ownership implies the power to transfer the property's title: the owning-implies-selling fallacy. This necessitated the convoluted and flawed impossibility-of-the-will argument in favor of body-inalienability. The modified title-transfer theory proposed here recognizes that the body is "owned" only in the sense that a person has the sole right to control the body and repel invasions of its borders. But the body is not homesteaded and acquired, and cannot be abandoned by intent in the same way that homesteaded property can.

1. Addendum: Rothbard's Mistake?

As pointed out in note 45, above, in the years since I published the original article upon which this chapter is based, I have rethought some of my criticism of Rothbard's take on inalienability. In this chapter, I have retained my original criticism, above, from the original article, and will now try to explain my current perspective.[50]

In other chapters I argued that rights in our bodies stem from the fact of our direct control of our bodies, drawing on Hoppe's arguments, while property rights in external, previously unowned resources arise from original appropriation or title transfer from a previous owner by contract or for purposes of rectification.[51] I have a better claim to my body than others since I have direct control over it, which gives me a more objective link to the resource of my body than to anyone else, who compared to me can at best have only indirect control of my body. Now when someone commits an act of aggression, he therefore, in effect, gives irrevocable permission to the victim to use force against the aggressor's body for purposes of self-defense or proportionate retaliation or rectification.

But in the case of an attempted voluntary slavery contract, the promisor, by saying, "I promise to be your slave," or "I give my body

---

[50] I discuss this also in "Selling Does Not Imply Ownership, and Vice-Versa: A Dissection" (ch. 11), the section "Fallacy 1: You Can Sell What You Own," and in Kinsella, "Thoughts on Walter Block on Voluntary Slavery, Alienability vs. Inalienability, Property and Contract, Rothbard and Evers."

[51] See "How We Come to Own Ourselves" (ch. 4) and "Goods, Scarce and Nonscarce" (ch. 18). See also Hoppe's pithy summary of these basic rules, in "A Realistic Libertarianism," *LewRockwell.com* (Sept. 30, 2013; https://www.hanshoppe.com/2014/10/a-realistic-libertarianism/) and in *idem*, "Of Common, Public, and Private Property and the Rationale for Total Privatization," pp. 85–87.

to you" does not commit an act of aggression. It does not create any victim who has a right to retaliate against him. So if the would-be slave decides to renege on his promise and run off, the would-be master has no right to use force to stop him. It is always current consent that matters. If a girl promises a kiss at the end of the date and the boyfriend an hour later kisses her, she cannot claim it was nonconsensual. In effect, she communicated her consent, she set up a standing presumption that is reasonable to rely on—until and unless she changes her mind. If at the end of the date she announces she no longer wants a kiss, it is *that* consent that matters. It is always the most recent consent that matters since this is the best evidence for what was consented to. There is nothing in libertarianism that says people cannot change their minds. To simply state that you can make an irrevocable, binding promise is just question-begging since it is just another way of sneaking in the assumption that our bodies are alienable, even though our rights to our body do not stem from homesteading or acquisition but rather from our direct control of them.

In other words, the fundamental argument against the enforceability of voluntary slavery contracts is that ownership of bodies is based on the person's direct control over their body. But this is similar to the "will" that Rothbard relies on in his opposition to voluntary slavery. So, as noted in the section above, when Rothbard says voluntary slavery contracts are illegitimate since it is impossible to alienate one's will—he is basically right. Without committing an act of aggression, that is. And promising to be a slave is not an act of aggression.[52]

D. Theft and Debtors' Prison

Although he rejects the enforceability of voluntary slavery contracts, Rothbard inconsistently views failure to pay a debt or other agreed upon future title transfer as "implicit theft." Writes Rothbard:

---

[52] I suspect Rothbard would have come around on this issue had he lived longer. After all, he accepted Hoppe's argumentation-ethics defense of rights as an improvement on his natural law-based defense. I believe he also would have come around on intellectual property. Alas.

I respond further to disagreements with Walter Block on this subject in "Selling Does Not Imply Ownership, and Vice-Versa: A Dissection" (ch. 11).

> The debtor who refuses to pay his debt has stolen the property of the creditor. If the debtor is able to pay but conceals his assets, then his clear act of theft is compounded by fraud. But even if the defaulting debtor is not able to pay, he has *still* stolen the property of the creditor by not making his agreed-upon delivery of the creditor's property.[53]

Rothbard is partly correct here. If, on the due date, the debtor is able to pay, then refusal to pay is theft. This is because the title to some of the money held by the debtor transferred to the creditor on the due date. At that moment, the debtor is in possession of the creditor's property. Failure to turn it over is tantamount to theft or trespass—it is a use of the creditor's property without his permission.

But Rothbard's view that it is theft "even if the defaulting debtor is not able to pay" is confused. Rothbard senses that this could justify debtors' prison, which is tantamount to voluntary slavery, which he has already rejected. So he tries to avoid this result by arguing that imprisoning a defaulting debtor goes "far beyond proportional punishment" and, thus, is "excessive."[54] But why? If failure to pay a debt is "implicit theft," why can't the "thief" be treated as such and punished?

One reason Rothbard has to come up with a convoluted argument to avoid the voluntary slavery implicit in debtor's prison is that he didn't follow his own contract theory to its logical conclusion. He writes:

> [W]hen a debtor purchases a good in exchange for a promise of future payment, the good cannot be considered his property until the agreed contract has been fulfilled and payment made. Until then, it remains the creditor's property, and nonpayment would be equivalent to theft of the creditor's property.[55]

---

53 Rothbard, "Property Rights and the Theory of Contracts," p. 144; also see pp. 137–38. Evers has a similar view: "Once the money falls due, the debtor who does not pay up is defrauding the creditor and is unjustly detaining his property… *even if* the debtor does not have the funds on hand to pay the creditor." Evers, "Toward a Reformulation of the Law of Contracts," p. 11 n. 5 (emphasis added). This analysis is confused. What "property" is "detained" if the debtor has no funds? And where is the "fraud"? David Boaz, *The Libertarian Mind: A Manifesto for Freedom* (Simon & Schuster, 2015), chap. 3, the section "*Freedom of Contract*," mirrors Rothbardian contractual analysis, as well as the Rothbardian error that it is implicit theft for a debtor to fail to pay a debt on the due date. See also Rothbard, *Man, Economy and State*, pp. 176–80.

54 Rothbard, "Property Rights and the Theory of Contracts," p. 144.

55 Rothbard, *Man, Economy, and State, with Power and Market*, p. 177.

This is the mistake that leads him to also classify failure to repay a debt as "implicit theft." Suppose creditor-lender *A* loans $1000 to debtor-borrower *B* in exchange for *B* paying $1100 (principal plus interest) to *A* in a year. Now the very purpose of loaning money is to enable the borrower to *spend* it on some project. For example, *B* needs to pay *C* for supplies to start his snow-cone stand business. The hope is that the business is successful, *B* makes a profit, and is able pay *A* $1100. But for *B* to use or spend the money, to pay *C*, he has to fully own the money, unconditionally. In this bilateral and mutual arrangement, there are two title transfers: a present, unconditional transfer of $1000 now; a future, uncertain, and conditional payment of $1100 in the future. Why is the second transfer conditional? Because the future is uncertain. Future things don't yet exist. They might never come to exist. *B*'s business may fail. He may be dead. He may be bankrupt. *A* is well aware of this and, in fact, this is one reason he charges interest.

Rothbard has lost sight here of the necessity that any property rights schema be able to answer the question of who can use what resource *now*, rather than waiting for some future information, otherwise people would not be able to survive because they could not use resources to produce and consume in the present.[56] So the idea of implicit theft leads Rothbard to assume that debtor's prison is in principle justifiable, which then forces him to wriggle out of it by simply declaring it to be disproportionate punishment. The entire concept of "implicit theft" must be rejected as hopelessly muddled and incompatible with libertarian principles of property rights and justice.

Fortunately, we do not need such a convoluted argument to condemn debtor's prison. The real reason the defaulting debtor may not be punished is that he is simply not a thief at all. If the debtor is bankrupt, there is no property to steal. The debtor is not "refusing" to turn over "the" money owed. There *is* no money to be turned over. How can there be theft of a non-existent thing? As discussed above, all future title transfers are necessarily conditioned on the thing's existing at the specified transfer time. Failure to transfer something that does not exist

---

56 See, on this, the comments by Hoppe and others in "How We Come to Own Ourselves" (ch. 4), n.14 and "Defending Argumentation Ethics" (ch. 7), n.31.

cannot be theft; rather, one of the conditions for the title transfer has simply not been satisfied.[57]

Of course, contracts would normally contain default or explicitly spelled out ancillary title transfers to address the unavoidable possibility of future default. For instance, a default title transfer that is ancillary to the main title transfers might be that the debtor also transfers title to $1100 plus accrued interest at any time after the original due date if he is unable to repay on the due date, if and when he gets a paycheck or otherwise comes into money. Such ancillary provisions can be explicit in written contracts or be assumed as default provisions in accordance with custom and context.

E. Fraud

As noted earlier,[58] libertarians often claim to believe in the non-aggression principle, or NAP, and that the NAP prohibits not only the initiation of force against the person of someone else (self-ownership) but also prohibits the use of force against the *property* of someone else—*or threats* thereof, *or fraud.*[59] But including owned resources under the NAP rubric is somewhat awkward, since aggression would seem to literally refer to physically attacking another's body. And then threats and fraud are just tacked on. As I previously noted, using the NAP as

---

[57] For similar reasons, Rothbard is also incorrect that a prospective employee who receives advance payment for future performance is necessarily a thief if he does not return the money. Only if the prospective employee still possesses the money and then refuses to pay it is he a thief. Similarly, I believe Rothbard is incorrect in assuming that failure to meet a performance bond (monetary damages payable in the event of non-performance) is "implicit theft" from the promisee. Ibid., pp. 137–38. See also the quote from Evers in note 53, above, misusing the concept of fraud.

[58] See "What Libertarianism Is" (ch. 2), n.4; also "Selling Does Not Imply Ownership, and Vice-Versa: A Dissection" (ch. 11) and "On Libertarian Legal Theory, Self-Ownership and Drug Laws" (ch. 23).

[59] Writes Rothbard:

Defensive violence, therefore, must be confined to resisting invasive acts against person or property. But such invasion may include two corollaries to actual physical aggression: *intimidation*, or a direct threat of physical violence; and *fraud*, which involves the appropriation of someone else's property without his consent, and is therefore "implicit theft."

Rothbard, "Self-Defense," in *The Ethics of Liberty* (https://mises.org/library/right-self-defense), at p. 77.

a shorthand for this cluster of relative rights is fine as long it is kept in mind that the justifications for these are different. I argued in chapters 2, 4, and elsewhere that self-ownership rights (and thus the prohibition on aggression) stem from each person's direct control of his body; but that actors also acquire property rights in external, previously-unowned resources by original appropriation or contractual acquisition from a previous owner. I argued in chapter 5 (section IV.F) why threats are also types of aggression under libertarian principles.

The theory of contract espoused here demonstrates that fraud is properly viewed as a type of theft, if defined properly. The problem is that even some libertarians use the term loosely, which leads to error. Sometimes it is just used to mean dishonesty; other times in support of the idea of "implicit theft," a concept I have criticized above.[60] But because of the sloppy use of the term, failure to provide clear definitions, and lack of appreciation of Rothbard's and Evers's groundbreaking title-transfer theory of contract elaborated, refined, and extended in this chapter, libertarian theory is left vulnerable to criticism, such as that of James Child and others, discussed below.

The only type of "fraud" that can count as a violation of libertarian principles, is when it amounts to a type of theft. The Rothbard-Evers title-transfer of contract (after being pruned of its confused "implicit theft" branches) can help to make this clear. Suppose Karen buys a bucket of *apples* from Ethan for $20.[61] Ethan represents the things in the bucket as being apples, in fact, as apples of a certain nature, that is, as being fit for their normal purpose of being eaten. Karen conditions the transfer of title to her $20 on Ethan's not knowingly engaging in "fraudulent" type activities, like pawning off rotten apples. (Good faith is also a default background interpretative condition to the contractual title transfers.)[62] If the apples are indeed rotten and Ethan knows this,

---

[60] See, e.g., the quote from Evers in note 53, above.

[61] Let's put aside for now the problem with owning fiat money (see note 31, above); let's assume $20 represents something ownable, like some amount of gold.

[62] On good faith as it pertains to contractual matters, see Louisiana Civil Code, art. 1759: "Good faith shall govern the conduct of the obligor and the obligee in whatever pertains to the obligation" and art. 1983: "Contracts must be performed in good faith." See also Levasseur, *Louisiana Law of Obligations in General: A Comparative Civil Law Perspective, A Treatise*, ¶¶ 39–43; *idem, Louisiana Law of Conventional Obligations: A Précis*, § 8.1.2; Litvinoff, *The Law of Obligations*, § 1.8.

then he knows that he does *not* receive ownership of or permission to use the $20, because the condition "no fraud" is not satisfied. He is knowingly in possession of Karen's $20 without her consent, and is, therefore, a thief.

This is akin to the legal notion of larceny by trick:

> Under common law, larceny is the trespassory taking and carrying away of the personal property of another with the intent to steal. Larceny by trick is distinguishable in that a defendant who commits larceny by trick *obtains only possession of the personal property of another, not title of that property*. Also, the defendant who commits larceny by trick obtains possession of the property by intentionally making a false statement to the victim.[63]

This libertarian take on fraud is also more or less compatible with conventional legal doctrines: "In law, fraud is intentional deception to secure unfair or unlawful gain, or to deprive a victim of a legal right."[64]

The reason this conception of fraud follows from libertarian property rights principles and the title-transfer theory of contract is that ownership of a resource (including one's body) gives one the right to exclude others from using the resource. The owner can grant permission or deny permission by communicating his consent to others. In the case of alienable, owned things, the owner can allow someone to use the thing temporarily (loaning my car to a friend for a day), give it outright (a gift), or agree to give up title to it in exchange for some act or other title transfer from the other party. This is what contracting *is*: the exercise of property rights by the owner communicating his consent about who can use the property and under what conditions. If I loan you my car, you are the temporary possessor, not the owner. Possession and ownership are distinct. I can transfer ownership but not possession, or vice-versa; or both; or neither. In the example above, when Ethan takes possession of Karen's $20, he only has possession,

---

[63] "Larceny by trick," *Legal Information Institute* (Cornell Law School; www.law.cornell. edu/wex/larceny_by_trick) (emphasis added). See also "Larceny: Larceny by Trick" (Wikipedia; https://en.wikipedia.org/wiki/Larceny#Larceny_by_trick). For a somewhat similar approach to fraud as the one I advance here, see Gary Chartier, *Anarchy and Legal Order: Law and Politics for a Stateless Society* (Cambridge University Press, 2013), chap. 2, § IV.E.3 (p. 73) and chap. 5, § II.C.2.vi (p. 278–79).

[64] "Fraud" (Wikipedia; https://en.wikipedia.org/wiki/Fraud).

not ownership, since Karen made the transfer of title to the money conditional upon the apples being genuine.[65]

Once understood this way, the criticisms of libertarianism for being unable to justify fraud law can be seen as confused and flawed. James W. Child, for example, is wrong in asserting that "the basic moral principles of libertarianism do not support a prohibition of fraud."[66] Benjamin Ferguson argues that Child is correct that libertarianism does not prohibit fraud, but that we can oppose fraud by "appealing to an external theory of moral permissibility."[67] Ferguson is also incorrect, like Child, in his first point, so the second part of his thesis is unnecessary; libertarianism already prohibits fraud and does not need patching with external theories.

IV. CONCLUSION

The title-transfer theory of contract avoids the problems of detrimental reliance and consideration-based defenses of contract. It permits gratuitous contracts without inventing arcane doctrines or burdensome formalities and provides a conceptually elegant theory of contract that can provide damages for breach of promises to perform, similar to modern legal systems.

---

[65] See also the discussion of trademarks and fraud in "Reply to Van Dun: Non-Aggression and Title Transfer" (ch. 12). For further discussion of the law of fraud, see Barnett, "Rational Bargaining Theory and Contract"; *idem*, "The Sound of Silence: Default Rules and Contractual Consent"; and Rothbard, "Property Rights and the Theory of Contracts," p. 143. For further commentary on the points made in this section, see Kinsella, "KOL044 | 'Correcting some Common Libertarian Misconceptions' (PFS 2011)," *Kinsella on Liberty Podcast* (May 2, 2013); *idem*, "Fraud, Restitution, and Retaliation: The Libertarian Approach," *StephanKinsella.com* (Feb. 3, 2009); and *idem*, "The Problem with 'Fraud': Fraud, Threat, and Contract Breach as Types of Aggression," *Mises Economics Blog* (July 17, 2006).

[66] James W. Child, "Can Libertarianism Sustain a Fraud Standard?", *Ethics* 104, no. 4 (July 1994): 722–38, at 722.

[67] Benjamin Ferguson, "Can Libertarians Get Away With Fraud?", *Economics and Philosophy* 34 (2018; https://perma.cc/HL4Z-S2KC; pdf: https://perma.cc/799P-Y8SP): 165–84. Will Wilkinson also argues that standard libertarian principles can't prohibit fraud. See the discussion in Bryan Caplan, "Fraud and Punishment," *EconLog* (Feb. 1, 2009; https://perma.cc/67YF-XMEZ).

This view of contract also solves the problems of voluntary slavery contracts and debtors' prison and avoids convoluted arguments for inalienability. Finally, the framework presented herein provides a justification for outlawing fraud.

10

Inalienability and Punishment:
A Reply to George Smith

George H. Smith published "A Killer's Right to Life" in *Liberty* magazine in 1996, making various arguments and claims about inalienability.[*] I responded in the *Journal of Libertarian Studies*,[†] in a piece which complements and supplements my previous articles on the inalienability and punishment issues, now chapters 5 and 9 in the present volume. Despite my disagreements with Smith on this issue, I respect and have learned from his work, such as his great essay "Justice Entrepreneurship in a Free Market."[††]

It can reasonably be argued that capital punishment is immoral or problematic because of the danger of executing an innocent person by mistake.[1] George Smith, in a recent *Liberty* magazine article in which

---

[*] George H. Smith, "A Killer's Right to Life," *Liberty* 10, no. 2 (Nov. 1996; https://perma.cc/8U8C-ZTAR): 49–54 & 68–69.

[†] Stephan Kinsella, "Inalienability and Punishment: A Reply to George Smith," *J. Libertarian Stud.* 14, no. 1 (Winter 1998–99): 79–93. Smith's article was also criticized in the May 1997 issue of *Liberty*. See John C. Goodman, "Do Inalienable Rights Outlaw Punishment?", *Liberty* 10, no. 5 (May 1997; https://perma.cc/4TMF-2S5R): 47–49; Timothy Virkkala, "The Hollow Ring of Inalienability," *Liberty* 10, no. 5 (May 1997; https://perma.cc/4TMF-2S5R): 49–50. Smith's response was "Inalienable Rights?," *Liberty* 10, no. 6 (July 1997; https://perma.cc/48NM-UAPK): 51–56; Virkkala's response was "The Stilted Logic of Natural Rights," *Liberty* 10, no. 6 (July 1997; https://perma.cc/48NM-UAPK): 56.

[††] George H. Smith, "Justice Entrepreneurship in a Free Market," in *Atheism, Ayn Rand, and Other Heresies* (Buffalo, N.Y.: Prometheus Books, 1991). Smith, who passed away in 2022, was a thoughtful and provocative libertarian theorist. See, for example, *idem, Atheism: The Case Against God* (Buffalo, N.Y.: Prometheus Books, 1979); *idem, Atheism, Ayn Rand, and Other Heresies*.

---

[1] See "A Libertarian Theory of Punishment and Rights" (ch. 5), n.84 and Kinsella, "Fraud, Restitution, and Retaliation: The Libertarian Approach," *StephanKinsella.com*

he argues against capital punishment, does not take this approach. Instead, Smith states that capital punishment is never permissible, even where *"reasonable doubt is impossible* and where the crimes have been especially heinous."[2] In other words, even if we know beyond all doubt that someone has committed murder, it is impermissible to execute him (and also, presumably, to inflict less severe punishment).

Smith bases his argument on the concept of "inalienable rights," rights that "cannot be transferred, surrendered, or forfeited."[3] The argument runs roughly as follows. Libertarians must adopt one of two positions: (1) everyone has inalienable rights, in which case even a (known) murderer may not be executed; or (2) certain crimes may be punished with death, in which case the theory of inalienable rights must be abandoned. In Smith's opinion, position (2) "would be catastrophic, for we cannot construct a libertarian theory of justice except on a foundation of inalienable rights."[4]

Smith's entire argument, then, rests on the notion that libertarianism and justice require inalienable rights. There are either "inalienable" rights, or there are no rights at all. Yet Smith's arguments for why libertarianism requires that rights be inalienable are unpersuasive.

STANDING THREATS

One of Smith's approaches is to provide an argument for capital punishment based on the notion of self-defense and then to attack this argument as insufficient. Smith writes:

> Some years ago during a summer conference, Randy Barnett and I sat down to see whether we could manufacture a defense of capital punishment. The best we could come up with was the notion of a "standing threat." This is based on John Locke's treatment of reparation and restraining, which

---

(Feb. 3, 2009). For a related commentary related to disputes in general, see Kinsella, "On the Obligation to Negotiate, Compromise, and Arbitrate," *StephanKinsella.com* (April 6, 2023).

[2] Smith, "A Killer's Right to Life," p. 46 (emphasis added).

[3] Ibid.

[4] Ibid., p. 48.

"are the only reasons, why one Man may lawfully do harm to another, which is that we call punishment."[5]

Thus, according to Locke, we may kill an aggressor in self-defense, since he has placed the victim and aggressor in a "state of war." Similarly, a case could be made that a convicted aggressor may be executed, on the grounds that he is a "standing threat" to others.

Rejecting this argument, Smith notes:

> To kill someone as a "standing threat" in the name of self-defense may amount to little more than a surreptitious effort to smuggle capital punishment in through the back door of libertarian theory, having denied it entrance through the front.[6]

Smith is correct here: it is not for reasons of self-defense that a victim has a right to punish an aggressor.[7] However, this does not mean punishment (retribution or retaliation) is impermissible, only that self-defense is not sufficient to justify punishment.

BARNETT ON PUNISHMENT

Let me briefly note the following. Smith states:

> For years [Barnett] has brilliantly elaborated on the pure theory of restitution as the only acceptable model of libertarian punishment, and he recognizes that the death penalty cannot be incorporated within this model."[8]

Admittedly, Barnett does appear to believe that even guilty aggressors have a right against punishment. But he does not claim to have justified such a right in his writings on restitution. In his published works on this issue, Barnett opposes a punishment-based system because he

---

⁵ Ibid., p. 68.

⁶ Ibid., p. 69.

⁷ That said, I do agree that in certain cases someone who *is* a standing threat to others may be dealt with appropriately, in which case self-defense principles come into play. See "A Libertarian Theory of Punishment and Rights" (ch. 5), Part IV.F. But not everyone who has committed an act of aggression is necessarily a standing threat.

⁸ Smith, "A Killer's Right to Life," p. 68.

believes it may deter crime less than would a restitution-based system, and also because the unavoidable possibility of error can lead to "infliction of harm on the *innocent*."[9] He does not, however, provide a strong argument that punishing an actual aggressor violates his rights. Indeed, in his book *The Structure of Liberty*, Barnett states: "this analysis *cannot conclusively prove* that no combination of compensation or punishment can ever address effectively the compliance problem."[10] And further: "I do not claim to have completely demonstrated this proposition [that justice requires restitution, not punishment] either in my earlier writings, or in this book."[11]

Thus, although Barnett opposes punishment for a variety of reasons,[12] those that are given to buttress his case in favor of restitution do not rest on viewing rights as inalienable and, in my view, Barnett has never demonstrated that rights are inalienable in the sense used by Smith.[13]

---

[9] Randy E. Barnett, *The Structure of Liberty: Justice and the Rule of Law*, 2d ed. (Oxford, 2014), p. 228 (emphasis added).

[10] Ibid., p. 237 (emphasis added).

[11] Ibid., p. 186 n. 36. See also p. 321: "If men were gods, then perhaps imposing rewards and punishments on the basis of desert would be a workable theory." Also: "It has been noted that one who wishes to extinguish or convey an inalienable right may do so by committing the appropriate wrongful act and thereby forfeiting it." *Idem*, "Contract Remedies and Inalienable Rights," *Social Pol'y &Phil.* 4, no. 1 (Autumn 1986; https://tinyurl.com/44adafte): 179–202, p. 186, and *idem*, "Rights and Remedies in a Consent Theory of Contract," in Frey & Morris, eds., *Liability and Responsibility: Essays in Law and Morals*, pp. 156–57, both citing Diana T. Meyers, *Inalienable Rights: A Defense* (New York: Columbia University Press, 1985), p. 14. But if a criminal has forfeited his rights (to not be punished, say), then it does not violate his rights to punish him.

[12] As pointed out in note 33, below, I also oppose institutionalized punishment for many of the pragmatic reasons given by Barnett, though it is not because rights are inalienable, and it is not because (proportional) punishment would violate the rights of actually guilty criminals.

[13] A second, less significant point, relates to Smith's doubts about the propriety of killing or imprisoning someone who has shown himself to be a "standing threat" to others. Smith notes: "Objective standards and procedures seem problematic in this case, to say the least. (Perhaps I am lacking in imagination; if so, I have little doubt that more imaginative libertarians will come to my aid with ingenious solutions.)" Smith, "A Killer's Right to Life," p. 69. Barnett seems to have done just this. Barnett argues that the principle of "extended self-defense" justifies imprisoning (sometimes for life) those who have made a sufficiently unambiguous communication of a threat to another. Barnett, *The Structure of Liberty*, pp. 188–193. On pp. 213–14, Barnett points out that because of problems of enforcement abuse and rule of law considerations, however, this remedy should be limited to those persons who have communicated a threat to others by their past *criminal* behavior (i.e., those who have been convicted, perhaps multiple times, of a crime), and only if the previous

DEFENSE, RESTITUTION, AND INALIENABILITY

Another problem with Smith's assertion that rights are inalienable is just that: it is merely an assertion. Simply labeling rights over and over again with the modifier "inalienable" does not make it so.[14] Libertarians do not typically view rights as "inalienable" in Smith's sense, or put much weight on this concept. In fact, viewing rights as alienable is perfectly consistent with—indeed, implied by—the libertarian non-aggression principle.[15]

---

crimes had been proven beyond a reasonable doubt. See also Randy E. Barnett, "Getting Even: Restitution, Preventive Detention, and the Tort/Crime Distinction," *Boston U. L. Rev.* 76 (February/April 1996; www.randybarnett.com/pre-2000): 157–68. I believe this limitation on the principle of extended self-defense is unduly restrictive, but that is neither here nor there. See, e.g., my post "Stalking and Threats as Aggression," *StephanKinsella.com* (Jan. 10, 2021).

[14] Smith says Jeremy Bentham held the theory of "inalienable rights" to be "nonsense upon stilts," and thus wonders if anyone who rejects inalienable rights must follow Bentham to his anti-libertarian conclusions. Smith, "Inalienable Rights?", p. 51. Yet Bentham said that *rights* were nonsense, and that *natural* rights were nonsense upon stilts. He did not use the modifier "inalienable" that Smith subtly puts in his mouth (though he does use the adjective "imprescriptible"). Jeremy Bentham, "Anarchical Fallacies," in *Human Rights*, A.I. Melden, ed. (Belmont, Calif.: Wadsworth Publishing, 1970), p. 28. Bentham opposed natural rights on the grounds that they were anterior to government, and thus his criticism is applicable to both alienable and inalienable natural rights. Thus, one can oppose Bentham's rights-skepticism by being in favor of *alienable* natural rights, which means that rejecting inalienability does not mean following Bentham down a non-libertarian path, as long as one advocates *natural* rights.

[15] Many, probably most, libertarians maintain that rights are strictly "alienable," i.e., *some* actions are sufficient to alienate rights (although they usually also maintain that rights are "inalienable" *sometimes*, e.g., promising to be another's slave, as opposed to the commission of an act of aggression, does not serve to alienate rights; see section "Inalienability," and note 34, below. In fact, any libertarian who advocates the right to punish (or, really, even the right to self-defense) at least implicitly endorses that rights can be alienated, to some extent. See, e.g., Murray N. Rothbard, "Self-Defense," in *The Ethics of Liberty* (New York: New York University Press, 1998; https://mises.org/library/right-self-defense), p. 81, where he says "the criminal ... loses his right *to the extent* that he has deprived another man of his" (emphasis in original); Barnett, "Contract Remedies and Inalienable Rights," p. 186 (quoted in note 11 above); Roger Pilon, "Criminal Remedies: Restitution, Retribution, or Both?," *Ethics* 88, no. 4 (July 1978): 348–57, 353 ("The criminal act has created rights in the victim; in the criminal it has both alienated rights and created obligations correlative to the newly created rights of the victim."); John Locke, *Second Treatise on Civil Government* (1690; https://www.johnlocke.net/2022/07/two-treatises-of-government.html), § 172 (power over one man's life "is the effect only of forfeiture which the aggressor makes of his own life when he puts himself into the state of war with another"); Auberon Herbert, "Part XI," in Auberon Herbert & J. H. Levy, *Taxation and Anarchism: A Discussion between the Hon. Auberon Herbert and J.H. Levy* (London: The Personal Rights Association, 1912;

Under this principle, only the *initiation* of force is prohibited; defensive, restitutive, or retaliatory force—more generally, "responsive" force—is not. One *does* alienate or forfeit certain rights by committing acts of aggression.[16] This is exactly why it is permissible to use force to defend against or punish aggression, or to obtain restitution. One has a natural, not inalienable, right to be free from aggression.

Both defensive and restitutive force, like punitive (retributive or retaliatory) force, imply some alienation of rights. This is just why defensive or restitutive force is considered to be permissible: because the aggressor has alienated his right to be free of such force. If one is opposed to punishment on inalienability grounds, how can one then endorse defensive or restitutive force? As John Goodman correctly notes, Smith's argument against the death penalty is an argument against punishment as such, and even against defensive or restitutive force.[17] Thus, to be consistent, Smith has to either object to *any* use of force against an aggressor, including even self-defense, or admit that rights are not truly inalienable.[18]

---

https://perma.cc/LX8H-MZFH), p. 38 ("Am I right in saying that a man has forfeited his own rights (to the extent of the aggression he has committed) in attacking the rights of others? ... It may be very difficult to translate into concrete terms the amount of aggression, and of resulting restraint; but all just law seems to be the effort to do this. We punish a man in a certain way if he has inflicted an injury which lays me up for a day; in another way if he takes my life.... [T]he punishment or redress ... should be measured by the amount of aggression; in other words that the aggressor—after a rough fashion—loses as much liberty as that of which he has deprived others."), also ibid., pp. 39–40; also other sources quoted in "A Libertarian Theory of Punishment and Rights" (ch. 5), n.43; also Kinsella, "Quotes on the Logic of Liberty," *StephanKinsella.com* (June 22, 2009).

[16] For more on forfeiture or alienation of rights, see "Knowledge, Calculation, Conflict, and Law" (ch. 19), n.81 and "A Libertarian Theory of Punishment and Rights" (ch. 5), n.88 and Appendix: The Justice of Responsive Force; also "What Libertarianism Is" (ch. 2), n.17; "How We Come to Own Ourselves" (ch. 4), n.15; also, in general, "A Libertarian Theory of Punishment and Rights" (ch. 5) and "Dialogical Arguments for Libertarian Rights" (ch. 6).

[17] Goodman, "Do Inalienable Rights Outlaw Punishment?", p. 47.

[18] The following thought-experiment, from the ever-fertile libertarian mind of Walter Block (as relayed to me by Joe Salerno), illustrates why a proponent of restitution must, in principle, be willing to support capital punishment as well. Block asks, what if it were possible to actually provide true restitution to a murder victim—to restore his life—by connecting a "life-sucking" machine to the murderer and transferring his life essence to the dead victim? This would bring the dead victim back at the cost of the killer's life. Surely, a restitutionist would have to be in favor of this, as it is simply a type of force used to enforce restitution, and the purpose of restitution is to "restore" the victim. But what is the difference, in principle, between killing the aggressor to "restore" the victim and killing the aggressor as punishment? In both cases, the aggressor is intentionally killed, against his

So which is it? Is Smith inconsistent, or does he consistently object to all force? Smith has apparently flip-flopped on this issue. At first, he seems to acknowledge that rights are not really inalienable: "I agree with Locke that reparation (restitution) and restraint (self-defense) are the only justified uses of violence in a free society."[19] But a justified use of violence implies some alienation of rights. Yet later, Smith appears to change his mind:

> Goodman argues that my case against capital punishment, if consistently applied, would militate against all forms of punishment, *such as fines and imprisonment*. I freely concede that this is a major problem for the libertarian theory of restitution.... Can we imprison someone and compel him to work off his debt? ... These and other questions have not been adequately examined, much less answered, by libertarians, and I remain uncertain about how to deal with them.[20]

Smith's view of the inalienability of rights has clearly led him down a dead end. If he is consistent, he must condemn all uses of force, even defensive and restitutive. (Such a position might be referred to as "stupid," or, perhaps, "Darwinian," pacifism.)[21] If, however, he admits that defensive and restitutive force are permissible, he has admitted rights are not inalienable, and thus, he cannot oppose punishment on grounds of inalienability.

---

will, in response to his earlier aggression. It would seem that in this case, the restitutionist, like the retributionist, supports executing murderers, and thus cannot claim that a murderer has, in principle, an inalienable right to life. See Walter Block & Roy Whitehead, "Taking the Assets of Criminals to Compensate Victims of Violence: A Legal and Philosophical Approach," *Wayne State U. L. Sch. J. Law Soc.* 5 (2003, www.walterblock.com/publications): 229–53, pp. 249–51; Walter E. Block, "The Death Penalty," *LewRockwell.com* (November 11, 2003; www.lewrockwell.com/2003/11/walter-e-block/the-death-penalty).

19 Smith, "A Killer's Right to Life," p. 69

20 Smith, "Inalienable Rights?," p. 55 (emphasis added). Note that Smith here confusingly refers to "fines and imprisonment"—presumably forms of restitution—as "punishment," even though a supposed advantage of restitution is that it is *not* punitive.

21 Libertarian Robert LeFevre has been accused of holding such views. But his pacifism was perhaps a bit more nuanced. In revising this chapter, this footnote grew to unmanageable length. I have placed the relevant commentary in the Appendix, below.

THE RIGHT OF PROPORTIONAL PUNISHMENT

As I have argued at greater length elsewhere,[22] an individual has a right to use force against an aggressor in response to aggression. This right to use force can be utilized for a variety of purposes: for self-defense during or before the act of aggression, for revenge, to obtain restitution (or rectification), to prevent the aggressor from committing further crimes, or to deter others from committing crimes. What the victim wants to use the right *for* is his business. But the reason *why* a victim has a right to retaliate or defend against an aggressor is that the aggressor cannot coherently withhold his consent to retaliatory, defensive, or restitutive force (these may be considered different types of *responsive* force, that is, *non-initiated* force, force which is *in response to* initiated force). To use related legal terminology, the aggressor is "estopped," or precluded, from denying the victim's right to use (proportional) responsive force, since such a denial would contradict the aggressor's view that the use of force *is* permissible (the view ineluctably demonstrated by the act of aggression).[23]

Thus, eye-for-an-eye type proportional punishments are legitimate in response to aggression. A murderer, therefore, is estopped from objecting to his own capital punishment. He can no longer claim a right to be free from such treatment. Since he previously had such a right, the right that he previously had must have evaporated. We may say, then, that his right to not have force used against him has been alienated (or forfeited, waived, abandoned, relinquished, surrendered, or lost; the terminology is not important).[24]

---

[22] See "A Libertarian Theory of Punishment and Rights" (ch. 5) and "Dialogical Arguments for Libertarian Rights" (ch. 6).

[23] For a discussion of proportionality, see "A Libertarian Theory of Punishment and Rights" (ch. 5), Part IV.A

[24] Another error lies in the very title of Smith's article: "A Killer's Right to Life." Under libertarianism, one has a right against the *initiation* of force—against aggression. But punishment is not *initiatory* force; it is force *in response* to initiated force. Part of Smith's confusion here lies in thinking that libertarianism upholds some actual right to *life*. There is no right to life. There is no right to "free speech." The ability to enjoy your life or engage in speech is a consequence of a system where your property rights are respected. As I wrote previously:

If I own ... 100 acres of land, I can prance around naked on it, not because the land is imbued with some "right-to-prance-naked," but because I own the land

THE UTILITY OF PUNISHMENT

There are further errors in Smith's article. Consider, for example, Smith's view that restitution is superior to punishment as a basis for criminal justice. Smith argues that punishing an aggressor "does not restore or equalize rights; it simply wipes out another set of rights," and that allowing retaliation only provides, at most, "a sense of emotional balance" to the victim. Several responses to this argument can be made. First, Smith here begs the question of whether rights are inalienable by assuming that the aggressor *has* a set of rights to be violated. If the aggressor's rights were alienated, proportionally punishing him does not "wipe out his rights," as he had none left to wipe out.

Second, just because punishment does not restore rights, it is not clear why restitution is automatically superior, since restitution does not restore rights either. It is true that the consequences and fact of an act of aggression can never be undone. The indignity will always have been suffered. Any response by a victim, including restitution and retribution, will always be an imperfect remedy. Indeed, this is one reason why aggression is impermissible: because the harm done thereby is literally undoable, incalculable, and not subject to an adequate remedy.[25] A victim will always remain, to some extent, a victim.

---

and it does not (necessarily) violate the property rights of others for me to use my property in this fashion.

Kinsella, *Against Intellectual Property* (Auburn, Ala.: Mises Institute, 2008), p. 53. See also Rothbard's criticism of the "right to free speech" in Murray N. Rothbard, "Human Rights as Property Rights," in *The Ethics of Liberty* (https://mises.org/library/human-rights-property-rights).

Likewise, there is no abstract "right to life." There is a right against aggression, that is, to not have one's property rights violated. That is why libertarians advocate the non-aggression axiom or principle, not the "life axiom." An innocent person can use his right against aggression to protect his life, if he so chooses; or he may commit suicide or waste his life in other ways. Thus, an innocent person may be said to have a right to life, if it is kept in mind that the so-called "right to life" is merely derivative of—a consequence of—the primary right against aggression, just as the right to free speech is derivative of the right to own private property and the right against aggression. An aggressor, on the other hand, no longer has a right against the imposition of force, and thus his life is in peril. The aggressor, therefore, no longer has a "right to his life," such that it was.

[25] Barnett, an advocate of restitution and opponent of punishment, recognizes this, and for this reason emphasizes the importance of crime *prevention*. See Barnett, *Structure of Liberty*, pp. 185–92. As does LeFevre, as discussed in the Appendix.

This does not, however, dictate that the victim should be artificially restricted in choosing among various imperfect remedies. Admittedly, both inflicting punishment on an aggressor (retribution) and extracting monetary damages from him (restitution) are imperfect remedies. But why not let the victim decide which one, or which combination of these, he prefers?[26] After all, the victim did not ask to be made a victim. He did not ask to be put in the position of having only two imperfect possible remedies available to him. If a victim prefers to torture his torturer, who is Smith to say that the victim's preference is not rational? Unlike Smith, I am not so unwilling to allow victims to attempt to attain "a sense of emotional balance," if that is all that is possible to them. (Like Barnett, however, I am concerned about the unavoidable possibility of mistakenly punishing the innocent, and thus admit the appeal of a restitution-based system in order to avoid punishing innocents, but not for reasons of inalienability.)[27]

The right to inflict (proportional) punishment on one's aggressor can be useful in other ways as well. Most significantly, perhaps, it may be utilized to reach a more objective determination of the proper amount of restitution. For example, the victim may trade all or part of his right to retaliate for a payment ("ransom") or other service by the aggressor, i.e., the aggressor buys his way out of punishment.[28] A serious aggression leads to the right to inflict more severe punishment on the aggressor, which would thus tend to be traded for a higher average amount of ransom or restitution than for comparatively minor crimes. Further, a victim especially offended or traumatized by aggression (and thus subjectively "damaged" more severely) will tend to bargain for a higher ransom. Also, richer aggressors will tend to be willing to pay more ransom to avoid the

---

[26] On giving victims the option of what type of punishment to apply or whether to seek restitution or some blend of punishment and restitution, see "A Libertarian Theory of Punishment and Rights" (ch. 5), Part IV.B; Pilon, "Criminal Remedies," p. 356; Barnett, *Structure of Liberty*, p. 184 n.32; Joseph Ellin, "Restitutionism Defended," *J. Value Inquiry* 34, no. 2 (Sept. 2000): 299–317.

[27] See note 33, below.

[28] For previous suggestions of the possibility of criminals buying their way out of punishment, see Rothbard, "Punishment and Proportionality," in *The Ethics of Liberty*, pp. 86, 89; Pilon, "Criminal Remedies," p. 356.

punishment the victim has a right to inflict.[29] Thus, allowing punishment to be traded for damages solves the so-called millionaire or billionaire problem faced under a pure restitution system, where a rich man may commit crimes with impunity, since he can simply pay easily-affordable restitution after committing the crime.

For these reasons, allowing the option of punishment can help arrive at a more objective measure of restitution damages.[30] And even if punishment is banned and is not an actual option—because of the possibility of mistakenly punishing innocents, say—an award of restitution can be *based* on the model of punishment. E.g., a jury could be instructed to award the victim an amount of money it believes he *could* bargain for, given all the circumstances, *if* he could threaten to punish the aggressor. This can lead to more just and objective restitution awards than would result if the jury is simply told to award the amount of damages it "feels" is "fair."[31]

The right to retaliate could also be used to justify "enslaving" the aggressor and putting him to work for a time to generate income for the victim (restitutionists like Barnett support this use of force against the aggressor, but do not consider it to be punitive, but rather necessary

---

[29] See "A Libertarian Theory of Punishment and Rights" (ch. 5), Part IV.G. See also Randy E. Barnett, "Restitution: A New Paradigm of Criminal Justice," *Ethics* 87, no. 4 (July 1977; https://scholarship.law.georgetown.edu/facpub/1558/): 279–301, pp. 297–98, reprinted in *Assessing the Criminal: Restitution, Retribution, and the Legal Process*, Randy E. Barnett & John Hagel III, eds. (Cambridge, Mass.: Ballinger, 1977), pp. 379–380; Roger Pilon, "Criminal Remedies," p. 351. For a "law-and-economics" discussion of this issue, see David D. Friedman, "What Is 'Fair Compensation' for Death or Injury?", *Int'l Rev. L & Econ.* 2 (1982; https://perma.cc/W5BU-K6PL): 81–93; *idem*, "Reflections on Optimal Punishment, or: Should the Rich Pay Higher Fines?," *Research in L. & Econ.* 3 (1981): 185–205; *idem*, "Why Not Hang Them All: The Virtues of Inefficient Punishment," *J. Pol. Econ.* 107, no. S6 (December 1999; https://perma.cc/3M2H-68N2), pp. S259–S269.

[30] On the issue of determination of the proper amount of damages, see Bruce L. Benson, "Restitution in Theory and Practice," *J. Libertarian Stud.* 12, no. 1 (Spring 1996; https://mises.org/library/restitution-theory-and-practice): 79–83; Rothbard, "Punishment and Proportionality," pp. 88–89. See also references in the preceding note.

[31] I believe this latter approach is consistent with and supplements Barnett's theory of a restitution-based justice system, since Barnett nowhere specifies any objective standards or criteria by which a judge or jury is to determine the amount of restitution a victim is to receive for a non-economic crime like murder, rape, and the like. He specifies only that the aggressor must "compensate" the victim for the "harm caused," to "restore" the victim. Barnett, *Structure of Liberty*, pp. 161, 187. Of course, how much compensation is needed to compensate for various violent crimes is a difficult question, and, of course, no amount of restitution can ever "restore" a murdered victim, nor can it "undo" other types of battery.

to enforce restitution).[32] Or suppose an aggressor is very poor and otherwise unable to pay monetary damages to the victim. In this case, the threat of inflicting severe punishment on the aggressor may induce the aggressor's relatives or friends to pay off the victim to spare the aggressor from being punished. The victim would thereby be compensated even though the aggressor is penniless, whereas the victim would be totally uncompensated if no threat of punishment were available to motivate the aggressor's relatives to chip in. (In a restitution-based system, a poor aggressor who is imprisoned in a work-facility designed to generate income payable to the victim may also find friends and relatives to pay off part of his debt to have him released earlier. However, as the aggressor in this case faces only a limited and usually temporary form of "slavery" and not more severe punishment, the motivation for others to bail him out would probably be reduced.)[33]

INALIENABILITY

The theory of inalienability has been plagued by confusion, vagueness, and inconsistency. The concept is typically applied to the issue of whether a *non-aggressor* can alienate his rights by a mere contract or promise, i.e., by a peaceful action. For example, may one sell oneself into slavery or enter into a binding, enforceable contract to perform services? Libertarians come down on both sides of this question, but tend to say that rights are "inalienable," i.e., one may not sell oneself into slavery.[34] Most libertarians hold this view of inalienability, which

---

[32] Barnet, *Structure of Liberty*, pp. 176–86.

[33] Note: although I still believe Smith is wrong about this aspect of inalienability of rights, and that it does not violate the rights of an aggressor for the victim or his agents/heirs to proportionately punish him for his crime (for more on this, see "Defending Argumentation Ethics" (ch. 7), text at notes 35–36), I nonetheless sympathize with the idea of a restitution-based system being preferable and even likely in any free society, as noted in "A Libertarian Theory of Punishment and Rights" (ch. 5), n.85, and Kinsella, "Fraud, Restitution, and Retaliation: The Libertarian Approach." For related discussion about disputes in general, see Kinsella, "On the Obligation to Negotiate, Compromise, and Arbitrate."

[34] See, e.g., Barnett, *Structure of Liberty*, pp. 78–83; *idem*, "Contract Remedies and Inalienable Rights," pp. 186–95; Rothbard, "Interpersonal Relations: Voluntary Exchange," in *The Ethics of Liberty*, pp. 40–41 (https://mises.org/library/crusoe-social-philosophy)

I will refer to as the standard or "limited" view of inalienability, since adherents of this view usually also maintain that acts of aggression *do* alienate rights.[35] In this view, only violent actions serve to alienate rights. Smith has used the label "inalienability" in an idiosyncratic way to mean that even *aggressive* actions do not alienate rights.

What, then, is the correct, libertarian view of inalienability and rights? Consent is the crucial element to focus on here. If a person consents to an action that would otherwise violate his rights, there is no rights violation. Boxers in a ring, or duelers dueling, do not have their rights violated when struck by fist or bullet. This is because they consented to these exchanges of force.[36] To alienate one's right *means that* one is *unable* to withhold consent to some action that would otherwise infringe the right if there were no consent. Thus, a right is alienated by somehow rendering it impossible to object to the action that the alienated right would otherwise prohibit. One does something *now* that prevents one from withholding consent in the future, thereby effectively alienating the relevant right. To alienate a right, then, is to *irrevocably* grant the relevant consent to another.

Is it possible to irrevocably grant consent? Smith, an advocate of what may be called the "strong" view of inalienability, would say it is not possible under any circumstances (except, perhaps, for defensive or restitutive

---

and "Property Rights and the Theory of Contracts," 134–136 (https://mises.org/library/property-rights-and-theory-contracts); Tibor R. Machan, *Human Rights and Human Liberties* (Chicago: Nelson Hall, 1975), pp. 116–17; Smith, "A Killer's Right to Life," p. 49; *idem*, "Inalienable Rights?," p. 54.

[35] See note 15 above.

[36] As Richard Epstein explains,

> The case for the recognition of consent as a defense in case of the deliberate infliction of harm can also be made in simple and direct terms. The self-infliction of harm generates no cause of action, no matter why inflicted. There is no reason, then, why a person who may inflict harm upon himself should not, prima facie, be allowed to have someone else do it for him.

Richard A. Epstein, "Intentional Harms," *J. Legal Stud.* 4 (1975): 391–442, p.411. See also "A Libertarian Theory of Punishment and Rights" (ch. 5), Part II. For an unorthodox libertarian view that duelers do not actually "consent" since a duel is only engaged in due to the "threat of disgrace," see T. Patrick Burke, *No Harm: Ethical Principles for a Free Market* (New York: Paragon House, 1994), pp. 192, 268 n.15, which I criticize in my "Book Review," *Reason Papers* No. 20 (Fall 1995; https://reasonpapers.com/archives/): 135–46, and Kinsella, "'Aggression' versus 'Harm' in Libertarianism," *Mises Economics Blog* (Dec. 16, 2009). See related comments in "A Libertarian Theory of Punishment and Rights" (ch. 5), n.16 and "Dialogical Arguments for Libertarian Rights" (ch. 6), n.3.

force). Proponents of the limited view of inalienability, by contrast, hold that it is possible to do this by aggressing, but not by merely making an agreement or promise. (Those rare libertarians, like Walter Block, who believe rights may be alienated even by a non-violent action like agreement, hold what may be viewed as a "weak" view of inalienability.)[37]

Let us examine the three ways that consent possibly could be irrevocably granted: by physical means, by aggression, and by voluntary agreement. The physical, or physiological, means refers to a person voluntarily undergoing some process that literally places him under the power of another (e.g., drugs, surgery, technology).[38] This is akin to committing an act of suicide or "zombicide," and is not of particular interest, since after the zombicide is complete, the zombie presumably does not even try to run away or withhold consent from his master.

---

[37] I critique Block's views in "Selling Does Not Imply Ownership, and Vice-Versa: A Dissection" (ch. 11).

[38] See, e.g., discussions of this in Smith, "Inalienable Rights?," p. 54:

Moral agency is inalienable, and so must be the right to exercise that agency.... This does not mean, however, that moral agency cannot be extinguished, which brings us to another kind of slavery contract. Suppose that Murphy agrees to have a computer chip implanted in his brain, which will enable me to control him with a joystick, moving him around like a robot. (Perhaps in exchange for this dubious privilege, I have agreed to pay one million dollars to his destitute family.) Here, Murphy has voluntarily extinguished his moral agency, not transferred it to me. What he has transferred is physical control over his body, which becomes my property after he has taken leave of it. Therefore, since the body, like all physical objects, is transferable, I regard this kind of slavery contract as possible and valid.

See also Barnett, *Structure of Liberty*, 78 & n. 39, who writes:

Suppose that Ann consented to transfer partial or complete control of her body to Ben. Absent some physiological change in Ann (caused, perhaps, by voluntarily and knowingly ingesting some special drug or undergoing psycho-surgery) there is no way for such a commitment to be carried out.... Arthur Kuflik offers these examples to undercut this type of argument for inalienability. See Arthur Kuflik, "The Inalienability of Autonomy," *Philosophy and Public Affairs* 13, no. 4 (1984): 271–98, p. 281: "This suggests that the impropriety of an autonomy-abdicating agreement has more to do with the impropriety of autonomy-abdication itself than with some general fact that we have no right to make commitments we know we will be unable to keep." But arguments based on impropriety and one based on the impossibility of such agreements are not mutually exclusive. Kuflik's examples only show that this reason for inalienability is *limited* to those commitments to alienate the future control over one's person which are not made possible by mind-altering drugs, brainwashing techniques, or psychosurgery.

Committing an act of aggression is a clear-cut means for alienating (some of) one's rights. As explained above,[39] an aggressor is estopped from withholding consent to the victim's proposed use of (proportional) retaliatory force, since such a denial would contradict the aggressor's view that the use of force is permissible. An act of aggression is a way of irrevocably granting consent to punishment. This is exactly why an act of aggression serves to alienate rights: because the act of aggression conclusively demonstrates the aggressor's view that aggression is proper, thus precluding him from consistently objecting to the victim's use of (proportional) retaliatory force. The strong view of inalienability (Smith's view) is, for this reason, untenable.[40] So which view is correct, the limited view or the weak view?

This depends on the answer to the following question: Can one irrevocably grant consent by voluntary agreement, such as a promise or contract to be another's slave? Barnett recognizes the importance of consent here:

> The crucial question … is whether Ann's current consensual choices can limit her right to revoke her consent in the future. Having consented to let Ben touch her or to enter the [boxing] ring with him, may she be forced to carry through with her commitment after she has changed her mind?"[41]

This is a difficult and complicated question. Some argue that a contract is a contract, and may be enforced.[42] This view is based on the theory that one is a self-owner, entitled to full control of all of one's property, including one's body, and that this control comprises the ability to sell one's body.[43] Most libertarians, however, seem to hold the limited view of inalienability, whereby aggression does alienate rights, but promising to be someone's slave does not. Advocates of this view typically argue that

---

[39] See note 22 above, and accompanying text.

[40] See notes 11 and 15 above.

[41] Barnett, *Structure of Liberty*, p. 81. Rothbard also realizes the importance of being able to change one's mind. In a discussion about voluntary slave contracts, he writes: "The problem comes when, at some later date, Smith *changes his mind* and decides to leave. Shall he be held to his former voluntary promise?" Rothbard, "Property Rights and the Theory of Contracts," p. 136 (emphasis added).

[42] But see, of course, the dissenting view expressed in chapter 9.

[43] A view I criticize in "Selling Does Not Imply Ownership, and Vice-Versa: A Dissection" (ch. 11).

such contracts are not enforceable because there is some sort of logical impossibility involved in voluntarily alienating all of one's rights in this manner.[44] For example, some argue that it is literally impossible to transfer one's actual will to another, and thus a promise to do so is null and void; title thereto cannot be transferred. It is like contracting to sell the sun to someone. Such a contract, having an impossible object, would be null and void from the outset.

My view is that the impossibility reasoning typically given to argue that consent cannot be irrevocably granted is fallacious and has helped to muddle the issue of inalienability. For example, if the "impossibility" of literally alienating one's will means that it is impossible to be bound by contract to act as someone's slave, why is it not "impossible" to imprison an aggressor to enforce restitution? After all, even a convicted aggressor still has a will. Why is it not "impossible" to defend oneself with force? And yet it is *not* impossible for consent to be irrevocably granted, as we have seen; this condition exists for a justly imprisoned aggressor. Recipients of defensive, restitutive, or retaliatory force all retain a will, which is overwhelmed with some type of responsive force.

The key here is to focus on force and consent, for to keep someone as a slave, it is not necessary that the will be physically alienated. Rather, in order to enslave someone, the slave-owner must be *entitled* to use (justified in using) force against the slave if the slave disobeys or tries to run away. The impossibility of actually alienating one's faculty of volition is irrelevant. It is the legitimacy of using force that matters, and this depends on consent.

Putting the issue this way, however, provides a different argument why consent cannot irrevocably be granted by mere agreement or promise— why the prospective slave may change his mind in the future and withdraw his consent. If *A* promises (or contracts, or agrees; the terminology is not important) to be *B*'s slave, this is no doubt an attempt to consent *now* to force inflicted in the future. If *A* later changes his mind and tries to run away, may *B* at that point use force against *A*?

This is the crucial question. If the answer is yes, this means that *A* has no right to object and has effectively alienated his rights. I would say

---

[44] See note 34 above; also "A Libertarian Theory of Contract: Title Transfer, Binding Promises, and Inalienability" (ch. 9), Part III.C.

no, however, simply because there is no reason why *A cannot* withdraw his consent. Libertarianism does not say one cannot change one's mind. When we ask about consent, it is the most recent expression of consent that is most relevant. Unlike the case of aggression, where the aggressor's prior aggression estops him from objecting to the use of retaliatory force, *A has not committed aggression* against *B*. Thus it is not inconsistent for *A* to later object to the use of force. All *A* did previously was utter words to *B* such as "I agree to be your slave." But this does not aggress against *B* at all, any more than does uttering the insult, "You are ugly." Words per se do not aggress, which is one reason there is a (derivative, not independent) "right" to free speech. In a nutshell, a would-be slave-owner must be entitled to use force against the would-be slave in order for the slavery agreement to be enforceable and for rights to be alienated in this manner; but the would-be slave has simply not initiated force against the would-be slave-owner. The would-be slave-owner is thus *not* entitled to use force against the slave; hence no rights were alienated.[45]

Thus, I conclude that a slavery agreement is not enforceable. Rights are not completely inalienable, as Smith contends, for aggression can alienate rights. We must reject the strong view of inalienability. However, rights are inalienable in the limited (and more conventional) sense that one cannot irrevocably grant consent to aggression in the future by way of a mere promise or agreement. This is not because of any impossibility in alienating one's will, but because a promisor has not committed aggression. One retains the right to change one's mind, absent special circumstances.[46] The limited view of inalienability seems to be the most sensible.

---

[45] Proponents of the weak view of inalienability, like Walter Block, on the other hand, would argue that the sale of one's body confers ownership of it to another person and that subsequent violence against the sold body by the new owner is no more aggression than is self-mutilation. I remain to be convinced by this line of argument, primarily because there seems to be a relevant difference between the rights related to one's body and rights in homesteaded resources, due to the different justifications for and nature of these rights. For more on this, see "Selling Does Not Imply Ownership, and Vice-Versa: A Dissection" (ch. 11).

[46] E.g., an airplane pilot may be forcibly restrained by passengers from parachuting out in mid-flight. See Barnett, *Structure of Liberty*, p. 81; also *idem*, "Rights and Remedies in a Consent Theory of Contract," in R.G. Frey & Christopher W. Morris, eds., *Liability and Responsibility: Essays in Law and Morals* (Cambridge University Press, 1991), p. 163 n.52. The reason the parachuting is arguably aggression is that this action can be considered to

The right to alienate external resources is not limited, however, because of crucial differences between rights pertaining to one's body and rights of ownership in previously-unowned, homesteaded resources. The right to appropriate external resources is derivative of and distinct from the basic right against non-aggression (self-ownership). External scarce resources are appropriated and acquired, and held by intention (it is this that distinguishes ownership from possession),[47] and thus can be abandoned or alienated by a sufficient expression of intention, e.g., a contract or act of abandonment. For this reason, under the libertarian title-transfer theory of contract, one can alienate particular property titles, i.e., titles to external (homesteadable) scarce resources. In this sense there is a distinction between title to property, which is alienable by mere contract; and rights related to one's body, which are not alienable by promise or contract (speech act) but are alienable by acts of aggression.[48]

---

be the *cause* of the physical harm that will befall the passengers, much like one who shoots a gun or drops a bomb is an aggressor. Alternatively, in the airplane example, it could be argued that the ownership of the airplane is contractually granted in common to the passengers for the duration of the flight, and they could thus use force to stop the pilot from opening the door since they "own" it and do not grant him permission to use it for this purpose.

For more on causation, see "Causation and Aggression" (ch. 8). Arguments could be constructed for other special cases, such as agreeing to donate an organ which causes the recipient to rely on this, or enlisting in a volunteer army at a time of peril. I do think there is room for more development of ideas related to such issues by future scholars.

[47] See "A Libertarian Theory of Contract" (ch. 9), at n.40 and accompanying text.

[48] See also Barnett, *Structure of Liberty*, p. 82. There has been great confusion in the area of contract theory, which has perhaps contributed to the confusion in inalienability reasoning. For example, the "impossibility" reasoning seems to be based on the groundless assumption that contracts are based on the concept of "binding promises" or on an improper analogy between homesteadable scarce resources, which can be acquired or abandoned, and rights against aggression, which relate to one's body. However, contracts need have nothing to do with promises, and there is a difference between rights to acquired external resources and rights to one's body. For more on the libertarian theory of contracts, see Randy E. Barnett, "A Consent Theory of Contract," *Colum. L. Rev.* 86 (1986; www.randybarnett.com/pre-2000): 269; Rothbard, "Property Rights and the Theory of Contracts"; Williamson M. Evers, "Toward a Reformulation of the Law of Contracts," *J. Libertarian Stud.* 1, no. 1 (Winter 1977; https://mises.org/library/toward-reformulation-law-contracts): 3–13. Thus, the framework for rights, punishment, and consent put forward herein also has implications for other aspects of libertarian theory, which cannot be addressed in detail here. For example, the view of the unenforceability of slavery contracts also applies to contracts for personal services, and, indeed, to all promises in general, and thus to the theory of contracts. The theory of detrimental reliance is also relevant here. In my view, promises *per se* are not

To summarize, then, one may object to certain acts of aggression; or one may grant consent to allow the otherwise-prohibited action to take place. The right against aggression may be alienated, but only by *irrevocably granting* consent, which may be done only by committing an act of aggression. A non-violent action such as a promise or agreement to do something with one's body, on the other hand, does not alienate rights, because the consent may be withdrawn at any time in the future, with certain exceptions. This is because a promise now to consent in the future to violence does not commit aggression against the promisee, and because a future change of mind revokes the consent.

CONCLUSION

If Smith is right that even a murderer has a right to not be killed, then it is wrongful aggression to kill the aggressor, just as it is wrongful aggression for a murderer to kill the victim. Then it is no longer the initiation of force that is impermissible; it is force in general, even re-taliatory, defensive, or restitutive force. Without a right to respond to aggression, the non-aggression principle goes out the window, as does the distinction between aggressor and victim. Smith's defense of the strong version of inalienable rights thus undermines what is surely the heart of libertarianism, the non-aggression principle.

---

enforceable, and contracts are not best viewed as enforceable promises but as exchanges or alienations of titles to acquired tangible property external to one's body. Some promises may be enforceable, due to detrimental reliance, but only in cases where the reliance is not circular, and thus plays a causal role in harming another, and such enforceable promises are something different from contract itself. This view of contracts, inalienability, and rights presented herein also has implications for the distinction between the alienability of homesteadable property versus the (limited) inalienability of rights related to one's body. Elaboration of these ideas will have to await a subsequent article.

Author's note (2023): I have chosen to retain the above note instead of updating it. The original article was written in 1998–99, when I anticipated I would need to elaborate on these ideas subsequently. This is what I did. The next year, in 1999, I started developing the ideas noted above, which ultimately became "A Libertarian Theory of Contract (ch. 9).

APPENDIX
LEFEVRE'S PACIFISM

As noted above, the material here was originally intended to appear in footnote 21, above. Due to its length, I include this material in this appendix.

As noted in the text, the consistent pacifist must condemn all uses of force, even defensive and restitutive, and that libertarian Robert LeFevre has been accused of holding such views. However, as alluded to above, it is not clear that LeFevre took his pacifism so far. As LeFevre writes:

> *Protection* is what we do *prior* to the commission of a criminal act which does, in fact, *prevent* such an act from occurring....

> Protection, because of the fact that it prevents a trespass from occurring, is *always moral*....

> *Defense*, on the other hand, is what we do during an attack by someone else. It is what takes place in what is called the "hot encounter." You are walking down the street and a man comes up to you, sticks a gun in your face, and demands your money. Now you are face to face with an attacker. You cannot *protect* yourself (i.e., prevent the attack); it is too late for that. Now you must defend yourself (i.e., ward off the attack).

> As long as your actions are for the sole purpose of *warding off* the attack, you would not be guilty of an immoral act yourself. But if your actions serve the purpose of *attacking* the criminal, you are guilty of a trespass even though the other man initiated the attack....

> Suppose, in the situation outlined above, the other man takes a swing at you. Clearly, you can raise your arm to ward off his blow. This is *defense*. If, however, you then bring your arm down upon his head and begin attacking him, you are no longer defending yourself, but attacking the other man. This would be immoral, as it is a trespass upon the other person.[49]

Although I disagree with this pacifist view, it seems some libertarians mischaracterize LeFevre as opposing violence in self-defense. E.g., writes Rothbard:

---

[49] Robert LeFevre, *Fundamentals of Liberty* (Santa Ana, California: Rampart Institute, 1988; https://archive.org/details/LeFevre-TheFundamentalsOfLiberty), pp. 354–55.

If every man has the absolute right to his justly-held property it then follows that he has the right to *keep* that property—to defend it by violence against violent invasion. Absolute pacifists who also assert their belief in property rights—such as Mr. Robert LeFevre—are caught in an inescapable inner contradiction: for if a man owns property and yet is denied the right to defend it against attack, then it is clear that a very important aspect of that ownership is being denied to him. To say that someone has the absolute right to a certain property but lacks the right to defend it against attack or invasion is also to say that he does *not* have total right to that property.[50]

This implies LeFevre opposes the right to self-defense, to "defend … against attack." See also the comments of Todd Lewis:

While most libertarians view the right to use lethal force to defend one's body and physical property as naturally flowing from a strict reading of the Non-Aggression Principle, there is at least one little-known libertarian, the late great Robert LeFevre, who took an even more radical position on violence. Not only did he eschew the initiation of violence; he also eschewed the use of violence in one's own self-defense.[51]

Neither Rothbard nor Lewis provide any citations to LeFevre to back up this characterization of his views on violence used in self-defense.[52] Thus, in the absence of any further writing by LeFevre on this subject (which may well exist), I have to conclude that the accusations of him adopting such an extreme pacifist view are unfounded.

---

[50] Rothbard, "Self-Defense," p. 77.

[51] Todd Lewis, "Protection, Defense, Retaliation, and Self-Ownership," *Libertarian Christian Institute* (July 11, 2021; https://perma.cc/9SB2-XJC7).

[52] Lewis did not respond to an email I sent him asking for further clarification or support of his accusation of LeFevre.

11

Selling Does Not Imply Ownership, and Vice-Versa: A Dissection

I delivered this speech at the Property and Freedom Society's 16th Annual Meeting, in Bodrum, Turkey, in 2022.[*] It takes aim, in part, at some of my friend Walter Block's views on voluntary slavery and body-alienability, a topic we've disagreed about for a long time.[†] The transcript was lightly edited for clarity and to add some headings, references, and links, but the colloquial and informal tone has largely been preserved. I published it on my old, mostly defunct site *The Libertarian Standard*, to which Walter responded in due course.[††] This chapter is a lightly-edited version of that article.[§]

TWO RELATED FALLACIES

I want to explore two related beliefs, which I think are fallacious, and they stem from confusions about core libertarian principles and confusions introduced by the sloppy use of language and overuse of metaphorical thinking. And, by the way, I did touch on this topic in less detail at the

---

[*] Kinsella, "KOL395 | Selling Does Not Imply Ownership, and Vice-Versa: A Dissection (PFS 2022)," *Kinsella on Liberty Podcast* (Sept. 17, 2022).

[†] See Kinsella, "KOL004 | Interview with Walter Block on Voluntary Slavery and Inalienability," *Kinsella on Liberty Podcast* (Jan. 27, 2013).

[††] Kinsella, "Selling Does Not Imply Ownership, and Vice-Versa: A Dissection," *The Libertarian Standard* (Oct. 25, 2022). Walter's response: "Rejoinder to Kinsella on Ownership and the Voluntary Slave Contract," *Management Education Science Technology Journal* (MESTE) 11, no. 1 (Jan. 2023; https://perma.cc/H3AL-WBQJ): 1–8. See also *idem*, "Toward a Libertarian Theory of Inalienability: A Critique of Rothbard, Barnett, Gordon, Smith, Kinsella and Epstein," *J. Libertarian Stud.* 17, no. 2 (Spring 2003; https://perma.cc/79AC-34BZ): 39–85.

[§] Some of this material is also discussed in "*Against Intellectual Property* After Twenty Years: Looking Back and Looking Forward" (ch. 15), Part IV.G.

PFS [Property and Freedom Society] here in 2011, when I talked about a bunch of libertarian misconceptions, and also in a "Libertarian Controversies" lecture from Mises Academy about 10 years ago.[1]

So, the first fallacy: *Ownership implies selling*. Walter Block uses this a lot. In fact, I heard him say it explicitly last week again in Nashville at the Libertarian Scholars Conference. So the idea is this: if you own yourself—that is, you own your body—you should be able to sell it. So, a voluntary slavery contract should be enforceable. And if the legal system does not permit voluntary slavery, then it means you really don't own yourself. So the implicit assumption behind this argument is that one inherent aspect of ownership is the right or ability to sell.[2] In other words, it is assumed that "ownership" necessarily includes the ancillary "right to sell." It's taken for granted that "if you own something, you can sell it." This is a mistaken assumption, as I shall explain presently.

Fallacy two: *Selling implies ownership*. So, some contracts that we're used to are exchanges of *owned things*. Consider some simple ones: an apple for an orange, 10 chickens for a pig, 1 ounce of gold for a horse, or $3 for a cup of coffee. Now, we also have labor contracts, where it's considered to be a sale of a service, which implies that you "own your labor" because, after all, you "sold" it. And also there's the sale of knowledge, information, or know-how—like teachers who get paid to give information, publishers, speakers, contracts for transfer of know-how, and so on. And this argument is also used to argue for intellectual property. People say, "Well, if you can sell your idea, you must have owned it, so intellectual property is a legitimate concept." Similarly

---

[1] See Kinsella, "KOL044 | 'Correcting some Common Libertarian Misconceptions' (PFS 2011)," *Kinsella on Liberty Podcast* (May 2, 2013), at slide 7 and *idem*, "KOL049 | 'Libertarian Controversies Lecture 5' (Mises Academy, 2011)," *Kinsella on Liberty Podcast* (May 4, 2013), at slide 15. See also *idem*, "KOL092 | Triple-V: Voluntary Virtues Vodcast, with Michael Shanklin: Can You Trade Something You Don't Own?," *Kinsella on Liberty Podcast* (Oct. 30, 2013); *idem*, "The 'If you own something, that implies that you can sell it; if you sell something, that implies you must own it first' Fallacies," *StephanKinsella.com* (June 1, 2018); *idem*, "On the Danger of Metaphors in Scientific Discourse," *StephanKinsella.com* (June 12, 2011).

[2] See Kinsella, "KOL004 | Interview with Walter Block on Voluntary Slavery and Inalienability" and *idem*, "Thoughts on Walter Block on Voluntary Slavery, Alienability vs. Inalienability, Property and Contract, Rothbard and Evers," *StephanKinsella.com* (Jan. 9, 2022).

with Bitcoin: people say that Bitcoin can be possessed, and sold, so Bitcoins must be owned and ownable things.[3]

SCARCITY AND PROPERTY RIGHTS

Now, let's revisit some elementary categories of libertarian thought. So first of all, action is when humans in the world employ means or scarce resources as tools to help achieve their ends or goals. When there's society—other human actors—there's a possibility of conflict in the use of these resources. Now, it's good that we live in society, because we have the division and specialization of labor, trade, and intercourse with other people. But there can also be conflict among human actors in the use of these scarce resources, including our bodies, because of the nature of these resources.

So what this means is the scarce resources, which we employ as human actors in a purely economic sense, are precisely *things over which there can be conflicts*. So sometimes, to avoid confusion, I will refer to these things as rivalrous, or *contestable* or *conflictable* resources.[4] They are the types of things over which there can be conflict. I find I sometimes need to emphasize this aspect and avoid the term "scarce resources" because, quite often, an intellectual property proponent will say something like, well, "I don't know about you, but good ideas is pretty scarce." They can't easily say that good ideas are *conflictable* (or rivalrous), though. The point is information is not the type of thing that can be subject to property rights or ownership.[5]

---

[3] See Kinsella, "KOL274 | Nobody Owns Bitcoin (PFS 2019)," *Kinsella on Liberty Podcast* (Sept. 19, 2019).

[4] See "*Against Intellectual Property* After Twenty Years" (ch. 15), Part III. On the term "conflictable," see Kinsella, "On Conflictability and Conflictable Resources," *StephanKinsella. com* (Jan. 31, 2022); see also "How We Come to Own Ourselves" (ch. 4), text at n.10; "A Libertarian Theory of Punishment and Rights" (ch. 5), at n.62 and accompanying text; "Dialogical Arguments for Libertarian Rights" (ch. 6), at n.6 and accompanying text; "Causation and Aggression" (ch. 8), n.19 and accompanying text.

[5] See Kinsella, *Against Intellectual Property* (Auburn, Ala.: Mises Institute, 2008); "*Against Intellectual Property* After Twenty Years" (ch. 15). To avoid any doubt: I think patent and copyright law should be abolished. In about 20 years. Daddy's got to put food on the table. Just kidding. "Do it now." I don't think they are listening to me anyway.

Property Rights

Now, in civilized society, property or ownership rights are assigned to reduce this conflict.[6] So what are property rights? All rights are human rights, and all human rights just are property rights,[7] because the very purpose of property rights is to avoid conflict over scarce (rivalrous, conflictable) resources. So ownership means property rights. To own a thing is to have a property right in the thing. So it's actually better to refer to property as the *relationship between* a person and a thing, although, over time, we sometimes are careless with language, and we will refer to the thing itself as property. Like we'll say, "That car is my property." But precise language would be, "I have a property right in that thing, in that car," or "I own that car."[8]

All right: so, ownership and property rights. A property right in a thing gives the owner the right to use it. This is what property rights are. Now, to be more precise, which is—this precision is not necessary for today's discussion, but—owning a thing actually does not literally give you the *right to use it*, but it gives you the *right to prevent others from using it*. It's an exclusionary right.[9] As a practical matter, that *usually* gives you the *ability* to use the thing. So, for example, if you own a gun, that means you can prevent anyone else from using the gun. But it doesn't mean you have the unlimited right to use the gun, because other people have property rights, and their property rights proscribe your actions. So I can't use the gun to shoot someone.

---

[6] See Hoppe, "Of Common, Public, and Private Property and the Rationale for Total Privatization," in *The Great Fiction: Property, Economy, Society, and the Politics of Decline*, Second Expanded Edition (Auburn, Ala.: Mises Institute, 2021; www.hanshoppe.com/tgf).

[7] See Rothbard, "'Human Rights' as Property Rights," in *The Ethics of Liberty* (New York: New York University Press, 1998, http://mises.org/rothbard/ethics/fifteen.asp); see also Kinsella, "KOL259 | 'How To Think About Property', New Hampshire Liberty Forum 2019," *Kinsella on Liberty Podcast* (Feb. 9, 2019).

[8] See "What Libertarianism Is" (ch. 2), n.5; and text accompanying note 39, below.

[9] See "*Against Intellectual Property* After Twenty Years" (ch. 15), n.62 and Part IV.H n.74. Ironically (and as noted in "What Libertarianism Is" (ch. 2), n.5), this is how the patent system works (having a patent on an invention doesn't give you the right to make, use, sell, or practice it, but only to stop others from doing those things), although almost no one except patent specialists really grok this. We patent lawyers like that it's arcane and no one but us gets it. Keeps us employed.

Property Rights as Limits on Action

Now, most people make the mistake of saying, well, this shows that property rights are limited. But this is actually incorrect. The reason I can't shoot the gun at my neighbor is *because* he has a property right in his own body. His property rights are a limitation on what *actions* I can perform. They are *not* a limitation on my property rights in my gun. In fact, if I had a stolen gun, which I didn't own, I still couldn't shoot my neighbor. Ownership of the gun—the means employed—has nothing to do with why am prohibited from shooting him. So the ownership of the gun is not limited by property rights. I can't shoot an innocent person with a gun that I own *or* with a stolen gun. The innocent person's *property rights in his body* limit what *actions* I can perform, with whatever causally efficacious scarce means, whether it's a resource I own or not. It's a limit on my actions, not on property rights. Because the essence of a property right is the right to exclude others, not the right to use.

This mistake is used also to argue for intellectual property because people will say—well, I'll point out that intellectual property rights restrict other property rights, so they're actually an infringement of property rights because they're effectively a nonconsensual negative servitude because, if I have a patent, I can prevent you from using your factory to make iPhones. So that's a limitation on your use of your property.[10]

And the response will be, "Well, all property rights limit other people's property rights." The implicit argument here is that just because patents limit property rights, that's no problem to patents being genuine property rights, because all property rights limit other property rights.[11] But that's not true. Property rights limit only actions. And the owner of a factory making iPhones is not committing any action that invades the borders of anyone else's property. So that's

---

[10] See *"Against Intellectual Property* After Twenty Years" (ch. 15), Part IV.B and note 39, below.

[11] Imagine a woman being assaulted and complaining that this violates her property rights in her body. "Don't complain," the aggressor says, "after all, all property rights are limited by others' property rights, and I'm asserting an ownership claim in your body." See also *"Against Intellectual Property* After Twenty Years" (ch. 15), Part IV.H.

why that's another fallacy. It's a related fallacy but not the one I'm addressing directly today.

So: libertarianism and property rights. The purpose of property rights is to permit conflicts over the use of scarce resources to be avoided. So they assign these exclusive rights so that others can avoid the conflict.

Property Rights and Objective Link

So how does this work? The property rights are assigned in accordance with whichever actor has the *best link* or connection to the resource.[12] This is the only way you can have a workable system of property rights, because any system of property rights has to be voluntarily respected, and for it to be voluntarily respected, it has to be seen as objectively fair, which means it can't be based upon arbitrary differences like "I have the right to rule you, and you don't have the right to rule me because I'm me, and you're you." That's a *particularistic* rule.[13] Or "I have the right to your land because I'm stronger."

Those types of arguments and reasons are not justifications. There has to be an objective best link.[14] So how does that work out? In Western

---

[12] In this sense, all property rules are relative: the owner is the person who has a better claim than all other possible claimants. See, on this, "What Libertarianism Is" (ch. 2), at notes 33, 36; and "Law and Intellectual Property in a Stateless Society" (ch. 14), at n.41 *et pass.* This is why "taints" or original sin in the history of land in the distant past do not render current property rights insecure. See also "Libertarianism After Fifty Years: What Have We Learned?" (ch. 25); and "What Libertarianism Is" (ch. 2), at n.36.

In a recent talk, one legal scholar claims that Rothbard, in *Ethics of Liberty*, propounded a view of "absolute" property titles, as contrasted with the "relative" property titles of the common law. See Wanjiru Njoya, "Defending Private Property: Principles of Justice" (YouTube, March 27, 2023; https://youtu.be/jzamN_8l77k). However, I believe the best reading of Rothbard is that the position he supports is basically the relative property title system indicated above. See Kinsella, "Rothbard on the 'Original Sin' in Land Titles: 1969 vs. 1974," *StephanKinsella.com* (Nov. 5, 2014); *idem*, "Mises, Rothbard, and Hoppe on the 'Original Sin' in the Distribution of Property Rights," *StephanKinsella.com* (Oct. 7, 2014). See also Jeff Deist's breakdown of Rothbard's approach to such property issues in "A Libertarian Approach to Disputed Land Titles," *Mises Wire* (June 3, 2021; https://mises.org/wire/libertarian-approach-disputed-land-titles).

[13] See, on this, "What Libertarianism Is" (ch. 2), n.23 and accompanying text; "How We Come to Own Ourselves" (ch. 4), n.15; "A Libertarian Theory of Punishment and Rights" (ch. 5), n.45 and accompanying text; and "Dialogical Arguments for Libertarian Rights" (ch. 6), n.43 and accompanying text.

[14] See "How We Come to Own Ourselves" (ch. 4).

private law and in libertarianism, which is a far more consistent working out of this, there are basically two types of links—the type of link applied to your body, which is a unique scarce resource; and the type of link applied to external resources in the world, which were *previously unowned* scarce resources. For the body, the link is a self-ownership link. You own your body, and the reason is because of your direct control over it, which I will get to in a minute.

And then for scarce resources in the world, they're always owned first by someone first using them from their unowned state. That's called *homesteading* or *original appropriation*. And then ownership can be *transferred* for two reasons: *contractually*—that's a voluntary transfer of your ownership title of the resource to someone else, either by sale or by gift; or for purposes of *rectification*, which can be seen as a subset of contract because it's also a transfer of title from an owner to someone, but it's because the owner committed a tort against the victim and thus gave him a right to recover some of the aggressor's property as damages.

So *original appropriation*, *contract*, and *rectification* are basically the only three principles to determine ownership of external resources in case of a dispute. So these four principles—body-ownership due to direct control, with an exception made for forfeiture of this right due to committing aggression,[15] plus the three principles for external resources—are how we determine the best link, and this is the core of all property rights, and of all just law. A developed body of private law, to be just, has to be based on these core principles, and just entails working out the details as the law develops.[16] And every socialist

---

15 See "Inalienability and Punishment: A Reply to George Smith" (ch. 10) and note 18, below. See also the Libertarian Party Platform language quoted in note 27, below.

16 See "Legislation and the Discovery of Law in a Free Society" (ch. 13), in general, and "Knowledge, Calculation, Conflict, and Law" (ch. 19), the section "Abstract Rights and Legal Precepts." See also Hoppe's pithy summary of these basic rules, in "A Realistic Libertarianism," *LewRockwell.com* (Sept. 30, 2013; https://www.hanshoppe.com/2014/10/a-realistic-libertarianism/) and in "Of Common, Public, and Private Property and the Rationale for Total Privatization," at pp. 85–87, and the LP Platform language mentioned in note 27, below. As Hoppe writes in "A Realistic Libertarianism":

But who owns what scarce resource as his private property and who does not? First: Each person owns his physical body that only he and no one else controls *directly* (I can control your body only in-directly, by first directly controlling my body, and vice versa) and that only he directly controls also in particular when

system, and every law not based on these core principles, including IP law, always ends up deviating from these core private property law principles in one way or another.

Self-Ownership

Now, so we commonly use the term "self-ownership." This is another phrase that can be misleading because you can have people object to it and say, well, how can you own yourself, because that's a religious view because it implies that your "self" is different than your body or something like that, and they'll criticize it that way.[17]

So to be precise, self-ownership is just a shorthand for body ownership, because your body is a scarce resource. Your "self" is not a scarce resource. The notion of "self" is bound up with the concept of personality and the person that you are, your identity as a person in the world, as an actor, as an agent. So *every person is the presumptive owner of his body.* That's the basic libertarian rule. We don't need to get into controversial metaphysics to understand this basic norm or rule.

Now, by the way, I say "presumptive" because it's not absolute; it's defeasible. The self-ownership right can be lost by committing aggression, because the victim has the right to defend himself during a crime or to retaliate after.[18] And when they do that, they're using the body of the aggressor without his consent.[19] So he's, in a sense, lost ownership of his body to the extent that the victim needs to be able to use force against him to obtain justice.

---

discussing and arguing the question at hand.... [A]s for scarce resources that can be controlled *only* indirectly (that must be appropriated with our own nature-given, i.e., un-appropriated, body): Exclusive control (property) is acquired by and assigned to that person, who appropriated the resource in question *first* or who acquired it through voluntary (conflict-free) exchange from its *previous* owner. For only the *first* appropriator of a resource (and all later owners connected to him through a chain of voluntary exchanges) can possibly acquire and gain control over it without conflict, i.e., peacefully.

[17] See "How We Come to Own Ourselves" (ch. 4), n.1.

[18] See "Inalienability and Punishment: A Reply to George Smith" (ch. 10), n. 11 *et pass.*

[19] Alternatively, it could be said that his prior act of aggression was an irrevocable grant of consent to the victim to retaliate; the aggression is a substitute for manifested consent later.

So the basis here of self-ownership, or body-ownership, is not homesteading, but it's the direct control over your body. This is the *best link* between the given actor and the resource of his human body. And actually, I think the first person who explicitly recognized this was Professor Hoppe in a German publication in 1987.[20] You actually weren't explicit about this in your later English book, but it's implicit in there.[21] And if you remember, you told me about that passage, and you translated it for me for my article.

And so Hoppe's argument is that you own your body because you directly control it. So this gives each person or actor logical-temporal priority or precedence as compared to anyone's indirect control. What that means is, if you were to enslave someone or claim to own their body, the only way to control that body is by coercion, by directing threats of force to get them to act the way you want them to act. But in that case, they're the ones still directly controlling it, and that always has precedence, and it's a better link than the indirect control I can exert over you by coercion. Not to mention that the coercer himself would be in contradiction because he claims ownership of his body for the purpose of being the one who can punish you or threaten you.

So this is what the best link means here. It's not homesteading, although people think it's homesteading. It can't be homesteading because to homestead means you're an actor in the world, already a self-owner, or body-owner, and you find an unowned resource, and you appropriate it to yourself. But this presupposes there's already a person with a body, so it's impossible to imagine that you homestead your body unless you have some religious view where the soul goes down there and grabs it. But that's not the domain of science as I think Guido [Hülsmann] and Mises would agree.[22] We could make an analogy. We could say that when a child "wakes up" at the moment when he becomes

---

20 See "How We Come to Own Ourselves" (ch. 4).

21 Professor Hoppe was in the audience, and I briefly addressed my comments to him, so have left the text unchanged here.

22 Here I am referring to the talk given earlier on the day of my talk, Jörg Guido Hülsmann, "The Ultimate Foundation of Economic Science," *YouTube* (Sept. 17, 2022; https://youtu.be/C3Oglpv47Fg) which itself discussed the book by Mises of the same title (Ludwig von Mises, *The Ultimate Foundation of Economic Science: An Essay on Method* (Princeton, N.J.: D. Van Nostrand Company, Inc., 1962; https://mises.org/library/ultimate-foundation-economic-science)), which happens to also be my own favorite book by Mises.

sapient enough to be said to have rights, he homesteads himself. But it's really a loose analogy. It just means that's the point in time in which he's a person with rights. It's not like his body was unowned, and he just homesteaded it.

External Resources

Now, as for external resources, these are things that were *previously unowned*. This is a key point, and they're external to the human body, so they're not part of people's bodies. So in this case, as I said earlier, the best link is determined by the three principles. First, we have original appropriation or homesteading. What this means is you *possess* something, which is an *economic category*. It means to be able to use or manipulate. Mises—I'll get to this later, but Mises calls it catallactic or sociological ownership, but what he really means is *possession*, which is—and this is important—an *economic* category. So mere possession, like Crusoe on an island—in a Robinsonade—he can never "own" anything because there's no society to have norms with respect to. He controls, and he uses things. He *possesses* these things as means, he exercises "factual authority" over these things—but he doesn't own them.[23]

In society, where there are property rights norms, you can also do the same thing. You can just possess something and not intend to own it—you pick up a stick and throw it away. Or you can possess it with the intent to own, and you take certain steps to transform it or to put a barrier up around it, or to, as Hoppe calls it, emborder it, which basically means to put up a visible public link between you and the thing demonstrating to everyone that this thing is no longer unowned, to say, "I'm claiming ownership of it."[24]

This requires the merger or the combination of actual possession or transformation or embordering—with then intent to own.[25] So those

---

[23] See note 36 and related text, below.

[24] See Hans-Hermann Hoppe, *A Theory of Socialism and Capitalism: Economics, Politics, and Ethics* (Auburn, Ala.: Mises Institute, 2010 [1989], www.hanshoppe.com/tsc), chaps. 1–2.

[25] For a related notion, see my Book Review of Rosalyn Higgins, *Problems and Process: International Law and How We Use It* (1994), *Reason Papers* No. 20 (Fall 1995): 147–53, p. 147: "Law, far from being authority battling against power, is the interlocking of authority with power." Similarly, ownership stems from the interlocking of possession and intent.

two things are essential to owning a thing that was previously unowned. And then, once you own a thing, you can contractually transfer it to someone by your intent, your consent, and I'll get to the mechanics of that in a moment. And then, again, there can also be a transfer as rectification—if you have to transfer something to someone to compensate them for damages you caused them by a tort (an uninvited use of their property).

Okay. Oh, and by the way, this formulation of rights that I just went through, this way of looking at the best link and the breakdown between the body, I'm happy that I was able to help the Mises Caucus in the US get this basic formulation put into the Libertarian Party Platform[26] last May at the "Reno Reset," as we call it. Up until this time, there was no definition of aggression in the Libertarian Party platform. It was just implied.[27]

Contract, Selling and Ownership: External Scarce Resources

Getting back to the problem of confusing selling and ownership, of thinking there's a necessary relationship between them. *How* do we sell an external resource that we own, like the contractual title transfer we talked about early? So: when you own a resource, because the ownership

---

See also, on this, "A Libertarian Theory of Contract: Title Transfer, Binding Promises, and Inalienability" (ch. 9), n.40.

[26] See Libertarian Party Platform, at https://www.lp.org/platform/, and https://perma.cc/GF6J-GPWV.

[27] See Kinsella, "Aggression and Property Rights Plank in the Libertarian Party Platform," *StephanKinsella.com* (May 30, 2022). Modified Plank 2.1 reads, in part:

2.1 Aggression, Property and Contract

Aggression is the use, trespass against, or invasion of the borders of another person's owned resource (property) without the owner's consent; or the threat thereof. We oppose all acts of aggression as illegitimate and unjust, whether committed by private actors or the state.

Each person is the presumptive owner of his or her own body (self-ownership), which right may be forfeited only as a consequence of committing an act of aggression. Property rights in external, scarce resources are determined in accordance with the principles of original appropriation or homesteading (whereby a person becomes an owner of an unowned resource by first use and transformation), contract (whereby the owner consensually transfers ownership to another person), and rectification (whereby an owner's property rights in certain resources are transferred to a victim of the owner's tort, trespass, or aggression to compensate the victim).

requires the merger of possession and the intent to own, you can lose ownership by losing the intent to own, by making it clear you no longer intend to own the resource. This is abandonment. So if you acquire a thing, you can "unacquire" it, so to speak. And because of this, it gives you the ability to sell because you can basically abandon it "in favor" of someone else.[28]

Imagine you're in a tree, and you have an apple, and there's people walking by, below you. You can kind of toss the apple to whoever you want. You can drop it so that whoever you want will catch it. You can direct this—you can direct the re-homesteading, in effect. So if I have an apple and I give it to you to hold temporarily, you're the possessor, but you're not the owner. I'm the owner, but I'm not the possessor. So ownership and possession are distinct concepts and statuses. But if you're holding my apple, and if I then abandon it, now you're holding an unowned apple, and you can just re-homestead it right away. So that's the mechanics, the juristic or legal mechanics, of why and how you can sell things.[29] So the way that we come to own unowned resources is *the reason why* they can be sold. So it's not an incident or aspect of ownership *per se*. It's an aspect of the way external things come to be owned.

Fallacy 1: You Can Sell What You Own

Now, what about selling yourself, your "self," i.e., your body, like Walter Block thinks we can do? Keep in mind: external things can be sold because they were *previously unowned* and *acquired* by an actor-owner who is *already a self-owner*, and he can abandon it. But your body rights don't arise by homesteading or by your intent to own yourself. They arise because of the best link based upon your direct control.

---

[28] But see my posts "Inability to Abandon Property in the Civil Law," *StephanKinsella.com* (Aug. 3 2009) and "Homesteading, Abandonment, and Unowned Land in the Civil Law," *StephanKinsella.com* (Aug. 28, 2021). The positive law ignores the very possibility of unowned or abandoned land. I am not aware of any deep scholarly exploration of this curious feature of modern law, but suspect it stems from a combination of statism and legal positivism, or do I repeat myself. I may explore this issue in further legal scholarship at some point.

[29] See "A Libertarian Theory of Contract" (ch. 9).

So if I try to make a contract, "I promise to sell" or "I promise to be your slave forever," *those words do not change the fact that I still have the best link to my body.* And because my words are not an act of aggression—which is the only way to come to own someone else's body, by them forfeiting their rights by committing a crime—then promising to be someone's slave is simply not enforceable because it doesn't transfer any title to anything. You still own your body because you still have direct control and thus the better link. You can always change your mind, in other words.

So Rothbard seems to notice this in his kind of convoluted arguments in his contract theory. But it's implied, perhaps unknowingly, and later clarified by Hoppe. In any case, Rothbard wrote:

> It is true that man, being what he is, cannot absolutely guarantee life-long service to another under a voluntary arrangement. Thus, Jackson, at present, might agree to labor under Crusoe's direction for life, in return for food, clothing, etc., but he cannot guarantee that he will not change his mind at some point in the future and decide to leave. In this sense, a man's own person and will is "inalienable," i.e., cannot be given up to someone else for any future period.[30]

So I think the reason he focuses on the fact that the will is inalienable is that Rothbard senses that that's *the reason* you own your body, although he never quite says it explicitly, but he gets really close. I mean, what's the relevance of the fact that your will is inalienable to the legitimacy or enforceability of a voluntary slavery contract? The only relevance could be that your direct control, or your will, is the reason you own your body.[31]

Okay, so again, after you promise to be a slave, you still have direct control, so you're still the owner, and you have not committed aggression, so you can always *change your mind* (in contrast to an aggressor who, as noted above, has *irrevocably* granted consent, since he cannot undo the historical fact of the aggression).

---

[30] Murray N. Rothbard, *Man, Economy, and State, with Power and Market*, Scholars ed., second ed. (Auburn, Ala.: Mises Institute, 2009; https://mises.org/library/man-economy-and-state-power-and-market), p. 82 n.2. As noted previously, this was later expanded on and clarified by Hoppe. See note 2, above.

[31] For elaboration, see "A Libertarian Theory of Contract" (ch. 9), Part III.C.

Fallacy 2: You Own What You Sell

Okay, now what about the other fallacy—owning what you sell? In a simple exchange, for two material resources that are both owned by two different people like an apple for an orange or an apple for a silver coin, the sellers do own what they sell. There are two title transfers: The orange changes ownership, and the apple changes ownership.

But in a "sale" of service, labor, or information, the contract *in legal terms*[32] only involves *one title transfer*. This is in legal terms—whatever is "paid" to the person performing the service. So if I give you a chicken to pay you for giving me a haircut, the title to the chicken transfers to you. But you don't transfer title to any labor to me. It's not like there's a bucket of labor, which I'm handing over to you. So these are *actions*, not things that can be owned.[33] So labor or services or actions are what we *do with* things that we own like our bodies or other owned resources. They're not themselves owned resources. So you don't really sell labor, in a legal sense. So why do we describe it this way?

Economic vs. Normative Realms of Analysis: Ownership vs. Possession

Now, here's what I think is the reason for the confusion. There are different modes of understanding for different realms of phenomena and different conceptual frameworks. So, for example, in the teleological versus causal realms, we have human action and purposive behavior on the one hand versus causal laws of nature on the other. We have praxeology versus the empirical method, the scientific method. We have apodictic or *a priori* versus tentative or contingent knowledge. We also have normative or juristic, legal, types or realms of understanding versus factual. And human laws and norms versus empirical facts.

---

[32] I am referring to libertarian law here, not to modern positive law, which views contracts as enforceable, binding obligations. For more on this see "A Libertarian Theory of Contract" (ch. 9).

[33] See "A Libertarian Theory of Contract" (ch. 9) and Kinsella, "Cordato and Kirzner on Intellectual Property," *C4SIF Blog* (April 21, 2011). As Kirzner writes: "Laboring, Day contends, is an activity, 'and although activities can be engaged in, performed or done, they cannot be owned.'" See also *"Against Intellectual Property* After Twenty Years" (ch. 15), Part IV.D.

I'm getting to the point. So, now, Mises was careful to distinguish the juristic or the legal or the *should* from the factual, but he used the word "ownership" in both, which is potentially confusing. So he said: "Regarded as a sociological category"—this was in *Socialism* in 1922, he changed the word to catallactic later, probably because he hadn't come up with the term catallactics yet. I don't know. But he calls it the sociological or economic category of ownership, which is the *power to use a good*. Now, that's possession. That's what we would call possession or control.[34] The "factual authority" mentioned previously.

And then he says the sociological and juristic (by which he means legal or normative) concepts of ownership are different. "Ownership" (really: possession) from the sociological (economic; descriptive) point of view is the *having* of a good. It's just what Crusoe could do. So that's natural or original "ownership," and it's a purely physical relationship of man to goods. But the legal is the "should have." Who should have it? Who has a right to it? This is where property rights and law come in. And later in *Human Action*, he goes on in a similar vein.[35]

---

[34] For more on this, see "What Libertarianism Is" (ch. 2), notes 28–29 and accompanying text, *et pass.*; and "Law and Intellectual Property in a Stateless Society" (ch. 14), n.36. Economists often muddle this issue by either reducing ownership to possession or conflating the terms. See, on this, Geoffrey M. Hodgson, "Much of the 'economics of property rights' devalues property and legal rights," *J. Inst. Econ.* 11, no. 4 (2015; https://perma.cc/9VV3-8DX3): 683–709; and Boudewijn Bouckaert, "From Property Rights to Property Order," *Encyclopedia of Law and Economics* (Springer, forthcoming 2023), the section "Reduction to Mere Possession."

[35] As Mises observed:

Regarded as a sociological category ownership appears as the power to use economic goods. An owner is he who disposes of an economic good.

Thus the sociological and juristic concepts of ownership are different. This, of course, is natural, and one can only be surprised that the fact is still sometimes overlooked. From the sociological and economic point of view, ownership is the *having* of the goods which the economic aims of men require. This *having* may be called the natural or original ownership, as it is purely a physical relationship of man to the goods, independent of social relations between men or of a legal order. The significance of the legal concept of property lies just in this—that it differentiates between the physical *has* and the legal *should have*. The Law recognizes owners and possessors who lack this natural *having*, owners who do not have, but ought to have. In the eyes of the Law "he from whom has been stolen" remains owner, while the thief can never acquire ownership. Economically, however, the natural having alone is relevant, and the economic significance of the legal *should have* lies only in the support it lends to the acquisition, the maintenance, and the regaining of the natural *having*.

So as I said earlier, it's better to distinguish ownership and possession, to use those words rather than two senses of the word ownership,
because it could be potentially confusing because people say they own
Bitcoins, but what they really mean is they possess Bitcoins. People say
they own their minds, but your mind is just an epiphenomenon of your
physical brain—you own your brain; you can change your mind, but
you can't change your brain. They're different concepts. A dead body has
a brain, but it doesn't have a mind. The brain weights three pounds; the
mind doesn't weigh anything.

There's a well-known Roman law, civil law scholar who passed away
a couple years ago, from Greece, but he was a Louisiana law professor,
A.N. Yiannopoulos. And he defines, and the Louisiana Civil Code also
defines, possession as actual control or the "factual authority" a person
has over a corporeal or a material thing.[36] I like these phraseologies.
And again, calling Bitcoin possession "ownership" is one reason for the

---

Ludwig von Mises, *Socialism: An Economic and Sociological Analysis*, J. Kahane, trans.
(Indianapolis, Ind: Liberty Fund, 1981; https://oll.libertyfund.org/title/kahane-socialism-
an-economic-and-sociological-analysis), chapter 1, §1. See also related discussion in
"What Libertarianism Is" (ch. 2), n.29 and n.45, and similar distinctions made in Eugen
von Böhm-Bawerk, "Whether Legal Rights and Relationships Are Economic Goods,"
George D. Huncke, trans., in Eugen von Böhm-Bawerk, *Shorter Classics of Eugen von
Böhm-Bawerk* (South Holland, Ill.: Libertarian Press, 1962 [1881]), p. 57 *et pass.*, discussed in Gael J. Campan, "Does Justice Qualify as an Economic Good?: A Böhm-Baw-
erkian Perspective," *Q. J. Austrian Econ.* 2, no. 1 (Spring 1999; https://perma.cc/G3CK-
B8WB): 21–33, p. 24.

See also *idem*, Ludwig von Mises, *Human Action: A Treatise on Economics*, Scholar's ed.
(Auburn, Ala.: Mises Institute, 1998; https://mises.org/library/human-action-0), chap.
XXIV, § 4:
> Ownership means full control of the services that can be derived from a good.
> This catallactic notion of ownership and property rights is not to be confused
> with the legal definition of ownership and property rights as stated in the laws
> of various countries. It was the idea of legislators and courts to define the legal
> concept of property in such a way as to give to the proprietor full protection by
> the governmental apparatus of coercion and compulsion, and to prevent anybody
> from encroaching upon his rights. As far as this purpose was adequately realized,
> the legal concept of property rights corresponded to the catallactic concept.

[36] Possession is "the *factual authority* that a person exercises over a corporeal thing."
A.N. Yiannopoulos, *Louisiana Civil Law Treatise, Property* (West Group, 4th ed. 2001),
§ 301 (emphasis added); see also Louisiana Civil Code (https://www.legis.la.gov/legis/
Laws_Toc.aspx?folder=67&level=Parent), art. 3421 ("Possession is the *detention* or *enjoyment* of *a corporeal thing*, movable or immovable, that one holds or exercises by himself or
by another who keeps or exercises it in his name"; emphasis added). For further discussion
of these matters, see "What Libertarianism Is" (ch. 2), text at notes 28–29 *et pass.*

confused idea that it's ownable. So if you say I possess a Bitcoin, that's fine. But it doesn't imply that you own it. Plus, Bitcoins can be sold, and so people think if you sell something, you must own it, so that's why they make that mistake. But they are referring to the economic description of the actions—saying I "sold" a bitcoin is a way of describing why the buyer gave me money: to obtain possession of "my" bitcoin—not to the juristic nature of the transaction, which is a one-way title transfer (of the money).[37]

Yiannopoulos also points out something I mentioned earlier—that the accurate use of the word *property* should be the designation of rights people have with respect to things. In other words, property is not the thing itself. It's the relationship between you and the thing.[38] I have a property right in the thing. I'm the owner of the thing.[39] (And by thing I mean an ownable, conflictable resource.)

So: why do we refer to a sale of labor or information when, as I already pointed out, there's only a one-way title transfer of the payment made to the labor performer? Why do we call it that? What happens is, just like in the way the word ownership is used in both senses sometimes to mean possession or economic "ownership," or juristic ownership or real ownership, we use the word sale in that way

---

[37] Using possessives like "my" is just descriptive; it does not imply ownership. Likewise, Robert LeFevre observed:

> It is quite common for one or both spouses in a marriage contract to presume that their opposite number is actually a possession of theirs. Our language gives credence to this supposition for it is usual to hear a man refer to his partner as "my wife." She is not his in a property sense.

Robert LeFevre, *The Philosophy of Ownership* (1966; https://mises.org/library/philosophy-ownership).

[38] Technically speaking a property right is not a right to control a resource but a right to *exclude* others from using the resource; and it is not exactly a relationship between owner and thing, but between owner and other people, *with respect to* the thing owned. But these nuances are not pertinent here. See "What Libertarianism Is" (ch. 2), n.4; "A Libertarian Theory of Contract" (ch. 9), n.1.

[39] See references and quotes in "What Libertarianism Is" (ch. 2), n.5. As discussed there, the civil law has a broad understanding of the concept of a "thing," which can be owned or the subject of legal rights; see Louisiana Civil Code, art. 448: "Division of things. Things are divided into common, public, and private; corporeals and incorporeals; and movables and immovables." Incidentally this exhaustive classification schema implies that intellectual property rights are (private) "incorporeal movables." See *"Against Intellectual Property* After Twenty Years" (ch. 15), Part IV.B, and Kinsella, "Are Ideas Movable or Immovable?", *C4SIF Blog* (April 8, 2013).

too. Sometimes we use it as economists to *describe* the structure of a given human action; and sometimes we use it as lawyers to describe the rights that are transferred.[40]

So in (libertarian) law, "sell" refers to transferring title to an owned thing. So you don't literally sell your labor. You just perform your labor. You perform some action. But in economics, it can be used to describe or characterize an action. So all action from an economic point of view involves an actor using scarce means to pursue some goal or purpose. So when we try to describe what someone does, we try to discern their goals and purposes, and also the means that they're using.[41] So that's what history does as well, right, which Guido was mentioning earlier.[42] We try to understand or characterize the actions of people within a means-ends (praxeological) framework.

So when we say as an economist, "*A* sold his labor to *B*," this is just a concise way of explaining the praxeological nature of that action. We're explaining *why A* performed the action, his labor. Well, he performed it to get money from *B*. So we're describing his goal. His goal was to get money from *B*. That's why he engaged in the means of using his body

---

40 For example, in Israel M. Kirzner, "Producer, Entrepreneur, and the Right to Property," *Reason Papers* No. 1 (Fall 1974; https://reasonpapers.com/archives/): 1–17, p. 6, Kirzner uses the term "own" in the economic sense:

> Day is sharply critical of Locke, denying that one can talk significantly of owning labor (in the sense of "working"). Laboring, Day contends, is an activity, "and although activities can be engaged in, performed or done, they cannot be owned." However, economists will find Locke's use of terms quite familiar and acceptable. Economists speak of agents of production (in the sense of *stocks*), and of the "services" of agents of production (in the flow sense). A man who "owns" an agent of production is considered by economists to own, by that token, also the services flowing from that agent. Again, by hiring the services of a productive agent, a producer is considered by economists to have acquired ownership of the service flow, by purchase from the previous owner of that flow (i.e. the owner of the agent "itself"). In speaking of owning the services of an employee, therefore, the economist does not in fact have in mind the ownership of the *activity* of working, nor the ownership of that which the activity of working produces, nor even the ownership of the *capacity* for working. Rather the economist is perceiving the employee as a stock of human capital, capable of generating a flow of services. [citations omitted]

41 See, on this, Hans-Hermann Hoppe, "A Note on Preference and Indifference in Economic Analysis" and "Further Notes on Preference and Indifference: Rejoinder to Block," both in *The Great Fiction*.

42 Hülsmann, "The Ultimate Foundation of Economic Science."

to perform an action, which he knew would satisfy *B*. And why did *B* transfer ownership of his money to *A*—he actually did legally sell his money to *A* because he transfers title to the money to *A*—to induce him to perform an action. So there's only one title transfer.

So in this case, the economic and the juristic uses of the word "sell" are different because, in legal terms, *B* transfers money to *A* conditional on him performing an action. There's only one title transfer—the money that was transferred. But in economic terms, *A* sells his labor to *B* "in exchange" for money, and *B* sells his money to *A* "in exchange" for A's action. So we can use selling (or exchange) in an economic sense, but we should be careful. Otherwise, you might end up justifying intellectual property.[43]

Thank you very much.

---

[43] In *International News Service v. Associated Press*, 248 U.S. 215, 246 (1918; https://supreme.justia.com/cases/federal/us/248/215/), the Supreme Court recognized a *quasi-property* right in the fruits of one's labor, what is sometimes called the "sweat of the brow" doctrine (a doctrine later rejected in the copyright context in *Feist Publications, Inc. v. Rural Tel. Serv. Co.*, 499 U.S. 340 (1991; https://supreme.justia.com/cases/federal/us/499/340/)). In dissent, Justice Holmes recognized in passing that "Property, a creation of law, does not arise from value, although exchangeable—a matter of fact." Ibid., p. 246. In other words, just because something can be exchanged, a matter of "fact"—i.e., a matter of description and economics—does not imply that the thing sold is property, or owned.

12

Reply to Van Dun: Non-Aggression and Title Transfer[*]

In a recent issue of *The Journal of Libertarian Studies*, Fran van Dun commented on my views on intellectual property and Walter Block's views on blackmail.[1] In this reply, I will concentrate on two aspects of Van Dun's comments: the non-aggression principle and libertarianism, and trademark and contract.

[*] Originally published as Kinsella, "Reply to Van Dun: Non-Aggression and Title Transfer," *J. Libertarian Stud.* 18, no. 2 (Spring 2004): 55–64.

[1] Frank van Dun, "Against Libertarian Legalism: A Comment on Kinsella and Block," *J. Libertarian Stud.* 17, no. 3 (Summer 2003; https://mises.org/library/against-libertarian-legalism-comment-kinsella-and-block-0): 63–90, commenting on Kinsella, "Against Intellectual Property," *J. Libertarian Stud.* 15, no. 2 (Spring 2001): 1–53 and Walter Block, "Toward a Libertarian Theory of Blackmail," *J. Libertarian Stud.* 15, no. 2 (Spring 2001; https://mises.org/library/toward-libertarian-theory-blackmail): 55–88. Block's reply is Walter Block, "Reply to 'Against Libertarian Legalism' by Frank van Dun," *J. Libertarian Stud.* 18, no. 2 (Spring 2004; https://mises.org/library/reply-against-libertarian-legalism-frank-van-dun): 1–30. In this chapter I focus on Van Dun's criticism of my views. However, I agree with Block's blackmail views and with his response to Van Dun and, in fact, have co-authored with Block on the blackmail topic. See Walter Block, Stephan Kinsella & Hans-Hermann Hoppe, "The Second Paradox of Blackmail," *Business Ethics Q.* 10, 3 (July 2000): 593–622.

Van Dun is a longtime friend whom I greatly respect. This is a friendly disagreement. We agree on other issues, such as argumentation ethics. See, e.g., Frank van Dun, "Argumentation Ethics and the Philosophy of Freedom," *Libertarian Papers* 1, art. no. 19 (2009; www.libertarianpapers.org), and "Dialogical Arguments for Libertarian Rights" (ch. 6), "Defending Argumentation Ethics" (ch. 7), and "The Undeniable Morality of Capitalism" (ch. 22). I have also disagreed with another article of Van Dun's, "Freedom and Property: Where They Conflict," in *Property, Freedom, and Society: Essays in Honor of Hans-Hermann* Hoppe, Jörg Guido Hülsmann & Stephan Kinsella, eds. (Auburn, Ala.: Mises Institute, 2009; https://mises.org/library/property-freedom-and-society-essays-honor-hans-hermann-hoppe);

THE NON-AGGRESSION PRINCIPLE
AND LIBERTARIANISM

Van Dun criticizes Block and me for using "the so-called Rothbardian non-aggression rule as the foundation or axiom for libertarian jurisprudence." For although "[n]on-aggression is an important and valid rule of libertarian jurisprudence," it is "inadequate from a libertarian point of view." Rather than being the foundation of libertarian theory, Van Dun argues, it is only an implication of the libertarian philosophy of law.[2]

After such a claim, one might expect Van Dun to provide a critique or denial of the principle of non-aggression followed by an explanation of the contours of the proper theory of law. However, Van Dun seems to accept the non-aggression rule. He uses the concept of "aggression in the traditional sense of a physically invasive, non-defensive use of force (violence) against another person or his property,"[3] just as Rothbardians do. He writes:

> I have no problem with the thesis that, in a libertarian legal order, no individual or group—least of all those who are engaged in the administration of justice—should aggress against any person or any person's property. Aggression, in the libertarian sense of the word, is the physical invasion of another person's domain without that person's consent and without lawful justification. As such, aggression is unlawful and should therefore be illegal in a libertarian legal order (because such an order is intended to be as true to law as is humanly possible). Nor do I have a problem with the thesis that violent border crossings are lawful and therefore legally permissible if and only if they are committed in self-defence, to bring a criminal to justice, or to exact restitution or compensation for an unlawfully inflicted harm. They are permissible to the extent that they are themselves compatible with the requirements of justice.[4]

However:

> It does not follow from those theses that defensive use of force is justified or lawful only in response to aggressive violent invasions of persons or

---

see Kinsella, "Van Dun on Freedom versus Property and Hostile Encirclement," *StephanKinsella.com* (Aug. 3, 2009).

[2] Van Dun, "Against Libertarian Legalism," pp. 63–64.

[3] Ibid., p. 65 n. 4

[4] Ibid., p. 65.

property. It does not follow that only aggression against another person or his property is unlawful. There may be unlawful acts that are not invasions of a person's physical domain, yet justify the defensive use of force to prevent, stop, or exact compensation for such acts.[5]

Van Dun goes on to state even more explicitly his view of the relation between aggression and what is properly regarded as "unlawful":

> Block and Kinsella proceed with their arguments on the supposition that such acts are not unlawful because they are not aggressions. Accordingly, they also suppose that the use of force in retaliation against such acts must itself be an aggression, and therefore unlawful. *In their system of thought, the dichotomy of aggression and non-aggression coincides with the logical opposition between unlawful and lawful acts.*[6]

As Van Dun explains in a brief outline at the end of the paper, in his view, libertarian theory tells us what should be *unlawful,* by which term he seems to mean a rights violation or against natural law.[7] For Van Dun, "unlawful" means the type of conduct that should be made illegal (against positive law). As he writes, "aggression is unlawful and should *therefore* be illegal in a libertarian legal order."[8] Thus, libertarianism is concerned with what is *lawful* and *unlawful,* or with what should be made illegal.

Van Dun states that while physical aggression is one type of unlawfulness, it is not true "that *only* physical invasions of another's person or property are unlawful."[9] Because aggression is only one type of unlawfulness, he writes, other unlawful things may also be made illegal. Such things include trademark infringement, libel, or blackmail.

I hope that I have accurately summarized this aspect of Van Dun's thought. Now I do not deny that the non-aggression principle might not be an "axiom" in the Randian sense and that it might be the result of, or dependent on, more basic truths or reasons.[10] But a given theory of law either is or is not compatible with the rule. It seems that Van

---

[5] Ibid.

[6] Ibid., pp. 65–66, emphasis added.

[7] Ibid., pp. 83–89.

[8] Ibid., p. 65, emphasis added.

[9] Ibid., p. 73, emphasis in original.

[10] In other chapters I have pointed out that the non-aggression principle, or NAP, is merely a concise shorthand for the libertarian conception of property rights, namely

286 | PART 3: Libertarian Legal Theory

Dun wants to have it both ways. He is quite correct that, as Block and I see it, "the dichotomy of aggression and non-aggression coincides with the logical opposition between unlawful and lawful acts."[11] The reason for this is that to declare something "unlawful" means it should be made illegal, meaning that force may be used to oppose the unlawful action. The libertarian believes, I submit, that the only case in which force is justified is if it is in response to an initiated act of force. Otherwise, the outlawing of the conduct is itself an initiation of force.

Van Dun, though, says that the category of unlawful conduct is broader than aggression. This means conduct other than aggression may be—nay, should be—outlawed. Which means that violence should be wielded against innocent people who have not engaged in aggression. However, since it is not in response to aggression, this is initiated force. For this reason, I fail to see how one can admit that aggression should be unlawful but maintain that things other than aggression are also unlawful. If aggression is unlawful, then nothing else can be, because outlawing non-aggression is itself aggression.

In my view, Van Dun cannot really agree with the non-aggression principle if he is going to adhere to his "broader" view of unlawfulness. Rather, to follow this line of reasoning, it would be more consistent to state that many, even most, acts of aggression are unlawful, but that some types of aggression are not unlawful—namely, the violent suppression of some types of non-aggressive conduct (e.g., libel). But then it would be plain that this theory supports, at least in some cases, the infliction of violent force against those who have not themselves initiated force. This does not seem very libertarian.

Before I turn to Van Dun's critique of some of my intellectual property views, a brief digression. Van Dun states:

> A libertarian legal theory must be founded on a sound philosophy of law if it is to have any chance of holding its ground in serious intellectual debate. Block and Kinsella do not provide such a philosophy. They assume instead that it can be found in Rothbard's writings.[12]

---

self-ownership and property rights in scarce resources acquired by original appropriation or contract. See e.g. "What Libertarianism Is" (ch. 2).

[11] Van Dun, "Against Libertarian Legalism," p. 66.

[12] Ibid., p. 83.

However, Van Dun continues, "Rothbard explicitly warned his readers that he himself was merely presupposing the validity of the theory of natural law and would not attempt 'a full-scale defense of that theory.'"[13]

Now, just as Van Dun cannot set forth his entire legal theory in his article, so I did not in mine, but I did not and do not rely only on Rothbard. To the contrary, I cited my own work and that of Hans-Hermann Hoppe, which elsewhere set forth a defense of the non-aggression principle.[14] Hoppe's argumentation or discourse ethics approach, in particular, is a powerful defense of the standard non-aggression-based libertarian view. And it is one Van Dun and I both agree with.

If I am right, Van Dun must reject the non-aggression principle in favor of his view that unlawfulness is not based on or equated with aggression, so that not only aggression may be outlawed. But what I find a bit puzzling is that Van Dun himself employs discourse ethics, in a way similar to Hoppe, to show that "principles of private property and uncoerced exchange" are also presupposed by participants in discourse.[15] In other words, as Hoppe argues, the non-aggression principle does have a justification in the nature of peaceful discourse; it is not simply an arbitrary "axiom." Therefore, it is unclear to me why Van Dun refuses to embrace the non-aggression principle and opposes building a foundation on it. It seems that his own "dialogue ethics" theory, like that of Hoppe, also shows that the non-aggression rule is, in fact, justified and correct.

TRADEMARK AND CONTRACT

Van Dun seems to agree with the main portion of my paper on intellectual property, that patent and copyright laws are unlibertarian. However,

---

13 Ibid.

14 See, e.g., "Dialogical Arguments for Libertarian Rights" (ch. 6); "Defending Argumentation Ethics" (ch. 7); "The Undeniable Morality of Capitalism" (ch. 22); Hans-Hermann Hoppe, *A Theory of Socialism and Capitalism: Economics, Politics, and Ethics* (Auburn, Ala.: Mises Institute, 2010 [1989], www.hanshoppe.com/tsc); *idem, The Economics and Ethics of Private Property: Studies in Political Economy and Philosophy* (Auburn, Ala.: Mises Institute, 2006 [1993]; www.hanshoppe.com/eepp).

15 See "Dialogical Arguments for Libertarian Rights" (ch. 6), text at n.31, discussing Van Dun.

he takes issue with my comments with respect to trademark, the relevant portions of which are provided here:

> Suppose some Lachmannian changes the name on his failing hamburger chain from LachmannBurgers to RothbardBurgers, which is already the name of another hamburger chain. I, as a consumer, am hungry for a RothbardBurger. I see one of the fake RothbardBurger joints run by the stealthy Lachmannian, and I buy a burger. Under current law, Rothbard, the "owner" of the RothbardBurgers trademark, can prevent the Lachmannian from using the mark RothbardBurgers to sell burgers because it is "confusingly similar" to his own trademark. That is, it is likely to mislead consumers as to the true source of the goods purchased. The law, then, gives a right to the trademark holder against the trademark infringer.
>
> In my view, it is the *consumers* whose rights are violated, not the trademark holder's. In the foregoing example, I (the consumer) thought I was buying a RothbardBurger, but instead got a crummy LachmannBurger with its weird kaleidoscopic sauce. I should have a right to sue the Lachmannian for fraud and breach of contract (not to mention intentional infliction of emotional distress and misrepresentation of praxeological truths). However, it is difficult to see how this act of fraud, perpetrated by the Lachmannian on *me*, violates *Rothbard's* rights. The Lachmannian's actions do not physically invade Rothbard's property. He does not even convince others to do this; at most, he may be said to convince third parties to take an action within their rights, namely, to buy a burger from the Lachmannian instead of Rothbard. Thus, it would appear that, under libertarianism, trademark law should give *consumers*, not trademark *users*, the right to sue trademark pirates.[16]

Van Dun maintains that "it is ... difficult to see how trademark piracy could violate the consumer's rights if it was not a violation of the trademark holder's right."[17] Van Dun mounts an escalating series of criticisms of the alleged implications of my trademark views. Most seem to rest on his conclusion that, under my theory, one cannot say that the consumer has a fraud or breach of contract claim. He reasons:

> According to Kinsella, the consumer supposedly is defrauded because the L-Burger chain misrepresented itself to the consumer. The latter

---

16 Kinsella, "Against Intellectual Property," pp. 43–44.
17 Van Dun, "Against Libertarian Legalism," p. 68.

therefore should have a right to sue the L-Burger chain for "fraud and breach of contract." That is a strange conclusion, for it is not at all clear what contract L-Burger breached. The consumer presumably got what he paid for: a burger. If L-Burger acted within its legal rights under the Kinsella Code in using the R-Burger trademark, the consumer should know that a trademark carries no legally relevant information. Kinsella's argument—the consumer thought he bought an R-Burger, but instead got a crummy L-Burger—is simply irrelevant. The consumer's expectations would have been equally frustrated if he had bought at R-Burger when, unbeknownst to him, that chain had hired another chef with the same tastes as his counterpart at L-Burger or had changed its production processes or suppliers. Should any of these things also constitute a violation of the consumer's rights?[18]

I acknowledge the reasoning was somewhat compressed. In a 53-page paper devoted primarily to patent and copyright, I devoted only three paragraphs to the issue of whether trademark law can be justified. My view that the consumer has a fraud or breach of contract claim is obviously based on a theory of contract contained in an article published after the intellectual property article.[19] I believe Van Dun is incorrect that my non-aggression-principle-compatible legal theory cannot support a fraud or breach of contract claim in the context noted above.

As explained more fully in my contract theory chapter, libertarianism maintains that the owner of a scarce resource has the right to use the resource and to dispose of it. The owner is the first possessor (homesteader) or someone who legitimately acquired the property from the first possessor (contract). Having the right to use property implies one may choose to exclude others from it, permit them to use or borrow it, give or sell title to another, or abandon it. If you own something, you can use it, hoard it, share it, destroy it (abuse), sell it (alienate) or give or lend it to another, or abandon it. One's choice whether to sell something or lend it, for example, obviously must be manifested in some way. Clearly, social interaction and property exchanges presuppose the ability of the parties to *communicate* with each other.

---

[18] Ibid., p. 68.
[19] "A Libertarian Theory of Contract: Title Transfer, Binding Promises, and Inalienability" (ch. 9), in particular Part III.E.

It is the owner's consent that distinguishes permitted use from trespass. If my neighbor walks to my front door to borrow a cup of sugar, she has implied permission to use my sidewalk and doorknocker for this purpose because of default rules in the community that can be relied on if not contradicted. This is how language and communication work. But if I tell her she is not welcome on my property, then she is a trespasser if she steps on it. Clearly, the manifested or communicated consent of the owner is relevant as to whether the use of property is permissible—whether it is a form of trespass or theft.

This is also true for loans and exchanges of title. If I lend my car to someone, the permission must be communicated to him somehow. For example, I can lend my car to my brother. His use is not trespass since I consented to it. If a random stranger takes my car and uses it, we call that theft because I did not consent to it.

But since consent is communicated and can be withheld, it need not be all or nothing—a loan need not be a permanent gift. The consent given to others to use one's property can be conditional. For example, it can be limited in time or in other ways. If I lend my car to my brother to go to lunch and he drives off to Canada in it for a month-long vacation, he is now using my car without my consent, and he knows this. At this point, he is identical to the thief or other trespasser. The question to be asked is always: Did the owner consent to the other's use of the property? If so, it is permissible and rightful, since an owner can allow others to use his property. But if not, it is a type of theft or trespass. And clearly, determining whether consent was granted presupposes the *possibility of communication.*

Now, when someone sells or buys an item, the sale or purchase can be, and usually is, conditional. For example, if I buy a candy bar for a shilling from a vendor, I transfer title to my shilling to the vendor, and he transfers title to the candy to me. Other customary assumptions are viewed as implied conditions on the title transfers, but they can also be made explicit or they can contradict default assumptions (sometimes called suppletive law). I might state that the title to my coin transfers *only* if the candy bar has such-and-such property (e.g., it is unopened or fresh, or not laced with poison; although these would probably be default or implied conditions anyway). Therefore, the vendor receives my consent to use and take title to the coin *only* if these conditions are met.

If the vendor knowingly sells me a five-year-old piece of chocolate, then the condition for transferring title to the coin to him has simply not been met, and he is aware of this. So the vendor would be aware that he does *not* have the right to use or keep the coin—just as, in the example above, my brother knows he may use my car to go to lunch, but that he has no right to use it to drive to Canada.

Likewise, in the R-Burger/L-Burger example I gave, I assumed a hypothetical situation in which the customer wanted an R-Burger. That is, he wanted a burger having certain characteristics—it is fresh, has meat and bread, and was made by a certain, identifiable company (the R-Burger chain). When he paid for the fake R-Burger, then title to his coin transfers to the vendor only if the conditions are met. They are not met, because the burger was not made by the R-Burger chain, and that was one of the customer's conditions. Therefore, the L-Burger chain is taking and using his coin without his consent. It is for this reason that he should have a claim against them for trespass (which may be couched in fraud, breach of contract, or theft terms).[20]

Van Dun might argue that it is not possible to identify the R-Burger chain if it does not have a trademark right and that the L-Burger chain can just rename itself "R-Burgers" too, so that when the customer asks for an R-Burger (i.e., conditions the title transfer to the money on it being made and sold by R-Burger), he is actually getting one. He is just getting it from the second R-Burger company, not the first R-Burger company.

However, this response would be easy to overcome. *It need only be possible for the customer to adequately identify what the condition is.* Language is not infinitely malleable, and communication is (undeniably) possible. If pressed, the customer could specify that the purchase is conditioned on the current store he is in being owned by the same R-Burger company first started at such and such date and address, and so on. There is no reason it would be impossible to identify a given vendor without traditional trademark law, just as it is not impossible to identify fellow humans, despite the fact that we do not usually have

---

[20] Such as "larceny by trick." See "A Libertarian Theory of Contract" (ch. 9), Part III.E and, in particular, text accompanying n.63, *et pass.*

trademarks on our names (in fact, humans often have identical names, e.g., John Smith).

Van Dun's implicit assumption here is really that communication and identification of individuals or entities is literally impossible in the absence of trademark rights. I believe this is one of his central mistakes here. Van Dun seems to be so accustomed to the positive law's trademark framework being relied on by modern businesses and consumers that he seems to believe accurate communication is impossible without it. This is obviously absurd.[21]

Accordingly, I submit that Van Dun is incorrect. Under libertarian principles, property owners are free to condition the transfer of title to their property. In a typical exchange, there are many implied conditions, and others may be expressly added or changed. These conditions specify when the other party has the right to take and use the property to be transferred, just as when one lends property or invites a guest to one's home, the manifested consent of the owner governs which uses by the invitee are permissible and which are tantamount to trespass. From here, it is easy to see how selling an item to a customer with a falsely-labeled characteristic can result in title to the monetary payment not passing due to failure of one of the conditions. If title does not pass, then the vendor does not have a right to take, use, or spend the money; it is still the property of the customer.

---

[21] To the contrary. Not only is trademark law not necessary for humans to be able to communicate with each other, but trademark law, like copyright, *impedes* the ability to communicate. See, e.g., Wendy J. Gordon, "A Property Right in Self-Expression: Equality and Individualism in the Natural Law of Intellectual Property," *Yale L. J.* 102, no. 7 (1993; https://scholarship.law.bu.edu/faculty_scholarship/1981/): 1533–1610, at 1585, discussing the U.S. Olympic Committee's attempt to use trademark law to prevent an organization from calling its games the "Gay Olympics." As Gordon writes:

> When the courts have to choose between depriving the trademark owners of some of the "fruits of their labor," on the one hand, or depriving the public and competing manufacturers of the *ability to communicate simply and accurately on the other*, the courts opt to sacrifice the creators' reward in favor of securing *the public's liberty of communication*. Thus, if the word "Olympic" is a generic communicative term, it would not be protectable as a trademark.

Ibid. (emphasis added; citations omitted).

13

Legislation and the Discovery of Law in a Free Society

Originally published in the *Journal of Libertarian Studies* in 1995, this was one of my earliest scholarly publications and my first in that journal, written just a year after I had met Hans-Hermann Hoppe and Murray Rothbard; Hoppe was then the new editor of the *JLS* after Rothbard's passing in January 1995.[*]

I had become fascinated with the Roman/civil law (the law of Louisiana and continental Europe) and the English common law and its possible connections to libertarian political and legal philosophy. I conceived of this project in law school (1988–91) at LSU, a civil-law law school, when I was still more under the thrall of Ayn Rand and her type of rationalism. At first I thought the more "rationalist" civil law was more compatible with a reason- and deductivist-based approach to politics and law than was the common law. One of my law professors, John Devlin, suggested I read Oliver Wendell Holmes's *The Common Law* to counterbalance some of these views. This helped me gain an appreciation of the English common law and decentralized legal systems in general. I ended up concluding that decentralized legal systems—the original Roman law, and its offspring, European civil law and the later English common law—were more compatible with natural principles of justice favored by libertarianism than legislated law. This article was an attempt to highlight what is good in these ancient systems of law and what we can draw on and use in our libertarian theorizing.[†]

---

[*] Stephan Kinsella, "Legislation and the Discovery of Law in a Free Society," *J. Libertarian Stud.* 11, no. 2 (Summer 1995): 132–81. See "How I Became a Libertarian" (ch. 1) for further details.

[†] I later studied and wrote about international law and have also written and spoken about aspects of international law of interest to libertarians. See, e.g., Noah D. Rubins, Thomas N. Papanastasiou & Stephan Kinsella, *International Investment, Political Risk, and Dispute Resolution: A Practitioner's Guide*, Second Edition (Oxford University Press, 2020); Kinsella, "KOL250 | International Law Through a Libertarian Lens (PFS 2018)," *Kinsella on Liberty Podcast* (Sep. 26, 2018); *idem*, "International Law, Libertarian Principles, and the Russia-Ukraine War," *StephanKinsella.com* (April 18, 2022).

For a condensed version of this chapter, see "Legislation and Law in a Free Society," *Mises Daily* (Feb. 25, 2010). For later talks based on the content of this chapter, see "KOL001 | "The (State's) Corruption of (Private) Law" (PFS 2012)," *Kinsella on Liberty Podcast* (Jan. 11, 2013), "KOL221 | Mises Brasil: State Legislation Versus Law and Liberty," *Kinsella on Liberty Podcast* (May 17, 2017), and "KOL020 | "Libertarian Legal Theory: Property, Conflict, and Society: Lecture 3: Applications I: Legal Systems, Contract, Fraud" (Mises Academy, 2011)," *Kinsella on Liberty Podcast* (Feb. 21, 2013).

The original author's note thanked "Professor Saúl Litvinoff and Jack Criss, Jr. for helpful comments on an earlier draft of this article."

> *Justice must stand quite still, or else the scales will waver*
> *and a just verdict will become impossible.*
> —Franz Kafka[1]

I. INTRODUCTION

Libertarians' devotion to individual rights, and to laws in support of those rights, is unquestionable. Most of the laws favored by libertarians can be shown to be consistent with our individual rights—unlike the blatantly illegitimate laws advocated by socialists. Despite this, however, many libertarians overlook important procedural or structural requirements that must accompany any legal system in which substantively justifiable law can develop and last.

In particular, the danger and futility of making law by *legislation* is too often ignored, even by libertarians (other than anarcho-capitalists, who oppose the existence of any government on principle, including its legislature).[2] Libertarians often, for example, advocate that the legislature

---

1 Kafka, The Trial (New York: Schocken Books, Definitive ed. 1984, Willa and Edwin Muir, trans. 1956), at 146.

2 In this book, I sometimes use the term government to refer to what should more precisely be referred to as the state, although, as I have argued elsewhere, to be precise, government (or the institutions of governance) is conceptually distinct from the state. The state commandeers various natural and private institutions in society, such as communication, transportation, defense, education, healthcare, and law and order (institutions of governance), and over time the populace associates these institutions with the state. But just as libertarians are only against state-provided roads and education, but not against roads and education, we are not against "government," meaning institutions or law and order. We are against the state. We anarchist libertarians are not for chaos and do not think law is impossible without the state; indeed, we think true, just law is only really possible without the state. Thus we anarchist libertarians do not oppose law and order, or even "government," properly understood. Nonetheless, I sometimes use "government" in this book in the conventional sense to more or less mean the state, to avoid tedium. See, on this, "Libertarianism After Fifty Years: What Have We Learned?" (ch. 25); Kinsella, "The Nature of the State and Why Libertarians Hate It," *StephanKinsella.com* (May 3, 2010); *idem,* "The State is not the government; we don't own property; scarcity doesn't mean rare; coercion is not aggression," *StephanKinsella.com* (Dec. 19, 2022);

Likewise, in this book I try to avoid or minimize using "property" to refer to the object of property rights (the scarce resource owned) (see "What Libertarianism Is" (ch. 2), n.5) and using "coercion" as a synonym for aggression (Kinsella, "The Problem with 'Coercion,'"

enact this or that law, or they at least support many statutes that are already in force, such as statutes prohibiting murder. The concept of separation of governmental powers into the legislative, executive, and judicial branches, which many libertarians support, implies that legislation can be a valid function of a libertarian government. But as Italian legal theorist Bruno Leoni noted in 1961:

> It is … paradoxical that the very economists who support the free market at the present time do not seem to care to consider whether a free market could really last within a legal system centered on legislation.[3]

Leoni argued that legislation as such is incompatible with freedom. If this is correct, then even statutes that seem to embody libertarian principles simultaneously subvert those principles.

There is another way of forming law, however—in which law is "found" or discovered, rather than "made"—which does not depend on legislation or legislators. This is the way of decentralized legal systems such as customary law, Roman law, and the English common law.

In this chapter I will examine the two ways of forming law—centralized (i.e., legislation-based) and decentralized—and will argue that only the latter is compatible with libertarian principles. I will also examine the proper role for legal codification in light of this conclusion.

II. CENTRALIZED AND DECENTRALIZED LEGAL SYSTEMS

A. Civil Law and Common Law

In modern times the two dominant legal systems in the world are the common law and the continental civil law. Based on the body of English

---

StephanKinsella.com (Aug. 7, 2009) and "The State is not the government; we don't own property; scarcity doesn't mean rare; coercion is not aggression"), but sometimes retain the less-precise usage due to the older usage employed in the source material and to avoid tedium.

[3] Bruno Leoni, *Freedom and the Law* (Indianapolis: Liberty Fund, expanded 3d. ed. 1991 [1961]; https://oll.libertyfund.org/title/kemp-freedom-and-the-law-lf-ed), at 23; see also p. 89.

case law that developed gradually over the centuries, the common law spread to English colonies and commonwealths like America, Canada, Australia, New Zealand, and India. Modern civil law systems are based in part on Roman law, which, like the common law, developed many of its important legal principles in the accumulated decisions of jurists in thousands of cases over centuries (and which predates the common law by centuries).[4] Virtually all of Europe and many other jurisdictions, including Louisiana, Puerto Rico, Quebec, Scotland, and Latin America, have a civil-law system. The civil law systems are usually based on civil codes, such as in Japan. The earliest of these codes was the French Napoleonic Code of 1804.

In the common law and Roman law, there eventually evolved very sophisticated bodies of legal principles, concepts, methodology, and precedents. Because the classical common law and Roman law developed the large bulk of their legal principles through the decision and discussion of cases, they serve as rough examples of decentralized systems of "judge-found" law, as do largely private customary law systems like the Law Merchant.[5]

Unlike Roman law and the common law, however, modern civil law principles are embodied in a statute called a Civil Code, and the civil law enshrines legislation as the primary source of law.[6] In these systems, legal scientists elegantly codify the preceding body of legal principles developed mostly in a decentralized fashion (via the Roman law) and customary European law, but then the legislature enacts this code as a statute and makes legislation the primary source of law. The modern civil law is thus a good example of an explicitly centralized legal system, even though much of the substantive provisions of civil codes are based on legal principles discovered in decentralized fashion in Rome many

---

[4] See notes 37 and 81, below, and accompanying text.

[5] The expression "judge-found" will be used throughout this chapter, rather than the more popular and positivistic phrase "judge-made." I will use the generic phrase "judges" often to refer to the relevant expert decision maker, whether judge, jurist, or private arbitrator, in situations where the relevant discussion applies to decentralized legal systems such as the common law, Roman law, and private law. Although Roman and common law were not based solely on the decisions of judges, for illustrative purposes I will focus on this characteristic as their primary way of finding law.

[6] In revising this chapter, this footnote grew to unmanageable length. I have placed the relevant commentary in the Appendix, below.

centuries ago. Roman law thus has more in common with the common law and customary law than with the Roman law's offspring, modern civil law, since the former were decentralized law-finding systems, while the latter are centralized, legislation-based law-*making* systems.[7] Today's common law, while based on the classical and mostly decentralized Anglo-American common law, is also coming to be more and more dominated by legislation and, to that extent, is gradually being centralized as well.

Thus, previously, law was thought of as a body of true principles ripe for discovery by judges, not as whatever the legislator decreed. Nowadays, however, legislation has become such a ubiquitous way of making law that "the very idea that the law might not be identical with legislation seems odd both to students of law and to laymen."[8] And, one might add, to many libertarians. As discussed below, however, a legislative system is incompatible with libertarian principles and destroys true Law. This holds true for all legislation-based legal systems, even civil law systems, which typically embody fairly libertarian principles, much as the original body of common law does. Although the civil codes of civil law systems codify, in elegant form, principles developed in the relatively decentralized Roman legal system, civil codes are still merely statutes in a system in which legislation is the primary source of law. Thus even civil codes, the most elegant and liberal exemplars of centralized legislation, are subject to the general criticism of legislation presented in this chapter.

B. Civil Law, Rationalism, and Libertarianism

Before concluding this section and proceeding to general criticisms of legislated law, I want to briefly note the tendency of civilians to regard the civil law as a great "rationalist" system.[9] Civilians consider

---

7 For more discussion of the gradual method of developing law in the Roman and common law and of these systems' relative similarity, see Stein, "Roman Law, Common Law, and Civil Law," p. 1592; Buckland & McNair, *Roman Law and Common Law*, at xiv.

8 Leoni, *Freedom and the Law*, p. 6.

9 Rationalism has been defined as:

[T]he doctrines of a group of philosophers of the 17th and 18th centuries, whose most important representatives are Descartes, Spinoza, and Leibniz. The characteristics of this kind of rationalism are: (a) the belief that it is possible to obtain by reason alone a knowledge of the nature of what exists; (b) the view that knowledge

modern civil law to be "rational" or even "rationalistic" for various reasons, including the views that civil law: is rationally and systematically codified,[10] rather than "unscientifically" developed in an uncoordinated fashion by decentralized judges; is "certain" and clear because the rules are written;[11] and is proclaimed by the legislator. Civil law systems such as the Louisiana and French systems are also praised as being drafted "in the spirit of the Enlightenment,"[12] and as resting on an ideological commitment to democracy,[13] economic liberalism,[14] private property,[15] freedom of contract,[16] individualism,[17] natural law,[18] and justice.[19]

Most libertarians would agree that such virtues are genuinely justifiable and thus ought to be supported by any legitimate legal system.

---

forms a single system, which (c) is deductive in character; and (d) the belief that everything is explicable, that is, that everything can in principle be brought under the single system.
Antony Flew, *A Dictionary of Philosophy*, 298–99 (New York: St. Martin's Press, rev'd 2d ed., 1984). See also Hans-Hermann Hoppe, "In Defense of Extreme Rationalism," in *The Great Fiction: Property, Economy, Society, and the Politics of Decline* (Second Expanded Edition, Mises Institute, 2021; www.hanshoppe.com/tgf). See also note 6, above.

[10] See, e.g., Shael Herman, *The Louisiana Civil Code: A European Legacy for the United States* (Louisiana Bar Foundation, 1993), pp. 11–16; Shael Herman & David Hoskins, "Perspectives on Code Structure: Historical Experience, Modern Formats, and Policy Considerations, *Tul. L. Rev.* 54 (1980): 987–1051, p. 996 *et seq.* (discussing in Part III "The Contribution of the Enlightenment: A Drive to Systematization"); Stein, "Roman Law, Common Law, and Civil Law," pp. 1594–95; and Julio C. Cueto-Rua, "The Future of the Civil Law," *La. L. Rev.* 37, no. 3 (1976–77; https://digitalcommons.law.lsu.edu/lalrev/vol37/iss3/2/): 645–79, pp. 646, 652. See also Giovanni Sartori, *Democratic Theory* (Westport, Connecticut: Greenwood Press, 1962), pp. 231–37, 245–56 (discussing the political rationalism of the continental legal system).

[11] See Part III.B, below.

[12] See, e.g., Herman, *The Louisiana Civil Code: A European Legacy for the United States*, p. 12.

[13] See, e.g., ibid. p. 12. However, "democracy" is nothing more than majoritarianism—i.e., mob rule—which does not deserve unqualified praise and thus does not belong in the same class as the other virtues listed above. See notes 22 and 86, below, and accompanying text (discussing some deficiencies of democracy).

[14] See, e.g., ibid. p. 12.

[15] See, e.g., ibid. p. 15.

[16] See, e.g., ibid.

[17] See, e.g., Cueto-Rua, "The Future of the Civil Law," p. 652.

[18] See, e.g., Alan Watson, *The Making of the Civil Law* 68 (Cambridge, Massachusetts and London: Harvard University Press, 1981); Cueto-Rua, "The Future of the Civil Law," p. 652.

[19] See, e.g., Cueto-Rua, "The Future of the Civil Law," p. 677. I call these generally praiseworthy things, values, and conditions "virtues" for lack of a more generic description.

Moreover, civilians are also correct that these liberal principles are consistent with rationalism, because libertarian principles can also be justified with rationalist arguments.[20]

Under the libertarian conception of individual rights, the virtues typically cited in favor of the civil law are certainly necessary requirements of a just legal system. The virtues of economic liberalism, private property, freedom of contract, individualism, natural law, and justice are really only secondary derivations of the basic individual rights to person and property. Natural law is nothing more than the objective truth that each individual has certain rights—i.e., to own himself and to homestead unowned property or acquire it by contractual transfer. Justice is nothing more than giving a person his due, but what a person's "due" is depends upon what his rights are.[21] Individualism has meaning and validity, because it is *individuals* that have rights. Economic liberalism, private property, and freedom of contract are only the playing out of the fact that individuals have a right to own, and thus trade, private property, and indeed have a right to do *anything* that is not aggression. Economic liberalism is only a consequence of the government's lack of authority to hamper free trade and association between individuals.[22]

---

[20] See, e.g., Hans-Hermann Hoppe, *A Theory of Socialism and Capitalism: Economics, Politics, and Ethics* (Auburn, Ala.: Mises Institute, 2010 [1989], www.hanshoppe.com/tsc), chap. 7, and *The Economics and Ethics of Private Property: Studies in Political Economy and Philosophy* (Auburn, Ala.: Mises Institute, 2006 [1993], www.hanshoppe.com/eepp), chap. 13; "A Libertarian Theory of Punishment and Rights" (ch. 5); "Dialogical Arguments for Libertarian Rights" (ch. 6).

[21] "Justice is the constant and perpetual wish to render every one his due.... The maxims of law are these: to live honestly, to hurt no one, to give every one his due." J.A.C. Thomas, ed., trans., *The Institutes of Justinian: Text, Translation, and Commentary* (Amsterdam: North-Holland Publishing Company, 1975).

[22] Almost all of the virtues acclaimed by civilians—as understood here as necessarily compatible with and supportive of individual rights—are genuine, objectively valid virtues or standards that the civil law must be judged by. However, the concept of "democracy" is not in the same class as the other alleged virtues of the civil law. Although the term "democracy" is widely misused today to represent things such as self-determination, economic liberties, or civil liberties, it actually denotes a type of polity whereby certain rules are made by majority vote. Under democracy, nothing prevents a majority from voting for whatever sort of tyrant or tyrannical laws that they like. There is no guarantee, or even likelihood, that laws enacted by a majority or their elected representatives will tend to be just—in fact, it is unlikely, as argued below. *See* Part III.C.3, below and Hans-Hermann Hoppe, *Democracy: The God That Failed* (Transaction, 2001; www.hanshoppe.com/democracy).

Any system of law must be compatible with the rights that individual humans have, and, to that extent, law should be "certain"—that is, we should be certain that law will protect our rights and will not infringe them. The more general goal of "certainty" in the law is merely an aspect of the rule of law, which is necessary for any civilization to survive. Without certainty and the *rule of law*, individuals are not able to predict the results of their actions and are thus unable to rationally plan for the future.

In Part III, below, I argue that centralized legal systems like the civil law and, increasingly, the legislation-dominated common law systems are antithetical to the values of justice, natural law, individual rights, and certainty. Civilians generally support these values, yet they also support the idea of the primacy of legislation which will tend to destroy these values. But how can the civil law be the great system of reason and rationalism, how can it support economic liberalism and individualism, if the civil law is based on legislation, which undercuts these things? Although worshipers of legislation claim to be rationalists, only a naive sort of rationalism, the same naivety that is behind the desire of socialists to "scientifically" plan market activity, can underlie such claims.[23]

Civilians are correct that reason and even rationalism justify the tenets of individualism, individual rights, economic liberalism, private property, and natural law. Contrary to claims of civilians, however, it is a completely private, decentralized law-finding system that is compatible with and that fosters such virtues and principles. Therefore, as will be shown, it is non-legislative, decentralized law-finding systems that are imbued with the spirit of reason and true rationalism. Legislation-based systems are not compatible with either libertarianism or rationalism, or with our natural human rights.

III. LAW, LEGISLATION, AND LIBERTY

In this Part, I explain the various reasons why legislation is incompatible with individual rights and the related standards that any valid legal order must uphold. Each criticism of legislation applies equally to the civil

---

[23] See Part IV, below.

law, because the civil law is a centralized (i.e., legislative) law-making system, and also applies to modern common law systems to the extent that legislation has supplanted (decentralized) case law as the primary source of law.

A. Anarcho-Capitalism

In the opinion of many libertarians, a principled and consistent application of libertarian principles invalidates not only most of today's (legislated) laws, but also the state itself, since government is an agency of institutionalized aggression.[24] The state, by its mere existence, rests on aggression and necessarily initiates violence against innocent individuals (e.g., taxation; monopolizing law). The state cannot exist without aggression, and if aggression is illegitimate, then so is the state.[25]

As most libertarians are aware, this view is known as "anarcho-capitalism" or anarchist libertarianism, since this form of anarchism follows

---

[24] See "What It Means to Be an Anarcho-Capitalist" (ch. 3) and "What Libertarianism Is" (ch. 2).

[25] Regarding the possibility of a system of anarchy that is ordered, not chaotic, see Hans-Hermann Hoppe, "The Private Production of Defense," in *The Great Fiction*; Randy E. Barnett, "Imagining a Polycentric Constitutional Order: A Short Fable," in *The Structure of Liberty: Justice and the Rule of Law*, 2d ed. (Oxford, 2014); Robert P. Murphy, *Chaos Theory: Two Essays on Market Anarchy*, Second Edition (Auburn, Ala.: Mises Institute, 2010; https://mises.org/library/chaos-theory-two-essays-market-anarchy-0); Gerard Casey, *Libertarian Anarchy: Against the State* (Continuum International Publishing Group, 2012); Bruce L. Benson, *The Enterprise of Law: Justice Without the State* (San Francisco, Ca.: Pacific Research Institute for Public Policy, 1990); David Friedman, *The Machinery of Freedom: Guide to A Radical Capitalism*, 3d ed. (2014); Morris & Linda Tannehill, *The Market for Liberty* (Auburn, Ala.: Mises Institute, 2007 [1970]; https://mises.org/library/market-liberty-1); Murray N. Rothbard, *For a New Liberty*, second ed. (Auburn, Ala.: Mises Institute, 2006; https://mises.org/library/new-liberty-libertarian-manifesto), esp. chap. 12; George H. Smith, "Justice Entrepreneurship in a Free Market," in *Atheism, Ayn Rand, and Other Heresies* (Buffalo, N.Y.: Prometheus Books, 1991); Jeffrey Rogers Hummel, "National Goods Versus Public Goods: Defense, Disarmament, and Free Riders," *Rev. Austrian Econ.* 4 (1990; https://mises.org/library/national-goods-versus-public-goods-defense-disarmament-and-free-riders): 88–122; and Terry Anderson & P.J. Hill, "An American Experiment in Anarcho-Capitalism: The Not So Wild, Wild West," *J. Libertarian Stud.* 3, no. 1 (1979; https://mises.org/library/american-experiment-anarcho-capitalism-not-so-wild-wild-west): 9–29. Additional references are listed in Kinsella, "The Greatest Libertarian Books," *StephanKinsella.com* (Aug. 7, 2006) and Hans-Hermann Hoppe, "Anarcho-Capitalism: An Annotated Bibliography," *LewRockwell.com* (Dec. 31, 2001; https://archive.lewrockwell.com/hoppe/hoppe5.html).

from a respect for individual rights that are also a feature of laissez faire capitalism. It almost goes without saying that, if government may not exist, neither may legislation, because only a governmental legislature can enact statutes. There is simply no room for government and legislation in the moral universe. This does not mean, however, that there would be no law if there were no government. Certainly law can develop in a decentralized court system, whether a government-based common-law system or a private system. As Rothbard explains:

> [I]t is perfectly possible, in theory and historically,[26] to have efficient and courteous police, competent and learned judges, and a body of systematic and socially accepted law—and none of these things being furnished by a coercive government.[27]

The remainder of this Part is devoted to additional critiques of legislation that do not depend on anarcho-capitalism but only on the general rights and principles accepted by libertarians in general. In other words, one does not need to be an anarchist libertarian to oppose legislation as a means of making, developing, or identifying law.

B. Certainty

1. Certainty, the Rule of Law, and Legislation

Certainty, which includes clarity and stability in the law, is a necessary feature of any just legal order, as it is a crucial component of the rule of law itself. "The rule of law" is a phrase that is used with varying meanings:

> (1) the absence of arbitrary power on the part of the government to punish citizens or to commit acts against life or property; (2) the subjection of every man, whatever his rank or condition, to the ordinary law of the

---

26 See Rothbard, *For A New Liberty*, pp. 286–89, discussing the largely successful, anarchic system that lasted for roughly 1,000 years in ancient Celtic Ireland. *See also* Benson, *The Enterprise of Law*, discussing historical examples and theoretical bases for privately-produced justice; Friedman, *The Machinery of Freedom*, chap. 45 (discussing anarchy in ancient Iceland); and Casey, *Libertarian Anarchy*, chap. 5 (discussing anarchy in ancient Ireland and other societies).

27 Rothbard, *For A New Liberty*, p. 290.

realm and to the jurisdiction of the ordinary tribunals; and (3) a predominance of the legal spirit in English institutions....[28]

The rule of law is necessary because a government with arbitrary power to inflict violence on its subjects is a standing threat to individual liberty. And if laws are not equally applicable to all men and women, some individual rights will not be respected, because all men and women have certain inalienable, natural rights by their very nature as humans. Clearly, then, the rule of law must be maintained by any just legal system. But the rule of law "cannot be maintained without actually securing the certainty of the law, conceived of as the possibility of long-run planning on the part of individuals in regard to their behavior in private life and business."[29] Thus, a direct implication of rationalism is that the law should be certain.

Even those favoring legislation recognize the importance of certainty; indeed, certainty is one of the purported hallmarks of the civil law. In the words of Professor Vernon Palmer:

> What enduring objectives underlie the relentless drive toward codification in the twentieth century? In my view, this may be explained in three words—certainty, justice, and modernity.... An unchanging purpose of codification and recodification is to overcome an existing fragmentation of law and legal sources in order to create the conditions necessary for *legal certainty.*[30]

Yet, as Leoni points out, there is much more certainty in a decentralized legal system, than in a centralized legislative system. When the legislature has the ability to change the law from day to day, we can

---

[28] Leoni, *Freedom and the Law*, p. 61.

[29] Ibid., p. 95.

[30] Vernon Palmer, "Celebrating the Québec Codification Achievement: A Louisiana Perspective," *Loy. L. Rev.* 38 (1992; https://perma.cc/JK8T-HX4J): 311–27, p. 315 (emphasis added). *See also* Herman & Hoskins, "Perspectives on Code Structure: Historical Experience, Modern Formats, and Policy Considerations," pp. 1001–1002; Herman, *The Louisiana Civil Code: A European Legacy for the United States*, p. 11; *idem*, "Minor Risks and Major Rewards: Civilian Codification in North America on the Eve of the Twenty-First Century," *Tul. Civ. L. Forum* 8 (1993): 63–80, p. 65 ("Civilians presuppose as a fundamental tenet that the fountainhead of stability is their legislation."); and Leoni, *Freedom and the Law*, pp. 73, 142–43 (a desire for certainty in the law, in the sense of verbal precision, was one of the chief reasons for the continental codification efforts).

never be sure what rules will apply tomorrow.[31] As Leoni observes, in a system of legislative supremacy:

> [N]obody can tell whether a rule may be only one year or one month or one day old when it will be abrogated by a new rule. All these rules are precisely worded in written formulae that readers or interpreters cannot change at their will. Nevertheless, all of them may go as soon and as abruptly as they came. The result is that, if we leave out of the picture the ambiguities of the text, we are always "certain" as far as the literal content of each rule is concerned at any given moment, but we are *never certain* that tomorrow we shall still have the rules we have today.[32]

Thus:

> [A] legal system centered on legislation, while involving the possibility that other people (the legislators) may interfere with our actions every day, also involves the possibility that they may change their way of interfering every day. As a result, people are prevented not only from freely deciding what to do, but from foreseeing the legal effects of their daily behavior.[33]

We may have, then, either rule by legislators or the rule of law, but not both.[34] In the words of the Italian scholar Giovanni Sartori, "Mass fabrication of laws ends by jeopardizing the other fundamental requisite of law—certainty."[35]

---

[31] As the not-quite-trite bumper sticker or plaque reads, "No man's life, liberty or property is safe while the legislature is in session." (Attribution: Gideon J. Tucker; Wikipedia, https://perma.cc/PB8G-DP4J.)

[32] Leoni, *Freedom and the Law*, p. 75.

[33] Ibid., p. 10.

[34] See Giovanni Sartori, *Liberty and Law* (Menlo Park, Ca.: Institute for Humane Studies, 1976), at 15–16 *et pass.* The "other" fundamental requisite of law is that law be based on rules of general application, a requisite that special statutes tend to undermine. I am grateful to Leonard Liggio for calling Sartori's works to my attention. But having statutory, artificial law be predictable, known ahead of time, and of "general applicability" is not sufficient for law to be just. If this is your only criteria, you can support all manner of statist laws, as Hayek does. See Walter E. Block, "Hayek's Road to Serfdom," *J. Libertarian Stud.* 12, no. 2 (Fall 1996; https://mises.org/library/hayeks-road-serfdom), pp. 327–50.

[35] Ibid. at 38. *See also* Ridgway K. Foley, Jr., "Invasive Government and the Destruction of Certainty," *The Freeman* (Jan. 1988; https://fee.org/articles/invasive-government-and-the-destruction-of-certainty/); Peter H. Aranson, "Bruno Leoni in Retrospect," *Harv. J. L. & Pub. Pol'y* 11 (1988): 661–711, pp. 672–73 & 681–82; Leonard P. Liggio & Tom G. Palmer, "Freedom and the Law: A Comment on Professor Aranson's Article," *Harv. J. L. & Pub. Pol'y* 11 (1988; http://tomgpalmer.com/selected-publications/): 713–25.

2. Decentralized law-finding systems

a. Limits of Courts' Decisions: Jurisdiction, Scope of Decision, and Precedent

By contrast, judicial decisions—whether by private arbitrators in an anarcho-capitalist society or by judges in a government-established common-law system—are much less able to cause legal uncertainty than is legislation. This is because, as Leoni explains, the position of common-law or decentralized judges "is fundamentally different from that of legislators, at least in three very important respects."[36] First, judges can only make decisions when asked to do so by the parties concerned. Second, the judge's decision is less far-reaching than legislation because it primarily affects the parties to the dispute, and only occasionally affects third parties or others with no connection to the parties involved.[37]

Regarding this second point, let me point out that this is true only for the plaintiff, however, in systems where a verdict may be enforced against a defendant regardless of his consent to the court's jurisdiction—i.e., where courts have compulsory jurisdiction over certain individuals. But even this power is of a drastically lesser scope than the ability of legislators to enact statutes at any time, without being requested by anyone, and that affect everyone, not just plaintiffs and defendants. Further, in a totally private court system, courts do not necessarily have to have the ability to assert jurisdiction over unwilling defendants.[38]

---

[36] Leoni, *Freedom and the Law*, p. 22. *See also* Aranson, "Bruno Leoni in Retrospect," pp. 669–71 and Rothbard, *For a New Liberty*, pp. 283 *et seq.* (discussing Leoni's views with respect to these issues).

[37] As Professor Benson explains, without legislative interference by non-judges, the common law would grow gradually. It would grow and develop in the same way that all customary law grows and develops, particularly as a consequence of the mutual consent of parties entering into reciprocal arrangements. For example, two parties may enter into a contract, but something then occurs that the contract did not clearly account for. The parties *agree* to call upon an arbitrator or mediator to help lead them to a solution. The solution affects only those parties in the dispute, but if it turns out to be effective and the same potential conflict arises again, it may be *voluntarily* adopted by others. In this way, the solution becomes part of customary law.
Benson, *The Enterprise of Law*, p. 283 (endnote omitted).

[38] See Benson, *The Enterprise of Law*, p. 33 *et pass.*; Tannehill & Tannehill, *The Market for Liberty*, p. 66 *et seq*; Bruce L. Benson, "Customary Law as a Social Contract: International

And even in a government court system such as the common law, it is not absolutely necessary that the courts have compulsory jurisdiction over unwilling participants. By contrast, legislation by its nature arrogates to itself jurisdiction over all the government's subjects.

Third, a judge's discretion is further limited by the necessity of referring to similar precedents.[39] This does not necessarily mean that a judge is automatically bound by a prior judicial decision on similar facts, but that at least such precedents are influential. When law is viewed as being *found* rather than *made*, it makes sense that one court would refer to principles already discovered and developed over the centuries by other judges. Because individuals crave certainty and predictability, they will tend to prefer decisions of courts that respect the wisdom of established custom and precedent, where possible. Thus, even a government court will feel a necessity to refer to similar precedents, so that its judgments and reasoning will be respected. A private court will have even more incentive to respect relevant precedents so as to gain and retain customers.

But a court's essential job is to issue a just decision rather than automatically following precedents through blind obedience. Indeed, under the Roman law, and under the common law as it existed at the time of Blackstone, an individual decision was not absolutely binding on future courts.[40] Even the great common-law advocate "Blackstone was not a slavish adherent of the principle of *stare decisis* (decision according to precedent)—a prior decision could be overruled if 'contrary to reason'...."[41] But Blackstone did favor *stare decisis* as a means of subordinating judges to law and for stability in the law:

> For it is an established rule to abide by former precedents, where the same points come again in litigation: as well to keep the scale of justice even and steady, and not liable to waver with every new judge's opinion; as also because the law in that case being solemnly declared and determined, what

---

Commercial Law," *Constitutional Political Economy* 3 (1992): 1–27, p. 9.

[39] See Benson, *The Enterprise of Law*, pp. 17 & 364.

[40] Gordon Tullock, "Courts as Legislators," in Robert L. Cunningham, ed., *Liberty and the Rule of Law* (College Station, Texas: Texas A&M University Press, 1979), chap. 5, p. 142.

[41] Richard A. Posner, "Blackstone and Bentham," *J. Law & Econ.* 19 (1976): 569–606, p. 584 (citing 1 William Blackstone, *Commentaries on the Laws of England* § 83, at *70).

before was uncertain, and perhaps indifferent, is now become a permanent rule, which it is not in the breast of any subsequent judge to alter or vary from, according to his private sentiments....[42]

In this sense, the civilian concept of *jurisprudence constante* is more likely to be adhered to by private courts than *stare decisis*. (*Stare decisis* contemplates adherence by a court to a principle of law announced and applied in a single occasion in the past. Under the doctrine of *jurisprudence constante*, the rule of law upon which repeated decisions in a long line of cases is based is entitled to great weight in subsequent decisions.[43]) In any event, it is very likely that judges will always attempt to distinguish or at least criticize similar precedents even if they choose not to follow them.[44] As mentioned above, this will tend to limit the judge's discretion to "make" law.

b. Government Courts: Extra-Market Powers and Disguised Legislation

Thus, decentralized law-finding systems offer more certainty than centralized law-making systems. As the discussion above shows, however, in a government-backed *common-law* type of decentralized system (as opposed to a wholly private court system), the common law itself can develop legislative characteristics that tend to undermine certainty just as legislation does. This is because common-law courts are government courts and thus have extra-market powers, such as the power to subpoena, the power of compulsory jurisdiction over defendants, and the power of judicial review.

Supreme courts, for example, may engage in what is really disguised legislation. The United States Supreme Court does this all the time.[45] However, this is not a problem of decentralized law itself, but of involving

---

[42] 1 Blackstone, *Commentaries on the Laws of England* § 83, at *69, also quoted in Posner, "Blackstone and Bentham," at 582.

[43] See *Johnson v. St. Paul Mercury Ins. Co.*, 236 So.2d 216, 218 (La. 1970).

[44] See Rothbard, *For a New Liberty*, at 282 *et seq.*

[45] See, e.g., Robert H. Bork, *The Tempting of America: The Political Seduction of the Law* (New York: The Free Press, 1990); Henry Mark Holzer, *Sweet Land of Liberty: The Supreme Court and Individual Rights* (Costa Mesa, Calif.: Common Sense Press, 1983); Bernard H. Siegen, *Economic Liberties and the Constitution* (Chicago: University of Chicago Press, 1980); and James A. Dorn & Henry G. Manne, eds., *Economic Liberties and the Judiciary* (Fairfax, Va.: George Mason University Press, 1987).

government in the court system. Under anarcho-capitalism, with a system of totally private courts and judges, these problems would be minimized as much as is possible in the real world. And, as Leoni points out:

> [E]ven supreme courts are not at all in the same practical position as legislators. After all, not only the inferior courts, but also the supreme courts, may issue decisions only if asked to do so by the parties concerned; and although supreme courts are in this respect in a different position from inferior courts, they are still bound to "interpret" the law instead of promulgating it…. [Further,] under a system of "binding" precedent, supreme courts too may be bound … by their own precedents…. [T]his makes for a considerable difference between judges of supreme courts and legislators as far as the unwelcome imposition of their respective wills on a possibly great number of other dissenting people is concerned.[46]

Thus, even under a government-based decentralized legal system such as the common law, judges' ability to "legislate" is radically different from that of legislators. The possibility of judges acting like legislators is not necessarily implied in the nature of decentralized law-finding systems, but "is rather a deviation from it and a somewhat contradictory introduction of the legislative process under the deceptive label of lawyers' or judiciary law at its highest stage."[47]

Although law developed in a decentralized legal order is an "unplanned," spontaneous order, it results in certainty, while a centralized legal system tends to destroy certainty. In a decentralized legal system:

> Law develops in a case by case manner during which judges fit and adapt existing law to circumstances so as to produce an overall order which, although it may not be "efficient" in a technical, rationalistic sense, … is more stable than that created by statute…. [S]tatute law is in fact much more capricious [than common law] precisely because, in the modern world especially, statutes change frequently according to the whims of legislatures…. *A structure of law which is not the result of will and cannot be known in its entirety, paradoxically, displays more regularities than a written code.*[48]

---

[46] Leoni, *Freedom and the Law*, p. 181.
[47] Ibid., at 24.
[48] Norman Barry, "The Tradition of Spontaneous Order," *Literature of Liberty* 5, no. 2 (Summer 1982; https://perma.cc/Y7X3-S8WY): 7–58, p. 44 (emphasis added), quoted in Aranson, "Bruno Leoni in Retrospect," p. 723, n.40.

3. Civil Codes

a. The "Special" Status of a Civil Code

Can legislation be made more stable so that it does not engender uncertainty? Written constitutions such as the United States Constitution are, after all, difficult to explicitly amend,[49] although the Supreme Court has amended the Constitution *de facto* hundreds of times.[50] The more stable a written statute is, however, the less it resembles legislation, and vice-versa. Civilians contend that the civil law's core is the civil code, which is not meant to change on a daily basis. Rather, a code is more like a constitution, which changes only rarely, in response to greater urgency. The code is not a normal sort of legislation; it is more stable than legislation, and therefore is not subject to the criticism that it engenders uncertainty in the same way as does a mere legislative system.

> [C]odification has for its object the creation of a permanent framework and direction of the evolution of the law. It has a prospective life, and it is not limited to a short-lived or cyclical legislation.... [C]odification is to be contrasted with simple legislation tailored to the circumstances.[51]

A civil code is more like a constitution than mere legislation:

> It is a commonplace that a civil code enjoys a more exalted status than an ordinary statute. The higher dignity accorded to a code is traditional in the civil law world. This respect is due originally to the special qualities of the legislation—its relative permanence, imposing structure, and inner coherence. Statutes may be ad hoc, scattered, and temporary, but the civil code in our tradition has attained something close to the stature enjoyed by a constitution or a Magna Carta in the common-law world.[52]

Note: if writing this now, I would avoid the term "spontaneous" since it is problematic and intermixed with some of Hayek's views that I now disagree with on the knowledge problem and how the market functions. See the "Introductory Note" to Part III.C, below. I have left the term "spontaneous" in the text since it was in the original. I believe the term "spontaneous" as used by Hayekians can be confusing and misleading.

49 In over 200 years, the U.S. Constitution has been amended only 27 times.

50 See note 45, above, and references cited therein.

51 Jean Louis Bergel, "Principal Features and Methods of Codification," *La. L. Rev.* 48, no. 5 (May 1988; https://digitalcommons.law.lsu.edu/lalrev/vol48/iss5/3/): 1073–1097, at 1079.

52 Vernon Palmer, "The Death of a Code—The Birth of a Digest," *Tul. L. Rev.* 63, no. 2 (December 1988): 221–64, at 235. Although it must be admitted that even a written constitution, such as that of the United States, is nothing but a statute, albeit a special

However, such flattery cannot change the fact that the civil code itself provides that legislation is the primary source of law. It does not provide that *codal* legislation, which conforms to certain code-like requirements (e.g., generality, natural law, and the like), is the only source of law. It does not abolish mere statutes and does not take precedence over any subsequently-enacted conflicting statutes, as the U.S. Constitution does; and neither does it provide for a supermajority requirement for its amendment. From a legislator's point of view, the civil code and more mundane legislation are on the exact same horizontal level. (Moreover, even a higher piece of legislation like the U.S. Constitution is still just legislation: written decrees announced by a government committee and enforced by the state, whether just or not.)

Thus the code itself is subject to continual revision and, indeed, is continually revised. It may not in practice be revised as drastically or as often as the other statutes, but the legislature retains the ability to change the code from day to day. For, "a code is a special kind of statute, but a statute nevertheless."[53]

b. Diluting Effect of Special Statutes

What is worse, even if the civil code itself were to be immutably etched in stone—and civil codes are, admittedly, amended much less frequently in some regimes than are "normal" statutes—it would tend to be swamped by subsequent special statutes. Civilians do not disagree with this point. Once a code has been produced and the laws codified, as Professor Palmer recognizes:

> Fragmentation continues inexorably. Special legislation lying outside of the code piles up on all sides, as caselaw and jurisprudence create a thicker and thicker gloss upon the code texts….[T]his inflation of redundant and overlapping laws … is the true enemy of a scientific codification and *the true nemesis of legal certainty*.[54]

---

form of statute and often not as problematic as is normal legislation, as it is more abstract and tends to be partly a codification of earlier customary and private law norms.

[53] Julio C. Cueto-Rua, "The Civil Code of Louisiana Is Alive and Well," *Tul. L. Rev.* 64, no. 1 (1989): 147–76, 158.

[54] Palmer, "Celebrating the Québec Codification Achievement" at 316 (emphasis added). See also ibid. at 317 (discussing the phenomenal growth of special laws in Louisiana since 1825); Leoni, *Freedom and the Law*, p. 6 (discussing the submersion of continental civil

The inexorable production of specialized legislation thus dilutes any stabilizing effect of a civil code and makes the code less relevant. Given the unwieldy hodge-podge of arcane, special-interest statutes that we are faced with today, is it any wonder that uncertainty—both in what the law is today and in what it might be tomorrow—is engendered? Yet we would not have reached such a chaotic state if not for the legislature's ability to enact its will into law.

4. Negative Effects of Uncertainty

a. Sanctity of Contract

As discussed above,[55] without certainty of the law, individuals are less able to make long-range plans. The uncertainty resulting from legislative supremacy also has the negative side effect of weakening the sanctity of contract. Legislation:

> ...destroy[s] established rules and [nullifies] existing conventions and agreements that have hitherto been voluntarily accepted and kept. Even more disruptive is the fact that the very possibility of nullifying agreements and conventions through supervening legislation tends in the long run to induce people to fail to rely on any existing conventions or to keep any accepted agreements.[56]

When legislation becomes supreme and statutes are fruitful and multiply, our very conception of what the law is changes. Unlike in the past, "we are used to having our rights modified by the sovereign decisions of legislators. A landlord no longer feels surprised at being compelled to keep a tenant; an employer is no less used to having to raise the wages of his employees in virtue of the decrees of Power. Nowadays it is understood that our subjective rights are precarious and at the good pleasure of authority."[57]

---

codes in thousands of specialized statutes); Merryman & Pérez-Perdomo, *The Civil Law Tradition*, chap. XX (same). See also Kinsella, "The Mountain of IP Legislation," *C4SIF Blog* (Nov. 24, 2010).

[55] See Part III.B.1, above.

[56] Leoni, *Freedom and the Law*, p. 18.

[57] Bertrand de Jouvenel, *Sovereignty: An Inquiry into the Political Good* (Chicago: University of Chicago Press, 1957), at 189. See also Leoni, *Freedom and the Law*, pp. 145–46.

When contractual reliance becomes more risky, "contractual exchanges requiring temporally separated future performance become less attractive, leading the parties to develop costly alternatives, such as contractual hostages (if that is possible at all under the statute), otherwise unwarranted vertical integration of production processes, or the foregoing of such exchanges entirely."[58] Such alternatives impoverish us all by imposing unnecessary costs on production and exchange.

b. Time Preference and the Structure of Production

Another extremely pernicious but subtle effect of the increased uncertainty of legislative systems is the increase of man's time preference. Individuals invariably demonstrate a preference for earlier goods over later goods, all things being equal. This is the phenomenon of time preference.[59] Time preference explains the advent of interest payments, payments made to someone who loans money. When a loan of money is made, the lender gives up (more-valued) present dollars and receives (less-valued) future dollars, and thus the loan will go forward only if the lender is compensated with interest.

Men prosper materially when time preferences are lower, since when this is the case, they are more willing to forego immediate benefits such as consumption and invest their time and capital in more indirect (i.e., more roundabout, lengthier) production processes, which yield more and/or better goods for consumption or for further production.[60] We forego picking bananas to eat them now (consumption) and devote some of our present time to the building of fishing nets (capital) so we

---

58 Aranson, "Bruno Leoni in Retrospect," pp. 681–82 (footnote omitted).

59 Hans-Hermann Hoppe, "Time Preference, Government, and the Process of De-Civilization—From Monarchy to Democracy," *J. des Economistes et des Etudes Humaines* 5, no. 2/3 (June/September 1994; https://www.hanshoppe.com/publications/): 319–49, at 319–21 (also included in *Democracy: The God That Failed* and in John Denson, ed., *The Costs of War: America's Pyrrhic Victories* (New Brunswick: Transaction Publishers, 1997; https://mises.org/library/costs-war-americas-pyrrhic-victories)). See also Ludwig von Mises, *Human Action: A Treatise on Economics*, Scholar's ed. (Auburn, Ala.: Mises Institute, 1998; https://mises.org/library/human-action-0), chaps. 18–19; Murray N. Rothbard, *Man, Economy, and State*, in *Man, Economy, and State, with Power and Market*, Scholar's ed., second ed. (Auburn, Ala.: Mises Institute, 2009; https://mises.org/library/man-economy-and-state-power-and-market), chap. 1, §4 and chap. 6, §3.

60 Hoppe, "Time Preference, Government, and the Process of De-Civilization—From Monarchy to Democracy," pp. 320–21.

can catch more fish in the future, which can feed more people for the same amount of work as it took to search for bananas.

Any artificial raising of the general time preference rate tends to impoverish society by pushing us away from production, long-term investments, and roundabout production processes and towards consumption and more short-term investments which produce fewer and/or worse quality goods. In other words, instead of foregoing picking bananas to eat them now and instead of spending time building fishing nets to produce goods in the future, we tend to eat more bananas now and live only for the moment, and reduce our investment in the future. Clearly, when the general time preference rate is artificially raised, the populace becomes materially poorer and worse off.

Yet increased uncertainty causes an increase in time preference rates. With the very possibility of legislation, the future is made more unpredictable than it would be without the possibility of legislation. Future goods are always less desirable to individuals than present goods. But if the future becomes more unpredictable, future actions and goods become less certain to occur, and thus future goods become relatively even *less* desirable, and present goods therefore become relatively more desirable. As explained by Hoppe:

> [T]he mere fact of legislation—of democratic law-making—increases the degree of uncertainty. Rather than being immutable and hence predictable, law becomes increasingly flexible and unpredictable. What is right and wrong today may not be so tomorrow. The future is thus rendered more haphazard. Consequently, all around time preferences degrees will rise, consumption and short-term orientation will be stimulated, and at the same time the respect for all laws will be systematically undermined and crime promoted (for if there is no immutable standard of "right," then there is also no firm definition of "crime").[61]

Leoni anticipated a similar effect of legislation. Leoni called the illusory certainty generated by written legislation the short-run certainty of the law, as opposed to genuine, long-run legal certainty. The desire for short-run certainty over long-run certainty corresponds to an immature desire for immediate gratification. Leoni writes:

---

[61] Ibid., at 340.

> I am reminded of a conversation I had with an old man who grew plants in my country. I asked him to sell me a big tree for my private garden. He replied, "Everybody now wants big trees. People want them immediately; they do not bother about the fact that trees grow slowly and that it takes a great deal of time and trouble to grow them. Everybody today is always in a hurry," he sadly concluded, "and I do not know why." [62]

The answer is, in part, because an increased climate of uncertainty increases the general time preference rate.

c. Time Preference and Crime

There is also a fascinating relationship, as Hoppe above alludes to, between higher time preference and increased crime. This is because earning a market income requires more patience than does the immediate gratification that criminals seek: "one must first work for a while before one gets paid. In contrast, specific criminal activities such as murder, assault, rape, robbery, theft, and burglary require no such discipline: the reward for the aggressor is tangible and immediate whereas the sacrifice—possible punishment—lies in the future and is uncertain."[63] As a person becomes more present-oriented, immediate (criminal) gratifications become relatively more attractive, and future, uncertain punishment becomes less of a disincentive. Thus many people on the margin—those who are just deterred from committing crimes by the threat of possible future punishment under normal time-preference conditions in a free society—will not be deterred from committing crimes in a society with legislation and its concomitant increase in time preference. In other words, there are individuals today who are committing violent crimes solely because of the increased uncertainty in society caused by the existence of legislation.[64] Further, when the increased uncertainty tends to

---

[62] Leoni, *Freedom and the Law*, p. 80.

[63] Hoppe, "Time Preference, Government, and the Process of De-Civilization—From Monarchy to Democracy," at 340 n.31. On the relationship between time preference and crime, Hoppe cites J.Q. Wilson & R.J. Herrnstein, *Crime and Human Nature* (1985), pp. 49–56, 416–22; E.C. Banfield, *The Unheavenly City Revisited* (Boston: Little, Brown, 1974); and *idem*, "Present-Orientedness and Crime," in Randy E. Barnett & J. Hagel, eds., *Assessing the Criminal, Restitution, Retribution, and the Legal Process* (Cambridge: Ballinger, 1977).

[64] Regarding "the increase in criminal activity brought about by the operation of democratic republicanism in the course of the last hundred years as a consequence of steadily increased legislation and an ever expanding range of 'social,' as opposed to private, responsibilities"

impoverish us by shortening the structure of production, more people are poor and impoverished, which also tends to increase the amount of crime in society.

When law is based on legislation, uncertainty is increased, not decreased, even in the supposedly "certain" civil law systems. This hampers the ability of individuals to engage in private calculation, i.e., in planning for the future and in knowing the legal consequences of their future actions. It makes contractual reliance more risky and thus imposes further costs on otherwise-beneficial economic transactions. And the unavoidable uncertainty caused by legislation also raises our time preference rate, which "necessarily exerts a push away from more highly capitalized, and hence more productive production processes, and into the direction of a hand-to-mouth existence,"[65] and thus tends to impoverish us all.

C. Central Planning and Economic Calculation

Introductory Note: In this section (Part III.C), I relied heavily on Bruno Leoni's interpretation of Mises's and Hayek's views on the economic calculation problem and his related criticism of legislation by analogy to central economic planning. Subsequently, I gained a deeper understanding of the difference between Mises's and Hayek's approach to this issue, after Joseph Salerno initiated the "dehomogenization" debate.[66] At

---

(Hoppe, "Time Preference, Government, and the Process of De-Civilization—From Monarchy to Democracy," n.31), Hoppe cites R.D. McGrath, *Gunfighters, Highwaymen, and Vigilantes: Violence on the Frontier* (Berkeley: University of California Press, 1984), esp. chap. 13, and *idem*, "Treat Them to a Good Dose of Lead," *Chronicles* (January 1994), pp. 17–18.

[65] Hans-Hermann Hoppe, "The Economics and Sociology of Taxation," in Hoppe, *Economics and Ethics of Private Property*, at 34.

[66] See Joseph T. Salerno, "Postscript" [1990], in Ludwig von Mises, *Economic Calculation in the Socialist Commonwealth*, S. Adler, trans. (Auburn, Ala.: Mises Institute, 1990 [1920]; https://mises.org/library/economic-calculation-socialist-commonwealth); *idem*, "Ludwig von Mises as Social Rationalist," *Rev. Austrian Econ.* 4 (1990; https://mises.org/library/ludwig-von-mises-social-rationalist): 26–64 Joseph T. Salerno, "Ludwig von Mises as Social Rationalist," *Rev. Austrian Econ.* 4 (1990; https://mises.org/library/ludwig-von-mises-social-rationalist): 26–64, at 31 (also published in Jeffrey M. Herbener, ed., *The Meaning of Ludwig von Mises: Contributions in Economics, Sociology, Epistemology, and Political Philosophy* (Norwell, Mass.: Kluwer Academic Publishers, 1993; https://mises.org/library/meaning-ludwig-von-mises)); and especially *idem*, "Mises and Hayek Dehomogenized,"

the time I wrote the original article, I did not appreciate this distinction and thus too-uncritically accepted Leoni's arguments, many of which are summarized or relied on in this section, even though Austrian economist Jeffrey Herbener had sent me helpful comments on an early manuscript, pointing this out.[67] I did not at the time (1995) fully appreciate his criticisms. I now believe there are many flaws in Leoni's reliance on Hayek to criticize legislation, when he analogizes the problems of legislation to the economic calculation problem faced by a central economic planner, because Hayek's own approach to the calculation problem and his focus on "knowledge" is flawed. By the time I wrote the article which would become chapter 17 of this volume, in 1999, I had realized my error, and discussed the flaws with the Hayekian approach in the section "Knowledge vs. Calculation." In sum, as several Misesian Austrians have pointed out:

Rothbard: "the entire Hayekian emphasis on 'knowledge' is misplaced and misconceived"

Hülsmann: discussing "the irrelevance of knowledge problems"

Salerno: "[t]he price system is not–and praxeologically cannot be—a mechanism for economizing and communicating the knowledge relevant to production plans. The realized prices of history are an accessory of appraisement"

Hoppe: "Hayek's contribution to the socialism debate must be thrown out as false, confusing, and irrelevant."[68]

Rev. Austrian Econ. 6, no. 2 (1993; https://mises.org/library/mises-and-hayek-dehomogenized): 113–46; and other material collected at Kinsella, "The Great Mises-Hayek Dehomogenization/Economic Calculation Debate," *StephanKinsella.com* (Feb. 8, 2016).

67 Herbener's letter is available at Kinsella, "Legislation and the Discovery of Law in a Free Society," *StephanKinsella.com* (Jan. 8, 2021).

68 See Murray N. Rothbard, "The End of Socialism and the Calculation Debate Revisited," *Rev. Austrian Econ.* 5, no. 2 (1991; https://mises.org/library/end-socialism-and-calculation-debate-revisited-0): 51–76, at 66; Jörg Guido Hülsmann, "Knowledge, Judgment, and the Use of Property," *Rev. Austrian Econ.* 10, no. 1 (1997; https://mises.org/library/knowledge-judgment-and-use-property): 23–48, at 39; Salerno, "Ludwig von Mises as Social Rationalist," at 44; Hans-Hermann Hoppe, "Socialism: A Property or Knowledge Problem?", *Rev. Austrian Econ.* 9, no. 1 (1996; https://mises.org/library/socialism-property-or-knowledge-problem): 143–49, at 146. See also Kinsella, "Knowledge vs. Calculation," *Mises Economics Blog* (July 11, 2006). See also related discussion in "Knowledge, Calculation, Conflict, and Law" (ch. 19), at n.34, and *idem*, "Second Thoughts on Leoni, Hayek, Legislation, and Economic Calculation," *The Libertarian Standard* (May 9, 2014).

In this chapter I have retained the following section from the original article since it still contains some useful insights and also is a good summary of Leoni's position on this matter.

Besides the fact that the possibility of legislation breeds uncertainty and is thus harmful for this reason alone, legislators face a problem that central economic planners also face. It is an information problem, and this unavoidable problem makes it unlikely that any body of legislation will develop substantively legitimate law—i.e., a body of law consistent with principles such as justice, individualism, and economic liberalism. For the same reason that central economic planning is impossible, centrally-planned laws cannot hope to be truly based on the true interests or needs or situation of the populace. I first discuss the reason why central planning—i.e., socialism—is impossible, before analogizing socialism to legislation.

1. Central Planning and the Impossibility of Socialism

With the collapse of communism/socialism, mainstream opinion is finally starting to realize that socialism, in addition to being incredibly immoral and wasteful of human life, simply does not work. But this comes as no revelation and no surprise to the Austrian school of economics following in the footsteps of Ludwig von Mises. As far back as 1920, Mises explained why socialism is *impossible*. Although Mises's amazingly prescient ideas were arrogantly and unfortunately ignored for decades by establishment thinkers, Mises has finally been vindicated by the universally (if belatedly) acknowledged failure of socialism,[69] and I will not re-argue the obvious here, especially in a libertarian journal.

However, Mises's explanation of why socialist central planning is doomed to failure has, as pointed out by Leoni, important ramifications for *legislation* as well. Thus, in this subsection I briefly discuss the so-called "economic calculation debate" before exploring its implications for legislation.

---

[69] See Gertrude E. Schroeder, "The Dismal Fate of Soviet-Type Economies: Mises Was Right," *Cato J.* 11 no. 1 (Spring/Summer 1991; https://www.cato.org/cato-journal/spring/sumer-1991): 13–25; Mark Skousen, "'Just Because Socialism Has Lost Does Not Mean That Capitalism Has Won': An Interview with Robert L. Heilbroner," *Forbes* (May 27, 1991): 130–35.

In 1920 Mises published his devastating critique of socialism, "Economic Calculation in the Socialist Commonwealth."[70] Mises showed that, besides the incentive problem of socialism (e.g., "Who will take out the garbage?"),[71] the central planner cannot know what products or how much of them to order to be produced without the information provided by prices on a free market. In a free market, in which there is by definition private ownership of property, the free exchange of goods by individual human actors in accordance with their subjective utilities establishes relative prices, in terms of money (which historically was gold and other precious metals). These money prices are the indispensable tool of calculation for rational coordination of scarce resources, since "monetary economic calculation is the intellectual basis of the market economy."[72] Without market prices, how can a central planning board know what or how many products to produce, with which techniques and raw materials, and in which location? These and a practically infinite number of questions are simply unanswerable without the information provided by monetary prices. As Rothbard explains:

> Mises demonstrated that, in any economy more complex than the Crusoe or primitive family level, the socialist planning board would simply not know what to do, or how to answer any of these vital questions. Developing the momentous concept of *calculation*, Mises pointed out that the planning board could not answer these questions because socialism would lack the indispensable tool that private entrepreneurs use to appraise and calculate: the existence of a market in the means of production, a market that brings about money prices based on genuine profit-seeking exchanges by private owners of these means of production. Since the very essence of socialism is collective ownership of the means of production, the planning board would not be able to plan, or to make any sort of rational economic decisions. Its decisions would necessarily be completely arbitrary and chaotic, and therefore the existence of a socialist

---

[70] Mises, *Economic Calculation in the Socialist Commonwealth*; idem, *Socialism: An Economic and Sociological Analysis*, J. Kahane, trans. (Indianapolis, Ind: Liberty Fund, 1981; https://oll.libertyfund.org/title/kahane-socialism-an-economic-and-sociological-analysis), at 95–130; Mises, *Human Action*, at 200–31, 695–715; Murray N. Rothbard, "The End of Socialism and the Calculation Debate Revisited," in *Economic Controversies* (Auburn, Ala.: Mises Institute, 2011; https://mises.org/library/economic-controversies).
[71] Rothbard, "The End of Socialism and the Calculation Debate Revisited," at 828.
[72] Mises, *Human Action*, at 259.

planned economy is literally "impossible" (to use a term long ridiculed by Mises's critics).[73]

Defenders of socialism often countered with the bare fact of the Soviet Union's existence and "success" as disproof of the contention that socialism is impossible. However, as Rothbard points out, Soviet GNP and other production figures relied upon as evidence of the USSR's success were wholly inaccurate and deceitful—as the final collapse of socialism has made manifest. Further, the Soviet Union and other socialist countries have never enjoyed complete socialism, for despite their best efforts to stamp out individual initiative, free trade, and private property, the existence of black (i.e., free) markets and bribery is widespread, which prevent socialism from completely controlling and thus strangling the economy.

Also, these socialist economies existed in a world containing many (relatively) capitalist markets, such as that in the United States. Thus, the socialist planners were able to parasitically copy the prices of the West as a crude guideline for pricing and allocating their own capital resources.[74] To the extent true socialism was able to be imposed on the populace, economic calculation thereunder was impossible and the people suffered accordingly.

In the words of Mises, "Where there is no market there is no price system, and where there is no price system there can be no economic calculation."[75] "The paradox of 'planning' is that it cannot plan, because of the absence of economic calculation. What is called a planned economy is no economy at all."[76]

2. Legislation as Central Planning

One of Bruno Leoni's greatest achievements was to teach us that Mises's criticism applies not only to a central planning board of a socialist economy, but also to a legislature attempting to "centrally plan" the laws of a society. Leoni notes that several economists in the early '20s,

---

[73] Rothbard, "The End of Socialism and the Calculation Debate Revisited," at 829.

[74] Ibid., pp. 854. See also Mises, *Human Action*, at 702 (discussing the use of western price systems by socialist governments).

[75] Mises, *Socialism*, at 113 (p. 131 of the 1936 J. Kahane translation).

[76] Mises, *Human Action*, at 700.

but especially Mises, demonstrated "that a centralized economy run by a committee of directors suppressing market prices and proceeding without them does not work because the directors cannot know, without the continuous revelation of the market, what the demand or the supply would be...."[77] Leoni recognized that:

> ...this demonstration may be deemed the most important and lasting contribution made by the economists to the cause of individual freedom in our time. *However, its conclusions may be considered only as a special case of a more general realization that no legislator would be able to establish by himself, without some kind of continuous collaboration on the part of all the people concerned, the rules governing the actual behavior of everybody in the endless relationships that each has with everybody else.* No public opinion polls, no referenda, no consultations would really put the legislators in a position to determine these rules, any more than a similar procedure could put the directors of a planned economy in a position to discover the total demand and supply of all commodities and services.[78]

What does this mean? Leoni is pointing out that legislators, even if they wanted to enact rules that truly take into account the actual situation, customs, expectations, and practices of individuals, simply can never collect enough information about the near-infinite variety of human interactions. The legislator, like a communist central planner, can only grope in the dark. And unlike a blind man who literally has to grope in the dark but at least knows when he has finally run into a wall or found the door, the legislator (or central planner) has no reliable guide for knowing whether they have constructed the "right" law (or economic allocation) or not. Further, not only can legislators not know the actual situation of the individuals they intend to cast their legislative net over, but they cannot predict the often far-reaching effects of legislation. Legislation routinely has unintended consequences, a fact that cannot be gotten around since it is necessitated by the systematic ignorance that legislators face.[79]

---

[77] Leoni, *Freedom and the Law*, p. 19.

[78] Ibid. at 19–20 (emphasis in original). See also ibid. at 89; Aranson, "Bruno Leoni in Retrospect," p. 676.

[79] On the unintended consequences that flow from various governmental programs and laws, see William C. Mitchell & Randy T. Simmons, *Beyond Politics: Markets, Welfare, and the Failure of Bureaucracy* (Boulder: Westview Press, 1994).

The ultimate reason that the legislator and central planner are both ultimately doomed to failure is that *"there is more than an analogy between the market economy and a judiciary or lawyers' law, just as there is much more than an analogy between a planned economy and legislation."*[80] There is "more" than an analogy because legislation and central planning are really the same thing: coercively-backed commands emanating from the government that order individuals to act in certain ways that the government prefers.

In a common-law process, law develops spontaneously, much as prices arise spontaneously on a free market. Mises showed that only when individuals remain free to trade and own private property can genuine prices be discovered. Similarly, true law is discovered in a process that "can be described as sort of a vast, continuous, and chiefly spontaneous collaboration between the judges and the judged in order to discover what the people's will is in a series of definite instances—a collaboration that in many respects may be compared to that existing among all the participants in a free market."[81] True law cannot be designed or imposed top-down on society. The form of a legal system, like a price structure or like a language, must evolve naturally, from the bottom up. This is why the artificial language Esperanto failed to take hold.[82] The naive belief that Law can be discovered by means of government employees' dictates is reminiscent of the joke about the new English public school, in which the headmaster announced to the students one day, "from now on, it will be a tradition at the School to wear hats on Fridays." Legislation is artificial law and is no substitute for evolved law.

A crucial reason for the systematic ignorance of central planners and legislators alike is "the decentralized, fragmentary character of knowledge."[83] This makes central planners and central law-makers systematically unable to ever have enough knowledge to make informed decisions that affect entire economic or legal systems. Moreover, not only is a central planner "unable" to gather information only present in a dynamic price structure, but the attempt to plan actually *destroys*

---

[80] Leoni, *Freedom and the Law*, p. 23 (emphasis in original).
[81] Ibid. at 22; see also p. 104; Aranson, "Bruno Leoni in Retrospect," pp. 668–69; and note 37, above, and accompanying text.
[82] See Leoni, *Freedom and the Law*, p. 218 (discussing similarities between evolved systems like language and law).
[83] Aranson, "Bruno Leoni in Retrospect," p. 675.

the price structure because the private property system at the base of a price structure is outlawed. Similarly, not only does a legislator face a severe ignorance problem—he could never hope to have a comprehensive and continually updated view of all the interactions, rules, relationships, and customs that exist among the people—he also subverts the very spontaneous legal order that would form in the absence of legislative interference. Customs change, for example, because of the uncertainty introduced, because people become more suspicious and rely less on contracts, and because their time preference increases, as discussed above.[84] As Professor Aranson puts it, "Legislation saps the social order of spontaneity."[85]

Just as a decentralized, free market economy is essential to the coordination of resources and the production of wealth, so a decentralized law-finding system is a prerequisite to allowing true law to develop. This does not guarantee that the law will be just—there are no guarantees—but at least it is possible in a decentralized law-finding system, while in a legislated system it is not.

---

[84] See Part III.B.4, subsections b. and c.

[85] Aranson, "Bruno Leoni in Retrospect," p. 675. See also Lawrence M. Friedman, *A History of American Law* (New York: Simon & Schuster, Inc., 2d ed. 1985), p. 404 (discussing James Carter's view that legislated "[c]odes impaired the orderly development of the law; they froze the law into semipermanent form; this prevented natural evolution.... A statute drafted by a group of so-called experts was bound to be an inferior product, compared to what centuries of evolution, of self-correcting growth, could achieve.... [T]he social and economic legislation of the late 19th century ... were doomed to failure; they were hasty intrusions, and they contradicted the deeper genius of the law."); and Benson, *The Enterprise of Law*, p. 282 ("public production of law undermines the private property arrangements that support a free market system"). An interesting discussion of, *inter alia*, the debate on whether to legislatively codify the common law is found in Mark D. Rosen, "What Has Happened to the Common Law?—Recent American Codifications, and Their Impact on Judicial Practice and the Law's Subsequent Development," 1994 *Wisc. L. Rev.* (1994): 1119–1286. For more on James Carter's opposition to Field's attempt to legislatively codify the common law of New York, see Kinsella, "Another Problem with Legislation: James Carter v. the Field Codes," *Mises Economics Blog* (Oct. 14, 2009).

For further discussion of Leoni's ideas in this regard and related issues, see Gottfried Dietze, "The Necessity of State Law," in *Cunningham, ed., Liberty and the Rule of Law* (chap. 3, p. 74); Tullock, "Courts as Legislators"; Sartori, *Liberty and Law*, and *idem, Democratic Theory*, chap. 13; Leonard P. Liggio, "Law and Legislation in Hayek's Legal Philosophy," *Southwestern U. L. Rev.* 23 (1994; https://perma.cc/5GHM-T8KU): 507–29; Murray N. Rothbard, "On Freedom and the Law," *New Individualist Review* (Winter 1962, vol. 1, no. 4) 37, *reprinted in New Individualist Review* omnibus volume at 163 (1982; https://oll. libertyfund.org/title/friedman-new-individualist-review) (reviewing Leoni, *Freedom and the Law*).

3. Special Interests and the Unrepresentative Character of Legislation
A problem of a legislative system that is related to the central planning problem is its unrepresentative character. Although democracy is not without problems,[86] a representative democracy is better than one that is not. Because of the information problem faced by centralized law-makers, they cannot know the people's wishes with any accuracy or detail. *"[A] legal system centered on legislation resembles … a centralized economy in which all the relevant decisions are made by a handful of directors, whose knowledge of the whole situation is fatally limited and whose respect, if any, for the people's wishes is subject to that limitation."*[87]

Italian legal scholar Giovanni Sartori puts the point forcefully:

> [W]e make the inference that when a person who allegedly represents some tens of thousands contributes … to the lawmaking process, then he is making the thousands of people whom he is representing free, because the represented thereby obey norms that they have freely chosen…. How absurd! … In empirical terms, from the premise that I know how to swim it may follow that I can cross a river, but not that I can cross the ocean.[88]

Similarly, even if citizen involvement and participation in a small community can produce liberty, "we cannot draw the conclusion that the same amount of participation will produce the same result in a large community; for in the latter an equally intense participation will entail diminishing consequences."[89] Leoni argues that "the more numerous the people are whom one tries to 'represent' through the legislative process and the more numerous the matters in which one tries to represent them, the less the word 'representation' has a meaning referable to the actual will of actual people other than that of the persons named as their 'representatives.'"[90]

---

[86] For a discussion of some problematic tendencies of democracies, see Hoppe, "Time Preference, Government, and the Process of De-Civilization—From Monarchy to Democracy" and "On Free Immigration and Forced Integration," in *Democracy: The God That Failed.*

[87] Leoni, *Freedom and the Law*, p. 22 (emphasis in original). See also ibid. at 89; Aranson, "Bruno Leoni in Retrospect," p. 675.

[88] Sartori, *Liberty and Law*, at 31–32.

[89] Ibid. at 32.

[90] Leoni, *Freedom and the Law*, p. 19. See also Aranson, "Bruno Leoni in Retrospect," pp. 676–77.

Legislators cannot discover the will of their constituents, and, as explained above,[91] cannot know very much at all about the actual interactions and circumstances of those who they seek to regulate. At best, then, a legislator will produce rather neutral, if bumbling, intrusive, and ineffectual, laws. But we all know about lobbyists and special interest groups, and their existence ensures that legislators will not be merely ignorant idiots. Instead, they will actively seek to enact invidious statutes that benefit a select few at the expense of others and, in the long run, at the expense of all of society.

In the political process, statutes are enacted that reflect the will of a contingent majority of legislators. This provides an opportunity for various groups to demand special treatment, such as protectionism or blatant wealth transfers. Those with a vested interest in a given piece of legislation are willing to invest much time, effort, and money (e.g. for bribes) to persuade legislators to enact the legislation. Each individual in the large group outside the special interest group feels the pain of the legislation much less than the special interest group will benefit, so that there is relatively little incentive for many people to oppose the special group's lobbying efforts, or even to educate themselves as to which lobbying efforts are taking place. Escalating efforts at forming special interest groups to lobby for specialized statutes results in "nothing less than a potential *legal war of all against all*, carried on by way of legislation and representation."[92] Any legislative system in a large, modern society is doomed to succumb, to a large extent, to special interest groups rather than representing the general will of the populace.

4. Decentralized Law-Finding Systems

As discussed above, legislative systems such as the civil law are centralized law-making systems and face many of the problems faced by central planners in general. Decentralized law-finding systems like the

---

91 See Part III.C.2, above.

92 Leoni, *Freedom and the Law*, pp. 21, 158. See also Aranson, "Bruno Leoni in Retrospect," pp. 677–79; Mitchell & Simmons, *Beyond Politics* (discussing the large number of special interest groups that accompany big government), and Frederic Bastiat, *The Law* (Irvington-on-Hudson, N.Y.: Foundation for Economic Education, Dean Russell trans. 1950 [1850]; https://fee.org/resources/the-law), pp. 17–18 (discussing ever-escalating conflicts among disparate special interest groups).

common law, on the other hand, are analogous to free markets in that a spontaneous order arises in both.[93] Unlike a legislator imposing his will on society, when a judge decides a case he attempts "to discover and make explicit the rule that is implicit in the practices, customs, and institutions of the people.... Law then develops through the application of the rule to new situations."[94] But as Liggio and Palmer note:

> This process reveals another analogy with the decentralized market process, for the decision of a judge in a particular case is subject to review by other participants in the legal process. One judge cannot impose his personal will or idiosyncratic interpretation of the law on the entire legal system; similarly, innovations in the market process arise through the decentralized activities of entrepreneurs and firms and are then subject to the review of consumers, investors, and other market participants. In both the market process and the common law process there is little danger of having "all your eggs in one basket," as is the case with both socialism and legislation.[95]

Judges in a decentralized law-finding system are also less likely to be influenced by special interests than are legislators. Professor Epstein argues:

> that structural features limit what the manipulation of common law rules can achieve. The more focused and sustained methods of legislation and regulation are apt to have more dramatic effects than does alteration of common law rules and thus will attract the primary efforts of those trying to use the law to promote their own interests.[96]

To the extent a court-based legal system displays legislative characteristics, which often occurs in government-based court systems,[97] it faces the same central planning problems as does legislation.[98] For example,

---

[93] See notes 37 and 81, above, and accompanying text.

[94] Liggio & Palmer, "*Freedom and the Law:* A Comment on Professor Aranson's Article," at 720–21.

[95] Ibid. at 721, n.30.

[96] Richard A. Epstein, "The Social Consequences of Common Law Rules," 95, no. 8 *Harv. L. Rev.* (June 1982; https://chicagounbound.uchicago.edu/journal_articles/1276/): 1717–51, pp. 1718–19.

[97] See Part III.B.2, above.

[98] Aranson, "Bruno Leoni in Retrospect," p. 697; Peter H. Aranson, "The Common Law as Central Economic Planning," *Const. Pol. Econ.* 3 (1992): 289–320, pp. 297–99 *et pass.*

judges that attempt in their decisions to "maximize society's wealth" [99] face the same information problems as a central economic planner.[100]

Judges, then, especially government-employed judges, can run into the legislator's ignorance problem when they act like legislators and pretend they are omniscient.

D. The Proliferation of Laws

Legislation is nothing more than controls, and it is evident that controls breed yet more controls. And invariably, because of government propaganda combined with public ignorance, the inevitable failures of the nostrum of legislation are blamed, not on the interventionist government, but on freedom and unregulated human conduct. Thus even more controls are imposed to solve problems caused by controls in the first place, and the process accelerates. For example, the well-known boom-bust business cycle, with its recurrent depressions and recessions (such as the Great Depression and recent recessions), is caused not by capitalism but by government manipulation of the money supply (which is, of course, only possible with legislatively-created institutions such as the Federal Reserve).[101] When such government-caused calamities strike, the current Roosevelt or Clinton milks the disaster as an excuse for more government intervention and power.[102] Thus, legislation has a ratcheting effect whereby statutes tend to lead to further statutes, and the government sphere expands outward as these statutes cascade down from generation to generation.

Such a continual outpouring of laws has many insidious effects. As has wisely been said, "The more corrupt the Republic, the more the laws."[103] But the reverse is also true. As special interest groups become

---

[99] Aranson, "Bruno Leoni in Retrospect," p. 692.

[100] Ibid. at 697–98 (emphasis added) (footnotes omitted). See also Aranson, "The Common Law as Central Economic Planning," p. 314.

[101] See Murray N. Rothbard, *America's Great Depression* (New York: New York University Press, revised ed. 1975); *idem, Man, Economy, and State*, chap. 12, §11.B; *idem, For a New Liberty*, at chap. 9; Mises, *Human Action*, chap. XX, esp. p. 561.

[102] See Robert Higgs, *Crisis and Leviathan: Critical Episodes in the Growth of American Government* (New York: Oxford University Press, 1987).

[103] Tacitus, *Annals*, III, 27, quoted in Sartori, *Liberty and Law*, at 3. For example, in the case of legislation related to intellectual property law, see Kinsella, "The Mountain of IP

successful, others become necessary for self-defense, and soon a legal war of all against all begins to emerge, as already discussed.[104] The ability of legislators to change laws reduces legal certainty, which makes contractual reliance more risky and hampers useful economic transactions. Uncertainty also increases the general time preference rate, which shortens the structure of production, thereby impoverishing society. The ensuing higher time preference also increases the prevalence of criminal activity.[105]

Additionally, when so many laws exist, and with such arcane, vague, complex language, it becomes almost impossible for each citizen to avoid being a law-breaker, especially when we have the perverse rule that "ignorance of the law is no excuse." Even government officials cannot seem to obey federal tax laws regarding household help. Almost everyone has violated a tax law, securities regulation, "racketeering" law, drug law, handgun law, alcohol law, customs regulation, anti-sodomy law, or at least traffic ordinance.[106] But when we are all law-breakers the law is discredited[107] and, what is worse, the government can selectively and arbitrarily enforce whatever law is convenient against whichever "trouble-maker" it wishes.

Furthermore, "the legislative conception of law accustoms those to whom the norms are addressed to accept any and all commands of the State, that is, to accept any *iussum* as *ius*."[108] People become more accustomed to following orders, and thus become more docile, servile, and less independent. Once people become docile and lose their rebellious spirit, "[t]he road is cleared for the legal suppression of constitutional legality. Whoever has had the experience of observing, for example, how fascism established itself in power knows how easily

---

Legislation," *Mises Economics Blog* (Nov. 24, 2010).

[104] See note 92, above, and accompanying text.

[105] See Part III.B.4, subsections b. and c.

[106] In the case of copyright, for example, see Kinsella, "We are all copyright criminals: John Tehranian's 'Infringement Nation,'" *Mises Economics Blog* (Aug. 22, 2011).

[107] Professor Benson notes that such a proliferation of laws "leads to selective enforcement, corruption, *and* open tolerance of illegal acts. Clearly a negative externality is created as respect for and fidelity to all law is harmed when large numbers of such largely unenforceable laws are openly defied." Benson, *The Enterprise of Law*, p. 286.

[108] Sartori, *Liberty and Law*, at 38–39.

the existing juridical order can be manipulated to serve the ends of a dictatorship without the country's being really aware of the break."[109]

Legal inflation cheapens and dilutes law, just as money inflation by the Federal Reserve dilutes dollars and causes price inflation. True law becomes smothered by legislation.

IV. NAIVE RATIONALISM AND THE PRIMACY OF LEGISLATION

If the arguments made herein are correct, no centralized legal system can be a rationalist system, because legislation undermines the rationalist, libertarian virtues of individualism, individual liberty, and the rule of law. Why, then, is the civil law proclaimed as the great rationalist legal system, even though it sets up legislation as the primary source of law? Why are legislation and codification hailed as superior, scientific, and rational? Why, for that matter, is legislation so popular today even in common-law regimes, as well as in our federal system? It seems somewhat strange that those who support individual liberty, justice, and the rule of law would also support the very thing that opposes and erodes these things.

In Hayek's view, there are two types of rationalism: evolutionary rationalism (or, in Karl Popper's terminology, critical rationalism) and constructivist rationalism (Popper's naive rationalism).[110] Each of these two variants of rationalism is associated with a unique view of liberty. Critical rationalism, i.e., true rationalism, relates to a "British" theory of

---

[109] Ibid. at 39. See also Benson, *The Enterprise of Law*, p. 282 ("it appears that the increasing centralization of law-making has been associated with increasing transfers of property rights from private individuals to government or perhaps, more accurately, to interest groups.") (endnote omitted).

[110] F.A. Hayek, I. *Law, Legislation and Liberty: Rules and Order* (Chicago: University of Chicago Press, 1973), pp. 5–6; see also pp. 72, 118; *idem, The Fatal Conceit: The Errors of Socialism*, vol. I of *The Collected Works of F.A. Hayek* (Chicago: University of Chicago Press, W.W. Bartley, III, ed., 1989); *idem, The Constitution of Liberty* (Chicago: University of Chicago Press, 1960), p. 38 *et seq.*; Eugene F. Miller, "The Cognitive Basis of Hayek's Political Thought," in Cunningham, ed., *Liberty and the Rule of Law*, chap. 11, pp. 242, 245 (discussing the two kinds of rationalism and their political consequences); John Gray, *Hayek on Liberty* (Oxford: Basil Blackwell, 1984), p. 10; Sartori, *Democratic Theory*, at chap. 11 (discussing rationalism vs. empiricism).

liberty that derives from thinkers such as Locke, Hume, Smith, Burke, Montesquieu, de Tocqueville, and Lord Acton, while the "French" version of rationalism, i.e., naive rationalism, derives from Rousseau, Condorcet, Hobbes, and Descartes.[111] Hayek believed that "all modern socialism, planning and totalitarianism derive" from the naive rationalism of the French tradition.[112]

Like the socialists who naively believe that the delicate order of the market, coordinated by millions of individual interactions, can be replaced by the brute force of a central planning board, naive rationalists have an almost superstitious faith in the ability of reason to impose law on society.

> In Hayek's view, the decisive influence on the French Enlightenment political theory was the philosophy of Descartes, with its extravagant assumptions about the powers of human reason. Cartesian [i.e., naive] rationalism lead to the belief that everything which men achieve, including liberty, is the direct result of reason and therefore should be subject to its control. It traced all order to deliberate human design and expressed contempt for institutions that were not consciously designed or not intelligible to reason.[113]

But naive rationalists fail to appreciate the true role of spontaneous order in human society. Because they did not understand, for example, that resources are allocated rationally only in a decentralized free market, a free market appears chaotic and unruly, as something that should be tamed and replaced with "scientific" central planning.

The belief of civilians and other proponents of centralized lawmaking that true law ever could be made by a legislature stems from a naive rationalism because it assigns too broad a role to deductive reason. This is not surprising, given the French influence on the development of modern civil law. Reason is our only means of knowledge, but we would not attempt, for example, to take a sick person's temperature by closing our eyes and deducing it. Instead, we would measure it, if we

---

111 Miller, "The Cognitive Basis of Hayek's Political Thought," at 245.
112 Ibid. at 246.
113 Ibid. at 246–47 (footnote omitted).

realized that a pure exercise of deductive thinking cannot hope to give us this information.[114] This would be naive.[115]

A genuine market order can only be generated from the bottom up by the free interaction of private property owners. Given this fact, it is rational not to destroy this order by the top-down commands issued by a sovereign central planner. A detailed body of law, while based on fundamental norms established by and compatible with true rationalism, can only be discovered and established in a decentralized fashion; and it is clear that centralized legislative commands can only disrupt and distort the spontaneous and rational development of Law. The championing of legislation, not to mention central economic planning, thus irrationally ignores the reality that Law is compatible only with a decentralized law-finding system, and it ignores the inevitable negative effects of attempting to legislate (i.e., uncertainty, proliferation of the laws, special interest wars, unintended effects). The civil law worships legislation because of a desire to impose "order" on a field where there is already spontaneous order. This naive rationalism is not really rationalism at all: it is anti-rationalism or irrationalism.

The desire to plan, to impose order—whether economic or legal—on others, is dangerous because, in the name of reason and freedom, individual freedom is smothered. As Thomas Sowell writes:

> At its most extreme, [rationalism] exalts the most trivial or tendentious "study" by "experts" into policy, forcibly overriding the preferences and convictions of millions of people. While rationalism at the individual level is a plea for more personal autonomy from cultural norms, at the social

---

[114] *See* Hayek, I. *Law, Legislation and Liberty: Rules and Order*, at 29 ("to make reason as effective as possible requires an insight into the limitations of the powers of conscious reason.... [O]ne of the tasks of reason is to decide how far it is to extend its control or how far it ought to rely on other forces which it cannot wholly control.").

[115] Hayek himself has been criticized for assigning too little role to reason on the part of individuals within a spontaneous free market order. *See* Hans-Hermann Hoppe, "F.A. Hayek on Government and Social Evolution: A Critique," in *The Great Fiction*. Hayek's teacher Mises, as opposed to Hayek, viewed laws, morals, market customs, and the price system as products of individual, rational, human action. "While these institutions were not created out of whole cloth by a single mind, political fiat or 'social contract,' they are indeed the products of rational and intentional planning by human beings, whose thoughts and actions continually reaffirm and reshape them in the course of history." Salerno, "Ludwig von Mises as Social Rationalist," at 31.

level it is often a claim—or arrogation—of power to stifle the autonomy of others, on the basis of superior virtuosity with words.[116]

Bentham is a good example of the dangerous arrogance of naive rationalism. Bentham longed to (legislatively) codify his utilitarian "greatest happiness principle" and, thus, to use legislation as necessary to sweep aside any common law in his way. He:

> ...evinced no misgivings about the power of reason—in particular Bentham's reason—to decide any questions of policy *de novo*, without benefit of authority, consensus, precedent, etc.... Bentham is not a little the fanatic whose willingness to sweep aside the obstacles to implementation of his proposals draws sustenance from a boundless confidence in his own reasoning powers.... Bentham's blind spot about the problem of social order is of a piece with his enthusiasm for social planning. He worried about all monopolies except the most dangerous, the monopoly of political power.[117]

Because the civil law and, indeed, all modern law, gives license to legislators, it is irrationalistic, and does not promote, but hinders, individual liberty and the true development of Law.

V. THE ROLE OF LEGISLATION AND CODIFICATION

A. The Role of Legislation

1. The Secondary Role of Legislation
Does all this mean that there is absolutely no room for legislation? If anarcho-capitalism is accepted, of course there may be no legislation because there may be no government. Relaxing this assumption, if there

---

[116] Thomas Sowell, *Knowledge and Decisions* (New York: Basic Books, Inc., 1980), pp. 102–03.

[117] Posner, "Blackstone and Bentham," at 594, 603–606. For a discussion of Bentham and David Dudley Field, another proponent of common-law codification, and of anti-codifiers such as James C. Carter, see Friedman, *A History of American Law*, at 391–92, 403–406; and Kinsella, "Another Problem with Legislation: James Carter v. the Field Codes."

is a government, then even if it is a minimalist one, it seems that there must effectively be some legislation, if only to determine the structure and function of the government itself. In this case, the points made in this paper militate against any legislation at all other than that strictly necessary to govern the government itself (e.g., a written constitution).

Even if there is a state, the body of law in society should be fashioned by a decentralized court system. The courts should be part of a private system of courts to the extent possible, for example, a competing system of arbitral tribunals rather than government-backed common-law courts. But whether law-finding fora are government courts or private courts, the legislature should have no ability to enact "laws" that have any effect on the decisions that courts make.[118]

If we relax the anarchist/minimal state assumption once more, and admit that a legislature should in some special cases be able to enact statutes to override court decisions, clearly legislation should never be seen as even *a* primary source of law, much less *the* primary source of law, lest all the law-destroying features described herein arise.

As the renowned legal scholar Alan Watson has pointed out, in previous eras, legislation was not widely used to alter the private law or to impose some imagined social order on society, but rather to make the law clearer or more accessible.[119]

Even Leoni was not a complete anarchist and believed in the necessity of at least some legislation.[120] According to Leoni, the role of legislation should be kept very small and applied very carefully:

> Substituting legislation for the spontaneous application of nonlegislated rules of behavior is indefensible unless it is proved that the latter are

---

[118] This is not, however, to say that the judicial branch of a government should have the power of judicial review with respect to other branches of the government. Ideally, the legislative, judicial, and executive branches each have an equal and independent power to interpret the constitution. See William J. Quirk & R. Randall Bridwell, "Angels to Govern Us," *Chronicles* (March 1995), p. 12 and *idem, Judicial Dictatorship* (New Brunswick, N.J.: Transaction Publishers, 1995).

[119] Alan Watson, *Failures of the Legal Imagination* (University of Pennsylvania Press, 1988; https://archive.org/details/failuresoflegali0000wats), pp. 47 et seq.

[120] Leoni, Freedom and the Law, pp. 10 and 129–31.

uncertain or insufficient or that they generate some evil that legislation could avoid while maintaining the advantages of the previous system. [121]

Not much, if any, of today's legislation could survive this test. Thus, legislation must be restricted to a strictly secondary role, at most, for a system based on the *primacy* of legislation will inevitably subvert the spontaneous order and substitute pernicious and chaotic rules in its stead.

2. Alleged Deficiencies of Decentralized Law-Finding Systems

Hayek, another advocate of the spontaneous order of decentralized systems, also believed that legislation is called for in certain situations.[122] Hayek maintained that the fact that a "grown" system of law has some desirable characteristics that legislation usually:

> ...does not mean that in other respects such law may not develop in very undesirable directions, and that when this happens correction by deliberate legislation may not be the only practicable way out. For a variety of reasons the spontaneous process of growth may lead into an impasse from which it cannot extricate itself by its own forces or which it will at least not correct quickly enough. The development of case-law is in some respects a sort of one-way street: when it has already moved a considerable distance in one direction, it often cannot retrace its steps when some implications of earlier decisions are seen to be clearly undesirable. The fact that law that has evolved in this way has certain desirable properties does not prove that it will always be good law or even that some of its rules may not be very bad. It therefore does not mean that we can altogether dispense with legislation.[123]

Hayek also maintained that the judicial, evolutionary growth of law may be "too slow" to bring about the "desirable" rapid adaptation of the law to wholly new circumstances. Further, according to Hayek, a judge would have to upset "reasonable expectations created by his earlier decisions" to

---

[121] Ibid. at 14; see also p. 178 ("Whatever is not positively proved worthy of legislation should be left to the common-law area.").

[122] Hayek, I. *Law, Legislation and Liberty: Rules and Order*, at 88, subsection entitled "Why grown law requires correction by legislation."

[123] Ibid. at 88 (also citing Leoni, *Freedom and the Law*).

overturn an erroneous line of cases, whereas a legislator can promulgate a new rule which is to be effective only in the future.[124]

Objectivists are also in favor of legislation if it is the only way to have intellectual property rights. For example, Objectivist attorney Murray Franck writes (in response to my criticism that intellectual property rights cannot arise on the common law, or organically, and require legislation):

> [J]ust as the common law evolved to recognize "trespass by barbecue smoke," it would have evolved to recognize property in the airwaves and in intellectual creations. But even if it could be established somehow that the common law would never have recognized intellectual property rights, this would not be an argument against such rights. The common law often requires legislation to correct it (for example, in recognizing the rights of women). Indeed it is a myth that the common law evolves to reflect, and that legislation always is in conflict with, the requirements of human nature. The same minds that employ induction and deduction to decide a particular case, making common law, can employ those methods to legislate universal laws.[125]

Richard Epstein, a brilliant proponent of the common law, also feels that legislation is sometimes desirable, for example, when courts cannot come up with a number, such as a statute of limitations, which might be very desirable.[126] Without legislation, courts would likely bar lawsuits after some length of time. But it is possible that different courts would have different limitations periods, and some judges may decide each case on its own merits. According to Epstein, without a statute of limitations, no court would develop a hard and fast, arbitrary number.[127] Rather, in a pure court system, individuals could only estimate the probability of being able to sue (or to be sued) after a given number of years. By contrast, the number is certain under a statute of limitations. Because certainty is desirable, and because people are

---

124 Ibid. at 88–89.

125 See references in Kinsella, "Letter on Intellectual Property Rights," *IOS Journal* (June 1995)," *C4SIF Blog* (Aug. 31, 2022). Talk about naïve rationalism.

126 Richard A. Epstein, "Past and Future: The Temporal Dimension in the Law of Property," *Wash. U. L. Q.* 64, no. 3 (1986; https://openscholarship.wustl.edu/law_lawreview/vol64/iss3/3/): 667–722, at 680–81.

127 Ibid. at 680.

risk-averse, "A single number stated in advance truncates the risk [by] making it clear that some actions cannot be brought."[128]

Even Blackstone was not "an uncritical opponent of statutory law.... Blackstone assigned a limited role to statutory law: its proper office was to resolve conflicts between common law precedents and otherwise to supplement and patch common law doctrine." [129]

But is the common-law's development "too slow," at least on occasion, as Hayek claimed? The U.S. Supreme Court has praised the common law's "flexibility and capacity for growth and adaptation" as "the peculiar boast and excellence of the common law."[130] For example, as Blackstone points out, judges under the common law were able to reform the system of feudal land law without legislation. [131]

It would seem, then, that decentralized systems are able to adapt to new situations when it is called for.[132] Additionally, it is not always desirable that basic rules (such as that contracts should be fulfilled) should change just because societal conditions change. Professor Epstein has explained that:

> Social circumstances continually change, but it is wrong to suppose that the substantive principles of the legal system should change in response to new social conditions. The law should not be a mirror of social organization. In private law matters, it can best perform its essential function only if it remains constant.[133]

Further, one wonders how any external observer, such as Hayek or any legislature, could ever know what rate of legal change is "too slow,"

---

[128] Ibid. at 681.

[129] Posner, "Blackstone and Bentham," at 585 (citing 3 Blackstone, *Commentaries on the Laws of England*, at *328, and 1 Blackstone, *Commentaries on the Laws of England*, § 432, *365).

[130] *Hurtado v. People of California*, 110 U.S. 516, 530 (1884). However, a private court system is an unadulterated decentralized system, unlike the common law, which is backed by government force. *See* Part III.B.2, above. Therefore, it will adapt more efficiently and more quickly to change than a common-law system would. See also Benson, "Customary Law as a Social Contract," at 17, discussing the superior ability of the (private) Law Merchant, compared to the common law, to adapt and change in response to rapid changes in the commercial system.

[131] 3 Blackstone, *Commentaries on the Laws of England*, at *268.

[132] See also Benson, *The Enterprise of Law*, p. 283, n.42, and works cited therein.

[133] Richard A. Epstein, "The Static Conception of the Common Law," *J. Legal Stud.* 9, no. 2 (March 1980): 253–89, at 254.

or even what change is "desirable," any more than a central planning board can know what is the "right" price to charge for a gallon of milk. Indeed, Hayek's own insights into the virtues of spontaneous order and the problems of central economic planning demonstrate the ignorance of any central planner in this regard.

I admit that, in some circumstances, a decentralized body of law can err and seem to need "patching"; and indeed, all things being equal, a statute of limitations might be better than none at all. Unfortunately, however, all things are *not* equal, because of the problems that inevitably accompany legislation. The choice is between a fallible system of decentralized law with no legislature and an even more fallible and dangerous legislative means of making law. To "patch" common law by legislation, you have to first empower a legislature. As Mises wisely put it:

> No socialist author ever gave a thought to the possibility that the abstract entity which he wants to vest with unlimited power—whether it is called humanity, society, nation, state, or government—could act in a way of which he himself disapproves.[134]

As Mises here warns, a legislature will not be content to merely fix one bad law. Rather, legislation will eventually overwhelm and suffocate the naturally-developed body of law and engender uncertainty; special interest warfare and quick fix laws will proliferate; and the government will eventually abuse its sovereign position by engaging in economic and human planning.

Epstein may well be correct that not having a definite period for liberative prescription may inject uncertainty into the legal process. Unfortunately, the attempt to cure this by empowering a legislature also increases the general uncertainty in society. Which uncertainty is greater? And what about the liberty of individuals who have their right to sue artificially limited by a statute of limitations? How can we know that the benefit to them (or even others) is greater than the harm done to them? Because values are subjective to the individual, and because of the economic calculation problem, no central governmental legislature can know whether the benefits of a statute of limitations are

---

[134] Mises, *Human Action*, at 692 (emphasis added).

worth the cost of such legislation.[135] Furthermore, why is it justifiable to harm one individual to benefit another?

Another problem with urging legislation as a solution to common law gone astray is that this assumes that the legislature can be convinced to make the correct legal reform. First, this is a very dubious assumption, especially given the special interest lobbying that legislators face, and also given the fact that legislators tend to be people who are interested in power rather than philosopher-kings who want to do the right thing.[136] Second, if a proponent of legislation assumes that reasonable and humane legislators can see the light of reason and correctly reform the law, why is it not at least as likely that judges can be persuaded as well?

Especially in an anarcho-capitalistic system—i.e., in a free society—in which all courts are private and compete for business by selling and producing "justice," the courts at least have an incentive to continually refine the rules in a just direction. If Epstein and legislators can see the value of a fixed time limit to instituting a lawsuit, so can the public, which would create a demand for such a rule. Private court systems that offered such rules to cater to consumer demand would tend to draw more customers and lawsuits than relatively unjust competitor-courts. Thus there is a natural incentive for courts, at least competing courts in a free society, to search for justice and to strive to adopt it, so as to cater to a justice-seeking consumer base.

3. Structural Safeguards to Limit Legislation

For all these reasons, I do not believe that legislation is a legitimate or practical means of creating law, or even of patching it. If a legislature can be convinced to recognize and respect the right law, so can a decentralized court system, especially one competing with other courts for customers. Courts do not face the same pernicious and systematic incentives that legislators do to make bad laws, and many of them. And courts, if they go bad, at least have a more limited effect on society;

---

[135] On the subjective theory of value, see Mises, *Human Action*, at 94–97, 200–206, 331–33 *et passim*; Rothbard, *Man, Economy, and State*, chap. 1, § 5.A; and Alexander H. Shand, *The Capitalist Alternative: An Introduction to Neo-Austrian Economics* (New York: New York University Press, 1984), chap. 4, esp. §2.

[136] For a related discussion, see Friedrich A. Hayek, *The Road to Serfdom* (Chicago: University of Chicago Press, 1944), at chap. 10, "Why the Worst Get on Top."

whereas when legislatures go bad, there is no end to the evil that they can perpetrate.[137]

If legislation can be considered valid at all (given a governmental system), it can only be occasional or spurious legislation that modifies the body of law which is *primarily* developed by a court-based, decentralized law-finding system—or legislation that controls how the state itself is limited and organized. If we must have legislation, several constitutional safeguards should accompany its exercise, to attempt to restrict legislation to a purely secondary role in the formation of law. Certainly, a supermajority,[138] and maybe a referendum, should be required in order to enact any statutes whatever, except perhaps for statutes that repeal prior statutes or that limit governmental power.

In addition to a supermajority requirement, another reform that might be considered would be for all legislation to be limited to replacing the opinion of a given court decision with a new decision, which would have purely prospective effect. Then, if a given case or line of cases were issued that had particularly egregious reasoning or results, a supermajority could form in the legislature that would rewrite the unfortunate opinion in purportedly better form and enact this into law, as if the court had first issued the rewritten decision. The rewritten opinion would then assume the status of a judicial precedent, at least for that court.

The benefit of this limitation is that it would prevent legislatures from enacting huge legislative schemes out of whole cloth. There would simply be no way for the legislature to enact an Americans with Disabilities Act, since any statute would really be a rewritten judicial opinion, and to the extent the legislated substitute opinion strayed from the facts of the particular case, it would be merely *dicta*. If a judge in a battery case, for example, ruled that the spotted owl or the intelligent socialist was now an endangered species, such language would be completely irrelevant, since it is beyond a judge's power to enact an Endangered Species Act in any judicial opinion. Such a mechanism for legislation would allow very bad

---

137 Government power is always subject to abuse. The greater government's role in society, the greater the chance for serious abuse. As Professor Epstein notes, "The smaller downside of a small government is perhaps its greatest virtue." Richard A. Epstein, *Simple Rules for a Complex World* (Cambridge, Mass.: Harvard University Press, 1995), p. 316.

138 See Leoni, *Freedom and the Law*, p. 178 n.5 (discussing a supermajority requirement as a way to tame legislators).

case law developments to be overcome, but would also severely restrict the ability of legislatures to radically restructure the law, and thus would reduce the incidence of vote-buying and special interest lobbying, the amount of uncertainty, the proliferation of statutes, and the amount of social planning and other mischief that a legislature might otherwise be inclined to engage in.

Other provisions that could help to limit the dangerous effects of having a legislature include a line-item veto by the executive branch and sunset provisions that automatically repeal legislation unless re-enacted after a given number of years. Another useful prophylactic measure would be an absolute right to jury trials in *all* cases, civil or criminal (so that government could not escape the jury requirement by calling truly criminal sanctions "civil"), in which the application of a statute is involved. This should be combined with a requirement that the jury be made aware of their right to judge the *law*'s validity as well as the defendant's liability or guilt.[139]

The right of law-abiding citizens to own weapons of any sort, without any registration requirement, is also essential so that an armed public can stand as a last bulwark against a tyrannical government. Even with such safeguards, the power of a government armed with the power to legislate, the power to create and rewrite "law," is awesome, and fearsome, to behold.

B. *The Role of Commentators and Codes*

The criticisms of legislation apply even to civil codes, the most impressive component of modern civil law. Admittedly, the civil law, at least

---

[139] The latter concept is advocated by many libertarians, and is often called the Fully-Informed Jury Amendment, or FIJA. *See* Don Doig, "New Hope for Freedom: Fully Informed Juries," pamphlet published by the International Society for International Liberty. For discussion of the historical and natural right of jurors to judge the law's validity, see also Comment, "The Changing Role of the Jury in the Nineteenth Century," *Yale L.J.* 74 (1964; https://perma.cc/72RE-WDSK): 170–92; and Lysander Spooner, "An Essay on Trial by Jury," in *The Lysander Spooner Reader* (San Francisco: Fox & Wilkes, 1992; version available online at http://www.lysanderspooner.org/works), at 122.

For other suggestions, see "Taking the Ninth Amendment Seriously" (ch. 21); Kinsella, "Constitutional Structures in Defense of Freedom (ASC 1998)," *StephanKinsella.com* (June 25, 2021); and *idem*, "Structural Safeguards to Limit Legislation and State Power," *StephanKinsella.com* (Jan. 23, 2015).

as embodied in a civil code, is superior to the common law in many ways. The civilian system of property rights, not mired in feudalistic form as is the British common law, is much cleaner and conceptually more sound than common law real property.[140] Common-law real property concepts are almost painful to the mind. As another example, the irrational common-law requirement of "consideration" to create a binding obligation[141] is replaced in the civil law with the more sensible prerequisite of "cause."[142] However, these superior qualities of the civil law are not due to its legislated character but to the superior legal concepts that evolved in the Roman law.

But the civil code also contains many illiberal and thus illegitimate provisions, which are a problem only because the code is legislated into law. If the civil code were a private, unlegislated codification, judges could simply ignore its illiberal provisions. A particularly egregious example of an unjust law is Louisiana's forced heirship regime,[143] which limits individuals' ability to dispose of their own property as they wish upon death. Also, in the civil law, certain sales may be annulled if "too low" a price was paid by the buyer,[144] which violates the rights of property owners

---

[140] See also Herman, *The Louisiana Civil Code: A European Legacy for the United States*, pp. 46–47 (discussing the civil code's "highly stylized, streamlined system of ownership"). Jacques du Plessis writes:

[T]he civil law of property, which does have an internal logic … does not easily correspond to anything known in the complex common law of property, with its "veritable jungle of concepts, many of which seemed to be merely the doubles of other concepts."

Jacques du Plessis, "Common Law Influences on the Law of Contract and Unjustified Enrichment in Some Mixed Legal Systems," *Tul. L. Rev.* 78, nos. 1 & 2 (December 2003): 219–56, at 249–50 (quoting F.H. Lawson, *The Rational Strength of the English Law* (1951), at 75, and also citing Ben Beinart, "The English Legal Contribution in South Africa: The Interaction of Civil and Common Law," *Acta Juridica* 1981 (1981): 7–64, at 30–31).

[141] See Randy E. Barnett, "A Consent Theory of Contract," *Colum. L. Rev.* 86 (1986; http://www.randybarnett.com/pre-2000): 269–321, at 287–91 (1986) (discussing problems with the theory of consideration).

[142] Louisiana Civil Code (https://www.legis.la.gov/legis/Laws_Toc.aspx?folder=67&level =Parent), art. 1967. For a discussion of the differences between cause and consideration, see Christian Larroumet, "Detrimental Reliance and Promissory Estoppel as the Cause of Contracts in Louisiana and Comparative Law," *Tul. L. Rev.* 60, no. 6 (1986): 1209–30.

[143] Louisiana Civil Code, art. 1493.

[144] Louisiana Civil Code, art. 2589: "Rescission for lesion beyond moiety: The sale of an immovable may be rescinded for lesion when the price is less than one half of the fair market value of the immovable."

to dispose of their property, and which also foolishly assumes that the government knows better than the seller and buyer what the right price is for an item.[145]

Ignoring relatively minor problems such as these, the civil code in and of itself is largely commendable, especially insofar as it embodies and systematizes a naturally grown body of law.[146] But the civil law is more than the civil code: it is legislation made paramount. Legislation is considered the primary source of law—indeed, the civil code itself is legislated—and thus all the problems of legislation discussed above apply to the civil law. When the civil code is enacted as a statute, it is no wonder that proponents of the civil code would naturally view legislation as supreme and tend to view legislation as the primary source of law. And then even the civil code itself tends to develop legislative characteristics, such as code articles enacted at the behest of special interests; illiberal provisions such as those cited above; and specialized, detailed articles out of place in a generalized code.

The civil law would be much improved if the civil code were more like a constitution, in that its provisions would prevail over any contrary statute, and in that some sort of supermajority requirement would be needed to amend it. But we already have constitutions, both state and federal. I do believe that the basic libertarian principles specified herein— the individual rights to self-ownership and to own property, as embodied in the libertarian non-aggression axiom—should be followed by any judge, but this does not necessarily mean there must be a statute or constitution specifying these principles. It is only important that judges recognize them and, in the long run, this can only happen if a consensus in society recognizes the validity of such principles in the first place. Our task is always education. If the public were ever to become libertarian

---

[145] Another egregious provision in blatant contradiction to the individual right to absolute ownership of property is contained in articles 2626–27, which provide for expropriation of private property "wherever it becomes necessary for the general use." Louisiana Civil Code, art. 2626. Of course, the United States Constitution suffers from the same defect. U.S. Const. Vth Amendment.

[146] *See* Thomas W. Tucker, "Sources of Louisiana's Law of Persons: Blackstone, Domat, and the French Codes," *Tul. L. Rev.* 44 (1970): 264–95; Rodolfo Batiza, "Origins of Modern Codification of the Civil Law: The French Experience and its Implications for Louisiana Law," *Tul. L. Rev.* 56 (1982): 477–601, at 585 *et seq.* (discussing Blackstone's influence on Louisiana's civil code).

enough to adopt a libertarian constitution, one would probably not be needed, since private justice supplied on the market, or even in govern-ment-based common-law courts, would veer in a libertarian direction in response to the people's sense of justice.

But if a libertarian constitution or code were in place, it would be relatively sparse. It would specify as first principles that the initiation of force is illegitimate and that the individual rights to own one's own body and any property one homesteads or acquires voluntarily from other owners are absolute and inviolable. As deductions therefrom, it could specify that rape, murder, theft, assault, battery, and trespass are also rights-violations. As Rothbard states:

> The Law Code of a purely free society would simply enshrine the liber-tarian axiom: prohibition of any violence against the person or property of another (except in defense of someone's person or property), property to be defined as self-ownership plus the ownership of resources that one has found, transformed, or bought or received after such transformation. The task of the Code would be to spell out the implications of this axiom (e.g., the libertarian sections of the law merchant or common law would be co-opted, while the statist accretions would be discarded). The Code would then be applied to specific cases by the free-market judges, who would all pledge themselves to follow it.[147]

(I would add that the "libertarian" sections of Roman law, e.g., as embod-ied in modern civil codes, could be adopted in developing Rothbard's

---

[147] Rothbard, *Power and Market*, in *Man, Economy, and State, with Power and Market*, p. 1053 n.4. See also *idem, The Ethics of Liberty* (New York: New York University Press, 1998), at xlviii–xlix ("While the book establishes the general outlines of a system of libertarian law, however, it is only an outline, a prolegomenon to what I hope will be a fully developed libertarian law code of the future. Hopefully libertarian jurists and legal theorists will arise to hammer out the system of libertarian law in detail, for such a law code will be necessary to the truly successful functioning of what we may hope will be the libertarian society of the future."); *idem, For a New Liberty*, second ed. (Auburn, Ala.: Mises Institute, 2006; https://mises.org/library/new-liberty-libertarian-manifesto), at 282. On the limits of armchair theorizing, see Kinsella, "The Limits of Armchair Theorizing: The Case of Threats," *Mises Economics Blog* (Jul. 27, 2006); also "Knowledge, Calculation, Conflict, and Law" (ch. 19), the section "Abstract Rights and Legal Precepts" and the following section; and "On Libertarian Legal Theory, Self-Ownership and Drug Laws" (ch. 23).

See also See Kinsella, "Roman Law and Hypothetical Cases," *StephanKinsella.com* (Dec. 19, 2022) and "Knowledge, Calculation, Conflict, and Law" (ch. 19), at n.64, discussing the practice of Roman jurists developing the Roman law by exploring and answering hypothetical cases.

libertarian Law Code, or at least could be referred to by private courts in fashioning legal rules to handle actual disputes.)

But because of the near-infinite variety of ways in which humans can interact, such a code could never be made all-comprehensive. Any codifier who attempted to do this would face the information problems discussed herein. At some point judges need to consider the particular facts of a controversy and, keeping principles of justice in mind, eke out the applicable rule. Judges will sometimes make mistakes, but, then, the fact that individuals are fallible can never be escaped, so this criticism is moot.

It is true that a decentralized, gradually-developed body of case law can become unwieldy and difficult to research. But it is not more so than the modern morass of statutes. I cannot see how either a lawyer or the average layman would have an easier time discerning what law applies to him in a given situation under today's statute-ridden laws, as opposed to in a decentralized legal system, having a body of judge-discovered principles. Surely in both cases laymen may resort to specialists such as attorneys and explanatory treatises to tell them what the law is. At least in a decentralized system the law is less likely to change from day to day, so that when a person knows what the law is today he is more certain it will be the law tomorrow. And there are likely to be far fewer laws regulating far fewer aspects of our daily lives in a judge-based system, which should make it easier to determine what the relevant law is concerning a given situation.

There is, for these reasons, a significant role for codification in a free society, but only for private, not legislative, codification. To the extent such private codes are systematic and rational, they can both influence the rational development of the law and present or systematize it in concise form for lawyers and laymen alike. We already have treatises such as the American Law Institute's *Restatements* of the law, *Texas Jurisprudence Third*, *American Jurisprudence Second*, and *Corpus Juris Secundum*. These treatises would be far more rational and systematic, and shorter, if they did not have to take an unwieldy and interfering body of legislation into account; if they could focus primarily on common-law developments. Legal scholars who currently draft civil code articles for consideration and enactment by a legislature could surely dedicate their energies to privately codifying and systematizing the body of case law that has been developed. [148]

Even a true codification of existing case law can make mistakes. If the code is private, judges can ignore the lapses in the commentator's reasoning. Of course, this has the extra benefit of giving an incentive to private codifiers not to engage in dishonest reasoning or meddlesome social planning. If a codifier wants his work to be used and acknowledged, he will attempt to accurately describe the existing body of law when he organizes and presents it, and will likely be explicit when recommending that judges adopt certain changes in future decisions.

Law codes should thus be strictly private. We have long seen the wisdom of keeping church and state separate. Theorists like Mises, and the collapse of socialism, teach the virtues of the separation of economy and state. True advocates of a libertarian social and legal order should favor the separation of law and state. [149]

C. Common Law vs. Civil Law

While in this chapter I argue for the superiority of decentralized law discovery systems such as the Roman law and common law over modern legislation-dominant systems, many libertarians in the past have tended to favor the English common law over competing systems, including modern civil law, even though the civil codes, although legislated, are elegant codifications of private law principles that themselves evolved in the decentralized Roman Law legal system. The fact that modern civil codes are enacted as statutes and enshrine legal or legislative positivism is indeed a negative. [150] This does not detract from

---

[148] Lawrence Friedman, *A History of American Law*, at 406, states that the Field "codes are the spiritual parents of the Restatements of the Law—black letter codes of the 20th century, sponsored by the American Law Institute, but meant for persuasion of judges, rather than enactment into law." See also 3 Blackstone, *Commentaries on the Laws of England* at *267 (discussing problems that arise when a new system of law is legislatively codified rather than built upon the evolved wisdom of courts). For a fascinating discussion of the significance of both private and legislated codes for the development of law, see Alan Watson, "The Importance of 'Nutshells,'" *Am. J. Comp. L.* 42, no. 1 (Winter 1994; https://digitalcommons.law.uga.edu/fac_artchop/668): 1–23.

[149] See Rothbard, *For a New Liberty*, p. 282 *et seq.* (discussing the separation of law and state).

[150] See note 6, above, and accompanying text.

the value of having an elegant written summary of the law prepared by legal scholars distilling and summarizing the body of private law developed in more or less decentralized systems over the ages.

Moreover, the common law itself, as noted, has been increasingly submerged in a sea of legislation, ever since the rise of the administrative state and democratic law-making in the 20th century. And as noted above, Alan Watson has pointed out that in the past, legislation was used mainly to make the law clearer or more accessible, not to make drastic change or impose a new social order.[151] This is in contrast to modern democratic law-making—legislation—that has increasingly become the dominant source of law and is used for widespread social engineering.

Hans-Hermann Hoppe has also commented on the relative merits of the English common law versus the European continental and Romanesque civil law:

> This is the structure that the initial founding cantons in Switzerland had, where all free men swore an oath that they would come to mutually assist each other in case of an attack against them. And these cities frequently had written law codes, that is, Magdeburg Law or Hamburg Law or Hanover Law or Lübeck Law, etc., so that people who moved to these cities knew what law code would apply to them, and when new cities were founded, the normal thing to do was to adopt one of the already existing law codes and maybe make a few amendments to it. That is, some law codes became the law codes, not just of one city, but of many, many cities, who adopted the initial example of a place that first took the initiative to write these laws down.
>
> In this connection, let me make a little side remark. In English-speaking countries, America and England, there is a certain amount of pride in having the so-called common law, which is, in a way, noncodified law, or case law. The Continental tradition, as you know, has been for a long time different. There, we have had codified law taken from the Romans, especially from the East Romans who had codified this law for the first time in an extensive manner and then, of course, in modern times, the Napoleonic Code, which has been taken over by most Continental European states in one form or another with some modifications. And, as

---

[151] Watson, *Failures of the Legal Imagination*, p. 47 *et seq.* See also Watson, "The Importance of 'Nutshells,'" on the significance of both private and legislated codes for the development of law.

I said, Anglo-Saxons looked down on codified law and hailed their own noncodified common law. I want to just remark that, for instance, Max Weber has a very interesting observation regarding this. He sees the reason for the noncodification of the common law in the self-interest of the lawyers to make the law difficult to understand for the layman and thus make a lot of money. He emphasizes that codified law makes it possible for the layman on the street who can read to study the law book himself and go to court himself and point out, here, that this law is written down. So, maybe this excessive pride that the Anglo-Saxons have in their common law might be a little bit overdrawn.[152]

I tend to agree with this. What is admirable about the common law is that it is decentralized. But so was the Roman law. Today's world is dominated by legislation and legal positivism, so the common view is that the civil law and common law are distinct. But this fails to recognize that the civil law, although legislated as a statute, is still a codification of a body of private law principles developed largely in the decentralized Roman law system, plus European custom that developed in intervening centuries—and that the common law of today is being overwhelmed with a growing body of statutory law (as are the continental civil codes).

---

[152] Hans-Hermann Hoppe, *Economy, Society, and History* (Auburn, Ala.: Mises Institute, 2021; www.hanshoppe.com/esh), p. 111 (based on his lecture "The Production of Law and Order: Natural Order, Feudalism, and Federalism" (2004; https://mises.org/library/6-production-law-and-order-natural-order-feudalism-and-federalism), starting at 1:07:30). See also the quote from Hadley in note 153, below. On the Weber reference, see generally, Max Weber, *Max Weber on Law in Economy and Society*, edited with introduction and annotations by Max Rheinstein, trans. from Max Weber, *Wirtschaft und Gesellschaft*, 2d ed. (1924), by Edward Shils & Max Rheinstein (Clarion, 1967); in particular, see Rheinstein, "Introduction," and chaps. VII and IX. See also note 30, above, regarding one goal of codification efforts being legal certainty.

Moreover, as noted above, the differences between the modern common law and civil law systems are sometimes exaggerated. As one legal scholar notes: "As common law systems become more systematized and civil law systems more focused on jurisprudence as an authoritative source of law, the two systems are coming together more closely than one might guess." Andrea B. Carroll, "Examining a Comparative Law Myth: Two Hundred Years of Riparian Misconception," *Tul. L. Rev.*, 80 (2006; https://perma.cc/CEP2-Z2BC): 901–45, at 942, citing, re the systematization of the common law, William D. Hawkland, "The Uniform Commercial Code and the Civil Codes," *La. L. Rev.*, 56, no. 1 (1995; https://digitalcommons.law.lsu.edu/lalrev/vol56/iss1/6/): 231–47, and, re the increasing focus of the civil law on jurisprudence, Vernon Valentine Palmer, "The French Connection and The Spanish Perception: Historical Debates and Contemporary Evaluation of French Influence on Louisiana Civil Law," *La. L. Rev.* 63, no.4 (2003; https://digitalcommons.law.lsu.edu/lalrev/vol63/iss4/11/): 1067–1126, at 1118 n.148.

It is not so clear that the *substance* of the English common law is significantly better or more libertarian than the substance of the Roman law as embodied in the modern continental civil codes. In fact, as noted in this chapter, in many respects the Roman legal concepts are arguably superior to common law principles (for example, the Roman law has a more conceptually elegant and streamlined system of property rights, as opposed to the cluttered common law system, which is mired in feudalistic concepts; and the Roman law's concept of contract is in some ways superior, since it does not have the unnecessary and formalistic doctrine of consideration).[153]

What we should be wary of is legal and legislative positivism, of relying on legislation as a dominant means of making law. And while we can appreciate the civil codes, along with private "codifications" of the law or treatises such as the ALI's *Restatements* of the law, and older treatises such as those by Blackstone and Coke, we should oppose efforts to codify the common law in various jurisdictions and enact them as positive legislation, such as David Dudley Field's attempt to (legislatively) codify New York's common law in the late 1800s. This was vigorously fought by New York lawyer James C. Carter. Carter opposed replacing case law with centralized legislation. He notes that caselaw precedents are flexible and allow the judge to do justice, while statutes are applied literally, even where injustice is done or the legislator did not contemplate the result. Thus, Carter argues, one of the worst effects of legislatively codifying law—replacing organically developed law with artificial statutes—is that it changes the role of courts and judges from one in which the judge searches for justice into mere squabbles over definitions of words found in statutes. As Carter wrote:

> At present, when any doubt arises in any particular case as to what the true rule of the unwritten [i.e., judge-found, common-law developed] law is, it is at once assumed that the rule most in accordance with justice and

---

[153] On property law, see note 140, above, and accompanying text; on consideration, see notes 141–142, above, and accompanying text. See also James Hadley, *Introduction to Roman Law* (Littleton, Colo.: Fred Rothman, 1996; https://archive.org/details/introductiontoro029387mbp), p. 66 ("A recent able lecturer on ancient law, Mr. Maine, finds in this fact an explanation of the more thorough scientific development which distinguishes the Roman law from the English."); and "Knowledge, Calculation, Conflict, and Law" (ch. 19), at n.64.

sound policy is the one which must be declared to be the law. The search is for that rule. The appeal is squarely made to the highest considerations of morality and justice. These are the rallying points of the struggle. The contention is ennobling and beneficial to the advocates, to the judges, to the parties, to the auditors, and so indirectly to the whole community. The decision then made records another step in the advance of human reason towards that perfection after which it forever aspires. But when the law is conceded to be written down in a statute, and the only question is what the statute means, a contention unspeakably inferior is substituted. The dispute is about *words*. The question of what is right or wrong, just or unjust, is irrelevant and out of place. The only question is what has been written. What a wretched exchange for the manly encounter upon the elevated plane of principle![154]

---

[154] James C. Carter, *The Proposed Codification of Our Common Law: A Paper Prepared at the Request of The Committee of the Bar Association of the City of New York, Appointed to Oppose the Measure* (1884), pp. 85–86; text available at Kinsella, "Another Problem with Legislation: James Carter v. the Field Codes." When the job of judges is primarily to interpret statutes—as is the case for most federal judges interpreting federal law and the written Constitution, since there is no federal common law (see *Erie Railroad Co. v. Tompkins*, 304 U.S. 64 (1938; https://en.wikipedia.org/wiki/Erie_Railroad_Co._v._Tompkins)—then they are acting as mere functionaries interpreting words, not doing justice, since there is no reason to expect a document written by a government committee (legislation, the Constitution) to have anything to do with justice or natural rights. Thus, I have pointed out before that in this sense, and to this extent, these "judges" are really fake judges, not real judges.

See also the comments of Samuel Read on legal positivism, quoted in Kinsella, "Samuel Read on Legal Positivism and Capitalism in 1829," *StephanKinsella.com* (Nov. 4, 2011):

... we observe every day men, and even legislators, pretending to reason concerning political justice and the general principles of law, as if there were no such distinction as that which has been here pointed out, and who seem to have scarcely the most distant comprehension that there is a *natural code* discoverable by the light of reason, to which alone reference ought to be had when any law ... is brought into question either for the purpose of enactment or repeal. Instead of *reasoning like legislators*, such persons merely *contend as lawyers*; they but inquire *what is*, or *what has been*, not *what ought to be*; and, provided they can find a *precedent*, think they have no need to trouble themselves with any farther investigation as to right or wrong. They pronounce the two cabalistic words, "vested right," and think themselves at once entrenched behind an impregnable fortress, without considering it as at all incumbent upon them to show that the investiture is consistent with real and natural right.

VI. CONCLUSION

Virtues such as individual liberty and legal certainty, understood as aspects of a just, libertarian polity, are indeed objectively valid standards that any legal system must uphold. Centralized legal systems—even those that attempt to embody libertarian virtues, such as the civil law—undercut individual rights, because in them legislation is made supreme and valid; because law-finding is replaced with law-making.

Both the Roman law and common law have been corrupted into today's inferior legislation-dominated systems. The primacy of legislation should be abandoned, and we should return to a system of judge-made law—a private system, ideally, but in the direction of systems like the old common law and Roman law, at least. Scholars who codify naturally-evolved law have a vital function to serve, but they should not ask for governmental imprimatur on their scholarly efforts.

Ultimately, the form of a legal system does not guarantee that just laws will be adopted. We must always be vigilant and urge that individual freedom be respected, whether by legislator or judge.

APPENDIX
LEGISLATIVE SUPREMACY IN THE CIVIL CODE

As noted above, the material here was originally intended to appear in footnote 6, above. Due to its length, I include this material in this appendix.

Legislative supremacy is announced in the very first articles of the Louisiana Civil Code. Article 1 provides that "The sources of law are legislation *and* custom," but article 3 makes it clear that legislation is dominant and supreme: "Custom may not abrogate legislation."[155]

---

[155] See also Herman, *The Louisiana Civil Code: A European Legacy for the United States*, p. 17; John Henry Merryman & Rogelio Pérez-Perdomo, *The Civil Law Tradition: An Introduction to the Legal Systems of Western Europe and Latin America*, 4th ed. (Stanford, California: Stanford University Press, 2018), discussing legislative supremacy in the civil law. N.b.: Louisiana's civil law is derived in large part from Spanish and Roman sources, though using the French code's style, organization, and sometimes text as the means to codify this Spanish-Roman law. This, by the way, is a controversial and complicated issue among Louisiana legal scholars; I tend to agree with Pascal and Levasseur, and disagree

Yet some scholars note that the Louisiana code is not quite as "rationalistic" or legal positivistic as the French code, since it also admits custom as a source of law and, importantly, also provides: "When no rule for a particular situation can be derived from legislation or custom, the court is bound to proceed according to equity. To decide equitably, resort is made to *justice, reason*, and prevailing usages."[156]

For discussion of the Louisiana Civil Code, its history, and related issues, see various works by Herman, Yiannopoulos, et al.[157] Differences in terminology between Louisiana's civil-law system and common-law legal systems are detailed in Rome & Kinsella, *Louisiana Civil Law Dictionary*.[158] A general comparison of civil and common law is found in Buckland & McNair, *Roman Law and Common Law: A Comparison in Outline*.[159]

---

with Batiza and Herman, as a *legal* matter, despite disagreeing *normatively* with Pascal's opposition to individualism and economic liberalism and despite agreeing with Herman's more liberal and individualist inclinations. See Robert A. Pascal, "*The Louisiana Civil Code: A European Legacy for the United States.* By Shael Herman," *La. L. Rev.* 54, no. 3 (Jan. 1994; https://digitalcommons.law.lsu.edu/lalrev/vol54/iss3/17/): 827–32; and Alain A. Levasseur, "Grandeur or Mockery?", *Loy. L. Rev.* 42, no. 4 (Winter 1997; https://digitalcommons.law.lsu.edu/faculty_scholarship/321/: 647–725.)

[156] Louisiana Civil Code, art. 4 (emphasis added). See also commentary on this issue by Yiannopoulos and Pascal: A.N. Yiannopoulos, "The Civil Codes of Louisiana," *Civil Law Commentaries* 1, no. 1 (Winter 2008; https://perma.cc/59DZ-KGSE): 0–23 (also included in *idem, Civil Law System: Louisiana and Comparative Law: A Coursebook: Texts, Cases and Materials*, 3d ed. (Baton Rouge, La.: Claitor's Publishing Division, 2000)); and Pascal's review of Herman cited previously, both as quoted in Kinsella, "Legislative Positivism and Rationalism in the Louisiana and French Civil Codes," *StephanKinsella.com* (April 4, 2023). See also *idem*, "Logical and Legal Positivism," *StephanKinsella.com* (June 23, 2010). Re rationalism, see also note 9, above. The 1804 French Civil Code, in English, may be found at *Code Napoleon: or, The French Civil Code* (London: William Benning, 1827; https://perma.cc/7CEZ-Q2D5).

[157] Herman, *The Louisiana Civil Code: A European Legacy for the United States*; Alain A. Levasseur "The Major Periods of Louisiana Legal History," *Loy. L. Rev.* 41, no. 4 (Winter 1996; https://perma.cc/XB9F-WQYX): 585–628; Yiannopoulos, "The Civil Codes of Louisiana"; Richard Holcombe Kilbourne, Jr., *A History of the Louisiana Civil Code: The Formative Years, 1803–1839* (Baton Rouge, La.: Center for Civil Law Studies, Louisiana State University, 1987). See also Merryman & Pérez-Perdomo, *The Civil Law Tradition* and Peter G. Stein, "Roman Law, Common Law, and Civil Law," *Tul. L. Rev.*, 66, no. 6 (1991–92): 1591–1604.

[158] Gregory Rome & Stephan Kinsella, *Louisiana Civil Law Dictionary* (New Orleans, La.: Quid Pro Books, 2011).

[159] W.W. Buckland & Arnold D. McNair, *Roman Law and Common Law: A Comparison in Outline* (Cambridge, England: University Press, 2d ed., revised by F.H. Lawson, reprinted with corrections, 1965).

PART IV

INTELLECTUAL PROPERTY

14

Law and Intellectual Property
in a Stateless Society

I've written a large number of articles on intellectual property, or IP, over the years, starting with *Against Intellectual Property*, first published in 2001.* This chapter, originally intended for a symposium issue of the *Griffith Law Review* but withdrawn/rejected because of a dispute with the editors, was originally published in my journal *Libertarian Papers* in 2013. It was the most comprehensive article I'd written on IP since *AIP*.[†] It incorporates much of the material from that work and includes some additional material that I had published in the intervening decade or so. Chapter 15 contains additional arguments developed subsequently and complements this work and *AIP*. These two chapters, together, contain a good presentation of my current views and arguments related to IP.[††]

* *Journal of Libertarian Studies* 15, no. 2 (Spring 2001): 1–53. Hereinafter, *AIP*. In this chapter I will cite the 2008 edition of *AIP* (www.c4sif.org/aip). In *AIP* I thanked "Wendy McElroy and Gene Callahan for helpful comments on an earlier draft." My article "In Defense of Napster and Against the Second Homesteading Rule," *LewRockwell.com* (September 4, 2000) presented a summary version of the argument later elaborated in *AIP*. I thanked Gil Guillory for helpful comments on that piece.

> a long habit of not thinking a thing *wrong*, gives it a superficial
> appearance of being *right*, and raises at first a formidable
> outcry in defense of custom. But the tumult soon subsides.
> Time makes more converts than reason.
>
> —Thomas Paine[1]

I. INTRODUCTION

It is widely recognized that the institutional protection of property rights was a necessary (though probably not sufficient)[2] condition for the radical prosperity experienced in the West since the advent of the industrial revolution. And property rights include so-called "intellectual

---

† Stephan Kinsella, "Law and Intellectual Property in a Stateless Society," *Libertarian Papers* 5, no. 1 (2013): 1–44. The publication history is detailed at Kinsella, "Kinsella, 'Law and Intellectual Property in a Stateless Society,'" *C4SIF Blog* (March 1, 2013). The structure of the article is similar to the more concise "Intellectual Property and Libertarianism," *Mises Daily* (Nov. 17, 2009). The title is slightly misleading because the article was really about why IP is unjust and had little to do with anarchy or stateless societies; the title and the slight emphasis on stateless societies in the text was intended to make the article fit the theme of the symposium issue it was intended for, which was "Law and Anarchy: Legal Order and the Idea of a Stateless Society." I've chosen to retain the original title here.

†† For those interested in reading my original *AIP*, I suggest instead the similar version "The Case Against Intellectual Property," in *Handbook of the Philosophical Foundations of Business Ethics* (Prof. Dr. Christoph Lütge, ed.; Springer, 2013) (chapter 68, in Part 18, "Property Rights: Material and Intellectual," Robert McGee, section ed.).

For other articles and blog posts related to IP, see Kinsella, *You Can't Own Ideas: Essays on Intellectual Property* (Papinian Press, 2023); also: the *AIP* Supplementary Material linked at www.c4sif.org/aip; the Resources page at www.c4sif.org/resources; Kinsella, "A Selection of my Best Articles and Speeches on IP," *C4SIF Blog* (Nov. 30, 2015); and my six-lecture Mises Academy course on IP, available at Kinsella, "KOL172 | "Rethinking Intellectual Property: History, Theory, and Economics: Lecture 1: History and Law (Mises Academy, 2011)," *Kinsella on Liberty Podcast* (Feb. 14, 2015). For criticism of IP by other writers from a libertarian or free market perspective, see Kinsella, ed., *The Anti-IP Reader: Free Market Critiques of Intellectual Property* (Papinian Press, 2023).

---

1 Thomas Paine, "Introduction," *Common Sense* (1776).

2 See Hans-Hermann Hoppe, "From the Malthusian Trap to the Industrial Revolution: An Explanation of Social Evolution," in *The Great Fiction: Property, Economy, Society, and the Politics of Decline*, Second Expanded Edition (Auburn, Ala.: Mises Institute, 2021; www.hanshoppe.com/tgf); see also *idem*, "PFP041 | Hans-Hermann Hoppe, From the

property" (IP) rights which emerged in their modern form around the same time.[3] Or so we have been told. The idea that IP rights are a legitimate type of property right, and a necessary part of a free market economy, has been taken for granted since the dawn of modern patent and copyright approximately two centuries ago.

Despite the widespread assumption that IP is legitimate, even its proponents seem somewhat uneasy with it. Thus most of them favor limited terms for patent and copyright—about 17 years for the former and usually over 100 years for the latter—unlike the potentially perpetual ownership of traditional forms of property.[4] And there is continual dissatisfaction with the state of the law, its ambiguities and arbitrary

---

Malthusian Trap to the Industrial Revolution: An Explanation of Social Evolution (PFS 2009)," *Property and Freedom Podcast* (Jan. 20, 2022; https://propertyandfreedom.org/pfp).

[3] In this chapter, IP refers primarily to patent and copyright unless the context indicates otherwise. For arguments against other forms of IP, such as trademark and trade secret, see *AIP*. Although defamation (libel and slander) is not usually considered a type of IP, I believe it should be, since arguments in favor of the "reputation rights" that this law protects are similar to those of other forms of IP, like trademark. See Kinsella, "Defamation Law and Reputation Rights as a Type of Intellectual Property," in Elvira Nica & Gheorghe H. Popescu, eds., *A Passion for Justice: Essays in Honor of Walter Block* (New York: Addleton Academic Publishers, forthcoming). For a criticism of defamation law as being incompatible with libertarian property rights principles, see Murray N. Rothbard, "Knowledge, True and False," in *The Ethics of Liberty* (New York: New York University Press, 1998; https://mises.org/library/knowledge-true-and-false); Walter E. Block, "The Slanderer and Libeler," in *Defending the Undefendable* (2018; https://mises.org/library/defending-undefendable).

[4] Yet some defenders of IP go so far as to support perpetual terms, such as Lysander Spooner, Andrew J. Galambos, some Randians (though not Rand herself), Robert Wenzel, Victor Yarros, possibly J. Neil Schulman, etc. See, e.g., Lysander Spooner, "A Letter to Scientists and Inventors, on the Science of Justice, and their Rights of Perpetual Property in their Discoveries and Inventions" and "The Law of Intellectual Property or an Essay on the Right of Authors and Inventors to a Perpetual Property in Their Ideas," in Charles Shively, ed., *The Collected Works of Lysander Spooner*, vol. 3, reprint ed. (Weston, Mass.: M&S Press, 1971 [1855]; www.lysanderspooner.org/works); discussion of Galambos in *AIP*; Kinsella, "Transcript: Debate with Robert Wenzel on Intellectual Property," *C4SIF Blog* (April 11, 2022). Re Yarros, see Kinsella, "Benjamin Tucker and the Great Nineteenth Century IP Debates in *Liberty* Magazine," *C4SIF Blog* (July 11, 2022) and *idem*, "James L. Walker (Tak Kak), 'The Question of Copyright' (1891)," *C4SIF Blog* (July 28, 2022); "Conversation with Schulman about Logorights and Media-Carried Property" (ch. 17). See also Jeffrey A. Tucker, "Eternal Copyright," *C4SIF Blog* (Feb. 21, 2012); and Wendy McElroy, "Intellectual Property," in *The Debates of Liberty: An Overview of Individualist Anarchism, 1881–1908* (Lexington Books, 2002; https://perma.cc/ZQM2-82B9), reprinted without endnotes as "Copyright and Patent in Benjamin Tucker's Periodical," *Mises Daily* (July 28, 2010; https://mises.org/library/copyright-and-patent-benjamin-tuckers-periodical).

standards, and with patent office efficiency and competence, or lack thereof. There are incessant calls for "reform," and for curbs on "misuse" or "abuse" of patent and copyright. But in these complaints and debates, it is almost always taken for granted that some form of copyright and patent are essential, even if reform is needed.

In recent years, however, increasing numbers of libertarians have begun to doubt the very legitimacy of IP.[5] In this chapter I argue that patent and copyright should be abolished entirely, not merely reformed.

As a preliminary matter, it is necessary to describe the libertarian view of property rights. As this discussion will make clear, IP rights such as patent and copyright are inconsistent with the private property order that would characterize a stateless, private-law society. I will follow with a discussion of what practices or laws might prevail in the absence of IP.

II. THE LIBERTARIAN FRAMEWORK[6]

A. Property, Rights, and Liberty

Libertarians tend to agree on a wide array of policies and principles. Nonetheless, it is not easy to find consensus on what libertarianism's defining characteristic is, or on what distinguishes it from other political theories and systems.

Various formulations abound. It is said that libertarianism is concerned with individual rights, property rights,[7] the free market, capitalism,

---

[5] See Kinsella, "The Death Throes of Pro-IP Libertarianism," *Mises Daily* (July 28, 2010); *idem*, "The Four Historical Phases of IP Abolitionism," *Mises Economics Blog* (April 13, 2011); *idem*, "The Origins of Libertarian IP Abolitionism," *Mises Economics Blog* (April 1, 2011); Kinsella, ed., "The Anti-IP Reader."

[6] The issues in this section are elaborated on in other chapters, e.g. "What Libertarianism Is" (ch. 2) and "How We Come to Own Ourselves" (ch. 4).

[7] As noted in "What Libertarianism Is" (ch. 2), n.1, the term "private" property rights is sometimes used by libertarians, yet property rights are necessarily public, in the sense that the borders or boundaries of property must be *publicly visible* so that nonowners can avoid trespass. For more on this aspect of property borders, see Hans-Hermann Hoppe, *A Theory of Socialism and Capitalism: Economics, Politics, and Ethics* (Auburn, Ala.: Mises Institute,

freedom, liberty, justice, or the nonaggression principle. But are any of these ideas truly fundamental or foundational? "Capitalism" and "the free market," for example, describe the catallactic conditions that arise or are permitted in a libertarian society, but they do not encompass other aspects of libertarianism.[8] And individual rights, justice, and nonaggression collapse into property rights. As Murray Rothbard explained, individual rights are property rights.[9] And justice simply means giving someone his due, which depends on what his (property) rights are.[10]

The nonaggression principle is also dependent on property rights, since what aggression is depends on what our (property) rights are. If you hit me, it is aggression *because* I have a property right in my body. If I take from you the apple you possess, this is trespass—aggression—only *because* you own the apple. One cannot identify an act of aggression without implicitly assigning a corresponding property right to the victim. "Freedom" and "liberty" face difficulties similar to that of the concept of aggression, as indicated in the common saying, "Your freedom ends where my nose begins!"

2010 [1989]; www.hanshoppe.com/tsc), pp. 167–68; "A Libertarian Theory of Contract: Title Transfer, Binding Promises, and Inalienability" (ch. 9), at n.38; *AIP*, pp. 30–31, 49; also Randy E. Barnett, "A Consent Theory of Contract," *Colum. L. Rev.* 86 (1986; www.randybarnett.com/pre-2000): 269–321, at 303.

[8] "Catallactics" is a term used by the Austrian economist Ludwig von Mises to refer to the economics of an advanced free market system which employs money prices and entrepreneurial calculation, as opposed to a barter or Crusoe economy. See the Wikipedia entry on "Catallactics" at https://en.wikipedia.org/wiki/Catallactics and the Introduction *et pass.* in Ludwig von Mises, *Human Action: A Treatise on Economics*, Scholar's ed. (Auburn, Ala.: Mises Institute, 1998; https://mises.org/library/human-action-0).

[9] Murray N. Rothbard, "'Human Rights' as Property Rights," in *The Ethics of Liberty* (http://mises.org/rothbard/ethics/fifteen.asp); *idem*, *For A New Liberty*, 2d ed. (Auburn, Ala.: Mises Institute, 2006; https://mises.org/library/new-liberty-libertarian-manifesto), pp. 42 *et pass.*

[10] "Justice is the constant and perpetual wish to render every one his due...The maxims of law are these: to live honestly, to hurt no one, to give every one his due." J.A.C. Thomas, ed., trans., *The Institutes of Justinian: Text, Translation, and Commentary* (Amsterdam: North-Holland Publishing Company, 1975). See also Thomas Aquinas, *Summa Theologica*, I–II, Q 64, art 2, in Anton C. Pegis, ed., *Basic Writings of St. Thomas Aquinas* (New York: Random House, 1945), 2: 491 ("the act of justice is to render what is due"), quoted in Tom Bethell, *The Noblest Triumph: Property and Prosperity through the Ages* (New York: St. Martin's Griffin, 1998), p. 161. See also Thomas Aquinas, *Summa Theologica* (New Advent, https://www.newadvent.org/summa), *Secunda Secundæ Partis*, Question 58, arts. 1, 11.

So capitalism and the free market are too narrow, and justice, in-dividual rights, liberty, freedom, and aggression all boil down to, or are defined in terms of, property rights.

What of property rights, then? Is this what differentiates libertarian-ism from other political philosophies—that we favor property rights, and all others do not? Surely such a claim is untenable. After all, a property right is simply the *exclusive right to control a scarce resource*. As Professor Yiannopoulos explains:

> *Property* may be defined as an *exclusive right to control an economic good…*; it is the name of a concept that refers to the rights and obligations, priv-ileges and restrictions that govern the relations of man with respect to *things of value*. People everywhere and at all times desire the possession of things that are necessary for survival or valuable by cultural definition and which, as a result of the demand placed upon them, *become scarce*. Laws enforced by organized society control the competition for, and guarantee the enjoyment of, these desired things. What is guaranteed to be one's own is property… [Property rights] *confer a direct and immediate authority over a thing*.[11]

In other words, property rights specify which persons own—that is, have the right to control—various scarce resources in a given region or jurisdiction. Yet every political theory advances *some* theory of prop-erty. None of the various forms of socialism deny property rights *per se*; each system will specify an owner for each contestable scarce resource.[12] If the state nationalizes an industry, it is asserting ownership of those means of production. If the state taxes you, it is implicitly asserting

---

[11] A.N. Yiannopoulos, *Louisiana Civil Law Treatise, Property* (West Group, 4th ed. 2001), §§ 1, 2 (first emphasis in original; remaining emphasis added). See also Louisiana Civil Code (https://www.legis.la.gov/legis/Laws_Toc.aspx?folder=67&level=Parent), art. 477 ("Ownership is the right that confers on a person direct, immediate, and exclusive authority over a thing. The owner of a thing may use, enjoy, and dispose of it within the limits and under the conditions established by law"). See also "What Libertarianism Is" (ch. 2), Appendix I.

[12] For a systematic analysis of various forms of socialism, such as Socialism Russian-Style, Socialism Social-Democratic Style, the Socialism of Conservatism, and the Socialism of Social Engineering, see Hoppe, *A Theory of Socialism and Capitalism*, chaps. 3–6. Recognizing the common elements of various forms of socialism and their distinction from libertarianism (capitalism), Hoppe incisively defines socialism as "an institutionalized interference with or aggression against private property and private property claims." Ibid., p. 2. See also the quote from Hoppe in note 18, below.

ownership of the funds taken. If my land is transferred to a private developer by eminent domain statutes, the developer is now the owner. If the law allows a recipient of racial discrimination to sue his employer for a sum of money, he is the owner of the money.[13]

Protection of and respect for property rights is thus not unique to libertarianism. What is distinctive about libertarianism is its *particular property assignment rules*: that is, the rules that determine who owns each contestable resource.

B. Property in Bodies

As indicated above, every legal system assigns a particular owner to each scarce resource. These resources obviously include natural resources such as land, fruits on trees, and so on. Things found in nature are not the only scarce resources, however. Each human actor has, controls, and is identified and associated with a unique human body, which is also a scarce resource.[14] Both human bodies and nonhuman, scarce resources are desired for use as *means* by actors in the pursuit of various goals.[15]

---

[13] Even the private thief, by taking your watch, is implicitly acting on the maxim that *he* has the right to control it—that he is its owner. He does not deny property rights—he simply differs from the libertarian as to *who the owner is*. In fact, as Adam Smith observed: "If there is any society among robbers and murderers, they must at least, according to the trite observation, abstain from robbing and murdering one another." Adam Smith, *The Theory of Moral Sentiments* (Indianapolis: Liberty Fund, 1982 [1759]), II.II.3.2.

[14] As Hoppe observes, even in a paradise with a superabundance of goods:
> [E]very person's physical body would still be a scarce resource and thus the need for the establishment of property rules, i.e., rules regarding people's bodies, would exist. One is not used to thinking of one's own body in terms of a scarce good, but in imagining the most ideal situation one could ever hope for, the Garden of Eden, it becomes possible to realize that one's body is indeed the prototype of a scarce good for the use of which property rights, i.e., rights of exclusive ownership, somehow have to be established, in order to avoid clashes.

Hoppe, *A Theory of Socialism and Capitalism*, 19. See also "Causation and Aggression" (ch. 8) (discussing the use of other humans' bodies as means). See also "How We Come to Own Ourselves" (ch. 4).

[15] This analysis draws on Ludwig von Mises's "praxeological" view of the nature of human action, in which actors or agents employ scarce means to causally achieve desired ends. See the section "The Structure of Human Action: Means and Ends" in Kinsella, "Intellectual Freedom and Learning versus Patent and Copyright," *Economic Notes* No. 113 (Libertarian Alliance, Jan. 18, 2011) and *idem*, "Ideas Are Free: The Case Against Intellectual Property," *Mises Daily* (Nov. 23, 2010). See also "*Against Intellectual Property* After Twenty Years" (ch. 15), Part IV.E.

Accordingly, any political theory or system must assign ownership or control rights in human bodies as well as in external things.[16] However, there are relevant differences between these two types of scarce resources that justify treating them separately.

Let us consider first the libertarian property assignment rules with respect to human bodies, and the corresponding notion of aggression as it pertains to bodies. Libertarians often vigorously assert the "non-aggression principle." As Ayn Rand said, "So long as men desire to live together, no man may *initiate*—do you hear me? No man may *start*—the use of physical force against others."[17] Or, as Rothbard put it:

> The libertarian creed rests upon one central principle, or "axiom": that no man or group of men may aggress against the person or property of anyone else. This may be called the "nonaggression axiom." "Aggression" is defined as the initiation of the use or threat of physical violence against the person or property of anyone else. Aggression is therefore synonymous with invasion.[18]

---

[16] The term "thing" here is used as a synonym for scarce resources, including not only material objects but also human bodies. This usage draws on the civil law, in which the term "things" refers to "material objects" that are "susceptible of appropriation"—that is, to "the objects of patrimonial rights." *See* Yiannopoulos, *Louisiana Civil Law Treatise, Property*, §§ 12, 201; Louisiana Civil Code, arts. 448, 453, *et pass.* For more discussion of the concept of "things," see "What Libertarianism Is" (ch. 2), Appendix I.

[17] Ayn Rand, "Galt's Speech," in *For the New Intellectual*, quoted in the "Physical Force" entry, *The Ayn Rand Lexicon: Objectivism from A to Z*, Harry Binswanger, ed. (New York: New American Library, 1986; https://perma.cc/L4YA-96CC). Ironically, Objectivists often excoriate libertarians for having a "context-less" concept of aggression—that is, that "aggression" or "rights" are meaningless unless these concepts are embedded in the larger philosophical framework of Objectivism—despite Galt's straightforward definition of aggression as the initiation of physical force against others. However, there are distinctions to be drawn between property rights in an actor's body and in external resources homesteaded by that actor or some previous owner. See, on this, Kinsella, "The Relation between the Non-aggression Principle and Property Rights: a response to Division by Zer0," *Mises Economics Blog* (Oct. 4, 2011). See also the related discussion in "What Libertarianism Is" (ch. 2), at n.13.

[18] Rothbard, *For a New Liberty*, 23. See also *idem, The Ethics of Liberty*: "The fundamental axiom of libertarian theory is that each person must be a self-owner, and that no one has the right to interfere with such self-ownership" (p. 60), and "What…aggressive violence means is that one man invades the property of another without the victim's consent. The invasion may be against a man's property in his person (as in the case of bodily assault), or against his property in tangible goods (as in robbery or trespass)" (p. 45). Hoppe writes:
> If … an action is performed that uninvitedly invades or changes the physical integrity of another person's body and puts this body to a use that is not to this

In other words, at least when it comes to human bodies, libertarians maintain that the only way to violate rights is by *initiating* force—that is, by committing aggression. And, correspondingly, that force used *in response* to aggression—such as defensive, restitutive, or retaliatory/retributive force—is justified.[19]

Now in the case of the body, it is clear what aggression is: invading the borders of someone's body, commonly called battery, or, more generally, using the body of another without his or her consent.[20] The very notion of interpersonal aggression presupposes property rights in bodies—more particularly, that each person is, at least *prima facie*, the owner of his own body.[21] And the notion of self-ownership corresponds to the non-aggression principle. Both imply each other, or are alternate ways of stating the same basic idea: that no person may use another's body without his or her consent; to do so is unjustified and impermissible aggression.

Non-libertarian political philosophies do not accept the libertarian self-ownership principle. According to them, each person has *some* limited rights in his own body, but not complete or exclusive rights. Society—or the state, purporting to be society's agent—has certain rights in each citizen's body, too. The state may limit or override the individual's control over his own body. This partial slavery is implicit

---

very person's own liking, this action … is called *aggression*.… Next to the concept of action, *property* is the most basic category in the social sciences. As a matter of fact, all other concepts to be introduced in this chapter—aggression, contract, capitalism and socialism—are definable in terms of property: *aggression* being aggression against property, *contract* being a nonaggressive relationship between property owners, *socialism* being an institutionalized policy of aggression against property, and *capitalism* being an institutionalized policy of the recognition of property and contractualism.

Hoppe, *A Theory of Socialism and Capitalism*, pp. 22–23, 18.

[19] See "Punishment and Proportionality" (ch. 5).

[20] The following terms and formulations may be considered as roughly synonymous, depending on context: aggression; initiation of force; trespass; invasion; unconsented to (or uninvited) change in the physical integrity (or use, control or possession) of another person's body or property.

[21] "*Prima facie*," because some rights in one's body are arguably forfeited or lost in certain circumstances, e.g., when one commits a crime, thus authorizing the victim to at least use defensive force against the body of the aggressor (implying the aggressor is to that extent *not* the owner of his body). For more on this see "What Libertarianism Is" (ch. 2), at n.17; "How We Come to Own Ourselves" (ch. 4); "A Libertarian Theory of Contract" (ch. 9); "Inalienability and Punishment: A Reply to George Smith" (ch. 10).

in state actions such as taxation, conscription, drug prohibitions, and other regulations and laws.

The libertarian says that each person is the *full owner* of his body: he has the right to control his body, to decide whether or not he ingests narcotics, joins an army, and so on. Others, however, maintain that the state, or society, is at least a partial owner of the bodies of those subject to such laws—or even a nearly complete owner in the case of conscriptees or nonaggressor "criminals" incarcerated for life or those killed by government bombs. Libertarians believe in *self*-ownership. Non-libertarians—statists—of all stripes advocate some form of slavery. This is virtually implicit in the nature of the state as an agency that asserts the right to be "the ultimate arbiter in every case of conflict, including conflicts involving itself, [and that] allows no appeal above and beyond itself."[22] This arrangement permits the state to override individuals' self-ownership rights—to, in effect, become their master or overlord.

As an illustration, consider this exchange between a communist party official and a farmer in China in 1978, when farmers were prohibited from private ownership of their crop yields: "At one meeting with communist party officials, a farmer asked: 'What about the teeth in my head? Do I own those?' Answer: No. Your teeth belong to the collective."[23]

Libertarians believe the farmer should own his teeth, his body, his home, his farm, and his crop yields.

---

[22] See Hans-Hermann Hoppe, "The Idea of a Private Law Society," *Mises Daily* (July 28, 2006; https://mises.org/library/idea-private-law-society):

> Conventionally, the state is defined as an agency that possesses two unique characteristics. First, the state is an agency that exercises a territorial monopoly of ultimate decision-making. That is, it is the ultimate arbiter in every case of conflict, including conflicts involving itself, and it allows no appeal above and beyond itself. Furthermore, the state is an agency that exercises a territorial monopoly of taxation. That is, it is an agency that unilaterally fixes the price private citizens must pay for its provision of law and order.

See also Hoppe's definition of the state in note 52, below.

[23] David Kestenbaum & Jacob Goldstein, "The Secret Document That Transformed China," NPR's *Planet Money* blog (Jan. 20, 2012; https://perma.cc/C4SP-XSC7).

C. Self-Ownership and Conflict-Avoidance

There is always the possibility of conflict over contestable (scarce, con-flictable)[24] resources. This is in the very nature of scarce, or rivalrous, resources. By assigning an owner to each resource, the legal or prop-erty rights system establishes objective, publicly visible or discernible boundaries or borders that nonowners can avoid. This makes conflict-free, productive, cooperative use of resources possible. This is true of human bodies as well as of external objects.[25] If we seek rules that permit peaceful, productive, and conflict-free use of our very bodies, some rules allocating body ownership must be established. These basic values, or *grundnorms*—peace, conflict-avoidance, prosperity—and related ones such as justice, cooperation, and civilization, are the reason that liber-tarians, indeed any civilized person who adopts these basic values, seek property assignment rules in the first place.[26] We prefer society and

---

[24] On the term "conflictable," see See *Against Intellectual Property* After Twenty Years" (ch. 15), text at n.29 *et pass.*; Kinsella, "On Conflictability and Conflictable Resources," *StephanKinsella.com* (Jan. 31, 2022); see also "What Libertarianism Is" (ch. 2), Appendix I; "How We Come to Own Ourselves" (ch. 4), text at n.10; "A Libertarian Theory of Punish-ment and Rights" (ch. 5), at n.62; "Dialogical Arguments for Libertarian Rights" (ch. 6), at n.6; "Causation and Aggression" (ch. 8), n.19.

[25] On the importance of the concept of scarcity and the possibility of conflict for the emergence of property rules, see Hoppe, *A Theory of Socialism and Capitalism*, 160; and the discussion thereof in Kinsella, "Thoughts on the Latecomer and Homesteading Ideas; or, Why the Very Idea of 'Ownership' Implies that only Libertarian Principles are Justifiable," *Mises Economics Blog* (Aug. 15, 2007).

[26] "Grundnorm" was legal philosopher Hans Kelsen's term for the hypothetical basic norm or rule that serves as the basis or ultimate source for the legitimacy of a legal system. See Hans Kelsen, *General Theory of Law and State*, Anders Wedberg, trans. (Cambridge, Mass.: Harvard University Press, 1949). I employ this term to refer to the fundamental norms presupposed by civilized people, e.g., in argumentative discourse, which in turn imply libertarian political norms.

That the libertarian *grundnorms* are, in fact, necessarily presupposed by all civilized people to the extent they are civilized—during argumentative justification, that is—is shown by Hoppe in his argumentation-ethics defense of libertarian rights. On this, see Hoppe, *A Theory of Socialism and Capitalism*, chap. 7; "What Libertarianism Is" (ch. 2), at n.2; "Dialogical Arguments for Libertarian Rights" (ch. 6); "Defending Argumentation Ethics" (ch. 7).

For discussion of why people (to one extent or the other) *do* value these underlying norms, see Kinsella, "The Division of Labor as the Source of Grundnorms and Rights," *Mises Economics Blog* (April 24, 2009), and *idem*, "Empathy and the Source of Rights," *Mises Economics Blog* (Sept. 6, 2006). See also "Punishment and Proportionality" (ch. 5), at Part I and IV.G:

civilization to mayhem and fighting and violence. Libertarians believe that self-ownership (and other property acquisition rules discussed further below) is the only property assignment rule compatible with these *grundnorms*; it is implied by them.

As noted above, the libertarian view is that the appropriate body-ownership rule is that each person is, *prima facie*, a self-owner: each person owns his own body. It might be argued, however, that *any* property assignment rule would suffice to permit conflict-free use of resources, that the libertarian self-ownership rule is not necessary. As long as everyone knows who owns a given resource—even if it is a king or tyrant—then people can avoid conflict by respecting existing property boundaries. In the case of bodies, this would mean some form of slavery, where some people are owned partially or completely by others.[27] Whether a person *A* is a self-owner, or owned by some other

---

Civilized people are also concerned about *justifying* punishment. They want to punish, but they also want to know that such punishment is justified. They want to be able to punish legitimately.... Theories of punishment are concerned with justifying punishment, with offering decent people who are reluctant to act immorally a reason why they may punish others. This is useful, of course, for offering moral people guidance and assurance that they may properly deal with those who seek to harm them.

[27] As Rothbard argues, there are only two alternatives to self-ownership either:
1. a certain class of people, A, have the right to own another class, B; or
2. everyone has the right to own his equal quota share of everyone else.

The first alternative implies that, while class A deserves the rights of being human, class B is in reality subhuman and, therefore, deserves no such rights. But since they are indeed human beings, the first alternative contradicts itself in denying natural human rights to one set of humans. Moreover, allowing class A to own class B means that the former is allowed to exploit and, therefore, to live parasitically at the expense of the latter; but, as economics can tell us, this parasitism itself violates the basic economic requirement for human survival: production and exchange.

The second alternative, which we might call "participatory communalism" or "communism," holds that every man should have the right to own his equal quota share of everyone else. If there are three billion people in the world, then everyone has the right to own one-three-billionth of every other person. In the first place, this ideal itself rests upon an absurdity—proclaiming that every man is entitled to own a part of everyone else and yet is not entitled to own himself. Second, we can picture the viability of such a world—a world in which no man is free to take any action whatever without prior approval or indeed command by everyone else in society. It should be clear that in this sort of "communist" world, *no one would be able to do anything, and the human race would quickly perish.*

Murray N. Rothbard, "Justice and Property Rights," in Samuel L. Blumenfeld, ed., *Property in a Humane Economy* by (LaSalle, Ill.: Open Court, 1974; https://mises.org/library/

person or group *B*, everyone can know who gets to decide who can use *A*'s body, and thus conflict can be avoided so long as everyone respects this property right allocation.

The libertarian view is that only its particular property assignment rule—*self*-ownership, as opposed to *other*-ownership (slavery)—fulfills the conflict-avoidance role of property rights. This is so for several inter-related reasons.

First, as Professor Hoppe has argued, the assignment of ownership to a given resource must not be random, arbitrary, particularistic, or biased if the property norm is to serve the function of conflict-avoid-ance.[28] This is because any possible norm designed to avoid conflict must be justified in the context of argumentation, in which partici-pants put forth *reasons* in support of their proposed norms. The norms proposed in genuine argumentation claim universal acceptability, i.e. they must be universalizable. Reasons must be provided that can in principle be acceptable to both sides as grounded in the nature of things, not merely arbitrary or "particularistic" rules such as "I get to hit you, but you do not get to hit me, because I am me and you are you."

---

property-humane-economy), at 107–108 (emphasis added) (also published in Murray N. Rothbard, *Economic Controversies* (Auburn, Ala.: Mises Institute, 2011; https://mises.org/library/economic-controversies)). A similar version of this article under the same ti-tle was published in Rothbard, *Egalitarianism as a Revolt Against Nature and Other Essays*, 2d ed. (Auburn, Ala.: Mises Institute, 2000 [1974]; https://mises.org/library/egalitarian-ism-revolt-against-nature-and-other-essays). Interestingly, the former piece, published shortly after the latter piece, appended a crucial final paragraph distancing Rothbard from some of the more leftish implications from the latter piece. See Kinsella, "Justice and Property Rights: Rothbard on Scarcity, Property, Contracts...," *The Libertarian Standard* (Nov. 19, 2010) and *idem*, "Rothbard on the 'Original Sin' in Land Titles: 1969 vs. 1974," *StephanKinsella.com* (Nov. 5, 2014). See Hoppe's similar argument, discussed in "How We Come to Own Ourselves" (ch. 4), n.14, and similar comments in David Boaz, *The Libertarian Mind: A Manifesto for Freedom* (New York: Simon & Schuster, 2015), p. 140.

On Rothbard's critique of this "communist" approach to property rights assignment, see also "How We Come to Own Ourselves" (ch. 4), at n.14; "Defending Argumentation Ethics" (ch. 7), at n.31; and Kinsella, "Argumentation Ethics and Liberty: A Concise Guide," *Mises Daily* (May 27, 2011), at n. 1.

[28] See Hoppe, *A Theory of Socialism and Capitalism*, 157–65; "What Libertarianism Is" (ch. 2), at n.23; "How We Come to Own Ourselves" (ch. 4), n.15; "A Libertarian Theory of Punishment and Rights" (ch. 5), Parts III.C and III.D; "Dialogical Arguments for Libertarian Rights" (ch. 6), at n.43; "Defending Argumentation Ethics" (ch. 7); and Kinsella, "The problem of particularistic ethics or, why everyone really has to admit the validity of the universalizability principle," *StephanKinsella.com* (Nov. 10, 2011).

Such an arbitrary assertion fails to even attempt to justify the proposed norm. For another example, B's claim that he owns his own body and also owns A's body, while A does not get to own his own body, is an obviously particularistic claim that makes arbitrary distinctions between two otherwise-similar agents, where the distinction is not grounded in any objective difference between A and B. Such particularistic norms or reasons are not universalizable; that is, they are *not reasons at all*, and thus are contrary to the purpose and nature of the activity of justificatory argumentation.

When assigning property title to a disputed or contested resource, such as A's body, some objective link must be found between the claimant and the resource, so that ownership can be established that can be recognized publicly by others and also acceptable as fair and as grounded in the nature of things. As I wrote elsewhere:

> [T]here are only two fundamental alternatives for acquiring rights in unowned property: (1) by doing something with the property with which no one else had ever done before, such as the mixing of labor or homesteading; or (2) by mere verbal declaration or decree. The second alternative is arbitrary and cannot serve to avoid conflicts. Only the first alternative, that of Lockean homesteading, establishes an objective link between a particular person and a particular scarce resource; thus, no one can deny the Lockean right to homestead unowned resources.[29]

Thus, as Hoppe has argued, property title has to be assigned to one of competing claimants based on "the existence of an objective, intersubjectively ascertainable link between owner and the" resource claimed.[30] In the case of one's own body, it is the unique relationship between a person and his body—*his direct and immediate control* over his body and the fact that, at least in some sense, a body is a given person and vice versa—that constitutes the objective link sufficient to give that person a claim to his body superior to those of typical third party claimants.

Moreover, any outsider who claims another's body cannot deny this objective link and its special status, since the outsider also necessarily presupposes this in his own case. This is so because, in seeking dominion over the other and in asserting ownership over the other's body, he has

---

[29] "Punishment and Proportionality" (ch. 5), Part III.F.
[30] Hoppe, A Theory of Socialism and Capitalism, 23.

to presuppose his own ownership of his body. In so doing, the outsider demonstrates that he *does* place a certain significance on this link, even as (at the same time) he disregards the significance of the other's link to his own body.[31]

For these reasons, libertarianism recognizes that only the self-ownership rule is universalizable and compatible with the *grundnorms* of peace, cooperation, and conflict-avoidance. We recognize that each person is *prima facie* the owner of his own body because, by virtue of his unique link to and connection with his own body—his direct and immediate control over it—he has a better claim to it than anyone else.[32]

---

31 For elaboration on this point, see "How We Come To Own Ourselves" (ch. 4), the sections "Direct Control" and "Summary"; "Defending Argumentation Ethics" (ch. 7), text following n.36; Hoppe, *A Theory of Socialism and Capitalism*, chaps. 1, 2, and 7. See also Hoppe, "The Idea of a Private Law Society":

> Outside of the Garden of Eden, in the realm of all-around scarcity, the solution [to the problem of social order—the need for rules to permit conflicts to be avoided] is provided by four interrelated rules... First, every person is the proper owner of his own physical body. Who else, if not Crusoe, should be the owner of Crusoe's body? Otherwise, would it not constitute a case of slavery, and is slavery not unjust as well as uneconomical?

32 See "How We Come to Own Ourselves" (ch. 4). Note that if an agent *A* has committed an act of aggression against *B*, as discussed in note 21, above, then *B*'s claim to be able to do things to *A*'s body without *A*'s permission *would* be making a distinction between *A* and *B*, but one grounded in the nature of things. As long as *A* and *B* have not attacked each other, there is no *relevant* distinction between them, rendering any unequal allocation of rights between them (such as *B* can own or hit *A*, but not vice-versa) non-universalizable, particularistic, and unacceptable in genuine argumentation. But matters are different if *A* has forcefully invaded *B*'s body without *B*'s consent. In this case we could say *A* is estopped from denying *B*'s similar right to invade *A*'s body, that is, to retaliate or defend himself. For similar reasons, critics of Hoppe's argumentation ethics who claim that the very possibility of a master arguing with his slave invalidates argumentation ethics are incorrect. In the case of chattel slavery, the master would be unable to argumentatively justify his use of force against the slave. He would be engaged in a contradiction: only peaceful, mutually-rights respecting norms can be argumentatively justified, because of the normatively peaceful presuppositions of argumentation itself; yet at the same time the master would be employing dominating force against the slave. The implicit logic of his stance in argumentation would condemn his enslaving actions. If he is consistent, he would have to quit arguing and simply behave like a brute, or release the slave. But if the "master" is a victim who is employing some kind of force in response to aggression, such as retaliatory force, then in this case there would be no contradiction involved if the master/victim were to engage in discourse with his slave/aggressor, since he could point to a justification for treating the slave/aggressor as a slave. I discuss this point also in "Defending Argumentation Ethics" (ch. 7).

D. Property in External Things

Libertarians apply similar reasoning in the case of other scarce resources—namely, external objects in the world. One key difference between bodies and external resources—and the reason for their separate treatment—is that the latter were at one point *unowned* and are *acquired by* human actors who are *already necessarily body-owners*. This difference implies a related distinction: as noted above, in the case of bodies, the idea of aggression being impermissible immediately implies (*prima facie*) self-ownership. In the case of external objects, however, we must identify who the owner of the object is before we can determine what uses of it constitute aggression.

As in the case with bodies, humans need to be able to use external objects as means to achieve various ends. Because these things are scarce (rivalrous), there is also the potential for conflict. And, as in the case with bodies, libertarians favor assigning property rights so as to permit the peaceful, conflict-free, productive use of such resources. Thus, as in the case with bodies, property is assigned to the person with the best claim or link to a given scarce resource—with the "best claim" standard based on the shared *grundnorms* of permitting peaceful, cooperative, conflict-free human interaction and use of resources.

Unlike human bodies, however, external objects are not parts of one's identity, are not directly controlled by one's will, and—significantly—they are *initially unowned*.[33] Here, the relevant objective link is *appropriation*—the transformation, possession, or embordering of a previously unowned resource, i.e., Lockean homesteading.[34] Under

---

[33] For further discussion of the difference between bodies and things homesteaded for purposes of rights, see "A Libertarian Theory of Contract" (ch. 9), Part III.B; "What Libertarianism Is" (ch. 2), the sections "Property in Bodies" and "Property in External Things," and, in particular, n. 26; and "How We Come to Own Ourselves" (ch. 4).

[34] On the nature of appropriation of unowned scarce resources, see Hoppe's and de Jasay's ideas quoted and discussed in Kinsella, "Thoughts on the Latecomer and Homesteading Ideas," and note 39, below, and accompanying text. In particular, see Hoppe, *A Theory of Socialism and Capitalism*, 24, 160–62, 169-71; and Anthony de Jasay, *Against Politics: On Government, Anarchy, and Order* (London & New York: Routledge, 1997), pp. 158 *et seq.*, 171 *et seq.*, *et pass.* (De Jasay is also discussed extensively in "Review of Anthony de Jasay, *Against Politics: On Government, Anarchy, and Order*" (ch. 20). See also "What Libertarianism Is" (ch. 2), at n.27.) De Jasay's argument presupposes the value of justice, efficiency, and order. Given these goals, he argues for three principles of politics: (1) if in doubt, abstain from

this approach, the first (prior) user of a previously unowned thing has a *prima facie* better claim than a second (later) claimant solely by virtue of his being earlier.

Why is appropriation the relevant link for determination of ownership? First, keep in mind that the question with respect to such scarce resources is: who is the resource's *owner*? Recall that ownership is the *right* to control, use, or possess,[35] while possession is *actual* control—"the *factual* authority that a person exercises over a corporeal thing."[36] The question is not who has physical possession, it is who has ownership. Asking who is the owner of a resource presupposes a crucial *distinction* between ownership and possession—between the right to control and actual control. And the answer has to take into account the nature of previously unowned things—namely, that they must at some point become owned by a first owner to become goods at all.

The answer must also take into account the presupposed goals of those seeking this answer: rules that permit conflict-free use of resources. For this reason, the answer cannot be whoever *has the resource or whoever is able to take it* is its owner. To hold such a view is to endorse might-makes-right, where ownership collapses into possession for want of

---

political action (pp. 147 *et seq.*); (2) the feasible is presumed free (pp. 158 *et seq.*); and (3) let exclusion stand (pp. 171 *et seq.*). In connection with principle (3), "let exclusion stand," de Jasay offers insightful comments about the nature of homesteading or appropriation of unowned goods. De Jasay equates property with its owner's "excluding" others from using it, for example by enclosing or fencing in immovable property (land) or finding or creating (and keeping) movable property (corporeal, tangible objects). He concludes that since an appropriated thing has no other owner, *prima facie* no one is entitled to object to the first possessor claiming ownership. Thus, the principle means "let ownership stand," i.e., that claims to ownership of property appropriated from the state of nature or acquired ultimately through a chain of title tracing back to such an appropriation should be respected. This is consistent with Hoppe's defense of the "natural" theory of property. *See* Hoppe, *A Theory of Socialism and Capitalism*, 21–25 and chap. 7. For further discussion of the nature of appropriation, see Jörg Guido Hülsmann, "The A Priori Foundations of Property Economics," *Q.J. Austrian Econ.* 7, no. 4 (Winter 2004; https://mises.org/library/priori-foundations-property-economics-0): 41–68, at 51.

[35] See note 11, above, and accompanying text.

[36] Yiannopoulos, *Louisiana Civil Law Treatise, Property*, § 301 (emphasis added); see also Louisiana Civil Code, art. 3421 ("Possession is the *detention* or *enjoyment* of a *corporeal thing*, movable or immovable, that one holds or exercises by himself or by another who keeps or exercises it in his name" [emphasis added]); and "What Libertarianism Is" (ch. 2), notes 28–29 and accompanying text, *et pass.*

a distinction.[37] Such a system, far from avoiding conflict, makes conflict inevitable.[38]

An aspect of ownership and property rights that is not often made explicit is what has been called the "prior-later distinction." This is the idea that it *makes a difference* who came first.[39] The prior-later distinction is implicit in the very idea of ownership, as the owner has a better claim—again, *prima facie*—to his resource than "latecomers."[40] If the owner did not have a better claim to the resource than someone who just comes later and physically wrests it from him, then he is not an owner, but merely the current user or possessor, and we are operating under the amoral might-makes-right principle instead of property rights and ownership.

More generally, latecomers' claims are inferior to those of prior possessors or claimants, who either homesteaded the resource or who can trace their title back to the homesteader or earlier owner.[41] The

---

[37] See, in this connection, the quote from Adam Smith in note 13, above.

[38] This is also, incidentally, the reason the mutualist "occupancy" position on land ownership is unlibertarian. See Kinsella, "A Critique of Mutualist Occupancy," *Mises Economic Blog* (Aug. 2, 2009); and "What Libertarianism Is" (ch. 2), at n.31.

[39] See Hoppe, *A Theory of Socialism and Capitalism*, 202; *idem*, "Of Common, Public, and Private Property and the Rationale for Total Privatization," in *The Great Fiction*; also Kinsella, "Thoughts on the Latecomer and Homesteading Ideas"; also "What Libertarianism Is" (ch. 2), n.32.

[40] See Kinsella, "Thoughts on the Latecomer and Homesteading Ideas."

[41] See Louisiana Code of Civil Procedure (https://www.legis.la.gov/legis/Laws_Toc.aspx?folder=68&level=Parent), art. 3653, providing:

To obtain a judgment recognizing his ownership of immovable property … the plaintiff … shall:
1. Prove that he has acquired ownership from a previous owner or by acquisitive prescription, if the court finds that the defendant is in possession thereof; or
2. Prove a *better title* thereto than the defendant, if the court finds that the latter is not in possession thereof.
When the titles of the parties are traced to a common author, he is presumed to be the previous owner. [emphasis added]

See also Louisiana Civil Code, arts. 526, 531–32; Yiannopoulos, *Louisiana Civil Law Treatise, Property*, §§ 255–79 and 347 *et pass.*; and "What Libertarianism Is" (ch. 2), at n.33.

One could make an analogy here between the prior-later distinction and how current title can, in principle, be traced back to the original act of appropriation of a given resource and Mises's regression theorem that explains the origin of the value of a commodity money by explaining its value today based on the change from its value yesterday, and so on, back to the original use of the commodity as money. On the latter, see Mises, *Human Action*, chap. 17, § 4. In fact, some of Mises's comments suggest this analogy. As he writes: "When we consider the natural components of goods, apart from the labour components they contain,

crucial importance of the prior-later distinction to libertarian theory is the reason Professor Hoppe repeatedly emphasizes it in his writing.[42]

and when we follow the legal title back, we must necessarily arrive at a point where this title originated in the appropriation of goods accessible to all." Ludwig von Mises, *Socialism: An Economic and Sociological Analysis*, J. Kahane, trans. (Indianapolis, Ind: Liberty Fund, 1981; https://oll.libertyfund.org/title/kahane-socialism-an-economic-and-sociological-analysis), chap. 1, §2, p. 32.

[42] See, e.g., Hoppe, *A Theory of Socialism and Capitalism*, p. 202; *idem*, *The Economics and Ethics of Private Property: Studies in Political Economy and Philosophy* (Auburn, Ala.: Mises Institute, 2006 [1993]; www.hanshoppe.com/eepp), pp. 327–30; see also discussion of these and related matters in Kinsella, "Thoughts on the Latecomer and Homesteading Ideas; "Defending Argumentation Ethics" (ch. 7); and "How We Come to Own Ourselves" (ch. 4). As Hoppe explains in "The Idea of a Private Law Society":

> every person is the proper owner of all nature-given goods that he has perceived as scarce and put to use by means of his body, *before* any other person. Indeed, who else, if not the first user, should be their owner? The second or third one? Were this so, however, the first person would not perform his act of original appropriation, and so the second person would become the first, and so on and on. That is, no one would ever be permitted to perform an act of original appropriation and mankind would instantly die out. Alternatively, the first user together with all late-comers become part-owners of the goods in question. Then conflict will not be avoided, however, for what is one to do if the various part-owners have incompatible ideas about what to do with the goods in question? This solution would also be uneconomical because it would reduce the incentive to utilize goods perceived as scarce for the first time.

See also, in this connection, de Jasay, *Against Politics*, further discussed and quoted in Kinsella, "Thoughts on the Latecomer and Homesteading Ideas." See also de Jasay's argument (note 34, above) that since an appropriated thing has no other owner, *prima facie* no one is entitled to object to the first possessor claiming ownership. De Jasay's "let exclusion stand" idea, along with the Hoppean emphasis on the prior-later distinction, sheds light on the nature of homesteading itself. Often the question is asked as to what types of acts constitute or are sufficient for homesteading (or "embordering" as Hoppe sometimes refers to it); what type of "labor" must be "mixed with" a thing; and to what property does the homesteading extend? What "counts" as "sufficient" homesteading? We can see that the answer to these questions is related to the issue of what the thing in dispute is. In other words, if *B* claims ownership of a thing possessed (or formerly possessed) by *A*, then the very framing of the dispute helps to identify what the thing is that is in dispute and what counts as possession of it. If *B* claims ownership of a given resource, he wants the right to control it, to a certain extent, and according to its nature. Then the question becomes, did someone else previously control it (whatever is in dispute), according to its nature; i.e., did someone else already homestead it, so that *B* is only a latecomer? This ties in with de Jasay's "let exclusion stand" principle, which rests on the idea that if someone is actually able to control a resource such that others are excluded, then this exclusion should "stand." Of course, the physical nature of a given scarce resource and the way in which humans use such resources will determine the nature of actions needed to "control" it and exclude others. See also on this Murray N. Rothbard's discussion of the "relevant technological unit" in "Law, Property Rights, and Air Pollution," in *Economic Controversies*; also B.K. Marcus, "The Spectrum Should Be Private

To sum up, the libertarian position on property rights is that in order to permit conflict-free, productive use of scarce resources, property titles to particular resources are assigned to particular owners. As noted above, however, the title assignment must not be random, arbitrary, or particularistic; instead, it has to be assigned based on "the existence of an objective, intersubjectively ascertainable link between owner" and the resource claimed.[43] As can be seen from the considerations presented above, the link is the physical transformation or embordering by the original homesteader, or a contractual chain of title traceable back to him (or to some previous possessor whose claim no one else can defeat).[44]

E. Consistency and Principle

Most people give some weight to some of the above considerations. In their eyes, a person is the owner of his own body—usually. A homesteader owns the resource he appropriates—unless the state takes it from him "by operation of law."[45] This is the principal distinction

---

Property: The Economics, History, and Future of Wireless Technology," *Mises Daily* (Oct. 29, 2004; https://mises.org/library/spectrum-should-be-private-property-economics-history-and-future-wireless-technology), and *idem*, "Radio Free Rothbard," *J. Libertarian Stud.* 20, no. 2 (Spring 2006; https://mises.org/library/radio-free-rothbard): 17–51.

[43] Hoppe, A Theory of Socialism and Capitalism, 23.

[44] On the title transfer theory of contract, see "A Libertarian Theory of Contract" (ch. 9). See also references in note 41, above, including art. 3653 of the Louisiana Code of Civil Procedure, providing that, in the case of a dispute over immovable property (land or realty), "When the titles of the parties are traced to a common author, he is presumed to be the previous owner." See also "What Libertarianism Is" (ch. 2), at n.33.

[45] State laws and constitutional provisions often pay lip service to the existence of various personal and property rights, but then take it back by recognizing the right of the state to regulate or infringe the right so long as it is "by law" or "not arbitrary." See, e.g., *Constitution of Russia*, art. 25 ("The home shall be inviolable. No one shall have the right to get into a house against the will of those living there, except for the cases established by a federal law or by court decision") and art. 34 ("Everyone shall have the right to freely use his or her abilities and property for entrepreneurial or any other economic activity not prohibited by the law"); *Constitution of Estonia*, art. 31 ("Estonian citizens shall have the right to engage in commercial activities and to form profit-making associations and leagues. The law may determine conditions and procedures for the exercise of this right"); *Universal Declaration of Human Rights*, art. 17 ("Everyone has the right to own property alone as well as in association with others... No one shall be arbitrarily deprived of his property"); art. 29(2) ("In the exercise of his rights and freedoms, everyone shall be subject only to such limitations as are determined by law solely for the purpose of securing due

between libertarians and typical non-libertarians (excluding crimi-nals, sociopaths, tyrants, government leaders, and so on): libertarians are consistently opposed to aggression, defined in terms of invasion of property borders, where property rights are understood to be assigned on the basis of self-ownership in the case of bodies. And in the case of non-bodily external objects, rights are understood on the basis of prior possession or homesteading and contractual transfer of title.

This framework for rights is motivated by the libertarian's consis-tent and principled valuing of peaceful interaction and cooperation—in short, of civilized behavior. Consider the Misesian view of human action. According to Mises, human action is aimed at alleviating some *felt uneasiness.*[46] Thus, the actor employs scarce means, according to his understanding of causal laws, to achieve various ends—ultimately, the removal of uneasiness.

Just as felt uneasiness in general is the cause of action aimed at alle-viating it, a certain type of "moral" uneasiness gives rise to the practice of normative justification aimed at its alleviation. To-wit, civilized man (evidently) feels morally uneasy at the prospect of violent struggles with others. On the one hand, he wants, for some practical reason, to control a given scarce resource and to use violence against another person, if nec-essary, to achieve this control. On the other hand, he also wants to avoid a wrongful use of force. Civilized man, for some reason, feels reluctance and uneasiness at the prospect of conflict or violent interaction with his fellow man. Perhaps he is reluctant to violently clash with others over certain objects because he has empathy with them.[47] Perhaps the instinct to cooperate is a result of social evolution. As Mises noted:

> There are people whose only aim is to improve the condition of their own ego. There are other people with whom awareness of the troubles of their

---

recognition and respect for the rights and freedoms of others and of meeting the just requirements of morality, public order and the general welfare in a democratic society"). Even the Thirteenth Amendment to the US Constitution, said to have abolished slavery, makes an exception for "crimes" (which, of course, the state can arbitrarily decree, such as drug crimes, tax evasion, evading conscription, etc.): "Neither slavery nor involuntary ser-vitude, *except as a punishment for crime whereof the party shall have been duly convicted,* shall exist within the United States, or any place subject to their jurisdiction." (Emphasis added.)

[46] Mises, *Human Action*, pp. 13–14, *et pass.*

[47] For further discussion of the role of empathy in the adoption of libertarian *grund-norms*, see note 26, above.

fellow men causes as much uneasiness as or even more uneasiness than their own wants.[48]

Whatever the reason, because of this uneasiness, when there is the potential for violent conflict, the civilized man *seeks justification* for the use of force or violence to control or defend the use of a desired scarce resource that some other person opposes or threatens. Empathy—or whatever spurs man to adopt the libertarian *grundnorms*—gives rise to a certain form of uneasiness, which gives rise to the attempt to justify violent action.

Civilized man may be thus defined as *he who seeks justification for the use of interpersonal violence.* When the inevitable need to engage in violence arises—for defense of life or property—civilized man seeks justification. Naturally, since this justification-seeking is done by people who are inclined to reason and peace (justification is after all a peaceful activity that necessarily takes place during discourse),[49] what they seek are rules that are fair, potentially acceptable to all relevant parties, grounded in the nature of things, and universalizable, and which permit conflict-free use of resources.

As noted in foregoing sections, libertarian property rights principles emerge as the only candidate that satisfies these criteria. We favor *prima facie* self-ownership of bodies as the only fair and justifiable body ownership rule that permits conflict-free use of the resources of our bodies. And in the case of resources external to human bodies, we favor property rights on the basis of prior possession or homesteading and contractual transfer of title. That is, the libertarian position on property rights in external objects is that in any dispute or contest over any particular scarce resource, the original homesteader—the person who appropriated the resource from its unowned status by embordering or transforming it (or his contractual transferee)—has a better claim than latecomers, those who did not appropriate the scarce resource. This is the only fair and justifiable property assignment rule that permits harmonious, productive, conflict-free use of such external scarce resources.

---

[48] Mises, *Human Action*, p. 14.

[49] As Hoppe explains, "Justification—proof, conjecture, refutation—is *argumentative* justification." Hoppe, *The Economics and Ethics of Private Property*, p. 384; see also ibid., p. 413 and Hoppe, *A Theory of Socialism and Capitalism*, p. 155, *et pass.*

Thus, if civilized man is he who seeks justification for the use of violence, the libertarian is he who is *serious* about this endeavor. He has a deep, principled, innate opposition to violence and an equally deep commitment to peace and cooperation.

For the foregoing reasons, libertarianism may be said to be the political philosophy that *consistently* favors social rules aimed at promoting peace, prosperity, and cooperation.[50] It recognizes that the only rules that are compatible with the *grundnorms* of civilized men are the self-ownership principle and the Lockean homesteading principle, applied as consistently as possible.

F. The State

Libertarians oppose all forms of crime (aggression). Thus we oppose not only private aggression: we also oppose *institutionalized* or public aggression. The opposition to institutionalized aggression is based on the view, espoused by Bastiat, that an act of aggression that is unjust for a private actor to perform remains illegitimate when performed by agencies, institutions, or collectives.[51] Murder or theft by ten, or a hundred, or a million, people is not better than theft by a lone criminal. It is for this reason that libertarians view the state itself as inherently criminal. For the state does not just happen to engage in institutionalized

---

[50] See also "What Libertarianism Is" (ch. 2). For this reason, Henry Hazlitt's proposed name "cooperatism" for the freedom philosophy has some appeal. See Henry Hazlitt, *The Foundations of Morality* (Irvington-on-Hudson, New York: Foundation for Economic Education, 1994 [1964]; https://fee.org/resources/foundations-of-morality/), p. xii; Kinsella, "The new libertarianism: anti-capitalist and socialist; or: I prefer Hazlitt's 'Cooperatism,'" *StephanKinsella.com* (June 19, 2009).

[51] As Bastiat writes:
Sometimes the law defends plunder and participates in it. Thus the beneficiaries are spared the shame and danger that their acts would otherwise involve... But how is this legal plunder to be identified? Quite simply. See if the law takes from some persons what belongs to them and gives it to the other persons to whom it doesn't belong. See if the law benefits one citizen at the expense of another by doing what the citizen himself cannot do without committing a crime. Then abolish that law without delay—No legal plunder; this is the principle of justice, peace, order, stability, harmony and logic.
Frederic Bastiat, *The Law*, 17–18 (Irvington-on-Hudson, N.Y.: Foundation for Economic Education, Dean Russell trans. 1950 [1850]; https://fee.org/resources/the-law/).

aggression; it necessarily does so on a systematic basis as part of the very nature of the state. As Hoppe notes:

> What must an agent be able to do to qualify as a state? This agent must be able to insist that all conflicts among the inhabitants of a given territory be brought to him for ultimate decision-making or be subject to his final review. In particular, this agent must be able to insist that all conflicts involving himself be adjudicated by him or his agent. And implied in the power to exclude all others from acting as ultimate judge, as the second defining characteristic of a state, is the agent's power to tax: to unilaterally determine the price that justice seekers must pay for his services.[52]

Such an agency necessarily commits aggression against either human bodies or owned property (usually both), either by taxing or by outlawing competition (usually both).[53] For these reasons, the consistent libertarian, in opposing aggression, is also anarchist.[54]

This also implies that legislation is illegitimate—as legislation requires a state—and that a law that is purely a result of legislation, and that cannot emerge in a decentralized legal order, is also invalid.[55]

---

[52] See Hans-Hermann Hoppe, "Reflections on the Origin and the Stability of the State," *LewRockwell.com* (June 23, 2008; https://www.lewrockwell.com/2008/06/hans-hermann-hoppe/to-battle-the-state/); also Kinsella, "The Nature of the State and Why Libertarians Hate It," *The Libertarian Standard* (May 3, 2010; http://libertarianstandard.com/2010/05/03/the-nature-of-the-state-and-why-libertarians-hate-it/).

[53] States invariably claim both powers, but either one alone is sufficient to give the state its unique status, and in fact each power implies the other. The power to tax alone would provide the agency with the ability to outcompete competing agencies that do not have this power, in the same way that public (government) schools outcompete private schools. Thus, the power to tax gives the taxing agency the practical ability to monopolize the field and outlaw or restrict competition. And the power to exclude competition alone would permit the monopolizing agency to charge monopoly prices for its services, akin to a tax.

[54] See "What It Means To Be an Anarcho-Capitalist" (ch. 3); also Jan Narveson, "The Anarchist's Case," in *Respecting Persons in Theory and Practice* (Lanham, Md.: Rowman & Littlefield, 2002; https://web.archive.org/web/20140914044736/www.arts.uwaterloo.ca/~jnarveso/articles/Anarchist's_Argument.pdf) and Hans-Hermann Hoppe, "Anarcho-Capitalism: An Annotated Bibliography," *LewRockwell.com* (Dec. 31, 2001; https://archive.lewrockwell.com/hoppe/hoppe5.html); Kinsella, "The Greatest Libertarian Books," *StephanKinsella.com* (Aug. 7, 2006); and other references in "Legislation and the Discovery of Law in a Free Society" (ch. 13), n.25.

[55] See "Legislation and the Discovery of Law in a Free Society" (ch. 13).

III. LIBERTARIANISM APPLIED TO IP

Given the foregoing libertarian (and Austrian-economics-informed) understanding of property rights, it is clear that the institutions of patent and copyright are simply indefensible. Here is why.

Copyrights pertain to "original works," such as books, articles, movies, and computer programs. They are grants by the state that permit the copyright holder to prevent others from using their own property—e.g., ink and paper—in certain ways. Thus copyright literally results in censorship—not surprising given its origins in suppressing the spread of ideas not favored by crown and church.[56] For example, shortly before his death, author J.D. Salinger, author of *Catcher in the Rye*, convinced U.S. courts to actually ban the publication of a novel called *60 Years Later: Coming Through the Rye*, based on copyright claims. And when a grocery store in Canada mistakenly sold 14 copies of a new Harry Potter book a few days before its official release on Saturday, July 16, 2005, a Canadian judge "ordered customers not to talk about the book, copy it, sell it or even read it before it is officially released at 12:01 a.m. July 16."[57]

Patents grant rights in "inventions"—useful machines or processes. They are grants by the state that permit the patentee to use the state's court system to prohibit others from using their *own property* in certain

---

[56] The Stop Online Piracy Act (SOPA), defeated a few years back through widespread Internet-based outrage, is a good example of a threat to freedom of expression in the name of copyright law. See Kinsella, "SOPA is the Symptom, Copyright is the Disease: The SOPA wakeup call to ABOLISH COPYRIGHT," *The Libertarian Standard* (Jan. 24, 2012). Regarding the origins of copyright, see Karl Fogel, "The Surprising History of Copyright and The Promise of a Post-Copyright World," *Question Copyright* (2006; https://perma.cc/DV92-TEH3); Michele Boldrin & David K Levine, *Against Intellectual Monopoly* (Cambridge University Press, 2008; www.againstmonopoly.org), ch. 2; Eric E. Johnson, "Intellectual Property and the Incentive Fallacy," *Florida State U. L. Rev.* 39 (2012; https://papers.ssrn.com/sol3/papers.cfm?abstract_id=1746343): 623–79, at 625 ("[T]he monopolies now understood as copyrights and patents were originally created by royal decree, bestowed as a form of favoritism and control. As the power of the monarchy dwindled, these chartered monopolies were reformed, and essentially by default, they wound up in the hands of authors and inventors."); Tom W. Bell, *Intellectual Privilege: Copyright, Common Law, and the Common Good* (Arlington, Virginia: Mercatus Center, 2014; https://perma.cc/JLC2-396Y), chap. 3. For more on the origins of IP, see references in "Introduction to *Origitent*" (ch. 16), n.3.

[57] See Kinsella, "The Patent, Copyright, Trademark, and Trade Secret Horror Files," *Mises Economics Blog* (Feb. 3, 2010).

ways—from reconfiguring their property according to a certain pattern or design described in the patent, or from using their property (including their own bodies) in a certain sequence of steps described in the patent.[58]

Both patent and copyright are simply state grants of monopoly privilege. In both cases, the state is assigning to *A* a right to control *B*'s property: *A* can force *B* not to engage in certain actions with *B*'s resources. Since ownership is the right to control, IP grants to *A* a co-ownership right (a negative servitude) in *B*'s property.[59] This clearly cannot be justified under libertarian principles. *B* already owns his property. With respect to him, *A* is a latecomer. *B* is the one who appropriated the property, not *A*. It is too late for *A* to homestead the resource in question—*B*, or his ancestor in title, already did that. The resource is no longer unowned. Granting *A* ownership rights in *B*'s property is quite obviously incompatible with basic libertarian principles. It is nothing more than redistribution of wealth. IP is therefore unlibertarian and unjustified.

Why, then, is this a contested issue? Why do some libertarians still believe in IP rights?

There are various arguments advanced for IP. Professor Nance notes that IP arguments:

> ... generally fall into two broad categories, deontological and consequentialist. The latter category embraces all theories that purport to justify property rights on the basis of the *good consequences* of their legal recognition, as distinct from their *moral rightness*.[60]

The consequentialist approach is implied by the Constitution's authorization for IP law, which reads:

---

[58] For examples, see ibid.

[59] See "*Against Intellectual Property* After Twenty Years: Looking Back and Looking Forward" (ch. 15), Part IV.B. As I noted in *AIP*, "ownership of an idea, or ideal object, effectively gives the IP owners a property right in every physical embodiment of that work or invention." See *AIP*, the section "IP Rights and Relation to Tangible Property," following n.29.

[60] Dale A. Nance, "Foreword: Owning Ideas," *Harv. J. L. & Pub. Pol'y* 13, no. 3 (Summer 1990): 757–74, p. 763.

The Congress shall have power ... To promote the progress of science and useful arts, by securing for limited times to authors and inventors the exclusive right to their respective writings and discoveries.[61]

Nance argues that most deontological arguments for IP—which fall into the "moral rights" tradition:

> ... fall into one of two sub-categories. First, they can be based upon the creator's deserving to own the fruits of her labors. This "labor theory" of property is generally associated with John Locke, whose influence on American thought is undeniable. An alternative theory, less familiar to Anglo-American thought, is that such rights are based upon respecting the creator's extension or reification of personality by the occupation of tangible or intangible things. The "personality theory" of property is most commonly attributed to the German philosopher Hegel and is better established in continental law.[62]

Consequentialist (incentive-based) arguments also have two major sub-categories: utilitarianism (maximizing preference satisfaction by

---

[61] U.S. Constitution, Art. I, Sec. 8, Cl. 8. Nance comments that "the reference to 'securing' (rather than, say, 'granting') the 'right' to authors and inventors suggests a deontological element as well." Nance, "Foreword: Owning Ideas," p. 763.

[62] Nance, "Foreword: Owning Ideas," p. 764 (citations omitted). Tom G. Palmer, who points out that Wilhelm von Humboldt also linked property rights to personality, critiques the personality justification for IP in "Are Patents and Copyrights Morally Justified? The Philosophy of Property Rights and Ideal Objects," *Harv. J. L. & Pub. Pol'y* 13, no. 3 (Summer 1990; https://perma.cc/J8LY-L4MQ): 817–65, at pp. 819–20 and Part III, esp. pp. 843–49). See also Justin Hughes, "The Philosophy of Intellectual Property," *Georgetown L.J.* 77, no. 2 (Dec. 1988; https://perma.cc/U4XX-5DZV): 287–366, p. 290 ("Properly elaborated, the labor and personality theories together exhaust the set of morally acceptable justifications of intellectual property. In short, intellectual property is either labor or personality, *or* it is theft."). See also Peter S. Menell, Mark A. Lemley, Robert P. Merges & Shyamkrishna Balganesh, *Intellectual Property in the New Technological Age: Volume I: Perspectives, Trade Secrets & Patents* (Clause 8 Publishing, 2022), chap. 1, § A, "Philosophical Perspectives."

The European reception to the personality justification for IP is one reason continental IP systems often include "moral rights," which, at least until recently, had been less common in Anglo-American jurisdictions. See, on the connection between personality rights in the civil (continental) law and moral rights, John Henry Merryman, "The Refrigerator of Bernard Buffet," *Hastings L. J.* 27, no. 5 (May 1976; https://repository.uclawsf.edu/hastings_law_journal/vol27/iss5/3/): 1023–49, p. 1025. For a more recent illustration of the application of such principles, see Daniel Grant, "Artist's lawsuit against school that sought to cover up his murals heads to appeals court," *The Art Newspaper* (Feb. 1, 2023; https://perma.cc/9EE3-49SA). See also Palmer, "Are Patents and Copyrights Morally Justified?", p. 820, n.6 and 841–43.

incentives) and teleology (using incentives to pursue values that deserve government support or encouragement). There are also other theories, sometimes overlapping with each other, such as contract-based arguments and those related to fairness, welfare, and culture.[63] I will address and criticize some of these arguments in the following sections.

A. Utilitarianism

One reason many libertarians favor IP is that is that they approach libertarianism from a utilitarian perspective instead of a principled one. They favor laws that increase general utility, or wealth. And they believe the state's propaganda that state-granted IP rights actually do increase general wealth.

The utilitarian perspective itself is bad enough, because all sorts of terrible policies could be justified this way: why not take half of Henry Ford's fortune and give it to the poor? Wouldn't the total welfare gains to the thousands of recipients be greater than Ford's reduced utility? After all, he would still be a billionaire afterwards. To take another example: if a man is extremely desperate for sex, could not his gain be greater than the loss suffered by his rape victim (say, if she is a prostitute), thus justifying rape, in some cases, on utilitarian grounds? Most people will recognize that there is something wrong with utilitarian reasoning if it could lead to such results.

---

[63] See, e.g., Hughes, "The Philosophy of Intellectual Property" (discussing the Lockean and Hegelian justifications); William Fisher, "Theories of Intellectual Property," in Stephen Munzer, ed., *New Essays in the Legal and Political Theory of Property* (Cambridge University Press, 2001; https://perma.cc/4YLX-P8JF); *idem*, "IP Theory" (https://perma.cc/Y48K-HCTV); Mick Soepboer, "Libertarian views on intellectual property law: An analysis of laissez-faire theories applied on the modern day IP system," University of Cape Town, School for Advanced Legal Studies, Master Dissertation Commercial Law (July 2009; https://perma.cc/4HR6-743V), §3.3; Edwin C. Hettinger, "Justifying Intellectual Property," *Philosophy & Public Affairs* 18, no. 1 (Winter 1989): 31–52; Vallabhi Rastogi, "Theories of Intellectual Property Rights," *Enhelion Blogs* (Feb. 27, 2021; https://perma.cc/U9D5-9V4U); Oishika Banerji, "Theories of protection of intellectual property rights," *IPleaders. in Blog* (Oct. 24, 2021; https://perma.cc/M2BU-T7BC); Kahsay Debesu Gebray, "Justifications for Claiming Intellectual Property Protection in Traditional Herbal Medicine and Biodiversity Conservation: Prospects and Challenges," *WIPO-WTO Colloquium Papers* vol. 4 (2013; https://perma.cc/3TXQ-LNFX); Adam D. Moore & Kenneth Einar Himma, "Intellectual Property," in Edward N. Zalta, ed., *Stanford Encyclopedia of Philosophy* (Stanford University, 2011; https://papers.ssrn.com/sol3/papers.cfm?abstract_id=1980917), §3.

But even if we ignore the ethical and methodological problems[64] with the utilitarian or wealth-maximization approach, what is bizarre is that utilitarian libertarians are in favor of IP when they have not demonstrated that IP does increase overall wealth. They merely assume that it does and then base their policy views on this assumption.

It is beyond dispute that the IP system imposes significant costs, in monetary terms alone, not to mention costs in terms of liberty.[65] The usual argument, that the incentive provided by IP law stimulates additional innovation and creativity, has not even been proven.[66] It is entirely possible (even likely, in my view) that the IP system not only imposes many billions of dollars of cost on society but actually impedes innovation, adding damage to injury.

But even if we assume that the IP system does stimulate some additional, valuable innovation, no one has established that the value of the purported gains is greater than the costs.[67] If one asks advocates of IP how they know there is a net gain, the result is silence (this is especially true of patent attorneys). They cannot point to any study to support their utilitarian contention; they usually just point to Article 1, Section 8 of the Constitution (if they are even aware of it), as if the backroom dealings of politicians two centuries ago are some sort of empirical evidence in favor of state grants of monopoly privilege.

In fact, as far as I am able to tell, *every* study that attempts to tally the costs and benefits of copyright or patent law concludes either that these schemes cost more than they are worth, that they actually reduce

---

[64] On the defects of utilitarianism and interpersonal utility comparisons, see the sources cited in *AIP*, at n. 40. See also Ronald M. Dworkin, "Is Wealth a Value?", *J. Legal Stud.* 9, no. 2 (March 1980; https://perma.cc/6WS4-LPPB): 191–226; *idem*, "Why Efficiency? — A Response to Professors Calabresi and Posner," *Hofstra L. Rev.* 8, no. 3 (Spring 1980; https://scholarlycommons.law.hofstra.edu/hlr/vol8/iss3/5/): 563–90.

[65] See studies cited in references in note 68, below; also Kinsella, "Reducing the Cost of IP Law," *Mises Daily* (Jan. 20, 2010); *idem*, "What Are the Costs of the Patent System?," *Mises Economics Blog* (Sep. 27, 2007); Julio H. Cole, "Patents and Copyrights: Do the Benefits Exceed the Costs?", *J. Libertarian Stud.* 15, no. 4 (Fall 2001; https://mises.org/library/patents-and-copyrights-do-benefits-exceed-costs-0): 79–105, the section "Costs of the Patent System," p. 89 *et seq.*

[66] See Kinsella, "Yet Another Study Finds Patents Do Not Encourage Innovation," *Mises Economics Blog* (July 2, 2009).

[67] See Boldrin & Levine, *Against Intellectual Monopoly*; Kinsella, "Yet Another Study Finds Patents Do Not Encourage Innovation"; and references in note 65, above and in note 68, below.

innovation, or that the research is inconclusive. There are no studies unambiguously showing a net societal gain.[68] There are only repetitions of state propaganda.

The Founders only had a hunch that copyrights and patents might "promote the Progress of Science and useful Arts"[69]—that the cost of this system would be "worth it." But they had no serious evidence. A hundred and fifty years later there was still none. In an exhaustive 1958 study prepared for the U.S. Senate Subcommittee On Patents, Trademarks & Copyrights, economist Fritz Machlup concluded:

> No economist, on the basis of present knowledge, could possibly state with certainty that the patent system, as it now operates, confers a net benefit or a net loss upon society. The best he can do is to state assumptions and make guesses about the extent to which reality corresponds to these assumptions… If we did not have a patent system, it would be irresponsible, on the basis of our present knowledge of its economic consequences, to recommend instituting one.[70]

And the empirical case for patents has not been shored up at all in the last fifty years. As George Priest wrote in 1986, "[I]n the current state of knowledge, economists know almost nothing about the effect on social welfare of the patent system or of other systems of intellectual property."[71] Similar comments are echoed by other researchers. François Lévêque and Yann Ménière, for example, of the Ecole des Mines de Paris (an engineering university), observed in 2004:

> The abolition or preservation of intellectual property protection is… not just a purely theoretical question. To decide on it from an economic viewpoint, we must be able to assess all the consequences of protection

---

[68] See Kinsella, "The Overwhelming Empirical Case Against Patent and Copyright," *C4SIF Blog* (Oct. 23, 2012); *idem*, "Legal Scholars: Thumbs Down on Patent and Copyright," *C4SIF Blog* (Oct. 23, 2012); *idem*, "KOL364 | Soho Forum Debate vs. Richard Epstein: Patent and Copyright Law Should Be Abolished," *Kinsella on Liberty Podcast* (Nov. 24, 2021); and *idem*, "Yet Another Study Finds Patents Do Not Encourage Innovation," *Mises Economics Blog* (July 2, 2009).

[69] U.S. Constitution, Art. I, Sec. 8, Cl. 8. For more background on the origins of copyright in America, see references in note 56, above.

[70] Fritz Machlup, *An Economic Review of the Patent System* (1958; https://mises.org/library/economic-review-patent-system), pp. 79–80.

[71] George Priest, "What Economists Can Tell Lawyers About Intellectual Property: Comment on Cheung," *Research in Law & Econ.* 8 (1986): 19–24.

and determine whether the total favorable effects for society outweigh the total negative effects. Unfortunately, this exercise [an economic analysis of the cost and benefits of intellectual property] is no more within our reach today than it was in Machlup's day [1950s].[72]

More recently, Boston University Law School Professors (and economists) Michael Meurer and Jim Bessen conclude that on average, the patent system discourages innovation. As they write: "[I]t seems unlikely that patents today are an effective policy instrument to encourage innovation overall" (p. 216). To the contrary, it seems clear that nowadays, "patents place a drag on innovation" (p. 146). In short, "the patent system fails on its own terms" (p. 145).[73]

And in a recent paper, economists Boldrin and Levine state:

> The case against patents can be summarized briefly: there is no empirical evidence that they serve to increase innovation and productivity.... This disconnect is at the root of what is called the "patent puzzle": in spite of the enormous increase in the number of patents and in the strength of their legal protection, the US economy has seen neither a dramatic acceleration in the rate of technological progress nor a major increase in the levels of research and development expenditure...
>
> Our preferred policy solution is to abolish patents entirely to find other legislative instruments, less open to lobbying and rent seeking, to foster innovation when there is clear evidence that laissez-faire undersupplies it.[74]

The Founders' hunch about IP was wrong. Copyright and patent are not necessary for creative or artistic works, invention, and innovation. They do not even encourage it. These monopoly privileges enrich some at the expense of others, distort the market and culture, and impoverish

---

[72] François Lévêque & Yann Ménière, *The Economics of Patents and Copyrights* (Berkely Electronic Press, 2004; https://papers.ssrn.com/sol3/papers.cfm?abstract_id=642622), at 102.

[73] James Bessen & Michael J. Meurer, Patent Failure: How Judges, Bureaucrats, and Lawyers Put Innovators at Risk (Princeton University Press, 2008).

[74] Michele Boldrin & David K. Levine, "The Case Against Patents," *J. Econ. Perspectives* 27 no. 1 (Winter 2013; https://perma.cc/Q5NT-9CGA): 3–22.

us all.[75] Given the available evidence, anyone who accepts utilitarianism should be *opposed* to patent and copyright.[76]

B. Libertarian Creationism[77]

Another reason why many libertarians favor IP is their confusion about the origin of property and property rights. They accept the careless observation that an individual can come to own things in three ways: through homesteading an unowned thing, by contractual exchange, and by creation. Therefore, they reason, if you own what you create, this is especially true for useful ideas. For example, libertarian philosopher Tibor Machan has stated: "[I]t would seem that so called intellectual stuff is an even better candidate for qualifying as private property than is, say, a tree or mountain."[78] And Objectivist philosopher David Kelley writes:

---

[75] See, e.g., Kinsella, "Leveraging IP," *Mises Economics Blog* (Aug. 1, 2010); *idem*, "Milton Friedman (and Rothbard) on the Distorting and Skewing Effect of Patents," *C4SIF Blog* (July 3, 2011); Matt Ridley, *How Innovation Works: And Why It Flourishes in Freedom* (Harper, 2020), p. 347 ("patents tend to favour inventions rather than innovations: upstream discoveries of principles, rather than downstream adaptation of devices to the market.").

[76] Another problem with the wealth-maximization approach is that it has no logical stopping point. If adding (and increasing) IP protection is a cost worth paying to stimulate additional innovation and creation over what would occur on a free market—that is, if the amount of innovation and creation absent IP law is *not enough*, then how do we know that we have enough now, under a system of patent and copyright? Maybe the penalties or terms should be increased: impose capital punishment, triple the patent and copyright term. And what if there still is not enough? Why don't we expropriate taxpayer funds and set up a government award or prize system, like a huge state-run Nobel prize with thousands of winners, to hand out to deserving innovators, so as to incentivize even more innovation? Incredibly, this has been suggested, too—even by Nobel Prize winners. See Kinsella, "$30 Billion Taxfunded Innovation Contracts: The 'Progressive-Libertarian' Solution," *Mises Economics Blog* (Nov. 23, 2008); *idem*, "Libertarian Favors $80 Billion Annual Tax-Funded 'Medical Innovation Prize Fund,'" *Mises Economic Blog* (Aug. 12, 2008).

[77] See also Part IV.C in *"Against Intellectual Property* After Twenty Years: Looking Back and Looking Forward" (ch. 15).

[78] Tibor Machan, "Intellectual Property and the Right to Private Property," Mises.org working paper (2006; https://mises.org/wire/new-working-paper-machan-ip), discussed in Kinsella, "Owning Thoughts and Labor," *Mises Economics Blog* (Dec. 11, 2006), and in *idem*, "Remembering Tibor Machan, Libertarian Mentor and Friend: Reflections on a Giant," *StephanKinsella.com* (April 19, 2016). See also the similar "ontology" based argument of J. Neil Schulman, mentioned in "Conversation with Schulman about Logorights and Media-Carried Property" (ch. 17).

> [T]he essential basis of property rights lies in the phenomenon of cre-
> ating value… [F]or things that one has created, such as a new product,
> one's act of creation is the source of the right, regardless of scarcity.[79]

The mistake is the notion that creation is an independent source of
ownership, independent from homesteading and contracting. Yet it is
easy to see that "creation" is neither necessary nor sufficient as a source
of ownership. If you carve a statue using your own hunk of marble,
you own the resulting creation because you already owned the marble.
You owned it before, and you own it now.[80] And if you homestead an

---

[79] Quoted in Kinsella, "Rand on IP, Owning 'Values', and 'Rearrangement Rights,'"
Mises Economics Blog (Nov. 16, 2009). The idea that you own what you "produce" or "create"
is widespread. See, e.g., Kirzner on Mill:

> "The institution of property," John Stuart Mill remarked, "when limited to its
> essential elements, consists in the recognition, in each person, of a right to the
> exclusive disposal of what he or she have produced by their own exertions, or re-
> ceived either by gift or by fair agreement, without force or fraud, from those who
> produced it. The foundation of the whole is the right of producers to what they
> themselves have produced." The purpose of this paper is to point out the ambiguity
> of the phrase "what a man has produced", and to draw attention, in particular, to
> one significant, economically valid, meaning of the term,—a meaning involving
> the concept of entrepreneurship—which seems to have been overlooked almost
> entirely…. Precision in applying the term "what a man has produced" seems to be
> of considerable importance.

Israel M. Kirzner, "Producer, Entrepreneur, and the Right to Property," *Reason Papers*
No. 1 (Fall 1974; https://reasonpapers.com/archives/): 1–17, p.1, quoting J.S. Mill, *Prin-
ciples of Political Economy* (Ashley Edition, Londen, 1923), p. 218. As another example,
patent attorney Dale Halling writes: "A patent is a property right it is not a monopoly.
Like all property the source of the property right is creation." See comments in Kinsella,
"Pro-IP Libertarians Upset about FTC Poaching Patent Turf," *Mises Economics Blog*
(Aug. 24, 2011).

[80] See, on this point, Sheldon Richman, "Intellectual 'Property' Versus Real Property:
What Are Copyrights and What Do They Mean for Liberty?," *The Freeman* (12 June 2009;
https://fee.org/resources/intellectual-property-versus-real-property):

> If someone writes or composes an original work or invents something new, the
> argument goes, he or she should own it because it would not have existed without
> the creator. I submit, however, that as important as creativity is to human flourish-
> ing, it is not the source of ownership of produced goods… So what is the source?
> Prior ownership of the inputs through purchase, gift, or original appropriation.
> This is sufficient to establish ownership of the output. Ideas contribute no neces-
> sary additional factor. If I build a model airplane out of wood and glue, I own it
> not because of any idea in my head, but because I owned the wood, the glue, and
> myself. If Howard Roark's evil twin trespassed on your land and, *using your materi-
> als*, built the most creatively original house ever seen, would he own it? Of course
> not. *You* would—and you'd have every right to tear it down.

unowned resource, such as a field, by using it and thereby establishing publicly visible borders, you own it because this first use and embordering gives you a better claim than latecomers.[81] Thus, creation is not necessary for ownership to arise.

But suppose you carve a statue in someone else's marble, either without permission or with permission, such as when an employee works with his employer's marble by contract. You do not own the resulting statue, even though you "created" it. If you are using marble stolen from another person, your vandalizing it does not take away the owner's claims to it. And if you are working on your employer's marble, he owns the resulting statue. Thus, creation is not sufficient for ownership rights to arise.

This is not to deny the importance of knowledge, or creation and innovation. Human action, which necessarily employs (ownable) scarce means, is also *informed* by technical knowledge of causal laws or other practical information. An actor's knowledge, beliefs and values affect the ends he chooses to pursue and the causal means he selects to achieve the end sought (as discussed further in the next section).

It is true that creation is an important means of increasing *wealth*. As Hoppe has observed,

> One can acquire and increase wealth either through homesteading, *production* and contractual exchange, or by expropriating and exploit-

See also Dan Sanchez, "The Fruit of Your Labor... is a good, not its form," *Medium* (Oct. 30, 2014; https://perma.cc/GD28-JS44).

[81] See "What Libertarianism Is" (ch. 2); Hoppe, *A Theory of Socialism and Capitalism*, chaps. 1, 2, and 7; David Hume, *A Treatise of Human Nature*, Selby-Bigge, ed. (Oxford, 1968), Book III, Part II, Section III n16:
> Some philosophers account for the right of occupation, by saying, that every one has a property in his own labour; and when he joins that labour to any thing, it gives him the property of the whole: But, 1. There are several kinds of occupation, where we cannot be said to join our labour to the object we acquire: As when we possess a meadow by grazing our cattle upon it. 2. This accounts for the matter by means of accession; which is taking a needless circuit. 3. We cannot be said to join our labour to any thing but in a figurative sense. Properly speaking, we only make an alteration on it by our labour. This forms a relation betwixt us and the object; and thence arises the property, according to the preceding principles.

See also *"Against Intellectual Property* After Twenty Years: Looking Back and Looking Forward" (ch. 15), at notes 56–57.

ing homesteaders, producers, or contractual exchangers. There are no other ways.[82]

While production or creation can certainly increase *wealth*, it is not an independent source of ownership or rights. Production is not the creation of new matter; it is the transformation of things from one form to another—the transformation of things someone already owns, either the producer or someone else. Using your labor and creativity to transform your property into more valuable finished products gives you greater wealth, but not additional property rights.[83] (If you transform someone else's property, he owns the resulting transformed thing, even if it is now more valuable.)

In other words, creation is not the basis for property rights in scarce goods. Creating something does not make you its owner. A mother who creates a child does not own it. A vandal who creates a mural on someone else's property does not own it. An employee who creates a consumer device using his employer's facilities and materials does not own it. Creation is not sufficient to generate rights. And those who

---

[82] Hans-Hermann Hoppe, "Banking, Nation States, and International Politics: A Sociological Reconstruction of the Present Economic Order," in *The Economics and Ethics of Private Property*, at 50 (emphasis added).

[83] See Kinsella, "Locke on IP; Mises, Rothbard, and Rand on Creation, Production, and 'Rearranging,'" *Mises Economics Blog* (Sep. 29, 2010). See also Pierre-Joseph Proudhon, "Les Majorats littéraires," Luis Sundkvist, trans. (1868), in Lionel Bently & Martin Kretschmer, eds., *Primary Sources on Copyright* (1450–1900; www.copyrighthistory.org/cam/index.php), at pp. 11 *et seq.*:

> The masters of science instruct us all—and the supporters of literary property are the first to argue this—that man does not have the capability of creating a single atom of matter; that all his activity consists of appropriating the forces of nature, of channeling these and modifying their effects, of composing or decomposing substances, of changing their forms, and, by this steering of the natural forces, by this transformation of substances, by this separation of elements, of making nature [*la création*] more useful, more fertile, more beneficial, more brilliant, more profitable. So that all human production consists (1°) of an expression of ideas; (2°) a displacement of matter.

This is essentially Spooner's mistake: he has a broad definition of "wealth," which includes knowledge, ideas, inventions, etc., and then assumes that property is just wealth that can be possessed. Thus, ideas can "be property." See Spooner, "The Law of Intellectual Property or an Essay on the Right of Authors and Inventors to a Perpetual Property in Their Ideas," §§ 2–3, *et pass.* This also highlights the importance of using the term property to refer to the property rights individuals have with respect to owned resources, as I note in "What Libertarianism Is" (ch. 2), Appendix I.

transform their own property to create a more valuable product own the resulting product because they already owned the original material, not because of creation. The creator of an idea does not thereby own the idea.[84]

C. The Contractual Approach

Many libertarians also argue that some form of copyright or patent could be created by contractual techniques—for example, by selling a patterned medium (book, CD, etc.) or useful machine to a buyer on the condition that it not be copied or revealed to others. For example, Brown sells an innovative mousetrap to Green on the condition that Green not reproduce it.[85]

For such contractual IP to emulate statutory IP, however, it has to bind not only seller and buyer, but all third parties. The contract between buyer and seller cannot do this—it binds only the buyer and seller. In the example given above, even if Green agrees not to copy Brown's mousetrap, Black has no agreement with Brown. Brown has no contractual right to prevent Black from using Black's own property in accordance with whatever knowledge or information Black has.

Now if Green were to sell Brown's watch to Black without Brown's permission, most libertarians would say that Brown still owns the watch

---

[84] In fact, as Proudhon notes:

[I]n the strict sense of the term, we do not produce our ideas any more than we produce physical substances. Man does not create his ideas—he receives them. He does not at all make truth—he discovers it. He invents neither beauty, nor justice—they reveal themselves to his soul spontaneously, like the conceptions of metaphysics, in the perception of the phenomena of the world, in the relations between things. The intelligible estate [*fonds*] of nature is, in the same way as its tangible estate, outside of our domain: neither reason, nor the substance of things are ours. Even that very ideal which we dream about, which we pursue, and which causes us to commit so many acts of folly—this mirage of our understanding and our heart—we are not its creators, we are simply those who are able to see it.

Proudhon, "Les Majorats littéraires," at p. 12. Or as Isaac Newton put it, "If I have seen further it is only by standing on the shoulders of giants." Letter to Robert Hooke (February 15, 1676).

[85] This is Rothbard's example, from "Knowledge, True and False," in *The Ethics of Liberty*, which is discussed at pp. 51–55 in *AIP*. See also Kinsella, "Richard O. Hammer: Intellectual Property Rights Viewed As Contracts," *C4SIF Blog* (June 13, 2021).

and could take it from Black. Why doesn't a similar logic apply in the case of the mousetrap design?

The difference is that the watch is a scarce resource that has an owner, while the mousetrap design is merely information, which is not a type of thing that can be owned. The watch is a scarce resource still owned by Brown. Black needs Brown's consent to use it. But in the mousetrap case, Black merely learns how to make a mousetrap. He uses this information to make a mousetrap, by means of his own body and property. He doesn't need Brown's permission, simply because he is not using Brown's property.

The IP advocate thus has to say that Brown owns the information about how his mousetrap is configured. This move is question begging, however, since it asserts what is to be shown: that there are intellectual property rights.

If Black does not return Green's watch, Green is without his watch precisely because the watch is a scarce good. But Black's knowing how to make a mousetrap does not take away Green's own mousetrap-making knowledge, highlighting the nonscarce nature of information or patterns. In short, Brown may retake his property from Black but has no right to prevent Black from using information to guide his actions. Thus, the contract approach fails as well.[86]

D. Learning, Emulation, and Knowledge in Human Action

Another way to understand the error in treating information, ideas, recipes, and patterns as ownable property is to consider IP in the context of human action. Mises explains that "[t]o act means: to strive

---

[86] See also Wendy McElroy's perceptive comments on the "copyright by contract" approach in her note to me reprinted in Kinsella, "McElroy: 'On the Subject of Intellectual Property' (1981)," *C4SIF Blog* (March 19, 2013); also Boudewijn Bouckaert, "What is Property?", *Harv. J. L. & Pub. Pol'y* 13, no. 3 (Summer 1990): 775–816, pp. 795 & 804–805. On the title-transfer theory of contract, see "A Libertarian Theory of Contract" (ch. 9). For criticism of Rothbard's attempt to justify something he confusingly calls "common-law copyright" (since that is something totally different in the common law) by use of contracts, see Kinsella, *AIP*, the section "Contract vs. Reserved Rights." Schulman also seems to think that IP, or "logorights," is somehow "an intellectual artifact of contract law," whatever that means. See "Conversation with Schulman about Logorights and Media-Carried Property" (ch. 17).

after ends, that is, to choose a goal and to resort to means in order to attain the goal sought."[87] Knowledge and information of course play a key role in action as well. As Mises puts it, "Action … is not simply behavior, but behavior begot by judgments of value, aiming at a definite end and *guided by ideas concerning the suitability or unsuitability of definite means.*"[88]

Rothbard further elaborates on the importance of knowledge to *guide* actions:

> There is another unique type of factor of production that is indispensable in every stage of every production process. This is the "technological idea" of how to proceed from one stage to another and finally to arrive at the desired consumers' good. This is but an application of the analysis above, namely, that for any action, there must be some *plan* or idea of the actor about how to use things as means, as definite pathways, to desired ends. Without such plans or ideas, there would be no action. These plans may be called *recipes*; they are ideas of recipes that the actor uses to arrive at his goal. A *recipe* must be present at each stage of each production process from which the actor proceeds to a later stage. The actor must have a recipe for transforming iron into steel, wheat into flour, bread and ham into sandwiches, etc.[89]

Moreover, "[m]eans are necessarily always limited, i.e. scarce, with regard to the services for which man wants to use them."[90] This is why property rights emerged. Use of a resource by one person excludes use

---

[87] Ludwig von Mises, *The Ultimate Foundation of Economic Science: An Essay on Method* (Princeton, N.J.: D. Van Nostrand Company, Inc., 1962; https://mises.org/library/ultimate-foundation-economic-science), p. 4.

[88] Mises, *Human Action*, 93.

[89] Murray N. Rothbard, *Man, Economy, and State, with Power and Market*, Scholars ed., second ed. (Auburn, Ala.: Mises Institute, 2009; https://mises.org/library/man-economy-and-state-power-and-market), p. 11. See also See also Guido Hülsmann, "Knowledge, Judgment, and the Use of Property," *Rev. Austrian Econ.* 10, no. 1 (1997; https://perma.cc/DKQ8-JX45): 23–48, p. 44 ("The quantities of means we can dispose of—our property—are always limited. Thus, choice implies that some of our ends must remain unfulfilled. We steadily run the danger of pursuing ends that are less important than the ends that could have been pursued. We have to choose the supposedly most important action, though what we choose is how we use our property Action means to employ our property in the pursuit of what appears to be the most important ends.… *In choosing the most important action we implicitly select some parts of our technological knowledge for application.*"; emphasis added). See also the related discussion in "Goods, Scarce and Nonscarce" (ch. 18), text at n.32.

[90] Ibid.

by another. Property rights are assigned to scarce resources to permit them to be used productively and cooperatively, and to permit conflict to be avoided. In contrast, ownership of the information that guides action is not necessary. For example, two people who each own the ingredients (scarce goods) can simultaneously make a cake with the same recipe.

Material progress is made over time because information is *not* scarce. It can be infinitely multiplied, learned, taught, and built on. The more patterns, recipes, and causal laws that are known, the greater the wealth multiplier as individuals engage in ever-more efficient and productive actions. It is *good* that ideas are infinitely reproducible. There is no need to impose artificial scarcity on ideas to make them more like physical resources, which—unfortunately—*are* scarce.[91]

E. IP, Legislation, and the State

A final problem with IP remains: patent and copyright are statutory schemes, schemes that can be constructed only by legislation, and therefore *have always* been constructed by legislation. A patent or copyright code could no more arise in the decentralized, case-based legal system of a free society than could the Americans with Disabilities Act or Medicare. IP requires both a legislature and a state. For libertarians who reject the legitimacy of the state,[92] or legislated law,[93] this is the final nail in the IP coffin.

IV. IMAGINING AN IP-FREE WORLD

It is fairly straightforward to explain what is wrong with IP: patent and copyright are artificial state-granted monopoly privileges that undercut and invade property rights, as elaborated above. But the consequen-

---

[91] For elaboration on the ideas discussed in this section, see Kinsella, "Intellectual Freedom and Learning Versus Patent and Copyright" and "*Against Intellectual Property* After Twenty Years: Looking Back and Looking Forward" (ch. 15), the section "The Separate Roles of Knowledge and Means in Action."

[92] See note 54, above, and accompanying text.

[93] See "Legislation and the Discovery of Law in a Free Society" (ch. 13).

tialist and utilitarian mindset is so entrenched that even people who see the ethical problems with IP law sometimes demand that the IP opponent explain how innovation would be funded in an IP-free world. How would authors make money? How would blockbuster movies be funded? Why would anyone invent if they could not get a patent? How could companies afford to develop pharmaceuticals if they had to face competition?

When I see such demands and questions, I am reminded of John Hasnas's comments in his classic article "The Myth of the Rule of Law."[94] After arguing against the state and for anarchy, Hasnas observes:

> What would a free market in legal services be like?
>
> I am always tempted to give the honest and accurate response to this challenge, which is that to ask the question is to miss the point. If human beings had the wisdom and knowledge-generating capacity to be able to describe how a free market would work, that would be the strongest possible argument for central planning. One advocates a free market not because of some moral imprimatur written across the heavens, but because it is impossible for human beings to amass the knowledge of local conditions and the predictive capacity necessary to effectively organize economic relationships among millions of individuals. It is possible to describe what a free market in shoes would be like *because we have one*. But such a description is merely an observation of the current state of a functioning market, not a projection of how human beings would organize themselves to supply a currently non-marketed good. To demand that an advocate of free market law (or Socrates of Monozizea, for that matter) describe in advance how markets would supply legal services (or shoes) is to issue an impossible challenge. Further, for an advocate of free market law (or Socrates) to even accept this challenge would be to engage in self-defeating activity since the more successfully he or she could describe how the law (or shoe) market would function, the more he or she would prove that it could be run by state planners. Free markets supply human wants better than state monopolies precisely because they allow an unlimited number of suppliers to attempt to do so. By patronizing those who most effectively meet their particular needs and causing those who do not to fail, consumers determine the optimal method of supply. If it were pos-

---

94 John Hasnas, "The Myth of the Rule of Law," *Wis. L. Rev.* 1995, no. 1 (1995; https://www.copblock.org/40719/myth-rule-law-john-hasnas/): 199–234.

sible to specify in advance what the outcome of this process of selection would be, there would be no need for the process itself.

In other words: the answer such a challenge might be, as Leonard Read said, "I don't know."[95]

To return to the current subject: with the advent of state IP legislation, the state has interrupted and preempted whatever other customs, business arrangements, contractual regimes and practices, and so on, that would no doubt have arisen in its absence. So it is natural for those accustomed to IP to be a bit nervous about replacing the current flawed IP system with… a vacuum. It is natural for them to wonder, "Well, what would occur in its absence?" As noted above, the reason we are not sure what an IP-free world would look like is that the state has snuffed out alternative institutions and practices.

Consider the analogous situation in which the FCC preempted and monopolized the field of property rights in airwaves just as they were starting to develop in the common law. Nowadays people are used to the idea of the state regulating and parceling out airwave or spectrum rights and might imagine there would be chaos if the FCC were abolished. Still, we have some idea as to what property rights might emerge in airwaves absent central state involvement.[96]

In any case, because people are bound to ask the inevitable: we IP opponents try to come up with some predictions and solutions and answers. Thus, in the end we must agree with Hasnas:

> Although I am tempted to give this response, I never do. This is because, although true, it never persuades. Instead, it is usually interpreted as an appeal for blind faith in the free market, and the failure to provide a specific explanation as to how such a market would provide legal services is interpreted as proof that it cannot. Therefore, despite the self-defeating nature of the attempt, I usually do try to suggest how a free market in law might work.

---

95 Leonard Read, "I Don't Know," *Mises Daily* (Nov. 2, 2011 [1965]; https://mises.org/library/i-dont-know).

96 For more on this see David Kelley & Roger Donway, *Laissez Parler: Freedom in the Electronic Media* (1985), as discussed in Kinsella, "Why Airwaves (Electromagnetic Spectra) Are (Arguably) Property," *Mises Economics Blog* (Aug. 9, 2009).

So, how would content creators be rewarded in an IP-free market? First, we must recognize that what advocates of IP want is a world where competition is tamed. Their view is that:

> Governments adopt intellectual property laws in the belief that a privileged, monopolistic domain operating on the margins of the free-market economy promotes long-term cultural and technological progress better than a regime of *unbridled competition*.[97]

Thus, they favor the grant of monopolies by the state that shelter various market actors from competition. But in a free society with no IP rights, content creators and innovators would face competition just as others do.

It must be recognized that the position of the creator of content that is easily copied or imitated is no different in kind from that of any other entrepreneur on the market. Every producer faces competition. If a given entrepreneur makes profit, competitors notice this and start to compete, eroding the initial profits made. Thus market actors continually seek to innovate and find new ways to please consumers in the pursuit of elusive profits. Most producers face a variety of costs, including costs of exclusion. For example:

> Movie theaters, for example, invest in exclusion devices like ticket windows, walls, and ushers, all designed to exclude non-contributors from enjoyment of service. Alternatively, of course, movie owners could set up projectors and screens in public parks and then attempt to prevent passers-by from watching, or they could ask government to force all non-contributors to wear special glasses which prevent them from enjoying the movie. "Drive-ins," faced with the prospect of free riders peering over the walls, installed—at considerable expense—individual speakers for each car, thus rendering the publicly available visual part of the movie of little interest .... The costs of exclusion are involved in the production of virtually every good imaginable.[98]

---

[97] Jerome H. Reichman, "Charting the Collapse of the Patent-Copyright Dichotomy: Premises for a Restructured International Intellectual Property System," *Cardozo Arts & Ent. L.J.* 13 (1995; https://scholarship.law.duke.edu/faculty_scholarship/685/): 475 (emphasis added), quoted in Kinsella, "Intellectual Property Advocates Hate Competition," *Mises Economics Blog* (July 19, 2011).

[98] Tom G. Palmer, "Intellectual Property: A Non-Posnerian Law and Economics Approach," *Hamline L. Rev.* 12, no. 2 (Spring 1989; https://perma.cc/DH7K-ZCRV): 261–304, at 284–85, quoted in *AIP*, n.67.

What this means is that it is the responsibility of entrepreneurs whose products are easily imitated to find a way to profit, and that they may not use state force to stop competitors. In a sense, this is already the situation facing content creators. Piracy is real and is not going away, unless the big media special interests succeed in having the Internet shut down. Even in the face of widespread file sharing and disregard for copyright, creativity is at an all time high.[99] The only solution to piracy and file sharing is to offer a better service.[100] For example, offering DRM-free movies or music for a reasonable price, as comedian Louis C.K. did, earning $1M in about two weeks.[101] Or use crowd-source fundraising mechanisms like Kickstarter—computer game company Double Fine Productions recently used Kickstarter to raise $400,000 to fund a new adventure game ($300,000 for game development, and $100,000 to make a documentary about the process). In fact, as of this writing, $1,095,783 had been raised, from 28,921 backers, in *one day*.[102]

And there are a variety of tactics people can adopt in different industries. A singer or musician can garner fans from his recordings, even if they are distributed for free, and charge fees for concerts. Movie studios can sell tickets to movies that have advantages over home viewing, such as better sound, 3D, large screens, and the like. Most non-fiction authors—such as bloggers or law professors publishing law review articles for free—do not get paid now, but engage in this activity to enhance their reputation and employability, for ad revenues, or for other reasons. A novelist could become popular with her first

---

[99] Mike Masnick, "We're Living In the Most Creative Time In History," *Techdirt* (Feb. 12, 2012; https://perma.cc/F6HY-QHG9).

[100] See, e.g., Mike Masnick, "Hollywood Wants To Kill Piracy? No Problem: Just Offer Something Better," *Techdirt* (Feb. 6, 2012; https://perma.cc/73TB-YQX8); Paul Tassi, "You Will Never Kill Piracy, and Piracy Will Never Kill You," *Forbes* (Feb. 3, 2012; https://perma.cc/23W2-E2FT).

[101] Kinsella, "Comedian Louis C.K. Makes $1 Million Selling DRM Free Video via PayPal on his own website," *C4SIF.org* (Dec. 22, 2011).

[102] See Kickstarter, https://perma.cc/MYH4-G38W. See also Mike Masnick, "People Rushing To Give Hundreds Of Thousands Of Dollars In Just Hours For Brand New Adventure Game," *Techdirt* (Feb. 9, 2012; https://www.techdirt.com/2012/02/09/people-rushing-to-give-hundreds-thousands-dollars-just-hours-brand-new-adventure-game/); Kyle Orland, "Double Fine seeks to cut out publishers with Kickstarter-funded adventure," *ars technica* (Feb. 9, 2012; https://arstechnica.com/gaming/2012/02/double-fine-seeks-to-cut-out-publishers-with-kickstarter-funded-adventure/).

few books and then get fans to pre-purchase the sequel before releasing it or get paid to be a consultant on/endorser of a movie version.[103]

We cannot forecast all the ways human entrepreneurial creativity will discover to profit and flourish in a free society with no state-granted protections from competition. But there is every reason to think that in a private-law society, we would be unimaginably richer and freer, with more diversity and intellectual creativity than ever before. The state is nothing but a hindrance to everything good about human society.

---

[103] Kinsella, "Conversation with an author about copyright and publishing in a free society," *C4SIF.org* (Jan. 23, 2012); see also idem, "Examples of Ways Content Creators Can Profit Without Intellectual Property," *StephanKinsella.com* (July 28, 2010); *idem,* "Innovations that Thrive Without IP," *StephanKinsella.com* (Aug. 9, 2010); and *idem, Do Business Without Intellectual Property* (Liberty.me, 2014).

15

Against Intellectual Property After Twenty Years: Looking Back and Looking Forward

This chapter is previously unpublished, other than a working draft posted on c4sif.org. It provides a perspective on the IP debates since my *Against Intellectual Property* (*AIP*) was published in 2001, and provides an overview of newer arguments about IP that I've made in the twenty-plus years since the publication of *AIP*. It also discusses changes I would make to the original arguments presented in *AIP*. This chapter complements chapter 14, which itself was originally published about a decade after *AIP*.

I. BACKGROUND

Against Intellectual Property originated as a *Journal of Libertarian Studies* article in 2001.[1] At the time there was less interest among libertarians

---

[1] "Against Intellectual Property" first appeared as part of the symposium Applications of Libertarian Legal Theory, published in the *Journal of Libertarian Studies*, vol. 15, no. 2

in the topic of intellectual property (IP) than there is now. Libertarian attention was more focused on issues such as taxes, war, central banking, the drug war, government education, asset forfeiture, business regulations, civil liberties, and so on. Not so much on patent and copyright, the two primary forms of IP.

I had no reason to think it was an especially important issue, but I had always been dissatisfied with various libertarian arguments for IP, and it kept nagging at me throughout college and law school. Ayn Rand's brief article on patent and copyright, for example, included strained arguments as to why a 17 year patent term and a life-plus-50 year copyright term were just about right.[2] She also offered a confused argument as to why it was fair for the first guy to race to the patent office to get a monopoly that could be used against an independent inventor just one day behind him.[3]

(Spring 2001): 1–53; it was later published as a monograph by the Mises Institute in 2008 and again by Laissez-Faire Books in 2012 (hereinafter *AIP*, citing the 2008 version). The 2001 article was based on "The Legitimacy of Intellectual Property," a paper presented at the Law and Economics panel, Austrian Scholars Conference, Ludwig von Mises Institute, Auburn, Ala., March 25, 2000. It has also been translated into various languages, including, to date, Czech, French, Georgian, German, Italian, Polish, Portuguese, Romanian, and Spanish. See www.stephankinsella.com/translations. *AIP* and many other works cited herein are available at www.stephankinsella.com/publications and www.c4sif.org/aip. And yes, it's actually been 22 years, not 20.

2 Ayn Rand, "Patents and Copyrights," in *Capitalism: The Unknown Ideal* (New York: New American Library, 1967), p. 133. The term is now life plus 70 years, thanks to the Sonny Bono Copyright Term Extension Act of 1998, aka the Mickey Mouse Protection Act (https://en.wikipedia.org/wiki/Copyright_Term_Extension_Act).

3 As Rand wrote there:

As an objection to the patent laws, some people cite the fact that two inventors may work independently for years on the same invention, but one will beat the other to the patent office by an hour or a day and will acquire an exclusive monopoly, while the loser's work will then be totally wasted. This type of objection is based on the error of equating the potential with the actual. The fact that a man *might* have been first does not alter the fact that he *wasn't*. Since the issue is one of commercial rights, the loser in a case of that kind has to accept the fact that in seeking to trade with others he must face the possibility of a competitor winning the race, which is true of all types of competition.

As it turns out, Rand was incorrect about the US patent law she thought she was defending. At the time she wrote, under US patent law, in the case of two inventors who independently invented and filed patent applications for the same invention, the *first to invent* (the first to conceive of the invention) won, *not* the first to file. It was not until the Leahy-Smith America Invents Act, signed into law by President Obama in 2011, that the US switched to the first-to-file standard common in most other countries. See, e.g., "Leahy–Smith America

It made no sense to me and didn't seem to fit in well with other aspects of libertarian theory and individual rights. I believed Rand's approach was wrong, or at least flawed, since natural property rights can't expire at an arbitrary time, much less one decreed by legislation, but I still assumed IP rights were, somehow, legitimate property rights. Since I was increasingly interested in libertarian theory (my first scholarly libertarian article was published in 1992)[4] and was beginning to specialize in IP in my law practice (in 1993),[5] I figured that I might be

---

Invents Act," *Wikipedia* (https://en.wikipedia.org/wiki/Leahy%E2%80%93Smith_America_Invents_Act); and Kinsella, "KOL164 | Obama's Patent Reform: Improvement or Continuing Calamity?: Mises Academy (2011)," *Kinsella on Liberty Podcast* (Dec. 9, 2014). Rand's argument defending what she thought was current US patent law was clearly makeweight; if she had known it was first-to-invent, she would no doubt have cobbled together some flimsy, disingenuous argument to justify that. Likewise, the patent term of 17 years is now 20 years from the date of filing, and the copyright term of life of the author plus 50 years has been extended to life of the author plus 70 years; there is little doubt she would have found a way to justify that, too. In other words, according to the US-Constitution-worshipping Rand, whatever the nearly infallible US Congress decrees just happens to mirror natural rights. Just so happens. One may recall the scene near the end of *Atlas Shrugged* (1957) in which Judge Narragansett had to make only a few amendments to the Constitution:

> He sat at a table, and the light of his lamp fell on the copy of an ancient document. He had marked and crossed out the contradictions in its statements that had once been the cause of its destruction. He was now adding a new clause to its pages: "Congress shall make no law abridging the freedom of production and trade...."

Ah, that almost-perfect US Constitution! One can understand Rand's enthusiasm for the relative superiority of the US system over the communist system of the USSR that she fled, but that doesn't make it presumptively libertarian in absolute terms. Let's not be naïve.

As I point out in "Ayn Rand Finally Right about the First-to-File US Patent System," *C4SIF Blog* (Sep. 9, 2011), Rand was also incorrect in stating "An idea as such cannot be protected until it has been given a material form. An invention has to be embodied in a physical model before it can be patented ...." No working model needs to be made to get a patent. For other mistakes she made about how the actual IP system works, see Kinsella, "Ayn Rand and *Atlas Shrugged, Part II*: Confused on Copyright and Patent," *C4SIF Blog* (Oct. 21, 2012).

4 See "Estoppel: A New Justification for Individual Rights," *Reason Papers* No. 17 (Fall 1992): 61–74; elaborated in "A Libertarian Theory of Punishment and Rights" (ch. 5). See also Kinsella, "The Genesis of Estoppel: My Libertarian Rights Theory," *StephanKinsella.com* (Mar. 22, 2016).

5 I started practicing law in 1992, initially specializing in oil & gas law and started transitioning to patent law in 1993, taking and passing the US Patent Bar Exam in 1994. See "On the Logic of Libertarianism and Why Intellectual Property Doesn't Exist" (ch. 24); also Kinsella, "The Start of my Legal Career: Past, Present and Future: Survival Stories of Lawyers," *KinsellaLaw.com* (Dec. 6, 2010) and www.stephankinsella.com/about. I became interested in libertarianism in 10th grade, around 1980, after reading

able to come up with a better defense of IP than previous libertarians had managed, since most of them really didn't have a good grasp of how actual patent and copyright law worked. So I dove deep into the literature and tried to find a way to justify IP rights, only to keep hitting dead ends.[6] Every argument I could come up with was as flawed and shaky as Ayn Rand's.

And in my research I came across libertarian and other criticisms of IP,[7] and also deepened my understanding of the crucial role of *scarcity* to property rights, as emphasized in particular by Hans-Hermann Hoppe.[8] I began to see that older criticisms of IP, such as the writings of Benjamin Tucker, Wendy McElroy, Sam Konkin, and Tom Palmer, were correct, even if their criticisms were not comprehensive or complete.[9]

Ayn Rand's *The Fountainhead*. See "How I Became a Libertarian" (ch. 1); Kinsella, "Faculty Spotlight Interview: Stephan Kinsella," *Mises Economics Blog* (Feb. 11, 2011); *idem*, "What Sparked Your Interest in Liberty?", *FEE.org* (April 21, 2016); and other biographical pieces at www.stephankinsella.com/publications/#biographical.

6 See also the discussion in "Conversation with Schulman about Logorights and Media-Carried Property" (ch. 17) of how both J. Neil Schulman and I tried to find arguments to justify IP, given our dissatisfaction with previous attempts.

7 Some of the works that influenced me and helped me change my mind on IP include Tom G. Palmer, "Intellectual Property: A Non-Posnerian Law and Economics Approach," *Hamline L. Rev.* 12, no. 2 (Spring 1989; https://perma.cc/DH7K-ZCRV): 261–304 and *idem*, "Are Patents and Copyrights Morally Justified? The Philosophy of Property Rights and Ideal Objects," *Harv. J. L. & Pub. Pol'y* 13, no. 3 (Summer 1990; https://perma.cc/J8LY-L4MQ): 817–65; Wendy McElroy, "Contra Copyright," *The Voluntaryist* (June 1985), included in *idem*, "Contra Copyright, Again," *Libertarian Papers* 3, art. no. 12 (2011; http://libertarianpapers.org/12-contra-copyright); Boudewijn Bouckaert, "What is Property?", *Harv. J. L. & Pub. Pol'y* 13, no. 3 (Summer 1990): 775–816; and *idem*, "From Property Rights to Property Order," *Encyclopedia of Law and Economics* (Springer, forthcoming 2023). Some of these, and others, are included in Kinsella, ed., *The Anti-IP Reader: Free Market Critiques of Intellectual Property* (Papinian Press, 2023).

8 See Hans-Hermann Hoppe, *A Theory of Socialism and Capitalism: Economics, Politics, and Ethics* (Auburn, Ala.: Mises Institute, 2010 [1989], www.hanshoppe.com/tsc); also *idem*, "Of Common, Public, and Private Property and the Rationale for Total Privatization," in *The Great Fiction: Property, Economy, Society, and the Politics of Decline* (Second Expanded Edition, Mises Institute, 2021; www.hanshoppe.com/tgf).

9 See Kinsella, "The Origins of Libertarian IP Abolitionism," *Mises Economics Blog* (April 1, 2011) and *idem*, "The Four Historical Phases of IP Abolitionism," *C4SIF Blog* (April 13, 2011). On Benjamin Tucker, see also Wendy McElroy, "Intellectual Property," in *The Debates of Liberty: An Overview of Individualist Anarchism, 1881–1908* (Lexington Books, 2002; https://perma.cc/ZQM2-82B9), reprinted without endnotes as "Copyright and Patent in Benjamin Tucker's Periodical," *Mises Daily* (July 28, 2010; https://mises.org/library/copyright-and-patent-benjamin-tuckers-periodical); See also Kinsella, "Benjamin Tucker and the Great Nineteenth Century IP Debates in *Liberty* Magazine,"

With a relief similar to the one I felt when I finally gave up minarchism and ceded the ground to anarchism, I finally concluded that patent and copyright are completely statist and unjustified derogations from libertarian principles and property rights. No wonder I had been failing in my attempts: I had been trying to justify the unjustifiable!

So I sought to build on the work done by previous thinkers, and clarify and expand it. I gave a few local talks and wrote some short articles on the topic starting in 1995,[10] often with a somewhat tentative tone as I was initially concerned that publicly opposing IP law might harm my budding IP law practice (turns out, it never caused a problem). I then wrote a lengthier treatment, which became *AIP*, mostly to get it out of my system, intending to then turn my attention back to other fields that interest me more, like rights theory, contract theory, causation, and other aspects of libertarian legal theory.[11]

I presented the paper, then entitled "The Legitimacy of Intellectual Property," at the Ludwig von Mises Institute's Austrian Scholars Conference in March 2000. This was the year Objectivist George Reisman started attending Mises Institute events, after having been ousted from Objectivist circles over his favorable remarks about Barbara Branden's biography of Rand, and had reunited with his old friend Ralph Raico, from whom he had been estranged for many years. I remember Reisman asking me, after I delivered my paper, something like, "Let me make sure I understand you. Are you saying all patent and copyright law should be abolished?" I answered yes and, seeming somewhat stunned, he slowly walked away. In any case, I submitted the paper to the *JLS*, where it was published as "Against Intellectual Property," a title suggested by Professor Hans-Hermann Hoppe, then the journal's editor.

AIP, and some other articles around the same time, argues that all forms of intellectual property—including patent, copyright, trademark,

---

StephanKinsella.com (July 11, 2022). See also the writings by these and others in Kinsella, ed., "The Anti-IP Reader."

    10 See, e.g., Kinsella, "Letter on Intellectual Property Rights," *IOS J.* 5, no. 2 (June 1995), pp. 12–13 (see references in *idem*, "Letter on Intellectual Property Rights," *IOS Journal* (June 1995)," *C4SIF Blog* (Aug. 31, 2022)); and *idem*, "Is Intellectual Property Legitimate?", *Pennsylvania Bar Association Intellectual Property Newsletter* 1 (Winter 1998): 3, republished in the Federalist Society's *Intellectual Property Practice Group Newsletter*, 3, no. 3 (Winter 2000); available at www.stephankinsella.com/publications/#againstip.

    11 See, e.g., various chapters in this book.

and trade secret, but especially the first two—are unjust and unlibertarian laws and should be abolished.[12]

II. THE INTERNET ERA AND THE GROWING IP THREAT

As noted above, IP had not received a great deal of attention from libertarians before the internet era. But IP's wallflower status was about to change. Some were starting to sense that the IP issue was becoming more important. The need to shine a light on patent and copyright, heretofore relegated to the shadows and the bailiwick of specialists, was becoming more apparent. An early sign of this among Austro-libertarians, perhaps, was the Mises Institute's awarding me the O.P. Alford III Prize for 2002 for *AIP*.[13]

The Internet is the reason for IP emerging from the shadows. The Internet—and digital information and file sharing, social media, and related technologies like cell phones, texting, and ubiquitous video cameras—was at this time gaining steam and becoming a huge social force. It was becoming one of the most important tools to fight statism and to preserve and extend human freedom and prosperity. And this is why it has been under attack by the state, in the guise of anti-pornography, anti-gambling, and anti-terrorism, as well as anti-piracy/copyright protection efforts.

The Internet became the world's biggest copying machine, leading to a dramatic increase in the amount of copyright infringement, and

---

[12] My article "In Defense of Napster and Against the Second Homesteading Rule," *LewRockwell.com* (September 4, 2000), presented a summary version of the argument also made around the same time in the original version of *AIP*. "Law and Intellectual Property in a Stateless Society" (ch. 14) restates the basic case against IP; a more concise version may be found in Kinsella, "Intellectual Property and Libertarianism," *Mises Daily* (Nov. 17, 2009).

For more extensive criticism of trademark law, see Kinsella, "Defamation Law and Reputation Rights as a Type of Intellectual Property," in Elvira Nica & Gheorghe H. Popescu, eds., *A Passion for Justice: Essays in Honor of Walter Block* (New York: Addleton Academic Publishers, forthcoming).

[13] https://perma.cc/E33D-JST6.

thus in the amount of copyright lawsuits and penalties.[14] At the same time, news of shockingly excessive, absurd, and outrageous copyright persecutions were instantly and widely communicated over the Internet—college students and single mothers sued for millions of dollars for sharing a few songs.[15] No longer were these lawsuits hidden in the dark; Internet users were starting to be made aware of them. Writes Siva Vaidhyanathan:

> By 1991 I noticed that [hip-hop] music had changed. The new work lacked the texture and richness that had marked the finest albums of the late 1980s, such as Public Enemy's *It Takes a Nation of Millions to Hold Us Back* and the Beastie Boys's *Paul's Boutique*. Instead, the digital samples of others' music that made up the intricate bed of sound in those great albums was replaced by a thinner, less interesting, less intricate collection of more obvious samples. The language of sampling seemed to become simpler and less interesting. There was less play and less depth to the music by 1992. I knew that several hip-hop artists had faced copyright suits over sampling in 1990 and 1991. So I wondered if the law had had such a profound effect on the art. After a bit of research, I concluded that it had. With a bit more research, I sought to explain the larger, longer relationship between copyright and creativity in American history. That project ... became the germ of my first book, published in 2001, *Copyrights and Copywrongs: The Rise of Intellectual Property and How It Threatens Creativity.*

> By 2001 copyright had exploded into public consciousness, largely through the remarkable rise and fall of Napster, the first easy-to-use

---

[14] In fact, one of my earliest publications on IP concerned one of the first streaming-music services, which was killed by the copyright industry. See Kinsella, "In Defense of Napster and Against the Second Homesteading Rule." Napster "originally launched on June 1, 1999, as a pioneering peer-to-peer (P2P) file sharing software service with an emphasis on digital audio file distribution.... As the software became popular, the company ran into legal difficulties over copyright infringement. It ceased operations in 2001 after losing a wave of lawsuits and filed for bankruptcy in June 2002." "Napster," *Wikipedia* (retrieved May 11, 2022; https://en.wikipedia.org/wiki/Napster).

[15] See, e.g., Kinsella, "The Patent, Copyright, Trademark, and Trade Secret Horror Files," *StephanKinsella.com* (Feb. 3, 2010); *idem*, "KOL364 | Soho Forum Debate vs. Richard Epstein: Patent and Copyright Law Should Be Abolished," *Kinsella on Liberty Podcast* (Nov. 24, 2021); and *idem*, "First Amendment Defense Act of 2021," *C4SIF Blog* (Jan. 17, 2021). See also *idem*, "We are all copyright criminals: John Tehranian's 'Infringement Nation,'" *Mises Economics Blog* (Aug. 22, 2011); *idem*, "The tepid mainstream 'defenses' of Aaron Swartz," *C4SIF Blog* (Jan. 29, 2013); and *idem*, "Tim Lee and Lawrence Lessig: 'some punishment' of Swartz was 'appropriate,'" *C4SIF Blog* (Jan. 13, 2013).

digital file-sharing service. The United States had radically expanded copyright law in the 1990s in anticipation of the "digital moment." But nothing had prepared the copyright industries for the torrent of unauthorized peer-to-peer distribution over the Internet, starting in about 2000. Meanwhile, computer software had blossomed from a mere hobby to a multibillion-dollar global industry in the 1980s and 1990s without any clear sense of how intellectual property would work for it (or against it). At about the same time that U.S. courts ruled that software could enjoy the protection of patent law as well as copyright, the movement to lock computer code open for the benefit of security, stability, quality, and creativity (and, to some, humanity) grew to be called the "Free and Open-Source Software" movement. As someone thrown into the copyright battles of the early twenty-first century despite my training as a nineteenth-century cultural historian, I felt compelled to make sense of these and other trends that were remaking our global information ecosystem. Those interests are reflected in my second book, published in 2004, *The Anarchist in the Library: How the Clash between Freedom and Control Is Hacking the Real World and Crashing the System.*

The copyright wars of the first decade of the twenty-first century yielded a global "Free Culture" movement, with law professor Lawrence Lessig as its intellectual leader. Globally, others concerned with issues beyond copyright and creativity, including biopiracy and the cost of pharmaceuticals in developing nations, launched the "Access to Knowledge" movement. During the decade the industries devoted to expanding and strengthening intellectual property succeeded in legislatures and courts around the world. And the United States embedded intellectual property standards into trade treaties with other nations. The issues were becoming more interesting and important every week.

Then, in late 2004 Google announced it would begin to scan into electronic form millions of books from dozens of university libraries—many of which would still be covered by copyright. The ensuing debate and lawsuits drew me into the fascinating world of search engines, Internet policy, and the future of libraries and books. That research generated my third book, published in 2011, *The Googlization of Everything and Why We Should Worry.*[16]

---

16 Siva Vaidhyanathan, *Intellectual Property: A Very Short Introduction* (Oxford University Press, 2017), at xviii–xx. See also Justin Hughes, "The Philosophy of Intellectual Property," *Georgetown L. J.* 77, no. 2 (Dec. 1988; https://perma.cc/U4XX-5DZV): 287–366, p. 288 (citations omitted):

In the centuries since our founding, the concept of property has changed dramatically in the United States. One repeatedly mentioned change is the trend

Or as Declan McCullogh writes:

> Over the past few years, intellectual property has morphed from an arcane topic of interest mostly to academicians and patent attorneys to the stuff of newsmagazine cover stories. Courtrooms' klieg lights have illuminated how copyright law has been stretched in ways unimaginable just five years ago. Software patents have roiled the computer industry and alarmed developers of open-source programs. Meanwhile, displaying all the temperance of a methadone addict, Congress keeps handing more and more power to copyright owners.[17]

Patent outrages and abuse also increased along with a growing tech sector and economy and were also communicated at light speed to blogs and RSS feeds. And in the meantime the traditional content-producers, ever-resistant to new technologies that disrupt comfortable, established business models, kept lobbying Congress to ratchet up patent and copyright scope and terms and penalties and enforcement,[18] while at the same time the US bullied other countries to keep ratcheting up their own IP laws and enforcement.[19] This culminated in the attempt to

---

towards treating new things as property, such as job security and income from social programs. A less frequently discussed trend is that historically recognized but nonetheless atypical forms of property, such as intellectual property, are becoming increasingly important relative to the old paradigms of property, such as farms, factories, and furnishings. As our attention continues to shift from tangible to intangible forms of property, we can expect a growing jurisprudence of intellectual property.

And: Ejan Mackaay, "Economic Incentives in Markets for Information and Innovation," *Harv. J. L. & Pub. Pol'y* 13, no. 3 (Summer 1990): 867–910, p. 868 (citation omitted):

Recent advances in reprography and computer technology have once more brought the issue of the theoretical status of intellectual rights into question. These advances greatly facilitate and reduce the cost of copying information from one medium to another. Information has become less dependent on the vehicle through which it is conveyed; it has become "purer."

[17] Declan McCullagh, "Foreword," in Adams Thierer & Wayne Crews, Jr., eds., *Copy Fights: The Future of Intellectual Property in the Information Age* (Cato, 2002), p. xi.

[18] See Kinsella, "The Mountain of IP Legislation," *C4SIF Blog* (Nov. 24, 2010); Mike Masnick, "How Much Is Enough? We've Passed 15 'Anti-Piracy' Laws In The Last 30 Years," *Techdirt* (Feb. 15, 2012; https://perma.cc/TG7U-768F); and Timothy B. Lee, "Copyright enforcement and the Internet: we just haven't tried hard enough?", *ars technica* (Feb. 16, 2012; https://perma.cc/75P9-KM7E).

[19] See, e.g., the following posts from the *C4SIF Blog*: "Intellectual Property Imperialism" (Oct. 24, 2010); "Covid-19 Relief Bill Adds Criminal Copyright Streaming Penalties and IP Imperialism" (Dec. 22, 2020); "*Intellectual Property Rights: A Critical History* and US IP Imperialism" (Dec. 31, 2014); "Blowback from IP Imperialism: Chinese Companies Again

enact anti-piracy legislation such as the Stop Online Piracy Act (SOPA) and Protect IP Act (PIPA), which was—at least for the moment—derailed by a historic Internet uprising.[20]

For these reasons, in the last couple decades, as IP becomes a more apparent threat to property rights, freedom of expression, and the Internet, the issue became more prominent, and libertarians of various stripes—Austrians, anarchists, left-libertarians, civil libertarians, and the young and Internet dependent—started to become more interested in the IP issue and more receptive to anti-IP arguments.[21] And more and more libertarians are writing on this important topic and building on, incorporating, or extending previous analyses, calling for significant reform of IP law or even outright abolition.[22] In addition, outside of

---

Using Patents To Punish Foreign Competitors" (July 14, 2012); "'Free-trade' pacts export U.S. copyright controls" (Oct. 17, 2011); "China and Intellectual Property" (Dec. 27, 2010); "Wikileaks cables reveal that the US wrote Spain's proposed copyright laws" (Dec. 3, 2010); and other posts at www.c4sif.org/tag/ip-imperialism. See also Michael Geist, "U.S. Copyright Lobby Takes Aim at Canadian Copyright Term Through Trans-Pacific Partnership," *MichaelGeist.com* (Aug. 7, 2013; https://perma.cc/9NW4-EMAN); *idem*, "Japan Considering Copyright Term Extension, Canada Next?," MichaelGeist.com (July 15, 2013; https://perma.cc/G4R8-SDEF); *idem*, "The Canadian Government Makes its Choice: Implementation of Copyright Term Extension Without Mitigating Against the Harms," *MichaelGeist.com* (April 27, 2022; https://perma.cc/3DER-JUK2); Declan McCullagh, "Free-trade pacts export U.S. copyright controls," *CNET* (Oct. 14, 2011; https://perma.cc/7LJE-PG4J).

20 See, e.g., Kinsella, "SOPA is the Symptom, Copyright is the Disease: The SOPA wakeup call to ABOLISH COPYRIGHT," *The Libertarian Standard* (Jan. 24, 2012). See also *idem*, "Where does IP Rank Among the Worst State Laws?", *C4SIF Blog* (Jan. 20, 2012); *idem*, "Masnick on the Horrible PROTECT IP Act: The Coming IPolice State," *C4SIF Blog* (June 2, 2012); *idem*, "Copyright and the End of Internet Freedom," *C4SIF Blog* (May 10, 2011); and *idem*, "Patent vs. Copyright: Which is Worse?", *C4SIF Blog* (Nov. 5, 2011).

21 See Kinsella, "The Death Throes of Pro-IP Libertarianism," *Mises Daily* (July 28, 2010); *idem*, "'We, The Web Kids': Manifesto For An Anti-ACTA Generation," *C4SIF Blog* (March 3, 2012). Even many Randians are now anti-IP. See, e.g., *idem*, "An Objectivist Recants on IP," *C4SIF Blog* (Dec. 4, 2009); *idem*, "Yet another Randian recants on IP," *C4SIF Blog* (Feb. 1, 2012); Timothy Sandefur, "A Critique of Ayn Rand's Theory of Intellectual Property Rights," *J. Ayn Rand Stud.* 9, no. 1 (Fall 2007; https://papers.ssrn.com/sol3/papers.cfm?abstract_id=1117269): 139–61. *But see* Kinsella, "Does Cato's New Objectivist CEO John Allison Presage Retrogression on IP?", *C4SIF Blog* (Aug. 27, 2012).

22 See, for example, Butler Shaffer, *A Libertarian Critique of Intellectual Property* (Auburn, Ala.: Mises Institute, 2013; https://mises.org/library/libertarian-critique-intellectual-property); Jacob Huebert, "The Fight against Intellectual Property," in *Libertarianism Today* (Santa Barbara, CA: Praeger, 2010; https://mises.org/library/fight-against-intellectual-property); Walter Block, "The Intellectual-Property Denier," in *Defending the Undefendable II: Freedom in All Realms* (UK and USA: Terra Libertas Publishing House,

libertarianism proper, a host of economists, empirical researchers, and legal scholars, most notably economists Michele Boldrin and David Levine, authors of the groundbreaking *Against Intellectual Monopoly*, have expressed deep skepticism, on empirical grounds, of the claimed pro-innovation effects of patent and copyright.[23]

The issue continues to receive attention from a variety of institutions and outlets. I have myself, lectured, debated, and been interviewed countless times on this topic, including on the *Stossel* show and the *Reason.tv*-sponsored Soho Forum debate.[24] I also gave a six-part lecture

---

2013; reprint edition Auburn, Ala.: Mises Institute, 2018; https://mises.org/library/defending-undefendable-2); Jeffrey A. Tucker, "Ideas, Free and Unfree," and other chapters in the "Can Ideas Be Owned?" section of *idem*, *It's a Jetsons World: Private Miracles & Public Crimes* (Auburn, Ala.: Mises Institute, 2011; https://mises.org/library/its-jetsons-world-private-miracles-and-public-crimes) (chaps. 37–41); *idem*, several chapters in the "Technology" section of *idem*, *Bourbon for Breakfast: Living Outside the Statist Quo* (Auburn, Ala.: Mises Institute, 2010; https://mises.org/library/bourbon-breakfast); Adam Kokesh, "Intellectual Property," in *Freedom!* (2014; https://archive.org/details/FREEDOMEbook), §VI; Sandefur, "A Critique of Ayn Rand's Theory of Intellectual Property Rights"; Chase Rachels, "Property," in *A Spontaneous Order: The Capitalist Case For A Stateless Society* (2015; https://archive.org/details/ASpontaneousOrder0), section "Intellectual Property"; Vin Armani, "The Ownable and the Unownable," in *Self Ownership: The Foundation of Property and Morality* (2017); Tom W. Bell, "Copyright, Philosophically," in *Intellectual Privilege: Copyright, Common Law, and the Common Good* (Arlington, Virginia: Mercatus Center, 2014; https://perma.cc/JLC2-396Y); Jerry Brito, ed., *Copyright Unbalanced: From Incentive to Excess* (Arlington, Va.: Mercatus Center, 2013); Jack Lloyd, "Property Rights," in *The Definitive Guide to Libertarian Voluntaryism* (2022); Isaac Morehouse, "How I Changed My Mind on Intellectual Property," *FEE.org* (Sept. 27, 2016; https://perma.cc/324H-TPRY), also in Keith Knight, ed., *The Voluntaryist Handbook: A Collection of Essays, Excerpts, and Quotes* (2022; https://perma.cc/N8UX-4PX4). See also various resources collected at www.c4sif.org/resources and Kinsella, ed., "The Anti-IP Reader."

[23] Michele Boldrin & David K. Levine, *Against Intellectual Monopoly* (Cambridge University Press, 2008; https://tinyurl.com/bdkn5885). See also Kinsella, "The Overwhelming Empirical Case Against Patent and Copyright," *C4SIF Blog* (Oct. 23, 2012); *idem*, "Legal Scholars: Thumbs Down on Patent and Copyright," *C4SIF Blog* (Oct. 23, 2012); and *idem*, "Yet Another Study Finds Patents Do Not Encourage Innovation," *Mises Economics Blog* (July 2, 2009).

[24] See Kinsella, "KOL308 | Stossel: It's My Idea (2015)," *Kinsella on Liberty Podcast* (Dec. 29, 2020) and *idem*, "KOL364 | Soho Forum Debate vs. Richard Epstein"; and dozens of speeches and appearances on radio shows and podcasts, collected on the Kinsella on Liberty podcast feed at www.stephankinsella.com/kinsella-on-liberty-podcast.

course on IP for the Mises Academy in 2010 and reprised in 2011,[25] and I have continued to write on this topic.[26]

What about the prospects for reform of patent and copyright law? While more and more libertarians have come to see IP law as unjust, it is unlikely there will be much legislative progress on this matter due to widespread confusion about property rights and entrenched special interests, in particular Hollywood and the American music industry, which rely on copyright, and the pharmaceutical industry, which profits from the patent system. That said, it seems unlikely that copyright terms—once 14 years extendable to 28, and then life of the author plus 50 years, and now life of the author plus 70 years—will be extended any further. And while patent and copyright law will stay on the books for a long time, technology will make them increasingly harder to enforce. Piracy of copyrighted works is already rampant due to the Internet and encryption. As 3D printing technology advances, we may see an increased ability of consumers to evade patent law as well.[27]

III. CHANGES

I've been asked from time to time what changes I would make to *AIP*. In my assessment, the basic arguments in *AIP* are sound. I have yet to see a valid criticism.[28] I might change the structure somewhat, or an emphasis or wording here and there. For example, I would clarify that *scarcity* is meant in the technical economics sense of rivalrousness.

---

[25] See Kinsella, "KOL172 | 'Rethinking Intellectual Property: History, Theory, and Economics: Lecture 1: History and Law' (Mises Academy, 2011)," *Kinsella on Liberty Podcast* (Feb. 14, 2015).

[26] See, e.g., Kinsella, "A Selection of My Best Articles and Speeches on IP," *C4SIF Blog* (Nov. 30, 2015), *idem, You Can't Own Ideas: Essays on Intellectual Property* (Houston, Texas: Papinian Press, 2023; www.stephankinsella.com/own-ideas), and other material at www.stephankinsella.com/publications and www.c4sif.org/aip.

[27] See Kinsella, "Gary North on the 3D Printing Threat to Patent Law," *C4SIF Blog* (Jan. 31, 2022), and links and references therein.

[28] See Kinsella, "There are No Good Arguments for Intellectual Property," *Mises Economics Blog* (Feb. 24, 2009); *idem*, "Absurd Arguments for IP," *C4SIF Blog* (Sep. 19, 2011); *idem*, "KOL367 | Disenthrall with Patrick Smith: Fisking Strangerous Thoughts' Critique of 'Intellectual Communism,'" *Kinsella on Liberty Podcast* (Dec. 20, 2021); *idem*, "KOL076 | IP Debate with Chris LeRoux," *Kinsella on Liberty Podcast* (Aug. 30, 2013).

I might even propose the use of the term "conflictable," to emphasize the nature of resources that gives rise to property rights in the first place, and to head off silly arguments like, "Well, IP is justified since good ideas are scarce."[29] Also, I might use "corporeal" or "material" instead of "tangible."[30] I would try to be more careful to use the term *property* to refer *not* to the owned resource that is the subject of property rights, but only to the relationship between the owner and the resource owned, although this can be tedious if overdone.[31] I would streamline the initial section providing a positive legal description of the main forms of IP and eliminate the Appendix providing examples of obvious IP abuse, since this can be done now in an easily updated online page or post.[32] I would now be a bit harsher on trademark than I was in *AIP*; all trademark law is evil and should be abolished. The aspects of it that can be defended are already present in contract and fraud law.

---

[29] See Kinsella, "On Conflictability and Conflictable Resources," *StephanKinsella.com* (Jan. 31, 2022).

[30] In *AIP* I sometimes used the term "tangible" to indicate scarce resources that can be subject to property rights. (I've also sometimes used the term corporeal, a civil-law term.) Hardy Bouillon argues that it might be more precise to focus on the difference between material vs. non-material goods, rather than tangible vs. non-tangible goods, as the touchstone of things subject to property rights. As Bouillon writes:

> Though some speak exclusively of tangible and non-tangible goods, I prefer to talk of material and immaterial goods.... The point about material goods is not that they are tangible, for some are not. For instance, atoms and many other small material units are not tangible; they are identifiable only indirectly, though this does not prevent us from calling them material.

Hardy Bouillon, "A Note on Intellectual Property and Externalities," *Mises Daily* (Oct. 27, 2009), previously published in Jörg Guido Hülsmann & Stephan Kinsella, eds., *Property, Freedom and Society: Essays in Honor of Hans-Hermann Hoppe* (Auburn, Ala.: Mises Institute, 2009). I see some merit in his argument, though as noted above I think the essence of what makes some thing a possible subject of property rights is whether it is conflictable or not.

[31] See "What Libertarianism Is" (ch. 2), n.5; also Kinsella, "Property: Libertarian Answer Man: Self-ownership for slaves and Crusoe; and Yiannopoulos on Accurate Analysis and the term 'Property,'" *StephanKinsella.com* (April 3, 2021).

[32] As I did in a later article based on *AIP*, "The Case Against Intellectual Property," in *Handbook of the Philosophical Foundations of Business Ethics*, Prof. Dr. Christoph Lütge, ed. (Springer, 2013) (chapter 68, in Part 18, "Property Rights: Material and Intellectual," Robert McGee, section ed.).

IV. ADDITIONS

But I would not change much, substantively speaking. However, since writing *AIP* over 20 years ago, I have found additional ways of explaining the fundamental problem with IP law—additional arguments, examples, and evidence.[33] So I would add some material, as I did to some degree in a later paper.[34] I'll briefly outline below some of the arguments developed after the initial publication of *AIP*.

A. Empirical Evidence

In the "Utilitarian Defenses of IP" section of *AIP*, I explained various defects in the utilitarian case for IP. First, as Austrians have explained, value is not a measurable, cardinal quantity that can be interpersonally compared.[35] Second, even if violating someone's rights by taking their resources and redistributing them to someone else makes the recipient better off, it is still a rights violation. And third, the proponent of IP, arguing that IP laws lead to net utility gains, has the burden of proof.[36]

---

[33] See, generally, Kinsella, "A Selection of My Best Articles and Speeches on IP."

[34] "Law and Intellectual Property in a Stateless Society" (ch. 14) restates the basic case against IP and incorporates some new arguments developed after *AIP*.

[35] See *AIP*, n.41; also Murray N. Rothbard, "Toward a Reconstruction of Utility and Welfare Economics," in *Economic Controversies* (Auburn, Ala.: Mises Institute, 2011; https://mises.org/library/economic-controversies). For a recent article debunking David Friedman's scientist and confused contention that "Von Neumann proved" that utility can be measured or expressed cardinally, see Robert P. Murphy, "Why Austrians Stress Ordinal Utility," *Mises Wire* (Feb. 3, 2022; https://mises.org/wire/why-austrians-stress-ordinal-utility).

[36] See Kinsella, "There's No Such Thing as a Free Patent," *Mises Daily* (Mar. 7, 2005); Palmer, "Are Patents and Copyrights Morally Justified?", pp. 849–50 (emphasis added):

> [U]tilitarian arguments of a certain class can cut for or against intellectual property rights claims. As dealt with in much of the economics literature, for example, the utility gains from increased incentives for innovation must be weighed against the utility losses incurred from monopolization of innovations and their diminished diffusion. Some have argued that the first part of the comparison may be either *negative* or positive; *patents or copyrights may actually decrease innovation, rather than increase it.*

As Matt Ridley writes:

> A further problem is that patents undoubtedly raise the costs of goods. That is the point: to keep competition at bay while the innovator reaps a reward. This slows the development and spread of the innovation. As the economist Joan Robinson put it: "The justification of the patent system is that by slowing down the diffusion

And it has become increasingly clearer, in the last 60+ years, that those arguing for IP on empirical grounds have not yet satisfied and cannot satisfy their burden of proof that IP makes us better off.[37] As I wrote in a subsequent paper, "Given the available evidence, anyone who accepts utilitarianism should be *opposed* to patent and copyright."[38]

B. IP Rights as Negative Easements[39]

Additionally, I have come to understand that IP rights can be properly classified as *non-consensual negative easements* (or servitudes),[40] which makes plain exactly how they infringe justly-acquired property rights.[41] All property rights are enforceable rights in material, scarce—conflictable—resources, the type of (causally efficacious) scarce means that human actors can possess and manipulate and employ to causally interfere in the world. It is not that assigning property rights in infor-

---

of technical progress it ensures that there will be more progress to diffuse." But this does not necessarily happen. Indeed, history is replete with examples of bursts of innovation that follow the ending of a patent.

Matt Ridley, *How Innovation Works: And Why It Flourishes in Freedom* (Harper, 2020), p. 347. The Robinson quote is from Joan Robinson, *The Accumulation of Capital*, 3d ed. (Palgrave Macmillan, 2013 [1969]), p. 87. This quote is paraphrased (with approval) by free-market economist William Shughart. See William F. Shughart II, "Ideas Need Protection: Abolishing Intellectual-property Patents Would Hurt Innovation: A Middle Ground Is Needed," *Baltimore Sun* (December 21, 2009); Kinsella, "Independent Institute on The 'Benefits' of Intellectual Property Protection," *C4SIF Blog* (Feb. 15, 2016).

[37] See Boldrin & Levine, *Against Intellectual Monopoly*; Kinsella, "The Overwhelming Empirical Case Against Patent and Copyright"; *idem*, "Legal Scholars: Thumbs Down on Patent and Copyright."; *idem*, "Tabarrok, Cowen, and Douglass North on Patents," *C4SIF Blog* (March 11, 2021).

[38] "Law and Intellectual Property in a Stateless Society" (ch. 14), text at n.76.

[39] See also Part IV.F, below.

[40] Servitude is the civil law term; easement the common law term. *See* Gregory W. Rome & Stephan Kinsella, *Louisiana Civil Law Dictionary* (New Orleans, La.: Quid Pro Books, 2011). These rights are also "nonapparent." See Kinsella, "Intellectual Property Rights as Negative Servitudes," *C4SIF Blog* (June 23, 2011). IP rights can also be classified legally as incorporeal movables, although this classification has no relevance here. See Louisiana Civil Code (https://www.legis.la.gov/legis/Laws_Toc.aspx?folder=67&level=Parent), arts. 461, 462, 475; Kinsella, "Are Ideas Movable or Immovable?", *C4SIF Blog* (April 8, 2013). See also related discussion in "Selling Does Not Imply Ownership, and Vice-Versa: A Dissection" (ch. 11), n.39 and references and quotes in "What Libertarianism Is" (ch. 2), n.5, related to the nature of "things" in the civil law.

[41] Kinsella, "Intellectual Property Rights as Negative Servitudes."

mation or knowledge is *wrong*, but that it is *impossible*.[42] Force cannot be applied to "ideas" or information, but only to scarce resources. Any IP right is just a disguised reassignment of property rights in existing scarce resources. One reason for the confusion here is that people are not careful in distinguishing between motivations and means.

For example, it is sometimes said that people "fight over religion." But this is not accurate. Religion is not a scarce resource over which there can be conflict. Any interpersonal human conflict is *always* over scarce, material, *conflictable* resources. If *A* kills *B* or takes his land or cows in a religious dispute, the religious disagreement is merely the *motivation* or reason for the conflict or clash—the explanation for why parties act as they do—but the clash itself is always over the material things that are the real subject of property rights. We can *explain* a given human action by reference to the ends aimed at and the means employed. One's motivations and goals factor into the ends; but the actual means employed and the actions taken are what property rights concern.[43]

All rights are human rights, and all human rights are property rights,[44] and property rights just are rights to the exclusive control of certain conflictable resources.[45] In the end, every law, every dispute, boils down to some actor being assigned ownership rights in a given contested (conflictable) resource. A copyright grant gives the holder a partial property right in the printing press and computers of other people. A patent grant gives the holder a partial property right in the

---

[42] See also Part IV.G, below, and "Selling Does Not Imply Ownership, and Vice-Versa: A Dissection" (ch. 11).

[43] For more on this, see the various discussions of what it means to have a "fight over religion," in "On the Logic of Libertarianism and Why Intellectual Property Doesn't Exist" (ch. 24); also Kinsella, "The Limits of Libertarianism?: A Dissenting View," *StephanKinsella.com* (April 20, 2014); and the comments in the transcripts to these episodes of the *Kinsella on Liberty Podcast*: "KOL337 | Join the Wasabikas Ep. 15.0: You Don't Own Bitcoin—Property Rights, Praxeology and the Foundations of Private Law, with Max Hillebrand" (May 23, 2021); "KOL154 | 'The Social Theory of Hoppe: Lecture 2: Types of Socialism and the Origin of the State'" (Oct. 16, 2014); "KOL076 | IP Debate with Chris LeRoux" (Aug. 30, 2013); and "KOL038 | Debate with Robert Wenzel on Intellectual Property" (April 1, 2013).

[44] See Murray N. Rothbard, "'Human Rights' as Property Rights," in *The Ethics of Liberty* (New York: New York University Press, 1998; https://mises.org/library/human-rights-property-rights).

[45] See Hoppe, *A Theory of Socialism and Capitalism*, chaps. 1–2 & 7.

factories and raw material already owned by others. Such rights are negative easements that permit the holder to veto or prevent certain uses by the owner. Negative easements are legitimate when consented to, but in the case of IP, the state grants these rights to the IP holder *without the consent* of the owner of the burdened property (the so-called "servient estate"). As I noted in *AIP*, "ownership of an idea, or ideal object, effectively gives the IP owners a property right in every physical embodiment of that work or invention."[46] Thus, IP rights amount to a taking or infringement of property rights otherwise established in accordance with the principles of original appropriation and contract.[47] This insight buttresses the argument in *AIP* that "a system of property

---

[46] See *AIP*, the section "IP Rights and Relation to Tangible Property," p. 15. Rothbard recognizes this in a limited way when he writes: "[P]atents actually invade the property rights of those *independent* discoverers of an idea or invention who made the discovery after the patentee. Patents, therefore, *invade* rather than defend property rights." Murray N. Rothbard, *Man, Economy, and State, with Power and Market*, Scholar's ed., 2d ed. (Auburn, Ala.: Mises Institute, 2009; https://mises.org/library/man-economy-and-state-power-and-market), chap. 10, §7, p. 749. Yet patents invade not only the rights of those who independently discover the same invention; they also invade the rights of competitors and copiers who have every right to use publicly available information to guide their actions and to manipulate their own resources. And as noted in "Law and Intellectual Property in a Stateless Society" (ch. 14), Part III.C, and Kinsella, *AIP*, the section "Contract vs. Reserved Rights," Rothbard does not really oppose patents. He defends what he erroneously calls copyright or "common law copyright," with a flawed contract-based argument that contradicts his own contract theory and his criticism of defamation law (another type of IP; see Kinsella, "Defamation Law and Reputation Rights as a Type of Intellectual Property"). But the copyright Rothbard advocates is not like current, legislated copyright, and it also includes inventions, like Brown's mousetrap (which is the domain of patent law). (For Rothbard's mousetrap example, see Murray N. Rothbard, "Knowledge, True and False," in *The Ethics of Liberty* (New York: New York University Press, 1998; https://mises.org/library/knowledge-true-and-false), p. 123.) So what he really advocates is a contractual version of patent law (and presumably copyright law, if his argument extends not only to inventions but also to artistic works and things like books). And his contract-based IP/copyright idea is not "common law copyright"; that was doctrine in the common law that was similar to trade secrets and had nothing to do with this contractual IP argument Rothbard is making, or to actual copyright that was not at all rooted in contract. See Wikipedia, https://en.wikipedia.org/wiki/Common_law_copyright. Writes Rothbard: "Violation of (common law) copyright is an equivalent violation of contract and theft of property." Ibid. I criticize this view in *AIP*, the section "Contract vs. Reserved Rights." His reasoning here also makes some of the same mistakes as his view of "implicit theft" that I criticize in "A Libertarian Theory of Contract" (ch. 9), Part III.D.

[47] For further discussion of the principles of original appropriation, contractual title transfer, and the relation principle of transfer for purposes of rectification, see "What Libertarianism Is" (ch. 2), n.11 and accompanying text *et pass.*

rights in 'ideal objects' necessarily requires violation of other individual property rights, e.g., to use one's own tangible property as one sees fit."[48]

C. Lockean Creationism[49]

In the "Creation vs. Scarcity" section of *AIP*, I pointed out that one mistake made by many proponents of IP is the notion that *creation is a source of property rights*. But it is not. I have elaborated on this topic in subsequent writing, pointing out that creation—i.e., production,

---

[48] *AIP*, text at n.94; and Roderick T. Long, "The Libertarian Case Against Intellectual Property Rights," *Formulations* (Autumn 1995):

> It may be objected that the person who originated the information deserves ownership rights over it. But information is not a concrete thing an individual can control; it is a universal, existing in other people's minds and other people's property, and over these the originator has no legitimate sovereignty. *You cannot own information without owning other people.*

(Emphasis added) See also note 65, below, and Roderick T. Long, "Owning Ideas Means Owning People," *Cato Unbound* (Nov. 19, 2008; https://www.cato-unbound.org/2008/11/19/roderick-t-long/owning-ideas-means-owning-people); Palmer, "Intellectual Property: A Non-Posnerian Law and Economics Approach," p. 281 and *idem*, "Are Patents and Copyrights Morally Justified?", pp. 830–31, 862, 863, 865. *See also* John M. Kraft & Robert Hovden, "Natural Rights, Scarcity & Intellectual Property," *N.Y.U. J. L. & Liberty* 7, no. 2 (2013; https://perma.cc/HLW8-YNVQ): 464–96, p. 480: "What is clear *is* that the observance of such 'rights' *does* interrupt and infringe on others' natural right to self-ownership" (citing Palmer, "Are Patents and Copyrights Morally Justified?", pp. 834, 862); also Wojciech Gamrot, "The type individuation problem," *Studia Philosophica Wratislaviensia* 16, no. 4 (2021; https://wuwr.pl/spwr/article/view/13718): 47–64, p. 49 ("*IP rights are about the control of matter*" (emphasis added), citing Hughes, "The Philosophy of Intellectual Property," pp. 330–50; Hugh Breakey, "Natural intellectual property rights and the public domain," *Modern L. Rev.* 73 (2010; https://papers.ssrn.com/sol3/papers.cfm?abstract_id=2856883): 208–39; and Radu Uszkai, "Are Copyrights Compatible with Human Rights?," *Romanian J. Analytic Phil.* 8 (2014; https://philarchive.org/rec/USZACC): 5–20)). See also Bell, writing:

> By invoking state power, a copyright or patent owner can impose prior restraint, fines, imprisonment, and confiscation on those engaged in peaceful expression and the quiet enjoyment of tangible property. Because it thus gags our voices, ties our hands, and demolishes our presses, *the law of copyrights and patents violates the very rights Locke defended.*

Tom W. Bell, "Indelicate Imbalancing in Copyright and Patent Law," in Thierer & Crews, Jr., eds., *Copy Fights* (https://papers.ssrn.com/sol3/papers.cfm?abstract_id=984085), p. 4 (citations omitted, emphasis added).

[49] See also the discussion of "rearrangement" in Part IV.F, below, and also Part III.B, "Libertarian Creationism," in "Law and Intellectual Property in a Stateless Society" (ch. 14).

transformation, or rearrangement[50] of existing resources—is a source of *wealth* but not a source of property rights. After all, transforming a set of input resources into a more valuable output product requires that the input factors already be owned. The resulting product is thus owned according to standard property rights and contract principles.[51]

Property rights in one's body are based in one's direct control over one's body.[52] Property rights in external, previously unowned scarce resources come from original appropriation, or homesteading—first use and transformation or embordering—of an *unowned* scarce resource or by contractual transfer from a previous owner.[53] Production or transformation of existing, already-owned resources may increase or create wealth, but is not a source of rights. This is a common confusion among libertarians, especially Randians and those influenced by the confused labor theory of property and the related labor theory of value,

---

[50] For more on this concept, see Kinsella, "Locke on IP; Mises, Rothbard, and Rand on Creation, Production, and 'Rearranging'," *C4SIF Blog* (Sep. 29, 2010); also Kinsella, "KOL037 | Locke's Big Mistake: How the Labor Theory of Property Ruined Political Theory," *Kinsella on Liberty Podcast* (March 28, 2013).

[51] See also the section "Creation of Wealth versus Creation of Property" in Kinsella, "Intellectual Freedom and Learning Versus Patent and Copyright," *Economic Notes* No. 113 (Libertarian Alliance, Jan. 18, 2011) (also published as "Intellectual Freedom and Learning Versus Patent and Copyright," *The Libertarian Standard* (Jan. 19, 2011)); "Law and Intellectual Property in a Stateless Society" (ch. 14), Part III.B; and Kinsella, "KOL012 | 'The Intellectual Property Quagmire, or, The Perils of Libertarian Creationism,' Austrian Scholars Conference 2008," *Kinsella on Liberty Podcast* (Feb. 6, 2013). And see Gary Chartier, *Anarchy and Legal Order: Law and Politics for a Stateless Society* (Cambridge University Press, 2013), at 78 ("the ability to control a possession means that one can *transform it* as needed in a way that may *enhance its value* either *to the possessor, to others*, or to both"; emphasis added); and Israel M. Kirzner, "Producer, Entrepreneur, and the Right to Property," *Reason Papers* No. 1 (Fall 1974; https://reasonpapers.com/archives): 1–17, p. 1 ("Precision in applying the term 'what a man has produced' seems to be of considerable importance."). See also Uszkai, "Are Copyrights Compatible with Human Rights?," p. 13, discussing my argument in *AIP* that creation:

... is neither necessary nor sufficient to establish ownership. The focus on creation distracts from the crucial role of first occupation as a property rule for addressing the fundamental fact of scarcity. First occupation, not creation or labor, is both necessary and sufficient for the homesteading of unowned scarce resources.

[52] "How We Come to Own Ourselves" (ch. 4).

[53] See note 47, above.

as can be seen in nonsensical sayings like, "You have a right to the fruits of your labor."[54]

D. *The Labor Metaphor*

Overreliance on "labor" metaphors also leads to confusion about IP. Locke correctly argued that the first person to "mix his labor with" an unowned resource owns it, since he thereby establishes an objective link to the resource which gives him a better claim to it than latecomers.[55] However, Locke based his argument on the confused and unnecessary idea that a person "owns" his labor and "therefore" owns resources that he mixes it with. But labor is not owned—it is an *action*, something a person performs with his body, which he does own—and this assumption is not needed for the Lockean labor-mixture argument to work.[56] This mistaken notion leads some people to favor IP because they figure that if you own a scarce resource because you mix your labor with it, you also own useful ideas that are produced with your labor. The related

---

[54] See references in Part IV.D, below. See also *International News Service v. Associated Press*, 248 U.S. 215 (1918; https://supreme.justia.com/cases/federal/us/248/215/), where the Supreme Court recognized a *quasi*-property right in the fruits of one's labor, what is sometimes called the "sweat of the brow" doctrine (a doctrine later rejected in the copyright context in *Feist Publications, Inc. v. Rural Tel. Serv. Co.*, 499 U.S. 340 (1991; https://supreme.justia.com/cases/federal/us/499/340/)).

[55] See Hoppe, *A Theory of Socialism and Capitalism*, chaps. 1–2 & 7.

[56] As J.P. Day, in a critique of Locke's homesteading argument, correctly observes:

[O]ne cannot talk significantly of *owning labour$_1$*. For labour$_1$, or labouring, is an activity, and although activities can be engaged in, performed or done, they cannot be owned.

J.P. Day, "Locke on Property," *Philosophical Quarterly* 16 (1966): 207–220, p. 212 (also reprinted in Gordon J. Schochet, ed. *Life, Liberty, And Property: Essays on Locke's Political Ideas* (Belmont, California: Wadsworth Publishing Company, 1971), p. 113). By "labour$_1$," Day is referring to the activity or action of working or labouring, as opposed to a task (labour$_2$), an achievement (labour$_3$), force times distance (labour$_4$), or workers themselves (labour$_5$) (see the Appendix, p. 220). Day's comments are briefly discussed in Kirzner, "Producer, Entrepreneur, and the Right to Property," p. 6. See also Kinsella, "Cordato and Kirzner on Intellectual Property," *C4SIF Blog* (April 21, 2011). See also the Hume quote in the following note.

In Kirzner's words, Day summarizes Locke's theory of property argument thusly: "(1) Every man has a (moral) right to own his person; therefore (2) every man has a (moral) right to own the labor of his person; therefore (3) every man has a (moral) right to own that which he has mixed the labor of his person with." Kirzner, *op. cit.*, p. 5, citing Day, *op. cit.*, p. 208 (and p. 109 of the Schochet book).

Smith-Ricardo-Marx labor theory of value, which underlies Marxism and socialism, is also sometimes used to support IP, as when people argue that if you work or labor, you "deserve" some kind of reward or profit. All this focus on labor must be rejected as overly metaphorical and confused, and, frankly, Marxian.[57]

E. *The Separate Roles of Knowledge and Means in Action*

The purpose of property rights is to permit conflict-free use of resources, the scarce means of action that humans employ to causally interfere with the course of events in an attempt to achieve their ends. But this applies only to *conflictable* resources. Human action also implies the *possession of knowledge* by the actor—knowledge of what ends are possible and knowledge of what scarce means might be employed to *causally achieve* the desired end. Thus all successful human action requires *two separate components*: the availability of scarce means or resources and knowledge to guide one's action.[58] Property rights apply *only* to the

---

[57] See Kinsella, "Locke, Smith, Marx; the Labor Theory of Property and the Labor Theory of Value; and Rothbard, Gordon, and Intellectual Property," *StephanKinsella.com* (June 23, 2010); *idem*, "KOL 037 | Locke's Big Mistake: How the Labor Theory of Property Ruined Political Theory," *Kinsella on Liberty Podcast* (March 28, 2013); and *idem*, "Cordato and Kirzner on Intellectual Property." As Hume observes, "We cannot be said to join our labour to any thing but in a figurative sense." David Hume, *A Treatise of Human Nature*, Selby-Bigge, ed. (Oxford, 1968), Book III, Part II, Section III, n.16; discussed in "Law and Intellectual Property in a Stateless Society" (ch. 14), n.81. On the perils of metaphors see also note 83, below. See also Dan Sanchez, "The Fruit of Your Labor … is a good, not its form," *Medium* (Oct. 30, 2014; https://perma.cc/GD28-JS44).

[58] For elaboration, see Kinsella, "Intellectual Freedom and Learning Versus Patent and Copyright"; also *idem*, "The Death Throes of Pro-IP Libertarianism" and "Intellectual Property and the Structure of Human Action," *Mises Economics Blog* (Jan. 6, 2010). I also discuss these issues in "Law and Intellectual Property in a Stateless Society" (ch. 14), Part III.D and in "Goods, Scarce and Nonscarce" (ch. 18), n.28.

As Hoppe explains, Carl Menger pointed out four requirements for objects to become goods:

> The first is the existence of a human need. The second requirement is such properties as render the thing capable of being brought into a causal connection with a satisfaction of this need. That is, this object must be capable, through our performing certain manipulations with it, to cause certain needs to be satisfied or at least relieved. The third condition is that there must be human knowledge about this connection, which explains, of course, why it is important for people to learn to distinguish between *goods* and *bads*. Thus, we have human knowledge about the object, our ability to control it, and the causal power of this object to

scarce means or conflictable resources that humans employ, but not to the knowledge or information people possess, which guides their behavior, since anyone can use the same or similar knowledge to guide their own actions without conflict. In fact, it is the accumulation of this technological knowledge over time that enables increasing material prosperity. Property rights are needed to permit conflict-free use of scarce resources, but imposing restrictions on the emulation, learning, and use of knowledge, which is what IP attempts to do, impoverishes the human race.[59] This is why I concluded one article with these words:

> It is obscene to undermine the glorious operation of the market in producing wealth and abundance by imposing artificial scarcity on human knowledge and learning…. Learning, emulation, and information are good. It is good that information can be reproduced, retained, spread, and taught and learned and communicated so easily. Granted, we cannot say that it is *bad* that the world of physical resources is one of scarcity—this is the way reality is, after all—but it is certainly a challenge, and it makes life a struggle. It is suicidal and foolish to try to hamper one of our most important tools—learning, emulation, knowledge—by imposing scarcity

---

lead to certain types of satisfactory results. And the fourth factor is, as I already indicated, that we must have command of the thing sufficient to direct it to the satisfaction of the need. Hans-Hermann Hoppe, *Economy, Society, and History* (Auburn, Ala.: Mises Institute, 2021; www.hanshoppe.com/esh), p. 9; see also Carl Menger, *Principles of Economics* (Auburn, Ala.: Mises Institute, 2007 [1871]; https://mises.org/library/principles-economics), chap. I, §1, p. 52 *et pass.* The second requirement corresponds to the means being *causally efficacious*; the third to the actor's *knowledge* of causal laws; and the fourth to the *availability* of the means. See also related discussion in "Goods, Scarce and Nonscarce" (ch. 18), n.28, and in Eugen von Böhm-Bawerk, "Whether Legal Rights and Relationships Are Economic Goods," George D. Huncke, trans., in Eugen von Böhm-Bawerk, *Shorter Classics of Eugen von Böhm-Bawerk* (South Holland, Ill.: Libertarian Press, 1962 [1881]), p. 57 *et pass.*, discussed in Gael J. Campan, "Does Justice Qualify as an Economic Good?: A Böhm-Bawerkian Perspective," *Q. J. Austrian Econ.* 2, no. 1 (Spring 1999; https://perma.cc/G3CK-B8WB): 21–33, p. 24.

[59] For elaboration, see Kinsella, "Hayek's Views on Intellectual Property," *C4SIF Blog* (Aug. 2, 2013) and "Intellectual Property and the Structure of Human Action," discussing Hayek's comments about how the accumulation of a "fund of experience" helps aid human progress and the creation of wealth. See also Kinsella, "Tucker, 'Knowledge Is as Valuable as Physical Capital,'" *C4SIF Blog* (March 27, 2017) and George Reisman, "Progress In a Free Economy," *The Freeman* (July 1, 1980; https://perma.cc/2HW6-JJ8J). See also Julio H. Cole, "Patents and Copyrights: Do the Benefits Exceed the Costs?", *J. Libertarian Stud.* 15, no. 4 (Fall 2001; https://mises.org/library/patents-and-copyrights-do-benefits-exceed-costs-0): 79–105, p. 84 *et seq.*, discussing the importance of technical progress (not to be confused with patents) to economic growth. Cole cites several studies in n.12.

on it. Intellectual property is theft. Intellectual property is statism. Intellectual property is death. Give us *intellectual freedom* instead![60]

F. Resources, Properties, Features, and Universals[61]

As noted above (see note 31), confusion about the IP issue sometimes stems from identifying "property" with the owned resource. People then get bogged down in loaded or confused questions like, "Are ideas property?" If one keeps in mind that the question is not what is property, but rather who is the owner of a conflictable resource, then the IP mistake is harder to make. A related mistake stems from the failure to understand that all human rights are property rights and all property rights *just are* rights to the exclusive control of a given scarce (conflictable) resource.[62] But every property right is an ownership right held by a particular person or owner with respect to a particular conflictable resource. It is the actual resource itself which is owned, *not* its characteristics.

For example, if you own a red car, you own that car, but you do not own its color; you do not own red or redness. If owning a red car meant you owned its characteristics, you would own not only that particular car, but its age, weight, size, shape, color, and so on, and, thus, would thereby have an ownership claim over any other object that is red, and so on. This would amount to reassigning ownership rights in someone

---

[60] Kinsella, "The Death Throes of Pro-IP Libertarianism."

[61] See also Part IV.B, above.

[62] To be even more precise, I would say that a property right is not a *right to use* a resource, but a *right to exclude others* from using a resource. In practical terms this gives the owner the ability to use it as he sees fit so long as he is not using trespassing on others' property rights. This follows from the analysis in Kinsella, "The Non-Aggression Principle as a Limit on Action, Not on Property Rights," *StephanKinsella.com* (Jan. 22, 2010) and *idem*, "IP and Aggression as Limits on Property Rights: How They Differ," *StephanKinsella.com* (Jan. 22, 2010). However, this nuance need not concern us here. See also "What Libertarianism Is" (ch. 2), p. 32; George Mavrodes, "Property," in Samuel L. Blumenfeld, *Property in a Humane Economy* (LaSalle, Ill.: Open Court, 1974; https://mises.org/library/propertyhumane-economy), p. 184; "A Libertarian Theory of Contract" (ch. 9), n.1; *Connell v. Sears, Roebuck Co.*, 722 F.2d 1542, 1547 (Fed. Cir. 1983; https://casetext.com/case/connell-v-sears-roebuck-co) ("the right to exclude recognized in a patent is but the essence of the concept of property"), citing *Schenck v. Nortron Corp.*, 713 F.2d 782 (Fed. Cir. 1983; https://casetext.com/case/carl-schenck-ag-v-nortron-corp). Further, property rights are rights *as between human actors*, but *with respect to particular resources*. See "A Libertarian Theory of Contract" (ch. 9), n.1.

else's red car to you, even though he owns that car and you did not homestead it or obtain it by contract. Likewise, information cannot be owned since it is not an *independently existing thing*; information is *always* the *impatterning* of an underlying medium or carrier or substrate, which is itself a scarce resource that has an owner.[63] If I own a copy of *Great Expectations*, I own that physical object: paper and glue and ink. It has various characteristics: an age, a size, a shape, and a certain arrangement of ink on its pages—the way the ink is impatterned so that it represents letters and words and meanings to someone who can read and who can observe the features of the book. But just as you don't own the color of your car, you don't own the way an object is arranged or shaped.[64]

As Roderick Long explains:

> It may be objected that the person who originated the information deserves ownership rights over it. But information is not a concrete thing an individual can control; it is a *universal*, existing in other people's minds and other people's property, and over these the originator has no legitimate sovereignty. You cannot own information without owning other people.[65]

---

[63] J. Neil Schulman argued for years for a form of IP known as "logorights." Oddly, perhaps partially in response to my relentless criticism of his flawed argument, he eventually changed his argument to argue for "media-carried property," thus implicitly acknowledging that he was in favor of property rights in characteristics, or features, of owned objects, i.e., universals. See "Introduction to Origitent" (ch. 16) and "Conversation with Schulman about Logorights and Media-Carried Property" (ch. 17).

[64] Even the pro-IP Ayn Rand implicitly acknowledged this. As she wrote:
The power to rearrange the combinations of natural elements is the only creative power man possesses. It is an enormous and glorious power—and it is the only meaning of the concept "creative." "Creation" does not (and metaphysically cannot) mean the power to bring something into existence out of nothing. "Creation" means the power to bring into existence an arrangement (or combination or integration) of natural elements that had not existed before.
See Kinsella, "Locke on IP; Mises, Rothbard, and Rand on Creation, Production, and 'Rearranging,'" quoting Ayn Rand, "The Metaphysical and the Man-Made," in *Philosophy: Who Needs It* (New American Library, 1984), p. 25. See similar quotes by Rothbard, J.S. Mill, and Mises in ibid; and Reisman, "Progress In a Free Economy."
Neil Schulman and I bat these ideas around in "Conversation with Schulman about Logorights and Media-Carried Property" (ch. 17).

[65] Long, "The Libertarian Case Against Intellectual Property Rights" (emphasis added). See also *idem*, "Owning Ideas Means Owning People" and *idem*, "Bye-Bye for IP," *Austro-Athenian Empire Blog* (May 20, 2010; https://perma.cc/HD5A-TTX8), and Part IV.B,

G. Selling Does Not Imply Ownership[66]

As noted in Part IV.B, above, it is literally impossible to own or have property rights in information or knowledge. People only manipulate and have conflict over scarce resources (they are means of action, after all), so that IP rights are just disguised reassignments of property rights in existing conflictable or scarce resources. And as noted in Part IV.F, above, information cannot be owned since it is not an *independently existing thing*; information is *always* the *impatterning* of an underlying medium or carrier or substrate, which is itself a scarce resource that already has an owner, in accordance with principles of original appropriation, contract, and rectification.

Yet IP proponents sometimes point out that information, ideas, know-how, and so on (as well as labor), can be *sold*. And so, the reasoning goes, something that can be *sold* must have been *owned* by the seller. Therefore, information can, in fact, be owned. As I have explained elsewhere, this reasoning is fallacious and based on conflation of two senses of the word "sell."[67] When *A* and *B* exchange two owned objects, such as an apple for an orange, then there are two title transfers. *A* sells his apple to *B*, and *B* sells his orange to *A*.

But other contracts only involve one title-transfer. Suppose *B* pays *A* to perform some action (labor, a service, providing information, etc.). In this case, *B*'s owned resource (money or something else) transfers to *A*, but nothing that *A* owns transfers to *B*. It is simply that *A* performed some action that *B* desired, and was induced to do so by *B*'s payment.

---

above, and Kinsella, "Mr. IP Answer Man Time: On Steel and Swords," *C4SIF Blog* (Feb. 4, 2022); *idem*, "How To Think About Property," *StephanKinsella.com* (April 25, 2021); *idem*, "Libertarian Answer Man: Mind-Body Dualism, Self-Ownership, and Property Rights," *StephanKinsella.com* (Jan. 29, 2022); *idem*, "KOL337 | Join the Wasabikas Ep. 15.0: You Don't Own Bitcoin—Property Rights, Praxeology and the Foundations of Private Law, with Max Hillebrand"; *idem*, "KOL219 | Property: What It Is and Isn't: Houston Property Rights Association," Kinsella on Liberty Podcast," *Kinsella on Liberty Podcast* (April 28, 2017); and *idem*, "Nobody Owns Bitcoin," *StephanKinsella.com* (April 21, 2021). See also *idem*, "Patrick Smith, Un-Intellectual Property," *C4SIF Blog* (March 4, 2016).

[66] The ideas in this section are developed more fully in "Selling Does Not Imply Ownership, and Vice-Versa: A Dissection" (ch. 11).

[67] See ibid.; also Kinsella, "The 'If you own something, that implies that you can sell it; if you sell something, that implies you must own it first' Fallacies," *StephanKinsella.com* (June 1, 2018); "A Libertarian Theory of Contract" (ch. 9).

In this case, the end of B's act of agreeing to pay A was not the attainment of a property right or title transfer, but the achievement of a new state of affairs in which A performed some action desired by B.[68] A is sometimes said to "sell" his labor or information to B because of the analogy to a normal exchange of title, but here the word "sell" is used in the economic sense to simply explain A's motivations and to properly characterize his actions: to understand his ends or goals. In order to get B's payment, A performed the action desired by B. A does not "sell" his labor or knowledge in a juristic or legal sense, and thus did not "own" it in a legal sense. Thus, "selling" in the economic sense does not imply owning. Information is unownable.[69]

H. All Property Rights Are Limited

One final argument may be addressed, which is touched on in some of the above sections.[70] When explaining why IP rights violate property rights, we IP opponents explain that the grant of an IP right is tantamount to a nonconsensual negative easement on someone else's property—it limits what the owner of a resource may do with the resource.[71] Or, as Roderick Long would say, "Owning Ideas Means Owning People."[72]

A common response runs something like this:

> Yes, IP rights limit what you can do with your own property. But this is true of all property rights. My ownership of a home, or my body, means you can't shoot your gun at it. So my property rights limit your property rights. Therefore, just because intellectual property rights limit your property rights doesn't mean they are illegitimate any more than my self-ownership limits your property rights in your gun.

---

[68] See also Kinsella, "Human Action and Universe Creation," *StephanKinsella.com* (June 28, 2022).

[69] As is bitcoin. Bitcoins are just abstract informational entries on a distributed ledger, that is, the impatternings of the memory devices of many people's computers; but they own those computers; nobody owns "how they are arranged." See Kinsella, "Nobody Owns Bitcoin."

[70] See, e.g., the discussion in Part IV.F, above.

[71] See Part IV.B, above.

[72] See Long, "Owning Ideas Means Owning People."

There are many problems with this argument, as I have detailed elsewhere.[73] First, even if we grant that in some cases property rights can be limited, it does not imply that just *any* limit is legitimate. If a woman objects to being raped, it will not do to say "stop complaining that we are violating your property right in your own body; after all, all property rights are limited." You would need to articulate why it's justified to limit property rights. In the examples given by IP proponents, someone's property rights are limited as needed to keep them from exercising those rights to commit aggression against others' property rights. But IP rights limit the owner's property rights (again, in the form of a negative servitude), even though the owner, in rearranging *his own resources* in a certain way, does not invade the borders of the inventor's or author's property. In response to this, the IP proponent will say, "Yes, by making a copy of the author/inventor's creation, the copier is infringing the author/inventor's property rights." But this is question-begging. It presupposes that there *are* rights to universals, when this is the issue under dispute.

Second, it is simply not true that property rights limit other property rights. Rather, property rights limit *actions*. If *A* owns his body, then *B* may not shoot it with a gun, *whether he owns the gun or not*. The point is that *B* may not use or invade the borders of *A*'s body—his owned resource—with *any* means at all, whether it be the use of *B*'s hands, or some other means such as a gun, even if he stole the gun from *C* and is not its owner. People are responsible for their *actions*, and actions always employ some means to achieve the end. The means may be simply the actor's own body, or it may be some external object, one that may be owned by the actor, or not.[74]

---

[73] See Kinsella, "The Non-Aggression Principle as a Limit on Action, Not on Property Rights"; *idem*, "IP and Aggression as Limits on Property Rights: How They Differ"; and "Selling Does Not Imply Ownership, and Vice-Versa: A Dissection" (ch. 11), n.11 and accompanying text.

[74] Likewise, many libertarians, having in mind some form of "strict liability," advance the confused idea that we are responsible for harms done with property (resources) that we own. This is incorrect. We are responsible only for our actions, not for uses to which inanimate objects are put. If I possess a stolen knife, I am liable if I stab an innocent person with it, even though I don't own the knife, since it is my *actions* that I am responsible for. And if some thief steals a knife and uses it to harm an innocent victim, it is the thief that is responsible, not the owner of the knife. One common confusion held even by many libertarians is the idea (which underlies many assertions about "strict liability") that ownership implies responsibility (some have even confusingly said that you "own your actions," which

Therefore, it *is* a valid criticism of IP that it unjustly limits others' use of their own resources.

I. *The Structural Unity of Real and Intellectual Property*

Another argument made in support of IP is that it is, legally, structurally similar to normal property rights in scarce resources, such as property rights in realty (land or immovables) or personalty (corporeal movables).[75]

---

is incoherent). It does not. Ownership means the *right to control* (or, more precisely: the right to exclude others from controlling) a given resource; it does *not* imply responsibility. We are responsible only for our actions, regardless of whatever means are employed by the actor to achieve the illicit end. It is misleading and confusing for libertarians to carelessly use expressions such as "I own that action" to mean "I am responsible for harm I cause." The term ownership should be restricted to property rights in conflictable resources—and should be used as a synonym for possession, either, as I point out in "Selling Does Not Imply Ownership, and Vice-Versa: A Dissection" (ch. 11), the sections "External Resources" and "Economic vs. Normative Realms of Analysis: Ownership vs. Possession."

On negligence and strict liability, see Kinsella, "The Libertarian Approach to Negligence, Tort, and Strict Liability: Wergeld and Partial Wergeld," *Mises Economics Blog* (Sep. 1, 2009); "A Libertarian Theory of Punishment and Rights" (ch. 5), at n.78; "Causation and Aggression" (ch. 8), at n.60; and "A Libertarian Theory of Contract: Title Transfer, Binding Promises, and Inalienability" (ch. 9), n.6.

[75] See, e.g., Richard A. Epstein, *The Structural Unity of Real and Intellectual Property* (The Progress and Freedom Foundation, 2006; archived version at https://perma.cc/B8JP-4MWQ); *idem*, "The Disintegration of Intellectual Property? A Classical Liberal Response to a Premature Obituary," *Stanford L. Rev.* 62, no. 2 (2010; https://perma.cc/79X2-9CS8): 455–523; Wendy J. Gordon, "An Inquiry into the Merits of Copyright: The Challenges of Consistency, Consent, and Encouragement Theory," *Stan. L. Rev.* 41 (1989; https://papers.ssrn.com/sol3/papers.cfm?abstract_id=3581843), Part I; Adam Mossoff, "Commercializing Property Rights in Inventions: Lessons for Modern Patent Theory from Classic Patent Doctrine," in Geoffrey A. Manne & Joshua D. Wright, eds., *Competition Policy and Patent Law Under Uncertainty: Regulating Innovation* (Cambridge University Press, 2011; https://perma.cc/SD7Q-F7U9); *idem*, "The Trespass Fallacy in Patent Law," *Florida L. Rev.* 65, no. 6 (2013; https://papers.ssrn.com/sol3/papers.cfm?abstract_id=2126595): 1687–1711; Roger E. Meiners & Robert J. Staaf, "Patents, Copyrights, and Trademarks: Property or Monopoly," *Harv. J. L. & Pub. Pol'y* 13, no. 3 (Summer 1990): 911–48, pp. 915, 923, 940, *et pass*. Mackaay unpersuasively argues that something resembling patent and copyright can emerge through private legal arrangement like trade secret and contractual structures, a "simulated property right," which the legislator can then "complement" by "by adding the possibility of systematically ensuring exclusivity against third parties." Mackaay, "Economic Incentives in Markets for Information and Innovation," p. 904; see also p. 899–901 *et pass*. Or, as summarized by Dale Nance, Mackaay sees IP rights:

> ... as representing a compromise that appears relatively warranted because they do not have the kind of features associated with the worst kinds of governmental meddling in the economy, and because their functional equivalents could, to a considerable extent but perhaps at greater cost, be achieved by carefully protected trade

This is an odd argument. It is true that the state, via legislation, is able to set up positive rights that, in modern legal systems, are treated similarly to property rights in scarce resources (land and personalty). But so what? In antebellum America, under chattel slavery, slaves—innocent human beings—were legally ownable and thus subject to the various legal incidents of property, such as sale, mortgages, and so on. The fact that the state, by artificial legislation, can make inventions and artistic creations the subject of contracts, sales, and so on does not show that the law is just. This is just a facile argument.[76]

First, patent and copyright were not originally called property rights. They were referred to accurately as state-granted privileges or monopolies.[77] Referring to patent and copyright as "property rights" was a later

---

secrets combined with contractually imposed restrictions on copying by buyers or licensees of the information in question. In other words, he sees patents and copyrights as little more troublesome than state-provided form contracts.

Dale A. Nance, "Foreword: Owning Ideas," *Harv. J. L. & Pub. Pol'y* 13, no. 3 (Summer 1990): 757–74, p. 770. Easterbrook makes a similar, and similarly untenable, claim, when he writes: "[I]n the end intellectual property may be understood as the result of voluntary undertakings, which the government simply enforces." Frank H. Easterbrook, "Intellectual Property Is Still Property," *Harv. J. L. & Pub. Pol'y* 13, no. 1 (Winter 1990; https://chicagounbound.uchicago.edu/journal_articles/309/): 108–118, p. 114.

And many other proponents of IP argue for parallels between IP rights and normal property rights. See, e.g., "Conversation with Schulman about Logorights and Media-Carried Property" (ch. 17).

Yet elsewhere, Epstein concedes there are some significant differences between IP and real property. As he writes, "There are in fact no 'natural' boundaries here [in patent and copyright law], similar to the metes and bounds of land." Richard A. Epstein, "Why Libertarians Shouldn't Be (Too) Skeptical about Intellectual Property," Progress & Freedom Foundation, *Progress on Point*, Paper No. 13.4 (February 2006; https://perma.cc/6F5S-7KNS), p. 8. So much for the "structural unity."

[76] See my posts "Yet more disanalogies between copyright and real property," *C4SIF Blog* (Feb. 4, 2013); "Mossoff: Patent Law Really Is as Straightforward as Real Estate Law," *C4SIF Blog* (Aug. 17, 2012); "Classifying Patent and Copyright Law as 'Property': So What?", *Mises Economics Blog* (Oct. 4, 2011); and "Richard Epstein on 'The Structural Unity of Real and Intellectual Property,'" *Mises Economics Blog* (Oct. 4, 2006). Anyone who thinks there can be a straightforward analogy between normal property rights and property rights in intangibles should consult Peter Drahos, *A Philosophy of Intellectual Property* (Ashgate, 1996; https://press-files.anu.edu.au/downloads/press/n1902/html/cover.xhtml), pp. 16–19 *et pass.*, and Alexander Peukert, *A Critique of the Ontology of Intellectual Property Law*, Gill Mertens, trans. (Cambridge University Press, 2021), p. 101 *et pass.*

[77] See Kinsella, "Intellectual Properganda," *Mises Economics Blog* (Dec. 6, 2010). See also the discussion of Böhm-Bawerk on the use of inaccurate terms, in "On the Logic of Libertarianism and Why Intellectual Property Doesn't Exist" (ch. 24), n.32.

innovation, engaged in for propaganda purposes. This was observed by Fritz Machlup and Edith Penrose in a seminal study in 1950:

> There are many writers who habitually call all sorts of rights by the name of property. This may be a harmless waste of words, or it may have a purpose. It happens that *those who started using the word property in connection with inventions had a very definite purpose in mind: they wanted to substitute a word with a respectable connotation, "property," for a word that had an unpleasant ring, "privilege."*[78]

And as Machlup wrote in a later study commissioned by the US Congress:

> While some economists before 1873 were anxious to deny that patents conferred "monopolies"—and, indeed, had talked of "property in inventions" chiefly in order to avoid using the unpopular word "monopoly"—most of this squeamishness has disappeared. But most writers want to make it understood that these are not "odious" monopolies but rather "social monopolies", "general welfare monopolies", or "socially earned" monopolies. Most writers also point out with great emphasis that the monopoly grant is limited and conditional.[79]

---

[78] Fritz Machlup & Edith Penrose, "The Patent Controversy in the Nineteenth Century," *J. Econ. History* 10, no. 1 (May 1950): 1–29, p. 16 (footnotes omitted; emphasis added). They go on (ibid.; footnotes omitted):

> This was a very deliberate choice on the part of politicians working for the adoption of a patent law in the French Constitutional Assembly. De Bouffler, reporting the bill to the Assembly, knew that "the spirit of the time was so much for liberty and equality, and against privileges and monopolies of any sort" that there was no hope of saving the institution of patent privileges except under an acceptable theory. Thus, according to Rentzsch, De Bouffler and his friends in deliberate insincerity "construed the artificial theory of the property rights of the inventor" as a part of the rights of man. De Bouffler obviously knew "what's in a name." As monopoly privileges, the patents for inventions would be rejected by the Assembly or, if accepted, would be disdained by the people; as natural property rights, they would be accepted and respected.

[79] Fritz Machlup, U.S. Senate Subcommittee On Patents, Trademarks & Copyrights, *An Economic Review of the Patent System* (85th Cong., 2nd Session, 1958, Study No. 15; https://mises.org/library/economic-review-patent-system), p. 26 (footnotes omitted). As explained in Machlup & Penrose, "The Patent Controversy in the Nineteenth Century," and as summarized in Machlup, *An Economic Review of the Patent System*, free market economists began to object to the patent system in the mid-1800s, leading some countries to repeal or delay adopting patent laws. The primary criticism was that protectionist patent grants are incompatible with free trade. However, the "Long Depression" starting in 1873 turned public opinion against free trade, leading the anti-patent movement to collapse and

Professor Michael Davis also explores the strategy of those who insist on erroneously classifying patents as property rights. He calls this tactic "the trump of property," which is

> a strategy of defining patents according to property law concepts far removed from debates over the public interest in the issuance of patents …. [T]he foregoing description of patent law as a form of competition regulation, let alone as a form of national industrial policy, is obviously not the conventional one. Organized patent interests (the patent bar, patent proprietors, and their sponsors) do not espouse that view, but instead habitually offer a more cramped description of patent law. One might call that description the trump of property—a strategy to secure the claim that proprietors can exclusively own patents, and to eliminate any argument that the public has a continuing interest in issued patents. That description promotes patents as just another kind of property, but firmly rejects any suggestion that patent law represents either a form of competition regulation or a national industrial policy. With a firm foundation in free market theories, the strong claim that patents are just another form of property implicitly rejects the idea that patent law serves any regulatory function….[80]

Davis also notes, of the attempt by defenders of patents to deny that they are monopolies:

> This "debate" seemingly has only one point: to sanitize the patent monopoly so that it more closely resembles simple property. A monopoly, of course, virtually compels the public interest. Thus, the trump of property depends on asserting not only that a patent is simple property, but also that it does not constitute an economic phenomenon, like a monopoly, in which the public has a particular interest.[81]

---

for modern patent systems to eventually become dominant world-wide. See also, on this, Meiners & Staaf, "Patents, Copyrights, and Trademarks: Property or Monopoly," p. 911–12.

[80] Michael H. Davis, "Patent Politics," *S. Carolina L. Rev.* 56, no. 2 (Winter 2004; https://scholarcommons.sc.edu/sclr/vol56/iss2/6): 337–86, pp. 338–39 & 373–74 (footnote omitted); discussed in Kinsella, "Patent Lawyers Who Don't Toe the Line Should Be Punished!" *C4SIF Blog* (April 12, 2012). Amusingly, the left-leaning Davis, somewhat perplexed, writes "Many libertarians, practically wedded to the free market system, surprisingly oppose patent rights," citing my *AIP*. Davis, *op cit.*, p. 374, n.142.

[81] Ibid., p. 374, n.141. See also Kinsella, "Are Patents and Copyrights 'Monopolies'?", *C4SIF Blog* (Aug. 13, 2013). As Hayek wrote:

> Perhaps it is not a waste of your time if I illustrate what I have in mind by quoting a rather well-known decision in which an American judge argued that "as to the suggestion that competitors were excluded from the use of the patent we answer

It is clear that, despite the assertions of defenders of IP, these rights are *not* like normal property rights in scarce resources. First, unlike property rights in scarce resources like personalty (movables) and real estate or land (immovables), IP rights in inventions (patents) and creative works (copyright) expire after a finite term—about 17 or so years for patents, and life of the author plus 70 years for copyright (say, about 120 years for a 40 year old author who lives to age 90). Second, the "borders" or boundaries defined by copyright law in "works" and by patent law for "inventions" is inherently murky, vague, arbitrary, and non-objective.

Scholars have noted other differences between IP and normal property rights. Writes Professor Tom Bell:

> Copyrights and patents differ from tangible property in fundamental ways. Economically speaking, copyrights and patents are not rivalrous in consumption; whereas all the world can sing the same beautiful song, for instance, only one person can swallow a cool gulp of iced tea. Legally speaking, copyrights and patents exist only thanks to the express terms of the U.S. Constitution and various statutory enactments. In contrast, we enjoy tangible property thanks to common law, customary practices, and nature itself. Even birds recognize property rights in nests. They do not, however, copyright their songs.
>
> Those represent but some of the reasons I have argued that we should call copyright an *intellectual privilege*, reserving *property* for things that deserve the label. Another, related reason: Calling copyright *property* risks eroding that valuable service mark.[82]

---

that such exclusion may be said to have been the very essence of the right conferred by the patent" and adds "as it is the privilege of any owner of property to use it or not to use it without any question of motive." It is this last statement which seems to me to be significant for *the way in which a mechanical extension of the property concept by lawyers has done so much to create undesirable and harmful privilege.* F.A. Hayek, "'Free' Enterprise and Competitive Order," in *Individualism and Economic Order* (Chicago: University of Chicago Press, 1948; https://mises.org/library/individualism-and-economic-order), p. 114 (emphasis added; citation omitted). See also *idem, The Fatal Conceit* (Chicago: University of Chicago Press, 1988), pp. 36–37; and Cole, "Patents and Copyrights: Do the Benefits Exceed the Costs?", at 82–83.

[82] Tom Bell, "Copyright Erodes Property^SM," *Agoraphilia* (July 14, 2011; https://perma.cc/L25V-A8X8). See also *idem,* "Copyright as Intellectual ~~Property~~ Privilege," *Syracuse L. Rev.* 58 (2007; https://perma.cc/7ZLM-CDWA): 523–46. Bell also writes elsewhere: "to call copyright 'property' risks vesting copyright holders with more powers than they deserve. To call it 'privilege' offers a rhetorical counterbalance, reminding copyright holders of what

Regarding Epstein's contentions about the "structural unity" between IP and real property rights, Professor Peter Menell concludes that:

> [T]he Property Rights Movement is too limited and grounded in absolutist ideology to support the needs of a dynamic, resource-sensitive intellectual property system. Professor Epstein's simplistic equation of real and intellectual property generates more heat than light. It is not particularly helpful to think of real and intellectual property as structurally unified. The differences matter significantly and resorting to rhetorical metaphors distracts attention from critical issues. As Judge (later Justice) Cardozo cautioned in 1926, "[m]etaphors in law are to be narrowly watched, for starting as devices to liberate thought, they end often by enslaving it."[83]

There are even further dissimilarities between IP rights and normal property rights. For example, as Professors Dorfman and Jacob write:

> In these pages we seek to integrate two claims. First, we argue that, taken to their logical conclusions, the considerations that support a strict form of protection for tangible property rights do not call for a similar form of protection when applied to the case of copyright. More dramatically, these considerations *demand*, on pain of glaring inconsistency, a substantially weaker protection for copyright. In pursuing this claim, we show that the form of protecting property rights (including rights in tangibles) is, to an important extent, a feature of certain normal, though contingent, facts about the human world. Second, the normative question concerning the

---

they owe to the public and recalling lawmakers to their duties." Bell, *Intellectual Privilege*, p. 98 (footnote omitted).

[83] Peter S. Menell, "The Property Rights Movement's Embrace of Intellectual Property: True Love or Doomed Relationship?", UC Berkeley Public Law Research Paper No. 965083 (Feb. 26, 2007; https://perma.cc/F6X9-5L9D), quoting *Berkey v. Third Ave. Ry. Co.*, 155 N.E. 58, 61 (N.Y. 1926; https://casetext.com/case/berkey-v-third-avenue-railway-co). See also *idem*, "Intellectual Property and the Property Rights Movement," *Regulation* 30, no. 3 (Fall 2007; https://perma.cc/F6X9-5L9D): 36–42, at 42 ("Suggesting that 'intellectual property' must be treated as part of a monolithic "property" edifice masks fundamental differences and distracts attention from critical issues"); and Christina Mulligan & Brian Patrick Quinn, "Who are You Calling a Pirate?: Shaping Public Discourse in the Intellectual Property Debates," Brandeis University Department of English Eighth Annual Graduate Conference (2010; https://perma.cc/7SCS-8P3J), pp. 7–8 (regarding overuse of the "piracy" metaphor for copyright infringement).

On the perils of misuse of metaphors, see Kinsella, "On the Danger of Metaphors in Scientific Discourse," *StephanKinsella.com* (June 12, 2011) and *idem*, "Objectivist Law Prof Mossoff on Copyright; or, the Misuse of Labor, Value, and Creation Metaphors," *Mises Economics Blog* (Jan. 3, 2008).

selection of a desirable protection for creative works is most naturally pursued from a tort law perspective, in part because the normative structure
of copyright law simply is that of tort law.[84]

Thus, as Wendy Gordon writes,

> The "property" portion of the "intellectual property" label has caused
> practical as well as conceptual difficulties. Too many courts have assumed
> that all things called "property" should be treated similarly, ignoring the
> important physical, institutional, and statutory differences that distin-
> guish intellectual "property" from the tangible kind.[85]

Incidentally, I should note that, to my knowledge, none of the
above-quoted scholars is an IP or patent abolitionist, except perhaps

---

[84] Avihay Dorfman & Assaf Jacob, "Copyright as Tort," *Theoretical Inquiries* in Law 12,
no. 1 (Jan. 2011; https://perma.cc/4HZM-QPHU): 59–97, p. 96–97.

[85] Wendy J. Gordon, "Intellectual Property," in *Oxford Handbook of Legal Studies* (Peter
Cane & Mark Tushnet ed., 2003; https://perma.cc/59GP-HRD8), § 1.1.3. *But see idem*,
"An Inquiry into the Merits of Copyright," at 1353, 1354, 1378 ("The noncontractual
restraints imposed by copyright are of the same nature as those imposed by other areas of the law.... [T]he commonalities in structure predominate over the differences....
[I]ntellectual and tangible property serve similar economic roles.... [T]he tangible and
intangible property structures are quite similar.... [C]opyright is functionally as well as
structurally consistent with tangible property."). Perhaps the apparent difference in Gordon's views is due to some evolution of views, as they were published fourteen years apart.
See also Adam Mossoff, "Patents as Constitutional Private Property: The Historical Protection of Patents Under the Takings Clause," *Boston U. L. Rev.* 87 (2007; https://perma.
cc/G7JW-NZNE): 689–724, at pp. 698–99 (mentioning some scholars who, accepting
the "claim that patents and copyrights were special, limited monopoly grants in the early
American Republic ... today condemn recent expansions in intellectual property rights,
which they refer to as 'propertizing' intellectual property. They also criticize the use of
'property rhetoric' in intellectual property doctrines today, which they consider both a
novel practice and a contributing factor in the 'propertization' of intellectual property
doctrines"; footnotes omitted); and Mulligan & Quinn, "Who are You Calling a Pirate?,"
p. 1 (arguing that the "analogy between physical property and intellectual property is
troubled for a number of reasons"). See also Lawrence Lessig, *Free Culture: How Big
Media Uses Technology and the Law to Lock Down Culture and Control Creativity* (New
York: Penguin Press, 2004; https://perma.cc/J8ZM-FT46), pp, 117–18, who argues that
the desire to treat IP rights the same as other property rights has:
> ... *no* reasonable connection to our actual legal tradition. ... While 'creative prop-
> erty' is certainly 'property' in a nerdy and precise sense that lawyers are trained
> to understand, it has never been the case, nor should it be, that 'creative property
> owners' have been 'accorded the same rights and protection resident in all other
> property owners.' Indeed, if creative property owners were given the same rights
> as all other property owners, that would effect a radical, and radically undesirable,
> change in our tradition.

for Davis re patents. But they are honest scholars who recognize IP as being an unnatural legal regime distinct from natural, common law property rights.

In sum, IP rights, especially patent and copyright, are not like property rights in scarce resources. And even if they were, this would not make them just, any more than the ability to make human slaves property justifies that institution.

J. John Locke and the Founders on IP as a Natural Right

In what seems to be nothing more than an appeal to authority, some defenders of IP argue that IP rights are not artificial state-granted monopoly privileges, but rather natural property rights, and that this was recognized by Locke and the Founders of the US Constitution and various constitutional interpretations of patent and copyright.[86]

First, it must be said that it is irrelevant whether Locke and some Founding Fathers thought of IP as a natural right or not. If they did, they were just wrong.

It is clear that Jefferson did not.[87] He was not opposed to patent and copyright, but clearly viewed them as grants of monopoly privilege, a policy tool. After all, during the drafting of the Bill of Rights, Jefferson, in a Letter to James Madison, proposed an amendment to

---

[86] See, e.g., Adam Mossoff, "Who Cares What Thomas Jefferson Thought About Patents? Reevaluating the Patent 'Privilege' in Historical Context," *Cornell L. Rev.* 92 (2007; https://perma.cc/UZ9H-RK77): 953–1012; *idem*, "Saving Locke from Marx: The Labor Theory of Value in Intellectual Property Theory," *Social Philosophy and Policy* 29, no. 2 (2012; https://perma.cc/QG87-BAMY): 283–317; *idem*, "The Constitutional Protection of Intellectual Property," Heritage Foundation (March 8, 2021; https://perma.cc/8ZUN-L4XZ); *idem*, "Life, Liberty and Intellectual Property by Adam Mossoff," Ayn Rand Institute, YouTube (Sep. 21, 2021; https://youtu.be/CfMd1fHc2mE); Randolph J. May & Seth L. Cooper, *The Constitutional Foundations of Intellectual Property: A Natural Rights Perspective* (Carolina Academic Press, 2015).

As can be seen, there are a variety of arguments in favor of IP: the utilitarian or consequentialist or incentive-based argument implied by the Constitution's authorization for IP law ("to promote the progress...") (see ch. 16, the section "IP in the Industrial Age"; ch. 14, Part III.A); natural rights, and "creationism" (Part IV.C, above; ch. 14, Part III.b); and others, such as theories related to personality or personhood, fairness, welfare, and culture. See references in "Law and Intellectual Property in a Stateless Society" (ch. 14), n.76.

[87] See, e.g., Mossoff, "Who Cares What Thomas Jefferson Thought About Patents?"

the draft Bill of Rights to limit the terms of "monopolies" (patent and copyright) to a fixed number of years, to-wit:

> Art. 9. Monopolies may be allowed to persons for their own productions in literature and their own inventions in the arts for a term not exceeding — years but for no longer term and no other purpose.[88]

In another letter, to Isaac McPherson, he wrote:

> Accordingly, it is a fact, as far as I am informed, that England was, until we copied her, the only country on earth which ever, by a general law, gave a legal right to the exclusive use of an idea. In some other countries it is sometimes done, in a great case, and by a special and personal act, but, generally speaking, other nations have thought that these monopolies produce more embarrassment than advantage to society; and it may be observed that the nations which refuse monopolies of invention, are as fruitful as England in new and useful devices.[89]

As for Locke, he did favor copyright for authors, but only as a policy tool. He did not view IP rights as natural property rights. As Professor Tom Bell explains, Locke's:

> … labor-desert justification of property gives authors clear title to the particular tangible copy in which they fix their expression. If an author has already acquired property rights in paper and ink by dint of creating them or, more likely, consensual exchange, and then mixes those two forms of chattel property, tracing ink words on cellulose paper, then the author enjoys natural and common-law rights in the newly arranged physical property. But it remains a separate—and contestable—question whether that argument establishing rights in *atoms* also justifies giving an author property rights to a parcel in the imaginary realm of ideas. Locke himself did not try to justify intangible property. He appears, in fact, to have viewed copyright as merely a policy tool for promoting the public good. Modern commentators who would venture so far beyond the boundaries of Locke's thought, into the abstractions of intellectual property, thus go further than Locke ever dared and further than they should in his name.…

---

[88] See "Letter From Thomas Jefferson to James Madison, 28 August 1789," *Founders Online* (https://founders.archives.gov/documents/Jefferson/01-15-02-0354); also Kinsella, "Thomas Jefferson's Proposal to Limit the Length of Patent and Copyright in the Bill of Rights," *C4SIF Blog* (Dec. 1, 2011).

[89] See "Thomas Jefferson to Isaac McPherson 13 Aug. 1813," *Founders Online* (text formatted; emphasis added; https://founders.archives.gov/documents/Jefferson/03-06-02-0322).

Unlike Epstein, I find that natural property rights theory can help fully explain a broad range of human behavior and offers a useful tool for assessing the justifiability of social institutions. Like him, however, I doubt that Locke's theory can justify copyright. To Epstein's trenchant critiques, I add one targeted at any supposed natural property right in expressive works: copyright contradicts Locke's own justification of property. Locke described legislation authorizing the Stationers' Company monopoly on printing—the nearest thing to a Copyright Act in his day—as a "manifest … invasion of the trade, liberty, and property of the subject." Today, by invoking government power a copyright holder can impose prior restraint, fines, imprisonment, and confiscation on those engaged in peaceful expression and the quiet enjoyment of tangible property. Copyright law violates the very rights—the tangible property rights—that Locke set out to defend. …

As our careful review of the historical record has showed … the Founders probably did not regard copyright as a natural right.[90]

In support of his contentions here, Bell cites Ronan Deazley, who "reads Locke's correspondence to indicate that 'Locke himself did not consider [that] his theory of property extended to intellectual properties such as copyrights and patents,' and instead recognized that it could exist only [by] grace of parliamentary action."[91]

In sum, IP rights, especially patent and copyright, have always been viewed as mere policy tools, not as natural property rights. These laws cannot be justified by appeals to authority.

---

[90] Bell, *Intellectual Privilege*, pp. 69–71 (footnotes omitted).
[91] Ibid., p. 192 n.52, quoting Ronan Deazley, *Rethinking Copyright: History, Theory, Language* (Cheltenham, UK: Edward Elgar, 2006)), at 144 n.32. See also Seana Valentine Shiffrin, "Lockean Arguments for Private Property," in Munzer, ed., *New Essays in the Legal and Political Theory of Property* (https://perma.cc/3TWB-4Z8A), p. 141:
> Despite the attractions of a Lockean approach and its apparent amenability to intellectual property, I side with Jefferson. I will challenge the claim that Lockean foundations straightforwardly support most strong natural rights over intellectual works—such things as articles, plays, books, songs, paintings, methods, processes, and other inventions. I will also challenge the related claim that Lockean foundations for strong property rights come easier for these forms of intellectual property than for real property. As Jefferson observed and as I hope to explain, the nature of intellectual works makes them less, rather than more, susceptible to Lockean justifications for private appropriation.

V. CONCLUSION

I may someday provide such an updated treatment, tentatively to be entitled *Copy This Book*, building on *AIP* and taking into account more recent arguments, evidence, and examples.[92] In the meantime, those interested in reading further on this topic may find useful the additional material suggested in "Law and Intellectual Property in a Stateless Society" (ch. 14), n.‡.

---

[92] *See* www.copythisbook.com.

16

Introduction to *Origitent*

Libertarian sci-fi author J. Neil Schulman, an old friend, and I agreed on most political matters, except for intellectual property (IP), over which we've had a decades-long disagreement.[*] Neil modified his theory over time, moving from "logorights" to "media-carried property," and eventually published *Origitent: Why Original Content is Property* in 2018, which included debates and discussions with IP abolitionists Wendy McElroy, Sam Konkin III, and me, and included my Introduction.[†] I have updated my Introduction, but retained the somewhat breezy and informal style.

"INTRODUCTION"

"Hey, Kinsella, why would you write an introduction for a pro-intellectual property book?" my friends might ask me. I mean, did ask me.

---

[*] See Kinsella, "On J. Neil Schulman's Logorights," *Mises Economics Blog* (July 2, 2009); *idem*, "KOL208 | Conversation with Schulman about Logorights and Media-Carried Property," *Kinsella on Liberty Podcast* (March 4, 2016). Neil passed away in 2019. See Kinsella, "J. Neil Schulman, R.I.P.," *StephanKinsella.com* (Aug. 10, 2019).

[†] See Stephan Kinsella, "Introduction," in J. Neil Schulman, *Origitent: Why Original Content is Property* (Steve Heller Publishing, 2018; https://perma.cc/2E6G-WWPE). For related and background material, see Kinsella, "On J. Neil Schulman's Logorights," *Mises Economics Blog* (July 2, 2009); *idem*, "KOL208 | Conversation with Schulman about Logorights and Media-Carried Property."

WHY DO THIS?

I could think of a few possible responses. First—I might say—it's not an introduction. It's really a foreword. Hence my scare quotes.[1] But the publisher insisted on calling my contribution an introduction. Much to my aplomb. Or chagrin. Whatever the word is. But let's face it, this is a weaselly response. What does it matter whether it's a foreword or introduction?

Second, Neil objects to the term "intellectual property" to describe his views, as you'll find in the pages that follow. He argues for property rights in what he used to call logorights but now refers to as "media carried property" (MCP). He tends to say that he opposes modern IP law—patent and copyright. But though he says he's not for IP law, he has sometimes gotten upset at my suggestion that patent and copyright law should be abolished. Hey, Neil, if you're not in favor of IP law then why do you bristle at my call to abolish it? Confuses the hell out of me. I think he does that just to keep me off balance. But it's cool, it's cool, I do the same to him.

Third, this is my chance to "come out"—to announce that I have finally changed my mind about IP and am now an ardent supporter of a certain form of legal protection for products of the mind. Because of the power and clarity of Neil's revised arguments, I've finally seen the light! As many know, as a newly-minted libertarian, I was initially in favor of IP (Ayn Rand ensnares a lot of us newbies), before developing some doubts about the notion. As a young patent attorney, I diverted my libertarian efforts towards finding and developing a good argument for IP. I pored through the literature, reading and studying tons of articles and books by legal scholars, political philosophers, economists, and libertarians of various stripes, searching for a way to justify patent and copyright. Hey, I did the work, so you don't have to. Anyway. I finally gave up and became an atheist. Sorry, I mean an opponent of IP. Despite my upbringing. I mean career. I became an anti-IP IP attorney. I became a self-hating patent lawyer. (But a *damn good* one.)

---

[1] See Pat McNees, "What is the difference between a preface, a foreword, and an introduction?" (March 16, 2023; https://perma.cc/72AK-MJPX).

But keep in mind that I was always looking for proof of God. Sorry—I mean a good argument for IP. I *wanted* to find a justification for patent law, after all—it was my career. Just like I wanted to find an argument for God after being a lifelong Catholic and altar boy. But I failed in my quest (both of them, not that they are connected, exactly). I was unable to square the circle. So I finally became the IP version of atheist, because I just couldn't find a good argument for IP.

But Neil never gave up. His original "logorights" argument (first published in 1983) didn't persuade me. But then, after repeated sparring with me, he reformulated his argument. He adjusted it. He tweaked it. Now, it's about "media carried property." And *mirabile dictu!*, he has done it! He has finally found a solid footing for a type of IP, one that has persuaded even me, Kinsella, arch-enemy of IP! Finally, my whole career is actually justified! All I need do is recant my IP heresy here, in this *soi-disant* "Introduction."

Coming Clean

Okay, time to come clean. I can't keep up pretenses anymore. As the punchline to the joke goes, "I'm just f*cking with you—she's dead."[2] In other words—I was joking. I'm not "coming out." I'm still anti-IP. So everybody just relax. I still think Neil is wrong. And he thinks I'm wrong. And we're cool with that. That's how libertarian bros do.

One thing you can say: Neil's given this issue repeated valiant efforts. Maybe it just takes him longer than me to give up. I gave it up after a good ten-plus years of diligent study and effort. Neil's been steadfast in his support for his version of IP for maybe 35 years now. That takes a special kind of stupid. I mean dedication.

So scratch the third reason. And let's face it, my first two "points" were really not very good arguments at all.

So back to the first question: why would I write this introduction? What's my purpose? What's the purpose of this book? Okay. Let me try this angle. The historical angle. The setting. The context.

---

2   See "Grieving Husband," *eBaum's World* (Sep. 29, 2006; https://perma.cc/5XHM-KVWS).

THE HISTORICAL SETTING OF
INTELLECTUAL PROPERTY

Look. Here's what happened. IP existed in scattered/proto forms hundreds of years ago, in the form of monopoly grants of privilege by the state. It goes back a long way, probably as far back as nascent forms of protectionism and proto-state-granted monopoly privilege. We see traces of it as far back as 2,500 years ago: in about 500 B.C., in the Greek city of Sybaris, located in what is now southern Italy, there were annual culinary competitions. The victor was given the exclusive right to prepare his dish for one year.[3] Sort of like a copyright. Or patent. Some kind of right to his origitent. And then, over the ensuing centuries, there were various

---

[3] See "History of patent law," Wikipedia (https://en.wikipedia.org/wiki/History_of_patent_law); Michael Witty, "Athenaeus describes the most ancient intellectual property," *Prometheus* 35, no. 2 (March 2018; https://perma.cc/4J2J-ZNDU): 137–43; Kinsella, "Food Patents in Greece in 500 BC," *StephanKinsella.com* (Aug. 8, 2010). For another example, about a millennium later, see Michael H. Roffer, "The Irish Copyright War," in *The Law Book: From Hammurabi to the International Criminal Court, 250 Milestones in the History of Law* (New York: Sterling, 2015).

For more on the origins of IP law, see, e.g., Oren Bracha, "Owning Ideas: A History of Anglo-American Intellectual Property" (June 2005; https://law.utexas.edu/faculty/obracha/dissertation/) (unpublished Ph.D dissertation, Harvard Law School); Karl Fogel, "The Surprising History of Copyright and The Promise of a Post-Copyright World," *Question Copyright* (2006; https://perma.cc/DV92-TEH3); Fritz Machlup, U.S. Senate Subcommittee On Patents, Trademarks & Copyrights, *An Economic Review of the Patent System* (85th Cong., 2nd Session, 1958, Study No. 15; https://mises.org/library/economic-review-patent-system), Part II, "Historical Survey"; Tom G. Palmer, "Intellectual Property: A Non-Posnerian Law and Economics Approach," *Hamline L. Rev.* 12, no. 2 (Spring 1989; https://perma.cc/DH7K-ZCRV): 261–304, Part II, "Historical Origins of Intellectual Property Rights"; Christopher May & Susan K. Sell, "The Emergence of Intellectual Property Rights," in *Intellectual Property Rights: A Critical History* (Boulder and London: Lynne Rienner Publishers, 2006); Brad Sherman & Lionel Bently, *The Making of Modern Intellectual Property Law: The British Experience, 1760–1911* (Cambridge University Press, 1999); Ronan Deazley *et al.*, eds., *Privilege and Property: Essays on the History of Copyright* (Cambridge: OpenBook Publishers, 2010); Maximilian Frumkin, "The Origin of Patents," *J. Pat. Off. Soc'y* 27, no. 3 (1945; https://perma.cc/Y575-ZR2A): 143–49; Benedict Atkinson & Brian Fitzgerald, *A Short History of Copyright: The Genie of Information* (Springer, 2014); Ronan Deazley, Rethinking Copyright: History, Theory, Language (Cheltenham, UK: Edward Elgar, 2006); Adam D. Moore & Kenneth Einar Himma, "Intellectual Property," in Edward N. Zalta, ed., *Stanford Encyclopedia of Philosophy* (Stanford University, 2011; https://papers.ssrn.com/sol3/papers.cfm?abstract_id=1980917), §1; Carla Hesse, "The Rise of Intellectual Property, 700 B.C.–A.D. 2000: An Idea in the Balance," *Daedalus* 131, no. 2 (Spring, 2002), pp. 26–45; Tom W. Bell, *Intellectual Privilege: Copyright, Common Law, and the Common Good* (Arlington, Virginia: Mercatus Center, 2014; https://perma.cc/

forms of protectionism, and also attempts to promote or protect or "incentivize" innovation and creativity. These controls were intermixed with mercantilism (protectionism) and censorship.[4]

Patents

Let's consider the origins of patents, property rights in inventions—techniques or machine designs that accomplish some practical purpose. A mousetrap, a method for threshing corn. But the original grant of patents did not usually involve some innovative machine or process. In England, the king would hand out monopoly privilege rights to cronies, maybe in exchange for helping the king out, by helping to collect taxes, and so on. These grants were called "letters patent"—patent meaning "open." "Only John Smythe may sell playing cards in ye olde town of Bluxsome-on-Thames" or whatever (and then government goons would raid his competitors on occasion to ensure they were not selling counterfeit or "pirated" cards... a bit ironic given that one of the early uses of Letters Patent by the British Crown was to entice pirates to become "privateers" [a fancy name for legitimized piracy], by giving them a monopoly over some of the spoils of their piracy for a given time).[5]

Real Pirates

A notorious example is Francis Drake, who was given a Letter Patent on March 15, 1587, to authorize his piracy, such as attacking Spanish ships sailing back from South America laden with silver, handing it over to the Queen after taking his share. Sir Francis Drake:

> ... made the first English slaving voyages, taking Africans to the New World. Drake attacked Spanish ships sailing back from South America laden with silver. He took their treasure for himself and his queen. He

---

JLC2-396Y), chap. 3. See also the references in Dale A. Nance, "Foreword: Owning Ideas," *Harv. J. L. & Pub. Pol'y* 13, no. 3 (Summer 1990): 757–74.

  [4] As Tom Palmer writes, "[m]onopoly privilege and censorship lie at the historical root of patent and copyright." Palmer, "Intellectual Property: A Non-Posnerian Law and Economics Approach," p. 264 (footnote omitted).

  [5] See Kinsella, "Rothbard on Mercantilism and State "Patents of Monopoly," *C4SIF Blog* (Aug. 29, 2011).

also raided Spanish and Portuguese ports. He undertook a circumnaviga-
tion of the world in 1572 and 1573. He discovered that Tierra del Fuego
was not part of the Southern Continent and explored the west coast
of South America. He plundered ports in Chile and Peru and captured
treasure ships. He sailed up to California and then across the Pacific
Ocean to the East Indies. He returned to England with his ship full of
spices and treasure, so gaining great acclaim."[6]

In other words, patents were originally used to *authorize* actual piracy, in
addition to protecting favored court cronies from competition and thus
restricting the free market. So it is a bit ironic that modern defenders of
IP claim to be opposed to IP "pirates"—even though *real* pirates (like
Francis Drake) kill people, break things, and take things from people
(and deliver slaves into bondage), while "information pirates" do none
of these things.

The Statute of Monopolies of 1623

In any case, "Letters Patent" began to be used widely by monarchs to grant
monopoly privileges to favored cronies on a certain trade or industry
or product in a certain region. When this protectionism and restraint
on free trade became too noticeably abusive, Parliament stepped in and
passed the Statute of Monopolies of 1623 (notice the name: "monopolies"; they were at least honest back then), which restricted the King's
power to issue letters patent, since they were basically trade restrictions,
protectionism, privileges, *monopolies*. But the statute made an exception:
monopoly privileges could still be granted for genuine "inventions"—i.e.,
for technical innovations.

Copyright

As for copyright—until the printing press, the Church and Crown
held a nice monopoly over controlling published thought, by means of
scribes and guilds like the Stationer's Company, which held a monopoly
over publishing from about 1557 until the Statute of Anne of 1710.

---

6 See Wikipedia, "Maritime History of England" (https://en.wikipedia.org/wiki/
Maritime_history_of_England). See also my post "The Real IP Pirates," *C4SIF Blog*
(Oct. 16, 2010).

During this time the printing press emerged and disrupted the state and church's control over printed works, leading to the Statue of Anne 1710, which recognized authors' copyrights in their works. But because, as a practical matter, authors still had to appeal to regulated presses to publish their works, the state and church were able to maintain their censorial control over what could be published, and the modern publishing system arose where publishing houses served as gatekeepers and the middlemen between authors and consumers.[7]

IP IN THE INDUSTRIAL AGE

Fast-forward to the dawn of the Industrial Revolution. The United States of America managed to break free from England in 1776 and established its own Constitution in 1789, which drew, of course, upon English legal principles and practices. And so Article 1, Section 8, Clause 8 of the US Constitution authorizes Congress "to promote the progress of science and the useful arts by securing for a limited time to authors and inventors the exclusive right to their respective writings and discoveries." Basically, this is the authorization for modern patent and copyright law. And thus emerged the modern system of patent and copyright that dominate the world today. Modern patent law, anchored in protectionist grants of monopoly privilege; and copyright law, rooted in censorship, gatekeepers, and control of thought and freedom of the press.

And of course world GDP, flat for thousands of years, began to exponentially increase right around this time.[8] Those who mistake correlation with causation argue that the wealth and might and prosperity of the West are linked to our adoption of European/

---

[7] See Fogel, "The Surprising History of Copyright and The Promise of a Post-Copyright World."

[8] See Figure 2 in Hans-Hermann Hoppe, "From the Malthusian Trap to the Industrial Revolution: An Explanation of Social Evolution," in *The Great Fiction: Property, Economy, Society, and the Politics of Decline,* 2d expanded ed. (Auburn, Ala.: Mises Institute, 2021; www.hanshoppe.com/tgf).

English-style patent and copyright law, though studies backing up these claims are wanting.[9]

And so the narrative was put in motion. The previous gatekeeper publishing industries seized on the new copyright system and quickly internationalized it apace with the progress of the Industrial Revolution (google "Berne Convention"). And new industries, captured by the monopoly profits possible by using institutionalized patents granted by an inept state bureaucracy, became entrenched and started defending patents.

And then the free market economists emerged in the 1800s and started to become alarmed at the proliferation of widespread, institutionalized grants of IP—which was obviously a restraint on trade, protectionism, censorship, and infringement of free market property rights. They basically emerged from their slumbers and said, "What the hell? You people have got to stop this." And they correctly referred to these state-initiated practices as "grants of monopoly privilege."[10] In response, the publishers, the gatekeepers, and industries now increasingly reliant on patent and copyright, intentionally, and deceitfully, bent the language of "natural property rights" to serve their purpose. Patent and copyright became "intellectual property rights" instead of monopoly privilege grants.[11] Much like health care is thought of as a "right" today.[12] And thus the ideological battle for IP was won by means of cheap semantics. Plus pressure groups (big Pharma, Hollywood, music,

---

[9] See Kinsella, "The Overwhelming Empirical Case Against Patent and Copyright," *C4SIF Blog* (Oct. 23, 2012); *idem*, "Legal Scholars: Thumbs Down on Patent and Copyright," *C4SIF Blog* (Oct. 23, 2012).

[10] See Fritz Machlup & Edith Penrose, "The Patent Controversy in the Nineteenth Century," *J. Econ. History* 10, no. 1 (May 1950): 1–29; Machlup, *An Economic Review of the Patent System*, Part II, "Historical Survey"; Palmer, "Intellectual Property: A Non-Posnerian Law and Economics Approach," Part II, "Historical Origins of Intellectual Property Rights."

[11] See Kinsella, "Intellectual Properganda," *Mises Economic Blog* (Dec. 6, 2010); and comments by Machlup and Penrose in "*Against Intellectual Property* After Twenty Years" (ch. 15), n.78; also Machlup, *An Economic Review of the Patent System*, Part II.D, "The victory of the patent advocates (1873–1910)."

[12] See Charles A. Reich "The New Property," *Yale L. J.* 73, no. 5 (April 1964): 733–87; and David A. Super, "A New New Property," *Colum. L. Rev.* 113 (2013; https://columbialaw review.org/content/a-new-new-property): 1773–1896, p. 1780, noting that the US Supreme Court has adopted Reich's understanding of entitlements as a form of property:

Reich's article reshaped legal debate to a degree that most scholars can only dream about. Its influence reached its apogee in 1970 when, in *Goldberg v. Kelly* [397 U.S.

software), and some confusion spawned by Locke himself about the labor theory of property.[13]

Nowadays virtually everyone assumes that the innovation that accompanied the spectacular prosperity in the modern West was due, at least in part, to patent and copyright law. And that if you are in favor of innovation or artistic creativity, you must be in favor of property rights for "products of the mind," or "the fruits of one's labor," or other metaphors that serve only to distort and deceive and lie and confuse thought.

HISTORICAL AND MODERN ARGUMENTS ABOUT IP

We can say that institutionalized IP rights began at the dawn of the Industrial Revolution, for example in the American and then European patent and copyright systems, which traced back to European institutions and practices such as the Statute of Monopolies of 1623 and the Statute of Anne of 1710. As these modern, institutionalized IP systems began to take hold in the 1800s, this provoked, first, a backlash from free market economists and then a defensive response from the entrenched IP interests. By the 1870s, the IP side had won.[14]

254, 262 n.8 (1970)], Justice Brennan relied on it to recognize welfare benefits as property interests protected by the Due Process Clauses.
Interestingly, Super notes:

> The half century since Reich wrote has produced a mixed verdict on the concerns animating *The New Property*. His worst fears have not been realized: The country is not approaching the point at which "most private ownership is supplanted by government largess." [Reich, op cit., p. 771] Yet the steady erosion of independent property rights has continued. The greatest expansion in property rights has been in the form of intellectual property, which rights come as an act of government largesse.

Super, *op cit.*, pp. 1780–81, citations omitted. For the IP point, Super cites Lea Shaver, "The Right to Science and Culture," *Wis. L. Rev.* 2010, no. 1 (2010; https://papers.ssrn.com/sol3/papers.cfm?abstract_id=1354788): 121–84, pp, 124 & 132–33 (contending IP "transform[s] creativity, information, science, and technology from public goods into private ones" and describing expansion of IP protections in 1970s and 1980s).

[13] See "*Against Intellectual Property* After Twenty Years" (ch. 15), Part IV.C; Kinsella, "KOL037 | Locke's Big Mistake: How the Labor Theory of Property Ruined Political Theory," *Kinsella on Liberty Podcast* (March 28, 2013).

[14] See Machlup & Penrose, "The Patent Controversy in the Nineteenth Century"; Machlup, *An Economic Review of the Patent System*, Part II, "Historical Survey."

Among proto-libertarians, and especially some anarchists, the chief figures debating IP, in the late 1800s, were Lysander Spooner and Benjamin Tucker. Spooner proposed a radically pro-IP theory, rooted in the Lockean labor theory of property, while Tucker opposed IP, on grounds similar to his arguments against other forms of monopoly.[15]

Amongst libertarians and proto-libertarians, the issue lay mostly dormant until the mid-1980s, when thinkers such as Sam Konkin, Wendy McElroy, and J. Neil Schulman entered the fray again. Konkin and especially McElroy provided the first systematic arguments against IP rooted in modern libertarian property rights principles, while Schulman was one of the first to attempt to provide a principled (as opposed to utilitarian or empirical) argument for a type of IP also rooted in libertarian propertarian principles.[16]

With the dawning digital age and the Internet of the mid-late 1990s making copying and "piracy" far easier than ever before, copyright and related IP issues began to attract more attention from libertarians. Libertarians have long recognized that the main issues that confront us are war, taxation, state education, the drug war, and central banking. Many of us now believe that IP lies in the baleful company of these other horrible institutions and, in a sense, is worst of all: because war, taxation, etc., are seen, at least by some libertarians, as *necessary evils*; but patent and copyright are labeled "intellectual property" and thus fly under the banner of "property rights," which are supposed to be good things, by libertarian lights. Thus, IP is far more insidious because, while you might want to minimize war and taxation as much as possible even if you think they are necessary evils—they are evils, after all—all good libertarians support robust legal support for strong property rights. And if IP is a legitimate property right, it's not a necessary evil at all; it's a good thing.

With patent law threatening, impeding, and distorting innovation and technological growth and human prosperity, and with copyright distorting culture, censoring thought and speech and freedom of the press and indeed threatening Internet freedom, it is no wonder that

---

[15] See references in "Law and Intellectual Property in a Stateless Society" (ch. 14), n.4 *et pass.*
[16] See my posts "The Four Historical Phases of IP Abolitionism," *Mises Economics Blog* (April 13, 2011); "The Origins of Libertarian IP Abolitionism," *Mises Economics Blog* (April 1, 2011); and "Classical Liberals and Anarchists on Intellectual Property," *C4SIF Blog* (Oct. 6, 2015).

IP has become an issue of interest and overwhelming importance amongst libertarians.[17]

This is why it is crucial for libertarians to understand modern IP and its relationship to property rights. To think about whether and how anything like patent or copyright can be justified. This issue is crucial. Innovation and creativity are essential for human survival, and so are property rights. And the state and its laws are dangerous. So it's important that we get this right: whether there should be any form of intellectual property rights, or not, and, if so, what and why. Unprincipled, utilitarian, empirical thinking will not help us figure this out. You can't just say that a 120 year copyright term is "too much" but we "need something greater than zero."[18] You need a principled approach. And though I disagree with Neil's conclusions, I respect the fact that he has for over three decades fought to figure out these issues with libertarian property rights principles in mind.

One final note. One argument we IP abolitionists use is that copyright is a form of censorship, and we oppose censorship. We applaud the communication and publication of ideas, arguments. Those of us interested in libertarian ideas about justice and property rights, and innovation and creativity, should applaud Neil for providing to the public, in accessible form, his sincere and interesting thoughts about these matters.

Stephan Kinsella
Houston, June 2018

---

17 See, e.g., my posts: "Legal Scholars: Thumbs Down on Patent and Copyright"; "The Overwhelming Empirical Case *Against* Patent and Copyright"; "Death by Copyright-IP Fascist Police State Acronym," *C4SIF Blog* (Jan. 30, 2012); "SOPA is the Symptom, Copyright is the Disease: The SOPA Wakeup Call to Abolish Copyright," *The Libertarian Standard* (Jan 24, 2012); "Where does IP Rank Among the Worst State Laws?", *C4SIF Blog* (Jan. 20, 2012); "Masnick on the Horrible PROTECT IP Act: The Coming IPolice State," *C4SIF Blog* (June 2, 2012); "Copyright and the End of Internet Freedom," *C4SIF Blog* (May 10, 2011); and "Patent vs. Copyright: Which is Worse?", *C4SIF Blog* (Nov. 5, 2011).

18 See, e.g., my posts "Tabarrok: Patent Policy on the Back of a Napkin," *C4SIF Blog* (Sept. 20, 2012); "Optimal Patent and Copyright Term Length," *Mises Economics Blog* (June 16, 2011); "Tom Bell on copyright reform; the Hayekian knowledge problem and copyright terms," *C4SIF Blog* (Jan. 6, 2013); "Yaron Brook on the Appropriate Copyright Term," *C4SIF Blog* (July 29, 2013); see also Cory Doctorow, "What's the objectively optimal copyright term?", *Boing Boing* (Oct. 6, 2015; https://perma.cc/UMJ3-4JHH).

[Note from JNS: I just got off the phone with Stephan, who's approved my making this bracketed comment about his Introduction: Stephan is aware that I do not take an historical approach to the question of logorights/MCP/origitent, but a theoretical approach based on natural law and natural rights. —J. Neil Schulman, June 15, 2018]

17

Conversation with Schulman about Logorights and Media-Carried Property

This edited transcript of a conversation between libertarian sci-fi author J. Neil Schulman and me was in his book *Origitent: Why Original Content is Property* (2018).* My introduction to *Origitent* is included as chapter 16 in this volume.

Stephan Kinsella: Hey, this is Stephan Kinsella doing an episode of the *Kinsella on Liberty* podcast. This should be number 208. I've got my old friend, Neil Schulman, online. We've actually met in person, haven't we Neil?

J. Neil Schulman: Yeah. As I recall, it was at Libertopia a few years ago.[1]

Kinsella: How are you doing?

Schulman: I'm doing well. How about you?

---

* J. Neil Schulman, *Origitent: Why Original Content is Property* (Steve Heller Publishing, 2018; https://perma.cc/2E6G-WWPE). This chapter of his book was based on Kinsella, "KOL208 | Conversation with Schulman about Logorights and Media-Carried Property," *Kinsella on Liberty Podcast* (March 4, 2016), which was transcribed by Rosemary Denshaw and edited for clarity for use in Schulman's book. I have further improved the transcript and added some references and comments in footnotes.

---

[1] See my talks at Libertopia that year (all at the *Kinsella on Liberty Podcast*): "KOL236 | Intellectual Nonsense: Fallacious Arguments for IP (Libertopia 2012)" (Feb. 10, 2018); "KOL237 | Intellectual Nonsense: Fallacious Arguments for IP—Part 2 (Libertopia 2012)" (Feb. 12, 2018); "KOL238 | Libertopia 2012 IP Panel with Charles Johnson and Butler Shaffer" (Feb. 14, 2018). Neil was in the audience for my talk (KOL236) and asked some questions during the Q&A session.

Kinsella: It's all right. Today is March 4th, 2016. You and I have known each other for maybe, what, 30+ years now?

Schulman: It's been a while. And I must say a lot friendlier now than we used to be.[2]

Kinsella: Well, in the beginning it was friendly. Remember on the GEnie Forums in the old days before the internet?

Schulman: My God, I didn't remember that we met on GEnie. That goes back to the early 90s.

Kinsella: Yeah, that's where I sent you the review of your *Heinleiniana* book.[3]

Schulman: Oh yes, yes. And it's one of the many interests we have in common.

Kinsella: Yeah, Heinlein. Of course, you knew him better than I did.[4]

Schulman: Well, I was very lucky to be able to interview him for the *The New York Daily News,* which led to our meeting and subsequent friendship.

Kinsella: Right. Right. Well, I think we're friendly when we're not threatening to convert each other to IP socialism. It depends on our definitions.

Schulman: Ha ha. Actually, it's amazing how much we agree on. And there's just one bone of contention which has occupied 90% of our energy.

Kinsella: Yeah and probably it's only because, as I have dug into this IP issue over the years, I get more and more into meticulous details

---

[2] See Kinsella, "Schulman: 'If you copy my novel, I'll kill you,'" *C4SIF Blog* (June 6, 2012). Or this Facebook post comment by Neil: "Stephan, let me make this as plain as I can. You're the foremost enemy of property rights because you masquerade as a defender of them while putting forward the proposition that the unique thing which an author or composer creates is the one thing that cannot be owned because of your misplaced test for non-rivalrousness." (March 22, 2011; https://www.facebook.com/nskinsella/posts/198807836808078.) See also Kinsella, "Libertarian Sci-Fi Authors and Copyright versus Libertarian IP Abolitionists," *C4SIF Blog* (June 14, 2012).

[3] See Kinsella, "Book Review of Schulman, *The Robert Heinlein Interview and Other Heinleiniana* (1991)," *StephanKinsella.com* (Dec. 12, 2013).

[4] This was tongue in cheek. I didn't know Heinlein at all.

because I keep seeing what I think are the errors that cause some mistakes to keep being perpetrated. So I get more and more into minutiae, but anyway. Do you remember a few years ago, I think I dug up the old information and got the tapes from someone, from that IP debate you had done with Wendy McElroy back in like '83 I think, right?

Schulman: Yes. And that was my first entry into this controversy.

Kinsella: And I think Wendy's was '81 with some newsletters in California and then '83. So I really think the modern debate on this started around then, to be honest.[5]

Schulman: Well, actually for me, it went back even further in time, because I was part of the close circle of Samuel Edward Konkin, III and his magazines: *New Libertarian Notes, New Libertarian Weekly, New Libertarian* and various other publications. And of course I was also good friends with Robert LeFevre. Both Sam and Bob LeFevre were opposed to the idea of state copyright and state patents.[6] And where I was coming in was a very early attempt to justify not statist concepts—being an anarchist, an agorist, I'm opposed to that—but to see if there was a natural law and natural right basis for a concept of ownership of content which existed only as what today I now call media-carried property,[7] but back then I called logorights.

The idea being that something didn't have to be made out of atoms and molecules in order to satisfy the requirements for a copyright claim. Now Sam allowed copyrights for individual writers in his publications. So he was not *so* opposed to it that he said, no, it has to be without copyright. And at that time, I don't even think there were Creative Commons licenses to enter the discussion.

---

5 See Wendy McElroy, "Contra Copyright," *The Voluntaryist* (June 1985), included in *idem*, "Contra Copyright, Again," *Libertarian Papers* vol. 3, art. no. 12 (2011; http://libertarianpapers.org/12-contra-copyright/); Kinsella, "The Origins of Libertarian IP Abolitionism," *Mises Economics Blog* (April 1, 2011) and *idem*, "The Four Historical Phases of IP Abolitionism," *C4SIF Blog* (April 13, 2011).

6 See Samuel Edward Konkin, III, "Copywrongs," *The Voluntaryist* (July 1986), reprinted at *LewRockwell.com* (Nov. 15, 2010; https://archive.lewrockwell.com/orig11/konkin1.1.1.html); Kinsella, "LeFevre on Intellectual Property and the 'Ownership of Intangibles,'" *C4SIF Blog* (Dec. 27, 2012).

7 See "MCP," in *Origitent*.

Kinsella: Well …[8]

Schulman: And Bob LeFevre, while he was opposed to copyright, he actually endorsed my concepts of logorights as worth considering, beginning right after my debate with Wendy McElroy.[9] I would say that if I were to boil it down to my position today, is that I am not so much discussing the question of intellectual property, or ideas as property, two concepts which I reject out of hand, but that I am exploring that property *itself* is an intellectual artifact. And as I posted on your Facebook wall today, I think that it comes closest to being an intellectual artifact of contract law.[10] Whether or not, as you posted, contract law is a subset of property law or whether property law is a subset of contract law is a debate I don't think is really worth spending a lot of time on. But I do think that property itself is an intellectual concept which falls under both a discussion of legal rights and a discussion of natural law and natural rights as libertarians would understand it.

Kinsella: Well before we get into your theories, let's talk a little bit more about the background because I think we have another thing in common. Maybe you would agree or not on this, but my suspicion is you had—I know you had sort of a Randian approach to some issues in your libertarianism, and you also were, and are, a writer and a successful career writer, right, a novelist. So you had an interest in trying to find a way to justify something that you had like a financial interest in, right?

And I did, too, in a way, because I was a patent attorney, and I still am. That's one reason I started searching as well. And the reason I was searching was because Ayn Rand influenced me early on. And one of the arguments she made that never did persuade me was her argument for IP. Something about it was just not like her other arguments. It was sort of arbitrary and utilitarian. It just didn't make sense like her other arguments did. But I was going to do patent law and copyright law for my career, and I'm a libertarian. So I started thinking, let me find

---

8 Well before the advent of creative commons (https://creativecommons.org), the generally anti-IP libertarian Leonard Read would publish FEE works with the notice "Permission to reprint granted without special request." See Kinsella, "Leonard Read on Copyright and the Role of Ideas," *C4SIF Blog* (Sept. 12, 2011).

9 See Schulman, "My Unfinished 30-Year-Old Debate with Wendy McElroy," in *Origitent*.

10 See this Facebook post: https://www.facebook.com/nskinsella/posts/10153462577483181 (March 4, 2016).

a better solution for this. So I was searching as well. It's just you came up with logorights and I came up with skepticism.

Schulman: It's ironic that you, as a patent lawyer, are probably one of the leading scholars today opposed to the very field you are operating in, which is patent law. But, in my case, I think you have the cause and effect reversed. My being a writer was not the reason why I felt it worth pursuing. It was my interest primarily as a libertarian natural law/natural rights believer which led me to this. And, in fact, I would say that I was probably more influenced by Robert LeFevre's approach to property rights *per se* than I was to Ayn Rand's.

Kinsella: Okay, I accept that. But you would admit there is, there tends to be some correlation. I tend to find …

Schulman: Well, let me let you off the hook by saying that in my original article, "Informational Property: Logorights,"[11] I did quote from Ayn Rand because I found that parts of her argument were expressive, but in terms of the basic theory of property which I was pursuing, I thought that Robert LeFevre made a more comprehensive case.

Kinsella: No, but what I was going to say it seems to be no coincidence that there's a disproportionate number of libertarian novelists who *happen to* support copyright, just like almost all patent lawyers *happen to* support patent and copyright. Do you follow me? I don't think it's quite a coincidence.

Schulman: But you see, it seems to me that that's starting off with, if I may use a term that Ludwig von Mises liked a lot, paralogia. In other words, it transfers the argument from a debate of the merits to a debate on the motivation of the people who are arguing it.[12]

Kinsella: Yeah, I don't mean to argue substance *by* psychologizing, but I do find psychologizing fun sometimes. I can't deny it. And I do think

---

[11] Schulman, "Informational Property: Logorights" (1983, 1989; https://perma.cc/ ECB9-KZQ9) (also in *Origitent*), responding to Konkin, "Copywrongs."

[12] I am unfamiliar with Mises talking about "paralogia," which appears to have something to do with schizophrenia. I suspect this might have been a mistake by Neil; he may have been thinking of polylogism, even though it is not quite related to the error of psychologizing, but rather to a different, Marxian error. See Jeffrey A. Tucker, "Marxism Without Polylogism," in Jörg Guido Hülsmann & Stephan Kinsella, eds., *Property, Freedom and Society: Essays in Honor of Hans-Hermann Hoppe* (Auburn, Ala.: Mises Institute, 2009).

that at least, at the very least, we should be aware of our biases and try to be sure that if you're advocating something that happens to be in your favor, that you have good reasons for it anyway. But, of course, the arguments stand on their own merits, I think.

But, by the converse, I get attacked quite often for *being* an IP lawyer and for opposing it,[13] as if, if my arguments, if they were correct, it's as if you wouldn't expect an IP lawyer to be one of the people that would recognize that. I mean it's possible to actually know something about the field that is unjustified and corrupt and to come to those conclusions, even though it's not in your personal, immediate interest.

Schulman: Well, look, just switching to somewhere else just as a for instance, because what I'm noting is not what I call hypocrisy but merely irony, okay? Wouldn't you find it at least ironic if you had a medical doctor, an obstetrician, say, who said that he was opposed to abortion who then, as part of his practice, performed abortions.

Kinsella: Yes. In fact, I think that might be hypocritical. It could be. But, first of all, I don't think there is anything wrong with pointing out irony any more than psychologizing, it's kind of interesting—and it may be ironic. I don't think it happens to be ironic. Let's suppose that there is a healthy difference of agreement among the population as a whole or among academics or scholars about IP; 30/70, whatever. I don't know. I mean it would be ironic if *some* percentage of patent lawyers didn't take that side, if everyone *automatically* agreed with it. As for the hypocrisy or the irony issue, it would be more ironic if I were out there *suing* people in the name of IP. So I agree that would be more difficult. But if you understand the way …

Schulman: Then let me establish this. I have never filed a lawsuit on behalf of any of my literary rights.

Kinsella: Right. No, I understand that … most copyright holders don't have those scruples. You have your anarchist and your voluntaryist

---

[13] See, e.g., my posts: "Are anti-IP patent attorneys hypocrites?" *C4SIF Blog* (April 22, 2011); "Patent Lawyers Who Don't Toe the Line Should Be Punished!" *C4SIF Blog* (April 12, 2012); "Is It So Crazy For A Patent Attorney To Think Patents Harm Innovation?" *StephanKinsella.com* (Oct. 1, 2009); "An Anti-Patent *Patent* Attorney? Oh my Gawd!" *StephanKinsella.com* (July 12, 2009).

scruples. So that tamps down the excesses that you might otherwise go to. So I understand that.

Schulman: Okay and now let me also make clear that in practice, when I have opposed pirating of my rights, I've only done so vocally in instances where I felt that it was damaging to a third party.

Kinsella: Right. Like more of a fraud type argument or something like that?

Schulman: Well, not even fraud. But let me give you an example. There was supposedly, I'm not sure, and I'm being told now that this never happened, but there was a representation that there was going to be a pirate screening of the *Alongside Night* movie at PorcFest to compete with the official screening that I went to a lot of trouble to sell at a movie theater ...

Kinsella: Right. I heard about that.

Schulman: ... nearby Roger's Campground. Okay? And I was upset about it because the whole purpose of the screening was set up as a fundraiser for the Free State Project. And so, I felt that a pirate screening competing with a fundraiser for the Free State Project was damaging to the Free State Project, and that upset me.

Kinsella: I understand that. Of course, that has nothing to do with the validity of copyright or even logorights, but I understand.

Schulman: Right. And, again, all of this is sort of like, as I say, paralogia. It's an interesting background discussion, but really it doesn't speak to the actual question of whether under a general theory of property rights which I maintain is a moral and a legal construct—it's a subset of a theory of natural law leading to natural human rights—that I consider property rights to be primarily an ontological and moral issue. And then you get to it as a legal issue.

But let me start by conceding to you that, as I observe it right now, the mainstream position of the libertarian movement, as I perceive it, is anti what they perceive as artistic rights in things which are not physical objects.[14]

---

[14] On this, see Kinsella, "The Death Throes of Pro-IP Libertarianism," *Mises Daily* (July 28, 2010); *idem*, "The Origins of Libertarian IP Abolitionism"; *idem*, "The Four Historical Phases of IP Abolitionism"; and other references and discussion in "Law and Intellectu-

Kinsella: Okay.

Schulman: So, in essence, I'm fighting an uphill battle, a battle in which you have the high ground, the strategic high ground.

Kinsella: Well, I understand that, but I think there's also, especially among anarchists, right, we are generally skeptical of existing statutory schemes. And so someone like you who supports some kind of, I don't want to call it intellectual property. You call it informational property or now material-carried property and we can get into the details in a second.

Schulman: Media-carried property.

Kinsella: Sorry, media-carried property. You shouldn't be in the position of having to defend the existing patent and copyright system.

Schulman: No, and I find it frustrating that most of the vitriolic attacks on me assume that I am supporting what is being portrayed as a monopolistic grant of privilege from the State. In my very first debate with Wendy, I started off by saying if the concept I was putting forward could not be defended other than as a monopolistic grant of privilege from the State, then I would immediately abandon it.

Kinsella: Well, but the problem is, I would say, and see if you agree with this, the vast majority of pro-IP libertarians *would* oppose the abolition of patent and copyright, at least until we could replace it with their ideal system. So they do not have this abolitionist view towards …

Schulman: And this is where I go into my usual spiel about how I don't think that any kind of property, if there is in fact a property, that there should be—there's a statist phrase, but it's a legal term of art, mostly [where the nation state is].[15]

If you're going to say that a copyright is statist, then why isn't a deed from the county clerk just as statist? And if you're going to say that we need to abolish now one, why not the other?

Kinsella: But you see, then I see that you're trying to have that both ways because you act, on the one hand, like you're not in favor of defending

---

al Property in a Stateless Society" (ch. 14), at n.5 and *Against Intellectual Property* After Twenty Years: Looking Back and Looking Forward" (ch. 15), at n.21.

15 Neil's words are not quite clear here in the recording.

the existing patent and copyright system, but when someone calls for abolishing it, then you sort of say, well, if we abolish that, why not abolish real property titles?

Schulman: But that's the thing. In other words, presumably you drive a car which is registered with the Department of Motor Vehicles and which you're not allowed to operate without that license from the State. And presumably the land deed issued by your county is in the same situation, if you are in fact a homeowner. Or, if not, at one remove as a renter from somebody who does have property which has a deed issued by the county. And so I just don't see the difference.

Kinsella: Okay. Well, so the problem I have with that argument, that analogy, is you and I as libertarians don't have much disagreement on the basic notion that there ought to be property titles recognized in scarce resources like land. We oppose *the state* from monopolizing …

Schulman: Well, scarcity is only one of the things.

Kinsella: Okay.

Schulman: And I don't see scarcity as absolute, as I discuss in my article, "Human Property."[16] Scarcity is not absolute. I'll refer people to that article rather than repeat myself.

Kinsella: I'm just trying to pick something uncontroversial. We both agree there should be property rights in land, right?

Schulman: Yes. I'm not a Henry Georgist.

Kinsella: And the basic function of the existing property title records offices in the counties around the country is to just keep track of that. Now we oppose the State monopolizing that function, but it's basically a correct function, a libertarian function. You can't just leap from that and say that similarly the copyright system does something—crudely, perhaps—but it does a similar function because—well, for several reasons. We don't agree that these kinds of things should be property. That's what we dispute. And, you know, the property title system itself

---

[16] Schulman, "Human Property," *Agorist.com* (2012; https://perma.cc/E9W5-T7UA); also in *Origitent*.

is not terrible, the way the State runs it. It's just that the State has the right to come in and seize your property because of eminent domain.

Schulman: Okay. Well, you see here we can get into another agreement immediately. I think that the way that the laws have been lobbied for by large corporations to extend and protect their claims of copyright and patent are egregiously anti-property rights. For example—I will give you one example in patents and another in copyright. What Monsanto did in suing farmers whose crops were *invaded* by Monsanto's seeds from adjoining property …

Kinsella: Patented seeds, right.[17]

Schulman: … and then sued the small farmers who had no ability to legally defend themselves against this mega-giant corporation, I think is one of the most horrific misuses of patent law that I can imagine.

Similarly, the way that corporations such as Disney have taken things that are traditional fairytales and copyrighted them and then aggressively attacked people who wanted to use this stuff which originated long before Disney got to it and sued the heck out of them to restrict their doing so is equally egregious. Getting images and taking paintings which hang in the Louvre and then pursue claims against people who reproduce them, things that go back hundreds of years, is similarly egregious. So if you are looking for Schulman to agree with Kinsella, that the way that the State handles this is egregious, we have no disagreement.

Kinsella: Well, let me disagree a little bit about on that. I wouldn't, I mean this is a quibble, but I wouldn't call it a misuse at all. And I wouldn't blame Monsanto and Getty. I mean maybe they're immoral, but they're using the legal rights the system gives them. In every one, all three of the cases you mentioned, you can explain why what they're doing is basically supported by the copyright and patent systems. What they're doing is totally legitimate.[18]

---

17 See my posts "Monsanto wins lawsuit against Indiana soybean farmer," *C4SIF Blog* (Sep. 24, 2011) and "Farmers and Seed Distributors Defend Right to Protect Themselves From Monsanto Patents," *C4SIF Blog* (Aug. 24, 2011).

18 *"The Thing! the Thing itself is the Abuse!"* Edmund Burke, "A Letter To Lord****," in *A Vindication of Natural Society* (Liberty Fund, 1756; https://oll.libertyfund.org/title/burke-a-vindication-of-natural-society) (emphasis added).

Schulman: And I'm not going to disagree with you, but that is the problem with all statist law. None of it supports a pure libertarian concept of property.

Kinsella: Right.

Schulman: And, in fact, one of the historical reasons why libertarians have opposed such law is that they started out with grants from kings and other royalties. So there is an historical parallel that the development of this body of law was corrupt going back to its root.[19] But, to me, that is an artifact of statism itself. In other words, I would say that, in fact, the Robin Hood story of how you have the king's land being poached on, okay, is just as much of an argument not to have privately held land as the argument for grants of privilege from kings being one of the earliest uses of artistic creation. It's equivalent. In other words, the problem here is not that we don't have something which deserves to be treated as a property right. The problem is we have the State.

Kinsella: I don't think that the argument that IP is unjust is the same as arguing that current property rights and land are unjust because of some corruption back in the old days, because we all agree there ought to be property rights in land and we have to have some system for determining who the best owner is. So that's not really controversial.

Schulman: Hold on. You can't say that we all agree.

Kinsella: All us libertarians, yeah.

Schulman: There are, in fact, communists who don't agree.

Kinsella: Well, you and I agree, okay? You and I agree on the land issues. That's one difference. The other thing is, if someone asks a libertarian, well, what would roads be like and would land title registry be like in a free market, we would say, well, it would be similar to what we have now. You'd have roads. It's just they'd have private owners and that would have different economic effects in how they're run and all that. We would have land title records.

---

[19] I disagree with criticisms of the legitimacy of current property titles because of injustice or taint in the title back in history. See "What Libertarianism Is" (ch. 2), at n.36; and "Selling Does Not Imply Ownership, and Vice-Versa: A Dissection" (ch. 11), at n.12.

Schulman: If you go to Cato and Reason, you're going to find scholars who found out that some of the earliest highways and turnpikes were, in fact, privately created. Then you get to the long history of the railroads where you have all sorts of statist interference.

Kinsella: But my point is you could use some of the existing common law-based and other systems that we have as a rough model as to what the libertarian system would look like, but it would be better. But you cannot say that [re IP]. So in terms of IP, I could give 50 or 100 or 1,000 examples and you might call them misuses of the system. I would just say this is just the implications of the current substantive law of patent and copyright that the State has created and you would probably agree with me on every one of those.

Schulman: I will immediately concede your historical point. What I represented in 1983, beginning with my debate with Wendy, is that I was putting forward a new natural rights theory that did not have an historical base.

Kinsella: Right. I understand. So let's get to something a little bit … you and I have gone back and forth over the years, mostly in writing. One reason that I just pinged you today was I was talking with another gentleman, and he was questioning the IP issues, and we were talking about it. And I was trying to explain something to him. And I made the point, which is *my* view, which I don't know if you completely agree with, but I was arguing that, look, one of the fundamental mistakes in the IP argument, or in your logorights argument I believe, is this idea that you can own an attribute or a characteristic or a feature of an object separate from the object itself, okay? And then I said …

Schulman: And that …

Kinsella: Hold on …

Schulman: And that comes directly out of Robert LeFevre's theory of property.

Kinsella: Okay, it may be. It's also somewhat of an implication of Locke. I think Locke was confused on his labor comments, etcetera, but, … and then I said actually that Schulman has modified his logorights characterization. You call it material-carried property, right?

Schulman: No, media-carried property.

Kinsella: Sorry, I keep messing it up—media-carried property. And I said, so basically, you view it the same as I. You just have a different conclusion. That's why I said, well, let's just talk about it. And let me just summarize quickly what I think the mistake is and you can tell me where you think I'm wrong or what I'm missing.

To my mind, if you own an object, and that's the media, that's the physical thing that is owned, that is always impatterned with some information or some attributes. And, in fact, information cannot be a free floating abstraction. Information, to exist and to be perceived and to persist, has to be embodied in some media. Wouldn't you agree with that part?

Schulman: Yes, but let me tell you where I think you're going where I think that you're not seeing what I'm seeing.

Kinsella: Go ahead.

Schulman: In my view, something intangible can't be owned, okay? For something to be ownable, it has to be something observable in the world and it has to be distinct and definite. Now the question which I pose, which you said that you agreed with my formulation …

Kinsella: No, I don't agree that is sufficient. That might be necessary.

Schulman: Let me get this out as concisely as I can.

Kinsella: Alright, go ahead.

Schulman: If you have an alphanumeric sequence which retains its material identity, in going from physical object to physical object, and is a commodity separate from the things on which it is carried, which give value, trade value, to the objects on which it is carried, but it is transferrable from one physical entity to another, I maintain we have now identified an object, a thing, something observable and distinct in the real world, which is in fact a property separable from the objects on which it is carried.

Kinsella: I got it but what …

Schulman: … and the example I gave in my debate with Wendy and have used ever since is, you buy a book with the title *Atlas Shrugged*. You take it home and start reading. And what you read is, "It was the best of times. It was the worst of times". Obviously—*A Tale of Two Cities* by Charles Dickens. It's not the same novel.

But if you're a reductionist saying that what can be owned is only a physical object, then you have something which—for the sake of argument—has the same number of pages, has ink impressions, has the same binding. And so, if you were going to reduce it and say that only a physical object can be owned, then the question arises: did you get what you paid for? Or, if you say yes, okay, then you have now eliminated the possibility of a novel being an existent, a thing, an entity; not an existent so much as an entity. You're saying that it cannot be a thing.

But if you're saying that you're entitled to the composition of words of *Atlas Shrugged* and not of *A Tale of Two Cities*, then you're saying that the composition of words, the alphanumeric sequence itself which is separable from the thing on which it is carried, the media-carried property, is the economic good which is being traded. And therefore you have an economic good which is a thing separable from the media on which it is carried.

Kinsella: I get your chain of reasoning. Let me see if I can summarize it. You tell me if I've got it right. You start off with the presumption that if you can identify something as an existent, entity, as a thing, as you call it, something that is—what was your word? Specific and definite? You're presupposing that that is sufficient for ownership. Like as long as something is specific and definite and you can give it some kind of ontological category or name and call it a "thing," and especially if it is valued in commerce and therefore it's a "commodity"—which I guess is only economic goods, not other kinds of goods—then that's sufficient for ownership. I just don't see the argument for the starting point here …

Schulman: No, I would say necessary but not sufficient.

Kinsella: Okay but …

Schulman: There are other things. In my original debate with Wendy and then in my subsequent 1983 treatise, "Informational Property: Logorights," I go through a whole bunch of other things that are necessary, but they're the same sets of questions that have to be satisfied for any other claim of ownership.

Kinsella: Well, the way you just stated it though, you only specified what was sufficient for ownership. I'm sorry, what was necessary for ownership, not what was sufficient. Just because …

Schulman: No, I'm saying that I've identified a category of things that can be owned if the same questions can be answered in the affirmative that you would have to answer for any claim of ownership of anything else.

Kinsella: See, I just don't think, to me that doesn't make sense, for several reasons. Number one, and I tried to give you an example in writing today, just as a pure contract situation. You could have a contract and the concept of fraud, even, if you want. You don't need to bring fraud into this, just contract. Contract theory and property rights alone explain why you're not getting what you asked for when you get the book that has the wrong pattern of information on it. In other words, if I give you money conditioned upon the book having a certain pattern in the book, and I don't get that, then the money that I paid you didn't transfer to you because it was conditioned upon a certain …

Schulman: Well, you see, it doesn't have to be fraud. Look, I'm a book publisher, okay? And I have in my possession an accidental artifact of a book which I received from Lightning Source. The cover is the cover of my novel, *The Rainbow Cadenza*, but the interior of the book is volume one of Robert LeFevre's autobiography. Now there was no deliberate fraud when this was manufactured …

Kinsella: Let's forget fraud, right. Let's just assume it's a contract.

Schulman: I'm not making a legal argument so much as I'm making an ontological argument. I'm saying that if, in fact, the composition, the alphanumeric sequence in this particular case is different, then you have a different thing, a different commodity.[20]

---

[20] Tibor Machan advanced a similar "ontology" based argument for IP. See Tibor Machan, "Intellectual Property and the Right to Private Property," Mises.org working paper (2006; https://mises.org/wire/new-working-paper-machan-ip), discussed in Kinsella, "Owning Thoughts and Labor," *Mises Economics Blog* (Dec. 11, 2006), and in *idem*, "Remembering Tibor Machan, Libertarian Mentor and Friend: Reflections on a Giant," *StephanKinsella.com* (April 19, 2016); see also "Law and Intellectual Property in a Stateless Society" (ch. 14), at n.78.

Kinsella: Right. But the different commodity is the physical book which is different than another physical book because of the way it's impatterned. The question is: can you own the attributes of the book in addition to the book itself? That's the question. Can you own …

Schulman: Well, this is the case even when there were no copyright laws to be enforced. In fact, you can argue … look, I will tell you right now that the argument you're making is one which is generally accepted by the film and television industry. The Writers Guild treats writing as if it's an act of labor, but they're much less specific on whether the labor produces something which can be owned. And I'll tell you that this is something which the Writers Guild calls separation of rights. In other words, if I as a screenwriter were to write for, let's say, *Gunsmoke*, it's a work for hire because I'm basically creating new stories based on their existing characters. But when I write an original episode of the *Twilight Zone*, an anthology series, they say I have separated rights unless it's a remake of an earlier *Twilight Zone*, such as the 1980s *Twilight Zone* that I worked on; remade some episodes from the original Rod Serling *Twilight Zone* from the 50s and 60s.

So, if I were the writer who was creating a new script based on an original script by Richard Matheson or Charles Beaumont or Rod Serling, then there are no separated rights because it's a work for hire. But if I create an original script with original story, not based on that, then there's a separation or rights.

Kinsella: Yeah, but these are just legal terms based on current copyright. I don't really see how that's relevant.

Schulman: These are legal terms of art.

Kinsella: It's not really relevant to what we're discussing, philosophy of what natural property rights would be. I mean you wouldn't have all these arcane arrangements.

Schulman: I am arguing, first of all, that all property exists only as an *intellectual artifact*. And where I make this argument the most concisely is in my essay, "Human Property."

Kinsella: But didn't you just say earlier that you don't believe in property in intangible things?

Schulman: Nothing found in nature is property. That it is basically a human intellect which creates the concept of property itself.

Kinsella: Well, that's true. But you could say human desire creates it too, but that doesn't mean desire gives rise to property rights absent other features.

Schulman: No, but what we're talking about is how human beings interact with each other. Unlike non-intellectual animals, we do it on the basis of intellectual construct.

Kinsella: Okay. Let me try to summarize a different way to look at it and get your take on this. It seems to me like your argument is basically this. You want to say, look, here's a book. There are two books that look identical on the outside. They have different patterns on the inside. You would be upset if you wanted one and you got the other. Therefore, it's a commodity or some kind of economic good. And because it's an economic good, that shows that the pattern, the logos as you call it, is an ontological thing that has existence.

Schulman: That's my argument.

Kinsella: I don't disagree with that as a philosophical exercise. It's just that you want to leap from that to saying, aha, because I've identified that there's a "thing" that has ontological existence, therefore it can have an owner. That, to me, is the entire mistake you're making because you haven't shown that that's …

Schulman: … I approach this a number of different ways in my original "Informational Property Rights," 1983, article. And one of the ways I approach is a *reduction ad absurdum*, using praxeology. In my reply to Konkin, his article, "Copywrongs," I basically deconstruct several of his premises in which I show, using Austrian economics—a praxeological approach—how, in fact, if you eliminate that concept, then you basically run into the contradiction of saying that that which you are arguing about doesn't exist.

I think that it is not a coincidence that literary contracts, regardless of whether we're talking about copyright or not, refer to something as the "work." In other words, it's a noun.

Kinsella: Because the copyright statute defined it that way.

Schulman: It's not arguing labor. It's arguing that there is a *thing* that is being traded called the "work." It is referred to in the contracts granting rights, which I have signed—there is a term of art called the work.

Kinsella: That's just how it's defined in the copyright statute, though, Neil.

Schulman: I am saying that is a thing which is, in fact, being traded or licensed in the same way that there is a right of occupancy which is being traded in a rental agreement for a car or an apartment.

Kinsella: Well, okay. So the copyright statute defined that term "work" and that's why contracts use it now.

Schulman: The copyright statute is beside the point as far as I'm concerned.

Kinsella: I don't think they would use the term work if not for the copyright statue.

Schulman: We're talking plain language.

Kinsella: But they wouldn't use that word if the copyright statue hadn't introduced it and defined it. That's a new innovation.

Schulman: I'm not sure that that's true. In other words, what you're arguing is which is the cart and which is the horse, and so am I. And I'm maintaining that there is a common-sense observation in these contracts which would survive the demise of the State and its admittedly mucked up copyright laws.

Kinsella: Well, let me ask you this. Would you agree with me that for your argument to work, you need to show that something having ontological existence is sufficient for there to be property rights possible in it? Don't you think you need to establish that?

Schulman: I think that given that you need to establish the same boundary issues that you would with other forms of property and contracts, that, yes, it qualifies as being entered into the running as a possible type of property.

Kinsella: My point is you have to show it, though. That is a presupposition of your argument, that establishing that something is of ontological existence, is an existent, is sufficient for it to be ownable. You have to prove that.

Schulman: It is necessary to qualify it for the debate on whether or not it is a property.

Kinsella: I mean, my view on this, I'm very Randian in my epistemology, my concept theory. I just think what you're doing, is you are doing reification in a sense. You're conflating the efficiency and the usefulness and the practicality of certain concepts with calling something "existing" and then leaping to the point where it can be owned.

Like, so for example, I think the concept of love is a valid concept. It has a referent in the world. You can say there "is" love. But just because we have identified an ontological type of thing that exists—love—doesn't mean it's a type of thing that can be owned. You have to do more than establish the validity of a concept to show that the referent of the concept is an ownable thing. I mean we have time. We have motion.

Schulman: I agree with that, but that, in fact, when you're identifying something which exists … look, love is something which is an expression, okay? And it is something which may be observable in human behavior but it is not something which you can identify as existing outside of human behavior in the way that an alphanumeric sequence is. I maintain that an alphanumeric sequence is, in fact, a thing.

Kinsella: Hold on a second. Earlier you said …

Schulman: An array of photographic frames is an observable thing in the real world.

Kinsella: Not outside of human behavior … you said earlier that property doesn't even exist, right?

Schulman: Just in the real world.

Kinsella: Hold on. You said property doesn't even exist outside of human intentions and human subjective evaluation. So how could alphanumeric sequences in something called a movie exist without regard for human intention?

Schulman: Okay, because "thingness" is one of the necessary, but not sufficient, conditions for a claim of ownership. Ownership is about action and intellectual creation of identity and … look, I would say that the identity exists independent, the thing exists. This is why it's both an ontological and an epistemological question before you get to the moral and legal questions. What I think that my work has done is establish the ontological and epistemological basis for these media-carried objects to be identified as ownable in the same way that other things can be ownable according to the general common sense principles of contract.

Kinsella: No, I understand your general thrust, but you seem to be agreeing because you say it on occasion. You seem to be agreeing with me that "thingness," which is just another way of saying something exists—or in my view it just means it's a valid concept—thingness is a necessary but not sufficient condition. That's why I keep saying … I just want to make sure you agree with me …

Schulman: Yes, that's what I'm saying.

Kinsella: But you need to …

Schulman: Necessary but not sufficient. But the sufficiency is by applying the exact same question that you would for any other claim of property.

Kinsella: Yes, I understand. We don't have time to get into that, but in your argument, in your logorights article and, I think, in your … what's the other, "Human Rights"? What's it called? "Human Property"?

Schulman: Property.

Kinsella: Yeah, in that one I think you try to give reasons why you think it is sufficient. I don't agree with you on that, but I think that's really the crux of our disagreement. But before …

Schulman: Can we at least come to the point where you think it is debatable, within the realm of possibility?

Kinsella: Honestly, I don't, Neil. But it's only because I've thought about it so much and I can see no way that you can own the characteristic of an object without that being a universal that gives you property rights in other people's owned resources.[21] In other words, to my mind, information …

---

[21] For discussion of the "universals" problem of IP law, see *Against Intellectual Property After Twenty Years*" (ch. 15), Part IV.F.

Schulman: And here's where I'm saying, that the defining distinction, which makes it possible, is that it is something outside of one human being. It's something that now exists in the world. At the point where it exists in the world, separate from the person who brought it into existence, now you have something real.

Kinsella: Let me ask you this. Is your view here, is it Platonic or mystical at all? Because I know you're a little bit mystical, more than I am, on some spiritual issues.[22] So does this view, because it seems to me …

Schulman: Back in 1983 when I was making these arguments, I was an atheist.

Kinsella: I'm asking about now though. I understand. But do you think there is anything mystical or Platonic about what you're saying? You seem to envision these …

Schulman: Only in the sense that Ayn Rand used the term "spiritual."

Kinsella: No, I don't mean that. I mean it's like you're envisioning the separate sort of ghostly existence of these Platonic objects that are out there, independent, ontologically separate from the…

Schulman: I don't accept a Platonic metaphysics.

Kinsella: Well would you agree that information has to be … hold on. Let me ask you this.

Schulman: Let me say this. I have made the argument that there is no such thing as a virtual reality, that either something is real or it isn't. You go back to the movie *The Matrix*, okay? And in fact there were these bodies …

Kinsella: Yeah, yeah, yeah, of course. There's always an underlying media or underlying …

Schulman: That was a reality.

Kinsella: Yeah, there is a substrate. I understand. I agree with you on that. But my point is, wouldn't you agree that information—these alphanumeric sequences you're talking about—they're always embedded

---

[22] See Neil's novel *Escape from Heaven* (Pulpless.com, 2017).

in some substrate or some media. They have to be just the impatterning *of a thing*. Wouldn't you agree with that?

Schulman: Yes, yes. And that's why I talk about media-*carried* property.
And the question is whether or not there is something separable which
can be transferred from physical object to physical object to physical
object. And that is the distinction which makes it a thing in and of itself.

Kinsella: Well, let's forget about whether it's separable. Let me ask you
this. If all information has to be embodied or impatterned in a media,
don't you agree the media has an owner? That physical thing that is the
media has some owner.

Schulman: Yes. And the ownership of that can be separated from the
ownership of the thing which is carried.

Kinsella: It *can* be .... I suppose it could be. But how does the fact that
someone writes a novel give them the ability to control the media that
other people own?

Schulman: Because there is a thing being carried for which property
rights have not been transferred.

Kinsella: Hold on, hold on. Give me thirty seconds. Hold on. Neil, hold
on. I've got to answer the door. Hold on thirty seconds. Neil, thirty
seconds.

Schulman: If you book a ride with Uber, your claim to a ride is a usage
which is separable from ownership of the vehicle.

Kinsella: Neil, sorry. I had to answer the door. Sorry. Go ahead.

Schulman: I'll repeat that because I don't know if you heard it. I'm saying that it is separable in the same way that if you book a ride with Uber,
what you're buying is a use, but you're not buying the Uber vehicle itself.

Kinsella: Well, I agree some things are separable, mostly by contract
or by co-ownership arrangements. But that doesn't mean that you can
control what other people do with their property unless you have a good
reason. I go with the Lockean and Rothbardian theory of property.

Schulman: Hold on. You're making an assumption. You're begging the
question. You're saying you're restricting what other people can do with
their property. I'm maintaining that what is being argued over is, in fact,

what is not being transferred to somebody else and what they cannot do because it is not their property.[23]

Kinsella: Well, but there's not always a transfer. So, for example, let's take the patent case. Okay, if you claim a property right in being the owner of this mousetrap design, alright? Now if I am toiling away in my garage with my own wood and steel, my own substrate, and I configure it into a certain shape, you can use the patent system to tell me I can't sell that. I can't even make that device. Now where was the transfer?

Schulman: You know, Stephan, I have to say that over the years I have become a lot less sanguine over arguing about patent rather than copyright.

Kinsella: Okay.

Schulman: I think the case for a patent is a harder case than arguing for what I've been calling media-carried property.

Kinsella: Well, let me do kind of a lightning round with you because there are some things I want to talk to you about because you know a lot of things about the history and Konkin and these things. Not to dwell too much on them. Let me just get your take on some things.

Number one, let's just stick with copyright, because you think that is some rough system that approximates something like, might, could exist in a free society. Do you think that the time limits on copyrights should be finite and arbitrary, or perpetual?

Schulman: I think that for media-carried property, you ask the exact same question that you would for ownership of any other kind of property.

Kinsella: So the problem with the copyright system is that it expires at about 120 years. In your view, it should last forever.

Schulman: Yeah, but again you're talking about a statist defined system.

Kinsella: I understand but one defect of the system is that …

Schulman: They could also arbitrarily say that land ownership ends with death and can't be carried …

---

[23] Neil is here implicitly making an argument that I criticize elsewhere. See "*Against Intellectual Property* After Twenty Years: Looking Back and Looking Forward" (ch. 15), Part IV.H.

Kinsella: I know. I just want to get you on record and see what you think. I mean you do realize the original copyright act was about fourteen years.

Schulman: All I'm saying is that when approaching this question, I think you need to satisfy the same requirements that you would for ownership and transfer of any other kind of property.

Kinsella: Are you aware, by the way, that Jefferson, when the Bill of Rights was being considered, he wrote a letter to Madison and he proposed ... because at that time the copyright clause was already in the Constitution, right, 1789. But for the Bill of Rights, Jefferson proposed amending the Bill of Rights, or adding a provision to the Bill of Rights saying that the State can grant these monopolies, by which he meant copyright and patent, but only for x years. So he wanted to put a time limit in there. You know, probably fourteen years.[24]

Schulman: Yeah, Jefferson, like Locke, was taking a utilitarian approach. I'm not. I wrote an entire novel, *The Rainbow Cadenza*, attacking the concept of utilitarianism being sufficient to come up with fairness. I'm an absolute believer in theories of natural law and natural rights. And I would say that would separate me from Jefferson and Locke.

Kinsella: So in your system, you couldn't even republish the Bible or Shakespeare's plays or Homer's works without getting some permission from some long lost descendent down the line. You would have to permission for everything. There would be a complete permission culture for all ideas.

Schulman: Well, I mean, again, I expand the question to every other sort of property.

Kinsella: So that's a yes.

Schulman: In other words, do we need to get permission from the heirs of the Roman emperors before we can take a tour of the Colosseum?

Kinsella: Okay. So let me ask you this one, about Konkin. You mentioned that he didn't oppose people using copyright, or in some cases,

---

24 See Kinsella, "Thomas Jefferson's Proposal to Limit the Length of Patent and Copyright in the Bill of Rights," *C4SIF Blog* (Dec. 1, 2011).

and LeFevre either. I mean, of course, I don't either. I've gotten copyrights on my works and used it before ...

Schulman: Sam did not copyright his own works and Robert LeFevre
did not copyright his own works.

Kinsella: Well, you realize that copyright is automatic. So that is actually
not true. They do have copyright in their work. As soon as you write
something, you have a copyright.

Schulman: Well, according to the State. But, I mean, are we ... these are
two people who did not recognize the authority of the State to define
these questions.

Kinsella: Well, but they had copyright in their works, whether they
wanted it or not.

Schulman: According to the State but not according to their own preferences.

Kinsella: Well, yeah, but someone couldn't, someone can't go publish
one of LeFevre's books right now without getting permission from
someone, even though LeFevre himself might have opposed copyright,
unless he put some kind of license ...

Schulman: That would be the case if it were an unpublished work. Then
that argument could be made. In fact, I will tell you where this arises
in a practical sense. As far as I know, the only copy of the manuscript
for Samuel Edward Konkin, III's *Counter-Economics* is in the hands of
Victor Koman. And Victor Koman has published other of Sam's works
which were first published when Sam was alive. And Sam explicitly
published them without a copyright.

Kinsella: No, that's not true. You can't publish something without a
copyright.

Schulman: The legal rights to this are held by the Konkin estate, which
devolves upon Sam's brother, Alan Konkin, in which Alan has made
me the literary executor. So Victor is in the position of having the only
manuscript, the only physical manuscript, which he refuses to provide
to the estate. But he cannot legally publish it himself ...

Kinsella: Correct.

Schulman: ... without permission from the estate.

Kinsella: Right. Well, this is just the kind of bizarre logic that comes from any type of IP system, I believe. You can blame the State's copyright system but I think it's just the logic of copyright. You're going to get these absurd and obviously unjust and obscene results. It's just an inevitable part of separating the idea of ownership from scarce resources.

I wanted to ask you. You mentioned earlier that in your earlier arguments you tried to rely on praxeology to support your case. I think praxeology …

Schulman: In my original 1983 article, "Informational Property: Logorights," Sam makes what he represents as a praxeological case and so I responded with a praxeological case.

Kinsella: Right. And then what I was going to say is I think that praxeology, especially Mises's version of the Austrian economics, is absolutely crucial, and indeed essential, to getting these issues straight. But I think it points in the other direction. I think that praxeology, basically, regards human action as the employment, right, the conscious, purposeful *employment of scarce means* to achieve something in the world, *guided by knowledge*.[25] So praxeology views human action …

Schulman: Let's start out with the first premise of Austrian economics, which I almost parodied in the first line of my novel, *Alongside Night*.[26] Mises argues human beings act to remove felt unease.

Kinsella: Correct. That's their purpose. That's their motivation, right.

Schulman: First line of the novel: "Elliot Vreeland felt uneasy the moment he entered his classroom."

Kinsella: Right. And I think that's a brilliant aspect of praxeology, but it only goes to the motives or the purpose. What human action *is*, is the *employment of scarce means*, which you can call scarce resources, *guided by*

---

[25] Here I was trying to explain to Neil why successful action requires both availability of scarce (conflictable) resources and information or knowledge to guide one's action, but that only the former is subject to property rights and ownership, since information cannot be owned. However we started having technical glitches so ended the discussion before we could make much headway on this. I discuss this issue in "Law and Intellectual Property in a Stateless Society" (ch. 14), Part III.D, and *"Against Intellectual Property* After Twenty Years" (ch. 15), Part IV.E.

[26] Schulman, *Alongside Night*, 20th anniv. ed. (Pulpless.com, 1999).

knowledge. So there are two important components to successful human action. One is the availability …

Schulman: Mises then goes on, through a whole series of deductive derivations on that premise.

Kinsella: I know. I'm just focusing on the bare structure … I just want to get your take on this okay? My argument is very simple. And I think Mises is right. When we act in the world, we're trying to achieve an outcome, right, to remove felt uneasiness or to achieve something at the end of the process, but we do it by employing scarce means that are causally effective in the world, and we do it by using our knowledge to decide what to do. So you have to have knowledge *and* you have to have scarce means. Property rights apply to the second …

Schulman: But you see, again, and I think that I made this argument in one of my other articles responding to that video, *Copying is Not Theft*.[27]

Kinsella: By Nina Paley.

Schulman: I responded to that … I think it's linked in an article called *The Libertarian Case for IP*. I'm basically saying that scarcity is itself a limited concept. In other words, that it is a relative concept … That there is no requirement for absolute scarcity. It merely needs to be scarcity within a particular context.

Kinsella: But what do you mean when you say you're opposed to intangible property and that you think all information is in a media? A media is a scarce physical resource. Land is a scarce, physical resource.

Schulman: I'm arguing that if there is an alphanumeric sequence, for example, then that alphanumeric sequence is a unique object. There's only one of it …

Kinsella: I know you think it's a unique object.

Schulman: … therefore, if there's only one of something, it's by definition scarce.

Kinsella: Okay, but let's go back. I want to just finish this very short praxeological argument and see what you think is wrong with it, because

---

[27] See Nina Paley, "*Copying Is Not Theft*," YouTube (https://youtu.be/IeTybKL1pM4; April 1, 2010). Neil's reply to the video is in *Origitent*.

you keep stopping me before I get to the end, and it's very simple. We employ scarce means. That is, you manipulate things in the world that can have a cause and effect. But to do that, you have to have some idea of what causality is, what physics laws are. And you have to have some idea of what's possible and what you're going to achieve. So knowledge is in your head. It guides your choice of means and your choice of ends. So every action is the employment of scarce means *and* the use of knowledge. Would you agree with that?

Schulman: I would say that that is a chain of reasoning which precedes the possibility of property, yes.

Kinsella: Yeah, I'm just saying that it's inconceivable to imagine human action that doesn't employ scarce means and that isn't guided by knowledge. Correct?

Schulman: Well, … uh … yes, but there's the possibility of human action acting on something which is ubiquitous.

Kinsella: Yeah right. That's the general condition of human action.

Schulman: In doing so, converting something from ubiquitous to scarce.

Kinsella: That's possible. I'm just saying the structure of action is that *every* single human action *has* to employ scarce means and *has* to be guided by knowledge. It's just inconceivable without it.

Schulman: In a sense …

Kinsella: But wait. Do you agree with that or not?

Schulman: Hold on. Let me try to answer your question. I think that human action is itself a scarcity [Kinsella sighs] and therefore the employment of human action on something else has at least the potential to satisfy the conditions of creating a scarce something.[28]

Kinsella: That's fine but I'm not talking about the end results of your action. The end result of an action *does not need to be the acquisition of a scarce resource or the ownership of some object.* The end of an action can be

---

[28] Here Neil is making an argument I call libertarian creationism, which I explain and criticize in "Law and Intellectual Property in a Stateless Society" (ch. 14), Part III.B and "*Against Intellectual Property* After Twenty Years" (ch. 15), Part IV.C.

anything. It can be totally subjective, right? It might be to get a little girl to smile after you do a card trick for her.[29]

Schulman: No, no. Hold on. The reason that the human mind affects an action is not the same thing, and I would say that there is a disconnect. Once the results of that action produce an etching in the real world, which is separate from the actor and observable by other actors.

Kinsella: I know. Okay, but you're getting … I'm not trying … I'm just talking about—if you view human action praxeologically as the employment of scarce means to achieve an end, and the action that you take is guided by knowledge, that that shows that knowledge, or information …

Schulman: We're having a communication artifact problem at the moment. What you just said verbally. Can you say it again please?

Kinsella: Oh sorry. What I'm trying to say is my understanding of the way property norms arise and the way they relate to Mises's economic understanding of …

Schulman: Oh geez. I'm sorry Stephan. What you're talking I'm not hearing verbally … try saying it one more time.

Kinsella: Test, test, test. Can you hear me now? Hello? Test. Neil?

---

[29] See, e.g,. Israel M. Kirzner, *Market Theory and the Price System* (Princeton, N.J.: D. Van Nostrand Co., Inc., 1963; https://mises.org/library/market-theory-and-price-system-0), p. 46–47:

> In the actuality of the everyday world, human beings are able to satisfy their wants only through directing their efforts toward appropriate *means* for such satisfaction. A man who wishes to eat may purchase food, cook food, or simply put on a hat and coat and go to a restaurant. His actions have been intermediary to the goal of eating. "Eating" is the *end* of his present endeavors; the *means* that he adopts for the attainment of his end can be an act of purchase, cooking, or walking to the restaurant.

In a sense, the actual end of action is *always* the attainment of some new state of affairs, some want-satisfaction, and never the acquisition or ownership of a corporeal good since, as Böhm-Bawerk has observed, such goods are valued *only because of the renditions of service they provide*. See Eugen von Böhm-Bawerk, "Whether Legal Rights and Relationships Are Economic Goods," George D. Huncke, trans., in Eugen von Böhm-Bawerk, *Shorter Classics of Eugen von Böhm-Bawerk* (South Holland, Ill.: Libertarian Press, 1962 [1881]), pp. 73, 77 *et pass.*, discussed in Gael J. Campan, "Does Justice Qualify as an Economic Good?: A Böhm-Bawerkian Perspective," *Q. J. Austrian Econ.* 2, no. 1 (Spring 1999; https://perma.cc/G3CK-B8WB): 21–33, pp. 23–24.

Schulman: Yeah, I'm not really getting anything. Do you want to stop the recording and call me back and start it again?

Kinsella: … Sure. I'll do that right now. Sorry about that. Yeah, let's just finish it up quickly. What I'm doing is calling you on one iPhone and I'm recording it over the air on another. A very low tech solution because everything is always glitchy in technology. In fact, why don't we wrap it up. Yeah, let's just wrap it up. I told you what I wanted. I was just running an alternative praxeological theory by you. The basic argument is that you need property rights in the scarce means that are essential to human action, but you *cannot* have property rights in the knowledge that guides human action because that's not a scarce human resource.

Schulman: I agree with you. I'm not making a knowledge argument.

Kinsella: Well, you do believe in informational property. So you think there are property rights in information.

Schulman: I believe that information *per se* cannot be owned but an information *object* can be. And that is a crucial distinction.

Kinsella: Okay. Okay. Well, I think …

Schulman: In the same way that you can't own matter, but you can own things made out of matter. You can't own information but you can own things made out of information.

Kinsella: So like, if you own a horseshoe, you don't own the matter in the horseshoe. You only own the way the matter is shaped?

Schulman: I'm sorry. Say that again please.

Kinsella: So like, if you own a horseshoe, you don't own the metal matter of the horseshoe. You only own the way the horseshoe is shaped?

Schulman: Well, again, you own the *thing* which is the horseshoe. You own the thing which is the horseshoe, in the same way that, if you own a novel, you own the thing that is the novel.

Kinsella: Let me ask you this …

Schulman: Which is the part of the thing on which it is in the same way that you can own the horseshoe without owning the horse.

Kinsella: Yeah, but … so let's suppose lightning strikes the horseshoe and melts it. And now you have a puddle of molten iron. Do you own that or have you lost the ownership of it because it's not a horseshoe anymore?

Schulman: Let me ask you this. If you own a house and the house burns down, do you own the ashes?

Kinsella: Yes, I would say that because I don't believe that the ownership of the house is dependent upon its shape.

Schulman: Well, here we have an interesting thing because unless the sole copy of a thing is destroyed, then you have something which is durable. And destroying a carrier of it does not necessarily destroy the thing which is carried.

Kinsella: But it does, because you can't have information without some media that it's carried in.

Schulman: Yes and …

Kinsella: Yeah, there could be multiple copies of it. I know.

Schulman: And here is a case where there needs to be at least one surviving carrier.

Kinsella: Right, but this also implies there could be multiple copies of it. You see, you want to call it one object.

Schulman: There could be multiple copies. But the way that I would phrase that is, what is the variable is the number of carriers. There is still only unique object which is being carried.

Kinsella: Yeah. So it's a universal or it's a Platonic … that's why I say it's a Platonic object, to me, it seems like.

Schulman: No, I can understand why, from a philosophical standpoint, this concept could be regarded by Plato as Platonic. However, I am not a Platonist and I'm not making a Platonic argument. There it is. I believe that Aristotle had the concept of the atom but later science started talking about electrons and neutrons and protons and sub-particles called quarks. So just because the language seems to say something which was said by the ancients doesn't mean it's equivalent.

Kinsella: Sure. Sure. Anyway, I'm going to tie it up now. I'm a little upset with you because I asked you to keep this to thirty minutes and you insisted on going a whole hour, Neil.

Schulman: I'm sorry. How much did we actually use?

Kinsella: [Laughs] No, I'm just joking. I don't know because I have it broken up. Probably about an hour and five minutes.

Schulman: Well, I don't have a problem with that.

Kinsella: No, no, I'm joking.

Schulman: But then again, you and I have no problem being loquacious.

Kinsella: That's true. That's true. Well, I appreciate your time and your sincerity on this issue. I think for now we'll have to agree to disagree, but at least people can listen to this and see where you're coming from and evaluate the different ways of looking at this stuff.

Schulman: I appreciate it very much. Thank you.

Kinsella: All right Neil. Hold on, hold on after I stop and we'll chat. Talk to you later. Thanks man.

Schulman: Okay.

18

Goods, Scarce and Nonscarce

Originally published in 2010, with co-author Jeffrey Tucker.* This emerged out of many discussions he and I had about intellectual property and our respective writings on this topic. I have revised and updated the original article,† which included this authors' note: "Special thanks to BK Marcus, Doug French, Jeffrey Herbener, Raymond Walter, David Gordon, Robert Murphy, and Joseph Salerno for comments."

Everyone who is serious about ideas now has to deal with the issue of "intellectual property," especially given the advent of digital media and the state's war on the supposed violators of the intellectual rights of others. The situation has at once become very hopeful, with more sharing of ideas than ever before in history, and extremely grim, with the federal government pressuring every internet-service provider to act as proxy enforcers of an unjust law—and twisting the arms of developing countries to adopt draconian, Western-style IP law.[1]

This debate, however, involves more than just IP issues. The discussion surrounding this topic has further clarified other issues, like the character of goods and property, the existence and centrality of nonscarce goods

---

* Jeffrey A. Tucker & Stephan Kinsella, "Goods, Scarce and Nonscarce," *Mises Daily* (Aug. 25, 2010).
† My co-author has reviewed the changes made in this chapter and fully agrees with them.

---

[1] See Kinsella, "Stop the ACTA (Anti-Counterfeiting Trade Agreement)," *StephanKinsella* (April 11, 2010). For other and more recent material on IP imperialism, see "*Against Intellectual Property* After Twenty Years: Looking Back and Looking Forward" (ch. 15), at n.19.

in economic life, and the role of learning in the evolution of society. This partially accounts for why the IP topic is so hot: it causes us to revisit fundamental issues over property, ownership, competition, and other areas we've mistakenly taken for granted. What follows is a summary of some fundamental ideas many of us batted around this summer.[2]

SCARCITY AND SCARCE GOODS

"Why are tangible goods property?" This is a central question of *Against Intellectual Property*. Or more precisely: why are there, or why should there be, property rights in material, corporeal, scarce resources? The reason for property rights is:

> ... the fact that there can be conflict over these goods by multiple human actors. The very possibility of *conflict* over a resource renders it scarce, giving rise to the need for ethical rules to govern its use. Thus, the fundamental social and ethical function of property rights is to prevent interpersonal conflict over scarce resources.[3]

On this point, we can cite Hoppe's *Theory of Socialism and Capitalism*, where Hoppe writes with singular clarity: "only because scarcity exists is there even a problem of formulating moral laws; insofar as goods are superabundant ('free' goods), no conflict over the use of goods is possible and no action-coordination is needed."[4] The logic for this insight Hoppe draws from Rothbard, and the term "free goods" he takes from Mises.[5]

---

[2] For some of these discussions, see the comment threads to the following *Mises Economics Blog* posts: Kinsella, "The Death Throes of Pro-IP Libertarianism" (July 28, 2010); "Kinsella: Ideas are Free: The Case Against Intellectual Property: or, How Libertarians Went Wrong" (Nov. 23, 2010); "The L. Neil Smith–FreeTalkLive Copyright Dispute" (June 14, 2010); "Replies to Neil Schulman and Neil Smith re IP" (July 19, 2010); "Leveraging IP" (Aug. 1, 2010); "The Creator-Endorsed Mark as an Alternative to Copyright" (July 15, 2010); "Locke, Smith, Marx and the Labor Theory of Value" (June 23, 2010).

[3] Kinsella, *Against Intellectual Property* (Auburn, Ala.: Mises Institute, 2008), p. 29. See also the related discussions in *"Against Intellectual Property* After Twenty Years" (ch. 15), Parts II.C and II.D, and "What Libertarianism Is" (ch. 2), *passim*.

[4] Hans-Hermann Hoppe, *A Theory of Socialism and Capitalism: Economics, Politics, and Ethics* (Auburn, Ala.: Mises Institute 2010 [1989]; www.hanshoppe.com/tsc), p. 158 n.120.

[5] Ludwig von Mises, *Human Action: A Treatise on Economics*, Scholar's ed. (Auburn, Ala.: Mises Institute, 1998; https://mises.org/library/human-action-0), chap. IV, § 1, p. 93, *et pass.* (discussing free goods and the general conditions of human welfare).

(As for the term "goods" itself, it is used by Austrians more or less as a synonym for the *scarce means of action*.)[6]

Hoppe writes:

> To develop the concept of property, it is necessary for goods to be scarce, so that conflicts over the use of these goods can possibly arise. It is the function of property rights to avoid such possible clashes over the use of scarce resources by assigning rights of exclusive ownership. Property is thus a normative concept: a concept designed to make a conflict-free interaction possible by stipulating mutually binding rules of conduct (norms) regarding scarce resources.[7]

Even in the case of the Garden of Eden, where superabundance would mean that all things we ever wanted were in our grasp, Hoppe explains that there would still be a need for property rights. This is because the human body itself is scarce: choices about who can use it and how it can be used necessarily exclude other choices. One cannot simultaneously

---

[6] This is explicit in Rothbard. He writes:
The *means* to satisfy man's wants are called *goods*. These goods are all the objects of economizing action. Such goods may all be classified in either of two categories: *(a)* they are immediately and *directly serviceable* in the satisfaction of the actor's wants, or *(b)* they may be transformable into directly serviceable goods only at some point in the future—i.e., are *indirectly serviceable* means. The former are called *consumption goods* or *consumers' goods* or *goods of the first order*. The latter are called *producers' goods* or *factors of production* or *goods of higher order*.
Murray N. Rothbard, *Man, Economy, and State, with Power and Market*, Scholars ed., 2d ed. (Auburn, Ala.: Mises Institute, 2009; https://mises.org/library/man-economy-and-state-power-and-market), chap. 1, § 3 (citations omitted). This equivalence between means and goods is also implicit in Mises's writings, as well. See, e.g., Mises, *Human Action*, chap. IV, § 1, p. 93:
Economic goods which in themselves are fitted to satisfy human wants directly and whose serviceableness does not depend on the cooperation of other economic goods, are called consumers' goods or goods of the first order. Means which can satisfy wants only indirectly when complemented by cooperation of other goods are called producers' goods or factors of production or goods of a remoter or higher order.
[7] Hoppe, *A Theory of Socialism and Capitalism*, p. 18. Note here the focus on the possibility of *conflict* and its connection to the concept of scarcity and the need for property rights. Thus, as noted elsewhere in this volume, in recent years I (Kinsella) sometimes use terms like rivalrous or "conflictable," instead of, or as an augment to, the concept of "scarce," to avoid equivocation from IP socialists. See *"Against Intellectual Property* After Twenty Years"* (ch. 15), n.29 *et pass.*; Kinsella, "On Conflictability and Conflictable Resources," *StephanKinsella.com* (Jan. 31, 2022); "What Libertarianism Is" (ch. 2), n.5; "How We Come to Own Ourselves" (ch. 4), n.10. In this chapter I have retained our original use of the term "scarce" but it should be understood to mean "conflictable."

eat an apple, smoke a cigarette, climb a tree, and build a house. Likewise, as Hoppe notes:

> … because of the scarcity of body and time, even in the Garden of Eden property regulations would have to be established. Without them, and assuming now that more than one person exists, that their range of action overlaps, and that there is no preestablished harmony and synchroniza-tion of interests among these persons, conflicts over the use of one's own body would be unavoidable. I might, for instance, want to use my body to enjoy drinking a cup of tea, while someone else might want to start a love affair with it, thus preventing me from having my tea and also reducing the time left to pursue my own goals by means of this body. In order to avoid such possible clashes, rules of exclusive ownership must be formulated. In fact, so long as there is action, there is a necessity for the establishment of property norms.[8]

A property right in one's scarce body is a precondition for action even in the face of superabundance. Hoppe goes so far as to say that the body is the "prototype of a scarce good."[9] Here he agrees with Jefferson's teacher Count Destutt de Tracy: "property exists in nature: for it is impossible that every one should not be the proprietor of his individuality and of his faculties."[10]

As Hoppe writes:

> The answer to the question what makes my body "mine" lies in the ob-vious fact that this is not merely an assertion but that, for everyone to see, this *is* indeed the case. Why do we say, "This is my body"? For this, a twofold requirement exists. On the one hand it must be the case that the body called "mine" must indeed (in an intersubjectively ascertainable

---

[8] Hoppe, *A Theory of Socialism and Capitalism*, p. 20–21. Thus: This "ownership" of one's own body implies one's right to invite (agree to) another person's doing something with (to) one's own body: my right to do with my body whatever I want, that is, includes the right to ask and let someone else use my body, love it, examine it, inject medicines or drugs into it, change its physical appearance and even beat, damage, or kill it, if that should be what I like and agree to. [p. 22]

[9] See "What Libertarianism Is" (ch. 2), at n.9; "How We Come to Own Ourselves" (ch. 4), at n.2; "A Libertarian Theory of Punishment and Rights" (ch. 5), at n.60; "Dialogical Arguments for Libertarian Rights" (ch. 6), at n.6 *et pass.*

[10] The Count Destutt Tracy, *A Treatise on Political Economy*, Thomas Jefferson, trans. (Auburn, Ala.: Mises Institute, 2009 [1817]; https://mises.org/library/treatise-political-economy-0), p. 125. For further elaboration on Hoppe's views on body-ownership, see Kinsella, "How We Come to Own Ourselves" (ch. 4).

way) express or "objectify" my will. Proof of this, as far as my body is concerned, is easy enough to demonstrate: When I announce that I will now lift my arm, turn my head, relax in my chair (or whatever else) and these announcements then become true (are fulfilled), then this shows that the body which does this has been indeed appropriated by my will. If, to the contrary, my announcements showed no systematic relation to my body's actual behavior, then the proposition "this is my body" would have to be considered as an empty, objectively unfounded assertion; and likewise this proposition would be rejected as incorrect if following my announcement not my arm would rise but always that of Müller, Meier, or Schulze (in which case one would more likely be inclined to consider Müller's, Meier's, or Schulze's body "mine"). On the other hand, apart from demonstrating that my will has been "objectified" in the body called "mine," it must be demonstrated that my appropriation has *priority* as compared to the possible appropriation of the same body by another person.

As far as bodies are concerned, it is also easy to prove this. We demonstrate it by showing that it is under my *direct* control, while every other person can objectify (express) itself in my body only *indirectly*, i.e., by means of their own bodies, and direct control must obviously have logical-temporal priority (precedence) as compared to any indirect control. The latter simply follows from the fact that any indirect control of a good by a person presupposes the direct control of this person regarding his own body; thus, in order for a scarce good to become justifiably appropriated, the appropriation of one's directly controlled "own" body must already be *presupposed* as justified. It thus follows: If the justice of an appropriation by means of direct control must be presupposed by any further-reaching indirect appropriation, and if only I have direct control of my body, then no one except me can ever justifiably own my body (or, put differently, then property in/of my body cannot be transferred onto another person), and every attempt of an indirect control of my body by another person must, unless I have explicitly agreed to it, be regarded as unjust(ified).[11]

---

[11] Quoted in "How We Come to Own Ourselves" (ch. 4), text at n.17. See also *idem, Economy, Society, and History* (Auburn, Ala.: Mises Institute, 2021; www.hanshoppe.com/esh), pp. 7–8 (discussing each human's unique connection to his own body). See also Emanuele Martinelli, "On Whether We Own What We Think" (draft, 2019; https://perma.cc/LQ98-HSAB), p. 3: regarding Locke's notion of self-ownership, "the basic intuition is that no one could metaphysically control another one's body and mind." See also John Locke, *Second Treatise on Civil Government* (1690; https://www.johnlocke.net/2022/07/two-treatises-of-government.html), chap. 5, "Of Property."

But let's be clear what we do *not* mean by the term scarce in the sense that it applies to this discussion. Something can have zero price and still be scarce: a mud pie, soup with a fly in it, a computer that won't boot. So long as no one wants these things, they are not economic goods. And yet, in their physical nature, they are scarce because if someone did want them, and they thus became goods, there could be contests over their possession and use. They would have to be allocated by either violence or market exchange based on property rights.

Nor does scarcity necessarily refer to whether a good is in shortage or surplus, nor to whether there are only a few or whether there are many. There can be a single "owner" of a nonscarce good (a poem I just thought of, which I can share with you without your taking it away from me) or a billion owners of scarce goods (paperclips, which, despite their ubiquity, are still an economic good).

Nor does scarcity necessarily refer to tangibility only, to the ability to physically manipulate the thing, or to the ability to perceive something with the senses; airspace and radio airwaves[12] are intangible scarce goods and therefore potentially held as property and therefore priced, while fire is an example of a tangible good of potentially unlimited supply.

Instead, the term scarcity here refers to the possible existence of conflict over the possession of a finite thing. It means that a condition of contestable control exists for anything that cannot be simultaneously owned: my ownership and control excludes your control.

REPLICATION AND NONSCARCE GOODS

In contrast, there are nonscarce goods. A classic statement on them comes from Frank Fetter's *Economic Principles*:

> [S]ome things, even such as are indispensable to existence, may yet, be-
> cause of their abundance, fail to be objects of desire and of choice. Such
> things are called *free goods*. They have no value in the sense in which the

---

12 See B.K. Marcus, "The Spectrum Should Be Private Property: The Economics, History, and Future of Wireless Technology," *Mises Daily* (Oct. 29, 2004; https://perma. cc/9VMQ-5VE2); Kinsella, "Why Airwaves (Electromagnetic Spectra) Are (Arguably) Property," *Mises Economics Blog* (Aug. 9, 2009).

economist uses that term. Free goods are things which exist in superfluity; that is, in quantities sufficient not only to gratify but also to satisfy all the desires which may depend on them.[13]

An example of a necessarily nonscarce good is a thing in demand that can be replicated without limit, so that I can have one, you can have one, and we can all have one. This is a condition under which there can be no contest over ownership. As Hoppe observes, under these conditions, there would be no need for property norms governing their ownership and use.

This nonscarce status might apply to many things but it always applies to nonfinite things, that is, goods that can be copied without limit, with no additional copy having displaced the previous copy and with no degradation in the quality of the copied good from the original good.

Jefferson himself made the lasting statement that clearly distinguishes the two types of goods:

If nature has made any one thing less susceptible than all others of exclusive property, it is the action of the thinking power called an idea, which an individual may exclusively possess as long as he keeps it to himself; but the moment it is divulged, it forces itself into the possession of every one, and the receiver cannot dispossess himself of it. Its peculiar character, too, is that no one possesses the less, because every other possesses the whole of it. He who receives an idea from me, receives instruction himself without lessening mine; as he who lights his taper at mine, receives light without darkening me. That ideas should freely spread from one to another over the globe, for the moral and mutual instruction of man, and improvement of his condition, seems to have been peculiarly and benevolently designed by nature, when she made them, like fire, expansible over all space, without lessening their density in any point, and like the air in which we breathe, move, and have our physical being, incapable of confinement or exclusive appropriation. Inventions then cannot, in nature, be a subject of property.[14]

---

13 Frank A. Fetter, *Economics—Vol. 1: Economic Principles* (NY: The Century Co., 1915; https://mises.org/library/economic-principles), chap. 3, §2. See also the Mises citation in note 5, above.

14 See "Thomas Jefferson to Isaac McPherson 13 Aug. 1813," *Founders Online* (text formatted; https://founders.archives.gov/documents/Jefferson/03-06-02-0322).

The idea is not just the spawn of Enlightenment thought. St. Augustine also took note of the peculiar goods quality of words.

> The words I am uttering penetrate your senses, so that every hearer holds them, yet withholds them from no other. ... I have no worry that, by giving all to one, the others are deprived. I hope, instead, that everyone will consume everything; so that, denying no other ear or mind, you take all to yourselves, yet leave all to all others. But for individual failures of memory, everyone who came to hear what I say can take it all off, each on one's separate way.[15]

Imagine if Jefferson's and Augustine's descriptions of ideas applied to finite things. Let's say that someone owns a magic bagel. He could give a friend a bagel and another would magically appear in its place, allowing him to keep his bagel at the same time. The very act of giving it away would create an exact copy of it. A neighbor could do the same. Potentially, everyone in the world could have an identical bagel—all equally delicious.

This magic bagel would then constitute what has been traditionally called a free good or what we are now calling a nonscarce good—something that can be possessed unto infinity and by an unlimited number of people without displacing or degrading the original. With free goods, or nonscarce goods, there is no conflict over ownership.

You could say that you have a property right in the magic bagel, but it would be meaningless because anyone could "take it" by the act of replicating it. It cannot be owned in the traditional sense. I could of course keep my magic bagel under wraps and never let anyone know about it. But that changes nothing about its magic properties. It remains a good that can be copied without limit. And my ability to keep the secret is a result of my property right in—my ability to control—the scarce resource of my body.

Under these conditions, the status of the bagel as a free good is due to its *replicability*. If it could not be so replicated, if its magic went away, it would become a scarce good. Once it became public, there would be a contest over ownership of that bagel (if I have it, you can't have it).

---

15 Garry Wills, *St. Augustine: A Life* (Viking Penguin, 1999), p. 145.

So it is with all things: if there is a zero-sum contest over its possession, it is scarce; if there need not be rivalry over its ownership, and its capacity for copying and sharing is infinite, it is nonscarce.

Does that sound fanciful? With regard to bagels, it is. But what if something like the magic-bagel example becomes real? Yesterday we could replicate information with photocopiers and print any number of perfect copies with a laser printer; and now we can copy and reproduce documents and files digitally. What if so-called 3D printers become widespread? These are devices that can fabricate various material objects by using a "recipe." In principle one could see a bagel (or car) that he likes, find or create a blueprint or recipe for it, and have a copy printed using one's own 3D printer, energy, and raw materials.

One can only imagine the IP police stopping people from using their 3D printers to make useful tools and goods based on the idea that doing so is somehow "stealing" the property of others that is still sitting in their homes.[16]

In any case, for now the technology for 3D copying and printing is in its infancy. Not so for digitally encoded information. For example, consider a file on your hard drive. It can be packaged up and sent via email. The file does not disappear. A perfect copy of that file appears in someone else's email. That person could similarly forward (a copy of) the file to another person. This can happen billions and trillions of times without compromising the integrity of the first file. In effect, this file is like the magic bagel, a nonscarce good. If the file is on a server, it can be accessed by billions of people, each of whom could similarly host the file until it multiplies without limit.[17]

Consider the power of this nonscarce good. That file might contain a database with all the world's financial transactions for last month. The record of those transactions would be nonscarce. The file could contain

---

[16] See *"Against Intellectual Property* After Twenty Years" (ch. 15), at n.27, for further discussion of this issue.

[17] For further discussion of why it is impossible to own information (or things like Bitcoin) precisely because it is replicable and always has to be stored on an underlying, already-owned medium, see "A Libertarian Theory of Contract: Title Transfer, Binding Promises, and Inalienability" (ch. 9), at n.31; "Selling Does Not Imply Ownership, and Vice-Versa: A Dissection" (ch. 11), at notes 3 and 5; *"Against Intellectual Property* After Twenty Years" (ch. 15), at n.69; and "Conversation with Schulman about Logorights and Media-Carried Property" (ch. 17).

images of all the paintings in the National Gallery of Art. These images would be nonscarce. It could contain videos of all college lectures given in the United States last semester. Again, nonscarce.

All of this is possible and practicable. We experience this every day. We do this every day. All the files on the World Wide Web, unless they have been specially coded to be otherwise, constitute free goods.

It seems clear that we are moving into a world in which we have to account for the existence of massive and growing numbers of goods that are not scarce, in the sense that they are potentially replicable into infinity. These goods fall outside the strict confines needed for rationing. There need be no conflict and hence no need for traditional property rights for them.

GOODS, SCARCE AND NONSCARCE

One helpful way to understand this is to classify all goods as either finite and therefore normally scarce or nonfinite and therefore naturally nonscarce. This distinction appears from time to time in the history of thought.[18] Property rights are essential for scarce goods. It is these scarce goods that serve as means for action, while nonscarce goods that can be copied without displacing the original are not *means* but *guides* for action.[19] It would be ridiculous to speak of some kind of "social ownership" over scarce goods.[20] Scarce goods can only be owned by one person at a time. Sure, you can share them, but that is just a means of allocating a scarce good that changes nothing about the intrinsic nature

---

[18] An example is Armen Alchian and William Allen, who write: "A *good* is anything desired by at least one person. Goods may be either *free* goods or *economic* (that is, scarce) goods." Armen Alchian & William R. Allen, *Exchange and Production: Competition, Coordination, & Control*, 3d ed. (Belmont, California: Wadsworth, 1983), p. 14. See also the Mises reference in note 5, above.

[19] For further discussion of why property rights apply to scarce resources or means of action but not to the knowledge that guides action, see *"Against Intellectual Property* After Twenty Years" (ch. 15), Part IV.E, at notes 58–59 *et pass.*; "Law and Intellectual Property in a Stateless Society" (ch. 14), Part III.D. See also the Mises and Rothbard quotes at notes 32 and 33, below.

[20] On Rothbard's critique of the "communist" approach to property rights assignment, see "How We Come to Own Ourselves" (ch. 4), at n.14 and "Law and Intellectual Property in a Stateless Society" (ch. 14), at n.27; also "Defending Argumentation Ethics" (ch. 7), n.31.

of the good. In the end, all attempts at socializing scarce resources lead to state ownership and the well-known chaos associated with it.

But let us return to the bagel, this time one without magic properties. What about the recipe and skills that made it? The recipe and skills can be copied by anyone. Anyone can watch and learn. The recipe can be shared unto infinity. Once the information in the recipe and the techniques of making it are released, they are free goods, nonscarce goods, or nonfinite goods.

What are some more examples of such naturally nonscarce goods? One person can share an idea and it can spread unto infinity, never reducing or degrading the quality of the original. Fire might be considered another example (as Thomas Jefferson said). A match can light a log without displacing the fire from the match. The times tables are another example: the grade-school teacher doesn't "give up" this knowledge when drilling it into the students. An image of anything qualifies too. One person can look at another and memorize what he or she sees, without somehow taking or replacing the original. A tune is the same way. It can be shared and replicated without limit. I can sing a song, and you can sing the same song without taking the song from me.

These goods are all nonscarce and thereby require no economization, and no property rights, as no conflict is possible. Once they are released, they need not be priced. There is no "structure of production" attached to their reproduction or allocation (hence there is no "structure of production" for the dissemination of ideas).

To be sure, nonscarce goods *can* be economized and thereby commercialized by rationing the scarce means of their distribution. For example, a professor, whose time and body are scarce, is paid to share nonscarce ideas. This is a service, but once the professor's ideas are shared, they enter into the realm of all nonscarce goods. What is paid for in fact is not the idea itself but the presentation, the time required to share, the labor services of teaching, all of which are scarce goods.[21]

It is the same with a book or article. What is scarce is the medium through which the idea is expressed, which is why books, articles, and

---

[21] Technically speaking, a service is a type of labor, which is just a type of action; and actions and services are not ownable things. For discussion of the proper classification of contracts for the "sale" of labor services, see "A Libertarian Theory of Contract" (ch. 9), Part II.C; also "Selling Does Not Imply Ownership, and Vice-Versa: A Dissection" (ch. 11).

web access cost money. The ideas conveyed in them, however, are copyable without limit.

This is not an insight that applies to digital media alone. This is true regardless of the technology involved. Whether we are talking about a scribe working on velum in the 8th century or a writer working on a web-based document in the 21st century, the ideas conveyed in the words, and the image of the words themselves, are nonscarce goods, while the medium through which they are conveyed is scarce. The range and importance of nonscarce goods has been vastly expanded by the existence of digital media.

As to whether a good is naturally scarce or nonscarce, the test here is simple. If the good can be taken (shared) without displacing the original, it is always nonscarce. If taking the original means that it can no longer exist in the possession of the original owner or possessor, it is a scarce good. All goods fall into one or the other category. All nongoods (unwanted things, necessarily a contingent category)[22] can of course be similarly classified. See Table 1, below.[23]

	Scarce	Nonscarce
Good	Bagel, Factory, Shoes, People, Desk	Recipe, Idea, Tune, Image, Skill, Fire
Nongood	Mud Pie, Poison Soup, Slug, Road Kill	Bad Idea, Awful Sound, Gibberish Text

Table 1: Scarce and Nonscarce Goods and Nongoods

---

[22] As Hoppe writes:

… man learns that some of the [scarce] means, some of the things that he can control, that he can move, that he can manipulate, can be referred to as "goods" and others can be referred to as "bads." *Goods* would obviously be those means that are suitable in order to satisfy some needs that we have, and *bads* would be objects that we can control, but that would have negative repercussions on us, that would not satisfy any needs but, to the contrary, may harm us or even kill us.

Hoppe, "Lecture 1: The Nature of Man and the Human Condition: Language, Property, and Production," in *Economy, Society, and History* (Auburn, Ala.: Mises Institute, 2021; www.hanshoppe.com/esh), p. 9. See also ibid., p. 143; *idem, The Great Fiction: Property, Economy, Society, and the Politics of Decline* (Second Expanded Edition, Mises Institute, 2021; www.hanshoppe.com/tgf), pp. x, 107, 191; *idem, The Economics and Ethics of Private Property*, p. 309 (mentioning "bads").

[23] The matrix in Table 1 is presented as a tool for mental experiment only—if anything is a nongood (necessarily a subjective idea), it is also by definition nonscarce, since all (nonexistent) demand for it is satisfied. Nonetheless, the typology illustrated in the matrix helps in categorizing the attributes of goods discussed in this article.

At the same time, it is also true that most things are bundles of scarce and nonscarce goods. A book is a nonscarce text conveying non-scarce ideas on scarce paper and taking up scarce space on a shelf. A key that unlocks a door is made of scarce metal, but its functioning is due to the nonscarce shape of the cut of the key, a shape that is infinitely copyable. A concert by Lady Gaga is a scarce human body backed by scarce instruments and microphones producing music and sound, which immediately become nonscarce in the performing and hearing. Tying a shoe employs scarce laces with scarce hands guided by replicable (non-scarce) skills and techniques.

REPLICATION AND CIVILIZATION

Nonscarce goods do not need the assistance of prices to ration their availability. They are free gifts that can be shared the world over. How important are these goods? Given that they are inclusive of all infor-mation, art, know-how, and anything else that can be possessed and copied without displacement, they are hugely important. Without these gifts, the whole of learning, imitation, and world culture would come crashing down.[24]

We are not truly human without being part of human civilization; and there can be no civilization and progress without the spread, dis-semination, and accumulation of knowledge. To be human is to be part of a learning society, a communicating society, an information-sharing society. Society is emulation-based.

As it stands, the existence of the nonscarce good is the basis of all intellectual progress, the foundation of technological and artistic prog-ress, and thereby a boon to civilization. It is also at the core of enterprise. Entrepreneurs succeed by imitating others who have succeeded. Their nonscarce experience and ideas are first copied and then improved, with the goal of profit. The example of success that entrepreneurs follow is itself a nonscarce good. Anyone with the means to do so is free to copy

---

[24] See the citations to Hayek's comments about how the accumulation of a "fund of experience" helps aid human progress and the creation of wealth in "*Against Intellectual Property* After Twenty Years" (ch. 15), at n.59

the successful idea and replicate it. The nonscarce good is the fuel of the competitive process.

In contrast, a scarce good cannot be shared without limit. It is necessarily owned and controlled by only one person at a time; even the attempt to share implies *displacement* (while I have it, you do not). To acquire it requires either homesteading unowned resources or stealing, transforming, or contractually acquiring (trading for) already-existing resources.[25] Trading is what gives rise to rationing and allocating by the price system.

Again, it would be preposterous to speak of socialism in scarce goods, because it is physically impossible to imagine two simultaneous owners of the same scarce good.[26] However, it is possible to speak of something like "socialism" for a good that is nonscarce by its nature, precisely because it can be infinitely copied.

The nonscarce good is private so long as it is never revealed; so long as it remains a secret. Once the secret is out, the good becomes part of the commons (or socially shared, if you will) because everyone who encounters it can use it. Technology has worked to create ever more goods

---

[25] As Hoppe has explained, "One can acquire and increase wealth either through homesteading, production and contractual exchange, or by expropriating and exploiting homesteaders, producers, or contractual exchangers. There are no other ways." Hans-Hermann Hoppe, "Banking, Nation States, and International Politics: A Sociological Reconstruction of the Present Economic Order," in *The Economics and Ethics of Private Property: Studies in Political Economy and Philosophy* (Auburn, Ala.: Mises Institute 2006 [1993]; www.hanshoppe.com/eepp), p. 50. See also related discussion in "Law and Intellectual Property in a Stateless Society" (ch. 14), text at n.82. But production presupposes the producer already owns the property that he transforms into something more desirable or useful. The only ways to *acquire* a particular scarce resource is to either homestead it, acquire it contractually, or steal it. (One may also transform already-owned property into the desired configuration.)

[26] As Hoppe observes, "Two individuals *cannot* be the exclusive owner of one and the same thing at the same time." Hoppe, "How is Fiat Money Possible?," in *The Economics and Ethics of Private Property*, p. 197. See also Hans-Hermann Hoppe, Jörg Guido Hülsmann & Walter Block, "Against Fiduciary Media," in Hoppe, *The Economics and Ethics of Private Property*, p. 210 n.8:

> Even partners cannot simultaneously own the *same* thing. A and B can each own half of a household, or half the shares in it, but they each own a *different* 50 percent. It is as logically impossible for them to own the same half as for two people to occupy the same space. Yes, A and B can both be in New York City at the same time, but only in different parts of it.

See also note 20, above.

that have become part of the nonscarce category, and this might be seen as a major feature of technological development for all time.

AUSTRIANS ON "FREE GOODS"

Austrians have always, if sometimes only implicitly, recognized the existence of the nonscarce good, which is precisely the good in question with regard to intellectual property. Menger's 1871 book, *Principles of Economics*,[27] begins with the definition of a good that excludes the concern over scarcity. Something is a good, in Menger's view, when it is causally capable of satisfying a human need. This is a very broad definition.

Hoppe summarizes Menger's four requirements for objects to become goods:

> The first is the existence of a human need. The second requirement is such properties as render the thing capable of being brought into a causal connection with a satisfaction of this need. That is, this object must be capable, through our performing certain manipulations with it, to cause certain needs to be satisfied or at least relieved. The third condition is that there must be human knowledge about this connection, which explains, of course, why it is important for people to learn to distinguish between *goods* and *bads*. Thus, we have human knowledge about the object, our ability to control it, and the causal power of this object to lead to certain types of satisfactory results. And the fourth factor is, as I already indicated, that we must have command of the thing sufficient to direct it to the satisfaction of the need.[28]

---

[27] Carl Menger, *Principles of Economics* (Auburn, Ala.: Mises Institute 2007 [1871]; https://mises.org/library/principles-economics).

[28] Hoppe, *Economy, Society, and History*, p. 9; see also Menger, *Principles of Economics*, chap. I, §1, p. 52 *et pass.* The second requirement corresponds to the means being *causally efficacious*; the third to the actor's *knowledge* of causal laws; and the fourth to the *availability* of the means. See also related discussion in *"Against Intellectual Property After Twenty Years"* (ch. 15), n.58, and in Eugen von Böhm-Bawerk, "Whether Legal Rights and Relationships Are Economic Goods," George D. Huncke, trans., in Eugen von Böhm-Bawerk, *Shorter Classics of Eugen von Böhm-Bawerk* (South Holland, Ill.: Libertarian Press, 1962 [1881]), p. 57 *et pass.*, discussed in Gael J. Campan, "Does Justice Qualify as an Economic Good?: A Böhm-Bawerkian Perspective," *Q. J. Austrian Econ.* 2, no. 1 (Spring 1999; https://perma.cc/G3CK-B8WB): 21–33, p. 24.

Thus, for Menger, for something to be a good, there must be human knowledge of this cause-and-effect connection, along with command over the thing so that the relationship between cause and effect can be realized. Among these goods he includes goodwill, family connections, friendship, love, religious and scientific fellowships—all of which fall into the class of things that can be replicated without displacement. Only later in the opening chapter, when discussing the issue of property, does Menger introduce the notion of scarcity and hence the need for economizing.

Seeing property as a subclass under the larger division of goods implies the existence of what Ludwig von Mises called a "free good"—something that is "available in superfluous abundance which man does not need to economize."[29] Mises says that though they are "not the object of any action," they are useful and even essential for production.[30] Giving the example of a recipe, he writes that these free goods, or nonscarce goods, render "unlimited services." A free good "does not lose anything from its capacity to produce however often it is used; its productive power is inexhaustible; it is therefore not an economic good."

But it is no less important than normal goods: "These designs—the recipes, the formulas, the ideologies—are the primary thing; they transform the original factors—both human and nonhuman—into means."[31] Ideas and information are nonscarce goods, but they serve as *guides to action* in the use of scarce means, to transform scarce things in the world to achieve the actor's desired end. As Mises wrote, "Action is purposive conduct. It is not simply behavior, but behavior begot by judgments of value, aiming at a definite end and *guided by ideas concerning the suitability or unsuitability of definite means.*"[32]

---

[29] Mises, *Human Action*, p. 93
[30] Ibid., p. 93; see also p. 128, re formulas and recipes.
[31] Ibid., p. 142.
[32] Ludwig von Mises, *The Ultimate Foundation of Economic Science: An Essay on Method* Princeton, N.J.: D. Van Nostrand Company, Inc., 1962; https://mises.org/library/ultimate-foundation-economic-science), p. 34 (emphasis added). See also Guido Hülsmann, "Knowledge, Judgment, and the Use of Property," *Rev. Austrian Econ.* 10, no. 1 (1997; https://perma.cc/DKQ8-JX45): 23–48, p. 44 (emphasis added):

The quantities of means we can dispose of—our property—are always limited. Thus, choice implies that some of our ends must remain unfulfilled. We steadily run the danger of pursuing ends that are less important than the ends that could have been pursued. We have to choose the supposedly most important action,

Murray Rothbard elaborated:

There is another unique type of factor of production that is indispensable
in every stage of every production process. This is the "technological idea"
of how to proceed from one stage to another and finally to arrive at the
desired consumers' good. This is but an application of the analysis above,
namely, that for any action, there must be some *plan* or idea of the actor
about how to use things as means, as definite pathways, to desired ends.
Without such plans or ideas, there would be no action. These plans may
be called *recipes*; they are ideas of recipes that the actor uses to arrive at
his goal. A *recipe* must be present at each stage of each production process
from which the actor proceeds to a later stage. The actor must have a recipe
for transforming iron into steel, wheat into flour, bread and ham into
sandwiches, etc.[33]

As Rothbard (and Mises) recognize, once the idea comes about, it no
longer has to be produced or economized. It is an "unlimited factor of
production that never wears out or needs to be economized by human
action." This is precisely what a nonfinite, nonscarce good is: an unlimited
factor of production.

Fetter also glimpses that ideas themselves are nonscarce goods:

The gain to the general welfare, however, can result only when the new
inventions are actually embodied in machines. An invention is only an
immaterial idea, and the machines in which inventions are incorporated
are wealth which has a capital value. Further, a gain can result only when
the usance of the machines is not so high as to absorb the larger part
of the gain in efficiency. Not all labor-saving inventions call for more
elaborate or more costly machines. Some are merely better methods, and
require no more equipment—or even less. Some of them are simpler
and less costly than the forms they displace. These (unless patented) are
free goods, uplifting the efficiency of production "without money and
without price."[34]

---

though what we choose is how we use our property. Action means to employ
our property in the pursuit of what appears to be the most important ends.... *In
choosing the most important action we implicitly select some parts of our technological
knowledge for application.*
On this issue, see also "Law and Intellectual Property in a Stateless Society" (ch. 14), Part
III.D, and *"Against Intellectual Property After Twenty Years"* (ch. 15), Part IV.E.
[33] Rothbard, *Man, Economy, and State, with Power and Market*, p. 11.
[34] Fetter, *Economic Principles*, 465.

Although Fetter assumes the existence of patent rights and does not question their legitimacy, he recognizes that methods—which are merely recipes, a type of information—are nonscarce goods (he calls them "free goods") that are freely available and increase efficiency and productivity—that is, unless they are patented, thus making them *artificially* scarce.

One of the longest and most searching essays on this topic is by Eugen von Böhm-Bawerk, in his article "Whether Legal Rights and Relationships are Economic Goods."[35] In this piece, Böhm-Bawerk points to several features of things that make them economic goods, among them physical possession and "the power of disposal and control." The notion of scarcity as a precondition for calling something an "economic good" is presumed but never stated outright. However, Böhm-Bawerk added critical elements to the idea of the good, noting that personal services must also be included in this category. Whether such are truly goods is not inherent in the service itself but depends on the subjective response to that service, thus introducing to the idea of a good a subjective component.[36] Here Böhm-Bawerk keenly observes the interplay between materially scarce and subjectively nonscarce goods:

> Be it granted that the poet's soul must have originated thought and emotion, and be it further granted that only in another soul and through intellectual powers can those thoughts and emotions be reproduced,

---

[35] Böhm-Bawerk, "Whether Legal Rights and Relationships Are Economic Goods," discussed in Campan, "Does Justice Qualify as an Economic Good?: A Böhm-Bawerkian Perspective."

[36] See also Hoppe, "Fallacies of the Public Goods Theory and the Production of Security," in *The Economics and Ethics of Private Property*, pp. 8–9:

> … looking into the distinction between private and public goods more thoroughly, we discover that the distinction turns out to be completely illusory. A clear-cut dichotomy between private and public goods does not exist, and this is essentially why there can be so many disagreements on how to classify a given good. All goods are more or less private or public and can—and constantly do—change with respect to their degree of privateness/publicness as people's values and evaluations change, and as changes occur in the composition of the population. In order to recognize that they never fall, once and for all, into either one or the other category, one must only recall what makes something a good. For something to be a good it must be recognized and treated as scarce by someone. Something is not a good as such, that is to say; goods are goods only in the eyes of the beholder. Nothing is a good unless at least one person subjectively evaluates it as such.

but the path from soul to soul leads through the physical world for one stretch of the journey and on that stretch the intellectual element must make use of the physical vehicle, that is to say, of the forces or powers of nature. The book is that physical material vehicle.[37]

As Joseph Salerno notes, "Böhm-Bawerk employed the example of the production and consumption of a poem to illustrate that the good is inextricably bound up with the want-satisfaction process that traverses and links the objective and subjective realms."[38]

SCARCE GOODS, NONSCARCE GOODS, PROGRESS, AND INTERVENTION

Why does all of this matter? It is interesting on the level of theory, but it is also critically important as a practical matter. Enterprise in our time is increasingly dependent on a clear understanding of the difference between scarce and nonscarce goods. In the current recession, for example, the bust hit scarce goods, and it is the scarce-goods sector that the government is attempting to stimulate.[39] But the nonscarce sector, which is not subject to the structure of production, and therefore is resistant to business-cycle effects, continues to thrive and has been unaffected by the machinations of bad macroeconomic policy. (But it is affected by "intellectual property" regulation, which imposes artificial scarcity where there is none naturally present.)

Institutions such as Google and the Mises Institute have discovered the secret of giving away nonscarce goods (search services and digital books) and restricting commercial operations to allocating only scarce goods (teacher services, physical books, and advertising space on screens).[40] This combination of giving away the nonscarce good

---

[37] Böhm-Bawerk, "Whether Legal Rights and Relationships Are Economic Goods," p. 91.

[38] Joseph T. Salerno, "Böhm-Bawerk's Vision of the Capitalist Economic Process: Intellectual Influences and Conceptual Foundations," *New Perspectives on Political Economy* 4, no. 2 (2008; https://perma.cc/7XV4-2KQA): 87–112, p. 101.

[39] This was written in 2010, in the aftermath of the Great Recession from 2007–2009.

[40] See Doug French, "The Intellectual Revolution Is in Process," *Mises Daily* (Dec. 12, 2009; https://mises.org/library/intellectual-revolution-process); Jeffrey A. Tucker,

and selling the scarce good has permitted both institutions to grow through service.

But this distinction is also exceedingly helpful for understanding economic theory. It clarifies the absolute necessity of property rights and free movement of prices for all scarce goods—exactly as classical economists have said. It also illustrates the need to completely de-control access to nonscarce goods and to permit the voluntary learning and sharing process to take its own course.[41]

Nonscarce goods are a great gift, courtesy of the structure of reality, a boon to humankind, a vast treasure of resources—tools for making the world a relentlessly better place.[42]

The failure to understand the distinction between scarce and intrinsically nonscarce goods might also help to explain the persistence of socialist ideology. For example, one possible explanation of the predictable socialist impulse of religious leaders, intellectuals, and artists is that their primary work consists in the production and distribution of nonscarce goods (salvation, ideas, and art) and that this accounts for the failure of the people in these professions to come to terms with the relentless reality of scarcity.

In summary, the world has given us two types of goods, one type that demands allocation through property and prices and one type that can be infinitely copied. In the production and distribution of scarce goods, there is no substitute for the commercial marketplace. And the notion that government should ever restrict replicable nonscarce goods or grant protection to a single monopolistic producer of nonscarce goods is contrary to freedom, material advancement, and social peace.

"A Theory of Open," *Mises Economics Blog* (Jan. 7, 2010; https://mises.org/wire/theory-open); and Gary North, "A Free Week-Long Economics Seminar," *LewRockwell.com* (July 24, 2010; www.lewrockwell.com/2010/07/gary-north/mises-u/).

41 The distinction between scarce and nonscarce goods is crucial. A signal example of the importance of making careful distinctions in fundamental economic concepts is Menger's clarification of price and value theory, which has profound implications with respect to other aspects of economics.

42 For elaboration, see the last three paragraphs of Kinsella, "The Death Throes of Pro-IP Libertarianism"; see also note 24, above.

PART V

REVIEWS

19

Knowledge, Calculation, Conflict, and Law

Originally published as Stephan Kinsella, "Knowledge, Calculation, Conflict, and Law," *Q. J. Austrian Econ.* 2, no. 4 (Winter 1999): 49–71, a review essay of Randy E. Barnett, *The Structure of Liberty: Justice and the Rule of Law* (Oxford: Oxford University Press, 1998). In this chapter, I have updated the references to refer to the second edition, *The Structure of Liberty: Justice and the Rule of Law*, 2d ed. (Oxford: Oxford University Press, 2014), hereinafter cited as *Structure* (apparently no changes were made to the main text, so the page numbers between the first and second editions are in most cases the same).

PERVASIVE SOCIAL PROBLEMS

Libertarian theorists have made significant contributions to the fields of economics, politics, and philosophy. Intimately bound up with libertarian and political theory is the question of what laws and legal systems are appropriate. Law and legal theory, therefore, have also been subjected to libertarian scrutiny. One might even say libertarianism is all about law: which laws are just, which are not. The writing in this area, however, is usually focused on narrow legal topics, such as contract or constitutional law.[1] Moreover, many libertarian authors are economists

---

[1] Williamson M. Evers, "Toward a Reformulation of the Law of Contracts," *J. Libertarian Stud.* 1, no. 1 (Winter 1977; https://mises.org/library/toward-reformulation-law-contracts): 3–13; Randy E. Barnett, "A Consent Theory of Contract," *Colum. L. Rev.* 86 (1986; www.randybarnett.com): 269–321; *idem*, Randy E. Barnett, "Getting Normative: The Role of Natural Rights in Constitutional Adjudication," *Constitutional Commentary* 12 (1995; http://www.randybarnett.com/pre-2000): 93–122; *idem*, "The Intersection of Natural Rights and Positive Constitutional Law," *Conn. L. Rev.* 25 (1993; www.randybarnett.com/pre-2000): 853–68; Lysander Spooner, "No Treason No. 4: The Constitution of No Authority,"

or philosophers who are not sufficiently familiar with the workings of real legal systems; others are not completely or consistently libertarian in their approaches.[2] Jurisprudence has yet to receive the attention it deserves from libertarians (and, one might say: vice-versa).

The publication of Randy Barnett's latest book, *The Structure of Liberty: Justice and the Rule of Law*, helps to fill this lacuna. Barnett, as a former criminal prosecutor and now law professor at Boston University School of Law,[3] is intimately familiar with the operation of the American legal system and also with the arcana of academic jurisprudence. His libertarian credentials are also impeccable: he has published important libertarian-oriented works on topics as diverse as contract law, constitutional theory and natural rights, restitution and criminal

---

in *The Lysander Spooner Reader* (San Francisco, Calif.: Fox and Wilkes, 1992; also available at http://www.lysanderspooner.org/works); and Robert W. McGee, "The Theory of Secession and Emerging Democracies: A Constitutional Solution," *Stanford J. International L.* 28, no. 2 (1992; https://papers.ssrn.com/sol3/papers.cfm?abstract_id=2177439): 451–76.

[2] Various works with at least a semi-libertarian approach to legal and constitutional theory include Marshall L. DeRosa, *The Ninth Amendment and the Politics of Creative Jurisprudence: Disparaging the Fundamental Right of Popular Control* (New Brunswick, N.J.: Transaction Publishers, 1996); Raoul Berger, *The Fourteenth Amendment and the Bill of Rights* (Norman, Okla.: University of Oklahoma Press, 1989); Robert H. Bork, *The Tempting of America: The Political Seduction of the Law* (New York: Free Press, 1990); William J. Quirk & R. Randall Bridwell, *Judicial Dictatorship* (New Brunswick, N.J.: Transaction Publishers, 1995); Bruno Leoni, *Freedom and the Law* (Indianapolis: Liberty Fund, expanded 3d. ed. 1991 [1961]; https://oll.libertyfund.org/title/kemp-freedom-and-the-law-lf-ed); F.A. Hayek, *Law, Legislation, and Liberty*, 3 vols. (Chicago: University of Chicago Press, 1973, 1976, 1979); Richard A. Epstein, *Takings: Private Property and the Power of Eminent Domain* (Cambridge, Mass.: Harvard University Press, 1985); *idem*, *Simple Rules for a Complex World* (Cambridge, Mass.: Harvard University Press, 1995); *idem*, *Principles for a Free Society* (Reading, Mass.: Perseus Books, 1998). Richard Epstein has contributed enormously to libertarian and legal theory, but is not a completely consistent libertarian and is certainly not an anarcho-capitalist. He also favors intellectual property. See Kinsella, "KOL364 | Soho Forum Debate vs. Richard Epstein: Patent and Copyright Law Should Be Abolished," *Kinsella on Liberty Podcast* (Nov. 24, 2021). Moreover, Epstein adheres more to mainstream, neoclassical economics, in which interpersonal utility is both relevant and comparable (see, e.g., *Simple Rules for a Complex World*, p. 141), than to Austrian economics, which does not suffer the many theoretical deficiencies of neoclassical economics, e.g., interpersonal utility comparisons, logical positivism and scientism, etc.

[3] As of 1999. At present (2023), Barnett is a law professor at Georgetown. http://www.randybarnett.com.

law, and drug prohibition.[4] Barnett was thus well-positioned to write *The Structure of Liberty*, the first broad and systematic treatise on legal theory written from a thoroughly libertarian perspective.

Barnett's aim in this ambitious book is to determine the type of legal system, laws, and rights which are appropriate *given* the widely-shared "goal of enabling persons to survive and pursue happiness, peace, and prosperity while living in society with others."[5] Happiness, peace, and prosperity are fine principles to select and quite compatible with libertarianism, but Barnett does not attempt to try to justify these basic norms or values. His argument is thus hypothetical and consequentialist, though not, he maintains, utilitarian.[6]

According to Barnett, the goals of social happiness, peace, and prosperity cannot be achieved unless society's politico–legal system somehow solves certain *problems* which stand in the way of this happy state. These are "the serious and pervasive social problems of knowledge, interest, and power."[7] Libertarianism enters the picture because the libertarian (Barnett prefers the term "liberal") conceptions of *justice* and the *rule of law* provide the "structure of liberty" that addresses these problems. These principles include the "natural background rights to acquire, possess, use, and dispose of scarce resources (and other rights as well)."[8] Barnett's argument thus proceeds by showing how and why libertarianism is the best way to overcome the problems of knowledge, interest, and power.[9]

---

[4] See, e.g., Randy E. Barnett, "Getting Even: Restitution, Preventive Detention, and the Tort/Crime Distinction," *Boston U. L. Rev.* 76 (February/April 1996; www.randybarnett. com/pre-2000): 157–68; *idem*, "Consent Theory"; idem, "Natural Rights and Positive Constitutional Law"; *idem*, "Getting Normative"; *idem*, "Necessary and Proper," *UCLA L. Rev.* 76 (1997; www.randybarnett.com/pre-2000): 745–93 and others cited in the Bibliography to *Structure*. See also *idem*, Randy E. Barnett & John Hagel III, eds., *Assessing the Criminal: Restitution, Retribution, And the Legal Process* (Cambridge, Mass.: Ballinger, 1977); Randy E. Barnett, *The Rights Retained by the People: The History and Meaning of the Ninth Amendment* (George Mason Univ. Press, 1991)

[5] *Structure*, p. 23.

[6] Ibid., pp. 8, 12, 17–23, esp. 22–23.

[7] Ibid., p. 3, emphasis added.

[8] Ibid., p. 16.

[9] *Structure* contains excellent summaries provided throughout the book at the end of many chapters and sections.

THE FIRST-ORDER PROBLEM OF KNOWLEDGE

Parts 1, 2, and 3 of the book respectively describe the three fundamental problems and how they are solved by libertarian rights and institutions. Barnett's first topic, discussed in Part 1, is the problem of knowledge, which is broken down into separate first-order, second-order, and third-order aspects.

The first aspect—basically the Hayekian "knowledge problem"[10]—concerns how individuals make "knowledgeable" use of physical resources.[11] This analysis starts out by presuming that an individual needs to "be able to act on the basis of [his] own personal knowledge," and "when so acting [he] must somehow *take into account* the knowledge of others."[12]

Alas, this is difficult to achieve, because such knowledge is "dispersed" or "fragmented," and each individual has "ever-changing and potentially conflicting personal and local knowledge of potential resource use."[13] Each person is thus rendered "hopelessly ignorant" of the "knowledge of others." So the alleged problem is this: given the dispersed, often inaccessible, and potentially "conflicting" nature of such knowledge, how can individuals act on the basis of their own knowledge while avoiding conflicts over resource use? And how can they take into account the knowledge of others?[14]

According to Barnett, libertarian rights are necessary because they facilitate the sharing and dissemination of knowledge.[15] They include the natural rights of "several" property (Hayek's term for private property), Lockean first possession (homesteading), and freedom of contract.[16] If individuals are accorded these rights, the first-order problem of knowledge is solved. One of the main ways this happens is that prices arise

---

[10] F.A. Hayek, "Economics and Knowledge" and "The Use of Knowledge in Society" in *Individualism and Economic Order* (Chicago: University of Chicago Press, 1948; https://mises.org/library/individualism-and-economic-order). I explain my disagreement with the Hayekian "knowledge" approach in the "Introductory Note" to Part III.C of "Legislation and the Discovery of Law in a Free Society" (ch. 13).

[11] *Structure*, p. 29.

[12] Ibid., p. 36 (emphasis added).

[13] Ibid., p. 40.

[14] Ibid., p. 36.

[15] Ibid., p. 44.

[16] Ibid., p. 83.

under such a private-property order, and prices themselves convey, in "condensed" form, personal and local knowledge.

Knowledge vs. Calculation

There is, unfortunately, much to be desired in Hayek's emphasis on the role of knowledge in the economy, as opposed to Ludwig von Mises's stress on the more fundamental role of money prices in *economic calculation*.[17] Hayek's and Mises's differing views have been improperly conflated,[18] and Barnett makes the same error by attributing to Mises Hayek's views on the information-conveying role of prices.[19]

What, then, are the differences between Mises and Hayek on the role of prices in the economy? Hans-Hermann Hoppe has ably summarized Mises's original calculation argument as follows:

> If there is no private property in land and other production factors, then there can also be no market prices for them. Hence, economic calculation,

---

[17] This has been pointed out in recent debates among Austrian economists, published primarily in the pages of the *Review of Austrian Economics*. See Jörg Guido Hülsmann, "Knowledge, Judgment, and the Use of Property," *Rev. Austrian Econ.* 10, no. 1 (1997; https://mises.org/library/knowledge-judgment-and-use-property): 23–48; Hans-Hermann Hoppe, "F.A. Hayek on Government and Social Evolution: A Critique," "F.A. Hayek on Government and Social Evolution: A Critique," in *The Great Fiction: Property, Economy, Society, and the Politics of Decline*, Second Expanded Edition (Auburn, Ala.: Mises Institute, 2021; www.hanshoppe.com/tgf); *idem*, "Socialism: A Property or Knowledge Problem?", in *The Economics and Ethics of Private Property*; Joseph T. Salerno, "Ludwig von Mises as Social Rationalist," *Rev. Austrian Econ.* 4 (1990; https://mises.org/library/ludwig-von-mises-social-rationalist): 25–54; idem, "Mises and Hayek Dehomogenized," *Rev. Austrian Econ.* 6, no. 2 (1993; https://mises.org/library/mises-and-hayek-dehomogenized): 113–46; *idem*, "Reply to Leland B. Yeager," *Rev. Austrian Econ.* 7, no. 2 (1994; https://mises.org/library/reply-leland-b-yeager-mises-and-hayek-calculation-and-knowledge): 111–25; Jeffrey M. Herbener, "Ludwig von Mises and the Austrian School of Economics," *Rev. Austrian Econ.* 5, no. 2 (1991; https://mises.org/library/ludwig-von-mises-and-austrian-school-economics): 33–50. For recent, related papers less critical of Hayek's position, see Steven Horwitz, "Monetary Calculation and Mises's Critique of Planning," *History of Political Economy* 30, no. 3 (1998; https://perma.cc/9HXZ-T36L): 427–50 and Bruce Caldwell, "Hayek and Socialism," *J. Econ. Literature* 35 (December 1997): 1856–90. For further discussion, see "Legislation and the Discovery of Law in a Free Society" (ch. 13), the "Introductory Note" to Part III.C. See also Kinsella, "The Great Mises-Hayek Dehomogenization/Economic Calculation Debate," *StephanKinsella.com* (Feb. 8, 2016); "Introductory Note" to Part III.C of "Legislation and the Discovery of Law in a Free Society" (ch. 13).

[18] Salerno, "Mises and Hayek Dehomogenized."
[19] *Structure*, p. 54, n. 21.

i.e., the comparison of anticipated revenue and expected cost expressed in terms of a common medium of exchange (which permits *cardinal* accounting operations), is literally impossible. Socialism's fatal error is the absence of private property in land and production factors, and by implication, the absence of economic calculation.[20]

The theories of Hayek on which Barnett and others have relied, however, downplay calculation and appraisement in favor of communication of knowledge. For Hayek, as Hülsmann notes:

> ... the impossibility of socialism stems from its inability to *communicate dispersed knowledge*.... [I]nformation about the particular circumstances of time and place can never be centralized. It necessarily exists in dispersed form and yet it can be communicated by the market prices of capitalist societies. Only capitalism is thus capable of solving the knowledge problem.[21]

But any informational function of prices is, at best, only secondary in comparison to the primary role of private property and money prices. The fundamental economic role of private property, along with money prices arising from exchanges of such property, as Mises showed, is to permit *economic calculation*. And, socially speaking, private-property rights serve to prevent conflict over resources. *This* is why private-property rights serve Barnett's goals of peace and prosperity: private property rights permit conflicts to be avoided (peace) and allow genuine, free-market money prices to form which can be used for economic calculation and hence rational resource allocation (prosperity). Concentration on the information-conveying role of prices instead of calculation obscures this role.[22] For example, Hayekians claim that prices "contain" economic

---

[20] Hoppe, "Socialism: A Property or Knowledge Problem?", p. 255.

[21] Hülsmann, "Knowledge, Judgment, Property," p. 23, emphasis added.

[22] Leoni seems to similarly attribute Hayekian knowledge-related concepts to Mises: [T]hat the central authorities in a totalitarian economy lack any knowledge of market prices in making their economic plans is only a corollary of the fact that central authorities always lack a sufficient knowledge of the infinite number of elements and factors that contribute to the social intercourse of individuals at any time and at any level.

Leoni, *Freedom and the Law*, p. 89 *et pass.*

See also "Legislation and the Discovery of Law in a Free Society" (ch. 13). As noted in the "Introductory Note" to Part III.C, in the original 1995 article upon which that chapter is based, I, too, influenced by Leoni, conflated Hayekian and Misesian ideas in overstating

information in "condensed" (or encrypted, encoded, or abridged) form.[23] Barnett follows the Hayekians when he states that "the knowledge-disseminating function of prices is largely unknown … the knowledge embedded in prices is not explicit…. It is encoded knowledge."[24]

There are several problems with viewing prices as encoding information. For one thing, concepts such as encoding, encryption, and the like *imply an encoder*—a person who actively and consciously *encodes* information in some communication medium, in accordance with some encoding scheme (i.e., the code). Yet there is clearly no intentional encoding of whatever knowledge may be embedded in prices; there is no encoding scheme and no way to decode the information. I buy a car for $30,000 because I think it is worth it, not to convey some secret message to someone.[25] Knowledge that I paid this price for the car does not reveal any information about the underlying objective conditions that give rise to this price (e.g., the intensity of my demand or the relative scarcity of the car). Such knowledge reveals only that I valued the car more than $30,000, and the seller had the opposite valuation.

---

the analogies between central economic planning and central law-creation. See also note 63, below, and accompanying text, concerning the possibility of deducing more concrete legal principles from (themselves deduced) abstract rights.

[23] The term "data compression" is often used synonymously by engineers with terms such as data encoding or encryption, so I suppose it is only a matter of time before Hayekians say that prices convey, in "compressed" form, fragmented and dispersed local knowledge of the particular circumstances of time and place.

[24] *Structure*, p. 54.

[25] The encoding metaphor seems to be a pseudoscientific and scientistic attempt to give this kind of economic theorizing a patina of scientific respectability by borrowing engineering terminology. It is scientistic because, in vainly trying to borrow natural sciences terminology, there is an assumption that only the "hard" or natural sciences have true validity. It is akin to using such inapt phrases as the "momentum" of the leading team in a basketball game, the "energy" of crystals and astral forms, or, even worse, "revving the engine" of the economy. Both economics and ethics can be sciences, but not in the same way as the causal, natural sciences. On scientism and empiricism, see Murray N. Rothbard, "The Mantle of Science" in *Economic Controversies*, and Hans-Hermann Hoppe, "In Defense of Extreme Rationalism," in *The Great Fiction*. On epistemological dualism, see Ludwig von Mises, *The Ultimate Foundation of Economic Science: An Essay on Method* (Princeton, N.J.: D. Van Nostrand Company, Inc., 1962; https://mises.org/library/ultimate-foundation-economic-science); *idem*, *Epistemological Problems of Economics*, 3d ed., George Reisman, trans. (Auburn, Ala.: Mises Institute, 2003; https://mises.org/library/epistemological-problems-economics); and Hans-Hermann Hoppe, *Economic Science and the Austrian Method* (Auburn, Ala.: Mises Institute, 1995; www.hanshoppe.com/esam).

Prices result from the subjective evaluations of goods by seller and buyer, but prices *are* exchange ratios. Besides these ratios, what other information *could* money prices communicate? What information can a mere price ratio convey? Take Hayek's famous tin example, which assumes:

> ... that somewhere in the world a new opportunity for the use of some raw material, say, tin, has arisen, or that one of the sources of supply of tin has been eliminated. *It does not matter* for our purpose—and it is significant that it does not matter—*which* of these two causes has made tin more scarce. All that the users of tin need to know is that some of the tin they used to consume is now more profitably employed elsewhere and that, in consequence, they must economize tin. There is no need for the great majority of them even to know where the more urgent need has arisen, or in favor of what other needs they ought to husband the supply. If only some of them know directly of the new demand, and switch resources over to it, and if the people who are aware of the new gap thus created in turn fill it from still other sources, the effect will rapidly spread throughout the whole economic system and influence not only all the uses of tin but also those of its substitutes and the substitutes of these substitutes, the supply of all the things made of tin, and their substitutes, and so on; and all this without the great majority of those instrumental in bringing about these substitutions *knowing anything at all about the original cause of these changes.*[26]

In this example, what information, *exactly*, is supposed to be conveyed by prices? Let us explore the possibilities. Can the original *cause* of the price increase (i.e., the change in demand or supply) itself be conveyed via prices? Well, no. Prices are the *result* of action. Thus, action that changes the prices must *already be informed by* knowledge.[27] Entrepreneurs *first* see the changed conditions and *then* bid prices up or down. They do not learn about the changed conditions *from* the resulting prices. Rather,

---

[26] Hayek, "The Use of Knowledge in Society," p. 85 (emphasis added).

[27] In other words, the prices generated on the market are *past* prices, which are always the *outcome* of action, not its cause. Hülsmann explains that "all information that this action was based upon had to be acquired beforehand. The price itself could not have communicated the knowledge that brought it [the price] about." Hülsmann, "Knowledge, Judgment, Property," p. 26. With regard to the tin example, "tin does not become scarcer and *then* this fact can come to be known to someone and lead to adaptations. Rather is it the other way around. The very fact that demand increases means that someone *already knows* of a more value-productive employment of tin." Ibid., p. 28.

they *cause* the prices to change, *based on* their appraisement of tin and knowledge or judgment of underlying conditions. Hayek seems to recognize that those entrepreneurs who "know directly of the new demand, and switch resources over to it" do not learn from prices, but rather help to form prices based on their own preferences, knowledge, evaluations, and judgments.

What about users of tin who merely observe the change in prices paid for tin—do these persons learn anything, from observed past prices, about the underlying conditions or "original cause" of the change in prices? No, because any of a variety of causes results in higher or lower prices (e.g., changes in demand by buyers or sellers, decrease in supply, changes in demand for money on the part of sellers or buyers, etc.). For these reasons, Hayek says that mere users of tin do not know "anything at all about the original cause of these changes."

Then what possible information can prices convey? Hayek writes: "All that the users of tin *need to know* is that some of the tin they used to consume is now more profitably employed elsewhere and that, in consequence, they must economize tin."[28] But the users do not *need* to know this; if tin is scarcer, there is less of it to go around.[29] Whether the prospective users know of the increased scarcity or not, they cannot use what does not exist. Their plans will have to conform, sooner or later, to this increased unavailability of tin.

At most, one could argue that the existence of prices enables prospective users to recognize the good's relative scarcity somewhat earlier than they would in the absence of prices (that is, sooner rather than later). And even this cannot be stated to be true as an economic law, simply because *all* prices are *speculative* and based on entrepreneurial judgments and anticipations about future (uncertain) conditions. An entrepreneur, for example, may bid the price of a good up based on a *mistaken* judgment about relevant future conditions, such as supply and demand. What do prices then convey in such a case—misinformation?

---

[28] Hayek, "The Use of Knowledge in Society," p. 85 (emphasis added).

[29] Notes Hülsmann in "Knowledge, Judgment, Property," p. 28:

An increased scarcity of tin implies that some market participants who otherwise could have benefited from tin are now of necessity prevented from using it. If a quantity of tin is sold, then the seller cannot sell it again, *regardless of the exchange rate*. There is simply no more of this left.

In any event, even granting that observers can learn of relative scarcity of a good from prices, emphasis on this aspect of prices distracts from the crucial role that prices play in economic calculation. That is, even if prices do tend to help users to become aware of a good's relative scarcity somewhat earlier than they would otherwise, it is not this function of prices which addresses the insurmountable problems of production and human action that are faced in the absence of private property. The fundamental problem faced by acting man is not the fact that information is dispersed.[30] Rather, it is deciding how to rationally allocate resources in the face of an uncertain future and given the subjective nature of value, which makes it impossible to compare alternative projects or plans in the absence of a cardinal set of prices.

Thus, as Rothbard explains, "what acting man is interested in, in committing resources into production and sale, is *future* prices."[31] The primary role of prices in a productive, advanced economy is not to communicate information, but to serve as the *starting point* for estimating what *future* prices will be.[32] The forecasted future prices are

---

[30] In fact, as Salerno points out in "Reply to Leland B. Yeager," p. 114–15, "dispersed knowledge is not a bane but a boon to the human race; without it, there would be no scope for the intellectual division of labor, and social cooperation under division of labor would consequently, prove impossible."

[31] Murray N. Rothbard, "The End of Socialism and the Calculation Debate Revisited," in *Economic Controversies* (Auburn, Ala: Mises Institute, 2011; https://mises.org/library/economic-controversies). As Mises notes: "Appraisement is the anticipation of an expected fact. It aims at establishing what prices *will be paid* on the market for a particular commodity or what amount of money will be required for the purchase of a definite commodity" (emphasis added). Ludwig von Mises, *Human Action: A Treatise on Economics*, Scholar's ed. (Auburn, Ala.: Mises Institute, 1998; https://mises.org/library/human-action-0), p. 329. "The essential elements of economic calculation are speculative anticipations of future conditions," and the entrepreneur calculates based on "an understanding of future conditions, necessarily always colored by the entrepreneur's opinion about the future state of the market." Ibid., p. 349.

[32] See Hülsmann, "Knowledge, Judgment, Property," p. 44, discussing the secondary importance of any possible information communicated through prices. But as Mises points out, in an intriguing and neglected passage, future prices are not only not dependent on past prices, but in principle could be forecasted by entrepreneurs even before there are existing money prices. As Mises writes:

> If the memory of all prices of the past were to fade away, the pricing process would become more troublesome, but not impossible as far as the mutual exchange ratios between various commodities are concerned. It would be harder for the entrepreneurs to adjust production to the demand of the public, but it could be done nonetheless. It would be necessary for them to assemble anew

then used to quantitatively compare various projects and to select the most profitable—and thus most value-productive—use of resources under consideration.[33] Prices are thus important because they serve as an *accessory of appraisement*. "Current" (immediate past) prices tell only what the current price structure is, and thus serve as a basis for forecasting what the future array of prices will be, given the current starting point. Thus, present prices "can have no communicative function because they are only the, if indispensable, starting point for our understanding of the future."[34]

---

all the data they need as the basis of their operations. They would not avoid mistakes which they now evade on account of experience at their disposal. Price fluctuations would be more violent at the beginning, factors of production would be wasted, want-satisfaction would be impaired. But finally, having paid dearly, people would again have acquired the experience needed for a smooth working of the market process.

Mises, *Human Action*, chap. XVI. Some people, who are anti-bitcoin, etc., are alarmed by this comment by Mises, since it undercuts their view of the nature and function of money and prices, but I think it gets to the heart of the matter: that all action is aimed at changing the future, which is uncertain; and it is *future* (uncertain) prices which are used in economic calculation. See Kinsella, "Human Action and Universe Creation," *StephanKinsella.com* (June 28, 2022). "Current"—or, immediate past—prices cannot determine future prices, but they can serve as a starting point, an "accessory of appraisement," since it can be easier to take stock of the current price array and envision the change, the delta, between now and the future, based on one's forecast of how human interactions will change, than to forecast a future price starting from chaos. But in principle, there is no reason an actor in a barter society could not forecast the emergence of money in the near future and try to predict the prices that would emerge thereafter. This *Gedankenexperiment* helps to highlight that prices do not convey knowledge or information, but rather reflect the knowledge, preferences, forecasts, and judgments of actors.

[33] Barnett gives an example of a consumer using prices to decide whether or not to purchase an airline ticket to fly to France. *Structure*, p. 55. But this example ignores the role of prices in entrepreneurial appraisal in favor of its economically less essential role in consumer choices. See Ludwig von Mises, *Economic Calculation in the Socialist Commonwealth* (Auburn, Ala.: Mises Institute, 1990 [1920]; https://mises.org/library/economic-calculation-socialist-commonwealth), pp. 4–6, 24. As Rothbard notes, "consumers goods are not the real problem.... The real problem ... is in all the intermediate markets for land and capital." Rothbard, "The End of Socialism and the Calculation Debate Revisited," pp. 56–57. He goes on: "the crucial decisions in the capitalist economy are the allocation of capital to firms and industries." Ibid., pp. 58–60. See also Mises, *Human Action*, p. 325: "The driving force of the market process is provided neither by the consumers nor by the owners of the means of production ... but by the promoting and speculating entrepreneurs." See also Salerno, "Ludwig von Mises as Social Rationalist," pp. 45–46.

[34] Hülsmann, "Knowledge, Judgment, Property," p. 47. Horwitz also notes that current "prices ... do serve as the starting point for the next round of entrepreneurial appraisement," but then adds, "*because they do provide (imperfect) information about scarcity, wants,*

The problem faced in a society without libertarian property rules is that there can be no money prices and there can thus be no economic calculation. Talk of a knowledge-disseminating role for prices is flawed and misses the point. Accordingly, Hoppe concludes that "Hayek's contribution to the socialism debate must be thrown out as false, confusing, and irrelevant."[35]

Barnett on Knowledge

Barnett's attempt to make knowledge the central inquiry, instead of calculation, scarcity, and interpersonal conflict, leads, not surprisingly, to confusion. Barnett maintains that the problem to be solved is "potentially conflicting personal and local knowledge of potential resource use"[36] or conflicting "preferences."[37] He then claims that private property and related liberal rules would minimize such conflicts, because it would lead to *you* "taking into account" *my* information and vice-versa, and to a general spreading of information (in "encoded" form).

As an example, Barnett hypothesizes that "there is a particular tree between my neighbor's house and mine."[38] One neighbor wants to keep

---

and opportunity costs." Horwitz, "Monetary Calculation and Mises's Critique of Planning," p. 441. The latter part of the sentence seems to be superfluous and not logically connected to the first. Current prices are the starting point in appraisement because today's prices will change in various ways to result in future prices, which are of interest to entrepreneurs. For a discussion of the connection of current prices to previous prices, see Mises's regression theorem (*Human Action*, p. 405 *et pass.*; *idem*, *The Theory of Money and Credit* (New Haven: Yale University Press, 1953), pp. 408 *et seq.*) and Murray N. Rothbard, *Man, Economy, and State, with Power and Market*, Scholars ed., 2d ed. (Auburn, Ala.: Mises Institute, 2009; https://mises.org/library/man-economy-and-state-power-and-market), chap. 4, §5.B.

35 Hoppe, "Socialism: A Property or Knowledge Problem?", p. 259. See also Rothbard, "The End of Socialism," p. 66: "the entire Hayekian emphasis on 'knowledge' is misplaced and misconceived;" Hülsmann, "Knowledge, Judgment, Property," p. 39, discussing "the irrelevance of knowledge problems;" and Salerno, "Ludwig von Mises as Socialist Rationalist," p. 44: "[t]he price systems is not—and praxeologically cannot be—a mechanism for economizing and communicating the knowledge relevant to production plans. The realized prices of history are an accessory of appraisement." See also related quotes in "Legislation and the Discovery of Law in a Free Society" (ch. 13), at n.68.

36 *Structure*, p. 40

37 Ibid., p. 38. One wonders why Barnett does not refer instead to "problems of preference." But this may have been a more obviously faulty notion, as it does not garner automatic respectability due to association with Hayek and other intellectuals.

38 Ibid.

the tree; yet the other wants to cut it down because it blocks his view of the sunset. Although Barnett acknowledges that it is these proposed *actions* (keeping the tree; cutting it down) which conflict with each other, he awkwardly and unnecessarily tries to fit this within the knowledge framework. He writes:

> In my example, my neighbor and I both have personal knowledge of how the tree affects the view from our respective windows. My neighbor and I have personal knowledge of each of our preferences concerning the use of this particular tree. Finally, and most significantly, these preferences conflict or, more precisely, each of us subjectively prefers to use the tree in physically incompatible ways.... Notice that there is no problem of scarcity in the absence of an incompatibility of subjective preferences.[39]

Now assigning property rights to the tree, as Barnett advocates, does solve the problem of conflict over use of the tree: Whichever neighbor owns the tree gets to decide whether to cut it down or not. But this solution has nothing to do with knowledge—except to the extent that non-owners must of course *know* someone else *owns* the tree in order to avoid conflicts over use of the tree.[40] The true way to avoid conflict is to establish, and promote respect for, property rights, not to disseminate "local" knowledge or information about others' preferences.

Barnett's account implicitly recognizes this. He says, for example, that the "radical dispersion of knowledge … leads to a knowledge problem when people seek to act on the basis of their differing knowledge in incompatible ways."[41] Note that the phrase "on the basis of their differing knowledge" is completely superfluous here; if it is eliminated, then this says that a problem arises "when people seek to act—*in incompatible ways*"—that is, when there are conflicting *actions* in the *use* of scarce resources. But conflicts are not caused by lack of knowledge, and thus cannot be solved by the spreading of knowledge. Conflicts arise because of the fundamental fact of scarcity and the lack of property rights allocating control of resources to specified owners.[42]

---

[39] Ibid.

[40] See note 58, below, and accompanying text, discussing the boundary-defining role of property rights and its relation to Barnett's second-order problem of knowledge.

[41] *Structure*, p. 41.

[42] Hayek's model leads Barnett into further error, as can be seen in his statement that "there is no *problem* of scarcity in the absence of an incompatibility of subjective

That is why property rights are the only way to prevent conflicts over scarce resources.

Why would anyone think knowledge *could* prevent conflict? Even omniscient actors, who are fully aware of each other's preferences and intentions, may struggle for control of a given scarce resource. If lack of knowledge is the reason for conflict over the tree in Barnett's tree example, surely the two neighbors would be able to learn of each other's conflicting preferences—by speaking with or watching each other—more easily than they learn similar facts in "condensed" form from the general price system! How will prices tell owners who *owns* the tree, i.e., who may control it? In fact, the existence of prices *presupposes* a system of private property, which itself *already* resolves conflicts over the use of scarce resources. As Hoppe puts it, "[p]rivate property is the necessary condition—*die Bedingung der Möglichkeit*—of the knowledge communicated through prices."[43] In any private-property system, whether or not prices have yet arisen, the private-property rules themselves suffice to promote peace and cooperation.

And a deeper difficulty looms in Barnett's account. For how can knowledge, or even preferences, of two individuals "conflict"? If we use the term "preference" in the precisely defined meaning it has in praxeology, where it concerns only one's demonstrably preferred use of one's own property,[44] there *can* be no conflict in preferences. The non-owner simply cannot have demonstrated preferences with regard to his neighbor's property, because these preferences would have to be demonstrated in action with another's property, which is prohibited. And if, instead, Barnett means only to use "preferences" in some colloquial, imprecise sense, how can information prevent conflicting preferences? In this loose sense of preference, individuals can have different preferences, even if they are "aware" of the other's wants.

---

preferences." Ibid., p. 38. But this gets it backwards. We cannot even meaningfully say that preferences "conflict" *unless* they are manifested in conflicting *actions* regarding the use of particular scarce resources. Thus the concepts of scarcity and conflict are more fundamental than the notion of conflicting preferences or knowledge. On the theory of demonstrated preference, see Rothbard, "Toward a Reconstruction of Utility and Welfare Economics," in *Economic Controversies*; and Mises, *Human Action*.

43 Hoppe, "Socialism: A Property or Knowledge Problem?", p. 258.
44 Rothbard, "Toward a Reconstruction of Utility and Welfare Economics."

And such a casual conception of preference cannot hope to be used to establish a rigorous case for private property, anyway.

Libertarians (and Misesian–Austrians) recognize that it is only *actions* that can conflict; it is the very possibility of conflict over the use of things that renders these things *scarce* resources and thus possible economic goods. Again, when the rubber hits the road, Barnett recognizes this truth: he notes that "there would be no knowledge *problem* with respect to resource use in the absence of scarcity."[45] He also notes that:

> The *actions* of some, not their preferences, are what interfere with the ability of others to pursue happiness by acting on the basis of their own personal and local knowledge. What is sought is a social order in which such knowledgeable actions by everyone are possible.[46]

Thus, when he actually has to formulate operational rules for guiding conduct, Barnett appropriately focuses on conflicting *actions* directed at scarce resources and shows that property rights are necessary to prevent such conflicts. Talk about knowledge and preference conflicts, and about the need for "knowledgeable actions" (instead of successful action), is superfluous and distracting window dressing.

Instead of the misplaced emphasis on knowledge, Barnett could have more straightforwardly noted that there indeed is a problematic potential for interpersonal conflict over scarce resources (including one's body), which would interfere with his assumed goals of peace and happiness. He could then have argued that private-property rights and the libertarian principles of self-ownership and Lockean homesteading solve this problem of interpersonal conflict.[47] Libertarian homesteading and property rules give rise to peace and prosperity, because in such a system conflicts can be avoided and prices can arise to allow economic calculation and thus rational resource allocation.

---

[45] *Structure*, p. 37.

[46] Ibid., p. 43. Barnett's conception of rights is also consistent with this emphasis on scarcity and action (p. 77). "[R]ights are construed as enforceable claims to acquire, use, and transfer resources in the world-claims to control one's person and external resources." Such rights are thus *operational* and can serve to guide action so that conflicts are avoided. See also pp. 100–101.

[47] As Hoppe does. See Hans-Hermann Hoppe, *A Theory of Socialism and Capitalism: Economics, Politics, and Ethics* (Auburn, Ala.: Mises Institute, 2010 [1989]; www.hanshoppe. com/tsc), p. 157; "What Libertarianism Is" (ch. 2).

In fact, this more direct approach could have led Barnett to recognize that it is possible to give much more than a merely hypothetical or consequentialist defense of libertarian principles by using Hoppe's pathbreaking argument that advocacy of any social ethic other than private property *contradicts* peace- and happiness-conducive norms such as cooperation and conflict-avoidance, which are necessarily presupposed by all participants in argumentation.[48] In fact, in other writings Barnett argues, in a way compatible in approach with Hoppe's argumentation ethics, that those who claim that the U.S. Constitution justifies certain government regulation of individuals are themselves introducing normative claims into discourse and thus cannot object, on positivist or *wertfrei* grounds, to a moral or normative criticism of their position.[49]

What about the goal of prosperity? Here Barnett could have pointed out, following Mises, that the private-property order and its accompanying price system also permits economic calculation and thus is the only way to achieve this goal. "Knowledge" would have been recognized as merely a technical problem that confronts any individual when choosing means to achieve certain ends and when deciding which ends to pursue.[50]

As for the right to contract (contractually transfer resources to others), Barnett provides a Byzantine argument that such a contract-based system is desirable because it requires the buyer to take the current owner's

---

[48] Hoppe, *A Theory of Socialism and Capitalism*, p. 157 *et pass*; "Dialogical Arguments for Libertarian Rights" (ch. 6). Hoppe's discourse ethics would appear to be a natural complement to Barnett's own views and previous writings, especially given that Barnett has in the past been heavily influenced by Hoppe's mentor Rothbard, who claimed that Hoppe "has managed to establish the case for anarcho-capitalist-Lockean rights in an unprecedentedly hard-core manner, one that makes my own natural law/natural rights position seem almost wimpy in comparison." See Murray N. Rothbard, "Beyond Is and Ought," *Liberty* (Nov. 1988; https://perma.cc/6HMQ-7CVQ): 44–45, 44, discussed in "Dialogical Arguments for Libertarian Rights" (ch. 6), n.15.

[49] Barnett, "Getting Normative," p. 100. See also *idem*, "The Intersection of Natural Rights and Positive Constitutional Law"; and *Structure*, p. 122 *et seq.*, following Fuller in arguing that the common law usefully requires parties to state their claims in terms of rights, thus necessarily asserting (presupposing) some principle or standard by which the claim of right can be tested.

[50] Hülsmann, "Knowledge, Judgment, Property," p. 44. The need to acquire knowledge faces even Crusoe alone on his island, who has no need for private property rules because there are no other people and thus no possibility of interpersonal conflict.

knowledge "into account."[51] Barnett also favors freedom of contract because it allows a price system to emerge, which serves as a powerful engine for the encoding and transmission of knowledge. Again, knowledge need not be even mentioned to support the institution of contracting. First, Barnett has already argued that the rights to homestead and use property are necessary to solve conflicts and promote prosperity. But the right to contract is implicit in the rights to acquire and use property. This is because if one has the right to acquire property, one has the right to abandon it (i.e., one has to be permitted to get rid of it, e.g., give it to another). And if one has the right to use property, this implies that others cannot take the property without obtaining the owner's consent.

Second, as Barnett notes, the right to exchange titles to property allows a price system to arise. Yet as already noted, the price system promotes Barnett's goal of prosperity not because of knowledge dissemination but because of the crucial role of prices as accessories of appraisement. Third, permitting contractual transfer of resources promotes prosperity because both parties to a voluntary exchange are made better off.[52]

Thus, it is the potential for interpersonal conflict and lack of objectively and justly defined property rights that endangers liberty, peace, and prosperity, not ignorance of others' preferences and local knowledge. Barnett's various "knowledge problems" are therefore better reformulated as "conflict problems." Libertarian principles would then be seen as ways to promote harmony and prosperity and to avoid conflict, instead of remedying the non-problem of deficiencies in knowledge.

THE SECOND-ORDER PROBLEM OF KNOWLEDGE AND THE RULE OF LAW

"The *second-order problem of knowledge* is the need to communicate knowledge of justice in a manner that makes the actions it requires accessible to everyone."[53] This is where the rule of law comes in. The rules

---

[51] *Structure*, pp. 53–54.
[52] Rothbard, "Toward a Reconstruction of Utility and Welfare Economics."
[53] *Structure*, p. 85.

of justice (i.e., substantive laws concerning private-property rights, etc.) must be adequately *communicated* to individuals so that they can serve as guides to action and thus prevent conflicts. To ensure adequate communication, various "formal" requirements must be satisfied. These formal requirements—the rule of law—govern both the *form* of laws and *processes* by which they are generated and promulgated.[54]

For example, rules of conduct must be communicated ahead of time (*ex ante*); and they must also be sufficiently concrete to be applied in a variety of situations. These and other considerations lead to the conclusion that laws must be: "(a) general rules or principles that are (b) publicized, (c) prospective in effect, (d) understandable, (e) compossible, (f) possible to follow, (g) stable, and (h) enforced as publicized."[55] Otherwise, a rule cannot serve as an operational guide to conduct or will not be just.

Abstract Rights and Legal Precepts

As Barnett insightfully explains, principles such as private property, first possession, and freedom of contract are very *abstract*, and thus cannot serve to guide conduct except in relatively rare situations.[56] (Barnett refers to such abstract natural rights as "background" rights, as opposed to the actually existing or enforced laws or rights, which he refers to as legal rights. It is background rights to which legal rights *should* conform.)[57] Thus, any legal system must develop a body of specific or concrete legal rules or principles, based on or at least compatible with more abstract background rights. Barnett refers to the particular, concrete rules or principles that serve as guides to action as *legal precepts*.[58]

---

[54] Ibid., p. 84.
[55] Ibid., p. 107.
[56] Ibid., pp. 84–85, 94–97, and 109–117.
[57] Ibid., p. 16.
[58] Ibid., pp. 94–95. On the objective function of property rules, see Hoppe, *A Theory of Socialism and Capitalism* and *idem*, *The Economics and Ethics of Private Property: Studies in Political Economy and Philosophy* (Auburn, Ala.: Mises Institute, 2006 [1993]; www.hanshoppe. com/eepp); "Selling Does Not Imply Ownership, and Vice-Versa: A Dissection" (ch. 11), at n.16; "Legislation and the Discovery of Law in a Free Society" (ch. 13), n.147. See also *Structure*, p. 101: "Only a general reliance on objectively ascertainable assertive conduct will enable a decentralized system of rights to perform its allotted boundary-defining function."

This analysis is on the mark, because it is true that legal principles must be known (communicated or published) and *operational* (sufficiently concrete) if they are to be used to avoid conflicts. The common tie between Barnett's second-order and first-order problems is therefore not *knowledge* but rather *conflict-avoidance*. A private-property order helps to avoid conflicts because each scarce resource is assigned a specified proper owner (reformulated first-order analysis). For conflicts to actually be avoided by individuals respecting these rules, however, the various rules as well as actual property boundaries must of course be *known*: I cannot consciously avoid trespassing on your property unless I know it is property and that trespassing is impermissible.

As a practical matter, this requires the rule of law be followed and that legal rules be concrete enough (Barnett's legal precepts) to serve as operational guides to action. This problem is in a sense inherent in the very idea of a private-property order, because the latter cannot exist if no one *knows* what conflict-avoidance rules to follow, but it is a real problem nonetheless and deserves the attention Barnett gives it.

THE THIRD-ORDER PROBLEM OF KNOWLEDGE AND THE COMMON LAW

What kind of legal and political system guarantees (or at least makes it possible) that the rule of law will be followed? How will concrete legal

---

See also Saúl Litvinoff, *The Law of Obligations: Part I: Obligations in General*, 2d ed. (St. Paul, Minn.: West Publishing Company, 2001), §1.9 (footnotes omitted):

… the law of obligations is one area of the vast region of the law of patrimony, which comprises, precisely, property and obligations.

The *theory* of obligations appears as a peculiar intellectual phenomenon in the evolution of legal thought. No doubt, it belongs together with the *law* of obligations but the theory does not reach as far as the law itself. The theory of obligations concerns itself only with an analysis of the component parts, the blueprint, of a certain mechanism, but without exploring the ways in which that mechanism works in concrete situations. Thus, the theory of obligations concerns itself with contract as the general scheme of all sorts of accords of the will of parties, without looking into the variations to which that scheme is susceptible according to the different needs it must satisfy. The theory leaves these variations to be explored elsewhere, in the sphere of special contracts, or contracts in particular, such as sale, lease, loan, and the many others that exist.

precepts be developed? (Barnett does not ask how the abstract natu-ral or background rights are to be developed; presumably through the writings of academic specialists like Barnett.) Clearly, some institutional means of providing such concrete private-property rules is needed. This is where a decentralized law-generation process such as the common law steps in.

In chapter 6, Barnett expands the conception of the rule of law to include the way in which a body of legal precepts is developed. Ac-cording to Barnett, the *"third-order problem of knowledge* is the need to determine specific action-guiding precepts that are consistent with both the requirements of justice and the rule of law."[59] Again, I would characterize this as related to conflict-avoidance rather than knowl-edge. In order to avoid conflicts, concrete private-property rules must be developed by some institution, and the institution must be such that the rules developed are just.[60]

Barnett first maintains that there are limits to the ability to deduce specific legal precepts from abstract principles of justice (natural rights), in part because many sets of legal precepts are consistent with the gener-al parameters of the abstract principles of natural rights.[61] He argues that a common-law type decentralized legal system, unlike law professors and philosophers, can develop legal precepts, because, in such a system, they gradually develop and evolve from the outcomes of thousands of actual cases.

Yet, Barnett does not provide a rigorous argument showing where the exact *limits* of the ability to deduce concrete rules are. He evi-dently feels that the more abstract principles can, for some reason, be established by armchair theorists. If denizens of the ivory tower can do this, why can they not deduce or establish more concrete rules by simply considering more and more contextual facts?[62] In the Roman

---

[59] *Structure*, p. 108.

[60] Just rules are those that conform to the type of private-property order that serves to permit conflict avoidance and enable prosperity. As Hoppe has shown, such a private-property order is based on Lockean type homesteading since the first-possessor rule is the only objective rule that can be intersubjectively and universalizably agreed upon by potential disputants. See Hoppe, *A Theory of Socialism and Capitalism*, p. 157.

[61] *Structure*, pp. 109–11.

[62] But see Kinsella, "The Limits of Armchair Theorizing: The Case of Threats," *Mises Economics Blog* (Jul. 27, 2006).

law system—a somewhat decentralized legal system superior in many ways to the common law—Roman jurists (jurisconsults) helped develop the great body of Roman law by providing opinions on the best way to resolve disputes. These disputes were often purely hypothetical or imaginary cases, in which the jurists asked, "Under such and such a possible or conceivable combination of circumstances, what would the law require?"[63] It is conceivable that a large part or even all of the legal code existing in a given society can be "deduced" in this fashion and then these rules applied like precedents to actual controversies as they arise. As a libertarian (and, I confess, a lawyer), I must say that I believe I would be more comfortable living under a set of concrete rules deduced by libertarian philosophers than the (perhaps more concrete) set of rules developed under the actual common law, although, as noted, there are limits to armchair theorizing.

---

[63] James Hadley, *Introduction to Roman Law* (Littleton, Colo.: Fred Rothman, 1996; https://archive.org/details/introductiontoro029387mbp), p. 66. Hadley notes that "A recent able lecturer on ancient law, Mr. Maine, finds in this fact an explanation of the more thorough scientific development which distinguishes the Roman law from the English." Ibid. On the use of hypotheticals by Roman jurists, see also the following sources, quoted more extensively in Kinsella, "Roman Law and Hypothetical Cases," *StephanKinsella.com* (Dec. 19, 2022): H.F. Jolowicz & Barry Nicholas, *Historical Introduction to the Study of Roman Law*, 3d ed. (Cambridge, U.K.: University Press, 1972), pp. 95 & 97; Bruce W. Frier, *The Rise of the Roman Jurists* (Princeton, N.J.: Princeton University Press, 1985), pp. 163–71, esp. p. 167; W.W. Buckland & Arnold D. McNair, *Roman Law and Common Law: A Comparison in Outline* (Cambridge, England: University Press, 2d ed., revised by F.H. Lawson, reprinted with corrections 1965), pp. 6–15, esp. p. 9; Peter Stein, *Roman Law in European History* (Cambridge University Press, 1999), pp. 8–9, 18, and 67–68; A. Arthur Schiller, *Roman Law: Mechanisms of Development* (Mouton Publishers, 1978), § 137; Alan Watson, "Justinian's Corpus Iuris Civilis: Oddities of Legal Development; and Human Civilization," Lecture 2 in *Authority of Law; and Law: Eight Lectures* (Stockholm: Institutet fr̈ Rtshistorisk Forskning, 2003; https://perma.cc/2BD5-4P4K), p. 65; James Gordley, *The Jurists: A Critical History* (Oxford University Press, 2013), p. 17; John P. Dawson, *The Oracles of the Law* (Thomas M. Cooley Lectures, Ann Arbor: University of Michigan Law School, 1968), pp. 116–17, 63–64, 71–72 (commenting on the use of hypotheticals in the Roman law as well as English common law); Barry Nicholas, *An Introduction to Roman Law* (Oxford University Press, 1962), pp. 33–34; Alan Watson, *Roman Law and Comparative Law* (University of Georgia Press, 1991), pp. 261, 250–51; and Wolfgang Kunkel, *An Introduction to Roman Legal and Constitutional History*, J.M. Kelly, trans (Oxford University Press, 1966), p. 86. I cite so many sources here because the comments of these various authors on the issue of hypothetical cases do not always seem fully consistent with each other, though the overall general thrust in this regard seems clear.

Still, Barnett's argument in favor of a common-law system makes sense, even to libertarians who favor a deductive approach to rights.[64] Legal rules must be concrete in the sense that the rules must take into account the entire relevant factual context. Since there are an infinite number of factual situations that could exist in interactions between individuals, a process which focuses on actual cases or controversies is likely to produce the most "interesting" or useful rules.[65] It probably makes little sense devoting scarce time and resources to developing legal precepts for imaginary or unrealistic scenarios. If nothing else, a common-law type system that develops and refines legal precepts as new cases arise serves as a sort of filter that selects which disputes (i.e., real, commonly-encountered ones) to devote attention to.

Barnett thus makes a convincing case that, in a decentralized legal system such as the English common law (or the early Roman law, the Law Merchant, and even modern arbitral systems)—especially one in which judges or arbitrators attempt to apply fundamental notions of justice to concrete situations—it is reasonable to expect a body of concrete legal concepts and precepts to develop which are more or less compatible with fundamental notions of justice.[66]

If and when unjust legal precepts do arise, they are not necessarily permanent, because a common-law process allows them to be modified or replaced when this becomes apparent. However, unless it is clear that a given legal precept is inconsistent with justice, then there should be reluctance to jettison established legal rules or precedents. This thus

---

[64] Hoppe, *A Theory of Socialism and Capitalism*, p. 157; Murray N. Rothbard, *The Ethics of Liberty* (New York: New York University Press, 1998); "A Libertarian Theory of Punishment and Rights" (ch. 5); "Dialogical Arguments for Libertarian Rights" (ch. 6).

[65] This is analogous to Mises's method selecting certain empirical assumptions (e.g., assuming there is money instead of barter) to develop "interesting" laws based on the fundamental axioms of praxeology, rather than irrelevant or uninteresting (though not invalid) laws. See Mises, *The Ultimate Foundation of Economic Science*, p. 41; *idem*, *Epistemological Problems of Economics*, pp. 14–16, 30–31, 87–88; *idem*, *Human Action*, pp. 64 *et seq*. See also Hoppe, *A Theory of Socialism and Capitalism*, p. 142, as quoted in "Causation and Aggression" (ch. 8), n.4. See also "A Libertarian Theory of Punishment and Rights" (ch. 5), n.36.

[66] Barnett does note the similarity between common law and civil law systems. *Structure*, p. 116 n.10. The civil law was derived from principles developed in a common-law fashion in the Roman law. It is the Roman law, more than the more positivistic and legislation-worshiping civil law, that bears a similarity with the common law. For further discussion on decentralized legal systems and related matters, see "Legislation and the Discovery of Law in a Free Society" (ch. 13), at n.153.

gives rise to the legal doctrine of *stare decisis* (or *jurisprudence constante* in continental or civil-law systems).[67]

This leads Barnett to make the provocative (for libertarians) argument that the "legal rights generated by a sound legal process may even be entitled to *presumptive legitimacy*"[68] and thus can even assist in determining the content of our background rights. We can always subject concrete legal precepts developed by courts to the scrutiny of the more abstract principles of justice and natural rights. This can help identify legal precepts "that are ... inconsistent with either justice or the rule of law or both."[69]

One question that bears exploring in this regard is exactly *how libertarian* are the abstract principles of justice that have been followed throughout the ages by judges and jurists of the common law, Roman law, and Law Merchant? In other words, just how libertarian are the legal precepts actually developed historically, and just how strong is the presumption of legitimacy which is to be accorded to these extant bodies of law? Which concepts of the common law are illiberal enough, when compared to Barnett's carefully-developed abstract principles of justice, to overcome the presumption of legitimacy? And how did the common law happen to employ more or less correct abstract principles of justice even before modern libertarian theory? Are these principles intuitive? Was it luck? Natural selection? Barnett does not answer these questions, but cannot be criticized for not doing everything.[70] Libertarian law students and scholars looking for topics to research, pay heed!

---

[67] See "Legislation and the Discovery of Law in a Free Society" (ch. 13), n.43; also Gregory Rome & Stephan Kinsella, *Louisiana Civil Law Dictionary* (New Orleans, La.: Quid Pro Books, 2011).

[68] *Structure*, p. 22, emphasis added; also p. 130. For conventional views regarding the duty to obey laws promulgated by the state, see M.B.E. Smith, "Is There a Prima Facie Obligation to Obey the Law?," *Yale L. J.* 82 (1973; https://perma.cc/MF3A-LBEV): 950–76 and Leslie Green, "Who Believes in Political Obligation?" in *For and Against State*, John T. Sanders & Jan Narveson, eds. (Lanham, Md.: Rowman and Littlefield, 1996), p. 15.

[69] *Structure*, p. 110.

[70] But see his discussion at ibid., pp. 122–23.

PROBLEMS OF INTEREST AND POWER

After discussing the problems of knowledge (better characterized as conflict-avoidance, as noted above), Barnett turns to problems of *interest* and *power*. The problems of interest concern how individuals balance questions of incentive, compliance, and partiality in access to resources. The problems of power are the possibility that there will be error and abuse in applying or enforcing legal precepts. Barnett elaborates on these challenges, and shows how each of them is addressed by the libertarian conception of justice and the rule of law.

Most of Barnett's arguments concerning interest and power are more straightforward than those regarding knowledge in Part 1, even where Barnett tries to support his arguments by referring to various knowledge-related aspects of the issue at hand. Barnett's discussion of the "problem of partiality," however (the first problem of interest), seems overly muddled due to the preoccupation with knowledge. Barnett claims that there is a "partiality problem" which "arises from the fact that people tend to make judgments that are partial to their own interests or the interests of those who are close to them at the expense of others."[71] This partiality "leads to a tendency to favor ones own interest"; partiality "is judgment affected by interest." Maybe I am slow, but I cannot see what is the alleged problem here. This seems to be nothing more than the unavoidable fact of self-interest. Of course people are "partial" to themselves. What is wrong with this? I see no need for people to take "into account the partial interests of others."[72] So long as others' property rights are respected, it seems to me that one ought to be able to be as "partial" as one likes without others complaining about it.

Barnett's discussion of the other problems of interest and the problems of power, though, are much more fruitful and less tainted by the occasional and vain attempt to link it to the Hayekian knowledge paradigm. For example, it is certainly true that the incentives which are provided under capitalism are very useful and are missing under socialism.[73] And there is indeed a need to ensure *compliance* [74] with

---

[71] Ibid., p. 136.
[72] Ibid., p. 137.
[73] Ibid., chap. 8.
[74] Ibid., chap. 9.

private-property rules, e.g., by using force for self-defense, restitution, and punishment.[75] I see no strong reason to call these problems of "interest," although the label seems harmless enough.

And (Part 3), there are indeed dangers involved in the use of power, such as the possibility of *error* in enforcement and punishment[76] and abuse of the power of law enforcement.[77] Many of Barnett's arguments here are very insightful and persuasive (some discussed below), although again, I find most of them to be so *despite* the superfluous comments on knowledge. In fact, I found the last half of the book,[78] which bears less and less on the knowledge paradigm introduced at the beginning, to be the most fascinating and best part of the book (plus the discussion of the common law in chapter 6).

Restitution vs. Retribution

One interesting argument that Barnett makes, with regard to enforcement error and abuse, is that all criminal justice should be restitutive, not punitive or retributive. As I have argued elsewhere,[79] I believe Barnett is mistaken that retribution (punishment) violates the *rights* of (actually guilty) aggressors.[80] However, in keeping with his consequentialist approach, which avoids questions of justification of fundamental norms, Barnett does not pretend to make a strong theoretical case for the rights of aggressors to be free from punishment.[81]

---

[75] Ibid., pp. 176, 184, 191.

[76] Ibid., chaps. 10 and 11.

[77] Ibid., chap. 12.

[78] Ibid., chaps. 9–15.

[79] "Inalienability and Punishment: A Reply to George Smith" (ch. 10); for more on the theory of inalienability, including discussion of Barnett's views in this regard, see "A Libertarian Theory of Contract: Title Transfer, Binding Promises, and Inalienability" (ch. 9). See also Walter E. Block, "Toward a Libertarian Theory of Inalienability: A Critique of Rothbard, Barnett, Smith, Kinsella, Gordon, and Epstein," *J. Libertarian Stud.* 17, no. 3 (Spring 2003; https://perma.cc/79AC-34BZ): 39–85, and my discussion of Block's views in "Selling Does Not Imply Ownership, and Vice-Versa: A Dissection" (ch. 11).

[80] For justification of the right to punish aggressors, see "A Libertarian Theory of Punishment and Rights" (ch. 5); "Dialogical Arguments for Libertarian Rights" (ch. 6); and Hoppe, *A Theory of Socialism and Capitalism*, p. 157 *et pass.*

[81] As Barnett acknowledges, "this analysis cannot conclusively prove that no combination of compensation or punishment can ever address effectively the compliance problem." *Structure*, p. 237. And further: "I do not claim to have completely demonstrated this proposition

Indeed, most of Barnett's concerns regarding punishment are warranted: he opposes it because he believes it may deter crime less than would a restitution-based system and also because the unavoidable possibility of error can lead to "infliction of harm on the *innocent*."[82] Like Barnett, I am concerned about the unavoidable possibility of mistakenly punishing the innocent, and thus admit the appeal of a restitution-based system in order to avoid punishing innocents. Moreover, Barnett makes a powerful and original argument for why the *standard of proof* should be higher if a victim seeks to punish a purported aggressor rather than merely obtain restitution.[83] Thus, a victim seeking to punish the aggressor must prove guilt beyond a reasonable doubt, whereas the lower standard of preponderance of the evidence is more appropriate for a civil trial for damages. It is therefore *more costly* to seek punishment than to seek restitution. For this and other reasons, restitution would probably become the predominant mode of justice in a free society.

Nevertheless, acknowledging (and justifying) the theoretical legitimacy of punishment can be useful. For example, punishment (or a theory of punishment) may be utilized to reach a more objective determination of the proper amount of restitution,[84] because a serious aggression leads

---

[that justice requires restitution, no punishment] either in my earlier writings, or in this book." Ibid., p. 185 n.36. See also pp. 228 & 320, and p. 321: "If men were gods, then perhaps imposing rewards and punishments on the basis of desert would be a workable theory." Also: "It has been noted that one who wishes to extinguish or convey an inalienable right may do so by committing the appropriate wrongful act and thereby forfeiting it." Randy E. Barnett, "Contract Remedies and Inalienable Rights," *Social Pol'y & Phil.* 4, no. 1 (Autumn 1986; https://perma.cc/P8JL-KAT2): 179–202, p. 186, citing Diane T. Meyers, *Inalienable Rights: A Defense* (New York: Columbia University Press, 1985). As I noted in "Inalienability and Punishment: A Reply to George Smith" (ch. 10), Smith is incorrect in claiming that Barnett's writings support Smith's view that all rights, even those of a murderer, are inalienable. See George H. Smith, "A Killer's Right to Life," *Liberty* 10, no. 2 (November 1996; https://perma.cc/AF2J-RAL9): 46–54. For more on forfeiture or waiver of rights, see also Herbert Morris, "Persons and Punishment," in *On Guilt and Innocence: Essays in Legal Philosophy and Moral Psychology* (Berkeley: University of California Press, 1976), pp. 31, 52, *et pass.*, discussing the right to bodily integrity and the waiver of this right; also "A Libertarian Theory of Punishment and Rights" (ch. 5), n.88 and Appendix: The Justice of Responsive Force.

82 *Structure*, p. 228, emphasis added; also pp. 197, 228.

83 Ibid., p. 212.

84 On the issue of determination of the proper amount of damages, see Bruce L. Benson, "Restitution in Theory and Practice," *J. Libertarian Stud.* 12, no. 1 (Spring 1996; https://mises.org/library/restitution-theory-and-practice): 79–83, and Murray N. Rothbard,

to the right to inflict more severe punishment on the aggressor, which would thus tend to be traded for a higher average amount of ransom or restitution than for comparatively minor crimes.[85] Especially offended victims will tend to bargain for a higher ransom; and richer aggressors will tend to be willing to pay more ransom to avoid the punishment the victim has a right to inflict, thereby solving the so-called "millionaire" problem faced under a pure restitution system (where a rich man may commit crimes with impunity, since he can simply pay easily-affordable restitution after committing the crime).

Moreover, even if punishment is banned (*de facto* or *de jure*) and is not an actual option—because of the possibility of mistakenly punishing innocents, say—an award of restitution can be *based on* the model of punishment. To-wit: a jury could be instructed to award the victim an amount of money it believes he *could* bargain for, given all the circumstances, *if* he could threaten to proportionately punish the aggressor. This can lead to more just and objective restitution awards than would result if the jury is simply told to award the amount of damages it "feels" is "fair." Barnett nowhere specifies any objective standards or criteria by which a judge or jury is to determine the amount of restitution a victim is to receive for a non-economic crime like murder, rape, and the like. He specifies only that the aggressor must "compensate" the victim for the "harm caused," to "restore" the victim.[86] Thus, a retribution-based system, even if used only as a model to help determine the amount or standard of restitutive damages, supplements Barnett's theory of a restitution-based justice system.

Preventative Force

Barnett makes a convincing case that the principle of "extended self-defense" justifies imprisoning (sometimes for life) those who have

---

"Punishment and Proportionality," in *The Ethics of Liberty* (https://mises.org/library/punishment-and-proportionality-0), pp. 88–89.

[85] For further discussion of criminals buying their way out of punishment, see "Inalienability and Punishment: A Reply to George Smith" (ch. 10); "A Libertarian Theory of Punishment and Rights" (ch. 5); Rothbard, "Punishment and Proportionality," pp. 86, 89; Roger Pilon, "Criminal Remedies: Restitution, Retribution, or Both?" *Ethics* 88, no. 4 (July 1978): 348–57, at 356.

[86] *Structure*, pp. 159, 185.

made a sufficiently unambiguous communication of a threat to another.[87] Because of the possibility of enforcement abuse and rule of law considerations, however, Barnett would limit this remedy to those persons who have communicated a threat to others by their past criminal behavior (i.e., those who have been convicted, perhaps multiple times, of a crime), and only if the previous crimes were proved beyond a reasonable doubt.[88]

This limitation on the principle of extended self-defense seems to me to be unduly restrictive, however. In my view, a threat can be viewed as a species of the crime of *assault*. Assault is defined as putting someone in fear of receiving a battery (physical beating).[89] A threat should count as a type of assault because the threatener puts the victim in fear of receiving a battery and also deliberately increases the likelihood of physical harm befalling the victim. As explained elsewhere,[90] assault may be punished because this is the only way the victim can reciprocate and put the aggressor–threatener in a like state of fear. I see no reason to allow extended self-defense only where the aggressor has previously been convicted of a crime. Even the first crime is a crime.

---

[87] Ibid., pp. 186–91.

[88] Ibid., pp. 213–14. See also *idem*, "Getting Normative," p. 157. One problem with Barnett's solution here is that, under his restitution-based system, previous crimes would have been proved by some standard less than the "beyond a reasonable doubt standard," such as the "preponderance of the evidence" standard, and thus it would be very difficult to jail threatening individuals.

[89] Louisiana Criminal Code §36 (https://www.legis.la.gov/legis/laws_Toc.aspx?older=75&level=Parent); *Black's Law Dictionary* (1994, p. 114; defining assault); *Mason v. Cohn*, 108 Misc. 2d 674, 438 N.Y.S.2d 462 (N.Y. Sup. Ct. 1981; https://casetext.com/case/mason-v-cohn-1) (defining assault). The Louisiana Criminal Code defines assault as "an attempt to commit battery, or the intentional placing of another in reasonable apprehension of receiving battery." A battery is defined as "the intentional use of force or violence upon the person of another; or the intentional administration of a poison or other noxious liquid or substance to another." Louisiana Criminal Code § 33. Assault can thus also include an attempted battery (which need not put the victim in a state of apprehension of receiving a battery—e.g., the victim may be asleep and be unaware that another has just swung a club at his head, but missed.

[90] "A Libertarian Theory of Punishment and Rights" (ch. 5).

POLYCENTRISM—I MEAN, ANARCHO-CAPITALISM

One of the best parts of *The Structure of Liberty* is its argument in favor of anarcho-capitalism. It is marred by its strict avoidance of the more appropriate terms anarcho-capitalism or anarchy; Barnett for some reason prefers to describe anarcho-capitalism as a "polycentric constitutional order," presumably to avoid unduly alienating statist readers. (If he feels polycentric is a better term than anarcho-capitalism, he does not offer reasons.)

Barnett notes that various types of structures have been tried "to deal with the problem of enforcement abuse by a coercive monopoly of power," i.e., government, including elections, federalism, and free emigration. Yet, he recognizes, these have failed to keep government in check. Thus, he argues that each of these three principles "reflects a more fundamental principle that needs to be more robustly incorporated into institutional arrangements: *reciprocity, checks and balances*, and the *power of exit*." [91]

Barnett elaborates on these in chapter 13, one of the best in the book. He notes that two constitutional principles are sufficient to achieve a polycentric order: *nonconfiscation* and *competition*. Under the former, "[l]aw-enforcement and adjudicative agencies should not be able to confiscate their income by force, but should have to contract with the persons they serve." Under the latter, they "should not be able to put their competitors out of business by force." [92] As is clear to libertarians, adherence to these two principles would indeed result in the anarcho-capitalist society, for no government can exist without the ability of a coercive monopoly over its services. [93]

Barnett makes several excellent points in chapter 13. He notes, for example, that if an individual refuses to contract with any legal system, force can still be used against him if he harms others. "The justice of using force against such a person is based on the fact that he or she violated the rights of the victim, not that he or she consented to the jurisdiction

---

[91] *Structure*, p. 256.
[92] Ibid., p. 258.
[93] Charles Murray, *What it Means to Be a Libertarian* (New York: Broadway Books, 1997), p. 64, makes a similar point when he argues that citizens should be able to opt out of certain government programs.

of a court."[94] It is refreshing to see this point emphasized, because many advocates of anarcho-capitalism seem to feel that an aggressor can be punished by a defense agency only if the aggressor somehow previously consented to the jurisdiction of the agency (if he did not consent, the only permissible remedy is presumably ostracism).

Another excellent point concerns the likelihood of a polycentric order actually embodying liberal norms. Barnett sensibly points out that:

> … it is difficult to imagine a society that did not adhere to some version of a liberal conception of justice ever accepting a polycentric constitutional order in the first instance. A societal consensus supporting these rights and remedies would seem to be a precondition for ever peacefully ending [monopoly government power]. And, once adopted, the inherent stability of the robust "checks and balances" provided by a competitive system is likely to preserve this initial consensus.[95]

Finally, my favorite part of the book is the well-written, thoughtful, and imaginative chapter 14, "Imagining a Polycentric Constitutional Order: A Short Fable," in which Barnett speculates on what a possible polycentric-ordered society might look like and how it might function. I mean, an anarcho-capitalist society.

TERMINOLOGY

It is clear that Barnett is a libertarian and that *The Structure of Liberty* is thoroughly infused with libertarian principles with regard to rights, government, and economics. He even goes so far as to advocate a polycentric—i.e., anarcho-capitalist—system. But one irritating aspect of the book is the unconventional and idiosyncratic use of terminology. Some of these terms seem to be used to try to avoid alienating statists. It is understandable—but ultimately futile, in my view—why Barnett might want to soften the blow of loaded terms like libertarian and anarchy and use the kinder, gentler (but blander, less descriptive, and more misleading) terms liberal and polycentric instead. In my view it is preferable to call

---

[94] *Structure*, p. 278.
[95] Ibid., p. 281–82.

a spade a spade.[96] We won't fool anyone into supporting anarcho-capitalism by using a fancier term.

Some of the terms employed, such as "several property" and "polycentric" order, clearly reveal the Hayekian influence on Barnett; other Hayekian terms such as "spontaneous" and "coordination" are also sprinkled throughout the book. Nothing seems to be gained except confusion and lack of clarity by replacing perfectly good terms like private property and anarcho-capitalism with inferior terms, or even with equally conceptually valid terms.[97]

Barnett also uses the expressions "background rights" instead of natural rights, and "legal precepts" instead of "concrete legal rules" or some other such descriptive term. I must admit that I like having a term for operational, concrete legal rules as distinct from more abstract principles; and "legal precepts" seems, I suppose, as good as any. But "background rights" does not seem to be an improvement over terms such as natural or moral or individual rights (or just plain "rights"). However, these quibbles mainly relate to Barnett's strategy or style, not to the substance or soundness of his arguments.

---

[96] See Ayn Rand, "Introduction," in *The Virtue of Selfishness: A New Concept of Egoism* (New York: Signet, 1964), p. vii:

> The title of this book [*The Virtue of Selfishness*] may evoke the kind of question that I hear once in a while: "Why do you use the word 'selfishness' to denote virtuous qualities of character, when that word antagonizes so many people to whom it does not mean the things that you mean?" To those who ask it, my answer is: "For the reason that makes you afraid of it."

Rand also unabashedly, and admirably, proclaimed herself to be a radical for capitalism.

[97] In the second edition of *Structure*, Barnett grants that the use of the term "several" in the first edition was a mistake:

> Were I writing the book today, however, I might change one term. I might use the term "private property" rather than the term "several property" that I borrowed from Hayek, who himself borrowed it from Scottish Enlightenment thinkers. I preferred "several property" because it emphasized the need to recognize jurisdiction over resources among the several or many individuals and associations that comprise a society. Were property held in the private hands of a very few, this type of "private property" would not address the problems of knowledge and interest. But in the interest of clarity and the avoidance of jargon, "private property" would have been clearer and, I now think, preferable.

Structure, p. 330–31.

PROBLEMS WITH THE PROBLEMS

A consequentialist analysis can be valuable, but one difficulty with Barnett's account is that he presumes that the universally shared goals of peace, prosperity, and happiness can be achieved if only we solve *three* main problems (of knowledge, interest, and power). I have already explained that the Barnettian problems of knowledge are better reformulated as aimed at conflict-avoidance, and thus peace (and perhaps at enabling economic calculation, and thus prosperity). A deeper question is why are these the only problems that get in the way of our goals? Why are these three problems exhaustive? What about other purported problems harped on by communitarians, socialists, or other consequentialists, such as inequality and poverty, commercialism and consumerism? Barnett's considers this issue,[98] but provides only a brief and somewhat unconvincing argument that addressing these other problems with legal coercion would undermine the "foundations" of the "structure of liberty" and thus prevent the three fundamental problems from being solved.[99]

CONCLUSION

As is often the case in a review of this sort, many of my comments have been critical, but this should not give the impression that I find fault with the bulk of Barnett's work. I have focused primarily on the aspects with which I disagree, and have emphasized economic calculation and the Hayekian knowledge paradigm, and have largely omitted discussion of the many valuable ideas in *The Structure of Liberty*. In fact, I have profited immensely from many of Barnett's previous theories, such as his views on constitutional interpretation, contract theory, and his tantalizing suggestion that there should be a presumption against the legitimacy of government statutes in derogation of common law or

---

[98] *Structure*, pp. 325–26.
[99] For a similar critique of Barnett's argument in this regard, see Lawrence B. Solum's review of *The Structure of Liberty* (first edition), "The Foundations of Liberty," *Mich. L. Rev.* 97, no. 6 (May 1999; https://repository.law.umich.edu/mlr/vol97/iss6/26/): 1780–1812, at 1791–92.

liberties—a "presumption of liberty."[100] Most of these are not included or discussed at length in this treatise. Luckily, Barnett's next book is reportedly *The Presumption of Liberty: Restoring the Constitution*.[101]

The Structure of Liberty is an important new work by one of libertarianism's most significant and thoughtful legal scholars. Its primary substantive deficiency is its over-reliance on the Hayekian knowledge paradigm, but the work nonetheless arrives at the private-property norms that address the more relevant issue of interpersonal conflict. The book is full of subtle insights regarding standards and burdens of proof, restitution, the workings of the common law, and the operation of anarcho-capitalism. It is must-reading for all those seriously interested in libertarian theory.

---

[100] Barnett, "Getting Normative"; idem, "Natural Rights and Positive Constitutional Law."

[101] Since the original review was written, this book has indeed been published; see Randy E. Barnett, *Restoring the Lost Constitution: The Presumption of Liberty*, 2d ed. (Princeton University Press, 2013).

20

Review of *Against Politics: On Government, Anarchy, and Order,* by Anthony de Jasay

Originally published as Stephan Kinsella, "*Against Politics: On Government, Anarchy, and Order.* By Anthony de Jasay. London and New York: Routledge, 1997," *Q. J. Austrian Econ.* 1, no. 1. (Fall 1998): 85–93. De Jasay's book will be referred to herein as *Against Politics*.

This is a wonderful collection of previously published articles by Anthony de Jasay who, it turns out, is an undiscovered Austrian, or at least a close cousin. The essays in *Against Politics*, published between 1989 and 1996, are united around a common theme, the economic and political aspects of government and "ordered anarchy." The book is full of sparkling insight and penetrating, calm dissections of pro-state arguments. Opponents of the state will find much ammunition here. Statists (even of the minimalist variety) will find much to ponder.

De Jasay's arguments pack quite a punch, and make it clear that he is a powerful, careful scholar. He also appears to be a quasi-Austrian economist and political theorist, which is surprising given that he does not appear to be very familiar with the work of Austrian theorists, such as Mises and Rothbard. Has he even read *Human Action*? One wonders. The primary well-known Austrians he cites are Hayek and Wieser, who represent the "Vienna School" instead of the Austrian school.[1] He has apparently come to many Austrian conclusions without the benefit

---

[1] *Against Politics*, p. 162.

of much exposure to Austrianism. For example, he makes good use of the observation that not only is utility not measurable, but interpersonal utility is also completely incommensurate.[2] He even writes that, "[u]nlike the physical sciences, inference presupposing purposiveness is proper to the study of reasoning beings and cannot be avoided without inordinate loss of content,"[3] which bears an uncanny similarity to Mises's own epistemology.[4]

The book is divided into two parts. The seven chapters of Part 1 are critical of statism, the view that political action is necessary, efficient, or desirable. In the four chapters of Part 2, our author somewhat tentatively proffers his own politico-economic theories, designed to show that various desirable social institutions are possible without political arrangements. The essays are well-ordered and generally fit together almost as well as chapters of an integrated work, although, as is to be expected in a collection of this kind, there is some repetition and redundancy. (A useful summary of the book's themes, structure, and arguments is found in the Introduction, at pp. 4–7.)

De Jasay is a master of criticism. A standard technique is to hold a statist's logic up to standards that the statist himself espouses. In a rare personal glimpse, he reveals an instance of applying this technique in his own life:

> The present writer, when a subject of a "people's democracy" [presumably the author's country of origin, Hungary], used to taunt his political masters that capitalism had never existed anywhere, that it was yet to come, it was the "wave of the future"—a taunt that reduced them to fury but naturally failed to provoke any refutation.[5]

Given his power of criticism, the critical pieces in Part 1 contain stronger arguments than Part 2, although for some (such as this reviewer),

---

[2] See, e.g., ibid., 81–81, 92, 98, 144

[3] Ibid., 74.

[4] See, e.g., Ludwig von Mises, *Human Action: A Treatise on Economics*, Scholar's ed. (Auburn, Ala.: Mises Institute, 1998; https://mises.org/library/human-action-0); *idem*, *The Ultimate Foundation of Economic Science: An Essay on Method* (Princeton, N.J.: D. Van Nostrand Company, Inc., 1962; https://mises.org/library/ultimate-foundation-economic-science); *idem*, *Epistemological Problems of Economics*, 3d ed., George Reisman, trans. (Auburn, Ala.: Mises Institute, 2003; https://mises.org/library/epistemological-problems-economics).

[5] *Against Politics*, pp. 108–9.

the essays in Part 2 will still be of at least as much or more interest. For although his positive theorizing is weakened by his own moral skepticism (more on this below), it is strengthened by his critique of statist alternatives; further, his basic intuitions and premises are largely sound. Combine this with a multitude of keen insights and critiques of opposing social theories, and Part 2 is of immense interest, even with its deficiencies.

Part 1 opens with "Self-Contradictory Contractarianism," which addresses the argument that various "intractable" problems of the state of nature, such as prisoner's dilemmas and free riding,[6] prevent systematic social cooperation. One way out of these dilemmas would be to make "binding" contracts. However, people cannot make binding contracts in the state of nature, since rational actors without fear of sanction will always default, thereby making contracting impossible and requiring the state to provide an effective contract enforcement mechanism.

But, de Jasay asks, "if contracts require an enforcer, how could there be a social contract creating an enforcer without *its* enforcement being assured by a meta-enforcer created by a meta-social contract, and so on in an infinite regress."[7] De Jasay recognizes that the proposed solution assumes that the state can act as an "enforcing agent acting as a programmed automaton."[8] Yet this is to "assume away the principal-agent problem,"[9] since the state has little reason to restrict itself to enforcing the contract. For these and other reasons, "[t]here is ... no contractual exit from the state of nature: if the state is to be created by contract, it cannot be created, since it is its own antecedent condition."[10] Thus this particular ground for the necessity of the state contradicts itself, and advocates of government are hoisted by their own petard.

De Jasay correctly recognizes that the real question is whether ordered anarchy (what we would call anarcho-capitalism) is possible or not, and this question "ultimately boils down to the issue of the enforcement

---

6 Ibid., pp. 11–12.
7 Ibid., p. 5.
8 Ibid., p. 19
9 Ibid.
10 Ibid., p. 22

of mutual promises without a final specialized enforcer."[11] De Jasay seems at home with the somewhat dubious field of game theory, but this helps to make him especially suited to criticize its irrelevance to the actual world. He argues that typical game-theoretical arguments are unrealistic and inapplicable to real life situations, since "[a]nyone who has a name, lives in a place, does something for a living—that is, anyone tied into the fabric of society—would think twice before treating mutual promise as the single-play prisoner's dilemma says he must."[12] We can, therefore, expect that contracts can be self-enforcing, without the aid of a central-ized enforcing agent, and thus at least some of the dilemmas that are claimed to be part of anarchy are chimerical.[13]

Indeed, as argued in chapter 2, "Is Limited Government Pos-sible?," it is not proponents of anarcho-capitalism but rather those who advocate limited government who hold unrealistic views. Our author recognizes that "[t]here is a plethora of constitutional devices for 'rigging' rules and procedures in such a way as to clip the wings of the state."[14] However, the real problem is not how to invent such devices but to find the conditions, if possible, that would be likely to be adopted and to stay intact long enough to do any good.[15] De Jasay's economic reasoning here persuasively demonstrates why no such arti-ficial restriction is likely to succeed, and why any government can be expected to have a tendency to grow.[16]

The other chapters of Part 1 are also interesting and insightful. "Frogs' Legs, Shared Ends, and the Rationality of Politics"[17] argues that political grounds generally cannot have rational grounds and cannot be

---

[11] Ibid., p. 29.

[12] Ibid., p. 33.

[13] Further, as Alfred G. Cuzán has insightfully pointed out, the existence of the state itself is evidence that anarchy is possible, for officials of the state "voluntarily" abide by certain hierarchies and rules, e.g., the American president is physically less powerful than his armies, yet they tend to obey him rather than vice-versa. Alfred G. Cuzán, "Do We Ever Really Get Out of Anarchy?," *J. Libertarian Stud.* 3, no. 2 (Summer 1979; https://mises.org/library/do-we-ever-really-get-out-anarchy): 151–58. See also *idem*, "Revisiting 'Do We Ever Really Get Out of Anarchy?'", *J. Libertarian Stud.* 22, no. 1 (2010; https://mises.org/library/revisiting-do-we-ever-really-get-out-anarchy): 3–21.

[14] *Against Politics*, p. 53.

[15] Ibid.

[16] Ibid., p. 57ff.

[17] Ibid., chap. 3.

rationally defended. This essay, however, seems more hastily written and more poorly organized than most others in the book. "The Twistable is Not Testable,"[18] a review essay of Popper's *The Open Society and Its Enemies*,[19] shows de Jasay at the height of his critical powers. In this piece, de Jasay subjects Popper's own (socialistic) propositions "to the acid of the very method of which he is the champion," the test of falsifiability.[20] Popper contended that "[g]enuine propositions are capable of being corroborated, and are criticized by a process of confrontation with the ascertainable facts of the case."[21] However, Popper advocated both democracy and socialism; yet, as de Jasay shows, this advocacy rests upon the completely unfalsifiable building block descriptions, concepts, and judgments, such as "weak" and "strong." For example, these concepts are essential to the Popperian proposition that social institutions must be constructed to protect the "economically weak" from the "economically strong."[22] Thus, de Jasay shows that Popper's socialism is indefensible by Popper's very own scientific standards.[23]

In the course of this essay, de Jasay also deflates the myth that Popper was a liberal.[24] Also of interest is de Jasay's critical treatment of other

---

[18] Ibid., chap. 5.

[19] Karl R. Popper, *The Open Society and Its Enemies*, vol. 2, 4th rev. ed. (London: Routledge and Kegan Paul, 1962).

[20] *Against Politics*, p. 105.

[21] Ibid.

[22] Ibid., pp. 114–15.

[23] As has been pointed out, logical positivism is inherently contradictory since it fails its own test, as it is not itself falsifiable. Mises, for example, writes:

The essence of logical positivism is to deny the cognitive value of a priori knowledge by pointing out that all a priori propositions are merely analytic. They do not provide new information, but are merely verbal or tautological, asserting what has already been implied in the definitions and premises. Only experience can lead to synthetic propositions. There is an obvious objection against this doctrine, viz., that this proposition that there are no synthetic a priori propositions is in itself a—as the present writer thinks, false—synthetic a priori proposition, for it can manifestly not be established by experience.

Mises, *The Ultimate Foundation of Economic Science*, p. 5. See also Hoppe, "Austrian Rationalism in the Age of the Decline of Positivism," in *The Economics and Ethics of Private Property*, p. 363; idem, *The Economics and Ethics of Private Property*, p. 271; idem, *Economic Science and the Austrian Method* (Auburn, Ala.: Mises Institute, 1995; www.hanshoppe.com/esam), pp. 33–34; idem, *A Theory of Socialism and Capitalism*, pp. 126–27; and Martin Hollis & Edward J. Nell, *Rational Economic Man: A Philosophical Critique of Neo-Classical Economics* (Cambridge, 1975), p. 110.

[24] *Against Politics.*, p. 114.

prominent liberal economists and political theorists, notably James Buchanan, F.A. Hayek, and Robert Nozick. In "Hayek: Some Missing Pieces,"[25] for example, de Jasay argues that Hayek "has no complete theory of the social order to back up his liberal recommendations."[26] In advocating that government should go beyond the maintenance of law and order to provide amorphous and endless "highly desirable" public goods, Hayek ends up supporting virtually unlimited government. De Jasay will have none of this:

> A theory of social order is incomplete if it makes no serious attempt at assessing the long-term forces that make the public sector grow or shrink. This can hardly be done without relying on a defensible theory of public goods. Hayek feels no necessity for one. Strangely, the question seems to have held no interest for him.[27]

In other words, Hayek has not done his homework and his half-baked political theory endangers the very freedom that he is viewed as upholding. (The critiques of Nozick and Buchanan are discussed below in the discussion of Part 2.)

I have mentioned above that de Jasay's work could be improved if it built more on and dealt more with contemporary Austrian theory, in particular Misesian economic theory as well as associated political theories, such as those of Rothbard. But this is unfair and somewhat ungrateful. We cannot rightfully criticize him for what he has not done, especially when what he has done is so significant. It might be better to say that, given his obvious acuity and talents, it seems a shame that he has not done so. One can only hope that we see more treatment and use of Austrian work in his further output.

For example, his discussions of the so-called public goods "dilemma"[28] could have profited from the trenchant insights of Austrians Murray Rothbard and Hans-Hermann Hoppe, among others.[29] His discussion

---

[25] Ibid., chap. 6.
[26] Ibid., p. 120.
[27] Ibid., p. 125. See also Walter Block, "Hayek's Road to Serfdom," *J. Libertarian Stud.* 12, no. 2 (Fall 1996; https://perma.cc/5NZM-QLCV): 327–50.
[28] Ibid., pp. 20, 124.
[29] See, e.g., Hans-Hermann Hoppe, *The Economics and Ethics of Private Property: Studies in Political Economy and Philosophy* (Auburn, Ala.: Mises Institute, 2006 [1993]; www.hanshoppe.com/eepp), chap. 1; *idem*, "The Private Production of Defense," in *The Great Fiction: Property,*

of why government will tend to grow[30] could also be usefully supplemented by recent Austrian politico-economic theory.[31] Rothbard (relying on Schütz) criticized the empiricist assumption that only "verifiable" (or falsifiable) propositions are "scientific," and thus the existence of human action and even other human actors cannot be scientifically maintained, on the grounds that the principle of verifiability itself requires other human beings to exist to replicate experimental results.[32] This insight could have been used with profit in de Jasay's Popper critique.[33] De Jasay's critiques of Nozick[34] (discussed below) and Hayek[35] could have also fit well with Austrian analysis.[36]

A more serious objection lies in de Jasay's moral skepticism. His general skepticism serves him well as a critic, since it leads him invariably to put the burden of proof on those who advocate the state and to find their proof wanting. However, his own skepticism goes too far and is itself unwarranted. It also undercuts his own positive theorizing, since even that, as tentative as it is, depends on some modicum of moral judgment or assumptions.

De Jasay seems to believe that the only meaningful propositions are those that are subject to rational criticism, and that only falsifiable

---

Economy, Society, and the Politics of Decline, Second Expanded Edition (Auburn, Ala.: Mises Institute, 2021; www.hanshoppe.com/tgf); Murray N. Rothbard, *Man, Economy, and State, with Power and Market*, Scholars ed., 2d ed. (Auburn, Ala.: Mises Institute, 2009; https://mises.org/library/man-economy-and-state-power-and-market); *idem*, "The Myth of Neutral Taxation," in Rothbard, *Economic Controversies* (Auburn, Ala.: Mises Institute, 2011; https://mises.org/library/economic-controversies).

[30] *Against Politics*, p. 57 *et seq.*

[31] See, e.g., Hoppe, "Time Preference, Government, and the Process of De-Civilization—From Monarchy to Democracy," in John Denson, ed., *The Costs of War* (New Brunswick: Transaction Publishers, 1997; https://perma.cc/N7NA-24C8).

[32] Murray N. Rothbard, "Praxeology as the Method of the Social Sciences," in *Economic Controversies*.

[33] *Against Politics*, chap. 5.

[34] Ibid., p. 170, 174.

[35] Ibid., chap. 6.

[36] On Nozick, see Rothbard, "Robert Nozick and the Immaculate Conception of the State," *The Ethics of Liberty* (New York: New York University Press, 1998; https://perma.cc/5BU9-YLXD); on the error in the Lockean proviso and Nozick's adoption thereof, see Hoppe, *The Economics and Ethics of Private Property*, p. 410. On Hayek, see Hoppe, "F.A. Hayek on Government and Social Evolution: A Critique," in *The Great Fiction*, and Block, "Hayek's Road to Serfdom." Hoppe also criticizes Nozick in "Murray N. Rothbard and the Ethics of Liberty," in Rothbard, *The Ethics of Liberty* (www.hanshoppe.com/publications).

propositions that can be corroborated or not, fall into this category. One exception is that "value judgments" that are not merely *ad hoc*, i.e., that fit into some coherent hierarchy or system, can also be criticized if they are not internally consistent.[37] I may be too hasty here and may be unfairly attributing to him a kind of Popperian scientism that he means to present and critique rather than adopt. However, over and over, de Jasay denigrates the idea that ends or values can be rational. Thus, "[w]hat is ultimately unfalsifiable, immune to rational criticism and useless except as a piece of gratuitous self-expression, is the stand-alone, ad hoc value judgment."[38]

Here is where perhaps the greatest improvement could be made to de Jasay's thought by careful consideration of important Austrian work. In particular, Hoppe's extension of praxeology into the field of ethics, the importance of which cannot be overstated, demonstrates that there is indeed an unchallengeable, rational basis for ethics.[39] In fact, in his skepticism and his subsequently deficient political theorizing, de Jasay has more in common with Mises than just economics. For Mises himself, as Rothbard has pointed out, as an opponent of objective ethics, presented a very weak, half-hearted, and, ultimately, unsuccessful, utilitarian defense of liberalism.[40]

The most important and interesting essay of Part 2 is "Before Resorting to Politics,"[41] which de Jasay admits is "the book's most ambitious."[42] In this chapter, he criticizes consequentialism and other problems that, as he sees it, plague modern liberal theory. In its stead he "proposes three, admittedly sketchy, 'principles of politics,'" which are

---

[37] *Against Politics*, p. 106.

[38] Ibid., p. 106; see also pp. 16–17, 36 n. 2, 66.

[39] See, e.g., Hoppe, *A Theory of Socialism and Capitalism: Economics, Politics, and Ethics* (Auburn, Ala.: Mises Instittue, 2010 [1989]; www.hanshoppe.com/tsc), chap. 7; *idem*, *The Economics and Ethics of Private Property*, chaps. 8–11; The Undeniable Morality of Capitalism" (ch. 22); "A Libertarian Theory of Punishment and Rights" (ch. 5); "Dialogical Arguments for Libertarian Rights" (ch. 6); Rothbard, *The Ethics of Liberty*; *idem*, *For A New Liberty: The Libertarian Manifesto*, 2d ed. (Auburn, Ala.: Mises Institute, 2006; https://mises.org/library/new-liberty-libertarian-manifesto).

[40] Rothbard, "Praxeology, Value Judgments, and Public Policy," in *Economic Controversies*.

[41] *Against Politics*, chap. 8.

[42] Ibid., p. 6.

"entailed in the liberal ethic" and which must be incorporated into the foundations of any coherent liberal theory.[43]

As noted above, however, de Jasay does not seem to believe that normative propositions can be justified, and he does not really try to do so. He just uses the occasional "should" and normative premise where it is unavoidable, and appears to simply presume that the reader shares these (uncontroversial) premises, perhaps counting on the reader's own good will or love of consistency. For example, he merely asserts that "[i]t is dubious in the extreme that a political authority is entitled to employ its power of coercion for imposing value choices on society ... and on individual members."[44] Yet the force of the normative concepts "dubious" and "entitled" here is diluted by the lack of even an attempt at justification.

De Jasay's argument is thus a hypothetical one—and I am not sure if he would disagree, for I am not sure he thinks anything better is possible—for it relies for its persuasiveness on the listener already valuing (for some reason) the goals of justice, efficiency, and order. Nevertheless, because most of these principles are certainly sound and justifiable anyway (for example, using Rothbard's or Hoppe's ethical theory), and because de Jasay's critical and analytical skills are so acute, much of interest emerges from this essay.

His three principles of politics are: (1) if in doubt, abstain from political action;[45] (2) the feasible is presumed free;[46] and (3) let exclusion stand.[47] The justification of principle (1) begins with a vigorous critique of consequentialism. De Jasay notes that most political action requires assessing the worth or value of various policies. Drawing on the idea that interpersonal utility and values are incommensurate, de Jasay points out that we can rarely know if any proposed government measure is really "worth it" or not.[48] Thus, government action, which necessarily employs the power of coercion, should be avoided where possible; the burden of proof should be on those agitating for it. This

---

[43] Ibid., p. 147.
[44] Ibid., p. 151.
[45] Ibid., pp. 147 *et seq.*
[46] Ibid., pp. 158 *et seq.*
[47] Ibid., pp. 171 *et seq.*
[48] Ibid., pp. 149, 151.

entails a corollary principle, "that applying coercion is legitimate when it is positively invited by the prospective coercee." [49]

Next, in principle (2), "the feasible is presumed free," de Jasay asserts that "[t]he basic rule is that a person is presumed free to do what is feasible for him to do," [50] as long as the proposed feasible action is not ruled out by his own obligations or the possibility of harm to others. We should live by right and not by permission, presumably in part because the former situation is more workable and efficient. If a feasible action is thus presumed free, then the actor need not prove that the action is permissible; rather, the burden is on he who challenges the permissibility of the action. [51] Otherwise, an actor might be unable to ever act since it would be essentially very difficult to prove a negative by showing that no one will be harmed. [52]

Incidentally, de Jasay offers an interesting critique of Nozick's conception of rights here. By viewing rights as "permissions" to do something, rather than as claims for performance by another, Nozick perhaps unwittingly endorses a system in which action is not presumed free, as action is undertaken with "permission" by others, which presumably must first be granted. [53]

I found the justification of principle (3), "let exclusion stand," to be of most interest, especially the discussion of homesteading or appropriation of unowned goods. [54] De Jasay equates property with its owner's "excluding" others from using it, for example by fencing in immovable property (land) or finding or creating (and keeping) movable property (corporeal, tangible objects). Thus, the principle means "let ownership stand," i.e., that claims to ownership of property appropriated from the state of nature or acquired ultimately through a chain of title tracing back to such an appropriation should be respected.

---

[49] Ibid., p. 156.
[50] Ibid., p. 160.
[51] Ibid.
[52] For criticism of norms that would not permit actors to act *now* because they would be unable to get permission, see "How We Come to Own Ourselves" (ch. 4), at n.14; "Defending Argumentation Ethics" (ch. 7), n.31; and "Law and Intellectual Property in a Stateless Society" (ch. 14), at n.27.
[53] *Against Politics*, p. 170.
[54] See also "What Libertarianism Is" (ch. 2), at n.27.

The basic defense of the Lockean proposition that the first or original appropriator of property is entitled to appropriate it draws on his previous "feasible" principle (2) as well as his distinction between rights and liberties. Others have objected to the idea that one can appropriate unowned property on the grounds that such an action unilaterally (and thus unjustifiably) imposes on others moral duties to refrain from interfering.

> The basic defense, however, is quite general and straightforward. It is that if a prospective owner *can* in fact perform it, taking first possession of a thing is a feasible act of his that is *admissible* if it is *not a tort* (in this case not trespass) and violates no right; but this is the case by definition, i.e., by the thing being identified as "unowned."[55]

Thus, by treating individuals as being free to act unless it contravenes a right (claim) of another, there is simply no reason *not* to allow a person to appropriate unowned property. For who could object, if not another, prior owner? To be entitled to object is to be able to "exclude" the claimant, but the right to exclude is an incident of ownership, and the property is by presumption unowned. No one can validly object to my appropriating unowned property, then, because, assuming feasible actions are free, any objection itself must claim a right, and this itself raises a type of ownership claim.[56]

The beauty of this approach is that it avoids the troublesome "Lockean proviso," which allows homesteading of unowned goods only so long as "enough and as good is left to others."[57] Nozick, on the other hand, allowed appropriation of an unowned object only if it did not worsen the situation of others. However, de Jasay points out, in a world with finite resources, this condition would make it impossible for any

---

[55] Ibid., p. 173.

[56] Similar reasoning is employed in my estoppel theory of rights to preclude someone from denying the rights that they necessarily presume exist in a certain context (punishment). This theory is related to and draws on Hoppe's argumentation ethics. See "A Libertarian Theory of Punishment and Rights" (ch. 5); "Dialogical Arguments for Libertarian Rights" (ch. 6), the section "Estoppel." Hoppe's insights into why the *first* appropriator has a better moral claim than latecomers is also of relevance here. See Hoppe, *A Theory of Socialism and Capitalism*, pp. 168 *et seq.*; *idem, Economics and Ethics of Private Property*, pp. 328–30.

[57] *Against Politics*, p. 188, n.15; see also p. 195.

unowned property to be ever used, since any appropriation causes a loss of opportunity for others to homestead the object and thereby worsens their situation. By contrast, de Jasay's position "does not require that nobody loses as a result of first possession, as long as the losses were not vested interests."[58]

De Jasay's application of his appropriation rule to two basic types of appropriation is also worth study. These two types are "finding and keeping" and "enclosure."[59] The former appears to apply primarily to movable objects that may be found, taken, and hidden or used exclusively. Since the thing has no other owner, *prima facie*, no one is entitled to object to the first possessor claiming ownership. Other grounds for opposing this might be that the thing was found at least partly by luck, and was thus undeserved. But for this to be relevant, there would have to be a general rule requiring the lucky in life to compensate the unlucky. But such a rule rests on a simply unsupportable assertion.

For immovable property (land), possession is taken by "enclosing" the land and incurring exclusion costs, e.g., erecting a fence. As in the case with movables, others' loss of the opportunity to appropriate the property does not give rise to a claim sufficient to oust the first possessor (if it did, it would be an ownership claim). However, for those who used to occasionally enjoy access to and use of the property, they do lose an actual benefit.[60] De Jasay admits that he cannot do full justice to this difficult issue, but offers a tentative solution. If some people previously used the property merely in passing, on an ad hoc basis, no right of theirs is violated by the homesteader enclosing it. However, if some identifiable, closed set of persons have used the property regularly enough to establish a precedent on which they rely, compensation must be paid them by the new owner.[61] (It is unclear why this regular use and "precedent" does not itself establish an ownership claim on behalf of the prior users; but de Jasay is here speaking of borderline cases.)

[58] Ibid., p. 188, n. 15. For other libertarian critiques of the Lockean Proviso, see the reference in note 36, above; Kinsella, "Down With the Lockean Proviso," *Mises Economics Blog* (Aug. 26, 2009); and Michael Makovi, "The 'Self-Defeating Morality' of the Lockean Proviso," *Homo Oeconomicus* 32, no. 2 (2015; https://perma.cc/G8PQ-LJ85): 235–74.

[59] Ibid., p. 174.
[60] Ibid., p. 176–77.
[61] Ibid., p. 177.

Other chapters in Part 2 argue that rational choices by individuals in the state of nature can be expected to lead to enforcement of property rights and contractual promises.[62] This chapter also shows that James Buchanan's interpretation of Hobbes and history is incorrect, and that proper understanding of both supports the idea that markets can exist prior to and without states, contra Buchanan.[63] In the last chapter, "Liberties, Rights, and the Standing of Groups,"[64] one has to agree with his conclusion that "group rights" are problematic, and the proper bearers of rights are individuals.

This is a thought-provoking book. I have only been able to touch upon some of the nuances and important insights it contains. This work is an important contribution to economic and political literature; it should be read and studied by the serious student.

---

[62] Ibid., chap. 9.
[63] Ibid., p. 198.
[64] Ibid., chap. 11.

21

Taking the Ninth Amendment Seriously

Originally published in 1997 in the *Hastings Constitutional Law Quarterly*, at the suggestion of Professor Randy Barnett.* The original article thanked "Paul Comeaux for helpful comments on an earlier draft of this Book Review."†

What we need is an amendment forbidding the circumvention of the Constitution. It could read: "The Constitution shall not be circumvented." I just got a big laugh from any lawyers who may be reading this.

—Joe Sobran[1]

I. INTRODUCTION: THE INSTRUMENTAL VALUE OF THE AMERICAN CONSTITUTION

We Americans are lucky indeed to have inherited our Constitution and our classical liberal tradition. For suppose we had inherited a totalitarian form of government, a government that did not respect property rights

---

* Stephan Kinsella, "Taking the Ninth Amendment Seriously: A Review of Calvin R. Massey's *Silent Rights: The Ninth Amendment and the Constitution's Unenumerated Rights*," *Hastings Const. L.Q.* 24, no. 3 (Spring 1997): 757–84, reviewing Calvin R. Massey, *Silent Rights: The Ninth Amendment and the Constitution's Unenumerated Rights* (Philadelphia: Temple University Press, 1995) (hereinafter, *Silent Rights*).

† Comeaux, currently an attorney in Dallas, was a law school and grad school friend, and a colleague, from 1992–94, at Jackson Walker in Houston.

---

1 Joe Sobran, "Constitutional Legerdemain," syndicated column of April 11, 1996 (reprinted in *Sobran's* 3, no. 5 (May 1996), page 12).

or other individual rights, that arbitrarily discriminated against—even executed or exterminated—certain classes of its subjects from time to time.[2] If such a government on occasion failed to implement its totalitarian "constitution" to the letter—say, it was slow to adopt a fully socialized agriculture policy or temporarily retreated from such a policy after causing the starvation of a few million people—it is unlikely even the strictest "originalists" in that society would complain that the government was shirking its duties under the totalitarian constitution. The totalitarian constitution itself—the basic plan underlying the government—would be seen by even the originalists as inherently illegitimate, with no purpose served by advocating stricter adherence to its precepts. No purpose in service of liberty, at least.[3]

Under a totalitarian system, proponents of liberty and individual rights[4] would be relegated to other tactics, such as fomenting revolution

---

[2] Examples of totalitarian governments include communist and fascist states, both of which are types of socialism. Socialism may be defined as a system of "institutionalized interference with or aggression against private property and private property claims." Hans-Hermann Hoppe, *A Theory of Socialism and Capitalism: Economics, Politics, and Ethics* (Auburn, Ala.: Mises Institute, 2010 [1989]; www.hanshoppe.com/tsc), p. 2.

[3] To put it even more starkly, suppose the government adopts a plan to exterminate all Hungarians at a rate of ten per day, but, for some reason, is bungling the job and is only executing one Hungarian per day. No sane person would admonish the government to speed up its executions or even to investigate the cause of the government's "inefficiency" in this regard. For a similar point, see Bruce L. Benson, "Third Thoughts on Contracting Out," *J. Libertarian Stud.* 11, no. 1 (Fall 1994; https://mises.org/library/third-thoughts-contracting-out): 44–78, which argues that privatization of governmental services should not always be favored, even by libertarians; for example, when the privatized service, such as the IRS, is unjust and increasing its efficiency would simply increase injustice. See also Randy E. Barnett, "The Relevance of the Framers' Intent," *Harv. J. L. & Pub. Pol'y* 19 (1995–96; http://www.randybarnett.com/pre-2000): 403–410, p. 410 (arguing that one reason we should interpret the Constitution in accordance with the Framers' original intentions is "because we today share their intentions to limit the power of government in a way that enhances and protects the liberty of the people.").

[4] By individual rights, I mean the specifically *libertarian* conception of individual rights, in which the only fundamental right is to be free from aggression, where "'[a]ggression' is defined as the *initiation* of the use or threat of physical violence against the person or property of anyone else." Murray N. Rothbard, *For A New Liberty*, 2d ed. (Auburn, Ala.: Mises Institute, 2006; https://mises.org/library/new-liberty-libertarian-manifesto), 27. (See also "What Libertarianism Is" (ch. 2).) The phrase "individual rights" is preferable to the phrase "human rights," since the latter expression, like the term "liberal" in American usage, has acquired a leftist or socialist tinge. *See, e.g.,* the United Nation's *Universal Declaration of Human Rights*, U.N. GAOR, 217A (III) (1948), at articles 22–26 (reciting, for example, "human rights" to "social security" and to "free" "education"). Libertarian individual rights

or civil disobedience, trying to persuade or educate society or government officials to see the light of liberty, or even advocating outright dishonest interpretation of the constitution to achieve better results. A constitution, then, has only instrumental value; it is worth supporting and interpreting honestly only if such an interpretation would tend to lead to desirable results. To a supporter of individual rights, for example, a constitution providing for an explicitly totalitarian system does not have instrumental value, and he would not seek to have such a constitution put into effect or put into effect more stringently.

Now imagine that there is a better constitution in place, one originally designed to undergird limited government and individual rights. Over the decades, however, the government has incrementally misconstrued this constitution, seizing more and more power not authorized by it. Imagine also that, for a variety of reasons, the population had acquiesced, and even grown somewhat accustomed, to this state of affairs.[5] Advocates

---

are roughly equivalent to the set of natural rights under older terminology. For libertarian justifications for the existence of individual rights, see Hoppe, *A Theory of Socialism and Capitalism* (especially chap. 7); Hans-Hermann Hoppe, *The Economics and Ethics of Private Property: Studies in Political Economy and Philosophy* (Auburn, Ala.: Mises Institute, 2006 [1993]; www.hanshoppe.com/eepp); Rothbard, *For a New Liberty; idem, The Ethics of Liberty* (Atlantic Highlands, NJ: Humanities Press, 1982); "A Libertarian Theory of Punishment and Rights" (ch. 5); "Dialogical Arguments for Libertarian Rights" (ch. 6); Roger A. Pilon, "Ordering Rights Consistently: Or What We Do and Do Not Have Rights To," *Georgia L. Rev.* 13, no. 4 (Summer 1979; https://perma.cc/C68C-C5HC): 1171–96; Ayn Rand, *Capitalism: The Unknown Ideal* (New York: Signet, 1967); *idem, The Virtue of Selfishness: A New Concept of Egoism* (New York: Signet, 1964); Leonard Peikoff, *Objectivism: The Philosophy of Ayn Rand* (New York: Plume, 1991); Tibor R. Machan, *Individuals and Their Rights* (Open Court, 1989); Douglas B. Rasmussen & Douglas J. Den Uyl, *Liberty and Nature: An Aristotelian Defense of Liberal Order* (Chicago: Open Court, 1991); Ludwig von Mises, *Liberalism: In the Classical Tradition*, 3d ed., Ralph Raico, trans. (New York: The Foundation for Economic Education, 1985; https://perma.cc/7KMG-X4DD); Jan Narveson, *The Libertarian Idea* (Philadephia: Temple University Press, 1988); Loren E. Lomasky, *Persons, Rights, and the Moral Community* (Oxford: Oxford University Press, 1987). For more recent works, see the list of books at Kinsella, "The Greatest Libertarian Books," *StephanKinsella.com* (Aug. 7, 2006).

5 Reasons for the populace's acquiescence might include: a sympathy with socialism over the years on the part of intellectuals and large portions of society; the corruption wrought by democracy itself, which breeds special interest wars and the willingness to use government to get one's piece of the pie before one is made victim by others; the welfare/warfare state, which provides recipients of redistributed tax dollars (in the form of welfare payments or government salaries) with an incentive to support ever-growing government; and public education, which inevitably results in the state propagandizing each generation of students in favor of its programs. *See generally* Frederic Bastiat, *The Law* (Irvington-on-Hudson, N.Y.:

of limited government and individual rights in this setting have an option available to them that those in our hypothetical socialist society do not: they can insist that the government respect the constitution's original meaning. They can argue, for example, that the supreme court has been misinterpreting the constitution and should now interpret the constitution in accordance with its original understanding.[6] Given the country's traditional respect for the constitution and at least some widespread sentiment that the government's very legitimacy depends

---

Foundation for Economic Education, Dean Russell, trans. 1950 [1850]; https://fee.org/resources/the-law/), pp. 17–18 (discussing ever-escalating conflicts among disparate special interest groups); Robert Higgs, *Crisis and Leviathan: Critical Episodes in the Growth of American Government* (New York: Oxford University Press, 1987) (discussing the public's acquiescence in expansions in government power during times of crisis, power which is never returned after the crisis is over, leading to a ratchet effect of growing government power with each new "crisis"); Bruno Leoni, *Freedom and the Law* (Indianapolis: Liberty Fund, expanded 3d. ed. 1991 [1961]; https://oll.libertyfund.org/title/kemp-freedom-and-the-law-lf-ed) (discussing special interest group warfare); William C. Mitchell & Randy T. Simmons, *Beyond Politics: Markets, Welfare, and the Failure of Bureaucracy* (Boulder, Colo.: Westview Press, 1994) (discussing the unintended consequences of governmental programs and the large number of special interest groups that accompany big government); Sheldon Richman, *Separating School and State: How to Liberate America's Families* (Fairfax, Va.: Future of Freedom Foundation, 1994) (tracing the history of government-sponsored education, its use as propaganda, and other pernicious effects); Giovanni Sartori, *Liberty and Law* (Menlo Park, Calif.: Institute for Humane Studies, 1976) (discussing the tendency of citizens ruled by increasing legislation and regulation to become more docile and accustomed to following orders and thus to allow fundamental rights to be trammeled by the government); Hans-Hermann Hoppe, "Time Preference, Government, and the Process of De-Civilization—From Monarchy to Democracy," *J. des Economistes et des Etudes Humaines* 5, no. 2/3 (June/September 1994; https://www.hanshoppe.com/publications/): 319–49, p. 319 (also included in *Democracy: The God That Failed* and in John Denson, ed., *The Costs of War: America's Pyrrhic Victories* (New Brunswick: Transaction Publishers, 1997; https://mises.org/library/costs-war-americas-pyrrhic-victories)) (discussing systemic features of democracy that make it likely to oppress liberty).

6 Judge Robert Bork's theory of original understanding is largely sound, although Bork himself occasionally misapplies his own theory, for example, with respect to the Ninth Amendment. *See* Robert H. Bork, *The Tempting of America: The Political Seduction of the Law* (New York: Free Press, 1990), pp. 143–45, 183–85. Original understanding should not be confused with original intent. The "original intent" of the Framers is relevant only insofar as it is evidence for the public's "original understanding" of the Constitution, the so-called "original public meaning," as agreed to by the people or their representatives. See also Louisiana Civil Code (https://www.legis.la.gov/legis/Law.aspx?d=111052), art. 9:

> When a law is clear and unambiguous and its application does not lead to absurd consequences, the law shall be applied as written and no further interpretation may be made in search of the intent of the legislature.

on its acting within limits proscribed by the constitution, this might be a reasonable, even hopeful, course to take.[7]

America is largely in this latter situation since our Constitution was originally designed to establish limited government. It is for this reason that I say that we Americans are lucky to have inherited our Constitution and our classical liberal tradition. We are not limited to the unattractive options of revolution or despairing resignation as our only responses to government tyranny. We can urge the Supreme Court and Congress to respect individual rights and limit government powers in accordance with the original design of the Constitution. Our Constitution has instrumental value—at least for those who support limited government and both personal and economic individual freedom.[8]

One problem with trying to persuade the Court to move towards a more originalist interpretation of the Constitution is that, even if the Court wants to do this, it may be too late. Given the entrenched and accumulated accretions of government power and court decisions that have resulted from over a century of misinterpretation of the Constitution,[9] the Supreme Court is unlikely to simply undo its own jurisprudence and interpret the Constitution anew. Further, even if the Court wanted to start reining in the federal government's powers, it would not be able to get away with it, at least not without a sufficiently sneaky or clever theory that would allow some incremental

---

[7] Regarding the presumption of governmental legitimacy, Professor Barnett makes the interesting and promising argument that the necessary assumption that citizens have a moral obligation to obey positive law presumes that there be some mechanism to ensure that such laws are legitimate. See Randy E. Barnett, "Foreword: The Ninth Amendment and Constitutional Legitimacy," *Chicago-Kent L. Rev.* 64 (1988): 37–65, reprinted in Randy E. Barnett, ed., *The Rights Retained by the People*, vol. 2 (Fairfax, Va.: George Mason University Press, 1993), p. 391. Under our system of government, this requires Ninth Amendment-based judicial review of legislation to provide a sort of "quality control" to ensure the promulgated laws do not infringe the citizens' enumerated or unenumerated rights. See ibid.; see also *idem*, "Getting Normative: The Role of Natural Rights in Constitutional Adjudication," *Constitutional Commentary* 12 (1995; www.randybarnett.com/pre-2000): 93–122, p. 100; *idem*, "Implementing the Ninth Amendment," in *idem*, ed., *The Rights Retained by the People*, vol. 2, p. 1; *idem*, "The Intersection of Natural Rights and Positive Constitutional Law," *Connecticut L. Rev.* 25 (1993; www.randybarnett.com/pre-2000): 853–68.

[8] Another option, of course, is to attempt to have the Constitution amended so as to better serve liberty. See U.S. Const. art. V.

[9] See sources cited in note 21, below.

movement toward liberty in a manner not obvious enough to catch the Leviathan's eye.

In his new book, *Silent Rights: The Ninth Amendment and the Constitution's Unenumerated Rights*, Professor Calvin R. Massey seeks to provide such a "stealth" theory (my words, not his) by providing a new way to read the Ninth Amendment. As Massey points out, this amendment has been largely ignored since its addition to the Constitution in 1791.[10] In this book, Massey proposes a novel and somewhat radical theory to reincorporate the Amendment and its original purposes into the current constitutional landscape. At the heart of Massey's theory is his proposed "constitutional cy pres doctrine"[11] and his contention that the Ninth Amendment incorporates rights based in state law.[12] Before further exploring this theory, it is necessary to delve into, as Massey does, the history and political context of the Ninth Amendment.

II. THE DUAL PURPOSES OF THE NINTH AMENDMENT

The Ninth Amendment provides as follows: "The enumeration in the Constitution, of certain rights, shall not be construed to deny or disparage others retained by the people."[13] It follows, of course, the various rights enumerated in the first eight amendments in the Bill of Rights, and it precedes the Tenth Amendment.[14] In a discussion of the original debate concerning the Ninth Amendment, Massey points out that there are many possible answers as to just what the Ninth Amendment means:

> Some, like former Judge Robert Bork, contend that the amendment has no discernible meaning whatever. Others ... suggest that the amendment is merely hortatory and duplicative of the axiomatic reminder in the Tenth Amendment that the states retain all powers not surrendered

---

10 See ibid., at 7 (citing Alex Kozinski & J.D. Williams, "It Is a Constitution We Are Expounding," *Utah L. Rev.* 1987, no. 4 (1987): 977–994, pp. 981 & 984).

11 Ibid., at 97–98; see also Part II, above.

12 See *Silent Rights*, at 122; see also notes 67–73, above.

13 U.S. Const. amend. IX.

14 The Tenth Amendment reads: "The powers not delegated to the United States by the Constitution, nor prohibited by it to the States, are reserved to the States, respectively, or to the people." U.S. Const. amend. X.

under the Constitution. Still others ... contend that the amendment prohibits the federal government from exercising any power with respect to the "rights retained by the people." ... Yet another view ... asserts that the Ninth Amendment was merely a cautionary device to check unwarranted extension of the powers of the federal government. Some ... suggest that the amendment is best regarded as a ... rule of interpretation [that] invalidates [the] argument that any given right (such as the right to use contraceptives) is not to be included within some enumerated right of the Constitution (such as due process) simply because the right to use contraceptives is not expressly enumerated in the Constitution.... Finally, [some] contend that the amendment ought to be treated as an independent source of substantive and judicially enforceable individual rights, determined without reference to any of the enumerated rights.[15]

As Massey explains, one of the objectives of the Ninth Amendment was to preserve the states' sovereignty and independence, in part so that the states could serve as a check on expansions of federal power.[16] To this end, the central government was vested only with a few defined powers, reserving other powers to the states.[17] Protection of the natural rights of citizens, for example, would be largely a matter for the states to handle.[18] Because of the limited delegation of power to the federal government, the Federalists did not believe an enumerated bill of rights to be necessary.[19] Without the granted *power* to invade rights, the federal government would simply be unable to do so.

The Antifederalists, nevertheless, demanded a bill of rights, fearing that without one, the federal government would both encroach on the states' sovereignty and violate the natural rights of the people.[20] History has proven the Antifederalists right; it would have been too dangerous to create the federal government without also providing a bill of rights. Although the current federal government has arrogated for itself vast powers not authorized by the Constitution,[21] it seems almost certain

---

[15] *Silent Rights*, at 10–11.
[16] Ibid., at 55.
[17] Ibid., at 56.
[18] Ibid.
[19] Ibid.
[20] Ibid., at 56–57.
[21] For discussions of the Supreme Court's various misinterpretations of the Constitution, see Raoul Berger, *The Fourteenth Amendment and the Bill of Rights* (Univ. Oklahoma Press, 1989); *idem, Government by Judiciary: The Transformation of the Fourteenth Amendment*

that things would have been worse had the Bill of Rights not been added as a precautionary measure.

On the other hand, as the Federalists countered, even if having no bill of rights would be dangerous, enumerating rights to limit a government of purportedly limited powers is also dangerous, for two primary reasons. First, the very declaration of a particular right (e.g., freedom of speech) might be construed to imply that some power had been given to the federal government to invade this right.[22] This could lead to the implication that the federal government possessed *un*enumerated powers, similar to the broad "police powers" exercised by states, rather than strictly limited, enumerated powers. These unenumerated powers of the central government could be used to invade any (unenumerated) rights of the citizenry as well as the sovereignty of the states.[23] Second, listing certain rights in the "bill of rights might raise the implication that the only rights possessed by the people were those enumerated,"[24] that is, that the listing of rights in the Constitution was exhaustive. Enter the Ninth Amendment, designed, as Massey shows, to combat both these dangers.

Some commentators acknowledge that the Amendment was meant only to address the first of these two dangers by serving as a rule of construction as to federal powers. Under this "single-purpose" interpretation, it is held that:

> [T]he amendment's function was merely to restrain constitutional interpreters from construing too broadly the powers delegated to the central government. By doing so, it had the secondary effect of preserving individual liberties, because the "residual rights" of the citizenry were protected by the sheer absence of governmental power to curtail them.[25]

(Cambridge, Mass.: Harvard Univ Press, 1977); Bork, *The Tempting of America*; James A. Dorn & Henry G. Manne eds. *Economic Liberties and the Judiciary* (Fairfax, Va.: George Mason Univ Press, 1987); Henry Mark Holzer, *Sweet Land of Liberty: The Supreme Court and Individual Rights* (Costa Mesa, Calif.: The Common Sense Press, 1983); and Bernard H. Siegan, *Economic Liberties and the Constitution* (Chicago: University of Chicago Press, 1980).

[22] See *Silent Rights*, at 60–61.
[23] See ibid., at 61–62; see also ibid., at 24.
[24] Ibid., at 62; see also ibid., at 23–24.
[25] Ibid., at 24.

Thus, the Amendment merely served as a rule of construction regarding federal powers, and "adherents to this view reject the idea that the Ninth Amendment is itself an independent source of human rights capable of judicial cognizance."[26]

Massey disagrees with such a single-purpose interpretation of the Ninth Amendment. He argues persuasively that the Ninth Amendment had dual, but complementary, purposes: To prevent the listing of rights from being used to imply that the federal government had powers beyond those enumerated, *and* to prevent the listing of rights from implying that the list is an exclusive and exhaustive one.[27] For example, as Massey notes, many states admitted to the Union in the nineteenth century added a version of the Ninth Amendment to their own constitutions:

> It is hard to understand why any group of state constitution makers would have done so if they had thought the Ninth Amendment was simply a device to confine federal legislative power.... The presence of Ninth Amendment analogues in state constitutions is reason to conclude that nineteenth-century legal actors continued to regard the federal Ninth Amendment as instantiating dual paths to a single end of preserving human liberty.[28]

The distinction between the dual purposes of the Ninth Amendment was not completely clear two hundred years ago. One reason for this, Massey claims, is that, in the Founding Fathers' generation, "rights were thought of as the absence of governmental powers,"[29] that is, individual rights were merely conceived of "as the complement of governmental powers."[30] Thus, to the Framers, the distinction between these two purposes was "blurry at best."[31] Individual rights could be secured simply by limiting government power, since "rights could not lawfully be invaded by a government lacking power to do so."[32] However, today's

---

[26] Ibid.

[27] See ibid., at 62, 93. Hereinafter, I will sometimes refer to these as the limited-powers purpose or function, and the unenumerated-rights purpose or function, respectively.

[28] Ibid., at 86–87.

[29] Ibid., at 93.

[30] Ibid., at 67.

[31] Ibid., at 93.

[32] Ibid., at 67.

conception of the relation between individual rights and governmental power is different. Massey claims that:

> Today we would be unlikely to converse in the same vernacular. We are likely to think of rights as trumping governmental powers. Thus, pursuant to the commerce clause Congress may have the *power* to enact a law forbidding the interstate shipment of Bibles, but its effective ability to do so is trumped by at least two First Amendment *rights*—freedom of speech and the right to free exercise of religion.[33]

Massey provides a brief survey of Supreme Court jurisprudence to document the changing conception of rights vis-a-vis powers.[34] Because of this "shift in perspective over the past two centuries," there is disagreement today over what the Framers originally meant by the Amendment.[35] Modern observers tend to ascribe to the Ninth Amendment merely the first objective, that of preventing the enumeration of rights from implying that the federal government must therefore possess unenumerated powers to invade rights, since this seems to be synonymous with the purpose of the Tenth Amendment, that is, to preserve a separate sphere of state powers. This view, however, ignores the Ninth Amendment's other purpose of ensuring "that the catalog of constitutional rights did not stop with the enumerated rights. As rights no longer were thought of as the absence of governmental powers, but rather as independent restraints upon governmental powers, it was inevitable that the lost function of the Ninth Amendment would again be perceived."[36]

Massey also argues that the interrelationship between the Ninth and Tenth Amendments can be better explained if one realizes that the founding generation viewed rights and powers as complementary, that is, merely two sides of the same coin.[37] In order to secure individual

---

[33] Ibid., at 67, see also ibid., at 79:
Today, ... we perceive rights as uncoupled from governmental powers. Limiting governmental powers may indeed preserve liberty obliquely, but creating enforceable rights is a far more direct way of preventing governmental abuse of individual liberty, given our modern conception that rights 'trump' powers.
[34] See Ibid., at 88–93.
[35] Ibid., at 67.
[36] Ibid., at 94.
[37] See ibid., at 79.

rights against infringement by the federal government, both Amendments were necessary to constrain the government's powers.[38]

> The Ninth would do so by guarding against either the inference of non-existent unenumerated rights or the inference of constructive powers. The Tenth would do so by an explicit statement that the central government possessed only its specified powers. The Tenth Amendment may be seen as performing the principal function of rebutting the Antifederalist concern that the new government might be presumed to possess all powers not specifically retained, while the Ninth Amendment may be seen as primarily addressing the Federalist concern that any enumeration of rights might be viewed as recognition of the existence of implied governmental powers. But both amendments are more complex. The Ninth Amendment also addresses, in part, the fear that rights enumeration would eliminate other rights, and the Tenth also preserves to the people their discretionary authority to allocate (or not) powers to their state governmental agents. The complex and dual nature of the two amendments is deeply rooted in the founding generation's perceptions of the inextricable relationship between rights and powers. Thus, the lack of either amendment would be inimical to the preservation of a zone of individual autonomy where governments could not intrude.[39]

As Massey points out, even if it is admitted that the Ninth Amendment "could be a proper constitutional basis for unenumerated rights[, this] does nothing to solve the enormous problem of selecting *which* unenumerated rights deserve designation as constitutionally protected."[40] Under Massey's theory of "constitutional cy pres doctrine," elaborated in Part III of *Silent Rights*, he lets the states do most of this work for us.[41] It is to this doctrine that we now turn.

III. CONSTITUTIONAL CY PRES

It is largely undisputed, even by single-purpose theorists, that the Ninth Amendment was intended to prevent the enumeration of rights from implying federal powers not explicitly granted in the Constitution.

---

38 See ibid., at 79–80.
39 Ibid., at 78, see also ibid., at 80, 106; note 80, below.
40 Ibid., at 94.
41 Ibid., at 97.

However, "apart from a radical reconstruction of existing doctrine, that intent can no longer be accomplished."[42] As Massey puts it:

> After two centuries of constitutional development, we no longer make any serious attempt to control the extent of the implied powers of Congress. If the Ninth Amendment's original intent was only to provide a rule of construction by which claims of implied congressional power would be rejected, that function has been irretrievably eclipsed by the awesome breadth of contemporary federal power.[43]

In other words, it is now, perhaps regrettably, "impossible" to achieve the Ninth Amendment's original function of limiting the implied powers of the federal government (the limited-powers function). The genie is, irrevocably, out of the bottle.

It is here that Massey borrows from the concept cy pres to announce his "constitutional" cy pres doctrine. Under the doctrine of cy pres, "[w]hen faced with the problem of an expressed testamentary intent that is impossible to achieve, courts seek to effectuate as nearly as possible (cy pres) the testator's intent."[44] Similarly, if we still wish to "preserve the supposed original function of preventing implied federal powers,"[45] a new interpretation must be given to the Ninth Amendment to attempt to limit governmental power.[46] In fact, "To effectuate the original intent as nearly as possible, it is necessary to constrain governmental power by reading the Ninth Amendment as a source of judicially enforceable individual rights that operate to limit the exercise of governmental power."[47] Thus, in today's context, even those who attribute only the limited-powers function to the Ninth Amendment must be willing to accept use of the Amendment to generate unenumerated rights if the amendment is to be at all effective in limiting the exercise and unwarranted expansions of governmental power:

---

[42] Ibid., at 98.

[43] Ibid., at 97.

[44] Ibid.; see also La. Rev. Stat. (https://www.legis.la.gov/legis/laws_Toc.aspx?folder=75& level=Parent), § 9:2331 (relating to cy pres).

[45] *Silent Rights*, p. 97.

[46] See ibid., at 97–98.

[47] Ibid., at 98.

> If the original intention of the amendment was to confine governmental power, the reason for doing so was entirely to preserve rights. We have failed to confine those powers, partly because we now regard the affirmative assertion of rights as the vehicle for controlling the unwarranted assumption of governmental power. Thus, the only way the Ninth Amendment can be applied in our times to accomplish its original purpose is to regard the amendment as an independent source of individual rights.[48]

Massey notes that the second (unenumerated-rights) purpose of the Ninth Amendment (preventing the implication that enumerated rights were the only rights capable of blocking governmental action) is not really impossible, as is the limited-powers purpose, "but the legitimacy of this endeavor is badly eroded by our undue reliance upon an inappropriate and ill-suited vehicle—the due process clause—for the task of providing constitutional recognition to unenumerated rights,"[49] that is, only a strained interpretation of the Due Process Clause allows it to be mined as a source for unenumerated rights. Therefore, "[s]traightforward recognition of the Ninth Amendment as the vehicle for this project would be consistent with the founding intentions as well as provide a more ready answer to those critics of unenumerated rights who loudly question the connection of those rights to the constitutional text."[50]

Massey consoles those who are uncomfortable with using a cy pres-type doctrine to interpret the Constitution by showing that this type of reasoning is not really without precedent, although Massey's jazzy term "constitutional cy pres" appears not to have been used before. For example, the Court gave "an expansive reading to the due process and equal protection clauses of the Fourteenth Amendment in order to accomplish the intended purposes of the privileges and immunities clause"[51] when the *Slaughter-House Cases*[52] decision, and the lack of will to overturn that decision, made it impossible to implement the original purposes of this clause. Other supposed examples of

---

[48] Ibid., at 98–99.
[49] Ibid., at 114.
[50] Ibid.
[51] Ibid., at 99.
[52] *Slaughter-House Cases*, 83 U.S. (16 Wall.) 36 (1873; https://en.wikipedia.org/wiki/Slaughter-House_Cases).

constitutional cy pres include cases involving the Eleventh and Fourteenth Amendments.[53]

But the utility of Massey's appeal to constitutional cy pres is unclear. In a standard cy pres situation where, for some external reason, it is actually impossible to achieve the testator's will, the court attempts to effectuate as nearly as possible the testator's intent. However, if today it is impossible to honestly interpret the Constitution and to give the Ninth Amendment its original reading, this is not due to some impersonal, external cause about which the Court is helpless to do anything. Instead, it is largely the Court's own twisting of the Constitution over the last two centuries, as well as its current unwillingness to return to a traditional reading of the Constitution, that lies behind the current impossibility of limiting the federal government's powers.[54] The government will be equally unable to implement a proposed law or regulation if it is declared by the Court to be unconstitutional on the grounds that (a) it did not have the power (an "impossible" result nowadays), or (b) unenumerated Ninth Amendment rights stand in the way (Massey's cy pres method). Thus, one wonders why the Court would overturn a law based on an unenumerated right, given its unwillingness to do so on the ground that there is a lack of legitimate governmental power to implement the law in the first place. It is not as if Congress or the President would be any less upset at being thwarted by the Court in the second manner as opposed to the first.[55]

Massey appears to believe that the reason for the current impossibility of using the Ninth Amendment to limit directly the federal government's powers is the aforementioned shift in how rights and powers are viewed.[56] He claims that "[w]e have failed to confine [the federal government's] powers, partly because we now regard the affirmative

---

[53] See *Silent Rights*, at 100–01 (discussing *Hans v. Louisiana*, 134 U.S. 1 (1890) (Eleventh Amendment)); ibid., pp. 102–104 (discussing *Brown v. Board of Education*, 347 U.S. 483 (1954) (Fourteenth Amendment)).

[54] See sources cited in note 21, above.

[55] In fact, given that these proposals would seem to be equally unacceptable to the ruling elites, the Framers' view of the complementary nature of rights and powers seems correct, not "sloppy thinking about the methodology of protecting human liberty." *Silent Rights*, at 79. As Massey claims, we now tend to regard the founding generation's view that "the distinction between rights and powers [is] of no consequence." Ibid.

[56] See ibid., at 98–99.

assertion of rights as the vehicle for controlling the unwarranted assumption of governmental power."[57] This claim is unconvincing, however, since Massey does not provide a clear case as to just how the alleged shift in viewing powers and rights has led to a failure to confine the government's usurpation of more and more powers. Massey's account makes decades of misinterpretation of the Constitution by the Court seem downright innocent, an honest mistake caused by simple confusion over the conceptual relation between rights and powers. More conventional, and less benign, explanations for the unfortunate state of the Court's modern jurisprudence seem more appropriate.[58]

Additionally, there are other, less serious, problems with Massey's cy pres approach. First, Massey's theory claims to work even if one adheres only to the limited-powers purpose. In this case, however, it is inexplicable why so much attention is given earlier in the book to proving that the Amendment had a dual purpose. After showing in Part II that the Ninth Amendment had dual purposes,[59] Massey largely omits the second purpose and assumes, for the sake of argument, only the limited-powers purpose.

Second, in Part II, prior to his cy pres analysis in Part III, Massey argues, *without* appealing to cy pres, that one function of the amendment was to generate enforceable, unenumerated rights.[60] It is, therefore, not clear why one needs to use cy pres to turn the limiting-powers function into the unenumerated-rights function. The unenumerated-rights function should stand alone and can apparently be reasonably argued without the aid of constitutional cy pres. In fact, in an earlier incarnation of Massey's theory, the doctrine of constitutional cy pres is not invoked at all.[61] As best I can tell, the primary purpose of constitutional

---

[57] Ibid., at 99.

[58] See sources cited note 21, above.

[59] See *Silent Rights*, at 53.

[60] See ibid., at 93–94.

[61] See Calvin R. Massey, "Antifederalism and the Ninth Amendment," *Chicago-Kent L. Rev.* 64 (1989; https://scholarship.kentlaw.iit.edu/cklawreview/vol64/iss3/13/): 987–1000, reprinted in Barnett, ed., *The Rights Retained by the People*, vol. 2, at 267, 277 (arguing "that individual liberties secured by state constitutions against state invasion were federalized by the ninth amendment," without resort to a "cy pres" theory, without even resorting to the argument that it is "too late" or "impossible" to now use the Ninth Amendment to limit government powers directly); idem, "Federalism and Fundamental Rights: The Ninth Amendment," *Hastings L.J.* 38, no. 2 (1987; https://repository.

cy pres is to convince those who favor the limited-powers function but who shun the unenumerated-rights function that, in today's constitutional landscape, the only way to achieve the limited-powers function is to allow the Ninth Amendment to be construed to protect unenumerated rights. Since Massey sets forth other, independent grounds for the unenumerated-rights function of the Ninth Amendment, it is not clear why constitutional cy pres is given such prominent attention in the book, nor why it is brought up again and again once this point is made. For example, Massey's application of constitutional cy pres to the unenumerated powers purpose of the Ninth Amendment is confusing. If the unenumerated powers purpose is not impossible to attain but has merely had its legitimacy eroded, why is cy pres applicable at all, since the doctrine has to do with impossible or unattainable purposes?

Third, it appears to be quite an ordinary and reasonable interpretive method to try to interpret difficult or ambiguous constitutional provisions in accordance with the provision's original objectives, just as was done in the cases cited by Massey as examples of "de facto" applications of constitutional cy pres. But this technique is just one of dozens of standard canons of interpretation of legislation or constitutional provisions,[62] and it is not clear why a new terminology and doctrine is needed for this one particular technique.[63]

Continuing with the development of his theory, Massey next argues that "there are three major ways in which constitutional cy pres

---

uchastings.edu/hastings_law_journal/vol38/iss2/2/): 305–44, reprinted in Barnett, ed., *The Rights Retained by the People*, vol. 1. Massey's first discussion of constitutional cy pres of which I am aware came after these two articles, in "The Natural Law Component of the Ninth Amendment," *University of Cincinnati L. Rev.* 61 (1992; https://repository. uchastings.edu/faculty_scholarship/1142/): 49–105.

[62] For example, a law should be interpreted, if possible, so as not to produce absurd or unconstitutional results. One explicit canon of interpretation in Louisiana is: "When a law is clear and unambiguous and its application does not lead to absurd consequences, the law shall be applied as written and no further interpretation may be made in search of the intent of the legislature." Louisiana Civil Code, art. 9.

[63] As Ayn Rand explained in her doctrine known as "Rand's Razor": "The requirements of cognition determine the *objective* criteria of conceptualization. They can be summed up best in the form of an epistemological 'razor': *concepts are not to be multiplied beyond necessity*—the corollary of which is: *nor are they to be integrated in disregard of necessity.*" "Rand's Razor" entry, Harry Binswanger, ed., *The Ayn Rand Lexicon: Objectivism from A to Z* (New York: New American Library, 1986; https://perma.cc/Z6QZ-CJW4); see also note 61, above, and accompanying text.

can be applied to the Ninth Amendment."[64] First, the amendment can be used to secure "against federal invasion individual rights having their origin in state constitutions."[65] Massey refers to this as the positive law component of the Ninth Amendment, or "positive Ninth Amendment rights."[66] Second, it can be read as a rule of interpretation in favor of generalizing explicitly enumerated constitutional rights to protect un-enumerated rights that are *consistent with* the enumerated rights. Third, the Ninth Amendment can be used "to locate and enforce rights having their origin in natural law."[67] Massey refers to this third approach as the natural law component of the Ninth Amendment, or "natural Ninth Amendment rights."[68]

The listing of these three proposals reveals further problems with Massey's theory. One is that this list of three ways to apply constitutional cy pres seems arbitrary. Further, it is unclear whether this list is exhaustive: Are there more ways to apply constitutional cy pres? Why, for example, could not his cy pres theory be used to argue that the Fourteenth Amendment and the incorporation doctrine should be reinterpreted to return more power to the states, to better accomplish the original constitutional function of federalism?

Another problem with Massey's constitutional cy pres theory is that the second and third proposals do not need constitutional cy pres to be recommended, and in fact have been advanced by others, without requiring Massey's innovative cy pres theory.[69] Massey himself has previously argued for the first proposal without even mentioning constitutional cy pres.[70] Massey seems to view the second proposal as largely subsumed by, and inferior to, the first and third proposals,[71] and

---

[64] *Silent Rights*, at 106.
[65] Ibid.
[66] Ibid.
[67] Ibid.
[68] Ibid., at 106, 182.
[69] See, *e.g.,* Laurence Tribe & Michael Dorf, *On Reading the Constitution* (Cambridge, Mass.: Harvard University Press, 1991), 54, 111, 110, cited in *Silent Rights*, at 245 n.20 (suggesting the second proposal); Barnett, *Getting Normative* and "The Intersection of Natural Rights and Positive Constitutional Law" (suggesting the third proposal).
[70] See note 61, above, and accompanying text.
[71] See Silent Rights, at 109–10.

thus devotes most of the remainder of the book—chapters 5 and 6—to elaborating positive and natural Ninth Amendment rights.

IV. POSITIVE NINTH AMENDMENT RIGHTS

The most innovative and controversial aspect of Massey's thesis is his view that the Ninth Amendment ought to be read to include judicially enforceable rights having their origin in state constitutions, as well as natural rights. Massey argues that the unenumerated rights contemplated by the Ninth Amendment were of the following two types: "natural" and "civil," or "positive," rights.[72] Natural rights include, in the words of Madison, "those rights which are retained when particular powers are given up to be exercised by the Legislature,"[73] and positive rights are those that "result from the nature of the compact."[74] For example, freedom of speech is a natural right; trial by jury is not a natural right, but results "from the social compact which regulates the action of the community."[75] However, Massey cleverly reasons that:

> … the founding generation did not use the distinction between natural and positive rights as a basis for selection of the rights worthy of constitutional enumeration. The package of rights expressly enumerated in the Constitution contains natural and positive rights. It is a fair inference, then, that the unenumerated rights of the Ninth Amendment were thought to consist of both varieties. Positive rights had their source in state common, constitutional, and statutory law. Natural rights stemmed from Lockean notions concerning the inalienable rights of the people.[76]

Thus, the Ninth Amendment's unenumerated rights contain both positive and natural rights.

As Massey notes, most of the Framers looked "to the states not only as the source of, but as the vehicle for, protection of their cherished liberties."[77] "The inclusion of the Ninth Amendment was, in

---

72 Ibid., at 118.
73 Ibid.
74 Ibid., at 118 n.6.
75 Ibid.
76 Ibid., at 118.
77 Ibid., at 118 n.5.

part, an attempt to be certain that rights protected by state law were not supplanted by federal law simply because they were not enumerated."[78] Since "the Ninth Amendment was as much an enumerated right for purposes of judicial enforcement as any other aspect of the Bill of Rights,"[79] both types of unenumerated rights—natural rights and positive rights having their source in state law—are subject to judicial protection. In other words, any federal law that violates an unenumerated positive (i.e., state law-based) right is subject to being stricken down by federal courts as violative of the Ninth Amendment.[80] In giving effect to the Ninth Amendment, then, the courts are to recognize that one source of the unenumerated rights protected by the Ninth Amendment is state constitutions.

One advantage that Massey sees in this understanding of the Ninth Amendment is that it would give "citizens of the states ... the power, through their state constitutions, to preserve areas of individual life from invasion by the federal Congress in the exercise of its delegated powers."[81] This, in turn, would "prevent Congress from using its delegated powers to contravene an unenumerated federal right contained within a state constitution."[82]

Massey recognizes that his theory "is radical stuff,"[83] and also admits that the implementation of his theory would give rise to "a number of

---

[78] Ibid., at 121–22.

[79] Ibid., at 119.

[80] See ibid., at 124. In support of this theory, Massey discusses the symbiotic relationship between the Ninth and Tenth Amendments:

The Tenth Amendment ... was intended to complement the power limiting aspect of the Ninth Amendment. If the Ninth Amendment was intended in part to prevent the accretion of federal power implied by virtue of the existence of enumerated rights exempt from the reach of federal power, the Tenth Amendment was designed to prevent the accretion of federal power by implication from any other source in the Constitution.... Both Amendments were intended to preserve to the people of the states the sovereign's prerogative to confer powers upon their state governmental agents (recognized in the Tenth Amendment) and to maintain all manner of individual rights secure from governmental invasion (recognized in the Ninth Amendment). An intended medium for doing so, in both cases, was the state constitution.

Ibid., at 106–107.

[81] Ibid., at 124–25.

[82] Ibid., at 124.

[83] Ibid., at 125.

difficulties," none of which, however, "are indisputably insuperable."[84] The first difficulty is whether state-sourced positive rights protected by the Ninth Amendment "are a set of rights antecedent to the federal Constitution and, thus, effectively frozen in time and content, or whether such rights are a dynamic, evolving list that change as sentiment shifts within the states."[85] Massey admits that there is much to be said for the static view, but ultimately concludes, albeit unsatisfactorily and confusingly,[86] that "a dynamic concept holds more promise."[87] (Interestingly, in an earlier version of his theory, Massey *rejected* the dynamic concept in favor of the static, on the grounds that the "more radical" dynamic conception "poses enormous practical problems" that make it "hopelessly unworkable."[88])

The dynamic view leads to further difficulties. For example, can these federalized, state-sourced rights be applied uniformly across the nation? Can such rights, once created, be altered or abolished by the states removing the rights from their constitutions?[89] Massey grapples mightily with these and other thorny problems that his own theory has engendered. On the one hand, positive Ninth Amendment rights could be uniformly applied across the entire nation, what Massey terms the "national concept" of positive Ninth Amendment rights.[90] Where state constitutional norms conflict, however, the Court would have to decide which one to prefer, a job "of considerable difficulty and uncertainty."[91] As for whether these rights are permanent or not, Massey concludes, for reasons that are not made entirely clear, that once such rights are recognized, "they would presumably be immune from elimination as a constitutional right at the hands of the state polity that sowed the seed of the federal right."[92]

On the other hand, it could be acknowledged that, because positive Ninth Amendment rights:

---

[84] Ibid., at 128.
[85] Ibid., at 129.
[86] See ibid., at 128–31.
[87] Ibid., at 131.
[88] Massey, "Federalism and Fundamental Rights," at p. 326 & n.109.
[89] See *Silent Rights*, at 131–32.
[90] Ibid., at 132.
[91] Ibid.
[92] Ibid., at 133.

... have their origin in state constitutions, the substance of federal positive Ninth Amendment rights varies with the differing state constitutions. On this view, Ninth Amendment decisional law would develop a richly variegated pattern. A federal Ninth Amendment right of privacy would be recognized with respect to Californians and Alaskans, for example, because both states explicitly recognize such a right. In contrast, Missouri does not recognize that right. As a result, the citizens of each state would be uniquely and separately entitled to define the nature of their relationship with all of their governmental agents. They would be able to do this immediately (with the state via the state constitution) and ... mediately (with the national government via the Ninth Amendment's incorporation of state constitutional guarantees).[93]

Although this state-specific concept of positive Ninth Amendment rights would effectively result in a different federal constitutional law (with respect to the content of such rights) for each of the fifty states, Massey quite correctly points out that such a scheme is similar to the current federal practice, under *Erie Railroad Co. v. Tompkins*,[94] by which the federal courts in diversity cases follow the law of the appropriate state.[95] Further, under the state-specific concept of positive Ninth Amendment rights, unlike under the uniform national concept, a state could eliminate a positive Ninth Amendment right by eradicating it from its own constitution (although the reason for this difference in treatment is unclear).[96]

One of the most serious disadvantages of the national concept of positive Ninth Amendment rights, Massey points out, is the Fourteenth Amendment and the incorporation doctrine. The Bill of Rights, when enacted in 1791, was intended to bind only the federal government, not the states.[97] Under the incorporation doctrine, most of the guarantees of the Bill of Rights have been held to be applicable to the states by reading them into the Due Process Clause of the Fourteenth Amendment. Although it is unclear whether unenumerated rights

---

[93] Ibid., at 134.

[94] *Erie Railroad Co. v. Tompkins*, 304 U.S. 64 (1938; https://en.wikipedia.org/wiki/Erie_Railroad_Co._v._Tompkins).

[95] See *Silent Rights*, at 134, 136.

[96] See Ibid., at 136.

[97] See U.S. Const. amend. XIV; Berger, *The Fourteenth Amendment and the Bill of Rights; idem, Government by Judiciary; Silent Rights*, at 138.

applicable against the federal government through the Ninth Amendment would be applied against states via the incorporation doctrine, it is possible, and even likely, at least under the national conception of positive Ninth Amendment rights.[98] This would mean that positive Ninth Amendment rights would be applied against states by the federal government. In the state-specific conception of positive Ninth Amendment rights, this would amount to the federal government's forcing the state to abide by its own law. Massey sees little problem with this, since "[s]urely, a requirement that a government abide by its own law is the essence of due process."[99] (So formulated, Massey's conception of due process is bizarre, and the "surely" here is surely misplaced. I fail to see how abrogating federalism and transforming the states from sovereign entities into mere administrative units of the federal government has anything to do with due process.)

Under the national conception, Massey notes, incorporating positive Ninth Amendment rights into the Fourteenth Amendment's Due Process Clause would be likely, and would result in the constitutional rights of one state being used to override contrary rights in other states.[100] For example, suppose Louisiana provides for a constitutional right of the fetus to life, while most other states provide for a constitutional right to abortion. Further suppose that the Supreme Court decides that the right to abortion is a positive Ninth Amendment right.[101] In this case, the local decision of some states with respect to the abortion issue would be used to trump the decisions of other states. For this reason, "[t]he incorporation problem would be experienced most acutely if a national concept of positive Ninth Amendment rights were adopted. The state-specific concept … avoids these problems."[102] In the end, after much vacillating and consideration of the myriad and complicated pros and cons of each of the national and

---

[98] See Silent Rights, at 138–41.
[99] Ibid., at 140.
[100] See ibid., at 142.
[101] My own example, not Massey's.
[102] Silent Rights, at 42.

state-specific concepts of positive Ninth Amendment rights, Massey tentatively comes down in favor of the state-specific conception.[103]

Before further assessing the merits of Massey's theory, I first turn to Massey's discussion, in chapter 6, of natural Ninth Amendment rights.[104]

V. NATURAL NINTH AMENDMENT RIGHTS

After the extensive discussion in chapter 5 concerning positive Ninth Amendment rights, Massey argues in chapter 6 that the Ninth Amendment should also be read to include natural rights, rights that are "prepolitical retained rights."[105] (Although Massey asserts, inexplicably and without support, that "the fact is that there is probably no such thing."[106]) As in his theory of positive Ninth Amendment rights, Massey's theory of natural Ninth Amendment rights also bears some innovative features.

Massey begins by noting that we should not "expunge natural law from the Constitution";[107] however, the attempt to inject natural law into constitutional adjudication must be tempered by the realization that "[n]atural law cannot be forced on an unwilling and disbelieving community."[108] Also, natural Ninth Amendment rights are difficult to determine, and judges and legislators are inherently fallible "as the prophets of natural Ninth Amendment rights."[109] Thus, there should be a role for natural Ninth Amendment rights, but they should given only "contingent" status, so as to provide "an iterative dialogue between the

---

[103] See ibid., at 137; 186. But see ibid., at 138 (stating that "it is not clear that the best concept of the substantive content of positive Ninth Amendment rights is state-specific").

[104] In the remainder of chapter 5, Massey addresses many other issues related to implementing positive Ninth Amendment rights. For example, a state-specific positive Ninth Amendment right could be incompatible with a constitutional right based in federal law. See ibid., at 147–73. In this case, Massey recommends that one right be chosen over another by examining the competing rights' "constitutional fundamentality" and by engaging in a complicated balancing test. See ibid.

[105] Ibid., 187.

[106] Ibid.

[107] Ibid., at 182.

[108] Ibid.

[109] Ibid., at 188.

courts and legislatures whenever the subject is the content or scope of natural Ninth Amendment rights."[110] This iterative dialogue is meant to ensure that there is "a sufficiently widely shared cultural understanding to support recognition"[111] of an asserted natural right.

Massey notes that there are several devices to accomplish this dialogue and to make sure that any declared natural Ninth Amendment rights are merely contingent. For example, in recognizing any natural Ninth Amendment right, the Supreme Court could make it clear that its decision is provisional and subject to congressional override.[112] Alternatively, the Court could weaken its usual rule of stare decisis with respect to natural Ninth Amendment rights so that it is free "to change its mind if it realizes that its earlier recognition of a natural Ninth Amendment right was inappropriate."[113]

As for identifying an asserted right in the first place as a natural Ninth Amendment right, Massey provides various methods that a court could use to make this decision. First, natural rights can be identified from the nature of rights already guaranteed (e.g., locating the right to privacy in the penumbra of other enumerated rights).[114] Second, a presumption of validity can be given to any asserted right that is consistent with rights enumerated in the Constitution.[115] The right would be recognized unless the government could overcome the presumption.[116] Finally, to recognize a natural Ninth Amendment right, "[i]n addition to demanding consistency with enumerated rights and some logical nexus with the themes that inform the enumerated rights, we might also require that any claimed natural Ninth Amendment right be consistent with our dynamic history and traditions."[117]

Whereas Massey is not quite sure whether state-specific positive Ninth Amendment rights would be applicable to the states via the incorporation doctrine,[118] he is not so hesitant regarding natural Ninth

---

[110] Ibid.; see also ibid., at 182.
[111] Ibid., at 193; see also ibid., at 187.
[112] See ibid., at 189.
[113] Ibid.
[114] See ibid., at 193.
[115] See ibid.
[116] Ibid., 194–95.
[117] Ibid., pp. 200-01.
[118] See ibid., at 186.

Amendment rights.[119] Since natural rights are "prepolitical entitlements," they are necessarily "fundamental" in the sense relevant to the Fourteenth Amendment.[120] Thus, any recognized natural Ninth Amendment rights presumably would be applicable against the states by the incorporation doctrine, since the Due Process Clause of the Fourteenth Amendment is seen as incorporating rights of sufficient fundamentality.[121]

VI. MASSEY'S NINTH AMENDMENT

I have mentioned above some problems with Massey's constitutional cy pres theory.[122] At this point, it is appropriate to address further weaknesses in Massey's theory. Most seriously, Massey's argument that the Ninth Amendment actually *does* incorporate state-sourced rights is unconvincing.[123] The contention seems to be pulled out of thin air, not rooted in the text or history of the Constitution. The Ninth Amendment does not *state* this, for example, and even if it were understood in 1791 to protect the set of natural rights, some of which happened to also be enumerated at the time in state constitutions, there is no reason to think that *new* positive rights *subsequently* added to various state constitutions were to be included in the original set of natural rights contemplated by the Ninth Amendment.

Furthermore, regardless of the merits of Massey's reasoning in support of the thesis that the Ninth Amendment protects state-sourced unenumerated rights, it is not clear how this reasoning is strengthened by appeal to the constitutional cy pres doctrine.[124] Both his theories of

---

[119] See ibid.
[120] Ibid.
[121] See ibid.
[122] See text accompanying notes 44–71, above.
[123] Thomas McAffee has concluded that:
Massey's claim that the Ninth Amendment secures state-created rights as affirmative limitations on federal power had not been advanced by a single commentator between 1789 and the 1980s. This reading, moreover, presents an incoherent amalgamation of diametrically opposed readings of the text and history of the Ninth Amendment.
Thomas B. McAffee, "Federalism and the Protection of Rights: The Modern Ninth Amendment's Spreading Confusion," *Brigham Young U. L. Rev.* 1996, no. 2 (1996; https://digitalcommons.law.byu.edu/lawreview/vol1996/iss2/3/): 351–88, p. 374.
[124] See note 61, above, and accompanying text.

natural and positive Ninth Amendment rights seem to be supported by quite respectable (though ultimately unpersuasive) reasoning that is independent of cy pres-type reasoning. Indeed, Massey's constitutional cy pres doctrine seems to be more of an afterthought, a sophisticated justification or overarching framework added after the fact—to his original insight that the Ninth Amendment might be read to directly incorporate state-sourced rights.

Additionally, even if we accept Massey's contention that the Ninth Amendment ought to incorporate state-sourced rights, why would this include only rights explicitly enumerated in state constitutions? As in the federal system, some rights might be protected by the states in other ways—by decisions of their state supreme courts, by legislation, by common law, or even by mere state practice.[125] In Louisiana, for example, a civil-law jurisdiction,[126] its Civil Code, according to the civilian tradition, is treated more like a constitution than like mere legislation.[127] Massey's focus on state constitutions does avoid the seemingly insurmountable problems that his theory would face if all of these potential state sources of rights were to be considered, but the focus seems arbitrary, nonetheless.

Massey's theory is also worrisome because it gives natural rights relatively short shrift in comparison to positive rights; Massey's discussion of the latter is much longer than the former.[128] Also, unlike positive Ninth Amendment rights, which would presumably be very large in number due to the potentially unlimited number of rights provided in state constitutions, Massey's natural Ninth Amendment rights would likely be very few in number.[129] Natural Ninth Amendment rights are granted reluctantly, and have only contingent status.[130] Massey does not

---

[125] Indeed, as Massey himself points out, "Positive rights had their source in state common, constitutional, and statutory law." *Silent Rights*, at 118.

[126] Puerto Rico is also a civil-law jurisdiction, although it is not, as of this writing, a state.

[127] In civil-law systems, a code is more like a constitution, which changes only rarely, relative to legislation. See Jean Louis Bergel, "Principal Features and Methods of Codification," *La. L. Rev.* 48, no. 5 (May 1988; https://digitalcommons.law.lsu.edu/lalrev/vol48/iss5/3/): 1073–1097, p. 1079; Vernon Palmer, "The Death of a Code—The Birth of a Digest," *Tul. L. Rev.* 63, no. 2 (December 1988): 221–64, p. 235.

[128] See *Silent Rights*, at 218.

[129] See ibid.

[130] Query: Under this approach, would previously recognized unenumerated rights suddenly become merely contingent?

similarly insist that the Court's recognition of *positive* Ninth Amendment rights be merely contingent. Further, Massey provides no method for resolving conflicts between incompatible natural and positive Ninth Amendment rights, and, indeed, does not even allude to the possibility of such a conflict. This is inexplicable, given Massey's extended discussions of how to resolve potential incompatibilities between Ninth Amendment rights and other (federal) constitutional rights.[131]

Consider, for example, the following conflict between natural and positive rights. Assume that the original understanding of Ninth Amendment rights is largely consistent with the libertarian conception of rights as being strictly negative rights, that is, rights against aggression, the initiation of force.[132] In this case, one could very well argue that there is a natural Ninth Amendment right against having one's property forcibly taken by the government and redistributed as welfare benefits to others. Now suppose that California enshrines various welfare rights in its constitution—a right to education, to housing, to a minimum income, and the like (in contravention to natural law). Under Massey's doctrine of positive Ninth Amendment rights, this could also result in a *federal* Ninth Amendment right to these things, at least for California citizens. This would be a disastrous result, if only because an illegitimate conception of rights, formerly localized to California—and such localization of policy is one of the benefits of federalism—is now imposed on the federal government.

Even worse, under the national concept of positive Ninth Amendment rights, the federal government (acting through its agent, the Supreme Court) could adopt this welfare right as a positive Ninth Amendment right of national scope, and force *all* the states to provide education and welfare rights, an even worse attack on the principle of federalism and an illegitimate result to boot (since there are, in truth, no such welfare rights). The only possible saving grace to this situation would be if the courts were to find that the natural Ninth Amendment right to not have one's property expropriated and redistributed to others somehow outweighed the positive Ninth Amendment welfare right. But

---

[131] See, e.g., *Silent Rights*, at 142–73, 193–94.

[132] See note 4, above (discussing the libertarian conception of rights and Rothbard's definition of aggression).

Massey does not address how such potential conflicts between natural and positive Ninth Amendment rights would be resolved; in any event, it is contrary to principles of federalism to allow the federal government to resolve such conflicts. Additionally, lest it be thought that my interpretation that Massey's theory would yield positive rights is paranoid, it should be noted that Massey himself explicitly states that the Ninth Amendment, when interpreted under today's conceptions of rights, might require non-negative rights such as welfare rights.[133]

In my view, if the Ninth Amendment is to be judicially enforceable, it is unnecessary to use a cy pres-type theory or to include positive rights in the Ninth Amendment. Rather, it ought to be recognized that the Ninth Amendment essentially protects unenumerated natural rights as long as the natural rights can be identified with sufficient certainty. By now, this reading of the Ninth Amendment has been adequately established.[134] For example, as Randy Barnett has pointed out, even if the Framers' view of natural rights was incorrect—even if there are no natural rights—it is relevant that the *Framers* believed in natural rights and embodied a certain conception of these rights in the Constitution. Thus, anyone who "allow[s] a role for [the] Framers' intent" and who "view[s] the Constitution as a kind of contract entered into at the time of ratification" should "make some effort to discern and protect at least the kinds of rights the Framers had in mind when they ratified the Ninth Amendment."[135]

---

[133] See *Silent Rights*, at 128.

[134] See, e.g., sources cited at note 7, above. For an (unconvincing) opposing view, see Raoul Berger, "The Ninth Amendment, As Perceived by Randy Barnett," *Northwestern U. L. Rev.* 88, no. 4 (1994): 1508–36.

[135] Randy E. Barnett, "Introduction: James Madison's Ninth Amendment," in Barnett, ed., *The Rights Retained by the People*, vol. 1, at 1, 33; see also note 7, above (discussing Randy Barnett's "constitutional legitimacy" argument for judicial enforcement of unenumerated Ninth Amendment rights). There is another argument in favor of protecting rights unenumerated by the Ninth Amendment. The Constitution was ratified in 1789 only on the understanding that a bill of rights would be added. However, since the Bill of Rights was not completed and adopted until 1791, at the time of ratification, the rights that were to be added by a bill of rights were unspecified. Since these rights were unspecified, but the Constitution was initially conceived as being limited by whatever these rights were, merely enumerating some of these rights at a later time in the Bill of Rights does not necessarily exhaust all the background rights that *could have been* enumerated in the Bill of Rights (i.e., there is no guarantee that the Bill of Rights captured all the enumerated rights on which the Constitution's ratification was dependent). Thus, for the ratification to be effective and

In *identifying* what these rights are, the various techniques proposed by Massey, Barnett, and others are useful. It seems reasonable that one way to discover the content of the natural rights included within the scope of the Ninth Amendment would be to examine the rights guaranteed by state constitutions, especially since, as Massey points out, protection of natural rights was to be left primarily to the states.[136] However, in this view, state-sourced rights are merely *evidence* of which natural rights are protected by the Ninth Amendment. Whether these rights are dynamic and ever-evolving and growing, as Massey maintains,[137] or static is another question, but I am unconvinced by Massey's argument that both positive and natural Ninth Amendment rights should be envisioned as changing with the times. It is a written constitution that we are interpreting, after all.

Further, given that the modern conception of rights and legitimate state power is thoroughly statist, the Framers' conception of rights is vastly preferable, at least for anyone who favors individual rights. For example, as mentioned above, the dynamic view of unenumerated rights might result in the cross-pollination and thus spreading of (illegitimate) welfare-type rights.[138] Interpreting the Constitution in accordance with its original, that is, static, understanding is therefore preferable to reading socialist rights into it, as it is a more honest interpretation and also more likely to be in accord with individual rights.

Finally, there is another serious weakness in Massey's theory. As Massey readily acknowledges, one of the original purposes of the Constitution was federalism, the sovereignty of each state.[139] Indeed, one of

---

for the Constitution to have validity, the rights enumerated in the Bill of Rights cannot be seen as an exhaustive list. For a complementary argument, see Randy E. Barnett, "Reconceiving the Ninth Amendment," *Cornell L. Rev.* 74, no. 1 (1988; www.randybarnett.com/pre-2000): 1–42, p. 29 ("Only a handful of the many rights proposed by state ratification conventions were eventually incorporated in the Bill of Rights. The Ninth Amendment was offered precisely to 'compensate' these critics for the absence of an extended list of rights.").

136 See *Silent Rights*, at 56.
137 See text accompanying notes 83–88, above.
138 See text accompanying notes 132–133, above.
139 See *Silent Rights*, at 56; see also Raoul Berger, *Federalism: The Founders' Design* (Norman, Okla.: University of Oklahoma Press, 1987); Bork, *The Tempting of America*, at 52–53; John C. Calhoun, *Union and Liberty: The Political Philosophy of John C. Calhoun*, Ross M. Lence, ed. (Indianapolis, Ind.: Liberty Fund, 1992) (discussing the advantages of federalism); Paul K. Conkin, *Self-Evident Truths: Being a Discourse on the Origins &*

Massey's reasons to support constitutional cy pres and positive Ninth Amendment rights is to help limit the powers (though indirectly, by trumping these powers with Ninth Amendment rights) that the federal government has illegitimately usurped over the years.[140] Yet there can be little doubt that, in this age of an untrustworthy federal government and Supreme Court, expanding the Court's jurisdiction to declare rights would result in the further weakening of federalism.[141]

Massey admits that Ninth Amendment rights would likely be applied to the states by the incorporation doctrine.[142] But the incorporation doctrine is one reason why Massey's theory should be rejected, for as long as that is in place, further federal judicial activism only imperils our rights, leading to further erosion of federalism by making state policy subject to federal control. One would think that Massey, since he is obviously willing to urge an innovative interpretation of the Ninth Amendment, would have used his constitutional cy pres doctrine, or at least ordinary reasoning, to build a rejection of the incorporation doctrine into his theory. Federalism, in the American constitutional system, is essential to the protection of individual rights, both enumerated and unenumerated ones.[143] The greatest violator of individual rights, even if measured by such a simple parameter as the overall level of taxation, is the federal leviathan; in comparison, the states are minarchist utopias. Although Massey's proposal is intended to increase the protection of individual rights, it involves ceding more power to the federal government to control and oversee the states and to define what rights are to apply at which level of government.[144] As Ludwig von Mises wisely observed in a related context, "No socialist author ever gave a thought

---

Development of the First Principles of American Government—Popular Sovereignty, Natural Rights, and Balance & Separation of Powers (Bloomington, Ind.: Indiana Univ. Press, 1974); Martin H. Redish, *The Constitution as Political Structure* (New York: Oxford University Press, USA, 1995); For Massey's own views of the importance of federalism, see Massey, "Federalism and Fundamental Rights."

140 See, e.g., notes 81–82, above, and accompanying text.

141 See, e.g., Marshall L. DeRosa, *The Ninth Amendment and the Politics of Creative Jurisprudence: Disparaging the Fundamental Right of Popular Control* (New Brunswick, N.J.: Transaction, 1996).

142 See text accompanying notes 97–103, 118–121, above.

143 See note 140, above.

144 See note 94, above, and accompanying text; see also McAffee, "Federalism and the Protection of Rights," at 386:

to the possibility that the abstract entity which he wants to vest with unlimited power—whether it is called humanity, society, nation, state, or government—could act in a way of which he himself disapproves."[145] In other words, the central government cannot be trusted to safely exercise any extra power that is given to it, even if the purpose of the power is ostensibly to protect rights. Accordingly, as Paul Conkin has noted, "Ironically, the tremendous expansion of federal power in all areas, including the expanded role in protecting individual rights, has finally transformed the often fantastic eighteenth-century fears of a federal leviathan into prophetic admonitions."[146] Handing more power to the federal government, as Massey's theory unfortunately does, would ill-serve the original understanding and purpose of the Ninth Amendment.

Unlike the Supreme Court, most modern constitutional scholars, and other intellectuals, Massey takes the Ninth Amendment seriously. He has written a provocative study of the Ninth Amendment, but, due to the problems with Massey's thesis detailed above, I believe a better approach to the Ninth Amendment may be found in the writings of other scholars, such as Randy Barnett[147] and Marshall DeRosa.[148]

VII. CONCLUSION: CONSTITUTIONAL INTERPRETATION OR POLITICAL THEORY?

If Massey is correct that it is too late to limit the federal government to its proper powers, it is unlikely that the Court will try to, or even want to, accomplish the same thing by trumping those powers with Ninth Amendment rights. The truth is, and I doubt Massey would demur, that Massey's theory stands no realistic chance of being adopted by the

---

Recognizing that the Supremacy Clause and structural analysis cannot do all of the work required to avoid unwelcome outcomes of his states' rights thesis, Massey eventually simply delegates to the Supreme Court the task of preventing potential state abuses that such a guarantee might permit.

[145] Ludwig von Mises, *Human Action: A Treatise on Economics*, Scholar's ed. (Auburn, Ala.: Mises Institute, 1998; https://mises.org/library/human-action-0), p. 692.

[146] Conkin, *Self-Evident Truths*, at 141.

[147] See sources cited note 7, above.

[148] See DeRosa, *The Ninth Amendment and the Politics of Creative Jurisprudence.*

Supreme Court. Most likely, from the Court's point of view, it is too radical, too academic, and at least has the potential of imposing some limits on federal power. So Massey's theory is not *really* a theory of how the Constitution should be interpreted. What, then, is it? In truth, it is a proposal to amend the Constitution.

There are, however, better and simpler alternatives available— alternatives that strengthen, rather than weaken, federalism. One such alternative is that of Marshall DeRosa, as explained in his recent book *The Ninth Amendment and the Politics of Creative Jurisprudence*.[149] DeRosa proposes an ingenious constitutional amendment, which would read as follows:

> When a national majority of each State's chief judicial official declares a decision by the U.S. Supreme Court to be inconsistent with the U.S. Constitution, the said decision shall thereby be negated and precedent restored. The States' designated chief judicial officers shall convey their declarations to the U.S. Solicitor General, who in turn will notify the Chief Justice of the U.S. Supreme Court to take appropriate measures consistent with this amendment.[150]

As DeRosa explains, this would allow controversial Supreme Court decisions to be overturned "more expeditiously and competently" than at present.[151] The states would not have to "resort[] to a cumbersome amendment process or the national congress that is significantly detached from states' interests."[152] Also, the amendment would have a chilling effect on the Supreme Court, making it more reluctant to issue unreasoned or unconstitutional decisions,[153] just as lower courts are reluctant to issue decisions that may be overturned by higher courts. In essence, this amendment would "heighten popular control

---

[149] Ibid.

[150] Ibid., at 192. This proposed amendment is preferable to an amendment recently suggested by Robert Bork, which would have little beneficial effect on federalism. See Robert H. Bork, *Slouching Towards Gomorrah: Modern Liberalism and American Decline* (New York: ReganBooks, 1996), 117 (proposing a constitutional amendment to make "any federal or state court decision subject to being overruled by a majority vote of each House of Congress.").

[151] DeRosa, *The Ninth Amendment and the Politics of Creative Jurisprudence*, at 192.

[152] Ibid., at 193.

[153] See ibid.

over unenumerated rights jurisprudence, and to that extent a significant portion of originalism would be recovered."[154]

As for other potentially useful amendments, unfortunately, Sobran's
proposed amendment, "The Constitution shall not be circumvented,"
would be easily circumvented, as Sobran recognized.[155] However, Sobran
proposes another "amendment that would actually restrain the federal
government. It would read: 'Any state may, by an act of its legislature,
secede from the United States.'"[156] Either Sobran's or DeRosa's proposed
amendment (or both) would straightforwardly enhance federalism and
increase the likelihood that our individual rights would be respected.[157]

And while we're at it, let us amend the Constitution to repeal the
incorporation doctrine. We also might as well eliminate judicial supremacy (sometimes confusingly referred to as "judicial review"), the idea that
the Supreme Court is the sole and final arbiter of the Constitution and
constitutionality. Instead, the original scheme of separation of powers
required concurrent review, sometimes referred to as Jefferson's tripar-
tite theory of constitutionalism.[158] Under concurrent review, each branch
(executive, legislative, judicial) has an equal right to determine the constitutionality of government action. But enough of making my wish list.
Any one of these changes would be enough to warm the heart of a true
constitutionalist.[159]

---

[154] Ibid., at 194.

[155] Sobran, "Constitutional Legerdemain," at 12.

[156] Ibid.

[157] The proposed amendments are also consistent with Jefferson's "belief that the states
were the prime interpeters of the federal compact." Conkin, *Self-Evident Truths*, at 72.

[158] See ibid., at 69–73; David N. Mayer, *The Constitutional Thought of Thomas Jefferson*
(Charlottesville, Va.: Univ of Virginia Press, 1994), 131, 259, 263, 269–72; William J. Quirk
& R. Randall Bridwell, *Judicial Dictatorship* (New Brunswick, N.J.: Transaction, 1995), pp.
xiv, 10–11, 13.

[159] I should reiterate that, as I said at the beginning, written constitutions and statutes,
such as the US Constitution, have only instrumental value for libertarians; they are useful
only insofar as they happen to embody some more or less liberty-friendly provisions or
can be used in state courts to limit the application of unjust state laws. That is, we should
only be "constitutionalists" insofar as insisting that the state should adhere to constitutional
limitations can be useful in restraining state power.

22

The Undeniable Morality of Capitalism

Originally published in 1994, this is one of my first scholarly articles.[*]
As noted in "How I Became a Libertarian" (ch. 1), I sent this article to Hoppe
and soon after met him and others at the Mises Institute. I have made only
minimal revisions to the original piece, except for deleting the initial section
"Criticisms," since, in retrospect, these criticisms now seem silly and trivial.[†]

[*] Stephan Kinsella, "The Undeniable Morality of Capitalism," *St. Mary's L. J.* 25, no. 4 (1994): 1419–47, a review essay of Hans-Hermann Hoppe, *The Economics and Ethics of Private Property* (Boston/Dordrecht/London, Kluwer Academic Publishers, 1993). In this chapter I will cite to the most recent edition, *The Economics and Ethics of Private Property: Studies in Political Economy and Philosophy* (Auburn, Ala.: Mises Institute, 2006 [1993]; www.hanshoppe.com/eepp); hereinafter "*EEPP.*"

I. INTRODUCTION

If Professor Hans-Hermann Hoppe's books and articles would come already-underlined and highlighted, it would save readers a lot of time. Or at least each book should come with a free pen attached. For when I follow my usual habit of underlining, circling, checking, starring, or highlighting important insights in the books I read, I find that my copies of Hoppe's books start to look as if a two-year-old with a crayon had gotten hold of them.

In 1989, Hoppe published *A Theory of Socialism and Capitalism*, in my eyes one of the most important books of the decade for its analysis of capitalism, socialism, and property rights, focus on scarcity in property and economic theory, and its revolutionary "argumentation ethic" defense of individual rights.[1] Over the past few years, Hoppe has produced a significant assortment of articles elaborating on his argumentation ethic and the epistemology that underlies it, as well as on his impressive economic writings. His new book, *The Economics and Ethics of Private Property*, is a collection of almost all of these related writings (not counting a large number of writings published previously in German). This may come as a disappointment to some, who, like me, were expecting a new treatise, building upon the prior one. The book is significant, nonetheless, for drawing together material previously published in such varied sources as *Liberty* magazine, the

---

† In the original article, I wrote that it was unfortunate that Hoppe's article "In Defense of Extreme Rationalism" was not included in *EEPP*. See Hoppe, "In Defense of Extreme Rationalism: Thoughts on Donald McCloskey's *The Rhetoric of Economics*," *Rev. Austrian Econ.* 3, no. 1 (1989; https://mises.org/library/defense-extreme-rationalism-thoughts-donald-mccloskys-rhetoric-economics): 179–214. This has now been remedied, as this article was later published in Hans-Hermann Hoppe, *The Great Fiction: Property, Economy, Society, and the Politics of Decline* (Second Expanded Edition, Mises Institute, 2021; www.hanshoppe.com/tgf).

---

1 See "The Ethical Justification of Capitalism and Why Socialism Is Morally Indefensible," chap. 7 in Hans-Hermann Hoppe, *A Theory of Socialism and Capitalism: Economics, Politics, and Ethics* (Auburn, Ala.: Mises Institute, 2010 [1989]; www.hanshoppe.com/tsc). Argumentation ethics is discussed in "Dialogical Arguments for Libertarian Rights" (ch. 6) and "Defending Argumentation Ethics" (ch. 7).

Journal of Libertarian Studies, the *Review of Austrian Economics, Ratio*, and others.[2]

---

[2] Hoppe's article, "The Ultimate Justification of the Private Property Ethic," *Liberty* 2, no. 1 (Sept. 1988; https://perma.cc/6TYM-BJRZ): 20–22 (included as chap. 13 of *EEPP*), was the subject of the symposium, "Breakthrough or Buncombe," *Liberty* 2, no. 2 (Nov. 1988; https://perma.cc/A5UU-P64A): 44–53, containing discussion of Hoppe's argumentation ethics by several libertarian theorists, many critical, and Hoppe's reply, "Utilitarians and Randians *vs* Reason" (53–54). This reply is included in "Appendix: Four Critical Replies" in *EEPP*; see also subsequent response to critics in *idem*, "PFP163 | Hans Hermann Hoppe, 'On The Ethics of Argumentation' (PFS 2016)," *The Property and Freedom Podcast*, ep. 163 (June 30, 2022).

In addition to the response to the *Liberty* symposium, "Appendix: Four Critical Replies" also includes responses to David Osterfeld, Loren Lomasky, and David Conway in other publications. See David Osterfeld, "Comment on Hoppe," *Austrian Economics Newsletter* 9, no. 3 (Spring/Summer 1988; https://perma.cc/4229-ZR7P): 9–10 (also including Hoppe's reply, "Demonstrated Preference and Private Property: Reply to Professor Osterfeld," pp. 10–12, and Sheldon Richman, "Comment on Osterfeld," p. 10). David Conway's review of Hoppe, *A Theory of Socialism and Capitalism* (pp. 11–14) and Hoppe's response, "On the Indefensibility of Welfare Rights: A Comment on Conway" (pp. 14–16), appeared in *Austrian Economics Newsletter* 11, no. 1 (Winter/Spring 1990; https://perma.cc/X2PR-H8BW). Loren Lomasky's criticism was "The Argument from Mere Argument," *Liberty* 3, no. 1 (Sept. 1989; https://perma.cc/38XS-ZDEL): 55–57. Hoppe's reply to Lomasky was "Intimidation by Argument—Once Again," *Liberty* 3, no. 2 (Nov. 1989; https://perma.cc/4382-RKSQ): 37–39, republished as "Intimidation by Argument," section III in "Appendix: Four Critical Replies." Rothbard's humorous response to Lomasky was "Hoppephobia," originally published in *Liberty* 3, no. 4 (March 1990; https://perma.cc/JT7K-YTUJ): 11–12, reprinted at *LewRockwell.com* (Oct. 4, 2014; https://perma.cc/5HH6-2P78. See also the discussion re Lomasky and others in "Defending Argumentation Ethics" (ch. 7), at n.4 *et pass.*, including excerpts from Hoppe's and Rothbard's responses to Lomasky's critique.

For more on argumentation ethics, see Kinsella, "Argumentation Ethics and Liberty: A Concise Guide," *StephanKinsella.com* (May 27, 2011); *idem*, "Hoppe's Argumentation Ethics and Its Critics," *StephanKinsella.com* (Aug. 11, 2015).

Regarding Yeager—in my view, he is wrong about several topics. First, he is wrong about Hoppe's argumentation ethics; see also "Defending Argumentation Ethics" (ch. 7), n.5. Also, he is wrong about self-ownership; see "How We Come to Own Ourselves" (ch. 4), n.1. And he is wrong about knowledge and the calculation problem. On this latter issue, see "Legislation and the Discovery of Law in a Free Society" (ch. 13), at n.66, and references in Kinsella, "The Great Mises-Hayek Dehomogenization/Economic Calculation Debate," *StephanKinsella.com* (Feb. 8, 2016), including Leland B. Yeager, "Mises and Hayek and Calculation and Knowledge," *Rev. Austrian Econ.* 7, no. 2 (1994; https://mises.org/library/mises-and-hayek-and-calculation-and-knowledge): 93–109; Joseph Salerno, "Reply to Leland B. Yeager on Mises and Hayek on Calculation and Knowledge," *Rev. Austrian Econ.* 7, no. 2 (1994; https://mises.org/library/reply-leland-b-yeager-mises-and-hayek-calculation-and-knowledge): 111–25, and Yeager, "Calculation and Knowledge: Let's Write *Finis*," *Rev. Austrian Econ.* 10, no. 1 (1997; https://mises.org/library/calculation-and-knowledge-lets-write-finis): 133–36.

II. INDIVIDUAL RIGHTS

A. The Reception of Hoppe's Ideas

This book is fascinating, stimulating, provocative, and ground-break-ing. In the September 1988 issue of *Liberty*, Hoppe published "The Ultimate Justification of the Private Property Ethic." This article gave rise to a symposium, "Breakthrough or Buncombe?", published in the November 1988 issue of *Liberty*, containing the critical comments of ten commentators, including Murray Rothbard, Tibor Machan, David Friedman, Leland Yeager, David Gordon, Douglas Rasmussen, David Ramsay Steele, Timothy Virkkala, and others.

To my surprise, almost all of these libertarian commentators were unimpressed by, if not downright hostile to, Hoppe's argument. Only Murray Rothbard gave Hoppe's thesis wholehearted endorsement and recognized its validity and significance:

> In a dazzling breakthrough for political philosophy in general and for libertarianism in particular, he has managed to transcend the famous is/ought, fact/value dichotomy that has plagued philosophy since the days of the scholastics, and that had brought modern libertarianism into a tiresome deadlock. Not only that: Hans Hoppe has managed to establish the case for anarcho-capitalist-Lockean rights in an unprecedentedly hard-core manner, one that makes my own natural law/natural rights position seem almost wimpy in comparison.[3]

Why Hoppe's ideas, which are such an important advance in politi-cal and libertarian thought, have failed to cause more excitement or gain more adherents than they have is baffling, but the best solution to this is the publication of further elaborations and defenses contained in Hoppe's newest book.

The book is divided into two parts, "Economics" and "Philosophy." Because *Part Two: Philosophy* contains Hoppe's most important ideas—his defense of individual rights—I will discuss this part first. The six chapters (chapters 6 through 11) in Part Two plus the "Four Critical Replies" in the Appendix present Hoppe's argumentation ethic and its

---

[3] Rothbard, "Beyond Is and Ought," p. 44.

underlying epistemology—often repeatedly and redundantly, because the chapters were first published as independent papers, and little editing, except in chapter 6, has been done to integrate them or to delete redundancies.

B. Argumentation Ethics

Hoppe's "argumentation ethics" theory, briefly stated, starts by noting that all truths, including ethics and normative statements, must be discoverable through the process of argumentation. This "a priori of communication and argumentation" is undeniable, as one would have to contradict oneself in using argument to deny this. Therefore, whatever facts or norms are postulated while engaging in argumentation cannot be contradicted by any proposed fact or norms.[4] As Hoppe writes:

> In analyzing any actual norm proposal reason's task is merely confined to analyzing whether or not it is logically consistent with the very ethics which the proponent must presuppose as valid insofar as he is able to make his proposal at all.[5]

In argumentation, the validity of certain implications cannot be disputed. For example, the universalization principle, as formulated in the Golden Rule of ethics or in the Kantian Categorical Imperative, states:

> … that only those norms can be justified that can be formulated as general principles which without exception are valid for everyone. Indeed, as it is implied in argumentation that everyone who can understand an argument must in principle be able to be convinced by it simply because of its argumentative force, the universalization principle of ethics can now be understood and explained in the wider a priori of communication and argumentation.[6]

---

[4] *EEPP*, pp. 314–15

[5] Ibid., p. 315.

[6] Ibid., p. 316. On universalizability, see Kinsella, "The problem of particularistic ethics or, why everyone really has to admit the validity of the universalizability principle," *StephanKinsella.com* (Nov. 10, 2011); "What Libertarianism Is" (ch. 2), at n.23; "How We Come to Own Ourselves" (ch. 4), n.15; "A Libertarian Theory of Punishment and Rights" (ch. 5), Part III.D.1; "Dialogical Arguments for Libertarian Rights" (ch. 6), at n.43; and "Defending Argumentation Ethics" (ch. 7), the section "Universalizability."

In other words, anyone who argues accepts the validity of the universalization principle implicitly.

"The universalization principle only provides one with a *purely formal* criterion for morality.... However, there are *other positive norms* implied in argumentation apart from" this principle.[7] First Hoppe points out three interrelated facts: "First, that argumentation is not only a cognitive but a practical affair. Second, that argumentation, as a form of action, implies the use of the scarce resource of one's body. And third, that argumentation is a conflict-free way of interacting."[8]

Therefore, anyone engaging in argumentation (or, indeed, any discourse at all, even with oneself) must accept the presupposed right of self-ownership of all listeners and even potential listeners: for otherwise the listener would not be able to consider freely and accept or reject the proposed argument, which is undeniably a goal of argumentation. "It is only as long as there is at least an implicit recognition of each individual's property right in his or her own body that argumentation can take place."[9] The libertarian nonaggression principle—"nobody has the right to uninvitedly aggress against the body of any other person and thus delimit or restrict anyone's control over his own body"—is implied in the concept of argumentative justification, because justifying *means* justifying without having to rely on coercion.

The concomitant right to homestead private property is also presupposed by anyone engaging in argumentation: since the use of natural resources, i.e., property rights in land, food, water, etc., is absolutely necessary for any listener to survive and be able to participate in an argument, and since homesteading unowned property is the only objective and conflict-free way to assign property rights, all arguers must also presuppose the validity of the homesteading of unowned property, the Lockean "mixing of labor" with scarce resources, for otherwise argumentation

---

[7] Ibid., pp. 316 & 317 (emphasis added).
[8] Ibid., p. 317.
[9] Ibid.

could not occur.[10] And, of course, the right to self-ownership plus the right to homestead are the bases of laissez-faire capitalism.[11]

C. Estoppel and Directions for Further Inquiry

Professor Hoppe's discovery of such a rock-solid defense of individual rights is a profoundly important achievement. Because so many of Hoppe's insights deserve further exploration and development, one welcomes future writing by Hoppe and by others building upon his work.[12]

For example, in my own article, "Estoppel: A New Justification for Individual Rights,"[13] I draw on Hoppe's work—especially his application of the principle of universalizability to the activity of argumentation—in making another argumentation-based or discourse-based defense of individual rights. Hoppe's main argument is that any person who argues must accept certain principles that must be implicitly acknowledged by any person engaged in the very activity of arguing, and that these principles imply the rights of self-ownership and homesteading, as they are incompatible with any other—"socialist"—ethic. In my estoppel theory, I argue that the existence of rights can be demonstrated by looking at the consistency of the arguments made by a rights violator at the moment when he is about to be punished for the rights violation.

Since what is important about rights is that they are (legitimately) *enforceable*, if an alleged rights-violator is unable to meaningfully object to his punishment or, indeed, if he implicitly consents to his punishment, then this is enough to justify the existence of the rights claimed. And it is indeed true that if *A* initiates violence against *B*, *A*

---

[10] Ibid., pp. 319–22. Hoppe makes it clear that, although he agrees with Locke's theory of homesteading by mixing one's labor with resources, he believes the Lockean proviso—Locke's limitation that the right to homestead extends only when "enough and as good" is left for others—is false and must be rejected (contra Lomasky). Ibid., p. 410.

[11] For further elaboration of these issues, see "What Libertarianism Is" (ch. 2) and "How We Come to Own Ourselves" (ch. 4).

[12] For subsequent discussion of argumentation ethics since the publication of the original article in 1994, see Kinsella, "Argumentation Ethics and Liberty: A Concise Guide" and *idem*, "Hoppe's Argumentation Ethics and Its Critics."

[13] Kinsella, "Estoppel: A New Justification for Individual Rights," *Reason Papers* No. 17 (Fall 1992): 61–74. See note 15, below.

592 | PART 5: Reviews

is estopped, or prevented, from complaining (i.e., objecting or with-holding consent) if *B* retaliates or punishes *A*. For *A* has admitted the validity of aggression, and it would be inconsistent for him to object to his own punishment, which is, after all, "only" aggression.

By the same token, however, laws that attempt to enforce "positive" rights (such as the right to food or a job) or to prohibit nonaggressive behavior (such as expression, prostitution, the use of drugs, or the offer to pay someone less than minimum wage) are not legitimate. For here the state, in enforcing such laws against nonaggressors, is itself an aggres-sor.[14] If the imprisoned, nonaggressive "criminal" asserts his *right* to be

---

[14] Rothbard has developed a useful classification or typology of aggressive intervention. If an aggressor's command or order involves only the commanded individual himself—i.e., the aggressor restricts the individual's use of his own property, when exchange with some-one else is not involved—this Rothbard calls *autistic intervention*. If the aggressor compels an *exchange* between the individual and himself, or coerces a "gift" from the individual subject, this may be called a *binary intervention*, since a hegemonic relation is established between two people: the aggressor and the individual subject. If the aggressor compels or prohibits an exchange between a *pair* of subjects, this is called *triangular intervention*.

Examples of autistic intervention are murder or compulsory prohibition or enforcement of a salute or speech. Taxation, conscription, slavery, and compulsory jury service are examples of binary intervention. Examples of triangular intervention are price controls, minimum wage laws, and licensing. Murray N. Rothbard, *Man, Economy, and State, with Power and Market*, Scholars ed., 2d ed. (Auburn, Ala.: Mises Institute, 2009; https://mises.org/library/man-economy-and-state-power-and-market), chap. 12, §2. In chapter 3, "Banking, Nation States and International Politics: A Sociological Reconstruction of the Present Economic Order," Hoppe makes similar distinctions among aggressive actions in pointing out why states with relatively more liberal internal economic policies are more successful in war against states with relatively less internal liberalization:

> The need for a productive economy that a warring state must have also explains why it is that ceteris paribus those states which have adjusted their internal re-distributive policies so as to decrease the importance of economic regulations relative to that of taxation tend to outstrip their competitors in the arena of in-ternational politics. Regulations through which states either compel or prohibit certain exchanges between two or more private persons as well as taxation imply a non-productive and/or non-contractual income expropriation and thus both damage homesteaders, producers or contractors i.e., those that cause wealth to come into existence. However, while by no means less destructive of productive output than taxation, regulations have the peculiar characteristic of requiring the state's control over economic resources in order to become enforceable without simultaneously increasing the resources at its disposal. In practice, this is to say that they require the state's command over taxes, yet they produce no monetary income for the state (instead, they satisfy pure power lust, as when *A*, for no material gain of his own, prohibits *B* and *C* from engaging in mutually beneficial trade). On the other hand, taxation and a redistribution of tax revenue according to the principle

freed and his concomitant right to use force against the aggressor-state to escape, the state cannot deny this asserted right nor the legitimacy of the prisoner's (proposed) use of force against the state, since the state, by being an aggressor, is estopped from denying the legitimacy of the use of force. Since the prisoner has a right to be freed, of course the state has no contrary "right" to imprison him. By this same logic, an aggressive criminal has a right to not be *disproportionately* punished. For example, someone who steals an ink pen may not be executed as punishment.[15]

It is hoped that others will also build upon or critique Hoppe's work. Murray Rothbard stated in the *Liberty* symposium that "a future research program for Hoppe and other libertarian philosophers would be (a) to see how far axiomatics can be extended into other spheres of ethics, or (b) to see if and how this axiomatic could be integrated into the standard natural law approach."[16] Also of interest would be a systematic cataloguing of just what is a priori axiomatic knowledge.[17]

Another tantalizing idea deserving further exploration is Hoppe's discussion of free will:

> [O]ne must regard one's knowledge and actions as uncaused. One might hold this conception of "freedom" to be an illusion, and from the point of view of a "scientist" with cognitive powers substantially superior to

---

"from Peter to Paul," increases the economic means at the government's disposal at least by its own "handling charge" for the act of redistribution. Since a policy of taxation, and taxation without regulation, yields a higher monetary return to the state (and with this more resources expendable on the war effort!) than a policy of regulation, and regulation with taxation, states must move in the direction of a comparatively deregulated economy and a comparatively pure tax-state in order to avoid international defeat.... A highly characteristic example of this connection between a policy of internal deregulation and increased external aggressiveness is provided by the Reagan administration.
EEPP, p. 102–103 & n.22.

[15] Kinsella, "Estoppel: A New Justification for Individual Rights." An expanded discussion of the estoppel theory will be presented in my work-in-progress, Estoppel: A Theory of Rights. (Author's note: This previous comment was included in the original 1994 article. Subsequently, I elaborated on this theory, albeit under different titles than previously envisioned. See "A Libertarian Theory of Punishment and Rights" (ch. 5) and "Dialogical Arguments for Libertarian Rights" (ch. 6).)

[16] Murray N. Rothbard, "Beyond Is and Ought," *Liberty* 2, no. 2 (Nov. 1988; https://perma.cc/8LZR-DN6Y; also https://mises.org/library/beyond-and-ought): 44–45.

[17] Although Hoppe demonstrates the a priori character of several concepts, he neither systematically nor exhaustively catalogues them. See Part IV, below, for a discussion of Hoppe's a priori concepts.

any human intelligence, from the point of view of God, for example, such a description may well be correct—but we are not God, and even if freedom is illusory from His standpoint, for we [sic] human beings it is a necessary illusion.[18]

D. Remaining Questions—Rights of Fetuses, Babies, and Defective Humans

Hoppe establishes the foundation for individual rights, but takes it no further. One almost salivates at the prospect of Hoppe writing more on this, answering the questions of exactly how to apply the rights of self-ownership and homesteading to the hard cases, such as fetuses, babies, children, and retarded people (who, after all, cannot argue). Hoppe deals only suggestively or obliquely with this problem: the question of what is just or unjust "does not arise vis-à-vis a stone or fish, because they are incapable of engaging in such exchanges and of producing validity-claiming propositions."[19]

What about fetuses, or even babies? Another related statement of Hoppe's fails to answer this question:

> Obviously, we could have conflicts regarding the use of scarce resources with, let us say, an elephant or a mosquito, yet we would not consider it possible to resolve these conflicts by means of proposing property norms. The avoidance of possible conflicts, in such cases, is merely a technological, not an ethical, problem. For it to turn into an ethical problem, it is also necessary that the conflicting actors be capable, in principle, of argumentation.[20]

Is a baby "in principle" capable of argumentation? Hoppe's view on this is unfortunately unrevealed.

---

[18] *EEPP*, p. 301. For an interesting discussion of neuropsychologist Roger W. Sperry's writing on the subject of free will, determinism, and causality, see Charles Ripley, "Sperry's Concept of Consciousness," *Inquiry* 27 (1990): 399–423; see also Leonard Peikoff, *Objectivism: The Philosophy of Ayn Rand* (1991), pp. 69–72 (discussing Ayn Rand's theory of volition and its relation to causality); and David Kelley, "The Nature of Free Will," *The Foundations of Knowledge*, Lecture 6 (Portland Institute Conference, 1986; YouTube; https://youtu.be/m8qeaxNl7jE).

[19] *EEPP*, p. 341.

[20] Ibid., pp. 333–34.

E. Hoppe, Rothbard, Rand, and Classical Natural Rights Theory

Hoppe never commits himself as to whether he believes other defenders of natural rights—such as Rothbard, whom Hoppe obviously admires greatly—are correct in their support of natural law and natural rights. He remains noncommittal, stating:

> Agreeing with Rothbard on the possibility of a rational ethic and, more specifically, on the fact that only a libertarian ethic can indeed be morally justified, I want to propose here a different, non-natural-rights approach to establishing these two related claims. It has been a common quarrel with the natural rights position, even by sympathetic readers, that the concept of human nature is far "too diffuse and varied to provide a determinate set of contents of natural law."[21]

Does Hoppe agree that natural law is hogwash? Is he a "sympathetic reader"? One gets the impression that he agrees with this criticism of natural law. If so, however, it is unclear how Rothbard, aligning himself with the natural law or natural rights tradition of philosophy, in "*The Ethics of Liberty* presents the full case [that] the libertarian property norms" are the rules that "can be discerned by means of reason as grounded in the very nature of man."[22]

Hoppe even attempts to define his own theory as being, really, a new type of natural rights theory:

> Nor, then, do I claim that it is impossible to interpret my approach as falling in a "rightly conceived" natural rights tradition after all.... What is claimed, though, is that the following approach is clearly out of line with what the natural rights approach has actually come to be, and that it owes nothing to this tradition as it stands.... Of course, then, since the capability of argumentation is an essential part of human nature—one could not even say anything about the latter without the former—it could also be argued that norms which cannot be defended effectively in the course of argumentation are also incompatible with human nature.[23]

---

[21] Ibid., p. 313 (Alan Gewirth, "Law, Action, and Morality," in *Georgetown Symposium on Ethics: Essays in Honor of Henry B. Veatch*, R. Porreco, ed. (New York: University Press of America, 1984), p. 73)). See also the related discussion in "Dialogical Arguments for Libertarian Rights" (ch. 6), the section "Argumentation Ethics and Natural Rights."

[22] Ibid.

[23] Ibid., pp. 314 n.15, 315 n.17.

Yet, Hoppe states:

> [T]his defense of private property is essentially also Rothbard's. In spite of his formal allegiance to the natural rights tradition Rothbard, in what I consider his most crucial argument in defense of a private property ethic, not only chooses essentially the same starting point—argumentation—but also gives a justification by means of a priori reasoning almost identical to the one just developed. To prove the point I can do no better than simply quote: "Now, *any* person participating in any sort of discussion, including one on values, is, by virtue of so participating, alive and affirming life. For if he were *really* opposed to life he would have no business continuing to be alive. Hence, the *supposed* opponent of life is really affirming it in the very process of discussion, and hence the preservation and furtherance of one's life takes on the stature of an incontestable axiom."[24]

---

[24] Ibid., pp. 321–22, quoting Murray N. Rothbard, "A Crusoe Social Philosophy," in *The Ethics of Liberty* (New York: New York University Press, 1998), pp. 32–33, also published as *idem*, "A Crusoe Social Philosophy," *Mises Daily* (December 7, 2021; https://mises.org/library/crusoe-social-philosophy). Ayn Rand's thought related to this subject is worth noting:

> [A]s Rand maintains, all "oughts" are hypothetical, based on valuing one's life.... The point is not that one has to be alive in order to act to achieve anything. The point is that being pro-life is what makes end states qualify as *values*. Only choosing to hold one's life as a value gives one the stake in one's actions that is required for the whole issue of evaluation to arise....
>
> Contrary to biological determinism, one does not *have* to pursue any goals or proclaim anything to be of value. But contrary to subjectivism, if one does, the action or proclamation logically depends on implicitly accepting one's life as one's ultimate value....
>
> The issue of *justifying* choices arises only in the context of having already chosen to live. The choice to live is not extra-moral, but pre-moral; it is a precondition of all moral evaluation.

Harry Binswanger, "Life-Based Teleology and the Foundations of Ethics," *The Monist* 75, no. 1 (Jan. 1992): 84–103, at 99–100. As Ayn Rand states:

> Life or death is man's only fundamental alternative. To live is his basic act of choice. If he chooses to live, a rational ethics will tell him what principles of action are required to implement his choice. If he does not choose to live, nature will take its course.

Ibid., at 100 (quoting Ayn Rand, "Causality Versus Duty," in *Philosophy: Who Needs It* (Signet 1984), pp. 95, 99. For further discussion of the structure of this Rothbard's argument for rights here, see David Osterfeld, "Natural Rights Debate: A Comment on a Reply," *J. Libertarian Stud.* 7, no. 1 (Spring 1983; https://mises.org/library/natural-rights-debate-comment-reply-0): 101–13, pp. 106–07.

F. Hoppe's Value-Free (?) Ethics

In addition to Hoppe's seeming unwillingness to criticize wholeheart-edly the natural rights tradition, he is also curiously reluctant to admit the ethical aspects of his argumentation ethic:

> Here the praxeological proof of libertarianism has the advantage of offer-ing a completely value-free justification of private property. It remains entirely in the realm of is-statements, and nowhere tries to derive an ought from an is. The structure of the argument is this: (a) justification is propositional justification—a priori true is-statement; (b) argumentation presupposes property in one's body and the homesteading principle— a priori true is-statement; and (c) then, no deviation from this ethic can be argumentatively justified—a priori true is-statement.[25]

Now I do not see how this is a "completely value-free justification of private property." Private property means *rights* in private property; and "rights" is indeed a normative, value-laden concept. Of course, in a triv-ial sense, any statement such as *"A* should do X" is an is-statement, because one is implicitly stating that "it is the case that *A* should do X." But this is still really an ought-statement, as is step (b) above, in making a statement about property rights. I do not see, however, why Hoppe is reluctant to admit this, as this is not a defect of his argument, but is in fact why it is so powerful—because it *does* justify the subset of ethics concerning rights.

G. Hoppe's Conception of "Rights"

Unfortunately, Hoppe never clearly defines what he means by "rights," which leads to some slight confusion in the presentation of aspects of his argument.[26] Primarily, he uses the word in a normative, ethical sense. He occasionally, however, seems to mean "power," which is value-neutral and non-normative: "[I]f no one had the right to acquire and control

---

[25] *EEPP*, p. 345.

[26] This is in marked contrast to Hoppe's normal habit of clearly defining key terms. For example, Hoppe has brilliantly demonstrated that socialism "must be conceptualized as an institutionalized interference with or aggression against private property and private property claims." Hoppe, *A Theory of Socialism and Capitalism*, p. 10.

anything except his own body … then we would all cease to exist…."[27]
It is true that we would all cease to exist if we had no power or ability to
acquire and control things; however, a "right" is not logically necessary
for this power to be exercised. For example, in a Robinsonade, Crusoe
alone on his desert island has no rights because rights are relevant only
socially, as they concern relationships between individuals. Yet Crusoe,
if he has the power to build a hut and gather fruit, can actually survive.

Certainly we have the ability to affect the world, otherwise we
would not continue to exist—and this may explain *why*, according to
Hoppe's theory, we must have the *right* to exercise this ability. But the
problem with switching to the power-sense of "rights" in a justification
of normative-rights is that one may end up justifying the former and
not the latter, or neither. And certainly it would be both useless and
futile to try to prove that we all have the actual ability and power to
control our bodies and to homestead; the very existence of the Internal
Revenue Service disproves this contention immediately. Hoppe's inconsistent use of "rights" is not fatal to his argument, but clarification
of this step in his argument and a precise definition of "rights" would
be welcome.[28]

H. Habermas's and Apel's "Discourse Ethics" and Gewirth's and Pilon's "Principle of Generic Consistency"

Much of Hoppe's argumentation ethics draws on the "discourse ethics"
theories of Jürgen Habermas and Karl-Otto Apel.[29] Hoppe's argumen-

---

[27] *EEPP*, p. 320.

[28] Lomasky makes a similar critique in "The Argument from Mere Argument."

[29] *EEPP*, p. 314 n.16. Jürgen Habermas's works, often in German, are cited frequently throughout the book. Habermas's work on "communicative action" is crucial in Hoppe's own argumentation ethics. See also discussion in "Dialogical Arguments for Libertarian Rights" (ch. 6), n.25 *et pass*. Habermas's writings published in English, or English-language discussions of Habermas's works, include: Seyla Benhabib & Fred Dallmayr, eds., *The Communicative Ethics Controversy* (Cambridge, Mass.: MIT Press, 1990); Douglas B. Rasmussen, "Political Legitimacy and Discourse Ethics," *International Philosophical Quarterly* 32 (1992; https://perma.cc/MK59-QEVV); Jeremy Shearmur, "Habermas: A Critical Approach," *Critical Rev.* 2 (1988): 39–50; Kenneth Baynes, *The Normative Grounds of Social Criticism: Kant, Rawls, and Habermas* (Albany: State University of New York Press, 1992), pp. 77–122; Jane Braaten, *Habermas's Critical Theory of Society* (1991); Jürgen Habermas, *Moral Consciousness and Communicative Action*, Christian Lenhardt & Shierry Weber Nicholsen,

tation ethic also bears some similarities to Alan Gewirth's "dialectically necessary method."[30] Applying this method and the principle of universalizability, Gewirth derives the precept "act in accord with the generic

trans.(Cambridge, Mass.: MIT Press, 1990 [1983]) (containing English translation of work originally published in German as "Moralbewusstsein und communikatives Handeln"); idem, Between Facts and Norms: Contributions to a Discourse Theory of Law and Democracy, William Rehg, trans. (Cambridge, Mass.: MIT Press, 1996; https://perma.cc/27K9-YWW2); idem, Communication and the Evolution of Society, Thomas McCarthy, trans. (Boston: Beacon Press, 1979); idem, Knowledge and Human Interests, Jeremy Shapiro, trans. (Boston: Beacon Press, 1972); idem, Legitimation Crisis, Thomas McCarthy, trans. (Boston: Beacon Press, 1975); idem, The Philosophical Discourse of Modernity : Twelve Lectures, Fredrick Lawrence, trans. (Cambridge, Mass.: MIT Press, 1987); idem, Theory and Practice, John Viertel, trans. (Boston: Beacon Press, 1973); idem, The Theory of Communicative Action, Thomas McCarthy, trans. (Boston: Beacon Press, 1984 & 1987) (two volumes); Thomas McCarthy, The Critical Theory of Jürgen Habermas (Cambridge, Mass.: MIT Press, 1981); idem, Ideals and Illusions: On Reconstruction and Deconstruction in Contemporary Critical Theory (Cambridge, Mass.: MIT Press, 1993); John B. Thompson & David Held, eds., Habermas: Critical Debates (London: Macmillan Press, 1982); Michael Pusey, Jürgen Habermas (London and New York: Routledge, 1987); Richard J. Bernstein, ed., Habermas and Modernity (Cambridge, Mass.: MIT Press, 1985); Jürgen Habermas, Jürgen Habermas on Society and Politics: A Reader, Steven Seidman, ed. (Boston: Beacon Press, 1989); David M. Rasmussen, ed., Reading Habermas (Wiley-Blackwell, 1991); Stephen K. White, The Recent Work of Jürgen Habermas (Cambridge University Press, 1988); Gary C. Leedes, "The Discourse Ethics Alternative to Rust v. Sullivan," U. Rich. L. Rev. 26 (1991; https://scholarship.richmond.edu/lawreview/vol26/iss1/4/): 87–143, at 108-11; Lawrence B. Solum, "Freedom of Communicative Action: A Theory of the First Amendment Freedom of Speech," Northwestern U. L. Rev. 83 (1989; https://scholarship.law.georgetown.edu/facpub/1954/): 54–135, at 86–106.

See also Karl-Otto Apel, "Is the Ethics of the Ideal Communication Community a Utopia? On the Relationship between Ethics, Utopia, and the Critique of Utopia," in Benhabib & Dallmayr, eds., The Communicative Ethics Controversy; idem, "The A Priori of the Communication Community and the Foundations of Ethics," in Towards a Transformation of Philosophy (London and New York: Routledge, 1980); idem, "The Problem of Philosophical Foundations Grounding in Light of a Transcendental Pragmatics of Language," in Kenneth Baynes, James Bohman & Thomas McCarthy, eds., After Philosophy: End or Transformation? (Cambridges, Mass.: MIT Press, 1986); Kim Davies, "Review of K-O Apel, Towards a Transformation of Philosophy (1980)," Radical Philosophy 30 (Spring 1982; https://www.stephankinsella.com/wp-content/uploads/texts/davies_apel-review.pdf); Michel Rosenfeld, "Book Review of Habermas, Between Facts and Norms: Contributions to a Discourse Theory of Law and Democracy," Harv. L. Rev. 108 (1995): 1163–89.

30 EEPP, p. 315 n.18. Gewirth's theory is presented in his book Reason and Morality (Chicago: University of Chicago Press, 1978). For a concise statement of Gewirth's theories, see his article "The Basis and Content of Human Rights," Georgia L. Rev. 13 (1979): 1143–70; also idem, Moral Rationality (The Lindley Lecture, Univ. of Kansas, 1972; https://core.ac.uk/download/pdf/213402925.pdf); idem, "Law, Action, and Morality," p. 73.

See also the discussion of Gewirth and his libertarian student Roger Pilon in "Dialogical Arguments for Libertarian Rights" (ch. 6).

rights of your recipients as well as of yourself," which he calls the "Principle of Generic Consistency" (PGC).[31] Gewirth holds that his theory shows that individuals have rights to "freedom and well-being," which in turn justify a welfare state.[32]

Hoppe criticizes Gewirth's "dialectically necessary method" because it is based on action in general as opposed to the specific communicative subcategory of action.[33] It is interesting to note that Gewirth's former student, Roger Pilon, believes Gewirth's PGC is correct, important, and pathbreaking, but that Gewirth himself has applied his own theories incorrectly in an attempt to justify the welfare state.[34] The libertarian Pilon believes he can reform his own teacher's work in order to justify libertarian principles.[35] Similarly, Hoppe believes his former teacher Habermas's discourse-ethics theories, while correct at core, are applied incorrectly by Habermas to yield a socialistic ethic; Hoppe feels that Habermas's theories, if correctly applied (as Hoppe himself does), yield the libertarian non-aggression norm.

Hoppe states:

> Apel and Habermas are essentially silent on the all-decisive question of what ethical prescription actually follows from the recognition of the "a priori of argumentation." However, there are remarks indicating that they both seem to believe some sort of participatory social democracy to be implied in this a priori. The following [i.e., argumentation ethics] explains why hardly anything could be farther from the truth.[36]

Although Habermas and Apel agree that argumentation implies that certain intersubjectively meaningful norms exist,[37] they would not agree with the next step taken by Hoppe. Hoppe next recognizes that argumentation, as a form of action, requires exclusive control of the scarce resources in one's body; this implies that "as long as there is

---

31 Gewirth, "The Basis and Content of Human Rights," p. 1155.
32 Ibid., at 1149, 1167-69.
33 *EEPP*, p. 315 n.18.
34 Roger A. Pilon, "Ordering Rights Consistently: Or What We Do and Do Not Have Rights To," *Georgia L. Rev.* 13 (1979; https://perma.cc/FYX4-CFNH): 1171-96, pp. 1178, 1187; see also *idem, A Theory of Rights: Toward Limited Government* (Ph.D. dissertation, University of Chicago, 1979; https://perma.cc/DGS3-W4UA).
35 Ibid at 1186-87.
36 *EEPP*, p. 335 n.2.
37 Ibid., p. 334.

any argumentation, there is a mutual recognition of each other's property right in his own body."[38] As Hoppe observes, "That Habermas and Apel are unable to take this step is, I submit, due to the fact that they, too, suffer, as do many other philosophers, from a complete ignorance of economics, and a corresponding blindness towards the fact of scarcity."[39] Presumably, just as Hoppe criticizes Gewirth's welfare-state-justifying theory, not only because of its results but also because of its action-based method, he would also find fault in Pilon's neo-Gewirthian theory and methods, despite Pilon's libertarian (i.e., correct) conclusions.

III. EPISTEMOLOGY

A. The Application of Praxeology to Epistemology and Ethics

Hoppe's epistemology is basically an extension of Ludwig von Mises's praxeology, which Mises had previously applied only to economics.[40] Mises inquired into the logical status of typical economic propositions such as the law of marginal utility. Mises showed that both empiricism and historicism are self-contradictory doctrines and justified the claims of rationalist philosophy by demonstrating the existence of a priori synthetic propositions.[41]

In the Kantian and Misesian framework, analytic truths like "all bachelors are unmarried" are true, but circular or tautological. Synthetic truths, like "all bachelors are unfulfilled" (if that were true), say something substantial about bachelors that is not already part of the definition of bachelors. We may know a synthetic truth through experience or empirically (or a posteriori). But these truths are not *necessarily* true, and might have been false if experience had been different. According to empiricism, synthetic truths can be known only through experience.[42]

---

[38] Ibid., p. 335.
[39] Ibid.
[40] Ibid., p. 278 *et seq.*
[41] Ibid., p. 271 *et seq.*
[42] Roger Scruton, *Kant* (Oxford University Press, 1982), pp. 18–19.

602 | PART 5: Reviews

A synthetic a priori proposition is significant because it is necessarily true yet is not a tautology, thus yielding certain unchallengeable real knowledge about the world.[43]

Mises shows that the propositions of economics are indeed knowledge that is *not* derived from observation and yet is constrained by objective laws. In the science of praxeology, the general theory of human action, the "axiom of action" (i.e., the proposition that humans act, that they display intentional behavior), qualifies as a priori synthetic knowledge because (a) the "axiom is not derived from observation—there are only bodily movements to be observed but no such thing as actions—but stems instead from reflective understanding"; and (b) this understanding is of a self-evident proposition, "for its truth cannot be denied, since the denial would itself have to be categorized as an action."[44] Mises shows that all of the "categories which we know to be the very heart of economics—values, ends, means, choice, preference, cost, profit and loss—are implied in the axiom of action."[45]

Hoppe's achievement is to explain how praxeology also provides the foundation for epistemology and ethics (the argumentation ethic has already been discussed above). To the a priori axiom of action, Hoppe adds a second a priori axiom, the "a priori of argumentation." This axiom:

> ... states that humans are capable of argumentation and hence know the meaning of truth and validity. As in the case of the action axiom, this knowledge is not derived from observation: there is only verbal behavior to be observed and prior reflective cognition is required in order to interpret such behavior as meaningful arguments. And the validity of the axiom, like that of the action axiom, is indisputable. It is impossible to deny that one can argue, as the very denial would itself be an argument....

> Recognizing, as we have just done, that knowledge claims are raised and decided upon in the course of argumentation and that this is undeniably so, one can now reconstruct the task of epistemology more precisely as that of formulating those propositions which are argumentatively indisputable in that their truth is already implied in the very fact of making one's argument and so cannot be denied argumentatively; and to delineate

---

[43] David Gordon, *The Philosophical Origins of Austrian Economics* (Auburn, Ala.: Mises Institute, 1993; https://perma.cc/AQ6N-VS4H), pp. 30–31.

[44] *EEPP*, pp. 275–76.

[45] Ibid., p. 277.

the range of such a priori knowledge from the realm of propositions whose validity cannot be established in this way but require additional, contingent information for their validation, or that cannot be validated at all and so are mere metaphysical statements in the pejorative sense of the term metaphysical.[46]

B. Hoppe and Kant Versus Rand

Hoppe offers a stunning justification and interpretation of Kant's controversial statement that "[so] far it has been assumed that our knowledge had to conform to reality," instead it should be assumed 'that observational reality should conform to our mind.'"[47]

> According to rationalist philosophy, a priori true propositions had their foundation in the operation of principles of thinking which one could not possibly conceive of as operating otherwise; they were grounded in categories of an active mind. Now, as empiricists were only too eager to point out, the obvious critique of such a position is, that if this were indeed the case, it could not be explained why such mental categories should fit reality. Rather, one would be forced to accept the absurd ideal-istic assumption that reality would have to be conceived of as a creation of the mind, in order to claim that a priori knowledge could incorporate any information about the structure of reality.[48]

The empiricists' critique seemed to be justified by statements such as that of Kant above. However, writes Hoppe:

> … recognizing knowledge as being structurally constrained by its role in the framework of action categories provides the solution to such a complaint. For as soon as this is realized, all idealistic suggestions of rationalist philosophy disappear, and an epistemology claiming that a priori true propositions exist becomes a realistic epistemology in-stead. Understood as constrained by action categories, the seemingly unbridgeable gulf between the mental on the one hand and the real, outside physical world on the other is bridged. So constrained, a pri-ori knowledge must be as much a mental thing as a reflection of the structure of reality, since it is only through actions that the mind comes

---

[46] Ibid., p. 280.
[47] Ibid., p. 282, quoting Immanuel Kant, *Kritik der Reinen Vernunft* [Critique of Pure Reason], in vol. 3 *Werke*, Wilhelm Weischedel, ed. (Frankfurt/M.: Suhrkamp, 1968), p. 45.
[48] *EEPP*, p. 282.

into contact with reality, so to speak. Acting is a cognitively guided adjustment of a physical body in physical reality. And thus, there can be no doubt that a priori knowledge, conceived of as an insight into the structural constraints imposed on knowledge qua knowledge of actors, must indeed correspond to the nature of things. The realistic character of such knowledge would manifest itself not only in the fact that one could not *think* it to be otherwise, but in the fact that one could not *undo* its truth.[49]

In Hoppe's pamphlet *Praxeology and Economic Science*,[50] which contains a discussion similar to the one in chapter 6 of his book, he makes it clear that he does not think that Kant himself meant that reality is created by the mind.[51] Indeed, Kant had hinted at the solution presented in Hoppe's interpretation above. Hoppe writes, "He thought mathematics, for instance, had to be grounded in our knowledge of the meaning of repetition, of repetitive operations. And he also realized, if only somewhat vaguely, that the principle of causality is implied in our understanding of what it is and means to act."[52]

As for the Objectivist or Randian denunciation of Kant for this statement that observational reality should conform to the mind, Hoppe states:

> Among some followers of Austrianism, the Kant interpretation of Ayn Rand (see, for instance, her *Introduction to Objectivist Epistemology* [1979]; or *For the New Intellectual* [1961]) enjoys great popularity. Her interpretation, replete with sweeping denunciatory pronouncements, however, is characterized by a complete absence of any interpretive documentation whatsoever. On Rand's arrogant ignorance regarding Kant, see B. Goldberg, "Ayn Rand's 'For the New Intellectual,'" *New Individualist Rev.*, vol. 1, no. 3 (1961).[53]

---

[49] Ibid., pp. 282–83.

[50] Hans-Hermann Hoppe, *Praxeology and Economic Science* (1988), later included in *idem*, *Economic Science and the Austrian Method* (Auburn, Ala.: Mises Institute, 1995; www.hanshoppe.com/esam).

[51] Ibid., pp. 17–18.

[52] Ibid., p. 18.

[53] Ibid., at 45 n.14. Goldberg's article, however, is poorly reasoned and largely unconvincing. See David Kelley, *The Evidence of the Senses: A Realist Theory of Perception* (1986), p. 27–31 (discussing the primacy of existence); Leonard Peikoff, *Objectivism: The Philosophy of Ayn Rand* (New York: Dutton, 1991), pp. 148–52 (discussing Ayn Rand and philosophy of objectivity). The notorious phrase of Kant's can be found in English in Immanuel Kant,

Critique of Pure Reason (Norman K. Smith trans. 1953 [1929]), pp. 21–22. As David Kelley, executive director of the Institute for Objectivist Studies, paraphrases Kant:

> Hitherto it has been supposed," Kant says in his major work, "that all our knowledge must conform to the objects," but, he argues, … under that supposition, every effort to establish the validity of consciousness has failed. So, "the experiment therefore ought to be made, whether we should not succeed better with the problems of metaphysics by assuming that the objects must conform to our mode of cognition.

Kelley perceptively criticizes Kant here with an analogy, that of Kant's thought applied to the driving of a car:

> Hitherto it has been supposed that our steering must conform to the road. But on this supposition it has proved impossible to establish the validity of our steering. The experiment therefore ought to be made, whether we should not have more success with the problem of driving by assuming that the road must conform to our steering.

David Kelley, "The Primacy of Existence," *The Foundations of Knowledge*, Lecture 1 (The Jefferson School Conference, San Diego; YouTube, 1985; https://youtu.be/AVBgfamJxFk).

Author's note (2023): As Hoppe has observed, Kant's meaning is ambiguous or murky enough because of his wording to cause some, such as Kelley, and other, primarily American, philosophers, to interpret Kant in this idealistic way, while others, primarily on the continent, have interpreted him in a more realistic way. See *EEPP*, p. 282 and 282 n.17, citing, as examples of the latter, Friedrich Kambartel, *Erfahrung and Struktur* (Frankfurt/M.: Suhrkamp, 1968), chap. 3 as well as Hoppe's own *Handeln und Erkennen: Zur Kritik des Empirismus am Beispiel der Philosophie David Humes* (Bern: Lang, 1976; www.hanshoppe.com/german). Some other books suggested to me in this regard, which I have not yet read (and I don't know German), include: Ralph C.S. Walker, *Kant* (London: Routledge and Kegan Paul, 1978) (suggested by Barry Smith); Paul Abela, *Kant's Empirical Realism* (Oxford: Clarendon Press, 2002) and J.N. Findlay, *Kant and the Transcendental Object: A Hermeneutic Study* (Oxford: Clarendon Press, 1981) (suggested by David Gordon); Paul Lorenzen, *Methodisches Denken* (Frankfurt/M.: Suhrkamp, 1968) and *idem*, *Normative Logic and Ethics* (Mannheim: Bibliographisches Institut, 1969) (suggested by Hoppe); Magdalena Aebi, *Kants Begründung der "Deutschen Philosophie": Kants Transzendentale Logik, Kritik Ihrer Begründung* (Basel: Verlag für Recht und Gesellschaft, 1947) (suggested by Kevin Mulligan).

But as Hoppe points out, "Whether or not such an interpretation of Kant's epistemology is indeed correct is a very different matter. Clarifying this problem is of no concern here, however." *EEPP*, p. 282 n.17. In any case, Kantians such as Mises, Kantian-Misesians such as Hoppe, and Aristotelean-Misesians such as Rothbard are in fact epistemological realists and not idealists as some philosophers construe Kant to be. To the contrary, the Misesian praxeological perspective helps to ground a realist epistemology. As Hoppe notes,

> Recognizing knowledge as being structurally constrained by its role in the framework of action categories provides the solution to such a complaint, for as soon as this is realized, all idealistic suggestions of rationalist philosophy disappear, and an epistemology claiming that a priori true propositions exist becomes a realistic epistemology instead. Understood as constrained by action categories, the seemingly unbridgeable gulf between the mental on the one hand and the real, outside physical world on the other is bridged.

C. A Priori Truths

Hoppe then ferrets out various truths that are implied in the very fact of arguing. The laws of logic, such as junctors ("and," "or," "if-then," "not"), quantors ("there is," "all," "some"), and the laws of identity and contradiction:

> ... are a priori true propositions about reality and not mere verbal stipulations regarding the transformation rules of arbitrarily chosen signs, as empiricist-formalists would have it. They are as much laws of thinking as of reality, because they are laws that have their ultimate foundation in action and could not be undone by any actor. In each and every action, an actor identifies some specific situation and categorizes it in one way rather than another in order to be able to make a choice.[54]

Hoppe goes on to show that arithmetic is an a priori and yet empirical discipline and "is rooted in our understanding of repetition—the repetition of action."[55] He even demonstrates the irrelevance of Gödel's Incompleteness theorem.[56] Euclidean geometry is a priori and yet incorporates empirical knowledge about space, "because it is not only the very precondition for any empirical spatial description, it is also

---

Ibid., pp. 282–83. For more on Hoppe's realistic, Misesian-based epistemology, see his *Economic Science and the Austrian Method*, pp. 68–70. On Rothbard's, see his "The Mantle of Science,""In Defense of 'Extreme Apriorism,'" and other chapters in Section One: Method, of *Economic Controversies* (Auburn, Ala.: Mises Institute, 2011; https://mises.org/library/economic-controversies). On Mises's realism, see Ludwig von Mises, "Epistemological Studies," in *Memoirs*, Arlene Oost-Zinner, trans. (Auburn, Ala.: Mises Institute, 2009; https://mises.org/library/book/memoirs) (formerly *Notes and Recollections*); Mises's dismissive remarks on Popper in *The Ultimate Foundation of Economic Science: An Essay on Method* (Princeton, N.J.: D. Van Nostrand Company, Inc., 1962; https://mises.org/library/ultimate-foundation-economic-science), chap. 4, §8 and chap. 7, §4; *idem, Theory and History: An Interpretation of Social and Economic Evolution* (Auburn, Ala.: Mises Institute, 2007 [1957]; https://mises.org/library/theory-and-history-interpretation-social-and-economic-evolution), chap. 1, §3. See also Edward W. Younkins, "Menger, Mises, Rand, and Beyond," *J. Ayn Rand Stud.* 6, no. 2 (Spring 2005; https://perma.cc/SM4J-TYBV): 337–74, p. 342 *et pass.* (also in Edward W. Younkins, ed., *Philosophers of Capitalism: Menger, Mises, Rand, and Beyond* (Lexington Books, 2005)), and Heidi C. Morris, "Reason and Reality: The Logical Compatibility of Austrian Economics and Objectivism," *Rebirth of Reason* (May 10, 2005; https://perma.cc/PSR5-MNFE).

54 *EEPP*, p. 284.
55 Ibid., p. 286.
56 Ibid., p. 286 n.20.

the precondition for any active orientation in space."[57] Einstein's non-Euclidean theories even presuppose the validity of Euclidean geometry: "After all, the lenses of the telescopes which one uses to confirm Einstein's theory regarding the non-Euclidean structure of physical space must themselves be constructed according to Euclidean principles."[58]

Hoppe also demonstrates the a prioristic character of causality and teleology. Significantly, Hoppe shows that "everything which is not an action must necessarily be categorized causally"; and, "in contrast, everything that is an action must be categorized teleogically."[59] Also, because the causality principle is a necessary presupposition even of the Heisenberg Uncertainty Principle in physics, there is a "fundamental misconception involved in interpreting the Heisenberg principle as invalidating the causality principle."[60]

IV. ECONOMICS

A. Public Goods Theory and the Production of Security

Part One: Economics contains five interesting and insightful chapters. In chapter 1, "Fallacies of the Public Goods Theory and the Production of Security," Hoppe shows that the distinction between "private" and "public" goods is completely illusory:

---

[57] Ibid., pp. 288.

[58] Ibid, p. 288 n.23; see Petr Beckmann, *Einstein Plus Two* (Golem Press, 1987), p. 27 *et pass.* (proposing theory implying that Einstein's work does not prove physical space is non-Euclidean). In the journal founded by Dr. Beckmann, who passed away in 1993, a recent article purports to have found evidence disproving part of Einstein's theory, thereby confirming Beckmann and Hoppe. Howard C. Hayden, "Stellar Aberration," *Galilean Electrodynamics* [https://perma.cc/JUY8-W7WS] vol. 4, no. 5 (Sept./Oct. 1993; https://perma.cc/GQY6-KUVK): 89–92. In this article, Hayden, a professor of physics at the University of Connecticut, claims that evidence shows that the phenomenon of stellar aberration is not due to the relative velocity of a star with respect to Earth, as is claimed by Einstein's theory of relativity. Ibid., at 91–92. The evidence thus casts doubt on the validity of Einsteinian relativity. *Galilean Electrodynamics* is now edited by Howard C. Hayden. (Author's note (2023): this original comment was written in 1994.)

[59] Ibid., pp. 291–92.

[60] Ibid., p. 290 n.25.

> A clear-cut dichotomy between private and public goods does not exist....
> All goods are more or less private or public and can—and constantly do—
> change with respect to their degree of privateness/publicness as people's
> values and evaluations change, and as changes occur in the composition
> of the population. In order to recognize that they never fall, once and for
> all, into either one or the other category, one must only recall what makes
> something a good. For something to be a good it must be recognized and
> treated as scarce by someone. Something is not a good as such, that is to
> say; goods are goods only in the eyes of the beholder. Nothing is a good
> unless at least one person subjectively evaluates it as such. But then, when
> goods are never goods-as-such—when no physico-chemical analysis can
> identify something as an economic good—there is clearly no fixed, ob-
> jective criterion for classifying goods as either private or public. They can
> never be private or public goods as such. Their private or public character
> depends on how few or how many people consider them to be goods, with
> the degree to which they are private or public changing as these evalua-
> tions change and ranging from one to infinity.[61]

Hoppe then applies this analysis to the production of security, commonly held to be a public good. Because the production of security is
no more a "public good" than goods and services such as cheese, houses,
or insurance, there is no special economic reason that prevents markets
from producing security, and thus no justification to require remedial
state action, such as state monopolization of police and defense.

B. The Economics and Sociology of Taxation

In chapter 2, "The Economics and Sociology of Taxation," Hoppe
argues that only three ways exist of acquiring or increasing wealth:
through homesteading, producing, or contracting. Since taxation implies a reduction of income a person can expect to receive from these
three activities, the opportunity cost for using one's time and body to
perform these activities is raised by taxation. Thus the marginal utility
of producing wealth is decreased, and the marginal utility of consumption and leisure is increased, leading to a shift away from the production
of wealth and towards consumption and leisure. Therefore taxation is
a means for the destruction of property and wealth-formation.[62]

---

[61] Ibid., pp. 8–9.
[62] Ibid., p. 35.

To the objection that taxation makes people actually work *harder* in order to earn the same income as before taxation, Hoppe replies that even if increased taxation causes:

> … [an] increase in workaholism, it is still the case that the income of value-productive individuals has fallen. For even if they produce the same output as previously, they can only do so if they expend more labor now than before. And since any additional labor expenditure implies foregone leisure or consumption (leisure or consumption which they otherwise could have enjoyed along with the same output of valuable assets), their overall standard of living must be lower now.[63]

Hoppe also explains "why the assumption that taxation can possibly leave the productive output of valuable assets unaffected and exclusively cripple consumption is fatally flawed."[64] This is because time preference—people's preference of present goods over future goods—combines with the increased marginal utility of leisure and consumption and the decreased marginal utility of production. Because people have an increased preference for consumption (in the present), and a relatively decreased preference for production (in the future), the length of the structure of production is shortened, and thus fewer valuable future assets are produced. "Every act of taxation necessarily exerts a push away from more highly capitalized, and hence more productive production processes, and into the direction of a hand-to-mouth existence."[65]

After showing that taxes reduce the standard of living of consumers, Hoppe discusses the sociological reasons *for* taxation, and ever more of it. This discussion is fascinating and insightful, but it comes down to the fact that there is taxation because the government can get away with it; the government can get away with it because a majority of the population either actively or passively support such governmental policies; and the majority support government because of the lack of (complete, principled) acceptance of a private property ethic.[66]

---

[63] Ibid., p. 39.

[64] Ibid.

[65] Ibid., p. 42.

[66] In this book I often use "government" more or less synonymously with "the state," although it is probably preferable to use the term state, when possible, as it is conceptually distinct from "government," as one can imagine "governing institutions" of law and order in

Government propaganda plays a role in influencing public opinion. Hoppe asks how the government could change public opinion from true ideas (i.e., the historical support in the United States for freedom and private property) to wrong ideas. He points out:

> It would seem that such a change towards falsehood requires the systematic introduction of exogenous forces: A true ideology is capable of supporting itself merely by virtue of being true. A false one needs reinforcement by outside influences with a clear-cut, tangible impact on people in order to be capable of generating and supporting a climate of intellectual corruption.[67]

(Objectivists who would criticize Hoppe because many of his ideas were influenced by Kant should note Hoppe's radical lack of epistemological and moral skepticism evident in this statement.)

Thus the government effectively buys support from the populace through a system of transfer payments, grants of privilege, and governmental provision of certain goods, e.g., education, which makes the populace increasingly dependent on the continuation of state rule.[68] By adopting democracy, the state "opens every government position to everyone and grants equal and universal rights of participation and competition in the making of state-policy."[69] Thus people gradually

---

a private-law society. In fact many statists and mini-statists (minarchists) often engage in equivocation on this point; they presuppose that there cannot be law and order, or "government," without the state, but if the anarchist claims to favor law and order, then the statist equates government with state and accuses the anarchist of being inconsistent. This is really simply disingenuous question-begging hidden behind an equivocation.

[67] Ibid., p. 65.

[68] Hoppe discusses some of these themes also in *Democracy: The God That Failed* (Transaction, 2001; www.hanshoppe.com/democracy).

[69] Ibid., p. 67. This calls to mind the words of Lysander Spooner, writing in 1870. Note especially Spooner's point 2:

The ostensible supporters of the Constitution … are made up of three classes, viz.: 1. Knaves, a numerous and active class, who see in the government an instrument which they can use for their own aggrandizement or wealth. 2. Dupes—a large class, no doubt—each of whom, because he is allowed one voice out of millions in deciding what he may do with his own person and his own property, and because he is permitted to have the same voice in robbing, enslaving, and murdering others, that others have in robbing, enslaving, and murdering himself, is stupid enough to imagine that he is a "free man," a "sovereign"; that this is a "free government"; "a government of equal rights," "the best government on earth," and such like absurdities. 3. A class who have some appreciation of the evils of government, but either do not see how to

lose sight of the immorality of the exploitation and expropriation in which they participate, and are lured "into accepting the view that such acts are legitimate as long as one is guaranteed a say over them...."[70]

> [W]hen everyone is potentially a minister, no one is concerned to cut down an office to which he aspires one day himself, or to put sand in a machine which he means to use himself when his turn comes. Hence it is that there is in the political circles of a modern society a wide complicity in the extension of power.[71]

Hoppe concludes that everything depends on a change in public opinion. Although this may appear hopeless, "ideas have changed in the past and can change again in the future ... and the idea of private property has certainly one attraction: it, and only it, is a true reflection of man's nature as a rational being."[72]

C. Banking, Nation States, and International Politics

Chapter 3, "Banking, Nation States, and International Politics: A Sociological Reconstruction of the Present Economic Order," is the best and most important chapter in Part One. Here Hoppe explores how and why the state monopolizes money and banking and shows the danger of the ever-approaching international monetary order.[73] Similarly to the discussion in chapter 2, this chapter argues that the state arises *despite* its inefficiencies and immorality and therefore depends

---

get rid of them, or do not choose to so far sacrifice their private interests as to give themselves seriously and earnestly to the work of making a change.
Lysander Spooner, "No Treason No. 4: The Constitution of No Authority," in *The Lysander Spooner Reader* (San Francisco, Calif.: Fox and Wilkes, 1992; http://www.lysanderspooner.org/works). Spooner (1808–1887), an anarchist, was a Massachusetts lawyer noted for his vigorous opposition to the encroachment of the state upon the liberty of the individual, such as the institution of slavery. In *No Treason*, Spooner demolishes the "consent" theory of the validity of the Constitution. Unfortunately, Spooner was a total crank and wrong on the important issue of intellectual property. See "Law and Intellectual Property in a Stateless Society" (ch. 14), n.4 *et pass.*

[70] *EEPP*, p. 68.
[71] Ibid., p. 69.
[72] Ibid., p. 75.
[73] See note 14, above (quoting Hoppe's explanation of why more liberal or free-market states are more successful in war or imperialism than more socialist states).

upon public support, either active or passive. To create legitimacy in the minds of the public, the state engages in propaganda:

> Much time and effort is spent persuading the public that things are not really as they appear: Exploitation is really freedom; taxes are really voluntary ... no one is ruled by anyone but we all rule ourselves; ... etc.[74]

Additionally, to garner public support, the state also engages in redistribution: it takes individuals' wealth, which individuals tend to resist, but redistributes some of it to individuals in order to corrupt them into assuming state-supportive roles. Because the state rests upon coercion, it must of course monopolize the police, defense, and courts.[75] In order to be able to regularly exploit the population, the state must also control traffic and communications, so it monopolizes these also. The state monopolizes the field of education to eliminate ideological competition. The state also adopts a democratic system that opens up potential government jobs and votes to all, giving the people a legal stake in the state in order to reduce resistance to state power.[76]

But "[t]he monopolization of money and banking is the ultimate pillar on which the modern state rests."[77] Thus the state monopolizes the minting of gold (to shift psychologically the emphasis from gold in universal terms like ounces to terms of fiat labels like "dollars"); passes legal tender laws; monopolizes the banking system; nationalizes gold; and finally cuts the last tie to gold by declaring paper notes irredeemable in gold.

But because there is still competition *among* states, which limits governments' abilities to inflate their currencies, governments have an incentive to expand their territories and to expand the territory in which each government's currency is in place. Historically, the tendency has been towards a one-world government, with a one-world paper currency, with the United States at the helm, and with no remaining limit on inflation of the money supply except hyperinflation and a collapse of the economy. This tendency is likely to continue unless public opinion:

---

[74] *EEPP*, pp. 86–87. Here one is reminded of government leaders referring to taxes as "contributions."

[75] Ibid., p. 88.

[76] Ibid., pp. 88–89.

[77] Ibid.

... the only constraint on government growth[,] undergoes a substantial change and the public begins to understand the lessons explained in this [chapter]: that economic rationality as well as justice and morality demand a worldwide gold standard and free, 100% reserve banking as well as free markets worldwide; and that world government, a world central bank and a world paper currency—contrary to the deceptive impression of representing universal values—actually means the universalization and intensification of exploitation, counterfeiting-fraud, and economic destruction.[78]

D. Marxism Reformed by Praxeology

Chapter 4, "Marxist and Austrian Class Analysis," is an interesting chapter that reinterprets the Marxist theory of history from an Austrian economics perspective. Hoppe argues that the hard-core tenets of the Marxist theory of history are essentially correct, but are derived in Marxism from a false starting point; and that the Mises-Rothbard brand of Austrianism can give a different justification for the validity of these theses.

The five hard-core Marxist beliefs are: (1) The history of mankind is the history of class struggles; (2) the ruling class is unified by its common interest in upholding its exploitative position and maximizing its exploitatively appropriated surplus product; (3) class rule manifests itself primarily in specific arrangements regarding the relations of production (i.e., the assignment of property rights); (4) internally, the process of competition within the ruling class generates a tendency toward increasing concentration and centralization; and (5) finally, with the centralization and expansion of exploitative rule gradually approaching its ultimate limit of world domination, class rule will increasingly become incompatible with the further development and improvement of "productive forces."[79]

Hoppe points out that Marx's theory of exploitation is flawed because, in maintaining that there is exploitation when a capitalist retains a surplus profit after paying a laborer, his theory does not take into account nor "understand the phenomenon of time preferences

---

[78] Ibid., p. 116.
[79] Ibid., pp. 117–19.

as a universal category of human action."[80] Of course, once time preference is considered, it can be seen that "contrary to the case of slave and slave master where the latter benefits at the expense of the former, the relationship between the free laborer and the capitalist is a mutually beneficial one."[81] It is logically absurd to regard homesteading of unowned goods, or voluntary agreements between different homesteaders, as exploitative, because nothing is taken away from anybody by these activities, and goods are actually created. "Instead, exploitation takes place whenever any deviation from the homesteading principle occurs…. Exploitation is the expropriation of homesteaders, producers and savers by late-coming non-homesteaders, non-producers, non-savers and non-contractors…."[82] Given this theory of exploitation, Hoppe analyzes the nature of government to justify the five Marxist theses above.

E. Mises Versus Keynes

The final chapter in Part One, "Theory of Employment, Money, Interest, and the Capitalist Process: The Misesian Case Against Keynes," contains an illuminating discussion of the Austrian theories of employment, money, and interest. After this discussion, Hoppe states that it is now "easy to recognize Keynes's 'new' *General Theory of Employment, Interest, and Money* as fundamentally flawed and the Keynesian revolution as one of this century's foremost intellectual scandals."[83] Hoppe then proceeds to eviscerate Keynes's theories against this backdrop.

V. CONCLUSION

Like *A Theory of Socialism and Capitalism* before it, *The Economics and Ethics of Private Property* contains cutting-edge economic theories and breakthroughs in epistemology and individual rights theories. Hoppe is indeed correct that, in the long run, immoral government policies

---

[80] Ibid., p. 122.
[81] Ibid.
[82] Ibid., pp. 125–26.
[83] Ibid., p. 155.

depend upon the tacit support of the majority of the population. The only way to win more recognition and enforcement of our individual rights is to educate the populace of the truth and wisdom of freedom. The publication of works like Hoppe's, with an uncompromising, hard-core (and, more importantly, correct) defense of liberty, certainly advances this cause.

PART VI

INTERVIEWS & SPEECHES

23

On Libertarian Legal Theory, Self-Ownership, and Drug Laws

This was an interview by Anthony Wile at *The Daily Bell*: "Stephan Kinsella on Libertarian Legal Theory, Self-Ownership and Drug Laws," *The Daily Bell* (July 20, 2014).

The Daily Bell: It's been a while since we interviewed you. Let's focus on some areas that you've been exploring lately. You've been thinking a lot about the essential basis of the libertarian idea lately, and the relationship between the non-aggression principle, property rights and related matters. Can you give us insight into your thinking? What specifically remains confused? What is the difficulty that people struggle with regarding the non-aggression principle and property rights?

Stephan Kinsella: The core insight of the founding generation of modern libertarian thinkers like Ayn Rand and Murray Rothbard is that *initiating* violence against others is wrong, unjustified, and should be prohibited by law—whether that is state law (in Rand's case) or private law (for anarchist libertarians like Rothbard and Hoppe).

Rand, in Galt's speech, sets out a "non-initiation of force" principle:

> So long as men desire to live together, no man may *initiate*—do you hear me? No man may *start*—the use of physical force against others.[1]

---

[1] Ayn Rand, "Galt's Speech," in *For the New Intellectual*, quoted in the "Physical Force" entry, Harry Binswanger, ed., *The Ayn Rand Lexicon: Objectivism from A to Z* (New York: New American Library, 1986; https://perma.cc/L4YA-96CC). See discussion in "What Libertarianism Is" (ch. 2), n.13 *et pass.*

Rothbard formulated a similar idea but called it an "axiom":

> The libertarian creed rests upon one central axiom: that no man or group of men may aggress against the person or property of anyone else. This may be called the "nonaggression axiom." "Aggression" is defined as the initiation of the use or threat of physical violence against the person or property of anyone else. Aggression is therefore synonymous with invasion.[2]

Rothbard goes on, in *The Ethics of Liberty*:

> The fundamental axiom of libertarian theory is that each person must be a self-owner, and that no one has the right to interfere with such self-ownership.... What ... aggressive violence means is that one man invades the property of another without the victim's consent. The invasion may be against a man's property in his person (as in the case of bodily assault), or against his property in tangible goods (as in robbery or trespass).[3]

(I provide elaboration on some of these issues in other articles and posts.[4])

Rand's non-initiation of force principle, and Rothbard's so-called "non-aggression axiom," are usually today referred to as the non-aggression principle, or NAP, by libertarians (some call it the zero-aggression principle, or ZAP). My impression is that "axiom" changed to "principle" over the last few decades for a couple reasons. First, "axiom" was a term heavily used by Objectivists, e.g., in their epistemological reasoning and terminology, and a growing number of libertarians are not Objectivists, and so shun that usage.

Second, calling the principle an "axiom" implies that it is either the primary or only principle, or self-contained or complete; or perhaps that it is simply an arbitrary postulate as in mathematical axioms; or

---

[2] Murray N. Rothbard, *For A New Liberty* 2d ed. (Auburn, Ala.: Mises Institute, 2006; https://mises.org/library/new-liberty-libertarian-manifesto), p. 23.

[3] Murray N. Rothbard, "Property and Criminality," p. 60, and "Interpersonal Relations: Ownership and Aggression," p. 45, both in *The Ethics of Liberty* (New York: New York University Press, 1998; https://mises.org/library/crusoe-social-philosophy).

[4] E.g., "What Libertarianism Is" (ch. 2), "How We Come to Own Ourselves" (ch. 4), and posts such as Kinsella, "The Relation between the Non-aggression Principle and Property Rights: a response to Division by Zer0," *Mises Economics Blog* (Oct. 4, 2011).

even that it is an undeniable, logically deduced starting point. Because libertarians are diverse in their views on the nature of rights and how they are justified, it seems better to refer to the non-aggression principle—a better way to define what views we all share in common, regardless of how they are arrived at. Randians, for instance, think that the individual rights implied by the non-initiation of force principle (i.e., the NAP) are validated by more fundamental philosophical insights about the nature of man, so they would not want to view non-aggression as some arbitrary or postulated math-type axiom. Utilitarian and empiricist type libertarians, intuitionists, religionists who ultimately base their political ethics on some divine or moral law or commands, etc., might not want to view non-aggression as some self-contained or logically deduced starting point. And so on. So the term "axiom" has become less common. Nonetheless, definitions and categories are necessary—there is something that makes us all libertarian, after all. And the idea of the "non-aggression principle" seems to best capture that, at least as a generally descriptive if shorthand term.[5]

However, one problem that has arisen is that aggression, as commonly thought of, has to do with interpersonal violence: invading another person's *body*: physical fighting or clashing. If you say you are opposed to aggression, this implies you favor self-ownership or, more precisely, body ownership. But it does not obviously, immediately imply property rights in *other* resources, such as land or movable objects. One would not think of stealing the owned resources of others as "aggression," as the term is used in everyday talk. Squatting on someone's land or using their hut while they are away might be trespass, but it does not seem like interpersonal violence that the term "aggression" seems to be aimed at.

Thus, libertarians tend to elaborate or define the NAP in a somewhat counterintuitive or idiosyncratic way, so that "aggression," as they mean it, covers both interpersonal bodily violence and theft or trespass against other owned resources. In their elaborations they say that we oppose aggression against the bodies *or property* of other people—and *also*, that this means *fraud* is also prohibited … as is *contract breach*. This is a lot to pack into the notion of aggression, into the NAP, which on its face

---

only prohibits attacking others' bodies without provocation. They take the idea that it is wrong to physically attack others' bodies and then pack into it related libertarian notions such as: homesteading (how property rights arise), trespass (use of someone's owned resource without permission), contract and abandonment (the capacity to transfer or alienate property rights in owned resources), and even fraud theory. This cluster of related ideas or principles is crucial to the libertarian political philosophy, but it is a lot to put under the rubric of "aggression." Both libertarians and our opponents have noticed this, and the former have sought to clarify our principles, and our terminology.

And, thus, the more sophisticated libertarians have recognized that property rights are more fundamental than the non-aggression principle. This is part of what Rothbard was getting at in his insistence that *all rights are essentially property rights.*[6] It is what Hoppe is getting at in his Misesian-Austrian influenced theory that property rights arise because of the fundamental fact of scarcity: the possibility of *conflict.*[7]

Why are property rights and how they are allocated more fundamental than the non-aggression principle? Well, in the case of bodies, the NAP is virtually *synonymous* with body-ownership; to say you oppose aggression is to *say that* you endorse self-ownership; and vice-versa. These are basically equivalent normative statements. We do not need a theory of property allocation for bodies, since opposing aggression automatically implies that each person is the owner of his body (libertarians differ on the rationale, but all consistent libertarians favor self-ownership and oppose interpersonal aggression, for whatever reason).

---

6 See Rothbard, "'Human Rights' as Property Rights," in *The Ethics of Liberty* (http://mises.org/rothbard/ethics/fifteen.asp).

7 See, e.g., Hans-Hermann Hoppe, *A Theory of Socialism and Capitalism: Economics, Politics, and Ethics* (Auburn, Ala.: Mises Institute, 2010 [1989]; www.hanshoppe.com/tsc), chaps. 1, 2, and 7; *idem*, "Of Common, Public, and Private Property and the Rationale for Total Privatization," in *The Great Fiction: Property, Economy, Society, and the Politics of Decline*, Second Expanded Edition (Auburn, Ala.: Mises Institute, 2021; www.hanshoppe.com/tgf); "What Libertarianism Is" (ch. 2), n.9 *et pass.*

But this is not so in the case of *external* resources—that is to say, scarce means or goods *that were once unowned*, unused, unclaimed, but that now are *regarded as means of action* by some human actors.[8]

For such resources, we need a theory of property *allocation* to determine the owner of the resource *before* we can judge a given use of the resource as "aggression"—i.e., trespass, theft—or not. If *A* enters into a hut that *B* claims, it is trespass, or "aggression," only if *B* is the owner of the hut. If *A* is the owner of the hut, then it is not trespass to use it, even if *B* objects. Contrast this with *A* using *B*'s body without *B*'s consent (hitting it, say); simply by being opposed to aggression, we take *B*'s side over *A*'s, because to oppose interpersonal, bodily aggression *means* that each person (at least presumptively) owns his own body.[9] But opposing "aggression" (trespass) for non-human resources requires us to identify who the owner of a given resource is. In the case of human bodies, it is obvious who the (presumptive) owner of the body is. Not so for external, previously-unowned, resources.

To be sure, there is definitely a *connection* between self-ownership and property rights in other resources. One's body is a *means of action*, as are other scarce means (resources, goods) in the world. There can be clashes or conflict over both, and because of the fundamental, unavoidable and undeniable fact of scarcity, only one person, one actor, can have the right, or ability, to use a body or other resource for a given purpose at a given time.

The libertarian principle, then, is based on recognizing this fundamental condition of human life, and it says that we ought to have property rights assigned in all scarce resources—any means over which there could be conflict—so that humans can peacefully, cooperatively, and productively employ scarce means to pursue their goals; and that property rights have to be determined in accordance with some objective criteria—some objective *link* between the claimant and the resource in question. It has to be a link that is objective so that various contestants

---

[8] For further discussion of the difference between bodies and previously unowned things, see "A Libertarian Theory of Contract" (ch. 9), Part III.B.

[9] See "What Libertarianism Is" (ch. 2), n.4 *et pass.*

who claim the resource can recognize it and come to an agreement about who has the better claim to the resource.

In the case of one's body, the obvious answer is: each person himself presumptively has the best link to his body, because of his direct control of it. It is only presumptive, since some actions, like violent attacks on others, can justify the victim using self-defense; but it is the default presumption.

And in the case of other resources, external resources, things that were once unowned, then obviously the first user of the resource has a better claim than a latecomer, since without what Hoppe calls the "prior-later" distinction, there can be no property rights at all, only a war of all against all and might-makes-right. This latter rule is supplemented by principles of contractual transfer and rectification. That is, the earlier user has a better claim to the resource than some latecomer—*unless* he did something to change this, such as contractually transfer (or abandon) the thing, or commit some offense (tort) against someone else, which obligates him to transfer some of his property to the victim to make restitution.[10]

I have no problem with using the concept of aggression, or the NAP formulation, as a shorthand summary of the basic libertarian idea, but it must be kept in mind that it is only shorthand, and its meaning can only be fully grasped by appreciating the nature and purpose of property rights and how they are allocated.[11] We cannot forget the fundamental fact of scarcity is what gives rise to the possibility of conflict and thus for the need for property rights to enable social cooperation.

In recent years some libertarians have objected to the NAP. I think there are a variety of reasons for this. One is that the relationship between property and scarcity and rights and aggression as sketched above has not been fully comprehended by everyone in our relatively young freedom philosophy (which basically started in the 1960s with Rand and

---

[10] These issues are discussed in other chapters, such as "What Libertarianism Is" (ch. 2), "How We Come to Own Ourselves" (ch. 4), and "A Libertarian Theory of Contract" (ch. 9).

[11] Again, see "What Libertarianism Is" (ch. 2), n.4 *et pass.*

Rothbard, in my view).[12] And, the movement has been growing in recent decades, with a lot of the newcomers coming in through Ron Paul and political activism rather than through more intellectual Randian or Rothbardian approaches. This has resulted in a large number of people with a fairly surface level understanding of the connections between liberty, property rights, aggression, and so on. And they sense that the NAP does not capture everything about the libertarian principles. So they reject it and seek some deeper connections or better formulations.

Another reason is that there are many minarchist or even classical liberal-type libertarians who do not oppose the state itself on principle, they do not oppose taxation, they accept the idea of public goods, market failure, and the need for state provision of law and justice and infrastructure and so on. In other words, they recognize that if we oppose all aggression, on principle, they have to oppose the state, and they do not want to do that. So they essentially do what conservatives and liberals do, which is to count the NAP as just one of many important moral or societal "values" that "matter." So they are against aggression, they will say—but they are also for or against other things too, and all these competing values must be "balanced" against each other. We can't be dogmatic or extreme or doctrinaire, you see. Yes, yes, we want to reduce aggression, but we want to defend the country, we want to fund the state and the police and the roads, we want to prevent people from racially discriminating against minorities and so on—so you have to compromise or bend the NAP. You have to permit the state to commit aggression—to tax, to put people in jail for reading the wrong books or using the wrong drugs or for refusing to fight for the country in a war—for the greater good. In other words, if you are going to make an omelet, you have to be willing to break a few eggs.

Some of these statist-"libertarians" are honest and admit they are in favor of aggression. They think it is unfortunate that we have to permit some aggression, but it's necessary to prevent some anarchist chaos. I can almost respect this type of "rights-utilitarianism," though I disagree with it. But others are more disingenuous about this. For example, they

---

[12] See "Libertarianism After Fifty Years: What Have We Learned?" (ch. 25); Kinsella, "Foreword," in Chase Rachels, *A Spontaneous Order: The Capitalist Case For A Stateless Society* (2015; https://archive.org/details/ASpontaneousOrder0).

will engage in equivocation—equating aggression to all forms of force, including self-defense, and saying that the anarcho-libertarian himself supports aggression (because he recognizes that self-defense is legitimate), so he makes an "exception" too, just like the minarchist-statist does. This is blatantly stupid, or dishonest, in my view, but I've seen it many times.

Then we have the emergence of the soi-disant "bleeding heart" libertarians, the "privilege" checkers and the "thickers," and so on, many of whom are in favor of the state and the promotion of values other than individual (property) rights. They don't want a rigid—i.e., principled—adherence to the NAP to get in the way of using the state or law to pursue their a-libertarian, or even unlibertarian, goals.

Now, as a human being, I, like every other libertarian, have values other than liberty. We are not just libertarians, ever. However, we do value liberty, and we oppose aggression. For us it is a "side-constraint," to use Nozick's phrase: we believe aggression is simply wrong, or unjustifiable. As Nozick wrote, "Individuals have rights, and there are things no person or group may do to them (without violating their rights)."[13] When the conservative, or liberal, or minarchist, or "bleeding heart" libertarian starts wagging their finger and tut-tutting that they oppose aggression but that unlike the "simpleminded" libertarian it is not their "only value," you can be sure they are setting the stage to propose or endorse or condone some kind of invasion of liberty—some act of aggression. That is, when I hear people, even some libertarians, condescendingly denounce our focus on aggression as the primary social evil, ... I want to hold onto my wallet, because they are coming after it. Or as Ayn Rand says in "Francisco's Money Speech," "Run for your life from any man who tells you that money is evil. That sentence is the leper's bell of an approaching looter."[14] Likewise, when someone says

---

13 See Robert Nozick, *Anarchy, State, and Utopia* (New York: Basic Books, 1974), p. ix.

14 See Ayn Rand, "Francisco's Money Speech," Capitalism Magazine (Aug. 30, 2002; https://perma.cc/J2G2-TU2U). See also Llewellyn H. Rockwell, Jr., "The Tax-Reform Racket," *Mises Daily* (Jan. 17, 2005; https://mises.org/library/tax-reform-racket):

Is there a need to reform taxes? Most certainly. Always and everywhere. You can always make a strong case against all forms of taxation and all tax codes and all mechanisms by which a privileged elite attempts to extract wealth from the population. And this is always the first step in any tax reform: get the public seething

aggression is not the only thing that matters, they are about to advocate aggression. Keep an eye on these people.

To be clear here, among some of these "leftish" type libertarians, I would distinguish two prominent groups very differently: the "bleeding heart" libertarians seem by and large to be mushy-headed, non-rigorous and pro-state while the anarchist left-libertarians are largely solid—they are against the state, they are mostly solid on economics and Austrianism (except perhaps for some of the mutualists), they are against war, they are against intellectual property, etc.

In my view, the bleeding heart types are by and large barely libertarian and promote horrible and statist ideas, such as a basic guaranteed income, an insane proposal that most libertarians for the last fifty years could have instantly recognized as a socialistic and unjustified positive right. By contrast, the anarchist left-libertarians are by and large great. That said, I personally think the best and most consistent approach to libertarianism is Misesian-Rothbardian-Hoppean anarcho-libertarianism, sometimes called anarcho-capitalism. Incidentally, that latter term is one I use less now than I used to, partly because of the damage done to the term "capitalism" by the left-libertarians' relentless campaign against it, and partly because it is somewhat misdescriptive: capitalism refers to only one aspect of the economy of an advanced free market society; and the economy itself is only one part of a libertarian society. Just as the NAP can be used as a convenient shorthand for the libertarian vision of a cooperative, property-rights respecting society, "capitalism" can also be used as a shorthand term to describe the libertarian society, though it's increasingly difficult to do this and the term is fraught with the potential for confusion. Anyway, this is somewhat of a tangent, now, but what I primarily disagree with the anarchist left-libertarians on is their "thickism," some of their cultural preferences and predictions about what a free society would look like, and their endorsement of the left-right spectrum or dichotomy in their use of the left prefix itself. I reject the left-right spectrum. I think the right or conservatism is virtually incoherent (why would there be an alliance of neocons, religious right, and

---

about the tax code, and do it by way of preparation for step two, which is the proposed replacement system. Of course, this is the stage at which you need to hold onto your wallet.

free market chamber of commerce types), and the left is soft-socialism, and ultimately the right is some variant of socialism too.[15]

The Daily Bell: Murray Rothbard insisted that all "human rights" are property rights—why?

Stephan Kinsella: He talked about this in his chapter "'Human Rights' As Property Rights," from his great work *The Ethics of Liberty*. Rothbard understood that all disputes—all real disputes—are ultimately about control of scarce means of action, i.e., physical resources. The right to freedom of speech or the press makes sense only if understood as a theory of property rights: the right of a publisher or person to use his own paper and ink and body as he sees fit. Rothbard was influenced not only by Rand, but by Mises (Hoppe was in turn influenced heavily by Rothbard and Mises).

Mises's praxeology provides an incredibly lucid and useful analysis of the nature of human action. When humans act, they employ scarce means (including their bodies) to attempt to causally interfere with the universe, so as to bring about a different future outcome than they predict or forecast would otherwise transpire without their acting intervention—a prospect that gives rise to uneasiness (Mises's term) that they seek to quell. In a magical world or the Garden of Eden or the Land of Cockaigne (Hoppe sometimes calls it Schlaraffenland)[16] there is no conflict possible, but human action is also virtually inconceivable. (Just as human action is virtually inconceivable in the unrealistic and

---

[15] See, e.g., Hans-Hermann Hoppe, "The Socialism of Conservatism," in *A Theory of Socialism and Capitalism. But see* Hoppe's article "A Realistic Libertarianism," *LewRockwell.com* (Sept. 30, 2013; https://www.hanshoppe.com/2014/10/a-realistic-libertarianism), arguing that "libertarian theory [is] compatible with the world-view of the Right," because the right is essentially "realistic"—it recognizes "the existence of individual human differences and diversities and accepts them as natural"—while the left is egalitarian and thus destructive and contrary to human nature since it "denies the existence of such differences and diversities or tries to explain them away and in any case regards them as something unnatural that must be rectified to establish a natural state of human *equality*."

[16] See, e.g., Hoppe, "Of Common, Public, and Private Property and the Rationale for Total Privatization," p. 86 (using "Schlaraffenland"); Hoppe, *A Theory of Socialism and Capitalism*, p. 219 (quoting Mises using the term "land of Cockaigne"). See also the Wikipedia entry for "Cockaigne" (https://en.wikipedia.org/wiki/Cockaigne).

hypothetical construct of the "evenly rotating economy" employed by Mises and Rothbard.)[17]

In our world, the real world, there is always scarcity, always the possibility of conflict between actors, always the need to employ scarce means to pursue ends or goals. Property rights are simply conflict-avoidance or conflict-reduction norms that civilized people adopt, respect, and abide by because of their basic values: pro-peace, pro-society, pro-prosperity, pro-cooperation and so on (I have referred to these basic values as "grundnorms," drawing on legal philosopher Hans Kelsen's terminology).[18] That is why every right, every human right, every individual right, is ultimately a property right. All property rights are ultimately enforceable by physical control of the possessor/user/claimant, and defendable by physical force (e.g., self defense) or the literal use of force implied by a *law* that protects such right.

All law, after all, ultimately is enforced by the use of force against the body or other possessions of the transgressor. (This is recognized in the so-called "bad man" theory of law espoused by Supreme Court Justice Oliver Wendell Holmes.)[19] Every conflict, every dispute, is always, ultimately, about who gets to control a given disputed resource. That is why every law, every right, is ultimately about property rights: deciding who the owner is, or should be. There is no way around this. This is why it is frustrating when mainstream thinkers and even some libertarians talk vaguely about "human rights"; it opens the door to legal invasions of property rights. People confusingly say that people fight over religion; they do not. They fight over others' bodies and the physical things, the scarce means (land and so on) that the others have or want to use. If I threaten to kill you if you do not convert to Islam, I am really asserting a property right in your body: I am asserting the right to decide whether to stick a sword into your belly. The libertarian says: you have the right to control what gets stuck into your body. Religion is just an excuse for

---

[17] See the criticism of the ERE in Jörg Guido Hülsmann, "A Realist Approach to Equilibrium Analysis," *Q. J. Austrian Econ.* 3, no. 4 (Winter 2000; https://mises.org/library/realist-approach-equilibrium-analysis): 3–51.

[18] See "What Libertarianism Is" (ch. 2), at n.22.

[19] See the Wikipedia entry for "Prediction theory of law" (https://en.wikipedia.org/wiki/Prediction_theory_of_law).

the property invasion; it is the motivation or reason for the invasion. But it is impossible to own religion and it is literally impossible to "fight over religion." It is always, always, always about property rights.[20]

The same goes for other false and positive rights, such as intellectual property (e.g., patent and copyright). The IP advocate says they support property rights in general but "also" in useful, valuable, "created" patterns and ideas. But what they really support is legal theft: using IP as an excuse to take others' money or to seize a "negative servitude" over others' already-owned scarce resources.[21]

Ultimately, every political philosophy, every legal system, is about property rights. They specify a set of rules that determines who the owner of any given scarce resource is, in the case of a dispute or contest to control that resource. The libertarian view simply has a unique way of allocating such property rights, different than other systems.[22] All other systems advocate some form of slavery or theft, since they endorse aggression against others, which is a form of slavery, or taking of owned resources from the owner when he does not contractually consent to this.[23]

The Daily Bell: Why is it crucial that libertarian theory have a sound basis for property rights and for its unique property assignment rules?

Stephan Kinsella: Property rights make sense only in a world where there is potential conflict over some identifiable scarce means (meaning: the real world). For humans to live in society, they need to acknowledge each other's existence and respect others' right to live. Every human society that has persisted has figured out a way for people to get along—to agree to certain rules that specify who has the recognized right to use or control a given resource. Humans need to use scarce means to achieve results. For those people who recognize that we exist in society, they recognize benefits of being social (trade, intercourse, division and specialization of labor) and drawbacks (you have to curtail certain appetites). The obvious result is the libertarian property assignment or

---

[20] See also *"Against Intellectual Property* After Twenty Years: Looking Back and Looking Forward" (ch. 15), at n.43 *et pass.*

[21] See *"Against Intellectual Property* After Twenty Years" (ch. 15), Part IV.B.

[22] See the first two sections of "What Libertarianism Is" (ch. 2).

[23] See "What Libertarianism Is" (ch. 2) at notes 19 & 21 *et pass.*

allocation rule: the owner of a resource is determined by inquiring into its origin: original appropriation or contract.[24]

The Daily Bell: Libertarianism rightly focuses on the concept of first use of a previously unowned scarce resource as the key test for determining ownership of it. But some say that land, for instance, can never be owned, only the improvements on the land. Any truth to this?

Stephan Kinsella: "Land" is just a referent to a particular scarce resource. It is surface area on the Earth. Land is just one type of scarce resource, so is not special in any fundamental sense (although the law classifies it as realty or immovable property, which has some different rules for transfer and alienation than does personalty or movable property, due to its different nature; but in principle it is just another ownable scarce resource). This is one problem I have with Georgists, who obsess about land as some special good.[25]

One argument against ownership of land is that the bulk of the value of the land is due to natural features that the user/homesteader did not cause, so he does not "deserve" the full value of the land, but only that which he himself worked on—the improvement. There are many problems with this argument. First, in a sense, the homesteader of a good is its creator—because of the subjective nature of values, the type of "good" a thing is and whether it is really even a "good," depends on how it is regarded by its user.[26]

Second, the argument is anchored in the flawed labor theory of property and value. It assumes that values are what property rights protect; that value can be owned. It cannot. Property rights have to do with the

---

[24] See Hoppe's pithy summary in "A Realistic Libertarianism"; and in "Of Common, Public, and Private Property and the Rationale for Total Privatization," at pp. 85–87; "What Libertarianism Is" (ch. 2), at n.37.

[25] See, e.g., Murray N. Rothbard, "The Single Tax: Economic and Moral Implications," in *Economic Controversies* (Auburn, Ala.: Mises Institute, 2011; https://mises.org/library/economic-controversies).

[26] See Hoppe's discussion of the public/private nature of goods based on subjective evaluations of users, in "Goods, Scarce and Nonscarce" (ch. 18), at n.35. This applies also to the classification of goods as consumer or capital goods, or even as goods vs. "bads," as well as the classification of a physical resource as a good at all, depending on whether it is valued by any given actor. On goods vs. "bads," see *Against Intellectual Property* After Twenty Years" (ch. 15), at n.58 and "Goods, Scarce and Nonscarce" (ch. 18), n.21.

physical integrity of scarce resources, since all conflicts are ultimately about incompatible uses of such resources. There is no property right in the value of resources one owns. Value cannot be owned.[27] Nor can labor.[28] Lockeans are wrong to say that the reason there is property rights in things like land is because a person owns his "self" and therefore he owns his "labor" and therefore he owns what unowned things he "mixes" his labor with.

Almost every part of this version of Locke is wrong. First, we do not own our "selves"; this is metaphorical nonsense. We own our bodies. Second, you do not own your labor any more than you own your actions. Owning your body gives you the *ability* and perhaps the *right* to use it as you see fit. Just as owning a home gives you the right to contemplate the stars at midnight, but we would not say there is some independent "right to contemplate the stars"; this ability is rather a *consequence* of having property rights respected in one's body, land, and other resources. And even if you owned your labor, mixing it with some resource—well, "mixing" is itself an ambiguous metaphor—but it might well simply result in the loss of ownership of the labor, rather than the acquisition of ownership of the thing the labor mixed with. If you spit in the ocean, you lose your spit, you do not homestead the ocean. That said, I think Locke's basic insight was right; it is just that it is too complicated and adorned by imprecise metaphors and unnecessary steps. Hume recognized this.[29] The reason you have a right to own a resource like land is not that you created its value, but that you staked out a claim before anyone else did. Hoppe calls this embordering.[30]

---

[27] See Hoppe, *A Theory of Socialism and Capitalism*, p. 23 n.11 & 165–68; also Hans-Hermann & Walter Block, "Property and Exploitation," *Int'l J. Value-Based Mgt* 15, no. 3 (2002; https://perma.cc/UQ8U-UM35): 225–36; Rothbard, "Law, Property Rights, and Air Pollution," in *Economic Controversies*, p. 375; *idem, Man, Economy, and State, with Power and Market*, Scholar's ed., second ed. (Auburn, Ala: Mises Institute, 2009; https://mises.org/library/man-economy-and-state-power-and-market), chap. 2, § 12, p. 183; Kinsella, "Hoppe on Property Rights in Physical Integrity vs Value," *StephanKinsella.com* (June 12, 2011).

[28] See "Selling Does Not Imply Ownership, and Vice-Versa: A Dissection" (ch. 11), at n.33 *et pass.*

[29] See "*Against Intellectual Property* After Twenty Years" (ch. 15), n.56.

[30] Hoppe, *A Theory of Socialism and Capitalism*, chaps. 1, 2.

For someone to object to my ownership of a plot of land is for them to assert a property right in the land. For only an owner of the resource has a ground for objecting to my use of it. But if they claim to own it, they have to have a basis. Yet *per assumption*, I was the first owner or user, not them. So I have a better claim to the land. This is the essential flaw in the state ownership of national forests and other undeveloped resources: state agents have not used or appropriated the resource, they have not done anything to establish a legitimate claim to the land (and I would argue no state ever can, since by its nature it is criminal, so that any property rights it ever acquires, either by contract, expropriation, or even homesteading, are owed as restitution to the state's victims), yet they prevent others from homesteading the resource. They are *acting as the owner* even though they are not a legitimate owner. Something similar is the case in the way the states of the world have coordinated via treaties to claim ownership of the seabeds, the moon, outer space, Antarctica and the like.

So the anti-land-ownership "libertarians," if we can call them that, are taking a line similar to that of statists and tyrants. In denying someone the ownership of a resource, they are themselves acting as owners. Only an owner of a resource can exclude someone else from using it.[31] Yet they have no basis for this ownership claim; it is just arbitrary verbal decree, the type of claim that cannot serve the function of property rights since it cannot prevent conflict.[32]

But there is another argument against land ownership that is more consistent with libertarian principles. This is the objection to the enclosure movement, e.g., in England. The argument is that when the state grants ownership rights in plots of land, they take away existing rights of people to use the land in certain ways, e.g., for passage. Or they assign the rights to their cronies. Or they take the land away from previous

---

[31] See "What Libertarianism Is" (ch. 2), Appendix I; "A Libertarian Theory of Contract: Title Transfer, Binding Promises, and Inalienability" (ch. 9), n.1.

[32] See "How We Come to Own Ourselves" (ch. 4), text at n.12; "Defending Argumentation Ethics" (ch. 7), the section "Objective Links: First Use, Verbal Claims, and the Prior-Later Distinction." See also Hans-Hermann Hoppe, *The Economics and Ethics of Private Property: Studies in Political Economy and Philosophy* (Auburn, Ala.: Mises Institute, 2006 [1993]; www.hanshoppe.com/eepp), pp. 320–21 (re the insufficiency of verbal decree).

634 | PART 6: Interviews & Speeches

owners (e.g., Native Americans in the US). Hoppe sketches a theory that partial property rights can be homesteaded by use.[33] For example, in a town a common path is used, establishing a collectively owned easement, a right of passage or right of way (a servitude or easement). Someone who builds a road later has to recognize the pre-existing passage rights, owned by residents of the town or their heirs. I believe I read not too long about some legally recognized right in Italy of the people to cross over privately owned property for purposes of hunting. One could argue this type of law is justified by the "partial homesteading" approach Hoppe outlines.

In this sense one could argue that the state recognition and enforcement of property rights in land sometimes amounts to a taking of pre-existing easements that had been privately homesteaded by others. But this only highlights the fact that the state, and its legislation-based legal system, inevitably violates rights and mucks things up. It does not mean that land is special or that property rights in land are not legitimate. It only means that sometimes there are partial usage-rights homesteaded by earlier users of the resource, which property rights must be respected by later comers. In other words, the only coherent objection to property rights in land rests on a recognition of the legitimacy of property rights in land (and on at least an implicit recognition that the state messes things up).[34]

The Daily Bell: Is ownership always defined by first use?

Stephan Kinsella: As indicated above, ownership in one's body is not based on first use, but on one's intimate connection to, and direct control over, one's body. That is, the objective link in the case of the body that connects a person-claimant-owner to "his" body is that it is *his* body; it houses his identity, and he directly controls it.

---

[33] See Hoppe, "Of Common, Public, and Private Property and the Rationale for Total Privatization."

[34] Likewise, arguments for IP based on the contention that IP limits on property are legitimate since "all property rights are limited by other property rights" fail because of a fundamental confusion. It is not property rights that property rights limit; it is *actions* that property rights limit. See *"Against Intellectual Property* After Twenty Years" (ch. 15), Part IV.H.

For other things—that is, scarce resources, scarce means, economic goods—"conflictable" things[35]—things that were previously unowned, unclaimed and unused—the objective link between a given claimant and the disputed resource in question is based upon three factors or principles: original appropriation (first use, or labor-mixing), contract, and rectification. In other words, being the original appropriator is not enough to show ownership, because the original owner might have abandoned the resource; or contractually transferred it to someone else, by gift or sale; or might have a debt to them due to some offense (rectification). So all three considerations play a role. But as between any two or more claimants to a given resource, we can in principle decide which one has the better claim by asking: who had it first; was any contractual transfer or abandonment done; is there a debt between the claimants that can or has to be satisfied by a property title transfer. So if *A* can show he was using the property before *B*, he has a presumptively better claim (note: *A* does not need to show that he was the first user of the property, only that he was using it before *B*).[36] But if *B* can show that *A* contractually transferred the property to *B*, then *B* has a better claim than *A*. Or if *A* harmed *B* and owes *A* restitution. Or, if *A* abandoned the property and then *B* re-homesteaded it.

The Daily Bell: What constitutes first use?

Stephan Kinsella: Some questions cannot be answered from the armchair.[37] There are more or less general or abstract legal precepts, and then more or less refined, developed and applied concrete rules that develop over time due to custom and the legal system of an advanced society. That said, we have had over two thousand years of such processes in the Roman law and English common law, so we are not totally in the dark. I would say that the essential principle here is what Hoppe identifies in chaps. 1-2 of *A Theory of Socialism and Capitalism*: the idea of *embordering*. If a resource is not yet claimed or used, then the person who somehow starts to use it in a way that is publicly visible has a better claim than others. There needs to be publicly visible borders or boundaries (one reason I sometimes think the term "private" property

---

[35] See "What Libertarianism Is" (ch. 2), Appendix I.
[36] Ibid., n.36.
[37] See "Legislation and the Discovery of Law in a Free Society" (ch. 13), n.147.

is somewhat inappropriate; all property rights are in some sense "public," as in publicly visible),[38] to serve the conflict-avoidance function of property rights. The purpose of property rights is to permit resources to be used without conflict, and the only way they can serve this function is if the boundaries or borders of the resource, or of the usage-right or property rights in the resource, are publicly visible—that is, objectively visible, or as some Kantian-inspired theorists like Hoppe might say, "intersubjectively ascertainable."

And then, also, we have to recognize that if the purpose of property rights is to permit conflict-free use of resources, and if there would be no need for property rights in a conflict-free world, then the only time a question about the scope and nature of particular property rights could ever arise, in the real world, is in an actual, real, dispute between two or more persons over a given scarce resource. And in that dispute, the very nature of the resource in question will be defined: it is whatever is being disputed or sought by the competing claimants. The very dispute itself helps define what is the resource in question. This, in turn, helps determine what type of usage "counts" for homesteading in the first place.[39]

The Daily Bell: When does a child become "first owner"?

Stephan Kinsella: I do not pretend to have a solid answer to this difficult issue. My view is that rights are bound up with human rationality and the capacity to understand, agree with and respect others' rights. Hoppe implies as much in the opening chapters of *A Theory of Socialism and Capitalism*. Rothbard and others imply that it is when the child has enough capacity to say "no" and try to run away.[40] My view is roughly along these lines, but different in some ways. My thinking is this. First, it seems obvious to me that a one-day old zygote has no rights yet, even though it is a potential human person, and biologically a "human life." It also seems obvious to me that infants have rights, so that infanticide is murder. And that there is little difference between late-term abortion

---

[38] See "What Libertarianism Is" (ch. 2), n.1.

[39] See "What Libertarianism Is" (ch. 2), n.34 *et pass.* and "Law and Intellectual Property in a Stateless Society" (ch. 14), at n.42; see also Rothbard's discussion of the "relevant technological unit" in "Law, Property Rights, and Air Pollution."

[40] Rothbard, "Children and Rights," in *The Ethics of Liberty* (https://mises.org/library/children-and-rights), p. 103.

and infanticide (even the pro-choice Ayn Rand recognized this: she wrote "A piece of protoplasm has no rights—and no life in the human sense of the term. One may argue about the later stages of a pregnancy, but the essential issue concerns only the first three months.").[41]

It seems to me that it is usually immoral or wrong to abort, even early on, but at a certain point it becomes tantamount to infanticide. However, I still think the state or even private law should not intervene, for a variety of reasons. Basically, the *jurisdiction* should remain with the mother or the family until birth. But I think that at least for a born human, it should be recognized as having full human rights. The parents can care for and make decisions on behalf of the child as its natural agent or guardian. So I think a child is a self-owner from at least the moment of birth, but it is helpless, and thus we presume the child implicitly consents to care by its guardians, presumptively its parents.[42] As for when the child reaches the capacity to be responsible for acts of aggression, or to run away and manumit himself, my feeling is roughly along the lines endorsed by common sense and the common law—at certain ages or stages of development in mid-childhood.

The Daily Bell: How does a child homestead himself, or reach adulthood?

Stephan Kinsella: This is interesting because the Montessori educational approach sees adulthood being reached after four six-year planes of development, or about age 24. Which seems about right to me, psychologically, but legally, I think the standard cultural norms on this get it about right. Eighteen years of age seems to be a good rule of thumb, though in my view, children younger than this ultimately have the right to declare independence, if they want to, so long as they have sufficient mental capacity and maturity so that it is clear the choice is a considered and real one.

The Daily Bell: Henry George believed that no land can be owned; only improvements on land. Can you comment? Was Henry George correct in any of his thinking in this area?

---

[41] See "Abortion" entry, *The Ayn Rand Lexicon* (https://perma.cc/CN8B-RGZ8).
[42] See "How We Come to Own Ourselves" (ch. 4) and Kinsella, "Objectivists on Positive Parental Obligations and Abortion," *The Libertarian Standard* (Jan. 14, 2011).

Stephan Kinsella: Well, as indicated above in the comments about land, I think this is complete nonsense and a deep confusion. First, land is not special; it is just one type of scarce resource. Second, the idea that you have a right to own resources only insofar as you improve them is based on the labor theory of property, which is itself deeply flawed and which is related to the Marxian labor theory of value.[43] Property rights allocate the legal right to control a resource when there is a conflict or potential conflict over the resource. The only question, then, is which of the two or more contestants or claimants has the better claim. The first user of a tract of land has a better connection than a latecomer, regardless of whether the first user can be said to have "created" or even "deserved" the land or not. His first use is better than that of latecomers, because without this principle there is no right to ever first use land; it would lie fallow forever.[44] Indeed, it would not exist, in a sense, because goods are things that are subjectively regarded as such as demonstrated in action, and if use of the thing is not possible, it in some sense does not "exist" as a good.[45] Notice that any institution or agency or person that tells you that you cannot homestead or use a piece of land is himself or itself asserting ownership rights in it. But based on what? Not even on first use. But on some arbitrary verbal decree. And property rights cannot be allocated based on verbal decree, because such a rule would permit any number of simultaneous claims of ownership with no objective way to distinguish therebetween, and thus would not serve the very purpose of property rights, which is to reduce conflict, to permit conflict-free and cooperative use of scarce resources.

The Daily Bell: You've called the following a fallacy: "If you own something, that implies that you can sell it; and if you sell something, that implies you must own it first. The former idea, which is based on a flawed idea about the origin and nature of property rights and contract theory, is used to justify voluntary slavery; the second, which is based on

---

[43] See *"Against Intellectual Property* After Twenty Years" (ch. 15), Part IV.D.

[44] On Rothbard's critique of the "communist" approach to property rights assignment, see "How We Come to Own Ourselves" (ch. 4), at n.14 and "Law and Intellectual Property in a Stateless Society" (ch. 14), at n.27; also "Defending Argumentation Ethics" (ch. 7), n.31.

[45] See note 26, above.

a flawed understanding of contract theory, is used to justify intellectual property." Can you elaborate please?

Stephan Kinsella: I discuss this in more detail elsewhere.[46] This is hard to elaborate in a quick interview. But here is a summary answer.

Ownership means the right to control (technically: the right to *exclude* others).[47] It is not automatically clear why this would imply the power or ability or right to *stop* having the right to control it. My view is that we own our bodies not because of homesteading but because each person has a unique link to his body: his ability to directly control it. Hoppe recognized this decades ago, as I point out in "How We Come to Own Ourselves" (ch. 4). I had to find an old German text of his and have it translated to find out his early insight on this, from 1987. This has implications for the idea of the voluntary slavery contract and the so-called inalienability debate. (See chapters 9 and 10.) In fact, the idea of homesteading one's body is obvious nonsense. A homesteader is an actor; an actor already has a body. It is inconceivable to imagine an actor homesteading his body. Homesteading, or original appropriation, has to do with the acquisition of property rights, by *already body-owning actors*, in external scarce resources in the world that were *previously unowned*. For these resources, they are *acquired* by intentional action and thus can be abandoned—or, thus, sold or given to others. So ownership of external resource *does* imply the capacity to contract, or sell, but self- or body-ownership does *not*, because they have different bases. The point is that ownership as a legal concept does not imply the right to sell. Too many libertarians just assume that it does. They are used to the right to sell in the case of ownership of external resources and thus assume that right to sell is some inherent right of ownership; it is not.

The converse mistake is the assertion that if you sell something you must have owned it. Otherwise you could not have sold it. So pro-IP advocates observe that people are paid to teach or to provide information or to invent. So they reason that the person being paid must have sold something. And to sell it, you must have owned it. You can

---

only sell things that you own, right? Well what was sold? It was the information that you were paid to come up with or transmit. Therefore, information is an object of a sale contract and must be an ownable thing. Of course, the argument is rarely put this explicitly, mostly because people making such arguments are legal naïfs, but if it was, it would be easier to show how ridiculous and flawed it is. Contracts are simply ways owners of resources grant, or deny, permission to others, to use the resource, whether the grant of control is temporary or permanent (as with a lease versus a sale) or whether it is partial or complete, or whether it is conditional or unconditional. Often this involves an exchange where two owners of two resources exchange title to these things: my apple for your pear. My coin for your milk. And so on. But some title transfers—contracts—are only one-way: a gift, or donation, say. Or if I agree to perform some action within my capability *on the condition* that you give me a monetary payment, this is a one-way title transfer: only the money is being transferred.

People confuse this because they analogize it to a normal bilateral exchange and wonder what is being exchanged in the service contract, and they assume the thing being sold is labor and that it must be ownable. This is just wrong. A careful study of Rothbard's truly revolutionary and path-breaking title-transfer theory of contract is a good idea for people who want to argue this way. (See chapters 9 and 11.) But the point is that you cannot use this confused legal reasoning to shore up the arguments for ownership of labor, or for ownership of the "fruits of one's labor," of or IP. Just because I can persuade someone to give me money on the condition that I invent something for them or teach or divulge to them some information does not mean that an invention or information is an ownable object.

The Daily Bell: Another major question for libertarians involves when and why agreements are legally enforceable or in other words, how rights are voluntarily transferred. Can you offer some insight?

Stephan Kinsella: As indicated above, I think the theory of Rothbard and Evers on this is the place to start. Contracts are just transfers of title, or ownership, to a scarce resource by the owner, by some sufficient communication of his consent (see chapter 9). Outside of this, actions that are crimes or torts—invasions of the borders of others' owned resources—can also be considered to be transfers of rights, via "rectification" or retaliation. For example if *A* attacks *B*, now *B* has a right to punch *A*. *A* has in a sense given up his right to object to this force. The right has been transferred, or forfeited. Or if *A* negligently harms *B*, now *B* is entitled to claim some of *A*'s money as damages; that too results in a transfer. But notice that intentional aggression, sometimes called "crime," and torts, are all *intentional* actions—as are contracts. These are all basically actions human actors can take that result in some kind of change in the rights landscape. This is one reason I am not hostile to the idea of positive rights—so long as they are the result of one's action. If you push someone in a lake, you now have an obligation to rescue them even though a stranger does not. If you create a dependent child by copulation, then you have certain parental obligations to care for this child. It's a positive obligation but one that you created by your free action. Libertarians, in my view, are not against positive obligations—we are just against *unchosen* positive obligations.[48]

The Daily Bell: Why does making a promise or agreeing or "committing" to do something result in a transfer of rights from the promisor to the promisee? To many—even to many libertarians—it seems elementary and obvious: If you promise to do something, you may be forced to do it.

Stephan Kinsella: We are used to thinking this way because the state's legal system has characterized it this way for some time. The idea now is that promises should be binding, if they are made with the right formalities. One theory that is used to back this up is that people rely on your promises and would be harmed, would suffer damage, if you were to be free to renege. But this reasoning is circular, of course—if the law did not enforce promises it would be unreasonable for promisees to "rely" on that promise.[49] So as Rothbard recognizes, the "binding promise" theory of contract is not coherent. Contract really simply means a transaction

---

[48] See "How We Come to Own Ourselves" (ch. 4) and Kinsella, "Objectivists on Positive Parental Obligations and Abortion." On forfeiting or waiving rights by acts of aggression, see "Knowledge, Calculation, Conflict, and Law" (ch. 19), n.81 and "A Libertarian Theory of Punishment and Rights" (ch. 5), n.88.

[49] See "A Libertarian Theory of Contract" (ch. 9), Part I.E.

or arrangement whereby the owner of a resource exercises his ownership power to grant permission or even to transfer ownership of the resource to someone else. That is all that contracts are: title-transfers, with various conditions (triggers) attached to the transfers.

The Daily Bell: By recognizing the legitimacy of defensive force, the non-aggression principle recognizes that you normally own your body but you can partially or completely forfeit this right by committing aggression. True? False?

Stephan Kinsella: In my view, this is correct. Each person owns his body—*presumptively*. But if he aggresses against others, they acquire the right to use force against him—in self-defense, first and foremost, but also, arguably, to obtain restitution or even for purposes of retribution. We must, however keep proportionality considerations in mind, so that aggressors are not "over-punished." I go into such matters in some detail in chapter 5.

The Daily Bell: Can we postulate that only by committing aggression can you lose rights in your body?

Stephan Kinsella: That is my view. It is a direct implication of the non-aggression principle. Force is justified in response to initiated force only. That is the reciprocity or symmetry of the libertarian ethos. You can do to someone what they do to you, meaning: you can only use force against someone if they have used force against you. Making a promise is not a use of force. So voluntary slavery contracts are not enforceable, as I point out in chapters 9 and 10.

The Daily Bell: Some argue that there are two ways you can forfeit or alienate your rights: aggression and saying certain words. Does this follow?

Stephan Kinsella: Well, I believe in general that speech is not a use of force and thus cannot be considered aggression. Which means force in response to such speech cannot be justified and would have to be characterized as aggression. But speech-acts can sometimes be aggression. Imagine a mafia captain saying to an underling, "Kill Mr. Jones." Or President Truman ordering a nuclear bomb to be dropped on civilian populations in Japan. And so on. (See chapter 8.)

The Daily Bell: To change the subject a bit ... we've been writing a lot about marijuana legalization here at *The Daily Bell*. High Alert, in fact, is involved in a marijuana venture. If marijuana is generally legalized, does the state owe compensation to those who were previously incarcerated?

Stephan Kinsella: Well, the state claims ownership of certain scarce resources, to which everyone who is a state victim has a legitimate claim for restitution—taxpayers, victims of regulation, prisoners incarcerated for victimless crimes, and so on. There can never, in principle, be enough resources in the state's hands to make full restitution, since the state always destroys wealth and wealth creation. So if the state dissolved, it could only pay one cent on the dollar to its victims, if that. But if a given person has the ability to get a higher restitution award, I believe they are justified in doing so.

The Daily Bell: Was there any justifiable reason to incarcerate them in the first place?

Stephan Kinsella: Well, finally, an easy one! Of course not. Drug laws are completely evil. I believe some day we will look back on this like we look back on the days of chattel slavery now.

The Daily Bell: As a matter of reality, will they receive compensation?

Stephan Kinsella: Of course not.

The Daily Bell: Any other points you want to make?

Stephan Kinsella: I would just encourage people to think consistently, use coherent and consistent terminology, and think about the liberty of your neighbors as well as your own.

The Daily Bell: Thanks again for your time.

AFTER THOUGHTS
by Anthony Wile

Stephan Kinsella makes many good and interesting points in this interview. He is an eloquent proponent for logical libertarianism and has offered significant theories on issues of property rights, copyrights, and ownership in general.

He's been attacked in the past for empyrean proposals—ones that are not entirely realistic. But to oppose his vision based on what is currently real and practical is to miss the point.

Kinsella is building an argument brick by brick for freedom and for how freedom works. There are others that concentrate on less hypothetical perspectives. We're partial to Stephan's vision because it's an uncompromising one.

There are plenty of people that can provide information on how government interacts with a "free" society but few who follow Ayn Rand's hyper-rigorous logic. Of course, Ayn Rand is controversial, especially in this day and age, but she's certainly inspired several generations of libertarian thinkers.

In statements such as "drug laws are completely evil," we can see clearly Kinsella's impatience with what he considers moral relativism. Again, he can be attacked by enemies for presenting a black and white vision. But in an era where so many are eager to proclaim shades of gray, we're happy to observe (and present) his arguments.

He is a steadfast and creative intellect at a time where it takes considerable courage to be either. One very obviously worth paying attention to whether you agree with him or not.

24

On the Logic of Libertarianism and Why Intellectual Property Doesn't Exist

This was an interview by Anthony Wile at *The Daily Bell*: "Stephan Kinsella on the Logic of Libertarianism and Why Intellectual Property Doesn't Exist," *The Daily Bell* (March 18, 2012). I would not word the title this way—the problem with intellectual property (IP) is not that it doesn't "exist" but rather that IP law is unjust. But I didn't choose the title, and have not changed it here.

Daily Bell: Give us some background on yourself. Where did you go to school? How did you become a lawyer?

Stephan Kinsella: I was from a young age interested in science, philosophy, justice, fairness, and "the big questions." In high school a librarian recommended I read Ayn Rand's *The Fountainhead*, which started me down that rabbit-hole. I ended up majoring in electrical engineering at Louisiana State University, from 1983–87. I liked engineering but over time became more and more interested in political philosophy, economics, philosophy, and so on.

In the late '80s, I started publishing columns in the LSU student newspaper, *The Daily Reveille*, from an explicitly libertarian perspective. As my interests became more sharply political and philosophical, my girlfriend (later wife) and friends urged me to consider law school. After all, I liked to argue. I might as well get paid for it! I was by this time in engineering grad school, pursuing an MSEE degree. Unlike many attorneys I now know, I had not always "wanted to be a lawyer." In fact, it had never occurred to me until my girlfriend suggested it over a family dinner, when I was wondering what degree I could pursue next—partly in order to avoid having to enter the workforce just yet. And also to make more money.

At the time I naively thought one had to have a pre-law degree and many prerequisite courses that engineers would lack; and I feared law school would be very difficult. I remember my girlfriend's chemical engineer father laughing out loud at my concern that law school might be more difficult than engineering.

So I walked across the LSU campus one day and talked to the vice chancellor about all this. He tried to dissuade me, saying that engineering undergrads tended to find law school difficult. But he conceded that a pre-law degree is not needed; all one needs is a bachelor's degree in *something*, in anything, really. I took the LSAT and did well enough to get accepted at LSU Law Center. (In the US, law is a graduate degree, the *Juris Doctor*, which requires an initial B.A. or B.S. degree. Because of ABA protectionism. But I digress.)[1]

I actually greatly enjoyed law school. Unlike many of my fellow law students, apparently, who seemed in agony. I was free to talk about laws, rules, human action and interaction. I wasn't stuck with mathematical equations. Norms and opinions were relevant. Human interactions interested me. I enjoyed the Socratic discussion method.

In one sense, it was unlike electrical engineering, which studies the impersonal behavior of subatomic particles. In law, the subject matter is acting humans and the legal norms that pertain to human action. On the other hand, I found it similar to engineering in that it was analytical and focused on solving problems. It is less mechanistic and deterministic than is engineering, but it is still analytical. So if you are the type of engineer who can shift modes of thought and who is able to write and speak coherently (not all engineers are), then law school is fairly easy. By contrast, many liberal arts majors are not used to thinking analytically. The first year of law school is meant to teach you to "think like a lawyer"—essentially, to break their spirit and remold them into the analytical, lawyer-thinking, problem-solving mold.

---

[1] I discuss some of this in "How I Became A Libertarian" (ch. 1); additional biographical material is at www.stephankinsella.com/publications/#biographical.

In any case, I became a lawyer and do not regret it. It can be lucrative and mentally stimulating. In my own case, my legal career has complemented my libertarian and scholarly interests. As Gary North has pointed out, for most people there is a difference between career and calling.[2] Your career or occupation is what puts food on the table. Your *calling* is what you are passionate about—"the most important thing you can do with your life in which you are most difficult to replace." Occasionally they are the same, but often not; but there is no reason not to arrange your life so as to have both. If you can manage it. In my case, my various scholarly publications and networks helped my legal career if only by adding publications to my CV. And my legal knowledge and expertise, I believe, has helped to inform my libertarian theorizing.

Daily Bell: You founded your own firm. Tell us how that came about.

Stephan Kinsella: After law school my first job was in oil and gas law at a large Houston-based law firm, Jackson Walker. I found the work fascinating; it was all about contract and property rights. Then I moved into patent law because it was more in demand at this time (mid '90s), and unlike state-based oil & gas law, it is a national legal field and so allows more geographic mobility. My wife's employer at the time was pushing her to take a job in the head office outside Philadelphia. So I switched to patent law in part to accommodate this and in part to capitalize on the then-burgeoning field of IP law.

I recall discussing my career choices at this time with my friend, LSU law professor Saúl Litvinoff, an old-world gentleman, who confessed that he was "nonplussed" that I, a man, a husband, would take into account my wife's career plans in my own career decisions. Oh, well. Different times.

I ended up taking a job with a Philadelphia law firm, Schnader Harrison, doing patents and related IP work. I and others there ended up moving later to Duane Morris, and when I moved back to Houston in 1997, I opened their Houston office and was eventually made partner. In 2000 I decided to join one of my clients, an optoelectronics company (think: lasers), as general counsel. At the time I had been at big law firms

---

2 Kinsella, "Career Advice by North," *StephanKinsella.com* (Aug. 12, 2009).

for about ten years and had learned a lot and enjoyed it but was ready for a change. And after about ten years as general counsel, I was ready for another shift, so I have recently formed my own legal practice, specializing in intellectual property, technology and commercial law.

Daily Bell: Why were you attracted to Austrian economics and why did libertarianism attract you?

Stephan Kinsella: I was always interested in science, truth, goodness, and fairness. I have always been strongly individualistic and merit-oriented. This is probably because I was adopted and thus have always tended to cavalierly dismiss the importance of "blood ties" and any inherited or "unearned" group characteristics. This made me an ideal candidate to be enthralled by Ayn Rand's master-of-universe "I don't need anything from you or owe you anything" themes.

Another factor is my strong sense of outrage at injustice, which probably developed as a result of my hatred of bullies and bullying. I was frequently attacked by them as a kid because I was small for my age, bookish, and a smartass. Not a good combination.

A librarian at my high school (Catholic High School in Baton Rouge, Louisiana), Mrs. Reinhardt, one day recommended Ayn Rand's *The Fountainhead* to me. (I believe this was in 1982, when I was a junior in high school—the same year Rand died.) "Read this. You'll like it," she told me. I devoured it. Rand's ruthless logic of justice appealed to me. I was thrilled to see a more-or-less rigorous application of reason to fields outside the natural sciences. I think this helped me to avoid succumbing, in college, to the simplistic and naïve empiricism-scientism that most of my fellow engineering classmates naturally absorbed. Mises's dualistic epistemology and criticism of monism-positivism-empiricism, which I studied much later, also helped shield me from scientism.

By my first year of college (1983), where I studied electrical engineering, I was a fairly avid "Objectivist" style libertarian. I had read Henry Hazlitt's *Economics in One Lesson* and some of Milton Friedman's works,[3] but I initially steered clear of self-styled "libertarian" writing. Since Rand was so right on so many things, I at first assumed she must be right in

---

[3] See Kinsella, "The Greatest Libertarian Books," *StephanKinsella.com* (Aug. 7, 2006).

denouncing libertarianism as the enemy of liberty. I eventually learned better, of course (for example, when I saw Libertarian Party pamphlets on campus before the 1988 Presidential election, and when I attended a Ron Paul appearance on campus as part of his campaign).

Daily Bell: How did you meet Lew Rockwell and become affiliated with Mises?

Stephan Kinsella: I eventually started reading more radical libertarians like Rothbard and Austrians like Mises and Hayek and soon became an Austrian and anarchist. The Austrian approach to knowledge made so much sense to me. It was rigorous without being mathematical and it was "Kantian" without succumbing to idealism: Like Rand's epistemology, the Misesian approach is also realistic.[4]

In 1988, when I was in law school, I read Hans-Hermann Hoppe's controversial and provocative article in *Liberty*, "The Ultimate Justification of the Private Property Ethic."[5] In this article Hoppe sets forth his "argumentation ethics" defense of libertarianism. This idea had a profound influence on me. I wrote several papers defending libertarian ethics based on this theory, and I wrote an in-depth review essay of Hoppe's *The Economics and Ethics of Private Property* (see chapter 22). I promptly sent it to Hoppe, who sent back a warm thank you note. This was around 1994.

Later that year, in October 1994, I attended the John Randolph Club meeting which was held near Washington, D.C., primarily to meet Hoppe, Rothbard, and Rockwell. While there I was able to get Rothbard to autograph my copy of *Man, Economy, and State*, which he inscribed "*To Stephan: For Man & Economy, and against the state—Best*

---

[4] Some of my favorite works in this regard are Ludwig von Mises, *The Ultimate Foundation of Economic Science: An Essay on Method* (Princeton, N.J.: D. Van Nostrand Company, Inc., 1962; https://mises.org/library/ultimate-foundation-economic-science); Murray N. Rothbard, "The Mantle of Science," in *idem*, *Economic Controversies* (Auburn, Ala.: Mises Institute, 2011; https://mises.org/library/economic-controversies); and Hans-Hermann Hoppe, *Economic Science and the Austrian Method* (Auburn, Ala.: Mises Institute, 1995; www.hanshoppe.com/esam). See also David Kelley's lecture series, "The Foundations of Knowledge" (YouTube playlist at https://www.youtube.com/playlist?list=PLnHOyZsmJrozETJ9zzryDhW0kliZkbIsu).

[5] See "Dialogical Arguments for Libertarian Rights" (ch. 6); "Defending Argumentation Ethics" (ch. 7); "The Undeniable Morality of Capitalism" (ch. 22).

regards, Murray Rothbard" (he died the following January). I started attending and speaking at various Mises Institute conferences such as their annual Austrian Scholars Conference.[6] I am now involved with Hoppe's Property and Freedom Society, which has annual meetings in Bodrum, Turkey, since its founding in 2006.[7]

Daily Bell: Tell us about your legal theory of property and how you came to believe that intellectual property doesn't exist.

Stephan Kinsella: My main interest has always been and remains the basics of libertarian ethics: What are individual rights and property, how is this justified, and so on. As I discuss in some previous writing, from the beginning of my exposure to libertarian ideas, the IP issue nagged at me.[8] I was never satisfied with Ayn Rand's justification for it, for example. Her argument is a bizarre mixture of utilitarianism with overwrought deification of "the creator"—not *the* Creator up there, but Man, The Creator, initial caps, who has a property right in what He Creates. Her proof that patents and copyrights are property rights is lacking.[9]

So I kept trying to find a better justification for IP and this search continued after I started practicing patent law, in 1993 or so.

Many libertarians abandon minarchy in favor of anarchy when they realize that even a minarchist government is unlibertarian. That was my experience.[10] And it was like this for me also with IP. I came to see that the reason I had been unable to find a way to justify IP was because

---

[6] It was eventually disbanded years later. In recent years, the Mises Institute has revived the Libertarian Scholars Conference and also hosts the Austrian Economics Research Conference.

[7] More at www.propertyandfreedom.org.

[8] See, e.g., Kinsella, "Intellectual Property and Libertarianism," *Mises Daily* (Nov. 17, 2009).

[9] See, e.g., my speeches "KOL012 | 'The Intellectual Property Quagmire, or, The Perils of Libertarian Creationism,' Austrian Scholars Conference 2008," *Kinsella on Liberty Podcast* (Feb. 6, 2013) and "KOL253 | Berkeley Law Federalist Society: A Libertarian's Case Against Intellectual Property," Kinsella on Liberty Podcast (Oct. 12, 2018); and my blog posts "Objectivist Law Prof Mossoff on Copyright; or, the Misuse of Labor, Value, and Creation Metaphors," *Mises Economics Blog* (Jan. 3, 2008); "Regret: The Glory of State Law," *Mises Economics Blog* (July 31, 2008); and "Inventors are Like Unto.... GODS....," *Mises Economics Blog* (Aug. 7, 2008).

[10] The old joke is: What's the difference between a minarchist and an anarchist? A: About six months.

it is, in fact, unlibertarian. As the anti-IP Benjamin Tucker said of his pro-IP opponent Victor Yarros, in the IP debate in the pages of *Liberty* in the late 1800s, "if he [Yarros] has failed [in his attempts to justify IP] and, so far as I know it, such is the nearly unanimous verdict of the readers of *Liberty*,—the fault is not with the champion, but with his hopeless cause."[11] So, too, was my attempt to justify IP a hopeless cause.

In coming to understand IP could not be justified, I was heavily influenced by previous thinkers, such as Tom Palmer and Wendy McElroy.[12] Perhaps the unlibertarian character of patent and copyright would have been obvious if Congress had not enacted patent and copyright statutes long ago, making them part and parcel of America's "free-market" legal system—and if early libertarians like Rand had not so vigorously championed such rights.

But libertarianism's initial presumption should have been that IP is invalid, not the other way around. After all, we libertarians already realize that "intellectual" rights, such as the right to a reputation protected by defamation law, are illegitimate.[13]

Why, then, would we presume that other laws, protecting intangible, intellectual rights, are valid—especially artificial rights that are solely

---

[11] Wendy McElroy, "Intellectual Property," in *The Debates of Liberty: An Overview of Individualist Anarchism, 1881–1908* (Lexington Books, 2002; https://perma.cc/ZQM2-82B9), p. 97, reprinted without endnotes as "Copyright and Patent in Benjamin Tucker's Periodical," *Mises Daily* (July 28, 2010; https://mises.org/library/copyright-and-patent-benjamin-tuckers-periodical). See also Kinsella, "Benjamin Tucker and the Great Nineteenth Century IP Debates in *Liberty* Magazine," *StephanKinsella.com* (July 11, 2022).

[12] See Kinsella, "The Four Historical Phases of IP Abolitionism," *Mises Economics Blog* (April 13, 2011); *idem*, "The Origins of Libertarian IP Abolitionism," *Mises Economics Blog* (April 1, 2011).

[13] See Murray N. Rothbard, "Knowledge, True and False," in *The Ethics of Liberty* (New York: New York University Press, 1998; https://mises.org/library/knowledge-true-and-false); Walter E. Block, "The Slanderer and Libeler," in *Defending the Undefendable* (2018; https://mises.org/library/defending-undefendable); "Law and Intellectual Property in a Stateless Society" (ch. 14), n.3; Kinsella, "Defamation as a Type of Intellectual Property," in Elvira Nica & Gheorghe H. Popescu, eds., *A Passion for Justice: Essays in Honor of Walter Block* (New York: Addleton Academic Publishers, forthcoming).

the product of legislation, i.e., decrees of the fake-law-generating wing of a criminal state?[14]

But IP is widely seen as basically legitimate. There have always been criticisms of existing IP laws and policies and many calls for "reform." But I became opposed not just to "ridiculous" patents and "outrageous" IP lawsuits, but to patent and copyright *per se*. Patent and copyright law should be *abolished*, not reformed. The problem is not "abuse" of the system, but, as Burke said, the "thing itself."[15] The basic reason is that patent and copyright are explicitly anti-competitive grants by the state of monopoly privilege, rooted in mercantilism, protectionism, and thought control.[16] To grant someone a patent or copyright is to grant them a right to control others' property—a "negative servitude" granted by state fiat instead of contractually negotiated.[17] This is a form of theft, trespass, or wealth redistribution.

So to answer your question: IP rights—patent and copyright—"exist," but are not legitimate any more than welfare rights are. There are many types of IP;[18] all are illegitimate, in my view. Not only because most of them are based on and require legislation (I view all legislation as unlibertarian; see chapter 13) but because they try to set up rights in non-scarce things, which in effect grants negative servitudes to some people at the expense of the property rights of others.

Daily Bell: According to Wikipedia and other sources, "In contract theory, you extend Murray Rothbard's and Williamson Evers's title transfer theory of contract linking with inalienability theory." What does that mean?

---

14 See "Legislation and the Discovery of Law in a Free Society" (ch. 13), and the James Carter quote at n.154.

15 "*The Thing! the Thing itself is the Abuse!*" Edmund Burke, "A Letter To Lord****," in *A Vindication of Natural Society* (Liberty Fund, 1756; https://oll.libertyfund.org/title/burke-a-vindication-of-natural-society) (emphasis added).

16 See, e.g., Kinsella, "Intellectual Property Advocates Hate Competition," *Mises Economics Blog* (July 19, 2011); Karl Fogel, "The Surprising History of Copyright and The Promise of a Post-Copyright World," *Question Copyright* (2006; https://perma.cc/DV92-TEH3); Kinsella, "Rothbard on Mercantilism and State "Patents of Monopoly," *C4SIF Blog* (Aug. 29, 2011). For more on the origins of IP, see references in "Introduction to *Origitent*" (ch. 16), n.3.

17 See "*Against Intellectual Property* After Twenty Years" (ch. 15), Part IV.B.

18 See Kinsella, "Types of Intellectual Property," *C4SIF Blog* (March 4, 2011).

Stephan Kinsella: I discuss these issues in various articles (see chapters 9 and 10). The basic idea is to root the entire idea of contract in a libertarian theory of property. The latter is based on the realization that the entire purpose of property rights is to solve the problem of incompatible uses of scarce resources. The fact that some things in the world are scarce (or conflictable) resources means that these resources can be used as means of action only if ownership is assigned and socially recognized. For things that are not scarce, there is no social problem to be solved. Hans-Hermann Hoppe addresses these issues in the opening chapters of his foundational treatise *A Theory of Socialism and Capitalism*.

Rothbard recognized that all individual rights are property rights and, therefore, that a theory of contract is not about enforceable or binding "promises" but simply about how owners of resources can contractually transfer title to others. As Rothbard recognized, this has implications for alienability or so-called "voluntary slavery" contracts. Many libertarians, assuming contracts are just binding promises, see no reason one could not bind oneself to be a slave. (See chapters 9–11.) But if you view contracts as simply transfers of title to owned objects, then the question arises: Is one's body alienable, or not? You cannot just assume that it is. Rothbard argued that it was not.

Daily Bell: You also attempted to clarify the theory. How so?

Stephan Kinsella: Rothbard sketched the theory in 1974; Evers elaborated on it in 1977, based on Rothbard's insights. Rothbard then built on Evers's pioneering article in his 1982 *Ethics of Liberty*.[19] But neither were lawyers and only took this analysis so far. I tried to incorporate their insights and integrate them with other Rothbardian, Misesian, and Hoppean insights about property rights and liberty and with established legal concepts, such as those developed under the Roman-influenced

---

[19] See "A Libertarian Theory of Contract: Title Transfer, Binding Promises, and Inalienability" (ch. 9); Murray N. Rothbard, "Property Rights and the Theory of Contracts," in *The Ethics of Liberty*; Williamson M. Evers, "Toward a Reformulation of the Law of Contracts," *J. Libertarian Stud.* 1, no. 1 (Winter 1977; https://mises.org/library/toward-reformulation-law-contracts): 3–13. Kinsella, "Justice and Property Rights: Rothbard on Scarcity, Property, Contracts...," *The Libertarian Standard* (Nov. 19, 2010), discusses the origins of the Rothbard-Evers contract theory.

continental or civil-law systems, which I regard as more libertarian, in some respects, than the more feudalistic common-law concepts.[20]

My basic approach is to recognize that mainstream legal theories of contract have been muddied by unlibertarian and positivistic conceptions of law and rights. Questions about what rights are "alienable" or not, loose talk about how promises should be "binding," etc., highlight the need for clarity in this area. In my view, to sort these issues out one needs a very clear and consistent understanding of the nature of property rights and ownership. First, we must recognize that only scarce resources are ownable; second, that the body is a type of scarce resource; third, that the mode of acquiring title to external objects is different from the basis of ownership of one's own body. The libertarian view is that human actors are self-owners, and these self-owners are capable of appropriating unowned scarce resources by Lockean homesteading—some type of first use or embordering activity. Obviously, an actor must already own his body if he is to be a homesteader; self-ownership is not acquired by homesteading but rather is presupposed in any act or defense of homesteading. The basis of self-ownership is the fact that each person has direct control over the scarce resource of his body and therefore has a better claim to it than any third party (and any third party seeking to dispute my self-ownership must presuppose the principle of self-ownership in the first place since he is acting as a self-owner).[21]

So there is a difference between body-ownership and ownership of external scarce goods. An actor is a self-owner; self-owners are able to acquire property rights in external, unowned objects by homesteading them—or by contractual acquisition from a previous owner. Many libertarians simply assume that if you own something, you can sell it. Thus, they conclude that if we are self-owners, we can sell our bodies. (Walter Block makes this argument.) My view is that we start with the nature of ownership: Ownership means the right to exclude others. It does not automatically imply the "right to sell," since this is actually moving from a situation where you have the right to exclude to one where you *do not*.

[20] See "Legislation and the Discovery of Law in a Free Society" (ch. 13) at n.153.
[21] See "How We Come to Own Ourselves" (ch. 4), text at n.15; see also "What Libertarianism Is" (ch. 2) and Kinsella, "The Relation between the Non-aggression Principle and Property Rights: a response to Division by Zer0," *Mises Economics Blog* (Oct. 4, 2011).

But in the case of formerly unowned resources, because of the way ownership is acquired, it can be undone, in effect. Homesteading an object requires more than just possession—it requires the intent to own. So if the intent to own is abandoned, then the thing is no longer owned, but merely possessed (if that). Thus, an owner of an object can transfer ownership to another by allowing the other to possess the object and then manifesting his intent to abandon ownership "in favor" of the new possessor. The new possessor then, in effect, re-homesteads the item, becoming its new owner. In other words, the nature of ownership in external objects means that it is possible to abandon ownership to them or use this abandonment method to transfer title to someone else. So ownership does not directly include the "right to sell," but it so happens to imply this power, for acquired property. However, the same is simply not true of one's body. There is no way to "undo" the homesteading of your body since you did not homestead it in the first place. There is no way to abandon your ownership of your body since it is rooted in your better claim to it based on your direct control over it. Merely stating "I promise to be your slave" doesn't change your status as having a better claim to your body, than third parties. (For more on this, see chapter 11.)

So in exploring the Rothbard-Evers title transfer theory of contract and in building on insights by Hoppe about the crucial importance of scarcity to property rights and his insights as to the nature of self-ownership and homesteading, I tried to identify the difference between body and external resource ownership, the basis and nature of acquisition of rights in each, and the nature of what contracts are (transfers of title to alienable owned objects) and what implications this has for body-alienability (namely, that voluntary slavery contracts are unenforceable and invalid).

Daily Bell: You advance a theory of causation that attempts to explain why remote actors can be liable under libertarian theory. Can you clarify this point, please?

Stephan Kinsella: I had long been dissatisfied with the approach various libertarians take to the issue of responsibility for aggression caused by leaders or groups. Too often libertarians made what seemed to me to be too simplistic or unjustified assumptions, which they relied on in their analysis. For example, some seemed to assume that there is a fixed amount of responsibility, so that if you say the mafia boss is responsible for ordering a hit, then the lackey who committed the killing is innocent. Or some would argue that a mafia boss or general or president is not responsible for the aggression committed by his underlings, unless he had coerced them or had a "contract" with them.

These all seemed confused to me. As for the latter: a contract is just a title transfer, so it is unclear why A hiring B to kill C means A is liable, but A persuading B through sexual favors to kill C is not. Focusing on *ad hoc* exceptions to the rule that A is not responsible for B's actions seemed confused to me. The Austrian theory of subjective value teaches us that there are many ways to incentivize or motivate or induce someone to commit an action for you: you can promise sexual favors, promise to pay money, hire someone, and so on. Also, there is no reason to think that both the boss and his underling cannot both be 100% responsible: in the law this is called joint and several liability.

So in developing a paper called "Reinach and the Property Libertarians on Causality in the Law" for a Mises Institute symposium in 2001 on Adolf Reinach and Murray Rothbard (see chapter 8), I relied on Mises's praxeological understanding of the structure of human action and cooperative action in general. Mises points out that in a market economy with the division and specialization of labor, people use others as *means* to achieve their ends. This is the essence of market cooperation.

When the aim is peaceful production of wealth, this is good. But people can cooperate to engage in collective aggression too. In this case the members of the group conspire to achieve an illicit end, such as theft or murder. Just as a man can use a gun (a means) to commit aggression, so people can employ others as means to commit crimes. Sometimes these other people are innocent (e.g., hiring a boy to deliver a bomb concealed in a package) and other times they are complicit (the mafia boss's underling). In the latter case, both actors are aggressors, as they play a causal role in action that uses efficacious means to achieve the end of invading the borders of the property of innocent victims. The argument is general and praxeological and focuses on the intent of the actor (which relates to the praxeological *end* or goal of the action) and the *means* employed, whether that means be an inanimate good or another human. Thus, there is no need to resort to *ad hoc* exceptions such as "the boss is liable because he was coercing the underling" or "the boss is liable because of a contract with" the underling. (For more on this, see chapter 8; also chapters 9–11.)

Daily Bell: You provide non-utilitarian arguments for intellectual property being incompatible with libertarian property rights principles. Can you explain this?

Stephan Kinsella: I alluded to this above in my discussion about negative servitudes. An IP right gives the holder the right to stop others from using their property as they wish. For example, George Lucas, courtesy of copyright law, can use the force of state courts to stop me from writing and publishing "The Continuing Adventures of Han Solo." J.D. Salinger's estate was able to block the publication of a sequel to *Catcher in the Rye*, for example. This is censorship.[22] And Apple can get a court order blocking Samsung from selling a tablet if it resembles an iPad too closely. This is just protection from competition.[23]

Daily Bell: You offer a discourse ethics argument for the justification of individual rights, using an extension of the concept of "estoppel." Can you expand please?

Stephan Kinsella: This approach is laid out in chapters 5 and 6. The libertarian approach is a very symmetrical one: the non-aggression principle does not rule out force, but only the *initiation* of force. In other words, you are permitted to use force only *in response to* some else's use of force. If they do not use force you may not use force yourself. There is a symmetry here: force for force, but no force if no force was used.

Now in law school I learned about the concept of estoppel, which is a legal doctrine that estops or prevents you from asserting a position in a legal proceeding that is inconsistent with something you had done previously (see chapters 1 and 9). You have to be consistent. I was at this time fascinated with Hoppe's argumentation ethics, which is

---

[22] See "Law and Intellectual Property in a Stateless Society" (ch. 14), n.57 *et pass.*

[23] See Kinsella, "Apple Secures Win Against Motorola Over 'Slide-to-Unlock' Patent," *C4SIF Blog* (Feb. 17, 2012); *idem*, "Intellectual Property Advocates Hate Competition." For a more recent example, see Blake Brittain, "US trade commission sides with iRobot, bans SharkNinja robot vacuum imports," *Reuters* (March 21, 2023; https://perma.cc/2MH9-2ZGG).

probably why it struck me that the basic reasoning of legal estoppel could be used to explain or justify the libertarian approach to symmetry in force: The reason you are permitted to use force against someone who himself initiated force is that he has already, in a sense, admitted that he thinks force is permissible, by his act of aggression. Therefore if he were to complain if the victim or the victim's agents were to try to use defensive or even retaliatory force against him, he would be holding inconsistent positions: His pro-force view that is implicit and inherent in his act of aggression and his anti-force view implicit in his objection to being punished. Using language borrowed from the law, we might say he should be "estopped" (prevented) from complaining if a victim were to use force to defend himself from the aggressor or even to punish or retaliate against the aggressor. I tried to work this into a theory of libertarian rights, relying heavily on insights from Hoppe's argumentation ethics and from his social theory in general.

Daily Bell: Please comment on and summarize the following books you wrote, with special emphasis on your IP theory:

- *Protecting Foreign Investment Under International Law: Legal Aspects of Political Risk* (with Paul E. Comeaux). Oceana Publications, 1997
- *Online Contract Formation* (with Andrew Simpson). Oxford University Press, 2004
- *International Investment, Political Risk, and Dispute Resolution: A Practitioner's Guide* (with Noah Rubins). Oxford University Press, 2005
- *Against Intellectual Property.* Ludwig von Mises Institute, 2008

Stephan Kinsella: The first three books are legal treatises that have little do with libertarianism or IP, although the first and third do examine practical ways for international investors to use international law to protect their property from takings from the host state.[24]

---

[24] These books and other strictly legal publications (not libertarian-related) are linked at www.kinsellalaw.com/publications. Since the original article upon which this chapter is based was published in 2012, a second edition of the third book listed above has been published: Noah D. Rubins, Thomas N. Papanastasiou & N. Stephan Kinsella, *International Investment, Political Risk, and Dispute Resolution: A Practitioner's Guide*, 2d ed. (Oxford University Press, 2020).

The latter monograph was first published as an article in the *Journal of Libertarian Studies* in 2001, with the title suggested by Professor Hans-Hermann Hoppe, then the journal's editor. My initial title had been "The Legitimacy of Intellectual Property," the name of the earlier paper I had delivered at the Austrian Scholars Conference the preceding year. (I discuss this in chapter 14.)

It was only 11 years ago [from 2012], but at the time there was not yet much interest among libertarians in intellectual property (IP). It was thought of as an arcane and insignificant issue, not as one of our most pressing problems. Libertarian attention was focused on taxes, war, the state, the drug war, asset forfeiture, business regulations, civil liberties, and so on, not on patent and copyright.

I felt the same way. I looked into this issue primarily because I had been, since 1993, a practicing patent attorney and had always been dissatisfied with Ayn Rand's arguments in favor of IP.[25] Her weird admixture of utilitarian and propertarian arguments raised red flags for me. It included tortuous arguments as to why a 17-year patent term and a 70-year copyright term were just about right and why it was fair for the first guy to the patent office to get a monopoly that could be used against an independent inventor just one day behind him.

I sensed Rand's approach was wrong, but I assumed there must be a better way to justify IP rights. So I read and thought and tried to figure this out. In the end, I concluded that patent and copyright are completely statist and unjustified derogations from property rights and the free market. So I wrote the article to get it out of my system and then moved on to other fields that interest me more, like rights theory, libertarian legal theory and the intersection of Austrian economics and law.

In the meantime, with the flowering of the Internet and digital information and with increasing abuses of rights in the name of IP, more and more libertarians have become interested in the IP issue and have realized that it is antithetical to libertarian property rights

---

[25] See "*Against Intellectual Property* After Twenty Years" (ch. 15), Part I.

and freedom.[26] It is in fact becoming a huge threat to freedom and increasingly used by the state against the Internet, which is one of the most important weapons we have against state oppression.[27]

Daily Bell: What is the reaction to your theory of IP? Hostility?

Stephan Kinsella: At first there was apathy. The few people who thought about it mostly thought my views were too extreme—maybe we need to fix copyright and patent, but surely the basic idea is sound. But my impression is that nowadays most libertarians are strongly opposed to IP.[28] And, in fact, scholars associated with the Mises Institute sensed the importance of this issue earlier than most—for example, the Mises Institute awarded my "Against Intellectual Property" paper the O.P. Alford III Prize for 2002.[29]

Laissez Faire Books is coming out with a new edition of my *Against Intellectual Property* later this year.[30] I also plan to someday write a new book on IP, tentatively entitled *Copy This Book*, taking into account more recent arguments, evidence and examples. In the meantime, those interested in this topic may find useful the additional material suggested in "Law and Intellectual Property in a Stateless Society" (ch. 14), n.‡.

Daily Bell: How do you think artists and writers feel about it? What do they do to make a living if they do not receive royalties?

Stephan Kinsella: Well, sharing is not piracy, and copying is not theft. (And competition is not theft, either.)[31] But people are used to thinking in these terms, due to state- and special interest-inspired propaganda

---

[26] See ibid., Part II; and "Introduction to *Origitent*" (ch. 16), the section "Historical and Modern Arguments About IP."

[27] See references in "*Against Intellectual Property* After Twenty Years" (ch. 15), at n.20 and "Law and Intellectual Property in a Stateless Society" (ch. 14), n.56.

[28] See references in "Law and Intellectual Property in a Stateless Society" (ch. 14), n.5.

[29] See Mises Institute Awards, archived at https://perma.cc/E33D-JST6.

[30] See the 2012 Laissez Faire Books edition linked at www.c4sif.org/aip.

[31] See Kinsella, "Stop calling patent and copyright 'property'; stop calling copying 'theft' and 'piracy,'" *C4SIF Blog* (Jan 9, 2012); Christina Mulligan & Brian Patrick Quinn, "Who are You Calling a Pirate?: Shaping Public Discourse in the Intellectual Property Debates," Brandeis University Department of English Eighth Annual Graduate Conference (2010; https://perma.cc/7SCS-8P3J); Nina Paley, "*Copying Is Not Theft*," YouTube (https://youtu.be/IeTybKL1pM4); Kinsella, "Intellectual Property Advocates Hate Competition."

to the contrary.[32] Most artists and writers do not make much money from copyright; if they are successful at all, they typically go through a publisher who makes most of the profits and owns the copyrights anyway. Luckily, technology is allowing writers and musicians to bypass the publishing and music industry gatekeepers.

There are any number of models artists can use to profit from their talent and artistry. It is not up to the state to protect them from competition. Musicians can obviously get paid for performing, and having

---

[32] See Kinsella, "Intellectual Properganda," *Mises Economic Blog* (Dec. 6, 2010); and comments by Machlup and Penrose in "*Against Intellectual Property* After Twenty Years" (ch. 15), n.78. As I note in "What Libertarianism Is" (ch. 2), I employ the term intellectual property or IP even though it is loaded, because these terms are so commonly employed one must adopt them in order to communicate about these topics with others. See also "*Against Intellectual Property* After Twenty Years" (ch. 15), Part IV.I. Böhm-Bawerk makes a similar point about the necessity of continuing to use some inaccurate terms in economics. As he writes:

> [I]f we undertake a theoretical examination of the sources of our well-being, we cannot but recognize the truly useful element when it is present, even in this area, in personal and material renditions of service, nor can we do aught but recognize that, from the economic viewpoint, such "goods" as family, church, love and the like are merely *linguistic disguises* for a totality of concretely useful renditions of service....
>
> No matter how clearly I may have proved that payment-claims and good-will relationships are not genuine goods, no matter how clearly I have therefore proved that, whenever, in practical economic life rights and relationships are bought and sold, it is not, in truth, those intangibles that are meant and are valued and transferred, but that actually it is material goods and renditions of service that are so dealt in; no matter, I say, how clear my proof, I am not going to pretend to believe that economic practice will submit to any slavish accuracy in the matter. It will in the future continue to be the custom, and rightly so, to say that *A*'s wealth consists in payment-claims, that *B* sold his good will for $50,000 to C, and that the state, the church and the family are valuable "goods." Yes, I believe even *economic theory* will, quite properly, continue talking that same language because it is the language that all the world talks and understands. For it would be an absurd undertaking to banish from the language of *economic theory* every manner of speaking that is not literally correct; it would be sheer pedantry to proscribe every figure of speech, particularly since we could not say the hundredth part of what we have to say, if we refused ever to take recourse to a metaphor.
>
> *One requirement is essential, that economic theory avoid the error of confusing a practical habit, indulged in for the sake of expediency, with scientific truth.*

Eugen von Böhm-Bawerk, "Whether Legal Rights and Relationships Are Economic Goods," George D. Huncke, trans., in Eugen von Böhm-Bawerk, *Shorter Classics of Eugen von Böhm-Bawerk* (South Holland, Ill.: Libertarian Press, 1962 [1881]), pp. 173–75 (first emphasis added).

their music copied and "pirated" helps them in this respect by making them more well known, more popular. As Cory Doctorow has noted, "for pretty much every writer—the big problem isn't piracy, it's obscurity."[33] Artists are just entrepreneurs. It's up to them to figure out how or if they can make a monetary profit from their passion—from their calling, as I discussed above. Sometimes they can. Musicians can sell music, even in the face of piracy. Or they can sell their services—concerts, etc. Painters and other artists can profit in similar ways. A novelist could use kickstarter for a sequel or get paid to consult on a movie version.[34] Authors of non-fiction such as academic articles do not even get paid today—but it enhances their reputations and helps them land jobs in academia, for example. Inventors have an incentive to invent to make better products that outcompete the competition—for a while. Or they are hired in the R&D department of a corporation that is always trying to innovate. And so on.[35] And if you cannot make your calling your career, then find a way. As director Francis Ford Coppola has observed:

> You have to remember that it's only a few hundred years, if that much, that artists are working with money. Artists never got money. Artists had a patron, either the leader of the state or the duke of Weimar or somewhere, or the church, the pope. Or they had another job. I have another job. I make films. No one tells me what to do. But I make the money in the wine industry. You work another job and get up at five in the morning and write your script.[36]

Daily Bell: We find your theories reasonable, but are you making headway? Are people generally hostile?

Stephan Kinsella: As I mentioned earlier, libertarians have, in my impression, generally become more opposed to IP, and generally on principled grounds. Most "mainstream" people are reluctant to take a

[33] Kinsella, "Cory Doctorow on Giving Away Free E-Books and the Morality of 'Copying,'" *Mises Economics Blog* (Sept. 16, 2008).

[34] See Kinsella, "Conversation with an author about copyright and publishing in a free society," *C4SIF Blog* (Jan. 23, 2012).

[35] See Kinsella, "Examples of Ways Content Creators Can Profit Without Intellectual Property," *StephanKinsella.com* (July 28, 2010); and references and discussion in "Law and Intellectual Property in a Stateless Society" (ch. 14), at n.102 *et pass.*

[36] See Kinsella, "Francis Ford Coppola, copyfighter," *C4SIF Blog* (Jan. 29, 2011).

principled or "extreme" position, instead recognizing that IP is "broken" and needs to be "reformed." They think IP abolitionism is too extreme, but really cannot articulate why. So they advocate "reform."[37] Those who stubbornly insist on defending IP have to keep coming up with increasingly absurd arguments to justify it.[38]

---

[37] Most libertarian or free-market oriented IP critics, or others who pose as critics of IP, are not actually IP abolitionists; they simply want to reform or tame the "excesses" of the system, e.g., Tom Bell, Jerry Brito, Alexander Tabarrok, Michael Masnick, Cory Doctorow, Larry Lessig, Mark Cuban (who has sponsored a chair at the EFF to fight "stupid patents"; see https://perma.cc/3K8N-8RMG), even leftists like Eben Moglen and Richard Stallman etc. who pose as opponents of corporate IP. But none of them want to abolish patent and copyright. They just want to reform it, and/or replace it with some other statist system, like taxpayer funded innovation awards or prizes. E.g., Tom Bell wants to return to the "Founder's Copyright." I mean, better than nothing, but thin gruel. As for the others, see Kinsella, "Tom Bell on copyright reform; the Hayekian knowledge problem and copyright terms," *C4SIF Blog* (Jan. 6, 2013). Tabarrok supports reducing the patent term, but not to zero, and also supports a tax funded innovation prize. Kinsella, "Tabarrok's *Launching the Innovation Renaissance*: Statism, not renaissance," *StephanKinsella.com* (Dec. 2, 2011). Lessig thinks "some punishment" of Aaron Swartz—the brilliant young co-creator of RSS, who committed suicide when facing decades in federal prison on copyright charges for uploading academic articles to the Internet—was justified. See Kinsella, "Tim Lee and Lawrence Lessig: 'some punishment' of Swartz was 'appropriate,'" *StephanKinsella.com* (Jan. 13, 2013), *idem*, "The tepid mainstream 'defenses' of Aaron Swartz," *C4SIF Blog* (Jan. 29, 2013), and *idem*, "Lessig on the Anniversary of Aaron's Swartz Death," *C4SIF Blog* (Jan. 10, 2014). See also *idem*, "Tabarrok: Patent Policy on the Back of a Napkin," *C4SIF Blog* (Sept. 20, 2012); *idem*, "'Intellectual Property' as an umbrella term and as propaganda: a reply to Richard Stallman," *C4SIF Blog* (Feb. 10, 2012); *idem*, "Stallman: An Internet-Connectivity Tax to Compensate Artists and Authors," *C4SIF Blog* (June 19, 2011); *idem*, "Eben Moglen and Leftist Opposition to Intellectual Property," *C4SIF Blog* (Dec. 4, 2011); *idem*, "Cory Doctorow, Victim of Fox Copyright Legal Bullying, Should Take A Stand Against Copyright," *C4SIF Blog* (April 27, 2013).

[38] For example:
- "Thank goodness the Swiss did have a Patent Office. That is where Albert Einstein worked and during his time as a patent examiner came up with his theory of relativity."
- "It is true that other means exist for creative people to profit from their effort. In the case of copyright, authors can charge fees for reading their works to paying audiences. Charles Dickens did this, but his heavy schedule of public performances in the United States, where his works were not protected by copyright, arguably contributed to his untimely death."
- If you are not for IP, you must be in favor of pedophilia.
- If you oppose IP, you are advocating slavery.
- "Patents are the heart and core of property rights."
- Song piracy and file-sharing are the cause of stage collapses at concerts.
- "To make a distinction between things which are ownable or not ownable with the difference being whether they're constructed out of molecules or

Daily Bell: We've come to the conclusion that copyright law and patent law are deterrents to progress and technology. Your view?

Stephan Kinsella: The empirical studies all point in this direction.[39] And this should not be surprising. Everything the state does, without exception, destroys (okay, it's good at propaganda as well—making people think it's necessary). Patent and copyright are pure creatures of state legislation. The origins of copyright lie in censorship and thought control; the origins of patents lie in mercantilism and protectionism. As Tom Palmer writes, "[m]onopoly privilege and censorship lie at the historical root of patent and copyright."[40] It should be no surprise that state interventions in the market lead to destruction of wealth, which of course will have an adverse effect on innovation.

Daily Bell: What would the world look like without patent and copyright law?

Stephan Kinsella: As far as copyright, I think it would look somewhat like what our current world is heading to since there is rampant "piracy" despite copyright law. Except there would be fewer outrageous, draconian results like jail terms and prison.[41] And there would be more freedom to engage in remixing and other forms of creativity and a richer public domain to draw on. We would still have a huge amount of artistic works being created, of course.

---

pixels is to create a new kind of apartheid, in which some kinds of property are just [n-words]."
- If IP isn't legitimate, then it's okay to steal other people's babies.
- Without IP you can't have money

See Kinsella, "Absurd Arguments for IP," *Mises Economics Blog* (Dec. 10, 2010); see also *idem*, "There are No Good Arguments for Intellectual Property," *Mises Economics Blog* (Feb. 24, 2009); *idem*, "There are No Good Arguments for Intellectual Property: Redux," *StephanKinsella.com* (Sep. 27, 2010).

[39] See references in *"Against Intellectual Property* After Twenty Years" (ch. 15), n.23.

[40] Tom G. Palmer, "Intellectual Property: A Non-Posnerian Law and Economics Approach," *Hamline L. Rev.* 12, no. 2 (Spring 1989; https://perma.cc/DH7K-ZCRV): 261–304, p. 264 (footnote omitted).

[41] See, e.g., references re Aaron Swartz in note 37, above; Kinsella, "Six Year Federal Prison Sentence for Copyright Infringement," *C4SIF Blog* (March 3, 2012); *idem*, "Man sentenced to federal prison for uploading "Wolverine" movie," *C4SIF Blog* (Dec. 21, 2011); *idem*, "British student Richard O'Dwyer can be extradited to US for having website with links to pirated movies," *C4SIF Blog* (Jan. 13, 2012).

Without patents, companies would be free to compete without fear of lawsuits—and without being able to rely on a state-granted monopoly privilege to protect them from competition. I believe that an IP-free world would have far more innovation and diverse creativity than today's world. And there would be fewer barriers to entry, so smaller companies could compete with the oligopolies that patent law has helped to create.[42]

Daily Bell: Can you explain how patent and copyright law evolved and why it was likely a reaction to the Gutenberg Press and a means of controlling information rather than protecting the public?

Stephan Kinsella: The roots of copyright lie in censorship. It was easy for state and church to control thought by controlling the scribes, but then the printing press came along, and the authorities worried that they couldn't control official thought as easily. So Queen Mary created the Stationer's Company in 1557, with the exclusive franchise over book publishing, to control the press and what information the people could access. When the charter of the Stationer's Company expired, the publishers lobbied for an extension, but in the Statute of Anne (1710), Parliament gave copyright to authors instead. Authors liked this because it freed their works from state control. Nowadays they use copyright much as the state originally did: to censor and ban books—or their publishers do, who have gained a quasi-oligopolistic gatekeeper function, courtesy of copyright law.[43] And now we see copyright being used, along with regulation of gambling, child pornography, and terrorism,

---

[42] Kinsella, "Google's Schmidt on the Patent-Caused Smartphone Oligopoly," *C4SIF Blog* (Dec. 5, 2012).

[43] See references in note 16, above; also Kinsella, "History of Copyright, part 1: Black Death," *C4SIF Blog* (Feb. 2, 2012); *idem*, "How Intellectual Property Hampers the Free Market," *The Freeman* (May 25, 2011). See also Justin Hughes, "The Philosophy of Intellectual Property," *Georgetown L. J.* 77, no. 2 (Dec. 1988; https://perma.cc/U4XX-5DZV): 287–366, p. 291 (citations omitted):

> One cannot call the history of intellectual property a purely proletarian struggle. While ancient Roman laws afforded a form of copyright protection to authors, the rise of Anglo-Saxon copyright was a saga of publishing interests attempting to protect a concentrated market and a central government attempting to apply a subtle form of censorship to the new technology of the printing press.

Regarding Roman law protecting a form of copyright, Hughes cites UNESCO, *The ABC of Copyright* (1981; https://unesdoc.unesco.org/ark:/48223/pf0000187677), p. 12. Yet this reference does not support the contention that copyright law was recognized, only that

as an excuse for the state to radically infringe Internet freedom and civil liberties.[44]

Patents originated in mercantilism and protectionism; the crown would grant monopolies to favored court cronies, such as monopolies on playing cards, leather, iron, soap, coal, books, and wine. The Statute of Monopolies (1623) eliminated much of this but retained the idea of a monopoly grant to an inventor of some useful machine or process.[45]

Daily Bell: Didn't Germany do better *without* strict copyright than Britain did *with* it? Isn't this the reason that Germany progressed so much in literature, philosophy, mathematics, etc., during the 17th and 18th centuries?

Stephan Kinsella: It probably had something to do with it. One study, by economic historian Eckhard Höffner, indicates that Germany's lack of copyright in the 19th century led to an unprecedented explosion of publishing, knowledge, etc., unlike in neighboring countries England and France, where copyright law enriched publishers but stultified the spread of knowledge and limited publishing to a mass audience.[46] Höffner's study claims that this is the main reason that Germany's production and industry had caught up with everyone else by 1900. This seems believable to me.

Daily Bell: Shouldn't the enforcement of copyright law be strictly civil? When did it become a criminal offence?

Stephan Kinsella: I am not sure exactly when the criminal penalties were added, but as I noted above, there are potentially severe civil

---

plagiarism was seen as dishonorable. Plagiarism has nothing to do with copyright law. See references in "Libertarianism After Fifty Years: What Have We Learned?" (ch. 25), n.39.

[44] See references in "*Against Intellectual Property* After Twenty Years" (ch. 15), n.20.

[45] See "KOL108 | 'Why 'Intellectual Property' is not Genuine Property," Adam Smith Forum, Moscow (2011)," *Kinsella on Liberty Podcast* (Dec. 11, 2013); also Kinsella, "How Intellectual Property Hampers the Free Market."

[46] See Frank Thadeusz, "No Copyright Law: The Real Reason for Germany's Industrial Expansion?," *Spiegel International* (Aug. 18, 2010; https://perma.cc/R3H7-6KG8). As indicated by Thadeusz, a new study by economic historian Eckhard Hoffner argues that the main reason that Germany's production and industry had caught up with everyone else by 1900 is the absence of copyright law. This seems plausible to me. See also Jeffrey A. Tucker, "Germany and Its Industrial Rise: Due to No Copyright," *Mises Economics Blog* (Aug. 18, 2010).

and criminal penalties for copyright infringement, including prison, extradition, being banned from the Internet, and so on.[47] Patent law can also be enforced not only by a damages award but also by a court injunction ordering a competitor to stop making a given product, on pain of contempt of court. And patent law literally kills people.[48]

Daily Bell: Why is Kim Dotcom in prison in New Zealand?

Stephan Kinsella: I've discussed this case in a number of posts on C4SIF.[49] Basically, he offered a service that permitted people to share files (information) with each other. This crackdown threatens any number of "legitimate" sites and services such as YouTube, Yousendit, Dropbox, and so on.[50]

Daily Bell: We've postulated a simpler solution than what you present. We've pressed the argument for private justice—clan and tribal justice as practiced for thousands of years. In this formulation no "authority" is present but those agreed upon by the two parties to the quarrel/crime. Thus, copyright issues would become incumbent on the copyright holder to enforce. In other words, the *copyright holder* not the state would have the expense of enforcement. What's your take on this?

Stephan Kinsella: I suppose this could be an improvement but I think it's still misguided. Any attempt to use force against people using information would be aggression. The only exception would be if someone

---

[47] As noted in note 36, above, there are serious criminal consequences for copyright violation, which led to Aaron Swartz's suicide, for example.

[48] Kinsella, "Patents Kill Update: Volunteers 3D-Print Unobtainable $11,000 Valve For $1 To Keep Covid-19 Patients Alive; Original Manufacturer Threatens To Sue," *C4SIF Blog* (March 18, 2020); *idem*, "Patents Kill: Millions Die in Africa After Big Pharma Blocks Imports of Generic AIDS Drugs," *C4SIF Blog* (Jan. 31, 2013); *idem*, "Patents Kill: Compulsory Licenses and Genzyme's Life Saving Drug," *C4SIF Blog* (Dec. 8, 2010); *idem*, "Killing people with patents," *C4SIF Blog* (June 1, 2015). Not to mention that IP is death. See the final lines of Kinsella, "The Death Throes of Pro-IP Libertarianism," *Mises Daily* (July 28, 2010), quoted in *"Against Intellectual Property* After Twenty Years" (ch. 15), text at n.60.

[49] See, e.g., Kinsella, "Two lessons from the Megaupload seizure," *C4SIF Blog* (Jan. 24, 2012).

[50] A recent copyright threat is to the Internet Archive. See Mike Glyer, "Judge Decides Against Internet Archive," *File 770* (March 24, 2023; https://perma.cc/K5UH-VCWT); Mike Masnick, "Publishers Get One Step Closer To Killing Libraries," *TechDirt* (March 27, 2023; https://perma.cc/BYG5-6MXL).

has contractually agreed to pay a fine if they use information in an unapproved way. But who would sign such a ridiculous contract?

In the end, I believe there is nothing wrong with using information. If you reveal information to the public by telling people or selling some product that embodies or otherwise makes evident some idea, you have to expect people to learn from this, compete with you, maybe emulate or copy it or even build on and improve on it. As Wendy McElroy has explained, quoting Benjamin Tucker:

> [I]f a man publicized an idea without the protection of a contract, then he was presumed to be abandoning his exclusive claim to that idea.
>
> "If a man scatters money in the street, he does not thereby formally relinquish title to it ... but those who pick it up are thereafter considered the rightful owners.... Similarly a man who reproduces his writings by thousands and spreads them everywhere voluntarily abandons his right of privacy and those who read them ... no more put themselves by the act under any obligation in regard to the author than those who pick up scattered money put themselves under obligations to the scatterer."
>
> Perhaps the essence of Tucker's approach to intellectual property was best expressed when he exclaimed, "You want your invention to yourself? Then keep it to yourself."[51]

Daily Bell: Why should the state enforce copyright on behalf of the individual?

Stephan Kinsella: It shouldn't. In fact, the only thing the state should do is commit suicide. Staticide. Whatever the word would be.

Daily Bell: Why should disinterested third parties pay for copyright enforcement?

Stephan Kinsella: They shouldn't and wouldn't. The whole idea is preposterous and flies in the face of human action. The market provides abundance in the face of physical scarcity. It's a good thing when we are more productive. Likewise more information and knowledge is good. To try to restrict the spread and use of knowledge is insane.

---

51 McElroy, "Intellectual Property," in *The Debates of Liberty: An Overview of Individualist Anarchism, 1881–1908* (Lexington Books, 2002), pp. 97–98.

Daily Bell: If people want to claim copyright and third party contracts, shouldn't it be up to them to enforce those contracts?

Stephan Kinsella: Sure. But you can't get IP from contracts. IP is an *in rem* or *erga omnes* right—something good against the world. Contractual rights are good only as between the parties—*in personam*—and can never result in *in rem* IP rights. I've explained this over and over.[52]

Daily Bell: Is the US legal system—which is a state-run, "public" judicial system—competent and fair in your estimation?

Stephan Kinsella: No. It is thoroughly unjust and illegitimate. It is just the facade of a criminal organization with a pretense to legitimacy.

Daily Bell: Why does the US have so many millions of prisoners, half the world's [prison] population?

Stephan Kinsella: Someone has to be first. But seriously—it's partly due to our insane war on drugs and also due to the devastation various state (mostly federal) policies have imposed on the Black population: minimum wage, welfare, inflation, unemployment, war, Jim Crow and other vestiges of slavery.

And the US regularly uses IP as an excuse to engage in imperialistic bullying of other nations, to benefit US industries such as Hollywood, the music and software industries, big Pharma, and the like.[53]

Daily Bell: Is there a power elite intent on moving toward one-world government, and are they behind copyright and patent laws?

Stephan Kinsella: I used to be fearful of a one-world state, but my current view is that the big powers, primarily the US, are the biggest threat. But yes, the Western powers are using copyright and patent to crack down on dissent and to influence other countries' policies at the behest of the MPAA, RIAA, and so on.

Daily Bell: What would be the best approach to socio-politics in your view?

Stephan Kinsella: As I explain in chapters 2 and 3, I am definitely an anarchist—have been since 1988 or so. I prefer the term "anarcho-libertarian"

---

52 See "Law and Intellectual Property in a Stateless Society" (ch. 14), Part III.C.
53 See references in *"Against Intellectual Property* After Twenty Years" (ch. 15), n.19.

nowadays, in part because of confusion spread by some left-libertarians about the connotations of "capitalism." But I am in favor of a free market and capitalism rightly understood. I am basically a Rothbardian-Hoppean in terms of politics.

Daily Bell: Do you think the Internet itself, via what we call the Internet Reformation, is having a big impact on the powers-that-be and their ability to control society and information?

Stephan Kinsella: As some earlier answers have indicated—yes. The Internet is one of the most significant developments in our lifetime, perhaps in the history of humanity.[54] The state is trying to control the Internet but I believe and hope that by the time the state is fully roused to the danger the Internet poses to it, it will be too late for it to stop it. As a *Salon* writer said about former congressman/now copyright lobbyist Chris Dodd after the Internet uprising that helped defeat the Stop Online Piracy Act (SOPA): "No wonder Chris Dodd is so angry. The Internet is treating him like damage, and routing around it."[55] My hope is that the Internet will find ways to treat the state like the cancerous damage that it is, and route around it and leave it in the dust.

Daily Bell: Where does the IP movement go now? What are the next moves? Are you content with theorizing about it? Is it having a real-world impact? What would that be?

Stephan Kinsella: Ultimately we have to try to highlight the illogic and injustices of the system so that people realize IP is illegitimate. This is an uphill battle, of course. Most people are unprincipled and utilitarian, influenced by state propaganda and economically illiterate. I have pondered trying to set up some kind of patent defense league but have not yet figured out how viable this is.[56] I would also like to urge some group like EFF or Creative Commons to come up with a simple, reliable, inexpensive way for people to abandon their copy-

---

[54] Though as of late (2023), the *Omni Magazine* types and space cadets seem to be overly obsessed with AI and ChatGPT. See Kinsella, "Rothbard on Libertarian 'Space Cadets,'" *StephanKinsella.com* (Sep. 23, 2009).

[55] See Kinsella, "Kevin Carson: So What if SOPA Passes?," *StephanKinsella.com* (Jan. 23, 2012). For more on SOPA, see "Law and Intellectual Property in a Stateless Society" (ch. 14), n.56 and *"Against Intellectual Property* After Twenty Years" (ch. 15), at n.20.

[56] See Kinsella, "The Patent Defense League and Defensive Patent Pooling," *C4SIF Blog* (Aug. 18, 2011).

rights. At present there is no easy way to do this.[57] And though it is not prudent to advocate that people flout the law, the widespread disregard for copyright and resort to piracy, torrents, and encryption will put some limits on how effective copyright enforcement can be.

Daily Bell: Any other points you want to make?

Stephan Kinsella: Let me close with a quote from Lew Rockwell:

> Let me state this as plainly as possible. The enemy is the state. There are other enemies too, but none so fearsome, destructive, dangerous, or culturally and economically debilitating. No matter what other proximate enemy you can name—big business, unions, victim lobbies, foreign lobbies, medical cartels, religious groups, classes, city dwellers, farmers, left-wing professors, right-wing blue-collar workers, or even bankers and arms merchants—none are as horrible as the hydra known as the leviathan state. If you understand this point—and only this point—you can understand the core of libertarian strategy.[58]

Daily Bell: Any references, web sites, etc., you want to point to?

Stephan Kinsella: As mentioned, I may someday write *Copy This Book*, and I also have another book in the works, *Law in a Libertarian World: Legal Foundations of a Free Society*, an edited selection of my rights and law-related articles [note: this is now the current book]. Also, I blog regularly at *The Libertarian Standard* [now defunct] and *C4SIF*. Finally, the slides and audio/video for the four Mises Academy lectures I delivered in 2011: Rethinking Intellectual Property, Libertarian Legal Theory, The Social Theory of Hoppe, and Libertarian Controversies, are also available.[59]

Daily Bell: Thanks for your time.

Stephan Kinsella: You're welcome. Thanks for your interest.

---

[57] See note 34, above.

[58] Kinsella, "Rothbard and Rockwell on Conservatives and the State," *The Libertarian Standard* (Jan. 26, 2012).

[59] See these *Kinsella on Liberty Podcast* episodes: "KOL172 | 'Rethinking Intellectual Property: History, Theory, and Economics: Lecture 1: History and Law' (Mises Academy, 2011)" (Feb. 14, 2015); "KOL018 | 'Libertarian Legal Theory: Property, Conflict, and Society, Lecture 1: Libertarian Basics: Rights and Law' (Mises Academy, 2011)" (Feb. 20, 2013); "KOL153 | 'The Social Theory of Hoppe: Lecture 1: Property Foundations' (Mises Academy, 2011)" (Oct. 16, 2014); and "KOL045 | 'Libertarian Controversies Lecture 1' (Mises Academy, 2011)" (May 2, 2013).

AFTER THOUGHTS
by Anthony Wile

We thank Stephan Kinsella for this interview and for the work he has done generally on this issue of copyright. Ideas have ramifications far beyond their apparent initial non-acceptance. What seems impractical now may be common sense tomorrow.

Human history seems to go in cycles. Right now we are seemingly at the top of the totalitarian arc. Cold comfort to most, but there has probably never been a time in human history when there was so much hidden totalitarianism and when a cabal of individuals controlling Money Power were likely making final moves to try to control the world

It is very hard to peer through the confusion purposefully laid by the dynastic families that apparently control central banking (and thus money) around the world. Monetary apologists are out in force these days, claiming that various forms of government money are an antidote to the abuse of mercantilism.

Of course, it is via mercantilism, the abuse of government laws and regulations by private parties, that Money Power retains its clout. Only by controlling the "democratic process" does a tiny group of people retain their hold on the levers of government. Behind the scenes these levers are pulled for their benefit. And *they* do the pulling.

It is mercantilism, the use of public law to reinforce private privilege, that bides at the base of Money Power. And those who are behind Money Power, the assorted apologists and enablers, will use *any* tool to buttress their privilege. Lately, in our view, they've been behind the resurgence of Georgism, Greenbackerism, Social Credit, and a number of other "movements" that claim "the people" need to take back government.

Of course, it is improbable, these days anyway, that people can "take back" their government. What is more likely is that the powers-that-be are encouraging these movements because they provide a fertile methodology for the continuance of mercantilism. Mercantilism is impossible to apply in the absence of government.

But so long as public nostrums are being peddled, it is fairly easy for Money Power to gain a foothold once again. This is why we are proponents of laissez faire and libertarianism. The solution to the problem of government is not to have more of it "properly controlled," but to have as *little* of it as possible. The less government there is, the less feasible it is to abuse it.

People like Stephan Kinsella do us a great favor when it comes to establishing this sort of argument. Any perspective that shows us how laws and regulations provide artificial benefits to some at the expense of others is of a larger benefit as well because it delegitimizes force.

Force, in fact, is at the heart of government, any government. A handful of people pass the laws that bind us to the state, and generations to come as well. But Rothbardian libertarianism (and Misesian libertarianism generally) has been all about providing an alternative narrative to the force of the state.

Logically, Rothbard, Mises, and other Austrian economists have shown us that force is the common currency of government and that voluntary, free-market societies have existed in the past and are likely the better alternative.

By opening up our minds to an alternative view of copyright, Kinsella continues this process. You don't have to agree with him, of course, and we ourselves have proposed a simpler solution: If people want to enforce copyright (or any other legal nostrum for that matter), let them do so out of their own pocket. That would put an end to the regulatory state in short order.

Beyond that, government doesn't work on a logical level. Every law and regulation, enforced by the threat of incarceration or even death, fixes prices by transferring wealth from those who earn to those who haven't. The more price-fixing you have, the more unfair, disorderly, and inefficient society becomes. Eventually, society falls apart entirely.

Of course, in the West, one could argue we're at that stage now. Humans badly need new solutions. People need to understand that they need to think for themselves and exercise their own "human action" in order to help themselves and their families to survive as the world continues its slow-motion spiral into depression and military destruction.

People like Stephan Kinsella are indispensible to this process. Austrian economics, generally, and the larger ambit of free-market thinking it encourages, are necessary in providing us with alternatives showing us that the current environment is not the "only alternative."

Whether you agree with Kinsella or not, we're happy he's around and has presented such thought-provoking ideas. It's people like Kinsella with exciting new ways of looking at sociopolitical and economic issues who provide us with a vision for the future. He is, in fact, part of the so-called "great conversation."

You can join it, too. Just study the great thinkers and come up with your own ideas. If the ideas are interesting enough, people will start to discuss them and write about them and respond to them. That's how the Austrian school succeeded and why its ideas are now part of the larger economic dialogue.

We know it's a real discipline because it builds on thousands of years of economic history. Don't let the sophists and the wily ones distract you from the truth. As free-market thinking succeeds, they are coming out in force. But the bottom line, unfortunately, is that government is force, no matter the "law" it is enforcing.

Of course, there is no absolute freedom, and human beings are innately tribal. But within this context, we choose to advocate for freedom above all. One travels toward minarchism via rigorous anarchic logic, not by advocating *more* government. We're glad that people like Kinsella give us additional intellectual tools to make persuasive arguments for a less coercive society.

25

Libertarianism After Fifty Years:
What Have We Learned?

This chapter is an edited transcript of my speech "Libertarianism After Fifty Years: What Have We Learned?", delivered at the NYC LibertyFest in Brooklyn in 2014. I was allotted only a short speaking time, so the speech was somewhat condensed. I expanded on the issues touched upon in a transcript posted on my site, which is the basis for this chapter.*

INTRODUCTION

Hello. I'm glad to be here. Thank you to Ian and Mike for the invitation. I do have my eleven-year-old son with me. It's the second or third time he's seen me speak. He's been to Auburn with me. I went to the New York Comic Con with him on Thursday. So turnabout's fair play although it was fun. Comic Con was great.

I have fifteen minutes. My topic is "Libertarianism After Fifty Years—What Have We Learned"? If I get cut off, I will continue this in a private podcast. You can find more information, if I run out of time, because this is a big topic for fifteen minutes.

This is my own view of libertarianism. It might not be shared by everyone here. But what I would like to talk about is—what is the libertarian

---

* My talk was originally billed as "Libertarianism After Fifty Years: A Reassessment and Reappraisal," NYC LibertyFest, Brooklyn, NY (October 11, 2014), but I changed the subtitle before speaking. The speech is available at "KOL152 | NYC LibertyFest: 'Libertarianism After Fifty Years: What Have We Learned?'", *Kinsella on Liberty Podcast* (Oct. 12, 2014); the transcript was posted as "Libertarianism After Fifty Years: What Have We Learned? (transcript)," *StephanKinsella.com* (Oct. 12, 2014). I have updated and reworked it for this chapter.

movement? How old is it? Where did we come from? What have we learned, and what's to come?

THE MODERN LIBERTARIAN MOVEMENT[1]

In my view, the modern libertarian movement is only about five or six decades old. The ideas that have influenced our greatest thinkers can be traced back decades and centuries to previous movements and thinkers[2]—to the Enlightenment, to classical liberal thinkers, to thinkers from the Old Right, to luminaries such as Hugo Grotius, John Locke, Thomas Paine, Herbert Spencer, David Hume, and John Stuart Mill, and to more recent and largely even more radical thinkers, such as Gustave de Molinari, Benjamin Tucker, Lysander Spooner, Bertrand de Jouvenel, Franz Oppenheimer, and Albert Jay Nock.[3]

The beginnings of the modern movement can be detected in the works of the "three furies of libertarianism," as Brian Doherty calls them: Rose Wilder Lane, Ayn Rand, and Isabel Patterson, whose respective books, *The Discovery of Freedom*, *The Fountainhead*, and *The God of the Machine*, were all published, rather remarkably, in the same year: 1943.[4] But in its more modern form, libertarianism originated in the 1960s and 1970s from thinkers based primarily in the United States, notably Ayn Rand and Murray Rothbard. There's a reason Jerome Tuccille's hilarious satirical memoir is entitled *It Usually Begins with Ayn Rand*.[5] Other significant influences on the nascent libertarian movement include Ludwig

---

[1] This section did not appear in my original talk for lack of time. It is an expanded version of my introductory remarks, and was included in a long footnote in the transcript posted on my site. I have adapted this section from Kinsella, "Foreword," in Chase Rachels, *A Spontaneous Order: The Capitalist Case For A Stateless Society* (2015; https://archive.org/details/ASpontaneousOrder0). For another interesting retrospective, see Mark Thornton, "Libertarianism: A Fifty-Year Personal Retrospective," *J. Libertarian Stud.* 24, no. 2 (2020; https://mises.org/library/libertarianism-fifty-year-personal-retrospective): 445–60.

[2] See Brian Doherty, *Radicals for Capitalism: A Freewheeling History of the Modern American Libertarian Movement* (New York: PublicAffairs, 2008); and David Boaz, ed., *The Libertarian Reader: Classic & Contemporary Writings from Lao Tzu to Milton Friedman* (Simon & Schuster, 2015).

[3] See Boaz, *The Libertarian Reader*.

[4] See Doherty, *Radicals for Capitalism*, chap. 3.

[5] Jerome Tuccille, *It Usually Begins with Ayn Rand* (New York: Stein and Day, 1971).

von Mises, author of *Liberalism* (1927) and *Human Action* (1949, with a predecessor version published in German in 1940); Nobel laureate F.A. von Hayek, author of *The Road to Serfdom* (1944); Leonard Read, head of the Foundation for Economic Education (founded 1946); and Nobel laureate Milton Friedman, author of the influential *Capitalism and Freedom* (1962).

The most prominent and influential of modern libertarian figures, however, were novelist-philosopher Ayn Rand, the founder of "Objectivism"—the political wing of which, dubbed "capitalism" by her, is more or less co-extensive with libertarian minarchism—and a "radical for capitalism"; and Murray Rothbard, the Mises-influenced libertarian anarcho-capitalist economist and political theorist. Rothbard's seminal role is widely recognized, even by non-Rothbardians. Objectivist John McCaskey, for example, has observed, that out of the debates in the mid-1900s about what rights citizens ought to have:

> ... grew the main sort of libertarianism of the last fifty years. It was based on a principle articulated by Murray Rothbard in the 1970s this way: No one may initiate the use or threat of physical violence against the person or property of anyone else. The idea had roots in John Locke, America's founders, and more immediately Ayn Rand, but it was Rothbard's formulation that became standard. It became known as the *non-aggression* principle or—since Rothbard took it as the starting point of political theory and not the conclusion of philosophical justification—the *non-aggression axiom*. In the late twentieth century, anyone who accepted this principle could call himself, or could find himself called, a libertarian, even if he disagreed with Rothbard's own insistence that rights are best protected when there is no government at all.[6]

We can date the dawn of today's libertarianism to the works of Rand and Rothbard: to Rand's *Atlas Shrugged* (1957), and to Rothbard's *Man, Economy, and State* (1962), *Power and Market* (1970), and *For a New Liberty* (1973), plus his journal *The Libertarian Forum* (1969–1984). *For a New Liberty* stands today as a brilliant, and early, bold statement of

---

[6] John P. McCaskey, "New Libertarians: New Promoters of a Welfare State," *JohnMcCaskey.com* (April 14, 2014; https://perma.cc/259E-K2AB). See also Wendy McElroy, "Murray N. Rothbard: Mr. Libertarian," *LewRockwell.com* (July 6, 2000; https://perma.cc/H7P2-P2YD). Writes Hoppe in the Foreword to this book, "through his work Rothbard became the founder of the modern libertarian movement."

the radical libertarian vision. By the mid-60s, the modern libertarian movement was coalescing, primarily behind the non-initiation of force principle and the "radical capitalism" of Ayn Rand and Rothbard's systematic libertarian corpus based upon the non-aggression principle, or axiom. It is no surprise that the Libertarian Party was founded in 1971, as these ideas, and the liberty movement, were gaining steam.

In the ensuing decades, many other influential works appeared expounding on the libertarian idea.[7]

---

[7] See various works listed in Kinsella, "The Greatest Libertarian Books," *StephanKinsella.com* (Aug. 7, 2006) and in Kinsella, "Foreword," including works by the Tannehills, Hospers, David Friedman, Henri Lepage, and many others.

Regarding the proliferation of books presenting or re-stating libertarian thought in the last couple decades, recall this comment by scholar A.H.J. Greenidge, in his "Historical Introduction" to Gaius's *Institutes of Roman Law*: "The Institutes of Gaius are a product of this activity; for *it is necessary that a great deal of detailed and special work shall be done in a science before a good handbook on the subject can be written for the use of students.*" A.H.J. Greenidge, "Historical Introduction," in Gaius, *Institutes of Roman Law*, with a translation and commentary by Edward Poste, 4th ed., revised and enlarged by E.A. Whittuck (Oxford: 1904; https://oll.libertyfund.org/title/gaius-institutes-of-roman-law), p. li (§ 20; emphasis added). This important work by Gaius was mostly lost until found in nearly complete form in a palimpsest in Verona in 1816. (See Wikipedia entry, "*Institutes (Gaius)*," https://en.wikipedia.org/wiki/Institutes_(Gaius)). The "activity" referred to by Greenidge above is described in the preceding section thusly:

> The literary activity in the domain of law, during the period which intervened between the accession of Augustus and the time of Gaius, was of the most varied character. Religious law (Jus Pontificlum) attracted the attention of Capito. Labeo wrote on the Twelve Tables. The Praetor's Edict was the subject of studies by Labeo, Masurius Sabinus, Pedius and Pomponius. The Edict of the Curule Aediles was commented on by Caelius Sabinus. Salvius Julianus, besides his redaction of the Edicts, produced a work known as Digesta, which perhaps assumed the form of detailed explanations of points of law systematically arranged. Comprehensive works on the Civil Law were furnished by Masurius Sabinus and Caius Cassius Longinus. Other jurists produced monographs on special branches of law, as the younger Nerva on Usucapion, Pedms on Stipulations, Pomponius on Fideicommissa. Some lawyers wrote commentaries on the works of their predecessors. It was thus that Aristo dealt with Labeo, and Pomponins with Sabinus. Other works took the form of Epistolae, which furnished opinions on special cases which had been submitted to their author, and collections of Problems (Quaestiones). Nor was history neglected. There must have been much of it in Labeo's commentary on the Twelve Tables; and Pomponius wrote a Handbook (Enehiridion), which contained a sketch of the legal history of Rome from the earliest times.

Greenidge, "Historical Introduction," § 19, pp. l–li.

On the issue of the preservation and transmission of bodies of knowledge, such as legal systems, see also Alan Watson: "The Importance of 'Nutshells,'" *Am. J. Comp. L.* 42, no. 1 (Winter 1994; https://digitalcommons.law.uga.edu/fac_artchop/668): 1–23.

So the movement is about fifty or sixty years old. It's a relatively young movement as far as ideologies and political philosophies go. We still have our disagreements over certain controversies like abortion and other issues. But a lot of progress has been made in the last fifty years. We've had a lot of development, partly because of incessant libertarian internal debate, criticism by outsiders, criticism by minarchists, criticism by insiders. But at the fifty year stage, I do think it is a good time to step back and reflect and think what have we learned over the last fifty years. How we could use this going forward to further *refine* and *develop* our ideas.

WHAT HAS BECOME CLEARER

So let's talk first about what has become clearer in the last fifty years. And, again, not everyone is going to agree with this—but this is my take. My take is from the position of an Austrian and anarchist influenced libertarian; from someone influenced greatly by Rothbard, Mises, Ayn Rand—and Hans-Hermann Hoppe, whom I regard as the greatest living libertarian theorist and Austrian economist.

This first insight may not be the most popular with everyone here, but I think the one thing we've learned is that political activism as a primary means of progress is limited at best.[8] I don't want to discourage people from doing it, but not everyone agrees with voting or that electoral politics is the way to go.[9] And the sort of sorry history and state of the Libertarian Party since 1971—incompetence, corruption, and inefficacy—shows that electoral politics has not succeeded very much so far.[10]

I would also say that we've learned that a *principled* libertarian position is preferred over an *ad hoc* or single purpose one like NORML or marijuana legalization or a utilitarian approach. Those have their

---

[8] Kinsella, "The Trouble with Libertarian Activism," *LewRockwell.com* (Jan. 26, 2006; https://archive.lewrockwell.com/kinsella/kinsella19.html).

[9] For a libertarian argument against voting, see Wendy McElroy, "Why I Would Not Vote Against Hitler," *Liberty* 9, no. 5 (May 1996; https://perma.cc/5NE3-BWES): 46–47.

[10] That said, since this speech, I have joined the LP. See Kinsella, "Aggression and Property Rights Plank in the Libertarian Party Platform," *StephanKinsella.com* (May 30, 2022).

purpose. They have their role. But a principled approach is superior and necessary. You really need to have a love for liberty, a love for libertarianism. You have to believe that aggression is really wrong, not just impractical.[11]

It has become clear that libertarianism has to be 100% anti-war, not merely against "unjust" wars—as even Rothbard said, in the history of America, there have only been two "just" wars: the Revolutionary War and the war to prevent the independence of the South. We need to condemn both of those wars, the Revolutionary War and the Civil War, on both the South's and the North's side. These are both wars waged by the state.

In the case of the Revolutionary War, it was a war that involved conscription, shooting deserters, tons of war crimes, taxation, inflation.[12] And it resulted in the current state that we have now. The American Revolution was a failure as well.[13]

Libertarianism is *anti-state,* or at least it is increasingly becoming so.[14] There's an increasing number of libertarians and an increasing number of those that get drawn to anarchy. What's the old joke? "What's the difference between a minarchist and an anarchist? About six months." To be against aggression, you have to be against *all* aggression: private aggression, that is, crime, and public aggression, or institutional aggression, which is what the state always does.

Libertarianism is *radical.* It's not incremental. There is nothing wrong with being incremental, but libertarianism is really a *radical* doctrine. And it's also *unique* and radical and different from, and superior to, the Left and the Right. We have to recognize that. We're not "of the Left." We're not "of the Right."

[11] Kinsella, "Why I'm a Libertarian—or, Why Libertarianism is Beautiful," *Mises Economics Blog* (Dec. 12, 2006).

[12] Kinsella, "The Murdering, Thieving, Enslaving, Unlibertarian Continental Army," *LewRockwell.com* (July 3, 2009).

[13] See Kinsella, "When Did the Trouble Start?", *LewRockwell.com* (Sep. 5, 2003); *idem*, "Happy We-Should-Restore-the-Monarchy-and-Rejoin-Britain Day!", *Mises Economics Blog* (July 2, 2009).

[14] Kinsella, "The Nature of the State and Why Libertarians Hate It," *StephanKinsella.com* (May 3, 2010).

Also, libertarianism is now increasingly, overwhelmingly, anti-intellectual property.[15] Intellectual property, patent and copyright law, and related laws like trademark and trade secret used to be the boring province of specialists and policy wonks, but with the advent of the internet and the increase of global trade and high tech, the so-called "abuses" of patent and copyright law have become evident to all of us.

We have to realize that *intellectual property* is one of the top five or six horrible things the state does to society. After war, public education, the drug war, central banking, taxation—intellectual property is up there.[16] It's one of the worst things that helps support the police state and suppress individual liberties and reduce innovation and impose hundreds of billions of dollars of cost on the globe every year.[17] This kind of view upsets a lot of the old guard libertarians, Objectivists and minarchists and utilitarians and "Constitutionalists," who still attempt to defend IP ... but modern libertarians, left libertarians, tech libertarians, young people, people who actually "use the Internet"—they all know that there's something wrong with a law that prevents you from *learning* and sharing in what we call, in the free market, "competition." There's nothing wrong with competition!

Another thing we've learned in the last fifty years, due to the work of writers like Bruno Leoni, Hayek, others: legislation is not the way to make law. Law has to arise from custom, from contract, from agreement, from decentralized processes like the common law or arbitration.[18]

---

[15] See "Law and Intellectual Property in a Stateless Society" (ch. 14), at n.5; *"Against Intellectual Property* After Twenty Years: Looking Back and Looking Forward" (ch. 15), at n.21.

[16] Kinsella, "Where does IP Rank Among the Worst State Laws?", *C4SIF Blog* (Jan. 20, 2012).

[17] Kinsella, "Copyright and Free Trade; Patents and Censorship," *C4SIF Blog* (Feb. 29, 2012); Kinsella, "Death by Copyright-IP Fascist Police State Acronym," *C4SIF Blog* (Jan. 30, 2012); "SOPA is the Symptom, Copyright is the Disease: The SOPA Wakeup Call to Abolish Copyright," *The Libertarian Standard* (Jan 24, 2012); *idem*, "Masnick on the Horrible PROTECT IP Act: The Coming IPolice State," *C4SIF Blog* (June 2, 2012); *idem*, "Copyright and the End of Internet Freedom," *C4SIF Blog* (May 10, 2011); *idem*, "Copyright Censorship versus Free Speech and Human Rights; Excessive Fines and the Eighth Amendment," *C4SIF Blog* (Sep. 6, 2011); *idem*, "The Overwhelming Empirical Case Against Patent and Copyright," *C4SIF Blog* (Oct. 23, 2012); *idem*, "Yet Another Study Finds Patents Do Not Encourage Innovation," *Mises Economics Blog* (July 2, 2009); *idem*, "Costs of the Patent System Revisited," *Mises Economics Blog* (Sep. 29, 2010).

[18] See "Legislation and the Discovery of Law in a Free Society" (ch. 13).

Also, I think we've learned, due to the work primarily of Hans-Hermann Hoppe and others ... we've had to recognize that democracy was not a step on the road to progress towards a libertarian society. Moving from monarchies in the ancient regimes to democracy might have been better in some ways, but it wasn't unambiguously better, and it's definitely not a simulation of a libertarian or a liberal society.[19]

And along those lines I think we also have to recognize that we need to quit thinking of America as some kind of proto-libertarian paradise back in the day of the Founders. The Constitution is not libertarian. It was a centralizing document. It was a power grab. It failed... or rather, it *succeeded* in what it was really meant to do, which is to centralize power in the hands of the federal government.[20] So we need to wipe these illusions from our eyes about the American Founders being proto-libertarians. They were not. The Constitution is not libertarian. America was not a libertarian country early on. There's any number of victim classes you could ask, and they would probably agree with this.

Another thing that has become clear, just in recent years, has been the libertarian approach to peace and cooperation as informing the issue

---

[19] See Hans-Hermann Hoppe, *Democracy: The God That Failed* (New Brunswick: Transaction, 2001; www.hanshoppe.com/democracy). As Hoppe notes in the Introduction: "although aware of the economic and ethical deficiencies of democracy, both Mises and Rothbard had a soft spot for democracy and tended to view the transition from monarchy to democracy as progress."

[20] Kinsella, "On Constitutional Sentimentalism," *StephanKinsella.com* (Jan. 16, 2011); *idem*, "Black Armbands for 'Constitution Day,'" *The Libertarian Standard* (Sept. 17, 2010); *idem*, "The Bad Bill of Rights," *LewRockwell.com* (Dec. 17, 2004; www.lewrockwell.com/lrc-blog/the-bad-bill-of-rights); *idem*, "Goodbye 1776, 1789, Tom," *StephanKinsella.com* (June 29, 2009); *idem*, "Rockwell on Hoppe on the Constitution as Expansion of Government Power," *StephanKinsella.com* (Aug. 3, 2009); *idem*, "Richman on the 4th of July and American Independence," *StephanKinsella.com* (July 2, 2009); *idem*, "The Murdering, Thieving, Enslaving, Unlibertarian Continental Army"; *idem*, "Napolitano on Health-Care Reform and the Constitution: Is the Commerce Clause Really Limited?", StephanKinsella.com (Sep. 17, 2009); *idem*, "Was the American Revolution Really about Taxes?", *The Libertarian Standard* (April 14, 2010); *idem*, "Bill Marina (R.I.P.) on American Imperialism from the Beginning," *StephanKinsella.com* (July 8, 2009); *idem*, "Happy We-Should-Restore-the-Monarchy-and-Rejoin-Britain Day!"; *idem*, "Revising the American Revolution," *StephanKinsella.com* (July 6, 2009); *idem*, "The Declaration and Conscription," *StephanKinsella.com* (July 6, 2009); *idem*, "Untold Truths about the American Revolution," *StephanKinsella.com* (July 7, 2009); *idem*, "Jeff Hummel's 'The Constitution as a Counter-Revolution,'" *StephanKinsella.com* (July 1, 2009).

of children. That is, there has been a reexamination of how we rear our children, how we discipline children and how we educate children. Thus we have the rise of the anti-spanking and the "peaceful parenting" movement. And we have an increasing resort to homeschooling and even so-called unschooling. So these are all things that we are starting to learn.[21]

The two most important things I think that have become clear—and some of these were known to earlier thinkers before—number one is the importance of a solid understanding of economics to inform your case. And I think that means Austrian Economics.[22] You have to be economically literate. And the rise in the popularity of Austrian Economics has been stunning to see.[23] There is a reason for that. You don't see the Chicago school or the Coasean school being passionately argued for by most libertarians now.

Finally, the most important point, it has become clear, and we need to return to this and emphasize this, libertarianism is essentially *about property rights*. That's really what it's all about.[24] Liberty is a consequence of property rights. It's what you can do when your property rights are respected.

---

[21] See Kinsella, "Montessori, Peace, and Libertarianism," *LewRockwell.com* (April 28, 2011); *idem*, "KOL059 | Libertarian Parenting—Freedomain Radio with Stefan Molyneux (2010)," *Kinsella on Liberty Podcast* (May 22, 2013); *idem*, "Stefan Molyneux's 'Libertarian Parenting' Series," *The Libertarian Standard* (July 21, 2010); *idem*, "Montessori and 'Unschooling,'" *StephanKinsella.com* (Oct. 16, 2010).

[22] Kinsella, "Afterword," in Hans-Hermann Hoppe, in *The Great Fiction: Property, Economy, Society, and the Politics of Decline*, Second Expanded Edition (Auburn, Ala.: Mises Institute, 2021; www.hanshoppe.com/tgf); Kinsella, "Foreword," in Hans-Hermann Hoppe, *A Theory of Socialism and Capitalism: Economics, Politics, and Ethics* (Auburn, Ala.: Mises Institute, 2010 [1989]; www.hanshoppe.com/tsc).

[23] For a recent example, the LP's Mises Caucus (https://lpmisescaucus.com) completely took over the US Libertarian Party at the 2022 convention. See Brian Doherty, "Mises Caucus Takes Control of Libertarian Party," *Reason.com* (May 29, 2022; https://perma.cc/US78-Y24C); Zach Weissmueller, Nick Gillespie & Danielle Thompson, "Inside the Mises Caucus Takeover of the Libertarian Party," *Reason.com* (June 15, 2022; https://perma.cc/QCK5-3HND). See also Kinsella, "Aggression and Property Rights Plank in the Libertarian Party Platform," *StephanKinsella.com* (May 30, 2022).

[24] Murray N. Rothbard, "'Human Rights' as Property Rights," in *The Ethics of Liberty* (New York: New York University Press, 1998; http://mises.org/rothbard/ethics/fifteen.asp); Hoppe, *A Theory of Socialism and Capitalism*, chaps. 1–2 *et pass.*

ISSUES THAT DIVIDE OR CONFUSE

Now there are still some issues that divide or confuse us. There is this left vs. right debate.[25] Are we of the left? Or are we of the right? There is the thick vs. thin debate. Should we be thick libertarians or thin libertarians?

There's the debate whether we should be activists or whether we should be theorists or whether we should just mind our own business and not work for the state.[26]

There are esoteric issues like voluntary slavery. Should I be able to sign a contract and sell my kidneys, or myself? This is the alienability issue.[27]

There is sometimes debate about whether you should be responsible for the actions of others. I have had people tell me that Adolf Hitler really never pulled the trigger, so he really didn't commit murder.[28] Only the henchmen are guilty. Truman didn't really drop the bomb on Japan. A mafia boss doesn't actually pull the trigger. His hit man does. So you have this kind of confusion, I would say.

And on the topic of intellectual property, even though libertarians are largely moving in our direction on this—there is still widespread confusion among people about this issue.

And there is also still confusion about the basis and the nature of property rights; about utilitarianism or consequentialism vs. deontological or natural rights thinking vs. intuitionism vs. Popperian conjecturalism.[29]

---

[25] Kinsella, "The Limits of Libertarianism?: A Dissenting View," *StephanKinsella.com* (April 20, 2014)

[26] Kinsella, "The Trouble with Libertarian Activism."

[27] See "A Libertarian Theory of Contract: Title Transfer, Binding Promises, and Inalienability" (ch. 9); "Selling Does Not Imply Ownership, and Vice-Versa: A Dissection" (ch. 11); and Kinsella, "KOL004 | Interview with Walter Block on Voluntary Slavery and Inalienability," *Kinsella on Liberty Podcast* (Jan. 27, 2013).

[28] See "Causation and Aggression" (ch. 8), at n.31 *et pass*; also Kinsella, "KOL149 | IP And Beyond With Stephan Kinsella—Non-Aggression Podcast," *Kinsella on Liberty Podcast* (Aug. 30, 2014).

[29] Hoppe's approach is not a standard natural rights argument, but he grants that it could be interpreted "as falling in a 'rightly conceived' natural rights tradition...." See Hoppe, *A Theory of Socialism and Capitalism*, pp. 156–57, n.118, quoted in "Dialogical Arguments for Libertarian Rights" (ch. 6), n.14. For Randy Barnett's argument distinguishing consequentialism from utilitarianism, and on Jan Lester's Popperian "conjecturalism," see references in "Dialogical Arguments for Libertarian Rights" (ch. 6), n.3.

DANGER OF UNCLEAR LANGUAGE AND METAPHORS

Now one reason for this confusion is the lack of careful attention to speaking clearly, thinking clearly, and being aware of the danger of the use of metaphors.[30] When libertarianism arose in the middle of the last century, it was so much superior to the prevailing thought that we could speak in sloppy terms. It was still better, even with imprecise language. After all, our competitors also employed, and still employ, vague and nonrigorous terms. But even though the libertarian approach seems obviously superior to statist alternatives, even in its early days, as it gets applied to more and more issues, harder issues arise and the older ways of thinking and reasoning don't always suffice. We need to revisit our foundations and we need to think more carefully about this.

Let me give some examples of metaphors or uncareful use of terms, things that can lead to equivocation by our opponents, things that can lead to confusion when we try to analyze difficult issues.

So one is, for example, most libertarians have always been against what we call "public schools." And in recent years, maybe in the last decade or two, I've heard libertarians say, they've used the term "government schools," because they want to make clear, "I'm against government schools." They're trying to call to the attention of the proponents of "public" schools that they're really in favor of the *government* being in charge of educating people.

Well, even the word "government," in my view, is a dangerous word to use. I use it from time to time but I increasingly try to use the word "state" to make it clear that I'm against *the state* because the state has a definition. It's a monopoly in a geographic area over the provision of

---

[30] See discussion and references at "Selling Does Not Imply Ownership, and Vice-Versa: A Dissection" (ch. 11), notes 1 and 33; "*Against Intellectual Property* After Twenty Years" (ch. 15), Part IV.D and n.83; "On Libertarian Legal Theory, Self-Ownership and Drug Laws" (ch. 23), n.29 *et pass.* See also Kinsella, "On the Danger of Metaphors in Scientific Discourse," *StephanKinsella.com* (June 12, 2011); *idem*, "Objectivist Law Prof Mossoff on Copyright; or, the Misuse of Labor, Value, and Creation Metaphors," *Mises Economics Blog* (Jan. 3, 2008); *idem*, "KOL044 | 'Correcting some Common Libertarian Misconceptions' (PFS 2011)," *Kinsella on Liberty Podcast* (May 2, 2013); *idem*, "KOL045 | 'Libertarian Controversies Lecture 1' (Mises Academy, 2011)," *Kinsella on Liberty Podcast* (May 2, 2013); *idem*, "KOL118 | Tom Woods Show: Against Fuzzy Thinking," *Kinsella on Liberty Podcast* (March 31, 2014).

law, justice, and force.[31] The word government has ambiguous meanings. And your opponent—either a minarchist, which we can call a mini-statist, or a regular statist—by the word government, they mean the governing institutions in society. And they also use it as an equivalent to the state because they believe the state is necessary for these governing institutions. So they are smuggling in their presuppositions, a type of question-begging.

So if you say, as an anarchist, I'm against the government (meaning: against the state), they will take you to mean you're against law and order. So if they ask you, "Well, do you believe in law?"

You say, "Yes."

Then they say, "Well, then you believe in government."

And I say, "Well, I believe in government as law and order."

And then they say, "Well, then you must believe in the state."

You see there's that trick there. So we have to stay focused on being opposed to the state, defined in a certain way.

Here's another one. It's the use of the word aggression in sloppy ways. Some libertarians, or some of our opponents, will use it just to mean force. So they'll say, "Well even you guys aren't against aggression. You believe in force to defend yourself."

---

[31] Writes Hoppe:

Let me begin with the definition of a state. What must an agent be able to do to qualify as a state? This agent must be able to insist that all conflicts among the inhabitants of a given territory be brought to him for ultimate decision-making or be subject to his final review. In particular, this agent must be able to insist that all conflicts involving *himself* be adjudicated by him or his agent. And implied in the power to exclude all others from acting as ultimate judge, as the second defining characteristic of a state, is the agent's power to tax: to unilaterally determine the price that justice seekers must pay for his services.

Based on this definition of a state, it is easy to understand why a desire to control a state might exist. For whoever is a monopolist of final arbitration within a given territory can *make* laws. And he who can *legislate* can also *tax*. Surely, this is an enviable position.

Hans-Hermann Hoppe, "Reflections on the Origin and the Stability of the State," *LewRockwell.com* (June 23, 2008; https://archive.lewrockwell.com/hoppe/hoppe18. html), quoted in in Kinsella, "The Nature of the State and Why Libertarians Hate It," *StephanKinsella.com* (May 3, 2010). Hoppe's article was based on his 2008 speech, available at Hoppe, "PFP020 | Hans-Hermann Hoppe, Reflections on the Origin of the State (PFS 2008)," *Property and Freedom Podcast* (Dec. 24, 2021; https://propertyandfreedom.org/pfp).

Well, aggression is the *initiation* of force. And then you see other sloppy terminology, like I'm against "the initiation of aggression." Well, that's saying I'm against the initiation of the initiation of force. It's just not clear terminology.

Another one, it's just a little issue, is the word "coercion." Coercion technically means the use of the threat of force to compel someone to do something. Now just like force or violence, which is sometimes justified if it's used defensively, coercion can be justified sometimes too. If I coerce a guy trying to rob me, there's nothing wrong with that. So we should quit using the word coercion as a synonym for aggression.[32] And we should never refer to defensive force as aggression.

There is also the labor theory of property and its close cousin, the labor theory of value.[33] This is what I think the fundamental mistake in a lot of libertarian thinking is, which is what led to intellectual property, and it also led to communism and the deaths of tens of millions of people in the 20th century.[34] It all started with John Locke who was responding to Filmer and understandably used this labor metaphor. But we have to stop thinking of labor as a special thing (it's just a type of action), and we have to get rid of this confused idea that we own our labor. You don't own your labor. Labor is what you do with something you own: your body. (You don't own your "self" by the way. That's another vague term. You own your body.)[35]

Property rights are rights to control scarce, or conflictable, resources in the world. These are the only *things that can be conflicted over.* Your

---

[32] See Kinsella, "The Problem with 'Coercion,'" *StephanKinsella.com* (Aug. 7, 2009); also "Legislation and the Discovery of Law in a Free Society" (ch. 13), n.2.

[33] See *"Against Intellectual Property* After Twenty Years" (ch. 15), Part IV.D.

[34] Kinsella, "KOL037 | Locke's Big Mistake: How the Labor Theory of Property Ruined Political Theory," *Kinsella on Liberty Podcast* (March 28, 2013); *"Against Intellectual Property* After Twenty Years" (ch. 15), Part IV.C, and other references in notes 51 & 57 *et pass.*

[35] See "What Libertarianism Is" (ch. 2) and "How We Come to Own Ourselves" (ch. 4). But admittedly, it is difficult to avoid using these terms, as I have indicated elsewhere in this book. Though it might be better to refer to the state instead of government; to an owned resource in which someone has a property right, rather than to calling the resource "property"; to aggression instead of coercion, it is sometimes more convenient to use more conventional or colloquial terms to avoid tedium. I don't even like referring to patent, copyright, trademark, trade secret as "intellectual property" rights, but if one is to communicate with normies, sometimes one has to accept conventional terminology, even if it is loaded or ambiguous.

body is an example, and other things in the world are examples. Property rules *always* specify the owner of that thing. Owning your body is *sufficient* to allow you to act as you please, but it doesn't mean you "own your actions." It doesn't mean you "own your labor." If you start thinking this way, you're going to get to intellectual property. This is what results. I own my labor. I own what I mix it with. I own my labor. I own whatever it creates that "has" "value." But there are no property rights in value, as Hans-Hermann Hoppe has pointed out. I could elaborate, but I would run out of time.[36]

Another issue is the word "contract." Libertarians are confused by contract. Rothbard and Bill Evers have written revolutionary work on this topic, viewing contract as the exercise of property rights in resources that are owned. It is not an "enforceable promise." That way of thinking leads also to confused conclusions like debtor's prison which leads to the idea of voluntary slavery, etc.[37]

Another one is the word "fraud."[38] Libertarians throw this word, fraud, around a lot, especially advocates of intellectual property; also the word plagiarism. They totally confuse fraud, contract, plagiarism, property rights, labor theory of value, and patent and copyright law.[39] They mix them together into a big gumbo of confusion. And, you know, they'll imply that if you're against patent law then you're in favor of fraud or you're in favor of dishonesty or you're not in favor of giving someone attribution for their ideas. These are all confused, and they're all disingenuous usually, or they're said in total ignorance of what these

---

[36] Kinsella, "Hoppe on Property Rights in Physical Integrity vs Value," *StephanKinsella. com* (June 12, 2011); "On Libertarian Legal Theory, Self-Ownership and Drug Laws" (ch. 23), n.7 *et pass.* As Justice Holmes recognized in passing in a dissent in a case establishing a quasi-property right in the product of the sweat of the brow, or the fruits of one's labor: "Property, a creation of law, does not arise from value, although exchangeable—a matter of fact." *International News Service v. Associated Press*, 248 U.S. 215, 246 (1918; https://supreme.justia.com/cases/federal/us/248/215/).

[37] "A Libertarian Theory of Contract" (ch. 9).

[38] See "A Libertarian Theory of Contract" (ch. 9), Part III.E.

[39] See Kinsella, "KOL207 | Patent, Copyright, and Trademark Are *Not* About Plagiarism, Theft, Fraud, or Contract," *Kinsella on Liberty Podcast* (Feb. 21, 2016); *idem*, "If you oppose IP you support plagiarism; copying others is fraud or contract breach," in "Hello! You've Been Referred Here Because You're Wrong About Intellectual Property" C4SIF (2023); Kinsella, "Common Misconceptions about Plagiarism and Patents: A Call for an Independent Inventor Defense," *Mises Economics Blog* (Nov. 21, 2009).

terms mean and how the law really works and what property rights really are.

There's another confusion, which is the common paired set of expressions which everyone takes for granted. There are two paired notions. "If you own something, well, you can sell it"—which is wrong actually. "And if you sell something, that must mean you had to own it to sell it." That's also wrong.[40] Those ideas lead to the idea of voluntary slavery on the one hand[41] and the idea of intellectual property on the other. And I've taken those apart in other contexts as well. I can revisit them at some point when I have more time.

Now another source of confusion is the idea about where property rights come from and the idea that just because we believe that the first user of an unowned resource, like Locke's idea of original appropriation or homesteading—just because we believe he is the proper owner of that resource, that because there's been this "original sin" or this "taint" of property titles throughout human history, because we can rarely trace our title to a resource back to the original owner, back to Adam, let's say, then that means our entire theory of property rights is flawed. And then what's the next step? Then we're going to say, well, we are going to have to have redistribution someday. The current allocation of resources, the property rights that the rich have, really came from conquests 700 years ago. So no one is really entitled to their wealth. "You didn't build that," as Obama might say. And that when we have a libertarian revolution, a left-libertarian revolution, we need to redistribute these titles and everyone is going to be equal. Egalitarianism is driving these people.[42]

So whenever I hear someone say that there's something wrong with your theory of property, I hold on to my wallet, because I know they're coming after it. The people that condemn materialism and rich people

---

[40] See "Selling Does Not Imply Ownership, and Vice-Versa: A Dissection" (ch. 11).

[41] See "Inalienability and Punishment: A Reply to George Smith" (ch. 10) and "A Libertarian Theory of Contract" (ch. 9).

[42] See related discussion in "What Libertarianism Is" (ch. 2), at n.36 and "Selling Does Not Imply Ownership, and Vice-Versa: A Dissection" (ch. 11), at n.12; also Hans-Hermann Hoppe, "A Realistic Libertarianism," *LewRockwell.com* (Sept. 30, 2013; www.hanshoppe.com/2014/10/a-realistic-libertarianism), discussed in "On Libertarian Legal Theory, Self-Ownership and Drug Laws" (ch. 23), n.15.

and money always want your money. So you have to be very wary of these people.[43]

Now there's another related problem which afflicts a lot of quasi-left libertarians, and that is this idea that if you are in favor of property rights, you're really in favor of "aggression." Now, how do they come up with this idea? Basically, they don't believe in *ownership*. They believe that if you are using a resource that you have the right to use it in an undisturbed fashion, but as soon as you set it down and walk away, it's up for grabs. And if you maintain the right to use force to retrieve your resource, or to get damages from them for damaging or using your property, you're committing aggression.[44] This is obviously confused and unlibertarian.

MOVING FORWARD

So this is the fundamental problem that we need to focus on here. We need to understand that aggression is not the fundamental concept of libertarianism. Aggression is a shorthand description of our view of property rights. Every political philosophy, every person on the planet, has an implicit or explicit view of property rights. Because property rights arise only because we live in a world of scarcity, a world of scarce resources, which means a world where *conflict is possible*.[45] If you understand Mises's praxeology and his analysis of human action and how human action is the purposeful employment of scarce means— things that are *causally efficacious* in the world to achieve your end, *guided* by your knowledge (which is why there are no property rights

---

[43] See "On Libertarian Legal Theory, Self-Ownership and Drug Laws" (ch. 23), at n.14.

[44] This is also similar to the views of some mutualists, who in effect basically conflate possession with ownership, since "absentee" owners lose title to squatters, tenants, employees, and so on. See "What Libertarianism Is" (ch. 2), n.31; also "Law and Intellectual Property in a Stateless Society" (ch. 14), n.38.

[45] See "What Libertarianism Is" (ch. 2), the section "Libertarian Property Rights"; "Selling Does Not Imply Ownership, and Vice-Versa: A Dissection" (ch. 11), at n.6 *et pass.*; "On Libertarian Legal Theory, Self-Ownership and Drug Laws" (ch. 23), at n.16 *et pass.* See also Hans-Hermann Hoppe, "Of Common, Public, and Private Property and the Rationale for Total Privatization," in Hoppe, *The Great Fiction*; Hoppe, "A Realistic Libertarianism."

in ideas)[46]—then you'll understand that property rights are *always* the right to control a given resource. It's about that.[47]

Aggression is just a *shorthand* for our particular view of how property should be assigned.[48] Communists, socialists, liberals, environmentalists all believe in a certain allocation of property rights. They believe the state should own the property or maybe the poor people should own the property. So the question is what makes libertarianism unique? It is our *particular property allocation scheme.*[49]

And I will conclude by just summarizing the way I think we need to view the libertarian paradigm and how, if you think about it consistently, it will answer all the questions I just went through that are confusing to people. That is this: the rule of libertarianism is very simple. It is that when two or more people—because if you only have only one person, then there's no dispute, there's no problem to be solved; there is no social problem—when two or more people both want to use a given resource, when there is a possible dispute or conflict, the question is simply, for the resource in question: which of those two or more people has the better claim to the resource?

We answer that question by resorting to some very simple and common sense and almost undeniably true rules.[50] In the case of a person's body, which is a resource over which there can be dispute, the rule is self-ownership, or self-body-ownership: each person is the presumptive owner of his own body. We oppose slavery, which is "other-ownership" and instead favor self-ownership. Controversial, I know.

And as for previously-unowned, external resources, the types of things that can serve as scarce means of action, there are three simple rules. The first one is: who had it first? Or as between those two, who

---

[46] See "Law and Intellectual Property in a Stateless Society" (ch. 14), Part III.D; and "*Against Intellectual Property* After Twenty Years" (ch. 15), Part IV.E.

[47] "What Libertarianism Is" (ch. 2); also "On Libertarian Legal Theory, Self-Ownership and Drug Laws" (ch. 23), text at notes 6–7 and 18–23 *et pass.*

[48] See "What Libertarianism Is" (ch. 2), n.4.

[49] See ibid.

[50] See ibid., the section "Libertarian Property Rights." See also "How We Come to Own Ourselves" (ch. 4) and "Goods, Scarce and Nonscarce" (ch. 18); as well as Hoppe's summary of these basic rules in "A Realistic Libertarianism" and in *idem*, "Of Common, Public, and Private Property and the Rationale for Total Privatization," pp. 85–87. See also Kinsella, "How To Think About Property (2019)," *StephanKinsella.com* (April 25, 2021).

had it first as far as we know? You don't have to trace back to Adam. You can trace it back to a common ancestor as the law has it.[51] This is original appropriation, or homesteading. This has to be the basic property allocation rule, because for people to survive, they must use resources, and there must be a first user. His use has to be rightful if we are to have ownership and property rights as a concept distinct from mere possession.

Second: was there a consensual transfer from an owner to someone else? That's contract, or contractual title transfer.

And third: did one person harm the other, commit a tort or a crime, so that he owes compensation or rectification or restitution to the other guy, leading to a transfer of money or some resource from one guy to the other.

So if you look at those three principles, that will tell you who owns the resource in question. If I had it first, I am the owner—*unless* I gave it to someone else, and then they own it. They have a better claim than me. Every other philosophy, other than libertarianism, violates one of those three rules. They ultimately believe that someone has the right to a resource even though they didn't obtain it by contract, even though they weren't harmed by the previous owner, and even though they may have never found the resource or started using it and put it to productive use.

Basically every philosophy, other than libertarianism, believes either in a lawless world, a world of might makes right—or in some form of slavery: owning the products of other people's efforts or owning their bodies.[52] That is why libertarianism is superior. And if we focus on property rights and this foundational view of looking at things, it helps us to move forward and improve the libertarian project. Thank you.

---

[51] See the discussion of the civil law's solution of tracing title back to a "common author" (meaning ancestor in title) at "What Libertarianism Is" (ch. 2), at n.33 and "Law and Intellectual Property in a Stateless Society" (ch. 14), at n.41.

[52] See "What Libertarianism Is" (ch. 2).

Bibliography

Abela, Paul. *Kant's Empirical Realism*. Oxford: Clarendon Press, 2002.

Adcock, Jon C. "Detrimental Reliance." *La. L. Rev.* 45, no. 3 (Jan. 1985): 753–70. https://digitalcommons.law.lsu.edu/lalrev/vol45/iss3/5.

Aebi, Magdalena. *Kants Begründung der "Deutschen Philosophie": Kants Transzendentale Logik, Kritik Ihrer Begründung*. Basel: Verlag für Recht und Gesellschaft, 1947.

Alchian, Armen and William R. Allen. *Exchange and Production: Competition, Coordination, & Control*, 3d ed. Belmont, California: Wadsworth, 1983.

American Law Institute. *Restatement (Second) of Contracts*. St. Paul, Minn.: American Law Institute Publishers, 1979, 1981.

American Law Institute. *Restatement (Second) of Torts*. St. Paul, Minn.: American Law Institute Publishers, 1965.

Anderson, Terry, and P.J. Hill. "An American Experiment in Anarcho-Capitalism: The Not So Wild, Wild West." *J. Libertarian Stud.* 3, no. 1 (1979): 9–29. https://mises.org/library/american-experiment-anarcho-capitalism-not-so-wild-wildwest.

Anding, Gregory Michael. "Comment: Does This Piece Fit?: A Look at the Importation of the Common-Law Quitclaim Deed and After-Acquired Title Doctrine into Louisiana's Civil Code." *La. L. Rev.* 55, no. 1 (Summer 1994): 159–77. https://digitalcommons.law.lsu.edu/lalrev/vol55/iss1/8/.

Apel, Karl-Otto. "The A Priori of the Communication Community and the Foundations of Ethics," in *Towards a Transformation of Philosophy*. London and New York: Routledge, 1980.

—. "Is the Ethics of the Ideal Communication Community a Utopia? On the Relationship between Ethics, Utopia, and the Critique of Utopia." In *The Communicative Ethics Controversy*, edited by Seyla Benhabib and Fred Dallmayr. Cambridge, Mass.: MIT Press, 1990.

—. "The Problem of Philosophical Foundations Grounding in Light of a Transcendental Pragmatics of Language." In *After Philosophy: End or Transformation?* edited by Kenneth Baynes, James Bohman and Thomas McCarthy. Cambridge, Mass.: MIT Press, 1986.

Aquinas, Thomas. *Summa Theologica*. New Advent. https://www.newadvent.org/summa.

Aranson, Peter H. "Bruno Leoni in Retrospect." *Harv. J. L. & Pub. Pol'y* 11 (1988): 661–711.

—. "The Common Law as Central Economic Planning." *Const. Pol. Econ.* 3 (1992): 289–320.

Arendt, Hannah. *Eichmann in Jerusalem: A Report on the Banality of Evil*. Penguin (2006).

Aristotle. *Metaphysics*. Translated by Richard Hope. New York: Columbia University Press, 1952.

Armani, Vin. "The Ownable and the Unownable." In *Self Ownership: The Foundation of Property and Morality*, 2017.

Atkinson, Benedict and Brian Fitzgerald. *A Short History of Copyright: The Genie of Information*. Springer, 2014.

Ayn Rand Institute. *The Ayn Rand Lexicon: Objectivism from A to Z*. Edited by Harry Binswanger. New York: New American Library. 1986. http://aynrandlexicon.com/ayn-rand-ideas/ari-q-and-a-on-libertarianism.html.

Bacon, Francis. *Maxims of the Law*.

Banerji, Oishika. "Theories of protection of intellectual property rights," *IPleadersin Blog* (Oct. 24, 2021). https://perma.cc/M2BU-T7BC.

Banfield, E.C. "Present-Orientedness and Crime." In *Assessing the Criminal, Restitution, Retribution, and the Legal Process*, edited by Randy E Barnett and J. Hagel. Cambridge: Ballinger, 1977.

—. *The Unheavenly City Revisited*. Boston: Little, Brown, 1974.

Barnett, Randy E. "A Consent Theory of Contract." *Colum. L. Rev.* 86 (1986): 269–321. http://www.randybarnett.com/pre-2000.

—. "Contract Remedies and Inalienable Rights." *Social Policy and Philosophy* 4, no. 1 (Autumn 1986): 179–202. https://tinyurl.com/44adafte.

—. "Foreword: The Ninth Amendment and Constitutional Legitimacy." *Chicago-Kent L. Rev.* 64 (1988): 37–65. Reprinted in *The Rights Retained by the People*, vol. 2, edited by Randy E. Barnett. Fairfax, Va.: George Mason University Press, 1993.

—. "Getting Even: Restitution, Preventive Detention, and the Tort/Crime Distinction." *Boston U. L. Rev.* 76 (February/April 1996): 157–68. www.randybarnett.com/pre-2000.

—. "Getting Normative: The Role of Natural Rights in Constitutional Adjudication." *Constitutional Commentary* 12 (1995): 93–122. http://www.randybarnett.com/pre-2000.

—. "Implementing the Ninth Amendment." In *The Rights Retained by the People*, vol. 2, edited by Barnett. Fairfax, Va.: George Mason University Press, 1993.

—. "The Intersection of Natural Rights and Positive Constitutional Law." *Connecticut L. Rev.* 25 (1993): 853–68. http://www.randybarnett.com/pre-2000.

—. "Introduction: James Madison's Ninth Amendment," in *The Rights Retained by the People*, vol. 1., edited by Barnett.

—. "Necessary and Proper." *UCLA L. Rev.* 76 (1997): 745–93. www.randybarnett.com/pre-2000.

—. "Of Chickens and Eggs—The Compatibility of Moral Rights and Consequentialist Analyses." *Harv. J. L. & Pub. Pol'y* 12 (1989): 611–36. http://www.randybarnett.com/pre-2000.

—. "Rational Bargaining Theory and Contract: Default Rules, Hypothetical Consent, the Duty to Disclose, and Fraud." *Harv. J. L. & Pub. Pol'y* 15 (1992): 783–803. www.randybarnett.com/pre-2000.

—. "Reconceiving the Ninth Amendment." *Cornell L. Rev.* 74, no. 1 (1988): 1–42. www.randybarnett.com/pre-2000.

—. "The Relevance of the Framers' Intent." *Harv. J. L. & Pub. Pol'y* 19 (1995–96): 403–410. http://www.randybarnett.com/pre-2000.

—. "Restitution: A New Paradigm of Criminal Justice." In *Assessing the Criminal*, edited Barnett and Hagel III.

—. *Restoring the Lost Constitution: The Presumption of Liberty*, 2d ed. Princeton University Press, 2013.

—. "Rights and Remedies in a Consent Theory of Contract." In *Liability and Responsibility: Essays in Law and Morals*, edited by R.G. Frey and C. Morris. Cambridge University Press, 1991.

—. *The Rights Retained by the People: The History and Meaning of the Ninth Amendment.* George Mason Univ. Press, 1991.

—. "The Sound of Silence: Default Rules and Contractual Consent." *Va. L. Rev.* 78 (1992): 821–911. www.randybarnett.com/pre-2000.

—. *The Structure of Liberty: Justice and the Rule of Law*, 2d ed. Oxford, 2014.

— and Mary E. Becker. "Beyond Reliance: Promissory Estoppel, Contract Formalities, and Misrepresentations." *Hofstra L. Rev.* 15 (1987): 443–97. www.randybarnett.com/pre-2000.

—, and John Hagel III, eds. *Assessing the Criminal: Restitution, Retribution, And the Legal Process.* Cambridge, Mass.: Ballinger, 1977.

Barry, Norman. "The Tradition of Spontaneous Order." *Literature of Liberty* 5, no. 27 (Summer 1982): 44. https://perma.cc/Y7X3-S8WY.

Bastiat, Frederic. *The Law.* Translated by Dean Russell. Irvington-on-Hudson, N.Y.: Foundation for Economic Education, 1950 [1850]. https://fee.org/resources/the-law.

Batiza, Rodolfo. "Origins of Modern Codification of the Civil Law: The French Experience and its Implications for Louisiana Law." *Tul. L. Rev.* 56 (1982): 477–601.

Baynes, Kenneth. *The Normative Grounds of Social Criticism: Kant, Rawls, and Habermas.* Albany: State University of New York Press, 1992.

Beckmann, Petr. *Einstein Plus Two.* Golem Press, 1987.

Beinart, Ben. "The English Legal Contribution in South Africa: The Interaction of Civil and Common Law." *Acta Juridica* (1981): 7–64.

Bell, Tom W. "Copyright as Intellectual Property Privilege." *Syracuse L. Rev.* 58 (2007): 523–46. https://perma.cc/7ZLM-CDWA.

—. "Copyright Erodes PropertySM." *Agoraphilia* (July 14, 2011). https://perma.cc/L25V-A8X8).

—. "Indelicate Imbalancing in Copyright and Patent Law." In *Copy Fights*, edited by Thierer and Crews, Jr. https://papers.ssrn.com/sol3/papers.cfm?abstract_id=984085.

—. *Intellectual Privilege: Copyright, Common Law, and the Common Good.* Arlington, Virginia: Mercatus Center, 2014. https://perma.cc/JLC2-396Y.

Benhabib, Seyla and Fred Dallmayr, eds. *The Communicative Ethics Controversy.* Cambridge, Mass.: MIT Press, 1990.

Benson, Bruce L. "Customary Law as a Social Contract: International Commercial Law." *Constitutional Political Economy* 3 (1992): 1–27.

—. *The Enterprise of Law: Justice Without the State.* San Francisco, Ca.: Pacific Research Institute for Public Policy, 1990.

—. "Restitution in Theory and Practice." *J. Libertarian Stud.* 12, no. 1 (Spring 1996): 79–83. https://mises.org/library/restitution-theory-and-practice.

—. "Third Thoughts on Contracting Out." *J. Libertarian Stud.* 11, no. 1 (Fall 1994): 44–78. https://mises.org/library/third-thoughtscontracting-out.

Bentham, Jeremy. "Anarchical Fallacies." In *Human Rights*, edited by A.I. Melden. Belmont. Calif.: Wadsworth Publishing, 1970.

Bergel, Jean Louis. "Principal Features and Methods of Codification." *La. L. Rev.* 48, no. 5 (May 1988): 1073–1097. https://digitalcommons.law.lsu.edu/lalrev/vol48/iss5/3/.

Berger, Raoul. *The Fourteenth Amendment and the Bill of Rights.* Norman, Okla.: University of Oklahoma Press, 1989.

—. *Federalism: The Founders' Design.* Norman, Okla.: University of Oklahoma Press, 1987.

—. *Government by Judiciary: The Transformation of the Fourteenth Amendment.* Cambridge, Mass.: Harvard Univ Press, 1977.

—. "The Ninth Amendment, As Perceived by Randy Barnett." *Northwestern U. L. Rev.* 88, no. 4 (1994): 1508–36.

Bernstein, Richard J., ed. *Habermas and Modernity.* Cambridge, Mass.: MIT Press, 1985.

Bessen, James and Michael J. Meurer. *Patent Failure: How Judges, Bureaucrats, and Lawyers Put Innovators at Risk.* Princeton University Press, 2008.

Bidinotto, Robert James, editor. *Criminal Justice? The Legal System Vs. Individual Responsibility.* Irvington-on-Hudson, New York: Foundation for Economic Education, Inc, 1994. https://perma.cc/KW2G-4JF5.

Binswanger, Harry. "Life-Based Teleology and the Foundations of Ethics." *The Monist* 75, no. 1 (Jan. 1992): 84–103.

Bissell, Sciabarra, and Younkins. *The Dialectics of Liberty.*

Bitlaw. "Rights Granted Under U.S. Patent Law." *https://www.bitlaw.com/patent/rights.html.*

Black, Henry Campbell. *Black's Law Dictionary,* 6th ed. St. Paul, Minn.: West Publishing, 1990.

Blackman, Rodney J. "There is There There: Defending the Defenseless with Procedural Natural Law." *Ariz. L. Rev.* 37 (1995): 285–353.

Blackstone, William. *Commentaries on the Laws of England* (Oxford Edition), bk 4. General Editor, Wilfrid Prest. Oxford, 2016.

Block, Walter. "Austrian Law and Economics: The Contributions of Adolf Reinach and Murray Rothbard." *Q. J. Austrian Econ.* 7, no. 4 (Winter 2004): 69–85. https://mises.org/library/austrian-law-and-economicscontributions-adolf-reinach-and-murray-rothbard-law-economics-and.

—. *Defending the Undefendable.* 2018. https://mises.org/library/defending-undefendable.

—. *Defending the Undefendable II: Freedom in All Realms.* UK and USA: Terra Libertas Publishing House, 2013; reprint edition Auburn, Ala.: Mises Institute, 2018. https://mises.org/library/defending-undefendable-2.

—. "Hayek's Road to Serfdom." *J. Libertarian Stud.* 12, no. 2 (Fall 1996): 327–50. https://mises.org/library/hayeks-road-serfdom.

—. "Libertarianism vs. Objectivism: A Response to Peter Schwartz." *Reason Papers* 26 (2003): 39–62. https://reasonpapers.com/archives/.

—. "Radical Libertarianism: Applying Libertarian Principles to Dealing With the Unjust Government, Part I ." *Reason Papers* No. 27 (Fall 2004): 113–30. https://reasonpapers.com.

—. "Rejoinder to Kinsella and Tinsley on Incitement, Causation, Aggression and Praxeology." *J. Libertarian Stud.* 22, no. 1 (2011): 641–64. https://mises.org/library/rejoinder-kinsella-and-tinsley-incitement-causation-aggressionand-praxeology.

—. "Rejoinder to Kinsella on Ownership and the Voluntary Slave Contract." *Management Education Science Technology Journal* (MESTE) 11, no. 1 (Jan. 2023):1–8. https://perma.cc/H3AL-WBQJ.

—. "Rejoinder to Murphy and Callahan on Hoppe's Argumentation Ethics ." *J. Libertarian Stud.* 22, no. 1 (2011). www.walterblock.com.

—. "Reply to 'Against Libertarian Legalism' by Frank van Dun." *J. Libertarian Stud.* 18, no. 2 (2004): 1–30. https://mises.org/library/reply-against-libertarianlegalism-frank-van-dun.

—. "Toward a Libertarian Theory of Blackmail." *J. Libertarian Stud.* 15, no. 2 (Spring 2001): 55–88. https://mises.org/library/toward-libertarian-theory-blackmail.

—. "Toward a Libertarian Theory of Guilt and Punishment for the Crime of Statism." *J. Libertarian Stud.* 22, no. 1 (2011): 665–75. https://mises.org/library/toward-libertarian-theory-guilt-and-punishment-crime-statism.

—. "Toward a Libertarian Theory of Inalienability: A Critique of Rothbard, Barnett, Gordon, Smith, Kinsella and Epstein." *J. Libertarian Stud.* 17, no. 2 (Spring 2003): 39–85. https://perma.cc/79AC-34BZ.

—, and Roy Whitehead. "The Death Penalty." *LewRockwell.com.* November 11, 2003. www.lewrockwell.com/2003/11/walter-e-block/the-death-penalty.

—. "Taking the Assets of Criminals to Compensate Victims of Violence: A Legal and Philosophical Approach." *Wayne State U. L. Sch. J. Law Soc.* 5 (2003): 229–53. www.walterblock.com/publications

—, and Stephan Kinsella and Hans-Hermann Hoppe. "The Second Paradox of Blackmail." *Bus. Ethics Q.* (July 2000): 593–622.

—, Roy Whitehead, and Stephan Kinsella. "The Duty to Defend Advertising Injuries Caused by Junk Faxes: An Analysis of Privacy, Spam, Detection and Blackmail." *Whittier L. Rev.* (2006): 925–49.

Boaz, David. *The Libertarian Mind: A Manifesto for Freedom.* New York: Simon & Schuster, 2015.

—, ed. *The Libertarian Reader: Classic & Contemporary Writings from Lao Tzu to Milton Friedman.* Simon & Schuster, 2015.

Böhm-Bawerk, Eugen von. *Shorter Classics of Eugen von Böhm-Bawerk.* Translated by George D. Huncke. South Holland, Ill.: Libertarian Press, 1962 [1881].

Boldrin, Michele and David K Levine. *Against Intellectual Monopoly.* Cambridge University Press, 2008. www.againstmonopoly.org.

—. "The Case Against Patents." *J. Econ. Perspectives* 27 no. 1 (Winter 2013): 3–22. https://perma.cc/Q5NT-9CGA.

—. *Patent Failure: How Judges, Bureaucrats, and Lawyers Put Innovators at Risk.* Princeton University Press, 2008.

Bork, Robert H. *Slouching Towards Gomorrah: Modern Liberalism and American Decline.* New York: ReganBooks, 1996.

—. *The Tempting of America: The Political Seduction of the Law.* New York: The Free Press, 1990.

Bouckaert, Boudewijn. "From Property Rights to Property Order." In *Encyclopedia of Law and Economics.* Springer, 2023.

—. "What is Property?" *Harv. J.L. & Pub. Pol'y* 13, no. 3 (Summer 1990): 775–816.

Bouillon, Hardy. "A Note on Intellectual Property and Externalities." *Mises Daily* (Oct. 27, 2009); previously published in *Property, Freedom and Society: Essays in Honor of Hans-Hermann,* edited by Hoppe, Jörg Guido Hülsmann, and Stephan Kinsella. Auburn, Ala.: Mises Institute, 2009.

Braaten, Jane. *Habermas's Critical Theory of Society.* 1991.

Bracha, Oren. "Owning Ideas: A History of Anglo-American Intellectual Property." Unpublished Ph.D dissertation, Harvard Law School, June 2005. https://law.utexas.edu/faculty/obracha/dissertation/.

Bradford, R.W. "A Contrast of Visions." *Liberty* 10, no.4 (March 1997): 57–63. https://perma.cc/7FDT-G7FD.

Bradley, F.H. *Ethical Studies,* 2d ed. Oxford: Clarendon Press, 1927.

—. *The Structure of Liberty: Justice and the Rule of Law,* 2d ed. Oxford, 2014.

Branden, Barbara. *The Passion of Ayn Rand*. New York: Anchor, 1987.

Breakey, Hugh. "Natural intellectual property rights and the public domain." *Modern L. Rev.* 73 (2010): 208–39. https://papers.ssrn.com/sol3/papers.cfm?abstract_id=2856883.

Brito, Jerry, ed. *Copyright Unbalanced: From Incentive to Excess*. Arlington, Va.: Mercatus Center, 2013.

Brittain, Blake. "US trade commission sides with iRobot, bans SharkNinja robot vacuum imports." *Reuters* (March 21, 2023). https://perma.cc/2MH9-2ZGG.

Buchanan, James M. *The Limits of Liberty: Between Anarchy and Leviathan in The Collected Works of James M. Buchanan*, Vol. 7. Indianapolis: Liberty Fund, 2000 [1975].

Buckland, W.W. *A Text Book of Roman Law from Augustus to Justinian*, 3d ed. Revised by Peter Stein, reprinted with corrections. Cambridge University Press, 1975.

—, and Arnold D. McNair. *Roman Law and Common Law: A Comparison in Outline*, 2d Ed., reprinted with corrections. Revised by F.H. Lawson. Cambridge, England: University Press, 1965.

Buckley, F.H. "Paradox Lost." *Minn. L. Rev.* 72 (1988): 775–827. https://scholarship.law.umn.edu/mlr/1293/.

Burke, Edmund. "A Letter To Lord****," in *A Vindication of Natural Society*. Liberty Fund, 1756. https://oll.libertyfund.org/title/burke-a-vindication-of-natural-society.

Burke, T. Patrick. *No Harm: Ethical Principles for a Free Market*. New York: Paragon House, 1994.

Calhoun, John C. *Union and Liberty: The Political Philosophy of John C. Calhoun*. Edited by Ross M. Lence. Indianapolis, Ind.: Liberty Fund, 1992.

Callahan, Gene. "Hans-Hermann Hoppe's Argumentation Ethic: A Critique." *Anti-state.com*. Sept. 19, 2002.

—. "Hans-Hermann Hoppe's Argumentation Ethic: A Critique." *J. Libertarian Stud.* 20, no. 2 (2006): 53–64. https://mises.org/library/hans-hermann-hoppes-argumentation-ethic-critique.

Caldwell, Bruce. "Hayek and Socialism." *J. Econ. Literature* 35 (December 1997): 1856–90.

Campan, Gael J. "Does Justice Qualify as an Economic Good?: A Böhm-Bawerkian Perspective." *Q. J. Austrian Econ.* 2, no. 1 (Spring 1999): 21–33. https://perma.cc/G3CK-B8WB.

Caplan, Bryan. "Fraud and Punishment." *EconLog*. Feb. 1, 2009. https://perma.cc/67YF-XMEZ.

Carnis, Laurent. "Pitfalls of the Classical School of Crime." *Q. J. Austrian Econ.* 7, no. 4 (Winter 2004): 7–18. https://mises.org/library/pitfallsclassical-school-crime-0.

Carroll, Andrea B. "Examining a Comparative Law Myth: Two Hundred Years of Riparian Misconception." *Tul. L. Rev.* 80 (2006): 901–45. https://perma.cc/CEP2-Z2BC.

Carson, Clarence B. *Free Enterprise: The Road to Prosperity*. New Rochelle: America's Future, 1985. https://fee.org/articles/free-enterprise-the-key-to-prosperity/.

Carson, Kevin A. "Carson's Rejoinders." *J. Libertarian Stud.* (Winter): 97–136.

—. 2004. *Studies in Mutualist Political Economy*. Fayetteville, Ark.: Self-published, 2006. http://mutualist.org/id47.html.

Carter, James C. *The Proposed Codification of Our Common Law: A Paper Prepared at the Request of The Committee of the Bar Association of the City of New York, Appointed to Oppose the Measure*. 1884.

Casey, Gerard. *Libertarian Anarchy: Against the State*. Continuum International Publishing Group, 2012.

Cataldo, Bernard F., et al. *Introduction to Law and the Legal Process*, 3d ed. New York: John Wiley and Sons, 1980.

Chartier, Gary. *Anarchy and Legal Order: Law and Politics for a Stateless Society*. Cambridge University Press, 2013.

Chevigny, Paul G. "The Dialogic Right of Free Expression: A Reply to Michael Martin." *N.Y. U. L. Rev.* 57 (1982): 920–31.

—. "Philosophy of Language and Free Expression." *N.Y. U. L. Rev.* 55 (1980): 157–94.

Child, James W. "Can Libertarianism Sustain a Fraud Standard?" *Ethics* 104, no. 4 (July 1994): 722–38.

Cloud, Michael. "The Late, Great Libertarian Macho Flash." *benbachrach.com*. 1978. https://perma.cc/KY9P-V7K7.

Cohen, G.A. *Self-ownership, Freedom, and Equality*. Cambridge University Press, 1995.

—. "Self-Ownership, World-Ownership, and Equality." In *Justice and Equality, Here and Now*, edited by Frank Lucash. Ithaca, N.Y.: Cornell University Press, 1986.

Cohen, Morris R. "The Basis of Contract." *Harv. L. Rev.* 46 (1933): 573.

Cole, Julio H. "Patents and Copyrights: Do the Benefits Exceed the Costs?" *J. Libertarian Stud.* 15, no. 4 (Fall 2001): 79–105. https://mises.org/library/patents-and-copyrights-do-benefits-exceed-costs-0.

Comment, "The Changing Role of the Jury in the Nineteenth Century." *Yale L. J.* 74 (1964): 170–92. https://perma.cc/72RE-WDSK.

Conkin, Paul K. *Self-Evident Truths: Being a Discourse on the Origins & Development of the First Principles of American Government—Popular Sovereignty, Natural Rights, and Balance & Separation of Powers*. Bloomington, Ind.: Indiana Univ. Press, 1974.

Conway, David. "Review of Hoppe, *A Theory of Socialism and Capitalism*." *Austrian Economics Newsletter* 9, no. 3 (Spring/Summer 1988): 11–14. https://perma.cc/4229-ZR7P.

Craswell, Richard. "Contract Law: General Theories, section 4000." In *Encyclopedia of Law & Economics*. Cambridge: Cambridge University Press, 2000.

Crocker, Lawrence. "The Upper Limit of Just Punishment." *Emory L. J.* 41 (1992): 1059–1110.

Cueto-Rua, Julio C. "The Civil Code of Louisiana Is Alive and Well." *Tul. L. Rev.* 64, no. 1 (1989): 147–76.

—. The Future of the Civil Law." *La. L. Rev.* 37, no. 3 (1976–77): 645–79. https://digitalcommons.law.lsu.edu/lalrev/vol37/iss3/2/.

Cuzán, Alfred G. "Do We Ever Really Get Out of Anarchy?" *J. Libertarian Stud.* 3 (2) (1979): 151–58. https://mises.org/library/do-we-ever-really-get-outanarchy.

—. "Revisiting 'Do We Ever Really Get Out of Anarchy?'" *J. Libertarian Stud.* 22: 3–21. https://mises.org/library/revisiting-do-we-ever-really-get-out-anarchy.

Davies, Kim. "Review of K-O Apel, Towards a Transformation of Philosophy (1980)." *Radical Philosophy* 30 (Spring 1982). https://www.stephankinsella.com/wp-content/uploads/texts/davies_apel-review.pdf.

Davis, Michael H. "Patent Politics." *S. Carolina L. Rev.* 56, no. 2 (Winter 2004): 337–86. https://perma.cc/4229-ZR7P.

Dawson, John P. *The Oracles of the Law*. Thomas M. Cooley Lectures, Ann Arbor: University of Michigan Law School, 1968.

Day, J.P. "Locke on Property." *Philosophical Quarterly* 16 (1966): 207–220; also reprinted in *Life, Liberty, And Property: Essays on Locke's Political Ideas*, edited by Gordon J. Schochet. Belmont, California: Wadsworth Publishing Company, 1971.

de Jasay, Anthony. *Against Politics: On Government, Anarchy, and Order*. London & New York: Routledge, 1997.

de Jouvenel, Bertrand. *Sovereignty: An Inquiry into the Political Good.* Chicago: University of Chicago Press, 1957.

Deazley, Ronan. *Rethinking Copyright: History, Theory, Language.* Cheltenham, UK: Edward Elgar, 2006.

—, *et al.,* eds. *Privilege and Property: Essays on the History of Copyright.* Cambridge: OpenBook Publishers, 2010.

Deist, Jeff. "A Libertarian Approach to Disputed Land Titles." *Mises Wire,* June 3, 2021. https://mises.org/wire/libertarian-approach-disputed-land-titles.

Denson, John, ed. *The Costs of War: America's Pyrrhic Victories.* New Brunswick: Transaction Publishers, 1997. https://mises.org/library/costs-war-americas-pyrrhic-victories.

DeRosa, Marshall L. *The Ninth Amendment and the Politics of Creative Jurisprudence: Disparaging the Fundamental Right of Popular Control.* New Brunswick, N.J.: Transaction Publishers, 1996.

Dietze, Gottfried. "The Necessity of State Law." In *Liberty and the Rule of Law,* edited by Cunningham.

Doctorow, Cory. "What's the objectively optimal copyright term?" *Boing Boing.* Oct. 6, 2015. https://perma.cc/UMJ3-4JHH.

Doherty, Brian. "Mises Caucus Takes Control of Libertarian Party," *Reason.com.* May 29, 2022. https://perma.cc/US78-Y24C.

—. *Radicals for Capitalism: A Freewheeling History of the Modern American Libertarian Movement.* New York: Public Affairs, 2008.

Doig, Don. "New Hope for Freedom: Fully Informed Juries." Pamphlet published by the International Society for International Liberty.

Dominiak, Łukasz, Igor Wysocki, and Stanisław Wójtowic. "Dialogical Estoppel, Erga Omnes Rights, and the Libertarian Theory of Punishment and Self-Defense." *J. Libertarian Stud.* 27, no. 1 (March, 2023): 1–24. https://perma.cc/RP8Z-VE3C.

Dorfman, Avihay and Assaf Jacob, "Copyright as Tort." *Theoretical Inquiries in Law* 12, no. 1 (Jan. 2011): 59–97. https://perma.cc/4HZM-QPHU.

Dorn, James A., and Henry G. Manne. *Economic Liberties and the Judiciary.* Fairfax, Va.: George Mason University Press, 1987.

Drahos, Peter. *A Philosophy of Intellectual Property.* Ashgate, 1996. https://press-files.anu.edu.au/downloads/press/n1902/html/cover.xhtml.

du Plessis, Jacques. "Common Law Influences on the Law of Contract and Unjustified Enrichment in Some Mixed Legal Systems." *Tul. L. Rev.* 78, nos. 1 & 2 (December 2003): 219–56.

Dworkin, Ronald M. "Is Wealth a Value?" *J. Legal Stud.* 9, no. 2 (March 1980): 191–226. https://perma.cc/6WS4-LPPB.

—. "Why Efficiency? A Response to Professors Calabresi and Posner." *Hofstra L. Rev.* 8, no. 3 (Spring 1980): 563–90. https://scholarlycommons.law.hofstra.edu/hlr/vol8/iss3/5/.

Eabrasu, Marian "A Reply to the Current Critiques Formulated Against Hoppe's Argumentation Ethics." *Libertarian Papers* 1 (20) (2009). www.libertarianpapers.org.

Easterbrook, Frank H. "Intellectual Property Is Still Property." *Harv. J.L. & Pub. Pol'y* 13 (1) (1990): 108–118. https://chicagounbound.uchicago.edu/journal_articles/309/.

eBaum. "Grieving Husband." *eBaum's World.* Sep. 29, 2006. https://perma.cc/5XHM-KVWS.

Egan, Thomas P. "Equitable Doctrines Operating Against the Express Provisions of a Written Contract (or When Black and White Equals Gray)." *DePaul Bus. L. J.* 5 (1993): 261–312.

Ellin, Joseph. "Restitutionism Defended." *J. Value Inquiry* 34, no. 2 (Sept. 2000): 299–317.

Ely, John Hart. *Democracy and Distrust: A Theory of Judicial Review*. Cambridge, Mass.: Harvard University Press, 1980.

Epstein, Richard A. "An Analysis of Causation." In *A Theory of Strict Liability: Toward a Reformation of Tort Law*. San Francisco: Cato Institute, 1980. https://perma.cc/PVV6-U3Y7.

—. "Defenses and Subsequent Pleas in a System of Strict Liability." *J. Legal Stud.* 3 (1974): 74–85.

—. "The Disintegration of Intellectual Property? A Classical Liberal Response to a Premature Obituary." *Stanford L. Rev.* 62, no. 2 (2010): 455–523. https://perma.cc/79X2-9CS8.

—. 1975. "Intentional Harms." *J. Legal Stud.* 4 (1975): 391–442.

—. "Past and Future: The Temporal Dimension in the Law of Property," *Wash. U. L. Q.* 64, no. 3 (1986): 667–722. https://openscholarship.wustl.edu/law_lawreview/vol64/iss3/3/.

—. "Pleading and Presumptions." *U. Chicago L. Rev.* 40 (1973): 556.

—. "Possession as the Root of Title." *Georgia L. Rev.* 13 (1979): 1221–43. https://chicagounbound.uchicago.edu/journal_articles/1236/.

—. *Principles for a Free Society*. Reading, Mass.: Perseus Books, 1998.

—. *Simple Rules for a Complex World*. Cambridge, Mass.: Harvard University Press, 1995.

—. "The Social Consequences of Common Law Rules." *Harv. L. Rev.* 95, no. 8 (June 1982): 1717–51. https://chicagounbound.uchicago.edu/journal_articles/1276/.

—. "The Static Conception of the Common Law." *J. Legal Stud.* 9, no. 2 (March 1980): 253–89.

—. *The Structural Unity of Real and Intellectual Property*. The Progress and Freedom Foundation, 2006; archived version at https://perma.cc/B8JP-4MWQ.

—. *Takings: Private Property and the Power of Eminent Domain*. Cambridge, Mass.: Harvard University Press, 1985.

—. *A Theory of Strict Liability: Toward a Reformation of Tort Law*. San Francisco: Cato Institute, 1980. https://perma.cc/PVV6-U3Y7.

—. "Why Libertarians Shouldn't Be (Too) Skeptical about Intellectual Property." Progress & Freedom Foundation, *Progress on Point*, Paper No. 13.4 (February 2006). https://perma.cc/6F5S-7KNS.

Evers, Williamson M. "Toward a Reformulation of the Law of Contracts." *J. Libertarian Stud.* 1 (1) (1977): 3–13. https://mises.org/library/toward-reformulation-law-contracts.

Ezorsky, Gertrude, ed. *Philosophical Perspectives on Punishment*. Albany: State University of New York Press, 1972.

Farah, Judy. "Crime and Creative Punishment." *Wall Street J.* (March 15, 1995): A15.

Ferguson, Benjamin. "Can Libertarians Get Away With Fraud?" *Economics and Philosophy* 34 (2018): 165–84. https://perma.cc/HL4Z-S2KC; pdf: https://perma.cc/799P-Y8SP.

Fetter, Frank A. *Economics—Vol. 1: Economic Principles*. NY: The Century Co., 1915. https://mises.org/library/economic-principles.

Findlay, J.N. *Kant and the Transcendental Object: A Hermeneutic Study*. Oxford: Clarendon Press, 1981.

Fisher, William. "IP Theory." https://perma.cc/Y48KHCTV

—. "Theories of Intellectual Property," in *New Essays in the Legal and Political Theory of Property*, edited by Stephen Munzer. Cambridge University Press, 2001. https://perma.cc/4YLX-P8JF.

Flew, Antony. *A Dictionary of Philosophy*, rev'd 2d ed. New York: St. Martin's Press, 1984.

—. "What is a 'Right'?" *Georgia L. Rev.* 13(1979): 1117–41.

Fogel, Karl. "The Surprising History of Copyright and The Promise of a Post-Copyright World." *Question Copyright* (2006). https://perma.cc/DV92-TEH3.

Foley, Ridgway K., Jr. "Invasive Government and the Destruction of Certainty." *The Freeman* (1988). https://fee.org/articles/invasive-government-and-thedestruction-of-certainty/.

Free Speech Center. "Case Categories: Commercial Speech." In *The First Amendment Encyclopedia* (https://perma.cc/QY39-K9NP).

French, Doug. "The Intellectual Revolution Is in Process." *Mises Daily* (Dec. 12, 2009). https://mises.org/library/intellectual-revolution-process.

Fried, Charles. *Contract as Promise*. Cambridge, Mass.: Harvard University Press, 1982.

Friedman, David. *The Machinery of Freedom: Guide to A Radical Capitalism*, 3d ed. 2014.

—. "Reflections on Optimal Punishment, or: Should the Rich Pay Higher Fines?" *Research in L. & Econ.* 3 (1981): 185–205.

—. "What Is 'Fair Compensation' for Death or Injury?" *Int'l Rev. L & Econ.* 2 (1982): 81–93. https://perma.cc/W5BU-K6PL.

—. "Why Not Hang Them All: The Virtues of Inefficient Punishment." *J. Pol. Econ.* 107, no. 6 (December 1999): 259–269. https://perma.cc/3M2H-68N2.

Friedman, Lawrence M. *A History of American Law*, 2d ed. New York: Simon & Schuster, Inc, 1985.

Frier, Bruce W. *The Rise of the Roman Jurists*. Princeton, N.J.: Princeton University Press, 1985.

Frumkin, Maximilian. "The Origin of Patents." *J. Pat. Off. Soc'y* 27, no. 3 (1945): 143–49. https://perma.cc/Y575-ZR2A.

Gaius. *Institutes of Roman Law*, with a translation and commentary by Edward Poste, 4th ed., revised and enlarged by E.A. Whittuck. Oxford: 1904. https://oll.libertyfund.org/title/gaius-institutes-of-roman-law.

Gamrot, Wojciech. "The type individuation problem." *Studia Philosophica Wratislaviensia* 16, no. 4 (2021): 47–64. https://wuwr.pl/spwr/article/view/13718.

Gebray, Kahsay Debesu. "Justifications for Claiming Intellectual Property Protection in Traditional Herbal Medicine and Biodiversity Conservation: Prospects and Challenges." *WIPO-WTO Colloquium Papers* vol.4 (2013). https://perma.cc/3TXQ-LNFX.

Geist, Michael. "The Canadian Government Makes its Choice: Implementation of Copyright Term Extension Without Mitigating Against the Harms." *MichaelGeist.com* (April 27, 2022). https://perma.cc/3DER-JUK2.

—. "Japan Considering Copyright Term Extension, Canada Next?" *MichaelGeist.com* (July 15, 2013). https://perma.cc/G4R8-SDEF..

—. "U.S. Copyright Lobby Takes Aim at Canadian Copyright Term Through Trans-Pacific Partnership." *MichaelGeist.com* (Aug. 7, 2013). https://perma.cc/9NW4-EMAN.

Gerlin, Andrea. "Quirky Sentences Make Bad Guys Squirm." *Wall Street J.*, (Aug. 4, 1994): B1, B12.

Gewirth, Alan. "The Basis and Content of Human Rights." *Georgia L. Rev.* 13 (1979): 1150.

—. "Law, Action, and Morality ." In *Georgetown Symposium on Ethics: Essays in Honor of Henry B. Veatch*, edited by. R. Porreco. New York: University Press of America, 1984.

—. "Moral Rationality." *The Lindley Lecture*. Univ. of Kansas. 1972. https://core.ac.uk/download/pdf/213402925.pdf.

—. *Reason and Morality*. Chicago: University of Chicago Press, 1978.

Glyer, Mike. "Judge Decides Against Internet Archive." *File 770* (March 24, 2023). https://perma.cc/K5UH-VCWT.

Goetz, Charles J., and Robert E. Scott. "Enforcing Promises: An Examination of the Basis of Contract." *Yale L. J.* 89, no. 7 (June 1980): 1261–1322. https://scholarship.law.columbia.edu/faculty_scholarship/249/.

Goodman, John C. "Do Inalienable Rights Outlaw Punishment?" *Liberty* 10, no. 5 (May 1997): 47–49. https://perma.cc/4TMF-2S5R.

Gordley, James. *The Jurists: A Critical History*. Oxford University Press, 2013.

Gordon, David. *The Philosophical Origins of Austrian Economics*. Auburn, Ala.: Mises Institute, 1993. https://perma.cc/AQ6N-VS4H.

—, and Roberta A. Modugno. "Review of J.C. Lester's Escape from Leviathan: Liberty, Welfare, and Anarchy Reconciled." *J. Libertarian Stud.* 17, no. 4 (2003): 101–109. https://mises.org/library/review-jc-lesters-escape-leviathan-liberty-welfare-and-anarchy-reconciled-0.

Gordon, Wendy J. "An Inquiry into the Merits of Copyright: The Challenges of Consistency, Consent, and Encouragement Theory." *Stan. L. Rev.* 41 (1989). https://papers.ssrn.com/sol3/papers.cfm?abstract_id=3581843.

—. "Intellectual Property." In *Oxford Handbook of Legal Studies*, edited by Peter Cane and Mark Tushnet. 2003. https://perma.cc/59GP-HRD8.

—. "A Property Right in Self-Expression: Equality and Individualism in the Natural Law of Intellectual Property." *Yale L. J.* 102, no. 7 (1993): 1533–1610. https://scholarship.law.bu.edu/faculty_scholarship/1981/.

Graf, Konrad. "Action-Based Jurisprudence: Praxeological Legal Theory in Relation to Economic Theory, Ethics, and Legal Practice." *Libertarian Papers* 3, art. no. 19 (2011). http://libertarianpapers.org/19-action-based-jurisprudence-praxeological-legal-theory-relation-economic-theory-ethics-legal-practice/.

Grant, Daniel. "Artist's lawsuit against school that sought to cover up his murals heads to appeals court." *The Art Newspaper* (Feb. 1, 2023). https://perma.cc/9EE3-49SA.

Gray, John. *Hayek on Liberty*. Oxford: Basil Blackwell, 1984.

Green, Leslie. "Who Believes in Political Obligation?" In *For and Against State*, edited by John T. Sanders and Jan Narveson. Lanham, Md.: Rowman and Littlefield, 1996.

Greenidge, A.H.J. "Historical Introduction" to *Gaius's Institutes of Roman Law*. Translation and commentary by Edward Poste, 4th ed.; revised and enlarged by E.A. Whittuck. Oxford: 1904. https://oll.libertyfund.org/title/gaius-institutes-of-roman-law.

Grupp, Stanley E., ed. *Theories of Punishment*. Bloomington: Indiana University Press, 1971.

Habermas, Jürgen. *Between Facts and Norms: Contributions to a Discourse Theory of Law and Democracy*. Translated by William Rehg. Cambridge, Mass.: MIT Press, 1996. https://perma.cc/27K9-YWW2.

—. *Communication and the Evolution of Society*. Translated by Thomas McCarthy. Boston: Beacon Press, 1979.

—. *Consciousness and Communicative Action*. Translated by Christian Lenhardt and Shierry Weber Nicholsen. Cambridge, Mass.: MIT Press, 1990 [1983]. (Containing English translation of work originally published in German as "Moralbewusstsein und communikatives Handeln.)

—. "Discourse Ethics: Notes on a Program of Philosophical Justification." In *The Communicative Ethics Controversy*, edited by Selya Benhabib and Fred Dallmayr. Cambridge, Mass.: MIT Press, 1990.

—. *Jürgen Habermas on Society and Politics: A Reader*. Edited by Steven Seidman. Boston: Beacon Press, 1989.

—. *Knowledge and Human Interests*. Translated by Jeremy Shapiro. Boston: Beacon Press, 1972.

—. *Legitimation Crisis.* Translated by Thomas McCarthy. Boston: Beacon Press, 1975.

—. *The Philosophical Discourse of Modernity: Twelve Lectures.* Translated by Fredrick Lawrence. Cambridge, Mass.: MIT Press, 1987.

—. *Theory and Practice.* Translated by John Viertel. Boston: Beacon Press, 1973.

—. The *Theory of Communicative Action.* Translated by Thomas McCarthy. Boston: Beacon Press, 1984 & 1987.

Hadley, James. *Introduction to Roman Law.* Littleton, Colo.: Fred Rothman, 1996. https://archive.org/details/introductiontoro029387mbp.

Hare, R.M. *Freedom and Reason.* New York: Oxford University Press, 1963.

Harris, J.W. "The Elusiveness of Property." In *Perspectives on Jurisprudence: Essays in Honor of Jes Bjarup,* edited by Peter Wahlgren. Stockholm Institute for Scandinavian Law. 2005. https://perma.cc/SW6Z-FYTV.

—. *Property and Justice.* Oxford: Oxford University Press, 1996.

Hart, H.L.A. *The Concept of Law,* 3d ed. Oxford: Oxford University Press, 2012 [1961].

—. *Punishment and Responsibility: Essays in the Philosophy of Law.* Oxford: Oxford University Press, 1968.

—, and Tony Honoré. *Causation in the Law,* 2d ed. Oxford: Clarendon Press, 1985.

Hasnas, John. "The Myth of the Rule of Law." *Wis. L. Rev.* no. 1 (1995): 199–234. https://www.copblock.org/40719/myth-rule-law-john-hasnas/.

Hawkland, William D. "The Uniform Commercial Code and the Civil Codes," *La. L. Rev.,* 56, no. 1 (1995): 231–47. https://digitalcommons.law.lsu.edu/lalrev/vol56/iss1/6/.

Hayden, Howard C. "Stellar Aberration," *Galilean Electrodynamics.* (https://perma.cc/JUY8-W7WS) 4, no. 5 (Sept./Oct. 1993): 89–92. https://perma.cc/GQY6-KUVK.

Hayek, F.A. *The Constitution of Liberty.* Chicago: University of Chicago Press, 1960.

—. *The Fatal Conceit: The Errors of Socialism, vol. I of The Collected Works of F.A. Hayek.* Edited by W.W. Bartley, III. Chicago: University of Chicago Press, 1989.

—. *Individualism and Economic Order.* Chicago: University of Chicago Press, 1948. https://mises.org/library/individualismand-economic-order.

—. *Law, Legislation and Liberty: Rules and Order,* Vol. 1. Chicago: University of Chicago Press, 1978.

—. *The Road to Serfdom.* Chicago: University of Chicago Press, 1944.

Hazlitt, Henry. *Economics in One Lesson.* New York: Three Rivers Press, 1988.

Hegel, G.W.F. "Punishment as a Right." In *Philosophical Perspectives on Punishment,* edited by Ezorsky.

—. *The Philosophy of Right.* Translated by T.M. Knox. New York: St. Martin's Press, 1969.

Herbener, Jeffrey M. "Ludwig von Mises and the Austrian School of Economics." *Rev. Austrian Econ.* 5, no. 2 (1991): 33–50. https://mises.org/library/ludwig-von-mises-and-austrian-school-economics.

—, ed. *The Meaning of Ludwig von Mises: Contributions in Economics, Sociology, Epistemology, and Political Philosophy.* Norwell, Mass.: Kluwer Academic Publishers, 1993. https://mises.org/library/meaning-ludwig-von-mises.

Herbert, Auberon, and J. H. Levy. *Taxation and Anarchism: A Discussion between the Hon. Auberon Herbert and J.H. Levy.* London: The Personal Rights Association, 1912. https://perma.cc/LX8H-MZFH.

Herman, Shael. "Detrimental Reliance in Louisiana Law—Past, Present, and Future (?): The Code Drafter's Perspective." *Tul. L. Rev.* 58 (1984): 707–57.

—. *The Louisiana Civil Code: A European Legacy for the United States.* Louisiana Bar Foundation. 1993.

—. "Minor Risks and Major Rewards: Civilian Codification in North America on the Eve of the Twenty-First Century." *Tul. Civ. L. Forum* 8 (1993): 63–80.

—, and David Hoskins. "Perspectives on Code Structure: Historical Experience, Modern Formats, and Policy Considerations." *Tul. L. Rev.* 54 (1980): 987–1051.

Hesse, Carla. "The Rise of Intellectual Property, 700 B.C.–A.D. 2000: An Idea in the Balance." *Daedalus* 131, no. 2 (Spring, 2002): pp. 26–45.

Hettinger, Edwin C. "Justifying Intellectual Property." *Philosophy & Public Affairs* 18, no. 1 (Winter 1989): 31–52.

Higgins, Rosalyn. *Problems and Process: International Law and How We Use It*, reprint edition. Clarendon Press, 1995.

Higgs, Robert. *Crisis and Leviathan: Critical Episodes in the Growth of American Government.* New York: Oxford University Press, 1987.

Hodgson, Geoffrey M. "Much of the 'economics of property rights' devalues property and legal rights." *J. Inst. Econ.* 11, no. 4 (2015): 683–709. https://perma.cc/9VV3-8DX3.

Hohfeld, Wesley N. *Fundamental Legal Conceptions as Applied in Judicial Reasoning.* Edited by W.W. Cook. New Haven, Conn.: Yale University Press, 1946.

Hollis, Martin and Edward J. Nell. *Rational Economic Man: A Philosophical Critique of Neo-Classical Economics.* Cambridge, 1975.

Holmes, Jr., Oliver Wendell. *The Common Law.* Boston: Little, Brown, 1881.

Holzer, Henry Mark. *Sweet Land of Liberty: The Supreme Court and Individual Rights.* Costa Mesa, Calif.: Common Sense Press, 1983.

Honoré, Tony. "Causation in the Law." In *The Stanford Encyclopedia of Philosophy*, edited by Edward N. Zalta, 2001. https://perma.cc/3JJ6-VD29/

Hoppe, Hans-Hermann. "Anarcho-Capitalism: An Annotated Bibliography." *LewRockwell. com*, Dec. 31, 2001. https://archive.lewrockwell.com/hoppe/hoppe5.html.

—. *Democracy: The God That Failed.* Transaction, 2001. www.hanshoppe.com/democracy.

—. "Demonstrated Preference and Private Property: Reply to Professor Osterfeld," *Austrian Economics Newsletter* 9, no. 3 (Spring/Summer 1988): 10–12. https://perma. cc/4229-ZR7P.

—. *Economic Science and the Austrian Method.* Auburn, Ala.: Mises Institute, 1995. www. hanshoppe.com/esam.

—. *The Economics and Ethics of Private Property: Studies in Political Economy and Philosophy*, 2d ed. Auburn, Ala.: Mises Institute, 2006 [1993]. www.hanshoppe.com/eepp.

—. *Economy, Society, and History.* Auburn, Ala.: Mises Institute. 2021. https://www. hanshoppe.com/esh/.

—. "Eigentum, Anarchie und Staat." *Manuscriptum Verlag*, 2005; originally published in 1987, informal translation. www.hanshoppe.com/eigentum.

—. "F.A. Hayek on Government and Social Evolution: A Critique." *Review of Austrian Economics*, 10(1) (1997): 23–48.

—. *The Great Fiction: Property, Economy, Society, and the Politics of Decline*, Second Expanded Edition. Auburn, Ala.: Mises Institute, 2021. www.hanshoppe.com/tgf.

—. *Handeln und Erkennen: Zur Kritik des Empirismus am Beispiel der Philosophie David Humes.* Bern: Lang, 1976. www.hanshoppe.com/german.

—. "The Idea of a Private Law Society." *Mises Daily* (July 28, 2006). https://mises.org/library/idea-private-law-society.

—. "In Defense of Extreme Rationalism: Thoughts on Donald McCloskey's *The Rhetoric of Economics.*" *Rev. Austrian Econ.* 3, no. 1 (1989): 179–214. https://mises.org/library/defense-extreme-rationalismthoughts-donald-mccloskys-rhetoric-economics.

—. "Intimidation by Argument—Once Again." *Liberty* 3, no. 2 (Nov. 1989): 37–39. https://perma.cc/4382-RKSQ. Republished as "Intimidation by Argument," section III in "Appendix: Four Critical Replies."

—. "On the Indefensibility of Welfare Rights: A Comment on Conway" *Austrian Economics Newsletter* 11, no. 1 (Winter/Spring 1990: 14–16. https://perma.cc/X2PR-H8BW.

—. "PFP020 | Hans-Hermann Hoppe, Reflections on the Origin of the State (PFS 2008)," *Property and Freedom Podcast*, Dec. 24, 2021. https://propertyandfreedom.org/pfp.

—. "PFP041 | Hans-Hermann Hoppe, From the Malthusian Trap to the Industrial Revolution: An Explanation of Social Evolution (PFS 2009)." *Property and Freedom Podcast*, Jan. 20, 2022. https://propertyandfreedom.org/pfp.

—. "PFP163 | Hans Hermann Hoppe, 'On The Ethics of Argumentation' (PFS 2016)." *The Property and Freedom Podcast*, June 30, 2022.

—. *Praxeology and Economic Science*. 1988. Later included in Hoppe, *Economic Science and the Austrian Method*. Auburn, Ala.: Mises Institute, 1995. www.hanshoppe.com/esam.

—. "The Production of Law and Order: Natural Order, Feudalism, and Federalism." 2004. https://mises.org/library/6-production-law-and-order-natural-order-feudalism-and-federalism

—. "Property, Causality, and Liability." *Q. J. Austrian Econ.* 7, no. 4 (Winter 2004): 87–95. https://mises.org/library/property-causality-and-liability-1.

—. "A Realistic Libertarianism." *LewRockwell.com*, September 30, 2013. https://www.hanshoppe.com/2014/10/a-realistic-libertarianism/.

—. "Reflections on the Origin and the Stability of the State," *LewRockwell.com*, June 23, 2008. https://www.lewrockwell.com/2008/06/hanshermann-hoppe/to-battle-the-state/.

—. "Socialism: A Property or Knowledge Problem?" *Rev. Austrian Econ.* 9, no. 1 (1996): 143–49. https://mises.org/library/socialism-property-or-knowledge-problem.

—. *A Theory of Socialism and Capitalism: Economics, Politics, and Ethics*. Auburn, Ala.: Mises Institute, 2010 [1989]. www.hanshoppe.com/tsc.

—. "Time Preference, Government, and the Process of De-Civilization—From Monarchy to Democracy." in *The Costs of War*, edited by John Denson. New Brunswick: Transaction Publishers,1997. https://perma.cc/N7NA-24C8. Also in *J. des Economistes et des Etudes Humaines* 5, no. 2/3 (June/September 1994): 319–49. https://www.hanshoppe.com/publications/. Also in Hoppe, *Democracy: The God That Failed*.

—. "Time Preference, Government, and the Process of De-Civilization—From Monarchy to Democracy." *J. des Economistes et des Etudes Humaines* 5, no. 2/3 (June/September 1994): 319–49. https://www.hanshoppe.com/publications.

—. "The Ultimate Justification of the Private Property Ethic." *Liberty* 2 (1) (1988): 20.

—. "Utilitarians and Randians vs Reason." *Liberty* 2, no. 2 (Nov. 1988): 53–54. https://perma.cc/A5UU-P64A.

—, and Walter Block. "Property and Exploitation." *Int'l J. Value-Based Mgt* 15, no. 3 (2002): 225–36. https://perma.cc/UQ8U-UM35.

Horwitz, Morton J. *The Transformation of American Law, 1780–1860*. Harvard University Press, 1977.

Horwitz, Steven. "Monetary Calculation and Mises's Critique of Planning." *History of Political Economy* 30, no. 3 (1998): 427–50. https://perma.cc/9HXZ-T36L.

Hospers, John. "Retribution: The Ethics of Punishment." In *Assessing the Criminal*, edited by Barnett and Hagel III, 1977.

Huebert, Jacob. "The Fight against Intellectual Property." In *Libertarianism Today*. Santa Barbara, CA: Praeger, 2010. https://mises.org/library/fight-againstintellectual-property.

Huemer, Michael. *Ethical Intuitionism*. Palgrave Macmillan, 2007.

Hughes, Justin. "The Philosophy of Intellectual Property." *Georgetown L.J.* 77, no. 2 (Dec. 1988): 287–366. https://perma.cc/U4XX-5DZV.

Hülsmann, Jörg Guido. "The A Priori Foundations of Property Economics." *Q.J. Austrian Econ.* 7 (4) (2004): 51–57. https://mises.org/library/priori-foundations-property-economics-0

—. "Editorial." *Q. J. Austrian Econ.* 7, no. 4 (Winter 2004): 3–6. https://mises.org/library/editorial-special-symposium-issue-austrian-law-and-economics-0.

—. "Facts and Counterfactuals in Economic Law." *J. Libertarian Stud.* 17, no. 1 (2003): 61–64. https://mises.org/library/facts-and-counterfactuals-economic-law-1.

—. "Knowledge, Judgment, and the Use of Property." *Rev. Austrian Econ.* 10, no. 1 (1997): 23–48. https://mises.org/library/knowledgejudgment-and-use-property.

—. "A Realist Approach to Equilibrium Analysis." *Q. J. Austrian Econ.* 3, no. 4 (Winter 2000): 3–51. https://mises.org/library/realist-approach-equilibrium-analysis.

—. "The Ultimate Foundation of Economic Science." *YouTube*, Sept. 17, 2022. https://youtu.be/C3Oglpv47Fg

Hume, David. *A Treatise of Human Nature*. Edited by Selby-Bigge. Oxford, 1968.

Hummel, Jeffrey Rogers. "National Goods Versus Public Goods: Defense, Disarmament, and Free Riders." *Rev. Austrian Econ.* 4 (1990): 88–122. https://mises.org/library/national-goods-versus-public-goods-defense-disarmamentand-free-riders.

International Risk Management Institute. "The History of Proximate Causation." https://www.irmi.com/articles/expert-commentary/the-history-of-proximate-causation.

Jefferson, Thomas. "Letter From Thomas Jefferson to James Madison, 28 August 1789." *Founders Online*. https://founders.archives.gov/documents/Jefferson/01-15-02-0354.

—. "Thomas Jefferson to Isaac McPherson 13 Aug. 1813." *Founders Online*. https://founders.archives.gov/documents/Jefferson/03-06-02-0322.

Johnson, Eric E. "Intellectual Property and the Incentive Fallacy." *Florida State U. L. Rev.* 39 (2012): 623–79. https://papers.ssrn.com/sol3/papers.cfm?abstract_id=1746343.

Jolowicz, H.F. and Barry Nicholas. *Historical Introduction to the Study of Roman Law*, 3d ed. Cambridge, U.K.: University Press, 1972.

Justinian. *The Digest of Justinian*. Translation by Alan Watson. Philadelphia: University of Pennsylvania Press, 1985.

Kafka, Franz. *The Trials*, Definitive Edition. Translated (in 1956) by Willa and Edwin Muir. New York: Schocken Books, 1984.

Kambartel, Friedrich. *Erfahrung and Struktur*. Frankfurt/M.: Suhrkamp, 1968.

Kant, Immanuel. *Critique of Pure Reason*. Translated by Norman K. Smith. 1953 [1929].

—. *The Philosophy of Law: An Exposition of the Fundamental Principles of Jurisprudence as the Science of Right*. Translated by W. Hastie. Edinburgh: T&T Clark, 1887. https://oll.libertyfund.org/title/hastie-the-philosophy-of-law.

Kaufman, Walter. "Retribution and the Ethics of Punishment." In *Assessing the Criminal*, edited by Barnett and Hagel III.

Kelley, David. *The Evidence of the Senses: A Realist Theory of Perception*. 1986.

—. *The Foundations of Knowledge* Lecture series. YouTube playlist. https://www.youtube.com/playlist?list=PLnHOyZsmJrozETJ9zzryDhW0kliZkbIsu.

—. "The Nature of Free Will." *The Foundations of Knowledge*, Lecture 6. Portland Institute Conference, 1986. *YouTube*. https://youtu.be/m8qeaxNl7jE.

—. "The Primacy of Existence." *The Foundations of Knowledge*, Lecture 1. The Jefferson School Conference, San Diego, 1985. *YouTube* https://youtu.be/AVBgfamJxFk.

—, and Roger Donway. *Laissez Parler: Freedom in the Electronic Media*. 1985.

Kelley, Patrick J. "Proximate Cause in Negligence Law: History, Theory and the Present Darkness." *Washington U. L. Q.* 69, no. 1 (Jan. 1991): 49–105. https://openscholarship.wustl.edu/law_lawreview/vol69/iss1/6/.

Kelsen, Hans. *General Theory of Law and State*. Translated by Anders Wedberg. Cambridge, Mass.: Harvard University Press, 1949.

Kestenbaum, David and Jacob Goldstein. "The Secret Document That Transformed China." NPR's *Planet Money* blog, Jan. 20, 2012. https://perma.cc/C4SP-XSC7.

Kilbourne, Richard Holcombe, Jr. *A History of the Louisiana Civil Code: The Formative Years, 1803–1839*. Baton Rouge, La.: Center for Civil Law Studies, Louisiana State University, 1987.

King, J. Charles. "A Rationale for Punishment." *J. Libertarian Stud.* 4 (2) (1980): 151–65. https://mises.org/library/rationale-punishment-0.

Kinsella, Stephan. "$30 Billion Taxfunded Innovation Contracts: The 'Progressive-Libertarian' Solution," *Mises Economics Blog* (Nov. 23, 2008).

—. "Afterword." In *The Great Fiction: Property, Economy, Society, and the Politics of Decline*, Second Expanded Edition, by Hans-Hermann Hoppe. Auburn, Ala.: Mises Institute, 2021. www.hanshoppe.com/tgf.

—. "Absurd Arguments for IP." *C4SIF Blog*, Sep. 19, 2011.

—. *Against Intellectual Property*. Mises Institute, 2008. Reprinted by Laissez Faire Books, 2012.

—. "Against Intellectual Property." *J. Libertarian Stud.* 15 (Spring 2001): 1–53. (Also: *AIP* Supplementary Material linked at www.c4sif.org/aip; the Resources page at www.c4sif.org/resources.)

—. "Aggression and Property Rights Plank in the Libertarian Party Platform." *StephanKinsella.com*, May 30, 2022.

—. "'Aggression' versus 'Harm' in Libertarianism." *Mises Economics Blog*, Dec. 16, 2009. www.stephankinsella.com/2009/12/aggression-versus-harm-in-libertarianism/.

—. "Another Problem with Legislation: James Carter v. the Field Codes." *Mises Economics Blog*, Oct. 14, 2009.

—, ed. *The Anti-IP Reader: Free Market Critiques of Intellectual Property*. Papinian Press, 2023.

—. "An Anti-Patent Patent Attorney? Oh my Gawd!" *StephanKinsella.com*, July 12, 2009.

—. "Apple Secures Win Against Motorola Over 'Slide-to-Unlock' Patent." *C4SIF Blog*, Feb. 17, 2012.

—. "Are anti-IP patent attorneys hypocrites?" *C4SIF Blog*, April 22, 2011.

—. "Are Ideas Movable or Immovable?" *C4SIF Blog*, April 8, 2013. https://c4sif.org/2013/04/are-ideas-movable-or-immovable/.

—. "Are Patents and Copyrights 'Monopolies'?" *C4SIF Blog*, Aug. 13, 2013.

—. "Argumentation Ethics and Liberty: A Concise Guide." *StephanKinsella.com*, May 27, 2011. https://www.stephankinsella.com/2015/01/argumentation-ethics-and-liberty-a-concise-guide-2011/.

—. "Ayn Rand and Atlas Shrugged, Part II: Confused on Copyright and Patent." *C4SIF Blog*, Oct. 21, 2012.

—. "Ayn Rand Finally Right about the First-to-File US Patent System." *C4SIF Blog*, Sep. 9, 2011.

—. "The Bad Bill of Rights." *LewRockwell.com*, Dec. 17, 2004. www.lewrockwell.com/lrc-blog/the-bad-bill-of-rights.

—. "Being a Libertarian." In *I Chose Liberty: Autobiographies of Contemporary Libertarians*, edited by Walter Block. Mises Institute, 2010.

—. "Benjamin Tucker and the Great Nineteenth Century IP Debates in Liberty Magazine." *C4SIF Blog*, July 11, 2022.

—. "Bill Marina (R.I.P.) on American Imperialism from the Beginning." *StephanKinsella.com*, July 8, 2009.

—. "Biographical pieces." *stephankinsella.com*. www.stephankinsella.com/publications/#biographical.

—. "Black Armbands for 'Constitution Day.'" *The Libertarian Standard*, Sept. 17, 2010.

—. "Blowback from IP Imperialism: Chinese Companies Again Using Patents To Punish Foreign Competitors." *C4SIF Blog*, July 14, 2012.

—. "Book Review." *Reason Papers* No. 20 (Fall 1995): 135–46. https://reasonpapers.com/archives/.

—. "Book review of Anthony de Jasay, *Against Politics: On Government, Anarchy, and Order*." *Q. J. Austrian Econ.* 1, no. 1. (Fall 1998): 85–93.

—. "Book Review of Rosalyn Higgins, *Problems and Process: International Law and How We Use It* (1994)." *Reason Papers* No. 20 (Fall 1995): 147–53.

—. "Book Review of Schulman, *The Robert Heinlein Interview and Other Heinleiniana* (1991)." *StephanKinsella.com*, Dec. 12, 2013.

—. "Book Review: *The Economics and Ethics of Private Property: Studies in Political Economy and Philosophy* by Hans-Hermann Hoppe." *Foundation for Economic Freedom*, Nov. 1, 1994. https://perma.cc/5J2V-R5R6.

—. "British student Richard O'Dwyer can be extradited to US for having website with links to pirated movies." *C4SIF Blog*, Jan. 13, 2012.

—. "Career Advice by North." *StephanKinsella.com*, Aug. 12, 2009.

—. "The Case Against Intellectual Property." In *Handbook of the Philosophical Foundations of Business Ethics*, edited by Prof. Dr. Christoph Lütge. Springer, 2013. Chapter 68, Part 18, "Property Rights: Material and Intellectual," Robert McGee, section ed.

—. "Causation and Aggression in symposium issue on Austrian Law and Economics: The Contributions of Reinach and Rothbard." *Q. J. Austrian Econ.* 7, no. 4 (Winter 2004).

—. "China and Intellectual Property." *C4SIF Blog*, Dec. 27, 2010.

—. "Classical Liberals and Anarchists on Intellectual Property." *C4SIF Blog*, Oct. 6, 2015.

—. "Classifying Patent and Copyright Law as 'Property': So What?" *Mises Economics Blog*, Oct. 4, 2011.

—. "Comedian Louis C.K. Makes $1 Million Selling DRM Free Video via PayPal on his own website." *C4SIF.org*, Dec. 22, 2011.

—. "Common Misconceptions about Plagiarism and Patents: A Call for an Independent Inventor Defense." *Mises Economics Blog*, Nov. 21, 2009.

—. "Constitutional Structures in Defense of Freedom (ASC 1998)." *StephanKinsella.com*, June 25, 2021.

—. "Conversation with an author about copyright and publishing in a free society." *C4SIF.org*, Jan. 23, 2012.

—. "Cool Footnote Policy." *StephanKinsella.com*, June 14, 2002.

—. "Copyright and Free Trade; Patents and Censorship." *C4SIF Blog*, Feb. 29, 2012.

—. "Copyright and the End of Internet Freedom." *C4SIF Blog*, May 10, 2011.

—. "Copyright Censorship versus Free Speech and Human Rights; Excessive Fines and the Eighth Amendment." *C4SIF Blog*, Sep. 6, 2011.

—. "Cordato and Kirzner on Intellectual Property." *C4SIF Blog*, April 21, 2011. https://c4sif.org/2011/04/cordato-and-kirzner-on-intellectual-property/.

—. "Corporate Personhood, Limited Liability, and Double Taxation." *The Libertarian Standard*, Oct. 18, 2011.

—. "Cory Doctorow on Giving Away Free E-Books and the Morality of 'Copying.'" *Mises Economics Blog*, Sept. 16, 2008.

—. "Cory Doctorow, Victim of Fox Copyright Legal Bullying, Should Take A Stand Against Copyright." *C4SIF Blog*, April 27, 2013.

—. "Costs of the Patent System Revisited." *Mises Economics Blog*, Sep. 29, 2010.

—. "Covid-19 Relief Bill Adds Criminal Copyright Streaming Penalties and IP Imperialism." *C4SIF Blog*, Dec. 22, 2020.

—. "The Creator-Endorsed Mark as an Alternative to Copyright." *Mises Economics Blog*, July 15, 2010.

—. "A Critique of Mutualist Occupancy." *StephanKinsella.com*, August 2, 2009.

—. "Death by Copyright-IP Fascist Police State Acronym." *C4SIF Blog*, Jan. 30, 2012.

—. "The Death Throes of Pro-IP Libertarianism." *Mises Daily*, July 28, 2010.

—. "The Declaration and Conscription." *StephanKinsella.com*, July 6, 2009.

—. "Defamation as a Type of Intellectual Property." In *A Passion for Justice: Essays in Honor of Walter Block*, edited by Elvira Nica and Gheorghe H. Popescu. New York: Addleton Academic Publishers, forthcoming.

—. "Defending Argumentation Ethics: Reply to Murphy and Callahan." *Anti-state.com*, Sept. 19, 2002.

—. "Dialogical Arguments for Libertarian Rights." In *The Dialectics of Liberty*, edited by Chris Sciabarra, Roger Bissell and Ed Younkins. Lexington Books, 2019. https://www.stephankinsella.com/2019/06/dialogical-arguments-for-libertarian-rights-in-the-dialectics-of-liberty/.

—. "The Division of Labor as the Source of Grundnorms and Rights." *Mises Economics Blog*, April 24, 2009.

—. *Do Business Without Intellectual Property*. Liberty.me, 2014.

—. "Does Cato's New Objectivist CEO John Allison Presage Retrogression on IP?" *C4SIF Blog*, Aug. 27, 2012.

—. "Down With the Lockean Proviso." *Mises Economics Blog*, Aug. 26, 2009.

—. "Eben Moglen and Leftist Opposition to Intellectual Property." *C4SIF Blog*, Dec. 4, 2011.

—. "Empathy and the Source of Rights." *Mises Economic Blog*, September 6, 2006.

—. "The Essence of Libertarianism? 'Finders Keepers,' 'Better Title,' and Other Possibilities." *StephanKinsella.com*, Aug. 31, 2005.

—. "Estoppel: A New Justification for Individual Rights." *Reason Papers* No. 17 (Fall 1992): 61–74.

—. "Examples of Ways Content Creators Can Profit Without Intellectual Property." *StephanKinsella.com*, July 28, 2010.

—. "Extreme Praxeology." *StephanKinsella.com*, Jan. 19, 2007. https://www.stephankinsella.com/2007/01/extreme-praxeology/.

—. "Faculty Spotlight Interview: Stephan Kinsella." *Mises Economics Blog*, Feb. 11, 2011.

—. "Farmers and Seed Distributors Defend Right to Protect Themselves From Monsanto Patents." *C4SIF Blog*, Aug. 24, 2011.

—. "First Amendment Defense Act of 2021." *C4SIF Blog*, Jan. 17, 2021.

—. "Food Patents in Greece in 500 BC." *StephanKinsella.com*, Aug. 8, 2010.

—. "Foreword." In *A Spontaneous Order: The Capitalist Case For A Stateless Society* by Chase Rachels. 2015. https://archive.org/details/ASpontaneousOrder0.

—. "Foreword." In *A Theory of Socialism and Capitalism: Economics, Politics, and Ethics* by Hans-Hermann Hoppe. Auburn, Ala.: Mises Institute, 2010 [1989]. www.hanshoppe.com/tsc.

—. "The Four Historical Phases of IP Abolitionism." *Mises Economics Blog*, April 13, 2011.

—. "Francis Ford Coppola, copyfighter." *C4SIF Blog*, Jan. 29, 2011.

—. "Fraud, Restitution, and Retaliation: The Libertarian Approach." *StephanKinsella.com*, Feb. 3. 2009.

—. "The Freeman: Ideas on Liberty." Nov. 1994. https://perma.cc/5J2V-R5R6.

—. "'Free-trade' pacts export U.S. copyright controls." *C4SIF Blog*, Oct. 17, 2011.

—. "Gary North on the 3D Printing Threat to Patent Law." *C4SIF Blog*, Jan. 31, 2022.

—. "The Genesis of Estoppel: My Libertarian Rights Theory." *StephanKinsella.com*, March 22, 2016.

—. "Goodbye 1776, 1789, Tom." *StephanKinsella.com*, June 29, 2009.

—. "Google's Schmidt on the Patent-Caused Smartphone Oligopoly" *C4SIF Blog*, Dec. 5, 2012.

—. "The Great Mises-Hayek Dehomogenization/Economic Calculation Debate." *StephanKinsella.com*, Feb. 8, 2016.

—. "The Greatest Libertarian Books." *StephanKinsella.com*, August 7, 2006.

—. "Happy We-Should-Restore-the-Monarchy-and-Rejoin-Britain Day!" *Mises Economics Blog*, July 2, 2009.

—. "Hate Crime—Intentional Action and Motivations." *StephanKinsella.com*, July 9, 2009. https://www.stephankinsella.com/2009/07/hate-crime-intentional-action-and-motivations/.

—. "Hayek's Views on Intellectual Property." *C4SIF Blog*, Aug. 2, 2013.

—. "History of Copyright, part 1: Black Death." *C4SIF Blog*, Feb. 2, 2012.

—. "Homesteading, Abandonment, and Unowned Land in the Civil Law." *StephanKinsella.com*, Aug. 28, 2021.

—. "Hoppe on Property Rights in Physical Integrity vs Value." *StephanKinsella.com*, June 12, 2011.

—. "Hoppe's Argumentation Ethics and Its Critics." *StephanKinsella.com*, August 11, 2015. https://www.stephankinsella.com/2015/08/hoppes-argumentation-ethics-and-its-critics/.

—. "How I Became A Libertarian." *LewRockwell.com*, December 18, 2002.

—. "How Intellectual Property Hampers the Free Market" *The Freeman*, May 25, 2011.

—. "How to Think About Property (2019)." *StephanKinsella.com*, April 25, 2021.

—. "How We Come to Own Ourselves." *Mises Daily*, Sept. 7, 2006.

—. "Human Action and Universe Creation." *StephanKinsella.com*, June 28, 2022.

—. "Ideas Are Free: The Case Against Intellectual Property." *Mises Daily*, Nov. 23, 2010.

—. "If you oppose IP you support plagiarism; copying others is fraud or contract breach." In "Hello! You've Been Referred Here Because You're Wrong About Intellectual Property." *C4SIF*, 2023.

—. "The 'If you own something, that implies that you can sell it; if you sell something, that implies you must own it first' Fallacies." *StephanKinsella.com*, June 1, 2018.

—. "Inability to Abandon Property in the Civil Law." *StephanKinsella.com*, Aug. 3, 2009.

—. "Inalienability and Punishment: A Reply to George Smith." *J. Libertarian Stud.* 14, no. 1 (Winter 1998–99): 79–93.

—. "In Defense of Napster and Against the Second Homesteading Rule." *LewRockwell.com*, September 4, 2000.

—. "Independent Institute on The 'Benefits' of Intellectual Property Protection." *C4SIF Blog*, Feb. 15, 2016.

—. "Innovations that Thrive Without IP." *StephanKinsella.com*, Aug. 9, 2010.

—. "Intellectual Freedom and Learning versus Patent and Copyright," *Economic Notes* No. 113 (Libertarian Alliance, Jan. 18, 2011); also published as "Intellectual Freedom and Learning Versus Patent and Copyright," *The Libertarian Standard*, Jan. 19, 2011.

—. "Intellectual Properganda." *Mises Economics Blog*, Dec. 6, 2010.

—. "Intellectual Property Advocates Hate Competition." *Mises Economics Blog*, July 19, 2011.

—. "Intellectual Property and Libertarianism." *Mises Daily*, Nov. 17, 2009.

—. "Intellectual Property and the Structure of Human Action." *StephanKinsella.com*, Jan. 6, 2010. https://www.stephankinsella.com/2010/01/intellectual-property-and-the-structure-of-human-action/.

—. "'Intellectual Property' as an umbrella term and as propaganda: a reply to Richard Stallman." *C4SIF Blog*, Feb. 10, 2012.

—. "Intellectual Property Imperialism." *C4SIF Blog*, Oct. 24, 2010. https://c4sif.org/2010/10/intellectual-property-imperialism/.

—. "Intellectual Property Rights: A Critical History and US IP Imperialism." *C4SIF Blog*, Dec. 31, 2014.

—. "Intellectual Property Rights as Negative Servitudes." *C4SIF Blog*, June 23, 2011.

—. "International Law, Libertarian Principles, and the Russia-Ukraine War." *StephanKinsella.com*, April 18, 2022.

—. "Introduction." In *Origitent: Why Original Content is Property* by J. Neil Schulman. Steve Heller Publishing, 2018. https://perma.cc/2E6G-WWPE.

—. "IP and Aggression as Limits on Property Rights: How They Differ." *StephanKinsella.com*, Jan. 22, 2010.

—. "The Irrelevance of the Impossibility of Anarcho-Libertarianism." *Mises Economics Blog*, Aug. 20, 2009.

—. "Is Intellectual Property Legitimate?" *Pennsylvania Bar Association Intellectual Property Newsletter* 1 (Winter 1998): 3. Republished in *the Federalist Society's Intellectual Property Practice Group Newsletter*, 3, no. 3 (Winter 2000); available at www.stephankinsella.com/publications/#againstip

—. "Is It So Crazy For A Patent Attorney To Think Patents Harm Innovation?" *StephanKinsella.com*, Oct. 1, 2009.

—. "J. Neil Schulman, R.I.P." *StephanKinsella.com*, Aug. 10, 2019.

—. "James L. Walker (Tak Kak), 'The Question of Copyright' (1891)." *C4SIF Blog*, July 28, 2022.

—. "Jeff Hummel's 'The Constitution as a Counter-Revolution.'" *StephanKinsella.com*, July 1, 2009.

—. "Justice and Property Rights: Rothbard on Scarcity, Property, Contracts...." *www.stephankinsella.com*. https://www.stephankinsella.com/2010/11/rothbard-justice-property-rights/.

—. "Kevin Carson: So What if SOPA Passes?" *StephanKinsella.com*, Jan. 23, 2012.

—. "Killing people with patents." *C4SIF Blog*, June 1, 2015.

—. "Kinsella: Ideas are Free: The Case Against Intellectual Property: or, How Libertarians Went Wrong." *Mises Economics Blog*, Nov. 23, 2010.

—. "Kinsella, 'Law and Intellectual Property in a Stateless Society.'" *C4SIF Blog*, March 1, 2013.

—. "Knowledge, Calculation, Conflict, and Law." *Q. J. Austrian Econ.* 2, no. 4 (Winter 1999): 49–71.

—. "Knowledge vs. Calculation." *Mises Economics Blog*, July 11, 2006. https://www.stephankinsella.com/2009/07/knowledge-vs-calculation/.

—. "KOL001 | "The (State's) Corruption of (Private) Law" (PFS 2012)." *Kinsella on Liberty Podcast*, Jan. 11, 2013. https://www.stephankinsella.com/paf-podcast/kinsella-pfs-2012-the-states-corruption-of-private-law/.

—. "KOL004 | Interview with Walter Block on Voluntary Slavery and Inalienability." *Kinsella on Liberty Podcast*, Jan. 27, 2013. https://www.stephankinsella.com/paf-podcast/kol004-interview-with-walter-block-on-voluntary-slaver-2/.

—. "KOL012 | 'The Intellectual Property Quagmire, or, The Perils of Libertarian Creationism,' Austrian Scholars Conference 2008." *Kinsella on Liberty Podcast*, Feb. 6, 2013.

—. "KOL018 | Libertarian Legal Theory: Property, Conflict, and Society: Lecture 1: Libertarian Basics: Rights and Law." *Kinsella on Liberty Podcast*, Feb. 20, 2013.

—. "KOL020 | 'Libertarian Legal Theory: Property, Conflict, and Society: Lecture 3: Applications I: Legal Systems, Contract, Fraud" (Mises Academy, 2011)." *Kinsella on Liberty Podcast*, Feb. 21, 2013.

—. "KOL021 | 'Libertarian Legal Theory: Property, Conflict, and Society, Lecture 4: Causation, Aggression, Responsibility' (Mises Academy, 2011)." *Kinsella On Liberty Podcast*, Feb. 21, 2013 [Feb. 21, 2011]. https://www.stephankinsella.com/paf-podcast/kol021-libertarian-legal-theory-property-conflict-and-society-lecture-4-causation-aggression-responsibility-mises-academy-2011/.

—. "KOL037 | Locke's Big Mistake: How the Labor Theory of Property Ruined Political Theory." *Kinsella on Liberty Podcast*, March 28, 2013.

—. "KOL038 | Debate with Robert Wenzel on Intellectual Property." *Kinsella on Liberty Podcast*, April 1, 2013.

—. "KOL044 | 'Correcting some Common Libertarian Misconceptions' (PFS 2011)." *Kinsella on Liberty Podcast*, May 2, 2013.

—. "KOL045 | 'Libertarian Controversies Lecture 1' (Mises Academy, 2011)." *Kinsella on Liberty Podcast*, May 2, 2013.

—. "KOL049 | 'Libertarian Controversies Lecture 5' (Mises Academy, 2011)." *Kinsella on Liberty Podcast*, May 4, 2013. https://www.stephankinsella.com/paf-podcast/kol-049-libertarian-controversies-lecture-5-mises-academy-2011/.

—. "KOL059 | Libertarian Parenting—Freedomain Radio with Stefan Molyneux (2010)." *Kinsella on Liberty Podcast*, May 22, 2013.

—. "KOL076 |IP Debate with Chris LeRoux." *Kinsella on Liberty Podcast*, Aug. 30, 2013.

—. "KOL092 | Triple-V: Voluntary Virtues Vodcast, with Michael Shanklin: Can You Trade Something You Don't Own?" *Kinsella on Liberty Podcast*, Oct. 30, 2013. https://www.stephankinsella.com/paf-podcast/kol092-triple-v-voluntary-virtues-vodcast-with-michael-shanklin-can-you-trade-something-you-dont-own/.

—. "KOL100 | The Role of the Corporation and Limited Liability In a Free Society (PFS 2013)." *Kinsella on Liberty Podcast*. https://www.stephankinsella.com/paf-podcast/kol100-the-role-of-the-corporation-and-limited-liability-in-a-free-society-pfs-2013/.

—. "KOL108 | "Why 'Intellectual Property' is not Genuine Property," Adam Smith Forum, Moscow (2011)." *Kinsella on Liberty Podcast*, Dec. 11, 2013.

—. "KOL118 | Tom Woods Show: Against Fuzzy Thinking." *Kinsella on Liberty Podcast*, March 31, 2014.

—. "KOL146 | Interview of Williamson Evers on the Title-Transfer Theory of Contract." *Kinsella on Liberty Podcast*, Aug. 5, 2014.

—. "KOL149 | IP And Beyond With Stephan Kinsella—Non-Aggression Podcast." *Kinsella on Liberty Podcast*, Aug. 30, 2014. https://www.stephankinsella.com/paf-podcast/kol149-ip-and-beyond-with-stephan-kinsella-non-aggression-podcast/.

—. "KOL152 | NYC LibertyFest: 'Libertarianism After Fifty Years: What Have We Learned?'" *Kinsella on Liberty Podcast*, Oct. 12, 2014.

—. "KOL153 | 'The Social Theory of Hoppe: Lecture 1: Property Foundations' (Mises Academy, 2011)." *Kinsella on Liberty Podcast*, Oct. 16, 2014.

—. "KOL154 | 'The Social Theory of Hoppe: Lecture 2: Types of Socialism and the Origin of the State.'" *Kinsella on Liberty Podcast*, Oct. 16, 2014.

—. "KOL161 | Argumentation Ethics, Estoppel, and Libertarian Rights: Adam Smith Forum, Moscow (2014)." *Kinsella on Liberty Podcast*, Nov. 7, 2014.

—. "KOL164 | Obama's Patent Reform: Improvement or Continuing Calamity?: Mises Academy (2011)." *Kinsella on Liberty Podcast*, Dec. 9, 2014.

—. "KOL172 | "Rethinking Intellectual Property: History, Theory, and Economics: Lecture 1: History and Law (Mises Academy, 2011)." *Kinsella on Liberty Podcast*, Feb. 14, 2015.

—. "KOL197 | Tom Woods Show: The Central Rothbard Contribution I Overlooked, and Why It Matters: The Rothbard-Evers Title-Transfer Theory of Contract." *Kinsella on Liberty Podcast*, Dec. 3, 2015. https://www.stephankinsella.com/paf-podcast/kol197-tom-woods-show-the-central-rothbard-contribution-i-overlooked-and-why-it-matter/.

—. "KOL207 | Patent, Copyright, and Trademark Are Not About Plagiarism, Theft, Fraud, or Contract." *Kinsella on Liberty Podcast*, Feb. 21, 2016.

—. "KOL208 | Conversation with Schulman about Logorights and Media-Carried Property." *Kinsella on Liberty Podcast*, March 4, 2016.

—. "KOL219 | Property: What It Is and Isn't: Houston Property Rights Association." *Kinsella on Liberty Podcast*. April 28, 2017.

—. "KOL221 | Mises Brasil: State Legislation Versus Law and Liberty." *Kinsella on Liberty Podcast*, May 17, 2017. https://www.stephankinsella.com/paf-podcast/kol221-mises-brasil-state-legislation/.

—. "KOL225 | Reflections on the Theory of Contract (PFS 2017)." *Kinsella on Liberty Podcast*, Sep. 17, 2017.

—. "KOL229 | Ernie Hancock Show: IP Debate with Alan Korwin." *Kinsella on Liberty Podcast*, Nov. 16, 2017.

—. "KOL236| Intellectual Nonsense: Fallacious Arguments for IP (Libertopia 2012)." *Kinsella on Liberty Podcast*, Feb. 10, 2018.

—. "KOL237 | Intellectual Nonsense: Fallacious Arguments for IP—Part 2 (Libertopia 2012)." *Kinsella on Liberty Podcast*, Feb. 12, 2018.

—. "KOL238 | Libertopia 2012 IP Panel with Charles Johnson and Butler Shaffer." *Kinsella on Liberty Podcast*, Feb. 14, 2018.

—. "KOL250 | International Law Through a Libertarian Lens (PFS 2018)." *Kinsella on Liberty Podcast*, Sep. 26, 2018. https://www.stephankinsella.com/paf-podcast/kol250-international-law-through-libertarian-lens-pfs-2018-2/.

—. "KOL253 | Berkeley Law Federalist Society: A Libertarian's Case Against Intellectual Property." *Kinsella on Liberty Podcast*, Oct. 12, 2018.

—. "KOL259 | 'How To Think About Property,' New Hampshire Liberty Forum 2019." *Kinsella on Liberty Podcast*, Feb. 9, 2019.

—. "KOL274 | Nobody Owns Bitcoin (PFS 2019)." *Kinsella on Liberty Podcast*. Sept. 19, 2019. https://www.stephankinsella.com/paf-podcast/kol274-nobody-owns-bitcoin-pfs-2019/.

—. "KOL278 | Bob Murphy Show: Debating Hans Hoppe's 'Argumentation Ethics'." *Kinsella on Liberty Podcast*, Nov. 24, 2019. https://www.stephankinsella.com/paf-podcast/kol278-bob-murphy-show-debating-hans-hoppes-argumentation-ethics/.

—. "KOL308 | Stossel: It's My Idea (2015)." *Kinsella on Liberty Podcast*, Dec. 29, 2020.

—. "KOL337 | Join the Wasabikas Ep. 15.0: You Don't Own Bitcoin—Property Rights, Praxeology and the Foundations of Private Law, with Max Hillebrand." *Kinsella on Liberty Podcast*, May 23, 2021.

—. "KOL345 | Kinsella's Libertarian "Constitution" or: State Constitutions vs. the Libertarian Private Law Code (PorcFest 2021)." *Kinsella on Liberty Podcast*, June 26, 2021.

—. "KOL354 | CDA §230, Being "Part of the State," Co-ownership, Causation, Defamation, with Nick Sinard." *Kinsella on Liberty Podcast*. Aug. 3, 2021. https://www.stephankinsella.com/paf-podcast/kol354-cda-230-being-part-of-the-state-nick-sinard/.

—. "KOL364 | Soho Forum Debate vs. Richard Epstein: Patent and Copyright Law Should Be Abolished," *Kinsella on Liberty Podcast* (Nov. 24, 2021).

—. "KOL367 | Disenthrall with Patrick Smith: Fisking Strangerous Thoughts' Critique of 'Intellectual Communism.'" *Kinsella on Liberty Podcast* (Dec. 20, 2021).

—. "KOL382 | FreeTalkLive at PorcFest: Corporations, Limited Liability, and the Reno Reset." *Kinsella on Liberty Podcast*. June 23, 2022. https://www.stephankinsella.com/paf-podcast/kol382-freetalklive-at-porcfest-corporations-limited-liability-and-the-reno-reset/

—. "KOL395 | Selling Does Not Imply Ownership, and Vice-Versa: A Dissection (PFS 2022)." *Kinsella on Liberty Podcast*. Sept. 17, 2022. https://www.stephankinsella.com/paf-podcast/kol395-selling-does-not-imply-ownership-and-vice-versa-pfs-2022/

—. "The L. Neil Smith–FreeTalkLive Copyright Dispute," *Mises Economics Blog* (June 14, 2010).

—. "Law and Intellectual Property in a Stateless Society." *Libertarian Papers* 5, no. 1 (2013): 1–44.

—. "LeFevre on Intellectual Property and the 'Ownership of Intangibles.'" *C4SIF Blog* (Dec. 27, 2012).

—. "Legal Scholars: Thumbs Down on Patent and Copyright," *C4SIF Blog* (Oct. 23, 2012).

—. "Legislation and Law in a Free Society." *Mises Daily*. Feb. 25, 2010. https://mises.org/library/legislation-and-law-free-society

—. "Legislation and the Discovery of Law in a Free Society." *J. Libertarian Stud.* 11, no. 2 (Summer 1995): 132–81.

—. "Legislative Positivism and Rationalism in the Louisiana and French Civil Codes." *StephanKinsella.com*, April 4, 2023.

—. "The Legitimacy of Intellectual Property." Paper presented at the Law and Economics panel, Austrian Scholars Conference, Ludwig von Mises Institute, Auburn, Ala., March 25, 2000.

—. "Leonard Read on Copyright and the Role of Ideas." *C4SIF Blog*, Sept. 12, 2011.

—. "Lessig on the Anniversary of Aaron's Swartz Death." *C4SIF Blog*, Jan. 10, 2014.

—. "Letter on Intellectual Property Rights." IOS Journal (June 1995); *C4SIF Blog*, Aug. 31, 2022.

—. "Leveraging IP." *Mises Economics Blog*, Aug. 1, 2010.

—. "Libertarian Answer Man: Mind-Body Dualism, Self-Ownership, and Property Rights." *StephanKinsella.com*, Jan. 29, 2022.

—. "Libertarian Answer Man: Self-ownership for slaves and Crusoe; and Yiannopoulos on Accurate Analysis and the term 'Property'; Mises distinguishing between juristic and economic categories of 'ownership." *StephanKinsella.com*, April 3, 2021.

—. "The Libertarian Approach to Negligence, Tort, and Strict Liability: Wergeld and Partial Wergeld." *Mises Economics Blog*, Sep. 1, 2009.

—. "The Libertarian Approach to Negligence, Tort, and Strict Liability: Wergeld and Partial Wergeld." *Mises Economics Blog*, Sep. 1, 2009. https://www.stephankinsella.com/2009/09/the-libertarian-approach-to-negligence-tort-and-strict-liability-wergeld-and-partial-wergeld/.

—. "A Libertarian Defense of Kelo and Limited Federal Power." *Southern U. L. Rev.* (2005).

—. "Libertarian Favors $80 Billion Annual Tax-Funded 'Medical Innovation Prize Fund.'" *Mises Economic Blog*, Aug. 12, 2008.

—. "Libertarian Sci-Fi Authors and Copyright versus Libertarian IP Abolitionists." *C4SIF Blog*, June 14, 2012.

—. "A Libertarian Theory of Contracts." *Austrian Scholars Conference*. Auburn, Ala.: Mises Institute. April 17, 1999.

—. "A Libertarian Theory of Contracts: Title Transfer, Binding Promises, and Inalienability." *J. Libertarian Stud.* 17, no. 2 (Spring 2003): 11–37.

—. "A Libertarian Theory of Punishment and Rights." *Loy. L.A. L. Rev* 30 (2) (1997): 607–45. https://digitalcommons.lmu.edu/llr/vol30/iss2/.

—. "Libertarianism After Fifty Years: What Have We Learned? (transcript)." *StephanKinsella.com*, Oct. 12, 2014.

—. "'Libertarians' Who Object to 'Self-Ownership'." *StephanKinsella.com*, July 19, 2022.

—. "The Limits of Armchair Theorizing: The Case of Threats," *Mises Economics Blog*, Jul. 27, 2006.

—. "The Limits of Libertarianism?: A Dissenting View." *StephanKinsella.com*, April 20, 2014.

—. "Locke on IP; Mises, Rothbard, and Rand on Creation, Production, and 'Rearranging.'" *Mises Economics Blog*, Sep. 29, 2010.

—. "Locke, Smith, Marx; the Labor Theory of Property and the Labor Theory of Value; and Rothbard, Gordon, and Intellectual Property." *StephanKinsella.com*, June 23, 2010.

—. "Logical and Legal Positivism." *StephanKinsella.com*, June 23, 2010.

—. "Man sentenced to federal prison for uploading "Wolverine" movie." *C4SIF Blog*, Dec. 21, 2011.

—. "Masnick on the Horrible PROTECT IP Act: The Coming IPolice State." *C4SIF Blog*, June 2, 2012.

—. "McElroy: 'On the Subject of Intellectual Property' (1981)." *C4SIF Blog*, March 19, 2013.

—. "Milton Friedman (and Rothbard) on the Distorting and Skewing Effect of Patents." *C4SIF Blog*, July 3, 2011.

—. "Mises: Keep It Interesting." *StephanKinsella.com*, Oct. 16. 2010. https://www.stephankinsella.com/2010/10/mises-keep-it-interesting/.

—. "Mises, Rothbard, and Hoppe on the 'Original Sin' in the Distribution of Property Rights." *StephanKinsella.com*, October 7. 2014.

—. "Mr. IP Answer Man Time: On Steel and Swords." *C4SIF Blog*, Feb. 4, 2022.

—. "Monsanto wins lawsuit against Indiana soybean farmer." *C4SIF Blog*, Sep. 24, 2011.

—. "Montessori and 'Unschooling.'" *StephanKinsella.com*, Oct. 16, 2010.

—. "Montessori, Peace, and Libertarianism." *LewRockwell.com*, April 28, 2011.

—. "Mossoff: Patent Law Really Is as Straightforward as Real Estate Law." *C4SIF Blog*, Aug. 17, 2012.

—. "The Mountain of IP Legislation." *C4SIF Blog*, Nov. 24, 2010. https://c4sif.org/2010/11/the-mountain-of-ip-legislation/.

—. "The Murdering, Thieving, Enslaving, Unlibertarian Continental Army" *LewRockwell.com*, July 3, 2009.

—. "Napolitano on Health-Care Reform and the Constitution: Is the Commerce Clause Really Limited?" *StephanKinsella.com*, Sep. 17, 2009.

—. "The Nature of the State and Why Libertarians Hate It" *The Libertarian Standard*, May 3, 2010. http://libertarianstandard.com/2010/05/03/the-nature-of-the-state-and-why-libertarians-hate-it/.

—. "The new libertarianism: anti-capitalist and socialist; or: I prefer Hazlitt's 'Cooperatism'." *StephanKinsella.com*, June 19, 2009.

—. "New Rationalist Directions in Libertarian Rights Theory." *J. Libertarian Stud.* 12, no. 2 (Fall 1996): 313–26.

—. "Nobody Owns Bitcoin." *StephanKinsella.com*, April 21, 2021.

—. "The Non-Aggression Principle as a Limit on Action, Not on Property Rights." *StephanKinsella.com*, Jan. 22, 2010.

—. "Objectivist Law Prof Mossoff on Copyright; or, the Misuse of Labor, Value, and Creation Metaphors." *Mises Economics Blog*, Jan. 3, 2008.

—. "An Objectivist Recants on IP." *C4SIF Blog*, Dec. 4, 2009.

—. "Objectivists on Positive Parental Obligations and Abortion." *The Libertarian Standard*, Jan. 14, 2011.

—. "On Conflictability and Conflictable Resources." *StephanKinsella.com*, Jan. 31, 2022.

—. "On Constitutional Sentimentalism." *StephanKinsella.com*, Jan. 16, 2011.

—. "On J. Neil Schulman's Logorights." *Mises Economics Blog*, July 2, 2009.

—. "On the Danger of Metaphors in Scientific Discourse." *StephanKinsella.com*, June 12, 2011.

—. "On the Obligation to Negotiate, Compromise, and Arbitrate." *StephanKinsella.com*, April 6, 2023.

—. "Optimal Patent and Copyright Term Length." *Mises Economics Blog*, June 16, 2011.

—. "The Origins of Libertarian IP Abolitionism." *Mises Economics Blog*, April 1, 2011.

—. "The Other Fields of Praxeology: War, Games, Voting… and Ethics?" *StephanKinsella.com*, Aug. 5, 2006. https://www.stephankinsella.com/2006/08/other-fields-of-praxeology/.

—. "The Overwhelming Empirical Case Against Patent and Copyright." *C4SIF Blog*, Oct. 23, 2012.

—. "Owning Thoughts and Labor." *Mises Economics Blog*, Dec. 11, 2006.

—. "The Patent, Copyright, Trademark, and Trade Secret Horror Files." *Mises Economics Blog*, Feb. 3, 2010.

—. "The Patent Defense League and Defensive Patent Pooling." *C4SIF Blog*, Aug. 18, 2011.

—. "Patent Lawyers Who Don't Toe the Line Should Be Punished!" *C4SIF Blog*, April 12, 2012.

—. "Patent vs. Copyright: Which is Worse?" *C4SIF Blog*, Nov. 5, 2011.

—. "Patents Kill: Compulsory Licenses and Genzyme's Life Saving Drug." *C4SIF Blog*. Dec. 8, 2010.

—. "Patents Kill: Millions Die in Africa After Big Pharma Blocks Imports of Generic AIDS Drugs." *C4SIF Blog*, Jan. 31, 2013.

—. "Patents Kill Update: Volunteers 3D-Print Unobtainable $11,000 Valve For $1 To Keep Covid-19 Patients Alive; Original Manufacturer Threatens To Sue." *C4SIF Blog*, March 18, 2020.

—. "Patrick Smith, Un-Intellectual Property." *C4SIF Blog*, March 4, 2016.

—. "The problem of particularistic ethics or, why everyone really has to admit the validity of the universalizability principle." *StephanKinsella.com*, Nov. 10, 2011.

—. "The problem of particularistic ethics or, why everyone really has to admit the validity of the universalizability principle." *StephanKinsella.com*, Nov. 10, 2011. https://www.stephankinsella.com/2011/11/the-problem-of-particularistic-ethics-or-why-everyone-really-has-to-admit-the-validity-of-the-universalizability-principle/.

—. "The Problem with 'Coercion." *StephanKinsella.com*, Aug. 7, 2009.

—. "The Problem with 'Fraud': Fraud, Threat, and Contract Breach as Types of Aggression." *Mises Economics Blog*, July 17, 2006.

—. "Pro-IP Libertarians Upset about FTC Poaching Patent Turf." *Mises Economics Blog*, Aug. 24, 2011.

—. "Property: Libertarian Answer Man: Self-ownership for slaves and Crusoe; and Yiannopoulos on Accurate Analysis and the term 'Property.'" *StephanKinsella.com*, April 3, 2021.

—. "Punishment and Proportionality: The Estoppel Approach." *J. Libertarian Stud.* 12 (1) (1996): 51–73. https://mises.org/library/punishment-and-proportialityestoppel-approach-0.

—. "Quotes on the Logic of Liberty." *StephanKinsella.com*, June 22, 2009. https://www.stephankinsella.com/2009/06/quotes-on-the-logic-of-liberty/.

—. "Rand on IP, Owning 'Values', and 'Rearrangement Rights.'" *Mises Economics Blog*, Nov. 16, 2009.

—. "The Real IP Pirates." *C4SIF Blog*, Oct. 16, 2010.

—. "Reducing the Cost of IP Law." *Mises Daily*, Jan. 20, 2010.

—. "Regret: The Glory of State Law." *Mises Economics Blog*, July 31, 2008.

—. "The Relation between the Non-aggression Principle and Property Rights: a response to Division by Zer0." *Mises Economics Blog*, Oct. 4, 2011.

—. "Remembering Tibor Machan, Libertarian Mentor and Friend: Reflections on a Giant." *StephanKinsella.com*, April 19, 2016.

—. "Replies to Neil Schulman and Neil Smith re IP." July 19, 2010.

—. "Reply to Van Dun: Non-Aggression and Title Transfer." *J. Libertarian Stud.* 18, no. 2 (Spring 2004): 55–64.

—. "Revising the American Revolution." *StephanKinsella.com*, July 6, 2009.

—. "Richard Epstein on 'The Structural Unity of Real and Intellectual Property.'" *Mises Economics Blog*, Oct. 4, 2006.

—. "Richard O. Hammer: Intellectual Property Rights Viewed As Contracts." *C4SIF Blog*, June 13, 2021.

—. "Richman on the 4th of July and American Independence." *StephanKinsella.com*, July 2, 2009.

—. "Rockwell on Hoppe on the Constitution as Expansion of Government Power." *StephanKinsella.com*, Aug. 3, 2009.

—. "Roman Law and Hypothetical Cases." *StephanKinsella.com*, Dec.19, 2022.

—. "Rothbard and Rockwell on Conservatives and the State/" *The Libertarian Standard*, Jan. 26, 2012.

—. "Rothbard on Libertarian 'Space Cadets.'" *StephanKinsella.com*. Sep. 23, 2009.

—. "Rothbard on Mercantilism and State "Patents of Monopoly." *C4SIF Blog*. Aug. 29, 2011.

—. "Rothbard on the 'Original Sin' in Land Titles: 1969 vs. 1974." *StephanKinsella.com*, November 5, 2014.

—. "Samuel Read on Legal Positivism and Capitalism in 1829." *StephanKinsella.com*, Nov. 4, 2011.

—. "Schulman: 'If you copy my novel, I'll kill you.'" *C4SIF Blog*, June 6, 2012.

—. "Second Thoughts on Leoni, Hayek, Legislation, and Economic Calculation." *The Libertarian Standard*, May 9, 2014. https://www.stephankinsella.com/2014/05/second-thoughts-leoni/.

—. "A Selection of my Best Articles and Speeches on IP." *C4SIF Blog*, Nov. 30, 2015.

—. "Six Year Federal Prison Sentence for Copyright Infringement." *C4SIF Blog*, March 3, 2012.

—. "SOPA is the Symptom, Copyright is the Disease: The SOPA wakeup call to ABOLISH COPYRIGHT." *The Libertarian Standard*, Jan. 24, 2012.

—. "Stalking and Threats as Aggression." *StephanKinsella.com*, Jan. 10, 2021.

—. "Stallman: An Internet-Connectivity Tax to Compensate Artists and Authors." *C4SIF Blog*, June 19, 2011.

—. "The Start of my Legal Career: Past, Present and Future: Survival Stories of Lawyers." *KinsellaLaw.com*, Dec. 6, 2010.

—. "The State is not the government; we don't own property; scarcity doesn't mean rare; coercion is not aggression." *StephanKinsella.com*, Dec. 19, 2022.

—. "Stefan Molyneux's 'Libertarian Parenting' Series." *The Libertarian Standard*, July 21, 2010.

—. "Stop calling patent and copyright 'property'; stop calling copying 'theft' and 'piracy.'" *C4SIF Blog*, Jan 9, 2012.

—. "Stop the ACTA (Anti-Counterfeiting Trade Agreement)." *StephanKinsella.com*, April 11, 2010.

—. "The Story of a Libertarian Book Cover." *StephanKinsella.com*, March 4, 2011.

—. "Supreme Confusion, Or, A Libertarian Defense of Affirmative Action." *LewRockwell.com*, July 4, 2003.

—. "Tabarrok, Cowen, and Douglass North on Patents." *C4SIF Blog*, March 11, 2021.

—. "Tabarrok: Patent Policy on the Back of a Napkin." *C4SIF Blog*, Sept. 20, 2012.

—. "Tabarrok's Launching the Innovation Renaissance: Statism, not renaissance." *StephanKinsella.com*, Dec. 2, 2011.

—. "Taking the Ninth Amendment Seriously: A Review of Calvin R. Massey's Silent Rights: The Ninth Amendment and the Constitution's Unenumerated Rights." *Hastings Const. L.Q.* 24, no. 3 (Spring 1997): 757–84.

—. "The tepid mainstream 'defenses' of Aaron Swartz." *C4SIF Blog*, Jan. 29, 2013.

—. "The Theory of Contracts." *Rothbard Graduate Seminar*. Auburn, Ala.: Mises Institute. July 28–Aug. 2, 2002. https://perma.cc/RQ5Z-S2GE.

—. "There are No Good Arguments for Intellectual Property." *Mises Economics Blog*, Feb. 24, 2009.

—. "There are No Good Arguments for Intellectual Property: Redux." *StephanKinsella.com*, Sep. 27, 2010).

—. "There's No Such Thing as a Free Patent." *Mises Daily*, Mar. 7, 2005.

—. "Thomas Jefferson's Proposal to Limit the Length of Patent and Copyright in the Bill of Rights." *C4SIF Blog*, Dec. 1, 2011.

—. "Thoughts on Intellectual Property, Scarcity, Labor-Ownership, Metaphors, and Lockean Homesteading." *Mises Economic Blog*, May 26, 2006.

—. "Thoughts on the Latecomer and Homesteading Ideas; or, Why the Very Idea of 'Ownership' Implies that only Libertarian Principles are Justifiable." *Mises Economics Blog*, August 15, 2007.

—. "Thoughts on Walter Block on Voluntary Slavery, Alienability vs. Inalienability, Property and Contract, Rothbard and Evers." *StephanKinsella.com*, Jan. 9, 2022.

—. "The Three Fusionisms: Old, New, and Cautious." *StephanKinsella.com*, January 16, 2022.

—. "The Trouble with Libertarian Activism," *LewRockwell.com*, Jan. 26, 2006. https://archive.lewrockwell.com/kinsella/kinsella19.html.

—. "Tim Lee and Lawrence Lessig: 'some punishment' of Swartz was 'appropriate.'" *C4SIF Blog*, Jan. 13, 2013.

—. "Tom Bell on copyright reform; the Hayekian knowledge problem and copyright terms." *C4SIF Blog*, Jan. 6, 2013.

—. "Transcript: Debate with Robert Wenzel on Intellectual Property." *C4SIF Blog*, April 11, 2022.

—. "Tucker, 'Knowledge Is as Valuable as Physical Capital.'" *C4SIF Blog*, March 27, 2017.

—. "Two lessons from the Megaupload seizure." *C4SIF Blog*, Jan. 24, 2012.

—. "Types of Intellectual Property." *C4SIF Blog*, March 4, 2011.

—. "The Undeniable Morality of Capitalism." *St. Mary's L. J.* 25 (4) (1994): 1419–47.

—. "Untold Truths about the American Revolution," *StephanKinsella.com*, July 7, 2009.

—. "Van Dun on Freedom versus Property and Hostile Encirclement." *StephanKinsella.com*, Aug. 3, 2009.

—. "Was the American Revolution Really about Taxes?" *The Libertarian Standard*, April 14, 2010.

—. "We are all copyright criminals: John Tehranian's 'Infringement Nation." *Mises Economics Blog*, Aug. 22, 2011.

—. "'We, The Web Kids': Manifesto For An Anti-ACTA Generation." *C4SIF Blog*, March 3, 2012.

—. "What Are the Costs of the Patent System?" *Mises Economics Blog*, Sep. 27, 2007.

—. "What it Means to Be an Anarcho-Capitalist." *LewRockwell.com*, Jan. 20, 2004. https://perma.cc/QAJ6-KHKN.

—. "What Libertarianism Is." In *Property, Freedom, and Society: Essays in Honor of Hans-Hermann Hoppe*, edited by Guido Hülsmann and Stephan Kinsella. Mises Institute, 2009.

—. "What Sparked Your Interest in Liberty?" *FEE.org*, April 21, 2016.

—. "When Did the Trouble Start?" *LewRockwell.com*, Sep. 5, 2003.

—. "Where does IP Rank Among the Worst State Laws?" *C4SIF Blog*, Jan. 20, 2012.

—. "Why Airwaves (Electromagnetic Spectra) Are (Arguably) Property)." *Mises Economics Blog*, Aug. 9, 2009.

—. "Why I'm a Libertarian–or, Why Libertarianism is Beautiful." *Mises Economics Blog*, Dec. 12, 2006.

—. "Wikileaks cables reveal that the US wrote Spain's proposed copyright laws." *C4SIF Blog*, Dec. 3, 2010.

—. "Yaron Brook on the Appropriate Copyright Term." *C4SIF Blog*, July 29, 2013.

—. "Yeager and Other Letters Re Liberty article 'Intellectual Property and Libertarianism'." *StephanKinsella.com*, Jan. 23. 2010.

—. "Yet another Randian recants on IP." *C4SIF Blog*, Feb. 1, 2012.

—. "Yet Another Study Finds Patents Do Not Encourage Innovation," *Mises Economics Blog*, July 2, 2009.

—. "Yet more disanalogies between copyright and real property." *C4SIF Blog*. Feb. 4, 2013.

—. *You Can't Own Ideas: Essays on Intellectual Property*. Papinian Press, 2023. www.stephankinsella.com/own-ideas.

— and Paul E. Comeaux. *Protecting Foreign Investment Under International Law: Legal Aspects of Political Risk*. Oceana Publications, 1997.

— and Robert P. Murphy. "Informal discussion." *Anti-state.com*. https://tinyurl.com/54rzjcnp and https://perma.cc/UU8S-2APB

— and Noah Rubins. *International Investment, Political Risk, and Dispute Resolution: A Practitioner's Guide*. Oxford University Press, 2005.

— and Andrew Simpson. *Online Contract Formation*. Oxford University Press, 2004.

— and Patrick Tinsley. "Causation and Aggression." *Q. J. Austrian Econ.* 7, no. 4 (Winter 2004): 97–112.

Kirzner, Israel M. *Market Theory and the Price System*. Princeton, N.J.: D. Van Nostrand Co., Inc., 1963. https://mises.org/library/market-theory-and-price-system-0.

—. "Producer, Entrepreneur, and the Right to Property." *Reason Papers* No. 1 (Fall 1974): 1–17. https://reasonpapers.com/archives.

Knight, Frank H. *On the History and Method of Economics*. Chicago: University of Chicago Press, 1956.

Knight, Keith, ed. *The Voluntaryist Handbook: A Collection of Essays, Excerpts, and Quotes*. 2022. https://perma.cc/N8UX-4PX4.

Kocourek, Albert. *Jural Relations*. Indianapolis: Bobbs-Merrill, 1927.

Kokesh, Adam. *Freedom!* 2014. https://archive.org/details/FREEDOMEbook.

Konkin, Samuel Edward, III. "Copywrongs." *The Voluntaryist*. July 1986. Reprinted at *LewRockwell.com*, Nov. 15, 2010. https://archive.lewrockwell.com/orig11/konkin1.1.1.html.

Koppelman, Andrew. *Burning Down the House*. St. Martin's Press, 2022.

Kozinski, Alex. "Of Profligacy, Piracy, and Private Property." *Harv. J.L. & Pub. Pol'y* 13 (1) (1998): 17–21. https://perma.cc/Z8AD-634V.

—, and J.D. Williams, "It Is a Constitution We Are Expounding." *Utah L. Rev.* no. 4 (1987): 977–994.

Kraft, John M. and Robert Hovden. "Natural Rights, Scarcity & Intellectual Property." *N.Y.U. J. L. & Liberty* 7, no. 2 (2013): 464–96. https://perma.cc/HLW8-YNVQ.

Kuflik, Arthur. "The Inalienability of Autonomy." *Philosophy and Public Affairs* 13, no. 4 (1984): 271–98.

Kunkel, Wolfgang. *An Introduction to Roman Legal and Constitutional History*. Translated by J.M. Kelly. Oxford University Press, 1966.

Larroumet, Christian. "Detrimental Reliance and Promissory Estoppel as the Cause of Contracts in Louisiana and Comparative Law." *Tul. L. Rev.* 60, no. 6 (1986): 1209–30.

Lawson, F.H. *The Rational Strength of the English Law*. 1951.

Lee, Timothy B. "Copyright enforcement and the Internet: we just haven't tried hard enough?" *ars technica*, Feb. 16, 2012. https://perma.cc/75P9-KM7E.

Leedes, Gary C. "The Discourse Ethics Alternative to Rust v. Sullivan." *U. Rich. L. Rev.* 26 (1991): 87–143. https://scholarship.richmond.edu/lawreview/vol26/iss1/4/.

LeFevre, Robert. *Fundamentals of Liberty*. Santa Ana, California: Rampart Institute, 1988. https://archive.org/details/LeFevre-TheFundamentalsOfLiberty.

—. *The Philosophy of Ownership*. 1966. https://mises.org/library/philosophyownership.

Legal Information Institute. "Larceny by trick." *Cornell Law School*. www.law.cornell.edu/wex/larceny_by_trick.

Leoni, Bruno. *Freedom and the Law*, 3d. ed. Indianapolis: Liberty Fund, 1991. https://oll.libertyfund.org/title/kemp-freedom-and-the-law-lf-ed.

Lessig, Lawrence. *Free Culture: How Big Media Uses Technology and the Law to Lock Down Culture and Control Creativity*. New York: Penguin Press, 2004. https://perma.cc/J8ZM-FT46.

Lester, J.C. *Escape from Leviathan: Liberty, Welfare and Anarchy Reconciled*. New York: St. Martin's Press, 2000.

Levasseur, Alain A. "Grandeur or Mockery?" *Loy. L. Rev.* 42, no. 4 (Winter 1997): 647–725. https://digitalcommons.law.lsu.edu/faculty_scholarship/321/

—. *Louisiana Law of Obligations in General: A Comparative Civil Law Perspective, A Treatise*. Durham, NC: Carolina Academic Press, 2020.

—. *Louisiana Law of Obligations in General: A Précis*, 3d ed. LexisNexis, 2009.

—. "The Major Periods of Louisiana Legal History." *Loy. L. Rev.* 41, no. 4 (Winter 1996): 585–6. https://perma.cc/XB9F-WQYX.

Lévêque, François and Yann Ménière. *The Economics of Patents and Copyrights*. Berkely Electronic Press, 2004. https://papers.ssrn.com/sol3/papers.cfm?abstract_id=642622.

Lewis, Todd. "Protection, Defense, Retaliation, and Self-Ownership." *Libertarian Christian Institute*, July 11, 2021. https://perma.cc/9SB2-XJC7.

Libertarian Party. "Libertarian Party Platform." https://www.lp.org/platform/, and https://perma.cc/GF6J-GPWV.

Liggio, Leonard P. "Law and Legislation in Hayek's Legal Philosophy." *Southwestern U. L. Rev.* 23 (1994): 507–29. https://perma.cc/5GHM-T8KU.

—, and Tom G. Palmer. "Freedom and the Law: A Comment on Professor Aranson's Article." *Harv. J. L. & Pub. Pol'y* 11 (1988): 713–25. http://tomgpalmer.com/selected-publications/.

Ligon, Cheyenne, Jack Schickler, and Nikhilesh De. "Hodlonaut Wins Norwegian Lawsuit Against Self-Proclaimed "Satoshi" Craig Wright ." *Coindesk.com*, Oct. 20, 2022. https://perma.cc/QLV9-VSLM.

Lippert-Rasmussen, Kasper. "Against Self-Ownership: There are No Fact-Insensitive Ownership Rights Over One's Body." *Philosophy & Public Affairs* 36 (1) (2008): 86–118.

Litvinoff, Saúl. *The Law of Obligations: Part I: Obligations in General*, 2d ed. St. Paul, Minn.: West Publishing Company, 2001.

—. "Still Another Look at Cause." *La. L. Rev.* 48, no. 1 (1987): 3–28. https://digitalcommons.law.lsu.edu/lalrev/vol48/iss1/5/.

Lloyd, Jack. "Justice and Voluntaryism." *Voluntaryist Association*, Dec. 7, 2022. https://perma.cc/2FZJ-U4EX.

—. "Property Rights," in *The Definitive Guide to Libertarian Voluntaryism*. 2022.

Locke, John. *Second Treatise on Civil Government*. 1690. https://www.johnlocke.net/2022/07/two-treatises-of-government.html.

Lomasky, Loren. "The Argument from Mere Argument." *Liberty* 3, no. 1 (Sept. 1989): 55–57. https://perma.cc/38XS-ZDEL

—. *Persons, Rights, and the Moral Community*. New York: Oxford University Press, 1987.

Long, Roderick T. "Bye-Bye for IP." *Austro-Athenian Empire Blog*, May 20, 2010. https://perma.cc/HD5A-TTX8.

—. "Getting Self-Ownership in View." *Paper presented to the PPE conference*. New Orleans, March 2019. https://perma.cc/U4AU-F996.

—. "Land-Locked: A Critique of Carson on Property Rights." *J. Libertarian Stud.* 20 (1) (2006): 87–95. https://mises.org/library/land-locked-critique-carson-property-rights.

—. "The Libertarian Case Against Intellectual Property Rights." *Formulations* (Autumn 1995).

—. "Owning Ideas Means Owning People." *Cato Unbound*, Nov. 19, 2008. https://www.cato-unbound.org/2008/11/19/roderick-t-long/owning-ideas-means-owning-people.

—. "This Self Is Mine." *Austro-Athenian Empire Blog*, July 8, 2014. https://perma.cc/VKP7-9F4D.

—. "Why Libertarians Believe There is Only One Right." *C4SS.org*, April 7, 2014. https://c4ss.org/content/25648.

Lorenzen, Paul. *Methodisches Denken*. Frankfurt/M.: Suhrkamp, 1968.

—. *Normative Logic and Ethics*. Mannheim: Bibliographisches Institut, 1969.

Ludwig von Mises Institute. "Reinach and Rothbard: An International Symposium." Auburn, Ala. March 29–30, 2001. https://perma.cc/396W-HJEL.

Machan, Tibor R. *Human Rights and Human Liberties: A Radical Reconsideration of the American Political Tradition*. Chicago: Burnham Inc Pub, 1975.

—. "Individualism and Political Dialogue." *Poznan Studies in the Philosophy of Science and the Humanities* 46 (June 1996): 45–55. https://www.stephankinsella.com/wp-content/uploads/texts/machan_dialogue.pdf.

—. *Individuals and Their Rights*. Chicago: Open Court Publishing, 1989.

—. "Intellectual Property and the Right to Private Property." Mises.org working paper. 2006. https://mises.org/wire/new-working-paper-machan-ip.

Machlup, Fritz. *An Economic Review of the Patent System*. 1958. https://mises.org/library/economic-review-patent-system.

—, and Edith Penrose. "The Patent Controversy in the Nineteenth Century." *J. Econ. History* 10, no. 1 (May 1950): 1–29.

Mackaay, Ejan. "Economic Incentives in Markets for Information and Innovation." *Harv. J. L. & Pub. Pol'y* 13, no. 3 (Summer 1990): 867–910.

MacIntyre, Alisdair. *After Virtue*. Notre Dame, Ind.: University of Notre Dame Press, 1981.

Mack, Eric. "The Natural Right of Property." *Social Philosophy and Policy* 27 (1) (2010): 53–78.

Madison, G.B. *Freedom and Reform*. Indianapolis: Liberty Press, 1982

—. *The Logic of Liberty*. New York: Greenwood Press, 1986.

Makovi, Michael. "The 'Self-Defeating Morality' of the Lockean Proviso." *Homo Oeconomicus* 32, no. 2 (2015): 235–74. https://perma.cc/G8PQ-LJ85.

Marcus, B.K. "Radio Free Rothbard." *J. Libertarian Stud.* (2) (2006): 17–51. https://mises.org/library/radio-free-rothbard.

—. "The Spectrum Should Be Private Property: The Economics, History, and Future of Wireless Technology." *Mises Daily*. October 29, 2004. https://mises.org/library/spectrum-should-be-private-property-economics-historyand-future-wireless-technology.

Martin, Michael. "On a New Argument for Freedom of Speech." *N.Y. U. L. Rev.* 57 (1982): 906–19.

Martin, Patrick H., and J. Lanier Yeates. "Louisiana and Texas Oil & Gas Law: An Overview of the Differences." *La. L. Rev.* 52, no. 4 (March 1992): 769–860. https://digitalcommons.law.lsu.edu/lalrev/vol52/iss4/3/.

Martinelli, Emanuele.. "On Whether We Own What We Think (draft)." 2019. https://www.academia.edu/93535130/On_Whether_We_Own_What_We_Think.

Masnick, Mike. "Hollywood Wants To Kill Piracy? No Problem: Just Offer Something Better." *Techdirt*, Feb. 6, 2012. https://perma.cc/73TB-YQX8.

—. "How Much Is Enough? We've Passed 15 'Anti-Piracy' Laws In The Last 30 Years." *Techdirt*, Feb. 15, 2012. https://perma.cc/TG7U-768F.

—. "People Rushing To Give Hundreds Of Thousands Of Dollars In Just Hours For Brand New Adventure Game." *Techdirt*, Feb. 9, 2012. https://www.techdirt.com/2012/02/09/people-rushing-to-give-hundreds-thousands-dollars-just-hours-brand-new-adventure-game/.

—. "Publishers Get One Step Closer To Killing Libraries." *TechDirt*, March 27, 2023. https://perma.cc/BYG5-6MXL.

—. "We're Living In the Most Creative Time In History." *Techdirt*, Feb. 12, 2012. https://perma.cc/F6HY-QHG9.

Massey, Calvin R. "Antifederalism and the Ninth Amendment." *Chicago-Kent L. Rev.* 64 (1989):987–1000. https://scholarship.kentlaw.iit.edu/cklawreview/vol64/iss3/13/. Reprinted in *The Rights Retained by the People*, vol. 2. edited by Barnett.

—. "Federalism and Fundamental Rights: The Ninth Amendment." *Hastings L.J.* 38, no. 2 (1987): 305–44. https://repository.uchastings.edu/hastings_law_journal/vol38/iss2/2/. Reprinted in *The Rights Retained by the People*, vol. 1., edited by Barnett.

—. "The Natural Law Component of the Ninth Amendment." *University of Cincinnati L. Rev.* 61 (1992): 49–105. https://repository.uchastings.edu/faculty_scholarship/1142/.

—. *Silent Rights: The Ninth Amendment and the Constitution's Unenumerated Rights.* Philadelphia: Temple University Press, 1995.

Mavrodes, George. "Property." in *Property in a Humane Economy*, edited by Samuel L. Blumenfeld. LaSalle, Ill.: Open Court, 1974. https://mises.org/library/propertyhumane-economy.

May, Christopher and Susan K. Sell. "The Emergence of Intellectual Property Rights." In *Intellectual Property Rights: A Critical History*. Boulder and London: Lynne Rienner Publishers, 2006.

May, Randolph J. and Seth L. Cooper. *The Constitutional Foundations of Intellectual Property: A Natural Rights Perspective*. Carolina Academic Press, 2015.

Mayer, David N. *The Constitutional Thought of Thomas Jefferson*. Charlottesville, Va.: Univ of Virginia Press, 1994.

McAffee, Thomas B. "Federalism and the Protection of Rights: The Modern Ninth Amendment's Spreading Confusion." *Brigham Young U. L. Rev.* 1996, no. 2 (1996): 351–88. https://digitalcommons.law.byu.edu/lawreview/vol1996/iss2/3/.

McCarthy, Thomas. *The Critical Theory of Jürgen Habermas*. Cambridge, Mass.: MIT Press, 1981.

—. *Ideals and Illusions: On Reconstruction and Deconstruction in Contemporary Critical Theory*. Cambridge, Mass.: MIT Press, 1993.

McCaskey, John P. "New Libertarians: New Promoters of a Welfare State." *JohnMc-Caskey. com*, April 14, 2014. https://perma.cc/259E-K2AB.

McCullagh, Declan. "Foreword." In., *Copy Fights: The Future of Intellectual Property in the Information Age*, edited by Adams Thierer and Wayne Crews, Jr. Cato, 2002.

—. "Free-trade pacts export U.S. copyright controls." *CNET*, Oct. 14, 201. https://perma.cc/7LJE-PG4J.

McElroy, Wendy. "Contra Copyright." *The Voluntaryist*, June 1985.

—. "Contra Copyright, Again." *Libertarian Papers* 3, art. no. 12 (2011) http://libertarianpapers.org/12-contra-copyright.

—. "Copyright and Patent in Benjamin Tucker's Periodical." *Mises Daily*, July 28, 2010. https://mises.org/library/copyright-and-patent-benjamin-tuckers-periodical.

—. *The Debates of Liberty: An Overview of Individualist Anarchism, 1881–1908*. Lexington Books, 2002. https://perma.cc/ZQM2-82B9.

—. "Intellectual Property." In *The Debates of Liberty: An Overview of Individualist Anarchism, 1881–1908*. Lexington Books, 2002. https://perma.cc/ZQM2-82B9.

—. "Murray N. Rothbard: Mr. Libertarian." *LewRockwell.com*, July 6, 2000. https://perma.cc/H7P2-P2YD.

—. "Why I Would Not Vote Against Hitler." *Liberty* 9, no. 5 (May 1996): 46–47. https://perma.cc/5NE3-BWES.

McGee, Robert W. "The Body as Property Doctrine." In *Handbook of the Philosophical Foundations of Business Ethics*, edited by Christoph Lütge. Springer, 2013.

—. "The Theory of Secession and Emerging Democracies: A Constitutional Solution." *Stanford J. International L.* 28, no. 2 (1992): 451–76. https://papers.ssrn.com/sol3/papers.cfm?abstractid=2177439.

McGrath, R.D. *Gunfighters, Highwaymen, and Vigilantes: Violence on the Frontier*. Berkeley: University of California Press, 1984.

—. "Treat Them to a Good Dose of Lead." *Chronicles* (January 1994): 17–18.

McNees, Pat. "What is the difference between a preface, a foreword, and an introduction?" *writersandeditors.com*, March 16, 2023. https://perma.cc/72AK-MJPX.

Meiners, Roger E. and Robert J. Staaf. "Patents, Copyrights, and Trademarks: Property or Monopoly." *Harv. J. L. & Pub. Pol'y* 13, no. 3 (Summer 1990): 911–48.

Menell, Peter S. "Intellectual Property and the Property Rights Movement." *Regulation* 30, no. 3 (Fall 2007): 36–42. https://perma.cc/F6X9-5L9D.

—. "The Property Rights Movement's Embrace of Intellectual Property: True Love or Doomed Relationship?" UC Berkeley Public Law Research Paper No. 965083. Feb. 26, 2007. https://perma.cc/F6X9-5L9D.

—, Mark A. Lemley, Robert P. Merges and Shyamkrishna Balganesh. *Intellectual Property in the New Technological Age: Volume I: Perspectives, Trade Secrets & Patents*. Clause 8 Publishing, 2022.

Menger, Carl. *Principles of Economics*. Auburn, Ala.: Mises Institute, 2007 [1871]. https://mises.org/library/principles-economics.

Merges, Robert Patrick, and John Fitzgerald Duffy. *Patent Law and Policy: Cases and Materials* (6th ed.). 2013.

Merrill, Thomas W. "Property and the Right to Exclude." *Neb. L. Rev.* 77 (1988): 730–55. https://scholarship.law.columbia.edu/faculty_scholarship/3553.

Merryman, John Henry. "The Refrigerator of Bernard Buffet." *Hastings L. J.* 27, no. 5 (May 1976): 1023–49. https://repository.uclawsf.edu/hastings_law_journal/vol27/iss5/3/.

—, and Rogelio Pérez-Perdomo. *The Civil Law Tradition: An Introduction to the Legal Systems of Western Europe and Latin America*, 4th ed. Stanford. California: Stanford University Press, 2018.

Meyers, Diana T. *Inalienable Rights: A Defense*. New York: Columbia University Press, 1985.

Miller, Eugene F. "The Cognitive Basis of Hayek's Political Thought." In *Liberty and the Rule of Law*, edited by Cunningham.

Mises, Ludwig von. *Economic Calculation in the Socialist Commonwealth*. Translated by S. Adler. Auburn, Ala.: Mises Institute, 1990 [1920]. https://mises.org/library/economic-calculation-socialist-commonwealth.

—. *Epistemological Problems of Economics*, 3d ed. Translated by George Reisman. Auburn, Ala.: Mises Institute, 2003. https://mises.org/library/epistemological-problems-economics.

—. *Human Action: A Treatise on Economics*, Scholar's ed. Auburn, Ala: Mises Institute, 1998. https://mises.org/library/human-action-0.

—. *Liberalism: In the Classical Tradition*, 3d ed. Translated by Ralph Raico. Irvington-on-Hudson, N.Y.: Foundation for Economic Education, 1985. https://mises.org/library/liberalism-classical-tradition.

—. *Memoirs*. Translated by Arlene Oost-Zinner. Auburn, Ala.: Mises Institute, 2009. (formerly *Notes and Recollections*). https://mises.org/library/book/memoirs.

—. *Socialism: An Economic and Sociological Analysis*. Translated by J. Kahane. Indianapolis, Ind: Liberty Fund, 1981. https://oll.libertyfund.org/title/kahane-socialism-an-economic-and-sociological-analysis.

—. *Theory and History: An Interpretation of Social and Economic Evolution*. Auburn, Ala.: Mises Institute, 2007 [1957]. https://mises.org/library/theory-and-history-interpretation-social-and-economic-evolution.

—. *The Theory of Money and Credit*. New Haven: Yale University Press, 1953. https://mises.org/library/theory-money-and-credit.

—. *The Ultimate Foundation of Economic Science: An Essay on Method*. Princeton, N.J.: D. Van Nostrand Company, Inc. 1962. https://mises.org/library/ultimate-foundation-economic-science.

Mitchell, William C., and Randy T. Simmons. *Beyond Politics: Markets, Welfare, and the Failure of Bureaucracy*. Boulder: Westview Press, 1994.

Moore, Adam D. and Kenneth Einar Himma. "Intellectual Property." In *Stanford Encyclopedia of Philosophy*, edited by Edward N. Zalta. Stanford University, 2011. https://papers.ssrn.com/sol3/papers.cfm?abstract_id=1980917.

Morehouse, Isaac. "How I Changed My Mind on Intellectual Property." *FEE.org*, Sept. 27, 2016. https://perma.cc/324H-TPRY. Also in *The Voluntaryist Handbook: A Collection of Essays, Excerpts, and Quotes*, edited by Keith Knight. 2022. https://perma.cc/N8UX-4PX4.

Morris, Heidi C. "Reason and Reality: The Logical Compatibility of Austrian Economics and Objectivism." *Rebirth of Reason*, May 10, 2005. https://perma.cc/PSR5-MNFE.

Morris, Herbert. *On Guilt and Innocence: Essays in Legal Philosophy and Moral Psychology*. Berkeley: University of California Press, 1976.

Mortellaro, Matt. "Causation and Responsibility: A New Direction." *Libertarian Papers* 1, art. no. 24 (2009). https://mises.org/library/causation-and-responsibility-new-direction.

Mossoff, Adam. "Commercializing Property Rights in Inventions: Lessons for Modern Patent Theory from Classic Patent Doctrine." In *Competition Policy and Patent Law Under Uncertainty: Regulating Innovation*, edited by Geoffrey A. Manne and Joshua D. Wright. Cambridge University Press, 2011. https://perma.cc/SD7Q-F7U9.

—. "The Constitutional Protection of Intellectual Property." *Heritage Foundation*, March 8, 2021. https://perma.cc/8ZUNL4XZ.

—. "Life, Liberty and Intellectual Property by Adam Mossoff." Ayn Rand Institute. *YouTube*, Sep. 21, 2021. https://youtu.be/CfMd1fHc2mE.

—. "Patents as Constitutional Private Property: The Historical Protection of Patents Under the Takings Clause." *Boston U. L. Rev.* 87 (2007): 689–724. https://perma.cc/G7JW-NZNE.

—. "Saving Locke from Marx: The Labor Theory of Value in Intellectual Property Theory." *Social Philosophy and Policy* 29, no. 2 (2012): 283–31. https://perma.cc/QG87-BAMY.

—. "The Trespass Fallacy in Patent Law." *Florida L. Rev.* 65, no. 6 (2013): 1687–1711. https://papers.ssrn.com/sol3/papers.cfm?abstract_id=2126595.

—. "Who Cares What Thomas Jefferson Thought About Patents? Reevaluating the Patent 'Privilege' in Historical Context." *Cornell L. Rev.* 92 (2007): 953–1012. https://perma.cc/UZ9H-RK77.

Moynihan, Ellen, and Larry McShane. "Bronx mom charged with luring ex-boyfriend to his shooting death by current beau." *New York Daily News*, Mar 15, 2023. https://perma.cc/79Z8-UV8L.

Mulligan, Christina and Brian Patrick Quinn. "Who are You Calling a Pirate?: Shaping Public Discourse in the Intellectual Property Debates." Brandeis University Department of English Eighth Annual Graduate Conference, 2010. https://perma.cc/7SCS-8P3J.

Mulligan, Kevin, ed. *Speech Act and Sachverhalt: Reinach and the Foundations of Realist Phenomenology*. Dordrecht/Boston/Lancaster: Martinus Nijhoff Publishers, 1987.

Murphy, Robert P. *Chaos Theory: Two Essays on Market Anarchy, Second Edition*. Auburn, Ala.: Mises Institute, 2010. https://mises.org/library/chaos-theory-two-essays-market-anarchy-0.

—. "Why Austrians Stress Ordinal Utility." *Mises Wire*, Feb. 3, 2022. https://mises.org/wire/why-austrians-stress-ordinal-utility.

—, and Gene Callahan. "Hans-Hermann Hoppe's Argumentation Ethic: A Critique." *Anti-state.com*, Sept. 19, 2002. https://tinyurl.com/5n62x6zc and https://perma.cc/D395-3JSW.

—, and Gene Callahan. "Hans-Hermann Hoppe's Argumentation Ethic: A Critique." *J. Libertarian Stud.* 20, no. 2 (Spring 2006): 53–64. https://mises.org/library/hans-hermann-hoppes-argumentationethic-critique.

Murray, Charles. *What it Means to Be a Libertarian*. New York: Broadway Books, 1997.

Nagel, Thomas. "Libertarianism Without Foundations." *Yale L. J.* 85 (1975): 136–49. https://perma.cc/SZP3-XPBM.

Nance, Dale A. "Foreword: Owning Ideas." *Harv. J. L. & Pub. Pol'y* 13, no. 3 (Summer 1990): 757–74.

Narveson, Jan. "The Anarchist's Case." In *Respecting Persons in Theory and Practice*. Lanham, Md.: Rowman & Littlefield, 2002. https://perma.cc/2P24-H4JL.

—. "Gewirth's Reason and Morality: A Study in the Hazards of Universalizability in Ethics." *Dialogue* 19 (1980): 651–74.

—. *The Libertarian Idea*. Philadelphia: Temple University Press, 1988. (Reissued Broadview Press, 2001).

Newton, Isaac. "Letter to Robert Hooke." February 15, 1676.

Nicholas, Barry. *An Introduction to Roman Law*, rev. ed. Oxford: Oxford University Press, 1962.

Njoya, Wanjiru. "Defending Private Property: Principles of Justice." *YouTube*, March 27, 2023. https://youtu.be/jzamN_8l77k.

North, Gary. "A Free Week-Long Economics Seminar." *LewRockwell.com*, July 24, 2010. www.lewrockwell.com/2010/07/gary-north/mises-u/.

Nozick, Robert. *Anarchy, State, and Utopia*. New York: Basic Books, 1974.

Orland, Kyle. "Double Fine seeks to cut out publishers with Kickstarter-funded adventure." *ars technica*, Feb. 9, 2012. https://arstechnica.com/gaming/2012/02/double-fine-seeks-tocut-out-publishers-with-kickstarter-funded-adventure/.

Osterfeld, David. "Comment on Hoppe." *Austrian Economics Newsletter* 9, no. 3 (Spring/Summer 1988): 9–10. https://perma.cc/4229-ZR7P.

—. "Natural Rights Debate: A Comment on a Reply." *J. Libertarian Stud.* 7, no. 1 (Spring 1983): 101–13. https://mises.org/library/natural-rights-debatecomment-reply-0.

Otsuka, Michael. *Libertarianism Without Inequality*. Oxford: Oxford University Press, 2003.

Paine, Thomas. *Common Sense*. 1776.

Paley, Nina. "*Copying Is Not Theft*." *YouTube*, April 1, 2010. https://youtu.be/IeTybKL1pM4.

Palmer, Tom G. "Are Patents and Copyrights Morally Justified? The Philosophy of Property Rights and Ideal Objects." *Harv. J. L. & Pub. Pol'y* 13, no. 3 (Summer1990): 817–65. https://perma.cc/J8LY-L4MQ.

—. "Intellectual Property: A Non-Posnerian Law and Economics Approach." *Hamline L. Rev.* 12, no. 2 (Spring 1989): 261–304. https://perma.cc/DH7K-ZCRV.

Palmer, Vernon. "Celebrating the Québec Codification Achievement: A Louisiana Perspective." *Loy. L. Rev.* 38 (1992): 311–27. https://perma.cc/JK8T-HX4J.

—. "The Death of a Code—The Birth of a Digest." *Tul. L. Rev.* 63, no. 2 (December 1988): 221–64.

—. "The French Connection and The Spanish Perception: Historical Debates and Contemporary Evaluation of French Influence on Louisiana Civil Law." *La. L. Rev.* 63, no.4 (2003): 1067–1126. https://digitalcommons.law.lsu.edu/lalrev/vol63/iss4/11/

—. "The Many Guises of Equity in a Mixed Jurisdiction: A Functional View of Equity in Louisiana." *Tul. L. Rev.* 69, no. 1 (1994): 7–70.

Pascal, Robert A. "*The Louisiana Civil Code: A European Legacy for the United States*. By Shael Herman," *La. L. Rev.* 54, no. 3 (Jan. 1994): 827–32. https://digitalcommons.law. lsu.edu/lalrev/vol54/iss3/17/.

Pauley, Matthew A. "The Jurisprudence of Crime and Punishment from Plato to Hegel." *Am. J. Jurisprudence* 39, no. 1 (1994): 97–152. https://scholarship.law.nd.edu/ajj/vol39/iss1/6/.

Peikoff, Leonard. *Objectivism: The Philosophy of Ayn Rand*. New York: Plume, 1991.

Pejovich, Svetovar. "Towards an Economic Theory of the Creation and Specification of Property Rights." In *Economics of Legal Relationships*, edited by Henry G. Manne. West Group, 1975.

Peukert, Alexander. *A Critique of the Ontology of Intellectual Property Law*. Translated by Gill Mertens. Cambridge University Press, 2021.

Pharr, Clyde, trans. *The Theodosian Code and Novels and the Sirmondian Constitutions*. Princeton, N.J.: Princeton University, 1952.

Phillips, R.P. *Modern Thomistic Philosophy: An Explanation for Students*, vol. 2. Westminster, Md.: The Newman Press, 1962 [1934–35].

Pilon, Roger A. "Criminal Remedies: Restitution, Retribution, or Both?" *Ethics* 88, no. 4 (July 1978): 348–57.

—. "Ordering Rights Consistently: Or What We Do and Do Not Have Rights To." *Georgia L. Rev.* 13 (1979): 1171–96. https://perma.cc/FYX4-CFNH.

—. "A Theory of Rights: Toward Limited Government." *Ph.D. dissertation, University of Chicago*, 1979. https://perma.cc/DGS3-W4UA.

Polanyi, Michael. *The Logic of Liberty*. Chicago: University of Chicago Press, 1980.

Popper, Karl R. *The Open Society and Its Enemies*, vol. 2, 4th rev. ed. London: Routledge and Kegan Paul, 1962.

Posner, Richard A. "Blackstone and Bentham." *J. Law & Econ.* 19 (1976): 569–606.

—. "An Economic Theory of the Criminal Law." *Colum. L. Rev.* 85 (1985).

Priest, George. "What Economists Can Tell Lawyers About Intellectual Property: Comment on Cheung." *Research in Law & Econ.* 8 (1986): 19–24.

Proudhon, Pierre-Joseph. *Les Majorats littéraires*. Translated by Luis Sundkvist; edited by L. Bently and M. Kretschmer. 1868.

Pusey, Michael. *Jürgen Habermas*. London and New York: Routledge, 1987.

Quirk, William J. and R. Randall Bridwell. "Angels to Govern Us." *Chronicles* (March 1995): 12.

—. *Judicial Dictatorship*. New Brunswick, N.J.: Transaction Publishers, 1995.

Rachels, Chase. "Property," in *A Spontaneous Order: The Capitalist Case For A Stateless Society*. 2015. https://archive.org/details/ASpontaneousOrder0.

Rand, Ayn. *Atlas Shrugged*. New York: Signet, 1992. New American Library, 1967.

—. *Capitalism: The Unknown Idea*. New York: Signet, 1967.

—. *For the New Intellectual*. New York: New American Library, 1961.

—. *The Fountainhead*. New York: Signet, 1996.

—. "Francisco's Money Speech." *Capitalism Magazine*, Aug. 30, 2002. https://perma.cc/J2G2-TU2U.

—. *Letters of Ayn Rand*. Edited by Michael S. Berliner. New York: Plume, 1995.

—. *Philosophy: Who Needs It*. New American Library, 1984.

—. *The Virtue of Selfishness: A New Concept of Egoism*. New York: Signet, 1964.

Rasmussen, Douglas B. "Arguing and Y-ing." *Liberty* 2, no. 2 (Nov. 1988): 50. https://perma.cc/A5UU-P64A.

—."Political Legitimacy and Discourse Ethics." *International Philosophical Quarterly* 32 (1992): 17–34. https://perma.cc/MK59-QEVV.

—, ed. *Reading Habermas*. Wiley-Blackwell, 1991.

—. *Norms of Liberty: A Perfectionist Basis for Non-Perfectionist Politics*. Pennsylvania State University Press, 2005.

—, and Douglas J Den Uyl. *Liberty and Nature: An Aristotelian Defense of Liberal Order*. La Salle, Ill: Open Court, 1991.

Rastogi, Vallabhi. "Theories of Intellectual Property Rights." *Enhelion Blogs*, Feb. 27, 2021. https://perma.cc/U9D5-9V4U.

Rawls, John. *Political Liberalism*, expanded ed. New York: Columbia University Press, 2005.

Re, Edward D. "The Roman Contribution to the Common Law." *Fordham L. Rev.* 29 (3) (1960): 447–94. https://ir.lawnet.fordham.edu/flr/vol29/iss3/2/.

Read, Leonard. "I Don't Know." *Mises Daily*, Nov. 2, 2011 [1965]. https://mises.org/library/i-dont-know.

Redish, Martin H. *The Constitution as Political Structure*. New York: Oxford University Press, USA, 1995.

Reich, Charles A. "The New Property." *Yale L. J.* 73, no. 5 (April 1964): 733–87.

Reichman, Jerome H. "Charting the Collapse of the Patent-Copyright Dichotomy: Premises for a Restructured International Intellectual Property System." *Cardozo Arts & Ent. L.J.* 13 (1995). https://scholarship.law.duke.edu/faculty_scholarship/685/.

Reinach, Adolf. "The A Priori Foundations of the Civil Law." *Aletheia* 3 (1983): 1–142. https://philarchive.org/rec/REITAP-9.

—. "On the Concept of Causality in the Criminal Law." *Libertarian Papers* 1, art. no. 35 (2009 [1905]). http://libertarianpapers.org/35-concept-causality-criminal-law/.

Reisman, George. "Progress In a Free Economy." *The Freeman*, July 1, 1980. https://perma.cc/2HW6-JJ8J.

Richman, Sheldon. "Intellectual 'Property' Versus Real Property: What Are Copyrights and What Do They Mean for Liberty?" *The Freeman*, 12 June 2009. https://fee.org/resources/intellectual-property-versus-real-property.

—. *Separating School and State: How to Liberate America's Families*. Fairfax, Va.: Future of Freedom Foundation, 1994.

Ricoeur, Paul. *Main Trends in Philosophy*. New York: Holmes and Meier, 1979.

Ridley, Matt. *How Innovation Works: And Why It Flourishes in Freedom*. Harper, 2020.

Charles Ripley. "Sperry's Concept of Consciousness." *Inquiry* 27 (1990): 399–423.

Robinson, Joan. *The Accumulation of Capital*, 3d ed. Palgrave Macmillan, 2013 [1969].

Rockwell, Llewellyn H., Jr. "The Tax-Reform Racket." *Mises Daily*, Jan. 17, 2005. https://mises.org/library/tax-reform-racket.

Roffer, Michael H. "The Irish Copyright War." In *The Law Book: From Hammurabi to the International Criminal Court, 250 Milestones in the History of Law*. New York: Sterling, 2015.

Rome, Gregory, and Stephan Kinsella. *Louisiana Civil Law Dictionary*. New Orleans, La.: Quid Pro Books, 2011.

Rosen, Mark D. "What Has Happened to the Common Law?—Recent American Codifications, and Their Impact on Judicial Practice and the Law's Subsequent Development." *1994 Wisc. L. Rev.* (1994): 1119–1286.

Rosenfeld, Michel. "Book Review of Habermas, *Between Facts and Norms: Contributions to a Discourse Theory of Law and Democracy*." *Harv. L. Rev.* 108 (1995): 1163–89.

Rothbard, Murray N. *America's Great Depression*, revised ed. New York: New York University Press, 1975.

—. "Beyond Is and Ought." *Liberty* 2, no. 2 (Nov. 1988): 44–45. https://perma.cc/8LZR-DN6Y; also https://mises.org/library/beyondand-ought.

—. "A Crusoe Social Philosophy." *Mises Daily*, December 7, 2021. https://mises.org/library/crusoe-social-philosophy.

—. *Economic Controversies*. Auburn, Ala: Mises Institute, 2011. https://mises.org/library/economic-controversies.

—. "Economic Thought Before Adam Smith and Classical Economics." In *An Austrian Perspective on the History of Economic Thought*, vols. 1 and 2. Aldershot, England and Brookfield, Vt.: Edward Elgar, 1995. https://perma.cc/3ABN-9FD2.

—. "The End of Socialism and the Calculation Debate Revisited." *Rev. Austrian Econ.* 5, no. 2 (1991): 51–76. https://mises.org/library/end-socialism-and-calculationdebate-revisited-0.

—. *Egalitarianism as a Revolt Against Nature and Other Essays*, second ed. Auburn, Ala.: Mises Institute, 2000 [1974]. https://mises.org/library/egalitarianism-revolt-against-nature-and-other-essays.

—. *Ethics of Liberty*. New York: New York University Press, 1998. https://perma.cc/5BU9-YLXD.

—. *For a New Liberty*, 2d ed. Auburn, Ala.: Mises Institute, 2006. https://mises.org/library/new-liberty-libertarian-manifesto.

—. "Hoppephobia." Originally published in *Liberty* 3, no. 4 (March 1990): 11–12. https://perma.cc/JT7K-YTUJ. Reprinted at *LewRockwell.com*, Oct. 4, 2014. https://perma.cc/5HH6-2P78.

—. "Human Rights" as Property Rights." In *The Ethics of Liberty*. New York: New York University Press, 1998. https://mises.org/library/human-rights-propertyrights.

—. "Justice and Property Rights." in *Property in a Humane Economy*, edited by Samuel L. Blumenfeld. LaSalle, Ill.: Open Court, 1974. https://mises.org/library/property-humane-economy.

—. "King on Punishment: A Comment." *J. Libertarian Stud.* 4, no. 2 (Spring 1980): 167–72. https://mises.org/library/king-punishment-comment-1.

—. "Law, Property Rights, and Air Pollution." In *Economic Controversies*. Auburn, Ala.: Mises Institute, 2011. https://mises.org/library/economiccontroversies.

—. *The Logic of Action*. Edward Elgar. 1997, later republished as *Economic Controversies*, Auburn, Ala.: Mises Institute, 2011; https://mises.org/library/economic-controversies

—. *Man, Economy, and State, with Power and Market*, Scholars ed., 2d ed. Auburn, Ala.: Mises Institute, 2009. https://mises.org/library/man-economyand-state-power-and-market.

—. "On Freedom and the Law." *New Individualist Review* vol. 1, no. 4 (Winter 1962). Reprinted in *New Individualist Review* omnibus volume. 1982. https://oll.libertyfund.org/title/friedman-new-individualist-review.

—. "On the Duty of Natural Outlaws to Shut Up." *New Libertarian*, April 1985. https://mises.org/library/duty-natural-outlaws-shut.

—. "Punishment and Proportionality." In *Assessing the Criminal*, edited by Barnett and Hagel III.

—. "The Single Tax: Economic and Moral Implications." in *Economic Controversies*. Auburn, Ala.: Mises Institute, 2011. https://mises.org/library/economic-controversies.

Rotunda, Ronald D. and John E. Nowak. *Treatise on Constitutional Law: Substance and Procedure*, vol. 4, 2d ed. St. Paul, Minn.: West Publishing, 1992.

Rubins, Noah D., Thomas N. Papanastasiou, and Stephan Kinsella. *International Investment, Political Risk, and Dispute Resolution: A Practitioner's Guide*, Second Edition. Oxford University Press. 2020.

Rychlak, Ronald J. "Society's Moral Right to Punish: A Further Exploration of the Denunciation Theory of Punishment." *Tul. L. Rev.* 65, no. 2 (1990): 299–338.

Sadowsky, James A. "Private Property and Collective Ownership." In *The Libertarian Alternative*, edited by Tibor R. Machan. Chicago: Nelson-Hall Co, 1974.

Salerno, Joseph T. "Böhm-Bawerk's Vision of the Capitalist Economic Process: Intellectual Influences and Conceptual Foundations." *New Perspectives on Political Economy* 4, no. 2 (2008): 87–112. https://perma.cc/7XV4-2KQA.

—. "Ludwig von Mises as Social Rationalist." *Rev. Austrian Econ.* 4 (1990): 26–64. https://mises.org/library/ludwig-von-mises-social-rationalist.

—. "Mises and Hayek Dehomogenized." Rev. Austrian Econ. 6, no. 2 (1993): 113–46. https://mises.org/library/mises-and-hayek-dehomogenized.

—. "Postscript." In *Economic Calculation in the Socialist Commonwealth*. Translated by S. Adler. Auburn, Ala.: Mises Institute, 1990 [1920]. https://mises.org/library/economic-calculation-socialist-commonwealth.

—. "Reply to Leland B. Yeager." *Rev. Austrian Econ.* 7, no. 2 (1994): 111–25. https://mises.org/library/reply-leland-b-yeager-mises-and-hayek-calculation-and-knowledge.

Sanchez, Dan. "The Fruit of Your Labor… is a good, not its form." *Medium*, Oct. 30, 2014. https://perma.cc/GD28-JS44.

Sandefur, Timothy. "A Critique of Ayn Rand's Theory of Intellectual Property Rights." *J. Ayn Rand Stud.* 9, no. 1 (Fall 2007): 139–61. https://papers.ssrn.com/sol3/papers.cfm?abstract_id=1117269.

Sartori, Giovanni. *Democratic Theory*. Westport, Connecticut: Greenwood Press, 1962.

—. *Liberty and Law*. Menlo Park, Ca.: Institute for Humane Studies, 1976.

Schafer, Stephen. *Compensation and Restitution to Victims of Crime*, 2d ed. Montclair, N.J.: Patterson Smith, 1970.

Scheiber, Harry N., ed. *The State and Freedom of Contract*. Stanford, Calif.: Stanford University Press, 1999.

Schiller, A. Arthur. *Roman Law: Mechanisms of Development*. Mouton Publishers, 1978.

Schroeder, Gertrude E. "The Dismal Fate of Soviet-Type Economies: Mises Was Right." *Cato J.* 11 no. 1 (Spring/Summer 1991): 13–25. https://www.cato.org/cato-journal/spring/sumer-1991.

Schulman, J. Neil. *Alongside Night*, 20th anniv. ed. Pulpless.com, 1999.

—. *Escape from Heaven*. Pulpless.com, 2017.

—. "Human Property." *Agorist.com*, 2012. https://perma.cc/E9W5-T7UA.

—. "Informational Property: Logorights." 1983, 1989. https://perma.cc/ECB9-KZQ9.

—. *Origitent: Why Original Content is Property*. Steve Heller Publishing, 2018. https://perma.cc/2E6G-WWPE.

Scruton, Roger. *Kant*. Oxford University Press, 1982.

Schwartz, Peter. "Libertarianism: The Perversion of Liberty." In *Ayn Rand, The Voice of Reason: Essays in Objectivist Thought*. Meridian, 1990.

Sciabarra, Chris Matthew. *Total Freedom: Toward a Dialectical Libertarianism*. Penn State University Press, 2000.

Sechrest, Larry J. "Praxeology, Economics, and Law: Issues and Implications." *Q. J. Austrian Econ.* 7, no. 4 (Winter 2004): 19–40. https://mises.org/library/praxeology-economics-and-law-issues-and-implications-0.

Shaffer, Butler. *A Libertarian Critique of Intellectual Property*. Auburn, Ala.: Mises Institute, 2013. https://mises.org/library/libertarian-critique-intellectualproperty.

—. "What Is Anarchy?" *LewRockwell.com*, Jan. 13, 2004. www.lewrockwell.com/shaffer/shaffer60.html.

Shand, Alexander H. *The Capitalist Alternative: An Introduction to Neo-Austrian Economics*. New York: New York University Press, 1984.

Shaver, Lea. "The Right to Science and Culture." *Wis. L. Rev.* 2010, no. 1 (2010): 121–84. https://papers.ssrn.com/sol3/papers.cfm?abstract_id=1354788.

Shearmur, Jeremy. "From Dialogue Rights to Property Rights: Foundations for Hayek's Legal Theory." *Critical Review* 4 (1990): 106–32.

—. "Habermas: A Critical Approach." *Critical Review* 2 (1988): 39–50.

Sherman, Brad, and Lionel Bently. *The Making of Modern Intellectual Property Law: The British Experience, 1760–1911*. Cambridge University Press, 1999.

Shiffrin, Seana Valentine. "Lockean Arguments for Private Property." In *New Essays in the Legal and Political Theory of Property*, edited by Munzer. https://perma.cc/3TWB-4Z8A.

Shughart II, William F. "Ideas Need Protection: Abolishing Intellectual-property Patents Would Hurt Innovation: A Middle Ground Is Needed." *Baltimore Sun*, December 21, 2009.

Siegen, Bernard H. *Economic Liberties and the Constitution*. Chicago: University of Chicago Press, 1980.

Skousen, Mark. "'Just Because Socialism Has Lost Does Not Mean That Capitalism Has Won': An Interview with Robert L. Heilbroner." *Forbes* (May 27, 1991): 130–35.

Slenzok, Norbert. "The Libertarian Argumentation Ethics, the Transcendental Pragmatics of Language, and the Conflict-Freedom Principle." *Analiza i Egzystencja* 58 (2022): 35–64. https://www.academia.edu/87163918/The_Libertarian_Argumentation_Ethics_the_Transcendental_Pragmatics_of_Language_and_the_Conflict_Freedom_Principle.

Slutskiy, Pavel. *Communication and Libertarianism*. Springer, 2021.

Smith, Adam. *The Theory of Moral Sentiments*. Indianapolis: Liberty Fund, 1982 [1759].

Smith, Barry. "An Essay on Material Necessity." In *Return of the A Priori (Canadian J. Philosophy*, Supplementary Volume 18, 1993): 301–322. https://philpapers.org/archive/SMIAEO-2.pdf.

—, and Wojciech Żełaniec. "Laws of Essence or Constitutive Rules? Reinach vs. Searle on the Ontology of Social Entities." In *Eidetica del Diritto e Ontologia Sociale. Il Realismo di Adolf Reinach*, edited by Francesca De Vecchi. Milan: Mimesis, 2012. https://perma.cc/LR2P-NLXW.

Smith, George H. *Atheism, Ayn Rand, and Other Heresies*. Buffalo, N.Y.: Prometheus Books, 1991.

—. *Atheism: The Case Against God*. Buffalo, N.Y.: Prometheus Books, 1979.

—. "Inalienable Rights?" *Liberty* 10, no. 6 (July 1997): 51–56. https://perma.cc/4CUE-KG7G.

—. "A Killer's Right to Life." *Liberty* 10, no. 2 (Nov. 1996): 49–54. https://perma.cc/8U8C-ZTAR.

Smith, M.B.E. "Is There a Prima Facie Obligation to Obey the Law?" *Yale L. J.* 82 (1973): 950–76. https://perma.cc/MF3A-LBEV.

Sobran, Joe. "Constitutional Legerdemain." Syndicated column of April 11, 1996. Reprinted in *Sobran's* 3, no. 5 (May 1996): 12.

Soepboer, Mick. "Libertarian views on intellectual property law: An analysis of laissez-faire theories applied on the modern day IP system." *University of Cape Town, School for Advanced Legal Studies, Master Dissertation Commercial Law* (July 2009). https://perma.cc/4HR6-743V.

Solum, Lawrence B. "The Foundations of Liberty." *Mich. L. Rev.* 97, no. 6 (May 1999): 1780–1812. https://repository.law.umich.edu/mlr/vol97/iss6/26/.

—. "Freedom of Communicative Action: A Theory of the First Amendment Freedom of Speech." *Northwestern U. L. Rev.* 83 (1989): 54–135. https://scholarship.law.georgetown.edu/facpub/1954/.

Sorensen, Roy A. *Blindspots*. New York: Oxford University Press, 1988.

Sowell, Thomas. *Knowledge and Decisions*. New York: Basic Books, Inc., 1980.

Spooner, Lysander. *The Collected Works of Lysander Spooner*, vol. 3, reprint ed. Weston, Mass.: M&S Press, 1971 [1855]. www.lysanderspooner.org/works.

—. *The Lysander Spooner Reader*. San Francisco: Fox & Wilkes, 1992. Available online at http://www.lysanderspooner.org/works.

—. *Poverty: Its Illegal Causes, and Legal Cure*, Part 1. 1846. http://www.lysanderspooner.org/works.

Stein, Peter G. "Roman Law, Common Law, and Civil Law." *Tul. L. Rev.*, 66, no. 6 (1991–92): 1591–1604.

—. *Roman Law in European History*. Cambridge University Press, 1999.

Steinberger, Peter J. "Hegel on Crime and Punishment." *Am. Pol. Science Rev.* 77, no. 4 (Dec. 1983): 858–70.

Stern, James Y. "The Essential Structure of Property Law." *Mich. L. Rev* 115 (7) (2017). https://repository.law.umich.edu/mlr/vol115/iss7/2/.

Super, David A. "A New New Property." *Colum. L. Rev.* 113 (2013): 1773–1896. https://columbialawreview.org/content/a-new-new-property.

Symposium. "Breakthrough or Buncombe." *Liberty* 2, no. 2. (Nov. 1988): 44–53. https://perma.cc/A5UU-P64A.

Tacitus. *Annals III*.

Tannehill, Morris and Linda. *The Market for Liberty*. Auburn, Ala.: Mises Institute, 2007 [1970]. https://mises.org/library/marketliberty-1.

Tassi, Paul. "You Will Never Kill Piracy, and Piracy Will Never Kill You." *Forbes*, Feb. 3, 2012. https://perma.cc/23W2-E2FT.

Thadeusz, Frank. "No Copyright Law: The Real Reason for Germany's Industrial Expansion?" *Spiegel International*, Aug. 18, 2010. https://perma.cc/R3H7-6KG8.

Thomas, J.A.C., ed. *The Institutes of Justinian: Text, Translation, and Commentary*. Amsterdam: North-Holland Publishing Company, 1975.

Thompson, John B. andand David Held, eds. *Habermas: Critical Debates*. London: Macmillan Press, 1982.

Thornton, Mark. "Libertarianism: A Fifty-Year Personal Retrospective." *J. Libertarian Stud.* 24, no. 2 (2020): 445–60. https://mises.org/library/libertarianism-fifty-year-personal-retrospective.

Tinsley, Patrick, Stephan Kinsella, and Walter Block. "In Defense of Evidence and Against the Exclusionary Rule: A Libertarian Approach." *Southern U. L. Rev.*, 32 no. 1 (2004): 63–80. www.walterblock.com/publications.

Torpman, Olle. "Mid-Libertarianism and the Utilitarian Proviso." *J. Value Inquiry*, Sept. 2, 2021. https://philpapers.org/rec/TORMAT-4.

Tracy, Destutt. *A Treatise on Political Economy*. Translated by Thomas Jefferson. Auburn, Ala.: Mises Institute, 2009 [1817]. https://mises.org/library/treatise-politicaleconomy-0.

Tribe, Laurence & Michael Dorf. *On Reading the Constitution*. Cambridge, Mass.: Harvard University Press, 1991.

Tuccille, Jerome. *It Usually Begins with Ayn Rand*. Stein and Day, 1971.

Tucker, Jeffrey A. *Bourbon for Breakfast: Living Outside the Statist Quo*. Auburn, Ala.: Mises Institute, 2010. https://mises.org/library/bourbon-breakfast.

—. "Eternal Copyright," *C4SIF Blog*, Feb. 21, 2012.

—. "Germany and Its Industrial Rise: Due to No Copyright." *Mises Economics Blog*, Aug. 18, 2010.

—. *It's a Jetsons World: Private Miracles and Public Crimes*. Auburn, Ala.: Mises Institute, 2011. https://mises.org/library/its-jetsons-worldprivate-miracles-and-public-crimes.

—. "Marxism Without Polylogism." In *Property, Freedom and Society: Essays in Honor of Hans-Hermann Hoppe*, edited by Jörg Guido Hülsmann and Stephan Kinsell. Auburn, Ala.: Mises Institute, 2009.

—. "A Theory of Open." *Mises Economics Blog*, Jan. 7, 2010. https://mises.org/wire/theoryopen.

—, and Stephan Kinsella. "Goods, Scarce and Nonscarce." *Mises Daily*, Aug. 25, 2010.

Tucker, Thomas W. "Sources of Louisiana's Law of Persons: Blackstone, Domat, and the French Codes." *Tul. L. Rev.* 44 (1970): 264–95.

Tullock, Gordon. "Courts as Legislators." In *Liberty and the Rule of Law*, edited by. Robert L. Cunningham. College Station, Texas: Texas A&M University Press, 1979.

UNESCO, *The ABC of Copyright*. 1981. https://unesdoc.unesco.org/ark:/48223/pf0000187677.

Uszkai, Radu. "Are Copyrights Compatible with Human Rights?" *Romanian J. Analytic Phil.* 8 (2014): 5–20. https://philarchive.org/rec/USZACC.

Vaidhyanathan, Siva. *Intellectual Property: A Very Short Introduction*. Oxford University Press, 2017.

van der Vossen, Bas. "What counts as original appropriation?" *Politics, Philosophy & Economics* 8 (4) (2009): 355–373.

Van Dun, Frank. "Against Libertarian Legalism: A Comment on Kinsella and Block." *J. Libertarian Stud.* 17, no. 3 (2003): 63–90. https://mises.org/library/against-libertarianlegalism-comment-kinsella-and-block-0.

—. "Argumentation Ethics and the Philosophy of Freedom." *Libertarian Papers* 1 (19) (2009.). www.libertarianpapers.org.

—. "Economics and the Limits of Value-Free Science." *Reason Papers* 11 (Spring 1986): 24.

—. "Freedom and Property: Where They Conflict." In *Property, Freedom, and Society: Essays in Honor of Hans-Hermann Hoppe*, edited by Jörg Guido Hülsmann and Stephan Kinsella. Auburn, Ala.: Mises Institute, 2009. https://mises.org/library/property-freed.

—. "On the Philosophy of Argument and the Logic of Common Morality." In *Argumentation: Approaches to Theory Formation*, edited by. E.M. Barth and J.L. Martens. Amsterdam: John Benjamins, 1982.

Veatch, Henry. *Human Rights: Fact or Fancy?* Baton Rouge: Louisiana State University Press, 1985.

Virkkala, Timothy. "The Hollow Ring of Inalienability." *Liberty* 10, no. 5 (May 1997): 49–50. https://perma.cc/4TMF-2S5R.

—. "The Stilted Logic of Natural Rights ." *Liberty* 10, no. 6 (July 1997): 56. https://perma.cc/48NM-UAPK.

Walker, Ralph. *C.S. Kant.* London: Routledge and Kegan Paul, 1978.

Watson, Alan. *Failures of the Legal Imagination.* University of Pennsylvania Press, 1988. https://archive.org/details/failuresoflegali0000wats.

—. "The Importance of 'Nutshells.'" *Am. J. Com* 42, no. 1 (Winter 1994): 1–23. https://digitalcommons.law.uga.edu/fac_artchop/668.

—. "Justinian's Corpus Iuris Civilis: Oddities of Legal Development; and Human Civilization." Lecture 2 in *Authority of Law; and Law: Eight Lectures.* Stockholm: Institutet fr̈ Ritshistorisk Forskning, 2003. https://perma.cc/2BD5-4P4K.

—. *The Making of the Civil Law.* Cambridge, Massachusetts and London: Harvard University Press, 1981.

—. *Roman Law and Comparative Law.* University of Georgia Press, 1991.

Weber, Max. *Max Weber on Law in Economy and Society*, edited with introduction and annotations by Max Rheinstein. Translated. from Max Weber, *Wirtschaft und Gesellschaft*, 2d ed. (1924), by Edward Shils and Max Rheinstein. Clarion, 1967.

Weissmueller, Zach, Nick Gillespie and Danielle Thompson. "Inside the Mises Caucus Takeover of the Libertarian Party." *Reason.com*, June 15, 2022. https://perma.cc/QCK5-3HND.

Wile, Anthony. "Stephan Kinsella on the Logic of Libertarianism and Why Intellectual Property Doesn't Exist." *The Daily Bell*, March 18, 2012.

White, Stephen K. *The Recent Work of Jürgen Habermas.* Cambridge University Press, 1988.

Whitehead, Roy, and Walter Block. "Taking the Assets of Criminals to Compensate Victims of Violence: A Legal and Philosophical Approach." *J. Law in Society* 5 (2003): 229–253. http://www.walterblock.com/publications/.

Wills, Garry. *St. Augustine: A Life.* Viking Penguin, 1999.

Wilson, J.Q., and R.J. Herrnstein. *Crime and Human Nature.* 1985.

Wittgenstein, Ludwig. *Tractatus Logico-Philosophicus.* Translated by D.F. Pears and B.F. McGuinness. London: Routledge & Paul Kegan, 1961.

Witty, Michael. "Athenaeus describes the most ancient intellectual property." *Prometheus* 35, no. 2 (March 2018): 137–43. https://perma.cc/4J2J-ZNDU.

Wood, Jeff. "The Triumphant Return of Libertarian Macho Flash." March 8, 2017. https://perma.cc/KE6W-WQK4.

Yeager, Leland B. "Book Review." *Rev. Austrian Econ.* 9, no. 1 (1996): 181–88. https://perma.cc/UDC3-UQ3Z.

—. "Calculation and Knowledge: Let's Write Finis." *Rev. Austrian Econ.* 10, no. 1 (1997): 133–36. https://mises.org/library/calculationand-knowledge-lets-write-finis.

—. "Mises and Hayek and Calculation and Knowledge." *Rev. Austrian Econ.* 7, no. 2 (1994): 93–109. https://mises.org/library/mises-and-hayek-and-calculation-and-knowledge.

—. "Raw Assertions." *Liberty* 2, no. 2 (Nov. 1988): 45–46. https://perma.cc/A5UU-P64A.

Yiannopoulos, A.N. "The Civil Codes of Louisiana." *Civil Law Commentaries* 1, no. 1 (Winter 2008): 0–23. https://perma.cc/59DZ-KGSE. Also included in Yiannopoulos, *Civil Law System: Louisiana and Comparative Law: A Coursebook: Texts, Cases and Materials*, 3d ed. Baton Rouge, La.: Claitor's Publishing Division, 2000.

—. *Louisiana Civil Law Treatise, Property*, 4th ed. West Group, 2001.

Younkins, Edward W. "Menger, Mises, Rand, and Beyond." *J. Ayn Rand Stud.* 6, no. 2. (Spring 2005). https://perma.cc/SM4J-TYBV: 337–74. Also in *Philosophers of Capitalism: Menger, Mises, Rand, and Beyond*, edited by Edward W. Younkins. Lexington Books, 2005.

Zailbert, Leo. "Toward Meta-Politics." *Q. J. Austrian Econ.* 7, no. 4 (Winter 2004): 113–28. https://mises.org/library/toward-meta-politics-0.

Index

About the Author

Stephan Kinsella, a libertarian since high school in the early 1980s, is a patent attorney and libertarian writer. Formerly a partner with Duane Morris LLP and General Counsel for Applied Optoelectronics, Inc., he has over thirty years' experience in patent, intellectual property, and general commercial and corporate law. He was founder and Executive Editor of *Libertarian Papers*, is Director of the Center for the Study of Innovative Freedom, and was adjunct professor at South Texas College of Law Houston. His libertarian publications include *Property, Freedom, and Society: Essays in Honor of Hans-Hermann Hoppe* (Mises Institute, 2009), *Against Intellectual Property* (Mises Institute, 2008), and numerous articles on the application of libertarian principles to legal topics. His legal publications include *International Investment, Political Risk, and Dispute Resolution: A Practitioner's Guide*, 2d ed. (Oxford University Press, 2020); *Trademark Practice and Forms* (Oxford/Thomson Reuters, 2001–2013); *Digest of Commercial Laws of the World* (Oxford, 1998–2013); and *Louisiana Civil Law Dictionary* (Quid Pro Books, 2011). He received an LL.M. (international business law) from King's College London, a JD from the Paul M. Hebert Law Center at Louisiana State University, and BS and MS degrees in electrical engineering from LSU.

A native of Prairieville, Louisiana, he lives with his wife, Cindy in Houston, Texas.